EXPLORING THE OLYMPIC MOUNTAINS

Accounts of the Earliest Expeditions
1878–1890

Compiled by Carsten Lien

THE
MOUNTAINEERS
BOOKS

Published by
The Mountaineers Books
1001 SW Klickitat Way, Suite 201
Seattle, WA 98134

Published simultaneously in Great Britain by Cordee, 3a DeMontfort Street, Leicester, England, LE1 7HD

Manufactured in Canada

Acquisitions Editor: Margaret Sullivan
Project Editor: Julie Van Pelt
Developmental Editor: Donna DeShazo
Copy Editor: Kris Fulsaas
Book Design and Layout: Mayumi Thompson
Set in Castellar MT, Futura, and Goudy

Cover photograph: Seattle Press *staff photo, June 7, 1889, the day after the Seattle Fire. The* Seattle Press *unknowingly assured its place in history by sponsoring and reporting on the 1890 Press Expedition to the Olympic Mountains. Assistant editor Edmond S. Meany is in the back row, second from the left.* Courtesy Manuscripts, Special Collections, University Archives, University of Washington Libraries, Seattle, UW18617

Grateful acknowledgement is given for help in securing permission to use previously unpublished material to the Bancroft Library, University of California, Berkeley, for Eldridge Morse's "Notes on the History and Resources of Washington Territory"; the Mazamas Club, Portland, Oregon, for Harry Fisher's diary, "Lt. Oneils [sic] Exploration of the Olympic Mountains"; Olympic National Park for the diary of Bernard J. Bretherton; and the Washington State Historical Society, Tacoma, for James Wickersham's journal "A Trip to the Olympic Mountains." Every attempt has been made to trace accurate ownership of copyrighted material in this book. In the event of errors or omissions, the publisher will be pleased to make corrections.

Library of Congress Cataloging-in-Publication Data
Exploring the Olympic Mountains: accounts of the earliest explorations,
1878-1890 / compiled by Carsten Lien.—1st ed.
     p. cm.
Includes bibliographical references and index.
    ISBN 0-89886-803-3
1. Olympic Mountains (Wash.)—Discovery and exploration—Sources. 2. Olympic
Mountains (Wash.)—History—19th century—Sources. 3. Explorers—Washington
(State)—Olympic Mountains—Biography. I. Lien, Carsten.
   F897.O5 E97 2001
   979.7'9403—dc21

                                      2001002403

Dedicated to Pacific Northwest historians, Robert L. Wood and Harry M. Majors. Without their meticulous research into the details of Olympic Mountains exploration, this compilation would have been greatly diminished.

CONTENTS

Part III: The O'Neil Expeditions 1885 and 1890

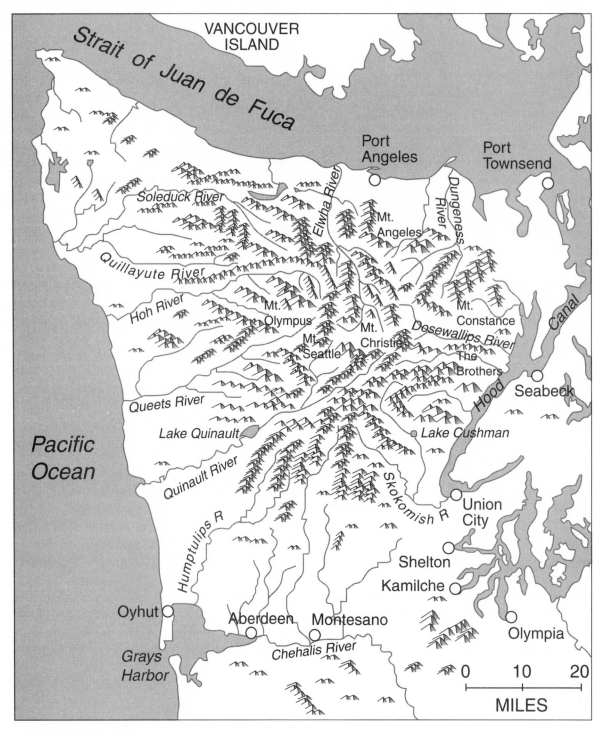

The Olympic Peninsula (Adapted from Wood, The Land That Slept Late, *25)*

PREFACE

My first exposure to the excitement of Olympic Mountains exploration was as a fifteen-year-old Boy Scout. Working in a home darkroom, two of my scouting friends and I printed a copy for each of us of U.S. Senate Document No. 59[1] containing Lt. Joseph P. O'Neil's official account of his 1890 Olympics exploration. I cannot now account for how copy negatives of this report happened to be available to us, or any other details about it. Because we were Olympics backcountry enthusiasts, however, anything relating to the wilderness there was embraced and added to each of our collections of Olympic Mountains ephemera. From time to time as I came across my personal pile of photocopied prints of O'Neil's account, I reread them with interest and tacitly understood that a source document such as this is gripping in a way that secondary accounts are not. Here was the story of a guy who had been there.

Two years later when I was a freshman at the University of Washington, I discovered in the Pacific Northwest Collection of the UW Library a nearly intact copy of the July 16, 1890, issue of the *Seattle Press* that contained the report of the explorers who were known as the Press Expedition. Although intact, it was on the verge of complete disintegration. Because the library had a bound photostatic copy of a miniaturized version, no one in the library was interested at that time in saving the original as a full-sized photostatic copy. I convinced the then head librarian of the Pacific Northwest Collection, Ronald Todd, that I should be allowed to take this fragile, disintegrating copy of the Press Expedition issue to have a last-chance original-sized photostatic negative and positive made for my use. I had no idea at the time how I would ever use it, but on the other hand, letting it disintegrate without making a copy did not seem to make much sense either.

Many years later, when I needed to face up to the fact that I did not yet really know how to use most efficiently my word processing program, I decided that I would reproduce the complete text of the Press Expedition report as a learning exercise. Stored in my basement for more than forty years, my copy of the expedition issue of the *Seattle Press* was now about to begin to serve some use. Day after day I typed away, returning from time to time to libraries to fill in the text that was missing because of the holes created by the crumbling that had already occurred before I made the photostatic copies. Fortunately, there were some microfilmed copies that had crumble holes in different places from my copy.

As my word processing program became available in newer, ever more flexible versions, I made the upgrades and kept on pecking out the words of the Press Expedition adventurers. When I finally finished the Press Expedition text, I realized that there were a number of other really interesting period documents out there relating to the Press Expedition that ought to be included. When I finished adding these, I found there were still more, including material on other expeditions. By default, I realized I was well on my way to including every original document of Olympics exploration known to exist. So I made the decision to do just that.

Moving on from the Press Expedition, I began to assemble the vast number of documents relating to the O'Neil Expeditions of 1885 and 1890. Here, I discovered that one of the most important pieces, the diary of Pvt. Harry Fisher, a member of the party, seemingly was available only as a microfilm copy of a huge handwritten manuscript. Even though I had devoted many months at the keyboard already, sitting in front of a microfilm reader for a great deal of the rest of my life, trying to decipher the handwriting of a not too literate soldier in the U.S. Army of 1890, had little appeal. I then remembered that Robert L. Wood, as the author of several books on Olympics exploration, must also have stumbled across Fisher's manuscript. Reasoning that Wood may well have transcribed at least some of it into typewritten copy in the process of producing his book on the O'Neil explorations, I went to see him.

I was pleasantly surprised to find that not only had Wood transcribed the whole manuscript from the microfilmed, handwritten copy into typed copy, but that he would give me a copy of his work. Wood had applied the skills and tools of a court reporter to the task that appeared so daunting to me. With the amount of work involved in that effort alone, he can claim legitimately to be a co-compiler of this volume. Wood enthusiastically ended up sharing many other things, including Press Expedition material. Many of the items in this book relating to the O'Neil Expedition of 1890 were included because Wood provided a citation or, in some cases, a copy of an item worthy of inclusion. He has enthusiastically given permission

7

---

[1] Senate, *Report on the Exploration of the Olympic Mountains* by Lt. Joseph P. O'Neil, Fourteenth Infantry, together with "Remarks on the Olympic Mountains," 54th Congr., 1st sess., 1896, S. Doc. 59, serial 3349, vol. 3.

for this volume to incorporate maps and other material from his own prior work on both the Press Expedition and the O'Neil Expedition.

Another historian who analyzed in depth what occurred on the Press Expedition is Harry M. Majors, writer for, as well as editor and publisher of, the highly regarded but now suspended journal *Northwest Discovery*. He accounted for each photograph taken on the expedition and established the date on which each was taken. He developed a numbering system for keeping track of them as well. Often with great insight, he commented by footnote on the events unfolding in the journals of Barnes and Christie, the two Press Expedition leaders. Majors also wrote some mini-essays analyzing aspects of the Press Expedition, including some tabulations from the text of the report listing the equipment and supplies hauled up the Elwha River by the men of the expedition. All of this appeared in *Northwest Discovery*, which was published in the early 1980s but is now, at least for the present, a journal of the past. Bound copies, however, are still available to researchers in many research libraries. This present book brings to the nonacademic reader some of Majors's contribution to the history of the Olympic Mountains. Majors graciously has permitted the use of his work on the Press Expedition, as it appeared in *Northwest Discovery*, to be included here.

Readers will find that many of the footnote citations come from three sources: Wood's Olympics volumes, *Across the Olympic Mountains: The Press Expedition of 1889–90* and *Men, Mules and Mountains: Lieutenant O'Neil's Olympic Expeditions*, as well as from various issues of the journal *Northwest Discovery*. These footnotes from other sources are in quotation marks. Notes that do not contain a source citation or another writer's tag are my comments.

Each of the short summaries that precede the original documents is written by me unless another author (usu-

ally Robert L. Wood) is identified by a tag line.

In reproducing the nineteenth-century documents herein, I chose to reprint them exactly as they appear in their original form, including all of the archaic spelling and punctuation conventions of the era. For instance, today's *Elwha River* appeared in the nineteenth century as *Elwha river*. *Quinault* was most often spelled then with a second *i*, which made it *Quinaiult*. Where that spelling appears in the original, it appears here. The only exception to this spelling rule is that whenever an obvious typographical error occurred, it was corrected. As an example, I saw no reason to confront the reader with numbers of (*sic*)s because the *t* was left out of the word *the*, making it appear as *he*. I corrected the error. In reproducing manuscript materials and other personal accounts, where the author struck out sentences and phrases I retained them as strikeouts so that the reader will be able to follow the author's thought processes. When an author underlined a word for emphasis, I have reproduced it that way. In other words, every effort was made to provide a complete, intact, and unedited reproduction of every original document or newspaper article included in this volume.

Readers will find many errors of fact in the narratives contained herein. For instance, the Press explorers believed that Mount Carrie was Mount Olympus and that Mount Anderson was The Brothers, making their accounts impossible to follow for those who do not know this but who know the Olympic backcountry from firsthand knowledge. In every case where this and similar errors occurred, I have attempted to alert the reader by including a footnote from the work of either Robert L. Wood or Harry M. Majors. So be forewarned: The footnotes are as important as the text.

With a salute to Harry M. Majors and to Robert L. Wood, who came before me and who now stand with me as compilers of this volume, let me say to you all: "Good reading."

8

INTRODUCTION

Modern-day readers of the Olympic Mountains exploration accounts that follow need to remember that the Seattle of the 1880s was a tiny place by present standards. At the beginning of the decade, two years after the first recorded venture into the Olympics—the Watkinson party in 1878—Seattle had a population of 3,533. Driven by an exploding economy, Seattle was experiencing explosive growth as well. The city increased in size twelve times over during the decade that was the golden era of Olympics exploration. The population was 33,500 in 1889, when the Press Expedition was being planned. By the time Lieutenant O'Neil began his major expedition in 1890, Seattle had grown to 42,837, an increase of nearly 10,000 in a year's time, much of it occurring while the Press Expedition was in the mountains.

As the decade neared its end, when the citizens of Seattle realized that no one really knew what lay in the range of mountains to the west of them, the Olympics became a community obsession. Politicians speculated about them, wild myths circulated openly about them, charlatans claimed to have seen what was there, and a general veil of mystery hung over them. No one could escape the Olympics because they glistened, bright and enticing, on Seattle's horizon to the west on every clear day, just as they do today. All the Seattle newspapers reported every detail of every exploration attempt.

In 1889, when the local evening paper, the *Seattle Press*, organized and financially supported an expedition to uncover, once and for all, the mystery of the mountains, it was inevitable that finally the Olympics would become an even greater focus of community attention. Seattle was exploding with activity. The Great Fire of June 6, 1889, had destroyed the town and Seattle was in the midst of a massive rebuilding campaign. Seattle was redefining itself in the process as well, not only physically, but also in many other ways. It was still trying to live down an ugly lynching of three men that had occurred in 1882, and the notorious anti-Chinese rioting in 1885 and 1886 in which cold-blooded murder went unpunished.

What no one in town was trying to live down, however, was that the Seattle establishment wanted a wide-open town and they got it. It was good for business, they said. There were more saloons than there were grocery stores. Gambling,

9

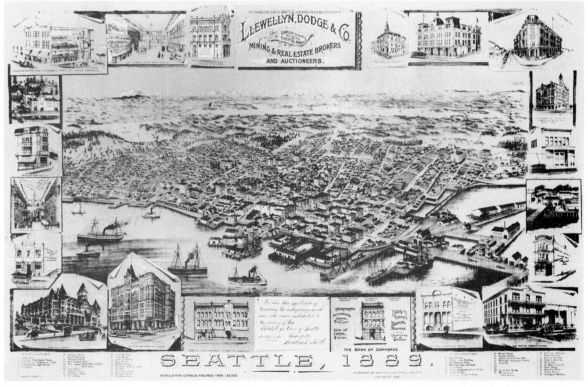

Seattle, 1889
Courtesy Manuscripts, Special Collections, University Archives, University of Washington Libraries, Seattle, UW553

unrestricted prostitution, prize fighting (then considered a vice), and every degrading activity anyone could think up provided every sailor, logger, and mill worker in western Washington with a way to separate his pay from his wallet. They all seemed to love Seattle and so did the pious businessmen who profited from it all.

In spite of Seattle's ever-expanding economy, money was in short supply. Continuous deflation had plagued the country for a long time, the value of the dollar having increased by 50 percent since the Civil War. Manpower was in short supply as well, resulting in the Northern Pacific Railroad importing vast numbers of Chinese to build the line's route through the Cascade Mountains east of Seattle. When the NP's tunnel through the mountains at Stampede Pass was completed in 1888, Puget Sound had a reliable direct rail connection to the East, allowing the railroad to abandon its previous route, an onerous crossing of the Columbia River at Kalama.

On top of all the other action going on in Seattle, Washington gained statehood on November 11, 1889, becoming the forty-second state of the union, with North Dakota, South Dakota, and Montana admitted just ahead of it. Elisha P. Ferry was elected governor, and the legislators chose Watson C. Squire as one of Washington's senators. Both Ferry and Squire were from Seattle. And both would have Olympic peaks named after them by the Press Expedition, which would be underway in the following month.

If not for the Olympics expedition it sponsored, the *Seattle Press* would be little remembered today. Because of that sponsorship, names assigned by the Press Party to a number of Olympic peaks and other features are in use today. The paper itself, however, turned out to be a short-lived blip on the local newspaper scene.

In 1886 local entrepreneur Homer M. Hill succeeded in acquiring two Seattle papers, the *Chronicle* and the *Call*, consolidating them under a new name, the *Seattle Press*. By 1889 the paper was free of debt and was making money for its owner, who decided to bank his profits by putting the paper up for sale. As luck would have it, twenty-nine-year-old William E. Bailey, a wealthy Philadelphian described as having large interests in Seattle, was bitten by an uncontrollable urge to run a newspaper. He paid Hill's asking price for the *Press*, somewhere between $20,000 and $25,000.[1] Bailey, with no shortage of resources, made important additions to the mechanical

department and engaged a large news and editorial force. In this group of new hires was twenty-seven-year-old Edmond S. Meany, a graduate of the Territorial University and a well-connected man about town who became an assistant editor.

With the whole region quietly obsessed with the Olympics, it was an easy move for Bailey to use his personal wealth to underwrite the costs of outfitting an expedition to find out what lay to the west of the familiar Olympics skyline. At the same time, such an expedition would put the *Press* at the forefront of local involvement in an issue of great interest to the public. Bailey assigned Assistant Editor Meany to the expedition in addition to his other duties. Meany became its treasurer, its chief correspondent, and very likely the dominant force in assigning the names to the features that the expedition uncovered. He later became the editor of the report that brought the expedition's findings to the *Seattle Press'* readers. And it was to Meany's ranch, at what is now the block between Roosevelt Way and Ninth Avenue Northeast at Northeast Forty-first Street, then considered far out of town,

Edmond S. Meany, circa 1889
Courtesy Manuscripts, Special Collections, University Archives, University of Washington Libraries, Seattle, UW3374

---

[1] In the months following the return of the Press Expedition, Bailey began to face the fact that two evening papers in a town the size of Seattle was too much. In February 1891, he purchased the *Times*, his competitor, and merged it with the *Press* under the name the *Press-Times*. The notorious crash of 1893 was just ahead. Circulation was not great, advertising was not enough to be more than a constant worry, and the depression by then underway forced him to give the paper up to his creditors. He lost $200,000 in his journalistic career, an incredible amount considering the value of the dollar in the 1890s.

The engine J. R. McDonald circa 1888 at North 34th Street and Stoneway in the contemporary Fremont/Wallingford neighborhood north of Seattle. Press Expedition members used the Seattle, Lake Shore, and Eastern Railway to haul gear and supplies from downtown Seattle to Edmond S. Meany's ranch on a route that today includes part of the Burke-Gilman Trail.
Courtesy Museum of History and Industry, Seattle, Washington

that all of the gear and supplies purchased for the trip were assembled. The goods were hauled by train on the Seattle, Lake Shore and Eastern Railway, whose nearby mainline is now the Burke Gilman Trail. In spite of not being an actual member of the exploring party, Meany was a key player in the expedition. At first glance, however, the record of the expedition renders nearly invisible the various roles played by Meany.

Just before the expedition departed, George Eastman had begun marketing his new roll-film camera, freeing photographers from the glass plates then in wide use. If not for this technological advance, there probably would not have been pictures at all from the Press Party. The halftone print process for reproducing photographs in newspapers, however, was not available in 1890. For pictures, the *Press* used the photoengraving process, as did most newspapers at the time. In this process, a highly skilled photoengraver sat with a zinc plate, a stylus, and the photograph to be reproduced. By scratching lines with the stylus onto the soft metal of the zinc plate, he reproduced, often with great clarity, the photograph involved. The engraver, however, had to create his plate as a mirror image of the photograph so that it would appear correctly when it came off the presses, a complicating factor to say the least. The pictures from the Press Expedition report were reproduced in this manner and appear in this volume as they appeared in the newspapers of their day. They offer a view of late-nineteenth-century newspaper technology as it was practiced in Seattle and around the country.

The floodgates of human interaction with the wilds of the Olympic Mountains were opened by the completion of the Press Expedition. In fact the knowledge that the Press Party was in the mountains inspired numbers of other parties to make their own forays; most of these focused not so much on exploration as they did on just going in where no one had been before. Too often their goals seemed to be centered on how many bears, elk, deer, cougars, wolves, and other large mammals could be slaughtered in the shortest possible period of time and left to rot. Within a decade of the return of the Press Expedition, the Olympics elk herd hovered on the edge of extinction. The estimated 8,000 to 9,000 animals present in 1890 were reduced to around 500 in 1900 by nothing more than what seems to be a driving need in nineteenth-century urban men to kill for the sake of killing. Only a total legislative ban in 1905 on hunting elk saved them from complete extinction. The Conrad/Olmstead party, which ultimately found the tracks of the Press Party by heading up the Dosewallips River, was typical of the macho, ill-prepared adventurers who shot everything in sight while demonstrating to themselves and everyone else how unready they were for the challenges that confronted them.

In contrast to the ne'er-do-wells mentioned above were two carefully planned expeditions that followed close on the heels of the Press Party's trip—the Wickersham Expeditions and the second O'Neil Expedition, both of which covered some of the same territory. Both parties cooperated with one

11

another, spending many hours around the campfire together, and both parties concluded that the Olympics should be made into a national park.

James Wickersham, a Tacoma probate judge, began his Olympics wanderings in the summer of 1889 with a trip up the Skokomish River with three good friends. They managed to push farther up the Skokomish valley than had any previous party. The following summer, 1890, with appetites whetted for more, Wickersham gathered up his friends and family and headed back into the Olympics, even though by then the mountains were crawling with people and activity.

Backed by two newspapers, the *Buckley Banner* and the *Tacoma News*, the Wickersham group was sometimes known as the Banner Party. Wickersham and his party became the first group to explore the headwaters of the Duckabush River and descend the Dosewallips. None of what Wickersham accomplished would have been possible, however, without the efforts the same year of Lieutenant O'Neil's party and the trail through the dense forest they left behind. By traveling without pack animals and not having to build a trail, Wickersham was able to move faster and quickly overtook and passed the military expedition. In the process of his explorations, Wickersham became a lifelong advocate of national park status for the Olympic Mountains. It was, however, his access to the pages of two newspapers that put his activities into the record and that exposed the public to his thoughts on national park status for the Olympics. In this concept he was almost exactly a half century ahead of his time.

Credit for really opening up knowledge of the Olympic Mountains has to go to U.S. Army Lt. Joseph P. O'Neil. He began his explorations from the north in 1885, an effort that was cut short by his transfer to Fort Leavenworth, Kansas, in the late summer of that year. Two years later, in 1887, he was transferred back to Vancouver Barracks. Coincidentally, shortly thereafter a number of local climbers founded the Oregon Alpine Club, the predecessor of the Mazamas, and O'Neil was elected club secretary. Immediately the club began agitating for a "scientific expedition" to explore the Olympic Mountains that, among other things, would give O'Neil a chance to complete the exploration he had begun in 1885 when he was twenty-two years old.

After the army approved further Olympics exploration, the Oregon Alpine Club appointed Will G. Steel and O'Neil to organize the effort. The army agreed to provide the leader,

several enlisted men, a pack train, and whatever equipment might be needed. The club would provide the scientists and some of the finances. By 1890 the effort was underway, with the twenty-seven-year-old O'Neil officially designated the commanding officer at the same time he remained a key officer in the civilian organization that would be the army's partner. It would be a joint military-civilian undertaking. No one saw a conflict of interest in O'Neil's role.

As soon as O'Neil's formal orders were posted in June 1890, authorizing his involvement, the Olympic Exploring Expedition, or the OEE as it became known, was underway. Ten enlisted men, all volunteers from the Fourteenth Infantry, were detailed to the expedition along with a civilian employed by the Quartermaster Department to manage the pack train of a dozen mules, plus several dogs. The Oregon Alpine Club provided the other civilians, who comprised the "scientific corps."

O'Neil's plan was to cross the Olympics from east to west, constructing a pack-train trail and exploring as the party did so. They managed to explore a major part of the Olympic Peninsula. The public was able to follow the expedition's progress during the summer of 1890 through the dispatches from "the front" that appeared in the newspapers.

The travels throughout the Olympic Peninsula of Arthur Dodwell and Theodore F. Rixon are not covered in this volume, even though it could be argued that they were the first to explore extensively many of the peninsula's high alpine areas as well as the lowland forested areas while preparing their official report on forest conditions in the Olympic Forest Reserve. Historian Harry M. Majors has started an in-depth study of their travels and surveys, which came too late in the decade of the 1890s to be included here. His or some other study will add this final piece later to the knowledge of Olympics exploration.

For those of us living in the twenty-first century, these accounts of trips into the Olympic Mountains, by those who were the first to go there in the nineteenth century, are a window into the thinking and attitudes of men who lived very different lives from those we live today. Their gift to us is that they wrote down what happened, providing us with a sharp sense of their time and place in the culture of the Pacific Northwest.

Here then is the primary source material from which history is written—the documents written at the time by those who were there when it happened.

12

PROLOGUE: FIRST STEPS—THE WATKINSON EXPEDITION 1878

Eleven years before the Press Party's north-south penetration of the Olympic Mountains, five young men from the logging camps of Hood Canal decided in September 1878 to cross over the mountains at their doorstep. This casual trip, well documented, very likely made this group the first to reach the ocean from the east and Hood Canal.

Several earlier claims, including one that Michael T. Simmons and Benjamin F. Shaw crossed the Olympic Mountains from Lake Cushman to Lake Quinault in the 1850s, have been discredited by historians. A report that Maj. John F. Sewell crossed from Port Townsend has never been accepted because he could have avoided the crossing by traveling along the northern edge of the peninsula. Most historians believe he did just that.

Following is a creditable report of the trip by the young loggers, however casually organized and carried out, that makes it a first in Olympics exploring history.

Robert L. Wood uncovered this report of the first east-west crossing of the Olympic Mountains, which includes portions of the diary of one of the participants, Melbourne Watkinson, by following a citation in Historic Resource Study for Olympic National Park by Gail E. H. Evans, on the unpublished work "Notes on the History and Resources of Washington Territory," volume 19, by Eldridge Morse (Hubert Howe Bancroft Library, University of California, Berkeley, n.d.). When Wood discovered the Morse volumes were available on microfilm at the University of Washington Library, he copied in Gregg shorthand the microfilmed handwritten material, from which in turn he transcribed this verbatim copy of the original. Bracketed notes in the text are Wood's. Wood's longer transcription notes are in footnotes.

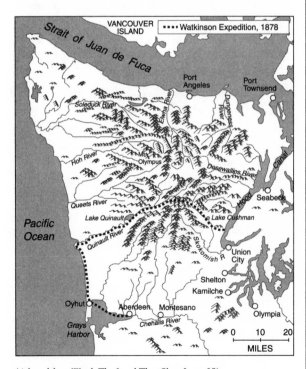

(*Adapted from Wood,* The Land That Slept Late, *25*)

NOTES ON THE HISTORY AND RESOURCES OF WASHINGTON TERRITORY[1]

By Eldridge Morse of Snohomish City, Snohomish County, Washington Territory

Book No. 19, Furnished H. H. Bancroft, of San Francisco, California

Account of the Only Trip Ever Made Over the Olympic Mountains. From Hood's Canal to the Ocean. Climate of Western Washington. Soil of the Sound.

Account of the <u>only</u> trip ever made by white men from Hood's Canal to the Ocean, over the top of the Olympic Mountains.

The Indians are not known to have ever crossed the wild Olympic Mountains, either from north to south, or from east to west, they always went around them. The accounts already given are of parties of white men, who simply penetrated into these mountains, and then returned.

Five young men on Hood's Canal, in Sept. 1878 determined to cross over their topmost points to the ocean. Some indications of gold found on the Canal, induced them to make this trip. None had any special knowledge of mineralogy or of gold mined; but all were experienced woodsmen, hardy, active, and used to outdoor life. The possible dangers of the trip, seemed to give it an additional attraction, and made them all the more eager to go.

The most active spirit in getting up the party was Melbourne Watkinson, whose father for many years had been sheriff of Mason county. His companions were Charles and Benjamin Armstrong, Geo. McLaughlin and Finley McRae.

13

[1] Unpublished manuscript, courtesy of the Bancroft Library, University of California, Berkeley.

Chas. Armstrong was a half breed Indian. He had worked for several years in the logging camps there. He was a very strong, active young man, well liked by his fellows. Each of these young men had had a similar experience in logging camps.

The party started from Sheriff Watkinson's residence on the Lilliwaup, on the west side of Hood's Canal Sept. 2, 1878. They went as far as Panther Creek and camped early at Burnt Bean Camp. This account is mainly drawn from Melbourne Watkinson's diary, kept by him while on the trip, with such additional information as was gathered from him at the time this was first written out.

It rained very hard on the first day. In the forenoon they killed two grouse, which went first rate for dinner.[2]

Sept. 3. Left camp at eight A.M. and arrived at Lake Cushman, or Skokomish Lake at 11 A.M. They caught some very fine trout at this lake for dinner, and at two P.M. started up the Skokomish river, traveling until six P.M. and killed three snipe and a pheasaint [sic], which they had for supper. Finley and Melbourne went a fishing and caught a fine string of fish for breakfast. On yesterday Melbourne fell and hurt his knee, which became very painful to day.

Sept. 4. Left camp at eight A.M., and waded up the river until eleven. The water was very cold. They found some very rough country and saw where the Indians had killed an elk. Stub (Chas. Armstrong) fired two shots at some ducks, but failed to kill any; stopped for dinner at 11 A.M., and then went across the river and found an old Indian trail, that had not been used recently, and went on this trail some four miles. They saw some beautiful waterfalls on the river, and camped at night on the upper forks of the Skykomish [sic] river. They killed no game to day; but start tomorrow up the mountain for the unknown country.

Sept. 5. They traveled west up a steep mountain;[3] the snow was on all sides of them; Watkinson killed two grouse; they saw fresh deer sign; got dinner by a snow bank, and had a great time snow-battling each other. All their way up the sides of the mountains, they found them covered with ripe blue huckleberries, and they eat these ripe berries as they passed along. At five o'clock in the evening they reached the top of a very high mountain. It was about as high as Mount Olympus and nearly due west of it.[4] Snow fields were all over its top. Wherever the ground was level on top of this mountain, the snow lay some 35 feet deep.[5] On the steeper places the rocks were bare, and all of them were covered with iron rust. Indications of iron ore were found on every hand. There appeared to be no regular range of mountains; each peak being separated from the rest. This high peak was on the divide between the waters which flowed to the eastward and to the westward. Two long spurs extended towards the west similar to those they had just came up from the east. The two western spurs seemed to extend some fifteen or twenty miles from the main mountain, with a river heading on this mountain, and flowing between them towards the Pacific Ocean. In looking backward from the summit of this mountain, Lake Cushman seemed also to be about fifteen miles distant from them, and can lie in a southeastern direction. The general course taken from this mountain to the ocean was a little south of west. Just before reaching the summit, the party had rare sport in killing an extra fine elk. He was seven feet four inches high from the top of its shoulders to the ground. He was three feet across his horns, which were three feet two inches long. This elk weighed not far from 800 pounds. The fat was three inches deep on his sides, and it took ten rifle shots to kill him; Watkinson firing five. Finley first saw the elk, and he cried to the boys; "Come here boys! Come quick! Here is a buffalo." They pitched their tents that night on the very spot where the elk fell dead, and they all feasted to their fill of this splendid meat. They first saw the elk in coming through a narrow pass, and in honor of Finley's discovery and to commemorate the name he gave the elk, they designated their camp for the night by the name of Buffalo Pass.

The scenery all around [several words obliterated in photocopying] was very grand. The snow lay in all directions, while the mountains were so steep and high as to make one dizzy to look at them. After supper they went a short way from their camp, and in looking down into a valley, they saw and counted sixteen fine elk. Having more meat than they could use, they did not disturb them. That evening they gave their boots and guns a great greasing with elk tallow, and filled Sheriff Watkinson's dog, who had accompanied them, thus far, so full of elk meat, that he snored all night.

Sept. 6. They made an early start; eating before starting all the elk meat possible, and taking some fifty pounds of it with them. They journeyed westward, over the divide, amid grand and beautiful mountain scenery, with snow all around, and little prairies scattered along their route. Through these prairies the elk had made their trails, the same as a herd of cattle. They saw two elk in the morning, and could easily have killed them, had they wished to do so. The dog fought

---

[2] Transcriber's note: Entries from Melbourne Watkinson's diary begin here.
[3] Transcriber's note: This was probably Six Ridge or possibly Seven Ridge.
[4] Transcriber's note: Obviously they were in error. They could not have been west of Olympus because they were about twenty miles southeast of it.
[5] Transcriber's note: This has to be a gross exaggeration, especially when one considers that they are reporting September conditions.

one of them. They passed the divide at 11 A.M. Here they could see Skokomish river running towards the southeast; while the unknown river before them, whose course they were about to follow towards the sea, ran to the westward. At 12 P.M., they started down the western slope toward the river bed, which appeared to be some four thousand feet below them. This was the roughest traveling, thus far experienced by them. They had to turn back three times, before they finally could make their decent [sic] to the river bed; which they reached at five P.M. The dog did not follow them. He remained on the mountain top. It was so rough, that he did not dare to travel after them. When they began their decent [sic], they helped him over some very rough places; but being accidentally separated from him, while going over some very steep places, he found it impossible to rejoin them. They supposed he would catch up with them; and they could hear him barking after they had reached the bottom. They saw no more of him on the trip, and knew not what had become of him, until after their return home, when the dog was there ready to welcome young Watkinson. When this dog found he could not follow his companions farther, he very sensibly made up his mind to go home again. He separated from them on the evening of the fourth day, and five days after, being on the ninth day from the time they started, the dog, all alone, reached home. These explorers, when they made their camp that evening, had no idea what stream they were on; but they were all determined to follow it, to its mouth. They saw plenty of fresh elk and bear sign. No fir timber was found near the head of this stream, but plenty of hemlock. Some of the hemlock trees were five feet in diameter. In going down this steep mountain, Finley lost his frying pan. It slid down the mountain side and he found it at the bottom. From this event, the trail was named, "Frying-pan Slide." They found great quantities of Salmon berries ripe along the route; Strawberries were in bloom and many flowers were to be seen. It seemed to them that spring had just come.

Sept. 7. They started down the river this morning and after going a short way, they came to a deep canyon, which was formed where the two western spurs from the main mountain come together. Here the river, which they had thus far followed, goes through a canyon, so narrow, that the mountain rose, almost perpendicularly, on each side of the river, for two thousand or more feet above its bed. They had to climb upwards of twenty-five hundred feet above the river's bed, to get around this point. The mountain sides were so icy and steep, that they found it to be the worst traveling thus far experienced. All around them, were to be seen the tracks of the avalanche. In places, they found the snow, packed in ravines, hundreds of feet in depth, and extending a half mile up the mountain side. It was two miles before they could get down to the river again. Finally, about four P.M., they struck a bear trail, and this helped them along first rate for a half a mile or more. At six P.M., they camped in a nice little valley. Above this deep canyon, in the basin between these two mountain spurs, the timber is all hemlock and spruce, while below it, is found cedar and fir. This cedar is of the finest quality.

Sunday, Sept. 8. They sleept [sic] poorly last night, as their bed was made at an angle of 45°, and they kept sliding down hill all night. Besides, the fire started in the moss and came near burning them out. Stub got up in the night and cut a tree down. This tree was on fire, and he was afraid it might burn down and fall on the camp. The rest were all asleep and were awakened by the falling of the tree, which startled them. They made a late start, and continued on their course down the river. At 10 A.M., they discovered a large branch coming into the river. Here, they first saw Indian sign west of the summit. There were plenty of fish in the river, but they did not bite. This day, they traveled about ten miles down a beautiful tract of fine bottom land. The bottom was about three miles wide, with a fertile soil. Two more branches of the river were seen, and indications of the Indians coming up to here, to fish, were noticed. The river was becoming too deep to ford. They saw what they supposed to be silver ore.

Sept. 9th. They had a good night's sleep, and were only disturbed by the howling of the wolves. There were many indications of very heavy freshets here. In some places, the bars are one quarter of a mile wide, with great drift piles on top of them. They crossed the river at 11 A.M. Stub and Watkinson each killed a deer. All were excited in crossing the river after the venison. Finley, while trying to ford the river, slipped and fell, and was washed some 50 yards down stream. He rolled over and over; some time he would be uppermost, and again his pack would be on top. He blowed like a porpoise, when out of danger. They had dinner where they killed the deer, and from thence they had good traveling down river that afternoon. At four P.M., they reached a beautiful lake. It appeared to be some twelve or fourteen miles long by five miles wide.[6] They found some Indians at the east side of this lake, who proved to be a portion of a large hunting party. From them, they learned that this lake was the Quinaielt river. These Indians were very much astonished at seeing white men here.

15

---

[6] Transcriber's note: This is another of the party's exaggerations, like their estimates of snow depth and elk height.

They were very sociable, and said it was only two days' journey to the coast; and that a white man, the Agent of the Quinaielt reservation, was up with the main party, hunting elk. (Compare this with Col. Woods account of the Lake). This lake, in length, stands nearly north and south; inclining a little from north east to south west. Its inlet, where the river flowed in, is near the center, on its eastern side. Its outlet is nearly due west, about six miles from its inlet, and across the lake, and near the center, north and south, on its western side.

Across the lake from their camp and a little north from the outlet is some fine prairie country, where the elk and deer are very plentiful. The Indians said that when the soldiers were stationed at Grey's Harbor or at Shoalwater Bay, they used to ride up from Grey's Harbor to hunt deer and elk. These Indians took this party to be soldiers also; they thought it very strange that anyone should come over the top of the mountains, and wished to know how many months it took to come over. A young Indian took Ben and Watkinson in his canoe, and paddled along the shore of the lake to see if he could see a bear. He said that his father was along the Shore of the lake packing in elk meat, and that he would be exceedingly glad to know who went there, and wanted them to fire their guns off, so his father would come in.

Sept. 10. The party stopped to day at the lake to hunt, fish, etc. Stub, Ben, and Watkinson each [several words obscured when photocopying] in a canoe. They discovered copper ore in a ledge on the lake shore. The Indians have some nice specimens of ores. One gave them a specimen of lead ore. The fish are very abundant in the lake. They can be seen jumping by the hundreds. There were several varieties of salmon, besides other fish. Geese and ducks were found around the lake in great numbers. Bear, also, come out in numbers on the shore of the lake to feed. That region may justly be called the Indians' happy hunting ground.

About four P.M., all of the Indian hunting party came in, headed down with meat. In that party were four bucks and three squaws. On their arrival, the Indians changed completely, in conduct, as well as the story they told. They demanded ten dollars a piece for taking white men to salt water. They scare them by saying that it would take fifteen days to walk there. It also appeared that the Agent had gone below two weeks before. All the white men were loggers, well used to river driving, and they offered the Indians only two dollars a piece to take them down. To show the Indians that they could get down without any help, they went to work and built a raft, then, they rolled small logs into the water, got on them and rode them. The Indians were astonished at this; as they could not stand on such small logs. They even examined the food of the white men, and said, it was

not enough to take them to the coast. But, when the Indians finally concluded that this party could take care of themselves, they became willing to take them all down in their canoes for the price first offered, two dollars each.

Sept. 11. Early in the morning, they all started together, in canoes across the lake, and down the river, except a few of the Indians, who awaited the return of one of the canoes, before they could go down. These canoes reached the river by nine A.M. This river is as large or larger than the Stillaguamish. Its banks are much more regular below the lake than above it. The bottoms are very wide and fertile from the lake down. In looking from the lake towards the Ocean, the low mountain spurs, which extend towards the west, on the north and south sides of the valley, appear to be some ten or twelve miles apart. About one half of the tract, enclosed by these mountain spurs, is, probably, alluvial bottom land; while the rest is <u>timber land</u>; so low, as not to be distinguished a short distance off, from bottom land. In Western Washington, where nearly all the country is very heavily timbered, the phrase "timbered land" is used to designate land covered with merchantable fir timber. Alluvial bottoms, although covered with a heavy growth of alder, spruce, cedar, maple, etc., are not usually spoken of as "timbered lands." These river bottoms, below the lake, appear to be subject to overflow, only in the high freshets of winter and spring. Some of the bottoms are, probably, rarely or never subject to overflow. The river is so very crooked that it is, probably, forty miles from the lake, by its channel, to salt water, while, in a straight line, it does not, in all probability exceed over one half that distance. At this time, the water was very low, and there were many dangerous riffles to shoot. There were seven persons in a small canoe, not over two inches, all round, on the canoe was out of water. It partially filled several times, and twice they had to haul it about one hundred yards. They stopped for dinner beside a large drift. At half past seven P.M. they camped for the night, after twelve hours ride in a canoe. That afternoon, they passed a number of ranches where the Indians were catching salmon. They also passed a number of burial grounds on the bluff. The dead were encased in big boxes, which were covered with all kinds of tinware, pots, kettles, etc. Enough of such articles were scattered around on these Memacluse [Memaloose?] Points to stock a common sized country store.

Sept. 12. While these explorers were getting breakfast, the Indians were away after a larger canoe, and having obtained it, the party started in this large canoe immediately after breakfast, and reached the Reservation at 11 A.M. A great band of Indians came out on the beach to receive them. All of them seemed pleased to receive these strangers from over the mountains, and they had a great Wason [?] over it. Some few of these Indians had visited Hood's Canal, going there by way of Olympia, but they could not understand how this party could have come from the Canal, over the top of the mountains, nor what their object could have been in coming. The Agency buildings are on a sandspit, which extends out into the ocean, at the mouth of the river. The Agent was away, gone to Montesano, but the employees likeably supplied these explorers with every thing they needed. On their arrival, the Indians had just bought a canoe 40 feet long, by seven feet beam. They purchased it for one hundred dollars from members of another tribe. The Indians catch a great many salmon after dark, at the edge of the breakwaters, near the mouth of the river, just where the fresh water spreads out. These salmon are considered inferior to the Columbia river kind. It is said that a Columbia river cannery has offered several thousand dollars for the privilege of fishing here, which the Indians have declined to accept. Finley bought from one of these Indians a thirty pound salmon for a half dollar.

Sept. 13. The party started on their return to the Canal. They walked down the ocean beach, toward Grey's Harbor, when the tide was out. This beach is smooth, hard and solid. It is one of the finest strips of ocean beach in the world. It is thirty miles from the Reservation to Grey's Harbor. They reached Grey's Harbor on the foremorning of the 14th, and crossed it in Indian canoes, and started up the Chehalis river the same day. They went as far as Montesano in canoes; from which place they walked to Union city, and reached it at 4 P.M., Sept. 19, 1878. They were eighteen days making the round trip. The incidents only are given of their trip across the top of the mountains. They received every courtesy that could be asked, while returning through the Chehalis country.

Part I: The Press Expedition 1889–90

None of the Olympics exploration efforts at the end of the nineteenth century captured the imagination of the public in the way that the Press Expedition did. After decades of speculation about what might lie beyond the peaks visible from Seattle, and at a time when exploration parties were beginning to push farther into the mountains, the Seattle Press offered to let everyone know what was out there. Wanting to be "the first," the Press Party felt the absolute necessity of beginning their trek in the dead of winter, a winter that turned out to be one of the worst on record. The public worried about them and speculated about what might have happened to them. Tensions rose as winter turned to spring and they had not yet been heard from.

There was nothing altruistic about the Seattle Press's involvement with the expedition. The quid pro quo for the proprietor of the newspaper was that the Seattle Press would scoop every other paper in presenting to the public a story of intense interest. The paper, in effect, bought the rights to the Olympics story by financing the expedition, hoping, of course, that the expedition would actually uncover the Olympics story. At the very least, the expedition would be creating a story about itself in the meantime. Not only that, but during the long period that the expedition was underway, the paper could hype the hiatus with occasional articles reminding readers that the big story was coming.

As it turned out, the story was so big that it ended up defining the Seattle Press itself. If it had not been for the expedition and the expedition report that followed, the Seattle Press would be no more remembered today than are its predecessor papers, the Call and the Chronicle. For a newspaper that existed for only five years, its decision to underwrite the cost of the expedition was a spectacularly good one, if measured by the place it earned for the paper in the history of the Pacific Northwest. Several names that ended up being permanently affixed to prominent features of the Olympics landscape came from the paper or from members of the expedition. Seattle Press owner William Bailey left his name for posterity on the Bailey Range, and Assistant Editor Edmond S. Meany had his name affixed to Mount Meany.

Chapters 1 through 4 comprise the complete, unedited text and accompanying graphics of the Press Expedition report as read by the readers of the Seattle Press on the afternoon of July 16, 1890. They had been waiting since the previous December for what was now in front of them. Unbeknownst to the Seattle Press staff at the time was that this would be the most important issue of the paper they would ever produce.

18

Seattle Press *staff, June 7, 1889. Assistant editor Edmond S. Meany is in the back row, second from left.*
Courtesy Manuscripts, Special Collections, University Archives, University of Washington Libraries, Seattle, UW18617.

"[F]irst group photograph of the Press Party, taken by a professional photographer [La Roche] in Seattle. In his journal entry for this day, Christie writes: 'Had photograph of party this afternoon. The artistic scenery made a very fine plate'" (Majors, vol. 2, 140). Left to right: John W. Sims and Daisy, Harris B. Runnalls, Charles A. Barnes, James H. Christie and Bud, John H. Crumback, Chris O. Hayes and Tweed.
Courtesy Manuscripts, Special Collections, University Archives, University of Washington Libraries, Seattle, La Roche 10018

CHAPTER ONE.
THE PRESS EXPEDITION UNFOLDS

SEMPLE'S STRIKING REPORT. [1]

Earthquakes Open Great Chasms in the Olympic Mountains.

The Convulsion of Nature Blocks up the Rivers and Kills Off the Innocent Inhabitants—He Adapts a Number of Indian Legends.

Hon. Eugene Semple, Governor of Washington territory, in his report forwarded to the secretary of the interior, for 1888,[2] has the following very striking description of a portion of the territory, which deserves to have a wider circulation than is given it in the public document that is filed away among the archives of a government department:

On the western side of Washington territory, facing the restless ocean and defying its angry waves with a rock-bound coast, stands the Olympic range of mountains. To the east of them is that magnificent spread of inland waters comprising Hood's Canal and Puget Sound, that has been called the Mediterranean of the Pacific.[3] These mountains, during nearly all the year, present a continuous array of snow-clad peaks for a hundred miles southward from the Straits of Juan de Fuca, which washes their northern end. They stand on the peninsula all in line, like soldiers up for inspection, while the mightier summits of Rainier and Baker, in the Cascade range, in Majestic isolation, appear in front, like officers of high rank reviewing the parade. The space between Hood's Canal and the ocean is almost entirely occupied by the Olympic range and its foothills. The mountains seem to rise from the edge of the water, on both sides, in steep ascent to the line of perpetual snow, as though nature had designed to shut up this spot for her safe retreat forever. Here she is entrenched behind frowning walls of basalt,[4] in front of which is Hood's Canal, deep, silent, dark, and eternal, constituting the moat. Down in its unfathomable waters lurks the giant squid, and

on its shores the cinnamon bear and the cougar wander in the solitude of the primeval forest. It is a land of mystery, awe-inspiring in its mighty constituents and wonder-making in its unknown expanse of canyon and ridge.

I can see these mountains from my window, and I often look at them. In the winter time they are lost to my sight, sometimes for weeks, behind the rain clouds, until I get homesick for them and sigh for them to bless my vision again. But I know that in the spring they will come forth bright and serene. One day they will look languid in the sunshine and the next they may present a savage aspect as they breast a raging storm, born of themselves. On the third, sunshine and cloud shadows may chase each other along their black sides alternately awakening hope and fear. When they are behind the leaden clouds one who loves them as I do will look in their direction and wish for the clouds to go away. When this occurs, as it often does, and the long line comes out in the clear, cold winter air, with its new-made coat of snow and its glint of freshness, and its undoubted purity, it seems like a realization of a dream of the resurrection; as if they had been in the grave and had come forth clad in the robes of innocence in obedience to a command of Jehovah.

When the air is clear they seem only a little way off. At the distance of 50 miles their angles are sharp cut and their forests are defined, almost tree by tree. If it is still you can imagine them to be the walls of paradise, enclosing scenes of bliss; but when awful clouds fly before the wind along their expanse, you can well believe that the homes of restless evil spirits are there. In autumn, when the air is filled with a delightful haziness, the mountains seem to have receded until their outlines are dim and uncertain. Everything is delightfully suggestive of rest and luxury. One can imagine that he has found the home of the Epicurean, and think that he can join Alciphron over there and sing and dream as long as he shall live. I have watched their shadowy outlines on a still,

---

[1] Territorial Governer Eugene Semple, *Seattle Press*, July 16, 1890.

[2] The *Seattle Press* published in its July 16, 1890, Olympic issue "The Olympic Mountains" section of Territorial Governor Semple's annual report for 1888 because of the profound impact it had on the thinking of the Press Party. Earlier, Chris Hayes had found the same piece in the August 1888 issue of *West Shore* (vol. 14, pp. 428–29). He showed it to Christie, which in turn resulted in Christie's contacting the *Press*. The Government Printing Office issued Semple's report as a pamphlet and as a part of the Report of the Secretary of the Interior, 50th Cong., 2nd sess., House Executive Document 1, serial 2638-1, vol. 3, pt. 5, pp. 925–27, "The Olympic Mountains."

[3] "The phrase 'Mediterranean of the Pacific' in reference to Puget Sound was first introduced in the article 'The Mediterranean of the Pacific,' in *Harper's New Monthly Magazine* (41 [September 1870]: pp. 481–98)." Harry M. Majors, ed., *Northwest Discovery* 2 (Feb. 1981): p. 94.

[4] "The region from the shore of Hood Canal west to Mount Constance and The Brothers consists of Crescent Basalt (Eocene), formed some 40 million years ago by the extrusion of a series of lava flows on the ocean floor by submarine volcanoes." Majors, ed., *Northwest Discovery* 2 (Feb. 1981): p. 94.

autumn night, and as the stars sank one by one behind the great western ridge, I could fancy they were fixed in the diadems of celestial beings, whose fleecy forms I could descry as they went down in groups, to sit at some feast or listen to the songs of the blessed.

Looking at the Olympic range from the eastern shore of Puget Sound[5] one can easily conceive how superstitious ideas could be fostered by them, in the minds of Indians and trappers who have to contend with the elements as well as with fanged and muscled beasts of prey that glare in their paths and menace their advance. Red men and white men have gone all around this section as bush men go all around a jungle in which a man eating tiger is concealed, but the interior is *incognito*. In tradition alone has man penetrated its fastness and trod the aisles of its continuous woods. Superstition lends its aid to the natural obstacles in preserving the integrity of this grand wilderness. The Indians have traditions in regard to happenings therein, ages ago, which were so terrible that the memory of them has endured until this day with a vividness that controls the actions of men. In those remote times, say the aborigines, an open valley existed on the Upper Wynoochee, above the canyon, in the heart of the Olympic range. This valley was wide and level, and the mountains hedged it in on every side. Its main extent was open land, matted with grass and sweet flowers, while the edge of the river and foot of the hills were fringed with deciduous trees.

This place was held sacred as a neutral ground by the tribes that hunted each other with murderous intent over every foot of the Northwest country. Here peace was enshrined and the warriors of the different tribes congregated once every year to engage in friendly rivalry in the games that were known to them, and to traffic with each other in such articles of commerce as they possessed. Coming from various directions at the appointed seasons, the bands of Indians threaded the mountain trails to the summits, gazed for a moment upon the entrancing scene below, then, throwing down their spears and dismissing the frowns from their brows, went forward with confidence and joy to repose upon the bosom of the valley. There they engaged in feats of strength and skill and in contests requiring courage and endurance akin to the Olympic games[6] of the ancient Greeks, with whom they may have been nearly contemporary.

No account exists of any violation of the neutrality, but

a great catastrophe occurred long, long ago during the continuance of one of their festivals, from which only a few of the assembled Indians escaped. According to the accounts of the Indians, the great Seatco, chief of all evil spirits, a giant who could trample whole war parties under his feet, and who could traverse the air, the water, and the land at will, whose stature was above the tallest fir trees, whose voice was louder than the roar of the ocean, and whose aspect was more terrible than that of the fiercest wild beast, who came and went upon the wings of the wind, who could tear up the forest by the roots, heap the rocks into mountains, and change the course of rivers with his breath, became offended at them and caused the earth and waters to swallow them up—all but a few who were spared that they might carry the story of his wrath to their tribes, and warn them that they were banished from the happy valley forever.

Doubtless an earthquake had opened chasms in the land and blocked the exits of the streams, thus spreading death among the peaceful delegations. Since then the river has again eroded a way through the rocks, and the upper valley of the Wynoochee has resumed its beauteous aspect, but the dreadful warning of the great Seatco has been passed from mouth to mouth of the uncounted generations, and the lake of the happy valley has not since reflected the image of an Indian. The white hunter and trapper not only acquires from the Indian his methods of taking game and his woodcraft, but also imbibes his superstitions, and he, too, has avoided the happy valley, so that the elk and deer roam there undisturbed to this day. The next person to stand upon the scene of the ancient convulsion will be the all-conquering "average man" of the Anglo-Saxon race, who will tear up the matted grass and the sweet flowers with his plow, and deprecate the proximity of the snow clad peaks because they threaten his crops with early frosts and harbor the coyote that tears his sheep.

The "Press" Explorations[7]

Today's edition of the *Press* presents, in addition to its regular complete telegraphic and local news-service, an elaborate illustrated account of the explorations made by the *Press* Olympic Mountain Expedition. The real, substantial purpose of the *Press* has at no time been lost sight of. The *Press* undertook to supply by actual investigation complete and de-

21

---

[5] "This phrase strongly suggests that Semple's description of his distant view of the Olympic Mountains applies to the vantage as seen from Seattle rather than from Olympia, most likely from his home or office in Seattle." Majors, ed., *Northwest Discovery* 2 (Feb. 1981): p. 94.
[6] "These so-called Indian 'Olympic Games' are almost certainly a fabrication, as no confirmation has been found concerning this in any of the Northwest historical or ethnologic literature." Majors, ed., *Northwest Discovery* 2 (Feb. 1981): p. 94.
[7] Edmond S. Meany, *Seattle Press*, July 16, 1890.

tailed facts about a vast area of the Northwest which, until now, was unknown to civilized and uncivilized man, and concerning which much curiosity has been excited by reports, chiefly fabulous, of the character of the country.

The party organized by the *Press* was made up of experienced and reputable men; it was thoroughly equipped in every respect for the work, and the *Press* unhesitatingly testifies to its entire confidence in the accuracy of the detailed report published today. There is no doubt whatever that this is the first time the country illustrated has ever been traversed by white men. Indeed, the reader will unhesitatingly believe that no party of men, less experienced in work of this kind and less elaborately equipped, could have conducted an expedition involving so great hardships and productive of so comprehensive results. The facts are detailed.

The path made by the *Press* explorers is indicated by indelible evidences that anyone can see and follow. There are no assumptions. No attempt, either directly or by ambiguity of expression, is made to mislead the reader into believing that more was done than was actually accomplished. The full page topographical map indicates the configuration of the country, the courses of the rivers and many minor streams, the location of the more important mountain peaks and the valleys, together with much other detailed information, so accurately and distinctly, that future expeditions that will be made will be enabled to escape many of the hardships incident to original investigations of the kind, and also, to devote themselves to a more thorough investigation of particular districts.

The main features of the country are now, for the first time, known. Illustrations drawn from photographs taken by the *Press* party of notable mountains and landmarks will be distinctly recognizable by everyone who traverses the explored country.

The public generally is informed that in addition to the illustrations which appear in this issue, the *Press* has in its possession nearly two hundred photographs, which are available to anyone who desires to inspect them, or who believes that they will aid him in contributing additional information to the public about a country that is now attracting general attention.

With pardonable pride the *Press* speaks of its presentation of this account. It is believed no handsomer paper was ever published on the Pacific coast. Certainly the illustrations have not been excelled by any newspaper.

To the Northwest Press

The *Press* today presents the results of its exploring expedition in the Olympic mountains to the public. The expedition had for its primary object, the wide dissemination of knowledge concerning a country about which nothing was positively known. The entire Northwest has an interest in the work accomplished by this journal and its exploring party.

The press of the Pacific coast is invited to still further aid in the mission undertaken by this paper by making copious extracts from the story of exploration presented, and by such comment as may appear appropriate.

The *Press* will appreciate the labors of independent explorers, who may turn in the direction of the Olympic mountains, and will be glad to add the product of their labors, with appropriate credit, to its own work, thus making the general result more complete and satisfactory.

THE OLYMPICS[8]

An Account of the Explorations Made by the Press Explorers.

A Topographical Map of the Region.

Many Illustrations From Photographs Taken by the Party.

Relation of the Explored Region to the State.

No Signs of White Men Ever Having Entered That District Before.

The "Press" Party Were Real Pathfinders.

They Put in Six Months of Toilsome Traveling Over Mountains of Snow and Ice.

A Good Trail Made for Future Explorers or Prospectors.

No Evidences of Human Life Were Found Except Some Very Old Indian Relics that Had Nearly Disappeared from Old Age—The Country Comprises One Mountain Range After Another With But Few Intervening Valleys—Many High Peaks Discovered as Well as Lakes, Rivers and Water Falls—Avalanches of Snow Portrayed and the Tracks of Snow Slides of Vast Proportions—

---

[8] This introduction to the narratives of expedition members Charles A. Barnes and James H. Christie was written by Edmond S. Meany, assistant editor of the *Seattle Press* (July 16, 1890).

Many Wild Adventures With Elk and by Grotesque Faces in Slate and Basalt—Two Big Geysers Heard—Mt. Seattle Ascended and Christened—Panoramic Views Taken from Its Summit—These Views of Surrounding Mountain Chains Reproduced—Rough Experiences in Camp and on the Trail—Loss of the Party Pack Animals—Shipwrecked on the Upper Quinaiult River—The Weary Homeward March—The Readers Will also Find Lieutenant O'Neil's Own Description of His Explorations in 1885—Also the Experiences of a Recent Expedition of Men Who Found the Trail and Marks of the "Press" Party—Minute Description of the "Press" Trail Through the Mountains for the Use of Future Travelers—Treatises on the Flora and Geology of the Mountains.

Following is a complete account of the exploration of the Olympic mountains made by the *Seattle Press* expedition. The account begins with the inception of the idea in an interview with Governor Ferry and ends with the return of the party after six months of hard climbing over snow covered mountains and through dangerous canyons. All details of the party's experiences are carefully recorded by Capt. Barnes, historian of the party, and Chief James H. Christie's journal gives a daily record of how the party moved and accomplished its work. The illustrations are zinc etchings from photographs taken by the party and the topographical map was made by Capt. Barnes from triangulations and field notes which were carefully preserved, even through the shipwreck on the Upper Quinaiult river. The map, photographs and trail made by the Press Party will be of invaluable service to all future travelers in that region.

The Party Organized

What Interested Chief Christie and Others in the Work

The *Press* exploring expedition was organized and fitted out by this paper for the purpose of exploring the hitherto unknown mountain region lying between Puget Sound and the Pacific ocean, and extending from the straits of Juan de Fuca to Lake Quiniault. All this region, with the exception of a narrow belt along the coast, which has been settled for years, has been a *terra incognita*.

This region was known to abound in large game, since the valleys putting up into the unknown region teemed with herds of elk, with cougars, bear and deer. Hunters have shipped in loads of elk horns and hides from the Quilayute region, and bear and cougar skins are common in all the huts at the mouth of that river. Some hunters claimed that the unexplored region consisted of rolling prairies on a huge plateau covering the whole area. Others asserted that bands of Indians claimed the land as their own and demanded tribute from all who desired to enter. One hunter who attempted to ascend the Qulayute was said to have been compelled to pay a tribute of tobacco and cloth to some Indians before he entered their domain.

One legend being handed down by the wise old Indians is to the effect that that region was once thickly peopled by a race of large, powerful Indians, who were adept as workers of iron and in carving, and who possessed fine horses and cattle. They prospered until a war called away the strong men, and in the severe winter that followed the bears and wild animals came down from the mountains and destroyed the camps, scattered the cattle and made desolate the homes of the red men. The plains were then deserted and the Indians now hold a superstitious dread of the whole district.

Lieut. O'Neil, in an interesting account[9] which appears elsewhere in these columns, gives a curious instance of these superstitions in his experience with the Indians. He says: "There is a legend among some Indians that a god, a bird of some kind, an eagle or a raven, makes his home in these mountains, and that it will inflict a terrible punishment on those who by entering them desecrates his home. When our copper colored friend [his guide] saw where we were and found out where he was going, neither big pay nor the fear of being shot—both were promised him—could detain him. He reluctantly camped with us, but during the night folded his tent and quietly stole away."

Ex-Governor Semple of the territory of Washington in his annual report for the year 1888—embodies some beautiful legends which are current regarding these unknown mountains.

Aside from such stories of hunters and legends of Indians there was nothing known of that large territory. The government charts contain but one of two elevations out of the

23

---

[9] "During July and August 1885, Second-Lieutenant Joseph Patrick O'Neil (1862–1938) led an army expedition into the high Olympic Mountains, from Port Angeles southward along Hurricane Ridge, and as far as the northwest side of Mount Anderson. Meany secured a copy of O'Neil's report, which was then included in the same newspaper issue as the Press Party narrative, as 'O'Niel's [sic] exploration' (*Seattle Press*, July 16, 1890)." Majors, ed., *Northwest Discovery* 2 (Feb. 1981): p. 104.

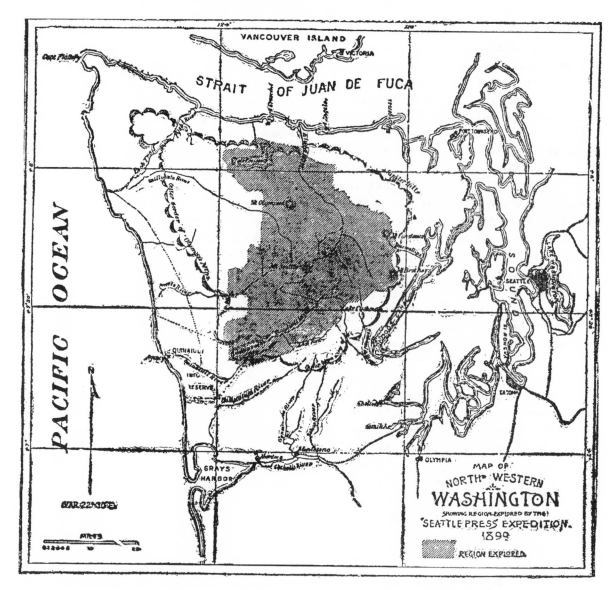

This map printed in the Seattle Press *on July 16, 1890, uses shading to show the area covered by the Press Expedition.*

whole range,[10] while there was absolutely no definite description of the kind of land, the possibility of minerals, stone or coal, the quantity and quality of timber found there or the feasibility of colonizing the region.

It was for the purpose of procuring accurate scientific information about all these things that the Press Expedition was organized. A short sketch of how the expedition came to be organized will prove interesting to readers of the *Press*.

In the course of a conversation with a reporter Governor Elisha P. Ferry expressed himself very forcibly about the advisability of having the area between the Olympic mountains and the Pacific ocean explored. The result of this talk with Governor Ferry was an item that appeared in the *Evening Press* of October 23, and was subsequently copied by newspapers in every part of the United States and especially in all the papers of the new state of Washington, the idea of exploring such an

---

[10] "The 'government charts' here referred to are most likely the two large maps published by the U.S. General Land Office, Territory of Washington (New York: 1887) and Territory of Washington (New York: 1889). On both these maps, only two elevation figures are presented for the entire Olympic Peninsula: 'Mt. Constance (7777)' and 'Mt. Olympus (8750).' The 7777 foot elevation value for Mount Constance (true altitude 7743 feet) was determined in 1855 by the U.S. Coast Survey, via distant triangulation from Hood Canal or Puget Sound." Majors, ed., *Northwest Discovery* 2 (Feb. 1981): p. 105.

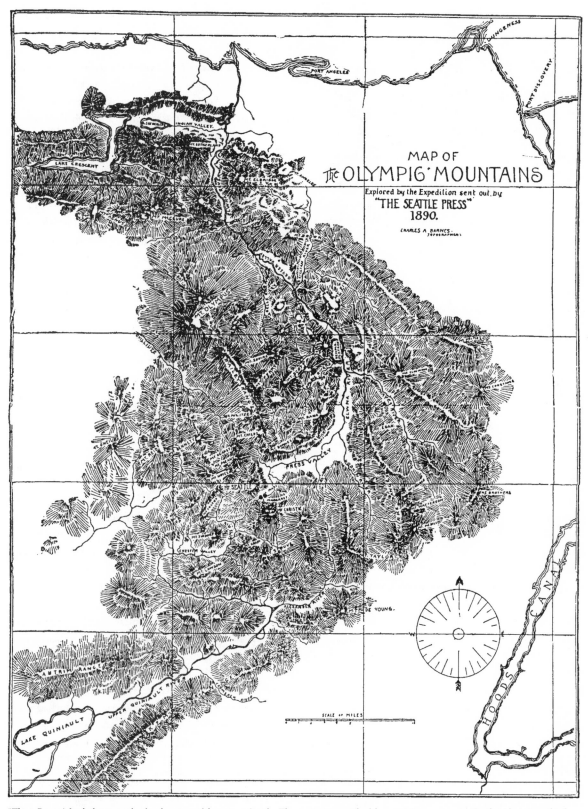

MAP OF
The OLYMPIC MOUNTAINS
Explored by the Expedition sent out by
"THE SEATTLE PRESS"
1890.

CHARLES A. BARNES.
TOPOGRAPHER

25

"This is Barnes' finished map, made after the return of the party to Seattle. The opening paragraph of the newspaper account specifies that 'the topographical map was made by Capt. Barnes from triangulations and field notes which were carefully preserved, even through the shipwreck on the Upper Quinault River.'" (Majors, vol. 2, 157)

This zinc engraving was published on the first page of the Seattle Press, *July 16, 1890. The limitations of the newspaper photo engraving process in the nineteenth century are evident when this illustration is compared to the actual photograph at the beginning of part 1.*

area of unknown lands within the confines of the commonwealth being especially forcible to them. The article which resulted from the talk with Governor Ferry and which finally led to the equipment of the Press Expedition was as follows:

A Chance for an Explorer[11]

A Section of Washington of 2500 Square Miles in the Olympic Mountains Which Has Never Been Trodden by the Foot of a White Man

Washington has her great unknown land like the interior of Africa. The country shut in by the Olympic mountains, which includes an area of about 2500 square miles, has never to the positive knowledge of old residents of the territory, been trodden by the foot of man, white or Indian. These mountains rise from the level country within 10 to 15 miles of the straits of San Juan de Fuca in the north, the Pacific ocean in the west, Hood's canal in the east and the basin of the Quinaiult lake in the south and, rising to a height of 6000 to 8000 feet, shut in a vast unexplored area. The Indians have never penetrated it, for their traditions say that it is inhabited by a very fierce tribe which none of the coast tribes dared molest. Though it is improbable that such a tribe could have existed in this mountain country without their presence becoming known to the white men, no man has ever ascertained that it did not exist. White men, too, have only vague accounts of any man having ever passed

through this country, for investigation of all the claims of travelers has invariably proved that they have only traversed its outer edges.

The most generally accepted theory in regard to this country is that it consists of great valleys stretching from the inward slopes of the mountains to a great central basin. This theory is supported by the fact that, although the country around has abundant rain, and clouds constantly hang over the mountain tops, all the streams flowing toward the four points on the compass are insignificant, and rise only on the outward slopes of the range, none appearing to drain the great area shut in by the mountains. This fact appears to support the theory that the streams flowing from the inner slopes of the mountains feed a great interior lake. But what drains this lake? It must have an outlet somewhere, and as all of the streams pouring from the mountains rise on their outward slopes, it must have a subterranean outlet into the ocean, the straits or the Sound. There are great discoveries in store for some of Washington's explorers.

A gentleman named Drew,[12] now residing at Olympia, states that he has climbed to the summit of the eastern range from Hood's canal, and looking down could see great valleys stretching toward the west. A party of railroad prospectors claim to have penetrated the interior, but could give no account of it, and appear only to have skirted the outer slopes 10 or 15 miles from Hood's canal. A party of United States soldiers is said to have traversed the country from Port Townsend, but no data is obtainable as to what they saw.

Numerous attempts have been made to organize exploring parties, but they have invariably fallen through, the courage of the projectors oozing out at the last moment. There is a fine opportunity for some of the hardy citizens of the Sound to acquire fame by unveiling the mystery which wraps the land encircled by the snow capped Olympic range.

Then started a steady stream of enquiries into this office. People wanted to join the party. They wanted to organize it. Some men had been all over the district mentioned, but when interviewed closely, they were willing to confess that they had not been in the immense district lying between the Quiniault and the Quilayute rivers and the Olympics and ocean. They had been along the edges, but not one had been over the summit of the mountains into the region named. Among the many letters and proposition was one that fi-

---

[11] This Elisha P. Ferry interview was probably conducted by and reported by Edmond S. Meany. It first appeared in the October 23, 1889, issue of the *Seattle Press* and was widely reprinted throughout the region; see the *Oregonian* [Portland], October 26, 1889, and *Public Opinion*, May 16, 1890. This article was considered so important to the expedition that the *Seattle Press* also ran it separately as a stand alone article in the July 16, 1890 issue. See also Majors, ed., *Northwest Discovery* 2 (Feb. 1981): pp. 88–89, 94.

[12] "This is likely Frederick Drew, who in 1888 was living at Olympia: *R. L. Polk & Co.'s Puget Sound Directory* 1888 (San Francisco: Polk, 1888), p. 214. Drew probably visited the mountainous region along the Skokomish River." Majors, ed., *Northwest Discovery* 2 (Feb. 1981): p. 94.

nally was acted upon. This proposition was made in the following letter:

To the Editor of the Seattle Press:

From your article upon the Olympics, I judge that we are both interested in the unveiling of the mystery which at present exists regarding the Olympic country. My interest, aroused by the fact that the mountains have not as yet been penetrated by white men and an ambition to accomplish what others may have failed in, backed by an inherent love of adventure, caused me to form the resolution to penetrate the depths of the unknown range. It is now my intention to act upon this resolution by entering the mountains this next month.

It is no ambitious, untried youth who now writes you, but a man tried in all the vicissitudes of mountain, forest and plain life, schooled in the great plain of the northwest territories during the Sioux and Nez Perces wars, having met with most of the reverses that fell to the lot of frontiersmen during the years between 1871 and 1878. Since then I have spent most of the time in the mountains prospecting for gain, exploring and hunting for pleasure. My explorations and hunting trips have varied from periods of one to three years beyond the limits of civilization, extending from the eastern boundary of the province of Quebec to the Hudson bay, and in the Northwest from the forty-ninth parallel to the Arctic circle, through the many ranges of Rocky mountains, from the chief mountains on the line to the unnamed mountains in the far north in the Peace, Laird and Mackenzie river districts on the eastern boundary of Alaska.

My object in thus writing you was to draw the attention of a few of the public men of the country to the object I had in view in thus seeking to open up this section of the country immediately adjacent to Seattle, and to ask them for their support in enabling us to push forward immediately a work that will benefit, pecuniarily, all parties that may be interested. I am sorry to say that the present state of my finances will not allow of our fitting out as fully or completely as we would wish to guarantee a possible lengthened stay in the mountains. This difficulty I am desirous of overcoming through the medium of your columns or of a few gentlemen who may be in any way interested in developing that country, publicly or privately, mill men, miners or others.

Why not let the *Press* give its countenance and support to an expedition for the clearing up of mystery lying at the very door of Seattle.

Respectfully,

J. H. Christie

North Yakima, November 6

It was promised that Mr. Christie and his comrades would be in Seattle about November 17, and they did so, arriving here during the last week of that month. All preliminary arrangements were hastily completed. Two more valuable members of the party, Dr. Runnalls and Capt. Barnes, were secured, and then the *Press* proceeded to equip the party with everything required to make a complete and careful exploration of the country and to provision the party for six months, and on December 8 the party left Seattle for Port Angeles, where all preparations were completed to ascend the mountains by way of the Elwha pass.

The reason for making the start in the winter was in order to be over the first ranges and into the central valleys ready for work when spring should open.[13] Nearly everyone expressing himself on the subject, however, said it was useless to undertake such a trip in the winter. They all predicted failure, and tried to dissuade the men from going. They did not know the mettle of the explorers. Those men had endured all kinds of tortures and hardships while fighting Indians and while traveling in the mountains, and some of them in the Arctic regions. They secured good snow shoes among their other stores, and as they started Chief Christie said: "If we can't reach a certain place of vantage today, we'll come as near as we can to it and then get there tomorrow."

That was the spirit which guided them. There was to be

27

---

[13] "This attempted justification for the mid-winter entry of the Press Party into the Olympic Mountains is not entirely convincing—especially when viewed in the light of certain contemporary events that Meany neglects to mention in his introduction. The true situation is that the Olympics were the focus of substantial publicity at this time, and at least two other expeditions had as their goal the exploration of the Olympic Mountains. The most important of these was the projected O'Neil expedition of 1890.

"In addition, a private party consisting of Charles Andrew Gilman (1833–1927) and his son Samuel C. Gilman, both of Minnesota, had already explored the East Fork Quinault River during October and November 1889. They would return again to the western Olympics in 1890 for further explorations—a partial report of which was published in the long established *Seattle Post-Intelligencer* for June 5, 1890 (a rival of the *Seattle Press*). Yet a third venture of 1890 was the party under Judge James Wickersham (1857–1939) of Tacoma, which visited the eastern Olympics in July 1890. In June 1889, prospectors J. L. Shelters and Dennis DeFord ascended the East Fork Quinault. And, in July 1889, the Olympic Mountains may have been entirely crossed by John Sherburn, Dan Andrews, and ____ Clark, via the North Fork Quinault and Elwha rivers. In 1890 several prospecting groups, such as the Olmstead-Conrad party and the Greenebaum party, also penetrated deep into the Olympic Mountains.

"Due to its widely-read article of October 23, 1889, the *Seattle Press* had been chiefly responsible for the wave of publicity concerning the unexplored Olympic Mountains; as a consequence, the *Seattle Press* may have had a proprietary outlook regarding Olympic exploration. Thus, a mid-winter expedition would have enabled the newspaper to get a jump on other projected Olympic expeditions, and consequently obtain a well-publicized 'scoop.'" Majors, ed., *Northwest Discovery* 2 (Feb. 1981): p. 106.

no rush to get through, and the work they were to do was to be done thoroughly. A short sketch of these men's lives will show where they have obtained the experience that has schooled them for such as undertaking:

The chief, James Hellbol Christie,[14] was born in Murrayshire, Scotland, in 1854. He was educated in the high school in Edinburg for a military life, but quitted the school before his term was finished, but he made this good by a subsequent service in Quebec in 1870. He was in the Canadian government's employ for six years, and served during the Reil rebellion.[15] He fought Indians, hunted and prospected "as far north as water will run," and a bare record of the thrilling incidents in his life would make a most wonderful story.

James H. Christie, Chief of the Party.

He returned last spring from a three years' trip to the Arctic region, taking in the Peace and McKenzie rivers and the Great Slave lakes. He is the best man in the Northwest to undertake an exploration requiring such skill and experience.

Capt. Charles Adams Barnes is the topographer of the party. He was born in the state of Illinois 1859, appointed cadet in the United States revenue marine in 1879, and commissioned a lieutenant in 1883. He was almost continuously on duty at sea from his entry into the service. He resigned from the service in 1887 to engage in business in California. He removed to Seattle about two years ago, where he is now engaged in several business

Charles A. Barnes

undertakings. He has explored the mountains and his experience in mountain life has specially fitted him for the work of this expedition. His topographical knowledge and practice obtained both at sea and ashore, fully qualify him for the special task of laying before the readers of the *Press* the first map of this interesting region.

Harry Boyle Runnalls, M.D., was the natural historian of the party. Owing to causes referred to in the proper place in the text he was unable to go through with the expedition, much to the regret of himself and of the *Press*.

John Henry Crumback was born in Ontario in 1856. He came west, and has been

John H. Crumback.

a cowboy, hunter, prospector and Indian fighter in the Northwest territory. He was in the Reil rebellion under Gen. T. B. Strange's party contingent from Calgary.

John William Sims was born in Essex, England, in 1861. In 1870 he joined the British army, in which he served for six years and 41 days. In 1881 he went to the Boer war in South Africa under Sir Evelyn Woods. In 1881 and 1882 he served under Sir Garnet Wolsey

John W. Sims.

[*i.e.*, Wolseley—Majors].[16] He came to America in 1866, and since that time has been hunting, trapping, prospecting and trading.

Christopher O'Connell Hayes is the youngest member of the party, being born in 1867. He is a great-grandson of the famous Irish patriot, Daniel O'Connell.[17] The last work he has been engaged in was riding on a cattle range in Yakima Valley.

All these men have endured hardship and privation

Christopher O'C. Hayes.

---

[14] "The *Seattle Press* incorrectly spells Christie's middle name as Hellbol. It should have been Halbold." Wood, *Across the Olympic Mountains*, p. 19.

[15] "The Riel insurrection, in which John Crumback also fought, takes its name from Louis Riel (1844–1885), a Canadian agitator of mixed French and Indian blood. There were actually two uprisings, the first (1870) taking place in the Red River valley in southern Manitoba, . . . The second Riel rebellion took place in 1885 on the North Fork Saskatchewan River. . . . Riel was captured, tried for treason, and executed on November 16, 1885." Majors, ed., *Northwest Discovery* 2 (Feb. 1981): p. 107.

[16] "The more famous Boer War of 1899–1902, in which the young Winston Churchill participated, was yet to come. This earlier Boer War of 1881, also known as the Transvaal Revolt, took place between the Boer colonists under Paul Kruger and British forces sent to suppress the fledgling but independent South African Republic." Majors, ed., *Northwest Discovery* 2 (Feb. 1981): p. 107.

[17] "Daniel O'Connell (1775–1847), one of Ireland's better known statesmen, received his training in France as a lawyer, and was elected to Parliament in 1828. . . . All four of O'Connell's sons were elected to Parliament." Majors, ed., *Northwest Discovery* 2 (Feb. 1981): p. 107.

28

at different times in their lives, and are hardy and rugged in their physical make up. They have abundance of grit and manly vim. The *Press* and the people of the country had reason to rest assured that these men would bring them a complete record of the unknown country within the Olympics.

"The Press Trail."[18]

It Can Be Used to Advantage by All Future Travelers

With the Following Explanation of Its Windings and Turns the Trail May Be Traced Out by Anyone—No Details Are Omitted—It Is the Path Made by the First Explorers in the Heart of the Olympics—The "Press" Trail Is One of the Most Important Parts of the Work Done by These Real Pathfinders.

For the benefit of settlers and prospectors, the following description of the trail made by the *Press* expedition will enable them to enter the mountains with little trouble. The trail is in general well blazed and defined in the lower Elwha to Lake Quinaiult.

The trail is blazed with the trademark of the expedition. It consists of three blazes, one above the other, thus:

Where time was an object, single blazes were occasionally made, but in general, and at all prominent points, the triple blaze was made clearly and distinctly.

Hundreds of logs were cut to make passage for the animals, and where necessary brush and undergrowth was removed. Many streams were bridged with trees.

From Port Angeles to McDonald's ranch one mile above the mouth of Indian creek, the trail is an old one, and consists of a wagon road as far as Meagher's ranch. From Meagher's ranch to McDonald's a well cut trail runs through the woods.

From McDonald's the trail follows the river through his bottom lands, skirts the lower slope of "McDonald's butte," passes through several small bottoms divided by small spurs, until it strikes into a long strip of bottom land, which constitutes Mr. Wariner Smith's claim. This part of the trail was cut and blazed in part by Mr. Smith, and improved by the *Press* expedition. His cabin is about two and one-half miles from McDonald's.

The trail extends onward one mile farther, to Dr. Lull's claim, upon which is a cabin in a clearing one hundred yards from the river.

This is the end of the old trail. From Dr. Lull's clearing the *Press* expedition found signs of an old Indian trail at intervals for three or four miles, but it was so closed up by time as to render the trail practically a new one. The *Press* blaze forms one unbroken line from here to Lake Quinaiult.

On the southern side of Dr. Lull's clearing the end of this line of blazes may be picked up. From there it runs diagonally away from the river, enters a section of low rolling hills one-half mile from the river, and two miles in length. So much trouble was here experienced in finding the lost route, that several blind trails will be found blazed off to one side or the other of the main trail, and some care must be taken to avoid them. A little care in following the trail at this place will be repaid on account of the dense underbrush, especially near the river. The trail then crosses a bottom half a mile wide to the lower slopes of Mount Eldridge, two hundred yards from where it forms a canyon at the river. Then it skirts the base to the river.

Devil's Backbone

An elk trail will here be observed leading up the Devil's Backbone, which is the name given to the western spur of Mount Eldridge. The trail around this spur ascends high above the river, is well blazed and is not difficult except at one or two places for pack animals. The expedition lost one of their mules here.

After crossing the "backbone" the trail keeps back a little from the river and runs for some distance across rolling hills, with dense underbrush, in which, however, the trail is cut out and blazed; two spurs from Mount Eldridge, in close succession, then forces the trail to the river's edge. The second spur is rather bad for pack animals but by unloading they can be gotten down the face of the rock without much trouble. This short descent of not more than twenty feet is really the only bad place on the trail.

The trail then enters bottom lands, crosses several sloughs or bayous, and keeps well out near the river's edge and avoids much underbrush and jungle. Three or four miles of this will bring the traveler to Goblin canyon. He will here find a good place to camp with plenty of dry wood and be the better prepared on the morrow for the climbing ahead of him.

The trail then crosses Wolf creek near its mouth and

29

---

immediately ascends the bluff. At 500 feet above the river our trail divides, one fork running along the top of the canyon bluff, the other running away from the river and upwards. The latter we made after exploration, and is beyond all comparison the better. The upper trail ascends the mountain side and avoids ravines, landslides and fallen timber.

Geyser Valley

This trail leads to a ledge of rock overlooking Geyser valley. We cut, by considerable labor, a zigzag trail from the ledge to the valley down the mountain side, which is very steep. It strikes the valley about one half mile from the lower end, opposite a large timbered island. Travel up the east bank of the river through the valley is bad, as the river washes the mountain side, forcing the trail up the side hill. We felled a tree across the river, just above the island. Found good travel without underbrush, and recrossed in the same manner a mile above. Dividing the valley into two parts at about the middle is a high bluff, up which the trail runs, and thence over rolling uplands covered with fallen logs of great size and a thicket of recent growth. We cut out so many logs here to let our own animal through that this once bad place is now in excellent condition for pack animals.[19] At the head of the valley the trail leads gradually down the side of Lillian river canyon by a carefully cut trail. At the bottom it crosses Lillian river, runs up the opposite bank several hundred yards and then commences the steep ascent on the south side of the canyon. All this is well blazed and earth cut out of the side hill and cannot possibly be missed.[20] Around the side of Mount Fitten the trail is equally distinct, and is as good as a wagon road. The climbing is heavy until the head of the great landslide is reached. Then it is an almost continuous descent for miles.

The Great Landslide

The first stream south of the slide is Kate creek, then comes a succession of ridges divided by deep ravines, which the trail crosses at right angles at some distance from the river. At about two miles above Kate creek the trail strikes straight down to the river bank, and follows a narrow shelf, not much wider at first than the trail itself, but which gradually wid-

ens into a broad bottom, half a mile in length. Beyond this the river is bordered by a bluff, which affords room, however, for a good trail between it and the water's edge, thereby enabling it to avoid the very rough and broken country above.

At length a rocky, impassable canyon is reached. From this point the trail, well blazed, climbs the bluff and gradually, to avoid ravines, runs quite a considerable distance from the river for a mile. Crossing a deep ravine there, it runs directly toward the river. Then turning upstream the trail passes over spurs and ravines, but is easily followed by the blazes.

The West Bank

Two miles below Semple plateau we found a good ford and crossed to the west bank, where the travel is better. The east bank becomes very rough a mile above this ford. Crossing the Elwha gives good travel to the very source of the river. From the ford our trail runs back a considerable distance from the river, but this was done to avoid the deep snow which covered the ground near the river. As the underbrush is not formidable in this valley, the traveler will do better to keep nearer the river than we did. A good trail can be found below and around the base of Semple plateau. Our trail crosses it however because it affords a shortcut to a good point at which to cross the Goldie river, just where it emerges from its canyon.

The route of the *Press* expedition was up the Goldie river, but this trail will be avoided by the future traveler. Press valley is the best of roads and extends to within a mile or two of the sources of the Quinaiult and the Quillayute rivers.

A few of our blazes will be found running up the valley several miles above Semple plateau. The underbrush in Semple valley is light, and after the plateau is left two miles behind the valley, is as level and open as possible.

The Road Forks

At the head of Press valley the traveler can choose between the Quinaiult and the Quillayute rivers. As shown on the map the river forks at the head of the valley, the stream coming in from the northward leads up a good practicable canyon and at once into the Quillayute watershed. The other fork leads toward the watershed of the Quinaiult. The trail follows this

30

---

[19] "A number of the original Press Party blazes have been found on trees in the area between Idaho Creek and the Lillian River. The Pratt party of prospectors crossed this old burn on August 6, 1890. George A. Pratt wrote that 'An old burn was traversed, the worst place for traveling I ever saw.'" Majors, ed., *Northwest Discovery* 5 (Aug. 1984): p. 274.

[20] "Five months later, in early September 1890, the Jones party of prospectors followed the Press Party route as far as the cache at Big Island Camp (camp 24). R. Jones describes the return trip northward from Big Island [see chapter 8, Other Explorations 1890]." Majors, ed., *Northwest Discovery* 5 (Sept. 1984): p. 306.

stream to Elizabeth falls, elsewhere described, and from there ascends to bluff which is 1700 feet in height. As our route led us into trouble and much hard climbing with life lines, it is suggested that a different route be tried.

A little beyond Elizabeth falls is the track of a great snow slide. This track seemed to us feasible, but we were prevented from following it by the great masses of snow which blocked it up at the time, but which will probably never occur again. At the worst, the climbing is not impossible.

The Divide

Having arrived at the top of the bluff, the travel for two or three miles southward is good. We crossed the two little lakes on the ice. Doubtless the travel is good on the banks. Below Lake Margaret, as soon as the river by its increasing size necessitates a choice of sides, take the eastern side regardless of marks or blazes. The snow was very deep when we passed this part of the canyon, the river being completely snowed under. For many miles down the river we made a few blazes. Keep the eastern side, gradually climbing the mountain side until the gap of Sims river is seen opposite. Then descend to a bottom which will be found here, and find good travel along the water's edge. At the lower end of the bottom land a perpendicular wall of rock obstructs progress. Our expedition crossed the river here by felling trees. If these trees are washed away, a good fording place will be found a few yards below the stumps. There is not much advantage in crossing, except for a short distance. We found travel on the west side so bad that the east can hardly be any worse. The occasional glimpses which we could gain of the east bank seemed to show better travel.

A Shortcut

A glance at the map will show a great bend in the river south of Chester valley. The gaps between the mountains in this bend appear easy to climb. This shortcut cannot possibly be worse than following the river, and will save several days of most fatiguing labor. Pack animals cannot travel on the west bank. The extremely steep mountain sides might be improved into a trail by much labor, but the rocky ravines are altogether impassable. The expedition had the greatest difficulty with them, having frequently to use life lines. If, however, the traveler prefers to follow the trail rather than the advice of the *Press* he will find it indicated by blazes on the west bank. On Mt. Zindorf it is quite high. It follows the length of Chester valley, occasionally touching the river. When it again

reaches the mountain it scrambles along the face of the naked rocks at the water's edge for some distance, and then climbs to a considerable altitude. Three or four miles before coming to Alexander river the expedition crossed the river on a tree—the river has now become too large to ford—and found a good elk trail and splendid travel to Alexander river. From Alexander river to Lake Quinaiult take the west bank if the traveler has any means of crossing. The sooner he crosses the better. If he cannot cross above he will find an opportunity of doing so at the double island, shown on the map, five miles below Alexander river. From the western end [of the] islands to the opposite shore, the expedition left a bridge which is probably still there. If not, the river can be forded at the upper end of the island. The expedition was informed by an Indian on the day of the shipwreck, that a good trail existed on the mountain sides north of the valley, from a point two miles below Crumback river and extending to the lake. The trail can probably be found on the spur which touches the river as shown on the map.

Lake Quinaiult

On the river, a few hundred yards above the lake is a settler, where the traveler can obtain the means to cross the river, and information regarding a pack trail which runs direct to Montesano or Aberdeen. If he has luck, Indians may be met with hereabouts, and canoe passage can be obtained to the Indian agency, whence a good road down the beach will be found.

From the mouth of the Elwha to the head of Press valley pack animals can be taken with ease. Between the head of Press valley and Alexander river the trail is impracticable for animals, either loaded or light. Between Alexander river and the lake, animals will go, but the trail will necessitate much clearing. The proper way to reach Alexander river is to ascend the Quinaiult river by canoe as far as the Indians can be persuaded to go.

A Suggestion

It is suggested by the *Press* that the easiest way to prospect the Olympics is to establish a cache of provisions at the head of Press valley, to which point pack animals can go. From this point as a base of supplies the prospector can reach any part of the mountains with ease.

The Olympic Geysers

The attention of explorers is especially called to the geysers described in the narrative. The first was heard in Geyser valley,[21] and is suspected of being in the canyon below the mouth of Lillian river.[22] The second was heard on the Quinaiult river between East fork, or Crumback river, and the lake. Who will find them?

General Description

Report on the Mountains, Valleys and Rivers of the Olympics

The Olympic mountains with their surrounding foothills, occupy the greater portion of the peninsula lying between Puget Sound and the Pacific Ocean. The Straits of Juan de Fuca separate it from the island of Vancouver on the north. Cape Flattery, the extreme northwestern point of this peninsula, is also the northwestern extremity of the United States.

A narrow belt of land, suitable for agriculture, skirts the coast, a belt which for its fertility and its wealth of timber is unsurpassed in the world.

One city and many small towns dot the coast, and many settlers are subduing the forest and bringing the land under the dominion of the plow. On the eastern side of this peninsula the shores of Puget Sound and Hoods canal constitute one continuous harbor. On the Straits of Fuca numerous harbors, Ports Townsend, Discovery, Angeles, Crescent and others, afford protection to vessels of the greatest draught. On the Pacific there is no haven north of Grays harbor. The larger rivers flow towards the north and west. None of the large streams flow toward and into Puget Sound. It is probably owing to this fact, the difficulty of access from the eastward, that the interior of the country has remained so long unexplored.

As viewed from the coast the Olympic mountains appear to lie in two ranges in form like the letter V, with the point or base toward the northeast. This, however, is only in appearance. Two ranges on the north lie parallel to the straits, but on the east, toward Puget Sound, the seemingly unbroken mountain range is in reality made up of the eastern ends of several ranges whose general direction is from northwest to southeast.

The backbone of the Olympics is Bailey range,[23] which together with Mounts Seattle and Christie have a general direction of north and south, and divide the watershed of the Elwha, which flows north, from the watersheds of the streams flowing south and west, the Quinaiult, the Quillayute and others. Mt. Olympus, the highest in this range, is also the highest in the Olympics. It has an altitude of 8550 feet, as near as could be ascertained by repeated observations. Mounts Seattle and Christie, which are practically a continuation of Bailey range, rise to an altitude of 7700 and 7450 feet, respectively.

Around this backbone as a center the other ranges which constitute the whole, lie with little regard to order. There seems to be something of the concentric in their general arrangement, but this is not very marked. The Burke range, a succession of lofty and precipitous peaks, divides the waters of the Elwha and its tributaries from the waters of the Skokomish. Holmes range, and the mountains which constitute the Sound range, separate the Elwha from the Dosewallips and other streams which flow toward the Sound. West of Bailey range the ranges, with the exception of that skirting the Straits, lie in a north and south direction, extending from the Quillayute river on the north, to what is supposed to the Queets river on the south.

It will be observed that none of the streams takes its rise from Mount Olympus, as has heretofore been supposed.

The apex of the Olympic roof is Mt. Seattle. Upon its sides or immediate vicinity rise the four principal rivers, the Elwha, the Quinaiult, the Queets and the Quillayute, which flow toward all points of the compass.

Lying along the streams are numerous valleys. Of those explored by the *Press* expedition the Quinaiult valley is the largest and most important. This valley begins at Alexander river and follows the Quinaiult river and lake in a southeasterly direction to the ocean. The upper valley above the lake, is 16 miles long, and from one to two miles in width, an area of about 15,000 acres of tillable bottom land. The soil is, in general, an alluvial loam, rich with decaying vegetable matter. Occasional sandy spots were observed, especially near the lake. The vegetation is very prolific. Besides the dense growth of large conifers, there is a great scattering growth of maple and alder of large size. A dense underbrush covers all the ground, consisting of salmon berry, raspberry and other similar bushes. The land is rather difficult to clear. The river is navigable by canoes as far as Alexander river. There are no

32

---

[21] "On some maps it appears as Geyser Basin." Robert L. Wood, *Across the Olympic Mountains: The Press Expedition of 1889–90* (Seattle: The Mountaineers Books, 1976), p. 112.

[22] "Between the confluence of the north and east forks of the Quinault and the lake, near their journey's end the men again heard the sounds of a 'geyser.'" Wood, *Across the Olympic Mountains*, p. 112.

[23] "The Press Expedition cannot actually be said to have 'discovered' the Bailey Range, for Lieutenant O'Neil discerned it from a distance on his exploration of the northern Olympics in 1885. The members of the Press Party were the first, however, to view it close up and actually to traverse some of its spurs." Wood, *Across the Olympic Mountains*, p. 203.

formidable rapids. The only dangers to navigation are the drift piles, but these are easily removed. The direction of the valley is such that it enjoys plenty of sun. The bounding mountain ranges although high, are not so near or steep as to shut out the sunlight in the morning.

Crumback river, or East fork, appears to be fairly navigable for canoes and to possess good bottoms for some little distance up. Alexander river is not navigable, and its several mouths are obstructed by timber. Several claims are located along the river near the head of the lake, of which, however, but two are bona-fide. Nine-tenths of the land above the river is still unclaimed by settlers.

Between the lake and the mountains, to the north and south, there are about 8000 acres of level, fertile land overgrown with heavy timber and underbrush, in all respects like that up the river.

We were told that all the land about the lake was taken up, but that only one claim is bona-fide. The lake shores therefore offer a most inviting spot to those who desire a home and who have the grit to clear the land. On the southern shore we were told that a town site was laid out but that there was not yet any clearing.

Below the lake the valley widens out and appears to contain upwards of about 50,000 acres of tillable land. For a description the reader is referred to the general narrative of the expedition. From Alexander valley to the ocean there are, therefore, 70,000 acres awaiting the settlers. For six or seven miles above Alexander river there are small fertile bottoms, varying from 10 to 50 acres in extent. Chester valley is five miles in width, and contains over 3000 acres of good land. The soil is rich. There is less underbrush but more fallen timber than in Quinault valley below. About one hundred acres of good land lies at the junction of Sims river with the Quinaiult.

The largest valley on the Elwha is Press valley. It is thirty miles long and from one to three miles in width, and contains about 14,000 acres. The lower and upper ends of the valley are respectively 1800 and 2500 feet above sea level. The timber is large and heavy. The ground is cumbered with neither underbrush or windfalls to any great extent. The soil is excellent. The surface is level at the upper end. At the lower end it is slightly rolling. Three miles above Semple plateau is a hundred acre piece of alder bottom. Smaller alder bottoms are frequent. The remainder of this valley is almost equally good. The timber is fir, spruce and hemlock. Very little cedar was observed.

North of the mouth of Hayes river, upon the mountain side, are several benches containing each several hundred acres of level land, with fair quality of soil and not heavily timbered. The southern slopes of Mt. Fitten are also tillable, the timber is, however, heavy, but the underbrush is light. Both Hayes and Godkin rivers contain good bottom land, but small in extent.

Geyser valley is fully described elsewhere. It contains about 2500 acres. A charming place for a tourists' hotel is facing Goblin gates in a miniature valley of 30 or 40 acres.

On Deer range are several excellent level benches with good soil. From Goblin canyon down the Elwha are many small bottoms, in which claims may be had containing 100 acres or more.

The course of the Quillayute in its headwaters is through a deep canyon. Its character, between the portion shown on the map and the settlements at its mouth, is unknown.

It will be observed that the headwaters of what is supposed to be the Queets river, lies through a large valley. From the summit of Mount Seattle this valley is seen to extend ten or twelve miles in a southwesterly direction, before the view is intercepted by Mount Frazier. It is from one to two miles in width. The photograph of this valley from Mount Seattle is one of the most beautiful in the *Press* collection. The valley is heavily timbered and lies well open to the sun.

These mountains and all the land described here, lying upon the Elwha river above Indian valley, and the entire Quinaiult watershed to the ocean, is unsurveyed. Title can therefore be obtained only by holding the land by the right of being a squatter until it is surveyed. It is expected that the survey of the more valuable portions will not be long delayed by the government.

Besides the two little lakes upon the height of the land, Lakes Mary and Margaret, three large lakes of importance to the state are shown on the map, two of which are for the first time correctly placed upon the map.

Lake Quinault is shown upon the maps issued by the United States land office as extending nearly north and south, with the outlet on the western side. It was found by the *Press* expedition to extend nearly at right angles to the direction given, and to have its outlet at about the middle of the southern side. It is between six and seven miles long, and two miles wide, having an area of about 12 square miles.

The Nomenclature

A List of the Names Given and in Whose Honor Named

Mount Agnus, after Gen. Felix Agnus, of the *Baltimore American.*

33

Alexander river, after Mr. Alexander Christie, of Edinburgh, Scotland.

Antrim range, after Mr. Frederick S. Antrim of Aberdeen, Washington.

Bailey range, after Mr. William E. Bailey of Seattle, Proprietor of the *Seattle Press.*

Mount Barnes, after Capt. Charles A. Barnes, of the *Press* expedition.

Mount Bennett, after Mr. James Gordon Bennett, of the *New York Herald.*

Mount Brown, after Mr. Amos Brown, of Seattle, Washington

Burke range, after Judge Thomas Burke, of Seattle.

Chester valley.

Mount Childs, after Mr. George Washington Childs, proprietor of the *Philadelphia Ledger.*

Mount Christie, after Mr. James H. Christie, chief of the *Press* expedition.

Crumback river, after John Crumback, of the *Press* expedition.

Mount Dana, after Mr. Charles A. Dana, editor and proprietor of the *New York Sun.*

Mount DeYoung, after Mr. M.H. DeYoung, editor and proprietor of the *San Francisco Chronicle.*

Mount Egan, after John G. Egan, city editor of the *Seattle Press.*

Mount Eldridge, after Mr. William C. Eldridge of Washington, D.C.

Elwha river, an Indian name signifying elk.

Mount Ferry, after Hon. E.P. Ferry, governor of Washington.

Mount Fitten, after Mr. DuBose Fitten of Seattle.

Mount Frazier, after Mr. S.R. Frazier, editor of the *Seattle Press.*

Mount Grady, after the late Henry Grady, editor of the *Atlanta Constitution.*

Geyser valley.

Godkin river, after Mr. E. L. Godkin, editor of the *New York Post.*

Mount Goodwin, after Judge C.C. Goodwin, of the *Salt Lake Tribune.*

Mount Holmes, after Mr. John H. Holmes, editor of the *Boston Herald.*

Hayes river, after C.O'C. Hayes of the *Press* expedition.

Mount Hearst, after W.R. Hearst, proprietor of the *San Francisco Examiner.*

Mount Hunt, after Mr. Leigh S.J. Hunt, proprietor of the *Seattle Post-Intelligencer.*

Mount Jones, after Mr. George F. Jones, editor of the *New York Times.*

Kemp range, after Mr. Alfred C.G. Kemp, of Montesano, Washington.

Mount Lawson, after Victor F. Lawson, editor of the *Chicago News.*

Mount McClure, after Col. A.K. McClure, of the *Philadelphia Times.*

Mount McCullough, after J.B. McCullough, of the *St. Louis Globe-Democrat.*

Mount Meany, after Edmond S. Meany, of the *Seattle Press.*

Mount Medill, after Joseph Medill, of the *Chicago Tribune.*

Mount Noyes, after Crosby S. Noyes, of the *Washington (D.C.) Star.*

Mount O'Neil, after Lieut. Joseph P. O'Neil, U.S.A.

Mount Pulitzer, after Joseph Pulitzer, proprietor of the *New York World.*

Mount Reid, after Whitelaw Reid, editor and proprietor of the *New York Tribune.*

Mount Seattle, in honor of the city of Seattle; altitude 7,700 feet.

Sims river, after John W. Sims of the *Press* expedition.

Mount Scott, after James W. Scott, of the *Chicago Herald.*

Mount Struve, after Judge H.G. Struve, of Seattle.

Mount Squire, after Senator Watson C. Squire, of the state of Washington.

Mount Taylor, after Col. Charles Taylor, of the *Boston Globe.*

Mount Watterson, after Henry Watterson, of the *Louisville Courier-Journal.*

Mount Zindorf.

34

CHAPTER TWO.
CAPTAIN BARNES'S NARRATIVE[1]

IT IS DIVIDED FOR CONVENIENCE INTO THREE PARTS

Following is the narrative by Capt. Charles A. Barnes, historian of the party. For convenience of the readers the narrative is divided into the following three parts:

Part One—From Seattle to Geyser Valley
Part Two—From Geyser Valley to the Water Shed.
Part Three—From the Water Shed to Lake Quinaiult.

Part One

The party starts from Seattle for Port Angeles—By boat up the Elwha River—Experiments With Sledges—Packing Through Heavy Snow—Cutting a Trail Through Fallen Timber—Snowbound In the Mountains—First Glimpse of Mount Olympus—A Field Day for Game In Camp—An Exploration of Goblin Canyon—Return for the Mules—Jennie Lost Over the Devil's Backbone—Arrival at Geyser Valley.

The *Press* exploring expedition left Seattle for Port Angeles by steamer on December 7, 1889. It was thoroughly equipped with everything necessary for making a complete exploration of the Olympic mountains. Game was depended upon as the principal means of subsistence, but flour, bacon, beans, coffee and other provisions were supplied to subsist the party until it should reach the game country, and afterwards to supplement the game supply. These provisions amounted to about 1500 pounds.[2] Winchester rifles, plenty of ammunition, a tent, canvas sheets, blankets, fishing tackle, axes, a whip saw for cutting out logs, a few carpenter tools, the necessary tools for mineral prospecting,[3] rope, snowshoes, a small but well selected assortment of cooking and other utensils, comprised a part of the general outfit.

All necessary instruments for topographical surveying and scientific observation, a camera with films for 250 exposures were provided. Fifty pounds of colored fire were taken along for the purpose of illuminating, if possible, some peak visible from Seattle.[4] No expense was spared in fitting out the expedition with everything that could contribute to its convenience or its chances of success.

By those who claimed knowledge, the difficulties in the path of the explorer were represented as being so great, the obstructions so varied in character, and failure foretold as being so certain, that many useless things were provided in order that every possible contingency might be met.

Mr. Christie's sole instructions were, "Succeed."

[1] Charles A. Barnes, *Seattle Press*, July 16, 1890. Assistant editor of the *Seattle Press* Edmond S. Meany was actively involved in preparing the *Press's* report of the expedition, as was Barnes. Certainly Meany, and probably Barnes as well, had a hand in editing both Barnes's and Christie's journals for publication.

[2] For a listing and analysis of these supplies, provisions, and equipment, see the Appendix to the Press Expedition Report (excerpted from *Northwest Discovery*) at the end of part 1. "Since the amount of food initially brought along amounted to about 100 days of full rations, this indicates that the Press Party set out with the expectation of spending a minimum of three months in the Olympic Mountains." Majors, ed., *Northwest Discovery* 2 (Feb. 1981): p. 126.

[3] "The fact that the Press Party carried 'the necessary tools for mineral prospecting,' and that they frequently prospected or panned for gold and silver during the expedition, suggests that the sponsor of the party, William E. Bailey, was interested in the potential mineral deposits of the Olympic Mountains. It is entirely possible that the men of the Press Party had instructions to stake claims to any promising mineral deposits they might find during the course of the expedition, with the understanding that these claims would then become the property of Bailey, who, in effect, was grubstaking the expedition out of his own pocket." Majors, ed., *Northwest Discovery* 2 (Feb. 1981): p. 126.

[4] "This 'fifty pounds of colored fire' became just another piece of useless baggage that had to be packed from camp to camp. It no doubt became an object of imprecation among the men who had to pack it, for they derisively referred to it as 'the hellfire.' One of the plans hatched in Seattle was that, on a pre-designated day during the expedition, the men would ascend a peak, light a huge bonfire at night, and then toss in the fifty pounds of 'colored fire'—hoping that the resulting pyrotechnics would be visible in Seattle.

"As things turned out, while crossing the Devils Backbone by the Elwha River on March 9, the mule (Jenny) carrying 150 pounds of flour and the 50 pounds of 'colored fire' slipped and fell 100 feet to her death. Christie and Sims descended to the lifeless pack animal and retrieved the precious flour. As for the 50 pounds of 'hellfire,' this was unceremoniously cut loose and, with the assistance of a good kick, it plunged 300 feet more straight down to the turbulent waters of the Elwha River.

"Meany alerted the people of Seattle to watch for the fire, in a now vanished issue of the newspaper (Edmond S. Meany, 'Watch For The Signals,' *Seattle Press*, December 20, 1889). (No copies of the *Seattle Press* have survived from October 1889 to July 1890.) However, as Meany later recalled, 'part of the program of that expedition was the sending of signals from the highest peaks. At the Seattle end, on the agreed night, I climbed to Seattle's highest building, the old University [near the present Olympic Hotel], and, with the fine telescope loaned by Arthur A. Denny, kept watch all night. There were no signals' (Meany, 'The Olympics in History and Legend,' *The Mountaineer Annual 1913*, vol. 6: 51–55, *cit* p. 52)."

"The chemicals that comprised the 'colored fire' likely included the chlorides, sulphates, and/or carbonates of copper (blue, green), potassium (violet), barium (yellow-green), lithium (red), strontium (red), and sodium (yellow)." Majors, ed., *Northwest Discovery* 2 (Feb. 1981): pp. 126–27.

On account of representations made to us at Port Angeles it was determined to build a boat on the Elwha, about four miles above its mouth, and to ascend as far as practicable in that manner.

The outfit was hauled from Port Angeles by wagon to the terminus of the county road, a distance of about five miles. Mr. Philip Meagher of Port Angeles tendered the use of his unoccupied farmhouse at this point to the party while preparing for advance. A vegetable garden, a cow, a wood pile, a farm well stocked with hay for the mules attest the hospitality of this gentleman and the comfort of his guests.

Cutting Out a Trail

The ranch was admirably situated for the purposes of the expedition. From it a trail leads through the woods nearly to the river, and over this trail the expedition had to pass, packing its outfit. The trail was rough and circuitous, over hills, gulches and canyons. Great trees lay across it so that for pack animals it was impassable, and even for a man it was little better than no trail at all. From the trail to the nearest point the river is distant about three-quarters of a mile, and across this interval a trail had to be cut through dense underbrush and fallen timber. Repairing and clearing the old trail and making the new one occupied a week, and for the most part it was ax work.

Sudden Rise in Horse Flesh

Great difficulty was met with in getting suitable pack animals, every person in the country round about having available animals, imagining that they had the expedition in a tight place, raised the price of their beasts several hundred per cent. For the meanest cayuse, that was worth at an honest valuation $25, $60, or $70 would be asked, and good animals were held in proportion. Even the Indians were posted and wanted fabulous prices for some broken down quadrupeds.

It was at last determined to try the country up the coast, back of Dungeness. We heard that about 12 miles south of Dungeness, in the foothills, lived one William Fogle, who had two mules to sell, and that at an Indian village near by some kind of animals might possibly be obtained. Mr. Fogel was found to be a worthy and hospitable man, got a fair price for his mules, and the *Press* two useful additions to its exploring staff. They arrived safely in camp after a hotly contested drive of two days, and were warmly welcomed by the whole party.

Meanwhile the trail was finished, and Thursday morning, December 19, the packing began. The mules—Jennie and Dollie—after several shrewd kicks, delivered with accuracy and precision from practice born of experience, and several unex-

pected attempts to bite, submitted to be "cinched up" to the tune of 250 pounds each, Mr. Christie, a veteran and connoisseur in these matters, reeving the diamond hitch with most artistic grace. Each man seized his 60 pounds, the dogs bounded ahead and moving camp to the river had begun.

In a Swamp

In half a mile was reached a swamp, upon which had been bestowed a world of pains in trying to make it passable for the mules. Brush, bark, rotten wood, everything that came handy had been tumbled into the trail, and there was some hope that the mules could get through it. But a dozen steps demonstrated the futility of the hope, and soon the wretched mules were floundering about in the bottomless morass. Packs were unloaded, and after much tugging, pulling and prying the mules were pulled out and reloaded. Several yards and in they went once more and unpacking had to be gone over again. Another trail with a lighter load produced similar results, this time the mules adding plaintive protests to the general tumult. Jennie in mud to the tail, beans, pork, snowshoes, frying pans, tobacco, and other bric-a-brac scattered about in profusion, joined her voice to Dollie, who, in her attempt to jump a log, got only half way, and hung there between wind and water, filling the air with lamentations. Christie and Barnes, their custodians, hatless and coatless, mud to their thighs, were struggling about, tugging at bridles, slacking cinches and calling for assistance temporal, and, it has since been affirmed about camp, spiritual. The splashing and plunging, the shouting and braying of man and beast was a spectacle for men and philosophers. The others of the party, who had got some distance ahead, hearing the outcry, came back. The animals were extricated, the bric-a-brac fished out, the mules recinched, and the caravan once more proceeded. But the swamp was attempted no more with the animals. Everything was packed on the backs of the human members of the party from the ranch through the swamp, and the mules packed there. It is extraordinary how the sure-footed animals will get over a trail like this one. When they come to a fallen tree three or even four feet through the brutes will rear and lift over it themselves, 250-pound pack and all, as lightly as a deer. But there is risk of their straining their backs and thus depriving us of their services, so we generally lightened them of their load, or which is better and involving no more work, where we passed over a trail so often, cut the log out.

One virtue of the mule must be noted, they will live and grow fat upon anything that grows in these woods. Greenstuff—to wit, ferns and cedar boughs—are devoured

36

by them with a great appetite. Grapevines twigs, and, in short, everything that can be chewed, furnishes them with sustenance. The only hay they ate for two weeks was what we packed through the swamp from the ranch, and that was necessarily very little. Oregon grape also furnished them with excellent feed.

A canyon about 200 feet in depth, with precipitous sides, tried their mettle. The trail cuts down one side and up the other in a zig-zag fashion. Soaked with water and with cut feet it became so slippery with mud that a man had to walk carefully to avoid sliding off. The mules passed it each time safely but it required much care on the part of both man and beast.

Canyon Camp Is Reached

The evening of December 23 saw all our outfit packed to Canyon camp, the name with which we christened our new camp. There remained only the lumber for the new boat, and this had been packed over the swamp. But that night it began to snow and by daybreak next morning there was a foot of snow on the ground. The storm continued all the next day and the night following, and while it continued we had all we could do to keep our camp from being snowed under. But Christmas morning broke cold and clear. We started out early with axes and mules, expecting to find the trail blocked by timber, brought down by the weight of snow. We were not disappointed, but the greater part of the trees across the trail were small trees, eight inches and under in diameter. Breaking the trail was laboriously performed.

By noon we commenced dragging the lumber for the boat, and by 4 o'clock we had it all—some 600 feet of lumber, for the most part 32 feet boards—at the gulch, both men and animals working hard. In dragging it along the crooked and tortuous trail, the lumber was sometimes bent like the letter "S." The first day both pack saddles were broken, rendering the animals useless, so that from the gulch we had to drag it all ourselves. The lumber, when it finally arrived in camp on the evening of the second day, was as smooth as if planed and the edges worn round. But for the snow we could never have transported it in so short a time.

Our pack-saddles we made while at the ranch, and are the ordinary Rocky mountain pack-saddles, consisting of two cross-trees of maple, shaped like the letter "X." They are easy on the mule and are very strong and serviceable.

Great Trees Falling Around Camp

Canyon camp was situated on a little bench on the precipitous banks of the Elwha, about 100 feet above the river. It was a wretched place to camp, but we had to camp as near as possible to the only good place on which to build our boat. There was a flat sand bank below. The distance over which to carry water, the scarcity of seasoned timber for camp fire, involved much extra work. During the night of December 23 we could hear great trees falling all around us, and one tree, a spruce, fell so near the camp as to be uncomfortable. So the next morning we went to work to get rid of another monster fir tree, six feet through at the base, which over hung the camp in a threatening manner. It struck another great tree in its fall, and for a few moments the whole forest seemed to be going down like a lot of ten pins. When the crash ended and the snow settled enough to see the result, we found four lying about the camp, one of them so close to the tent as to bury the side ropes, but gave us magnificent back-logs, and we sawed up much of the remainder and kept a monster fire going day and night.

The place selected for building the boat was the low bench of sand at the foot of a bluff immediately below the camp. There was a piece of ugly rapids at the point of launching, but this inconvenience could not be avoided, as suitable level banks are few on the Elwha.

Building the Boat

The boat was 30 feet in length, 5 feet beam, 2 feet in depth; flat bottomed, rounding up gradually at the bow and stern. Her sides were built with an out fall of six inches—that is, she was one foot wider at the tip or gunwale than the bottom or floor. She was decked forward and aft to afford a footing for the bowman and steersman. A "covering-board," 10 inches in width, extending along the side and connecting both decks, gave footing to the polemen. The hold or stowage space for cargo, occupied the entire portion between these decks and the sides—about twenty feet long by five wide. Strips of 2x4 scantling and sawed knees, constituted the framework of the little vessel, upon which was bolted the planking of inch cedar. We added a capstan for heaving her over heavy rapids, and a 50-fathom tow line. Good spruce poles and an 18-foot steering oar comprised her furniture.

The snow, which covered the ground to the depth of about a foot, was first removed. Each piece of lumber had first to be thawed out before being put into its place. The green lumber, from its long exposure on the trail, was sodden with water, and frozen hard and stiff. Cutting and packing in fuel, tending the fire and turning the lumber, required the services of two to three men. The weather was so cold that the thawing process was slow work, and after hours of cooking, and a plank became limber, it would freeze again before we could get it on the boat. The proper curvature was given them at the stem and stern by heaving them in with a lever arrangement.

Our stores furnished us with oakum and pitch for caulking her. The former we spun the evening before using. We caulked her as well as the wet and unseasoned condition of the wood permitted, but we awaited the result after launching with great anxiety, which the sequel well justified. We were four days building—four days of frosty fingers and frozen wood—constantly interrupted by flurries of snow.

The Launch

On December 31 she was ready for the launch. After the last touch, all hands clapped on, and she slid easily over the ways into the boiling water of the rapids, and was steered into the smooth water below by means of a line handled from shore. As she struck the water she was christened the "Gertie." No burst of music or libations of wine celebrated the launch of the "Gertie" but for all that it was considered about camp as being the most successful launch ever made, and we proceeded to make it as successful as the resources of the camp would permit. Pea soup, boiled ham, baked beans, corn bread and prune pie garnished the board, the roaring fire battled with the falling snow, and in deep potations of Java best, the "Gertie" entered upon her career.

Breaking Camp

This duty performed, the signal for breaking camp was given. In a moment all was bustle. The tent was struck, bags and boxes swung over the cliff by ropes, and Gertie was freighted with her cargo. But alas! as her upper seams came below water she began to take in water like a thirsty fish. But it was evident that with recaulking Gertie was a success. If she had no paint on her sides, at least she floated her cargo like a duck. It was determined to haul her out and give her green boards a thorough drying and try her again. We would drive oakum into her until her sides ached, and boil tar till the government interfered to save its timber, but Gertie must be tight.

Recaulking the Boat

The place selected for hauling out and recaulking the boat was a little bench about 10 feet above the river. To reach it we found it was necessary to haul the boat over a low bank of gravel 150 feet, then over a narrow arm of the river strewn with boulders, and up this bank to her resting place. The ground was covered with snow to a depth of four feet, bright, sparkling, glorious to look at, but to work in quite the re-

verse. We first made a passage through it by shoveling and trampling a lane about 12 feet wide. We cleared the little bench of a thick growth of young alder and maple that was upon it, and laid skids or ways 30 feet in length across the little water course and up the bank to the bench. This being done we laid hold of the Gertie and by hard work we got the ice-weighted little vessel out of the water and as far as the skids. All this consumed January 4th. The weather was still cold and frosty. The following day we rigged up a contrivance known to seamen as a Spanish windlass, and by its aid hove Gertie over the skids to her berth on the bench above. We turned her over and built fires under her and, in order to keep off the falling snow, with which we had constantly to battle, as well as the avalanches which descended from the overhanging firs, spread awning over her fore and aft. We moved camp to the riverside adjoining her, and for several days and nights we kept her hot. The ice dropped away, the sap stewed out. By day we cut and packed in wood, by night and day we smoked her by the watch. Through the long hours of the night the heavy masses of foliage above swing gently in the firelight. The heaps of snow around us, reaching up the great bluff on one side and sloping gradually away on the other to the river below, were lighted up by the ruddy glow. The swift-flowing flood of dark water and the towering wall of darker foliage beyond, bounded the circle of light, at the center of which was a poor *Press* explorer stoking fires, his eyes full of smoke, filling himself ever and anon with coffee—with the Gertie meanwhile getting as light as a cork.

The Gertie Once More Afloat

The boat was once more caulked and pitched, and once more launched. This time she behaved in a manner worthy of her name, and, we may say, creditable to her builders.

For the events of the next few days there are here given a few extracts from the journal of your correspondent.[5]

Extracts From a Diary.

Monday, January 13, 1890, weather clear and cold. After an early breakfast, commenced preparations for ascending the river, making portage of entire outfit from camp and cache to a point above first rapids. At 11 A.M. all was ready for this start, towline ran along left bank. Mr. Christie took the bow pole, assigned me to the steering oar and the other boys to the towline on the shore. She went over the rapids "like a Dutchman on a holiday," as Jack said. She made a pretty tough drag, empty too. Above the rapids we reloaded her

38

---

[5] "This sentence is obviously an editorial insertion, by Barnes or Meany." Majors, ed., *Northwest Discovery* 2 (Mar. 1981): p. 185.

and had dinner, after which we started again. From there to the camping place of this evening, about one mile, the river winds about a bluff with deep water on one side, and on the other alternately a gentle sloping shore of great boulders hidden beneath the deep snow. The fall of the river is great and the current swift, with rocks churning the water to foam; and in another place deep and swift like a mill race. The tow rope was manned on our side of the river, and the other alternately where foothold could best be secured.

During the afternoon Mr. Christie, stepping off the deck, took an involuntary header. He reported that the water was cold. All hands were nearly or quite as badly off, for every boot being leaky, the first step in the water filled them full. The boys on the rope are in over the tops about half the time, however, so it does not matter so much, a leak or two. Near the end of the day's trip the boat swung on a rock by the force of the current, and Mr. Christie and I had to jump overboard to save her. At 3 P.M. we hauled along shore to make camp, all hands suffering. Started fire under the lee of a great pile of drift timber. Cleared away snow and got a fire going, many of the logs joining in the conflagration. Night clear and cold, and the boys are rolling themselves in their blankets under the blue vault of heaven.

The Distance Honestly Won

Tuesday, January 14.—Cloudy and slightly warmer. Another good day. We have made today not more than a quarter of a mile, but every foot was worked for and honestly won. We have passed two series of heavy rapids, and cut out a big log lying across the stream. This log lay partly under water, and though only two feet through, took us an hour and a half to clear it away, making two cuts. The second series of rapids passed was quite difficult, the water being white for 150 yards and full of boulders. We made portage of the cargo. The snow is our greatest difficulty, as we are not able to get good foothold on account of it. Between the boulders, which are altogether covered, a man will frequently sink out of sight. We

had today a short but swift and difficult fall of rapids to drag through. We made three attempts to get over by towing, but the snow furnished such poor foothold that it was found impracticable to get her over that way. Finally the doctor was sent ahead to take a turn about a tree with the tow line while the rest of us plunged to our belts into the water filled with floating ice and snow, and gradually, foot by foot, we dragged her over. It was terribly cold. The air registered 16 degrees when we looked at the thermometer after it was over.

As we managed to get out of the freezing water the air changed our garments to ice in a moment. At one time we thought Crumback was going to faint, and all of us were of a livid blue for some time after it was over, until we got circulation started again. The sensation of having feet and legs as ours were is a very peculiar one. They were utterly devoid of sensation; so much so that we could scarcely preserve our balance to stand upright. We might have stuck a pin an inch into our legs without feeling it.

Over the Rapids

But we got Gertie over the rapids just the same and made her fast at the place for hauling her out the next day. What made her so hard to handle was the ice which she carried and the deep snow on the banks of the river. It was 4 o'clock when we had finished, and, after we had recovered a bit, supper was over and the boys were gathered about the glowing fire, all care was laid aside, and many was the joke that passed and pitiable was the state of the man who could not find something to laugh about in the day's adventures.[6] It seems marvelous that some one, if not all, were not crippled for life with rheumatism, or laid up with some of the afflictions guaranteed by works on hygiene and common sense. Not a man suffered from so much as a common cold, and with the exception of passing cramps in the legs, not one has suffered any of the consequences of this rashness.[7] Made camp tonight on terrace 15 feet above the river left bank at foot of second rapids.

39

---

[6] "This comment by Barnes, at the end of the most difficult and trying day thus far experienced, indicates that the sociologic crux of the expedition had been passed. After a month of close association under adverse conditions and within a hostile environment, the six men of the Press Party had psychologically adjusted to their environment and to each other, and they had become a compatibly functioning unit." Majors, ed., *Northwest Discovery* 2 (Mar. 1981): p. 185.

[7] "Today's entry displays the extraordinary physiological adaptation and stamina of the men of the Press Party. They had spent an entire winter's day plowing through snow, sometimes head deep, and wading up to their waists in a river 'filled with floating ice and snow,' with the air temperature at 16° Fahrenheit—sixteen degrees below freezing. The minute they stepped out of the water (which was 32–33°F.), their clothes instantly froze solid. Yet, no one suffered from frostbite, and none of the men succumbed to hypothermia. . . . Several factors probably contributed to their survival in so hostile an environment. First, they were young men in the prime of their lives, and likely in superb physical condition. Second, they almost certainly were wearing wool clothing, which provides a degree of warmth and insulation, even when wet. Third, in performing such heavy work today as cutting logs, thrashing through the snow, and having to haul a heavy boat, a considerable amount of thermal energy for their bodies was being generated in effect, for no matter how many degrees below freezing the ambient air temperature was, the moving fluid water of the river would always remain at slightly above 32°F. before it would undergo a phase change to the solid state. Since their clothes were already wet, it was 'warmer' to be wading in the Elwha River than to be standing on shore in those same wet clothes." Majors, ed., *Northwest Discovery* 2 (Mar. 1981): p. 185.

Another Day of Rapids and Wet Clothes

Wednesday, Jan. 15.—Cold and clear in morning, snow in afternoon and evening. A day of rapids and wet clothes. At 10 o'clock we stretched our tow-line and started over the rapids next following —between which and that of yesterday afternoon intervened smooth water for about 200 yards. With the windlass we succeeded in getting half way up with one half cargo, when the Gertie swung on a rock; her stern catching the water, she filled and lay with her after parts below water, which was swirling and boiling all around. It was all hands overboard in water to the waist, and cold. By much exertion we saved her entire cargo and passed it ashore, safe but wet—all our sugar, coffee, flour, tea, somewhat the worse for a quarter of an hour under water. When lightened we hove her stern up with the windlass, bailed her clear of water and completed the passage of the rapids. Then we made portage of the cargo around the rapids, 200 yards, loaded the boat and poled up stream as far as we could make headway in that manner. Made camp tonight behind a pile of driftwood, and a comfortable supper of pork and beans—those dear old standbys—made us forget the miseries of the day. Oh, for a day's hunt and some fresh meat. We will soon be among the elk and deer.

Entertained by a Lonely Settler

Thursday, January 16.—Clear and cold; warmer in the afternoon.[8] The whole forenoon was spent in drying cargo and camp outfit, which were soaked with water yesterday. The boys appreciated the occasion of rest, on account of the poor sleep of the night. We have sore bones this morning. After shoveling and melting out the snow last night for a bed place, the floor was found to be boulders the size of a man's head. No boughs available. Blankets made thin mattresses—hence, sore bones. While resting up we put in our time making portage of the cargo from the next rapids. These rapids are shoal, otherwise not formidable. We had much work forcing the boat over the stones in the river bed. At the head of the rapids a great, seven-foot tree lay across the stream, but this we were fortunately able to squeeze under, and we took in the cargo just above it. About 200 yards above the log we nearly had another shipwreck. The boat swung around in the strong current, striking a rock broadside. We recovered ourselves purely by the grit of Crumback, who managed to hold on to the towline after it had thrown everybody else off.

Dr. Runnalls was dragged over the rocks about 15 feet, bruising him badly. Half a mile further on we were hailed from shore by a settler, Lutz by name. His invitation to lodge with him was accepted, and we packed our camp utensils up the steep bluff to his cabin, 300 feet above the river. In his comfortable log cabin we are taking turns at his rocking chair and tasting the luxury of potatoes, and are about to roll ourselves up in our blankets on the floor of the first house we have slept in for six weeks.

A Day of Tiresome Wading

Friday, January 17.—Snow during night and morning, turning to rain in the afternoon. At 11 A.M. we loaded the boat and again started up stream. We cut away a fallen tree from the channel and made several hundred yards in smooth but swift running water, which required heavy hauling. A quarter of a mile up stream we passed heavy rapids. We tried the boat first with half cargo, but midway up became unable to force her further, but running her into the opposite shore, lightened her entirely and then got over with comparative ease. The portage this time was very laborious, being nearly all wading for 200 yards over round, smooth, slippery stones. These rapids have a fall of ten feet in a distance of 100 yards. Gertie is behaving well now, is comparatively water tight and has stood many severe strains without injury.

Above these rapids the river broadens to about 200 feet and breaks into shallow rapids, tumbling down among loose boulders, so that a man can wade across with ease. We hauled in immediately below them and discharged cargo on the left bank. It was almost dark and all of us wet to the waist and exhausted. Made camp and a good fire on a shelf 60 feet above.

The Settlers' Bridge Preserved

Saturday, January 18.—Clear and cold. All hands felt well this morning, resulting from a good night's sleep. Starting early. Began by clearing a channel among the boulders in the rapids. Made it about 15 inches deep and seven feet wide. Hauled boat through by wading and portaged cargo. This took most of the day. Again we manned the towline and at about 4 o'clock we arrived at the mouth of Indian creek,[9] through swift water and several minor rapids, encountering much sludge ice. Just above the mouth of the creek for a distance of 100 feet, are rapids having the character of a cataract, rather than of rapids. Above them another hundred feet

40

---

[8] "Barnes' weather entries are among the earliest meteorological observations made in the Olympic Mountains." Majors, ed., *Northwest Discovery* 2 (Mar. 1981): p. 185.

[9] "Today U.S. Highway 101 crosses the Elwha just above this point. It is impossible to explore the area below Indian Creek, where the struggles with the boat occurred, for it now lies beneath the waters of Lake Aldwell, a power reservoir." Wood, *Across the Olympic Mountains*, p. 50.

of quiet water frozen over, and then a jam of logs. This jam is used by the settlers in Indian valley as a means of crossing the river, so Mr. Christie decided to avail himself of the fact to obtain assistance from the settlers sufficient to carry the boat over and avoid the immense labor of cutting it. Word was sent up the valley therefore to those nearest requesting them to be on hand at noon on Monday to help us make the portage. In the meantime we unloaded Gertie below the rapids and hauled her up empty with labor and difficulty through the rapids and made her fast above them. Then we made camp. Evening cold and chilly, and at dark commenced snowing. We are sitting very close to the fire.

Slow But Steady Progress

The journal of the trips during the next few days is nearly a repetition of the foregoing. Considerable snow fell and progress up the river was slow. On Monday, January 20, we had five settlers and two Indians to assist us in crossing the jam of logs. The jam is six or seven feet out of the water. We placed inclined skids on each side, and with a good pull the 13 men hauled her over without difficulty. We had the visitors to dinner with us, and in the afternoon we made portage of the cargo. For the next three days we spent much time in the bone-chilling water, making progress slowly but steadily upward.

On the evening of the 23rd we arrived at McDonald's clearing, which is the outpost of civilization as well as the head of practicable navigation with a boat on the Elwha. As this was the last day with Gertie, as well as a memorable one for the hardships undergone, the journal for that day is here given entire:[10]

Last Day With the Boat

Thursday, January 23.—Cold and cloudy. At 11 A.M. loaded boat and shoved her into the current; towline taut. As she swung out from shore it was to begin our most severe experience with her. The rapids here are not heavy but so shoal and strewn with boulders, and the channel for the most part

so far from shore, that we were soon compelled to relinquish the use of the towline and to resort to wading. We were in the water continually for two hours, at one time to our armpits. As we would emerge from the water in the more shallow places our clothes would freeze in the air. We suffered terribly, and when we got to McDonald's and tied up to his landing place a sick-looking lot we were. But half an hour put all that right again. Hot coffee and blankets and a roaring fire in the old Scotchman's fireplace made us feel as though cold water had never been.

From McDonald's to Expedition Valley[11]

From January 24 to February 4 the expedition was detained at McDonald's by stormy weather. On the night of January 24 snow began to fall, and for three days it continued falling heavily and without cessation. At times the flakes, as large as an after-dinner coffee cup, filled the air so that it was scarcely possible to see 10 yards from the window. Meanwhile the air was so mild and warm that the depth of snow increased but little, and on the 27th there was barely five feet upon the ground. On the 27th the snow turned into rain, and all hands cheered themselves with the notion of a night frost, hard snow and good travel. But the night frost did not come until we had been at McDonald's for nearly two weeks. Intermittent rain, or a flurry of snow with a thawing temperature, kept the snow so soft and rotten that it was impossible to transport the outfit and supplies of the expedition.

The extraordinary depth of snow would prevent the use of the mules upon the next stage, and to take their place we built sledges and travvis. The idea was that if the snow should go away we could use the mules; if it formed a crust the sledges would be useful; if it remained soft then, as a last resort, we had snow shoes and could pack.[12]

Experiments With Sledging

Every man built his own vehicle after the fashion which suited him best. Mr. Christie decided upon a sledge as his means of

41

---

[10] "Not only does this sentence indicate the presence of an editorial hand, it also implies that not all portions of Barnes' original field journal were actually published in the newspaper narrative." Majors, ed., *Northwest Discovery* 2 (Mar. 1981): p. 187.

[11] "This is the only occasion on which the term Expedition Valley appears in the narratives. It most likely is not a true Press Party name, but one that originated with the editor (probably Meany) who supplied this headline." Majors, ed., *Northwest Discovery* 2 (Mar. 1981): p. 196.

[12] "The sleds, intended for hauling supplies on, were to be the third folly of the Press Party (after their winter departure, and the ill-advised boat venture). Sleds may have functioned well in such regions as Christie was familiar with as the Canadian interior plains, where persistent below-freezing temperatures would permit a snow pack suitable for this means of transportation. However, the mushy, barely freezing snow of lowland western Washington, combined with the frequent periods of rain and the unpacked nature of the early snowfall, rendered the use of sleds impractical both in this region as well as at this time of year. Christie belatedly became aware of this situation, for he wrote that 'judging from the weather of the past few months and the rotten state of the snow, I have little faith in anything beyond the pack rope.' In other words, the best means of packing was still a man with a backpack on snowshoes. However, the construction of the sleds maintained the interest of the men during their days of confinement, and thus buoyed up their morale. Christie may have been aware of this, for he noted that 'Cooped up in rather close quarters the party feels much like caged bears.'" Majors, ed., *Northwest Discovery* 2 (Mar. 1981): p. 197.

transport. Procuring from a neighboring slough two good pieces of vine maple he formed the runners three inches broad, bent upward at each end. The deck and stanchions he made of cedar. The sledge when completed was five feet and twenty inches wide, and had a tongue by which to drag it.

My vehicle was a travvis. A travvis[13] is somewhat like a wheelbarrow on runners and is very simple in construction. The runners are bent into the form of a bow. A stout stick is lashed in place of the cord. The runners being placed side by side a suitable distance apart, the deck is built upon the cordsticks. The runners extend forward four or five feet and form shafts, between which a man takes his place. Such fiery speed was expected of this product that it was christened the "go-devil." Mr. Christie named his the "Carry-all," a tribute to its supposed strength and capacity. Sims and Comstock settled upon a travvis which they might manage jointly. It was large and strong and received the name of "the go-cart."

A Sort of Snow Buggy

Lastly,[14] the "buggy," a nondescript contrivance, was built by Hayes. Light and airy, seemingly constructed from pleasure rather than for heavy hauling it deserved its name. More like a travvis than a sledge—more like a toboggan than a travvis, it defied all attempts at classification, and must be regarded as a new invention, too fearful for description.

The go-devil as it was expected to act.

"Probably February 4, 1890" (Majors, vol. 2, 141)

At last on Tuesday, February 4, the early morning found a thin crust on the snow. There had been heavy frost during the night, the air had cleared, and as the sun rose over the eastern tree tops and painted the old man's cabin a rosy hue, the expedition was astir.

Christie's Double-Ended Carry-All

Sims and Comstock pooling issues first came out. The "go-cart," their nondescript vehicle was warranted to carry 300 pounds. Next came Mr. Christie with his "carry-all." This double-ended product of human ingenuity was expected to surpass all estimates of its strength and endurance. Then came the "go-devil," light, airy and graceful. Lastly Hayes, who after many experiments and alterations exhibited to an astonished camp his completed "buggy."[15]

The train halted at the cache to load up. Three hundred pounds went aboard the "go-cart." Crumback seized the traces. Sims behind prepared to hold her back lest she should go too fast. A start was made. By using a stout sapling for a crowbar they got her several feet. Her load was reduced to 100 pounds, and by dint of great pulling and hard pushing the "go-cart" made a quarter of a mile. When last seen Sims was jumping with both feet up and down upon the wreck of the ill-fated "go cart" and Crumback was calling for an ax wherewith effectually to end its short but troubled career.

Forerunner of Many an Upset

Meanwhile Mr. Christie tossed upon the "carryall," bag after bag of flour and beans. A hand-pull and all but 100 pounds of this burden came off and she forged ahead. Two lengths and the "carryall" turned over on her side. This was the forerunner of many upsets, until finally at a distance of one half mile from the cache she went to join the angels. Her bones lie by the trailside, and the night wind mourns her untimely end.

Holding Back the Go-Devil

When these disasters were occurring your correspondent had loaded the Go-devil with 150 pounds, and with this he expected to have to hold him back by force. He soon found, however, that a 50 pound sack could be hauled easier than 150 and he lightened the load accordingly. He also found

---

[13] Travois.

[14] "Before he departed to visit his sick wife, Dr. Runnalls selected a travois as his vehicle, but it is not clear whether he completed it before leaving, or in fact, ever started its actual construction. Although he had been expected to return about February 4, he did not rejoin the expedition and the diaries are henceforth silent concerning his activities." Wood, *Across the Olympic Mountains*, p. 60.

[15] "Barnes' comment that both Christie and Hayes built separate sleds is in direct contradiction to Christie's own statement 'Chris Hayes and myself joining in for a light sleigh.' Perhaps Hayes and Christie initially worked on a sled together, and then Hayes later decided to build a sled on his own." Majors, ed., *Northwest Discovery* 2 (Mar. 1981): p. 198.

The go-devil as it really was.

"Probably February 4, 1890" (Majors, vol. 2, 141)

that the stern rope for easing the Go-devil down hill was superfluous, and might better have been employed as a tow rope with a good span of mules ahead. However, with the reduced load, the Go-devil managed to get half a mile.[16]

Going Back to Snow Shoes

The "buggy" still remains by the cache. It is its glory that it did not fail—it never started. Hayes, like a prudent man, profited by our experience and packed his load on his back. The fact was that the snow was too soft. The thin crust of the night had proved a delusion. The light crust disappeared before the sun was two hours high. The runners sank into the soft slush to the deck. There was nothing for it but to pack. With snow shoes some progress might be made, though slow.

We rigged up the pack straps, and each man shoulder-

ing his fifty pounds, the actual start was made. With fifty-pound packs even the snow shoes sank six or eight inches into the snow. By nightfall we had packed 800 pounds a mile and a half into the canyon. This over a trail that was not only rough but deep. The expedition returned that night to the ranch, quite tired from the first day's packing. It was the first of many days of similar labor. It was hard, but it was honest.[17]

Another Sharp Frost

During the night there was again a frost, so that the snow-shoe trail became quite firm, and we were able to do without snowshoes and pack in moccasins. We made this day three trips to the cache of the day before. Although the trail was good and packed hard by trampling, a mis-step over the side meant a plunge of five feet into soft snow. We used moccasins because our boots cut the trail and broke the crust. Moccasins, however, are little better than bare feet, so far as protection is concerned, and most of us began to suffer from "mal de moccasin," or foot lameness, from the unevenness and hardness of the icy trail.

Moccasins Give Way to Shoes

At the end of the second trip we substituted shoes for the moccasins, and managed to hobble over the third trip. But we were pretty well crippled up by night. The trail this day went through a bad country for packing. It wound about the base of a hog-back mountain,[18] steep and broken. Sometimes one had to scramble up on all fours, then slide down a distance on the slack of his pantaloons, a means of locomotion hardly more satisfactory than the toboggans.

It is easy enough when one has no pack, but with a pack there is no telling beforehand what the end will be. I am quite sure that if we had not been so carefully reared in childhood that we would at times use hasty expressions.

Sims Takes a Tumble

As I was plodding along one day thinking that if I was accomplishing nothing else, I was at least hardening my muscle

43

---

[16] "On page 10 of the July 16, 1890 Press Party issue of the *Seattle Press*, accompanying Christie's narrative, are two crude drawings entitled 'The go-devil as it was expected to act' and 'The go-devil as it really was,' which are both reproduced herein [i.e., in *Northwest Discovery*]. The coarseness of these two sketches, their marked difference in appearance from the other more realistic engravings (made from actual photographs), and the presence of the initials R.C. (for R. Cackly, staff artist of the *Seattle Press*) appearing on the latter view, all strongly indicate that these two pictures were sketched by the staff artist of the *Seattle Press*, rather than being taken from actual photographs. These two sketches probably represent the activity on February 4, the day when the sleds had their first good workout and were soon abandoned as useless." Majors, ed., *Northwest Discovery* 2 (Mar. 1981): p. 198.

[17] "This marks the first day of extensive backpacking of supplies by the Press Party, without assistance from the two mules. Barnes' entry also provides us with an estimate of the packing capability of the five men; five men packed a total of 800 pounds for $1\frac{1}{2}$ miles in 50-pound packs in one day. Thus today each man packed a total of 160 pounds for $1\frac{1}{2}$ miles in three round trips; this being equivalent to packing a single 50-pound pack for $4\frac{1}{2}$ miles and returning unloaded in one day." Majors, ed., *Northwest Discovery* 2 (Mar. 1981): p. 198.

[18] "This hogback is the western spur of MacDonald Mountain, which at this point descends directly to the bank of the Elwha River about $\frac{1}{2}$ mile north of the mouth of Madison Creek." Majors, ed., *Northwest Discovery* 2 (May 1981): p. 320.

and acquiring sore feet, I was suddenly shocked by hearing sundry strong expressions loudly and forcibly delivered. Upon looking about I found them to proceed from beneath the upturned roots of a great spruce tree. Sims had carelessly stepped outside the trail and in an instant had gone down and out of sight into a deep cavity formed between the snow and the roots. His cries were so appealing that I assisted him and his pack, which consisted mainly of bacon, to solid footing again, and he excused himself for his outrageous language and promised not to do so again, or until the necessity arose.

Extracts From Journal[19]

February 6.—Packed from McDonald's to a halfway cache, three loads each, and our bedding and kitchen kit clear through to Smith's cabin, two miles further on. My left foot is still quite painful so that I could not wear snowshoes, and had to wear leather boots, which made packing difficult. Smith's cabin is of logs with spaces between the logs from one to three inches with a loose sheeting inside of cedar shakes, a breezy and well ventilated cabin for this kind of weather. The cabin is uninhabited.

February 7, Smith's cabin.—Hard frost last night and I tried the go-devil again. She went well on the level places, so I used it as much as I could with a load of one hundred pounds, making portage of cargo and sledge over the rougher places. In the afternoon Mr. Christie went back and resurrected the "carry-all," patched up, and used it to good effect. From McDonald's to Smith's are packing two thousand pounds, which makes forty packs, of fifty pounds each."[20]

February 8, Smith's cabin.—Another fairly hard frost last night, so that all hands started out with snow shoes. Long before noon, however, the crust softened and then packing became very laborious. But by hard work we got everything to the cabin. As we were bringing up the last loads we were overtaken by four Indians from the mouth of the river, on the way up to kill elk. We had them at supper with us. The band of elk the Indians were after was a band which we our-

selves had planned to go for tomorrow, but this knocks all our plans in the head in all probability. We had been without fresh meat since leaving Port Angeles, and our poor dogs are almost starved. With a crowd of Indians chasing the elk we have precious little chance of overtaking them. We are getting into the game country now, however, and should get plenty of it from now on. Not fifty yards from Smith's cabin, where we now are, is a perfect stable for elk.[21] A band of 100 have evidently been wintering there and they left it only on our approach.

February 10, Smith's cabin.—This morning Mr. Christie, Sims and Hayes went up the river, reconnoitering, with two days grub. I went down the river to McDonald's for the purpose of getting some river courses for the map. The morning was crisp and sparkling with sunlight. The snow was hard and in perfect condition for the snow shoes. Leaving McDonald's on the return in the afternoon I followed the trail along his bottom land for nearly half a mile before striking the rugged hill side.[22] From there to camp steep side hills, dazzling white with snow, alternate with little level patches of land, overgrown with maple, alder and cedar. The soil in these bottoms, which occur occasionally on both sides of the river, is excellent and easy to clear. The hill sides are covered with a heavy growth of fir and spruce. Some of the cedar trees along the river measure 30 feet around—great giants, which were probably growing 2000 years. I cut a chip from one of them with my ax, and found 35 rings to the inch, which would have given the tree an age of 2100 years.[23] On my return to camp I found Crumback baking some beautiful white loaves of raised bread from yeast. We are using bark from the red fir trees for cooking. This kind of bark, which is in thickness from two to eight inches is full of pitch and makes a fire not unlike bituminous coal. It burns freely and with a bright blaze, with much heat.

February 12, Smith's claim.—Heavy rain and snow followed by clearing weather. Snow soft. Mr. Christie returned from up the river. He killed an elk, and brought back with

44

---

[19] "This headline indicates that today's entry is a verbatim quotation directly from Barnes' original field journal, with no editorial alteration, rewriting, or additions." Majors, ed., *Northwest Discovery* 2 (May 1981): p. 320.

[20] "A complete transfer by the five men from one camp or cache to another would thus involve eight round-trips per man. If the distance from one supply cache/camp to the next one was 1½ miles, then two days of packing were required to complete the transfer of the entire ton of material." Majors, ed., *Northwest Discovery* 2 (May 1981): p. 320. "The expedition left Seattle with about fifteen hundred pounds of supplies, but additional items were evidently procured at Port Angeles." Wood, *Across the Olympic Mountains*, p. 63.

[21] "This marks the first appearance in recorded history of the famed elk herds of the Elwha Valley. The specific variety found here is the Roosevelt or Olympic elk (*Cervus canadensis roosevelti*)." Majors, ed., *Northwest Discovery* 2 (May 1981): p. 320.

[22] "This distance of 'nearly half a mile' enables us to approximate the location of the MacDonald cabin from the point (near elevation marker 241 feet) where the northwest spur of MacDonald Mountain first reaches down to the Elwha River. MacDonald's cabin would thus have been located just south of the mouth of Little River." Majors, ed., *Northwest Discovery* 2 (May 1981): p. 320.

[23] "The current estimate for the age of the oldest living western red cedar trees is about 1000 years. Barnes' overestimate for the age of this particular tree may be explained by the fact that the annual increase in trunk diameter tends to decrease with age, thus the annual growth rings near the bark of older trees tend to be more closely spaced together than those present near the center of the trunk." Majors, ed., *Northwest Discovery* 2 (May 1981): p. 321.

him the liver and tenderloin. This is our first fresh meat for two months.

February 13 to 16, Smith's claim. These four days at Smith's claim were spent resting up and waiting for good weather. Weather variable, light flurries of snow, rain, and generally thawing weather by day, and a light frost at night. On the 13th, while resting and waiting, packed several loads and made cache in a valley on the river two miles above. On the 17th and 18th, taking advantage of night frosts, slightly harder than usual, the expedition finished packing the entire outfit to this point. Here we made camp on the little flat near the river. This packing was the hardest we have yet had. Through the deep snow with its thin crust of ice, one would often break through to his waist. There was many a struggle between Smith's claim and "little flat" camp. The angels in heaven shed many a tear before little flat camp was reached.[24]

February 19, Little Flat camp. Half a mile above camp a steep mountain comes down to the river, forming a deep canyon there. Mr. Christie took Sims and Hayes today and went ahead to overcome the engineering difficulties, and to make a passable trail if possible. This they succeeded in doing by cutting out much brush and digging out a shelf occasionally. While Crumback and I were in camp the dogs heard barking nearby. Thinking that the dogs had seen a squirrel we paid no attention. As we sat, Jack stirring the fire, and I preparing to go out, we were suddenly startled by a magnificent elk, who came into view followed by Tweed and Daisy, barking and nipping his heels as he ran. Distracted by the dogs the animal did not appear to notice the camp, but trotted across a little open space within thirty yards of where we were sitting. Jack and I jumped up and the way we looked for guns would surely have found one if there had been no elk in sight. By the time we had dragged a rifle out from under the stack of flour and beans, the elk had disappeared in the bush. I followed and caught sight of the elk just in time to see him disappear into the timber on the opposite side of the river. I crossed the river by fording and followed his elkship two miles, but the chase was fruitless. The elk was fresh and thoroughly alarmed. On my return to camp I found that the reputation of Jack and I as sportsmen was none the better for the elk passing camp without getting a shot. There was great fun in camp.[25]

February 20, Little Flat camp.—Moved our camp and outfit one-half mile, to the foot of the ridge, which is called by the settlers below the "Devil's Backbone."[26] Made camp and cache. A great cedar lay on the ground, and against this we made our fire. The cedar was dry and soon took fire. Rolling up in our blankets we passed a comfortable night. For three miles below the Devil's Backbone our trail has wound through broad bottoms, covered with timber, here and there with alder and maple, easy to clear and having a gentle slope from the mountain to the river. Several small tongues or spurs from the mountain breaks this valley land into pieces, each of which is large enough to make an excellent claim.

February 21 and 22.—Packed entire outfit over Devil's Backbone. Over the trail which we had made on the 19th we had no trouble in packing. In several places the mountain is quite steep, and in these we had to cut a little shelf in the side. By cutting out brush and a log here and there we had made a good trail. While making the first trip we were treated to the sight of a deer chase by the dogs. The dogs startled a deer some distance below us and all four gave chase. He struck down the river, and at a distance of about half a mile from us he emerged from the trees upon the river bank and plunged into the stream, followed by two of the dogs, Bud and Dike. The current was very strong at that place and full of rapids, and we became rather anxious as they were all—deer and dogs—swept down by the current. Fortunately for the deer he managed to get out on the opposite side some distance below, while the dogs crawled out on this side. But they showed spirit and pluck in staying with the chase so long.

In Camp Over Sunday

The 23rd was Sunday, and the expedition remained in camp. Christie went out for a reconnaissance, taking Hayes along. They killed a deer while out, and the evening was spent in eating liver and bacon and deer tenderloin.[27] The day had been pleasant, but during the night we had the pleasure of getting an addition to our bed clothes in the shape of five or six inches of snow. The snow we did not mind at all, but the air was warm and the snow melted, and the water soaking through our blankets made a rather uncomfortable camp.

---

[24] "This is a discrete [*sic*; discreet] reference to the profanities that today's difficult packing occasioned." Majors, ed., *Northwest Discovery* 2 (July-Aug. 1981): p. 472.

[25] "*Id est,* much fun was made by the other three members of the party at Barnes and Crumback having missed the opportunity to bag an elk a mere thirty yards from camp." Majors, ed., *Northwest Discovery* 2 (July-Aug. 1981): p. 472.

[26] "The term 'Devil's Backbone' thus originated with the local Elwha settlers, within 1888–1889, and not with the Press Party." Majors, ed., *Northwest Discovery* 2 (July-Aug. 1981): p. 472.

[27] "This was the first game killed since the elk of February 11, as well as being the first deer killed during the expedition." Majors, ed., *Northwest Discovery* 2 (July-Aug. 1981): p. 472.

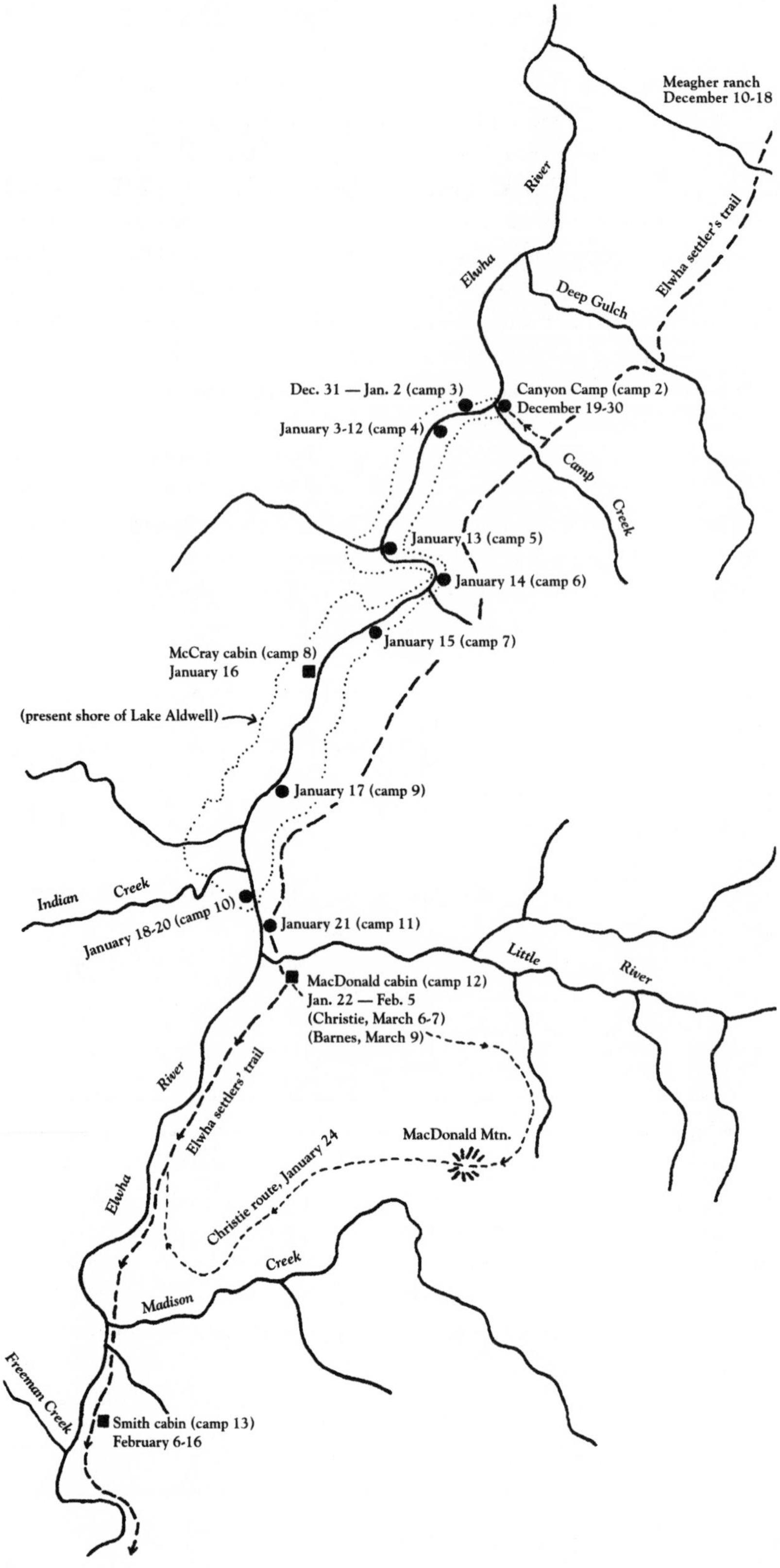

Meagher ranch
December 10-18

Elwha River

Deep Gulch

Elwha settler's trail

Dec. 31 — Jan. 2 (camp 3)

Canyon Camp (camp 2)
December 19-30

January 3-12 (camp 4)

Camp Creek

January 13 (camp 5)

January 14 (camp 6)

January 15 (camp 7)

McCray cabin (camp 8)
January 16

(present shore of Lake Aldwell)

January 17 (camp 9)

Indian Creek

January 18-20 (camp 10)

January 21 (camp 11)

Little River

MacDonald cabin (camp 12)
Jan. 22 — Feb. 5
(Christie, March 6-7)
(Barnes, March 9)

Elwha settlers' trail

River

MacDonald Mtn.

Christie route, January 24

Madison Creek

Elwha

Freeman Creek

Smith cabin (camp 13)
February 6-16

46

(Majors, vol. 5, 207)

The People's Ultima Thule

It took us half the next day to dig out. In the afternoon we moved a load four miles up the river to a point called by the people below "The Forks."[28] This is the *ultima thule*[29] of their exploration. But if their exploration is no better than their reports it is well that it went no further. The only fork we could find was a little creek that a man could jump over. The country passed over by us this day consists of some excellent bottom land. This bottom land alternates from one side of the river to the other. Many good claims can be had along here. The soil is good, and the clearing for the most part easy.

On the 25th we shifted camp to the "Forks," making one trip in the forenoon and one in the afternoon. The remainder of our outfit we temporarily cached at the "Backbone Camp." For this purpose we cut off four small trees, which were growing close together, about seven feet from the ground. On them we built a platform, piled our provisions, etc., upon it, and covered it with a tarpaulin.

At a point about the middle of our day's journey we had an excellent view of Olympus and obtained a photograph of the monarch. As seen from here it is a huge, spreading mountain, bell shaped, covering a great area. In the center rises the peak, snow crowned, regular in outline, clear cut against the dark blue sky beyond.

In the afternoon the sky became overcast; a cold raw wind began to blow from the southwest, chilling us to the very bone when we stopped to rest. Before we reached the "Forks" on the second trip, it was snowing furiously, the wind sweeping the flakes into one's face and clothing most unpleasantly. It was with hands chilled and blue that we made camp that evening, and the greatest fire we could make in that wind hardly took off the edge of discomfort. We pitched the tent and in the shortest possible time got into our blankets.

Following are more pages from the journal:

MOUNT OLYMPUS FROM ELWHA RIVER.

"February 25,1890. This view depicts the distant Mount Carrie massif, with the Elwha River in the foreground. It was taken somewhere near the mouth of Boulder Creek." (Majors, vol. 2, 142)

A Big Spruce Bridge

February 26.—We felled a large 200-foot spruce[30] today for a bridge across the river. It stood upon the bank and fell at right angles to the current, its topmost branch lying well upon the snow-covered beach opposite. This bridge is to enable us to explore the country lying west of the river. The day was for the most part devoted to the homely and necessary task of repairing clothes. The rough travel of the river has already begun to tell upon the clothes of the party, and a patch of canvas here and a piece of blanket sewed on there already gives the clothing a picturesque effect.

February 27.—Mr. Christie, accompanied by Crumback, made a trip up river this morning by the eastern side to reconnoiter.[31] He killed an elk about five miles up and left it for future use. I climbed the mountain back of camp for topographical purposes and was rewarded by obtaining an excellent view eastward and westward.[32] Mr. Christie returned late in the evening.

47

---

28 "The precise location of The Forks—another term that originated with the local Elwha settlers within 1888–1889—is nowhere specified in the Press Party account, . . . However, what the local Elwha settlers referred to as The Forks was most likely the confluence of the Elwha River with Boulder and Cat Creeks—the first two substantial streams encountered above Indian Creek and Little River." Majors, ed., *Northwest Discovery* 2 (July-Aug. 1981): p. 472.

29 "The Latin expression *ultima Thule*, meaning 'farthest Thule,' has come to signify the utmost limit of geographic knowledge or exploration." Majors, ed., *Northwest Discovery* 2 (July-Aug. 1981): p. 472.

30 "What Barnes refers to . . . was in all probability a Douglas-fir, which is far more common in the Elwha Valley, and which more frequently may reach heights of 200 feet in mature forests. Douglas-fir was at one time known as Douglas-spruce." Majors, ed., *Northwest Discovery* 2 (July-Aug. 1981): p. 473.

31 "February 27 was another significant day for the Press Party, as Christie and Crumback's reconnaissance represents the first exploration by the Press Party beyond the limits (The Forks) of previous journeys by local Elwha settlers. From this point onward, the Press Party was engaging in a true exploration of unknown territory." Majors, ed., *Northwest Discovery* 2 (July-Aug. 1981): p. 473.

32 "The mountain partially ascended by Barnes was Hurricane Hill (5757'), and his route probably followed the spur just south of Hurricane Creek. Though Barnes claims that he gained 'an excellent view eastward and westward,' he probably means southeastward and westward—for on his map of the Olympic Mountains, Barnes presents no correct geographical data for the area east of Hurricane Hill indicative that he reached the summit of this mountain. In all probability, Barnes ascended only part way up its west slope. It would have been from this vantage point that Barnes discovered Mount McClure and Mount Agnus; and from which he took bearings on 'Mount Sutherland' (Mount Baldy), Mount Hunt, and 'Mount Olympus' (Mount Carrie) for his map. However, mounts McClure, Agnus, and Hunt first appear in print only in Barnes' entry for March 20." Majors, ed., *Northwest Discovery* 2 (July-Aug. 1981): p. 473.

Field Day for Game

February 28.—Today was a field day for game. While we sat at breakfast about the fire, we caught sight of two large gray wolves on the opposite side of the river. The guns were handy and one of the wolves caught a bullet through the heart. The other trotted into the underbrush and escaped with a piece of lead somewhere in his carcass, for several drops of blood indicated the point of his disappearance. The dead wolf was brought over and skinned.[33] While the skinning was going on, Sims caught sight of a good sized wild cat also on the opposite side. It was a beautiful sight for a moment to see it stand as it did, surprised, wondering what kind of animals we were. Sims was the lucky man, and got it with the first shot. Tom made one jump of about five feet into the air and then doubled up in a heap. As Jack was fetching him across our tree bridge he seemed almost as large as Jack himself, but by actual measurement the cat was three feet nine inches in length from the front of the nose to the root of the tail. The tail measured eight inches. He was a dim color on the back, with grayish spots in stripes on the sides. We saved and stretched the skin.[34]

But this was not the end of the day's shooting. Wolves and cats are not grub, and the camp was almost out of meat. So in the afternoon Hayes was sent out to kill an elk, of which there were numbers on the hills around. He returned to camp after a couple of hours, having left a dead elk about a mile from camp, on the mountain side above. All hands were called, and with pack-straps and gunny-sacks we started off to fetch down the meat. We found a magnificent specimen of elk lying with his throat cut and a ball through his head, which accounted well enough for his death. We removed his hide for preservation,[35] and his tusks for mementos, and brought away all we could carry of the meat—some 300 pounds. We got many a tumble and roll in the soft snow before we reached the bottom of the 1500 foot slope, and were wet to the skin when we arrived in camp. But that is something we are accustomed to by this time. The weather is frosty and cold, but providing there is not wind blowing it is easy to be comfortable.

A Day at Drying Meat

March 1.—The day was spent in drying meat. The snow continues soft and deep. Almost impossible to travel in its present condition.

Goblin Gates Discovered

Record of Adventure in One of the Most Curious Canyons in the State

On March 2 Mr. Barnes was sent out to prospect for a trail ahead. He went up by the west bank of the river and returned by the east. The trip is interesting from the discovery of "The Goblin Gates." The following account is from his journal:[36]

March 2nd to 5th, inclusive.—Left camp[37] after an early breakfast. Carried gun, camera and some provisions, consisting of tobacco, coffee, bread and a handful or two of beans. Fifty yards above the crossing comes in a branch of the Elwha, which drains the northern sides of Olympus. This we called Cat creek, in honor of the cat killed March 1st on its banks. Opposite this torrent is another creek, which we called Wolf creek, from the wolf we killed on the same day. At this point, immediately above the two streams, the river issues from a canyon.[38] A steep climb of 300 feet took me to the top of the canyon walls. The walls are of broken rock, quite steep, gradually increasing in height as I traveled on. The hill side above me was overgrown with small firs, sufficiently dense to make it quite gloomy beneath them. After half a mile of tolerably good travel the mountain side is suddenly broken by a deep ravine, in the bottom of which is a stream, milk white from the melting snow mass which crowns the summit of Olympus. The ravine occupied by this little Alpine stream was filled with soft melting snow and a vast quantity of fallen timber, and I was quite a time getting across it.

A Large Wolf Killed

Just as I got up the other side I suddenly caught sight a little below where I was of an animal running swiftly. As my dog

48

---

[33] "This was the first wolf sighting by the Press Party. It resulted in tragedy for the wolves, for the two animals shot were probably a mated pair. The gray wolf (*Canis lupus*) is now regarded as being extinct in the Olympic Peninsula, and the Press Party report represents one of the few confirmed sightings of this species in the Olympic Mountains." Majors, ed., *Northwest Discovery* 2 (July-Aug. 1981): p. 473. "Apparently the pelt was taken down to MacDonald's and sent to Seattle by way of Port Angeles. On June 6, 1890, Edmond Meany received a bill for twenty dollars from a Seattle furrier, for dressing and mounting the skins of a deer, an elk, and a timber wolf." Wood, *Across the Olympic Mountains*, p. 73.

[34] "This was the only bobcat to be seen by the Press Party." Majors, ed., *Northwest Discovery* 2 (July-Aug. 1981): p. 474. "At another point in his narrative, Barnes states that the wildcat was shot on March 1." Wood, *Across the Olympic Mountains*, p. 74.

[35] "It was likely this same elk skin that was sent to Edmond S. Meany, along with the wolf skin and a deer skin." Majors, ed., *Northwest Discovery* 2 (July-Aug. 1981): p. 474.

[36] "This obvious editorial insertion, probably the work of Edmond S. Meany (assistant editor of the *Seattle Press*), presents direct evidence that the original field journals of Barnes and Christie were subjected to the editing process in Seattle prior to publication." Majors, ed,. *Northwest Discovery* 5 (Aug. 1984): p. 247.

[37] "Barnes' camp for March 2, 1890 was 0.4 mile southeast of FitzHenry Creek at elevation 1000 feet." Majors, ed., *Northwest Discovery* 5 (Aug. 1984): p. 247.

[38] "Goblin Canyon, they later called it, but today it is known as Rica Canyon." Wood, *Across the Olympic Mountains*, p. 75.

"Dike" had followed me half way across the tree bridge when leaving camp, it was my first impression that the moving animal was the dog. But the next instant it came into full view—a large gray wolf. He caught sight of me, stopped at the same time, double the size of Dike, although Dike was as large as a good-sized Newfoundland. I unslung my rifle and shot him through the lungs. As he jumped I gave him another one which laid him out. As he lay dead on the snow with his long tongue hanging out he was a horrible sight. I got a photograph of his carcass.

A River Madly Rushing

A third of a mile farther on, I found another and larger milky torrent, plunging down into a deep cut or gorge in the solid rock. After many minor cascades, a final grand plunge of a hundred feet amid much spray and foam, the torrent sank into a quiet pool and thence flowed noiselessly into the river. From a little point of rock on its right bank can be had a glimpse of the river below, at this point flowing in its canyon, deep, green, and quiet.

I found the canyon to continue and deepen all day. The eastern side of the canyon could be seen occasionally through the thicket, and it as well as the side upon which I was, was almost perpendicular for from nine hundred to a thousand feet. From the bottom came up the sounds of mad and roaring water, sometimes deafening. From the top of the cliff the mountain side slopes back at an angle of about forty degrees, broken by ravines and canyons and rough beyond description.

Camped at the Foot of a Tree

All day I clambered along this mountain side, sometimes through deep snow, and sometimes over little patches of bare ground protected by the foliage overhead, but always over fallen timber. Progress was slow and I was quite fatigued, when I at last found a suitable camping place, toward sundown. I chose a bare spot at the foot of a great fir tree on the mountain side, whose spreading roots made a capital fireplace, and enclosed a little shelf about ten feet square. Abundance of dry wood lay about, and all around was snow for water. So I unslung my pack and placed it in a dry place, with gun and photograph gallery. Then I gathered a quantity of wood.

Cutting up some of it with my ax—as much of it as I judged would keep the fire going through the night. I made a fire, put on a pail of snow to melt, and in a very few moments the aroma of coffee filled my solitary camp. After a frugal supper—for I had been disappointed in killing game today—I gathered an abundance of spruce boughs for my bed, and, having prepared my fire for the night and lighted my pipe, turned in just as it was beginning to grow dark.

A Science in a Spruce Bed

By the way, there is a science in laying spruce boughs,[39] if comfort is desired. Throw them down carelessly and the sensation of lying on a gridiron will be the result. They should be laid shingle fashion, the bushy foliage of one layer covering the sticks and stems of the lower. Given plenty of depth it rivals any bed that panders to the demands of luxurious civilization. The yielding springiness and aromatic odor of the spruce will transform a tired man into a fresh one in the shortest possible time. And how pleasant one's pipe tastes under such circumstances. Poets have sounded the glories of the chimney corner, the easy chair and comfortable dressing gown, but they know nothing of the roaring camp fire and the bed of boughs spread within its circle of warmth. Around about the fire-lighted snow, and, beyond and encircling all the gloomy blackness of the woods, encloses one like a cozy room. Soon the wet clothing is dry, the hard day's work contrasts with the present comfort, the burned-out pipe is refilled and one can drop into the pleasantest of dreams. The fire, replenished once or twice during the night lasts till morning, and at the first gray signs of dawn one can spring to his feet with the elasticity of boyhood.

Fresh Venison at Hand

March 3.—Yesterday I saw but one animal, a wolf, which treated me with scant ceremony by disappearing before I could get a shot.[40] I had seen numerous tracks of deer, but the game itself gave me not so much as a whisk of its tail, and that is rather short. I had brought no meat, as I had expected to kill all I required. For this reason I warmly welcomed a happy affair which occurred after breakfast. I had packed my kit and was just about to make a start when I was startled by a slight rustling in the bushes near by. I reached for my gun and waited. Presently another rustle, and, as I stood there

49

---

[39] "By spruce, Barnes in this instance probably means the Douglas-fir *Pseudotsuga menziesii* . . . rather than the true Sitka spruce. The needles of the Sitka spruce *Picea sitchensis* are painfully sharp to the touch, and would not have made a pleasant bedding to sleep on, unless cushioned with an intervening layer of blankets." Majors, ed., *Northwest Discovery* 5 (Aug. 1984): p. 247.

[40] "This is in direct contradiction to Barnes' entry for the previous day (March 2), wherein he describes how he shot a wolf through the lungs and then photographed the carcass. This discrepancy may be the result of the editorial alteration that Barnes' journal was subjected to prior to publication." Majors, ed., *Northwest Discovery* 5 (Aug. 1984): p. 247.

emerged from the thicket as beautiful a doe as ever leaped a mountain stream. I raised my gun. I had her sure and was in no hurry to shoot. I caught her eye for the first time and she stopped, her front half concealed by the clump of laurel not 20 yards away, and stood gazing from curiosity. As she stood I could not help admiring her—the light-brown coat, the graceful neck, the gentle eye—it seemed like murder to kill her. It was too bad. I felt sorry for the beautiful animal, but I needed meat. After what seemed a long time, but which was actually about a minute, she turned half around and I shot her through the heart. One spring and she was dead. I was at her side in a moment and cut her throat. Then I removed the liver and as much of the best meat as I could comfortable add to my pack and hung up the remainder of the meat for future camp use. It was still early when I got started. I blazed the trees as I went so that I might find the cache again.

Swimming a Mountain Torrent

Three quarters of a mile brought me to a large mountain torrent where I ticked the end of my blaze in the ground, so to speak, for it could be picked up easy here. Following the torrent down some 200 yards to where it made a bold jump into the river, I found a good place to climb up on the other side. The river was still a deep gorge below. I climbed up the other side of the torrent ravine. Here was little snow, the ground being protected seemingly by the dense foliage of the trees. For the next mile the mountain was a veritable elk pasture. The ground was bare of snow and covered with Oregon grape, affording excellent grazing, and it would be difficult to find a spot large enough to place a camp kettle which did not have the impressions of hoofs. Some of the tracks were not over a couple of days old. It was evident that a large herd of elk was not far off, so I proceeded carefully, looking out continually for still fresher tracks. It was slow work on this part of the journey, owing to the unevenness of the ground.

Surprised by Night and Rain

The slope gradually became less, however, and I began to expect the end of the canyon, and an improvement in the travel by finding valley or bottom land. But before I reached it I was surprised by the coming on of dusk. So dense had been the shade that I had scarcely all day caught a glimpse of the sun. Besides the gathering darkness it was beginning to rain. I had barely half an hour of dusk to find and make camp, and to prepare for a rainy night. I had to choose the spot where I

was,[41] there was not time for choice of place. The available wood was rotten and wet, and it was not until I had fumbled about for some time in the dark that I was able to boast a camp—and a wet camp at that. I potted the nearest patch of snow for coffee and had venison for my supper. A hasty thatch of cedar boughs shed a part of the rain, which was now falling in torrents. A good fire dried one side of me and then the other alternately as I would wake up and turn over during the night. Nevertheless I was quite wet when morning came.

Morning Breaks Clear and Bright

The morning broke clear and bright, so I dried out and folded my effects and stole again to the southward. A short distance brought me to the end of the canyon. I could see through the trees a lovely valley below. I followed downward a charming little ravine, radiant with the glories of this spring-like day, and reached the bottom after a descent of five or six hundred feet. It was at the bottom of the ravine that I caught the first glimpse of Goblin Gates, which must become famous among the natural marvels, not alone of the Olympics, but of the whole continent.[42] Along one side of a little valley the river thundered in great rapids, with a volume of sound, which, echoed by the bounding mountain walls, became almost stunning. The water of the river suddenly comes to a standstill in a deep, green pool,

THE GOBLIN GATES.

"March 4, 1890. This photograph was taken by Barnes on the west bank of the Elwha, looking downstream at the upper entrance to the canyon. The profiles of three 'goblin' heads are visible in the engraving that appears in the newspaper. The engraving is, on the whole, faithfully reproduced, as will be seen by a comparison of it with a modern-day photograph taken from the same vantage point. However, the profile that was once present on the lower part of the large boulder on the right has since eroded away." (Majors, vol. 2, 142)

---

[41] "Barnes' camp for March 3, 1890 was on the west side of the Elwha River, about 0.2 mile northwest of the confluence of Haggerty Creek, at the 1015 foot contour, on the crest of this small spur or ridge." Majors, ed., *Northwest Discovery* 5 (Aug. 1984): p. 247.
[42] "This is an undeservedly sweeping judgment which may be a later insertion." Majors, ed., *Northwest Discovery* 5 (Aug. 1984): p. 247.

or basin. On the opposite side of the pool the mountain is sheer perpendicular rock, smooth and bare. This rock is broken at right angles to the direction of the river, and down this cleft the water of the pool glides as noiselessly as a serpent. It is like the throat of a monster, silently sucking away the water. The whole river enters this canyon through portals not more than 12 feet in width.

Guarded by Two Heads

These portals are guarded by two gigantic heads of rock. It requires no imagination to see the features in the faces of these two heads, which are 15 feet in height.[43] About 30 feet inside of these heads is another pair of heads, making a kind of inner gateway, with a vestibule between the outer and inner. Upward and backward from the gateway, the canyon walls rise to a height of several hundred feet, as far as can be seen down the canyon, a multitude of faces appear in succession near the water's edge. One could conceive in them tortured expressions, which, with the gloomy and mysterious character of the whole, justified us in giving it afterwards the name of "The Goblin Gates."

Tilted Strata

The geographical strata here is tilted on edge and consists of alternate layers of hard slate and soft sandstone. The sandstone has worn away, leaving alternating slate projecting into the canyon and forming in profile the heads as they appear from the entrance.[44] The spectacle is one which alone would well repay a tourist for the trouble of a trip to see.

The little valley is about forty acres in extent, nearly encircled by the slopes of Olympus. It lies well to the sun, is bright and warm. The soil is a rich sandy loam. It is covered partly by a growth of maple and alder, and partly by fir trees.

Picking Out a Trail

From the Goblin Gates bottom land appeared to continue up the river some distance, affording good travel. The object of my trip, which was to find a trail, being therefore accomplished, I prepared to return to camp. Two hundred yards above the gateway the river is quite broad and shoal. At this

point I determined to ford. So I removed my clothing, packed everything on my shoulders, and with a pole in each hand, started carefully across. It was cold!

I gradually felt my way across, and reached the other side without mishap. In mid-stream the water reached above the waist. I then commenced the ascent of the hill. The stone wall of the gateway here broke into a steep hill side. About eight hundred feet in height, for the most part a sliding mass of thin, shaly, stones. But by dint of hard climbing and swinging to an occasional bush, with now and then some scrubby trees to rest in, I reached the top. The view was excellent. It was now four o'clock, and as dry wood was plenty I camped there exactly on the summit.[45] A good fire and some boughs made a very comfortable camp, and I boiled down some snow as usual and had venison stew for supper.

Return to Camp

After a good night's rest I made the trip to camp, down the right of the river, along the edge of the canyon. Half a mile from my camp of the night I killed a deer and hung him up for expedition use, when it should come along, which must be in a few days at most. The distance to camp on this side was not above five miles, being the chord of the arc made by the river. The snow was trying in places, deep and soft. Often I had to struggle out of holes into which I slid. I reached camp in about seven hours. This side was by far the best for travel. There are no cross ravines to scramble down and clamber out of.

In Camp Again

March 6 and 7, Camp at "Forks." Day clear and warm until evening. Colder weather and rain during the night. Snow soft and slushy. Impracticable to move camp. I returned to my eagle's nest camp[46] above the Goblin canyon to get observations. Arriving there in the afternoon I shifted my camp a few yards for a new backlog. About dark it came on to blow a steady gale. Rained and blew incessantly during night. Protected myself against it as well as I could. Cut a number of small fir saplings, stacked them up and weighted them with stones and sticks of wood for a windbreak.

In the morning, observing that the weather had signs

51

---

[43] "These head profiles are evident in the engraving of the Goblin Gates (made from a photograph by Barnes) that appears on page 2 of the *Seattle Press*, July 16, 1890." Majors, ed., *Northwest Discovery* 5 (Aug. 1984): p. 247.

[44] "Barnes has made a major error here in his geological description of the Goblin Gates, for it is the less resistant slates (not the harder sandstones) which have eroded away. The rock at this point consists of a series of resistant micaceous sandstones interbedded with softer micaceous slates, the whole comprising one unit of the Needles-Graywolf Lithic Assemblage. In Goblin Canyon, the softer slates have eroded away, leaving buttresses of harder sandstone projecting into the Elwha River." Majors, ed., *Northwest Discovery* 5 (Aug. 1984): p. 247.

[45] "Barnes' 'eagle's nest' camp for March 4 and 6, 1890, was at elevation contour 1275 feet, about 0.05 mile from benchmark 1300 (Benchmark Rock). This was the same site as the Press Party's Eagles Nest camp of March 18–19, 1890, on the east side of the Elwha River." Majors, ed., *Northwest Discovery* 5 (Aug. 1984): p. 248.

[46] "This was probably the present day 'elk overlook' just south of Whiskey Bend, near the Elwha trail." Wood, *Across the Olympic Mountains*, p. 83.

of holding bad for several days and that I would be unable to carry out the object for which I had come, determined to return to camp. I therefore cached my outfit under a log and covered them with an oil skin coat and canvas sheet. I went down the hill intending to cross the river and return to camp by the west side. Found river risen a foot and ford impassable. Returned up hill and traveled down the river by the east bank. Snow very rotten with rains and thawing. Laborious work tramping through it. Arrived in camp and found everybody gone down the river for the mules. Lighted fire, toasted some venison, and turned into the blankets to write some letters[47] and dry out. Still raining. Rain and snow all day and night. Built small fire this morning and rigged up teepee over it. Clothes drying all day under teepee.

March 9, Camp Forks.—Snow all day until evening. Turned out at day break. After breakfast started for McDonald's to mail letters. Still thawing and snowing. Two hundred yards below Devil's Backbone met the party returning to camp convoying the two mules laden with provisions. Arrived at McDonald's, 14 miles down the river, at 4:30, pretty well knocked out with heavy travel. Snow deep and too soft for snowshoes.

Sad Fate of the Mule Jennie

March 10, Camp at Forks.—Snow in early morning. Left McDonald's at 7 A.M.[48] and after a tiresome day's travel arrived in camp at 3 P.M. Here I learned that a sad accident had overtaken Jennie, one of the mules. It seems that about half an hour after I had passed them, they ascended the Devil's Backbone

and reached a point on the "bone" where the trail had been cut by us in the face of the precipice, a mere narrow ledge or shelf over a chasm 400 feet in depth. As they were passing, Mr. Christie in advance, followed by Crumback leading Jennie, a sudden slipping of earth occurred under the mule's hind feet. She made a spring to save herself, but with 200 pounds on her back she was dragged down. A plunge and all was over with poor Jennie. She struck the cleft between the cliff and a tree about 100 feet below. Here she stuck, her back broken and her head smashed to a jelly. Christie at once rigged up a rope from a tree growing above the trail, and by means of it he and Jack Sims swung themselves down, and in a few moments stood beside her. One cut of the knife and Jenny was parted from her pack. Another plunge straight downward for three hundred feet, a far away splash, and the body of poor Jennie was seen no more. It had plunged into the river below. One hundred and fifty pounds of flour and about fifty pounds of material for colored fire composed her load. The flour was hoisted to the trail by a rope. With a kick the "hell fire," as it was familiarly known in camp, was sent after Jennie and Mr. Christie and Sims ascended to the ledge above. The loss of poor Jennie to the expedition is greatly felt by us. She was the heaviest and strongest animal. Upon her we depended largely for the transport of our supplies. Without her we must do that work ourselves, so that the accident will result in great loss of time and expenditure of labor, which might be devoted to the objects of the expedition. After struggling through this long hard winter surrounded by mountains of ice and snow and seeing at last the snow disappearing and before us a practicable route to the other side,—after all this, is it any wonder that we all feel blue. Poor Jennie—*requiescat in pace.*

---

[47] "The letters which Barnes left with William D. MacDonald on March 10, 1890, to be forwarded to Seattle, mark the last word the outside world would hear of the Press Party until their arrival at Aberdeen on May 21. The opportunities of communication for the Press Party are as follows:

"December 12—Meany arrives at Port Angeles to visit Press Party at Meagher ranch.
"December 14—Meany leaves Port Angeles; he publishes an article on December 17.
"December 22—'Captain Barnes in camp at correspondence'
"December 27—Barnes and Runnalls visit Port Angeles on mules; return December 28.
"Janaury 26—'Received our first mail per Mr. W[arriner E.] Smith'
"February 2?—Runnalls receives word of his wife's illness.
"February 3—Runnalls departs for Seattle and Puyallup.
"March 6—Christie returns to the MacDonald cabin.
"March 7—Barnes writes some letters.
"March 8—Christie leaves the MacDonald cabin for the last time.
"March 10—Barnes leaves the MacDonald cabin for the last time.

"Thus, after Barnes' letters of March 7 were left at the MacDonald cabin on March 10, the Press Party had no communication with the outside world until their meeting with Frederick S. Antrim on May 18, 1890, along the Quinault River, just above Lake Quinault." Majors, ed., *Northwest Discovery* 5 (Aug. 1984): p. 248.

[48] "With Barnes' departure from William D. MacDonald's cabin on the morning of March 10, 1890, . . . the Press Party had now reached the point of no return. It is significant that none of the five men chose to return to Seattle. It is of interest to note that thus far, three months had been consumed in the short distance from Port Angeles to the mouth of Wolf Creek—the limit of exploration up the Elwha River previously reached by local settlers . . . a distance hardly 20 miles from Port Angeles. . . . However, it was to the advantage of the Press Party that so much time was spent on the lower Elwha River, within the confines of civilization, for this fortunately delayed their entry into the deep Olympic Mountains until spring. At any time up until mid-March 1890, there was little danger of the men starving, because food and help at William D. MacDonald's cabin were but a day's journey away. Had winter storms in January and February caught the men somewhere near the headwaters of the Elwha River, the expedition, as with John Franklin's ill-fated venture in the Canadian Arctic in 1847–1848, may very well have ended in disaster. As it was, the Press Party were saved from starvation by the timely emergence of bears from hibernation at the Low Divide." Majors, ed., *Northwest Discovery* 5 (Aug. 1984): p. 251.

Loss of the Mule Jennie Over the Devil's Backbone

"*March 9, 1890. This engraving is not based on a true photograph, but . . . was rather made from a hypothetical drawing made by the newspaper staff artist, R. Cackly.*" (Majors, vol. 2, 142)

Mount Eldridge Christened

The mountain above the Devil's Backbone we named Mt. Eldridge, in honor of Mr. William Eldridge, of Washington, D.C. It is snow-capped, and is connected by a ridge with Mt. Angeles.[49]

From March 11th to 14th the expedition made one round trip each day from the "Devil's Backbone" to the forks, packing up the stores cached there. On the 14th, on the return from below, camp was struck and moved to the bench 500 feet above, and about one half mile distant.[50] Then we packed up another load, all hands, and made camp there.

Heading Dollie Off

On the last trip up, Dollie broke of the trail and made down hill for home. With cries of "head her off" from those on the trail above, Jack and I, who were behind, rushed down packs and all, as Jack said, "to beat" his satanic majesty "on tan bark." We headed her off but in the tumble I tripped over a vine and went heels over head down the slope with my 50 pounds pack on my back. I went over three times to the consternation of all hands before bringing up in a heap under a fortunate log. On extricating myself I found that my stock of worldly possessions had been increased to the extent of a severe sprain in the groin. We are all ill at the present time caused, we think, by drinking the melting snow, with the water of which the streams are swollen.[51]

March 15, Camp No. 16.—Day cloudy with occasional showers. Heavy clouds hanging low in the gulches and canyons. Today we packed up the hill to camp two loads each and an extra mule load comprising the entire remaining outfit. We are all more or less "decomposed," as Sims put it, from our illness, and I additionally so from my sprain, so that it was a toilsome and laborious day and we are all glad for the coming rest tomorrow, Sunday. From the number of deer we call this bench and mountain side "Deer Range."[52]

March 16, Camp No. 16.—Christie and Crumback off for the day up the river reconnoitering, returned at dark

53

---

49 "This is the first 'newspaperman' type of geographic name to appear in the Press Party narrative, probably the self-serving creation of Edmond S. Meany. As with all such names of this type, they occur only in Barnes' narrative report. Nearly all of these are highly suggestive of being later editorial insertions by Meany." Majors, ed., *Northwest Discovery* 5 (Aug. 1984): p. 251.
50 "Camp 17 of the Press Party, for March 14–17, 1890, was located at or very near Whiskey Bend, on the northeast side of the Elwha River, at about 1150 feet elevation." Majors, ed., *Northwest Discovery* 5 (Aug. 1984): p. 251.
51 "In his journal entries for March 15 and 30, 1890 (note also April 1 and 2), Christie specifies 'All hands suffering from dysentery.' Several waterborne organisms could have produced this illness, particularly if the sanitary precautions necessary at an extended campsite were not well adhered to. Neither Christie nor Barnes describe their symptoms, thus a precise diagnosis cannot be advanced. . . . Nor can it be established whether the vector of infection was from the men themselves, or from the washed down pollution of animals upstream. Among the diseases the Press Party might have been susceptible to are dysentery, salmonella, and perhaps *Giardia lamblia*. However, it is highly significant that one of the many symptoms of malnutrition is diarrhea, which in Victorian times would have been euphemistically referred to as 'dysentery.'" Majors, ed., *Northwest Discovery* 5 (Aug. 1984): p. 252.
52 "Deer Range refers to the lower southwest side of Hurricane Hill, the gentle slope and benches immediately south of Wolf Creek. This is a genuine Press Party name, created in the field by the men of the expedition—as opposed to such 'newspapermen' names as Mount Eldridge, which were most likely created by Edmond S. Meany after the Press Party returned to Seattle." Majors, ed., *Northwest Discovery* 5(Aug. 1984): p. 252.
"I can find no evidence to substantiate such a claim, but abundant proof exists to the contrary. Barnes specifically mentions naming *by the explorers* of sixteen peaks, as well as other geographic features—ranges, creeks, rivers, waterfalls, lakes, and a plateau. Moreover, his map does not appear to have been tampered with, and the manner in which the hachure marks were drawn indicates the names were printed first as is customary in cartography.
"Let us consider the case of Mount Pulitzer. Not only does Barnes state [that] the explorers named this peak, but on July 16, 1890, the day the Press Party's story was published, Edmond Meany wrote Joseph Pulitzer, advising him that a copy of the account was being sent to him, and noting further: 'Your attention is also called to the fact that the Press explorers named a mountain peak in your honor.'
"What is the truth regarding the expedition's nomenclature? Obviously the explorers themselves did the naming, but where did they get the names? We have no direct evidence as such, but it is likely that, before the men left for the mountains, the *Seattle Press* provided them with a list of names (publishers and editors of various newspapers) to confer upon the peaks." Wood, *Across the Olympic Mountains*, Author's Note in paperback reprint, no page number.

54

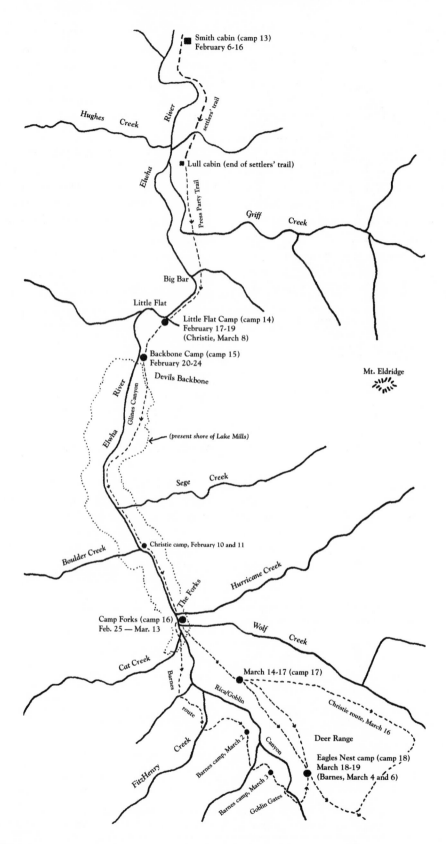

Smith cabin (camp 13)
February 6-16

Hughes Creek

settlers' trail

Lull cabin (end of settlers' trail)

Press Party Trail

Griff Creek

Big Bar

Little Flat

Little Flat Camp (camp 14)
February 17-19
(Christie, March 8)

Backbone Camp (camp 15)
February 20-24

Devils Backbone

Mt. Eldridge

Elwha River

Glines Canyon

(present shore of Lake Mills)

Sege Creek

Boulder Creek

Christie camp, February 10 and 11

The Forks

Hurricane Creek

Camp Forks (camp 16)
Feb. 25 — Mar. 13

Wolf Creek

Cat Creek

Barnes

March 14-17 (camp 17)

Rica/Goblin

Christie route, March 16

route

Deer Range

Creek

Barnes camp, March 2

Canyon

Eagles Nest camp (camp 18)
March 18-19
(Barnes, March 4 and 6)

FitzHenry

Barnes camp, March 3

Goblin Gates

(Majors, vol. 5, 229)

having shot four deer and an elk, leaving, as Christie said, venison on every stump. This gives us meat and will save the provisions of the pack.

A Camp on Eagle's Nest

March 17 to 20, on Deer Range.—Weather warm, with occasional showers on the 18th. Snow melting and very soft.[53] Expedition employed packing up the mountain side back of camp. Moved camp[54] to head of Deer range, five miles up the river, on a bluff overlooking the valley at the head of Goblin canyon. The trail follows old elk and deer runs and is over some considerable hills, but quite devoid of fallen timber, entirely free of underbrush and partially clear of snow. The ground is covered for the most part with small manzanita, ground laurel and Oregon grape. Timber medium size, fir, spruce and hemlock, averaging 2,000,000 feet per quarter section. We saw many deer, and the dogs were frequently heard running and barking at others. These hills are literally alive with them.

The bluff on which we camped is 870 feet in height by the aneroid above the valley below, and 1950 feet above the camp below the canyon. The fall of the river in the canyon therefore is about 1100 feet in a distance of four miles.[55] This bluff is crowned by a kind of eagle's nest of jutting slate and shale. On this eagle's nest we made the camp. The view is glorious. Mount Olympus, with many new crags and spurs unseen before, visible to the southward.[56] Many new and unnamed peaks bounded the horizon all about. At our feet lay a large valley extending to the southward and eastward.

Part Two

From Geyser Valley to the Watershed—John Crumback Takes Up a Claim, and the Event Is Celebrated in a Backwoods Feast—Making Pemmican—Exploration of

Elwha Pass—Evidences of Ancient Indian Life—An Old Wringing Post—Convulsion Canyon—Exploration of Belle River—A Cougar Hunt Backwards—Observations of the Geysers—Making a Temporary Base of Supplies—No More Spirits—A Substitute for Tobacco Discovered—Rough Starting—Scarcity of Provisions—Stalking the Elk—A Tame Cow—"Where Is Christie?"—An Ancient Indian Village—Exploration of Press Valley—Good-Bye to Dollie, the Last Surviving Mule—On Snowshoes Up Goldie River Canyon—Description of an Avalanche—Snow Getting Deeper—"The Quinaiult?"—First Glimpse of Mount Seattle—A Glorious Panorama—A Dangerous Camp—On Deception Divide—Press Valley Again—Scaling a Precipice—A Beautiful Lake—The Summit Reached at Last.

March 20, Geyser Valley.—Clear and warm. Cut trail down the side of the bluff through logs and young fir, and then packed down camp outfit. It took us one hour to make the descent without taking a rest. Made camp in valley, twenty yards from the river in a dense growth of large trees. Near camp[57] the river receives a large tributary from the south, which runs around and drains the eastern slope of Olympus, while the main stream extends in a southeasterly direction, evidently draining the eastern watershed of the Sound range.

From Deer Range can be seen to the westward a magnificent range of snowclad peaks, having a general direction east and west. The three notable peaks in the range we named mounts Hunt, McClure and Agnus.[58] Mount Hunt, after the Mr. L. S. J. Hunt, proprietor of the Seattle Post-Intelligencer, is the most easterly, and rises abruptly from the Elwha river, and has its head in the clouds. West of it is Mount McClure, in honor of Col. A.K. McClure of the Philadelphia Times, has a triple-peaked summit, and is equally imposing. Mount Agnus, after Gen. Felix Agnus of the Baltimore American, terminates

55

---

[53] "This is the first weather entry that indicates spring is at hand." Majors, ed., *Northwest Discovery* 5 (Aug. 1984): p. 272.

[54] "Camp 18 of the Press Party, for March 18–19, 1890, was at the Eagles Nest, a promontory on the east side of the Elwha River, 0.9 mile southeast of Whiskey Bend, at elevation 1275 feet, about 0.05 mile south of benchmark 1300 (Benchmark Rock). This campsite cannot have been at Elk Overlook promontory (about 1050 elevation), 0.5 mile southeast of Whiskey Bend, because: (a) Elk Overlook is not 'a ledge of rock overlooking Geyser Valley'; and (b) on March 20, the Press Party descended from Eagles Nest directly to the floor of Geyser Valley in 'one hour.' These conditions correctly apply only to the true Eagles Nest, at or very near benchmark 1300." Majors, ed., *Northwest Discovery* 5 (Aug. 1984): p. 272.

[55] "Barnes' aneroid barometer readings here are grossly inaccurate. The mean elevation of the floor of Geyser Valley is only 750 feet above sea level, whereas the elevation of their Little Flat camp of February 17–19 just below Glines Canyon was at about 375 feet. The total fall of the Elwha River from the Goblin Gates (650 feet elevation) to the embouchure of Glines Canyon (400 feet elevation) is only 250 feet, not '1100 feet'." Majors, ed., *Northwest Discovery* 5 (Aug. 1984): p. 272.

[56] "The peaks seen here would include those in the northern Bailey Range, Mount Carrie, as well as Ludden Peak and Dodger Point—all above 5000 feet in elevation." Majors, ed., *Northwest Discovery* 5 (Aug. 1984): p. 272.

[57] "Camp 19 of the Press Party, for March 20–27, 1890, was in Geyser Valley, on the north side of the Elwha River, opposite the mouth of Long Creek. This was also the site of Crumback's land claim of March 21, 1890." Majors, ed., *Northwest Discovery* 5 (Aug. 1984): p. 272.

[58] "Though Barnes does not mention it, these three peaks would have also been visible to him on February 27, when he ascended the spur on the south side of Hurricane Hill to take bearing for his map.... It was via triangulation intersections from both viewpoints that Barnes would have been able to plot the positions of these three peaks." Majors, ed., *Northwest Discovery* 5 (Aug. 1984): p. 272.

the striking series, to the westward, and has the shape of a long thin white wedge, in a north and south direction.

Formation of Goblin Canyon

The mountain sides east of Goblin canyon are of slate and sandstone formation. The exposed ledges of slate are excellent and accessible, rock strong and cleaving into thin plates of the best quality. The exposed sandstone frequently occurs in large measures and is yellow and brown in color, but apparently free from oxide of iron. The side hills are undulating, containing large benches, covered with strong clayey soil, and are suitable for agriculture.

To this mountain [Hurricane Hill 5757'] we gave the name of Mt. Brown, in honor of Mr. Amos Brown, of Seattle. It is a high mountain, its peak bare and covered with snow. Upon its long western slope is the succession of benches which were called Deer range. Goblin canyon [Rica Canyon] bounds it on the east and Geyser valley on the south.

Christening the Valley

The valley in which the expedition was encamped is about four miles long and one mile wide in its broadest part. To it we gave the name of "Geyser valley," for the reasons which will appear. We spent nearly two weeks in the valley. All hands needed rest, and an opportunity to repair clothes as well as physical fiber. We needed time to explore the surrounding country and to discover the best route or pass through the mountains to the southward. In addition to these causes Mr. Christie desired to add some pemmican to our stock of provisions. The elk, which he had killed while reconnoitering a week before, still lay undisturbed on the opposite side of the river near our present camp, and would furnish us with abundance of meat to dry for that purpose.

Poor Dollie, the survivor of the excellent pair of pack animals with which we started, had also suffered with overwork. So for a week she chewed the succulent Oregon grape in peace, and her sides took on flesh. Oregon grape and ground laurel are excellent food for fattening, and support the herds of elk and deer that cover the hills, but for a hard working mule they are a poor substitute for oats. But we had no oats for Dollie; she had to live on faith in the "bunchgrass coun-

try" ahead, of which we had heard so much and seen so little. We worked her as lightly as we could when packing, never loading her with more than 150 pounds, but even this she sometimes found difficult to lift over logs.

The little valley nestling in the mountains, an oasis in the desert of snow, won the affection of us all. So much so, in fact, that at least two of the party determined to return to it after the expedition had finished its labors, and to hold down a claim upon its fertile bottoms.[59] Peaceful and happy, covered with mammoth trees, through whose interlacing boughs gleamed the golden sunshine lighting up the long trailing vines, the creepers and mosses of many hues, it seemed a little paradise in contrast with the snowy peaks around us.

The enclosing mountains rising steeply on every side were alive with game animals, tame in the happy ignorance of the gun. The river, here broad and rippling, teemed with salmon, and its deeper pools were filled with trout.

"John Crumback. His Claim."

Crumback was one who determined to make this his home. The land is of course unsurveyed government land, and could only be held by "squatting" upon it and waiting for a survey. Undaunted, however, he decided to drive his stakes and lay the foundation of his cabin. So one afternoon we all lent a hand to start him. Each man took his ax and proceeded to the spot selected for the cabin. A few yards from the river, in the midst of a heavy growth of timber, four trees each a foot in diameter were selected. In a couple of minutes the four were on the ground. In 15 minutes from the first ax-cut, the four logs were of the proper length, saddles were cut in the ends, and the foundation of Crumback's log cabin was in place—dimensions 25x30 feet.[60] This was the first cabin in the Olympic mountains. A big blaze on a neighboring fir was made to bear the following notice to all comers: "John Crumback, his claim." An "expedition blaze" upon the opposite side of the tree was carved to give notice to all would-be claim jumpers and world in general, that behind "John Crumback, his claim," ready to make good the same, were five men, four dogs and a mule, armed with five guns, four rows of teeth and a pair of heels—let him on "jumping" bent beware! These formalities

56

---

[59] "John 'Jack' Henry Crumback (1856–date unknown) and John William Sims (1861–1909) never returned to their proposed homesteads in Geyser Valley. Crumback is reported to have settled near Lake Quinault in or shortly after 1890. However, Geyser Valley did later serve as the home site for such pioneer upper Elwha settlers as Krause, Addison 'Doc' Ludden, William 'Billy' Anderson, E. O. Michaels, and the two Humes brothers, Grant and Will. This pleasant site represented the absolute limit of human settlement on the Elwha River." Majors, ed., *Northwest Discovery* 5 (Aug. 1984): p. 273.

[60] "Five months later, on August 6, 1890, the foundation (four logs) of Crumback's cabin was seen by George A. Pratt's party of prospectors: 'Six of Christy's camps were passed on this day's march, and the party camped where Jack Crumback had staked a claim and put up the foundations of a house.'" Majors, ed., *Northwest Discovery* 5 (Aug. 1984): p. 273.

concluded, feeling that we had just had a hand in an event which might some day become historic in the annals of the Olympic mountains, we returned to camp to celebrate the occasion. Crumback was host, for we were now his guests, and on his claim. It was a royal banquet, and Crumback earned a lasting reputation for his hospitality.

The Important Event Celebrated

Elk tail broth, fresh trout[61] and roast venison comprised the menu as served. But some of the boys, not satisfied with these delicacies, said that, although it was not Sunday, we ought to have an extra allowance of bread, because the occasion was important enough to justify the indulgence and we needed something unusual to remember it by, and besides, they asked, what was a celebration without dessert, anyway. These reasons were deemed cogent, and we had bread with our coffee on this happy and memorable occasion.

For the benefit of history it may be well to state that the foundations of Crumback's cabin were laid with the ceremonies and festivities above mentioned on March 21, the opening day of spring, 1890.

Speaking of banquets, we were now living like princes and kings. For two months while in the lower country, the formula for meal calls came to be something like this: "Gentlemen, dinner is ready; pork and beans are on the table, venison on the hills and quail on the fence." But now we had plenty of game of all kinds. Elk, deer, quail,[62] grouse,[63] chicken and salmon trout[64] in plenty. The mountains were a game preserve. There was really no sport in shooting; the deer stood and gazed at the unaccustomed sight of man, until one could hit them with a stone. It was

no unusual thing to see a band of deer comprising 30 or 40 deer grazing on the hill side within sight of camp.[65] Hayes went out one day hunting and returned an hour afterwards having killed five deer out of such a band. They stood and gazed wonder, and he could have killed half of the band but for the rules strictly enforced in camp of killing no more than we actually needed. Mr. Christie returned to camp on day during the absence of all hands and killed a doe as it stood with its head inside the opening of the tent, probably wondering what kind of a cave it had found. One started them up singly or in pairs from behind every knoll, like jack rabbits on a desert. Owing probably to the severity of the winter, few bears were out of their hibernation as yet. We had seen none although we frequently came across traces of them in this valley where they had been feeding upon the kinnikinnick berries.[66] In consequence of the plentifulness of game, we were living now largely upon fresh meat, and with large camp appetites a vast quantity of it was consumed. It seems almost incredible and we could hardly believe it ourselves, when we calculated up the amount of venison consumed for six days ending on Saturday night while in Press valley. Four deer including one unusually large buck, had been hung up in camp during that period, and eaten besides all the salmon that was desired and a certain quantity of the provisions of the pack. The dogs meanwhile lived upon the bones, fish heads and other refuse.

Delicious Salmon Trout

A most delicious salmon trout abounded in the river. Mr. Christie, one day, took out 14 from a pool adjoining our camping place in less than half an hour. By actual weighing the

---

[61] "This is the first reference to fish being eaten by the Press Party." Majors, ed., *Northwest Discovery* 5 (Aug. 1984): p. 273.

[62] "Two species of resident quail would have inhabited the Olympic Peninsula in 1890, both of which had been recently introduced by man into the Puget Sound area from California. The California quail *Lophortyx californicus* was first brought to Puget Sound in 1857, when a shipment of these birds from San Francisco was let loose near Olympia. The California quail was also independently introduced several years later at Port Townsend, and by 1886 was thriving due to the receptive environment and mild winters. The other quail species, now a permanent resident of the Olympic Peninsula, is the mountain quail *Oreortyx pictus*. This bird was introduced into Washington State from California during the 1880s. Due to the late introduction of this bird, and its preference for the drier areas of Puget Sound (such as Orcas Island and the eastern Olympic Peninsula), it is less likely that the Press Party saw this species on the Elwha River in 1890." Majors, ed., *Northwest Discovery* 5 (Aug. 1984): p. 273.

[63] "Two species of grouse inhabit the Olympic Peninsula, both of which are natives and permanent residents. The varietal Olympic ruffed grouse *Bonasa umbellus castanea* is relatively common throughout this area, and can readily be distinguished during the mating season by the loud drumming or thumping noise made by the male. The mating process, with its accompanying drumming, can occur so early as March; and . . . it was this noise that gave rise to the misnomer 'Geyser Valley.' The sooty blue grouse *Dendragapus obscurus fuliginosus* is found throughout the Olympic Peninsula, from the coast up to sub-Alpine regions; during the winter their food consists largely of the needles and buds of fir trees. The mating call consists of several loud hoots, markedly different from that of the ruffed grouse." Majors, ed., *Northwest Discovery* 5 (Aug. 1984): p. 273.

[64] "'Salmon trout' was a term commonly applied to the steelhead or sea-run rainbow trout *Salmo gairdnerii*. This is the first reference to such migratory fish in the Press Party narratives. The Elwha River once held some of the greatest runs of salmon and steelhead on the Olympic Peninsula. These runs have been virtually obliterated by the construction of the Lake Aldwell and Glines Canyon dams." Majors, ed., *Northwest Discovery* 5 (Aug. 1984): p. 273.

[65] "This constitutes the first reference to the abundance of wildlife within the Olympic Mountains—a region now protected by Olympic National Park." Majors, ed., *Northwest Discovery* 5 (Aug. 1984): p. 274.

[66] "This is the first time that bear is mentioned by the Press Party. . . . Kinnikinnick or bearberry *Arctostaphylos uva-ursi* . . . is an evergreen shrub favored as a source of winter food by both bear and grouse. Indians would use the dried leaves as a form of substitute tobacco. Majors, ed., *Northwest Discovery* 5 (Aug. 1984): p. 274.

catch amounted to 42 pounds, and average weight of three pounds each. They measured from 22 to 26 inches in length. These, by the way, were the first fish we had caught.[67] They were the first of the season to ascend the river. But from this time on while we remained in Press valley we had abundance of them.

In order to have some fish when we should next move camp, which would take us away from the river, we partially smoked a quantity, splitting them down the back, and stringing them on poles behind the fire where they would dry and get an occasional whiff of smoke. About two days of this treatment made them ready to stow away for future use, and lightened them of considerable weight for packing. Toothsome as the fresh fish were, we were unanimous in preferring these half smoked fish to the fresh, and after the first trial hung up all we caught, if there was time, for a little touch of smoke before cooking.

Venison is also improved by being hung where the smoke can get at it now and then. It becomes dryer and more tender and takes on a new flavor, and when put into a pan with a bit of good bacon over a hot camp fire, it becomes a tid bit for an epicure.

The elk which lay on the other side of the river was packed into camp for pemmican. To make pemmican the meat is cut into strips as long and thin as possible and suspended on a rack near the fire where it will dry. It requires from two to three days to thoroughly dry it. When hard the meat is pounded into a kind of coarse meal and put into sacks. Into the sacks is then poured hot grease and it is slated to the taste. The mass hardens and makes excellent food. When one leaves camp for a day or two he puts a "chunk" of this into his pocket and off he goes. It can be eaten raw in its smoked condition, or cooked in almost any manner.

Bear grease is the proper fat to use in making pemmican, lacking that we were fortunate enough to obtain a moderate quantity from the elk himself, to which we added bacon fat. Three or four pounds of fresh meat will make one pound of pemmican. As the weight lost is the water evaporated, pemmican is much better to pack than meat. We

obtained from our elk about 100 pounds of good pemmican.[68] Meanwhile exploration was made of the adjoining region, with most interesting results.

Picking Out a Trail

An Exploration of Elwha Pass From "Geyser Valley" to Head of Convulsion Canyon.

On March 24, while the expedition were encamped in "Press Valley,"[69] Mr. Christie and I, accompanied by Hayes, left camp to explore a trail up the pass. We took with us two day's provisions, a gun, two axes, our blankets and the camera. We followed the river by the west bank for one mile along the valley. Then to avoid the river, which for half a mile washes the mountain side, we climbed the side hill for that distance. Then our course took us again along the bottom lands through tangled thickets and fern, through which in some places we had to cut our way, so dense did it become. At this place also we found a large tract of old brule or burnt timber. The burn had occurred so long ago that around the fallen trees young trees had grown in a thicket almost impassable. The logs lay

AN OLD INDIAN BLAZE.

"March 24 or 25, 1890. This illustration depicts a tree, supposedly blazed by Indians, near the head of Geyser Valley. Since Barnes was the photographer of the expedition, the man depicted in this photograph would be either Christie or Hayes." (Majors, vol. 2, 142)

[67] "The precise date when the first fish were caught cannot be determined. Obviously it was some time in the latter part of March, shortly after their arrival in Geyser Valley. According to Christie's diary, on March 26 he caught the fourteen 'salmon trout,' his first on the Elwha. Barnes also mentions this particular catch as being the first fish taken by the party, but he also states that 'fresh trout' were served at Crumback's dinner on March 21. Barnes further confuses things by twice mentioning the expedition being in Press Valley at this point in his narrative, when he must have meant Geyser Valley." Wood, *Across the Olympic Mountains*, pp. 95–96.

[68] "Barnes has here given one of the best accounts in the Northwest describing the process whereby pemmican is made." Majors, ed., *Northwest Discovery* 5 (Aug. 1984): p. 274. See Christie's journal in part 1, chapter 3, for his March 23 account of pemmican.

[69] "This slip—referring to Geyser Valley as Press Valley—occurs twice, in Barnes' narrative report, on March 21 (see March 28), and March 24. However, it is not until April 14 that Barnes mentions, for the first time, the naming of Press Valley. This earlier prescient use of the term 'Press Valley' constitutes further evidence that Barnes' original field journal was rewritten at a later date, prior to publication. As of March 21 and 24, the Press Party were still encamped in Geyser Valley, and had yet to enter Press Valley farther upstream." Majors, ed., *Northwest Discovery* 5 (Aug. 1984): p. 274.

upon the ground in every direction. This brule, seeing no way to avoid it, we clambered through. We found that it would be necessary to cut a number of the logs to let the expedition mule through and to make a good trail. Passing this we found a magnificent grove of curly maple,[70] each tree of which was worth hundreds of dollars.

Rich Carpet of Moss

Here, as elsewhere in this lovely valley, the ground is covered with a rich carpet of moss inches thick. Bright green with the sunshine of spring. This is a cozy spot and the warmth of spring was calling out the buds, and tender leaves were bursting on every tree. A lovelier valley cannot be in the mountains. Immediately beyond the maples the valley is broken by a bluff, which divides the valley into two nearly equal parts. As we neared the bluff we were so fortunate as to strike an elk trail leading up the steep ascent. Fresh tracks were visible, all going up. Elk had evidently preceded us by several days only. A steep climb of 300 feet took us to the summit of a ridge or spur, extending from the mountain to the river. Beyond this we could see a succession of similar ridges crossing our trail from the mountain on our left to the river on our right, and there forming a deep gorge, from which we could hear sounds of roaring waters. The rolling upland formed by these spurs is easy and gradual in its slopes, suitable for tilling, and with an excellent soil, strong with clay.

As we went on we found this entire upland to have been formerly burnt like that which we had before passed, and like it grown up with a dense growth of young timber.

First Signs of Old Indian Tribes

The elk trail held on over and under logs (for the beggars have long legs and can jump the side of a house), and continuously through the dense growth of young fir. Many times we had to cut to allow our passage. About one mile and a half of this brought us to noonday and we stopped and made coffee, filled our pipes and again went on. A few hundred yards further we made our first discovery of the former presence of man. It was that of a tree double-blazed, after the Indian fashion. Old friend Crusoe, when he discovered the footprints in the sand could not have been more surprised than we. It was the first evidence of the old Indian tribes now gone to the happy hunting grounds, who once hunted

and lived in the fastness of these mountains, and whose memory is now a legend. The tree, a spruce, twenty inches in diameter, bore two trail blazes, made when the tree was a sapling. The surrounding wood and bark of subsequent growth had grown to such a degree as to almost meet across the blaze-faces. Mr. Christie was of the opinion, from the shape of the blaze, that it could have been done only with one of the old Hudson Bay hatchets, which were shaped after the fashion of the Indian tomahawk, such, for instance, as the general reader will remember in the pages of Fenimore Cooper. This opinion was strengthened later in the day further on. By cutting the tree down and examining the rings and the blazes in cross sections it would be easy to arrive at the exact age of the blaze, but we were reluctant to destroy this ancient relic of a pre-historic race and besides, since we had found one, it was probable that we would fall in with others in the future, upon which we could carry our researches. The spruce of these mountains grows slowly; its rings at this period of growth averaging in number 30 years to the inch. This would make the tree 300 years old. The blaze must with certainty have been made before the tree was four inches in diameter, more probably less than three inches; hence we conclude that the blaze was made over 200 years ago,[71] a conclusion which we had opportunities to verify afterwards.

An Old Wringing Post

Half a mile beyond the blazed tree we came upon further and still more interesting evidences of ancient Indian life. Upon a little knoll a few feet to our left, as we followed the old elk trail, overhung by firs of enormous growth and wide spreading foliage, stood a post about six feet in height and 12 inches in diameter at the base. The base was about two feet high and covered with the decayed remains of what was once bark. The upper part of the post had been hewed down to a diameter of seven inches. This was at once identified as an Indian wringing post for dressing skins. The post bore signs of great antiquity. Although standing in a dry and sheltered place it was extremely rotten—so rotten it was that a hard blow with the back of an ax would had shattered it, and a hunting knife could be driven into it to the hilt. Further investigation was postponed until we should pass it while moving camp, for we had work of another kind on hand and hoped to make a number of miles before nightfall. It was proposed that we should

---

[70] "This, too, was undoubtedly big-leaf maple." Wood, *Across the Olympic Mountains*, p. 98.
[71] "This estimate of 200 years for the age of the blaze (dating it as 1690) would not agree with Christie's assertion that the blaze 'could have been done only with one of the old Hudson Bay hatchets.' The first physical contact of the Indians of Washington State with European man took place only in 1775, with the voyage of Hezeta and Bodega; the first overland contact from the east occurred in 1805 with the Lewis and Clark expedition. The actual influence of the Hudson's Bay Company in Washington State dates only from 1824, when it assumed control of the former North West Company fur posts in this region." Majors, ed., *Northwest Discovery* 5 (Aug. 1984): p. 274.

photograph it in place[72] and then remove and cache it nearby so that we could recover it for the benefit of antiquarians. The immediate surrounding would repay investigation and probably yield interesting results. Here the Indians, who are now gathered to their fathers, were accustomed to resort, for the purpose of dressing the skins taken in the chase, and the little knoll and its surroundings had furnished them with a camping place.[73]

A Talk With Indians Remembered

While on the subject it may be interesting to mention, that while we were at the mouth of the river we had an opportunity to converse with the Indians who have settled there. We were unable to gain from them any information regarding the interior of these mountains. Their fathers hunted the same foothills, and so far as we could learn, handed down no traditions, which would indicate more extended travel by their immediate ancestors, or any better knowledge of the country by them than is possessed by their living descendants. The only traditions, so far as our present information goes, relates to long ages ago, similar in character to those related by ex-Governor Semple in his article printed elsewhere in these columns. Therefore we were justified in believing that we were treading passes and gorges long accustomed to the presence of man.

An Excellent Hunting Ground

Two miles further over rough country and through the dense new growth brought us at about 3 o'clock in the afternoon to an elevated point overlooking the river, which here makes a slight bend to the southward. The higher portion of the valley through which we had just passed was literally alive with deer. Although we did not see the animals themselves, owing to the constant noise which we made with our axes, fresh tracks were constantly seen in the snow and mud. As a hunting ground this end of the valley is as good as Deer range.

At the point which we had now reached, opposite the bend of the river, the river receives the waters of a branch stream of considerable size, which we named Lillian river.[74] The triple canyon here is deep. Its almost perpendicular sides are 500 feet in depth. We followed the friendly elk trail some distance up the Lillian river and then down, fording its cold

waters to the knee, and then with much labor and shortness of breath, clambered up the opposite side to an altitude of eight hundred feet. "Poor Dollie" we thought "how she will suffer." It was evident that over this canyon we would have to pack everything on our backs. Dollie would get over, if at all, as the elk do, light. Once over, however, we found an excellent trail skirting the mountain, firm and even, and for the first time since leaving the maple trees free of snow. Fresh elk tracks were visible, a large band of fifty or sixty having passed ahead within a recent period. No fresh deer tracks were seen, however. This mountain side was timbered with a comparatively small growth of mountain fir, the first of this variety that we had seen. The slight underbrush consisted chiefly of Oregon grape.

Hearts Gladdened by a Little Discovery

One little discovery we made here, which we knew would gladden the hearts of the boys in camp. We had brought with us 48 pounds of tobacco. The unexpected delays which we had met incident to the extraordinary winter, and the difficulties apparent ahead, were beginning to create an apprehension in camp that our tobacco would not hold out. This worried the boys not a little. On this side hill we found, growing, beds of kinnikinnick, in some places covering the ground as a trailing vine for many square yards. The leaves of this plant, when fried, furnish an excellent substitute for tobacco. When smoked it has a peculiar flavor not at all unpleasant.

The elk trail here was three or four feet wide, cut deep into the steep slope of the mountain side. The elk had followed it for centuries. Two miles of good traveling on this excellent trail brought us to sunset, and we halted and hunted about and presently discovered on a little bench some 200 feet below a good camping place, with abundance of dry wood. We made ourselves comfortable, and after supper rolled up in our blankets and were soon asleep, with the starry heavens for a tent.

A Gorgeous Scene in a Mountain

This mountain, on whose side we now were, we called Mt. Fitten,[75] in honor of Mr. DuBose Fitten of Seattle.

---

[72] "Neither a print nor an engraving of the 'wringing post' have survived." Majors, ed., *Northwest Discovery* 5 (Aug. 1984): p. 274.

[73] "What the Press Party was observing here was likely the remnant of a former temporary summer elk hunting camp of the Elwha Indians." Majors, ed., *Northwest Discovery* 5 (Aug. 1984): p. 274.

[74] "Neither of the diaries mentions relatives of expedition members (other than the one reference to the illness of Dr. Runnall's wife). When they gave feminine names to natural features, they never indicated whether the name was given to honor a specific person or merely used in a general sense." Wood, *Across the Olympic Mountains*, p. 100.

[75] "The name does not appear on present-day maps, but the peak they intended to be so designated was probably the high point on the ridge northwest of Windfall Peak." Wood, *Across the Olympic Mountains*, p. 101.

60

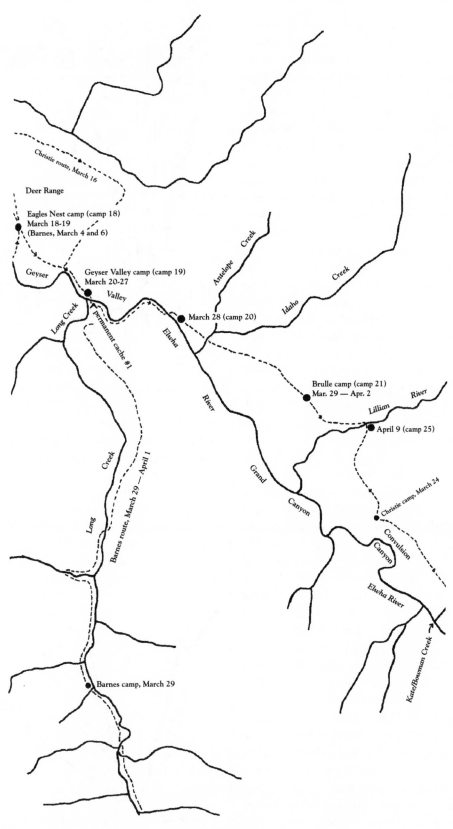

Christie route, March 16

Deer Range

Eagles Nest camp (camp 18)
March 18-19
(Barnes, March 4 and 6)

Geyser Valley camp (camp 19)
March 20-27

Geyser

Valley

Long Creek

Permanent cache #1

Long Creek

Antelope Creek

Idaho Creek

Elwha

March 28 (camp 20)

Barnes route, March 29 — April 1

Brulle camp (camp 21)
Mar. 29 — Apr. 2

River

River

Lillian

April 9 (camp 25)

River

Grand

Canyon

Christie camp, March 24

Convulsion

Canyon

Elwha River

Kate/Bowman Creek

Barnes camp, March 29

(Majors, vol. 5, 261)

As dawn appeared we were stirring, and from our perch on the mountain side there spread out before us a view which would gladden the heart of the most hardened explorer. The shelf overhung the river, which roared 800 feet below, and which appeared foamy white and light green with here and there the deep green so characteristic of these mountain streams. The canyon ran for miles up the river. Above the canyon the gap appeared to broaden into a beautiful valley with slopping sides clothed in the dark green of the conifer forests, extending southeastward for miles, terminating in the distance, perhaps 20 miles away, in a huge solitary mountain (afterwards named Mt. Dana) swathed in snow from base to summit, standing in the pale light of early morn like a great white specter, with outspread arms guarding the hidden and unknown region beyond. As the light increased we could gradually distinguish vague and shadowy outlines of other peaks, a cloud of specters hovering a ghostly throng behind the mighty chief. Suddenly as we gazed a ray of the rising sun swept the summit. In a moment the specters of the night vanished and in their stead stood mighty peaks, gilded with the rosy hues of morn seeming to welcome instead of repel. It was enough for us. Soon the aroma of coffee and the odor of venison steaks added their cheering influence to our already buoyant spirits and we were as eager to be off as school boys for a vacation.

A Great Land Slide

As we again followed the southward trail of the elk winding around the mountain side we arrived in about an hour at a great land slide, extending from the river below to the very trail on which we stood, a vertical height of 800 feet. The wild and rugged appearance of the slide and the peculiar character of the wall of rock on the opposite side of the canyon brought to our mind at once the legend related by Governor Semple, of the convulsion of nature or catastrophe which had overwhelmed the Indians while attending the last pow-wow in the mountains, in which the "Spirit of the Mountains" shook the earth, opened great chasms and swallowed up the returning bands. To one unacquainted with the record of the rocks as they tell their own history regardless of legends or traditions, here seems to be a confirmation of the Indian story. The canyon for about four miles is from 700 to 1000 feet in depth, with walls of solid rock inclined at an angle of eighty degrees. The slide is on the eastern side, is about 400 feet wide and inclined at about 45 degrees. There is little or no debris at the bottom, the slide having occurred gradually by the slipping down of material as it became loosened by natural causes. As the river passes the slide it makes

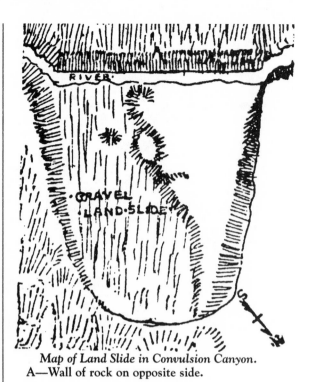

**Map of Land Slide in Convulsion Canyon.
A—Wall of rock on opposite side.**

"Probably March 25, 1890. Map sketched by Barnes." (Majors, vol. 2, 142)

a double bend, in form like a very flat letter "U," the bottom of the letter being towards the slide. The appearance of the wall on the opposite side of the canyon is that of a great flat rock, 800 feet high and 500 or 600 feet wide, standing on and leaning against the mountain side. A ravine 50 feet deep separated the top of the rock from the mountain, giving further color to the convulsion theory. It was as if it had been lifted from the slide cavity and tilted bodily across the canyon against the mountain opposite, the stream then changing its course and running around the rock.

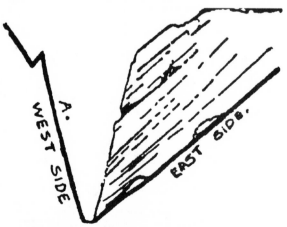

Sectional View of Canyon at Landslide.

"Probably March 25, 1890. Drawn by Barnes." (Majors, vol. 2, 142)

62

The Convulsion Theory Groundless

A moments examination, however, reveals the groundlessness of the convulsion theory. Aside from the fact that the rock would in that case have to be lifted upward to gain its present position, the stratification of the rock conforms to that of the mountain side behind it, while it does not conform with the side behind it, while it does not conform with the side upon which the slide occurs. The same peculiar conformation of rock is repeated in two other places in this canyon without any corresponding cavity opposite it.[76] Nevertheless out of respect to the old tradition we named this "Convulsion Canyon." We amused ourselves for a half an hour gazing into the great gulf below us, and rolled down a few boulders to see them dash to pieces at the bottom. A piece of rock started from the top would go bounding down detaching a hundred others on the way and rock and gravel would continue to clatter down for several minutes. It was great sport for the boys, but we could not remain for much of it.

We had by this time recognized the trail as an ancient Indian trail, which the elk continued to follow after it had been deserted by the Indians. Old blazes were seen at frequent intervals. They were correctly blazed and not to be confounded with the scars on the trees made by the horns of the elk as they brushed the bark. These blazes were all very ancient. Coming at last to the brow of a hill where we stopped and made coffee, we cut into one of these blazed trees. The tree, a white fir, was 32 inches in diameter. We found by actual count 210 rings, covering the edge of the blaze, indicating a probable age of over 200 years for the blaze. The blaze had grown with the tree, and was now about 10 feet long.[77]

Another Wringing Post Discovered

A few hundred yards further on we came upon another wringing post similar to the one already described. It was in a little glade by the side of a brook, an excellent place for a camp. It was like the other, very old and rotten, and had similarly been a standing tree dubbed down to the proper size. Our trail was thus becoming more and more interesting.

We had found a trail blazed by the old Indian and still kept fresh by his successor, the elk. Logs lay across it in every direction, but it was still well defined and could easily be made passable. Moreover, we were cheered by finding ourselves on a road. Roads lead somewhere, and this one possibly led into some beautiful valley with lakes, or perhaps a pass through the mountains. But our little party of three was now out of provisions and we had to turn back to camp. Eight hours at a rapid gait back over the trail which we had partially cleared, brought us in shortly after dark. And over our coffee and pipes we cheered the boys with the news of a good trail ahead.

Exploration of Belle River

No Glacier Found on Mount Olympus—Great Depth of Snow

Near the foot of Press Valley the Elwha river receives the waters of a considerable tributary, which winds around the eastern base of Olympus, and has its source in a majestic range of mountains to the southward, which we afterwards found to be a spur of the Bailey range.[78] Viewed from the mountain side north of our camp,[79] the course of the stream presented the appearance of a deep canyon with steep sides, formed by the easterly spurs of Olympus on the one hand and by the slopes of a lower range on the other. In the distance could be seen through the gap two remarkable peaks,[80] visible from base to summit, glittering white in the sun. Yet there was no certainty that the

63

---

[76] "Geologist Rowland Whitney Tabor (1932–) clarifies the origin of Convulsion Canyon: 'The peculiar knob of rock that seems to block the straight course of the river, throwing it into a U-bend, is a glacially carved boss of resistant pillow basalt. Most likely the river was diverted around the knob by ice or moraine at a much higher erosional level and has since entrenched itself in this convolute gorge. Forced to one side of the valley, the river undercuts the slope below the trail, creating the abyss below the viewpoint.' (Rowland Whitney Tabor, *Guide to the Geology of Olympic National Park*, Seattle: University of Washington Press, 1975, p. 91)." Majors, ed., *Northwest Discovery* 5 (Aug. 1984): p. 275.

[77] "This feature could not have been a true blaze, for such an injury to the bark of a tree would not have elongated so greatly . . . with advancing age." Majors, ed., *Northwest Discovery* 5 (Aug. 1984): p. 275. "This last statement raises considerable doubt as to whether the marks were, in fact, bona fide blazes, and arouses the suspicion that the men were drawing erroneous conclusions. A scar made on the trunk of a tree by an axe does not, of course, grow larger as the tree grows. The Press Party's 'Indian blazes' may have been scars cut on tree trunks by neighboring trees falling during winter storms, a not unusual occurrence in the Olympics. One should note that Barnes states the 'blazes' were not to be confused with marks made by elk antlers. Also, the explorers could have mistaken a rotting tree trunk—the remnant of a tree whose top had been broken off in some long past windstorm—for the Indians' 'wringing post.'" Wood, *Across the Olympic Mountains*, p. 105.

[78] "This is the first mention in Barnes' narrative of the Bailey Range. Actually, the name was given to the range at a later date by the expedition." Wood, *Across the Olympic Mountains*, p. 109.

[79] "This . . . is the slope above the Geyser Valley camp 19 for March 20–27, located opposite the mouth of Long Creek. This vantage point, visited by Barnes on March 27, provided a view southward, directly up the valley of Long Creek. It was likely on March 27, 1890, while making cartographic observations, that Barnes made his decision to explore Long Creek." Majors, ed., *Northwest Discovery* 5 (Aug. 1984): p. 284.

[80] Ludden Peak, 5828 feet, and the north peak of Mount Ferry, 6157 feet.

stream ended there. There was an appearance as of a pass[81] making to the westward between Olympus and the range containing the peaks observed, through which we might reach the watershed of the Quiniault. To settle the doubt I determined on the trip. Besides this reason it was reported that Olympus cradled a glacier on its eastern sides.[82] We had examined every stream draining its northern slopes without finding in their waters any evidence of its existence.[83] By this stream, then, if by any, the glacier must drain, and I wished to examine it.

Off With a Blanket and an Ax

Saturday morning, March 29, I left camp with my blanket and an ax and four day's provisions. Half an hour later I entered the canyon, and there found fairly good deer trails leading up the eastern side to a height of 700 or 800 feet. The canyon at its lower end is wild and rocky. On the left, looking up from the entrance, is a great rock towering up and overhanging the stream below, giving one the sense of its being about to roll out of its place. It bears a remarkable resemblance to the head of an enormous buffalo, the hill side as it swells upwards behind it resembling the hump on the shoulders of that animal. The stream is of considerable size and at this point is most romantic in its scenery. Little bridal veil, cascades leap into from 100 or 200 feet above, sparkling and bright, against the deep green of the mosses and ferns. The entrance being so near the river and so easily reached, is well worth the turning aside for half an hour to see. Scrambling along the mountain side in this way, many times holding on for dear life to keep from slipping. I arrived late in the afternoon at a large mountain torrent, which came down between the two great eastern spurs of Olympus. This was the only possible glacial stream. Its waters were clear as crystal and gave no evidence of a glacial origin. I ascended the stream for about 300 yards over a bed buried in logs and snow.[84]

The Press Blaze

It may be interesting to future explorers to observe that in cutting the blaze, which is the *sign manual* of the expedition, and which consists of three blazes, one above another, I took care to cut the lower one on a level of the surface of the snow. Future explorers will be able to note the depth of the snow and understand, as well, how the blazes came to be so far up the trees when I had no ladder. In some places the lower one will be found ten or twelve feet high. I made a practice of thus blazing the trees on the entire trip.

Crossing the tributary stream, I again climbed through much snow and reached a great land slide, down which was constantly falling fragments of rock and gravel, detached by the frost. I had to descend nearly to the bottom to cross, and when I did cross it, it was quickly, and with my heart in my mouth, for the falling rock made it ticklish business across a space of about two hundred feet. The sun by this time was down, and hastening up the mountain side again to a little space clear of snow I made camp for the night[85] and dried my clothing as well as circumstances permitted. The formation of the canyon and mountain sides observed during the day was mainly slate and sandstone, twisted and contorted to an astonishing degree, with here and there deposits of gravel and clay.

I had seen two deer and numberless tracks, including those of a bear. I was away again the next morning before the sun, traveling up the west side of the canyon. Sometimes at a considerable height, and at other times ascending to avoid heavy snow or jutting walls of rock, but the west side I found to be so cut up by side gullies and small torrents that I crossed the river to the east side.[86]

Fatigued With Travel

This day was a repetition of the preceding but worse. Toward evening I found myself painfully struggling around the

64

---

[81] "This . . . was likely the saddle in the Bailey Range between Stephen Peak and the north peak of Mt. Ferry 6157'." Majors, ed., *Northwest Discovery* 5 (Aug. 1984): p. 284.

[82] "This is a remarkable statement, for the eastern slope of Mount Carrie 6995' does indeed hold a substantial glacier. This information was likely derived ultimately from the trapper William Everett, or from the Elwha (Clallam) Indian Boston Charlie. Everett reportedly visited Cream Lake in 1885. Everett is known to have used both the Boulder Creek and the Cat Creek approaches to reach the northen Bailey Range, prior to 1908. Boston Charlie may also have used both of these approaches as early as 1893." Majors, ed., *Northwest Discovery* 5 (Aug. 1984): pp. 284–85.

[83] "Glacially fed streams do not normally present a milky appearance in winter or early spring, for it is still too early in the season for the actual ice of the glacier itself to melt and release the ground rock powder held within. Note that whereas Cat and Long creeks drain from glaciers on Mount Carrie, FitzHenry and Haggerty creeks (crossed by Barnes within March 2–4) do not." Majors, ed., *Northwest Discovery* 5 (Aug. 1984): p. 285.

[84] "It is this very stream that drains the largest glacier on Mount Carrie, situated on its eastern slope." Majors, ed., *Northwest Discovery* 5 (Aug. 1984): p. 285.

[85] "Barnes' camp for March 29, 1890, was on the west side of Long Creek, 0.8 mile above the Carrie Glacier tributary, at the south edge of a slide area." Majors, ed., *Northwest Discovery* 5 (Aug. 1984): p. 285.

[86] "Barnes' camp for March 30, 1890 was on the east side of Long Creek, about 2.3 miles northwest of Dodger Point, at about 2200 feet elevation." Majors, ed., *Northwest Discovery* 5 (Aug. 1984): p. 285.

face of the mountain side at the head of the canyon overlooking a little basin encircled by Olympus and the peaks of the Bailey range. I was so fatigued with travel through the heavy snow that when at last I found a spot from which the wind had blown the snow I could scarcely stand. I sketched the main features of the scene before me, took several observations for my chart and then made camp for the night.[87]

There was no pass here to the southward or westward. Across the little basin, which formed a head of the watershed of the stream up which I had been traveling, rose a solid wall of rock 5000 feet high,[88] with great precipices here and there of a thousand feet. The peaks formed at their base a little amphitheater, crescent-shaped, with one end touching Olympus and the other sweeping around the mountain, from the side of which I viewed it. From its seemingly narrow wall towered the pinnacle, and more conspicuous still was a thin wall-like peak, shaped like a great eagle's beak, clear cut against the dark blue sky. This remarkable mountain is visible from Deer range. We had first seen it from there and gave it the name of Mount Squire, after Senator Watson C. Squire of the state of Washington.

A Cougar Hunt Backwards

The next morning I arose very early. I had a down hill road homeward, and by starting on the early morning snow crust, I hoped to get out of the snow by noon before it should become softened by the sun. By the time it was light enough to see I had had my breakfast and was homeward bound, and here came my only advantage of the trip. As I followed back my trail of the night before, 50 yards from camp, I suddenly came upon the tracks of a large cougar. The tracks measured six inches across, and the animal had been following my trail. Fifty yards from camp, the animal having evidently sighted me, had left the trail, going up the mountain, apparently circling around my camp. The tracks, when made, were in soft snow, showing that they had been made before the night had hardened it, probably shortly after I had passed. Here was a surprise, and I challenge any man to find in the morning that a great cat probably five or six feet long has been prowling around him during the night, without twinges of con-

science. Then my mind went back to my fire, that I was sure had been my protection—but by what an accident! When I carry my blankets I am accustomed to neglect my fire. I had done so on the first night out. Rolled up snugly, and comparatively comfortable in them, I had permitted the fire to burn down and, finally, to go out, but last night, I was too tired to make a respectable fire. I had simply pulled from the bare spot selected, six or eight small cedar trucks, laid them parallel and made the fire at the lower end. Thus, quite by accident, the fire had an excellent opportunity to burn gradually uphill. This it did, and in the morning it was still smoldering. It was to this, I had no doubt, I owed my life. There is considerable question whether a cougar will attack a man unless driven to it by hunger, but fancy a great cat with such an opportunity as a sleeping man in the woods. As I studied that cougar track I had precious little doubt as to where I would have been that morning but for being close to a good fire. I was without my gun for I was traveling against time, as light as possible, but of course even a gun is of no use with a cougar clutching one's throat.[89] Following the trail homeward I found that the cougar had first struck my track where I had crossed the river the afternoon before and had followed them to camp.

Arrival Back at Camp

After some hours of down hill traveling I arrived in camp at about 3 P.M., glad to be once more in more lively society. On the western slope of the mountain, which lies east of the lower end of the canyon, I found at an elevation of 500 feet an excellent bench about two miles long and a mile wide, with excellent soil, and with running streams of water. The ground under the snow was covered with grass, and in patches, with Oregon grape and ground laurel.

On the western side of the canyon I discovered a stream, whose bed was full of a deposit of lime. The mosses and ferns which were exposed to the spray were covered with beautiful white concretions of the same material.

The formation is for the most part slate. The strata, like all observed before, is tilted almost to a vertical position. Several out-croppings of granite occur at high altitudes. There are good prospects for silver.

65

---

[87] "Barnes' camp for March 31, 1890, was on the east side of Long Creek, about 1.2 miles northwest of Ludden Peak, at about 2700 feet elevation (or somewhat higher up the hillside to the east)." Majors, ed., *Northwest Discovery* 5 (Aug. 1984): p. 285.

[88] "The wall was the face of Mt. Ferry 6157'. Barnes had entered a cul de sac on the eastern flanks of the Bailey Range, where its narrow spine widens perceptibly into a complex of cliffs and rugged mountain spurs. His statement about a 'wall of rock 5000 feet high' is understandable, if somewhat exaggerated—assuming that this was his mistake and not a printer's error in the published account of the expedition." Wood, *Across the Olympic Mountains*, p. 109. "... at the most the maximum relief at the head of Long Creek is about 3100 feet." Majors, ed., *Northwest Discovery* 5 (Aug. 1984): p. 285.

[89] Whether Barnes was truly in danger of being attacked by a cougar is a subject of disagreement: Wood feels an attack was improbable (Wood, *Across the Olympic Mountains*, p. 110), but Majors agrees with Barnes and notes that there are several recorded cougar attacks in Washington State (Majors, ed., *Northwest Discovery* 5, Aug. 1984: p. 285).

Observation of the Geyser

A Puzzling Phenomenon Which Gave a Name to the Valley

While camped in Geyser valley we heard, at intervals, certain sounds, which we attributed at first to snow or land slides, but on Saturday, March 29, early in the morning, these sounds were heard more distinctly, the wind being light. They were first heard in camp at about 8 A.M. On crossing the river at 9 o'clock, as I was starting out to explore Belle river, I could hear them much more distinctly than in camp. The sound was so remarkable that I returned to camp, and with Mr. Christie, crossed the river again to note them with greater care. After listening a while it was suggested that the sounds might be from a geyser. We timed the intervals between the reports and found them to be about four minutes. We were unable to remain at the spot long. At 10 o'clock, when I took my final departure for Belle river, the sounds still continued, and it was half an hour before I lost them as I entered the canyon.

On my return the following Tuesday I found that camp had been moved up the valley in my absence, but as I passed the place where the sound had been heard most distinctly, on the preceding Saturday, I heard the sounds once more. It was then 11 o'clock. I remained until noon, noting the characteristics, apparent direction, etc., hoping thereby to obtain some clue to its whereabouts, as well as to identify this particular geyser if we should afterwards find more than one.

The wind was light and variable. The clouds overhead drifting slowly westsouthwest; weather clear.

Intervals Between Reports

Time (hours, minutes, seconds)	Interval (minutes, seconds)
11:00:00	—:—
11:4:11	4:11
11:8:11	4:00
11:12:47	4:30
11:16:50	4:03
11:21:06	4:16
11:25:18	4:12
11:29:30	4:32
11:34:06	4:36
11:37:36	3:30
11:43:54	6:18
11:48:00	4:06
11:53:15	5:45
11:58:10	4:55

The sounds lasted exactly eight seconds, beginning slowly like the clicking of a ratchet on a cog-wheel, gradually increasing in rapidity, and at the end becoming too rapid for the ear to distinguish, and ceasing abruptly at the end of a few seconds. The direction seemed to be southeast—the direction of the head of the valley—but the high mountains by which the valley is surrounded rendered the real direction of the sound extremely uncertain. At noon I went on to camp, intending to return after dinner and observe the phenomenon until it should cease. As I departed, the sounds gradually became fainter, until half a mile away, at "Brule creek," they died out altogether. It was evident that the sounds were reflected to the spot where they were most distinctly heard from a considerable distance. I returned at 2 P.M., but the sounds had ceased.

The geyser was therefor in action on March 29 from 8 to 10:30 A.M., or two and one-half hours; and again on April 1 from 11 to 12:15, or one and one-quarter hours, with an interval of about three days between. Whether it were active within that three days could not be known, nor could it be known how long it continued in action, if more than two and one-half hours.

At our camp at the upper end of the valley nothing had been heard. Upon the next and the following days, while we were packing some supplies into camp which still remained below, during which we passed the point where the sound could be heard, the geyser was silent. On the third day it was again heard, this time by Crumback.

The geyser has therefore an interval between its times of activity of about three days. Acting upon the knowledge thus gained, we were particularly on the alert thereafter on every third day. At length, on April 13, we again heard the geyser, between the hours of 4 and 5:30 in the morning. We were then in camp opposite a large island on the Elwha four miles below Lillian river. On April 4, 7, and 10, it is probable that we would have heard it if our position had been favorable.

We did not hear the sounds again. Owing to the necessity for constant travel, we were unable to make any explorations for the geyser and were compelled to leave it for future explorers.

Camp Moved Up the Valley

While the explorations were in progress, camp was gradually removed from the lower end of the valley, up the bluff to a new camp on the rolling upland toward the head of the valley. Here much cutting of logs and clearing of brush was necessary to make packing at all feasible. The growth of small fir which covered the ground held in its protecting shade a great quantity of snow. In some places the snow was three feet deep, and extremely soft. We had showers nearly every night, so that while working, and afterwards while packing, through this portion of our route we suffered great discomforts. These small trees held the weather; upon every needle point trembled a tiny drop, and a touch would precipitate a quart of water upon us. Thus constantly drenched to the skin, and in snow which held water like a sponge, it was like a continual bath.

On April 2nd we commenced packing from the upper camp to Lillian river, and on the next day we struck camp and packed up the remainder. We had less difficulty getting Dollie over Lillian river than we anticipated.

A Cache at Lillian River

At Lillian river Mr. Christie decided to cache all of the supplies of the expedition for the present and to go on up the Elwha canyon, to reach the valley ahead and gain more knowledge of the country before moving up the supplies. If game were as plentiful above as it were below, we would have no difficulty in living upon the country. On March 25th, while on the exploring expedition whose history has been already narrated, we had observed, some 15 or 18 miles above the junction of the Lillian with the main stream, a valley larger by far than Geyser valley, and from which four passes or gaps appeared to radiate like the spokes of a wagon wheel. This valley seemed to be the key to the mountains, and would make an excellent base of supplies and center for exploration. This then was our present objective point.

Of the stores with which we started we now had remaining 250 pounds of flour, 60 pounds of beans, 30 pounds of bacon, 20 pounds of tea, 15 pounds of salt, 5 pounds of prunes, 7 pounds of tobacco, 20 pounds of sundries, with 50 pounds of pemmican, a total of provisions of over 400 pounds.

Besides the provisions we had remaining four Winchester rifles, 40-65, one shotgun, plenty of ammunition, fishing tackle and re-loading tools. One tent, 12x14, two large canvas sheets. Kitchen outfit, comprising a nest of sheet iron camp kettles, one large and two small frying pans, tin plates, etc. Tools: Several light carpenter's tools, two 6-pound axes, five 3-pound axes, one shovel, one spade, one pickax, one goldpan and a rock hammer. A 4x5 inch dry plate camera, with films for 250 exposures, instruments for topographical work, a field glass, an aneroid barometer, etc. A few medicines. Each individual was provided with a good, comfort-

able pair of blankets, cartridge belt, sheath knife, etc. The weight of this outfit was about 800 pounds.

No More Spirits

It will be observed that although greatly reduced in amount by the winter's consumption, we still had, with proper economy, provisions to last a considerable period. Our supply of ammunition would provide us with meat as long as we chose to stay or the meat consented to be killed. The sugar had been gone some time. We used the last of the coffee in Geyser valley, but we still had tea. We started with 50 pounds of salt, now reduced to 15, more by shrinkage than by use. Lest any evil minded person should imagine that "sundries" in the above list means *wet goods* it may be just as well to state that it does not. We had some excellent whisky in the medicine chest on starting, but during the first two or three weeks so much palliative was required for cramps in the stomach, nausea, sore thumbs, etc., that it was all consumed. Fortunately all recovered from these diseases and the camp has since had no necessity for the remedy.

Carrying Sour Dough

Baking powder was out, so that we relied upon raised bread, and carried with us from one camp to another a small lump of sour dough. We made bread whenever the opportunity presented, baking a large quantity at once. It was difficult at times to raise the bread as well as could be desired, out of doors, with cold weather and other unfavorable conditions, but once raised, our loaves, baked before the fire, made bread that was not to be despised. At other times, when unable to spend the time required for raising bread, we made thin cakes of flour and water, unleavened, and baked them in frying pans. These are familiarly known as "gillettes."

On the reconnoitering expedition upon which we now started we took with us the necessary camping outfit and provisions for a week. This consisted of 25 pounds of pemmican, 25 pounds of flour, some beans and bacon. A canvas shelter, guns, axes, cooking utensils and blankets completed our outfit.

Dollie went up the hill "Difficulty,"[90] eight hundred feet above the Lillian, with less trouble than was expected. Reaching the old elk trail we skirted the mountain side, passed above the great land slide in Convulsion canyon, and late in the afternoon went into camp at Kate creek.[91]

67

---

[90] "This is an allusion to the Hill 'Difficulty' in the great Christian allegory by the English Puritan author, John Bunyan (1628–1688), *The Pilgrim's Progress from This World to That Which Is to Come*, published in two separate parts in 1678 and 1684. Until now, this fact has totally escaped the notice of all historians and scholars on the Press Party." Majors, ed., *Northwest Discovery* 5 (Sept. 1984): p. 306.
[91] "This is probably the stream known today as Bowman Creek." Wood, *Across the Olympic Mountains*, p. 116.

Dollie Takes Many Headers

The next morning we were early astir, and our course took us over rougher country. We traveled until noon over rolling spurs, heavily timbered and deep in snow. The land is not too rough for farming, and if cleared would be excellent land, as the soil is good and upon a high bench, about 200 feet above the river, and well watered.

Finally, however, blocked by the deep snow that lay under the shelving trees, we could lead Dollie no farther on the bench, and were compelled to climb the mountain side behind. Reaching an elevation of about 1000 feet above the river we found better traveling for some two miles. This brought us to a deep gorge, at the bottom of which a mountain torrent was wearing still deeper its bed. It being impossible to cross this we descended, and finally reached the river one mile away. But the last 300 yards! Logs, snow and debris of the woods lay so heavy and deep toward the bottom that it was extraordinary how Dollie ever got through. A rough and headlong tumble and roll would carry her down 100 feet and land her over head and pack in a snow drift. We would dig her out—fortunately we had the shovel to do it with—and another tumble would put her down a little farther, until at last we reached bottom with a level space to camp.[92] But such a camp for April! Snow waist deep and no feed for Dollie after her exhaustive struggle. As for ourselves we were no less exhausted. But the shovel soon produced wonders. We shoveled out space for camp, spread our shelter, cut logs and made a fire. We managed to gather a handful of ferns for Dollie, and gave her a pound of our precious beans, but she got most of her provender that night by munching spruce boughs from our bed—filling, but indigestible.

"We'll Call This Sunday"

During the night it rained in torrents and continued during the forenoon of the next day. As we were all of us, including Dollie, badly knocked out by the preceding day, we called this Sunday and rested. Up the hill side we gathered some Oregon grape for Dollie, and so we were all comfortable. We were now out of meat, not having seen a deer for two days, except two which the dogs gave chase to, and which therefore we did not get. Mr. Christie tried the fishing in the river today, but evidently the fish have not ascended so far, for he did not get a bite.

Along the river bottoms the next day we found travel still bad for a mile and a half. We camped[93] in the first of a succession of little bottoms, which terminate in the large valley about six miles above.

More Pemmican Made

Below the Lillian we had plenty of game. Deer and trout were easily gotten, and we lived for the most part on fresh meat and fish. The greatest economy began to prevail at this time in camp with regard to reserve stores. When we left the Lillian we had expected to find game as easily as before, and had brought with us as meat only the pemmican already mentioned. But our experience at this stage of our exploration is illustrative of the vicissitudes of a hunter's life. With the exception of the two deer chased by the dogs we had not seen so much as a fresh track of any kind of animal since crossing the Lillian.[94] Pemmican was made to last us two days, so that when we reached the present camp we had been two days without fresh meat, and the inroads into the more valued provisions of the pack had been unfortunately great. Our stores were valuable—valuable from the amount of toil and hardship borne in getting them in, and also because they were dwindling to small proportions. Flour and bacon were a luxury, not to be eaten as common food.

Nero's Famous Luxury Outdone

Nero's dish of nightingales tongues seemed less extravagant to us than one of bacon and beans. As Jack said, as he dangled a couple of the succulent beans upon his fork preparing to masticate the same, "Many a millionaire has no beans for supper tonight." Until we reached the camp in the bottoms we had no time for hunting, unless the animals were considerate enough to come our way—which they had not been. It hurt our feelings, this extravagance, but there was not help for it, and we punished the stores with vigorous appetites. The result was that we must all go hunting the next day, and it was hunting for grub, no fancy sportsmanship. Meat we must have, for even of the precious company stores there was but two day's supply left in the advanced camp. But there is many a slip in hunting. During the night five inches of snow fell in the bottoms where we were encamped.[95] On the moun-

---

[92] "Camp 23 of the Press Party, 'Deep Snow Camp,' for April 4–5, 1890, was located at the confluence of Prescott Creek and the Elwha River, probably on the north side of Prescott Creek." Majors, ed., *Northwest Discovery* 5 (Sept. 1984): p. 306.

[93] See footnote on April 6 entry in Christie's journal in part 1, chapter 3.

[94] "Game was to remain scarce for the remaining six weeks of the expedition. The men never again encountered the abundance of elk met with in Geyser Valley. It was still too early in the season for the Elwha elk herds to move up valley from their wintering grounds in the Geyser Valley area, as the snow on the upper Elwha was yet too deep to allow easy travel and grazing." Majors, ed., *Northwest Discovery* 5 (Sept. 1984): p. 308.

[95] "This was the next to the last substantial snowfall of the winter." Majors, ed., *Northwest Discovery* 5 (Sept. 1984): p. 308.

tain side the snow was found to be still deeper. The morning grew warm and by 8 o'clock water was dripping from the trees and little pats of wet snow fell from the branches as they became heavy in melting. It became impossible to distinguish or follow any tracks and the hunters returned empty-handed toward evening. Not a single animal had been seen during the entire day. This was a state of things we were not used to, and as we looked at each other and the small amount of flour in the bag and thought of the distance back to the cache, the conviction came home to every man that tomorrow it must be an "elk or bust."

Starting on a Determined Hunt

So next morning early we got a good start with injunctions to shoot everything in sight from a herd of elk to a jay-bird on the fence. Two of the boys were sent up the mountain side back of camp and one down the river with fishing gear with letter of marque and full authority to catch fish. We had tried the fishing near camp the day before but without success. Mr. Christie and your correspondent took the river upstream. Climbing the lower slopes of the mountain we came upon a long and narrow glen about one mile from camp running up the mountain side. Sweeping this with the field-glass from above we saw in its lower part, about 800 yards distant, an elk.

He was lying upon the ground apparently asleep in the sun. His wide branching antlers lay against his back, his feet drawn up. That we had surprised his majesty asleep seemed certain. It was long range, but the wind was right for a successful stalk. I dropped behind a log, covered him with my rifle, while in an instant Christie divested himself of unnecessary hamper and disappeared in the bushes on the right. I waited, and the elk seemed entirely unsuspicious of our presence. Presently I saw Christie emerge from a clump of undergrowth and glide as silently as an Indian to the shelter of a fallen log. Now and then I could see him slowly and cautiously getting nearer and nearer until he reached a big stump covered with mosses and vines within easy range of his prey. Ten minutes had passed and I began to feel the tension relaxing a bit as I saw him take careful aim through the vines. Already broiled steak and marrow bones seemed to greet my hungry palate. But there came no report. I wondered if his rifle had jammed. Presently his gun slowly dropped and his head cautiously appeared as he seemed to survey the animal in surprise. Then he came out from his hiding place, walked up to the prostrate elk and beckoned to me. Was he dead? I came down in a hurry. Before I got there, however, it became so certain that he was dead that I slackened my speed some-

what. In fact, it became evident that he had been dead some time! As he lay upon the ground we could not but admire his mammoth proportions. It was a bull, and his antlers, which we saved, measured 5 feet 6 inches across, and the animal when alive must have weighed 600. He had evidently died of starvation—that was the conclusion we arrived at. With the hill side buried beneath the unusual snows he had starved to death.

Visions of marrow bones were more shadowy as we turned and climbed the hill once more. Half a mile further on we struck fresh elk tracks not an hour old, leading up the river. We resolved to stalk.

One of the Most Interesting Sports

Stalking the elk is one of the most interesting of sports. Wary, the animal is difficult of approach; fleet and tireless of foot, pursuit is impossible; watchful and timid, he is ever on the alert; armed with wide branching antlers and sharp cloven hoofs, he is a dangerous foe if brought to bay. Hastily preparing ourselves for what might prove a long trail we began the stalk. Absolute silence was necessary for we might at any moment come upon his lordship. For two hours, over ridge and spur, climbing logs and through the dense shade of the woods, we patiently followed his tracks, sometimes easily seen in the snow, and at others with difficulty as we passed over grassy or stony places. Then we became aware that it was after noon and with sharp appetites we sat down beside a tiny rivulet to lunch sparingly upon what we hoped would be the last gillettes we would be compelled to eat for some time. Quenching our thirst at the rivulet we again set out. Climbing the ridge bordering the stream we became aware that the hour old trail had suddenly become fresher. At the tip of the ridge and down the other side the animal had traveled with great leaps, going down twenty feet at a jump. We must have surprised him upon that very ridge, and he had gone down the other side as we approached the rivulet. Blaming ourselves for stopping to lunch, we hastened on, now hot for the game, but with little hope of seeing him again. At the foot of the ridge water was still trickling into the foot track he had made in the soft mud of a spring. Presently we saw where he had been joined by two other elk and they all traveled on together. It was probable that they were the scouts of a band which they were traveling to join. Now their tracks lay straight ahead as near as the nature of the woods and hills would allow. Instead of now and again stopping to take a bite from a tempting sprig of laurel, they hurried on with great strides. All our exertion seemed to bring us no nearer our supper. We had little hope now of getting anything better

69

than a snap shot, for the animals were on the alert, but even that was desirable in the reduced state of the camp larder.

At last the trail struck the river bottom, and passed over a wide space covered with cobble stones and boulders. We wore spikes on our boots, a necessary precaution in these log bestrewn forests, against slipping, for one is nearly half the time running along logs. In spite of the most careful stepping our spikes made a slight noise. We also found difficulty in tracing the trail here, which might lead across the river or up the mountain side at any point, and this necessary care delayed us.

The Famous Stag Sighted

Finally we reached a wooded tongue or low spur running quite to the water, and as we crossed this, bringing to our eyes a large valley beyond, we got just one glimpse of golden yellow disappearing in the brush, not 100 yards away. It was an elk and he had been on the alert. It was too bad. Giving up all hopes of elk now we seated ourselves on a log. Those elk would probably travel 10 miles now without stopping. Several minutes passed as we gazed up the river and in the direction of the disappearance. Suddenly there emerged from the thicket and quietly stepped down to the river's bank four or five hundred yards away, a magnificent elk—a stag as artists attempt them. But no brush can picture the splendor of that animal, as with head erect and wide branching antlers he appeared to be searching for his enemies. Carelessly I had leaned my gun against a tree four or five yards away. Mr. Christie's was in his hand, however, and hastily sighting his gun for the distance, fired. The shot seemed to strike. The animal turned, and with one bound was in the thicket again. Meanwhile I had got my rifle to bear as he started to leap and simultaneously Mr. Christie and I each gave him a snap shot, without, however, at that long range, bringing him down. We hastened around to his tracks and followed them for some time up the mountain side. From the manner in which the

animal turned after the first shot we were sure he had been hit, but his trail showed no blood. At one place the animal lay down for a moment. Several times he stopped and made tracks as if trying to lick a wound. So we were convinced that as he stood head toward us, the shot had entered his shoulder and passed inwardly, in which case he might not drop blood for miles.[96] As it was growing late and our devious track had led us seven or eight miles[97] from home we were compelled to give up the hunt. So we comforted ourselves with the thought that the boys had had better luck and that liver and marrow bones were awaiting us in camp. But as we entered camp tired and hungry from our exertions of the day we saw no meat hanging from the tree. Not a living thing had they seen all day, not a bird, beast or fish excepting one poor solitary duck.[98] We had this poor duck, together with our last handful of beans,[99] for supper. Our fisherman was out of luck, for after patiently fishing all day and smoking fifteen or twenty pipes,[100] he had not had a bite. It appeared that the salmon had not got up so far, although in Geyser Valley, they are plentiful. Having but a handful of grub in camp, we started back to the cache the very next morning.

Return to the Cache

Although compelled by lack of food to return to our cache the day after the unsuccessful hunt, it was only hastening matters by a day or two. For in the hunt up the river Mr. Christie and I had incidentally found that a fair trail for travel could be had, and that the valley ahead was what we expected and desired. The place at which we shot at the elk was the lower end of the valley, and we could see as we climbed the hill side searching for the wounded animal, it broadened out above to a considerable width, with gaps leading into the mountains. Here then was the place for a cache and base of supplies. We had on the morning of the return nothing for breakfast, but a little flour and some tea.[101] The flour we mixed with water, for

70

---

[96] "From the amount of space devoted in the Barnes and Christie narrative reports to detailed and lengthy descriptions of elk hunts, it is evident that this constituted the single most important activity of the men. Since supplies were short, and because the cold and strenuous physical activity required large amounts of phosphate-bond energy to sustain the various life processes of the body, it is easily understandable why elk hunting was foremost in the men's minds." Majors, ed., *Northwest Discovery* 5 (Sept. 1984): p. 308.

[97] "The direct distance from Stony Point to camp 24 (at the mouth of Evergreen Creek) is only 0.9 mile." Majors, ed., *Northwest Discovery* 5 (Sept. 1984): p. 308.

[98] "This was likely the common merganser *Mergus merganser*, which is a permanent resident of the Olympic Peninsula, and which frequents mountain rivers and lakes. It may also possibly have been a harlequin duck *Histrionicus histrionicus*, which at this time of year would be starting to migrate upriver from the Strait of Juan de Fuca." Majors, ed., *Northwest Discovery* 5 (Sept. 1984): p. 308.

[99] "The rest of the beans (an excellent source of protein) were at the Lillian River cache." Majors, ed., *Northwest Discovery* 5 (Sept. 1984): p. 308.

[100] "This is a rather large amount of tobacco to be smoked by one person in one day, particularly since supplies were so short at this point." Majors, ed., *Northwest Discovery* 5 (Sept. 1984): p. 308.

[101] "This was the Press Party's first real experience at food shortage. In this instance, the situation was not serious, due to the proximity of supplies at their Lillian River cache. However, in the days ahead there now would always loom the specter of starvation. As is evident in the Press Party narrative from this point onward, it was imperative that the men complete the exploration as soon as possible." Majors, ed., *Northwest Discovery* 5 (Sept. 1984): p. 308.

we had with us nothing to lighten it with, and baked it into gillettes before the fire. We made an insufficient meal of these, put by a remnant for lunch on the road, and started back. By good traveling, having no loads but a half blanket for each man and an ax and a rifle, and having now a knowledge of a better route to avoid the heavy snow, which we encountered on the second day coming up, we could make the cache in a day, for the real distance was not great.

Dollie's Rebellion

The day was marked by only two incidents of interest. The first incident was Dollie's rebellion. About two miles from camp while floundering through some heavy snow drift, she broke out of the path, which we were tramping for her, onto the river bank, and in spite of the honeyed and seductive promises swam across to the opposite side, and there stood regarding us with a "what are you going to do about it" expression in her peaceful eyes. The promises and threats, which we sent across, were alike disregarded, so that one of the boys had to ford the cold stream to his waist and catch her. Dollie has fewer tricks since the demise of her companion, but what they lack in number is usually made up in cussedness.

A Wonderously Tame Cow Elk

The second incident was one more worthy of note. The little caravan had passed the snows and was winding quietly and with quickened footsteps around the sloping mountain side above Convulsion canyon. Mr. Christie, with the only gun in the party[102] was on some distance ahead hoping to kill a deer. Suddenly those of us behind became aware of a rustling in the bushes below the trail, as of a deer. The dogs pricked up their ears. They were all fortunately at once held and prevented from giving chase. Almost at the same moment there came into sight not twenty-five yards away a great cow elk. Here was meat—but by all the angels where was Christie and the gun. The animal stood still and silently sized us up. Imagine our feelings. No meat for almost a week and here was three or four hundred pounds of it waiting to be put out of its misery. We were afraid to stir—almost to breathe. If we had had a club or a rock we could have struck her with it. We had involuntarily sunk to the ground on seeing the animal and there we squatted. "For God's sake, where is Christie," were the muttered feelings of each of us.

Great as my anxiety was I could scarcely refrain my laughter as I perceived our ridiculous situation. Here were hungry men and an elk quietly chewing her cud and waiting to be killed. After a couple of minutes, which seemed like hours, one of the boys could stand it no longer and uttered a half stifled cry—"Christie." Still the animal did not move. She was undoubtedly regarding us with curiosity and as we made no effort to molest her she appeared to feel no alarm. Encouraged by the continued standing of the animal another man called for "Christie," and the call was repeated by all hands several times with full strength of lung. But no answer came. Mr. Christie was some distance ahead, I was in advance of the party and nearest Christie, and as the only chance of getting the four-legged meat was to get the gun at any hazard, I laid down the ax which I was carrying and slowly crept away a few feet, then a few yards, and finally gaining my feet whipped over a knoll out of sight and ran, it need hardly to be said, break neck up the trail. I soon got within ear shot of Mr. Christie, called out to him and together we hurried back. The cow was still there. As the boys crouching upon the trail holding the struggling dogs caught sight of us we could see their excitement. With wild but half concealed gesticulations they indicated the direction of the elk, and with breathless lips formed the words "there—there—there." From a place within easy range Christie got in an excellent shot, and as she turned gave her another one. The logs were loosed in chase, but one hundred yards down the hill she fell dead. The first shot had entered the neck and passed out behind the right shoulder; the second had gone through her lungs.

Picture of a Band of Elk in Flight

Exciting as all this was, however, it was not quite the end of it. While the boys were skinning and cutting up the dead elk, I took the gun, ascended to the trail and arrived at the place where Dollie was standing just in time to see a small band of elk coming up from down the mountain side, but quite removed from the point where the dead elk lay. I dropped behind a fallen log, but I could see that the leader had my wind and the whole band crossed the trail and were traveling up the hill side as if forty devils were after them. One old bull, the leader, and 18 cows comprised the band, and as one after another they leaped up hill and crossed the

71

---

[102] "It is strange that at a time when fresh meat was so desperately needed, the men would neglect to carry their rifles with them. Barnes and Christie explain that the three rifles were left at the forward camp, and the five men traveled light with only an axe, one rifle, and five half-blankets, so that they could reach the Lillian River cache in one day. Moreover, they traveled light in order to be able to pack more supplies back from the Lillian River. Christie carried the single rifle, while Barnes packed an axe to chop firewood at camp that night." Majors, ed., *Northwest Discovery* 5 (Sept. 1984): p. 308.

trail within 100 feet of where I lay, they made a spectacle well worth looking at.

The leader, with wide-spreading horns, guided the advance, followed by the cows in single file. I had plenty of time to observe them closely as one by one they passed before me. They were of a dun color, graduating into a bright yellow on their flanks. Monstrously heavy they looked, but with what lightness and speed they sprang up the hill side! The old stag in advance seemed a monarch indeed. He was plainly alive to surrounding danger, but he showed none of the fear so evident in his convoy. He led his charge up the hill. They left behind a trail like a wagon road, so beaten with hoofs.

The Leader Elk Is Spied

I had plenty of time to pick out the youngest and most tender looking of the does and brought her down with a shot. It was hard to hold from shooting the leader he looked so majestic and tempting, but we did not want him for meat and it seemed a shame to kill so noble a beast.

The doe we had first killed evidently belonged to this band and had strayed off. A doe away from the band is very helpless. They will of course run if startled, but they do not possess the sagacity or cunning of the stag when pursued. The doe that we saw and killed was probably bewildered, and seeing strangers who did her no harm she was overcome with curiosity and would probably have stood still for an hour. The elk bands at this time of year separate, the cows to give birth to and suckle their young, and the bulls to wander about looking after and watching them, leaving the remainder of the band, consisting of does like the one seen this day, in charge of an old bull. This band may have numbered a hundred when full. The leader conducts the band from one feeding ground to another, and when traveling keeps well in advance of the rest, watchful for enemies. With wonderful sagacity he will keep his charge together, hunt good trails and feeding grounds, and in times of danger he will fight to the death to defend them.

The North American elk is, I believe, identical, or nearly

so, with the red deer of Scotland, described by Scott in the "Lady of the Lake." He is the royal stag of story and of song.[103]

Liver for Supper

We had liver for supper tonight. Continuing our return journey to the Lillian we crossed Coldfeet creek[104] and followed the old elk trail northward, arriving at Lillian river at about 4 o'clock in the afternoon. From our cache in the bottom of the canyon we packed up one load to the top, and made camp there.[105]

From Lillian River to Kate Creek

Thursday, April 10.—Weather raw and chilly. Flurries of snow in the afternoon. Packed second load up the hill this morning, comprising the whole of the remaining supplies. The bluff is very steep and about midway Dollie took a most remarkable tumble. She slipped off the side, crashed down over the snow, striking two or three logs, turned several somersaults, and brought up all standing about 50 feet below without injury. When we saw her going we were sure that she had gone to join Jennie. This feat was accomplished with 200 pounds on her back.

Brought both loads into camp[106] at Kate creek. At nightfall snowing heavily.

To Island Camp

Friday, April 11. Kate creek to Island camp.—Eight inches of snow fell last night.[107] Weather all day cloudy and chilly. Travel today very bad. Poor Dollie suffered much from the deep snow. The lower part of her hind legs is a mass of raw flesh, and every step she takes dyes the snow with blood. Late in the afternoon we arrived at our old camp opposite the island.

Saturday and Sunday, April 12 and 13.—Weather rainy and disagreeable. Expedition confined to camp.

Weather Clearing

Monday, April 14. Island camp to Press valley.—Weather clearing. Left camp early in the morning with full pack. As-

---

[103] "Formerly, the North American elk and the red deer of Europe were classified as two distinct species. However, at present taxonomists regard them as two distinct varieties of the same species *Cervus elaphus*." Majors, ed., *Northwest Discovery* 5 (Sept. 1984): p. 308.

[104] "From Christie's comment, . . . this creek would be Kate [Bowman] Creek, and not Dorothy Creek 'Coldfeet Creek.'" Majors, ed., *Northwest Discovery* 5 (Sept. 1984): p. 308.

[105] "Camp 25 of the Press Party, for April 9, 1890, was most likely at the site of the advance camp of March 24, 1890, at about elevation 1800 feet, about 0.05 mile SSW of benchmark 1923. This was halfway between the cache (at Lillian River) and the site of the elk kill (between Kate [Bowman] Creek and Windfall Creek)." Majors, ed., *Northwest Discovery* 5 (Sept. 1984): p. 308.

[106] "Camp for April 10, 1890, was at the same site as camp 22 of April 3, on the northwest side of Kate [Bowman] Creek, at elevation 1500 feet, 0.25 mile from its confluence with the Elwha River." Majors, ed., *Northwest Discovery* 5 (Sept. 1984): p. 309.

[107] "The 8-inch snowfall on the night of April 10–11, 1890 was the last substantial snowfall of the winter." Majors, ed., *Northwest Discovery* 5 (Sept. 1984): p. 309.

cended the foothills, passing a good bench one-half mile long and wide. Found a good elk trail running up the mountain side enabling us to cross several deep ravines at an advantage, but with much labor. Then descending toward the river to the brow of a deep canyon. From this canyon comes up a heavy booming sound, as of water pounding into a cave or hollow. From this point onward for two miles the timber is good. We made camp[108] late in the afternoon at the lower end of the large valley seen by us while hunting a few days ago. This valley we have named "Press Valley," in honor of the newspaper whose enterprise fitted out the expedition. While we were making camp Mr. Christie went on to reconnoiter and on the opposite side of the river, one mile above, he killed an elk.

The formation today observed is everywhere slate. Just abreast camp the formation is peculiar. The strata is nearly vertical and is bent into waves for one half mile along the river. The river following these waves curves like a snake. At other places on the river this slate projects in massive headlands a hundred or two hundred feet in height. At one point high up the mountain side, we found a sandstone ledge with quartz veins running through it. The timber today is everywhere excellent in quality, consisting for the most part of fir. In some places where the snow permitted us to see the ground there was little or no underbrush. In the bottoms the snow was very heavy.

Fording the River

April 15th. Lower end of Press valley.—Through snow to the river one-half mile above. Here we forded the river, which was three feet deep, broad and rippling. We were now fairly in the valley, which is at this end slightly rolling, heavily timbered with fir, but with here and there large patches of alder and maple. Soil excellent. Made camp for the night and went back for the elk, which was killed yesterday, skinned and dressed the meat and hung him up.

April 16th and 17th.—Drizzling rain. Returned to Is-

land camp and spent the night there. Next morning we cached a few unnecessary articles by hanging them in a bag up a tree, and resumed packing the remainder to Press valley, and arrived there at dark.

In Camp at Lower End of Press Valley

April 18th.—Clear and warm.[109] This morning I made a trip north and west, and climbing the mountain side, obtained an excellent view of the gap and mountains to the eastward.[110] All the formations we observed was slate. Some of it contained veins of quartz. After dinner Mr. Christie and I climbed a hill back of camp. Three hundred yards from camp we came to a level plateau about one and one-half miles long and three-quarters of a mile wide, rectangular in form. It is covered with a thin soil over a white, gravelly sand.[111] The growth is mountain fir, spruce and Douglas pine. Upon the plateau the trees are all small, there being hardly a tree over eight inches in diameter. The largest tree observed is not much over 200 years old. Fringing the edge and descending the bluff, which is everywhere very steep, the trees are very large. We were immediately struck with the number of trees upon the plateau which were blazed or otherwise injured. Examination of these scars showed the hand of man. The scars were old.

An Ancient Indian Village

Crossing the plateau we came upon a circular mound from which the snow was partially melted. Its perfect regularity would seem to indicate that it had been thrown up by artificial means. We soon became convinced that this had been an old Indian village or camping ground. The tokens are so generally distributed over it that it was evidently a large village as well as a permanent one.

The location is a good one for an Indian village. Three sides of the plateau descend steeply. The third side is an abrupt mountain side inaccessible except from the plateau itself. The place is therefore easily defended and its central position in this valley renders it convenient in times of peace.

---

[108] Probably at the mouth of Stony Creek.

[109] Compare to Christie's account: "An interesting item appears in Christie's diary under date of April 18: 'The boys drying bears' meat.' There is no explanation, no mention of their having shot a bear—or even having seen one thus far on the expedition." Wood, *Across the Olympic Mountains*, p. 127.

[110] "This view would have been to the southeast, up the valley of Hayes River to Mount Anderson 7365'." Majors, ed., *Northwest Discovery* 5 (Sept. 1984): p. 319.

[111] "The flat terrace of Semple Plateau represents the former outwash delta of Goldie River, formed during the time of the Fraser Glaciation (10,000 to 18,000 years ago). At this time, the west flank of the Puget Lobe of the continental ice sheet dammed the lower Elwha Valley, creating a massive Lake Elwha behind this. Into this now vanished lake, the Goldie River and its glaciers once discharged their sediment-laden waters, forming the delta now known as the Semple Plateau. Geologist Rowland Whitney Tabor describes this site: 'The Semple Plateau, named by the *Press* exploring party, is a strikingly flat series of terraces . . . mainly cut in bedrock slates and sandstone but . . . thickly mantled with gravels. . . . The Goldie [River] cuts an impressive gorge through these terraces' (Tabor, *Guide to Geology*, pp. 86, 91). At the most, the Semple Plateau could only have been the site of a temporary summer camp of the Elwha Indians. The stunted growth of the trees is due to the porous nature of the gravel soil which does not retain water. The tree 'blazes' were most likely due to damage inflicted by elk, deer, and bear." Majors, ed., *Northwest Discovery* 5 (Sept. 1984): p. 319.

There is scarcely a tree over seven or eight inches in diameter that does not bear a scar or mark of some kind, for the most part made with the ax. We could even see where children had stripped off the bark of the pines for the purpose of getting the gum.[112] The ground was covered with about a foot of snow. We found no fallen timber—this difference from the natural forest round about being very striking.

No Young Trees Blazed

Every particle of wood had evidently been gathered for fuel. None of the younger growth of timber, under six or seven inches in diameter, indication an age of 100 years or less, was scarred or blazed. The trees larger than this, having an age of say anywhere from 100 to 250 years, were, as already stated all scarred. Nothing older than that, none of the patriarchs of the surrounding forest, existed on the plateau.

We gathered from these facts that the original forest had been cleared off, either to admit the sunlight or to be used for fuel. The trees which are now scarred constituted the subsequent growth of saplings during the existence of the village, and were scarred by accident or by children. The smaller unscarred trees observed are the growth since the desertion of the village.

Probably a Large Village

The plateau was evidently the site of a large and permanent village. It is true that an occasional band of hunting Indians, camping at different times on different parts of the plateau, might in time scarify the trees over the whole surface, giving it the appearance of a large village. But a party of hunting Indians would never camp so far from water, as it must do if it camps near the mountains. With the choice of location the party would camp near the margin, where wood and water were convenient.

An Indian in his village, however, surrounded by his squaw and family, does not care how far his habitation is from the necessaries of existence, for the labor of fetching devolves upon the squaw. There is no water upon the plateau, but springs are numerous on all sides, just below the margin.

Will Repay Investigation

The snow prevented any extended investigation. We were accomplishing our purpose, however, if we discovered the ledge, and left to others the work of developing the mine. It is evident from the tokens observed that this plateau will repay careful investigation. In view of the fact that this ancient village may have furnished the basis for the legends of the Indian conventions and games so beautifully related by ex-Governor Semple, we named the place Semple plateau.[113]

Ascent to the Gallery

Crossing the plateau we arrived at the southwest corner. The mountain here comes down to a point. Leading up to the point of a mountain we found an old elk trail, which we followed up to the tip of a jutting rock about 300 feet above the plateau. From this rock we were afforded a magnificent view of the Sound range to the southeast. We named this rock the Gallery, from its excellent view and from the photographs[114] which we got there.

Saturday, April 19.—This morning Mr. Christie and I, accompanied by Crumback, started out to investigate the country ahead for a trail. We crossed the Indian encampment to the Gallery. From the gallery we climbed upwards. At first upon an easy slope, which gradually became steeper and steeper, as we mounted. After a weary climb we arrived at about one o'clock at a bench where we made fire and had lunch. Then removing our boots we slipped into moccasins and snowshoes and followed the bench around to the westward, upon the mountain side. After a half mile, however, the bench ended, and we proceeded upward in moccasins alone, and arrived at the summit of the mountain at about

---

[112] "These scars may have been made by bears." Wood, *Across the Olympic Mountains*, p. 127.

[113] "Despite the prominence given to Semple Plateau by the Press Party, as yet no extensive archaeological or botanical examination of the plateau and its trees has been conducted to ascertain the validity of their conjectures. Though this may have been the site of a temporary summer hunting camp of the Elwha Indians, it is extremely doubtful if the site was occupied all year." Majors, ed., *Northwest Discovery* 5 (Sept. 1984): p. 319.

"The benchland or 'plateau' in question is located along the west side of the Elwha River, immediately below the confluence of the large tributary stream later named Goldie River by the expedition. For unknown reasons, the name Semple Plateau has been shifted in subsequent years to the southern part of the Bailey Range, just north of Bear Pass. The validity of the Press Party's conclusions concerning this place being the site of an ancient Indian village is subject to serious doubt. The scars on the trees may have been made by elk or bear. Thin, poor soil on the benchland may explain why the trees were small, not large as on surrounding slopes. This would be a function of the 'edaphic factor,' where differences in the pattern of plant growth are a response to marked contrast in soil conditions. It may well be, however, that Semple Plateau constitutes a fruitful ground for competent archaeologists to explore. It is certainly not unknown terrain today, however, as an old trail crosses it, leading from the Elwha up to the Dodger Point fire lookout." Wood, *Across the Olympic Mountains*, pp. 129–130.

[114] "One of these photographs has survived through a print in the National Archives. This is a view to the southeast up the valleys of Hayes River and Godkin Creek, depicting Mt. Anderson, Mt. Norton, and Chimney Peak. An engraving of this appears on page 7 of the [*Seattle Press*, July 16, 1890]." Majors, ed., *Northwest Discovery* 5 (Sept. 1984): p. 319.

4 P.M., 2300 feet above camp.[115] From here the view was still better than from the Gallery. Press valley seemed to continue to the southward many miles.[116] To the westward extended a gap for eight or ten miles, and then appeared to sweep to the southward and to form a pass in that direction.

Westward Bound

We are desirous of getting westward. Press valley appears to extend southward, and if the maps already in existence are correct, the valley points toward the Skokomish river,[117] and that is not our destination. We are determined to come out by the Quinaiult, if possible.

So it was determined today that we take this westward gap. It seems practicable. Through this gap[118] is to be seen a great white range extending from the direction of Olympus, southward, seemingly the backbone of the mountains. We called it, provisionally, Bailey range, in honor of Mr. William E. Bailey, the proprietor of the *Seattle Press*.[119]

Press Valley, Below Semple Plateau

Monday, April 21.[120] —Weather clear and warm. This morning the boys were left to move camp to the "Gallery" above Semple plateau. Mr. Christie and I, taking our guns and two days' provisions, left camp to explore the valley southward.

We climbed the hill and reached the plateau. Crossing the plateau to its southwestern corner we paused a moment there to survey the glorious view at our feet. The valley stretched to the southward. Seemingly in its center Mt. Egan reared its snow white crest. The main valley, however, or the one

PRESS VALLEY FROM SEMPLE PLATEAU LOOKING SOUTH.

"April 18, 1890. This is apparently the only survivor of several photographs taken by Barnes at the Semple Plateau. The prospect is to the SSE up the valleys of Hayes River (left) and the Elwha River (right). The ridge of peak 5407 and Mount Norton (6319, 'Mount Egan') occupies the prominent center of the photograph. To the left, directly up the Hayes River valley, is the Mount Anderson massif (7365, 'The Brothers'). The engraving depicts Chimney Peak (6911, 'Old Snowback') to the right of Mount Norton." (Majors, vol. 2, 143)

75

---

[115] "This mountain is Dodger Point 5753', the ascent of which, via the entire southeast ridge, is accurately described by Barnes. This was one of the first major peaks to be climbed in the Olympic Mountains. Though the season was not astronomical winter, the snow conditions nonetheless qualify it as a winter ascent under true winter conditions. Because of its central location, Dodger Point offers a superb vantage point for viewing nearly all of the major peaks in the Olympic Mountains. Such a view would have been described in Barnes' journal entry for April 20, 1890, which unfortunately has not survived.

"I suspect that Christie, Barnes, and Crumback spent the night of April 19 at elevation 5100–5200 on the shoulder of the southeast ridge of Dodger Point. They had reached the summit of Dodger Point 5753' at 4 o'clock in the afternoon, which left insufficient daylight for a safe descent back down to camp. Moreover, the three men had . . . expected to spend one or two nights out away from camp 27. On the following morning, having selected the Goldie River valley as their future route, based upon their view from Dodger Point, the three men then retraced their route back to camp.

"April 19 was thus a crucial day for the Press Party, for on the basis of their prospect from Dodger Point, they made the fateful decision to head up the Goldie River instead of the Elwha River. This also explains why they returned from their brief reconnaissance one day early. The purpose of the excursion had been to scout out a route ahead. With this objective having been sighted and decided upon on April 19, 1890, from the summit of Dodger Point, there then was no reason to continue the reconnaissance any longer.

"From Dodger Point, the three men would have gained an excellent view of Mount Carrie 6995' to the northwest (their 'Mount Olympus'). However, because it is not mentioned by Barnes, I suspect that on this particular day the peak was partially obscured by clouds. Barnes confirms this in his journal entry for May 6, 1890, from near the summit of Mount Seattle, wherein he states that Mount Carrie 'Olympus' was visible to him: 'it was the first time it had been seen since we left Deer Range north of Geyser Valley, so completely is it hidden by other peaks.'" Majors, ed., *Northwest Discovery* 5 (Sept. 1984): p. 320.

[116] "Because the southern end of Press Valley was hidden from view by massive Mount Dana 6209', the Press Party were unaware of its westward bend, and thus deceived into selecting another, more rugged, course via the Goldie River, leading southwest to the sought-for headwaters of the Quinault River." Majors, ed., *Northwest Discovery* 5 (Sept. 1984): p. 320.

[117] "On the 1883 edition of the U.S. General Land Office map, *Territory of Washington*, a line drawn due south from the schematic head of the Elwha River will reach the schematic head of the Skokomish River; whereas the schematic head of the Quinault River lies to the southwest. This would elucidate the Press Party's decision to head southwest at this point, up the Goldie River, rather than continue southward up the Elwha Valley. Their objective was to cross the Olympic Mountains via the Elwha and Quinault rivers and emerge at the Pacific Ocean—not via the Elwha and Skokomish rivers, which would have led them back to the east side of the mountains at Hood Canal. This decision was a major mistake (as with the boat, and the winter departure), as the men realized. It might have cost a less experienced party their lives." Majors, ed., *Northwest Discovery* 5 (Sept. 1984): p. 320.

[118] "Barnes' use of the term 'gap' refers, not to a mountain pass or col, but rather to the gap formed by the Goldie River valley or canyon." Majors, ed., *Northwest Discovery* 5 (Sept. 1984): p. 320.

[119] Because Barnes employs the qualification "provisionally," this indicates that the Bailey Range was probably named by the Press Party themselves, while in the field, and not by Edmond S. Meany after the return of the party to Seattle. Barnes's entry for April 27 finalizes the term "Bailey Range."

[120] "There is no entry by either Barnes or Christie for April 20, 1890, in the printed Press Party narratives. This is the only day of the entire Press Party expedition that is unaccounted for. It was on this day that Christie, Barnes, and Crumback made their descent from the southeast shoulder of Dodger Point back to camp." Majors, ed., *Northwest Discovery* 5 (Sept. 1984): p. 320.

containing the river, seemed to sweep a little to the westward, between Egan and a great mountain on the right (Mt. Dana). Up this valley, far in the distance, could be faintly discerned a snow white peak. To this we gave the name of "Old Snowback." To the left, eastward of Mt. Egan, could be seen the distant peaks of the Sound range, most conspicuous of which towered "The Brothers."[121] We descended the hill, and there met the waters of Goldie river. Unslinging our axes, we felled a tree and crossed.

Traveling Up the Valley

We traveled bout three miles up the valley. The valley is rolling, possessing good soil and heavily timbered with spruce, fir and hemlock. A few Douglas pines are scattered here and there. We saw no cedar. There are occasional flats covered with maple. At about noon we touched the river, and found there an extensive bottom containing a hundred or more acres of alluvial soil, overgrown with alder. Here we had lunch, and then returned toward camp.

Surprised by a Number of Shots

We were still a mile from camp when we were startled by hearing two shots in quick succession. As we had noticed fresh elk trails in the morning on the plateau, we thought the boys had killed an elk, and we hastened our steps a little. A few minutes later from the top of a spur, or little ridge, which crossed the valley, we thought we could distinguish shouts. Then came another shot and unmistakable shouts. Surely they were not hunting elk in that unseemly fashion. Something had happened and they were trying to recall us, we thought. Acting on this hypothesis we gave them an answering shot. After listening for perhaps a minute, another shot came from the hill. Surely something had happened. The direction of the sound was the rendezvous of the day, the "Gallery," which was about seven hundred feet above us. It was a crag-like rock which jutted from the side of the mountain, above the plateau. It was a dangerous place but convenient for our purposes. The trail up to this lofty perch was zigzag and hazardous. Was it possible that one of the boys had tumbled over the rocks, or had a well meaning but undesired relief party come to camp. This last fear

mingled with the other as a misfortune second only to it. The progress of the expedition had been necessarily so slow, that we always had the fear of visitors in our minds. It was part of our mission to cut a trail into this region in order that the country might be opened to settlers. So thoroughly had we done it that a party leaving Port Angeles, could lope after us on horseback, and easily travel in a few days over a road which it had taken us months to come. So jealous were we of sharing our hard earned honors with exploiting and notoriety seeking strangers, that we would have regarded it as a catastrophe ranking next to the loss of one of ourselves.[122] Fearing one of these misfortunes, therefore, and unable to conceive any lesser reason for so much commotion, we hurried down the hill, crossed our bridge and scrambled up the opposite declivity with all the speed we could. Half way up, however, we were suddenly reassured by meeting with a deeply plowed trail of a descending band of elk, but a few minutes old. Frightened and evidently pursued, the animals had leaped down the hill 15 or 20 feet at a jump. We were now satisfied that the boys had been hunting elk, although in a most extraordinary manner, and were relieved of our anxiety. We arrived at the Gallery, and had been there several minutes when the boys came up with Dollie and the last of the camp outfit.

A Band of Elk Run Upon

They had indeed, while packing, run upon the band of elk, whose trail we had seen upon the hill side, and had killed one. But in the scrimmage, "Dike," one of the dogs, a large black retriever, had been killed also. It seems that the dog rashly attempted to head off one of the bulls. The bull striking "Dike" with his forefeet nearly cut the dog in two, killing him instantly. This explained the shouts that had so alarmed us. The boys perceiving the dog's danger had shouted at him in an endeavor to save him. We went down and visited poor "Dike's" remains. He was horribly mangled, and gave a most instructive object lesson upon the savage nature of the elk when brought to bay.[123] The elk that was killed lay near by. We took his liver and tenderloin for supplies, and gave the dogs a feed from his flanks, but we had sixty pounds of dried meat in the pack, so we hung up the remainder.[124]

---

[121] "The Press Expedition's Mount Egan is today known as Mount Norton; their Old Snowback is Chimney Peak; and the men mistook Mount Anderson—a peak lying far inland from the peaks facing Hood Canal—for The Brothers, one of the prominent peaks of the so called Sound Range." Wood, *Across the Olympic Mountains*, p. 133.

[122] "Barnes honestly admits that the Press Party were rather 'jealous' of the publicity and prestige associated with their expedition, thus suggesting that these factors were a significant source of motivation for the men of the expedition." Majors, ed., *Northwest Discovery* 5 (Sept. 1984): p. 336.

[123] "Barnes had acquired [Dike] during his visit to Port Angeles during December 9–13, 1889. This animal thereafter became known as Barnes' dog. See the section on 'The four dogs,' in *Northwest Discovery* 2 (Mar. 1981): pp. 174–75." Majors, ed., *Northwest Discovery* 5 (Sept. 1984): p. 337. See also Appendix to the Press Expedition Report at the end of part 1.

[124] "This would be the last game killed by the Press Party [for two weeks]." Majors, ed., *Northwest Discovery* 5 (Sept. 1984): p. 337.

76

A Climb for Water

There was no water at the Gallery, and it was necessary that we should take advantage of the hour of daylight still remaining to reach a suitable place for camp. So Dollie was loaded up. All hands shouldered their packs, and the expedition once more set forward. Immediately before us was a great land slide, above which it was necessary to pass. The exposed formation in the slide was slate, rock and gravel in places. After a vigorous climb we reached the tip of it. From there we worked gradually down through vast quantities of snow, carefully edging along the steep, sliding mountain side.

About half a mile from the starting place Dollie suddenly gave out and laid down. All our endeavors could not induce her to rise. Persuasion, couched in the most honied phases and emphasized by means of the large end of a fair-sized club, was unavailing. Poor Dollie was exhausted, so we unloaded her, made cache of her pack, and with the articles necessary for making a camp we went on without her to the foot of the hill. Here we reached a stream buried in snow, upon the bank of which we made camp in the dark. We named the stream Louise creek. It had been a hard day's work. We had hoped for a better camp, but the best we could do this night was to camp in our wet clothes on a wet snow bank.

Provisions Getting Low

By traveling as light as possible we could not hope to get through the mountains in less than a month, and it might take us double that time. Our provisions consisted of 150 pounds of flour, 10 pounds of bacon, 25 pounds of beans, 5 pounds of tea, and 5 pounds of salt. Of tobacco there was not two pounds in camp.[125] We had about 60 pounds of partially smoked meat. We had all the meat which it was considered necessary to carry, expecting, as we did, to be able to kill as

we wanted it. Therefore we had with us 10 day's full rations, an amount, however, which by economy and by putting ourselves upon an allowance, could be made to last indefinitely, and with this supply we now commence the search for the head of the Quinaiult.

The meat we now had was most villainously tough and dry, absolutely devoid of fat. It was only possible to eat it in the form of soup. We would fill a four-gallon kettle with meat, boil it all night, and in the morning not so much as a single globule of grease would be floating on the surface. Owing, as we supposed, to the want of grease, we were all suffering from dysentery,[126] and sometimes we would be so weak from this cause that we could hardly stagger. We had no remedy available. We used browned flour, mixed with a little of our precious bacon grease, which was better than nothing.

Turning Dollie Loose

After an uncomfortable night at Louise creek we started back the next morning to bring up the remaining stores. Dollie we expected to get, but the snow was becoming so heavy that it would be impossible to use her even if she were in good condition. We found her standing where we left her. Although hungry and without water the poor mule had been too exhausted to wander in search of food. We removed her halter, patted her on the back and turned her adrift to get her living as the elk do. Dollie had done us good service, her small feet made it possible for her to climb steep mountain sides where a horse would have failed.[127]

By 10 o'clock we had returned to Louise creek with our remaining stores in two loads, then striking up the canyon to the westward followed it until dark.[128] This stream being a large branch of the Elwha and worthy of a good name, we gave it that of Goldie river, in honor of Mr. R.H. Goldie of Seattle.

---

[125] "For an analysis of the food and supplies of the Press Party, see the section on 'Equipment and supplies of the Press Party,' in *Northwest Discovery* 2 (Mar. 1981): pp. 129–34." Majors, ed. *Northwest Discovery* 5 (Sept. 1984): p. 337. See also Appendix to the Press Expedition Report at the end of part 1.

[126] "This 'dysentery' was likely one of the symptoms of malnutrition." Majors, ed., *Northwest Discovery* 5 (Sept. 1984): p. 337.

[127] "It is not known for certain what became of Dollie. She did not follow the men, for thereafter no mention is made of her in the Press Party narratives. It is possible that she attempted to retrace her route back down the Elwha Valley. However, she could not have negotiated the ford just above Stony Creek, thus barring her from the east side of the river, where travel was far more feasible. Any further progress down the west side of the Elwha River was effectively blocked by Convulsion [Grand] Canyon. She thus could not have made it down even so far as the Lillian River. The 'trail' back down the Elwha was obscure and treacherous in places. Even the elk and deer, accustomed as they were to foraging and survival in the Olympic wilderness, were still staying down in Geyser Valley. The mule's condition, along with the deep snow, the lack of food (other than Oregon grape), the distance back home, and her domesticated background, make it very unlikely that she could have survived very long in the still inhospitable Elwha Valley. Considering the fact that the mule was starving, and her legs were severely cut and bruised from the crusty snow, it is likely that she either died of starvation (or hypothermia) soon after being turned loose, or was killed by a cougar. For information on the two mules of the Press Party, see the section on 'The two mules,' *Northwest Discovery* 2 (Mar. 1981): pp. 172–74." Majors, ed., *Northwest Discovery* 5 (Sept. 1984): p. 337. See also Appendix to the Press Expedition Report at the end of part 1.

[128] "Camp 29 of the Press Party, for April 22, 1890, was probably located on the northwest side of Goldie River, in a small flat on the valley bottom, 0.7 mile southwest of the mouth of Louise Creek." Majors, ed., *Northwest Discovery* 5 (Sept. 1984): p. 337.

IN GOLDIE RIVER CANYON.

"April 23?, 1890. This is one of the few illustrations that actually depicts the men of the Press Party—in this case being two fellows on snowshoes and carrying backpacks. One man is carrying the shovel, while the other holds what probably is a kettle. Both men are wearing caps and what may possibly be a rifle is protruding from the second man's pack." (Majors, vol. 2, 143)

Struggling Up the Canyon

During the next few days we spent our spare time struggling up this canyon. The remaining hours, principally those of night, were passed in sleeping on the snow. The canyon gradually became deeper and more difficult, and the river became smaller. At times we found little bottoms on which we could travel with snowshoes. But for the most part we were compelled to keep the mountain sides. The snow also became deeper as we advanced, and our daily progress slower. Beautiful scenery opened before us at every turn. At places the river was bridged with snow, so that we could cross with ease and safety. From the mountain sides magnificent cascades played hundreds of feet into the river below. Avalanches had at places stripped the mountain of its timber, and at these points the canyon was blocked up with a huge mass of mingled snow, rock and forest trees torn out by the roots.

Succession of Hard Days

These few days were a succession of hard working days. Fording the stream, plowing through short bottoms buried in snow, and climbing mountain sides that seemed to be set on edge, make up the history of this week.

Up the Goldie River

April 26.—Last night our outfit underwent another weeding. The canyon was getting rougher, the snow getting deeper, and the necessity for reducing our pack to the lightest possible weight was daily growing more evident.[129] A lot of bullets, a frying pan, two axes, a pick-ax, the large kettle and several other articles went over the fence. Some old clothes were discarded and we retained only those we wore. They were our best, but even they were ragged and torn. Tougher looking tramps never bummed along the roadside than the once well-dressed "Press Exploring Expedition." We had each started with good, strong suits of serviceable Scotch wool, a suit of overalls, a change of underclothing, stout flannel outside shirts, good leather boots and waterproof garments throughout. These were now reduced to the actual clothes we wore, all in rags. Our hats we threw away long ago as unnecessary and we were tiding over the winter bareheaded.[130] A piece of blanket served for a stocking; our boots there is little left but the soles. All other apparel has been left by the roadside, a prey to bears, cougars and other varmints. So much the less to pack over the mountains. At this rate, if we reach Grays harbor with our ammunition belts we will be doing well. We can hide in the woods while we negotiate a trade with some clothing merchant.

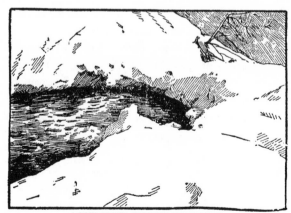

A SNOW BRIDGE OVER THE GOLDIE RIVER.

"April 26, 1890" (Majors, vol. 2, 143)

---

[129] See April 26 footnote in Christie's journal, chapter 3.

[130] "Barnes mentions that by now the Press Party . . . were at present traveling 'bare headed.' This means that in photographs the men are not wearing caps. Instead, they are most likely wearing headbands around their long hair. This has caused their hair to bunch up slightly above the band, giving the appearance in the engraving of a cap. Note that in the final group portraits of the expedition, taken on May 21, 1890 at Aberdeen, all five men are wearing headbands to restrain their long hair. They undoubtedly wore headbands throughout the duration of the expedition." Majors, ed., *Northwest Discovery* 5 (Sept. 1984): p. 338.

78

We left camp at 9 A.M., crossed a snow bridge a hundred yards above and followed the stream upwards. We got some excellent photographs of the snow bridges, and of Adeline cascade. This beautiful waterfall is about 100 feet in height, and falls from the north side of the canyon into the river, which was here buried in snow. At about 11 o'clock we put on snowshoes and followed a long bottom for half a mile, fording a creek from the northward,[131] which nearly shares the water with the Goldie. All day long we traveled without seeing a bare spot large enough to camp on, and we expected to have to make our beds in the snow bank again. But just as we were about to camp[132] we discovered a little bench above the trail, 15x20 feet in dimensions, enclosed by the hill side behind and two jutting rocks. Sunny and warm and bare of snow it was the cosiest little camping place imaginable. A low spreading spruce tree overhung it, which when cut down fell into camp and furnished us with a splendid bed. Two dead trees a little above also fell into camp and gave us an abundance of firewood. Twenty yards away ran the creek. It was the best camp that we had had. The boys wished that they could pack it along with us.

We were now at the base of the range which seemed to divide the watershed. From this camp we would begin the next day to climb the mountain side opposite, and camp for a week or two would be likely to be cold and disagreeable. If we could only have packed this camp along. We named this Lucky camp.

Mount Scott Named

The mountain on the north of the Goldie we named Mt. Scott, after Mr. James W. Scott of the Chicago Herald.

April 27th was Sunday, but we did not go to church. Grub was getting short and we must travel. So we shouldered 60 pounds each, crossed the raging Goldie, and struck up the mountain side, headed for the watershed of the Quinaiult. The lower slopes of the mountain incline at 55 to 60 degrees and we had to go at it side hill fashion, slowly and painfully, kicking a foothold into the snow, sometimes finding footholds five or six feet deep. We plowed through this deep snow on the mountain side for three hours and our packs made it laborious work. At an altitude of 4500 feet by aneroid we made cache of our pack. The snow was here 10 feet deep. In some places on the trail upward we had found it to be over 15. Around every tree a little well was melted, enabling us to see downward to the roots. The timber on this mountain side is heavy, and although the day was clear and warm, so impenetrable was the

MOUNT FERRY, LOOKING WEST.

"April 27?, 1890. This is a view taken through the trees from a low elevation, . . . from the Goldie River valley." (Majors, vol. 2, 144)

foliage overhead that a deep gloom pervaded the woods. Only one glimpse did we get of the sun on this mountain. Half way up there was a break in the timber, caused by a small landslide. Seated on a root, which projected from the top of the slide, we could catch a glimpse of the canyon below and a glorious range of mountains opposite us.

Naming a Snow Covered Range

Snow covered from base to summit, the range seemed to rise in a perpendicular wall. From its central position and lofty height it was evidently the backbone of the Olympic mountains. We called it Bailey range, after Mr. William E. Bailey, proprietor of the *Press*. Two splendid peaks in the range rose immediately opposite us. The peak to the northward we gave the name of Mount Ferry, after Governor E.P. Ferry of the state of Washington. The one to the southward we called Mount Pulitzer, after Mr. Joseph Pulitzer of the *New York World*.

Bailey range from where we sat seemed like a long thin wedge. Its edge, sharply defined against the sky, was covered with snow, through which sharp jagged rocks protruded like the teeth of a saw. The west wind which here prevails throughout the year, had drifted the snow along the summit in places into a huge overhang on our, or eastern side. It seemed in some places to project thirty or forty feet.

The Rumbling of Avalanches

All day long, as we traveled up the mountain side, we could hear the rumbling of avalanches. From the little opening

---

[131] "This is the stream that drains the west and southwest side of Mount Scott. The name Lucky Creek is herewith introduced for this feature for the first time." Majors, ed., *Northwest Discovery* 5 (Sept. 1984): p. 338.
[132] "Camp 31 of the Press Party, 'Lucky Camp,' for April 26–27, 1890, was located on the north side of the Goldie River, on the west side of Lucky Creek, the stream that drains the west and southwest sides of Mount Scott." Majors, ed., *Northwest Discovery* 5 (Sept. 1984): p. 338.

OLD CEDAR STUMP SHOWING THE SPIRAL GROWTH.

"April 28, 1890. This photograph was taken by Barnes on the west slopes of Low Mountain, near the head of the Goldie River." (Majors, vol. 2, 144)

where we stopped to rest and to observe the mountain range opposite us we had an opportunity to see one of them. As we sat there a low rumbling was heard. Looking quickly in the direction of the sound we perceived upon the face of Mount Pulitzer, directly opposite us at a distance of not over a mile, a great mass of snow slipping and rolling down the mountain side. A glance revealed the origin of the movement. A piece of the overhanging snow had broken from the crest. The snow below it lay upon the mountain side a hundred feet in depth. Dislodging a great quantity of this the combined mass began to descend the almost perpendicular descent, gathering momentum and fresh accumulation every moment. To us as we watched it from a distance it seemed to move slowly, but in fact it was plowing and plunging down the shining white plane at a great velocity. Before it bounded great balls of snow, like sputtering drops of oil on a heated surface. As it neared the timber line we watched it with increased interest. From the base of the mountain the timber belt extended up its sides some three thousand feet and lay directly across the path of the descending monster. We had not long to wait.

Like a Crashing Column Through the Timber

Before the head of the avalanche struck the timber the trees began to go down. It seemed as if a rushing column, or cushion, of air pressed forward, and sustained by the mighty down rush of the avalanche, struck the timber. It snapped them off like matches and hurled them before it hundreds of feet. Great forest trees gnarled with the hardy mountain growth of hundreds of years were torn up by the roots by the breath of the monster. Carrying destruction before it and leaving behind it a long, dirty yellow track extending up the mountain side it seemed like an angry come. The crash of timber and roar of the avalanche came to our ears like thunder—like the continued roar of artillery. It cut a swath through the timber hundreds of yards in width, and poured a dirty mass of snow, broken timber, rocks and earth into the canyon below. It was all over in about the space of a minute, but to us who watched it seemed an hour. The movement of a mountain side, the tearing up of rocks and crashing of trees made it a most thrilling spectacle. After it was over, we had time to observe the awful effects which ensued from that little break at the top. Broken and splintered stumps marked all that was left of the great trees in its path. The smaller trees had bent forward with the weight of the snow and had remained comparatively uninjured. Great patches of bare earth and naked rock showed here and there where there had been pure, white snow a few minutes before.[133]

Peculiar to This Range Only

This range is peculiarly liable to avalanches. In its higher altitudes it nearly approaches the perpendicular, and hence, whenever its burden of snow becomes heavy, a slip is the result.

Avalanches are not common in these mountains, as a whole. The timber extends everywhere in an unbroken belt along the lower slopes, unbroken, save by the present winter. Mountain slopes nearly approaching the perpendicular are everywhere heavily timbered, which would not be if such heavy snow were a common occurrence, or even happened once in a hundred years.[134]

After enjoying this remarkable spectacle, we again entered

---

[133] "This, incidentally, is one of the finest and most graphic descriptions of an avalanche in all the literature of Western Americana." Majors, ed., *Northwest Discovery* 5 (Sept. 1984): p. 338.

[134] "Weather Bureau records for four stations—Port Angeles, Tatoosh Island, Olympia, and Vancouver—reveal that the winter of 1889–90 was severe in western Washington. . . . Significantly at the two northern stations, Port Angeles and Tatoosh Island—which were nearest the expedition's location at that time—the mean temperature for [December through March] averaged 5.61 degrees colder than normal. . . . February was the coldest month, averaging 7.8 degrees colder than normal, with 1.70 inches more precipitation than usual. Although the precipitation was not greatly excessive, the low temperatures caused most of it to fall in the form of snow. This meant heavy snow in the valleys—such as the expedition experienced in December, January, and February—when normally the snow line would have been up two or three thousand feet. However, the amount of snow at the higher elevations probably did not greatly exceed the normal. Barnes was no doubt incorrect in his conclusion that 'such heavy snow' would not occur more than once in a hundred years. On August 14,1890, John P. McGlinn, United States Indian Agent at Neah Bay, reported: '. . . the past winter was the most trying and discouraging that I ever experienced. The rainy season (it is no Oregon mist) set in on the 1st of November, and it either snowed or rained incessantly till the middle of April. At times storms from the ocean were dreadful, and would shake the buildings to their foundation.' (*Reports of the Interior Department* [Washington, D.C.: Government Printing Office, 1890], pp. 222–25.)" Wood, *Across the Olympic Mountains*, pp. 145–46.

the gloom of the woods, followed our trail downward and arrive at "Lucky" camp in much less time than it had taken us to go up.

Loss of Valuable Bacon

Lucky camp, April 28.—Clear and warm. Last night the dogs got away with the bacon, leaving us only two or three pounds. In the remaining piece was very little fat, the only grease in camp. We have of late been very saving of bacon, and the loss amounts almost to a disaster. With the exception of minute allowance of bacon we have been for nearly two months past without grease, which is beginning to tell on the health of the expedition. As for the dogs they have had scarcely anything to eat since we left the dead elk at the Gallery, for we cannot pack for dogs. They are hardly to be blamed for last night's theft. We would probably steal ourselves if we were hungry.[135]

As the sun rose over the eastern mountains the expedition was on foot again, to commence, with the second pack, the ascent of the mountain. The snow was much better this morning to travel on, for we were able to follow the trail of yesterday, which was trampled hard by our feet, and climbing was quite a different matter. Still, it was long and hard work, and many a drop of perspiration fell and many a breath came short before the day was over. "I am leg weary of this job," quoth good Jack Crumback, before the tip was reached. Starting at about 8 A.M. we reached our altitude of yesterday at about noon. Stopping there we made a fire on the snow and had a little lunch and caught our breath. From here a bench makes along and upward at an easier grade, so we put on our snowshoes and proceeded at

an average of about twenty degrees rise. For two miles we got along excellently, occasionally having to slip our snowshoes at a steep place and go at it in bare moccasins. Snow everywhere. It was in vain to look for a bare camping place, so at about 3 o'clock we selected a spot having but six feet of snow for a camp, upon the side hill.[136] Cutting out a bench of ten feet square, we built the fire at the lower end. First we felled a tree about two feet in diameter, cut it into logs, and rolled them to the fire place, placed them parallel with each other and thus had a platform on which to build the fire. Before it, on the bench in the snow, we spread a layer of spruce boughs a foot thick for bed, and we were as comfortable as we had any right to be.

Peculiar Spiral Growth of Cedar

As soon as these preparations were in progress, Mr. Christie and I leaving the boys to complete them, went out for a reconnaissance. We followed the slope of the mountain for a couple of miles, finding good snowshoe traveling with an easy ascent. The woods continued so dense that in the short time at our disposal we were unable to find an opening in the trees from which a satisfactory outlook would be obtained, so Mr. Christie resolved to take the day for it tomorrow, and get above the timber belt, hoping to see over the divide ahead. There appears to be an excellent pass ahead of us. Returning, I made a photograph of an old cedar stump, which shows plainly the peculiar spiral growth of the cedar at this altitude.

This cedar was about three feet in diameter, and the spiral growth extends to the heart of the tree. Fir and

81

Mt. Barnes. Mt. Childs. Mt. Pulitzer. Mt. Ferry.
VIEW OF BAILEY RANGE.
Taken from "Table Top" near bed of Goldie River Canyon. Mt. Childs leans due West.

"April 29, 1890. This is a panorama of several photographs taken by Barnes from the summit of Table Top (5049), looking west and northwest toward the Bailey Range." (Majors, vol. 2, 144)

[135] "The loss of their precious and carefully rationed bacon was a severe loss to the Press Party larder, not to mention the effect on the morale of the men. Yet, Barnes could write of this incident with understanding and empathy for the famished dogs. Since the bacon supply totaled ten pounds on April 21, the dogs had consumed close to seven pounds. However, keep in mind that this providential feast on bacon was virtually the only food the three dogs had . . . [in] a period of two weeks. It was likely this bacon that kept the three dogs alive to enable them to participate in the bear hunt at the Low Divide on May 5. . . . Thus, the successful raid by the three dogs of seven pounds of the Press Party's bacon on the night of April 27–28 was in effect ultimately responsible for saving the lives of all five men." Majors, ed., *Northwest Discovery* 5 (Sept. 1984): p. 338.

[136] "Camp 32 of the Press Party, for April 28–30, 1890, was located on the west side of Low Mountain 4654', at elevation 3300 feet, at a point 0.8 mile WSW of the summit of Low Mountain. This was also the site of 'permanent cache #4' of the Press Party, 'up a tree.' This may possibly have been the cache where the shotgun and one rifle were left. Since this part of the Goldie River area has never since been visited by man, the rusting remains of permanent caches 3 and 4 of the Press Party are likely still there." Majors, ed., *Northwest Discovery* 5 (Sept. 1984): p. 338.

spruce, the predominating trees on this mountain side, are large, sound and close grained. There is much cedar interspersed, but differing from the cedar of the coast in being very tall and slender, and, for the most part, growing with a spiral grain as shown in the photograph of the old stump. In the cut given here, the tree at the left is a growing one of spiral grain, but concealed by its bark.

April 29.—Clear and warm. This morning the boys were sent back two miles to the cache made on the 27th, and Mr. Christie and I went ahead to prospect the country ahead for a trail and to endeavor to reach some high point. We climbed straight up the mountain side on the soft snow with snowshoes. We soon reached the summit of the low mountain we were on and found that it connected with a sharp snowclad peak directly south[137] by a "saddleback."[138]

Views of Mount Dana

The excellent view from here eastward induced us to rest and have a smoke while I made some negatives of a glorious mountain to the eastward. This mountain we recognized as being the great white peak previously observed from above Convulsion Canyon, but how different in appearance observed from here. Then we saw its northern side, pure white, glittering with snow, now, its western and southern slope came under our view, heavily timbered almost to the summit. Great

masses of snow however appeared near the summit, wind blown and curling over the summit to the northward and eastward, like a great wave breaking upon the beach. This mountain, though a part of Bailey range, is connected with that range by a low ridge only. It stands forth so independently and prominently that it reminded me of my favorite newspaper the *New York Sun.* So we called it Mount "Dana."

After having had our smoke and admiring the broad and generous proportions of Mount Dana, we descended a little to the saddleback with an easy grade. The snow here was as much as fifteen feet in depth covering the smaller trees whose heads peeped out through the covering. The trees were now becoming stunted and were for the most part mountain fir, with occasional cedars of small size similar in character to those of yesterday. Along the saddleback one mile brought us to the steep ascent of the great peak whose sides we wished to scale. Before attempting it we made a fire and had lunch, and thereby lightened our load of a little bread and dried venison.

A Most Difficult Ascent

Thus lightened and fortified, we began the ascent of 1100 feet at an angle of seventy-five degrees. The mountain side was partially bare of timber. A few tree tops only protruded through the deep snow. We made the ascent at considerable risk, for the snow, whose great depth we could only guess at, lay so soft

MOUNT DANA.
Looking Eastward.

"April 29, 1890. This is a panorama of four (possibly three) photographs taken by Charles Barnes from the summit of Low Mountain (4654). In the far left distance (looking northeast) is the ridge running northwest from McCartney Peak (6499). Mount Dana (6209) occupies the center, looking ESE. The far right of the panorama is a view SSE toward the east ridge of Mount Wilder (5928), which itself is obscured by the branch of a tree." (Majors, vol. 2, 144)

[137] This was Mount Wilder. Christie's diary entry for April 30 is headed "Mt. Barnes," and it is possible the peak now known as Wilder was the mountain that the expedition meant to bear the name Mount Barnes, after their historian and topographer. Present-day maps, however, indicate Mount Barnes as the northwestern of two peaks lying between the head of the Goldie and Dodwell-Rixon Pass, which peak does closely resemble the sketch of Mount Barnes in the *Press*'s story of the expedition. The men also gave the name Mount Childs to a peak in the Bailey Range. This could have been one of the two peaks adjacent to Dodwell-Rixon Pass; or it may possibly have been the higher summit about one mile north-northeast of Bear Pass.

[138] "From camp 32, the objective of Christie and Barnes on April 29 was, not the actual summit of Low Mountain 4654', but instead the higher peak of Mount Barnes [Wilder] 5928' to the southeast. Christie and Barnes therefore did not reach the actual summit of Low Mountain 4654', but merely gained the crest of the south ridge of Low Mountain at point 4500–4600, and then followed this ridged crest south to Table Top 5049'. A close examination of Barnes' panorama of Mount Dana reveals that it was taken, not from the 4654-foot summit of Low Mountain, but instead from point 4500–4600 on the south ridge of Low Mountain. The term 'Low Mountain' for peak 4654' . . . is herein introduced for the first time. The term 'Table Top' for peak 5049 was first introduced in the published Press Party narrative in the *Seattle Press* (July 16, 1890, p. 6) caption for the panoramic engraving *View of Bailey Range*." Majors, ed., *Northwest Discovery* 5 (Sept. 1984): p. 362.

and yielding on the mountain side that we constantly feared a slip of the entire mass. We made our way slowly up zigzag fashion. Mr. Christie went in advance, thrusting one snowshoe into the snow edgewise, carefully bringing his weight upon it, then thrusting in the other foot a little above and ahead of the other, sometimes making a short tack then a long one. Mr. Christie, followed closely by myself, gradually approached the top. After two hours of hard work we finally reached a flat-topped table, 1100 feet above the saddleback, which commanded a view of the entire horizon except about 40 degrees occupied by the main peak. The main peak towered a thousand feet above us, separated from our table-top upon which we now stood, so we gave up the idea of going further and concluded to take our observations from here. A few scattering trees thrust their stunted tops through the deep snow here and there, which we estimated to be 25 feet deep.[139] Mounting a small pinnacle of naked rock, we obtained a glorious view. The whole mountain system south of us came for the first time under our view, and for the first time under the view of any white man. Before us what a jumble of mountains. Range after range of peaks, snow-clad from base to summit, extended as far as the eye could reach, in splendid confusion.

"The Quinaiult!"

But our admiration was for the moment withheld. One thought was uppermost in both our minds. For a moment we were almost stunned by the sea of mountains across the pathway to our journey's end—and we had but twelve days' grub in camp by the utmost economy. For a moment only we gazed —then in one breath we cried, "The Quinaiult!" Yes, there was the watershed of the Quinaiult, the aim of all our travel, separated from us at a distance of not over six or seven miles by a "height of land" somewhat less than the height at which we stood. But what a watershed! What a route to travel! A deep gorge it seemed, its precipitous sides all rock and snow, rising gradually to the snow-capped, vapor-wreathed heights that formed its bounds. For some miles the pass appeared to run due south and then trended to the southwest, far away.

"One Pack!"

"One pack a man," said Mr. Christie, after several minutes of silence, during which we looked and pondered upon the situation—pondering in which pounds of flour and ounces of bacon largely figured.

"One pack," I assented.

This decision arrived at, the difficulties in the situation seemed to disappear, and we both felt relieved. By leaving behind all useless articles, by taking with us only what we could pack in a single load, and traveling right ahead, we might expect to reach Lake Quinaiult and a game country in ten or twelve days—sooner, if the road turned out better than it appeared; worse than it appeared, it could not be. All our slender stock of provision, our guns and ammunition, half a blanket each man, the camera and a few instruments—that was all we could take. Once near the lake, we had no doubt but that we could get plenty of game and fish. Our experience during the last 25 miles forbade us to expect any game before that.

A Group of Giant Pinnacles

To the left of the watershed or canyon of the Quinaiult rose a group of giant pinnacles, forming in their midst a great amphitheater in the clouds. On the right of the canyon rose the first as well as the highest and most majestic peak of a range which swept in a semicircle around to the westward. The peaks of this range differed so much in height from the mountains of the other ranges which we had yet seen, and possessed such strong individuality, varying each from the other, that they formed the most striking and interesting sight we had seen in the Olympics.

The first peak on the right of the canyon of the Quinaiult we named provisionally "Mount Seattle"—provisionally, because we might yet find a greater one.[140] From where we stood there did not appear to be a vestige of timber upon it. Pure white snow spread like a mantle from the double peak to the base. Its eastern and western sides seemed to slope gradually, but its northern was nearly up and down.[141]

83

---

[139] "This was not exaggerated. Snow in this part of the Olympics often reaches this depth in March and April." Wood, *Across the Olympic Mountains*, p. 149.

[140] "This is a rather interesting and revealing statement for only 1.65 miles directly northwest of Mount Seattle 6246', and visible from the Table Top, is the highest peak of this sub-range, Mount Meany 6695'. Here then, in full view of Christie and Barnes . . . was indeed 'a greater' peak—but it did not receive the name Mt. Seattle. Instead, it was named for an editor/reporter of the *Seattle Press*, Edmond S. Meany, who acted as treasurer and organizer of the Press Party Expedition. The name 'Mount Meany' was created in Seattle after the return of the Press Party, but not once is this term mentioned in the Barnes or Christie narratives. The name 'Mount Meany,' applied to the highest and most prominent peak in this sub-range southeast of Mount Olympus, may very well have been the creation of Edmond S. Meany himself, who was likely responsible for the creation of nearly all of the other 'newspapermen' names on Barnes' map of the Press Party. The name was certainly applied with Meany's acquiescence." Majors, ed., *Northwest Discovery* 5 (Sept. 1984): p. 362.

[141] "They were looking directly at the north face of Mount Seattle. Thus fore-shortened, it appeared to be vertical." Wood, *Across the Olympic Mountains*, p. 152.

Like Lions in the Path

Down the gap of the Quinaiult a second range appeared, and beyond it another range, crossing our proposed pathway like lions in the path. Beyond them, sky—thank heaven, there was an end to them.

But we had work to do. The sun was getting westward and the snow was getting softer as the afternoon advanced—how long we might be making the descent we did not know, and we were a long ways from home. One hour we had for work. First we made photographs of every part of the horizon—south, west, north, east—a splendid panorama was under our view; mountains on every side. For our map we had the bearings and altitudes of mountains to take, the positions and courses of canyons, valleys and streams; hasty sketches and outlines for future development, and much other work. We made a hasty examination of the rock upon which we stood. An hour never passed so quickly; we could have spent twelve with profit.

A Solitary Pansy Blossom

As we were reaching for our snowshoes, Mr. Christie exclaimed: "See, a pansy!" Sure enough, upon the very summit, growing in a cleft of the rock six thousand feet above level, surrounded by oceans of snow, baked in the warm sunlight, a little yellow flower.[142] It was the first we had seen. We pulled it tenderly and took it with us, a souvenir of our visit.

The rock upon which we had been standing was a needle-like mass of slate in place. The strata was nearly vertical having a slight dip to the northward. The strike east and west.

Before descending we named some of the peaks in sight. The Bailey range bounded our vision to the westward. In this range, due west of where we stood, rises to a considerable altitude above ourselves a grand old mountain clothed with snow, magnificent in its proportions. It seemed one solid mass of rock and snow. It deserved a good name and we called it Mount Childs[143] after George Washington Childs, the eminent philanthropist and proprietor of the *Philadelphia Ledger*. Northward appeared the beautiful pyramidal shaped peak, which we had already named Mount Scott.

Beyond Mt. Scott could be seen Mt. Squire which we had seen from Deer range which I had seen more clearly upon my trip up Belle river, and which is a spur from the Bailey range.

Going down was even worse than going up. The soft afternoon snow made dangerous work of that descent, where a little slip meant a plunge to the very bottom, unless the snow swallowed one up completely. But step by step, down the already nearly obliterated ladder of our former footsteps, we descended in safety to the saddleback. The sun was then setting, skirting the mountain side by a shorter route we arrived in camp soon after dark, hungry and tired. Pulling off our wet clothes and swaddling up in blankets, Indian fashion, we lighted our pipes, climbed down into the fire hole, in the snow and rested after the fatigues of the day.

Caching Away Superfluous Freight

April 30.—The result of our observations yesterday is that we spent today in stripping for the work ahead. From here we must carry not one superfluous ounce, and therefore we overhauled the entire cargo and divided what we would take into five packs and cached the remainder up a tree.

All day long at intervals we have been listening to the roaring of the avalanches. They are most common in the afternoons and evenings when the snow is softest. They sometimes average five or six in an hour and end only with the frost of night.

On our first night here our fire burned through the base logs, through the snow and reached the ground. It has since extended the hole by melting the snow so that there is space enough on bare ground to sleep tonight.

Homeward Bound at Last

Thursday, May 1.—This morning we broke camp for home. Homeward bound!—how the boys enjoyed the idea. We divided the outfit into five packs. The packs each weighed about 75 pounds, or in all, upwards of 400 pounds. This comprised all the provisions in camp, to wit: One hundred and twenty pounds of flour, one half pound of bacon, one half pound of dried venison and three pounds of tea. It included our snowshoes, a single blanket for each man, three axes, some rope, three guns, a supply of ammunition, fishing tackle, the scientific instruments of the expedition, etc. Seventy-five pounds was a rather heavy pack for the work before us, but we had the satisfaction of knowing that its weight would diminish every day as we consumed the provisions, and of believing that, as we descended the Quinaiult, the traveling would improve with every mile. The first day or two would be the worst. With the heavy packs we must climb the side of the mountain ahead to reach the division between the watersheds. But the magic phrase "homeward bound" made a trifle of the burden and a molehill of the mountain.

84

---

[142] "This . . . is the alpine buttercup *Ranunculus eschscholtzii*. . . . This little yellow-flowered plant is the first to bloom at alpine/Hudsonian elevations in the Olympic Mountains." Majors, ed., *Northwest Discovery* 5 (Sept. 1984): p. 363.

[143] "From Barnes' entry for May 1 (also April 29), the name Mount Childs applies to peak 6041." Majors, ed., *Northwest Discovery* 5 (Sept. 1984): p. 363.

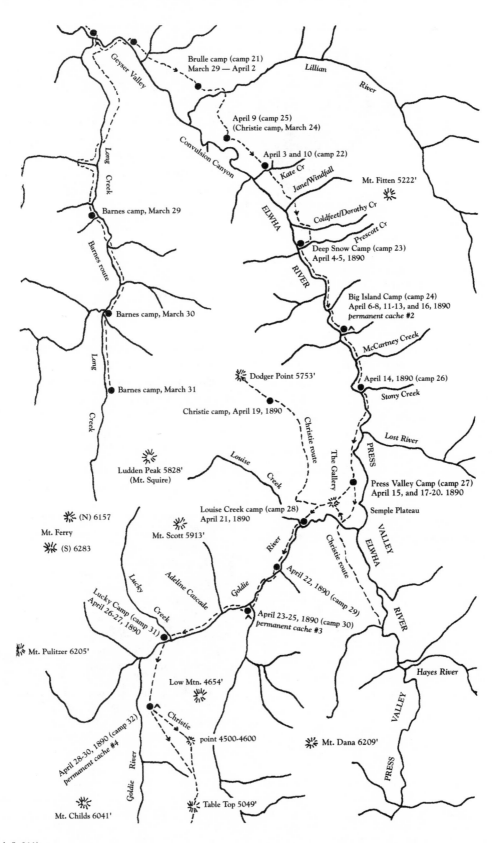

(Majors, vol. 5, 311)

A STEEP INCLINE.

"May 1, 1890. Probably taken by Barnes, depicts three men traversing a snowbank. . . .The last man holds what is probably one of the cooking kettles in his right hand. The leading man may be holding a shovel or an axe." (Majors, vol. 2, p. 146)

In Moccasins and Snowshoes

Leaving camp at 9 A.M. in moccasins and snowshoes, we began a gradual ascent of the mountain upon the side of which we were. After about two hours of travel, interrupted by frequent short intervals at rest, we reached the saddle connecting with the high peak adjoining. Half an hour later we were across the saddle and had reached the place where Mr. Christie and I had climbed up previously. We carefully skirted this mountain side, not without difficulty, working gradually around the face of the mountain. Sometimes we could use snowshoes, and sometimes when the side was too steep for this use, we were struggling along in moccasins. Without snowshoes the weight of the packs sank us deep into the snow and made painful work. On a little bench we made tea and divided up the last remaining half pound of venison.

All day long we passed steep inclines, bare of timber and heavy with snow. In two places avalanches had taken place, and we were in constant fear lest the jar of our weight would start others. For this reason we kept, as a rule, far apart, in order to bring as little weight as possible on any one point. The snow was soft and melting; little pieces started by our feet would go rolling or sliding sometimes thousands of feet, becoming great masses before reaching the bottom. We had to check the dogs from running above us on the slope, for even the small pieces of snow detached by them would often become dangerous by accretion by the time they reached us a little way below. Late in the afternoon we arrived at about the middle of the western slope, and there found a bare rock projecting through the snow below us. It was bare only on the outward face, and looking over we perceived little shelves or benches below. We were so weary of the snow that we selected these shelves, so warm and dry, for our camp. Upon one shelf we made the fire. Upon the ends of the shelf, and upon the shelves above and below, each man selected his berth and made himself as safe and comfortable as he could.

Magnificent View

The view from this rock was magnificent. Mount Seattle and Mount Childs were both in view. As the sun went down it flooded the mountains with a rosy glow, transforming this cold white drapery into soft garments of a warmer hue. This was again succeeded by white, then gray, until at length night obscured the view.

The vegetation at this altitude is stunted and gnarled. The trees are mountain pine and fir. We have seen no moss whatever since leaving the Goldie, but lichens now cover everything—trees and rocks, wherever it can get a hold.

Side Rock Camp

May 2.—This has been an eventful day all around. Our camp last night was neither comfortable nor safe, but it was "Hobson's choice."[144] It was the only relief from the steep slope of the

MOUNT CHILDS, LOOKING WEST.

"April 29?, 1890. This is a mid-elevation photograph, probably taken by Barnes . . .during the ascent of Low Mountain." (Majors, vol. 2, 144)

---

[144] "The archaic expression 'Hobson's choice' has since fallen into disuse. Thomas Hobson (1544?–1630) was an English stablemaster at Cambridge who . . . would rent only the horse, which at a given time, was tied nearest the stable door. It was either that horse or none at all. In this manner, Hobson could rotate his horses and thus ensure that no one of them received excessive use. Thus, it means 'this or nothing at all.'" Majors, ed., Northwest Discovery 5 (Sept. 1984): p. 363.

mountain side. None of us slept much, being kept awake more or less by the apprehension of falling off. My berth was not so very bad. I laid several good sized sticks from one jutting piece of rock to another, including one to keep me from rolling over. I could look down through the "slats" of my bed hundreds of feet below. Sims and Hayes sat up all night, not trusting themselves to sleep in their hazardous resting places. After the exhausting work of yesterday, the loss of sleep was unfortunate, but there was no help for it. And today was destined to be still more fatiguing than yesterday.[145]

A Scanty Breakfast

We finished our scanty breakfast of beans and were on our snowshoes at 6 o'clock. At first we made our way up the mountain side, the slope of which was gradual in some places, and at others very steep. Skirting around we crossed four or five deep canyons which scarify the mountain side. At 11 o'clock, all hands being about done up, we reached the apparent divide or watershed, and at length stood upon the summit. It was an interesting moment to us. We had no doubt that we would now have a down-hill pull for home.

It was a long, narrow ridge connecting the mountains that we had just skirted with Mount Childs.[146] Watershed it was for certain, but there was something wrong. At our feet far below was a broad and beautiful valley—but not the Quinaiult. What was it? Could it be the Elwha? Mr. Christie and I climbed a knoll 200 yards up the ridge to see. On our arrival there we saw at once what we had done. At our feet lay the beautiful Press valley, broader and larger than where we left it at the mouth of the Goldie. This old friend and the still older friend, the Elwha river, we still

ON DECEPTION DIVIDE.

"May 2, 1890. This photograph, probably taken by Barnes, depicts three men (wearing caps) gazing southward, one dog, and five packs lying on the snow. The man holding a pair of binoculars to his eyes, and wearing a plaid shirt is very likely Christie. One man holds what is probably a tilted rifle, the remaining man may be leaning on his rifle. Strewn among the packs is a wrapped rifle, the shovel, one of the three remaining axes, and a kettle. The two men in the foreground are on snowshoes." (Majors, vol. 2, 147)

had with us. But we felt toward them more like an enemy than a friend at this moment. Nevertheless it presented a pleasing contrast to the canyons we have of late been traveling through. It swept around the base of Mount Dana and ended at our feet, having an apparent width of two or three miles. In shape the valley is a crescent. We had left it at one horn, traveled over 20 miles of the roughest country and through the most rugged canyon in the mountains, and have experienced 12 days of the hardest work of the trip, only to find ourselves at the other horn of this crescent-shaped valley. We might have made the journey on snowshoes in a couple of days' easy traveling.

87

---

[145] "These two days and one night were the most difficult, exhausting, and trying that the Press Party would ever experience—both physically and emotionally." Majors, ed., *Northwest Discovery* 5 (Sept. 1984): p. 363.

[146] "It is impossible to determine exactly which peaks the Press Exploring Expedition meant to bear the names Mount Childs and Mount Barnes. There are four high peaks in the immediate area, any two of which could have been these. For the purpose of clarification in this footnote, these four summits will be referred to as peaks A, B, C, and D. Peak A, known today as Mount Wilder, is the easternmost of the four; Peak B, presently unnamed, is located about one mile southeast of Peak C, known today as Mount Barnes; Peak D, unnamed, is located in the Bailey Range about one mile NNE of Bear Pass.

"If the men were accurate in stating that Mount Childs was 'due west' of the 'table-top' from which they made observations on April 29, this would indicate that they were referring either to peak B or C; if so, the expedition gave the name Mount Barnes to Peak A (the mountain they were climbing on) or to Peak B. This conclusion is bolstered by Christie's diary entries for April 30, May 2, and May 3, all of which are headed 'Mt. Barnes.' Also Barnes' statement that they had reached 'a long, narrow ridge connecting the mountain . . . just skirted [i.e., Peak A or Mount Wilder] with Mt. Childs' indicates, again, that Mt. Childs was Peak B.

"It must be admitted, however, that the etching of Mount Barnes appearing in the official story of the expedition, which was made from an expedition photograph, greatly resembles Peak C. The evidence is not conclusive, however, that Peak C was, in fact, the one photographed, because Peak A has a similar configuration.

"The statement about Mount Childs being due west of the table-top is not necessarily accurate, for the men had made errors previously in regard to directions; i.e., they indicated Belle River as entering the Elwha from the southwest when, in fact, it flows directly from the south. Nor is Barnes' map conclusive, for it lacks the accuracy to determine this close question.

"Unfortunately, Barnes' map cannot be used for confirmation, for he was not consistent in placing the names of peaks either to the right or left of the cartographic indication of a summit. The name Mount Barnes lies between two peak designations, and thus it is impossible to determine which summit he was labeling. If he meant the one to the right—directly opposite Buckinghorse Creek—then the Press Party's Mount Barnes was undoubtedly Peak A. On the other hand, if he meant the peak shown to the left of the name, it was a minor spur of Peak A, or merely Deception Divide, the point at which the expedition had now arrived.

"The preponderance of the evidence indicated, however, that the Press Party's Mount Barnes was Peak A and that Peak B (or B and C considered as one) was their Mount Childs." Wood, *Across the Olympic Mountains*, pp. 159–60.

Just a Little Mad

Such is the fate of explorers. We are here to find these things out. Still we felt a little mad and may have on this occasion expressed it. The gap we have been taking for the Quinaiult is on the opposite side of the valley near the head. It still looked like the Quinaiult, that was one consolation. There was nothing to do but to go down into the valley and climb up the other side. After a frugal lunch and a short time for rest we started down at precisely noon. Our altitude by aneroid at this point was six thousand two hundred feet. The descent was very steep. We plunged down in our "moccasined" feet through the soft deep snow and while the slope remained nearly up and down we made rapid progress, which was about twelve hundred feet. Then as the mountain gradually became less precipitous it became heavier work in the snow where gravity had less to do with pulling us out. We shaped our course down a ravine for about twelve hundred feet further descent. Then the snow in the ravine began to get hollow underneath and the water running below us became unpleasantly evident. So we climbed out of the ravine and found a mountain side bare of snow, most delightful after a couple of weeks in the deep snow, but much harder to descend upon. When we reached the bottom it was 4 o'clock, so that we were four hours making the descent. By aneroid the head of the valley was twenty-four hundred feet elevation,[147] making our descent thirty-eight hundred feet. We called this Deception divide.

At the bottom of the hill we found five feet of snow in the valley beneath the trees. Selecting a favorable spot on the bank of the river we shoveled a space clear and made camp on bare ground.[148]

A New Kind of Soup

Camp at head of Press valley, May 3.—We spent today resting. We are all completely tuckered out by the experience of late, and particularly of the last few days. We are much in need of meat. Our sole food for the last few days has been flour soup. To make flour soup for five men one pound and a half of flour is added to three gallons of boiling water and well stirred. This is flour soup. It is not much of a dish for an epicure, nor is it found on the bill of fare at Delmonico, but it is very filling, and in the absence of anything else and with a good appetite is positively good.[149]

Rabbit Tracks Seen

In the afternoon Hayes went out to shoot something. He returned empty-handed, but said he saw rabbit tracks in the snow, and that he was going to polish up a club and try to get some of the tracks for supper if he couldn't get anything else.

Hayes is a good hunter, but sometimes he makes a mistake. He came in breathless a few days ago, and said he had seen bear tracks just outside of camp. It was a little rough on Mr. Christie's feet, but investigation showed that they were made by his new moccasins.

Camp at head of Press valley, May 4.—Clear and warm. Broke camp early, and on snowshoes headed up the valley, destination, the canyon or watershed discovered running to the southward. This canyon wherever it may turn out to lead is formed by the slopes of Mount Seattle on the one hand and the amphitheater shaped mountains on the other. A steep climb was ahead of us before we could reach it., and after breaking camp we headed directly for the foot of the declivity.

Elizabeth Falls

The timber in the upper end of the valley is large and dense. Pine, fir, spruce and hemlock predominate. The underbrush, if any, is buried in snow but the ground appears to be comparatively free of minor growth. We crossed a branch of the river coming in from the northwestward containing about one-third of the water.[150] The river now became small and was generally covered or bridged by the snow. At the foot of the declivity the stream again divides,[151] the main part pouring over rocks from above and forming beautiful falls about 50 feet high.

We named these Elizabeth falls. Beginning the ascent of the hill we put on our boots and kicked steps in the snow. For some distance we followed a recent snow slide and had

---

[147] Though Majors comments that "this is a correct elevation figure for the floor of the Elwha Valley at this point," (Majors, ed., *Northwest Discovery* 5, Sept. 1984: p. 363), according to Wood, "Apparently the aneroid was now funtioning better. Actual elevation at this point was about twenty-two hundred feet. Thus in descending they had lost elevation at the rate of about seven hundred feet an hour" (Wood, *Across the Olympic Mountains*, p. 162).

[148] "Camp 34 of the Press Party, for May 2–3, 1890, was located on the northeast bank of the Elwha River, 0.2 miles northwest of the mouth of Delabarre Creek. This was the later site of Chicago Camp." Majors, ed., *Northwest Discovery* 5 (Sept. 1984): p. 363.

[149] "This indicates that the party's supplies of dried beans was exhausted. . . . Delmonico's was the most famous restaurant in the United States during the latter half of the Nineteenth Century. Founded at New York City by the Swiss emigrant Lorenzo Delmonico (1833–1881), this restaurant catered to the gourmand, and did much to introduce French cuisine to America." Majors, ed., *Northwest Discovery* 5 (Sept. 1984): p. 363.

[150] "This is the true head of the Elwha River, draining from Dodwell-Rixon Pass. The Press Party, as can be seen from the next two sentences, applied the term 'Elwha River' to Delabarre Creek, instead of employing the convention in use today." Majors, ed., *Northwest Discovery* 5 (Oct. 1984): p. 396.

[151] "The east branch is known today as Delabarre Creek and the west is an unnamed creek descending from Martin's Park on the northern slopes of Mount Christie." Wood, *Across the Olympic Mountains*, p. 163.

ELIZABETH FALLS.

"May 4, 1890" (Majors, vol. 2, 147)

TRACK OF AN AVALANCHE.

"May 4, 1890. The precise date on which this photograph was taken is uncertain, as during the course of the expedition the men would have had the opportunity to cross several avalanche tracks. Barnes specifically mentions that on May 4, 1890, while ascending to the Low Divide, 'For some distance we followed a recent snow slide and had an opportunity of observing the effects of an avalanche.'" (Majors, vol. 2, 147)

an opportunity of observing the effects of an avalanche. The large trees had been broken off and carried down, the smaller ones bending forward. By noon we had made 1100 feet upwards. The hill side to this point, though steep, was easy climbing, the snow being firm and unbroken, but from this point upwards the ascent was broken and consisted of bare ledges of rock for 600 feet.

Hazardous Climbing Over Rocks

At extreme hazard one of us, generally Mr. Christie, would climb slowly up to some jutting splinter of rock or stunted tree whose roots had a firm hold in the crevices, and then throw down a line. One by one and from one niche or shelf to another we gradually scaled the face of the rocks, some time hand over hand, and at others by means of a loop around the body, each man worked up after the leader. Our baggage we hauled up in the same manner. As for the dogs we would tie the rope around their necks and pull them up. Fortunately the rock work was free of snow. It is not pleasant to trust one's entire weight to a cod line, and when we reached the top we were all quite exhausted, more from the expenditure of nervous force than by physical, but we arrived safely at the top at about 5 o'clock, and made camp right there.[152] Altitude by aneroid above the valley, 1700 feet.[153]

The formation of this bluff is slate, nearly vertical in stratification.

Part Three

89

From the watershed to Lake Quinaiult—On the Divide—Two Little Lakes—The First Water Flowing South—"A Bear!"—A Bear Hunt—Some Fat at Last— The Ascent of Mount Seattle—A Glorious View From the Summit—The Descent—More Bears—The Last Bit of Tobacco—Down the Quinaiult River Canyon—Rough Travel Over Rugged Mountain Sides—A Descent of Over Three Thousand Feet In Three Days—Chester Valley—Clambering With Ropes—Another Elk—Tracks of Game—Quinaiult Valley and a Broad River— Attempts at Crossing—Meeting the First Human Beings—The Raft—A Disaster—Nearly Everything Lost—The Records Safe—A Divided Camp—A Friend in Need—The First Taste of Civilized Food—Lake Quinaiult—Arrival at Aberdeen—Home Again.

Bluff Top Camp, May 5.—Clear and warm. We made an early start before sunrise, traveling on snowshoes. The water still flowed toward the Elwha, but it was a little brook

---

[152] "Camp 35 of the Press Party, Bluff Top Camp, for May 4, 1890, was located on the top of 'a small ledge of rock,' at elevation 3500 feet, 0.15 mile SSE of Lake Mary." Majors, ed., *Northwest Discovery* 5 (Oct. 1984): p. 396.
[153] "The elevation difference between the Low Divide 3600–3700' and the floor of the Elwha Valley (about 2200 feet) below, is about 1450 feet." Majors, ed., *Northwest Discovery* 5 (Oct. 1984): p. 396.

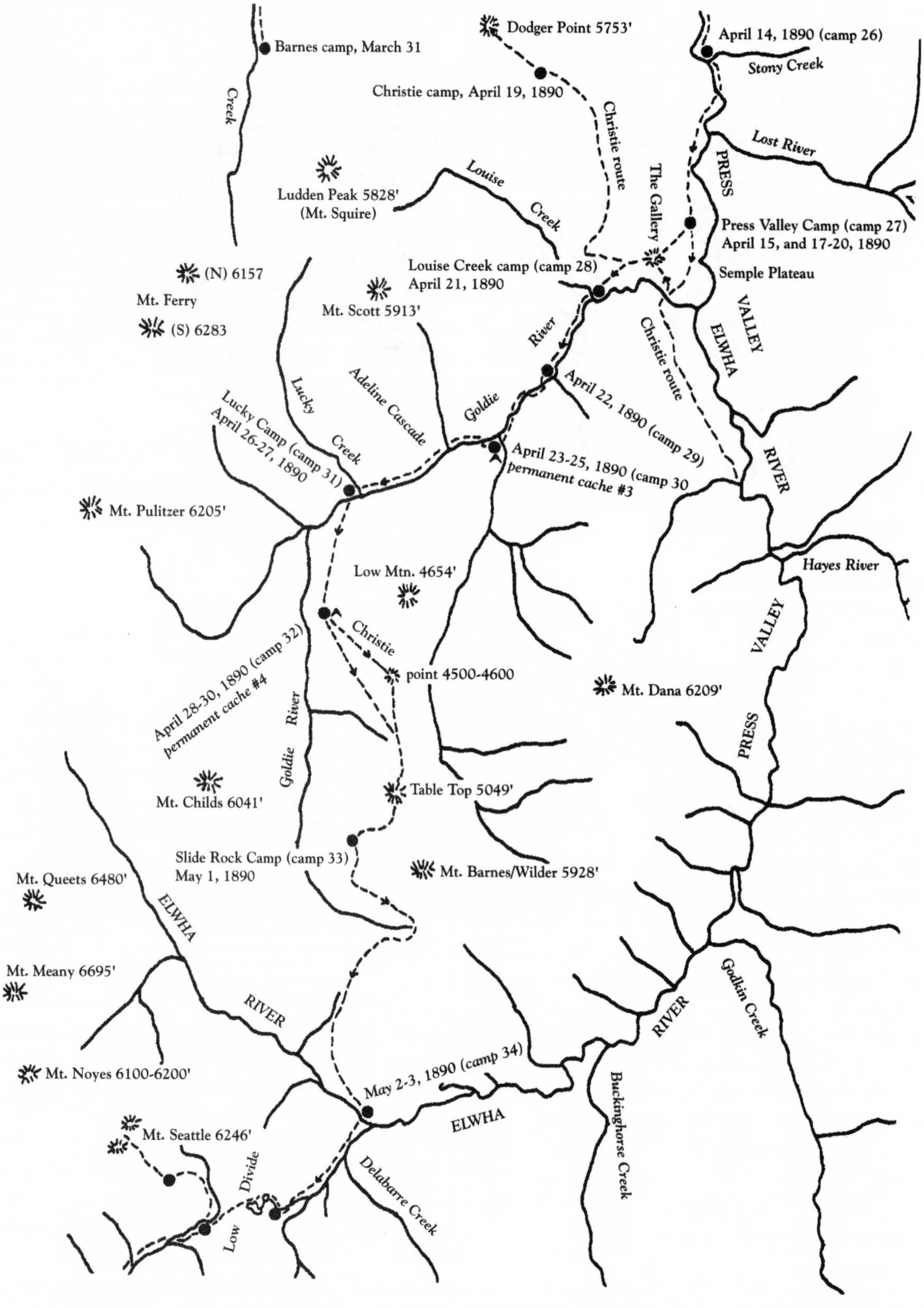

Barnes camp, March 31

Dodger Point 5753'

April 14, 1890 (camp 26)

Stony Creek

Christie camp, April 19, 1890

Lost River

Creek

Christie route

PRESS

Louise

Creek

Ludden Peak 5828'
(Mt. Squire)

The Gallery

Press Valley Camp (camp 27)
April 15, and 17-20, 1890

Semple Plateau

(N) 6157

Louise Creek camp (camp 28)
April 21, 1890

Mt. Ferry

Mt. Scott 5913'

(S) 6283

River

VALLEY

ELWHA

Christie route

April 22, 1890 (camp 29)

Lucky

Creek

Adeline Cascade

Goldie

Lucky Camp (camp 31)
April 26-27, 1890

April 23-25, 1890 (camp 30
permanent cache #3

RIVER

Mt. Pulitzer 6205'

Hayes River

Low Mtn. 4654'

VALLEY

90

April 28-30, 1890 (camp 32)
permanent cache #4

Goldie River

Christie
point 4500-4600

Mt. Dana 6209'

PRESS

Mt. Childs 6041'

Table Top 5049'

Slide Rock Camp (camp 33)
May 1, 1890

Mt. Barnes/Wilder 5928'

Mt. Queets 6480'

ELWHA

Godkin Creek

Mt. Meany 6695'

RIVER

Mt. Noyes 6100-6200'

May 2-3, 1890 (camp 34)

Buckinghorse Creek

Mt. Seattle 6246'

ELWHA

Low Divide

Delabarre Creek

(Majors, vol. 5, 340)

plunging over the precipice. The canyon between the two mountains was buried in snow, even trees, if there be any at all, were covered.[154]

Two Little Lakes Discovered

After half a mile of the first really good travel of the trip upon the hard snow, we came upon a beautiful little lake, frozen and snow covered. At the north end of the little lake, which was about 400 yards in diameter, the ice and snow were melted, affording us a glimpse of the water as we passed. We called this Lake Mary. Its outlet was northward. From its southern shore rose a little swell of ground, not 50 feet in height. Attaining this we looked down upon the other side and there lay another little lake. The little swell formed a complete barrier between them, and was evidently the divide, or height of land.[155] As we paused a minute there we felt that we had now attained the object of the expedition, and we could now say "homeward bound" in earnest. Crossing the second lake, which was quite similar to the first, and which we called Lake Margaret, we continued down the canyon. The canyon is from two to three hundred feet in width below Lake Margaret, the sides sloping gradually, with a broad sweeping curve up the mountains which form its sides. The snow covered everything and there was no obstacle to our progress. After an hour's travel we came, at about 6 o'clock to a great rock on the right hand, shaped like a vast cathedral, with spires and entrances. Through a hole in the snow at this point we caught our first sight of water running south.

As we stood looking at it, after having tasted its virtues—and it seemed to taste better than the Elwha—one of the dogs began to give tongue in a clump of trees about 300 yards down the canyon. The other two dogs were away like a shot.

An Exciting Bear Hunt

It Is Photographed From Beginning to the Finish

"A bear!" cried someone, and at that moment there emerged from the trees a bear, sure enough, worried by the three dogs.[156] We all seized our guns and started in chase. By a lucky thought, however, I dropped my gun and took instead the camera. By the time I got the camera out of its case, the others had gone over half the distance and I had to travel pretty hard to get there.

The bear was fighting the dogs, sometimes sitting back on his haunches and snapping at them and trying to reach them with his paws. Then one of the dogs would nip him behind and he would be off again. No sooner would he be off

THE FIRST SIGHT OF WATER RUNNING SOUTH.

"May 5, 1890. This probably depicts the stream that drains from an icefield on the upper east side of Mount Seattle. One of the three dogs is evident in the engraving." (Majors, vol. 2, 147)

"A BEAR!"

"May 5, 1890. This was the providential bear that saved the Press Party from starvation at the Low Divide. Three men (two with rifles) appear advancing in the foreground, but the dogs and bear are indistinct in the engraving." (Majors, vol. 2, 148)

[154] "This statement does not agree with the conditions depicted in the photograph taken at Low Divide wherein numerous trees, barren of snow, are visible." Majors, ed., *Northwest Discovery* 5 (Oct. 1984): p. 397.

[155] "In reality, both lakes drain into the Elwha River. The Press Party were led into this error because at this time of year the outlet of Lake Margaret was hidden beneath snow." Majors, ed., *Northwest Discovery* 5 (Oct. 1984): p. 396.

[156] "From the accounts of both Barnes and Christie on May 5, it is evident that the three dogs were directly responsible for (a) detecting the presence of the bear, and (b) keeping the bear occupied at one site until the men could reach there and kill the bear. Had not the three dogs eaten the seven pounds of bacon on the night of April 27, and had they died of starvation prior to May 5, then it is likely that the Press Party would not have been able to kill the providential bear at Low Divide that day—in which case, all five men would themselves have died of starvation and hypothermia." Majors, ed., *Northwest Discovery* 5 (Sept. 1984): p. 338.

THE FINISH

"May 5, 1890. This is the first of a series of three photographs taken, as identified by the two conifers on the left. The three dogs are engaged in worrying the ill fated bear, which appears to be partly slumped over in its death struggle, having been shot by Christie 'through the kidneys.'" (Majors, vol. 2, 148)

a few steps than one of the dogs would nip his heels, and that would bring him up all-standing once more, and the fighting and snapping would recommence. Meanwhile, the bear and dogs were nearing a little clump of trees, and to this we all hurried. I got three exposures while hastening toward them.

The others were some distance ahead of me and I was afraid they would shoot him before I got there, but they were afraid of hitting the dogs and did not, so that I got there in time to get several good negatives before the finish. A shot by Mr. Christie through the kidneys finally finished him. The bear made several rushes before concluding to give up the argument, one of which was made in my direction, which made me retire very quickly behind a tree, for I was not armed in precisely the right manner to cope with his bearship. At last he laid down and gave it up and a bullet through his head ended his sufferings.

After it was all over we could hardly believe our luck. Here was fat! It is impossible to convey an idea of the craving we had for fat at this time. After having lived on plain flour for a week and little besides flour for several weeks, and before that, plenty of meat,[157] but not an atom of fat, except a little dole from our precious bacon, for months, the prospects of grease seemed a delirious dream. It was not 15 minutes before

we had that bear skinned and dressed and his liver and slabs of fat frying over a fire. No food ever tasted so good to starving men as that fat tasted to us, for we were indeed starving for fat. So we sat around the fire and kept the frying pans going and drank the grease as fast as we could fry it out.[158] Mr. Christie decided right there to adopt the Indian custom of camping[159] alongside of our game and remaining there until it was all eaten. We made camp by the little south flowing stream. It seemed as if this little stream had brought us good fortune.

Plenty of Meat Changes Things

The killing of the bear made a great change in our plans. We now had meat and could take time to explore. As soon as it was settled that we should remain several days, I began to make preparations at once to ascend Mount Seattle.[160] I took the camera, instruments for topographical purposes, a blanket and meat enough for two days. On snowshoes I skirted the eastern base northward for one half a mile to a practicable canyon and then removing my snowshoes I commence the ascent of the canyon in bare moccasins. The ascent was easy for about four hundred feet, gradually becoming steeper until I passed the timberline at seven hundred feet. After that I had to zig-zag up the steep slope, which generally had an angle of 55 or 60 de-

AT CLOSER RANGE. AFTER THE FIRST SHOT.

"May 5, 1890. This [second bear hunt] photograph was taken next from the same position, for the wounded bear has managed to crawl closer to the 'little clump of trees.'" (Majors, vol. 2, 148)

---

[157] "The last game of the Press Party prior to May 5, was the elk killed on April 21 at Semple Plateau. Thus 14 days had elapsed without fresh meat, and one week without any meat at all. . . . By May 5, the five men were understandably famished, and perilously close to death by starvation. The timely emergence of this bear from hibernation had clearly saved the Press Party from disaster." Majors, ed., *Northwest Discovery* 5 (Oct. 1984): p. 396.

[158] "This reference to the Press Party's craving for fat . . . reveals the presence of a fundamental nutritional deficiency in their diet for the past several weeks. Fats and oils contain three known unsaturated fatty acids that are essential in the metabolism of a healthy animal: linoleic, linolenic, and arachidonic acids. . . . a severe deficiency of linoleic acid . . . can result in fatal damage to the kidneys." Majors, ed., *Northwest Discovery* 5 (Oct. 1984): p. 397.

[159] "Camp 36 of the Press Party, 'Bear Camp,' for May 5–8, 1890—one of the most historic sites in the Olympic Mountains—was located on the stream that drains from the icefield on the upper east slope of Mount Seattle, at a point 0.3 mile southwest of benchmark 3602, probably on the southeast side of the stream. Three months later, on August 2, 1890, the remains of this camp were seen by George A. Pratt's party of prospectors: 'A camp of the Christie party was found.'" Majors, ed., *Northwest Discovery* 5 (Oct. 1984): p. 397.

[160] "Christie's journal states that the captain ascended Mount Barnes, but this is obviously an error." Wood, *Across the Olympic Mountains*, p. 168.

THE END OF A SUCCESSFUL BEAR HUNT.

"May 5, 1890. For this final [bear hunt] photograph Barnes has now moved closer in to the moribund bear. The two trees evident on the left in the previous two photographs appear here from a different angle." (Majors, vol. 2, 148)

grees. The snow was extremely soft and yielding so I sank to my knees at every step, and sometimes sank bodily to my waist, and then had to struggle to extricate myself. As I got higher and could look down the long slope of a thousand feet or more at such an angle it was calculated to make a man proceed slowly and with caution—slowly, however, he had to.

At two thousand feet above the base, or sixty-three hundred feet above sea level, as indicated by the aneroid it was becoming late in the afternoon and I was greatly fatigued. So I determined to camp and go on in the early morning to the summit a thousand or more feet above. I had reached the back of a ridge and looking over the southern face I was gratified to find it an almost perpendicular rock wall with little shelves upon which grew stunted mountain pine, entirely free of snow

PRESS VALLEY AS SEEN FROM THE SIDE OF MOUNT SEATTLE.

"May 5?, 1890. This is a photograph looking northeast, . . . taken . . . by Barnes during his ascent of Mount Seattle. . . . Judging from the horizon and the caption, it very definitely was not taken on the crest of the mountain. This view depicts Mount Dana on the left, the upper end of Press Valley, with Mount Norton in the distance." (Majors, vol. 2, 148)

and exposed to the warm sunshine. After hunting along a little I presently discovered a suitable place to camp, about four feet below. The little bench there was three or four feet wide, and upon the margin grew several of the little pines, which branching inward, formed as cozy and snug a nook as can be imagined. My feet were wet and cold with the snow and the hot afternoon sun pouring upon my head for hours made me welcome the good fortune. Dropping into it and breaking from the pines a few dead branches I had a fire going in a very few minutes. I put dry duffels on my feet and soon had meat frying and tea brewing, and was as comfortable as in a drawing room. I spent the remainder of the afternoon and evening frying meat.

Breakfast on Mount Seattle

On Mount Seattle, Tuesday May 6.—At the first streak of light next morning I was up, made a fire and had breakfast. The snow was a little harder by the frost of the night than it had been in the afternoon before, and although the upper ascent was the most abrupt I had less difficulty in getting along. It was a ticklish thing though to plow along the face of a soft and yielding snow bank, which has its base half a mile below. I was glad when I approached the summit—or rather a kind of thin ridge or saddle, which connected two sharp unscalable spires of rock, which constituted the actual double summit of the mountain.[161] As I approached this saddle, the question of what was on the other side became of absorbing interest. This range, together with the Bailey range, divided the Olympic mountain region into two parts. Their height had shut off from us the view of anything beyond, so that the western portion was a *terra incognita*. Therefore at this height I anticipated a glorious view unless a range provokingly near should shut me off beyond. A final step brought my head above the sharp wedge like saddle and the curtain rose from before the unknown region.

The rising sun at my back swept over mountain ranges as far as the eye could reach and the view was all that I could have hoped for. At a distance of about two miles extending north and south was a range of mountains lower than the one upon which I stood. It was a range of solid rock nearly naked of soil and vegetation. The sides were so steep and precipitous that even snow could scarcely lodge, and it lay piled in sweeping curves from the base far up toward the summit.

93

---

[161] "Mount Seattle 6246' is one of the more prominent peaks at the head of the Elwha River. Though Barnes did not actually scramble the last 200 feet to reach the class 2–3 summit, his climb nonetheless constitutes essentially the first ascent of this peak. Barnes' route lay up the valley and basin on the east side to gain the ESE ridge, and finally the 6000–6100 foot saddle between the two summits of Mount Seattle. The second ascent of Mount Seattle (the first to reach the actual summit itself) occurred on August 4, 1890, by Asahel Curtis, Lorenz A. Nelson, and Grant W. Humes." Majors, ed., *Northwest Discovery* 5 (Oct. 1984): p. 397.

VIEW FROM SUMMIT OF MOUNT SEATTLE, LOOKING WEST.

Mt. Frazier.　　　　Sims River Canyon.　　　Mt. Noyes.　Mt. Bennett.　Mt. Meany.　Mt. Hearst.

"May 6, 1890. This panoramic engraving was prepared from six different photographs." (Majors, vol. 2, 148)

VIEW FROM MOUNT SEATTLE LOOKING EASTWARD.
Mount Christie.

"May 6, 1890. This montage depicts Mount Christie. The engraving was printed in the newspaper reversed [corrected here]. Either the print maker or the engraver reversed the negative or the plate. Four photographs were used in making the plate." (Majors, vol. 2, 152)

Higher Mountains to the Northwest

Over the top of this range to the northwest a higher range than it thrust its peaks heavenward. The highest peak of this range was a notable mountain of a peculiar gothic-like appearance (Mt. Bennett). Over the first range due west could be seen a large and beautiful valley,[162] sweeping the base of a superb range of mountains beyond (Mt. O'Neil).[163] Toward the southwest were low hills, evidently the lake country. These wooded hills of low, rounded form were in sharp contrast with the lofty snow-clad ranges of broken rock, which came down from the north. Toward the north could be seen the western side of the Bailey range, which swept around to the northward and westward until it culminated in "Olympus." Beyond Olympus it continued then to the westward as far as I had unobstructed vision. The valley and watershed of the Quillayute could be seen stretching along the southern base of this range, the head of the watershed lying almost at my feet.[164] The three ranges of mountains to the westward extended each from the Quillayute on the right to the valley before mentioned on the left.

The view to the eastward was more familiar. Comparing the mountains on the east and west sides, those on the

THE SUMMIT OF MOUNT SEATTLE, SHOWING ONE OF THE SPIRES.

"May 6, 1890" (Majors, vol. 2, 148)

94

---

[162] Queets Valley.

[163] "These place names, inserted editorially in brackets, probably by Edmond S. Meany, indicate that Barnes did not actually name these features in the field while on Mount Seattle." Majors, ed., *Northwest Discovery* 5 (Oct. 1984): p. 397.

[164] "This was actually the upper Hoh Canyon. In 1890, however, the Hoh River was virtually unknown, and Barnes understandably confused it with the Quillayute. Two early maps of the western portion of Washington Territory, however, show the Hoh as being distinct from the Quillayute. On James G. Swan's map, illustrating his book, *The Northwest Coast* (1857), the river is labeled the Hooch; on an 1874 map, the Ohalaats." Wood, *Across the Olympic Mountains*, p. 170.

west are arranged with more order, less confusion, and possess more greatness and sublimity than those on the east.[165]

Making Maps on a High Scale

After satiating myself with the view I made a number of exposures with the camera, and spreading out my chart, with my blanket upon the snow for a plane table, I worked for several hours upon my chart. The sight of Olympus was particularly interesting, inasmuch as it was the first time that it had been seen since we left Deer range north of Geyser valley, so completely is it hidden by other peaks. Constance and The Brothers were also in plain view to the eastward.[166]

Meanwhile the sun was becoming very hot, and finally became unendurable. The glare upon the snow from every direction was extremely painful to the eyes in spite of every precaution. At about 1 o'clock I descended from the summit and returned to my little camp under the scrub pines.

Up Again at Daybreak

On Mount Seattle, May 7.—Next morning I was up again at daybreak and returned to the summit. I finished my work in a couple of hours. The wind this morning was very strong from the southwest,[167] and while I remained there I was nearly frozen. It was necessary to ballast everything with pieces of rock.

Upon the western side of the summit the wind has exposed the rock, laying bare the formation. It consisted of slate, and like nearly all heretofore observed was nearly vertical. At the top it terminated in a sharp, jagged edge, between which and the deep snow covering the remainder were growing a few little stunted pine about two feet in height, leaning toward the eastward, as blown by the wind. The average reading of my aneroid while on the summit was 22 70–100 inches, which would make the altitude 7600 feet at the saddleback. Above the saddleback rose the sharp spires, the southern one of which I estimated as being 100 feet higher,

making the height of Mount Seattle 7700 feet.

Still More Bear Meat in Camp

Finishing my work I started downward, visiting my little camp en route. There occurred nothing of note on my down trip, and after about three hours of heavy travel, tumble and slide, I reached camp. I found that in my absence they had killed another black bear,[168] and both skins were stretched upon frames and were drying in readiness for the start next morning. The first bear, which was killed three days before, was all gone excepting a part of one of the hams. I could not say much for I had taken 15 pounds myself up the mountain, and that was all gone. Nothing tasted so good as bear meat fried in fat. We could sit around the fire all day, frying pans in hand.

Another Exciting Bear Hunt

I scarcely had time to cool my heated brow after my return, when Hayes came running into camp, breathless, crying, "A bear, a bear!" We sprang to our guns, got the dogs in hand and were soon hurrying across the snow. We could just see him up the canyon upon the open snow. Keeping close within the shelter of a little clump of timber, we hurried toward him. We gained the timber, passed through it and were some yards beyond before the bear got sight of us. We then instantly loosed the dogs and the race that ensued between the bear and the dogs was prettier than any steeplechase or handicap in the world. The bear had about 100 yards the start. He headed up the canyon toward a part of the hillside which was heavily timbered, the dogs hot after him. The bear was a large one and heavy and made poor work floundering through the soft snow, so that when he disappeared in the timber the dogs were close upon him. Soon the barking of the dogs indicated that they had rounded up their prey. In the race between ourselves to get there, Crumback and I, being lighter in weight than the others and therefore sinking less in the snow, succeeded in

95

---

[165] For a list and description of the mountains seen from this point, see "Nomenclature of the Press Exploring Expedition" in Appendix to the Press Expedition Report at the end of part 1.

[166] "Here again Barnes was in error. What he took to be The Brothers—the most conspicuous peak of the Olympic Mountains when viewed from Puget Sound—was actually another mountain further inland. A few months later Lieutenant O'Neil named it Mount Anderson, after Colonel T. M. Anderson of the Fourteenth Infantry. Barnes' error stemmed from the Press Party's belief that they were crossing the Olympics closer to Hood Canal than they actually were.

"Barnes obviously mistook Mount Anderson for The Brothers, but it is not clear which peak he believed to be Mount Constance. He may have been looking at Deception, Mystery or Wellesley. Lieutenant O'Neil later concluded he confused Mount Claywood for Constance. Detailed analysis of Barnes' map, however, leads one to conclude that he probably did, in fact, observe Mount Constance. The map was primarily based on observations taken from Mount Seattle. A line drawn on this map from the summit of Mount Seattle and passing through Mount Egan (known as Mount Norton today) points directly to Barnes' 'Constance'; a line similarly drawn on today's highly accurate United States Geological Survey maps does the same." Wood, *Across the Olympic Mountains*, p. 172.

[167] "This . . . was a harbinger of the rain that was to occur the following day. Storms and cloudy weather in this region generally blow in from the southwest, on counter-clockwise rotating cyclones moving into the Washington region from the Gulf of Alaska." Majors, ed., *Northwest Discovery* 5 (Oct. 1984): p. 398.

[168] "Christie's journal entry for that day, May 7, states: 'Capt. Barnes returned to camp this evening with the scalp of a fine full-grown bear, killed on his trip to the summit.' Barnes says nothing in his narrative about this, another example of the discrepancy between the stories of the two men." Wood, *Across the Olympic Mountains*, p. 173.

getting there first and at the same time. There was bruin up a tree and the dogs barking at the foot. Crumback and I fired simultaneously. The bear instantly dropped into the hole in the snow at the foot of the tree. The dogs tumbled in after him pell mell. We had to pull the dogs out first before we found out that old bruin was stone dead. On examination my shot was found to have gone through the brain below the ear. Crumback's passed through the heart, ranged upward and lodged in the spine. This made three vital points hit. It is no wonder that he dropped so quickly. It was a black bear, somewhat larger than the first one. His color was black, slightly tinged with gray. We dragged him into camp, skinned and dressed him. It was decided to defer moving for another day.

The Last Speck of Tobacco

There had been no time for talk between my return and the cry of "bear," so after camp had quieted down a little, someone inquired of me if I had any tobacco. I incautiously said, "Yes, a little" I had a piece about the size of my thumb and it proved to be the last small smoke. For the time being all other business was postponed that there might be no interruption to the last indulgence.

Bear camp, May 8.—Weather foggy and rainy all day. Laid over today to dry skin of yesterday's bear, but owing to bad weather were unable to dry it. Will dry tomorrow and move next day.

A Complete Change of Bill of Fare

We don't often change our bill of fare, but when we do it is radical. Flour last week, meat this. We have old bruin in every style, roast, boiled and fried. His sides thick with fat we rolled up and boiled and ate cold. One of his hams roasted would tempt the most pampered appetite. In vain we courted indigestion with the frying pan. Soup consumed a great amount. The choice tid

bits are the tail and the feet, which as Jack Crumback said beat "three of a kind." But the fat is the most highly prized in camp. It is the bear grease of commerce, pure white, the consistency of butter. Add a little salt and it has the taste of the purest dairy article, together with an indescribable flavor peculiarly its own. The first bear was consumed in three days, and a pretty good sized bear he was. Then all hands began to look fat and sleek, and before the second bear was all gone it would never be suspected that only a few days ago the party was on a diet of flour and salt, and a precious small allowance of flour at that.

Bear camp on the divide, 4300 feet[169] elevation, May 9.—The camp spent rather an uncomfortable night, on account of the rain. At noon the bear skin was pronounced dry, and a move was ordered. Our facilities for packing were limited, and for that reason we took only the best of the three bear skins. Our pack included 10 pounds of grease and as much meat as we could conveniently carry. We started on snowshoes and for a mile down the canyon had a continuation of the good travel which we had had from the lakes, the gulch being under snow from side to side, and the stream completely bridged. A mile below the stream emerged from its covering of snow and we had to keep the benches, climbing a little, but for the most part sliding down hill, an agreeable change in our mode of traveling. The mountain side, however, was very rugged, broken here and there by landslides, and obstructed by timber. It was only after four hours of steady work that we reached the end of this mountain side, at the point of junction of this stream with a larger branch from the westward, which we called Sims river, after John W. Sims, a member of the expedition.[170] It was now late and we made camp in a little bottom,[171] having descended by aneroid 1100 feet in three miles. The snow in this little bottom is eight feet deep, We flatter ourselves with the hope that by traveling steadily all day tomorrow we will reach a country with at least occasional spots of bare ground.

96

---

[169] "The crest of the Low Divide is close to 3650 feet elevation." Majors, ed., *Northwest Discovery* 5 (Oct. 1984): p. 410.

[170] "Of all the five features named by the Press Party for themselves (Mount Christie, Mount Barnes, Hayes River, Crumback River, Sims River), by far the most insignificant is Sims River, this being the present day Promise Creek. Of all the members of the Press Party, was Sims regarded with the least esteem? In contrast to Christie, Barnes, Hayes, and Crumback, the Christie and Barnes narratives are both marked by a paucity of references to Sims. Of the five members of the party, he is the one least mentioned. And, when two or three men set out on a hunting or reconnaissance trip, Sims is usually the person who is left out.

"As one example, on April 8, 1890, Christie and Barnes went out hunting together, and Hayes and Crumback formed another hunting party, whereas Sims was left by himself to fish on the Elwha River. In his journal entry for this day, Barnes remarks that while fishing all day, Sims had smoked 'fifteen or twenty pipes'—a comment that might be interpreted as a mild censure, considering how extremely short the Press Party was in their dwindling supply of tobacco at this point.

"If Christie and Barnes meant to name the entire North Fork Quinault River after Sims—which, in view of the application of the term 'Crumback River' to the East Fork Quinault River would have been the proper thing to do—then this would have indeed been a suitable feature to be named after a member of the Press Party. However, a careful reading of the Press Party narrative demonstrates that this was not the case. The term 'Sims River' was applied only to Promise Creek." Majors, ed., *Northwest Discovery* 5 (Oct. 1984): p. 411.

[171] "Camp 37 of the Press Party, 'Sims River Camp,' for May 9, 1890, was located . . . at the confluence of Promise Creek with the North Fork Quinault River, on the east side of the river, 'opposite' the mouth of Promise Creek. Ten weeks later, on August 1, 1890, the remains of this camp were seen by George A. Pratt's party of prospectors: '[we] came to another camp of Christy's expedition, where, judging by the appearance of the stumps, the snow must have been six feet deep' (George A. Pratt, 'Many Rich Mines. A Trip Through the Olympics Reveals Great Wealth,' *The Seattle Post-Intelligencer*, August 14, 1890, p.5, cols. 1–2). This agrees with Barnes' comment on the campsite." Majors, ed., *Northwest Discovery* 5 (Oct. 1984): p. 411.

Sims River Camp

May 10.—Cloudy and cool. Made start at 8 o'clock. We followed the river down by the left bank, climbing many rocky points to get from one little bottom to another. The stream was now getting quite large, owing chiefly to the addition of Sims river, which came in opposite our camp of last night, but also owing to the fact that at nearly every hundred yards came into it a torrent of greater or less size. One mile below the camping place of last night, finding it necessary to cross the river, we felled a large maple 30 inches in diameter at the base, but it failed to reach across the stream, which was here about 120 feet wide. Mr. Christie from the farther end of the bridge forded the remaining distance and dropped another tree from that bank to meet it. The remainder of the expedition then crossed dry shod.

Another Old Elk Trail Found

From this bridge we climbed the hillside above the right bank 200 or 300 feet and there found ground bare of snow in spots, and we ran upon an old friend once more, an elk trail. We followed this elk trail along the mountain side, sometimes up and sometimes down, over as rough a country as we had yet experienced. Presently we found that the trail was blazed like that upon the other side, but the blazed were very old, like those upon the Elwha. We were immediately pleased by this discovery, for it is the broad road to civilization again. Following this old trail we found that it differed in several respects from that on the Elwha. While the blazes themselves do not appear to be older they are invariably on older trees. We saw no blaze on any tree of less diameter than three feet. Fully half of the blazed trees are dead and broken off, say from 10 to 15 feet from the ground. These old yellow stumps, decayed and devoid of bark, are so numerous that they make a long line through the woods, which can be seen for some distance, marking the trail of the old Indian.

The Story of the Blazes

The blazes on the Elwha were generally made upon the trees when they were saplings. These upon full grown trees. This difference in the manner of blazing might indicate that they were made by a different tribe of Indians, and although con-

verging here near the height of land from different sides of the mountains, did not constitute a thoroughfare but rather hunting trails of the tribes living down the respective streams,—or if we accept the traditions, narrated by ex-Governor Semple, of an annual pow wow, these trails, so different in their characterics, would lend color to the theory that different tribes with different customs did meet there. In the neighborhood and for some distance on each side of the divide we failed to observe any trail, but for this there existed the excellent reason that from six to fifty feet of snow covered the ground. It is probable that if we had had the time to search for it we would have found some easier way of getting from Press valley to the watershed of the Quinaiult than by scaling the rock, and if we had found such easier place and free of snow we would there have found the Indian blazes.

The trail led downward and at last to the river. Here we found an excellent place to camp on the river bank,[172] free of snow in the midst of a pile of driftwood.

The side hills today were steep and rugged, heavily timbered. The timber is poor and for the most part rotten and conchy. We observed many cedar, but even these were crooked and knotty. There seems to be much greater moisture here than on the other side of the range, the vegetation is ranker and the undergrowth denser.[173] We made a distance today of five or six miles as the trail went, but not more than two miles of air line travel. We were, for the greater part of the day, passing a great slide on the opposite side of the river. It extended for a mile along the stream and reached nearly to the mountain side.

The mountain upon which the slide was we called Mount Grady, after the late Henry W. Grady of the *Atlanta Constitution*.[174] This great mountain is shaped like an old feudal castle, with battlements and towers crowned with snow.

Descended today 880 feet.

May 11.—This morning we started with the liveliest anticipations of getting out of the worst of the mountains and into better country for traveling. Below camp the river entered a deep and gloomy gorge. Scrambling up the steep side of Mount Zindorf, as we named this mountain, we followed the mountain side to the southward. The underbrush became gradually more rank. The mountain side also became more moist and wet. The ground was sodden, water oozed up by the pressure of every footstep. In

---

[172] "Camp 38 of the Press Party, for May 10, 1890, was located on the northwest side of the North Fork Quinault River, 0.3 mile northeast of benchmark 1546, at the later site of Big Fir Shelter. Ten weeks later, on July 31, this camp was seen by the Pratt party of prospectors: 'The Christy camp was reached at 10 o'clock'." Majors, ed., *Northwest Discovery* 5 (Oct. 1984): p. 411.

[173] "The Press Party have now entered the rain forest of the North Fork Quinault River, one of the better developed climax rain forests on the Olympic Peninsula." Majors, ed., *Northwest Discovery* 5 (Oct. 1984): p. 411.

[174] "The Press Expedition's Mount Grady is now called Mount Lawson. The party gave the name Mount Lawson to another peak about two miles to the southwest. In later years the terminology apparently became confused, like many of the names, with the application of the name to a different peak than the expedition intended." Wood, *Across the Olympic Mountains*, p. 180.

addition to this discomfort, which had to be borne in shoes of which by far the greater part, by weight, are worn away, it began to rain. We followed the side of the mountain until it curved to the westward, and then descended and found ourselves in a large valley. This valley is over a mile wide and five miles long, running about east and west, following the course of the river. The timber seen today is poor both upon the mountain side and in the valley. There is so much moisture that a stick begins to rot as soon as it falls, and any kind of scar or blaze seems to kill the tree. The ground is cumbered with rotting logs, for the most part so decayed that they crumble beneath a man's weight. Everything is rotten. We had the greatest difficulty in finding a place with enough tolerably dry wood to make a fire. In the afternoon half a mile before camping we came across a large mountain stream coming in from the northward. It had a deep rocky bed and poured over it in a raging torrent. We got a log across it. We gave it the name of "Lost Chord." We called this Chester valley.[175] It lies on both sides of the river, but principally upon the north side. It consists for the most part of benches, each of considerable width, and quite level. The soil is excellent, as we could see now and then where the snow would permit, though it must be confessed that this permission was rarely given. The valley is a beautiful one, lies well with reference to the sun, and would well repay the trouble and expense of clearing.

THE QUINAIULT AT UPPER END OF CHESTER VALLEY.

"May 11, 1890. This photograph was taken by Barnes probably within a mile above the mouth of Kimta Creek." (Majors, vol. 2, 156)

The rock seen all day in the outcrops is sandstone and slate.

The snow in the valley is deep and soft. For two miles we looked for a camp without finding the right combination of dry wood and a dry hole in the snow, until finally, just beside the river, we stumbled suddenly from winter and dampness into summer and dryness, sunshine, moss and dry wood.[176] Fortunate we felt as we dried our marrow. Net descent today, 900 feet [closer to 300 feet].

Chester Valley Camp

May 12.—Occasional showers throughout the day. One-half mile below we came to the second Lost Chord [Three Prune Creek] in the bottom of a deep gorge, and one mile further brought us to a third [Squaw Creek].[177] Here we had lunch on the banks of the latter, in a most charming alder bottom.

About here we began to be greatly puzzled by the outlook ahead. There is something much like exploring a dark rat hole in this following a stream in these woods, and enclosed by such hills as these. One can only see a few yards in any direction near the ground, and overhead the foliage shuts out even the sky. One cannot get a sight of the mountains or hills. At long intervals on approaching the river the most that can be seen is just sufficient to enable one by tracing the specks of light through the branches of the trees, to expect that the gap continues a little further in the given direction.

He Didn't Get a Bite

At about noon we came out upon a clear space on the river's bank from which at last a good view could be had. Just before us the stream turned to the southward. While we stopped to take lunch Mr. Christie tried his hand with the fishing rod, but owing to the river being turbid he did not get a bite. This space was at the lower end of the valley and our course now took us up a steep mountain side, and we spent the afternoon at hard labor. One stream [Three Prune Creek] in particular we were one hour in crossing. It tumbled down the mountain side through a deep gorge, which we were only able to pass by using ropes down one side and up the other. At about five o'clock we descended to the river and found a small bottom on which we made camp.[178]

---

[175] "The records do not state for whom Chester Valley and Mount Zindorf were named. Of the many masculine names given, these were the only ones not identified." Wood, *Across the Olympic Mountains*, p. 181. The latter may have been named for Mathew Zindorf, a Seattle contractor, who for some reason was not listed in *R.L. Polk & Co.'s Puget Sound Directory* of the era.

[176] "Camp 39 of the Press Party, 'Chester Valley Camp,' for May 11, 1890, was located at the confluence of Francis Creek and the North Fork Quinault River, probably on the south side of Francis Creek. This is nearly midway between Kimta Creek 'Lost Chord' and Three Prune Creek 'the second Lost Chord.' This is in accordance with Barnes' comment that Kimta Creek was crossed on May 11 'half a mile before camping,' while on the following morning Three Prune Creek was crossed 'One half mile below' camp 39. Francis Creek offers one of the best campsites in this immediate area; it was later the site of a shelter (now removed)." Majors, ed., *Northwest Discovery* 5 (Oct. 1984): p. 411.

[177] "Barnes neglects to mention the crossing of Elip Creek, which, like Kimta and Three Prune creeks, also flows through a gorge on its lower course. The previous day, May 11, Barnes similarly neglects to mention the crossing of Stalding Creek." Majors, ed., *Northwest Discovery* 5 (Oct. 1984): p. 411.

[178] "Camp 40 of the Press Party, 'Camp 39,' for May 12, 1890, was located on the southwest side of the North Fork Quinault River, at the confluence of Wild Rose Creek, probably on the northwest side of the creek's mouth." Majors, ed., *Northwest Discovery* 5 (Oct. 1984): p. 411.

QUINAIULT RIVER AT LOWER END OF CHESTER VALLEY.

"May 12, 1890. This photograph was taken by Barnes at the noon lunch stop at the mouth of Squaw Creek, where Christie did some unsuccessful fly fishing." (Majors, vol. 5, 406)

The river is now flowing due east, and we are very uncertain as to the identity of the river. It is away off the course laid down for the Quinaiult on the maps. The maps in our possession indicate the west fork of the Skokomish as draining this section,[179] and, as the river we are now on flows in the direction by them given to the Skokomish, we have much trouble on our minds tonight.

Joy Over the Killing of an Elk

Camp 39, on the Quinaiult, May 13.—Clear and warm. This morning, while we were preparing for another hard day's travel, Mr. Christie suddenly caught sight of an elk in the alders of the river bank immediately opposite. We ate the last of our bear meat yesterday, and had just risen from a repast of flour soup, and the appearance of the elk at once put life into every man in camp. All dropped flat on their faces and each man grabbed the dog nearest him. Mr. Christie crept to the bank, took deliberate aim, and putting his whole soul into the gun along with the cartridge, fired. The elk started, moved two or three yards and laid down, just as Mr. Christie put another shot into him; but the first shot killed. Then there was joy in camp, as well as meat. An hour was spent felling a tree across the river, and we were soon over. He was a magnificent buck, his new horns just sprouting. We had him dressed and his liver frying within half an hour after we got across the river. Then we moved camp over to his side,[180] cut him up and hung the

meat up to smoke. The day was welcome as a rest day, all hands being worn out by the hard travel of the preceding four days. We cannot help remarking on the fortunate way in which we have obtained meat on three occasions when we badly needed it: First, the elk at the lower end of Press valley; second, the bears; third, this elk. This morning we had only about 25 pounds of flour in camp. That was our whole provision. If this river should prove to be the Skokomish, we can now with our present supply of meat gain the Quinaiult, if there should be a dozen ranges to cross. We are anxious to explore the Quinaiult, if possible.

The formation on this side of the range seems to be identical with that on the other. Slate predominates. Strata of slate alternate with strata of sandstone, bent and tilted. Occasional dikes of trap appear. Basalt, or trap, is gradually becoming more common as we descend the river. Veins of quartz often appear, as on the other side of the mountains.

Meeting Human Beings

It Is Found That the Party Is Descending the Quinaiult

May 14, Upper Quinaiult.—Expedition drying meat and prospecting.

May 15.—Made a start at daylight, our pack once more replenished with meat. Our course took us up the mountain side, as we followed for a while an old elk trail. About one mile from camp we got a shot at an elk, but lost him. We could see before us, occasionally, through the trees, what seemed to be a little valley. At about 1 o'clock, descending the hill, we reached it. It was large and heavily timbered, with but little underbrush, and afforded good travel. We presently reached the river at a point where it received a stream from the eastward. This stream, which we named Alexander river,[181] is large but very shoal and rapid. At its mouth it is divided into three streams, forming a kind of delta, obstructed, however, with timber. We crossed it without difficulty and found ourselves in a large open bottom, enabling us to see up and down the valley. To our great satisfaction the river and valley turned to the westward and was undoubtedly the Quinaiult at last. The afternoon was delightful, warm and sunny. The valley was free from snow. For the first time in months, and finally, we hoped, we stood upon bare ground. We seemed to be near home now

99

[179] "One of these maps was almost certainly the 1883 edition of the U. S. General Land Office map, *Territory of Washington*, on which the schematic head of the Skokomish River lies due south of the schematic head of the Elwha River." Majors, ed., *Northwest Discovery* 5 (Oct. 1984): p. 412.
[180] See May 13 footnote in Christie's journal in part 1, chapter 3.
[181] "It is known today as the Rustler River, Rustler Creek, sometimes simply as The Rustler and even The Rusher." Wood, *Across the Olympic Mountains*, p. 184.

and the satisfaction of all hands was complete.[182] After resting up a little while and enjoying the novelty of the change in our circumstances we again shouldered our packs and followed the left bank of the stream.

The valley here is over a mile and a half in width, heavily timbered and possessing rich soil.

We made camp early under a large cedar log.[183]

Cedar Log Camp, Near Head of Quinaiult Valley

May 16.—Rainy all day. At 6 o'clock we were afoot after an early breakfast. One hundred yards below camp we forded a slough and traveled for a short distance on a bar. Recrossing to the mainland we came to a large island, over a mile long and about a mile wide. We crossed a deep stream separating it from the mainland, and traveled the length of the island through a dense jungle of underbrush. It is heavily timbered and possesses a fertile soil. At the west end of the island we dropped a tree across and took to the sidehill. The task now became very heavy, as for the remainder of the day we climbed up and down.

At one point descending to the river we found a small sandbar covered with driftwood. The land on the other side of the river was flat and we were desirous of getting there to avoid continuous climbing of these sidehills. The river was unfavorable, however, for fording, and the driftwood was too rotten and heavy for a raft, so that we had to give up the idea and take again to the sidehill. Toward evening, descending again to the river, we made two more attempts to cross. The first attempt was made with a rope lashed from man to man, but our united strength could not resist the strength of the current. At a short distance above we made another attempt, in water to our armpits, and succeeded in reaching an island in the middle of the river. We arrived there wet and tired, and

made camp[184] on the sand of the island. This has been one of the hard days of the trip. We are all sick again with dysentery.

Quinaiult Valley

May 17.—It rained all last night and when we turned out this morning we were but a little better off than we were when we made camp. The sun, however, soon came out after we started, and made things cheerful again. We felled a large tree from the island to the north bank and crossed. We continued all day down the river, through dense underbrush consisting of a tangled thicket of salmon berry bushes, vine maple and all other usual small growth that can be imagined. About noon we came to a big bend of the river with a fork from the eastward. This fork at the point of junction is about equal in size and in its possibilities for navigation with the main river. This is the East fork which is laid down on some of the maps. But it deserves a name, and gave it that of Crumback river, after John H. Crumback, a member of the party.[185] Below the fork we suddenly emerged upon a little clearing, in the middle of which was a log cabin, our first sign of civilized man for many months. It was empty. It proved to be the cabin of a white trapper. Carcasses of beaver, fisher and otter were scattered about, creating an awful stench. We did not stay long. The river was now large and broad. As we went onward we found frequent signs of man. We presently came upon a fisher trap, probably made by Indians. A little below that we came upon the cold embers of an Indian fire surrounded by a frame work of drying fish.[186] The bank of the river becoming now so dense with underbrush as to be almost impenetrable, we struck backward from the river and found dry sloughs, which we followed. They led us again to the river about one mile below and there we made camp on a sand bar.[187] For supper tonight we consumed the last of our flour in making

---

[182] "May 15 was one of the happiest and most satisfying days of the expedition, in that the snow was now gone; and, the goal of several months' work was now known, for the first time, to have been achieved." Majors, ed., *Northwest Discovery* 5 (Oct. 1984): p. 412.

[183] "Camp 42 of the Press Party, 'Cedar Log Camp,' was located on the east side of the North Fork Quinault River, 1.0 mile below the mouth of Alexander River [Rustler Creek]. This was at the north side of the mouth of a creek that enters the river from the east, 'One hundred yards' above the north end of Wolf Bar. Ten weeks later, on July 28, 1890, the remains of this camp were seen by the Pratt party of prospectors: 'Here the first indication of the Christy party was found—one of their camps.'" Majors, ed., *Northwest Discovery* 5 (Oct. 1984): p. 412.

[184] "Camp 43 of the Press Party, for May 16, 1890, was located on a temporary 'double island' in the North Fork Quinault River, 0.3 mile below/south of the present North Fork Ranger Station. At this point a bluff descends directly to the river's edge, and the Press Party had little choice but to cross the river." Majors, ed., *Northwest Discovery* 5 (Oct. 1984): p. 412.

[185] "John 'Jack' Henry Crumback (1856–?) never did return to his Geyser Valley claim. He did, however, return in late 1890 or early 1891 to the upper Quinault River, where he settled on a land claim at the junction of the North and East forks of the Quinault, near the land claim of William B. Wiser ['William Marsh'] of the 1890 O'Neil expedition. Wiser writes: 'Describing the north fork of the Quinault River, upon which [Wiser/Marsh] has located, the sergeant declares there is no grander spot on earth. It is at the junction of the east fork and south [north] fork of this river that Mr. Crumback has also a claim, he having relinquished a claim in one of 'the most beautiful spots on earth' in the valley of the Elwha—preferring the Quinault. Marsh is therefore a neighbor of an Olympic pioneer, who went out in the Press expedition, almost two years ago' (William B. Wiser ['William Marsh'], 'In From Quinault,' *Seattle Press-Times*, August 11, 1891, p. 6, col. 3)." Majors, ed., *Northwest Discovery* 5 (Oct. 1984): p. 424.

[186] "This site was likely Pino'otcan Tc'ta, or Pino'otcan's Village (named for a local Quinault Indian), which 'was a favorite place for drying fish and meat' for the Quinaults (Ronald L. Olson, *The Quinault Indians*, Seattle: University of Washington, Publications in Anthropology, 6, no. 1, 1936, pp. 18–19)." Majors, ed., *Northwest Discovery* 5 (Oct. 1984): p. 424.

[187] "Camp 44 of the Press Party, 'Camp Sandbank,' for May 17, 1890, was located . . . on the north side of the Quinault River, opposite the mouth of Bunch Creek." Majors, ed., *Northwest Discovery* 5 (Oct. 1984): p. 424.

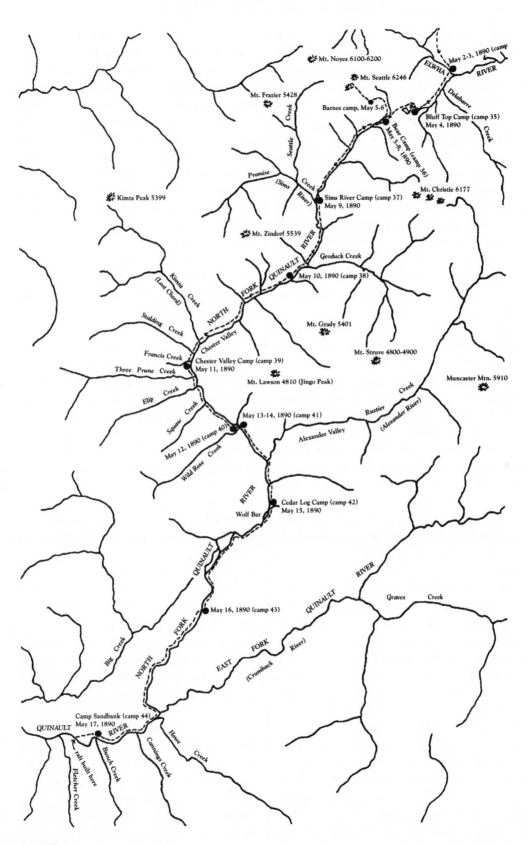

(Majors, vol. 5, 415)

soup. We have remaining sufficient meat for two days. We have observed today many tracks of bear, elk and fisher. There is a great many beaver signs. We observed both their habitations and small trees cut by them.

Good Fortune and a Disaster

Sunday, May 18th, Camp Sandbank.—Clear and warm. This has been the day, long looked forward to, of meeting white men and getting a taste of civilization, but coupled also with our greatest misfortune. At daylight broke camp. We had a spur to climb and follow, half a mile long, to reach the sand bars again. But the spur was so matted and jungled that we could penetrate only with difficulty, so we descended to the water's edge and scrambled along the rock, clinging to the overhanging foliage. Passing this we struck inland and followed a dry slough for a mile, which brought us out on the bank again.

For several miles back the river had been smooth and quiet, and the banks and channel free of drift timber. We were tired and foot sore, our packs were heavy and the lake seemed as far away as ever. So as we looked down the smoothly gliding stream, which would carry us in an hour a distance which it would take us two or three days to make along the bank, Mr. Christie was persuaded to build a raft.

So we set to work. While still cutting and rolling down logs, which lay upon the bank, we were suddenly surprised to catch sight of a man as he emerged from bushes on the opposite bank, several hundred yards below us. He caught sight of us at the same moment and stepped back again out of sight. After another moment he came out and we mutually signaled by waving our hands: "A settler!" cried one of the boys. "God help his plug of tobacco!"

Our pleasure on seeing him can be imagined. We stopped working on the raft and centered our attention on the stranger, who came down to the water's edge for hailing, as Mr. Christie reached a point opposite. The distance made communication difficult, but fortunately there came in sight around the bend from below his canoe paddled by his two Indian guides. The white man stepped into it, and in a few moments was alongside of us. He was evidently a little doubtful of us, for which we could hardly blame him, for we did look tough, but after a few moment's conversation he became convinced of our honesty and became most kind and cordial. His name was F. S. Antrim of Aberdeen. He apologized for jumping behind the brush when he first saw us, because, as he explained, he was looking for elk or bear, and, not expecting to meet any man up there, his momentary impression was that we were game.

Discovered Just in Time

Fortunately he discovered his mistake in time and did not "get" us. After we had enjoyed the joke for a little, he gave us much information concerning the river below, and offered us any assistance he could render us. He said the lake was eight miles down. We asked him if a raft would go down. He said he was ignorant of rafting, and turning to one of his Indian guides, asked him what he thought of it. The Indian nodded toward the hills on the north of the valley and said: "Good trail over there."

"Yes, but can these gentlemen go down on a raft?"

The Indian looked thoughtful for a moment and then said: "Yes, raft go down." But still he looked at the hills as he repeated: "Trail over there." But if a raft would go down we wanted no trail. We were weary and footsore and half sick. Now that we were so near our journey's end we wanted to finish it, and so it was little attention we paid to the hints of a trail "over there."

Tobacco and Coffee

We then came to the main point and broached the tobacco question. To our chagrin and disappointment Mr. Antrim informed us that he did not smoke. But learning our wants he secured for us a piece of tobacco from the Indians and presented us with a good brew of coffee and tea. He had a quantity of stores below at the mouth of the river and asked us to help ourselves to what we wanted. He was going up the river and would return in a few days and if we should still be about offered to share his canoe with us. He then left us and continued his voyage up the river.

The tobacco afforded a morsel for each man. How can it be expressed the satisfaction afforded by that morsel of tobacco? A fire was built and water put on for the coffee of which we partook as soon as the raft was ready. We set to work and finished the raft in short order. Seven good sized sticks rolled into the water and lashed to good solid cross pieces with rope lashings, made a comfortable raft of about eight by fifteen feet. Upon this we spread a few boughs to raise the cargo out of possible swash, provided her with a steering oar, and our vessel was complete.

Gliding Swiftly Down

Pushing out into the stream we were soon gliding quietly and swiftly down. The steering oar in Mr. Christie's experienced hands, assisted by an occasional check with the poles, served to keep us in mid channel. The river for over a mile continued as gentle as could be desired, and we congratulated ourselves on an early termination of our journey. It terminated earlier than we expected.

Shipwrecked and Nearly Drowned

As we rounded a sharp bend in the river we were suddenly horrified to see the whole current sweep in toward the right bank and pass under a great pile of drift timber which lay upon the bank and projected half way across the stream. We were then traveling at 10 to 12 miles an hour, and the poles were powerless. Mr. Christie, however with his oar was able to swing the raft so that it struck the drift pile broadside, thereby preserving it from instant destruction. The instant we struck, Crumback and Sims sprang from the raft to the driftpile and were safe. At the same moment a huge volume of water poured over the raft, sweeping from it Hayes, myself and all the baggage. When I came to the surface a few seconds later I had passed under the outer corner of the driftpile and was grasping the pack which contained the records, the loss of which we would have felt most. I managed to grasp a spar, which projected some distance out from the lower end of the driftpile. Mr. Christie meanwhile had succeeded in extricating young Hayes, who had been swept off the raft and was being borne directly under the timber. Mr. Christie grasped him by the arm just in time. It was a narrow shave for Hayes, for even if he had not met with an obstruction beneath, which would have terminated his career like a cat in a bag, the chances are a hundred to one that he would have bumped his head in the passage.[188]

Hayes then being safe ashore, Mr. Christie, not knowing but that I had gone on down the river, determined to follow with the raft. The raft had by this time swung out to near the point of the driftpile, and a strong effort on his part was sufficient to clear it entirely. I was, however, but 50 to 60 yards below, and fearing the raft might crush me, I let go the snag to which I was clinging. I was carried down the stream several hundred yards before I succeeded in getting out of the boiling waters which formed the current, and felt under my feet the gravel of terra firma on the opposite or left bank. Mr. Christie and the raft went on down a couple of hundred yards farther, and then he succeeded in getting to the same side on which I was.

Everything Lost

So ended the episode of the day. We lost everything except the contents of one pack and the clothes we were wearing. Guns, ammunition, bear skins, fishing tackle and most of the mineral and other specimens which we had collected.

All went.[189]

The loss to Mr. Christie of his box of flies and other fishing gear, the collections of a lifetime, can be appreciated only by a devotee of the gentle art of angling. It contained several hundred flies, many of them imported and very rare.

103

---

[188] "This was the closest brush with certain death that any member of the Press Party was to experience." Majors, ed., *Northwest Discovery* 5 (Oct. 1984): p. 424.

[189] "On August 21, 1890, as second-lieutenant Joseph Patrick O'Neil (1862–1938), private John Danton (b.1859), and private James B. Hanmore (alias Harry Fisher, b. 1856) descended the Quinault River, they witnessed the actual log jam on which the Press Party had wrecked three months earlier. In his journal, Hanmore mentions that a local settler named Clough informed the three men that 'Upon that pile of drift, the Seattle Press Party went to wreck.'

"Later that same day, August 21, 1890, farther down the river near Lake Quinault, O'Neil and privates Danton and Hanmore met newspaperman Harry West of Hoquiam, who had just explored the North Fork Quinault River with Samuel C. Gilman. They, too, had seen the Press Party log jam, at which point West and Gilman even found one of the packs that had been lost by the Press Party on the river (now evident due to low water in the river): 'a pack of material usually carried by explorers, with blankets, rifle [#5, the last Press Party rifle], coat, three camp kettles, two frying pans, elk meat, eighty-five cents in money and other materials.'" James B. Hanmore et al., "Lieutenant O'Neil's Olympic Expeditions" in *Men, Mules and Mountains*, Robert L. Wood, ed. (Seattle: The Mountaineers Books, 1976), p. 224.

"There is one additional account of this last Press Party rifle at the raftwreck site, which until . . . [now] has been totally unknown to all historians and scholars of the Olympic Mountains and the Press Party. In September 1890, English journalist F. Leather retraced the Press Party route across the Olympic Mountains, from north to south, and found one of the rifles (#5) that the Press Party had lost at the raftwreck site: 'A member of the party found the rifle that the Barnes exploring party had dropped in the river.'

"The disposition of the five Press Party rifles and one shotgun is of interest. When the men set out from Seattle, they had with them at least five Winchester rifles (40-65), and one shotgun (December 8 photo). On April 3, they had remaining 'four Winchester rifles, 40-65, one shotgun.' One rifle was thus left somewhere between Port Angeles and the Lillian River.

"On May 1, 1890, they were down to only 'three guns,' those of Christie, Barnes, and Crumback (May 7 and 5). One rifle and the shotgun, both probably broken, were left somewhere between the Lillian River and camp 32 on the lower west slope of Low Mountain 4654'. These could not have been cached at permanent cache #2 at the mouth of Evergreen Creek (camp 24), because this site was thoroughly rummaged through by the Olmstead, Pratt, and Jones parties of prospectors during the summer of 1890, none of whom mention these. The broken rifle and shotgun were most likely left either at permanent cache #3 (camp 30) on the Goldie River, or at camp 32 on the lower west slope of Low Mountain—in which case these would still be there, along with the other Press Party items left at these two caches.

"Two of the remaining three rifles of the Press Party (probably also broken by this time) were left at permanent cache #5 (camp 41) on the North Fork Quinault River on May 14, 1890, opposite the mouth of Wild Rose Creek, where they were found in 1891 by William B. Wiser ('William Marsh,' formerly with the 1890 O'Neil expedition): 'He tells of the finding of the snowshoes, ammunition and rifles left by the Press expedition on the North Fork [of the Quinault River], past which he traveled.'

"The fifth and last remaining rifle of the Press Party was lost during the raftwreck on May 18, 1890, at the large bend in the Quinault River 0.9 mile WNW of the mouth of Fletcher Creek (west half of land section 29). This rifle was seen on two different occasions during the summer of 1890, but was probably not picked up due to its by then useless condition. This fifth and last remaining Press Party rifle (probably Christie's) was first seen on August 21, 1890 by a small party under second-lieutenant Joseph P. O'Neil, during their descent of the Quinault River.

"This fifth and last Press Party rifle was also seen at the raftwreck site, by the Leather party of prospectors in September 1890: 'A member of the party found the rifle that the Barnes exploring party had dropped in the river.'" Majors, ed., *Northwest Discovery* 5 (Oct. 1984): pp. 424–25.

On account of the difficulty of packing we had brought down the river but few specimens of the flora and the fauna of the country, but the few which we had were lost. The same of minerals, although of them a part were preserved by being in the pack saved. The fact of their being there, however, nearly lost the remainder of the pack in the shipwreck, for partly owing to them the bundle was heavy, and had to be supported in the water. We lost also many little curios, such as bear's teeth, elk tushes, etc.

The pack saved contained most of the records of the trip—journals, the negative films, some 250 in number—and above all the map of the mountains which we had made.

The Party Safe

However it was all over now, and the party was safe: that was one consolation. The three boys on the opposite side of the river, and we on this, shouted inquiries and answers across the stream to the effect that, barring a few bruises, all were well. Then we set about straightening things out. Mr. Christie and I fired a large pile of brush near by, slipped off our few garments and spread them to dry, together with the contents of the pack saved. All was soaked excepting the films, each roll of which was separately packed in its case. The boys meanwhile were drying out also, and at length we all started down the stream. The boys had the best of the road, their side being for a large part along sandy bars. Our side was <u>covered</u> with thick woods, dense with underbrush, and cut with sloughs. The salmon berry bushes and bramble held us so that we did not make more than a mile in three hours of hard work. We had no food excepting the tender shoots of the raspberry bushes. There were plenty of these and we ate them as we went along. Finally we reached a sandbar and camped there with the boys opposite us.[190] We were better off than they because we had half a blanket while they had no shelter at all, nor any food except the green shoots.

We passed this afternoon two log cabins, both untenanted. The claims on which they are located are valuable ones. The mountains are more than half a mile from the river there. The houses are mere travesties on houses, are absolutely uninhabitable, being put together merely to enable the claimant to hold the land. It is an outrage that the law should make such a thing possible. The same thing is practiced on the lower Elwha, where valuable land is being acquired by men who are in business at some distant place, whose only improvements are similar to those

we saw today, and who do not ever make a pretense of visiting them.

"Split Camp"

May 19.—We made a fire last night and pulling our half blanket over us, were soon asleep. About midnight, however, it began to rain. The fire was then out, so we lay under the blanket until morning, but of course were wet to the skin. It was still raining this morning when we got up and looked around. The boys, on seeing us, came down the river bank, and we were able to communicate by shouting. They had sat around the fire all night, feeling, like us too mean to look for cover.

From the information furnished by Mr. Antrim, we estimated that we were about five miles from a settler's cabin at the head of the lake. We hoped to reach their cabin today and procure some "grub." The boys having permission to go on started at once, and it was as good as a joke to see the speed with which they disappeared into the woods. Mr. Christie and I made a fire to dry ourselves by, and while I was drying the blanket he went into the woods back of camp to see if he could not find an appetizing looking spruce tree for breakfast. The inner bark is sweet, and makes excellent food in the absence of better. He had not been gone five minutes when who should come around the bend from above but our benefactor of yesterday, Mr. Antrim, in his canoe, as handsome as ever,—indeed more handsome he appeared this morning to our famished eyes. In response to my call Mr. Christie emerged from the thicket. Mr. Antrim camped at the forks last evening. This morning he had left his camp at 4 o'clock, coming down the river, and thus we met him. It was a happy meeting. His offer of assistance was gratefully accepted, and we prepared to accompany him in the downward trip. He was, however, as wet as ourselves, and so we finished the drying out process and had the pleasure of adding to Mr. Antrim's wardrobe a pair of blanket "duffles" for his feet, an acquisition which, however comfortable, may create some amusement in the family circle at Aberdeen. Duffles are a style of hosiery not as yet prescribed by the tyrant, Fashion. Mr. Antrim killed a bear this morning, which was in the boat, and while we were drying out the Indians skinned it.

A Fine Canoe Ride

Once in the canoe we thoroughly enjoyed the day. The ruin ceased at about the same time, the clouds began to

---

[190] "Camp 45 of the Press Party, 'Split Camp,' for May 18, 1890, were two separate campsites, located on opposite sides of the upper Quinault River, in the north half of section 36. Christie and Barnes were encamped on the south side of the river, while Hayes, Crumback, and Sims camped on the north side—thus the name." Majors, ed., *Northwest Discovery* 5 (Oct. 1984): p. 425.

roll back upon the mountain tops and the sun came out. The river was a surprise to us. Piles of driftwood were frequent. In fact, it soon became evident to us that it would have been impossible for us to have descended the river on a raft. If we had not been wrecked where we were it would have been impossible to escape it half a mile below. As we neared the lake drift piles became still more numerous, and it required most skillful handling to clear them with the canoe. But in the hands of the Indians, who had been brought up from boyhood on the river, and had frequently traveled as high as the forks, the voyage was made in perfect safety. Their knowledge of the current is wonderful. They know every submerged sandbar, rock, and snag on the river, and just the right stroke of the paddle at the right time sends the canoe past dangers which to us were invisible until we were by them.

The Canoe Had a Big Load

About a mile down the river we picked up the boys who were stoutly trudging down the bank. Their surprise at seeing us may well be imagined. Eight men and three dogs made a large passenger list for the little canoe, but it arrived safely at last at the mouth of the river. Here we found a house, and an actual, bona fide, settler. Antrim's stores were cached here, and it was to them our first attention was directed. It was but a few moments before we had potatoes in the pot—real potatoes, and plenty of them. Baking powder biscuit on one side of the fire vied with more baking powder biscuit, light and flaky, on the other. Broiling ham and baking salmon mingled their savory odors with the aroma of coffee. But Mr. Antrim's treasures did not end here. He had butter, sugar, golden syrup, condensed milk, mustard, pickles—any single article of which we would have gladly and willingly have committed a homicide to attain. But murder was needless. Mr. Antrim was ours and we were his'n. He spared not his grub. If we paused a moment he felt our pulses and prescribed another biscuit or cup of coffee with plenty of milk. The feast was of long continuance, though hastened somewhat toward the end by the desire of the boys to get the tobacco burning, for of that precious weed we obtained another small supply from the Indians. When dinner was over it was 2 o'clock in the afternoon. There was still time to go a considerable distance before dark, and now that we were in touch with civilization again we became in a desperate hurry to get home. We had been nearly six months on the road. Taking our places in the small craft once more, a few minutes sufficed to carry us to the lake.

Lake Quinaiult is about seven miles long and three miles wide, extending in a direction from east-northeast to west -southwest. The river enters the lake at northeastern end. Its outlet is at about the middle of the southern side. It is on all sides surrounded by level land for a distance of from one to two miles from the lake. On the north and south this lake valley is surrounded by ranges of mountains, a continuation of the ranges which extend from Alexander river, broken only in the southern range, made by the East fork of the Quinaiult. The dense verdure which covers the mountain side and descends upon the valley, extends quite to the border of the lake, where the overhanging foliage conceals and hides the shore. The timber of the valley is large in growth and sound in quality, and consists of the varieties of conifer usual in this part of the state on level land and fertile soil. Fir and cedar predominate, mixed along the margin of the lake with maple and alder and other hard wood trees. There is not a clearing upon the lake, but it is all, we are told, taken up as squatters' claims, excepting that portion which is in the Indian reserve. The Quinaiult Indian reserve bounds the western side of the lake from a little east of the outlet to the northwest corner, and extends westward to the ocean. The outlet of the lake is entirely within the reservation. This broad lake, its wooded shores and high bounding mountains, its surface unruffled by storms, makes a peaceful picture of wild and entrancing beauty.

A New Experience of Traveling

After our experience in the mountains it was to us a new and delightful sensation, the crossing of the lake with the easy motion of the canoe, propelled by hands other than our own. The surface of the lake was dotted here and there with ducks and the shores are alive with game.

Crossing the lake we were soon gliding down its outlet. The lower Quinaiult river is broad, and for the first mile, smooth. Then it breaks into ripples or minor rapids, and at long distances apart rocks appear in the stream. In the first seven miles there were several of these slight rapids, hardly worthy of the name of rapids; they should rather be called swift flowing water. The water is deep and the channel free of obstruction. There is nothing to prevent steamboats of considerable size from navigating the river here. Seven miles below the outlet of the lake we came to a log jam. Here we had to get out and make portage of the canoe for about two hundred yards. Re-embarking we had another good stretch of water for two miles further. Here was another, but much smaller jam. It was now nearly dark, so we landed and made

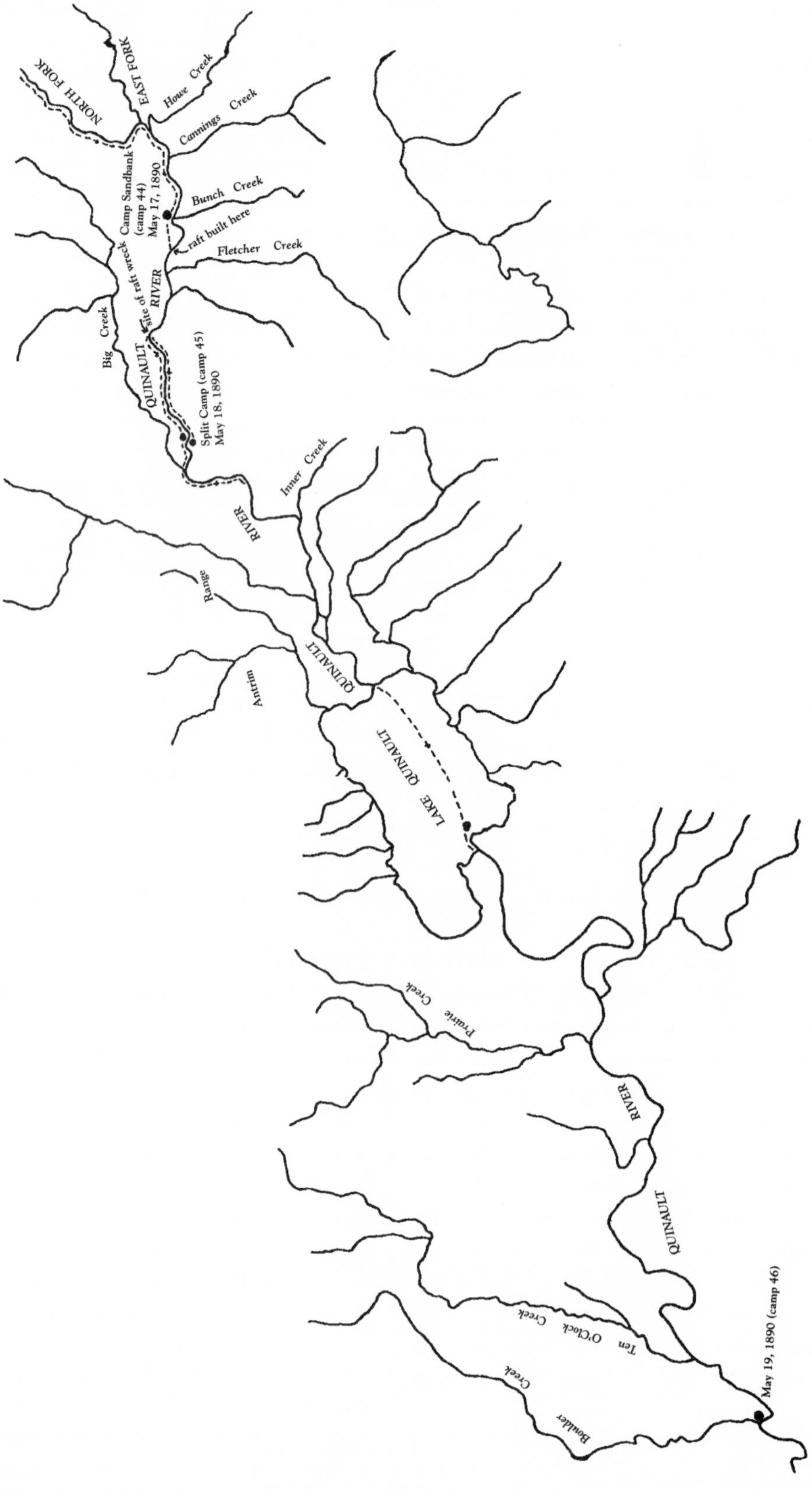

106

(Majors, vol. 5, 426–7)

camp on the river bank.[191] Mr. Antrim's stores furnished us with another wonderful feast.

The valley of the Quinaiult immediately below the lake through which we passed this afternoon is from seven to ten miles in width and seemingly as level as a floor, covered with the same dense verdure noticed at the lake.

Camp on the Lower Quinaiult

May 20.—This morning we were astir before daylight, had breakfast, and at 4 o'clock were underway. From this point to the mouth of the river the channel is free of obstruction. A bar is said to obstruct the mouth of the river, but from that point to the forks, 10 or 12 miles above the lake, the river channel is navigable for steamboats. The current is nowhere swift, and plenty of depth obtains. The only present obstacle is the occasional jam of logs or pile of drift timber, but these are small and easily cleared with a small quantity of dynamite.

The valley, generally speaking, is many miles in width. It is broken by two small spurs, or ranges of low hills, crossing the valley at right angles to the river.[192] Many Indians of the reservation are living along the river engaged in farming and fishing. Two fish weirs were noticed. Several miles above the mouth there is a salmon cannery, not, however, in present operation. We passed several canoes on the river paddled by Indians going up. Six miles from the mouth we stopped for a while at the house of the medicine man of the tribe.[193] The house, which is well built, is about 30 feet long by 25 in width. The interior consists of one room and is open in the center of the roof to let out the smoke. Ten or a dozen bunks lined the side walls. From the ceiling was suspended dried fish and jerked elk meat. The ground was bare excepting at the further end, where a raised platform marked the space devoted to the incantations and mysteries of the aboriginal medical profession. This platform and the wall behind it were covered with the apparatus of the profession, and are calculated to terrify unwelcome and undesired spirits.

We arrived at the reservation agency at the mouth of the river at 10 o'clock. There we procured lunch, hired a team, and were soon bowling down the beach. We arrived at Owyhut[194] soon after dark. There we took a sloop up to the head of Grays harbor and arrived at Aberdeen at 2 o'clock in the morning, having by 22 hours of continuous travel made a distance of 60 miles.

Arrival at Aberdeen

The remainder of the story is soon told. We arrived in Aberdeen at two o'clock in the morning and had great trouble in getting accommodations. But when we did touch real beds it was a luxury to be appreciated.

When we arose late the next morning we found that the news of our return to civilization had been sent abroad, and we found telegrams of congratulation from the *Seattle Press* and from many friends, and many kind inquiries after the health and welfare of the party.[195] As soon as we were awake[196] we had at our rooms interviews with various merchants of the town, and with the barbers, so that when at last we were able to resume a civilized appearance, we hardly recognized ourselves. Bronzed faces alone remained to remind us of what we had been through.

The people of the town were very kind and showed us every consideration. Unterrified by our tremendous appetites, they took us to their homes and gave us white folk's food.

107

---

[191] "Camp 46, the last camp of the Press Party, for May 19, 1890, was located on the lower Quinault River, at or very near the mouth of Boulder Creek, at a small log jam." Majors, ed., *Northwest Discovery* 5 (Oct. 1984): p. 433.

[192] "At several points steep bluffs occur near the lower Quinault River, which might present this appearance to a person descending the river: one mile above Ten O'Clock Creek; below the mouth of Chow Chow Creek; above and below Railroad Creek; and near the mouth of the river." Majors, ed., *Northwest Discovery* 5 (Oct. 1984): p. 433.

[193] "This may have been in the Quinault village *Pin'ilks*, where once 'was the home of the man [chief] who ranked above all others' by the name of Le'samats (Ronald L. Olswon, *The Quinault Indians*, Seattle, University of Washington, Publications in Anthropology 6, no. 1, 1936)." Majors, ed., *Northwest Discovery* 5 (Oct. 1984): p. 433.

[194] "Owyhut was a now vanished settlement on Damon Point, near the entrance to Grays Harbor." Majors, ed., *Northwest Discovery* 5 (Oct. 1984): p. 433.

[195] "At 12:50 P.M., on the afternoon of May 21, 1890, the following telegram was transmitted from James H. Christie at Aberdeen to Edmond S. Meany at Seattle: 'Expenses to Seattle will approximate one hundred-twenty five dollars. Please remit this morning by telegraph' (University of Washington Library, Manuscripts and University Archives Division, Edmond S. Meany papers box 10, folder 7)." Majors, ed., *Northwest Discovery* 5 (Oct. 1984): p. 433.

[196] "It was on the late morning of May 21, 1890, before the Press Party visited the 'barbers,' that photographer Charles R. Pratsch (who was also manager of the Hotel Del Monte, where the Press Party probably stayed) of Aberdeen took several group portraits of the Press Party, one of which was reproduced as an engraving on page 1 of the July 16, 1890 newspaper narrative report. On June 24, 1890, Charles K. (R.?) Pratsch wrote to the *Seattle Press* from Aberdeen: 'Sent your negatives this day By Express. My Bill is Five Dollars.' On June 25, Charles A. Barnes wrote to Meany that the group photograph had not yet arrived at Seattle (University of Washington Library, Manuscripts and University Archives Division, Edmond S. Meany papers, box 10, folder 8)." Majors, ed., *Northwest Discovery* 5 (Oct. 1984): p. 434.

Home Again

After two days of rest, which we needed so badly, we at length parted from our kind friends at Aberdeen and took the steamer for Montesano,[197] and thence to Seattle, where our arrival at the steamer's wharf ended our journey after an absence of six months.[198] Our exploration of the Olympics was completed.

Charles A. Barnes

108

---

[197] "On May 23, 1890, shortly after arriving at Montesano, James H. Christie sent the following telegram to Edmond S. Meany: 'Party left this morning & will arrive in Seattle this evening by Boat from Kamilchie.' Kamilchie was at the head of Totten/Skookum inlets (University of Washington Library, Manuscripts and University Archives Division, Edmond S. Meany papers, box 10, folder 7)." Majors, ed., *Northwest Discovery* 5 (Oct. 1984): p. 434.

[198] "The triumphal arrival back in Seattle of the Press Party on the evening of May 23, 1890, was totally ignored by all the other jealous Seattle newspapers. This is unfortunate, for practically no issues of the *Seattle Press* for 1890 have survived, this being the only newspaper that would have described the return to Seattle of the Press Party. After an extensive search of Washington newspapers for May and June 1890, I have discovered the only surviving account of the arrival of the Press Party back in Seattle, which was reprinted from a now vanished issue of the *Seattle Press*. Until this present issue of *Northwest Discovery*, both this and the Antrim account have been totally unknown to all historians and scholars of the Olympic Mountains and the Press Party:

"'The explorers, says the *Seattle Press*, have returned from their long examination of the hitherto mysterious region of the Olympic Range, and are now in Seattle. The result of their arduous and indefatigable researches will be given to the world in the columns of that paper without delay, and will prove of absorbing interest to many thousands of people.

"'The explorers did their work thoroughly. The unusual severity of the winter months delayed and hindered them materially, but they persevered with the courage and resolution of true pathfinders until their task was completed.

"'In some respects they have been destroyers of illusions. They found no wild and warlike tribes of dreadful savages, such as had been told about by the romancers. Their story will be a very interesting narrative of the actual condition of the extensive region now for the first time made known to the world, and will describe its advantages and merits.

"'The explorers made a topographical map of the country, took photographs and sketches of various natural features and made extensive notes of their travels and observations. These notes and illustrations will be reproduced in the above mentioned paper.

"'The timber and mineral resources, the botanical characteristics, agricultural possibility, the game, the grand scenery, and all the general features of the region will be described. The narrative will be so ample as to give all a good idea of the whole Olympic region.

"'The *Press* congratulates the gentlemen comprising the exploring party, and incidentally itself, upon the success of the expedition. The value of the work to the entire state will be very great. The extensive range of country so long suffered to remain in the realms of doubt and darkness, is now thrown open. Ere long it will be entered by hundreds of adventurous spirits, and homes and settlements will spring up. The Olympic region will be added to the productive territory of the state, and will increase the grand total of development and prosperity ('An Unknown Land No Longer,' *Daily Progress* [Anacortes], May 27, 1890, p. 2, col. 1)." Majors, ed., *Northwest Discovery* 5 (Oct. 1984): p. 434.

CHAPTER THREE.
CHRISTIE'S JOURNAL[1]

A Concise Record of Each Day's Work.

The Chief's Diary in Full.

It Shows Just How the Six Months of Time Passed.

How They Lived and Worked.

A Plain Account of the Most Adventurous and Exciting Experiences Yet Recorded in the History of Puget Sound Pathfinding—The Joy in Camp Over the First Elk Captured—A Magnificent View of a Monarch Elk— View of the Sound From McDonald's Butte—Fording Rivers, Climbing Mountains, Hunting Food—All Makes an Interesting Record for Sportsmen or Explorers.

Tuesday, December 8, 1889.—Another visit to *Press* office[2] made appointment to meet several gentlemen interested. Received letter from Dr. Runnalls, Puyallup, who wishes to accompany me as surgeon. Mr. Frazier, editor of the *Press* wishes a photographer to accompany the party. At the mention of this, I immediately bethought me of Capt. C.A. Barnes, mentioned it, and it is just possible he may accompany the party.[3] Had an interview with Mr. Bailey, proprietor of the *Press*. Received *carte blanche* to go on with my preparations. Ordered tents, covers, sheets, etc.

Received a number of letters from parties desirous of joining.

Packing Up the Provisions

Wednesday, December 4.—Moved the party out to Mr. Meany's ranch,[4] as we require room for fixing up. Busy in town. I secured a liberal supply of ammunition and fishing tackle, as my favorite sport must need be enjoyed. Rubber boots, oil skin, blankets were also secured. Spent the evening with Capt. Barnes, giving him some idea of the work and plans of the expedition. I fully expect he will join the party. Another batch of applicants who wish to join.[5]

Thursday, December 5.—Made arrangements with principals to secure the services of Capt. Barnes for the trip. Accepted Dr. Runnalls as a member of the party. He will join us here on the 7th.[6] Wired St. Paul for snowshoes,[7] completing purchase of stores, etc. We were hunting dogs, but failed to secure any.

Friday, December 6.—Party at Mr. Meany's ranch fixing and packing up. Had photograph of party this afternoon. The artistic scenery made a very fine plate. Completing all necessary arrangements the party will leave Seattle, tomorrow evening en route for Port Angeles. Met Mr. Bailey and several of his friends today and found all greatly interested in our trip, one gentleman advising me to pack nothing but pemmican and a liberal sprinkling of flour. Had the pleasure of meeting Mrs. Dr. Runnalls, who had come from Puyallup to see the party off.

Saturday, December 7.—Everything in readiness for a start. I had a last interview with Messrs. Bailey, Frazier

109

---

[1] James H. Christie, *Seattle Press*, July 16, 1890.

[2] "In 1889–1890, the office of the Press Publishing Company was located at 214 Columbia Street in Seattle. Edmond S. Meany was the secretary-treasurer of the Press Publishing Company." Majors, ed., *Northwest Discovery* 2 (Feb. 1981): p. 124. Meany was also assistant editor of the *Seattle Press*.

[3] "Christie's remark . . . suggests that Barnes had previously applied to accompany the expedition sometime between November 17 and December 2, and that Barnes had mentioned that he was skilled at photography. It is highly unlikely that Christie would have known Barnes from previous years. The rough prose of Christie's journal indicates that the version published in the 1890 newspaper is very close to (if not an exact rendition of) Christie's diary." Majors, ed., *Northwest Discovery* 2 (Feb. 1981): p. 124.

[4] "Though Meany's town residence in 1889 was at the northwest corner of Birch and Mercer, 'Meany's ranch' was a small tract of roughly one acre on the west side of what now is Roosevelt Way N.E., between N.E. 40th and N.E. 41st streets, directly at the north end of the present University Bridge." Majors, ed., *Northwest Discovery* 2 (Feb. 1981): p. 124.

[5] "The fact that . . . 'letters from . . . applicants' . . . were still pouring in, though the [Gov.] Ferry interview [about the need for Olympics exploration] had been published on October 23, 1889, suggests that the *Seattle Press* may have been promoting their proposed expedition with additional newspaper articles. Unfortunately, no complete file for this newspaper is known to have survived." Majors, ed., *Northwest Discovery* 2 (Feb. 1981): p. 124.

[6] "Runnalls arrived in Seattle from Puyallup on December 6, 1889, just in time to be included in the group portrait taken that afternoon. In his journal entry for the 6th, Christie mentions having met Runnalls that day for the first time. The day previous, Meany had published an article on the expedition as: 'Press Exploring Party' (*The Evening Press*, December 5, 1889). Regrettably, no copy of this or consecutive issues are known to have survived." Majors, ed., *Northwest Discovery* 2 (Feb. 1981): p. 124.

[7] "These snowshoes from St. Paul, Minnesota probably arrived in Seattle (via the Northern Pacific Railroad) after the Press Party had left for Port Angeles, and were brought there on December 12 when Barnes arrived with the remainder of the supplies and provisions." Majors, ed., *Northwest Discovery* 2 (Feb. 1981): p. 125.

and Meany. Final instructions and goodbyes.[8]

Starting From Seattle

Sunday, December 8.—I called the party together to meet at the rooms of Capt. Barnes, at 8:30, when we met and had a one-half hour enjoyable interview and planning. We made our way toward the Yesler wharf,[9] causing a good deal of remarks from the passersby on account of our show of arms and dogs.

At 7:30 we boarded the steamer Ferndale, there meeting Mr. Hodges[10] of the *Press* staff, with other friends, who had come down to see us off.[11] This meant an adjournment to a quiet corner of the cabin, and the expression of many opinions accompanied with promises made, the fulfillment of which will keep us all hustling. The last whistle warned our friends ashore and we had commenced our trip.[12]

Monday, December 9.—Daylight this morning found us on the way at Port Townsend. After a night on board of a Puget Sound steamer we wondered when the most beautiful body of water in the world would have passable boats on it. The boys looked after the dogs. I superintended the transfer of our baggage to the Port Angeles boat; then joined in search of a restaurant, fondly looking forward to the breakfast table. After breakfast we boarded the steamer Evangel, and a more

disreputable tub never carried a passenger. The pleasure of our journey was by no means enhanced by our being seated opposite a full grown girl chewing gum much like a cow chews her cud. Dinner was served on the boat much as well bred hogs are fed. We were all thankful when we pulled alongside the wharf and found ourselves at Angeles, under the shadow of the mountains we had undertaken to explore.[13]

They All Claim to Know the Country

Tuesday, December 10.—After a short night's rest, and a breakfast at the Central hotel we called on several of the leading citizens. Was introduced to Norman R. Smith,[14] a gentleman to the manor born. He claims to have traveled all through the Olympic country, knows the trend of every mountain range, the source of every stream, has located the paradise which Indian tradition says exists within the charmed circle of mountain peaks seen from the Sound and strait of Juan de Fuca. From inquiries, I found that it will be impossible for me to build our boat at the mouth of the river, as I am assured by the ancient inhabitants that there exists a canyon both dangerous and impassable some four miles up stream.[15] This is rather a disappointment, and means delay if I am compelled to pack everything above this point. From

110

[8] "The Press Party left Seattle with the intention of ascending the Elwha River as their route of entry into the Olympic Mountains. This decision was likely arrived at as a result of Christie's visit to Port Angeles within November 24 to December 2, 1889, at which time he spoke with such local residents as Norman R. Smith. Two other factors also likely influenced the decision.... Port Angeles was the nearest substantial community bordering on the Olympic Mountains, a town easily reached by steamer from Seattle. Any person in Seattle or Port Angeles who had traveled on a ship in the Strait of Juan de Fuca would have been impressed with the view up the Elwha Valley gained offshore, for at this point the Olympic Mountains appear to open up, revealing a valley leading directly into the heart of the range. Directly up the Elwha Valley, Mount Carrie (mistakenly referred to then as Mount Olympus) is prominently visible from offshore." Majors, ed., *Northwest Discovery* 2 (Feb. 1981): p. 125.

[9] "The Yesler Wharf was an extension of the sawmill built in 1852 by the Seattle pioneer Henry Leiter Yesler (1810–1892). The mill was located at what now is the junction of Yesler Way and Post Avenue (the site of the original shoreline), while the wharf was situated at the junction of Yesler Way and Western Avenue. The old shoreline has since been filled in and extended to Alaskan Way." Majors, ed., *Northwest Discovery* 2 (Feb. 1981): p. 125.

[10] "Lawrence K. Hodges later gained fame as a reporter for the *Seattle Post-Intelligencer*, when in 1896 he personally visited and wrote a series of articles on the various mining areas of the North Cascades. Hodges and Runnalls may possibly have met again in 1896 on Swauk Creek, where at that time Runnalls had a mining claim." Majors, ed., *Northwest Discovery* 2 (Feb. 1981): p. 125.

[11] "Among the many persons to see the Press Party off... from Seattle was Edwin Eells (1841–1917), the Indian Agent at the Puyallup Indian Reservation and a son of the pioneer Northwest missionary Cushing Eells (1810–1893). This is mentioned in a letter from Eells to Meany dated June 3, 1890 at Tacoma (University of Washington Library, Manuscripts and University Archives Division, Meany Papers, box 10, folder 8)." Majors, ed., *Northwest Discovery* 2 (Feb. 1981): p. 126.

[12] "Only five of the party departed from Seattle to Port Angeles on the evening of December 8, 1889. Charles Barnes remained in Seattle, likely awaiting the arrival of required equipment and supplies. Barnes later took a steamer to Port Angeles with these remaining supplies (with Meany coming along for the ride to check on the progress of the expedition), where he arrived and joined with the five other men on December 12, 1889." Majors, ed., *Northwest Discovery* 2 (Feb. 1981): p. 126.

[13] "In 1890, ... Port Angeles on the southern shore of the Strait of Juan de Fuca was bustling with activity from local lumbering and the Puget Sound Cooperative Colony (which went bankrupt in 1889 and finally dissolved in 1904). Port Angeles was first discovered on August 5, 1791 by the Spanish navigator Francisco de Eliza, who named it 'Puerto de Nuestra Señora de los Angeles.' The site was first settled in 1856 by a schooner captain, Alexander Sampson (1815–1893), ... The townsite itself was founded in 1862 by the notorious Victor Joseph Smith (1826–1865), who succeeded in having Abraham Lincoln sign a presidential proclamation on June 19, 1862 that established a five-square-mile townsite and proposed naval-military reservation.... In 1866, the U.S. Customs house was moved from Port Angeles to Port Townsend; as a result, the little community saw little activity until 1887, when the Puget Sound Cooperative Colony was established there and set up the town's first sawmill." Majors, ed., *Northwest Discovery* 2 (Feb. 1981): pp. 127–28.

[14] "Norman R. Smith (1857–date unknown) was one of the three sons of the founder of Port Angeles, Victor Joseph Smith.... Norman Smith possessed a modicum of intelligence regarding the geography of the fringe of the Olympic Peninsula, for in 1881 he undertook a preliminary survey for a potential road from Clallam Bay to the mouth of the Quillayute River. A few years thereafter, during July and August 1885, he accompanied the army expedition of Second-lieutenant Joseph Patrick O'Neil (1862–1938) from Port Angeles southward as far as Hurricane Hill.... Smith wrote a series of reminiscences covering the early history of Port Angeles during the period 1861–1887 (Norman R. Smith, 'Victory,' series of articles in the *Port Angeles Evening News*, June 9 to August 22, 1950)." Majors, ed., *Northwest Discovery* 2 (Feb. 1981): p. 128.

[15] "This ... canyon is now the site of the Lake Aldwell Dam." Majors, ed., *Northwest Discovery* 2 (Feb. 1981): p. 128.

information received I determined to move above the first canyon, build the boat there and from that point make a start for the mountains. The ideas regarding the interior of the country I find are rather misty, and from the thousand and one advices received I cannot get one sensible idea.

From the mass of rubbish that has been fully poured out for the education of our party, it is rather wonderful to hear that this section has been successfully explored, yet strange to say, I can get no information on which I can rely regarding the country beyond the mouth of Indian creek, about eight miles inland. Evidently some of our old-time settlers are jealous of our attempting to enlighten their darkness regarding the surroundings of their birthplace.

Hired teams to freight our provisions, etc., to Meagher's ranch, some six miles from this point. Sent the party ahead with teams. Remained in Angeles to make some final arrangements regarding material for boat, etc.

Followed party to Meagher's ranch this evening. Found the boys located comfortably, overhauling our provisions. They report everything first class.

First Call to Breakfast in Camp

Wednesday, December 11.—Was awakened this morning by Crumback's voice calling us to breakfast, a feast indeed compared with the food supplied us at the majority of restaurants we have visited lately. Bacon and beans baked in the approved fashion in a Dutch oven. Bread baked by the same oven, flanked by some superb coffee, was a meal to look forward to and then enjoy. Breakfast over I sent the boys on towards the river to find the possible trail to head of canyon, employing Hayes at home arranging stores and Crumback baking for a few days ahead. I started for the sawmill, about one mile below the ranch, to meet Warriner Smith,[16] and ordered lumber for the boat. Returning to camp Dr. Runnalls and Sims reported a rather hard outlook, as there is practically no trail towards the head of the canyon, distant some two and one-half miles. This does not agree with my information received that the "canyon was one-half mile from Meagher's ranch."

Capt. Barnes Loses Dike

Thursday, December 12.—Having inspected a part of the trail last night and sent the party forward to improve it somewhat, as it was in a most horrible condition, mud holes at every step and first mile through a veritable bogwater to the knees, I started for Port Angeles to meet Capt. Barnes and Mr. Meany, from Seattle. Messrs. Meany and Barnes arrived per steamer Evangel. Charlie having captured a big black dog had him in tow.[17] After the transaction of business we make tracks for camp, bidding Angeles good-bye. We made good time over a very indifferent road, reaching Smith's mill as the darkness began to be felt. Barnes fired his rifle as a signal for Meany and myself, who had dropped behind, to hurry up. The flash and report rather startled the black dog, who disappeared in the darkness, much as black cats are supposed to. And no amount of calling would bring him back. A mile of mud holes and water being got over in the darkness, we reached the boys and supper, wet to the waist.

Friday, December 13.—Arousing the boys at daylight to a truly backwoods breakfast, which was soon disposed of, the party began packing toward head of canyon.[18] Mr. Meany accompanying them to try a cast or two on the Elwha. Crumback remains in camp cooking, etc.

Met by Mr. Smith on appointment to try and arrange purchase of two pack animals from Indians located at the mouth of the river.

Mr. Meany returns. Had no luck fishing. Thinks we have rather a hard road to travel.

Bargaining for Pack Animals

Saturday, December 14.—The party packing towards the head of canyon. Met by Indians[19] by appointment with two ponies, who demanded $100 for a couple of plugs. Fifty dollars would have been a magnificent price. As Mr. Meany[20] returns to Seattle this afternoon, sent Capt. Barnes to Port Angeles with him to hunt up two pack animals. Improving trail this afternoon. Trail that is used by the settlers a disgrace to any community.

Sunday, December 15.—Our first Sunday on the trip.

111

---

[16] "Warriner Smith (1855–date unknown), another of Victor Smith's three sons. . . . Warriner and Norman were engaged in a joint sawmill business venture—the same sawmill from which the Press Party would soon purchase lumber from to constuct their boat." Majors, ed., *Northwest Discovery* 2 (Feb. 1981): p. 129.

[17] The . . . dog . . . was soon named Dike or Dyke." Majors, ed., *Northwest Discovery* 2 (Feb. 1981): p. 129.

[18] "Today's packing of supplies constitutes the first real physical work the Press Party was to engage in. It would last for nearly five months." Majors, ed., *Northwest Discovery* 2 (Feb. 1981): p. 129.

[19] "These would be the Elwha band of the Clallam Indian tribe, from the ancient village of *Elxwa* at the mouth of the Elwha River. Warriner Smith had mentioned them the day previous. Though Christie does not mention it, December 14 was his birthday." Majors, ed., *Northwest Discovery* 2 (Feb. 1981): p. 129.

[20] "Meany had arrived at Port Angeles from Seattle with Barnes on December 12, probably to check on the progress of the expedition, as well as to gather information for a newspaper article describing its efforts thus far . . . (Edmond S. Meany, 'Up the Elwha River,' *Seattle Press*, December 17 [possibly 19], 1889). Unfortunately, no copies of the *Seattle Press* for October 1889 to July 1890 have survived." Majors, ed., *Northwest Discovery* 2 (Feb. 1981): p. 129.

The party are engaged passing the time in divers ways, hunting, washing, cleaning guns, etc.

Monday, December 16.—Commencing a new week with good, healthy exercise, packing. Dr. Runnalls, Crumback, Hayes, Sims and myself wrestling with two packs toward the head of canyon. Towards midnight Dr. Runnalls was alarmed by the roar of a large cougar in the vicinity of the house. Succeeded in getting lumber hauled from mill.

He Lost His Commission

Tuesday, December 17.—The party at work packing. Tough work all around. Capt. Barnes arrived with two mules which he had purchased from a settler in the vicinity of Dungeness. He has had quite an experience on his trip and a good deal of hard wrestling, bringing with him the following note, which had been asked to present Mr. Eagle, the gentleman from whom he purchased the mules:

Mr. Fogle—Sir: I sent this man to look at your mules. Ask him $125 for them, and think he will give it as quick as $100.

There will be another up this week to see them if this one don't take them.

One of these big sharps of American trade. On the look out for a commission, but he was left on this deal.

Wednesday, December 18.—Rain. Dr. Runnalls, Crumback and Hayes at work on the trail. Sims and self at mill making up pack saddles.[21] Capt. Barnes at ropes for pack saddles. Capt. Barnes photographed mill and hands in the afternoon.

Sturdy Little Packers

Thursday, December 19.—The party moving camp to head of canyon.[22] Packed mules 250 pounds, but this I was compelled to reduce to 150 pounds, owing to the state of trail, the mules floundering belly deep through the swamps, necessitating the loading and unloading three different times; but the manner in which the little animals carried the load over every obstruction showed them as no new pilgrims in the brush. Made up a comfortable camp at head of canyon. The horrible state of the trail will necessitate the packing of stores by the party over the mud hole.

Friday, December 20.—Breakfast after rather an uncomfortable night. Barnes and I packed the mules, whilst the other boys packed across the swamps, and after a hard day's work we were all happy to see the Dutch oven full of delicious baked beans, to which ample justice was done ere we sought our spruce-bough bed.[23]

Packing hay from Meagher's barn to feed mules.

Saturday, December 21.—Packing to Canyon camp. Dr. Runnalls and Barnes, changing jobs as the doctor wishes to gain some experience in packing mules. Our supply of whisky well nigh exhausted, which is a good job.

The party gaining their second wind: do not find packing quite so heavy.[24]

Sunday, December 22.—Packing as usual. Captain Barnes in camp at correspondence.[25]

Monday, December 23.—Turned the boys out in a snowstorm[26] with axes to slaughter out a few of the wonderful crooks in the trail. Commenced packing lumber. Brought two thirty foot boards to deep gulch, leaving two at camp creek.[27] Packed the last of our stores to camp.

The boys were entertained by the Doctor rendering some

---

[21] "The two pack saddles (cinched with a diamond hitch) are described by Barnes in his journal for December 25, 1889." Majors, ed., *Northwest Discovery* 2 (Mar. 1981): p. 171.

[22] "This is Canyon Camp, the first real campsite of the Press Party, since the farmhouse at the Meagher ranch could hardly be considered a true wilderness camp." Majors, ed., *Northwest Discovery* 2 (Mar. 1981): p. 171.

[23] "Christie more probably refers to their use of young Douglas-fir (*Pseudotsuga menziesii*) branches; indeed, this tree was once known as 'Douglas spruce.' The present Sitka spruce (*Picea stichensis*) would have made rather unpleasant bedding—to gather as well as sleep on—for one of the distinguishing characteristics of its needles is that their tips are extremely sharp, even painful, to touch." Majors, ed., *Northwest Discovery* 2 (Mar. 1981): p. 171.

[24] "The men had first begun packing supplies on their backs on December 13; thus, in a little over a week's time, they had built up the requisite strength and stamina." Majors, ed., *Northwest Discovery* 2 (Mar. 1981): p. 171.

[25] "Barnes' letters were likely sent out on December 27, when he and Runnalls made a brief visit to Port Angeles. One of these letters was probably a report to Meany on the progress of the expedition; and, the information contained therein would have been used in the article: Edmond S. Meany, 'Beyond the Olympics' (*Seattle Press*, January 1, 1890). Unfortunately, no copies of this issue are known to have survived." Majors, ed., *Northwest Discovery* 2 (Mar. 1981): p. 171.

[26] "This was the first snow encountered by the Press Party. Winter had now set in for certain." Majors, ed., *Northwest Discovery* 2 (Mar. 1981): p. 171.

[27] "This lumber for constructing the boat had probably been ordered at Warriner Smith's sawmill on December 11, and was ready on the 23rd. The total amount was about 600 board-feet of lumber, probably consisting mostly of sixteen 32-foot length boards. The very length of these boards illustrates the nature, abundance, and availability of virgin timber in the 1890's. The idea of ascending the Elwha River in a boat was presented to Christie by Norman Smith during Christie's advance visit to Port Angeles within November 24 to December 2. At that time, Smith assured Christie that the Press Party 'would have water to spare for an eight-inch draft light scow for thirty miles up stream.' The plan was soon finalized on December 10, during Christie's second meeting with Smith. Christie was later to remark that 'This gentleman was certainly inspired, which caused some trouble and the delay of building a useless boat.' On the other hand, it was the long delay on the lower Elwha, from several causes, that was ultimately to save the lives of the Press Party. This . . . timed their arrival at the Low Divide at the moment hibernating bears were just beginning to emerge. Had the Press Party entered the deep Olympics directly in January 1890, they very well may have been caught on the upper Elwha by heavy snows and starved to death for lack of game.

"Neither 'deep gulch' nor 'camp creek' are capitalized. However, as with Cat Creek and Wolf Creek later on, the Press Party had evidently christened these features as such. The names were incipient and informal; and, as such, many geographic names are thus born." Majors, ed., *Northwest Discovery* 2 (Mar. 1981): pp. 171–72.

very difficult passages of high and ancient English. Apt quotations, all appertaining to the subject of driving mules.

My dog Bud, had a rather lively dispute with Dike regarding his behavior in camp.

Tuesday, December 24.—A heavy snow storm during the night brought down a number of the great trees in the vicinity, keeping all hands awake and their eyes fixed upon the ridge pole of the tent. The storm kept up until 11 A.M., and then showing some signs of clearing off we undertook to straighten up camp.

Sent Mr. Barnes for pack of hay to Meagher's ranch. Returning quite later he reported a foot of snow on the trail and a regular network of fallen timber. Several photos by Capt. Barnes.

Christmas in Camp

Wednesday, December 25.—Commenced snowing last evening again and kept it up until near midnight. Turning out this morning found things around camp in rather an uncomfortable condition, frozen stiff. Put in just half of the day chopping out the trail. Packed all lumber to the gulch above camp ere we returned to camp, six as hungry men as there is in the state, this night of Our Lord, doing ample justice to our Christmas dinner of bacon and beans.

Thursday, December 26.—Packed all the lumber for the boat to camp. The party putting as hard a day's work as one thoroughly under whip, but the party take hard work giving promise of staying powers, which will be called upon ere we reach Quinaiult.[28] The deep slush snow making the work of handling long, green, heavy lumber very disagreeable work indeed.

Friday, December 27.—Timbers all being packed to the beach. Gave Sims dimensions and the boat was laid on the stocks. The lumber was in a rather tough fix for boat building, the long 30 foot boards being thickened by one half inch of ice; this had to be thawed out ere they could be worked up, causing a good deal of work for the boys in providing fires.

Dr. Runnalls and Capt. Barnes left for Port Angeles, riding mules.[29] Sent invitation to Mr. W. Smith, to attend christening of boat Gerty.

Working on the Boat

Saturday, December 28.—More snow. Sims at work on boat, assisted by Crumback and Hayes. Capt. Barnes and Dr.

Runnalls returned from Angeles in the evening. I was engaged on steering oar and boat poles. Sparring oak during the evening.

Sunday, December 29.—Finished our work on boat, then packed and lowered all heavy stores over the bluff and stowed everything in cave below, ready for the launch "Gerty" in the morning. Gerty's dimensions: 30 feet over all, with five foot beam, twenty-two inches depth, flat bottom, rounding up bow and stem, sides six inches out, full in sections, bending inboard at bow on stern, with eight-inch covering inboard along journals, a windlass journal for heavy water, frame two feet apart, 2x4 clear.

Tuesday, December 31.—Snowing all day. A few last touches to the boat. Camp was struck and everything packed to beach. By 3 P.M. everything was ready for launching. Capt. Barnes took photographs. All ready, the boys stood by, and the Gerty was launched on the waters of the Elwha. She took to water kindly, sweeping into the deep water below the rapids. The boys stretched the tow line and we brought her up through her first rapid light.

The party in camp took hold and pulled her upstream and across on her trial trip. We tied up and made our first camp on our actual journey. I am sorry to find that she takes in a little too much water, which will compel a recaulking. Thus ends our labor for 1889.

New Year's Day on the Elwha

New Year's day on the Elwha, our first holiday.—On account of snow, which continued falling all day, the boys tried hunting, but were not successful, my fishing resulting in much the same way. Capt. Barnes took two views of the river and boat. I wonder when the snow will let up.

Thursday, January 2.—Still snowing, with little signs of a break. A small tree dropped across camp last night, slightly damaging our tent. Boys had to dig out from under snow drift this morning and we laid around camp all day.

Two Indians in Camp

January 3.—About three and a half feet of snow on a level this morning, entailing considerable shoveling to keep camp clear. Two Indians who had sought shelter with us last night, left for the camp at the mouth of the river,[30] the depth of the snow being something of a surprise to them as it is to myself.

---

[28] "From this statement, it appears that the Quinault River was indeed the goal of the Press Party, and that they hoped to reach it via the Elwha River." Majors, ed., *Northwest Discovery* 2 (Mar. 1981): p. 172.

[29] "The two mules were left in the care of William MacDonald (near the mouth of Little River) until March 8, at which time they were retrieved with the intention of bringing them up to the Press Party camp at the mouth of Wolf Creek." Majors, ed., *Northwest Discovery* 2 (Mar. 1981): p. 172.

[30] "This Indian camp . . . would be the old Clallam Indian village of *Elxwha* or *Elwha*. See Erna Gunther (1896–date unknown), 'Klallam Ethnography' (University of Washington Publications in Anthropology 1, 1927: pp. 171–314, *cit* pp. 174, 178)." Majors, ed., *Northwest Discovery* 2 (Mar. 1981): p. 172.

Chopped the ice from boat and cleaned her out to bring over the balance of our outfit. Crossing the river we broke a trail breast high through the snow. Afternoon pulled the boat up on bar above a rather swift rapid, which we crossed over with some rather hard language, as the water was uncomfortably cold. The boys saw their first buck this forenoon.[31] A short hunt through the deep snow satisfied them.

Saturday, January 4.—Devilish cold. All hands preparing a landing place for Gerty. Shoveling and tramping snow. Pounding and chopping a berth for her occupied us well into the afternoon. With a long pull and a heavy lift for six men, we succeeded in landing Gerty once more. Will raise her on the morrow.

A Fruitless Hunt

Sunday, January 5.—Raised the boat some four feet by building under and around. We mean to dry her out well this time. We will caulk her and give her room to shrink. River risen about twelve inches. Another disagreement between the boys, which made things lively in camp for awhile.[32]

Monday, January 6.—Cold. Snowing. Despicable weather. Fixing up a complete berth for Gerty. All hands chopping or packing firewood. I tried the hills back from camp for a shot, as I was assured that there was deer there. I had no luck. Found the snow something like five feet deep on the hills.

Tuesday, January 7.—At work on boat. Boys moved camp nearer the boat.

Wednesday, January 8.—At work on boat.

Thursday, January 9.—At work on boat.

Friday, January 10.—Commenced recaulking this morning. All hands at work. Spinning caulkum. Packing above camp some two hundred yards, where we will load up.

Saturday, January 11.—Finished caulking. Already for the pitch pot in the morning.

Sunday, January 12.—Finished Gerty. Again packed her to the river, and launched her. We were all happy to see that our labor had not been in vain, as she floated like a duck, and dry as a whistle.

They Began the Trip Up the Elwha

Monday, January 13.—Breakfast at daylight. The party packed all stores, etc., above first rapid. A few finishing touches was put on Gerty, and then pulled to cache above rapids. A hasty lunch and loading was commenced, and when sheets were spread over cargo, I found Gerty had her full cargo on board.

The tow line was stretched. Dr. Runnalls, Crumback, Sims and Hayes on the line, gave the steering to Capt. Barnes, myself acting as bowsman. In this order we commenced our journey up the Elwha.

The Elwha is quite a different stream I find from the Elwha of common report. After four hours' hard work we camped for the night at large drift pile. Devilish cold, and the party rather in a frozen-out condition. This was remedied just as soon as supper was ready.

Tuesday, January 14.—Another hard day's work on the Elwha. Moved camp some one fourth of a mile. Cutting away bridges thrown across by settlers in the vicinity delayed us considerable.[33] When just above a lovely salmon pool we ran into a stretch of white water that tried the temper of the boys as well as the strength of the tow line. The work on the shore towing is enough when a good foothold can be had, and the presence of two or three feet of snow renders it anything but pleasant.

Wednesday, January 15.—Another day on the Elwha. Cold, wet, disagreeable. White water and portages with the three hours work making camp in large drift pile put us to sleep, and though our bed was but the soft side of a gravel bar.

Thursday, January 16.—The forenoon spent drying our. Another portage above rapids and large tree, under which we forced the empty boat, loaded up and after a close shave from a wreck, only saved by the grit of Jack Crumback staying with the tow line, we made the pool below McCray's ranch, where we camped for the night, being hospitably entertained by Mr. Lutz, Mr. Lutz being engaged clearing and slashing on McCray's claim, during his absence.

Friday, January 17.—Portages, rapids and snow with a comfortable cabin for the night.[34]

Saturday, January 18.—Had to clear channel through

---

[31] "This marks the first time that deer had been sighted on the expedition. [Deer] would remain rather scarce throughout the next five months." Majors, ed., *Northwest Discovery* 2 (Mar. 1981): p. 172.

[32] "This is the first definite reference to bickering among the party. These were extremely trying and uncomfortable days for the Press Party, with no relief in sight; and tempers were beginning to flare. However, unless the Barnes and Christie narratives have suppressed incidents, the Press Party was a remarkably harmonious group, with compatible personalities. The two narratives commonly mention swearing during the difficult days on the lower Elwha; however, after today no reference is made to any disputes among or between the men themselves. Fortunately, for their own sake, the problems they had to face were those presented by the environment, and not by each other." Majors, ed., *Northwest Discovery* 2 (Mar. 1981): p. 172.

[33] "Rather than being true bridges, these were either trees felled across the Elwha River by nearby settlers, or mere log jams. Note, for instance, the entry for January 18." Majors, ed., *Northwest Discovery* 2 (Mar. 1981): p. 185.

[34] "Apparently a reference to the McCray ranch. Whether the expedition spent one or two nights in the cabin is not clear." Wood, *Across the Olympic Mountains*, p. 50.

rapids above camp. Cargo all aboard. The boys took the beach and through some rough water made the mouth of Indian creek,[35] camping immediately opposite a large jam of logs, which is used by the settlers as a bridge, being their only means of crossing. Sent the settlers in the vicinity word to the effect that if they turned out and assisted to run boat over it would save their bridge, as otherwise I would be compelled to cut it away. Capt. Barnes leaves for a visit to Indian creek and Lake Sutherland.

Sunday, January 19.—Another heavy fall of snow. Visited Mr. McDonald, some little distance above camp. Returned with Mr. Lutz. Passed the night with him at Craft's ranch. The boys had a hunt during the afternoon. Lots of cougar tracks in bush. Mr. McDonald visited camp, giving us much useful information regarding the river.

The Gerty Lifted Over a Bridge

Monday, January 20.—Five settlers from Indian creek[36] arrived this morning to assist in portaging boat across jam. This we accomplished with a good deal of heavy lifting. The Gerty was one more step towards Olympus.

Tuesday, January 21.—Made a move toward McDonald's ranch and was compelled to make cache on bar at the foot of a long shallow rapid, being unable to pull cargo owing to the wonderful low state of the river.[37] I am afraid that I will be compelled to give up the boat and take to the trail, as the depth of snow on the bank, through which the boys must plow their way makes progress devilish slow, tedious and disagreeable. After caching cargo went and paid a visit to Mr. McDonald and the mules. Jennie and Dolly seem to be in good hands.[38]

Wednesday, January 22.—Broke camp, with all outfit,

stores, etc., on board. Tried the rapids again, but was compelled to unload half the cargo, and haul the boat up through white water to McDonald's,[39] storing cargo in his cabin. After a change of clothing we found ourselves very comfortable squatting around McDonald's fireplace after seven hours' hard work in snow water to the waist. I intend to pull the boat out as soon as we can bring up the balance of the stores, as men cannot stand any such work as we have been compelled to undergo, through the unprecedented heavy fall of snow and low stage of water in the river.

Thursday, January 23.—Ran the Gerty down to the cache this forenoon and loaded her up for her last trip. Water was lower than yesterday (lower than McDonald has ever seen it) which caused us a good deal of hard work, in having to walk the boat up to McDonald's, zigzagging up and across the river, the boys at times up to their chins in water at our side of the boat, while the men lifting on the other would not be above their ankles. The thermometer showed several degrees of frost, and the clothing of the party would freeze as soon as any wet surface was exposed to the air above water. Several hours of this work chilled the men through and they gained but a small taste of future blessing. When we reached the comfortable cabin of our worthy host, McDonald, the nonchalance with which the members of the party accepts their present hardships bodes well for the future.

Friday, January 24.—Stripped out boat and stowed her in a comfortable berth, her future sphere of usefulness to be determined according to the will of Wariner Smith, whose property she becomes per agreement.

Capt. Barnes at work on chart.[40] Having made up my mind to continue our journey, by hand,[41] sent the other

115

---

[35] "Indian Creek received its name within 1879–1889, from the fact that the Elwha band of the Clallam Indians had a village here named *Sestie'tl* or *Stey'alh*, located at the confluence of this stream with the Elwha River. Some Elwha Indians were still living here, for on January 20 two nearby Elwha/Clallam Indians would assist the Press Party in portaging their boat around the Elwha log jam at the mouth of Indian Creek." Majors, ed., *Northwest Discovery* 2 (Mar. 1981): p. 185.

[36] "These . . . likely included Henry S. Hansen, Jake Hansen, two brothers from Norway, who first arrived on the Elwha River in 1888 and who homesteaded sites on both sides of Indian Creek a short distance above its mouth. See Jervis Russell, ed., *Jimmy Come Lately, History of Clallam County* (Port Angeles and Port Orchard: Clallam County Historical Society, 1971), cit. p. 322." Majors, ed., *Northwest Discovery* 2 (Mar. 1981): p. 186.

[37] "Today's campsite marks the first place on the Elwha River that the actual route of the Press Party can be retraced today. Below here, the length of the Elwha River down to Canyon Camp has now been inundated by the waters of Lake Aldwell, created in 1913 by the Lake Aldwell Dam (also known as the Elwha Dam)." Majors, ed., *Northwest Discovery* 2 (Mar. 1981): p. 186.

[38] "The two mules were sent up to William MacDonald's homestead on December 29 via Runnalls, 'there being nothing in the shape of food for them through the brush.' The mules would be retrieved on March 8, with the intention of bringing them up to the camp at the mouth of Wolf Creek. Since the mules were brought overland to the MacDonald cabin, the Press Party could similarly have packed their supplies along the same route used by the Indian Creek settlers to reach Port Angeles—rather than trying to bring a boat up the rugged and rapid-filled Elwha River." Majors, ed., *Northwest Discovery* 2 (Mar. 1981): p. 186.

[39] Even though the Press Party, maps, and other documents refer to "McDonald's," he actually spelled his name "MacDonald." Robert L. Wood found a letter from him to Edmond S. Meany in which he signed in clear, legible handwriting "MacDonald." Nonetheless, it seems that common usage will forever deny MacDonald the use of his actual name in history.

[40] "This is the first reference to Barnes having begun his duties as cartographer of the expedition." Majors, ed., *Northwest Discovery* 2 (Mar. 1981): p. 196.

[41] "Christie's comment here faintly suggests that there may possibly have been some thought about discontinuing or postponing the expedition at this point." Majors, ed., *Northwest Discovery* 2 (Mar. 1981): p. 196.

members of the party to hunt up a suitable tree from which we could construct toboggans.

A View From McDonald's Butte

McDonald's claim, where we are at present camped, is situated on the south branch of the little river[42] on the east side of the Elwha, and rising abruptly from the eastern line, some 1000 feet, towers McDonald's butte.[43] Leaving camp this morning I determined to climb to the summit and gain some information regarding the country to the southward, and possibly might run across a deer, as fresh meat would be appreciated in camp. Fitting on snowshoes three sizes too small for me I followed up the valley of the little river some two miles, then taking what appeared to be a very easy angle I commenced the ascent, but found the last 500 feet rather steep work for snowshoes. On the summit I found 10 feet of snow, packed hard and drifted to an immense depth in many places; met with many track of deer, fresh; but no deer until I reached the summit. I found a band of five head across a deep gorge, dividing the Butte from the base of Mount Angeles to the southeast, but altogether too far to attempt a shot. A short mile good snow shoeing to the westward brought me to the highest point overlooking McDonald's claim, which commanded a magnificent view north, west and south. Vancouver island in the distance northward, Brace Rock lighthouse lying serenely at my feet in the strait of Juan de Fuca, the water of the strait being lost in the far distant east and west; Lake Sutherland shining amidst the dark green forests which encircled its pure waters, the home of myriads of salmon trout, the great gray and mountain trout; a veritable paradise for any disciple of the gentle art of angling.

Beautiful Indian Creek Valley

The beautiful Indian creek valley extending from the lake to the west, gradually winding as it approached the Elwha, showed a lovely stretch of level country, which will be one of the valued spots of this fair state at no distant date. Splendid timber, well watered and magnificent soil, sheltered on every hand. The Indian creek valley will yet be heard from as a farming and fruit country, second to none of the famous valleys of vast California.[44] The Sutherland range bordering and sheltering this garden spot to the south rise ridge upon ridge many a water course until merging into the foot hills of Olympus towering to the south flanked by many other white capped summits on either hand. Rugged and grand ranges extending east and west through which we must soon force our way, ere we can hope to master the mystery which we have determined to solve.[45]

A Well Used Deer Trail

Leaving the Press party[46] blaze (three blazes, one above the other)[47] and taking the bearing of Mount Olympus[48] and Race Rock, leaving information for Capt. Barnes I sought for a gradual slope westward towards the river flowing from a well beaten deer track for some distance along the edge of the cliffs on the summit where the snow had been blown off. I found a rift through and down the face of the cliff, that evidently was used as a regular trail by the herds of deer, which inhabited these lower ranges, but the depths of snow had evidently driven all game to the lower plateaus. Sliding and plunging to my neck in the soft snow I reached a bench about half way down the butte, feeling much like a half drowned rat. With little prospect of getting a shot, I hurried on toward McDonald's as the sun disappeared. The twilight warned me to make tracks,

116

---

[42] "The Little River of today enters the Elwha from the east, near the confluence of which was located the MacDonald homestead. This . . . marks the first appearance of this geographic name, although in this and later entries Christie writes it without capitalization as 'the little river.' The name Little River was in formal use by the year 1892, for it appears as such on the U.S. General Land Office survey plat of that year. What Christie refers to as 'the south branch of the little river' is definitely not that which is today known as the South Branch, for this latter feature is situated a good $2\frac{1}{2}$ to $3\frac{1}{2}$ miles east of the MacDonald homestead, and therefore far beyond the limits of his claim." Majors, ed., *Northwest Discovery* 2 (Mar. 1981): p. 196.

[43] "This is present-day MacDonald Mountain (2250–2300'), a triple-peaked minor mountain situated between Little River and Madison Creek. This was the first of the few mountains climbed by members of the Press Party. This particular ascent . . . represents the first recorded winter ascent performed in the state of Washington. Christie's estimate of 'some two miles' is probably an overestimate for the distance he journeyed up the south side of the Little River valley. Christie's route most likely led . . . as far as the small tributary that drains into the Little River from the south through land sections 27 and 34. Christie then ascended along this tributary . . . and finally climbed the east peak of MacDonald Mountain. . . . From the east peak, Christie traversed westward across the middle peak to reach the west peak. . . . Christie then descended the mountain via its west (or possibly northwest) side to the Elwha River." Majors, ed., *Northwest Discovery* 2 (Mar. 1981): p. 196.

[44] "Christie's exuberant prophecies regarding the future agricultural development of Indian Valley have not been borne out. A similar adulative passage, praising the merits of the Elwha Valley, occurs in Christie's entry for February 24. These may possibly have been editorial insertions." Majors, ed., *Northwest Discovery* 2 (Mar. 1981): p. 196.

[45] "Christie's ascent of MacDonald Mountain provided him with the first good look at the mountainous country the Press Party had yet to traverse." Majors, ed., *Northwest Discovery* 2 (Mar. 1981): p. 196.

[46] "This marks the first time the term 'Press party' is used in the narratives." Majors, ed., *Northwest Discovery* 2 (Mar. 1981): p. 197.

[47] "This represents the first reference to the Press Party blaze to appear in the narratives. Since their boat journey had terminated, and they were at the limits of civilization, the Press Party henceforth would be marking their route with their distinctive triple blaze." Majors, ed., *Northwest Discovery* 2 (Mar. 1981): p. 197.

[48] "Throughout the expedition this peak was 'Olympus' to the party, none of the men ever detected their error. A decade later Theodore F. Rixon—who, together with Arthur Dodwell, made the original survey of the Olympic Forest Reserve—named the peak Mount Carrie, in honor of his wife, Carolina." Wood, *Across the Olympic Mountains*, p. 56.

and no sooner had I covered my rifle than a fine fat-looking doe sprang from the brush some 50 yards below, disappearing ere I had a chance to uncover my gun, but gave me a snap shot 200 yards below. Unfortunately the shot took effect too far back, and although evidently hard hit I was forced to give up the trail and seek camp, which I reached about 7 o'clock, to enjoy true bliss in the shape of a hearty meal and the pleasure of a comfortable pipe.

Saturday, January 25.—Snowing very hard.

Sunday, January 26.—Still snowing, harder if possible. Received our first mail per Mr. W. Smith.[49]

Snow Bound in Camp

Monday, January 27.—Commenced raining and I am perfectly satisfied of the fact now that it does rain here at times.

Monday, February 3.—For the last seven days we have been kept here as close prisoners. Practically unable to move any, owing to the extraordinary amount of rain and snow. Water fairly falling in sheets, as a rule, giving place to very heavy snow storms toward evening. There has scarcely been a single hour for the last week without a shower bath that went to the skin. Oil clothing seems to be of no use, and we have discarded it as useless. Cooped up in rather close quarters the party feels much like caged bears, but we must stand it, as the devil himself would not much relish a continued plowing through soft sodden snow to the waist, and a miniature creek coursing down his spinal column. During our enforced idleness I had given the party a few ideas regarding the construction of the various forms of sleighs in use among the tribes to be met with in the far north. For toboggans we found no suitable timber.[50] Go devils or carryalls come next best in order, being more simple in construction—but two long poles bent at one end, so as to form

arms held together by two cross bars, upon which the load is strapped. In the event of a difference in opinion, the old time travois can be relied upon as a means of transportation, and when all the other modes fail, then remains for the boys the never failing pack rope, but as each individual can suit his own taste and ideas regarding mode of transporting his load there is plenty of room for choice, but, judging from the weather of the past few months and the rotten state of the snow, I have little faith in anything beyond the pack rope.[51]

Sims and Crumback have employed their leisure in building up a sleigh to carry a double load. Dr. Runnalls and Capt. Barnes have adopted the travois rig as well. Chris Hayes and myself joining in for a light sleigh built from vine maple, which grows plentifully all through the valleys. It is not fit for anything in God's earth but to test the patience and temper of the hunter and voyager.

Tired of our enforced inaction we turned out on Saturday and broke a trail up stream as far as Wariner Smith's claim, chopping out and improving the trail to this point, returning to McDonald's at night soaked through; the boys swearing that the rain had gone clear through hide and hair. Monday Dr. Runnalls left us to visit his wife who had been attacked by some odd named new feature. Hope the doctor will find her quite recovered. He returns in ten days, and will overtake us about the fourth. [*id est*, the fourteenth][52]

Tuesday, February 4, McDonald's Ranch.—Daylight this morning gave promise of a change in the weather, and immediately after an early breakfast the boys were astir fixing the loads. Packed to Smith's claim, through three feet of snow; rained all day. The rotten state of the snow would not permit of sleighs being worked, so after a few attempts to

117

---

[49] "Today's mail constitutes the first contact the Press Party had with the outside world since the return of Barnes and Runnalls on December 28 from their short visit to Port Angeles." Majors, ed., *Northwest Discovery* 2 (Mar. 1981): p. 197.

[50] "To construct the classic Indian type of toboggan required the bending of the front end of a single piece of wood in nearly a 180° curve. The wood most commonly used by the Canadian interior Indians was birch (*Betula* spp.) and basswood or linden (*Tilia americana*), both of which possessed the requisite elasticity to permit them to be bent and gradually shaped without breaking. However, neither of these trees was available to the Press Party in the Elwha Valley." Majors, ed., *Northwest Discovery* 2 (Mar. 1981): p. 198.

[51] "Though Christie himself gave the men the ideas for sled construction, this very entry indicates that he had little faith in their feasibility. Christie may very well have encouraged these construction efforts so as to boost the interest and morale of the men during their confinement at the MacDonald cabin." Majors, ed., *Northwest Discovery* 2 (Mar. 1981): p. 198.

[52] "At this point, Runnalls terminated his association with the Press Party, for he never returned from Puyallup. . . . Just when Runnalls received word of his wife's illness is uncertain, since the last recorded time the Press Party received letters from Seattle was a week earlier, on January 26. This week's delay would not be congruent with a man's concern with his wife's illness. It would seem more likely that the Press Party received another mail delivery sometime during the intervening week—perhaps on the day previous, February 2, for which day neither Barnes nor Christie record an entry in their journals. William MacDonald may at this time have been serving as postmaster for the Elwha settlers, in which event the Press Party would have had immediate access to their mail.

"The nature of Mrs. Runnalls' illness is not specified. Runnalls did, however, return to the Olympic Peninsula, for by June 3, 1890 he was serving as physician to the Indian Agency at Neah Bay for the Makah Indian Reservation. On that date he wrote to Edmond S. Meany, asking for news concerning the Press Party, which had recently returned to Seattle: Harris B. Runnalls' letter to Edmond S. Meany, dated June 3, 1890 at Neah Bay (University of Washington Library, Manuscripts and University Archives Division, Edmond S. Meany papers, box 10, folder 8)." Majors, ed., *Northwest Discovery* 2 (Mar. 1981): p. 198.

drag them through they were thrown aside as useless and the pack shape resorted to.

Wednesday, February 5.—Packing to cache, about half way to Smith's claim.

Thursday, February 6.—Packed remaining stores as far as cache. Blankets and cooking outfit on to camp at Smith's claim. We found his cabin unoccupied, so took possession, and made ourselves as comfortable as possible. As the cabin has never been caulked we will have ventilation enough.[53]

Friday, February 7.—Finished packing from below. Having met with numerous signs of elk, I was anxious to get out for a hunt, and now that packing has been finished there arrives four Indians, and as they go up stream our chance of elk meat will be slim.[54]

The Indians on an Elk Hunt

Sunday, February 9.—Mr. Lutz arrived in camp last night to have a day's hunting with us. Was about to start this morning when the sound of shooting was heard upstream. Lutz and Sims struck out to see what was going on. Returning in the evening they reported the Indians having killed eight head. Our turn next.

Monday, February 10.—I left this morning accompanied by Sims and Hayes on a trip toward the forks[55] so often mentioned by our Port Angeles friends. One and a half miles brought us to a point on the river which afforded us a splendid view of the river and valley. A small slashing on the plat below us shows us the cabin of Dr. Lull, another absentee squatter.[56] The curl of blue smoke riding over the tree tops about a mile beyond the shanty told us where the Indians were camped. Following along the face of the bluff we soon reached the Indian camp,[57] though ere we had arrived at any satisfactory conclusion, we found the Indians in camp preparing their morning meal, with a quantity of fresh elk meat hung around on the trees.

Their Fathers Remembered

Being unable to speak Chinook and the Indians English, being rather mixed, I could gain very little information beyond the fact that a short distance beyond the present camp they were utterly ignorant of the country,[58] but that their fathers recollected that at one time one of the Quinaiult Indians had crossed the mountains and remained some time within the Clallams.

Bidding our Indian friends good-bye we struck out towards the foot of the bluff along which the Indians enjoined us we would find an old Indian trail, which led us to the foot of the Devil's Backbone,[59] the trail striking up the face of the bluff at an angle of seventy five degrees gave us several good excuses to smoke finding convenient resting places. The trail winding along the face of several places rendering it rather unsafe for any nervous youths to travel and which we will be compelled to improve a good deal before packing across. An odd glimpse of the mad water in the canyon could be had at different points along the trail.

A Barrier Against Canoeing on the Elwha

On gaining the upper end of the canyon we climbed out to the point of high rock which commanded a view of the river, roaring and tumbling through the narrow gorge at our feet. The whole of the water pouring through three

118

---

[53] "Warriner Smith's cabin and land claim were located on the east bank of the Elwha River, near the mouth of Madison Creek. This was merely an absentee land claim and not the actual home of Smith, whose true home lay much closer to his sawmill far downriver as well as the comforts of Port Angeles. Smith had filed for homestead rights on this fertile bottom land, not because he intended to live here, but probably with the intention of selling it at a later date for a good profit. This was one variation of the many fraudulent and speculative land schemes prevalent in the American West during the late Nineteenth Century. The Press Party would encounter the same situation on the Quinault River above Lake Quinault on May 18, 1890—thus indicative of how widespread this practice was in Washington State. The homestead laws were intended to help poor farmers settle uninhabited regions, but these laws were frequently abused by greedy land speculators." Majors, ed., *Northwest Discovery* 2 (May 1981): p. 320.

[54] "This is the first reference to elk in the expedition journals, a species that would soon constitute an important part of the Press Party diet while in the Elwha Valley." Majors, ed., *Northwest Discovery* 2 (May 1981): p. 320.

[55] "What the Press Party refer to as The Forks is nowhere precisely defined in the two narratives. However, from internal evidence, this site appears to be the confluence of Boulder and Cat creeks with the Elwha River. These two creeks constitute the first substantial tributaries of the Elwha River above Indian Creek." Majors, ed., *Northwest Discovery* 2 (May 1981): p. 321.

[56] "The cabin of Dr. A. B. Lull was situated somewhere near the mouth of Griff Creek. Lull's cabin represented the absolute limit of settlement in the Elwha Valley as of early 1890." Majors, ed., *Northwest Discovery* 2 (May 1981): p. 321.

[57] "This camp of Elwha Indians was located on the east bank of the Elwha River, just above [what is now] Altair Campground. This was not a permanent Indian village, but rather a temporary hunting camp set up by the four Elwha Indians who had passed the Press Party on February 7." Majors, ed., *Northwest Discovery* 2 (May 1981): p. 321.

[58] "Christie's entry today is of ethnographic interest, for it helps define the territorial boundaries of the Elwha Indians. This band or clan of the Clallam tribe confined itself to the lower Elwha River, and the coast near the mouth of this river. . . . From Christie's information, the Elwha Indians penetrated no farther up the Elwha River than the present Lake Mills dam, even though large herds of elk were present upvalley from here." Majors, ed., *Northwest Discovery* 2 (May 1981): p. 321.

[59] "The Devils Backbone is the extension of the northwest spur of Hurricane Hill which descends to the Elwha River at the present Lake Mills Dam, and which provides a footing for the east buttress of the dam. It is uncertain whether this name was a Press Party name, or, like The Forks, was one of the early Elwha settlers." Majors, ed., *Northwest Discovery* 2 (May 1981): p. 321.

small channels, the widest not over seven feet between the rocks, an effective barrier to canoeing on the Elwha.[60] The trail, for some distance, led through a comparative level country, crossing two small creeks, where we entered a good sized river bottom covered with a heavy growth of maple, about the center of which we found an old Indian smokehouse where we determined to camp for the night as we still had some hours of daylight. We cached our packs and took to the hills in hopes of getting shot. After an hour's tramp we found fresh elk signs and following them up we found the trail led down to the river, and as we expected, saw the elk feeding and quiet, where we left them for the night. As the sun had disappeared we sought our camp and hope to have fresh elk meat my noon on the morrow.

Tuesday, February 11.—Daylight found us rustling and while Sims attended to the beans and coffee, our packs were hung up to bide our return, rifles carefully looked over, and we were ready for anything that might turn up.

Off on an Elk Hunt

As soon as breakfast was over we struck the trail, which follows the river bank for some distance through a growth of young pine, then turning to the edge of first plateau for another half mile, affording us good, level snow shoeing. Reaching a rocky point on the river, we met with fresh signs of elk, and following the bank of the river, we found their trail leading on to a long gravel bar and across a wide slough into a large open plat above, very sparsely timbered, with an odd bunch of grass on the edge of the bank. The open character of the country compelled us to seek shelter in a strip of young pines which grew along the river bank. Through this young growth we worked our way to the upper end of the river, and crossing two small creeks we found that the herd of something like half a hundred of elk had plowed a deep, broad trail up the face of the butte, which rose abruptly from this point. (The fork of the Elwha, a crossing to the Angeles explorers.) Up the face of the butte on the well beaten trail we climbed to a height of some 600 feet, and on reaching the top we were glad enough to rest for wind. Here we found ourselves upon a broad level bench only partly timbered, showing the evidence of having been swept by fire in the long ago. A few minutes for a breathing spell, and we were on the trail again, straight way upstream for some half mile and then entering a bluff of heavy timber. This was carefully passed and the trail showed plain and broad straight up the face of the bench to the east. After a careful survey of the

country ahead we pressed on across the open space and commenced the scramble before us. After some hard scrambling and after a careful examination of the ground in front, we were rather disappointed at seeing no game in sight. The trail was followed for another one-third of a mile, then turning sharp to the left and entered a piece of low swamp land, and from signs we felt sure of our game. Quietly feeding, the sound of the bucks trampling and rubbing the trees, caught our ears, it sent the blood tingling to our finger tips. Cautiously working back from the swamp we divided our forces. Sims and Hayes went to work around toward the foot of the mountains to get a shot if possible, whilst I would attempt the same back towards the edge of the bench and out from the swamp.

A Magnificent Sight of an Elk

Ten minutes carefully stalking I reached my desired point, and carefully creeping around the roots of an upturned tree, my eyes were greeted with a sight that had warmed the heart of the coolest nimrod that had ever made moccasin tracks in a mountain side. Immediately fronting me stood one of the monarchs of the mountains—a stag royal with as fine a head as ever graced the trophied hall of any highland chief—some one hundred yards distant, with his nose well into the wind as if scenting danger to his harem. Grazing quietly around, scattered through the short brush of the swamp were some 50 or 75 elk, the young and graceful yearling, the more homely cows, now heavy with calf, with several royal heads of various ages. With all the pride of the hunter, I could not but gaze at the picture before me, reminding me forcibly of the not uncommon sights that I had met in mountains and around the chief mountains on both sides of the American boundary. Suddenly the simultaneous report of two rifles dispelled my dream as it suddenly awake the band of elk to a sense of danger. As they gathered in a complete mass for the brush, the great stag whom I had been admiring paused a few seconds as if uncertain which direction the sounds had come. Making a half turn towards the hill he turned again shot in his track, and dashed away through the swamp. Meanwhile having noticed one of the young bulls through the swamp restrained me from using my rifle, and although sorely attempted to take just one shot, allowed him to trot off in peace. They had hardly disappeared from the swamp when another shot from the boys put their game out of pain and gave us a good supply of fresh meat. Joining the boys we indulged in a pipe ere we cut up our game. Selecting a few choice pieces

119

---

[60] "Probably the Glines Canyon damsite." Wood, *Across the Olympic Mountains*, p. 65.

we made tracks for camp and enjoyed first meal of fresh elk meat, the forerunner of hopes of more to come.[61]

A Day's Discomfort Rewarded

Wednesday, February 12.—Rained very hard last night, thoroughly drenching us whilst curled up around the fire. As a consequence daylight found us ready for the pack trail, which we struck as soon as we could get a cup of coffee down us. Blazing the trail as we returned delayed us until well on toward night when we reached Smith's claim, but a supper of elk tenderloin steak, liver and bacon, with incomparable coffee, flanked by Crumback's bread, would well repay for a day's discomfort.

Sunday, February 16.—Smith's claim; 14th and 15th packed stores to cache on Lutz's claim. Finished up Saturday with the exception of camp outfit, one pack each.

Whilst packing on Saturday ran across fresh trail of very large cougar, and judging from large size of track, it must be "Johnnie," a large cougar of whom the settlers in the valley would fain be rid of, and being anxious to secure his pelt I determined to attempt it this morning. Hunting up the trail on the side hill, I put in three hours hard work following it up, being brought up the creek flowing between mountain angles and McDonald's ranch. This I was unable to cross as his catship the cougar, had to clear a good ten feet to the opposite rock. I concluded not to follow. Returning to camp I crossed a fresh cut undoubtedly made by the same animal, but there is no sign of cougar to be met with further.

Monday, February 17.—Packed camp outfit to large vine maple swamp, from which point we will have to cut out and make trail across Devil's Backbone, above the canyon. Packed from cache in the afternoon.[62]

Tuesday, February 18.—Packing from cache. Washed several pans on Big Barr with much the same result as my previous washing; no color.

The Dogs Herd Up an Elk

Wednesday, February 19.—Sims, Hayes and myself cut-ting and grading trail across Devil's Backbone. The dogs, during our work, herded a cow elk right close to camp, during our absence, much to the surprise of Capt. Barnes and Crumback. Barnes went out after the elk when we returned at night.

Thursday, February 20.—Moved camp to the foot of Devil's Backbone.

Friday, February 21, and Saturday, February 22.—Packing across Devil's Backbone.

Sunday February 23.—Leaving the boys in camp, they having well earned a day's rest, accompanied by Hayes, I struck up the river again in hopes of gaining some information regarding the country beyond. A good two hours' travel brought us to the lower end of a deep, black looking canyon, in which we did some prospecting. The formation is of black slate. On the east side it rose almost vertical from under the edge, showing several well defined veins of quartz formation, whilst the opposite wall of the canyon showed an angle of 85 degrees. On reaching the second and third benches to the east we found first class sandstone in place and no lack of good clay.

Returning to camp in the evening we started a deer. Both pulled our rifles on him and bowled her over in good shape. We hung him up for future use.

Monday, February 24.—About eight inches of snow last night accompanied by rain rendered it necessary to dry out blankets, etc. Constructed platform for cache.

Camp on Wildcat Creek

Tuesday, February 25.—Packed again for the road, making camp[63] in large flat on Wildcat creek. Eastern base of Mount Olympus, immediately opposite Wolf creek, which joins the Elwha here.[64]

Wednesday, February 26.—Put in the day felling large trees for bridge across river. The boys having a general washing and cleaning-up day. Preparing for a trip west toward the head of Wolf creek.[65]

---

[61] "This was the first game to be killed during the expedition. The detailed description by Christie of his elk hunt reveals that one of his principal interests and joys in life is hunting. Indeed, throughout his journal, Christie immediately perks up and engages in lengthy accounts whenever he narrates his hunting efforts. Several decades later, when asked by Edmond S. Meany in 1926 to recall some details of the 1890 expedition, Christie responded with a letter in which nearly half was devoted to a description of a single one of his elk hunts." Majors, ed., *Northwest Discovery* 2 (May 1981): p. 321.

[62] "Though no mention is made of it, today, February 17, was a momentous date for the Press Party, for this marked the first time they set up camp beyond the absolute limit of settlement in the Elwha Valley (as represented by A. B. Lull's cabin). They had now entered the true Olympic wilderness." Majors, ed., *Northwest Discovery* 2 (July-Aug. 1981): p. 472.

[63] "The Press Party would remain at this camp (now submerged beneath the waters of Lake Mills) until March 15—the longest period of time the expedition would remain at any one camp site." Majors, ed., *Northwest Discovery* 2 (July-Aug. 1981): p. 472.

[64] "Christie's use of two terms (Wildcat Creek and Wolf Creek) that at the very earliest came into existence on or shortly after February 28 demonstrates that portions of Christie's journal were re-written or augmented at a later date, probably after the return to Seattle." Majors, ed., *Northwest Discovery* 2 (July-Aug. 1981): p. 473.

[65] "This statement is contradictory, for on February 27 Christie and Crumback explored up the east side of the Elwha River. . . . Moreover, Wolf Creek heads to the east (not the west) of the Elwha. This confusion may have resulted from the fact that the term 'Wolf Creek' was a later addition to Christie's journal." Majors, ed., *Northwest Discovery* 2 (July-Aug. 1981): p. 473.

Two Large Wolf Visitors

Thursday, February 27.—Whilst enjoying a pipe after breakfast our attention was attracted to two large wolves quietly promenading the opposite bank of the river. The largest of the two advancing to the edge of the water to reconnoiter our camp. He was greeted by a Winchester pellet from Jack Sims' rifle, which did not agree with his digestive organs. They broke for the brush followed by Sims for 100 yards, where he found his wolfship and packed him to camp. His pelt now graces a friend's den in Seattle.[66]

Wednesday, March 5.—The last six days has been occupied in several different short trips up the various creeks entering the river in vicinity of camp from the west.

Heavily Timbered Mountains

The country lying between Olympus and the Indian creek valley is occupied by two magnificent ranges of heavily timbered mountains, intercepted by several small creeks and valleys. A section of country through which the elk and deer roam yet according to the bent of their own free will. The seclusion of their retreat being seldom disturbed by the foot fall of man, although within easy reach of Port Crescent and Port Angeles. These places hold great prizes in store for venturesome nimrods, else had the country been better known. Here miles on miles of magnificent timber stretch away from the river bank to the very summits of the mountains without a break in the dark confines. Here fortunes await the lumberations yet to be undertaken in the section, whilst there is room for many a happy homestead in the well sheltered valleys amidst the mountains. That is when the people think of running a good road through to this section, which can be done at a very small outlay of money considering the rare benefits which will accrue to them at no distant day.[67]

Capt. Barnes explored the great canyon and the base of Mount Olympus.

Sending Back for the Mules

Thursday, March 6.—Left camp this morning accompanied by Crumback, Hayes and Sims, for McDonald's ranch to bring up the mules, as there was a prospect of being able to use them. The trail, owing to the snow being so heavy, had to be cut almost the entire distance from camp to McDonald's, where we arrived on the evening of the 5th, and fixed up packs and saddles.

Friday, March 7.—Awoke this morning to find it raining as if a second flood were threatened. This kept up all day and detained us within the shelter of McDonald's cabin.

Saturday, March 8.—We packed the mules at daylight and left for camp, wishing Mr. McDonald good-bye. He seemed rather cut up at losing his pets, the mules.[68] We made what time we could, which was rather slow progress at best. The pleasure of plowing through slush and snow to the waist was somewhat heightened by being under a down pour of rain all day, compelling us to camp near a maple swamp all night.

Terrible Snow Storm

Sunday, March 9.—Rained and snowed all night. Daylight found a very heavy snow storm in full swing, the falling snow completely concealing objects at 15 paces distant. Shaking ourselves clear of the wet blanket, we packed up again and started, wet, miserable and just a little inclined to use bad language. Just on the north side of the Devil's Backbone, met Barnes in the bush en route to McDonald's to post some letters.[69] Pressing on through the blinding snow, we reached the Backbone and found the trail slippery with the mud and snow, which rendered extreme caution necessary in getting round some of the worst points.

Loss of Jennie

While ahead cutting away obstructions in the shape of falling trees I was brought to a sudden stop by a cry from

---

[66] "The friend referred to by Christie would be Edmond Stephen Meany (1862–1935), who on June 6, 1890 was billed by the Seattle furrier Ranko Petkovits (or Petkovitz, on Third Avenue, between James and Jefferson streets) the sum of twenty dollars, for one 'elk skin dressed and mounted,' one deer skin likewise dressed and mounted, and the pelt of one 'timber wolf' (University of Washington Library, Manuscripts and University Archives Division, Edmond S. Meany papers, box 10, folder 8). Both the wolf and elk skins were obtained from creatures killed on February 28. During the boat wreck of May 18, 1890, the Press Party 'lost everything except the contents of one pack' which contained the photographs and journals of the expedition. The 'few specimens of the flora and fauna of the country . . . were lost.' This indicates that the three skins in question were brought down to William MacDonald on March 6 (when Christie returned to retrieve the two mules), from whence they were subsequently shipped to Seattle. However, this does not explain the long delay presented by the June 6 date of the furrier's invoice." Majors, ed., *Northwest Discovery* 2 (July-Aug. 1981): p. 473.

[67] "As with Christie's previous (and unfulfilled) adulation of the Indian Creek valley on January 24, this extravagant praise of the merits of the Elwha Valley is so incongruent with Christie's normal style and content of writing, that the suspicion arises that it may have been an editorial insertion by the staff of the *Seattle Press*." Majors, ed., *Northwest Discovery* 2 (July-Aug. 1981): p. 472.

[68] "On April 21, William D. MacDonald wrote to Edmond S. Meany: 'A balance of twenty Dollars being due me for feed and care of mules for the winter, belonging to the Press Exploring Party, when taking the mules away J. H. Christie stated that he had written to you, and that you would forward the amount to me by mail. As I have not received the remittance would you please to write me and state if Christie had any authority for making such a promise, and oblige.'" Wood, *Across the Olympic Mountains*, p. 84.

[69] "This was apparently the last time the expedition was in contact with settlers in the Elwha Valley. From this point on they were out of touch with civilization." Wood, *Across the Olympic Mountains*, p. 84.

Crumback, and turned in time to see Jennie plunging down into the gulf below. The rattle of gravel was succeeded by the usual dull sickening thud, which greeted our ears as she struck the cleft of a tree below. I found that a portion of the trail had given away below her, thus causing the unfortunate accident. Hastily undoing our life lines and tying them to trees above, Sims and I lowered ourselves some hundred and fifty feet down the face of the cliff to find poor Jennie lying wedged between an enormous tree and the wall of rock. Her back broken and her poor body bruised in the last agony. A cut from my hunting knife released her from the pack saddle and trappings, and poor Jennie went thundering down 300 feet, bounding from ledge to ledge, until she disappeared in the bush. A few seconds passed and from below there came to us, who were watching her course, a repetition of heavy sounds as her body came in contact with the rock below told us the fate of a faithful mule. The sound of Jennie's plunge to the depth below had hardly died away when kicking the hell fire[70] after her it found a fitting resting place by her side. Raising the balance of the pack by rope to the summit of the cliff we clambered up and feeling keenly the loss of Jennie, we struck out for camp where we arrived at dark, cold and wet.

Monday, March 10.—By no means like nice weather. Drying out things around camp.

Tuesday, March 11.—All hands packing from cache below.

Wednesday, March 12.—Packing from cache below.

Thursday, March 13.—Packing from cache. Hayes brought in a deer this evening.

Capt. Barnes as a Tumbler

Friday, March 14.—Crumback and Hayes returned to cache for balance of stores, Barnes, Sims and self packing to top of butte; rather a tough pull up hill. Returning to camp, met the boys from below and packed camp outfit up during the afternoon. On the last trip we were treated to a circus by Capt. Barnes, as he plunged down the face of the butte to head off Dollie. He headed her off all right, but it took some

wonderful handsprings with a fifty pound pack to do it.

Saturday, March 15.—Another tough day packing to the top of the butte. All hands suffering from dysentery.[71]

Geyser Valley Sighted

Sunday, March 16.—Left camp this morning accompanied by Jack Crumback, to gain if possible some idea of the country ahead. The bench on which we are camped, extending upwards some two miles, was very promising to view and expecting to find a good trail across it, we struck out cheerfully enough. But we had not gone far before deep gulches and fallen timbers compelled us to take up the mountain side. After some rough work getting through the windfall we attacked the butte and found a very fair trail 500 feet above the bench, where we entered an excellent tract of timber, through which we traveled some two miles. Crumback got a snap shot at a very fine buck and brought him down in a very sportsman-like manner. Examining the buck we found him in a very fair condition, considering the hard winter. Hung him up for future use and again headed southward. Before leaving the hillside I succeeded in hanging two other deer on stumps along the trail. About 10 A.M. we reached a rocky point overlooking the river and valley (Geyser valley).[72] Immediately opposite a large stream enters the Elwha. Below lay a beautiful valley, stretching away up stream some four miles, a magnificent stretch of low river flats, comparatively open. A young paradise for some venturesome squatter. The course of the river could be traced far away to the southeast, whilst immediately opposite our lookout point, away to the south, arose a grand chain of peaks as far as the eye could reach, an exquisite panorama of mountain scenery to a lover of solitary natural grandeur. Enraptured with the scene before me I demanded of Crumback if he did not think it glorious, and was shocked to hear him give his opinion, low but impressive, that he considered it a "damned rough layout."

Having gazed our fill upon the mountains we sought a trail to the bottom lands below us and after some difficulty we reached the bank of the river. Fortunate in finding a place clear of snow we proceeded to make ourselves comfortable

122

---

[70] "One of the plans hatched in Seattle (prior to the departure of the expedition) was that on a pre-designated day during the venture, the men of the Press Party would ascend a peak, ignite a huge bonfire at night, and then toss in the fifty pounds of 'colored fire'—hoping that the colored flames would be visible at Seattle. Edmond S. Meany alerted the people of Seattle to watch for the fire in a now vanished issue of the newspaper: E. S. Meany, 'Watch For The Signals' (*Seattle Press*, December 20, 1889). However, as Meany later recounted,'part of the program of that expedition was the sending of signals from the highest peaks. At the Seattle end, on the agreed night, I climbed to Seattle's highest building, the old University, and, with the fine telescope loaned by Arthur A. Denny, kept watch all night. There were no signals' (Edmond Stephen Meany, 'The Olympics in History and Legend,' *The Mountaineer Annual* 6, December 1913, pp. 51–55, cit. p. 52)." Majors, ed., *Northwest Discovery* 5 (Aug. 1984): pp. 250–51.

[71] For an account of an elk encounter at about this time, see Christie's letter to Edmond S. Meany dated November 23, 1926, at Vernon, British Columbia. James Halbold Christie, "From the Leader of the Press Expedition," *The Mountaineer Annual* 19 (December 1926): pp. 37–39.

[72] "The appearance of the name *Geyser Valley* in the Press Party narrative for March 16, 20, and 22, 1890—a term that, at the earliest, came into existence on or shortly after March 29—indicates that portions of the Christie and Barnes journals were amended at a later date, probably after the return of the expedition to Seattle, when the two journals were being edited by Edmond S. Meany for publication." Majors, ed., *Northwest Discovery* 5 (Aug. 1984): p. 272.

and enjoy our lunch, having no qualms of conscience regarding our not having earned it. A smoke was next in order.

Studying a Fine Big Elk

Whilst quietly enjoying our pipes my ear caught the snort of an elk, acting on our nerve much like an electric shock in bringing us to our feet. A glance in the direction of the river and there in full view stood a magnificent specimen of the bull elk within a hundred and fifty yards of our resting place upon the bar on the opposite side of the river. Creeping back into the brush we sought better shelter and reached a stump, which completely covered us. We laid in wait watching his movements, feeling confident that he could not get away. I wished to give him an opportunity to come across before shooting. From his actions he had every intention of crossing as he advanced up the bar toward the head of a small ripple slowing step by step and sniffing the air as he came on; for fully 10 minutes he remained in front of us, giving us an excellent opportunity of studying his every movement. At times he seemed to make up his mind to step boldly across, whilst at others he would half turn toward the opposite bank and hesitate as if about to retrace his steps. His every motion was grace in itself. In spite of the wishes for stores of dried meat the thought would force itself upon me that it was barbarous to kill such a fine specimen of animal life. But by the time I had arrived at this conclusion a whiff of wind had carried to his sensitive nose a suspicion of danger, and one bound from two feet of water landed him on dry land, but ere he could gather himself for a second spring a 40.82 ball had pierced his lungs and furnished me with 400 pounds of good meat for pemmican.

Elk After Elk Plunge into the River

The report of my rifle had hardly died away when I was surprised to see elk after elk plunge into the river from a low point of the bank some 50 yards down stream. Running down the bank a little distance I covered what I considered the fattest buck in the band of some 75 head, and pulled the trigger, but no report following the action. I was chagrined to find my rifle had got out of fix. That is to say it had gone back on me, leaving me much in the position of a fool at a fair, gazing at the tail end of a procession of elk meat walking away from me down the stream. On examining my gun I found that the point of the trigger had broken off, thus rendering the arm useless. Whispering sundry compliments to the man who forged that particular trigger, we prepared to cross the river and dress our elk and hang it up. The day by this time was well nigh spent and we made what haste we could to reach camp. Hung up another deer on the trail. On reaching camp we horrified the boys when telling them of the amount of venison hung up; some 1500 pounds, but then 100 pounds of pemmican takes at least 600 pounds of fresh meat to make it.

Monday, March 17.—Cutting trail to bluff. Packing in the afternoon.

Tuesday, March 18.—Moved camp[73] to point of rock overlooking valley (Geyser). Will descend to the river in the morning.

Wednesday, March 19.—Packing from cache.

Thursday, March 20.—Capt. Barnes down stream visiting his old camp. The boys chopping a trail through young pine to the valley below.

A Log Cabin for Jack Crumback

Friday, March 21.—Capt. Barnes exploring the river toward the canyon below. The boys packing from Butte to camp. Left camp this morning to prospect the hills to the eastward. Ran across some fine sandstone and slate in place. At one of the creeks found the water heavily charged with lime. Leaving a deposit of pure lime from four to six inches deep. After supper cut four trees and laid foundation of log cabin for Jack Crumback.

Wonderful Growth of Bird's Eye Maple

Saturday, March 22.—Capt. Barnes crossed the river for a trip up Belle river canyon.[74] Sims accompanied me up the river to find the trail through brulle,[75] which I had seen in the distance yesterday. Crossing the river we found ourselves in a magnificent large river bottom, which we followed for some two miles, crossing to another fine flat comparatively clear. Timber in Geyser valley large. The upper end being covered by a wonderful growth of bird's eye maple.[76] Reaching the upper end of this we found a

123

---

73 "Camp 18 of the Press Party, for March 18–19, 1890, was at the Eagles Nest, a promontory on the east side of the Elwha River, 0.9 mile southeast of Whiskey Bend, at elevation 1275 feet, about 0.05 mile south of benchmark 1300 (Benchmark Rock). This campsite cannot have been at Elk Overlook promontory (about 1050 feet elevation), 0.5 mile southeast of Whiskey Bend, because: (a) Elk Overlook is not 'a ledge of rock overlooking Geyser Valley' and (b) on March 20, the Press Party descended from Eagles Nest directly to the floor of Geyser Valley in 'one hour.' These conditions correctly apply only to the true Eagles Nest, at or very near benchmark 1300." Majors, ed., *Northwest Discovery* 5 (Aug. 1984): p. 272.

74 "This is the first mention of the Press Party name 'Belle River' for Long Creek." Majors, ed., *Northwest Discovery* 5 (Aug. 1984): p. 274.

75 "*Brûlée* is a French term (the past participle of *bruler*, to burn) commonly used by French-Canadian traders and trappers to designate an area previously burned by a forest fire." Majors, ed., *Northwest Discovery* 5 (Aug. 1984): p. 274.

76 "This was undoubtedly big-leaf maple, a large deciduous tree that grows on river bottoms throughout the Olympics." Wood, *Across the Olympic Mountains*, p. 97.

river emerging from another great dark canyon.[77] Looking up this we could see a splendid falls. The river pouring over the ledges with a roar almost deafening. By this time it had begun to rain very heavily and in a few minutes we were saturated to the skin and when two hours had passed cowering under a rock, we thought camp was a much more comfortable place.

Making Pemmican

The boys today were occupied in drying the meat of the elk which we killed on the 16th inst.

Sunday, March 23.—The party attending to drying meat had most of it in condition for breading up in the manufacture of pemmican. The party, armed with butcher knives, attacked the carcass, cut the flesh clear from the bone. This meat is then dried on a rack built for the purpose and with the assistance of sun, air and fire, it is dried so it will break up easily. A large pot of liquid grease is ready and poured into the sack containing the dried meat, thus forming a compact mass. The Indians of the plains oft times introduce sundry condiments that are not always considered an improvement by the white man, but that is according to taste.

Monday, March 24.—Left camp this morning accompanied by Capt. Barnes and Hayes, to tackle the brulle and cut through if we cannot get round. Got through after a good deal of chopping and shoveling out the trail. Crossed and named the Lillian river;[78] camping for the night on a point near a great land slide.[79] Following up stream on the morning of the 25th we reached a point on the river some

twelve miles from camp in the valleys. Returned this evening, 25th, hungry as usual.

Some Excellent Fishing

Wednesday, March 26.—Sims, Crumback and Hayes, cutting trail through brulle at upper end of valley. Tried a cast in a lovely pool above camp and was happy to see a beauty rise to my first cast. Another twenty feet of line was run out and gently dropping a "Professor" and "Royal Coachman" beneath the shadow on the rock opposite, in a trice I had struck a fish. A fish which would fight, my first salmon trout on the Elwha. I landed him after five minutes of careful angling, the fish fighting to the end. Then followed one half hour of as fine fishing as any I ever enjoyed on the thousand streams I have had the pleasure of fishing in, carrying to camp fourteen splendid trout; weight about forty pounds; no mean basket from any water.[80]

Thursday, March 27.—Repairing in general. Cached several articles that are not considered necessary to take along.[81] Capt. Barnes out on hills hunting up bearing etc. He killed a deer and packed it home in the evening.

Friday, March 28.—Packed across river and cached there. Moved camp in the morning.[82] Caught another mess of beauties this evening. The river is fairly teeming with fish.

Saturday, March 29.—Capt. Barnes leaves for a trip up Belle river. Commenced moving toward the Brulle, where we have to camp[83] to make a trail for some two miles through desperate tough country. Made camp at a spring on bench, about 500 feet above river. Low rumbling noises,

---

[77] "Later called by them Convulsion Canyon, it is known today as the Grand Canyon of the Elwha." Wood, *Across the Olympic Mountains*, p. 97.

[78] "Lillian River is a genuine Press Party name, originating with the men of the expedition, and honoring a friend or relative of one of the men." Majors, ed., *Northwest Discovery* 5 (Aug. 1984): p. 274.

[79] "The reconnaissance camp of Christie, Barnes, and Hayes for March 24, 1890, was on the northeast side of the Elwha River, at about 1800 feet elevation, about 0.05 mile SSW of benchmark 1923." Majors, ed., *Northwest Discovery* 5 (Aug. 1984): p. 274.

[80] "This is the first reference to fishing in the Press Party narrative—one of Christie's favorite pastimes. One week earlier, 'fresh trout' is mentioned as being served on March 21 at the celebration over Crumback's land claim in Geyser Valley. The species of trout caught by Christie was rainbow/steelhead *Salmo gairdnerii*." Majors, ed., *Northwest Discovery* 5 (Aug. 1984): p. 275.

[81] "This was the first permanent cache of the Press Party. Christie's entry for March 28, 1890 . . . indicates that this cache was located on the south side of the Elwha River, immediately above the mouth of Long Creek, opposite camp 19. Nearly six months later, this Press Party cache in Geyser Valley was seen by the Jones party of prospectors: 'A little further on we came across their cache, where we found three sacks of something—apparently clothes—hung up, a pair of snowshoes and a pick and shovel. The two latter were not much the worse for wear.' This Long Creek cache was also seen by the Conrad/Olmstead party of prospectors in early July 1890: 'After an hour or two, as we emerge from the almost impenetrable jungle of a most precipitous gulch [Lost River], through which we had descended from the top of the mountain, we found ourselves upon a very distinctly and recently made trail. . . . We had no doubt now that we had struck the trail of the *Press* expedition, and after a mile or two more our conjectures were confirmed. We fell upon their cache [at Big Island Camp], and here I trust the gentlemen will pardon us, but honesty compels us to admit that never a sneak thief went through a private room with more celerity than we rifled those sacks, hoping against hope that we would find something to assuage the craving of empty stomachs, forgetful of the fact that it was not usual for expeditions of this character to embark with the commissary of a palace hotel. We were therefore somewhat disappointed when the quest produced nothing. Replacing everything carefully we again took up the trail, glad that we were once more upon a path that had been trod by our kind.' (A. D. Olmstead and John Conrad, 'They Found the Trail-A Party of Five Prospectors Return From the Olympics,' *Seattle Press*, July 16, 1890, p. 13, cols. 1–5.)" Majors, ed., *Northwest Discovery* 5 (Aug. 1984): p. 275.

[82] "Camp 20 of the Press Party, for March 28, 1890, was located on the northeast side of the Elwha River, about 0.25 mile northwest of the mouth of Idaho Creek. This was at or very near the Humes ranch." Majors, ed., *Northwest Discovery* 5 (Aug. 1984): p. 275.

[83] "Camp 21 of the Press Party, Brulle camp, for March 29 to April 2, 1890, was on the east side of the Elwha River, at about 1550 feet elevation, midway between Idaho Creek and Lillian River, about 0.15 mile southwest of benchmark 1600." Majors, ed., *Northwest Discovery* 5 (Aug. 1984): p. 284.

much like the sound of a geyser has been heard all day.[84]

Sunday, March 30.—Packing from cache below. The party suffering a good deal from dysentery.

Cutting Out a Trail

Monday, March 31.—Cutting a trail through brulle to Lillian river.

Tuesday, April 1.—Capt. Barnes returned from Belle river canyon. All hands packing to the Lillian river. I am quite ill today.

Wednesday, April 2.—Capt. Barnes and the boys made two trips to the cache at Lillian river, while I remained in camp and nursed myself.

Thursday, April 3.—Broke camp at daylight and packed to Lillian river, where we had lunch, built staging for cache, making everything snug, and headed again up the Elwha, with one hundred pounds on Dollie, the boys packing the camping outfit. Followed our trail, blazed a few days before and camped at Kate creek for the night.[85]

Friday, April 4.—Left Kate creek in the gray dawn. The first two miles, having crossed Jane creek, was very good traveling. If three feet of snow is considered an improvement, but on reaching Coldfeet creek we were confronted with a conundrum hard to solve. Dollie was suffering from skinned legs, and to take her on through snow such as we had passed meant sawing her legs off from the knees, and a good mule without legs is not worth much. Well on toward evening we met an-

CASCADE ON KATE CREEK.

"April 3 or 4, 1890. This stream is now known as Bowman Creek." (Majors, vol. 2, 142)

other mountain torrent, small but rough. We attempted to follow this creation of the devil toward the river, and after three hours' hard, tiresome work we climbed down into the river— a rough layout it looked, but before darkness overtook us and things looking comfortable, Dollie rather the worse for wear and tear and the rest of us pretty well played out.

Deep Snow Camp

Saturday, April 5.—All hands rather broke up. Making camp as comfortable as possible. Tried fishing, no luck.

Sunday, April 6, Deep Snow camp.—Moved camp[86]

125

---

[84] "These . . . 'noises,' . . . that the Press Party were to hear during the next few days in Geyser Valley, most likely were produced by the male Olympic ruffed grouse *Bonasa umbellus castanea.* During the mating season for this grouse, which had just begun, the male bird produces a drumming sound by rapidly beating his wings. However, it is inexplicable that such experienced outdoorsmen as the men of the Press Party could have made this mistake, particularly in view of the fact that the range of the ruffed grouse (a relatively common bird) extends almost entirely throughout Canada and into much of the northern United States. During his many years in Canada, Christie must have been familiar with, and likely even hunted, this common game bird. Ironically, judging from Barnes' entry for March 21, 1890, by this time (March 29) the Press Party had probably already dined on ruffed grouse, without recognizing it to be the source of the 'geyser' noises. There is no evidence that any men of the Press Party had ever visited Yellowstone National Park; they thus would have had no inkling of what a real geyser should have sounded like. At this time (1889–1890), Yellowstone was beginning to be the focus of a major publicity effort by the Northern Pacific Railroad in a effort to promote tourist travel to the Park. Some of the men of the Press Party may have read some promotional literature on Yellowstone, and could thus have learned about geysers." Majors, ed., *Northwest Discovery* 5 (Aug. 1984): p. 284.

[85] "Camp 22 of the Press Party, for April 3 and 10, 1890, was located at Kate [Bowman] Creek, probably on the northwest bank, at elevation 1500 feet, 0.25 mile from its confluence with the Elwha River. On either April 3 or 4, 1890, Barnes took the photograph from which the engraving 'Cascade on Kate Creek' [Bowman Creek] on page 10 of the newspaper was engraved." Majors, ed., *Northwest Discovery* 5 (Aug. 1984): p. 306.

[86] "Camp 24 of the Press Party, 'Big Island Camp,' for April 6–8, 11–13, and 16, 1890, was located on the east side of the Elwha River, probably on the north side of the mouth of Evergreen Creek (the stream between Wildrose and McCartney creeks). This was the site of permanent cache #2 of the Press Party. . . . It was also here, on April 17, that the Press Party shot a bear: 'The boys drying bears' meat.' Permanent cache #2 of the Press Party was seen by no less than three different parties of prospectors during the summer of 1890. The first of these was the Olmstead party of prospectors, who in early July 1890 journeyed from the head of the Dosewallips River to the Elwha River.

"On August 5, 1890, the remains of the Press Party cache at Big Island Camp, as well as the bones of the bear they had killed, were seen by the George A. Pratt party of prospectors: 'an old camp was found and a cache of Christy's party, where were signs of a bear having been killed. There camp was made [by us], the cache opened and some tea taken out. All the contents of the cache were found to be safe and undamaged' (George A. Pratt, 'Many Rich Mines. A Trip Through the Olympics Reveals Great Wealth,' *The Seattle Post-Intelligencer*, August 14, 1890, p. 5, cols. 1–2). For a number of years, George A. Pratt actively prospected the Snoqualmie Pass area. The Pratt River is named for him.

"In early September 1890, the R. Jones party of prospectors also came upon the Big Island Camp cache of the Press Party (R. Jones, 'A Trail That Is No Trail,' *The Seattle Post-Intelligencer*, September 30, 1890, p.9, cols. 3–4). Jones' account first appeared in *The Daily Reveille* (Whatcom), but no specimens of this particular issue have survived. 'A little further on we came across their cache, where we found three sacks of something—apparently clothes—hung up, a pair of snowshoes and a pick and shovel. The two latter were not the much the worse for wear.'

"Until now, the Pratt and Jones accounts of the prospecting parties of 1890 have been totally unknown to all historians and scholars of the Olympic Mountains and the Press Party." Majors, ed., *Northwest Discovery* 5 (Aug. 1984): p. 307.

to head of Big Island. Dike drove large buck elk into camp. As all hands were busy at the time he got away Scott free. Rained very heavy last night.

Monday, April 7, Big Island camp.—Hunting, but no game at night. No signs of any in the vicinity.

Tuesday, April 8, Big Island camp.—Hunting, and today's hunt means meat or go back to the cache for grub. Crumback and Hayes took the hills to the northeast in quest of deer, while Capt. Barnes and myself took the river bottom up stream for elk. About one mile and a half from camp we espied an elk lying on the hill side and enjoying the sunshine. Backing into cover we proceeded to kill that elk in the most approved fashion. Worked and sneaked around a full half hour, only to find that the elk had been dead for the last month or two—starvation in the deep snow. Whilst here examining the bed of a slough in which there was a great amount of float quartz of a very fine quality, walking along with a rustle in the brush, and looked up in time to see an elk disappearing in the thicket. Rushing up the bank in hopes of getting a shot, we found ourselves in a small flat, evidently a rendezvous for elk and deer, as the ground was literally plowed up with their hoofs. Whilst examining the signs, all that were left we were surprised to see a grand looking elk march from the willows into full view on a gravel bar some four hundred yards upstream, presenting a fair mark; we fired at him but missed him I think. Took another shot as he broke for the brush which had the effect only of making him run all the faster. Being short of grub I was compelled to make for Lillian cache for supplies. Taking the river bank in preference to another experience on the mountain, we found the first three miles was hard traveling.

An Elk Waiting to Be Shot

After lunch I went ahead hoping to get a shot, the other boys having left their rifles in camp while packing. I had well nigh reached the great land slide when I was overtaken by Capt. Barnes who informed me that an elk was back on the trail waiting to get shot. No further inducement was necessary to send me back on a run, some mile and a half, when I came in sight of the mule quietly munching her

favorite Oregon grape, the boys sitting in a row struggling with the dogs to keep them quiet, and making signs to attract my attention to the elk. There, sure enough, was a two year old elk gazing straight at the boys not 50 yards from where they sat in full view. I put a ball through her, and all hands were made happy at the prospect of liver and bacon for supper. While the boys were dressing the carcass, Capt. Barnes got a shot at a small band which was making uphill and killed a doe. Arrived at Lillian river toward evening.

Thursday, April 10, Lillian river.—Packed all supplies in two trips as far as Kate's creek.[87]

Friday, April 11, Kate creek.—Packed load to end of large bottom, returning to Kate creek, and packed to camp above island.

Saturday, April 12, Big Island Camp.—Packed cache from lower end of bottom to camp.

Rich Looking Float Rock

Sunday, April 13, Big Island Camp.—Packed again, another stage upstream. Below Thunder Canyon[88] was rather hard on Dollie, owing to the snow being crusted and heavy. After a scramble through a small vine maple swamp we reached the first bench, and found better traveling up some distance on an old elk trail. We finally camped near the river bank.[89] Seeing the boys settling camp, I took my rifle and started upstream for a hunt, and found that the snow by no means diminished. As I advanced, following the bank of the river, I found great quantities of good looking float rock, which gives promise of something rich in the hills.

Killing a Big Bull Elk

Struck fresh elk signs on entering the bush; following these for a short distance I saw a bunch of willows, which gave promise of game. Made a half circle to the left and on gaining the bank again I was pleased to see a grand bull elk break for the river. Allowing him to gain the opposite shore I dropped him in his tracks, and felt happy in the knowledge of having bacon and liver for supper once more.

Monday, April 14 [means 15th].—Broke camp this

[87] "In one trip, each man could normally pack 50 pounds (250 pounds total), while Dollie could carry 150–200 pounds (see *Northwest Discovery* 2, Feb. 1981: p. 130; the maximum per man was 75 pounds), making a grand total of 400–500 pounds per trip. Thus, the two packing trips on April 10, in which 'all supplies' were packed to Kate [Bowman] Creek, indicate that the total food, equipment, and supplies of the Press Party at this point came to 800 pounds. This figure is in agreement with Barnes' comment on April 3 that 'the [total] weight of this outfit was about 800 pounds'—consisting of 'over 400 pounds' of food/provisions, and nearly 400 pounds of equipment." Majors, ed., *Northwest Discovery* 5 (Sept. 1984): p. 309.

[88] "This canyon is located about a mile below the present day Elkhorn Ranger Station." Wood, *Across the Olympic Mountains*, p. 126.

[89] "Camp 26 of the Press Party, for April 14, 1890, was located on the east side of the Elwha River, probably at the mouth of Stony Creek." Majors, ed., *Northwest Discovery* 5 (Sept. 1984): p. 309.

morning and made tracks for the other side of the river,[90] just below gravel slide. We found good traveling on the south side of the river for a couple of miles and splendid bench and timber second to none. Having made camp[91] in the valley the boys returned to pack up the elk, and I started upstream to prospect. Obtained a magnificent view to the east, showing mountain peaks and open valleys.[92]

Press Valley Camp

Tuesday, April 15 [means 16th].—Left camp at daylight this morning to return to Island camp for stores. Forded the river with great difficulty; five feet deep. Bad weather prevented our return, and we had to remain below without blankets and with no meat, some limb of Satan having carried off our cache of deer hams[93] —cougars, I thought from the tracks.

Wednesday, April 16 [means 17th], Big Island Camp.—Overhaul camp and cached about 200 pounds of material.[94] The balance made one good heavy load of about 75 pounds to the man.[95] Reached Press Valley camp in the evening.

Friday, April 18, Press Valley Camp.—The boys drying bear's meat.[96] Capt. Barnes and myself hunting up specimens and examining the formation of the country in vicinity of camp. Semple Plateau was particularly interesting as showing every evidence of having been a favorite resort of original inhabitants. Crossing the plateau we scrambled up a ridge of outcropping sandstone to small bench above.

Saturday, April 19, Press Valley Camp.—Capt. Barnes, Crumback and I started this morning with three days' provisions and explored a trail through what we thought would be a good pass to the southwest. Following along the crest of a ridge on central plateau we reached the gallery by the same route followed yesterday. We reached an elevation of some 1200 feet.[97] There we had a good view up the canyon. Returned to camp.

Trip Up Goldie River

Monday, April 21, Press Valley.—Sent the boys on ahead with pack up the Goldie river as far as they could find decent traveling. Capt. Barnes and I left camp to go over as much as possible of Press valley. Our trail lay through the usual good timber across Semple plateau. Striking Goldie river about a mile from the mouth, we felled a large tree across and found some lovely alder spots partially bare of snow. We made good traveling and for eight hours continuous travel we found nothing but splendid soil through the valley, covered with incomparable timber and comparatively clear of brush.[98]

127

---

[90] "The Press Party forded the Elwha River at a point 0.3 mile SSE of the mouth of Stony Creek, where a bluff comes down to the east side of the river between benchmark 1397 and the Drum cabin. As a consequence, the Press Party failed to discover Lost River." Majors, ed., *Northwest Discovery* 5 (Sept. 1984): p. 318.

[91] "Camp 27 of the Press Party, 'Press Valley Camp' or Semple Plateau camp, for April 15, and 17–20, 1890, was located on the west side of the Elwha River, 0.8 mile north of the mouth of Goldie River, 0.25 mile west of the Elwha River, at elevation 1600 feet, just north of the Semple Plateau." Majors, ed., *Northwest Discovery* 5 (Sept. 1984): p. 318.

[92] "This is the only reference in the Press Party narratives to an apparent photograph taken by Christie. The 'view to the east' would have been east and southeast up the valley of Lost River to McCartney Peak, Cameron Peak, Lost Peak, and perhaps Mount Clay Wood." Majors, ed., *Northwest Discovery* 5 (Sept. 1984): p. 318.

[93] "This was elk (not deer) meat. The elk in question (which the cougar(s) ran off with) was that killed on April 14, which the men 'skinned and dressed the meat and hung him up' on April 15 at camp 26." Majors, ed., *Northwest Discovery* 5 (Sept. 1984): p. 318.

[94] "This, permanent cache #2 of the Press Party, was located at camp 24 'Big Island Camp,' at the mouth of Evergreen Creek." Majors, ed., *Northwest Discovery* 5 (Sept. 1984): p. 318.

[95] "This is the maximum pack load per man carried by the Press Party. The normal pack load for the men was fifty pounds. (See *Northwest Discovery* 2, Feb. 1981: p. 130.)" Majors, ed., *Northwest Discovery* 5 (Sept. 1984): p. 318.

[96] "No mention is made of when or how the 'bear' was killed. This is the first reference to a bear kill that appears in the Press Party narratives. However, this incident is confirmed by the George A. Pratt party of prospectors, who on August 5, 1890 visited the site of this Press Party camp and cache and noted the presence of 'a cache [#2] of Christy's party, where were signs of a bear having been killed.' The bear was probably killed on April 17 at camp 24 (at the mouth of Evergreen Creek), and the meat was then packed on April 18 to camp where it was dried." Majors, ed., *Northwest Discovery* 5 (Sept. 1984): p. 319.

[97] "This is likely a typographical error for '2200 feet,' since Barnes remarks that they reached a point some '2300 feet above camp.' Even Barnes' figure is not correct, for the true elevation difference is 4153 feet." Majors, ed., *Northwest Discovery* 5 (Sept. 1984): p. 319.

[98] "On April 21, 1890, Christie and Barnes ascended the Elwha River along its west side to a point 0.7 mile northwest of the mouth of Hayes River. Christie speaks of 'traveling . . . for eight hours continual travel,' but this refers to the round trip time, in order to perform and complete the trip during daylight hours. The Press Trail description mentions 'A few of our blazes will be found running up the [west side of Press] valley several miles above Semple Plateau . . . after the plateau is left two miles behind the valley is as level and open as possible.' Barnes is more specific, and states that 'We traveled about three miles up the [Press] valley' (actually 2.4 miles from camp 27). They reached a point 0.8 mile northwest of the mouth of Hayes River, where a bluff forced them down to the bank of the Elwha River. At this point, the massive east slope of Mount Dana still effectively blocks any view to the southwest, and thus the deception is conveyed that the course of the upper Elwha River (*id est*, Godkin Creek) continues due south. Above the confluence of the Hayes River, however, the southwest curve of the upper Elwha River becomes apparent.

"It is interesting to note that this same limit point, the mouth of the Hayes River, was probably that reached in August 1885 by H. Hawgood of the first O'Neil expedition, during his solo ascent of the Elwha River, from the mouth of the Lillian River to the mouth of Hayes River. As for the section of the Elwha River between the Low Divide and the mouth of Hayes River, this had been descended prior to the Press Party by the Sherburn party of prospectors in July 1889. Thus it was not until April 21, 1890, that the Press Party, by beginning their journey up the Goldie River, were now, for the first time, venturing into territory which had never before been visited by European man." Majors, ed., *Northwest Discovery* 5 (Sept. 1984): p. 336.

Retracing our steps, we camped[99] with the boys on a mountain stream entering Goldie river several miles from its mouth.

Good-Bye to Dollie

Tuesday, April 22.—The last day's travel of mule Dollie in our company. Poor Dollie has done her duty faithfully and well to the point, and where it becomes impossible to take her a mile further she fairly gave up. Played out. The boys left her on the track and have no doubt but that with fair luck she well be fat and fresh at the end of the month.

Wednesday, April 23, Goldie river canyon.—Packed this morning to fork on Goldie river.[100] Was compelled to ford the stream several times, breast high. Passed several beautiful water falls, traveling hard and disagreeable. Suffering from the old complaint of dysentery.

Goldie River Canyon

Thursday, April 24.—Work telling upon the boys, so have promised them every fourth day as Sunday. They lay over for a rest today. I left camp to get a look at the country ahead, if possible. I found it rough traveling all through, and was compelled to return to camp, having gained no definite knowledge of the route.

Friday, April 25, Goldie River Canyon.—Sent the boys ahead with Capt. Barnes with pack to make a cache above great snow slide. As I wanted a day off I remained in camp, selecting what I can possibly spare from the pack.

Saturday, April 26, Goldie River Canyon.—Had another dress parade of stores and camp outfit this morning. Cached quite a number of articles which I think I can dispense with.[101] Our trail lay along the river bank, which at best was hard work getting through. The snow was very deep, and overhanging drifts in many places made our journey rather precarious and kept us always on the alert for chances of a slide. Crawling up one spur to clamber down on the other side kept us engaged all day.

On arriving at a good looking place for a camp[102] I went

ADELENE CASCADE.

"April 26, 1890. This and the preceding [snow bridge] photograph [see pg. 78] were taken along the Goldie River. In the newspaper, this engraving was mistakenly printed upside down." (Majors, vol. 2, 143)

on ahead on a scout for a pass. About two hours from camp I discovered what I took for a good low pass through the hills. I reported to the boys, making them happy.

An Awe Inspiring Avalanche

Sunday, April 27, Goldie River Canyon.—Crumback and Hayes returned for two packs left at last camp. The rest of us packed up to what I believe will be an easy route to the summit. After crossing the Goldie we commenced an ascent and we found it quite steep enough by the time we reached the top of an old land slide. While resting we were surprised to see an immense body of snow begin to move from the summit of the mountain directly opposite our perch. A rumbling noise was heard soon to be swollen into a perfect hurricane of sound as the mass gained in volume and speed. The whole face of the mountain seemed to be in motion. But a very short interval before this enormous compact of snow met the line of timber, and the scene that followed beggars all description.

Any attempt to describe an avalanche in motion such as we saw is a task to which no language of which I am the master could do justice. Magnificently grand and inspiring

---

[99] "Camp 28 of the Press Party, Louise Creek camp, for April 21, 1890, was located on the north side of the Goldie River and on the east side of Louise Creek, probably at the confluence of Goldie River with Louise Creek. From here on, the Press Party would make relatively rapid progress, usually spending only one or two nights at a given campsite, and reaching Lake Quinault on May 19." Majors, ed., *Northwest Discovery* 5 (Sept. 1984): p. 336.

[100] "Camp 30 of the Press Party, for April 23–25, 1890, was located on the southeast side of the Goldie River, 1.65 miles southeast of Mount Scott, at the confluence of the south/east 'fork.' This south/east fork of the Goldie River is the stream that drains the northeast side of Mount Barnes [Wilder 5928'] and the west side of Mount Dana. This is also the site of permanent cache #3 of the Press Party: 'A lot of bullets, a frying pan, two axes, a pickaxe, the large kettle and several other articles went over the fence. Some old clothes were discarded.' The Press Party may have even left their shotgun and one of their rifles here (or at permanent cache #4 farther upstream)." Majors, ed., *Northwest Discovery* 5 (Sept. 1984): p. 337.

[101] "It is now apparent that the situation of the Press Party has become serious. It is now the source of some concern among the men. . . . Game was non-existent after entering the Goldie River valley; the mule had been abandoned; the snow was getting deeper; the terrain was becoming rougher; and most, if not all, the men were suffering from 'dysentery.' The men were becoming so exhausted that they had to rest every fourth day. The decision on April 25 (and April 30) to discard a number of superfluous items indicates that the Press Party now wished to complete the expedition and reach civilization as soon as possible." Majors, ed., *Northwest Discovery* 5 (Sept. 1984): p. 337.

[102] "Camp 31 of the Press Party, 'Lucky Camp,' was located on the north side of the Goldie River, on the west side of Lucky Creek, the stream that drains the west and southwest side of Mount Scott." Majors, ed., *Northwest Discovery* 5 (Sept. 1984): p. 338.

are but weak terms in which to describe the scene of awful destruction which lay outspread at our feet. This immense body of matter lay spread out in the valley of the Goldie river completely concealing it from view for the length of half a mile. Snow, ice, rocks and trees broken and twisted in every conceivable manner, piled high in one conglomerate mass. On the conclusion of the infernal din we found our tongues to exclaim, "Thank God that we were not on that side of the river!" Resuming our packs we held our way up the face of the mountain until arriving at a small spot just a trifle leveler than the balance of the side hill. We cached our packs[103] and returned to camp, where the other boys had arrived before us.

Adieu to Goldie River

Monday, April 28, Goldie River canyon.—Daylight found the boys arranging their packs for another trip up hill. Crossing the Goldie river we bade it an affectionate adieu, hoping to be across the divide in another three days. We struck up hill on our tracks of yesterday, and after many rests made the cache. The boys made fire and we had lunch. Tackling the side hill again pipes were filled up, (by the way tobacco is running short as well as bacon), during the afternoon we managed to make about a mile and a half, halting on finding a comfortable camp, lots of dry wood and about seven feet of snow.

Tuesday, April 29.—Crumback, Sims and Hayes returned to camp for what articles were left. Barnes and I ascended a peak to settle the question of the southern watershed.

We started on our way towards the great peak[104] on our right[105] which we had made up our minds to ascend. Following the ridge we found good traveling until we reached the steep sides of the crater, where our work really commenced. An hour's hard climbing brought us to a small ledge and the knowledge that we were both might hungry. Rustling a fire

MOUNT SEATTLE AND THE HEAD OF THE QUINAIULT RIVER LOOKING SOUTHWEST.

"April 29, 1890. This photograph was taken by Barnes from the Table Top (5049), looking over snow covered Deception Divide (4600-4700) in the foreground. The multi-peaked massif of Mount Christie (6177) lies to the left, with the Low Divide (3600-3700) in the center, and Mount Seattle (6246) on the right. Through the gap of the Low Divide, distant Mount Grady (5401, 'Mount Lawson') is visible." (Majors, vol. 2, 146)

of small twigs we soon had our kettle on, and but few minutes elapsed ere we were enjoying a cup of our fast going tea. Our lunch of dried elk meat and gillettes[106] was soon a thing of the past. Snowshoes arranged and once more on the way; as we neared the top we found the face of the mountain to become steeper at every step, and I am perfectly satisfied that the last 500 feet was done at an angle of fully 85 degrees— just about as steep climbing as there is any use for.[107]

After some more difficult climbing, we attained a height that permitted us to see what we had been longing for—the Quinaiult. It was about ten miles distant. Grand mountain peaks surrounded us. It was simply a grand, unequaled spectacle of mountain scenery.

129

---

[103] "This temporary cache was located at about 3100 feet elevation, close to 0.7 mile northwest of the summit of Low Mountain 4654'." Majors, ed., *Northwest Discovery* 5 (Sept. 1984): p. 338.

[104] "This . . . is the original Mount Barnes 5928' of the Press Party. In later years, a misreading of the Press Party map and narrative has resulted in the erroneous shifting of the name Mount Barnes to peak 5993, 2.8 miles to the northwest, and the renaming of the original Mount Barnes as 'Mount Wilder.' The true identity of the original Mount Barnes 5928', which had been totally unknown to all previous historians and scholars of the Olympic Mountains and the Press Party, was first revealed in Harry M. Majors, *Nomenclature of the Press Party* (Seattle: unpublished typescript, 1959), p. 6: 'The Mt. Barnes of the Press Party is illustrated [on Barnes' published map] as being east of Deception Divide in the crook of the upper Elwha River. This description fits perfectly Mt. Wilder, thus there can be no doubt as to the present day location [of the original Mount Barnes 5928'].'" Majors, ed., *Northwest Discovery* 5 (Sept. 1984): p. 362.

[105] "The term 'right' is relative. When, looking southeast from camp 32, to the 4100–4200 foot saddle between Low Mountain 4654' and Mount Barnes [Wilder 5928'], directly up the route taken by Christie and Barnes on April 29, Mount Barnes [Wilder] is indeed 'on our right.'" Majors, ed., *Northwest Discovery* 5 (Sept. 1984): p. 362.

[106] "Barnes' entry for April 3 describes gillettes: we made thin cakes of flour and water, unleavened, and baked them in frying pans. These are familiarly known as 'gillettes.'" Majors, ed., *Northwest Discovery* 5 (Sept. 1984): p. 362.

[107] "Here, as elsewhere on the expedition, the explorers were guilty of pardonable hyperbole. Except for cornices and similar structures, snow slopes seldom exceed an inclination of 50 degrees. Barnes' and Christie's exaggeration is understandable, however. Even experienced snow and ice climbers sometimes have the feeling that a 45-degree slope approaches the vertical, particularly if the slope is exposed. And a snow slope greater than 50 degrees almost brushes the climber's chin. The snow slope of the May 1st photograph, 'Side of Mountain,' has a 40 degree inclination." Wood, *Across the Olympic Mountains*, p. 149.

Only Ten Days' Grub

Wednesday, April 30, Mount Barnes.[108]—From the lookout ahead I determined that the packing should be as light as possible from this point. Overhauling provisions, I found that I had but ten days' provisions in camp; ordered all blankets, with exception of a single blanket for each man, to be cached with all surplus clothing, and otherwise reduced packs as much as possible, making a single pack for each member from this point.[109]

Thursday, May 1.—Struck camp this morning at daybreak. After some of the toughest kind of mountain climbing[110] we pitched camp[111] on a flat rock on the mountain side.

Ravines Increase the Distance

Friday, May 2, Mount Barnes.—Started from our rock perch at dawn this morning and as the snow was in first-class condition we made good traveling across the shoulder of the mountain. On rounding a low spur we found that the divide which we had journeyed to reach but two miles distant, but ravines necessitated a good six miles[112] of tough travel to

reach. Six hours of this work brought us to the divide. On reaching the crest of this packs were thrown off and the boys scattered in search of points from which they could gain a glimpse of the water flowing some two thousand feet below us. The glasses were brought to our aid and we were rather surprised to find the river running north instead of to the south, a disagreeable discovery which gave rise to sundry hard expressions not usually found in Webster, but quite excusable under the circumstances.

Barnes took a number of views while lunch was being prepared.

Press Valley

Saturday, May 3.—Resting in camp. Hayes hunting down stream. Self up stream looking up practicable trail towards summit of divide, some five miles southwest.

Sunday, May 4.—Made another break for the divide this morning. We arrived at the base of Mount Christie[113] and began again to climb for the divide, using boots instead of snowshoes.

"Homeward Bound Again"

After lunch we faced the music again. Another 500 or 600 feet of very hard climbing left us at the foot of what ap-

PEAK OF MOUNT BARNES FROM ONE OF ITS NORTHREN SPURS.

"April 29, 1890. This photograph was probably taken by Barnes from a point near Table Top." (Majors, vol. 2, 146)

GLIMPSE OF THE MOUNTAINS.

"May 4, 1890. The identity of this view is uncertain. It may depict Mount Dana and the upper Press Valley from the Low Divide." (Majors, vol. 2, 147)

---

[108] "These are the only two references to 'Mount Barnes' that appear in the Press Party narratives. The original Mount Barnes 5928' is also depicted and identified as such on Barnes' map, as well as on two engravings appearing in the newspaper. As such used and designated, the Press Party unquestionably applied the term Mount Barnes to peak 5928' (now named Mount Wilder)." Majors, ed., *Northwest Discovery* 5 (Sept. 1984): p. 363.

[109] "Vestiges of this cache might still be found by a lucky 'explorer' today. This is a remote, seldom-visited area. The exact spot of the cache may not have known the tread of a man's foot since 1890." Wood, *Across the Olympic Mountains*, p. 154.

[110] "As will be seen by comparison with Barnes' detailed entry, Christie's succinct journal doesn't even begin to adequately describe the ordeal of this day." Majors, ed., *Northwest Discovery* 5 (Sept. 1984): p. 363.

[111] "Camp 33 of the Press Party, 'Slide Rock Camp,' for May 1, 1890, was located on the northwest ridge of Mount Barnes [Wilder 5928'], 0.7 mile WNW of the summit, at elevation 4450 feet. This was at timberline, where the men could obtain firewood. This site has the distinction of being the highest camp of the entire Press Party expedition (except for Barnes' reconnaissance camp of May 5 and 6, 1890 at 5000 feet on Mount Seattle)." Majors, ed., *Northwest Discovery* 5 (Sept. 1984): p. 363.

[112] "Throughout their narrative reports, both Barnes and Christie nearly always overestimate distances, in some instances by factors from two to six." Majors, ed., *Northwest Discovery* 5 (Sept. 1984): p. 363.

[113] "This is the first and only reference to Mount Christie in the Press Party narratives." Majors, ed., *Northwest Discovery* 5 (Oct. 1984): p. 396.

THE FIRST GLIMPSE OF THE QUINAIULT.

"May 5, 1890. This view has not been identified with certainty. It likely was taken from the Low Divide looking southwest, with a spur from Mount Christie on the left." (Majors, vol. 2, 147)

MOUNT FRAZIER.

"May 6, 1890, pages 6 and 2. The flank of the higher southern summit of Mount Seattle (6246) appears at the left edge of the photograph with the upper valley of Seattle Creek on the right. Relatively insignificant Mount Frazier (5428) rises above the upper valley of Seattle Creek. In the far distance, the Kimta Peak (5399) group marks the horizon." (Majors, vol. 2, 148)

peared an impassable ledge of rock.[114] Some little exploring discovered a gap up which it seemed possible to climb, climbed to the summit of this, some 50 feet, and lowered hand line to raise pack and assist the boys. This operation was repeated some five times in all, as we found the summit was only to be reached by rope in this manner. Sundown found us on top, and I felt rather happy. All hands present for supper (flour soup), after a rather dangerous afternoon's work. Whilst the party prepared camp on a small ledge of rock,[115] I went ahead to assure myself that we were at last upon the Quinaiult. This I found as I had fondly hoped, returned and made the boys happy by the news, "Homeward bound again."

Monday, May 5.—Started from camp this morning at daybreak. Crossed Lakes Mary and Margaret, headwaters respectively of the Elwha and Quinaiult rivers.[116] Dogs scared up a fine, big, black bear which was secured and increased our stores at a critical point.[117]

Tuesday, May 6.—Barnes ascended to the summit of Mount Barnes and the rest of the boys attended to the meat.

Another Bear Hunt.

Wednesday, May 7.—In camp at the summit. The boys attending meat and drying hides. I had another bear hunt this forenoon, but had no luck. Capt. Barnes returned to camp this evening with the scalp of a fine full grown bear he killed on his trip to the summit.[118] Just after supper we were called out by Hayes for another bear hunt. A fine large fellow crossing the valley just above camp. Sent the boys after him and after a short scrimmage the bear sought refuge from them up a large tree, only to be brought down in a few seconds by well directed shots from the guns of Capt. Barnes and Crumback.

Thursday, May 8.—Spent forenoon in tanning the bear skins. Started in afternoon and made good progress down the mountain along the Quinaiult.[119]

Some Wonderful Canyons

Friday, May 9.—Continued our course down stream this morning,[120] side hill work for most of the day. Shinning old

131

---

[114] "At this point, the Press Party have crossed a concealed fault line, and have entered the Western Olympic Lithic Assemblage. The present trail up the northeast side of the Low Divide follows at or very near the same route taken by the Press Party in May 1890." Majors, ed., *Northwest Discovery* 5 (Oct. 1984): p. 396.

[115] "Camp 35 of the Press Party, 'Bluff Top Camp,' for May 4, 1890, was located . . . at elevation 3500 feet, 0.15 miles SSE of Lake Mary." Majors, ed., *Northwest Discovery* 5 (Oct. 1984): p. 396.

[116] "In reality, both lakes drain into the Elwha River. The Press Party were led into this error because at this time of year the outlet of Lake Margaret was hidden beneath snow." Majors, ed., *Northwest Discovery* 5 (Oct. 1984): p. 396.

[117] "In one terse sentence, Christie glosses over perhaps the single most important event of the entire expedition—the killing of the bear that saved the party from starvation." Majors, ed., *Northwest Discovery* 5 (Oct. 1984): p. 397.

[118] "Barnes, however, does not mention his shooting a bear in his journal entries for his Mount Seattle trip. Note also the discrepancy in Christie's journal entry for May 8." Majors, ed., *Northwest Discovery* 5 (Oct. 1984): p. 397.

[119] "Christie's entry does not agree with that of Barnes for this same day. Of the two, Barnes' entry is probably the correct one: the men did not move camp on May 8, but instead remained at the Low Divide due to rain. Christie may have written these entries at a later date, thus accounting for the discrepancy. This also indicates that Christie and Barnes did not collaborate with each other during the final preparation of their respective journals for publication after the arrival back at Seattle." Majors, ed., *Northwest Discovery* 5 (Oct. 1984): p. 398.

[120] "Barnes is more correct on this point, when he states that the party did not depart from camp until noon." Majors, ed., *Northwest Discovery* 5 (Oct. 1984): p. 410.

VIEW FROM THE WATERSHED, LOOKING EAST ACROSS PRESS VALLEY.

"May 4, 1890. This view was probably taken from the Low Divide, depicting Mount Norton in the distance." (Majors, vol. 2, 147)

GREAT SLIDE ON SIDE OF MOUNT GRADY.

"May 10, 1890. This is the true Mount Grady (5401), not 'Mt. Lawson' as has been termed erroneously in the past. This photograph was taken at a point about ¼ mile below the mouth of Geoduck Creek. The timberless swath of the rockslide is apparent in aerial photographs of this site taken in 1939." (Majors, vol. 2, 156)

logs or scrambling across rocks, which was hard on both back and knees, owing to the fact that the strata as a rule is standing on end; we found little or no good traveling. Saw some wonderful canyons and hard looking water. The river seems to be but one continuous long waterfall.

Signs of Richness in Minerals

Saturday, May 10.—Packs were slung bright and early this morning. We are headed once more for Lake Quinaiult. We made a couple of bridges and here found traces of ancient Indian life. The wash in the river shows a richness that bodes well for the hills.

Sunday, May 11.—This, without doubt, was the most dangerous day we have had for a month. Wet above, below and all around us. Another day of hard canyon and hill side work found us toward evening on a large river bottom, where we camped for the night. Hunted out toward the southwest

in hopes of seeing another bear, but returned to camp in the evening without meat.

Monday, May 12.—Packing as usual, down the west bank of the Quinaiult. Fine timber.

Camped Alongside an Elk

Tuesday, May 13.—Meat being rather short we were astir at dawn with the intention of making a record. Whilst preparing my pack I was surprised to hear the snort of an elk. A cautioning hush to the boys brought them on the ground. They seized the dogs to keep them silent. I grabbed my gun and on a short scout around saw a large buck elk stalk into view on the other side of the river. A couple of shots dropped him, and we had fresh meat again.[121] Cut two large trees for bridges, and moved camp[122] to the other side of the river alongside our game.

Wednesday, May 14.—Yesterday and today we were traveling through a magnificent country so far as timber and soil is concerned.

---

[121] "This was the first elk killed since that of April 21 at Semple Plateau, as well as the first fresh meat since the bear kill of May 7 at the Low Divide." Majors, ed., *Northwest Discovery* 5 (Oct. 1984): p. 412.

[122] "Camp 41 of the Press Party, for May 13–14, 1890, was located on the northeast side of the North Fork Quinault River, opposite the mouth of Wild Rose Creek, and directly opposite camp 40. This was also the site of permanent cache #5 of the Press Party. Ten weeks later, on July 29 and 30, 1890, the remains of the Press Party camps for May 12 and May 13–14 were found by the Pratt party of prospectors: 'Two camps of the Christy party were found by Messrs. [Theodore H.] Thompson and [Ira] Crawford, and the next day [July 30] Mr. Pratt joined them and found at one of the camps indications that the explorers had killed an elk there and devoured it in the eagerness of semi-starvation. There also they found a cache in which were 250 40-65 Winchester cartridges and a pair of snowshoes.' This cache, permanent cache #5, is of particular interest, in that it is mentioned by neither Christie nor Barnes. A year later, during the summer of 1891, William B. Wiser ('William Marsh,' formerly with the O'Neil expedition of 1890), encountered several Press Party items at this cache: [Wiser/Marsh] tells of the finding of the snowshoes, ammunition and rifles left by the Press expedition on the North Fork [of the Quinault River], past which he traveled (William B. Wiser ['William Marsh'], 'In From Quinault,' *Seattle Press-Times*, August 11, 1891, p. 6, col. 3)." Majors, ed., *Northwest Discovery* 5 (Oct. 1984): p. 412.

Pushing on Toward the Lake

Friday, May 16.—An early start was made this morning from camp as all hands were desirous of seeing Lake Quinaiult, and judging from the lay of the country ahead we cannot be far from it. Our course lay through a magnificent valley some two miles in length by one and one-half in width. On leaving this land we had some very fair travel on the bars with some rather hard side hill travel below. Crossing a river, which enters the Quinaiult above the island, Capt. Barnes took several views of the river and mountainous vicinity.

Saturday, May 17.—Another hard day's work through timber. Shot an eagle for Capt. Barnes.

A Man in Sight

Sunday, May 18.—Having rested, the ideas advanced by the boys pressed upon me—to build a raft. I was fain to give way for various reasons. We were getting rather short of grub; we were now almost naked. The continued hard work and travel which the party had undergone, backed by the fact that we were traveling or rather forcing our way along the bank of a magnificent stream, tended towards the making up of my mind to build a raft with which to reach the lake. On reaching a gravel beach some six miles below the east fork, dry wood being handy, I determined to collect timber and launch a raft at the point. Whilst chopping tim-

ANTRIM AND HIS GUIDES.

"May 18, 1890. This photograph was the last to be taken by Barnes prior to the loss of the camera in the Quinault River that same day. The view depicts three men in a canoe: Frederick S. Antrim of Aberdeen, his Quinault Indian guide Willie, and another Quinault Indian guide. Antrim is the central, seated, figure in the canoe, as the canoe was propelled by the two Indians." (Majors, vol. 2, 156)

ber on the bar we were startled by a shout from Crumback, that there was a man on the bar.[123] Sure enough, on the opposite side of the river a man was seen, half hidden in the willows.

We waved signals, and just saved ourselves from being shot, as they had mistaken us for an elk. On introducing ourselves to Mr. Antrim, we were soon plying him with questions varying from the grave to the gay. Suddenly the question of tobacco was brought forward, and to our horror we found that our angel was no smoker, but the Indian Willie immediately produced his plug, which he generously divided with us, Mr. Antrim kindly supplying us with a brewing of coffee, which was refreshing indeed. On making inquiry from the Indian we were assured that we could reach the lake all right by raft. Capt. Barnes took a photograph of the canoe. On completing our raft we stepped on board and put out into the stream, all going merrily for the first one and one-half miles, but soon after I was horrified to see the river gather into a narrow swift rapid channel and at a mad rate of speed the whole river rushed under a drift.[124]

The Shipwreck

We made an effort to save the raft and our packs, but there was little chance to do so, traveling at the rate of ten miles an hour. As the raft struck she was sucked down and an immense wave swept everything away. Capt. Barnes clung manfully to his records and as I hastily glanced at him over my shoulder I thought I saw the last of him, but he struggled ashore all right.

Saved From Drowning

Chris Hayes had been thrown into the water, and was now in a very dangerous position, being sucked under the drift and jammed by the raft. Giving him assistance to regain his feet upon the logs, and seeing that Crumback and Sims had succeeded in reaching the drift pile in safety, I turned my attention to Capt. Barnes, who was in a rather dangerous position. Climbing to a piece of timber about 50 yards below where we had struck and about midstream with the drift pile still menacing him below. After some hard work I succeed in turning the raft adrift and steering it towards Capt. Barnes, but he rather preferred to strike out and swim than run the risk of being struck by the raft. He succeeded in

133

---

[123] "This historic site, where the Press Party met Frederick S. Antrim—the first person they had encountered since departing from the William D. MacDonald cabin on the lower Elwha River on March 10—was located on the north side of the Quinault River, 0.5 mile above/ESE of the mouth of Fletcher Creek, at a point midway between Bunch and Fletcher creeks. Antrim was not a local pioneer settler of the Quinault River, but instead a resident of Aberdeen, who was out on a hunting excursion with two Quinault Indian guides." Majors, ed., *Northwest Discovery* 5 (Oct. 1984): p. 424.

[124] "This . . . is the bend in the Quinault River in the west half of section 26, located 0.9 mile WNW of the mouth of Fletcher Creek. . . ." Majors, ed., *Northwest Discovery* 5 (Oct. 1984): p. 424.

THE PRESS EXPLORERS UPON THEIR RETURN.

"May 21, 1890. This is the final group photograph of the Press Party, taken at Aberdeen by the professional photographer C.K. Pratsch, before the men visited 'the barbers.' This engraving is slightly different from the surviving photograph [see p. 158]." (Majors, vol. 2, 156)

gaining the bank some three hundred yards below and as I swept past him I was happy to see that he was safe, but evidently exhausted from his terrible fight with the river. Turning the raft I returned to assist him in spreading out his records and charts, saved by his exertion and at a very imminent risk of his life. We are indebted to his grit and pluck for preserving the records of our winter's work within the charmed circle of Olympus.

Mr. Antrim and his guides returned and rescued us next day and we then approached civilization once more. The trip home was uneventful except that the people at Aberdeen and especially Mr. Antrim were very considerate of our feeling. They did all they could to entertain us and took us to the homes where we enjoyed once more, "white folks food." The whole party were delighted when they reached home after nearly six months of rough work and wild adventure.

James H. Christie

CHAPTER FOUR.
GEOLOGY AND NATURAL HISTORY

GEOLOGY OF THE OLYMPICS.[1]

Observations Made by the Press Explorers

The Formation Is Slate and Sandstone—The Conditions Show the Olympics to Be the Youngest of the American Family of Mountains—Verical Stratification.

The coast strip and the foothills are basaltic in formation. Upon the Elwha this formation extends to the base of Olympus, including the two mountain ranges north of it. We observed here no rock in place other than basalt or trap. The formation then abruptly changes, and from and including Olympus southward, the formation is slate, sandstone, gravel and marl. Occasional dikes of trap were observed, but these were rare. Granite in place[2] was seen but once—on Belle river, high up the mountain side. The beds of several small streams were found encrusted with lime deposits, indicating lime rock or marble, but the rock itself was not seen.[3]

The stratification is much tilted and distorted. The inclination varies from the perpendicular to 45°. Between 70° and 85° are the most common angles. Less than 45° is very rare. The "strike" is, in most canyons, at right angles to the course of the river. The strata being set on edge, one of these canyons is therefore a geological panorama. Stratum succeeds stratum like books arranged upon a shelf. Any one of the canyons upon the Elwha is a paradise for the geologist or prospector. Nature can hide no secrets from him.

The most striking geological charcteristic of the Olympic mountains is the newness of their upheaval. This fact is evident on every hand. The sharp, jagged ranges, their unworn sides, the eater courses, the cascades and many other features all indicate that these mountains are the youngest of the American family of mountains.

The vertical stratification gives an extremely sharp outline to the ranges. Many of them have an outline like the teeth of a saw. From this saw-tooth edge there are frequently sheer

perpendicular precipices of from 1000 to 2000 feet of naked rock. Where the sides are less precipitous they are torn and broken beyond description. The effects of frost, and the wearing of the elements is conspicuously absent, indicating recent upheaval. The beds of the streams, even of the larger ones are but little worn. Deep canyons are frequent on the rivers, but these are fissures which the streams have followed and washed out.

In an old upheaval, or even in one comparatively recent composed of strata so nearly on edge, but few or no cascades would be expected. Yet in these mountains cascades are frequent, many of them plunging over soft slate rocks. The three illustrations given of waterfalls are all of this character. A recent geological period must therefore be assigned to the making of these mountains.

The following extract from the geological field notes will give an idea of the nature of the canyons in more detail. The canyon lies north of Geyser valley.

Rocks at Lower End of Goblin Canyon

Rocks at lower end of Goblin canyon are slate and sandstone, veined with quartz. The strata are distorted in every conceivable fashion, bending and folding back and forth. Thickness of slate layers from that of writing paper to six or seven inches. Some if it gritty; other, not grit. Hardness variable; steak white; easy cleaveage; color, black. Layers of sandstone are intermixed with the layers of slate in about equal proportion. Color streaked gray and red, very hard, texture fine, cleavage moderate.

The rocks on west side of canyon do not conform to those on east side, being almost at right angles to the other in dip and strike, those on the west side being less distorted than those on the east. East side, dip 75° to 85° east, strike north and south (true). West side, dip 75° to 85° west, strike east-southeast and west-southwest (true).

Quartz veins run through the rock very thickly. Thickness of a hair to one inch; color, white; hard. Direction of canyon, northwest to southeast. The sides of the canyon rise

135

---

[1] Charles A. Barnes, *Seattle Press*, July 16, 1890.

[2] "This is an impossibility, as nowhere in the Olympic Mountains is bedrock granite (referred to by Barnes as 'granite in place') exposed. What Barnes most likely observed was metamorphic schist of the Elwha Lithic Assemblage, which an untrained person might mistake for 'granite.'" Majors, ed., *Northwest Discovery* 5 (Aug. 1984): p. 285.

[3] "The rock at this point (Geyser Valley) consists of the Grand Valley Lithic Assemblage, a series of sandstones, siltstones, and slates. Occasionally present are small units or pods of silty marble, which would account for the 'lime' observed by Christie and Barnes, probably in Antelope Creek." Majors, ed., *Northwest Discovery* 5 (Aug. 1984): p. 273.

at an angle of about 75° several hundred feet, covered for the most part with soil and vegetation, from mosses to trees.

On each side of the canyon along the benches nothing was observed but sandstone and slate in place, with and without veins of quartz, principally without. Some coarse granite boulders, evidently glacial.[4] The walls of the canyon are perpendicular in places, where they are composed of rock. At other places the strata is of hard clay or gravelly clay, and the angle approaches 75°. There is, however, little of the clay walls. Chiefly slate and sandstone. Walls of canyon are from 500 to 1000 feet high. At the upper end of canyon formation is like that at lower end, but with less sandstone.

Two geysers were noted in the mountains. They are referred to in the main narrative.

The form of many of the peaks is that of a crater, but investigation invariably destroyed the theory. The peculiar shape of many of the peaks is due to the odd and fantastic breaks of the vertical strata. Indeed the fact of the vertical strata is alone sufficient to demolish the crater theory. Absence of lava or any volcanic matter except trap is one of the characteristics of the country gone through by the *Press* expedition.

Two geysers were heard in the mountains, but time did not permit any systematic search for them. The first was heard in Geyser valley, and is described in the narrative of the expedition. The second was heard in Quinaiult valley, from every point between Crumback river and the lake. The reports are about ten minutes apart, and it seems to be in action for several hours daily. Owing to the unfortunate disaster on the river, no record was kept of it.

Charles A. Barnes

FOUND IN THE OLYMPICS[5]

A Resume of the Natural Resources of Explored Region

The Kinds and Sizes of Trees Found—Good Timber on the Elwha—No Large Areas of Grass Country—Large Quantities of Berries—The Mountains Alive With Elk—Beaver and Fishers Numerous and Also the Big Black Bear—The Mineral Wealth of the Mountains.

Besides the two little lakes upon the height of land, Lakes Mary and Margaret, three large lakes of importance to the state are shown on the map, two of which are for the first time correctly placed upon the map.

Lake Quinaiult is shown upon the maps issued by the United States land office as extending nearly north and south, with the outlet on the western side.[6] It was found by the *Press* expedition to extend nearly at right angles to the direction given, and to have its outlet at about the middle of the southern side. It is between six and seven miles long, and two miles wide, having an area of about 12 square miles.

For the map of Lake Crescent we are indebted to a recent survey by the Port Crescent Land Company,[7] which is now published for the first time. This lake is not shown on any other map. In length it is about 12 miles, with an average width on one mile, giving it an area of about three square miles.[8] It is almost entirely surrounded by mountains. There is a small amount of bottom land on its eastern side, all settled. It empties into the straits by the Lyre river.

Lake Sutherland[9] is situated in Indian valley one mile east of Lake Crescent. It is two miles long and one and one-

136

---

[4] "These are likely glacial erratics brought down by the continental glacier from British Columbia. Within 10,000 to 18,000 years ago, a lobe of this massive ice sheet filled the Strait of Juan de Fuca and extended part way up the lowermost Elwha Valley. The Elwha River was dammed, thus forming ancient Lake Elwha. As fragments of glacial ice broke off from the edge of the glacier and floated on Lake Elwha, these ice fragments eventually melted and the granite rocks or boulders they contained sank to the bottom of the lake. These remain to this day as glacial erratics in the Elwha Valley." Majors, ed., *Northwest Discovery* 5 (Aug. 1984): p. 248.

[5] Charles A. Barnes, *Seattle Press*, July 16, 1890.

[6] "The fallacy of a north-south trending Lake Quinault (with an outlet on the middle of its western side) is a geographical misconception that was introduced on the 1862 U.S. General Land Office *Map of Washington Territory*. This error would persist through the 1883 map, but was corrected on the 1887 map." Majors, ed., *Northwest Discovery* 5 (Oct. 1984): p. 433.

[7] "More properly, this would be the Port Crescent Improvement Company, a land promotion corporation that in 1889 had purchased the townsite of Port Crescent on the Strait of Juan de Fuca, and were seeking to develop their land. One of the land speculation schemes of this corporation was an attempt to make Port Crescent a railroad terminus, and toward this end they hoped to promote a railroad route that would lead from Port Crescent to Lake Crescent, down the Soleduck River to the present site of Forks, and from thence southward across the Hoh and Queets rivers to eventually connect with a branch line of the Northern Pacific Railroad at Grays Harbor. This explains their interest in Lake Crescent, and why they had a survey made of the shoreline of that lake. See Jervis Russell, *Jimmy Come Lately, History of Clallam County* (Port Angeles and Port Orchard: Clallam County Historical Society, 1971), pp. 377–79." Majors, ed., *Northwest Discovery* 2 (Mar. 1981): p. 186.

[8] "The true surface area of Lake Crescent is 5127 acres, or nearly eight square miles. Barnes is correct in his assertion that this marks the first published appearance of Lake Crescent on a map, for although 'L. Sutherland' and the 'Lyre R.' appear on the 1889 U.S. General Land Office map of the *State of Washington*, Lake Crescent is conspicuously absent. Lake Crescent was discovered about 1865 by two fur trappers from Vancouver Island, John Sutherland (1841–date unknown) and John Everett (1831–date unknown), who settled on Freshwater Bay about 1863. The lake was named probably in 1889 by the Lake Crescent Improvement Company, not from the shape of the lake, but after nearby Port Crescent on Crescent Bay." Majors, ed., *Northwest Discovery* 2 (Mar. 1981): p. 186.

[9] "Lake Sutherland was also discovered about 1865 by the two fur trappers John Sutherland and John Everett, one of whom it honors." Majors, ed., *Northwest Discovery* 2 (Mar. 1981): p. 186.

half miles wide, and empties by Indian creek into the Elwha river. All of these lakes teem with fish, and during the proper season their surface is alive with waterfowl.

The mountains, as a whole, are well timbered. Hemlock, fir, spruce, cedar and pine are the chief varieties. On the Elwha there is but little straight-grained cedar above Goblin canyon, west of Mount Brown, about 1500 feet elevation. In the interior of the mountains much cedar is found of large size at an elevation between 3000 and 4000 feet. Fir, spruce and balsam clothe the mountain sides in general to 4000 feet. Above that the mountains are either bare or the timber is the hardy, close-grained varieties of fir. In Press valley is much white and yellow pine.[10]

The timber on the Elwha is generally good and sound, and will average as high as any timber in Washington. Four to five million feet to the quarter section is the average. In one place timber was observed which would run as high as 20,000,000 feet. The trees were medium size, very tall and straight, and perfectly healthy. There are several miles of this. There is enough lumber to justify considerable expense in getting it out. The most practicable way would be a flume down the river canyons.

On the Quinaiult river the timber is equally good as far up as Alexander river. About the lake the timber is unsurpassed. Above Alexander the timber is poor. It grows to a large size, but is rotten, conchy,[11] and crooked. The river could be cleared at slight expense, and logs driven with ease from as high as the head of Chester valley at all seasons of the year. The Elwha, it is thought, cannot be driven on account of the nature of its canyons.

There is no grass in these mountains, except some little on the lower Elwha upon old burnt mountain sides. The "bunch grass country" here is a myth. Oregon grape and ground laurel furnish an excellent substitute for grass for the use of animals while packing. They relish it, and if not worked too hard will keep in good condition. There is everywhere as abundance of it.

The mountains are full of berries. The salmon berry, the raspberry and blackberries and cranberries are also found in great quantities. In some parts the kinnikinick berry grows abundantly, and furnishes the chief food of the numerous bears.

The mountains are alive with elk, and for the most time very tame. Some bands, however, having been out upon the foothills, and having probably been chased, are more wild. Deer are also plentiful. One goat was seen by the party. Grouse, pheasant and chicken are undoubtedly plentiful, although we saw few, owing to the severity of the season.

Beaver and fisher are numerous on the Quinaiult. Black bear are plentiful during the proper season. We saw one track of a cinnamon bear on the Goldie river. The cougar, or mountain lion, are numerous. We frequently saw their tracks, but never the animal himself. The gray wolf and the wildcat are common.

The Mineral Wealth

Gold and Silver are Both Found in the Olympics

The unprecedented severity of the weather prevented much prospecting. The valleys and mountain sides were covered with snow. It was only occasionally that prospecting could be done.

There is no gold in the Elwha river where panned. Upwards of a dozen bars were washed without getting a color. Promising looking quartz was found in places but without gold. The float rock in the stream looks promising. For silver, however, the prospects are better. Silver was actually found in a ledge of rock, and indications of silver were often seen. On the upper Quinaiult silver was found but no gold. The sand in this river we had no opportunity to prospect. Below Lake Quinaiult the river is frequently bordered by gravel banks which it would pay to prospect. Oxide of iron was seen on both sides of the mountains.

No coal was found either upon the Elwha or the Quinaiult. The stratification is so inclined that even if it were found its value would be doubtful.

Galena was found in the silver rock. There were no traces found of copper or of tin. Silver seems to be the metal of the Olympics. A ledge of silver bearing rock was discovered four feet thick.[12] All the specimens from this ledge, except one, were lost in the shipwreck on the Quinaiult. The country will pay to prospect.

See article on the geological formation.

C. A. Barnes

137

---

[10] "Ponderosa pine is not at all common in the Olympic Peninsula, for this species prefers drier, well-drained areas. Several specimens grow in the vicinity of Lake Crescent and near Sequim. I suspect that the Press Party is in error here, for they frequently misuse the terms 'fir', 'spruce', and 'pine.'" Majors, ed., *Northwest Discovery* 5 (Sept. 1984): p. 318.

[11] "What is meant here is that the wood fractures or splits in a whorl-like or conchoidal (shell-like) manner, due to spiral growth or excessive knots." Majors, ed., *Northwest Discovery* 5 (Oct. 1984): p. 424.

[12] "The location of this supposed 'silver' deposit is uncertain. There are no known silver deposits along the Elwha River. What Barnes might possibly be referring to is the outcrop of Tertiary basalt (Tb) in the Needles-Graywolf Lithic Assemblage (Tnmu) at Windy Arm (Lake Mills). Mineralized contact zones are occasionally present at such sites." Majors, ed., *Northwest Discovery* 5 (Sept. 1984): p. 309.

CHAPTER FIVE.
THE RETURN OF THE PRESS EXPEDITION

Even before the explorers of the Press Party returned, the Alpine Club of Portland prepared to mount its own expedition into the Olympics. Lieutenant Joseph P. O'Neil had led an Army exploring excursion into the Olympics in 1885 and now, five years later, had gotten the Army to approve of a joint venture with the Oregon Alpine Club, of which he was secretary, for another exploring expedition. A cadre of enlisted men, a dozen mules, equipment, and other support would be provided by the Army, while the Alpine Club would supply the civilian scientists for the civilian/military joint effort. If the Press Expedition had not been in the mountains in the spring of 1890, the O'Neil Expedition would have been first. A contemporary report of the arrival of the Press Party at Aberdeen was not generally available until Northwest Discovery *published a reprint from the* Spokane Falls Review *(May 30, 1890)of an article that appeared first in the* Aberdeen Semi-Weekly Bulletin *(May 25, 1890). Harry Majors, editor and publisher of* Northwest Discovery, *surmises that the original article was most likely written by Frank H. Owen, owner and editor of the* Aberdeen Bulletin, *following an interview with Frederick S. Antrim, although the record neither supports nor disputes this conjecture. Antrim was the Aberdeen resident who was intercepted by the Press Party on the Quinault River, but he was not immediately at hand when their raft went to disaster in the log jam. The first two-thirds of the article were pure fabrication by the author of the piece, but the last part, describing the raft wreck on the Quinault, could only have been obtained from someone close at hand when it happened. It is through this newspaper interview with Antrim (if indeed it was him and not one of the Press Party) that this account of what happened in the raft wreck is available by way of papers in Spokane and Portland. No copies of the* Bulletin *have survived. The following articles either anticipate the return of the Press Party or report that event and set the stage for the O'Neil Expedition, then about to get underway.*

THE ALPINE CLUB OF PORTLAND[1]

The Alpine club of Portland, assisted by Gen. Gibbon, is actively preparing for its expedition into the Olympics. The action is timely. The early return of the Press exploring party is expected. The gentlemen composing that party have been in the Olympic range for several months, and it may be taken for granted that they have made a careful, thorough and intelligent exploration of the hitherto unknown region which has awakened so much romantic interest. It is probable that the Press party will emerge from their long exploration before the Alpine explorers are ready to set out. The information they will bring is eagerly awaited. It will give the world accurate knowledge of the characteristics and resources of the vast extent of country which has hitherto been no man's land, and will serve as a guide and map for the succeeding explorers. The Alpine party will, no doubt, faithfully and intelligently follow up these pioneer explorations, and their researches will make an interesting second chapter to the story of the Press exploration.—Press.

AN UNKNOWN LAND NO LONGER[2]

The explorers, says the *Seattle Press*, have returned from their long examination of the hitherto mysterious region of the Olympic range, and are now in Seattle. The result of their arduous and indefatigable researches will be given to the world in the columns of that paper without delay, and will prove of absorbing interest to many thousands of people.

The explorers did their work thoroughly. The unusual severity of the winter months delayed and hindered them materially, but they persevered with the courage and resolution of true pathfinders until their task was completed.

In some respects they have been destroyers of illusions. They found no wild and warlike tribes of dreadful savages, such as had been told about by the romancers. Their story will be a very interesting narrative of the actual condition of the extensive region now for the first time made known to the world, and will describe its advantages and merits.

The explorers made a topographical map of the country, took photographs and sketches of various natural features and made extensive notes of their travels and observations. These notes and illustrations will be reproduced in the above mentioned paper.

The timber and mineral resources, the botanical characteristics, agricultural possibility, the game, the grand scenery, and all the general features of the region will be de-

[1] Author unknown, *Mason County Journal* [Shelton], May 23, 1890. Reprinted from the *Seattle Press*.
[2] Author unknown, *Daily Progress* [Anacortes], May 27, 1890.

138

scribed. The narrative will be so ample as to give all a good idea of the whole Olympic region.

The *Press* congratulates the gentlemen comprising the exploring party, and incidentally itself, upon the success of the expedition. The value of the work to the entire state will be very great. The extensive range of country so long suffered to remain in the realms of doubt and darkness, is now thrown open. Ere long it will be entered by hundreds of adventurous spirits, and homes and settlements will spring up. The Olympic region will be added to the productive territory of the state, and will increase the grand total of development and prosperity.

IN THE OLYMPICS[3]

Return of a Brave Band of Explorers

Six Months in Wilderness

A Story of Hardship and Privation—Perilous Ride on a Raft

As the shades of night were falling Tuesday [May 20] a few people who happened near the wharf at the foot of H Street were surprised, not to say startled, by the appearance of five human beings clothed in tattered garments, bare-headed except [for] a strip of handkerchief or other cloth around their foreheads, dusty, unkempt beard and flowing hair like wild men of the woods. They were sunburned and tanned as by long exposure, and no feverish gold hunter of '49 could have presented a more utter absence of the outward civilization of man than did these strangers. Following them were three shaggy dogs such as might have trained with the Esquimaux or dragged the sledge of Arctic explorers. As quietly as they came these strange beings sought refuge from public gaze in one of our hotels, declining to talk or say who or what they were, and conducting themselves as though they knew their business and proposed to attend to it.

The following morning a *Bulletin* representative, who had noted their coming and believing they were returning from a prospecting and exploring expedition in a part of our state little known, sought an interview with their leader. This was granted, but proved of small avail, except that the men readily disclosed their identity and the nature of the voyage from which they had just returned. Having other sources of information [Frederick S. Antrim], however, ye scribe proceeded to learn something of their experience and of the country they had traversed.

Exploring the Olympics

The Olympic Mountains are a short range of precipitous, jagged, broken hills and peaks occupying a greater portion of that country north of Gray's Harbor basin between the Pacific Ocean, Puget Sound and the Straits of Fuca. But little of the land has been surveyed or settled, and with the exception of a rim a few miles wide near the water's edge, the country, its inhabitants, resources and characteristics [are] as little known to the general public as is the heart of Africa. Occasionally some venturesome spirit would wander back into its almost impenetrable fastnesses and returning tell of magnificent forests, verdant table lands and a soil rich in productive capacity, as well as coal and precious minerals, but his story would be merely an echo against the cliff of indifference and would soon be forgotten and lost in the whirr and clash of townsite booms, wild speculation and clamor of money getting.

But last fall a company of enterprising, patriotic and generous men, headed by Mr. Bailey, of the *Seattle Press*, conceived the idea of sending out an exploring party to see and know, and thereby publish to all the world what there was hid from civilization in these mountain reaches. In pursuance to this object they organized an exploring party, placing at the head Captain C. A. Barnes, a scientific gentleman long employed in geodetic survey and other similar work by the United States government. As first assistant he had Mr. J. H. Christie, who as hunter, trapper, guide and scout has traversed almost every uninhabited part of the North American continent, and long ago became famous for his skill as a woodsman and intrepidity and bravery in all kinds of peril. The others of the party were J. W. Sims, J. H. Crumback, and C. O. Hays [sic], tried and true men, selected for their fitness for the work before them.

Leaving Port Angeles the last of November [sic] they followed up the Elwha River and bade adieu to the haunts of the white man. To the left [right, west] was Mount Olympus,

Hoary and Majestic,

whose lofty top glistened with the eternal snow that made it seem almost like a beacon light at the harbor bar; north of Olympus could be seen Mount Constance [sic], silent and

139

---

[3] Author unknown, *Spokane Falls Review*, May 30, 1890. Reprinted from the *Aberdeen Semi-Weekly Bulletin*, May 25, 1890. Also in the *Oregonian* [Portland], June 3, 1890.

grim like a watchful sentinel, while further [*sic*] on lifting their heads above this jagged range were other peaks like soldiers in line of battle, as if guarding this unknown region from the intrusion of man.

Our adventurers had counted on an open winter, such as had preceded the last one, but were doomed to disappointment and consequent privation, as only a few days out they were met by a severe snow storm, followed by heavy rains and sleet. Some forty miles up the Elwha River, which is a precipitous stream flowing from a considerable altitude they emerged on to great table lands on which was but little timber, the soil of which was deep, rich and fertile, and produced wonderful growths of native grass and herbs. No trace of the white man's presence was visible, but Indians were frequently seen. These are "to the manor born," have lived there so long that the memory of the oldest of them knoweth not to the contrary, and many of them had never before seen a pale face. They were the stoical sort of North American natives, kind and willing to aid the strangers; guns they had, but war seemed an unknown occupation, and their living was gained principally by hunting and fishing, their agriculture being of the scantiest and crudest sort.

Striking southwesterly the explorers were soon lost in the impenetrable forest that clothes in evergreen the western slope of the Olympic range and from this time until Quinault Lake was reached they scarcely saw a human being and never a white man. By this time they realized something of their situation. Soon their flour and provisions were either devoured or ruined by the constant exposure to the elements, and their only subsistence was the wild game killed with their guns and the fish caught in the streams. Happily game was plentiful and easily killed, the wild animals seeming scarcely to be startled at the approach of man. Elk, deer and bear were met with in great numbers. Of the latter they met

A New Species

unknown elsewhere—an animal larger than the ordinary black bear with an almost red coat of short hair; a timid creature when first approached but ferocious and fierce when angered. The black Canada grouse were quite plentiful, but their flesh tasted quite strongly of spruce buds, on which they seemed to live. There was also much small game.

Careful examinations of the soil and the earth formation were made as the explorers proceeded. Good coal was found in many places, also iron, silver and lead, of which they saved many specimens. Perhaps the most important mineral discovery was the lead and silver, which was plentiful and quite rich, and when its quality is made known to the world will cause a sensation.

The hillsides and mountains almost up to the snow line were covered with timber all along the western coast, with dense underbrush in the valleys. The principal growth is spruce, fir, hemlock and cedar. Of the latter there was much of the yellow cedar, the most valuable finishing wood in the Northwest.

The winter was not so dry and open as the explorers had hoped for, yet it lacked much of the severity experienced in Puget Sound basin, or these brave men must have perished. Their garments were reduced almost to tatters, their hats were gone entirely and their shoes almost worn from their feet. They had long ago cast off their extra luggage, and were now struggling more to save life till Gray's Harbor could be reached than to explore the country. Not only had no white men been seen for months, but no Indian had a home or lodging place in this vast wilderness. Go back they could not, and their only hope was to push on to the southward. This was easier said than done. While their compasses pointed the way to keep it was well nigh impossible. Streams of water would be followed for a time only to see them disappear in the earth or under piles of drift or underbrush so dense that even the dogs would lose their way; the surface of the earth was torn and broken as if it had at some time been heaved up by a mighty volcano and settled back in dire confusion. To keep a straight course they could not, and it was often necessary to travel many miles to gain a point only a short distance ahead. But health and strength held out, no serious accidents occurred until they reached a stream, which they rightly judged to be the upper Quinault. This they followed down, and while in camp were overjoyed to see a canoe containing a white man and two Indians approaching. This welcome party proved to be Fred Antrim of Aberdeen, and his guides, who was [*sic*] out on tour for his own amusement. Henry M. Stanley, after years of submergence in the wilds of Africa, could not have been greeted with more joy than was Mr. Antrim received. After the first greeting was over, and inquiry made as to what the explorers were most in need of, the unanimous acclaim was—tobacco! In all his life Antrim had never chewed tobacco, yet by some strange guidance he had taken a pound plug of this great comforter with him[4] and soon produced it. Joy reigned unconfined.

---

[4] Probably for his two Indian guides.

Here the explorers had determined to build a raft and rest their travel-worn feet by floating to the lake on the primitive structure. Both Antrim and his Indian guides warned them that the river was too treacherous for such a venture, but the men seemed to have endured the privations of tramping the pathless forests so long that they could not be persuaded to give it up, and so, loading their traps on the frail structure, pushed off, the Aberdeen party going up as they went down.

Disaster

Soon these adventurous spirits saw that the warning was timely. They had entered on a rapid-running section of the stream, where its waters were confined to a narrow passage by encroaching hills, and by a sharp bend the force of the current drove the raft violently against a drift. Before they struck the men realized their peril and prepared to save their lives. Captain Barnes instantly resolved that the records of their trip should not be lost except he was, and taking a pack containing hundreds of photographic views and his notes and memoranda he leaped far out into the stream, hoping to reach the opposite [south] shore and thus keep from being sucked under the drift. In this he was successful, but lodged against a steep point where he almost succumbed before [being] rescued. The others jumped onto the drift safely except one man [Hayes], who fell in the stream, but managed to grasp a log, to which he clung until Captain Christie, at the risk of his own life, drew him from the water. This was the most difficult and dangerous feat, as the entire current of the rapid stream went under the drift at railroad speed and held the man [Hayes] under the water with such force as to almost take off his clothing. No lives were lost in this catastrophe, but all the personal effects except the one pack saved by Captain Barnes went to destruction. Now, indeed, they were anxious to return to civilization, and were soon overtaken by Mr. Antrim on his return and piloted safely to the Quinault agency, and then to Aberdeen, where they were furnished new clothing and other necessaries of life and comfort, and after two days' rest returned to Seattle. A full account of their wanderings, experiences, what they saw and discovered will be printed by the *Seattle Press*.

Thirty-six years after James Christie returned from the long winter trek of the Press Exploring Expedition, he had some final comments on the expedition and his experiences. Responding to a request from Edmond S. Meany for some comments on the expedition for The Mountaineer Annual *of 1926, he reviewed the trip in the light of the passage of decades of time. In 1890 Meany was a member of the Seattle Press staff and closely associated with the expedition. At the time of his request for Christie's comments, he was a professor at the University of Washington and president of The Mountaineers, a Seattle outdoor club that is still in existence.*

FROM THE LEADER OF THE PRESS EXPEDITION[5]

Vernon, B.C., November 23, 1926
Professor Edmond S. Meany,
Department of History, University of Washington
Seattle, Washington

Dear Friend Meany:
I have yours of the 17th, a request to jog my memory of the original Press Expedition through the then mysterious Olympic Mountains, the reputed home of a tribe of cannibals.[6] May I say that amongst the pleasantest of these memories was the meeting with yourself and others who were kindness itself to the stranger who had arrived amongst you.

At that time I had just returned from three years' travel and exploration through the Peace and McKenzie River districts, was then en route to Africa, remaining over on a short visit to old friends at North Yakima. Here at Yakima I first learned of the mystery of the Olympics. I met Christopher O'Connell Hays, a grandson of the great Dan O'Connell, the Irish Liberator.

Chris called my attention to a magazine article[7] expressing the opinion that a wild tribe of cannibal Indians lived within the Olympic Ranges, that rose so beautiful, so mystical and grand, just across the narrow Sound fronting your then rising port and city of Seattle.

I wrote to the "Press Times"[8] quoting my opinion as

141

---

[5] James H. Christie, *The Mountaineer Annual* 19 (1926): pp. 37–39.

[6] "The wild tales about cannibals in the Olympics may have stemmed, in part at least, from two incidents which occurred more than a century earlier. In 1775 Juan de la Bodega y Quadra landed a party of men at the mouth of the Hoh River to obtain fresh water and fuel. They were promptly killed by Indians. Twelve years later, in 1787, Charles William Barkley, commander of an East India Company ship, also sent a party ashore for fresh water at the same location, and his men met a similar fate at the hands of the natives residing along the coast." Wood, *Across the Olympic Mountains*, p. 203.

[7] This article was no doubt the reprint of Territorial Governor Eugene Semple's "The Olympic Mountains," which first appeared in his annual report for 1888, then as "In the Olympics: Return of a Brave Band of Explorers," *Spokane Falls Review*, May 30, 1888, then appeared with the report of the Press Expedition in the July 16, 1890, issue of the *Seattle Press*. Still later it appeared in the *West Shore* 14 (Aug. 1888): pp. 428–29. *West Shore* was a widely distributed periodical in the 1880s and '90s featuring life on the West Coast but particularly in Washington and Oregon.

[8] Christie wrote to the *Seattle Press*. The *Seattle Press-Times* did not come into being until February 1891, when the *Press* merged with the *Seattle Daily Times*.

against the possibility of the existence of this fierce tribe. Some discussion followed in the "Press" when I think Friend Meany, City Editor,[9] queried "Would I go see?"

I replied that I would, that I was on my way to Seattle with three friends, O'Connell Hays, Jack Sims, and Jack Crumlack[10], also, Bud and Tweed, bear dogs of quality.

Arriving at Seattle, we were met by Mr. Meany, City Editor of the "Press," were introduced to Mr. W.E. Bailey and friends, had one afternoon with Lieutenant Sawatka,[11] comparing notes regarding best methods of packing, making pemmican, etc., etc.

I received carte-blanche from Mr. Bailey for expenses and all equipment, and made a trip to Port Angeles for the purpose of examining the Elwha River. I was assured by the mayor,[12] that I would have water to spare for a eight-inch draft light scow for thirty miles up stream. This gentleman was certainly inspired, which caused some trouble and the delay of building a useless boat.

We were received by the settlers with much curiosity, but every kindness was shown and every assistance given as far as settlement then extended up stream.

Some twelve miles in from Angeles we adopted the old and reliable method of transport, pack straps. At this point we were sorry to part with Dr. Runnals who had to give up the trip on account of his wife's illness.

We packed, two packs a day, as far as convenient, starting next morning with packs of personal belongings to a day's packing beyond the previous day's pack. So we carried on till a base camp was formed some twenty-five or thirty miles up from Angeles. From this point several side trips were undertaken by Captain Barnes and myself in different directions with one packer accompanying.

These trips were really observation trips that a fair opinion of wild life in those wonderful mountains could be formed. On these trips Captain Barnes, the accredited historian of the party, collected some very interesting data for his Journal.

When changing camps as a rule I explored alone, without dogs, the route to be followed the next day. One

day on a quiet and slow scouting up stream some three miles from camp I arrived at a point where a fair sized stream came in from the west. Here I heard a peculiar, muffled sound. Listen and strain as I would, I could not determine the what or why of it. It was something. But what? A trifle uncertain I examined my gun, moved back from the water some fifty feet to a large boulder. Here I squatted to await a solution of the mystery. Tense and still as the rock I sat under, my eyes searching to the upper reaches of the river in view, at times I was conscious of the thought intruding, "Well is there some ground for a mysterious tribe?" A full half hour had passed without a movement, when from over my right shoulder came the distinct splash of a rock thrown into the stream.

Slowly, very slowly, my head turned toward the sound, when my eyes presently caught the form of a magnificent bull elk head up, standing mid-stream gazing full at me, not a hundred paces distant. He held me in gaze for some time. He moved slowly, cautiously testing the air which was in my favor. He slanted down and across the branch. Here he again held me in gaze for a full minute, when he moved on across the main stream, reaching my side of the river, some one hundred and fifty yards up from my resting place. Here he turned, head up, looked back from whence he came, giving a low gasp or cough and finishing by stamping the water.

Scarce had he struck the water the second time when a very torrent of elk poured down from the bench above the junction of the streams. Elk of all ages, bulls, cows, yearlings and calves, a truly magnificent sight this, a herd of fully three hundred had passed. When some ten or twelve splendid specimens brought up the rear and almost the last, a splendid head, had reached the bank of the stream, my promise to get some fresh meat for camp occurred to my mind. Slowly I raised my rifle to fire, as slowly let the muzzle drop again; another long look, and the gun was dropped to the crook of my arm. I returned to camp to tell the boys I had no fresh meat for them, the why of it I kept to myself.

The day following we had meat to spare. Numerous large

---

[9] At the time of the Press Expedition, the City Editor of the *Seattle Press* was John G. Egan. Edmond S. Meany was the treasurer of the Press Publishing Company and assistant editor of the paper.

[10] Time diminished the preciseness of Christie's memory. "Hays" spelled his name Hayes, and "Crumlack" was John H. Crumback.

[11] "Frederick Schwatka (1849–1892), a former cavalry lieutenant in the United States Army, gained a moderate degree of fame as an explorer of Arctic America during the late Nineteenth Century. In 1892, Schwatka was considering a visit to Mount Rainier with Frederick G. Plummer—a venture to be sponsored by the Tacoma Commercial Club to promote the creation of a Mount Rainier national park—but the project failed to materialize, and Schwatka died soon thereafter on November 2, 1892, at Portland, Oregon." Majors, ed., *Northwest Discovery* 2 (Feb. 1981): pp. 105–106.

[12] "This . . . was almost certainly Norman R. Smith, who at this time was acting in the capacity of unofficial mayor of the town. Some six months later, in June 1890, John Dyke (1842–date unknown) officially became the town's first legal mayor. After Dyke's brief term, Norman Smith again served as mayor of Port Angeles during 1891–1892. By way of coincidence, it was also largely due to information provided by Norman Smith in 1885 that Joseph P. O'Neil selected a route that led him into the Olympic Mountains south of Port Angeles directly via Yennis Creek." Majors, ed., *Northwest Discovery* 2 (Feb. 1981): p. 128.

bands were met with. Thus shooting when necessary, fishing, and packing, we held on our way to the summits. Across the summits the boys had their first bear hunt which they enjoyed. Then on down the western water shed, we had some experience with a raft. On the Quinault, a wreck and a rescue of the trip's records brought us again under our pack straps. A few days later we sighted a cruising party from Gray's Harbor, two Indians with canoe with Mr._____[13] from the mills at Aberdeen. Here was spice and variety, news and canoe, and with these friends we joined up and finally arrived at Aberdeen where we met the curious and went on, unshaven, to report that there were no wonderful discoveries made on the trip through and that there were also no cannibals.

Of the comrades who tramped, packed, and climbed with me then, I believe that gallant Charlie Barnes rests somewhere down at Panama;[14] Christopher O'Connell Hays I have met once since; Jack Sims, I heard of in Seattle; whilst Jack Crumlack accompanied me on the St. Elias expedition with Professor Russell the following year. But to the good friends if on top of the earth may they keep climbing, if below may they rest in peace.

To all mountain lovers,
Sincerely,

J. H. Christie,
Olympic Press Expedition.

[13] Christie could not remember the name of Frederick S. Antrim of Aberdeen as the white man in the canoe the party found on the Quinault near the end of the trip.

[14] Charles Barnes died of malaria in Colombia, where he was engaged in mining operations a few years after the conclusion of the Press Expedition. While Barnes was in South America, his mother and brother, Paul, homesteaded at Lake Crescent next to the creek that bears their name to this day. See Wood, *Across the Olympic Mountains*, p. 210.

APPENDIX TO THE PRESS EXPEDITION REPORT

Northwest historian Harry M. Majors, editor and publisher of Northwest Discovery, *has examined every reported detail of the Press Expedition as it wended its way through the Olympics in the winter and spring of 1889 and 1890. As a part of that effort (reported in* Northwest Discovery)*, Majors analyzed various aspects of the expedition, an analysis that provides a fascinating insight into the persons involved and the massive nature of the undertaking.*

Robert L. Wood, however, was the first historian to really examine in detail the activities of the Press Party as it crossed the Olympics. His "Nomenclature of the Press Exploring Expedition" is included here because of its usefulness in understanding the impact of the Press Expedition on present-day names in the Olympic Mountains.

Footnotes give the source location in Northwest Discovery *for each of the mini-monographs Majors presents. Footnotes also cite selections from Wood's book* Across the Olympic Mountains: The Press Expedition, 1889–90.

Some selected pages from the July 16, 1890, issue of the Seattle Press *conclude the appendix, allowing contemporary readers to see how the Press Expedition was presented to the 1890 readership.*

DETAILS AND TABULATIONS FROM THE EXPEDITION RECORD

Personnel[1]

The Press Party consisted of five men:
James Halbold Christie, age 35
Charles Adams Barnes, age 30
John "Jack" Henry Crumback, age 33
John William Sims, age 28
Christopher O'Connell Hayes, age 22

Also included in the party were four dogs:
Bud and Tweed (acquired in Yakima)
Daisy (acquired in Seattle)
Dike (acquired by Barnes in Seattle or Port Angeles)

Two mules, Jennie and Dollie, were purchased on December 15, 1889 from a settler south of Dungeness.

The Men of the Press Party[2]

Six men left Seattle in December 1889 on their way to the Olympic Mountains. However, due to the departure of Dr. Runnalls in January 1890 on the lower Elwha River, only five men constituted the actual Press Party that crossed the Olympic Mountains and arrived back at Seattle in May 1890.

Only one of the men, Charles Barnes, was a resident of Seattle when the expedition was organized. At that time, Christie was briefly visiting friends in North Yakima, on his way from Canada to Africa, Crumback, a Canadian resident, was probably accompanying Christie to the Dark Continent, and the two were evidently good friends. Both Christie and Crumback joined the Mount St. Elias expedition of Israel Cook Russell in 1890, after the return of the Press Party to Seattle.

Hayes, a Yakima cowboy, met Christie for the first time while at North Yakima; it was here that Christie learned of the unexplored Olympic Mountains, by accident, when Hayes brought the October 1889 Ferry interview to his attention. Sims, though English born, appears to have been living at Yakima at the time.

When Christie arrived in Seattle in late November 1889, he brought with him Crumback, Hayes, and Sims from Yakima. At Seattle, Barnes was added to the party on December 3 as photographer, topographer, diarist, and second in command. The last member to be added (and the only one to leave prematurely) was Runnalls on December 5, who was to serve as physician and naturalist to the party.

James Halbold Christie (1854–1942), the leader of the Press Party, was born on December 14, 1854 somewhere within the county of Moray, a district in northern Scotland bordering on the Moray Firth. Christie possessed a degree of intelligence, for he was admitted to the venerable Royal High School at Edinburgh, but his aspirations to become a military officer were thwarted by his dropping out of school.

Christie then migrated to Canada in or shortly before 1870, serving a period of six years first in Quebec and then elsewhere. Christie spent some twelve years hunting and prospecting in the wilds of western Canada, on trips that "varied from one to three years beyond the limits of civilization." During 1886–1889 he explored the vast reaches of the Peace River in northern Alberta, as well as the Great Slave Lake

[1] Majors, ed., *Northwest Discovery* 2 (Feb. 1981): p. 130.
[2] Majors, ed., *Northwest Discovery* 2 (Feb. 1981): pp. 108–115.

and Mackenzie River in the Canadian Arctic barrens.

Christie had evidently tired of the Canadian tundra, for in the fall of 1889 he was on his way to explore Africa, likely in the company of John Crumback. While in North Yakima in late October 1889, Christie first caught wind of the publicity surrounding the then unknown Olympic Mountains. He promptly volunteered his services to the *Seattle Press*, describing himself as "no ambitious, untried youth . . . but a man tried in all the vicissitudes of mountain, forest and plain life."

Christie's experience so highly impressed Edmond S. Meany , that it caused that newspaper editor to put forth the extravagant claim that Christie was "the best man in the Northwest to undertake an exploration requiring such skill and experience." The selection of Christie to head the expedition was indeed a wise choice, for it was largely due to his leadership and his wilderness expertise that the Press Party was able to withstand its nearly six month winter ordeal. Christie, through his leadership and experience, was, far more so than any other person, chiefly responsible for the success of the Press Party expedition. His peerless knowledge of wilderness techniques and survival, and the respect he drew forth from the other men, served to keep the party together in a hostile unexplored mountain region during the middle of winter, where other parties would almost certainly have retreated from or perished in.

From the very start of the expedition, we find Christie assuming undisputed command of the party—effortlessly knowing what to do, when and how to do it, as if it were innate to his character. He suggested the idea of such an expedition to the *Seattle Press*. His high degree of self-confidence also suggested that the expedition enter the mountains in winter, and the staff of the *Seattle Press* seconded him on this nearly fatal decision. The provisioning of the Press Party was likely under the direction of Christie, for he knew just what equipment and how many provisions would be required to sustain such an expedition.

Christie was as at ease in dealing with a newspaper publisher, editor, a doctor, military officer, or a mayor, as he was in speaking with a local Indian or a primitive settler. If packs for the mules were required, Christie knew how to construct them as well as how to cinch them. Despite Barnes' naval experience, the design and direction of construction of the boat appears to have been chiefly Christie's doing. And, when sleds were considered as a possible means of transportation across the snow, Christie's expertise suggested to the men the various ways in which such a device could be designed.

Christie was sensitive to the beauty of nature, as is evident in his letter of July 1, 1890 to Meany, describing the magnificent scenery at Yakutat Bay and Mount St. Elias. And, in a passage of March 16, 1890, when viewing the marvelous snow-clad peaks of the northern Bailey Range, Christie wrote: "a grand chain of peaks as far as the eye could reach, an exquisite panorama of mountain scenery to a lover of solitary natural grandeur. Enraptured with the scene before me I demanded of Crumback if he did not think it glorious."

After his return from the Olympic Mountains in May, Christie remained less than a month in Seattle. In June 1890, both he and Crumback accompanied the unsuccessful Mount St. Elias expedition of geologist Israel Cook Russell (1852–1906) to Alaska. After this, Christie settled in British Columbia and faded into obscurity. In 1920 he wrote a short letter to Edmond S. Meany.[3] By 1926, he was living in a log cabin near Vernon, British Columbia. In response to a letter from Meany, Christie replied in November 1926 with a letter that recounts several details of the Press Party not mentioned in the 1890 newspaper narrative.[4]

In 1936, Christie's published letter of 1926 caught the eyes of two young Seattle antiquarians, Gilbert Erickson and Robert B. Hitchman. A discrete inquiry directed to the Vernon postmaster, as to whether the old gentleman was still alive or not, elicited the pithy reply from Christie himself; "Who the hell says I'm dead?" Erickson's schedule did not permit him any free time that summer to visit Christie. However, Hitchman made plans for an automobile trip to eastern Washington with another companion, to visit the old explorer in British Columbia; and, after some difficulty (including a flat tire), finally arrived at Christie's cabin on September 10, 1936.

Christie was living in a modest log cabin in a clearing, with his dog Pat. He reportedly had an Indian common-law wife (who was nowhere to be seen), and he mentioned to Hitchman that he had adopted two part Indian boys. Christie was exuberant at the opportunity to talk with someone who displayed a genuine interest in his past life, and in his enthusiasm would jump from one topic to another.

Within his cabin, Christie had a large amount of papers stored away in boxes, along with various books and maps;

145

---

[3] Manuscripts, Special Collections, University Archives, University of Washington Libraries, Edmond S. Meany papers, box 35, folder 16.
[4] Christie, James H. "From the Leader of the Press Expedition." *The Mountaineer Annual* 19 (1926): pp. 37–39. This letter is reproduced here, at the end of chapter 5, The Return of the Press Expedition.

but there was almost nothing relating to the Press Party, other than a scrapbook and about six photographs. Equally disappointing to Hitchman was the fact that Christie could not recall sufficiently detailed memories in regard to specific questions concerning the Press Party expedition—in part because of his excitement at having someone to talk with, and in part due to the fact that he regarded it as only a relatively minor episode in his life. Hitchman later recalled of Christie, in 1951, "He was testy and stubborn. Pretty much of a remittance man, too, I think."[5]

After this brief visit, Hitchman saw Christie only once more, during a short visit in August 1937 (a dwarf Indian and his wife were looking after the old woodsman). Again, Hitchman was unsuccessful in attempts to draw forth any detailed or revealing reminiscences concerning the Press Party. James Christie finally died on June 15, 1942, and was buried near the town of Vernon, British Columbia.

About 1965, Mrs. Grace Worth of Vernon, British Columbia, prepared a short biography of Christie that was published only in mimeograph form.[6] In addition to the "before" and "after" group photographs of the expedition members, two other photographs of Christie have been published: one taken about 1887 in the Canadian West (about age 33); and the other taken in 1937 (about age 83) outside his cabin, with his dog Pat and the young Hitchman. These two photographs have been published in :

El Hult, Ruby, *The Untamed Olympics* (Portland: Binfords & Mort, 1954), opposite p. 54 (the 1887 photograph).

Wood, Robert L., *Across the Olympic Mountains: The Press Expedition 1889–90* (Seattle and London: The Mountaineers and the University of Washington Press, 1967), p. 18 (the 1887 photograph) and p. 209 (the 1937 photograph).

Four specimens of James Christie's handwriting and autograph signatures exist among the Edmond S. Meany papers, these being four letters from Christie to Meany dated March 7?, 1890 on the Elwha River (box 51, folder 16), June 28, 1890 at Yakutat Bay (box 10, folder 8), July 1, 1890 at Yakutat Bay (box 10, folder 9), and January 28, 1920 at Vancouver, British Columbia (box 35, folder 16).

Charles Adams Barnes (1859–*ca* 1900), second in command of the expedition, was born in 1859 in Illinois, the son of Sarah P. Barnes. He was a distant relative of the famous Adams family, his maternal grandfather being a cousin of president John Quincy Adams. Barnes brothers were Paul,

Pierre, Edward, and Horace. His adolescence was spent in Washington, D.C., and in 1879 he received his commission as a lieutenant in 1883. The Revenue Cutter Service was organized in 1790 as a branch of the Treasury Department; in 1915 this became the present U.S. Coast Guard. Resigning from this service in 1887, Barnes first settled in California, and then moved to Seattle about 1888. Sometime during 1887–1889, Barnes had found the time to explore "the mountains of Arizona and of Oregon and Washington," which he listed among the qualifications for joining the Press Party, along with his skill at photography.

It was largely due to Barnes' skill as a photographer that Christie was to recommend to the *Seattle Press* staff that he accompany the expedition. Barnes was the most highly educated member of the Press Party (after the departure of Runnalls), in light of his training at a military school and the fluent detailed prose of his narrative. It is to Barnes that we are indebted for most of the descriptive details of the Press Party expedition, the map of their explorations, as well as all the photographs of the expedition.

Barnes' specific duties were to act as photographer, cartographer, and diarist for the expedition. With the departure of Runnalls on February 3, Barnes then assumed the responsibility of being the naturalist of the party. Barnes was clearly second in command of the expedition, and assumed leadership during Christie's absence. Christie always courteously refers to Barnes in his journals as "Capt. Barnes."

During December 8–12, while the five men left Seattle for Port Angeles, Barnes remained in Seattle to finish the accumulation of equipment and supplies. Later, during December 15–17, Barnes was sent alone to secure the purchase of two mules, with the price and the selection of the animals left to his discretion. Barnes' position rank within the party is again illustrated on January 13, as the boat was being hauled up the icy Elwha River: Crumback, Sims, Hayes, and even Dr. Runnalls had to thrash on shore pulling the line, while on board the boat Christie served as bowsman (guide and director) and Barnes was in the stern as helmsman.

After his return from the Olympic Mountains, Barnes prospected for some time in Panama with his brother Pierre, before journeying to Colombia. Both brothers contracted malaria, and Charles Barnes soon died from this disease about 1900 along the Rio Magdalena.

The Barnes family has another close connection with the Olympic Peninsula, for his mother Sarah P. Barnes and

146

his brother Paul Barnes settled at the mouth of Barnes Creek on Lake Crescent. Paul Barnes also worked for the U.S. Revenue Cutter Service, and it was in the course of such duty, while stationed at Port Crescent, that he first learned of Lake Crescent. Paul visited the lake, and was so enchanted with it that he determined to settle there. During the 1890's, Paul owned and operated the small passenger steamer on Lake Crescent, the *Lady of the Lake*. Nearby Marymere Falls honor the sister of Charles and Paul, Mary Alice Barnes (later Mary A.B. Eldridge).

For a photograph of Barnes in his service uniform of captain, taken about 1885 (at about age 26), see:

Wood, Robert L. *Across the Olympic Mountains: The Press Expedition 1889–90*, 2d ed. (Seattle and London: The Mountaineers and University of Washington Press, 1976), p. 21. Biographical details appear on p. 210, obtained from his sister-in-law, Mrs. Pierre Barnes.

Further biographical details appear in:

Wood, Robert L., "Sleuthing in the Past," *The Mountaineer Annual* [Seattle] 71 (1977): pp. 49–57, cit. pp. 50–51.

Two specimens of Barnes' handwriting and autograph signatures exist among the Edmond S. Meany papers [Manuscripts Division, University of Washington Library, Seattle, Wash.], these being two letters from Barnes to Meany, dated June 25, 1890 at Seattle (box 10, folder 8), and a curious letter dated January 31, 1893 at Port Townsend (box 12, folder 3).

Christopher O'Connell Hayes (1867–date unknown), the youngest member of the Press Party at age 22, was born in 1867. Hayes was a great grandson of the Irish statesman and nationalist Daniel O'Connell (1775–1847), all of whose sons were elected to Parliament. Immediately prior to his joining the expedition, Hayes "was riding on a cattle range in Yakima Valley." It was Hayes who called an article on the then unknown Olympics to Christie's attention, thus initiating the Press Party.

Nothing is known of the later life of Hayes, other than the fact that in July 1890 he was living near Kiona in the lower Yakima Valley, probably working as a cowboy. In July 1890 Hayes wrote to Meany, inquiring as to the whereabouts of James Christie. The holograph letter, with Hayes' autograph signature, is now in the Edmond S. Meany papers [Manuscripts, Special Collections, University Archives, University of Washington Library, Seattle, Wash.] (box 10, folder 9). The only likeness of Hayes are the three line engravings appearing in the 1890 Press Party narrative.[7]

John "Jack" Henry Crumback (1856–date unknown) was born in 1856 in Ontario, probably at Galt. After moving to the Canadian West, he engaged in such various activities as "a cowboy, hunter, prospector and Indian fighter in the Northwest territory. He was in the Riel rebellion." When the Press Party was organized, Christie and Crumback had known each other longer than any other members of the group. It is likely that these two men were both on their way to Africa together, when the enticing news of the unexplored Olympics diverted them at North Yakima.

Crumback, who went by the nickname Jack, served as cook on the expedition. We first learn of him in this capacity on December 11, when he awoke everyone to a delectable breakfast of beans, bacon, freshly baked bread, and coffee. It was acclaimed "a feast indeed compared with the food supplied us at the majority of restaurants [in Seattle and Port Angeles] we have visited lately." Bread baking in the wilderness was an art unto itself, and Crumback soon found himself assigned the responsibility as official cook, for on December 13 when the rest of the men were laboriously packing supplies, "Crumback remains in camp cooking." On February 10, Crumback again remained in camp baking bread, while the four other men were out scouting the countryside.

Crumback was probably a friendly person, easy to get along with—particularly in view of the fact that Christie had originally selected him as a companion for the proposed African journey. Moreover, after the Press Party returned to Seattle in May 1890, Christie and Crumback set out together on the Mount St. Elias expedition of Israel Cook Russell.

On one occasion (January 16), Crumback displayed remarkable fortitude when, after all other members of the party had been overpowered, the boat was saved from imminent wreck only "by the grit of Jack Crumback staying with the tow line." Barnes adds that "We recovered ourselves purely by the grit of Crumback, who managed to hold on to the towline after it had thrown everybody else off."

Crumback appears to have been the humorist of the party, for several of his witty comments are recorded in the Press Party narrative. On May 8, he referred to certain tid-bits of bear meat as beating even "three of a kind" in poker. Crumback seems to have been a man of mundane interests, who was not particularly impressed with the beauty of nature. When Christie on March 16 viewed the splendid snow clad peaks of the northern Bailey Range, he "demanded of Crumback if he did not think it glorious, and was shocked

147

---

[7] This statement is factually incorrect. Hayes appears in the actual photograph from which the engravings were made, as well as in the engravings themselves. Copies of the photographs appear in Wood's book and are available in the Manuscripts, Special Collections, University Archives division of the University of Washington Libraries.

to hear him give his opinion, low but impressive, that he considered it a 'damned rough lay out'."

Upon the termination of the Press Party expedition in late May at Seattle, Christie and Crumback continued their friendship, for they both accompanied geologist Israel Cook on his Mt. St. Elias expedition. After his return from Alaska, Crumback is reported to have returned to the Olympic Peninsula and settled near Lake Quinault. See:

Cleland, Lucile H. (compiler), *Trails and Trials of the Pioneers of the Olympic Peninsula* (Humptulips, Wash.: The Humptulips Pioneer Association, 1959; facsimile reproduction, Seattle: Shorey Book Store, 1973).

No likeness of Crumback is known other than the three line engravings appearing in the 1890 newspaper narrative.

John William Sims (1861–1943) was born on July 10, 1861, in Essex, England. In 1870 he enlisted in the Royal Army, and was discharged in 1876. He migrated to South Africa, where he served during 1881–1882 in the Boer War. Sims moved to Alberta, Canada in 1886, where he engaged in "hunting, trapping, prospecting and trading." Soon thereafter, he settled near Yakima, where he met Christie in 1889. Sims may possibly have been one of the "old friends" whom Christie was then visiting at North Yakima, or they may have been introduced by a mutual acquaintance. Sims may have been able to provide Christie with information or suggestions concerning Africa and Christie's projected visit there.

After the return of the Press Party, Sims settled in Seattle as a carpenter. He later moved to Everett, he now being a United States citizen. Sims died near Yakima in 1943, and was buried in Marshland Cemetery near Snohomish. Details of Sims' later life, obtained from his daughter Mary Sims Buell and stepdaughter Mrs. Gladys Arnold—along with a photograph of him taken about 1883 (at about age 22)—appear in Wood, *Across the Olympic Mountains*, pp. 21 (photograph), 212, 213.

A compass carried by Sims on the 1890 Press Party expedition may have been presented to the Olympic National Park museum.

Harris "Harry" Boyle Runnalls (1854–1913), who did not complete the expedition, was born in 1854 at the seaport of Penzance, Cornwall, near the Land's End tip of England. He received his medical degree in 1880 from the Royal College of Surgeons at London, migrated to the United States in 1888, and soon settled at Puyallup. Runnalls was the last person to join the Press Party, he being accepted as a member on December 5, 1889, in the capacity of physician and naturalist.

Runnalls was likely the person least suited or prepared

for the expedition in view of his largely sedentary life at Puyallup as a physician, along with his lack of wilderness experience. Perhaps it had been felt that his usefulness as a doctor to the party would compensate for this lack of experience. Runnalls was the only married member of the expedition. As a consequence, this prolonged absence from his wife (which may or may not have been a boon), coupled with the burden of responsibility toward her in ensuring that he survived the expedition, may have placed him at a psychological disadvantage.

Nonetheless, Runnalls appears to have adjusted both to his new companions as well as to the harsh environment. His position as physician and naturalist conferred no immunity upon him from the strenuous daily labor of the expedition; thus on January 13 we find him on shore hauling a tow line with Crumback, Sims and Hayes, while Christie and Barnes rode on the boat. Runnalls was the first member of the party to suffer injury: this occurred on January 16, when the boat pulled loose and "Dr. Runnalls was dragged over the rocks about 15 feet, bruising him badly."

Runnalls' status as the only married member of the Press Party was to directly result in his termination with that venture. After receiving a letter that his wife was taken ill "by some odd named new feature," Runnalls left the Press Party on February 3, 1890 at the Macdonald homestead on the lower Elwha River, and returned to his home in Puyallup, never to rejoin the expedition. Interestingly enough, by June 3, 1890, Runnalls was now serving as Indian Agency physician on the Makah Indian Reservation at Neah Bay, for on that day he wrote to Meany asking for details concerning the just returned Press Party (Edmond S. Meany papers, box 10, folder 8).

Runnalls had a marked interest in mining, for by 1896 he had located the Bobtail and Mary Ellen claims in the Swauk Creek gold district northwest of Ellensburg. See:

Hodges, Lawrence K., *Mining in the Pacific Northwest* (Seattle: *Seattle Post-Intelligencer,* 1897), p. 70.

The following year he participated in the great Klondike gold rush, and soon gained prominence as the first postmaster of Skagway. Runnalls later moved back to Washington state, where he died in 1913.

A sample of Runnalls' handwriting and autograph signature appears in the June 3, 1890 letter cited above. A photograph of Runnalls, taken about 1900 during the Alaskan gold rush, appears in:

Wood, *Across the Olympic Mountains*, p. 21.

Details concerning Runnalls' life appear, briefly in Wood, "Sleuthing in the Past," *The Mountaineer Annual 71*

(1977): p. 51, as well as in a study by Runnalls' grand daughter, Mrs. Shirley I. Fager, *Doctor, Miner, Explorer: Dr. H. B. Runnalls* (unpublished pamphlet in the Robert L. Wood Collection, Manuscripts Division, University of Washington Library, Seattle, Wash.).

The Two Mules [8]

The two mules, Jenny (Jennie) and Dolly (Dollie), were purchased by Barnes on December 15, 1889 from a settler, William Fogle, who lived about twelve miles south of Dungeness. The price was probably about $40 or $50 each; and, "after a hotly contested drive of two days," Barnes finally succeeded in getting the two mules to the Meagher ranch entirely by himself.

The maximum load each mule could carry was 250 pounds apiece, but under very poor trail conditions this could be reduced to 150 pounds. Packing the mules required the patience and skill of an expert, as Barnes relates, for at first this could be accomplished only "after several shrewd kicks, delivered with accuracy and precision from practice born of experience, and several unexpected attempts [of the animals] to bite" (December 19). The men did, nonetheless, fully realize how dependent they were upon the mules to relieve them of the cumbersome responsibility to pack much of the provisions. Because of this, the animals were looked after with care: "But there is risk of their straining their backs [while leaping over a log] and thus depriving us of their services, so we generally lightened them of their load, or . . . cut the log out."

A decided advantage in the use of mules was their ability to forage for themselves, thus requiring a minimum of effort for their upkeep: "they will live and grow fat upon anything that grows in these woods. Greenstuff—to wit, ferns and cedar boughs—are devoured by them with a great appetite. Grapevines twigs, and, in short, everything that can be chewed, furnishes them with substenance [sic] . . . Oregon grape also furnished them with excellent food" (December 19).

The two pack saddles were made by Christie and Sims while at the Meagher ranch on December 18. These were "the ordinary Rocky Mountain pack-saddles, consisting of two cross-trees of maple, shaped like the letter 'X.' They are easy on the mule and are very strong and serviceable." The cinch used was the well known diamond hitch—a dependable method, but one that required experience to tie. On occasion, the mules could be ridden by the men for personal transportation, as during December 27–28 when Barnes and Runnalls visited Port Angeles.

On December 29, "there being nothing in the shape of food for them through the brush," the two mules were temporarily left in the care of William Macdonald. The two animals were retrieved on March 8, with the intent of bringing them up to the camp at the mouth of Wolf Creek. This effort, however, met with disaster on March 9, for while attempting to cross the Devils Backbone, a portion of the sodden trail gave way beneath Jenny, and she fell some 150 feet to her death.

The remaining mule, Dolly, was evidently not especially happy to be reunited with the expedition. On March 14 she made an opportune effort to return to the Macdonald place, only to be thwarted by a prompt sprint by Barnes and Sims, who were both wearing 50 pound packs. Shortly thereafter, Dolly benefited from a week's rest in Geyser Valley, at which time she feasted on Oregon grape (*Berberis nervosa*) and ground laurel (*Kalmia occidentalis*); but, this was a poor substitute for oats, and she never regained her initial strength. The men now "worked her as lightly as we could when packing, never loading her with more than 150 pounds, but even this she sometimes found difficult to lift over logs." By April 3, Dolly's load had been reduced to 100 pounds.

The value of the two mules to the Press Party may be demonstrated by the following: if no mules were used, it required the five men (each packing a 50 pound pack) eight round trips per man to completely transfer their 2000 pounds of equipment and supplies from one camp or cache to another. If one mule was added to the party, packing 150 pounds on her back, then a complete transfer would require only five round trips per mule and man. If two mules were employed, then this was reduced even further to 3.6 round trips per mule and man. The use of two mules could thus theoretically double the distance covered in a given time.

Even with her lightened load of 100 pounds, Dolly still experienced considerable difficulty in early April. By April 4, "she was suffering from skinned legs" due to the cutting action of crusted snow three feet deep; that evening she was "rather the worse for wear and tear." That day, the exhausted animal had successively stumbled and tumbled the last 900 feet down the hillside in deep snow while descending to camp. Since the only available fodder for Dolly was ferns and evergreen boughs, the men compassionately "gave her a pound of our precious beans."

However, Dolly was near the end of her endurance. On April 9 she was "floundering." The next day she tumbled down a 50 foot snow slope in a series of somersaults. On April

149

---

[8] Majors, ed., *Northwest Discovery* 2 (Mar. 1981): pp. 172–74.

11, the crusty snow was taking its toll: "Poor Dollie suffered much from the deep snow. The lower part of her hind legs is a mass of raw flesh, and every step she takes dyes the snow with blood." April 13 was similarly rather hard on Dolly, owing to the snow being crusted and heavy.

Finally, on April 21, 1890, near the mouth of the Goldie River, "Dolly suddenly gave out and laid [sic] down. All our endeavors could not induce her to rise . . . Poor Dolly was exhausted, so we unloaded her." The mule had reached her limit of endurance, and on April 22 she was turned loose to fend for herself.

In ascending the Goldie River, the Press Party was now entering a region of heavy snow, where even a mule in prime condition "would be impossible to use." The men returned to the place where Dolly had refused to move from the day previous, and here they "found her standing where we left her. Although hungry and without water the poor mule had been too exhausted to wander in search of food. We removed her halter, patted her on the back and turned her adrift to get her living as the elk do."

The Four Dogs [9]

The four dogs of the Press Party deserve notice here, for they were silent and enduring (though not always willing) partners in the six month enterprise. The mules were needed to haul heavy quantities of provisions and equipment, whereas the dogs, though not especially useful for hunting, nonetheless provided protection and companionship.

Bud was Christie's dog (December 23), Daisy belonged to Sims, Dike was picked up by Barnes, and Tweed was the pet of either Crumback or Hayes.

When Christie and his three companions arrived at Seattle from Yakima in late November 1889, they brought with them "Bud and Tweed, bear dogs of quality." Since Christie and Crumback were on their way to Africa at the time, and very likely not traveling with dogs, it is most probable that Bud and Tweed were obtained in Yakima (Tweed may possibly have previously been Hayes' pet). Bud became Christie's own dog.

After the four men reached Seattle, it was evidently felt that more dogs would be needed on the expedition, for on December 5 Christie mentions that "We were hunting [for] dogs, but failed to secure any." However, one additional animal had been secured by the following day, for in the group

photograph taken on December 6 a third dog is present—Sims' own dog, Daisy. On the 8th day of December, when the party tramped through town on their way to the steamer, this elicited "a good deal of remarks from the passers-by on account of the our show of arms and dogs."

Three dogs appear in the group photograph taken of the Press Party on December 6, 1889 at Seattle. Sims is kneeling astride his own dog, Daisy; while Bud and Tweed are in the center and on the left. The animals are evidently mixtures of several types, though Daisy has Labrador features, and the center canine may possibly have some English setter or Australian Shepherd blood in it. The features of the dog on the right (with Hayes) are indistinct, though it may bear a resemblance to the center animal. The dog with Hayes may be Tweed. None of the dogs are "brindle mastiffs," as Murray Morgan has stated. [10] The mastiff is a huge type of watch dog that originated in Great Britain, and weighs an average of 165 pounds—hardly consistent with the appearance of any of the modest sized Press Party dogs. Moreover, their color was likely black and white; not brindle, which is a combination of black spots on a gray or tawny background.

The two dogs on the right are the ones brought from Yakima, they appearing to be older, more imperturbable, and more at ease with the group. The dog on the left, Daisy, which Sims may very well be restraining, has the appearance of being younger, and is definitely curious as to the whole situation. It is likely that Sims acquired the dog as a young animal in Seattle, for Christie mentions only Bud and Tweed as having come with the four men from Yakima.

The last dog, Dike (Dyke), "a large black retriever," was "captured" by Charles Barnes sometime during December 9–13, and brought with him when he arrived at Port Angeles on December 12 to join the rest of the party. It is uncertain whether Barnes acquired the dog in Seattle or at Port Angeles. Dike was thereafter known as Barnes' dog (March 2).

The dogs, in general, got along with one another, though all four were likely males. [11] There was, as might be expected at first, an occasional fight, such as Christie relates on December 23, shortly after Dike arrived in camp: "My dog Bud, had a rather lively dispute with Dyke regarding his behaviour in camp." But, once the order of dominance and the subordinate group social structure was established among the four animals, the dogs thereafter lived in harmony.

The four dogs were important as a source of protection

---

[9] Majors, ed., *Northwest Discovery* 2 (Mar. 1981): pp. 174–75.
[10] Morgan, Murray, *The Last Wilderness* (New York: The Viking Press, 1956), p. 221.
[11] Many dog owners will challenge Majors's assertion that it is likely that all four dogs were males when one of them carried the name "Daisy."

and companionship in the wilderness. There were, however, minor shortcomings, for the dogs could not haul supplies, they competed with the men for what precious meat there was to eat, and they could frequently scare game away due to their lack of proper training in hunting.

It was through the efforts of two of the dogs, Tweed and Daisy, that the first elk were seen. On February 19, at the camp just below the present Lake Mills dam, the two dogs chased an elk nearby—much to the surprise of Barnes and Crumback, who, thinking that the dogs had only seen a squirrel, ignored their barking. The rifles were not readily at hand, and the two men thus missed an opportunity to add fresh meat to the camp larder.

Two days later, the dogs flushed a deer, which all four canines pursued even into the rapid waters of the icy Elwha River. The deer escaped across the river, but the dogs gained Barnes' respect because "they showed spirit and pluck in staying with the chase so long." On March 18, Barnes reports that "We saw many deer, and the dogs were frequently heard running and barking at others."

For the first two months, due to the absence of game and fresh meat, the dogs were compelled to live off scraps left by the men; on February 8, Barnes wrote that "our poor dogs are almost starved." The four animals fared best just after an elk or deer was killed, or several salmon were caught, such as in Geyser Valley on March 21 when the dogs "lived upon the bones, fish heads and other refuse" left over from cleaning and preparing game.

Rarely, the dogs might be of some use in hunting, such as on April 6 when Dike drove a large elk into camp. As the men were unprepared for this opportunity, the elk bounded off before they could get their rifles.

For the most part, however, due to their lack of training, the dogs were a nuisance in hunting elk. Thus on April 5 two deer escaped from being shot, because "the dogs gave chase to, and which therefore we did not get." On April 9, Christie succeeded in killing an elk, only because three of the men sat "in a row struggling with the dogs to keep them quiet." A similar situation occurred on May 13.

On April 21, Dike, Barnes' large black retriever, was killed during an elk hunt. The dog had "rashly attempted to head off one of the bulls. The bull striking 'Dike' with his forefeet nearly cut the dog in two, killing him instantly." The elk was soon butchered, and the men treated the remaining three dogs to "a feed from his flanks."

This elk was the last food the remaining three dogs had

for nearly a week. On the night of April 7, the famished dogs managed to get hold of the party's bacon supply, consuming perhaps seven pounds and leaving the men "only two or three pounds. In the remaining piece was very little fat, the only grease in camp." This was a serious loss; yet, displaying understanding and empathy, Barnes wrote: "As for the dogs they have had scarcely anything to eat since we left the dead elk at the Gallery, for we cannot pack for dogs. They are hardly to be blamed for last night's theft. We would probably steal ourselves if we were hungry."

The three surviving dogs are depicted in the group photograph of the Press Party taken at Aberdeen on May 21, 1890. However, the final disposition of the dogs is uncertain.

The Boat Gertie [12]

The decision to build a boat with which to ascend the Elwha River was likely made before the Press Party left Seattle, probably as a result of Christie's meeting with Norman R. Smith during the former's visit to Port Angeles within November 24 to December 2, 1889. At this time Christie "made a trip to Port Angeles for the purpose of examining the Elwha River. I was assured by the mayor [Norman R. Smith], that I would have water to spare for an eight inch draft light scow for thirty miles up stream. This gentleman was certainly inspired, which caused some trouble and the delay of building a useless boat." On December 10, the day after the expedition arrived at Port Angeles, Christie writes as though the decision had already been made: "I found that it will be impossible for me to build our boat at the mouth of the [Elwha] river."

The lumber for the boat was ordered by Christie on December 11 at Warriner Smith's sawmill on the lower Elwha River. Since Norman R. Smith (the person who advised building such a boat) was part owner of the sawmill with his brother Warriner Smith, the Smith brothers would thus have financially benefited by the construction of such a boat, and this factor may have entered into Norman Smith's advice to the Press Party.

The lumber was ready by December 23 when the Press Party began packing it, and on December 26 the last of it was packed through snow into Canyon Camp. There was a total of 600 board feet of lumber, most of this in the form of 16 boards 32 feet long. Barnes records that "In dragging it along the crooked and tortuous trail, the lumber was sometimes bent like the letter 'S'." The result of dragging the boards for four days was that they had become "as smooth as if planed

151

---

[12] Majors, ed., *Northwest Discovery* 2 (Mar. 1981): p. 188.

and the edges were worn round. But for the snow we could never have transported it in so short a time."

"The place selected for building the boat was the low bench of sand at the foot of a bluff immediately below the camp [Canyon Camp]. There was a piece of ugly rapids at the point of launching, but this inconvenience could not be avoided, as suitable level banks are few on the Elwha."

Despite Barnes' naval experience, the design and direction of building the boat appears to have been largely Christie's doing. The reason for this is that the design of the boat was of the type that would have been employed on the inland lakes and rivers of Canada, and which would therefore have been constructed differently from an ocean going vessel as Barnes would have had experience with. On December 10, Christie writes that "it will be impossible for me to build our boat at the mouth of the river." The dimensions were given to Sims on December 27, and construction began "while Barnes was away on a brief visit to Port Angeles." The boat was completed on December 30, and both Barnes and Christie give good detailed descriptions of its dimensions and appearance in their journal entries for that day.

The name *Gerty* (or *Gertie*) first appears in Christie's entry for December 27, the boat possible having been named after a friend or relative of some member of the Press Party. The vessel was launched on December 31, and was towed up the first rapids on the Elwha that same day. Unfortunately, the seams leaked, and during January 10–12, 1890, *Gertie* had to be recaulked. As it turned out, the Elwha River proved to have too steep a gradient and the water was too low for boat travel. On January 24, *Gertie* was abandoned, and the boat was given to Warriner Smith who thus profited doubly by this ill advised venture. During the last week in January 1890, the Press Party turned briefly to building sleds as a means of transportation.

Equipment and Supplies[13]

Barnes reports that "about 1500 pounds" of provisions (flour, beans, bacon, coffee) were carried by the Press Party when it departed from Seattle. These provisions were in addition to the equipment also carried along. Purchase of the supplies had been completed by December 5, 1889, as is noted by Christie in his diary.

On February 7, Barnes writes that the men were engaged in packing a total of 2000 pounds: this would include somewhat less than the initial 1500 pounds of foodstuffs, plus

a little more than 500 pounds of assorted impedimentia. ("Provisions" were regarded as foodstuffs, such as flour, beans, bacon, coffee, as is indicated by Barnes' entry for March 2, 1890.)

At first, each man was capable of packing 60 pounds of supplies (December 13). Little over a week later, the men had become accustomed to the load, for they "do not find packing quite so heavy." However, by February 4, the standard pack-load per man had been reduced to 50 pounds—probably because the flour and beans had been bagged in 50-pound sacks. The absolute maximum pack load per man mentioned in the journals is 75 pounds (April 17, May 1).

An estimate of the packing capability of the five men alone is given on February 4, the first day of extensive packing without the help of the two mules. On this day the five men packed a total of 800 pounds of supplies on their backs for a distance of $1\frac{1}{2}$ miles on snowshoes, "over a trail that was not only rough but deep [with snow]."

Barnes' entry for February 4 furnishes the following packing information: five men packed a total of 800 pounds for $1\frac{1}{2}$ miles in 50-pound sacks in one day. Thus today each man packed a total of 160 pounds for $1\frac{1}{2}$ miles in three round-trips. This is equivalent to packing a single 50-pound pack for $4\frac{1}{2}$ miles and returning unloaded, in one day.

Barnes also provides us with additional data to make yet another packing capability estimate, in his journal entry for February 7. At that time, the five men were packing a total of 2000 pounds of provisions and equipment via forty 50-pound packs. A complete transfer from one camp or cache to another would thus involve eight round trips per man. If the distance from one supply cache to the next cache or camp was $1\frac{1}{2}$ miles, then two days of packing would be required to complete the transfer of the entire tone of material.

The value and importance of the two mules can be understood by the following: If no mules were used, it required the five men (each packing a 50-pound load) eight round trips per man to completely transfer the 2000 pounds of equipment and supplies from one camp or cache to the next one. If one mule was added to the party, packing 150 pounds on her back, then a complete transfer would require only five round trips per man and mule (a total of 250+150 pounds per load per round trip). If two mules were used, then this figure was reduced even further to 3.64 round trips per men and mules (250+300 pounds per load per round trip). The use of the two mules could thus theoretically more than double the distance covered in a given time period.

152

[13] Majors, ed., *Northwest Discovery* 2 (Feb. 1981): pp. 129–30.

Food[14]

A total of 1500 pounds of food were carried along by the Press Party when it departed from Seattle. Most of this (about 930 pounds) consisted of flour, followed by approximately 225 pounds of beans, 113 pounds bacon, 75 pounds tea, 75 pounds "sundries," 56 pounds salt, 20 pounds dried prunes, and an assortment of several minor items.

The Press Party narrative also mentions that "Game was depended upon as the principal means of subsistence" (December 8).

The four most important food items consisted of: flour, probably close to 1000 pounds total, packed in 50-pound sacks, beans, about 250 pounds, packed in 50-pound sacks, bacon, roughly 113 pounds, coffee.

The flour carried initially probably amounted to 1000 pounds, packed in 50-pound sacks (February 4). On April 3 this had dropped to 250 pounds, on April 21 only 150 pounds were left, on May 1 there were 125 pounds, some was still left on May 3, and on May 13 there were 25 pounds left. The last of the flour was used up on May 17. The principal use of the flour carried along was to make bread.

Probably 250 pounds of beans were initially brought along, packed in 50-pound sacks (February 4, March 2). There was over 60 pounds left on April 3, 25 pounds on April 21, some left on May 2, and by May 13 all of the beans were gone.

Roughly 113 pounds of bacon were initially brought on the expedition. Over 30 pounds were left on April 3, 10 pounds on April 21, 2 or 3 pounds on April 28 (the dogs had consumed the remainder), ½ pound on May 1, and by May 13 the bacon was gone.

It is not known how much coffee was carried along. The last of the coffee was used up on April 3, while the party was still in Geyser Valley.

A rough estimate of the relative proportions of the provisions brought along may be derived from the following values: On April 3 there was over 250 pounds of flour, over 60 pounds beans, and over 30 pounds bacon. On April 21, there were 150 pounds left of flour, 25 pounds of beans, and 10 pounds of bacon.

Of the minor foodstuffs, on April 3 there were over 15 pounds of salt, over 20 pounds of "sundries," over 20 pounds of tea, and over 5 pounds of dried prunes.

Based on the above relative proportions, the Press Party may have initially started out with 1500 pounds of foodstuffs, consisting of: 937 pounds flour, 225 pounds beans, 75 pounds

tea, 75 pounds "sundries," 113 pounds bacon, 56 pounds salt (actually 50 pounds), and 19 pounds dried prunes. The close approximation of the estimated salt proportion (56 pounds) to the actual value (50 pounds) indicates that these relative proportions may not be too far off.

Rounding off these figures, it seems likely that the Press Party started out with: 1000 pounds flour, 250 pounds beans, 150 pounds bacon, 50 pounds tea, 50 pounds "sundries," 50 pounds salt, and 20 pounds dried prunes.

Included among the remaining foodstuffs (which by May 13 were entirely gone) were: dried peas (Dec.31), ham (Dec. 31) corn meal (Dec. 31), baking powder (gone by April 3), sugar (Dec. 15, gone by April 3), a lump of sour dough (April 3), salt, tea, and whiskey.

A total of 50 pounds of salt were initially carried along (April 3). There were over 15 pounds left on April 3, 5 pounds on April 21, and probably still some left on May 4 (May 8 entry). Perhaps 50 pounds of tea were initially brought along (Dec. 15), this dropping to 5 pounds on April 21, some left on April 29 and May 5, and 3 pounds left on May 1. Some "excellent" whiskey was carried along (April 3), but this was "well nigh exhausted" by December 21, less than a month after the start of the expedition.

The standard supper at first consisted of pork (bacon) and beans (December 15); however, when the game country was reached on the mid-Elwha River, "Game was depended upon as the principal means of subsistence" (December 8). Much of this was made into pemmican, thus on April 3 the party had 50 pounds of pemmican among their provisions.

So much time was spent packing supplies in the snow along the Elwha River, that the food of the Press Party inevitably dwindled away. After nearly five months in the mountains, the start of May found the Press Party still deep in the Olympic Mountains, with no game, and in danger of starvation. The men were saved by the timely emergence of several black bears from hibernation at the Low Divide.

On April 3, the Press Party had 400 pounds of provisions (food) left, in addition to some 800 pounds of equipment. By May 1, the total combined weight of food and equipment was 400 pounds (75 pounds per man). On April 21 there were ten days' full rations left. The journal entries subsequently record: April 29 "we had but twelve days' grub in camp by the utmost economy"; and April 30 "but ten days' provisions in camp." By May 13 all the food was gone, except the flour (which lasted until May 17).

The food items (considered "provisions", March 2)

153

---

[14] Majors, ed., *Northwest Discovery* 2 (Feb. 1981): pp. 131–32.

carried along by the Press Party included:

flour (Dec. 8, 15, Feb. 4, April 3, 21, May 1, 3, 13, 17)

beans (Dec. 8, Feb. 4, March 2, April 3, 21, May 2, 13)

bacon (Dec. 8, April 3, 21, 28, May 1, 13)

coffee (Dec. 8, 15, March 2, April 3)

tea (Dec. 15, April 3, 21, 29, May 1, 5)

dried peas (Dec. 31)

ham (Dec. 31)

dried prunes (Dec. 31, April 3)

corn meal (Dec. 31)

sugar (Dec. 15, April 3)

baking powder (April 3)

lump of sour dough (April 3)

salt (April 3, 21, May 4, 8)

whiskey (Dec. 21, April 3)

"sundries" (April 3)

pemmican (April 3, 21; made from game shot during the expedition)

Cooking Utensils [15]

"a small but well selected assortment of cooking and other utensils" (Dec. 8)

kitchen kit (Feb. 6)

one large and two small frying pans (Dec. 19, April 3, 26)

a nest of sheet-iron camp kettles (April 3)

tin plates (April 3)

a four-gallon kettle (April 21, p 10 engraving)

One frying pan and "the large kettle" were discarded on April 26 on the Goldie River.

Clothing, Bedding, Shelter [16]

one 12 x 14 foot tent (Dec. 3, 8, 24, 31, Feb. 25, April 3)

covers (Dec. 3)

tarpaulin (Feb. 25)

two large canvas sheets (Dec. 3, 8, March 7, April 3)

packs (March 2)

rubber boots (Dec. 4)

leather boots (Jan. 13, Feb. 6, April 26).

By January 13, every boot leaked water.

snowshoes (Dec. 5, 8, May 1)

waterproof oil-skin clothing (Dec. 4, Jan. 28–31, March 7, April 26)

bedding (Feb. 6, probably refers to blankets)

two blankets apiece (Dec. 4, 16, Feb. 25, March 24, April 3,

29, 30, May 1).

There were two blankets apiece on April 3; on April 29 there was only $\frac{1}{2}$ blanket apiece. On April 30 the extra blankets were discarded.

Scotch wool suits (April 26)

six suits of overalls (April 26)

"stout flannel outside shirts" (April 26)

six changes of underclothing (April 26)

hats (April 26)

On April 30 "all surplus clothing" was discarded on the upper Goldie River.

Tools [17]

axes (Dec. 8, March 2, 21, April 3, 26, May 1, May 2 engraving)

two 6-pound axes (April 3)

five 3-pound axes (April 3)

"a whip saw for cutting our logs" (Dec. 8)

"a few carpenter tools" (Dec. 8, April 3)

rope (Dec. 8, Feb. 4, May 1)

windlass journal (Dec. 30, Jan. 15, used for the boat)

two pack saddles (Dec. 18, 25, March 9)

hunting knife (March 9)

one shovel (April 3, p 10 engraving, May 2 engraving)

one spade (April 3)

one pickaxe (April 3)

On April 26, the Press Party discarded on the Goldie River: "A lot of bullets, a frying pan, two axes, a pickaxe, the large kettle and several other articles . . . Some old cloths were discarded." Four days later, on April 30, several more excess items were cached "up a tree" on the upper Goldie River, including "all surplus clothing."

Hunting and Fishing Items [18]

at least five Winchester rifles, 40-65 (Dec. 8, Dec. 6 photo)

four left on April 3, three left on May 1

one shotgun (April 3)

at least five cartridge belts (December 6 photo)

"a liberal supply of ammunition" (Dec. 4, 8, April 3, 26, May 1)

"plenty of ammunition" on April 3

"a lot of bullets" were discarded on April 26

40.82 ball ammunition (March 16)

re-loading tools (April 3)

154

[15] Majors, ed., *Northwest Discovery* 2 (Feb. 1981): p. 132.
[16] Majors, ed., *Northwest Discovery* 2 (Feb. 1981): p. 133.
[17] Majors, ed., *Northwest Discovery* 2 (Feb. 1981): p. 133.
[18] Majors, ed., *Northwest Discovery* 2 (Feb. 1981): p. 134.

six sheath knives (April 3)

fishing tackle (Dec. 4, 8, April 3, May 1)

Christie's "several hundred flies" (May 18)

Specialized Items[19]

"the necessary tools for mineral prospecting" (Dec. 8)

one gold pan (April 3)

a rock hammer (April 3)

one 4 x 5 inch camera (Dec. 8, April 3, 29, May 5)

"films for 250 exposures" (Dec. 8, April 3, May 18), "each roll . . . separately packed in its case" (May 18)

a field glass (April 3, 8, May 2, May 21 photo, survived the wreck)

compass (Dec. 6 photo, May 21 photo, survived the wreck)

an aneroid barometer (March 18, April 3, 19, 27, May 2, 5, 19)

thermometer (Jan. 14)

"a few medicines" (April 3)

"a plane table" (May 6, alidade visible in Mt. Seattle photo)

"All necessary instruments for topographical and scientific observations" (Dec. 8, April 3, April 29, May 1, 5, 6)

mineral specimens gathered during the trip (May 18, some preserved)

"specimens of the flora and the fauna" (May 18)

Also taken along were "Fifty pounds of colored fire were taken along for the purposes of illuminating, if possible, some peak visible from Seattle" (Dec. 8). This was jettisoned into the Elwha River on March 9.

Personal Items[20]

smoking pipes (Feb. 28)

Sims' smoking pipe (Dec. 6 photograph)

Christie's smoking pipe (Jan. 24)

Meany's pocket watch, lent to Christie (1913 *Mountaineer Annual* p. 53)

A total of 48 pounds of tobacco were initially brought along on the expedition (March 24, Dec. 19, March 2). There were 7 pounds left on April 3, less than 2 pounds on April 21, and the last tobacco was used up on May 7.

NOMENCLATURE OF THE PRESS EXPLORING EXPEDITION[21]

The men of the Press Exploring Expedition named many of the natural features they observed in the Olympic Moun-tains. Some of the names have endured with the passage of time; others have not. Those marked with an (*) appear on today's maps.

Rivers and Creeks

Alexander River After Alexander Christie of Edinburgh, Scot-land, apparently a relative of James H. Christie. (In Christie's scrapbook , there is a line drawn through "Edinburgh, Scot-land," and written above, in Christie's handwriting, "Montreal, Quebec.") This stream is known today as Rustler Creek or the Rustler; on some older maps, The Rusher.

Belle River Known today as Long Creek. The records do not disclose whom the name honored.

Crumback River For John Crumback, a member of the ex-pedition. This is the East Fork Quinault.

*Godkin River Known today as Godkin Creek; sometimes called The Godkin. Named for E. L. Godkin, editor of the *New York Post.*

*Goldie River After R. H. Goldie of Seattle.

*Hayes River Perpetuates the name of Christopher O'Connell Hayes, a member of the expedition.

*Lillian River The records do not state for whom this stream was named.

Sims River Known today as Promise Creek. Named after John W. Sims, a member of the expedition.

Six creeks were named: ***Cat, Coldfeet, Kate, Jane, Louise,** and ***Wolf.** Also a creek known today as Kimta was referred to as **The Lost Chord.**

Two waterfalls were named: **Adeline Cascade** and **Eliza-beth Falls.**

Valleys

Chester Valley Name given to portion of Quinault Valley west of Mount Lawson. The records do not indicate who Chester was.

*Geyser Valley Name applied to bottom lands along the lower Elwha contiguous with confluence of Belle River (Long Creek). The name—which still prevails—was given because the men thought they heard geysers while camped there. The valley sometimes called Geyser Basin. A few years after the expedition crossed the mountains, the valley was settled by homesteaders—the Humes, Michaels, Ludden, and Ander-son families. In this valley the expedition erected the foun-dation of Crumback's "cabin."

155

[19] Majors, ed., *Northwest Discovery* 2 (Feb. 1981): p. 134.

[20] Majors, ed., *Northwest Discovery* 2 (Feb. 1981): p. 134.

[21] Wood, *Across the Olympic Mountains,* pp. 215–20.

*Press Valley The upper Elwha Valley was named for the Seattle newspaper.[22] Today's maps show only that portion where the Hayes River joins the Elwha as being Press Valley, but the expedition intended the name to apply to the upper Elwha watershed from its headwaters in Elwha Basin to the juncture of the Goldie with the Elwha. Press Valley was described as being the largest valley on the Elwha, "30 miles long; 1 to 3 miles wide," and extending "to within a mile or two of the sources of the Quiniault and the Quillayute rivers." (The Hoh was mistaken for the Quillayute.)

Mountain Ranges

Three of the mountain ranges named by the expedition—the Bailey, Burke, and Holmes ranges—are rugged chains of peaks, snow-clad above timberline throughout the year.

Antrim Range This forest covered ridge north of Lake Quinault and west of Finley Creek was named for Frederick S. Antrim of Aberdeen, Washington, the first man the expedition members met as they emerged from the mountains.

*Bailey Range After William E. Bailey, proprietor of the sponsoring newspaper, the *Seattle Press*. This range was considered the "backbone" of the Olympics. The name is well established.

Burke Range "A succession of lofty and precipitous peaks," named for Judge Thomas Burke of Seattle, and bounded by the East Fork Quinault, Hayes River, and Godkin Creek. This name should be restored; the range is presently unnamed, and Burke was an important figure in western Washington at the time of the Press Exploring Expedition.[23]

Deer Range Name given to mountainsides bordering the Elwha on the east, between Devil's Backbone and Lillian River, because of many deer observed there.

Holmes Range Constituted some of the peaks to the east, dominated by Mount Holmes, which was probably Mount Deception: contiguous with the Sound Range—by which name the peaks facing Hood Canal and Puget Sound were generally known at that time.

Kemp Range After Alfred C. G. Kemp of Montesano, Washington; a forested ridge paralleling Lake Quinault on the south. Includes minor peaks such as Colonel Bob, Gibson Peak, and Mount O'Neil (not to be confused with the Mount O'Neil named by the Press Party).

Mountain Peaks

Thirty-six mountain peaks were distinguished with names. Only nine, or 25 percent, of the names appear on today's maps of the Olympics.

Mount Agnus After General Felix Agnus of the *Baltimore American*. One of the high points on Happy Lake Ridge.

*Mount Barnes Commemorates Captain Charles Adams Barnes of the expedition.

Mount Bennett Name given to Mount Olympus, after James Gordon Bennett of the *New York Herald*. Because the party mistook Mount Carrie for Olympus, they never realized that their Mount Bennett was the highest point in the Olympic Mountains.

Mount Brown For Amos Brown of Seattle. Known today as Lost Cabin Mountain.

Mount Childs A peak of the Bailey Range, named for George Washington Childs, proprietor of the *Philadelphia Ledger*.

*Mount Christie For James H. Christie, leader of the Press Exploring Expedition. It stands somewhat aloof from other peaks, as befits a leader.

*Mount Dana After Charles A. Dana, editor and proprietor of the *New York Sun*. An outlier of the Bailey Range.

Mount De Young For M. H. De Young, editor and proprietor of the *San Francisco Chronicle*. Known today as Muncaster Mountain, after a ranger of the United States Forest Service.

Mount Egan Named for John G. Egan, city editor of the *Seattle Press*. Now known as Mount Norton.

Mount Eldridge Named for William C. Eldridge of Washington, D.C. Known today as Hurricane Hill. At one time automobiles could be driven to the summit, but the road has been converted to a trail.

*Mount Ferry Honors E. P. Ferry, governor of Washington in 1890.

Mount Fitten For DuBose Fitten of Seattle. This peak may have been the mountain known today as Windfall Peak, but more likely was one of the unnamed high points on the ridge three or four miles to the northwest.

Mount Frazier For S. R. Frazier, editor of the *Seattle Press*. High point on the Queets-Quinault divide near Lake Beauty, possibly the peak known today as Kimta Peak.

Mount Goodwin For Judge C. C. Goodwin of the *Salt Lake Tribune*. This name does not appear on Barnes' map of the Olympics, and there is nothing to indicate its location.

156

---

[22] Robert Wood in *Across the Olympic Mountains* here attributed the name to the expedition, but on page 126 he correctly attributes the name to the newspaper. Wood states simply that he erred.

[23] In the era of 1990s environmentalism in the Pacific Northwest such a move would likely create great controversy, at the very least, in view of Burke's robber baron image and his vigorous antipreservation attacks on the environmentalists of his day.

Mount Grady For the late Henry Grady, editor of the *Atlanta Constitution*. Known today as Mount Lawson, a name given by the Press Party to a different peak.

Mount Hearst For W. R. Hearst, proprietor of the *San Francisco Examiner*. Known today as Mount Queets.

Mount Holmes After John H. Holmes, editor of the *Boston Herald*. Probably Mount Deception.

Mount Hunt For Leigh S. J. Hunt, proprietor of the *Seattle Post-Intelligencer*. Easternmost high point of Happy Lake Ridge.

Mount Jones After George F. Jones, editor of *The New York Times*. This name does not appear on Barnes' map; therefore, its location is unknown.

*Mount Lawson For Victor F. Lawson, editor of the *Chicago News*. In subsequent years the name was shifted to a peak one and one-half miles to the northeast, and the Press Party's Mount Lawson is presently unnamed.

Mount McClure For Col. A. K. McClure of the *Philadelphia Times*. A high point on Happy Lake Ridge; probably Lizard Head Peak.

Mount McCullough A peak in the Burke Range, named for J. B. McCullough of the *St. Louis Globe-Democrat*. Known today as Crystal Peak.

*Mount Meany After Edmond S. Meany of the *Seattle Press*, later president of The Mountaineers and a professor of history at the University of Washington.

Mount Medill Named for Joseph Medill of the *Chicago Tribune*. This is an unnamed peak today, in the Burke Range. A little to the northeast of Chimney Peak.

*Mount Noyes After Crosby S. Noyes, of the Washington, D.C. *Evening Star*.

"Old Snowback" Term used, while the expedition was in the lower end of Press Valley, to designate the mountain known today as Chimney Peak.

Mount O'Neil "after Lt. Joseph P. O'Neil, U.S.A." The spelling in the text is erroneous, but correct on the map. The mountain was possibly Hoh Peak, or one of The Valhallas of the Mount Olympus Range southwest of Mount Olympus.

Mount Pulitzer Name given to a prominent peak of the Bailey Range, after Joseph Pulitzer, proprietor of the *New York World*. Probably the peak called "Snagtooth" by fire lookout crews at the Dodger Point lookout.

Mount Reid Named for Whitelaw Reid, editor and proprietor of *The New York Tribune*. The present name is Mount Tom after Tom Martin, former treasurer of the state of Washington.

*Mount Scott For James W. Scott of the *Chicago Herald*.

*Mount Seattle "in honor of the city of Seattle." From this peak Barnes made the observations which enabled him to complete his map of the Olympics.

Mount Squire After Senator Watson C. Squire of the state of Washington. Later called Ludden Peak for a Geyser Valley settler.

Mount Struve After Judge H. G. Struve of Seattle. The peak is located slightly more than a mile southeast of the peak known today as Mount Lawson.

Mount Taylor After Colonel Charles Taylor of the *Boston Globe*. High point on the ridge at the head of Buckinghorse Creek, three miles southeast of Mount Christie.

Mount Watterson In the Burke Range, slightly southeast of Crystal Peak. This mountain, unnamed today, was named for Henry Watterson of the *Louisville Courier-Journal*.

Mount Zindorf This peak is almost encircled by the Quinault, Promise Creek, and Kimta Creek. The men failed to disclose the source of this name, one of the last chosen by the expedition. [Apparently it was named after Mathew Zindorff of Seattle.]

Other Names

Convulsion Canyon Name given to the Elwha Canyon at the site of the great landslide south of the Lillian.

Deception Divide The ridge running west from Mount Wilder toward Mount Barnes, where the expedition discovered that in following the Goldie it had been cutting a base line across a great curve of the Elwha.

Devil's Backbone Not really Press Party terminology, this was the local settlers' name for the western spur of Mount Eldridge (Hurricane Hill).

Difficulty Hill Probably not meant as a permanent name; merely the designation for the mountainside above the Lillian Canyon.

*Goblin Gates and **Goblin Canyon** Names given to the most unusual phenomenon discovered by the expedition. Goblin Gates designates the place where the Elwha right angles into a cliff; Goblin Canyon the gorge below the gate.

*Lakes Mary and **Margaret** These were names given to the two small lakes at Low Divide, where the expedition finally departed from the Elwha watershed and crossed over to the Quinault.

Semple Plateau For ex-governor Eugene Semple of Washington Territory, because of the evidence of former Indian life found there which reminded the explorers of the Governor's report in 1888 to the Secretary of the Interior. The "plateau" is actually a small bench above the Elwha just north of the confluence of the Goldie River, where it emerges from its canyon. For unknown reasons the name has been applied to the southern part of the Bailey Range, near Bear Pass.

Thunder Canyon The canyon on the Elwha near the present Elkhorn Ranger Station.

SELECTED PAGES FROM THE JULY 16,1890, EDITION OF THE *SEATTLE PRESS*

After the Press Party explorers returned to Seattle, the Seattle Press was confronted with the problem of what to do with the knowledge of the interior of the Olympic Mountains they had, but that no one else did. All of what they had—pictures, maps, journals, and details carried in the heads of individual members of the party—had to be rendered into readable copy.

The expedition photographs were sent off to San Francisco in order to get the very finest engravings that money could buy. The journals of the expedition leaders, James Christie and Charles Barnes, were edited and organized for presentation. No one will ever know how much they were embellished, if indeed their journals were embellished at all. Edmond S. Meany, expedition treasurer and assistant editor of the Seattle Press, set about to draft the attention-getting introductions and summaries that would entice the Press's readers

and at the same time create the journalistic scoop to which they were entitled. After all, the owner of the Press, William E. Bailey, had paid for the whole effort, cash up front, out of his own pocket. Meany anticipated sending copies to every major newspaper in the country after self-servingly naming peaks after all of their editors or owners.

Finally it all came together. The engravings were back from San Francisco, Barnes's map was as complete as he could get it, and the engraved plate for its full-page reproduction was finished. All of the additional pages of type for the expedition edition to come had been set. Everything awaited the arrival of Wednesday, July 16, 1890, the chosen publication date. On that evening, the citizens of Seattle were finally confronted with the end product of what they had been awaiting for eight months, ever since the Press Party had departed the previous December. Seattle's citizenry found an edition of the paper that summer evening that was almost entirely devoted to the Olympic Mountains, the returned explorers, and, at long last, the explorers' revelations of what lay behind the familiar skyline to the west.

A few of the pages of that famous edition of the Seattle Press follow.

158

The Press Party returns.
Courtesy Robert L. Wood

24 Pages. # THE SEATTLE PRESS. 24 Pages.

LUME XVIII. NO. 10.   SEATTLE, WASHINGTON, WEDNESDAY, JULY 16, 1890.   PRICE FIVE CENTS.

THE OLYMPICS

Account of the Explorations Made by the "Press" Explorers.

OPOGRAPHICAL MAP OF THE REGION.

oy Illustrations From Photographs Taken by the Party.

ATION OF THE EXPLORED REGION TO THE STATE.

Signs of White Men Ever Having Entered That District Before.

"PRESS" PARTY WERE REAL PATHFINDERS.

Put in Six Months of Toilsome Traveling Over Mountains of Snow and Ice.

D TRAIL MADE FOR FUTURE EXPLORERS OR PROSPECTORS.

THE PRESS EXPLORING PARTY BEFORE STARTING.

THE PRESS EXPLORERS UPON THEIR RETURN.

MOUNT OLYMPUS FROM ELWHA RIVER.

VIEW FROM SUMMIT OF MOUNT SEATTLE, LOOKING WEST.

Mt. Prader.   Mt. Noyes.   Mt. Brocott.   Mt. Meany.   Mt. Hearst.

Elwha River Canyon.

160

THE GOBLIN GATES.

VIEW FROM MOUNT SEATTLE LOOKING EASTWARD.

Loss of the Mule Jennie Over the Devil's Backbone

PART TWO.

AN OLD INDIAN BLAZE.

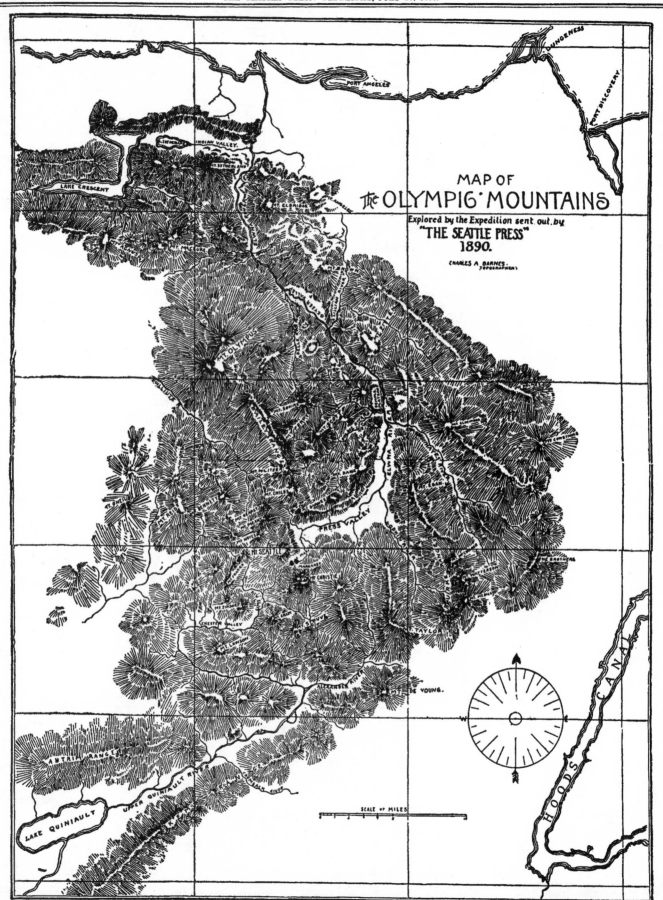

MAP OF
THE OLYMPIC MOUNTAINS

Explored by the Expedition sent out by
"THE SEATTLE PRESS"
1890.

CHARLES A BARNES,
TOPOGRAPHER

162

"THE PRESS TRAIL"

IT CAN BE USED TO ADVANTAGE BY ALL FUTURE TRAVELERS.

With the Following Explanation of Its Windings and Turns the Trail May be Traced Out by Anyone—Its Details Are Omitted—It Is the Path Made by the First Explorers in the Heart of the Olympics—The "Press" Trail Is One of the Most Important Parts of the Work Done by Those Real Pathfinders.

Christopher O'C. Noyes.

Charles A. Barnes.

James H. Christie, Chief of the Party.

John W. Sims.

John H. Crumback.

GENERAL DESCRIPTION.

Report on the Mountains, Valleys and Rivers of the Olympics.

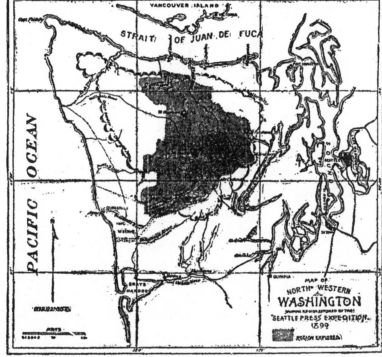

MAP OF NORTH WESTERN WASHINGTON
SHOWING ROUTES EXPLORED BY THE "SEATTLE PRESS EXPEDITION" 1899
REGION EXPLORED

THE NOMENCLATURE.

A List of the Names Given and to Whom Named.

CORRECTION.

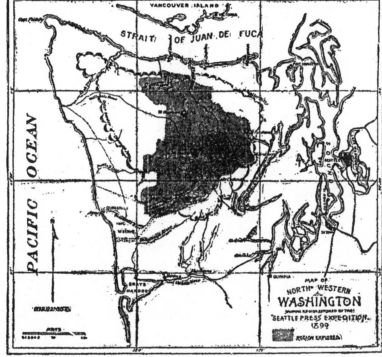

PRESS VALLEY AS SEEN FROM THE SIDE OF MOUNT SEATTLE.

PART TWO.

EXPLORATION OF DELLE RIVER.

(Continued from page three.)

GLIMPSE OF THE MOUNTAINS.

THE QUINAULT AT UPPER END OF CHESTER VALLEY.

VIEW OF DAILEY RANGE.

Taken from "Table Top" near head of Goldie River Canyon. Mt. Childs faces due West.

Mt. Barnes   Mt. Childs   Mt. Pulitzer   Mt. Perry

OBSERVATION OF THE GEYSER.

A Puzzling Phenomenon Which Gave a Name to the Valley.

MOUNT FRAZIER.
From summit of Mount Smith.

NO MORE SPIRITS.

VIEW FROM THE WATERSHED, LOOKING EAST ACROSS PRESS VALLEY.

CARRYING SOUR DOUGH.

CAMP MOVED UP THE VALLEY.

A CACHE AT LILLIAN RIVER.

DOLLIE TAKEN MANY HEADERS.

NERO'S FAMOUS LUXURY OUTDOORS.

STARTING ON A DETERMINED HUNT.

THE FAMOUS STAG SHORTEN.

A WONDROUS TAME COW ELK.

DOLLIE'S REBELLION.

PICTURE OF A KIND OF ELK IN FLIGHT.

THE LEADER ELK IS SPIED.

LIVED FOR SUPPER.

RETURN TO THE CACHE.

TO ISLAND CAMP.

WEATHER CLEARING.

FORDING THE RIVER.

PRESS VALLEY FROM SEMPLE PLATEAU LOOKING SOUTH.

A SNOW BRIDGE OVER THE GOLDIE RIVER.

OLD CEDAR STUMP SHOWING THE SPIRAL GROWTH.

MOUNT DANA.
Looking Eastward.

ADELENE CASCADE.

THE FIRST SIGHT OF WATER RUNNING SOUTH.

A STEEP INCLINE.

ON DECEPTION DIVIDE.
"Looking towards Home."

PART THREE.

AT CLOSER RANGE, AFTER THE FIRST SHOT.

"A BEAR!"

THE SUMMIT OF MOUNT SEATTLE, SHOWING ONE OF THE SPIRES.

ELIZABETH FALLS.

THE FINISH.

THE SEATTLE PRESS.

VOLUME XVIII. NO. 10. SEATTLE WASHINGTON, WEDNESDAY, JULY 16, 1890. PRICE FIVE CENTS.

PEAK OF MOUNT BARNES FROM ONE OF ITS NORTHERN SPURS.

GREAT SLIDE ON SIDE OF MOUNT GRADY.

MOUNT FERRY, LOOKING WEST.

MOUNT SEATTLE AND THE HEAD OF THE QUINAULT RIVER LOOKING SOUTHWEST.

MOUNT CHILDS, LOOKING WEST.

QUINAULT RIVER AT LOWER END OF CHESTER VALLEY.

TRACK OF AN AVALANCHE.

GEOLOGY OF THE OLYMPICS.

OBSERVATIONS MADE BY THE PRESS EXPLORERS.

The Formation in Slate and Sandstone—The Conditions Show the Olympics to Be the Youngest of the American Ranges of Mountains—Vertical Stratification.

CHRISTIE'S JOURNAL.

A Concise Record of Each Day's Work.

THE CHIEF'S DIARY IN FULL

It Shows Just How the Six Months of Time Passed.

HOW THEY LIVED AND WORKED.

THE FIRST GLIMPSE OF THE QUINAULT.

IN GOLDIE RIVER CANYON.

THE END OF A SUCCESSFUL BEAR HUNT.

ANTRIM AND HIS GUIDES

CASCADE ON KATE CREEK.

A VIEW FROM M'DONALD BUTTE.

Part II: Rivals, Controversies, and Steps Ahead, 1889–90

As soon as the Press Expedition's telegram reached Seattle advising that the explorers had arrived in Aberdeen, a rival newspaper, the Seattle Post-Intelligencer, responded with two articles that could only have been calculated to denigrate the Press's forthcoming scoop on Olympic knowledge. The first, by Charles A. Gilman, ex lieutenant-governor of Minnesota, was a reprint of an account that had appeared earlier in the Tacoma Ledger, covering Gilman's explorations the previous November with his son, Samuel C. of Gray's Harbor, just before the departure of the Press Expedition. For it to appear in the Post-Intelligencer on May 28, 1890, five days after the Press Party returned to Seattle, the Gilman account must have been prepared in advance, awaiting the news of the party from the rival Seattle Press. The second Gilman article appeared a week later, on June 5, 1890. Both seem to exist to minimize the forthcoming impact of what the Press was about to present, by trying to establish that all the basic knowledge of the Olympics had already been uncovered by others, even before the Seattle Press expedition got underway.

Two and a half months after the Seattle Press issue of July 16, 1890, in which the extensive report of the Press-sponsored expedition appeared, the Post-Intelligencer even went so far as to attack the integrity of the Press Expedition itself. In its September 30, 1890, issue, the Post-Intelligencer published a reprint from another paper of yet another exploring party's report (the Jones party), which claimed that there was in fact no trail left by the Press explorers in the Elwha Valley. By inference, the Post-Intelligencer seemed to question the veracity of the whole of the Press Party report.

The Press Party's return immediately spawned an explosion of Olympic penetration by adventurers, miners, hunters, opportunists, and anyone and everyone who could concoct a reason for going. Reports of the Gilman expeditions, as well as of the numerous parties that followed the Press Expedition, are presented here, ending with reports from the Wickersham expeditions of 1889–90. Wickersham's explorations were considerably more substantial than the others, and, along with the extensive explorations of Lieutenant Joseph P. O'Neil in the same time period, essentially led to the creation some years later of Olympic National Park.

CHAPTER SIX.
THE GILMAN EXPLORATIONS 1889–90

FARMS IN OLYMPICS[1]

Prospectors Told False Stories About Rugged Country.

It Is Full of Fine Valleys.

Matter-of-Fact Statement by a Man Who Has Been All Over the Alleged Impenetrable Region.

C. A. Gilman in *Tacoma Ledger.*

My son, S.C. Gilman, who is now making his headquarters at Gray's Harbor City, has been exploring Western Washington for more than a year past, and I was with him in the work during the last three months of 1889 in the Olympic country north of Gray's harbor, south of the straits and between the waters of Puget sound and the ocean. Three months' very hard work with suitable help, in which time we crossed that country both north and south and east and west, gave us an accurate knowledge of much of that region and a good general knowledge of the whole. The north, east and south sides of that peninsula are occupied and quite well known, but the great interior and the coast lands westerly therefrom were but little known and were supposed to be all mountains and uninhabitable. This is a great misapprehension, though the mountains are there in great form. They do not reach the ocean, however, except by a low spur which extends along the south side of the strait to Cape Flattery. South of that spur or extension and between the main body of the Olympic mountains and the ocean is a belt of fifteen miles or more in width of the finest country to be found anywhere. It is in all shapes, from moderately level to sharp hills, all in view of both the ocean and mountains.

Four large rivers, the Quinaiult, Queets, Hoh, and Quillyhute run from the easterly part of the mountains westerly to the ocean across the good belt, the first named river draining the mountains nineteen points within about twelve miles of Hood's canal. Upon various sections of these rivers, both in the mountains and west of them, are very fine bottom lands from one to four miles in width, timbered but lightly with very small cottonwood or brush, and very cheaply cleared for farms. These valleys are not excelled by any in the state for hop raising or for any kind of agriculture. Numerous smaller streams are also there, all bountifully supplied with salmon and trout. Being near the ocean and nearly surrounded by salt water the climate is the mildest on the coast north of San Francisco, the thermometer during the coldest of the winter registering 24 degrees above zero. The good belt lies well for a railroad north and south, and the river valleys leading into the mountains will no doubt be used for branch roads. With the exception of the lightly timbered bottom lands above mentioned, the whole country is heavily timbered with hemlock, fir, cedar and spruce, the most valuable being the cedar which excels in that region. There being no harbor on that part of the Pacific coast, the best of the country explored by my son and myself is quite difficult of access, but the tide of immigration is setting in that direction, and will soon open the way.

My son has made two trips into the interior this spring, and will soon make the third. It is my purpose to visit Tacoma in a few weeks and from thence to proceed to explore the

(*Wood*, The Land That Slept Late, *44*)

---

[1] Charles A. Gilman, *Tacoma Ledger*, no date. Reprinted in the *Seattle Post-Intelligencer*, May 28, 1890.

headwaters of the Queets, the Hoh and Quillyhute—the Quinaiult having been fully explored by us last year. I should have mentioned that all kinds of clay abounds, and at one point we found fine sandstone for building. A good country for elk, deer and bear. A small village of friendly Indians are located at the mouth of each of the four rivers named. It may be proper to add that there is no foundation whatever for the interesting romance published last year regarding the lake and prairie and the wild Indians located in the Olympic mountains. Quinaiult lake is a handsome body of water four and one half miles long, two miles wide, on Quinaiult river, where it emerges from the mountains, twenty-five miles from the ocean. It abounds in fine fish.

THE OLYMPICS OPENED[2]

We print this morning a record of explorations in the Olympic Peninsula, pursued during the past winter by Ex-Lt. Governor Gilman, of Minnesota, and his son Mr. S.C. Gilman, which clears away the mystery in which this region has hitherto been shadowed. No more important work of the kind, indeed no work of equal importance and value in a practical sense, has been accomplished on the American continent in the past quarter of a century. It opens up the last remaining bit of unknown country within the limits of the United States (excepting Alaska) and answers questions and speculations which have long interested geographers and the public at large. It is a singular fact that it has remained for two intrepid adventurers, acting solely on their own motion, employing only their own resources and prompted only by motives of laudable enterprise, to accomplish a task about which millions have talked and wondered for many years.

The record which we present this morning shows the exploration to have been most thorough as to its general lines. The Gilmans first entered the unknown region from the west by following up the course of the Quinaiult river, which empties into the Pacific north of Gray's Harbor. They reached the sources of this stream and far to the east climbed a summit of the Olympic chain from where they could view the land in all directions to the ocean at the west, to Puget sound at the east and to the Straits of Fuca at the north. Returning over the route by which they came, they again reached the ocean. Proceeding northward, they again entered the "unknown country," this time by following up the course of the Pysht river which flows northward into the Straits of Fuca.

The results of this second exploration are given in the record printed elsewhere.

The practical advantages of these discoveries are certain to be of the greatest value. The "unknown country" is found to be fertile, well watered and broken into fine valleys. It is rich in timber, coal, iron, and probably in precious minerals. It is described as a beautiful region, where the mountains tower in grandeur and where the valleys are pleasant and fertile, wanting only human population to make them smiling and bountiful.

Now that the mystery has been cleared away, that the trail has been "blazed," that there is neither difficulty nor danger in the way and that the country is attractive in all its features, it is reasonable to expect a rush of immigration. There is no great hazard in predicting that within five years the "unknown country" of the Olympic Peninsula will be as well populated, productive and as easily accessible as any part of Western Washington.

The official record of the explorations given in the story printed elsewhere, is a succinct, matter-of-fact statement which demonstrates that the work has been done with thoroughness and intelligence. It is a document rather important as the first complete and authentic narrative of a country destined to be the seat of great wealth and population. The Gilmans, father and son, have made for themselves a permanent and honorable place in the history of Washington. Others will come after them, but to them belongs the honor of "blazing" a trail through untrod wilds.

UNKNOWN NO LONGER[3]

The Olympic Range Easy of Access on all Sides.

Cut by Many Fine Valleys

Winter Explorations of Lieutenant-Governor Gilman and Son.

Up the Swift Quinaiult to the Crest of the Hills—Grand View From the Mountain-Top—Up Pysht River and Across to the Quinaiult Again—Game and Indians Abundant—The First Accurate Description of the Country—More Than Half the Land Fit for Settlement.

Gray's Harbor City, June 4.—Mr. S.C. Gilman, of Gray's Harbor City, and his father, Mr. C.A. Gilman, for several years

---

[2] Author unknkown, *Seattle Post-Intelligencer*, June 5, 1890.
[3] Samuel C. Gilman, *Seattle Post-Intelligencer*, June 5, 1890.

lieutenant governor of the state of Minnesota, are indisputably more intimately acquainted with the topography and characteristics of the mystic Olympic mountains than any other living men, and their knowledge was not acquired by any sensational methods of heroic exploration, or in any other fabulous manner, whereby a fine-spun tale, discounting the wild achievements of the daring Fremont of the more modern adventures of African Stanley, might be wrought. They just simply packed their blankets and a small store of provisions, donned serviceable suits of canvas clothing, hired a canoe and an Indian to paddle it, and traversed a great part of the unknown mountains in the dead of winter, without extreme hazard or excessive suffering. Nevertheless, their journeys were not unattended by great hardships, and the story recently told by Mr. S.C. Gilman, the son, to a Post Intelligencer correspondent, was both interesting and valuable.

Embarking for the Journey

S.C. Gilman came to Washington for the first time in February, 1889, and, during a journey in the region of the east fork of the Satsop river, heard a great deal about the unexplored Olympic mountains. He went back to Minnesota in the summer and, in talking with his father, they together decided to traverse the mountains and see what was really there. In the fall they came to Centralia, Lewis county, and embarked in a small boat down the Chehalis river. The trip by water began October 11, occupied but two days and was much easier than a journey by stage. At Gray's Harbor City they laid in a supply of provisions, and left on October 17 for Damon's point on the steamer Cruiser. Mr. Damon happened to be acquainted with friends of the senior Gilman, and treated both with great hospitality, the next day driving them up the beach to a place known as Griggsby's. That night they stretched their small tent which they had brought with them within seven miles of the Quinaiult agency and resuming their journey the next day they arrived about 2 P.M. They were received hospitably by Mr. Eels, the agent, and by others of the reservation. They made known their mission, saying they had studied the imperfect geography of the country pretty carefully and had concluded it was much easier and more practicable to enter the mountains from the west than from any other side. The outcome shows that their conclusions were entirely correct.

Up the Quinaiult

Rain had fallen almost steadily since they left Gray's harbor, and it was more than evident that winter was about to set in. On this account they found it impossible to secure a guide to take them up the Quinaiult river, whose course they had to follow to its origin. When their intention was made known to the Indians they shook their heads ominously, and muttered in their own peculiar, emotionless way something about the high waters and deep snows, sure to be encountered at that time of year. The undertaking was dangerous, they said, and no prudent Indian was willing to expose himself to the terrors of snow and ice and water. The Gilmans found one Indian, however, who agreed to take them to the forks of the river, well up in the mountains about thirty miles, in a north of easterly direction from the reservation. So, on October 20, at 11:30 A.M., they set out in great state for Lake Quinaiult, the two Gilmans, the Indian and his klootchman and their baby.

Lake Quinaiult and Environment

Lake Quinaiult is about twenty miles north of east of the agency, at the foot of the Olympic mountains. It is a surpassingly beautiful sheet of water, four and one-half miles long and two and one-half miles wide. It is located at the mouth of one of the fertile valleys into which the western Olympics are divided, and is surrounded by steep, abrupt shores and almost impenetrable forests. Its waters abound in fish, chief of which are salmon and salmon trout. The tributary country was at the time almost unsettled, though a number of settlers have gone in since and established an embryo city on the banks of the lake.

The journey from the reservation to the lake was not at all easy. The first few miles were upon tide water, but rapids were quickly reached and were encountered frequently before the lake appeared in sight. The country is described as very fertile, with numerous fine bottom lands, broken by an occasional wooded ridge. The bottoms were covered with cotton and alder, with dense underbrush of vine, maple and salmon berry. The hills were timbered with spruce and cedar. The character of the soil was such, however, that it gave rare promise of productiveness when its covering was removed.

Two days were occupied in going to the lake, the river, by its tortuous windings, making the journey from 30 to 35 miles in length. At the lake they found three hunters and trappers occupying a house that had been built and abandoned by a squatter the spring before. The three men received them well, but were very dubious when told of the mission of the Gilmans.

In the Shadow of the Mountains

The explorers were, however, not at all discouraged, and after stopping one day at the lake, set on bravely up the river,

172

the Indians and their canoe still accompanying them. The mountains, which had long been in the foreground, now rapidly closed in and swallowed them up. There were practically no foot hills, but the peaks on the east at once lifted themselves boldly into the sky at heights of from 4,000 to 5,000 feet. Their bases were distant not more than three-fourths of a mile. The adventurers found the river very swift and were constrained to walk most of the time, while the Indians pulled the canoe. Occasionally they would strike an obstruction on the bank and then the Indians would ferry them to the other side where they pursued their course until they were compelled to cross over again. They continued up the river until the afternoon of the next day, October 25, when they reached the forks about 4:30 P.M. Here was where it had been agreed that the Indians should leave them, but they remained there together for three days, the buck going up the East fork and killing four elk, which he salted down to take home with him.

Canoe Travel Abandoned

On October 28, they took the canoe and started on up the east fork, which came down from the direction of Mount Constance, in a course a little south of west; but they had hardly gone three miles before they encountered an immense log jam and had to abandon the canoe. Then they shouldered their blankets, weapons, provisions and camping outfit and set out on foot. They camped that night on the bank of the stream, and, staying there two days, climbed a neighboring peak, which their aneroid told them was 4,300 feet in height. They remained all night on top of the mountain. The weather was chilly but not severely cold. It was on this mountain that they struck their first snow.

In the Home of the Elk

Returning to the river, the journey was resumed and at the end of three days they were within two miles of the foot of Mount Constance. They were now in the heart of the mountains. Fierce overhanging peaks shut them in on every hand, and they found their way, during sunless days, over difficult paths and trails strewn with a profusion of rocks and logs. Elk trails became more numerous, and, to save labor, they followed them through the dense underbrush, only to return to the water and to continue their difficult way. Far upon the mountain sides the sun shone brightly, but its rays never pierced the gloom of that valley, or removed the moisture from the overhanging boughs and underbrush, upon which the frosts of the chilly nights hung in clots the live-long day. The ground and the very air was damp; and the

water dripping from the trees added much to their discomfort. The mountains were wildly rugged and broken, and it looked as if they would never dare climb their precipitous sides. Here and there on the mountain slopes, was a long, deep trail, showing where some gigantic land slide had torn in its irresistible course down to the valley below. It was easy to see where many of these great masses of rock and earth had started. Sometimes whole ledges, their hold becoming weakened by the action of the melting snows, had torn themselves loose, and dashed down into the valley with overpowering momentum, leaving exposed great barren patches in their stead. Often the track had begun so far up that they could not discover its origin, and it disappeared in the lofty distance. The scene with the surroundings was one of frightening grandeur; but the adventurers never faltered.

They concluded to ascend some of the peaks and get a view of the surrounding country. After much travel, they got to the summit of several in succession; but the skies were so thick with fog that nothing could be seen. Their provisions were getting a little low; so they shot an elk each, and cooked and ate its meat. They saw many others, but not needing them, did not molest them.

The Crest of the Range

For several days they had noticed a lofty peak to the south and on their right as they came up, and they determined to attempt its ascent. Its sides appeared very steep and they expected to have much work in climbing, nor were they disappointed. The mountain was so steep that they could make but little progress, and that with the most exhausting effort and labor. So slow was their march that night overtook them shortly after the snow line was passed. They made camp in the snow, and gathering some brush lighted their fire and cooked their supper. The slope was so steep that when they lay down to sleep they had to prop their feet against some logs to keep from rolling down the mountain—a means of descent, however easy, that they would not have relished. Next day they toiled on through the snow and reached the summit; and there the view that burst upon their bewildered vision was glorious beyond description. The morning was clear and beautiful and their sight was limited only by the far-distant horizon. To the northwest, eighteen miles, was Mount Olympus covered with glittering snow, and the last of a mighty range of hills extending in descending succession to the west, along the Straits of Juan de Fuca. Ten miles to the north was Mount Constance, abrupt and lonely, its lofty summit piercing the sky above all its immediate neighbors. On the east they could dimly see the range of wooded Cascades, with

173

Mount Rainier rising grandly to the right and Mount Baker on the extreme left. Hood's canal, its shores covered with evergreen, fir and cedar, was a shining thread at their feet; while beyond, Puget sound could just be discovered.

They Could Almost See Seattle

Seattle was lost in a haze, but they were quite sure they could locate the big city. Miles away to the west and south they described both Gray's harbor and Lake Quinault. In the background a rolling bank of thick fog shut off their view of the ocean. The whole vista was grand and unsurpassable, and impressed itself so fixedly upon the two lonely beholders that they will surely never forget it.

6,800 Feet Above the Sea-Level

The aneroid told them that they were 6,800 feet above the sea-level. The location of the mountain was singularly fortunate, for it enabled them not only to see a great distance, but it gave them a commanding view of the hills and vales and water courses around them. Loath to leave the scene, they tried to follow the crest of the mountain, but their course was soon impeded by insurmountable rocks and crevices. They decided to descend on the south side. The bluffs they found very steep, and in places they had to let themselves down with ropes. Camping again at night on the mountain side, they next day resumed the descent and finished during the day.

The Return to the Quinaiult

They reached a stream, plainly a branch of the Quinaiult, on November 9. That day it began to rain and continued without cessation for four days. Their sufferings during these days were very severe. Their blankets were saturated with water and nights were spent in extreme discomfort. The trees and the fallen timber were soaked with water, and one night they spent hours in unavailing attempts to light a fire. At last, however, they succeeded, and their gratitude knew no bounds.

At the end of the fourth day they got back to the main stream, exhausted and entirely out of provisions. They caught and cooked three salmon, and then spent two nights and a day in comparative comfort. Looking back upon the mountains they had left, they discovered that they were covered with heavy snow. If they had delayed their ascent of the mountain one day, doubtless they would have perished.

Impossible to Get Lost

The explorers were in the thick of the mountains, but at no time were they uncertain of their whereabouts. A man with ordinary intelligence could at any time tell what way to go by noting the course of the streams and following them.

On the second morning after reaching the east fork of the Quinaiult, they started down stream, in search of an old canoe they had noticed on their way up. They soon found it and spent some time in patching it up. Next morning, making an early start, they continued down to the forks, reaching them at noon; and at night they came to the lake. Here they found two trappers, and remained several days, fishing and recuperating. Then they resumed their journey, and reached in succession without incident, the Quinaiult agency, Damon's point, and Gray's Harbor City, arriving at the latter place on November 27, the day before Thanksgiving.

A Second Expedition, From the Sound

The Messrs. Gilman had penetrated the mountains to the great watershed visible best from Puget sound. They had gone over the most important part of the country and had acquainted themselves pretty well with its features, but they were not yet satisfied. They wanted to traverse the unknown land between the mountains and the ocean. Going around by way of Puget sound, they landed at the Pysht river, emptying into the straits of Juan de Fuca. They here announced their intention of going through the Quillyhute country, but it was in midwinter and they found no one willing to go through with them. Following the Pysht river and passing across to Beaver post office, on the Solduck, they found two men willing to accompany them. It had been raining and snowing and it was evident that a wearisome, if not dangerous, trip was before them. However they set out on December 11. The journey across to the Quinaiult reservation was anything but romantic and, indeed, with one exception, was not even very interesting. But they suffered much more from snow and rain than on their previous excursion. The result of the exploration is best contained in Mr. S.C. Gilman's own concise description of the Olympic country, which follows:

Over the Range to the Quinaiult

The country was in places settled by Indians who received them hospitably. On December 28 they reached the Quinaiult river, about fourteen miles above the coast, very tired and entirely without provisions. They began making a raft, but luckily some trappers from Quinaiult lake came along. Mr. Gilman, sr., went with them down to their reservation, and from there sent an Indian back after his companions. They reached the reservation December 31, 1889, happy that their arduous journey was ended. They came on to Gray's Harbor City, arriving January 4. Mr. S.C. Gilman has remained at Gray's harbor and at his claim on the Quinaiult since, while his father has returned to his home in St. Cloud, Minn.

Description of the Country[4]

The following, by Mr. S.C. Gilman, is probably the most complete and accurate description of the Olympic country that has yet been prepared:

Report of S.C. Gilman on the Olympic Peninsula, from personal observations as made by journeys in 1889 and 1890:

The Olympic peninsula is fifty miles wide on the south, ninety on the north side, and about eighty miles long. It contains about 5,600 square miles, or 3,585,000 acres. The Olympic mountains, from which the peninsula takes its name, commence in the form of a low range near Cape Flattery, and extend from there southeasterly, nearly parallel, and their summits, about sixteen miles distant from the straits, and gradually increasing in height until at Mount Olympus, eighteen miles south of Port Angeles, their greatest height, 8,150 feet, is reached. From Mount Olympus the summit of the range runs a little south of east to Mount Constance, 7,770 feet high, twelve miles west of Quilcene. Then it bears south about 30 degrees, west twenty miles, to a point near Lake Cushman, then west about eighteen miles to the Quinaiult river, just above the lake. Such is the general course of the main range that forms the divide between the waters flowing into the straits and Hood's canal and those flowing into Gray's harbor and the ocean. Of the 5,600 square miles in the peninsula there are about 2,060 square miles, or 1,890,000 acres of mountains, and 2,650 square miles, or 1,695,000 acres of land suitable for settlement, distributed as follows: Four hundred and fifty square miles, or 290,000 acres, mostly surveyed, on the north and east sides along the straits and Hood's canal, 900 square miles, or 575,000 acres, mostly surveyed, on the south side of the mountains, north of the Chehalis river and Gray's harbor, and drained by the Satsop, Wynoochie, Whishkah, Hoquiam and Humptulips rivers; and 1,300 square miles or 830,000 acres, 64,000 acres, surveyed, west of the mountains and on waters flowing direct to the Pacific ocean, the principal streams of which are the Osette, the Quillyhute and its four branches, the Dicky, the Solduck, Hoh and south fork of Quinaiult each drain a part of Mt. Olympus, the east fork of Quinaiult heading in Mt. Constance. The Queets penetrates the interior to a considerable distance. None of them are navigable at present for steamboats, although the four largest of them could be made so for fifteen or twenty miles each at a moderate expense. They can all be navigated with small boats and driven with logs to within a few miles of their head. Along them and their branches are in the neighborhood of 350 square miles or 224,00 acres of rich bottom land. The soil generally between the mountains and coast is good and well adapted, when cleared, for farming, grazing and fruit-raising. Among the mountains are many small rich valleys and much good grazing land. The peninsula as a whole is heavily timbered with fir, cedar, spruce and hemlock, the hemlock predominating on the western slope with cedar a good second. The prairies are small and few and far between. Coal float is found on a number of the streams, but has not been much prospected for. Iron crops out in considerable quantity in several places. Gold is found in the sand in nearly all the streams, and within the last year or two a few prospectors have penetrated the mountains and have met with fair encouragement, bringing out some very promising looking gold, silver and copper quartz. Tin ore, yielding a rich assay, is found on the Skokomish. On the western slope clay is abundant, some of it, notably some white and yellow banks, looking good enough to make most anything of, and I know of two very extensive croppings of elegant sandstone.

The streams teem with splendid fish and game is abundant. On the Quillyhute and its branches are between 300 and 500 settlers. Twenty-one claims have been settled on the Quillyhute this spring, about thirty on the Quinaiult, and the beach from the agency down to the harbor is all taken.

The Quinaiult Indian reservation extends from the Moclipse to the Queets along the ocean and back to Quinaiult lake, and contains about 220 square miles, or 140,000 acres. According to a census taken last fall there were then 453 Indians belonging to the reservation. That included quite a number of Indians at the Hoh and Queets and along the beach south. Most of the Indians live on the beach, a few families only living four or five miles up the streams. They seldom penetrate the interior, and then only for a few days at a time in pursuit of elk, which they kill for their hides and horns, seldom taking more than a few pounds of the meat. Quinaiult lake, eighteen miles northeast of the mouth of the river, is four and a half miles long, two miles wide and from seventy to 220 feet deep.

There is not a harbor on the coast between Neah bay and Gray's harbor.

S. C. Gilman.

GILMANS RETURN[5]

Ex-Lieutenant-Governor Charles A. Gilman, of St. Cloud, Minn., passed through Tacoma yesterday homeward-bound,

175

---

[4] This section of Gilman's report also appeared in *West Shore* 16, (August 2, 1890).
[5] Author unknown, in an unknown newspaper, 1889, attached to J. J. Banta's diary. See part 1, chapter 7, The Banta and Sharp Exploration 1889–90.

having just completed a most thorough and systematic exploration of the Olympic region. He and his son, S. C. Gilman, of Grays Harbor, started in October to explore this vast peninsula, of which little is positively known, and their reports of what they found are interesting. Unsurveyed and unexplored, it has generally been supposed to be mountainous and uninhabitable, but they report an entirely different condition.

The stormy season had already set in when they started, but the explorers persisted and traversed the entire region from north to south and from west to east, through its centre from the Pacific at the mouth of the Quinaiult, to the Quinaiult lake, thence northeasterly through the mountains on the several forks of that river to the divide, some dozen miles west of Hood's canal and down the valley of the Humptulip, climbing the mountains, affording views of the surrounding country, and generally exploring the timber, soil and lay of the land, reaching Grays harbor about December 1 and proceeding to Tacoma.

Recruiting here a few days they replenished their supplies and proceeded down the Sound by boat to the mouth of the Pysht river, on the straits of Juan de Fuca, where they again shouldered their packs and resumed their tramp, undaunted by the rigors of the weather. They followed the Pysht to its source, crossing the Olympic range to the headwaters of the Quillayute, explored its beautiful valleys down to the coast, then crossed the divide and explored, in their turn, the valleys of the Hoh, the Queet's, and the Raft, to the Quinault and thence to Gray's harbor again, a trip never before made, in any season of the year, by any person now known.

This exploration, carried out under great difficulties and very many hardships and privations, unavoidable in such a country in such weather, has demonstrated that between the Olympic mountains and the Pacific coast lies a belt of land varying in width from ten to twenty-five miles, unexcelled by any region in this state for agricultural and lumbering purposes. The most desirable bottom lands are abundant and well distributed, skirting the rivers from one to several miles in width, and extending far into the mountains. The rivers are all large, and, in many instances, are quite different in course and length from anything shown by any of the maps extant. Mr. Gilman and his son have taken full notes, accompanied by diagrams showing corrections of the map publishers, which will be valuable to future explorers of this region. The previous experience of the governor and his son

assures their competency for this work and fully guarantees the reliability of their reports.

The governor is much fatigued and shows the effects of the hardships of their trip by considerable lameness, but says he is much improved in general health by the outdoor experience.

THE OLYMPIC PENINSULA[6]

There is perhaps no portion of the United States, near a thickly settled center of country, so little known and which is misunderstood to such an extent as the great Olympic peninsula lying between the waters of Puget Sound and the Pacific ocean, in western Washington. This body of land is rectangular in shape, being ninety miles wide at its northern extension and about fifty miles in width at the south. The total length of the peninsula is about eighty miles, and the total area something like 5,600 square miles (3,585,000 acres). Of the entire 5,600 square miles of territory contained in the peninsula, about 2,950 square miles (1,890,000 acres) are mountainous lands, not suitable, perhaps, to many purposes of agriculture. In addition to the lands mentioned above, there are no less than 450 sq. miles (290,000 acres) mostly surveyed, on the north and east sides, along the straits and Hood's canal; 900 square miles, (575,000 acres) mostly surveyed, on the south side of the mountains and north of the Chehalis river and Gray's harbor, and drained by the Satsop, Wynoochie, Wishka, Hoquiam and Humtuleps rivers, and 1,300 square miles (830,000 acres), 64,000 acres of which are surveyed, west of the mountains and lying on the waters flowing directly into the Pacific. The principal streams of this area are the Osette, the Quillyute and its four branches, the Dicky, the Solduck, the Killiwan and the Baachiel, the Hoh, the Queets, the Ralt [Raft?], Quinault and the Chehalis. Three of these streams, viz: the Solduck, the Hoh and the north fork of the Quinault each drain a part of Mount Olympus, the last fork of the Quinault heading in Mount Constance. The Queets penetrates the interior to a considerable distance. No one of these streams is navigable for small boats, and driven with logs to within a few miles of their heads.

Along these streams are about 350 square miles, 224,000 acres of rich bottom lands. The soil between the mountains and coast is good, and generally adapted, when cleared, to farming, grazing and fruit raising. In the mountain districts are many small rich valleys, and a great abundance of good grazing lands. The peninsula as a whole is heavily timbered with fir, cedar, spruce and hemlock, the latter wood predominating on the

176

[6] Samuel C. Gilman, *Oregonian* [Portland], no date. Reprinted in the *Mason County Journal* [Shelton], June 13, 1890.

western slope, with cedar a good second. The prairies are small and far between.

The Quinault Indian reservation extends from the Moclipse to the Queets, along the ocean and back to the Quinault river lake. It contains about 220 square miles, or 114,000 acres. According to a census taken last fall there were then 453 Indians belonging to the reservation. This number included quite a number of Indians at the Hoh and Queets along the beach south. Most of the Indians live on the beach, a few families only living for a distance of four or five miles up the stream. These seldom penetrate into the interior, and then only for a few days at a time in pursuit of elk, which they kill for their hides and horns.

S. C. Gilman in Oregonian

Some time after Samuel C. Gilman had finished his Olympic explorations, he prepared a summary article on the Olympic Peninsula, including a map, which he submitted to National Geographic *magazine. By the time the magazine got around to publishing his article in 1896, Gilman was dead. Although Gilman did not purport that everything he said in his article was based on his own observations, that was the implication. His article erroneously reports the presence of mountain goats, pelicans, and minerals whose presence time has disclaimed.*

THE OLYMPIC COUNTRY[7]
By the Late S. C. Gilman, C. E.

[The following valuable article is based largely on the explorations of the writer in the comparatively unknown region he describes. A melancholy interest attaches to it, Mr. Gilman having been suddenly cut off, at the early age of thirty-six and in the midst of an increasingly useful and promising career, only a few days after the transmission of the article for publication and before he could be made aware of its acceptance.]

The Olympic peninsula, in northwestern Washington, forms the extreme northwest corner of the United States proper. It lies west of Puget sound, Admiralty inlet, and Hood's canal, commonly spoken of collectively as Puget sound, and extends over 90 miles along the south side of the straits of Juan de Fuca. Its west coast borders for 100 miles on the Pacific ocean, while Gray's harbor and the Chehalis river furnish deep-water navigation for 30 miles along its southern bor-

der, leaving only a neck of 25 miles in width connecting its southeastern part with the mainland.

As the northern, eastern, and southern sides of the peninsula, bordering on Fuca straits, Puget sound, and the Chehalis river and Gray's harbor, are partially settled and comparatively well known for six to ten miles back from those waters, this article will have reference almost exclusively to the interior and western portions of the peninsula. The whole peninsula contains an area of about 5,700 square miles, of which probably 3,000 square miles are occupied by the Olympic mountains, from which the peninsula takes its name.

The main watershed of these mountains begins at cape Flattery and extends southeasterly almost parallel with the straits and about 12 miles therefrom until nearly south of Port Angeles, where an abrupt turn to the south is made for about 6 miles; passing by the east end of mount Olympus; thence southeast 20 miles to Pyramid peak; thence southwest and gradually swinging to the west for 30 miles to mount Frances at the head of Quinault lake; thence southeast for about 18 miles, rapidly decreasing in height until it reaches its termination. Such is the general course of the divide between the waters flowing westward to the Pacific ocean and those flowing to the north, east and south in Fuca straits, Puget sound, and Gray's harbor. From the main divide, and in many places exceeding it in height, branch out in all directions spurs and ranges, they in their turn rebranching and branching again, until the complicated ramifications of mountain ridge and peak so completely cover the country with their rugged heights that there is hardly room for the gorges and canyons and ravines that lie between, and none at all for valley or plain. These mountains are a comparatively recent upheaval, and nature has not yet had time to round off their slopes or dull the jagged sharpness of their summits. She has, however, through the agency of an enormous rainfall, cut various gigantic sluices in the rocky face of the mountains, and through these a large amount of detritus is brought down.

Mount Olympus, the name peak, 8,150 feet high, is the highest and most conspicuous mountain in the range. It was first named La Sierra Santa Rosalia, by Perez, in 1774, but in 1788 Captain John Mears saw and described it under name of mount Olympus. It is about twenty miles south of Freshwater bay on the straits of Fuca, and is southwest of the main divide, with which it connects by a short, sharp, high ridge. It is a cluster of sharp, jagged rock peaks projecting upward through an accumulation of ice which forms a cap two miles

177

[7] *National Geographic* 7 (April 1896): pp. 133–40.

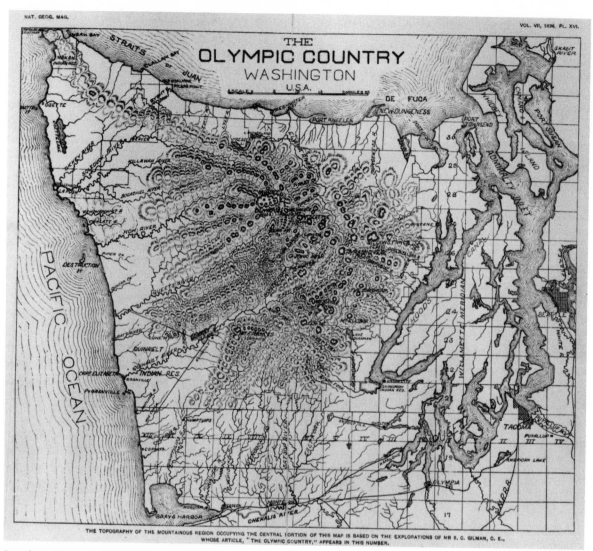

Samuel C. Gilman produced this map to accompany his 1896 article for National Geographic *magazine.*

wide and four miles long to the main body of the mountain. It is difficult to estimate the thickness of this ice cap. At the close of summer, when it is thinnest, there are places where it has the appearance of being at least 500 feet thick. It is built up many additional feet in thickness by the storms of winter, to be correspondingly melted away again by the succeeding warm summer months. The Queets, Hoh, and Solduck rivers head in mount Olympus, and Higley and Tunnel creeks, branches of the Elwha, have their sources in an ice-field two miles long and three-fourths of a mile wide close to the northeast end of Olympus. Tunnel creek has formed a beautifully arched tunnel 20 feet high and 40 feet wide (in summer), through which it flows for two and one-half miles under an accumulation of ice that fills the gorge to a depth of 100 to 300 feet. These accumulations of ice are very numerous among the higher peaks all through the range.

As for scenery, perched on one of the numerous accessible peaks, you are surrounded by towering, sky-piercing pinnacles and ragged, rocky ice-capped ridges that are plowed and harrowed by slides of rock and ice and chiseled and worn by ages of rushing water, mantled with snow and garlanded with great patches of roses and daisies and dainty mountain flowers and gowned with dense, dark evergreen forests, reaching far down into cavernous depths of canyon and ravine, across which on some opposite mountain side is rushing down from its icy fountain head a tumultuous mountain torrent which finally dashes over a lofty precipice and is lost in a veil of mist in the valley below. Away to the west is seen the ocean with its lazily rolling billows, the dark trail of a steamer's smoke, and the white sails of a ship just showing above the horizon. To the east lie Hood's canal and Puget sound, with their bays and arms and inlets spread out like silver leaf on a carpet of green. Beyond rise the dark, wooded slopes and snow-clad summits of the Cascades, with grand old Rainier standing guard to the southeast and the majestic Baker to the northeast.

Lakes Cushman, Crescent, and Quinault are all of considerable extent and great depth. At Quinault lake, nearly 20 miles from the ocean, the boom of the breakers on the beach is plainly heard during and after a storm, but the sound comes from the opposite direction to the ocean, being reflected from the slopes of mount Frances on the east.[8] For 25 miles north from the mouth of Gray's harbor is a stretch of broad, smooth, hard, sand beach reaching to point Grenville. From point Grenville to cape Flattery, bluffs 100 to 250 feet high border the ocean. Sometimes they stand a little back, leaving a narrow strip of loose sand, gravel, boulders, or slippery ledge between them and the sea. Sometimes they approach a little closer; the strip of sand or rock is correspondingly narrower and covered with water as the tide rises. Often they push boldly into the sea, which continually surges and dashes at their feet and leaps high up their face. About five miles southwest of the mouth of the Hoh river and four miles offshore is Destruction island, so called on account of the numerous wrecks that have occurred on its reefs and on the adjacent main shore. The island stands among many broad reefs, some of which are just visible at low tide, and over these the ocean swells foam and boil at high tide. It rises abruptly, with precipitous sides, 80 feet above the water, and then spreads out smooth and level about 60 acres in extent. The Hoh Indians have long cultivated several small potato patches on it and have also used it as a lookout station for whales, in the capture of which animal they have attained great proficiency. The United States Government has built on the island a lighthouse of the first order, 80 feet high, with a double fog-horn and the usual auxiliary building. It commands a fine view of the coast and mountains.

On the mountains, above 4,000 feet, the timber is very scrubby and infrequent, owing , probably, as much to the barrenness of the soil and the great depth of snowfall as to the elevation. At a lower altitude, among rocky crags, are thousands of acres of the finest grazing lands, well watered by innumerable rivulets and pools, fanned by the winds from the ocean, and free from flies, mosquitoes, and all other annoying insects. Of course, these grasslands would not be habitable during the winter, but they would be available from the first of June until December. Among the rocks at the edge of the grasslands, and just below the ice-fields, blueberries, huckleberries, and bearberries grow in profusion, and the season for them lasts from July to October, as they follow the snow up as it melts away, blossoming just below it and ripening a little lower down. These berries attract thither large numbers of black bear, and it is the exception when none are in sight among the peaks during the berry season. These open grasslands are also favorite ranges for large numbers of the elk that are common all over the peninsula and bands of fifty or more are often seen. From 4,000 feet down, the timber is good and thrifty. The Alaska cedar, from one and one-half to five feet in diameter and running up smooth and tall, is a very valuable variety of timber and is common down to 1,000 feet above sea level. The mountains and uplands of the peninsula generally are heavily timbered with hemlock, cedar, spruce, fir, balsam, pine, vine-maple, cottonwood, willow, box elder, crab-apple, ash, dogwood, and occasional immense bottom-land spruces. There is frequently also a very heavy undergrowth of sallal or salmon berry or of hazel or of mountain hemlock. It is also a great country for moss, which grows deep on the ground and down timber and on the trunks of standing trees and hangs in long streamers from the twigs and branches, and is always wet and slippery, except in the dry season. Many beautiful varieties of small, delicate ferns grow among the forests. On the prairies, which are neither numerous nor large, and which are often gravelly, though sometimes containing a very rich soil, a large and coarse variety of fern grows four to ten feet high.

Between the mountains and the coast are about 1,300 square miles, or 830,000 acres, of comparatively level valley and bench lands. Of this about 225,000 acres are rich bottom lands along the various streams. The soil of these bottom lands cannot be surpassed anywhere on the coast. The uplands are generally rolling, but there are several quite extensive and comparatively level tracts. The fact of these lands not draining readily has encouraged the growth of fine bodies of large cedar, with, in some places, tall, smooth, large, white pines scattered among them. These cedar lands are in no sense swamps or bogs. The soil is a heavy clay, into which the sluggish streams have not cut very deep channels, and they are frequently clogged or turned by fallen timber, so that during the rains the streams overrun their banks and spread pretty much all over the country, keeping the ground well soaked all through the rainy season. The soil is excellent, and there are numerous small openings sufficiently large for

179

---

[8] This incredible tale raises questions about how many other items in Gilman's article are fantasy as well.

nice farms. The soil of the rolling uplands is generally a rich, shot clay, but sometimes quite gravelly. The timber is generally very heavy and it will be many years before all the good land is under cultivation. There are, however, many open places and small creek bottoms and depressions among the hills that can be very easily cleared. In fact, there are few 160-acre tracts on which cannot be found ten or more acres of good land comparatively easy to clear, and the timber on all these lands will be valuable in a few years and be a help instead of a hindrance in establishing a home.

The principal streams draining this slope are the Quillyhute and its four branches, the Dickey, the Solduck, the Killawah, and the Bogachiel; the Hoh, Queets, Quinault, and Humptulips. They are all clear, cold, rapid streams, capable of floating logs and being canoed considerable distances. They teem with salmon and trout. The Quinault salmon, peculiar to that stream, is a short, thick fish, weighing from three to seven pounds and said to be the finest variety of salmon on this coast. Opportunities for developing good water-power at very small cost are numerous along these streams, and especially so in the mountains. Game is plentiful and it would be a paradise for the hunter were it not so difficult of access. In addition to elk and bear, before mentioned, are deer, mountain goat, cougar, beaver, otter, fisher, wildcat, marmot, geese, ducks, grouse, partridge, quail, pelican, and many smaller or less desirable birds and animals.[9] Off the beach from Gray's harbor to point Grenville is one of the few sea-otter ranges of the world. It still furnishes a few hides of that valuable fur to market each year.

The country rocks of the mountains are syenite, gneiss, quartzite, protogene, crystalline and chlorite schists, slate (hard black flinty to soft green tale) shale, sandstone, trap, and basalt. In the foothills on the west and along the coast the formation is principally shales, sandstone, cement gravel, conglomerate (in one place near Hoh Head, boulder conglomerate), clays and drift gravel and sand. Limestone much criss-crossed with small quartz seams is found in a few places. Clays are especially abundant and good-appearing, and, so far as tried, give very excellent analytic returns. Beds of partially formed lignite are abundant along the coast between the Quinault and Quillyhute rivers. In a bluff, a few miles south of the mouth of the Hoh river, four seams of such lignite, from 18 inches to 3 feet thick, show very distinctly, and occasionally pieces of wood, but little changed, are found. Small seams of very good coal crop out in several places in

sandstone and shale, but they are too small, so far as found, to be of any value. Between Pillar point and Clallam bay, on the straits of Fuca, is the abandoned Thorndike coal mine. There are said to have been "six leads of coal, ranging in thickness from 1 to 3 feet, dip 10 degrees, distance between coal leads, 12 to 100 feet, formation sandstone." This was said to have been one of the best coals found in Washington. It was mined for some time, until it pinched out or was cut off by a fault and the vein was lost and work abandoned.

In the valley of the Solduck river, among the mountains, is a group of springs which discharge quite a volume of hot water of undetermined medicinal value. Fine springs heavily charged with iron or sulphur are very numerous. On the coast just south of the Queets river, in the bluff along the beach, are several small alum springs. The alum is present in very small quantities, and cannot be detected during the rainy season, when the natural flow of the springs is reinforced by the numerous rains; but during the dry season, when the springs are at their lowest trickles down the cliffs exposed to the afternoon sun, the alum marks with white streaks the margin of the rivulets. There is also some borax present, and probably other chemicals might be found in measurable quantities.

Several varieties of iron ore are scattered promiscuously over the peninsula in limited quantities, and ocher and iron stains are numerous. Near Port Townsend is a deposit of limonite that has been worked for some time. On the headwaters of the Humptulips river is a vein of magnetite about one foot thick. On the coast south of the Raft river is a bed of clay ironstone of very low grade and so badly mixed with sulphurets as in all probability to be worthless. The traces of iron are so abundant and widespread that it would seem that there must be somewhere in the peninsula extensive deposits of a pure and valuable ore.

Colors of gold are found in the beach sands and along several of the streams in the mountains, and in a few places fair wages have been made washing it. Low grade silver and copper ore are found in good-sized veins in the mountains. Comparatively little prospecting has been done, owing to the inaccessibility of the region; not enough to determine its value as a mineral country.

It does not seem reasonable to suppose that the great upheaval of these mountains has been accomplished without bringing within reach some valuable mineral deposits. The principal apparent wealth of the peninsula is in the immense forests of fine timber, of which the Alaska cedar of

---

[9] There were no mountain goats on the Olympic Peninsula until 1929 when the Clallam County Game Commission released six from British Columbia on Storm King Mountain in return for some captured Olympic elk.

the mountains will soon be an important factor, and in the large area of fertile valley and benchland on its western slope.

The climate of the western slope of this peninsula is a little different from that of the rest of western Washington. Owing probably to its proximity to the ocean and its accessibility to the ocean breezes, there is more wind and much less foggy weather. The amount of rainfall on the average is in excess of that of the Sound country, but it comes in the shape of sharper showers and heavier storms, thus allowing a much greater proportion of fair weather. In the summer the nights are cool, but not cold, allowing tomatoes and corn to ripen perfectly and naturally, as they do not elsewhere west of the Cascades. Except in the mountains, ice or snow is seldom seen, and then only for a few hours at a time.

CHAPTER SEVEN.
THE BANTA AND SHARP EXPLORATION 1889-90[1]

In December 1889, while the Humptulips and Quinault Valleys were being settled via Hoquiam or the waterways, J. J. Banta and S. Price Sharp left Tacoma in search of a homestead somewhere west of Port Townsend.

After taking a boat to Pysht, they walked some twenty miles south to a beaver farm, and stopped with two men named Crosby and Harriss, proprietors of what Banta's diary called a "stopping place" or way place on the Soleduck River. There they overtook Charles A. Gilman and his son, Sam, whose trip is described in chapter 6, the Gilman Explorations 1889–90. The elder Gilman explained that they were mapping out a possible route for a railroad, and suggested that if Banta and Sharp would accompany the Gilmans to the Grays Harbor country, he would defray their expenses. As Banta and Sharp had no definite destination and were out to explore the country, they agreed to Gilman's proposition.

Accordingly, the four men, with sixty-pound packs on their backs, set out across the unexplored wilderness of the Duckabush Divide. Their daring trip through the Olympic Peninsula in winter led to the colonization of the Queets and Clearwater Valleys, as related in Banta's diary.[2]

DIARY OF J. J. BANTA[3]

Memorandum of our exploring trip from Tacoma around the Straits of Juan De Fuca to Pysht Bay, and through the country south to Grays Harbor. (S. P. Sharp, J. J. Banta) Dec. 3rd 1889 to Jan. 7th 1890.

Left Tacoma on board State of Washington Dec. 3, 1889 in company with S. A. Ayers, Fred Higbee, Geo. McDonald and Jacob Osborn.

Landed at Sea Home Dec. 4th about ten oclock A.M.

Ate our dinner. Went over to Fair Haven, found prices of Real Estate high. Also Rents. Could not get a building for Lodging House at any price. Small rooms 10' x 20' rent of $35.00 per month. At Port Townsend about an [sentence not completed]

Sea Home, Bellingham and Fair Haven will make a large City in the near future. They are virtuly one town now, though under seperate governments. They Have the finest Harbor on the Sound, and a good country to back them.

Dec. 5th. We took the Mail Boat, Point Arena [Aressa?] for Port Townsend and after cruising around all day among the Islands of the Sound, visiting Orcas Island, Roach Harbor, Friday Harbor, and several other small places, taking on board 1000 brls Lime at the Seattle Lime works, and going within ten miles of Victoria B.C. we landed at Port Townsend about ten Oclock that night.

Put up at the Olympic Lodging House. Stayed all day Dec. 6 there, looking oer the City, and in making preperations for our trip. While here I met an Old Friend of North Salem Ind. Mr Newton Orear, who I had not seen for five years. Had a good chat of Old Times. Left Port Townsend Dec. 7th..on Board the Evangel, for Pysht Bay, but found that the Boat only went as far as Port Angeles that day, that we would have to lay over there untill Dec. 9th. before we could go on to Pysh Bay.

Put up at the Bon Ton House.

Several persons wer seaSick on the trip down the straits. Our Fare on the Boat was $1.50. At the Bon Ton for supper bed and breakfast $1.00. We Concluded to walk to Crescent Bay Dec. 8th as Port Angeles was not much of a place and it being Sunday too, we thought it would be a dull place

---

[1] "Banta and Sharp had gone to the Olympic Peninsula from Tacoma in early December, 1889, 'in search of a homestead west of Port Townsend' [according to their diary]. They arrived in Port Angeles on December 7 (the day the Press Expedition left Seattle), and at a way place on the Soleduck River met the Gilmans. . . . On December 23, when the party reached a point on the Queets River about eight miles from the ocean, Banta decided this was the place where he wanted to take his homestead. The men ended their journey at Grays Harbor City on January 4, 1890. . . . Upon their return to Tacoma, Banta and Sharp began 'making arrangements to organize a colony' and that spring twenty-one claims were taken. The men worked feverishly to promote the project—known generally as 'the Tacoma settlement'—and Banta alone made six trips to the Queets in 1890 with prospective homesteaders. The following year they chartered a steamship which transported settlers to the Queets on two occasions." Wood, *Men, Mules and Mountains*, p. 399.

[2] This introduction was adapted from the introduction to the edited version of Banta's diary that appeared in Lucile Horr Cleland's compilation *Trails and Trials of the Pioneers of the Olympic Peninsula, State of Washington* (Humptulips, Wash.: The Humptulips Pioneer Association, 1959; facsimile reproduction, Seattle: Shorey Book Store, 1973).

[3] Banta's diary is presented here unedited as he wrote it, with spelling, grammar, and punctuation intact. The notes in brackets are by the compiler, Lucile H. Cleland, done to clarify when transcribing the handwritten original.

to stop in. Though I believe some day Port Angeles will be a Large City.

Accompanyed by a young Man, Seth Davis, from Missouri. We started early to walk to Crescent Bay, 12 miles down the Straits. It was raining and we did not know the Road and when night came on we found ourselves at an Old deserted House. At what is called Fresh Water Bay, about 2 miles from ~~Pysht~~, Crescent by the Beach, and five miles around the road.

We had had no dinner and our supper consisted of nice Fresh Baked Sea Biscuit, or Hard tack and water, but we had a good fire, and slept well. Our Breakfast was allee samee supper.

We reached Crescent Bay about noon next day, with wet feet and a good Appetite. Here we got a good square meal, warmed ourselves by the fire all afternoon. Ate our supper, Paid our fare, .50¢ and was ready for the Evangel when she came along.

She came about nine Oclock at night. The tide was out, and we had to wade quite aways in water over our Shoe tops, to get into the Boat, but we got there Just the same. We arrived at Pysht Bay at about eleven Oclock and here we again had to wade ashore, only we had to wade water kee [knee] deep in several places, for a about 40 rods. We didnot like that kind of Steam Boating. (Our Fare on the Evangel was $1.00.)

We stopped at the Lodging house there (the only house in the place), dried Ourselves before a big fireplace, went to bed and slept well. Ate our China cooked breakfast next morning, paid our 50¢ for Bed and Breakfast. We also left our Over Coats there, intending to go back that way.

Tuesday Dec. 10, 1889. We started early in the morning to walk over the divide twenty miles to Beaver Farm where there is a stoping place kept by Messrs Crosby and Harriss.

It was raining and snowing most all day, and we were pretty cold, tired and wet, when we arrived there about five Oclock in the evening.

But Mr. Harriss had a good fire and plenty to eat, and we was soon feeling allright.

At this place Mr. C. A. Gilman and Son, who had preceeded us one day, Made us a propasition that if we would go on through the Country to Grays Harber, That They would go with us. And as we was out Looking at the Country anyhow, We agreed to go.

The Country proposed to Explore is the Country of which the West Shore and the Seattle Post, each have written quite a long article—Stating that the country had never been entered by any White man. That there had been one or two men fare enough up the Olympic Mts. to look over into

this Country, And that They had said there was a beautiful Lake over there. Surrounded by Mountains. That there were beautiful valeys and beautiful Rivers emptying into this lake from all directions. And that the Lake was supposed to have an underground outlet.

Also that this beautiful place was inhabited by a fierce Band of Indians, who were certain death to anyone who might venture in there, and that all the other Indians were afraid to go there.

We didnot believe any of these storries and didnot think there was any particular danger, unless we might get hungry.

Sharp and I got some good heavy canvass from Mr Harriss and made us some good pack straps, and got ready for the Journey (of) three weeks.

Dec. 11th. We started after noon with about 60# pack to each man. Traveled about eight miles, and put up with Mr. Henry Farrill at night. The Land through here is comparitively level, and is covered with the best Fir timber I ever saw.

The Settlement is away ahead of the Survey, and land is being taken up very fast.

I think the land is most valuable for the timber here, though there is some fine bottom land on the Rivers.

The Quillayute is formed by three smaller rivers, the Solduc the Calawa and the Bogacheal. The Solduc being the Largest next the Bogacheal.

There is some Indications of Coal deposit here in several places. Some small prarie's one of about 2000 acres, near the Forks of these Rivers.

Dec. 12. We made the Forks Post Office by noon, and put up with Mr Peter Fisher. Mr Fisher has a fine farm located on a prairia of about 2000 Acres. The Prairia is all taken up, and is pretty well improved. Mr. Fisher has lived there twelve years, has a nice Orchard, gave us each an apple which he had raised. He said all kinds of fruit does well there.

There is a small Saw Mill there, Run by Water Power, cuts about 1200 ft per day. (The Mill is nearly all wood, except the Blade. (The Saw)

This prairia is between the forks or the Solduc and Bogacheal River.

Mr. Fisher has been nearly all over this Country, has followed the several Rivers to thear source, looking for gold and other Minerals, has not found any.

There is some fine bottom land along these Rivers, and is about all taken up, except on the Bogacheel, above the prairie. I think there is quite a lot of good land not yet taken.

At Mr. Fishers we hired the Women Folks to take our Wagon Sheets and splice them and make us a tent.

Bought some Bacon, Butter, Coffee and Flour of them. Also some Pans, spoons and knives and forks.

Started Friday noon (Dec. 13) with about 60 lbs. Pack to each man. Crossed the Bogacheel River about $1\frac{1}{2}$ miles from Mr. Fishers. Mr. F had gone that far with us to show us a vein of coal, that he had found. But couldnot find it anymore. He took us across the River in an Indian's Canoe. We bid Him good bye, and went up the river about $1\frac{1}{2}$ miles and camped in the woods.

The up land or seckond Bottom is comparatively level. good soil. Hemlock and Spruce Timber. Some Cedar in places.

Saturday 14, we made about 5 miles, and camped again in the woods, the soil & Timber, being about the same. Monday 16, we traveled all day over land pretty much the same as the day before, made about 4 miles, and camped on a hillside by a large Cedar Tree, measuring 28 ft. around the but.

Tuesday 17th. We Traveled over Mts. about 1200 ft high, reached the Ho River about noon. The Ho River is a good big River, and a very rappid River. Large piles of drift wood all over the bottom. Some great Trees 6 ft. through and 100 ft long, piled up in piles, Just as though they were sticks of kindling wood.

Some fine Bottom land where we came to the River. Think there is lots of it all along the River. We struck the River about two miles above the Mouth. This we think is the longest River of any we have crossed. That is heads away up on the north side of Mt. Olympus.

Wednesday 18th. Some Indians came along about two Oclock, and we gave them two dollars to take us down to the Ocean. We didnot know it was so short a distance, or we could have walked it easy. There are about 50 Indians at the River's mouth. They most all are barefooted, and One Old Man had nothing on but a thin Calico shirt. But some of them was well dressed. They seemed to think we were quite a Curious looking set of men. Some of them had been going to the School at Quinauilt Resurvation, and we could talk with them a little.

Hired one of them to go with us down the beach to the Quits River, to show us the way and to keep us from geting caught by the tide. Gave Him $3.00.

We Came to quite a Stream and he striped himself and Carried us all across. I think he made six trips across before he got us and our baggage all across.

We didnot expect this of Him but made no kick about it.

We camped on the Beach near this River. Coming down the beach this after noon, we had to Clime the bank and wait for the Tide to go out, for about 4 hours. This was opposite Destruction Island. They say there are two Farms on this Island. We can see quite a number of houses.

Friday l9th [20th] 1889. We had to wait untill nearly noon for the Tide to go down, Then we started for the Queits. Our guide said that he lived about one mile up the River and said if we would go up to his house that night, we was welcome to stay in his house. That he had plenty Flour, Salt Salmon Coffee and Potatoes. That He had a boat at the River to ride up in. This suited us, for we were wet through, and Cold, and I don't think I ever was much more tired than I was when we reached his boat. It was dark when we got to the Boat, and He said we would soon be there, but after we had sat still in the Boat for about one houre we were geting awful Cold. Would ask Him how near he was to His house. He would answer half mile. We would go about half mile ask again, and again get the same answer. Well, well! I think if anyone had been near and heard our teeth rattling, they would have thought it was a hundred frogs hollering. Well after we came very near being upset in the River, and had made two miles up the River, we pulled to shore, got out and followed a narrow path for about 40 rods. sometimes we had to hold on to one another to keep from getting lost. Expecting to come to the house every minute, but the first thing we knew we came out to the River again. Our walk had warmed us up some and we didnot feel so bad.

Our guide gave a war whoop and the Dogs began to bark. A light was lit up, and we see we were just across the River from the house. An Old Indian came over in a boat to take us over. But He not knowing there was so many of us, came over in one of thear small canues. And when he came up to the shore Our guide said get in Boys, and when we did get in the Boat began to sink. Our guide was in the front part of the boat, and pulled it to shore and got out. Now my Partner, S. P. Sharp, wanted out too, and I don't know wheather He thought he could walk on the water or not. But anyhow he steped out and and went to the bottom, about 3 ft. of cold water. He must a lost his faith, for he said somthing about the damed bank or something else, I did not just understand Him.

Well 3 men got out, and the rest of us went across, then the Old Indian went over after the other fellows. We all went into the house, which was about 30 ft. by 70 ft. divided.

There were 3 fires burning in the house, and 3 different Families crouched around them. In one corner was Just one old Woman, alone, who had allittle fire of her own. No one seemed to pay any attention to her, nor her to them. I suppose She had served Her day and was of no use any longer, and was Just waiting for the last fires of life to burn out.

Our Guide's (whose name is Charley Misp) Wife and all the Others seemed to be pleased with our Visit. The Land Lady flew around and Made some baking Powder Bread,

184

pealed some Potatoes and Boiled them with some salt Salmon, made some Tea, and when She had it all ready She spread a piece of Canvass down [on] a large platform, (which they use for all purposes), and set out each man a plate cup and saucer, knife and fork, and when She was done, I tell you the Table looked quite tempting to men who were hungry like we were. And I am sure we done it Justice.

And I thought that they were the best civilized Indians I have ever saw.

We dried ourselves by the fire and made our beds on Indian bedsteads went to bed and slept well.

Our Guide and Land Lord had agreed to take us up the River next day in his canue, to go as far up as he could go in two days time, and we thought we would start early next morning.

Saturday Morning, Dec 20 [Sat. 21st]. We layed in bed untill real late, waiting for our host to get up, but he was a better stayer then we. So we got up and pretty soon Misses Injun got up and after She got breakfast and we were all ready to go, Mr. Misp said that he couldnot go that day. Well it was late anyhow, and He said He could go next day early, we concluded to stop at the Misp House one day and night longer.

It was a rainy day and we stayed in doors most all day.

While Mrs. Injun was geting Supper I noticed that She had Elk Tallow put up in a gut (Just like we put up sausage), which She used to rub the end on the bread pan to keep the bread from sticking. and after She had greased the pan all good, and handed the grease to another Squaw. The Old gal tooke it and rubed it all over her face then over her hair, after She had herself well slicked up another took it and went through the same performance. I Just wondered if they had used the same gut for the same purpose before.

Again I saw a bright little girl about eight years old go up to a bucket that had some water in it where we had all been drinking, and where there was a tin cup seting on either side of the bucket, but instead of using the tins, She Just stuck her wooly head down into the bucket and supped the water from the bottom of the bucket.

Then I tried to think had I taken a drink or not? if so how long a go?

Sunday Dec. 22 1889. We hired two Indians to take us up the river ten miles. We have to pay them six dollars.

The Queits River doesnot head so high up in the Mts. but is formed among the foothills, and gathers its water's from a more level surface. Consequently it is not so swift as is the Ho or the Quinault. We think the bottom land will average one mile wide. it is level, and rich, does not overflow, is timbered with Cottonwood and Alder. We Camped

tonight about six miles up the river on a gravel bar.

Monday 23. We took dinner about 8 miles (Here is where I think I want to take my homestead), on North West side of River. Fine land Covered with small Cottonwood timber. Large Island on East side. Covered with Alder. Indians say there is a Prairia on both sides of the river about $1\frac{1}{2}$ miles. Camped at forks of River about ten miles from Oacean. There is still lots of fine land here yet, though the Valley is not so wide. We are about 150 or 200 ft. above the Sea level here.

The main Branch comes in from the north, And a branch about $\frac{1}{4}$ as large, comes from the East.

Tuesday 24 Dec 1889. Broke camp early in the morning. Started South. Come into heavy Cedar timber, and thick brush, shortly after we left the river.

Camped on Mountain Ridge about 4 miles from the River. Tomorrow is Christmas. Plenty of places to hang our socks, but not much prospect of geting them filled with Presents.

Christmas Morning. Clear and nice, Not very cold. About 2 inches snow on the ground. didnot leave camp untill about ten Oclock. Saw a band of about one dozen Elk, but didnot get a shot at them in time to get one.

About one Oclock we came to quite a Stream. We didnot know wheather it is Raft River or a branch of the Queits, that might empty into it near the Island.

Passed through some very fine Cedar timber.

We got a good view of the Country north and west, from a windfall on the Mt. Could see a long way north, and to the Ocean west. I dont think it is very hilly between the Queits and the Ho Rivers.

We judged it was 25 miles from Ocean to foothills.

Thursday 26. Traveled south East about 5 miles. Most of the way Over high hills and ridges. About one and ahalf miles into a Cedar swamp. Finest Cedar and most of it we have seen anywhere. Camped tonight right in the swamp. Our clothes wet through, and about 2 inches of wet snow on the ground. I would rather be in Tacoma. We are about out of Provisions, hope to reach the River tomorrow.

It is Raining now, will be wet traveling tomorrow.

Friday 27 Dec. 1889. We left Camp about ten Oclock in the Rain. Bushes wet with snow and water.

Traveled all day in a flat Cedar swamp. Awful fine cedar timber, and very hard to travel through on account of fallen timber and brush. Mad about five miles today, done without dinner, have only one more days grub. going on half rations now.

Saturday Dec. 28. Camped on the Quinaiult near the burned hill. We came to the River about 2 miles above here, and about 5 miles we suppose from the Lake. And 20 miles from the Ocean. We only made about 3 miles this morning. Saw some of the finest pile timber I ever saw anywhere, this morning. saw two large fir trees, on the hills near the River, the first we have seen since we crossed the Bogacheel river. Our Provisions has dwindled down to Just enough flour for half a meal in the morning. And a little slice of Bacon apiece. But plenty of Coffee and Tea. Begins to look like we would get pretty hungry before we can get anything to eat. The nearest Indians live about 15 miles down the river. We have concluded to dig us a log for a canue, and go down the river, as we could not stand it, to go on across the Country to the Humptulips settlement.

Sunday Dec. 29th. Commenced our canue this morning. S Gillman went hunting but got nothing. Worked hard on the old Log untilll one Oclock. The Log was a Spruce 2 ft through and 26 ft long. We found it very slow work to dig it out.

About one Oclock we noticed the Ducks comming down the River in droves. We guessed some one must be coming down the River, and quit work. We didnot feel much like work anyhow.

Sure enough, a boat came along with 4 white men in it, who had been up above the Lake Making Claims.

But They too had run out of Provisions, and couldnot spare us any, nor could they take us all down in thear boat. But Mr C. A. Gilman said that he would go down with them, to the nearest Indians house and hire them to come up after us the next day and bring us something to eat.

Well we quit work right then, we thought we could stand it longer if we didnot work. All we done was to keep a good Fire. It stormed hard all afternoon. We ate our last bread tonight, leaving our Bacon untill morning. But just about dark a Grouse came and lit in a tree near by, And Sam Gillman killed it. So now we will sleep late tomorn [sic], and have a good dinner anyhow. We have just a little flour left, and we will make some nice Grouse Soup.

Monday Dec. 30 1889. We had a fine breakfast. Bill of Fare—Grouse Soup, 3 cups full to each man, and plenty of Coffee. After Soup, Sharp and I took our gun and went to the top of the burned Hill. Where we had a good View of the whole country around. It was a fine sight.

We got back to camp wet and Cold and Hungry. We had nothing to do but keep up the fire, and go Hungry untill the Indians came, let it be one day or a week. But about 5 Oclock we heard the Indians shoot a gun off down the River, then we knew we were allright. They soon came in sight, Landed and gave us the grub Mr. Gilman had sent us. Potatoes, Flour, salt Salmon, & 3 loaves of Bread. Well the

Bread didnot last long, disappeared long before supper was ready.

The Indians, Jim Chow Chow, and Molex—something—I hav forgotten His name, Made a quick trip. Mr Gillman didnot reach thear House untill ten Oclock that day, Having stayed out all night before in the Storm, without any tent. stood around the fire allnight, but He told them that we were out Muck a Muck and that they must reach us that night, or they was not to have the full amount He had promised them—$7°° for bringing us down to the mouth of the River to the Agency.

Tuesday, Dec 31 1889. We left our camp about eight oclock. Had a nice trip down the River, for about 15 miles to the Indians Home [House?]. here We stoped and they ate thear dinner, and we warmed ourselves by the fire.

Then we went on down the river to the Agency. Arived there about 3 oclock. Here we met White People, and They were White Too.

Mr. Agers, the Agent, are [all?] Michigan people. They would have us take supper with them, and sleep in the Store Room. And would have us promise to take breakfast with them.

Had quite a pleasant chat with them. (Mr A is an I.O.O.F.). They Formly [formerly] came from Chipawa Co Michigan to Albany Or., then up Here.

Chas Mcintyer is Teamster for the government, and is a well informed man and We learned quite considerable from Him of the habits ect [etc.] of the Indians. We also met Dr Huston, the Physician there in charge.

met Mr Jackson [Cleve Jackson?] an Indian, Mr. Baker (Indian), Frank Hiason [Hyasman] (Indian).

We bid good bye to the Old Year, rolled ourselves in our blankets and went to sleep.

New Years Day. Jan 1 1890. Up early in the morning. Took Breakfast with Mr. Agers. We hired an Indian (Mr. Jackson) to haul us and our baggage down to the Oyhut, at the landing on the North West side of Grays Harber. Paid Him $6.00.

The distance from the Agency to the Oyhut is about 25 miles. We didnot leave the Agency untill halfpast ten Oclock. Had to wait until the tide was down, so we could pass a Point of Rock on the Beach. The day was windy and cold, and snow flying. We wraped ourselves each in a big double blanket, and then had to walk half the time to keep warm.

We took dinner at Mr Grigsby's about one mile from the Chepalis River, about 4 oclock. Had a splendid dinner, and warmed ourselves good and went on. (Paid 25¢ apiece for dinner). We arrived at the Oyhut about seven oclock. Mr Chas McIntyer had been kind enough to loan us the Key to

186

His house there, Where there was plenty of things to eat, and Stoves and beds ect. [etc.] And we was glad to get in out of the Storm.

The Beach between here and the Agency is fine, except about 1½ miles between the rocky Point and the Quinaiult. The Beach is all taken up by parties who think that it will be a grand Summer Resort some day. It is also mined considerable. The sand has gold in it. There is also quite a buisness Carried on there, Shooting Sea Otter. The Hunters have high dericks fixed up with alittle house on top of them large enough for aman to stand up in. and shoots the Otter away out in the Ocean, and Waits the Tide to bring them in. A good Sea Otter skin is worth one hundred dollars.

Jan 2 1890. It is snowing and blowing this morning to beat the Jews.

Mr Bull, the man who runs the sail boat from Here to the Terminus, is at the City now, And the ice is freezing on the flats here that He cannot land if He should come back. The Steamer which comes to Damons Point once aweek left last evening, and it will be a week before it will return. It looks now like we were pretty well boxed up.

We have of everything to eat here in the house and can stay here as long as we wish. And we would not mind being here if we had men who was not eather grumbling at Each other or else seting around grim [grum?] all the time. We don't know what is the matter with them. Wheather they are mad about something and afraid to say so, or what is the trouble with them.

My Opinion of Sam Gilman is, that He is an Arrogant, Selfish phool.

A Man who will contradict and dispute and quarrel with his Father over such trivial things as He does I dont Consider is any man at all.

Snow fell to the debth [depth] of two inches last night.

Price and I went out to the mud flats this evening and dug some Clams. had them cooked for supper. I don't go much on Clams.

Friday Jan 3 1890. Mr. Bull the Boat man came home this evening says he can take us to Grays Harber City tomorrow. He had to land his boat at Damons Point six miles south west of here, and we will have to walk that far in the morning.

It has been Clear and Cold here today. They say the Thermometer stood ten degrees above zero. Not so very cold if the wind didnot blow so strong from the East. Mr Blodget aman who lives here says it is the coldest it has been here for a long time. Nothing to do but eat, sleep, and grow fat. Mum is still the word with our Companions. The Old Man would

talk, but He is afraid that He will set that infernal Grumbling Mechine to going. So He holds his tonng. Ta Ta Sonny.

Saturday Jan 4th 1890. We left our Camp at 9 Oclock and walked to Damans Point, got there about eleven Oclock. Price Sharp and I both got our feet soaking wet, geting into the boat. The Wind was blowing strong and Cold from the East, which made it very hard for us to sail. By Constant Tacking we made out to arrive at the mud flats of the great Coming City of Grays Harbor, Just as the tide was going out, About 5 Oclock in the evening.

we pushed and pulled and Paddled untill we could go nofurther, and hung up, stuck tighter than blazes, about 40 rods from shore. Nothing to do but get out and wade ashore in mud two feet deep and some times deeper. And the slickest mud I ever did see. We left part of our packs on the Boat, Mr. Bull promising to bring them in early in the morning.

We got to the Hotel Grays Harbor, about six oclock, and was a [as] nasty looking set of men as had ever stoped there I reckon.

Our chuns [chums] left us here and I was glad of it. They going on to a Soninlaws place, up on the Hill. Sharp and I ate our supper, dried ourselves by the fire, and went to bed.

Sunday Jan 5th 1890. After eating our breakfast we took a walk over the City, up on the Hill on Summit Avenue. There are about one dozzen houses on this street and others on the hill. And about the same number down next to the landing. Summit Ave is graded, or partly graded, and They are at work now grading Broadway. donot stop for Sunday here. I think the Town Site is a very rough one and will require a wonderful amount of work to grade the streets and Excavating for buildings. They have a grade for a Rail Road made from Hoquaim to the foot of Broadway street. The Wharf is built one mile and a quarter long. The Ware House at the Wharf is Just about completed.

The snow is 3 inches deep. The Thermometer 20° above zero. I had to throw my shoes away here as they would hardly stay on my feet any longer. I could not buy any shoes Here, and a Man at the Hotel gave me a pair of old Rubber Boots to wear untill I could get some shoes.

We did not see Mr Bull the Boat man anymore. Mr C. A. Gillman came down to the Hotell, and bid us good bye. But Sam didnot. Mr C. A. Gillman promising to take care of some things left in the boat, for us and bring them to us at Hoquiam the next day.

In company with Mr Christman, a Barber who used to work at Centerville Oregon, we walked to Hoquiam this evening. Arrived at the Gamage House about five Oclock. This hotell is kept by Mr Chas Gardner and Wife ne Mrs

Abe Jones of Athera [Athena?]. Had a pleasant chat with them in the Parlor.

The City of Hoquiam is located on a low flat filled in with sawdust. Backed upby low hills on the north and northwest. I think it is a better place for a large City than Gray's Harbor City is.

Monday Jan 6th 1890. Left Hoquiam half past eight in the morning on board the Tillie [Tilley?] for Montesano, Stoped a [at] Aberdeen a few minutes.

Aberdeen is the Largest City on the bay. It is five miles from Hoquiam, and Situated on the banks of the Chehalis River.

It is eaquely as well located as Hoquiam and a nice town full of life.

Next came a small but beautiful little place called Cosmopolis, situated about half way between Aberdeen and Montesano. It is a Saw Mill town.

The Chehalis river is a mile from Montesano down to the Bay. Tide rises eight feet at Montesano.

We arrived at Montesano at noon, stoped at the Olympia Hotell.

This is a nice place, well layed out, on a nice prarie, Well Lighted with Electricity, New Court House to Cost $14,000 Just about finished, but somehow it is awful dull, the dullest place we have seen anywhere.

The snow is about 14 inches deep here. And people are out Sleigh riding with all manner of outfits, some with Horses and some with Oxen. There are very few roads in this country, and not many teams.

Our Hotell fare $1.00 per day.

Tuesday Jan 7th 1890. We left Montesano at ten Oclock, took the Train for Kamilche, Fare $2.25.

Passed through a small place called Elma, on the summit, which was a nice little town. It is 15 miles from Montesano.

Kamilche is on an arm of the Sound, not much of a place, and not much room to grow. Arrived here about noon. Went aboard the Multnoma. Ate dinner on the boat, 50¢. Fare to Tacoma $1.50. Stoped at Olympia a few minutes. Arived at Tacoma five Oclock in the evening, being out just five weeks. Total Expence per man $37.00.

Jan 8, 9 & 10 1890. S. P. Sharp and I kept ourselves buisy getting an Office (Room 14, 1002½ Tacoma Avenue) and in making arangements to organize a Colony to Settle on the Queits River.

We charge all parties who locate with us $50 for our services. They pay us nothing untill They see the land and are satisfied.

Feb 4th 1890. I and Mr Ed Grant and L. L. Carr Started from Tacoma and went to the Queits River to Mark out the land in claims of 160 acres each so it would be no trouble in locating.

We had some bad weather on our trip but arrived at Banta Station (Grant's name for it) about 4 Oclock in the evening.

Feb 11th 1890. I bought a bill of provisions at Hoquiam. Cost $31.50. Cost to get them to camp $37.00.

This is Indians Rate.

We employed Mr Walkitup to haul it from Damons Point to Agency. Dick & Chickamen man to carry it up to the Queits. Dick [Sharp] & Wife [Mary] & Jim (Fatty) to take us up the Queits.

I stayed with the Boys one week, helped Mark out claims and showed them where to build our Cabins, and came home.

I left Dick's Place at six in the morning and made The Agency by half past eleven on sunday left the next morning and made it [to] Mr Grigsbys one mile from Chepalis River, and stoped all night with him. Came to Damons next day, to Hoquiam the next day and home the next, arriving at Tacoma at five Oclock Feb 27 1890. Total cost of trip expenses and Provisions $86.00.

Tuesday March 11 1890. Sharp and I started with only eight men out of 34 names we had on our contract Paper. Most all of them were afraid they would be swindled. But we went out with the eight, and located 14 claims, and all were well satisfide except two.

The following are the names of those who went.

Adam Matheny
John Hollenbeck
J. E. Tisdale
B. Workman
F. H. Gardner
E. W. Grant
J. J. McGarry
F. R. Baker

The last two named didnt like the country, and wouldnot leave camp to look at the land. Though McGarry had first choise of Claims, having drawn no [number] one, when we drew for choice of claims. They said the country wouldnot be settled up in fifteen years.

They went back to Tacoma and told quite a string of lies.

But the Certificate of the others who did like the country, soon overcome the effect of thear lies. While I was gone the Portland, Port Angeles and Victoria R.R. was Incorpo-

188

rated, and now we will soon have a road and our country will boom.

We had quite a scaly [scary?] time coming home, in passing the Points of Rock on the beach. The wind had blown hard all night, and was still blowing that day, and kept the Tide in all day, and in going through a Tunnell in one of the Points, which was only about $4\frac{1}{2}$ ft high and about 20 ft long, some of the Boys thaught thear time had come, especially F. H. Gardner and J. E. Tisdale. The Tunnell would fill entirely full of water, when the tidal waves came in, and we had to watch our chance and go through when the wave receeded or went back. We all got wet up to our arms, and Tisdale and Gardner (Poor Fellows) They thaught would never get out of that hole. But thank the Good Lord we all came out safe, sound and well salted. And hope to live to see the Queits settlement the best in the land.

April 8 1890. I left Tacoma again with the following men to Locate.—Claims located:

Philip Mathews one
Geo. Cleveland one
C. S. Burnett one
A Strugle two
F. Schaupp one
G. W. Westfall one
We also located one for Capt Kopperhat.

We had a very good time going out. Cleveland (the Yankee) Worried the Reverend G. W. Westfall considerable and made lots of amusement for the rest of us.

We had to lay over one day at the agency, before we could get the Indians to carry our stuff for us. We had to pay $19.00 this trip to get our Mr [merchandise?] hauled from Damons Point [to the] Agency. But at the Agency is where the Indians begin to count the Quatters on us. Its Quatter for this and Quatter for that, and for crossing the river Quatter, Quatter, Quatter. (some of the Boys will remember this).

We made it up to the Queits allright, had to lay over sunday, went on up to the camp monday.

All the parties were well pleased with the Country. Found Dad Hollenbeck working like a Tiger in his garden.

Cleveland returned to Tacoma after about one week, after having built them each a log house.

I remained out there Just a month. Marking our more claims building houses ect.

Mr. G. W. W. worked about three weeks making a boat to cross the [Queets] in, and had just had it finished a few days. Crossed the river 3 times, fell out of the boat and into the River twice. The 3 [third] time he made preperations for it, Pulled off all his clothes except his shirt, so if he did get ducked he would have dry clothes when he came out anyhow, but came across allright.

Sharp and I and F. Schaupp left there tuesday eve went to Dick Hote11 that night, made to Grigsby's the next night, tired and hungry. next morning Mr Grigsby let us ride to the Oyhut, and we came to Hoquiam in a sail boat, and on home Friday, reaching Home at five Oclock.

Tuesday May 20 1890. S. P. Sharp started again for the Colony. Messrs Schaupp & Cleveland accompanying Him. there also was six other gentlemen going out to locate with him.

Mr. W. G. McRoberts & N. Nellis are the two who located and are staying with it.

E. Campbell, P. St. Louis and Mr Pete and one other Noyork [New York] Boy selected claims and afterwards threw them up.

Mr F. W. Boss gave out on the way up there and stoped at Mr Grigsby's and selected him a claim there.

June 10 I went out again with another crowd.

Mr H. B. Lyman, J. H. Dickerson, D. C. Burk, Chas Barnhart, Wm Maskell and Chas Crabb.

Mr Fred Mead also started with us, but for some reason he only went as far as Hoquiam.

Mr Lyman selected claims for E. Gregory 2, Mr Reed 2, one for his soninlaw Mr Randa 1, one for his son. One for Thom Craft and one for himself.

Came home to make a report, if he goes back all will go, if he fails to go, none of the party will go. Mr Burk took two Claims. one for his brother and one for himself. Barnhart took two. one for his friend Cushman and one for himself. Mr Crabb didnot locate.

I located a claim for Miss Dicky, Edward Belch, and 3 for Mr Bassett's Sons. Mr Dickerson located, and we put up his house for him, and he moved into [it] before we came away. We was there about two weeks and it rained some about every day the whole two weeks. And we had a very wet time of it. I upset our boat and spilled Mr Dickerson and myself into the River, lost Mr Lyman's ax and got a good ducking besides.

Rev. G. W. Westfall undertook to build his house on another mans claim, and when He found out that the Colonists would not alow that kind of buisness he sold his garden and came out with a very long lip about the timber being so very limy [limby] and no good, and the Soil no good, and the water muddy, and he dident like the country nohow. I was glad to get shut of such a man for a neighbor. I gave him $25 to leave the neighborhood and $5 for his garden.

189

Lyman, Westfall, Schaupp & Wm. Maskell came out together. Started home June 29th and land in Tacoma July 1st.

L. W. Carr & J. J. Banta came out July 9th at Tacoma. Carr had been up there just 4 months.

July 31. I started again for the Queets. H. B. Lyman, H. K. Mayhew, Chas Lawler, S. Thornton & F White accompaning me.

We had quite a time crossing the harbor in Mr. Conklings boat. We left Hoquiam about halfpast four in the morning. There was on board the boat besides our party Mr. Benne, Mr Burroughs, Mr Baldwin, Mr Schaupp and Wife and a box of Cherry bitters. We got badly stuck on the sand spit that day as well as on the box of bitters. Mrs S got very sick (sea sick) her husband was also troubled with the same sickness to. Mr Burroughs fell overboard, and such another puffing and blowing you never did hear. the Old Lady Schaupp soon had him out and in the boat allright again with the exceptions of wet cloths [clothes]. Then we landed on Damons point and waited for the Tide to come in. while there we had a regular old Clam bake, while Burroughs baked his shins. I made the quickest trip to the Queets this time that I ever made. Johny Johns took our provisions from the Oyhut to the Queets in his sail boat. Charged us $22.00.

Mr. Mayhew was well pleased with his claim I had selected for him. Mr Thornton and Lawler also liked the Country and located. Mr Mayhew Just spread himself for a few days, making the [woods] echo with his ax.

In about two weeks Mayhew, Thornton, Lawler, Dickerson, Hollenbeck and Sharp went out for Tacoma. I went as far as Hoquiam and brought back a boat load of provisions. We had about 2700 lbs and it cost me $55 to get it around. Mr Boss met me at hoquiam and Sent some grub along to. The Indinuns [Indians] were drunk at hoquiam and we had hard work to get them away with the stuff. Mr Lyman and myself were all alone up there for about three weeks, all having gone out except us, on the main river. Mr Boss was alone on the Nellis Creek for about a month. I came out Sept. 22ed, Sharp having come back upthere and Located Mr I. G. Digford, Mr Stewart [and] Mr Billings.

I left Tacoma again Oct 6 with Mr J L Thomas, W A Cushman, Chas Barnhart and Fred Brase. On a bet with J J Banta, W A Cushman walked barefooted from Damons Point to the agency. Left Damons at 12 oclock and arrived at the Agency at eight in the evening. He was to arrive at the Agency at the same time that Cultus Jim the Indian mail carrier did. Well he made it and won $2.00 off of J. B. But he said the Indian made Him hustle and made him run for three miles at a stretch. And we didnot disbelieve Him for his tracks in the sand was proof of his statement.

Messrs Barnhart, Thomas and Cushman were stoping in Barnhart's House, while up there, and the floods came and surrounded the house and the Boys took to the hills and landed on Mt Barnhart, half mile east, where they camped under a rubber blanket all night. In their haste to get on high land they only carried a small amount of flour and some bacon with them and the Boys say that that was a horrible night. It was reported that Thomas would cuss J. J. Banta a while, then he would pray a while. And when he got tired and would drop off to sleep, Cushman would do the praying for strength to hold up untill daylight came so they could get out of the country and get to Tacoma again.

When daylight did come they found that they had left the house for nothing, that if they had stayed there they would have been allright. so they went back and that day they selected a large spruce tree some twohundred feet high and intended to climb that the next night if the water came up again. but the floods went down and Thomas and Cushman made hast to get out of the country.

Dave Kerr said He intended to stay if he had to live with the Indians. Messrs Boss and Barnhart formed a partnership and was going to winter in Boss'is House. Barnhart, Lyman and J. J. B. went up to Quillyute to purchase goods for the winter. Had a pretty hard trip going up the Beach between the Ho and the Quillyute Rivers.

We left Mr Barnhart [at] the store (Mr Pullen's) to purchase thegoods and take them down in Indian canoes. Mr Lyman and Myself came on up to the Straits through the Quillyute and Solduck Valleys and down the Pysht River to the Straits. there we took the steamer and came on to Tacoma, landing at Tacoma Nov. 1 1890.

Jan 27, 1891. Messrs G. A. Martin, Eugene McGuire, Harry Hibberd, John Hanson, and I went up to the Queets River. Had a splendid trip. Made it in 5 days. Hibberd and I got pretty wet in going through the tunnell. All the Boys selected claims. Martin 3, Hibbert 2, Hanson and McGuire 1 each. H. Hermanns 1. The Queets River was very high about Jan 10th. Came very close to my house.

Two Germans lost nearly everything they had. Gun's, Blankets, Canoe, dog, ect. left their places, came down to my place and sold what provisions they did have to A. Matheney for $10 and left the Country broken Hearted. Several of the settlers lost their Canoes in the floods.

Snow fell about 3 inches deep Feb. 12th. But it melted nearly as fast as it fell. Other parties Reported the snow over one footdeep about the last of February.

A Meeting was called at Our Office, Mar 7th 7.30 P.M. J. J. Banta was made chairman of the meeting and J. E. Grant

190

secratary. A Committee was Appointed to make Inquirry of all the Steam Boat Companies to find out what we could charter a Steam Boat for, (at what price), to take us around to the Queets, about April 15th.

Another meeting is Called for Saturday Mar 14th.

The Committee appointed to see about the Boat are:

R. H. Stewart

F. W. King

J. E. Grant

April 22ed 1891. Our Colony set Sail today on Board the Lucy Lowe, chartered for the trip. We are to [pay] Seven hundred and fifty dollars. The Captain agreed to board our party and land us and our freight safely at our destination.

There are 56 of our party, consisting of the following named persons.

J. J. Banta

Nelson McKee, Wife and six children. H. K. Mayhew & Wife

John Powel & Wife & Daughter

E. Belcher, Wife and Daughter

F. W. King Wife & Son (Merle)

D. B. Ballard & Wife

Miss Dora Head

Miss Anna Dickey

N. A. McKinnon & Wife

W. S. Hartzell & Wife

B. Vanslyke, D. H. Lyman, L. S. Carr, G. McGuire, Fred Althen, J. W. [N.?] Grant, S. Hurst, P. Phelan, G. Phelan, E. W. Grant, Henry Hibbert and son George, E. McMartin, John Hanson, John Hollenbeck, Geo Martin, Leonard Martin, S. S. Glover, G. L. Fleming, Chas Byar, J. Smith, B. M. Bailey, Geo. Mannington, L. Hike, W. B. Connerly, John Kanode, L. S. Snow, F. Atwood, Frank Starling.

We had on board enough provisions to last three months. Some chickens, and 4 dogs, two or three cats. Hoisted the Flag and started about 9 A.M. We arrived at Neah Bay thursday night (23rd). Went out to the Cape, found the Wind blowing from S.E., and the Sea rough. put back to Neah Bay. Went out again friday afternoon, beyond the light House. the wind still S.E. returned again to the Bay. Waiting a day, we went out again to see how the wind blew. too rough. Returned again.

April 29. Made another unsuccessful attempt to get down to the Queets. The Captain thinking best not to go to far unless He saw that the wind was going to change, so that if He saw a storm was going to come up, He could run back to safety, there being no harbor along the coast there.

On the first day of May the wind changed to the N.E. and we had a splendid trip, nobody seasick. On the former trips going out to Sea, nearly all were sick. Some awful sick.

A great many Jokes were passed at the expense of some Sea Sick Soul. At the expressions they would make. Sample Oh my God, dont you smell that meat? Oh if I was only back to Indiana, Ide live on one meal a day and this country might go to thunder. N. McKee, Well Boys I cant allways be with you. This said as Ed Grant left the dinner table, Jumped over it, and flew up the ladder like a squirrel. Of course we all knew that he was going to throw himSelf overboard. Oh god what have I done to be punnished like this—L. W. Carr. Even the Cats and dogs were sick.

Well we landed off the mouth [of] the Queets river about 9 Oclock

Saturday morning May 2. The Breakers were rolling pretty high, And it was a question wheather we could unload or not. The Captain Couldnot go into the mouth of the River so He had to Anchor outside. And had to take our stuff ashore in small boats. This looked pretty scally [scary] but soon after our boat was anchored the Indians came out in one of their large Ocean Canoes. It was a very dangerous looking trip, to see them come over the breakers, Their canoe as it came over the swells would or seemed to shoot up 15 feet out of the water. When the Indians came up to the Steamer, They said that we could get ashore, or that they could unload it for us.

We thought best to have them take us off. Cap McDonald said to take the Ladies ashore first. When I steped into the Canoe and asked the Ladies to come on, They didnot come very fast. But after I got my Sister and her six children all in the Canoe I called for two more. And Miss Anna Dickey & Miss Dora Head came forward, and away we went. Well we went ashore without geting the least bit wet. After that it was not so hard to get them into the Canoes. We unloaded by Sunday noon without losing losing anything except one dozzen chickens belonging to N. A. McKinnon. One of the Sailors upset his boat but what we didnot get at the time washed ashore next day. Most everybody got their stuff allright. There was 4 sks [sacks] of flour, two or three sks potatoes, about 50# meat, was all that was lost.

We had to pay the Indians $2.50 per load for unloading, in all amounting to $91.00. When we landed on the Beach the River was so high that we was obliged to wait there for a week before we could go up the river to our claims.

We made a trail on the South side of the River up to the first cabin in the settlement.

Another trip to the Colony was made by the Lucy Lowe

191

July 12th. left Tacoma and landed there in [blank] days. Had on Board Mr John Powe[ll]. T. D. Turner, R. A. Tripple, L. McAdams, John Goodell & Jack the Ripper.

Sharp and I went up the river to Mt Olympus. We was four days going up in [a] Canoe, one half day climbing the mountain. We wrote our names on a small tree on the top of the mountain. Sharp tried to slide down the mountain on the seat of his pants, like a boy on the celler door, but only tried it once. He slid about 50 ft. and came down against some bushes, said it made him nervous. We were afraid we would have a time to get down, but we got down allright, without doing but little coasting.

As there was so much snow on the ground where we wished to prospect we concluded to go home, so we tied everything in the boat and started. went about 3 miles allright, then run upon a rock. I got my leg through a bale of wire that lay in the boat, and which was fast to the boat this threw me out and under the boat, and I thought for a few minutes that my time had come, but I broke the wire and came out allright. Our boat split from one end to the other, and we was obliged to take our stuff ashore, and dry our blankets and leave our tent and what stuff we could not carry. we had a sorry walk home. heavy packs to carry and I had no hat nor coat, having lost them in the swim. We was $4\frac{1}{2}$ days geting home, well near played out too. B. M. Bailey gave Sharp quite a ducking in the river as he was trying to put him across, in his dugout. I thought it safer to wade.

Shortly after this [the] Phelan Bros and Dave Kerr took a trip up to the Mts, and had just about such luck as we had. They had their Boat loaded down with Elk & Deer Meat. started home. boat went to the bottom with everything. I hear that the boys only saved their guns and blankets, and had to walk home. 2 days without anything atall to Eat.

About this time we let the Contract to Carry the Mail once a week to the Agency and back to the Settlement. The Contract was let to the lowest bidder. John Hansen was the lucky man. He agreeing to gether the mail at and deliver to the following named places in the settlement for $7.00 a trip. Chas Barnharts for all on Clearwater, D Karr's, F. Schaupp, Miss Dickey's and J. J. Banta's.

Mr H. K. Mayhew was selected as treasurer to collect the money from each member of the Colony and settle with the carrier.

Chas Barnhart & Stith Hurst made a trip to the Quillayute with the Indians to get some provisions. They say they dont want to go again. The Indns [Indians] ran to close to the rocks to suit them.

Mrs H. K. Mayhew, W. S. Hartzell and Myself came down

to the Agency with the Indians in a canoe the same day that Barnhart and Hurst went to [the] Quillayute, but we had a splendid trip. At the Oyhut we met Mr J. E. Tisdale and J. E. Grant and J. F. Hanks with a boat load of groceries for the Queets.

To Be Surveyed

Aug 27, 1891. Messrs. Noel, Taylor & Bailey, Surveyors, started out to make the Survey of two Townships. No's 24 North Range 12 & 13 West. Also to Make a survey of the Ind Reservation.

Aug 22, 1891. The Steam Schooner Mischief [with the] Following named persons on board, left Tacoma for the Queets.

H. B. Lyman & Wife
John Olson & Wife
Geo, Holms & Wife
S. A. Niver
W. H. Rathbun
James Irwin
John Kanode
Fred Tiessen
Jas. Hall
Jake Peters
Geo Petterson
Gus Carlson
D. H. Lyman
D. Groves

D H Lyman & Joe Hawthorn had on board quite a stock of groceries to start a Store up there. Several other parties also had frt. [freight]. We encountered high seas, layed over at Port Angles one day. Landed at cove four miles north of Queets River. Wednesday Aug 26th; didnot want to land frt at this point, so anchored steamer at Destruction Island that night next day the Indians after making one attempt and geting their canoe full of water and D. H. Lyman pretty well soaked with salt water, and returning to the shore. tried it again and made seven trips to the boat. One set of Indians upseting their boat, and dumping a load of goods into the Ocean, loosing Mr H. B. Lyman's Cook Stove but saved all other goods somewhat damaged by the water. the other Indians made another attempt to go to the boat. Met a heavy swell which stood them on end. Came down met another which turned them completely end over end, smashing the Canoe to pieces and the Indians was 20 minutes swiming ashore.

This ended the unloading to goods at that place. So the Boat pulled out for Grays Harbor. And Mr D. H. Lyman hired

192

Mr J F Hanks to take the rest of the frt up to the Queets in his Sail Boat. This made the freight come rather high. Str Machies [Mischief?] $8. per ton Hanks $10. Total $18. per ton. Mr D. H. Lyman had gone on board without coat, vest or shoes.

G. Cleveland & Phillip Mathews undertook to cross the River on a reft and they also like the Preacher got their shirts wet. in this case the old saying of Fishermans Luck ect was true with them. They lost all the fish (if they had any) and were as wet as any fisherman ever was.

[Several advertisements and an article, apparently from a Tacoma newspaper of that time, were attached to the J. J. Banta diary.]

Last Call! Last Chance! To Join Our Colony

We are going to locate in one of the finest River Bottoms in Western Washington. We will leave here about two weeks. We want about 20 more to join our colony. If you want a good farm in a good neighborhood, call and see us at our office.

Room 14, No. 1002½ Tacoma Avenue,

Sharp & Banta

Read This!

We are getting up a colony to locate Land in one of the finest river bottoms in Western Washington. Said land is easily cleared and of the best quality. If you want to get a good home and land that is worth something call and see us.

Room 14, No. 1002½ Tacoma Ave., Tacoma.

Sharp & Banta

Certificate

Whereas, we the undersigned have been located by Messrs. Sharp & Banta, and have found every thing just as represented by them in every respect, and that we are well pleased with our claims. We do heartily recommend them, as locaters, to all who are desirous of obtaining first class claims.

Signed,

E. W. Grant, Corner 7 and L Streets.
L. S. Carr, Tacoma,.
J. E. Tisdale, 1741 D Street
Adam Matheny, 1739 D Street
B. Workman, Center Street.
John Hollenbeck, 17 and G Streets.
F. H. Gardener, Hoquiam.

Certificate

Whereas, We, the undersigned, have been located by Messrs. Sharp & Banta and have found everything just as represented by them in every respect, and that we are well pleased with our claims. We do heartily recommend them as locators to all who are desirous of obtaining first-class claims.

Signed:

E. W. Grant, Cor, 17th & I Streets
J. E. Tisdale, 15th & I Streets
I. G. Bigford, 950 C Street
W. Maskell, 927 Tacoma Ave
J. S. Thomas, 950 C Street
F. H. Gardner, Hoquiam

Off for Homes!

We have chartered a steamer and will leave Tacoma for our settlement in the Queets River Country, Tuesday, April 21st, 1891. Anybody wishing to locate a Homestead, where they can get good Fruit, Hay & Hop Land, a good class of people to live amongst, where there is plenty of pure water, and in a climate that cannot be excelled, can now have the opportunity by calling on us at our office. No charges until satisfied. SHARP & BANTA, Room 18, 1311½ Tacoma Ave., Tacoma, Wash.

S. P. Sharp
J. J. Banta

Come Join Our Colony

We are locating in a beautiful River Valley on the route of Port Crescent and Chehalis Railroad. Splendid bottom land. Good climate and pure water. No charges until satisfied. IF YOU WANT A HOME Come and see us. Sharp & Banta, Room 18, 1311½ Tacoma Ave., Tacoma, Wash.

A FINE STRIP OF COUNTRY YET UNSETTLED.[4]

Comparatively Unknown, Owing to the Difficulty in Reaching It.

The Only Streams in Which Quinault Salmon are Found—Plenty of Game.

Port Townsend. Last summer the writer took a hunting trip to Neah Bay and the country along the Pacific coast as far as Flattery rocks. The coast is a very rugged one and is composed of one solid rock formation and is very difficult

193

---

[4] Tacoma newspaper? [unknown], date unknown, attached to J. J. Banta diary.

to travel. From Neah Bay to Flattery rocks it is a good day's travel. About a mile north of Flattery rocks the Ozette river empties into the Pacific. Here Charles Willoughby, a brother of the writer, and Walter Ferguson, have taken up claims. At the mouth of the river there is a large quantity of black sand, and it is their intention to wash it for the gold it contains the coming summer. The writer made his headquarters here. In the river fish of various varieties are plentiful. The little Quinault salmon runs in this river in the spring months. This salmon is considered, by those who have had the good fortune to test it, to be the finest salmon that swims. These fish are only known to run in three streams—the Quinault, from which they derive their name, the Nitnatt and Ozette. All of these streams have lakes at their head. Although there are quite a number of other streams along the coast where salmon run, these streams are the only ones in which the Quinault salmon are found. The lakes seem to have some attraction for them. Trout, "bone-sharks," salmon trout and a small red fish similar to the salmon trout are also very plentiful.

After stopping at the mouth of the river long enough to get over the effects of the hard travel down the coast a trip to the lake was in order. The lake is about five miles from the mouth of the river, and, after a three hours' tramp, we reached the "Lake of the Sun." This lake is named from an old Indian tradition. In early days the Indians claim that the sun made the lake, and that it did not wish anyone to bathe in the lake, but an Indian disobeyed the command. No sooner had he done so than the water got very rough and began to rise. The surrounding country was flooded, and all the Indians were drowned. It is possible that this lake did overflow in early days, and hence this tradition, as the land on the west side is very low until it reaches the coast, and here a line of hills stand about a hundred feet or more in height. One side of these hills form a part of the coast and are very steep on both sides. The lake is probably about thirty or forty feet above the level of the ocean and on the east side are small ranges which it drains. This lake is also called Swan lake, owing to the large number of those birds which migrate to it every year. The lake is about four miles wide and eight miles long and is cut up into bays and islands.

About half way down the east side of this lake a rich bottom land country begins. Up all the streams that empty into this lake are rich valleys. The soil in these valleys is of the rich-

est nature. There is very little underbrush. In these valleys or bottoms the elk, which are plentiful, make their feeding grounds. Anywhere in these bottoms a man can take up a claim and plant twenty acres of it the first season, as the alder are the only obstruction a settler will have in clearing the ground. This country is undoubtedly the finest left in the state for settlement, but it is comparatively unknown as yet, owing to the difficulty in reaching it. At present a few settlers have gone in there, and in the spring a big rush will probably be made for this section. There is room for a large settlement here, and if a few energetic people get in there and open a road, which is not a difficult matter, the finest section of land in the state will be thrown open. To cut a road from this lake is not near so difficult as it was to get a road from the Quillayute country fifteen miles further south. At the Indian village at Flattery rocks there is a good harbor where a vessel can lay in ease, and goods can be landed in large quantities and taken to the lake by way of the river until a road can be cut. A potato patch is all that a man needs in this country to live. The rest, such as meat, fish, wild fruits and berries, are already there. While the writer was there he helped his brother to salt down elk meat and salmon enough to last all winter.

Of late the writer has seen several reports in newspapers to the effect that the country lying between the Straits of Juan de Fuca and Grays Harbor had never been explored. This is entirely a mistake, and any one desiring any information regarding the country between these two points will be cheerfully accommodated by calling at this office.

The country for the most part is rough and mountainous, but the valleys in the foothills are numerous and would be excellent for grazing purposes, but of little use for agriculture, as they are situated, as a rule, in high altitudes and the frost does not leave the ground until late in the spring. In midsummer, when the grass is dried up on the Sound, in those valleys the grass is green and abundant.

Some minerals have been found in these foothills and in the Olympics, but as yet nothing in the nature of gold has been discovered in paying quantities, although all along the coast from Neah Bay to Gray's Harbor gold can be found by washing the sand or the banks. Gold croppings have been found near Swan Lake, and it has been discovered in large quantities further back in the mountains in the vicinity of the Quilayute country.

CHAPTER EIGHT.
OTHER EXPLORATIONS 1890

THE JONES PARTY 1890

A Trail That Is No Trail[1]

Bogus Olympic Explorers Exposed—A Sea of Rocky Mountains

R. Jones in *Whatcom Reveille.*

Starting early Wednesday morning and cutting out several bad places we struck the Elwha at 11 A.M. Here we concluded we were all right, because the Press party had said that a man could easily lope up from Port Angeles to the head of Press valley (some ten miles above us) in two days; also that their blazes formed one unbroken line clear through from Port Angeles to Lake Quiniault, and I may as well say here, at once, that a more misleading statement could not have been made. It is almost criminal in its reckless folly. Here we were with barely two days' food, trusting to their account of the trail they had made, when as a fact no trail existed beyond what had been made by the elk, with a bit of brushing here and a trifling bit of grading there. As for blazing they did not average three blazes to the mile, where there was any difficulty in finding the way, but where there was a good open elk trail on a side hill, or in their numerous camps you can see their blazes thick enough; in short, they had done just enough to let themselves and their pack animal through, and no more. It would be a poor pair of men who could not do more in one week than this party did in three months. Let no man be deceived again by the Press trail. It is a snare and a delusion. By the river we found a card of A. D. Armstedd's of Seattle, saying he was going on to Olympus, and dated 21st August, 1890. After lunch we crossed the river and found the Press blaze, but soon lost it again: crossed the river four times that afternoon, every now and again seeing the Press blaze, but finding no trail, and camped in the forest on the east side, opposite a big bluff (altitude 1,200 feet). The river here was from sixty to eighty feet across; named it Bluff camp.

Next morning, on very short rations, we started out and found a Press blaze and a log sawn through a quarter of a mile from camp, but as there was no other blaze for over half a mile, we had to cut our way through some thickly wooded country. Three miles down the river we came across a spot where they had done a few yards of brushing: the cuts were about three inches above the ground, and the brush had not even been thrown to one side. We looked in vain for any blazes ten feet up the trees where the snow had been ten feet deep. A little further on we came across their cache, where we found three sacks of something—apparently clothes—hung up, a pair of snowshoes and a pick and shovel. The two latter were not much the worse for wear.

After lunch we found no sign of any trail or blazes, and had to cut a way for ourselves again. One bad place kept us an hour, and Niblock, with six of his followers, caught us up. After that a good elk trail took us round Mount Fitten and we camped for the night close to the mouth of the Lillian river, Niblock's nine close to us. Altitude, 1,000 feet.

On Friday morning we had just food enough for one day, and no more. We crossed the Lillian river and found a fairly well blazed and cut out piece of [Press Valley] trail, which took us about four miles to the river and ended there [0.3 mile northwest of the mouth of Idaho Creek], this being the only piece on the whole way worthy of being called a trail. After reading the description of the Press route again carefully, we crossed the river where they had cut down a tree and from this point [on the south side of the Elwha River], although seventeen of us were hunting the trail the whole afternoon, we could not find it. Harris, however, after crossing the river several times, just before dark found their blazes about a mile inland from the river, and marking the spot by lighting a fire, returned to camp. Altitude, 700 feet.

Our dinner consisted of a small piece of bread and a fragment of bear meat, but Minerizhagen having shot an eagle on the wing with his Winchester in the afternoon, we decided to stew it for breakfast the following morning.

Saturday, the 13th, was a ticklish day for us. About an ounce of bread each and a smell at the eagle (that was enough) constituted our 5:30 A.M. breakfast, and after crossing the river [immediately above the mouth of Long Creek] and going

---

[1] *Whatcom Reveille* [Bellingham], no date. Reprinted in the *Seattle Post-Intelligencer*, September 30, 1890. Bracketed notes are by Majors. "R. Jones' account, 'A Trail That Is No Trail' (*The Seattle Post-Intelligencer*, September 30, 1890, p. 9), first appeared in *The Daily Reveille* [Whatcom], but no specimens of that particular issue have survived. Until now the Jones account of 1890 has been totally unknown to all historians and scholars of the Olympic Mountains and the Press Party." Majors, ed., *Northwest Discovery* 5 (Sept. 1984): p. 306.

through some open timber we found Harris' fire and picked up the Press blazes again, then commenced a very steep climb leading to a Press camp on the top of the hill overlooking Geyser valley [camp 18, Eagles Nest camp], through which we had just passed, and in which we had spent the night. We did not hear any geysers, either, at this point, or any other point on our trip, nor could we discover that any one else had, except the Press party, although we met several who had been there. At this camp the blazes stopped, and although we spent an hour hunting for them, and there were trees every ten or twelve feet, we could not find a single blaze; neither could Niblock's nine, who arrived on the scene shortly afterward, and we traveled a good mile before we saw any sign of them again. To get off the bench we had to climb down a steep spur which had been slightly graded, two miles of bottom land, and at 3 P.M., hungry and tired, we struck Mr. Hansen's ranch. Mr. Hansen was not at home, but his potatoes were, and we helped ourselves to a good square meal without any ceremony, knowing that we should meet Mr. Hansen afterward (which we did) and make it right with him. Gracious, how good those potatoes were, and what different being we felt afterward, so much so that we determined to push on and cross that terrible devil's backbone that afternoon. So taking a few more potatoes for next morning's breakfast, and bidding adieu to Niblock's nine, who determined to camp in the potato patch, we started off. The picture of the devil's backbone in the Seattle Press shows a perpendicular cliff of rock with a narrow ledge out in it, and a sheer fall below the ledge of about 500 feet, without a sign of any timber or brush. You may judge of our surprise, then, when we found it a very ordinary side hill, covered with trees and lots of brush, with plenty of rich black soil and no rock; so much so that in the worst place a horse could not roll down more than forty or fifty feet without being fetched up by a tree, and it would be absolutely impossible for him to drop into the river at all. At 6:30 we camped at Camp Trouble, as some one had named it before us. Ever since leaving Hansen's ranch we had been on a first-class trail, made by the settlers, so the following morning it was not long before we covered the two miles separating us from the next ranch belonging to Mr. Griffiths. His land is some of the most prolific I have ever seen, all made land, washed down by mountain streams from above. It grows peas, potatoes and other vegetables to an alarming size. Mr. Griffiths, fortunately for us, was at home, and insisted on showing us the way (which he did at the rate of about four and a half miles an hour), and carrying dinner for us on his back. Four miles of bottom land by giant

cedars, whose girth was certainly not less than fifty to sixty feet, brought us to McDonald's ranch, where we met the proprietor, who with kindly courtesy came out to show us the way through a big burn that had just been started by some careless persons. The flames were still burning fiercely along the trail, and we had to run hard to get through some of the places to avoid being choked by the smoke.

A couple more miles and we reached Mr. Daniel's ranch. Here we were taken in by Mr. Griffiths and introduced and most hospitably treated. The view from this house over the slope is as fine as anything we saw in the mountains. Two more miles brought us to a good wagon road, and another six into Port Angeles. How glad we were to see the bright blue sparkling sea, and feel that we were once more within coo-ee of a telegraph office. That we were friendly received in hospitable Port Angeles goes without saying, and to the numerous inquiries as to whether we had made any discoveries, we answered that we had seen quartz in abundance everywhere, in the valleys and on the mountain tops, but that so far as we could judge it did not look promising; that there were hundreds of acres of good grass land, but it all lay between 3,000 and 6,000 feet up, and was only good for summer food and difficult to get at. The grass itself could not be made into hay, because of the numerous stones and wind-falls lying amongst it.

We saw no indications of coal, though we noticed stains as of iron ore, and slate of good quality is there in large quantities, being especially good in the Dungeness valley. Generally speaking, the country is a sea of rocky mountains, not difficult for men to get through on foot, but owing to the large number of snowslides, difficult for horses, and in winter altogether too dangerous for cattle.

THE CONRAD/OLMSTEAD EXPLORATION 1890

THEY FOUND THE TRAIL[2]

A Party of Five Prospectors Return From the Olympics

Record of Their Trip From the Mouth of the Dosewallips River Over the Summit of the Mountains to the Elwha River and Thence to Port Angeles—Elk, Deer and Bear Killed—It is Reported a Great Country for Game, But of Little Worth for Anything Else.

196

---

[2] John Conrad, *Seattle Press*, July 16, 1890.

Below is given a record of 24 days in the Olympic mountains by a party of prospectors. It is written expressly for the *Press* by John Conrad from the diary kept by A.D. Olmstead. The members of the party are as follows: A.D. Olmstead, a prospector; John Conrad, a lawyer and prospector; Joseph B. Wilson, a teamster; James E. Lucky, a millman, who went to look up the timber prospects of that region, and Frank Ferguson, a miner. They are all practical men

A. D. Olmstead.

and were after wealth, if it was to be found in that region. They express themselves as having been overjoyed at finding the Press trail, and among themselves they called it the county road. Immediately on their arrival in Seattle they came at the *Press* office and reported having found the cache, which they broke

John Conrad.

open in search of food. They readily assented to prepare an account of their trip, to be given as supplementary to the records of the Press Expedition. Following is the account of their trip:

As the result of trifling banter during a social chat, four resolute and sturdy gentlemen, (and who were withal, expert shots, sagacious nimrods, skilled woodsmen and discriminating prospectors,) resolved, with myself to make an attempt of an exploration into that mythical region, and "terra incognito" and "awesome habitat of the thunder bolts," the Olympic mountains.

Our chief purpose, to be sure, was the quest of gold, but coupled with this was the irrepressible desire—a periodical relapse to barbarism and savage instincts and habits of our ancestry and clamber about the cliffs and heights, beneath the leafy shade in the seclusion of the wilderness. Therefore, disregarding the puns and ridicule of our friends who attempted by their frozen admonitions to make pale our cheek, we, on the morning of the 16th of June, at 6 P.M., embarked for Sebeck upon the

James E. Luckey.

good steamer Josephine and arrived at the eastern shore opposite the mouth of the Dosewallips. We engaged a boat of Mr. Henry Clark, of the general store at Sebeck, whom we found to be a gentleman most courteous and hospitable, but who very much questioned our ability to penetrate the solitudes from that point, giving us the benefit of this knowledge of previous attempts.

Joseph B. Wilson.

While awaiting the preparation of our boat we started to take a survey of Sebeck and its surroundings. We appreciated the sight of its former glory, the ruins of the vast mill and lumber enterprise that once made it such a stirring and active bee-hive,

Frank Ferguson.

but the fire fiend had devoured it in smoke and now a perpetual Sabbath reigns with its quietness, serenity and peace.

Sebeck has also another specimen of a lion in the shape of an old 12-pound piece of ordnance, marked 1846, formerly belong to an English man-of-war, but how they became possessed of it no one appeared to know. It had once been spiked.

Setting Sail Toward the Olympics

At 3 P.M. sail was set for the opposite shore, which we reached about 5 o'clock. We made our adieus to our boatsman, shouldered our packs and made over a pretty good trail, about two miles, when we most hospitably received and entertained by a settler and his wife at their homestead. Having rained frequently during the day, and the bushes wet, we were thoroughly saturated, and with the novelty of having to sleep upon the floor in our wet clothes, our rest was not the most refreshing and satisfactory. Nevertheless we accepted this but as a mild intimation of what was to follow, and the next morning at good time proceeded to verify it. Bidding our kind host and hostess good-bye we plunged immediately into the wilderness. It rained at intervals all day, making the trail over the fallen and dead timber and wet underbrush extremely disagreeable and fatiguing. We made about six miles. The bottoms being in places of first quality and having some excellent timber, though I think, mostly taken up.

197

Slight Accident With a Cartridge

We also met several of our party who had proceeded us a few days with the purpose of locating land, we searched one of their cabins and camped for the night. At this point we caught several trout, the finest I ever saw—18 inches long. Here also occurred a slight accident. A cartridge having fallen from one of the belts scraped from the floor of the cabin among the chips and thrown upon the fire exploding, a piece of the shell striking one of the party in the face, cutting quite a gash, though doing no more harm. At this point we rested all day, and prepared for the heavy apparent increasing difficulties of our trip.

Bright and early on the morning of the 20th we again started, but found the trails growing continually more obscure, indefinite and difficult, and the jungle growing denser, fallen timber more abundant, the hills steeper, spurs more numerous, slides more frequent, the bottom narrower, and the cliffs beginning to jut out to obstruct our way, and the small canyons and creeks multiplying. Amid this accumulation of difficulties one of the party stepping upon a rotten limb it gave away, letting his leg into a deep hole, he falling backwards, wrenching and almost breaking his leg and almost entirely disabling him. This rendered it necessary that we should pitch camp earlier than we had proposed and abridged our day's journey, yet it was still quite long enough to weary the most sturdy.

Here, after deliberation, it was determined that the disabled should struggle on, though it condemned him to unspeakable torture and his companions to additional fatigue, they having to assume the most of his pack. The pluvial deities were still hostile. It continued to rain, and all things had a sad, murky and lugubrious aspect, but we consoled ourselves with the philosophy that it was not the worst—we still survived.

The Dosewallips

July 21.[3] [sic]—Got an early start after a disagreeable night of damp and cold, though we tried to struggle on with unflagging spirits; at times following the indistinct deer and elk trails, the scenery continually growing cyclopean and grand with innumerable waterfalls, cascades and cataracts, some of them rolling and tumbling down prodigious heights. Just here let me remark parenthetically that this small river, the Dosewallips, is somewhat unique, in that up to this point it hardly has a curve from a direct line, with a most uniform fall and width, making it a complete millrace, whose power is

only limited by the number of wheels of a given diameter that could be placed between its mouth and the foot of the gorge or canyon which we are now approaching. This could be done by simply placing an abutment, upon each side of the narrow stream, for the journals, the wheels hanging in the water, it having sufficient velocity and volume to turn the largest waterwheel in the world; and here let me suggest to capitalists and electricians who want cheap power, that here is going to waste, at all times, sufficient power to operate all the electric motors that the region about the Sound will ever employ, and generate light sufficient to make it dazzle as the sun for all time. Here along its course could be operated an electric road, deriving its "motif" from the rapidly flowing stream beneath its wheels, to convey tourists to view the sublime beauties of these Tartarian solitudes—fir clothed, snow-capped and mist-veiled crags and peaks.

A Dangerous Cliff Ahead

After having made several miles under unusual difficulties, we camped at a prodigious height above the river and despatched a reconnoitering party to find, if possible, the least difficult pass around the gorge. After several hours they returned to report that, to accomplish the passage, the best they could find was both excessively difficult and extremely perilous, as we would have to circle a ledge of only a few inches width, at the foot of a towering cliff above, and upon the verge of a measureless abyss beneath. After building a roaring fire, having wood in abundance, to keep bears and cougars at a respectful distance, and consulting as to the best methods to surmount the obstacles to our progress, and without any very promising solution of the problem, we retire to the not very comforting or refreshing embraces of damp blankets, and the God Morpheus to dream of traversing cliffs and dark abysses, of falling through jagged rocks, and frightened by the very ghosts of our imagination, and hugged and torn by bears and cougars, but the sun rose all the same and we still survived.

Evidences of Cougar, Elk, Bear and Deer

June 22.—Getting an early start we are soon at the most difficult passage yet encountered, but we set about it with a determination to surmount it if possible, and after several hours of infinite toil and danger, came safely through congratulations and a lunch, we took a survey of our surroundings. We found a small valley, fairly well timbered, abundant fresh evidence of bear, cougar, deer and elk, and the skel-

198

[3] In view of the fact that the trip began on June 16, this date should obviously have been June 21.

etons and antlers of several of the latter stately denizens of the locality, that had evidently fallen victims to the craft of bruin or the savage agility of the cougar.

Resuming our packs we made another march of several miles over a much easier trail and through some excellent timber; pitched camp, made fire, dispatched a hunter, who, in a few minutes, brought down a couple of fine deer at one shot, and hallooed for help to drag them to camp, where we soon had them quartered and cut up and upon states jerking for future use. Subsistence rapidly diminishing, it behooved us to exercise some forethought; and raining, we therefore lay in camp all next day and cured as much venison as we could conveniently carry.

Crossing Many Small Rivers

Again on the line of march, we keep our course as near as possible to the largest tributary of the river, crossing many smaller ones, but as we approach its headwaters it becomes almost impassable from fallen timber, underbrush and frequent snow slides, that with prodigious force has swept thousands of trees from one to three feet in diameter as a mower sweeps the grass before his scythe, and grinding them to bits as though they had passed through a bark mill these great, snowy Anacondas. In many instances, with inconceivable momentum, passed completely over the river, rushed up the opposite mountain, and, when its progress was arrested, falling back into the stream, forming bridges and dams to the height of fifty and a hundred feet.

June 26.—Today's march has been the most tiresome since starting. Nature in her most savage aspect stares at us from every quarter. Toward evening, however, we emerge from the jungle, with its gloom and dampness, into a vast amphitheater under the full blaze of the sun. Immediately in the foreground is spread comparatively smooth, green hillocks, but at a short distance rises abrupt cliffs that reach almost to the clouds and surely bar farther progress in that direction, to the north and south also lofty mountains raise their bold and snowclad summits. The genial warmth of old Sol being inviting, we conclude to pitch camp and resolve ourselves into a "ways and means" committee to extricate us from this cul de sac.

The result was committees of investigation were sent, one to the southwest, the other northwest, carrying nothing but our alpenstocks. With perilous efforts we finally reached the summit, but with no possibility of getting our packs over by these trails. But here we found our compensation, and every man of us felt that we were fully repaid for the privation, discomfort, dangers and exhaustive labors of the last ten or twelve days.

Mute With Wonder

What a picture here spreads itself to our gaze? One stands mute in wonderment at the savage display, and our thoughts are completely bewildered, as they rise and struggle to comprehend the cosmic energy that did this mighty work. Here nature was in one of her most savage and termagant moods when she took upon her this sullen and forbidding aspect. From this center around the horizon is grouped an assemblage of mighty peaks and crags, as if assembled in mild obedience to the call of gigantic Olympus, which rears his snow-clad head to the clouds, several miles directly west, glittering cold and silent. Through the channel of the Elwha to the northwest, as it runs as an aisle between the seats of the titanic members here assembled, can be seen the Straits of Juan de Fuca. To the east, down the stream, which we followed to this point is a similar dale, but the Sound is obscured beneath a blanket of fog. To the southeast Mt. Constance raises her shaggy head above the enveloping fog, and still farther to the east and south Mt. Rainier through the haze, blue and gloomy, stands silent, majestic, awful. Down the numerous canyons can be seen innumerable gigantic and fantastic fog specters, arising from the many gorges and grottoes, flitting and scurrying away over trees and crags, sending their fleecy habiliments, as they pass and vanish these weird and spectral forms must be the ghosts of the departed genii of these mountain pastures, whose brooding silence and seclusion has been ruthlessly disturbed by this sacrilegious intrusion of the nineteenth century vandals, and they beat a hasty retreat in search of greater seclusion and obscurity.

Leaving Their Autographs

Whilst seated upon the very apex of the peak we fire a salute, eat our lunch, flatten the empty cartridges, scratch our names upon them and deposit them under a small stone to prevent blowing away. From here we look down into three of the several tributaries of the Elwha, which we descended a few days subsequent, also into the tributaries of the Dosewallips. We took handfuls of snow and threw some of it into each of the watersheds. These particles may again mingle upon the broad bosom of the mighty Pacific. We now commence the descent and retrace our steps to camp to hear and report what progress was made by the reconnaissance. Both parties reached the camp almost simultaneously, but the report soon evidenced the fact that no possible rout had been found to attempt with our packs. We therefore, "since the affairs of men rest still uncertain, fell to reasoning of the worst that may befall," and concluded to trust to luck and find, if we could, a path mapped out by the instinct of the brute and

199

follow that if possible. This, after Herculean efforts, succeeded, but it came very nearly being the end of our lives and the expedition.

Under the revivifying influence of a bright scene and a part of a day's rest we felt greatly refreshed, and in the morning cheerfully shouldered our burdens, and after considerable search finally found an old trail, but very little used, and that only by bears, running five or six hundred feet up a perpendicular cliff.

Only Two Horns to the Dilemma

The dilemma had but two horns, go up, or go back. We choose the former, with dangers, rather than the latter with discomfiture, but it was a foolhardy and perilous undertaking. A slip, a poor foothold, the giving way of a hand-hold, a weakening nerve or unsteady head and all would be over. One would be rolled into jelly or dashed to fragments at the bottom. So we agreed that if one lost his hold and fell, the rest would waste no time searching for his remains, for little he would need their tender offices, but to hasten and put themselves beyond the dangers that overtook their ill-fated companion. But fortunately none of these impending fates overtook us, and after incredible labor, and completely worn out, we reached the summit; and here, whilst resting, we had a consultation as to whether we should from here make our way out by the Elwha and Port Angeles, the Quillayute and Gray's harbor, or the Skokomish and Union City. The later, although, as we thought, the most difficult, since we would have to cross the watershed of the Quillayute and a long series of spurs spreading from Mount Constance before reaching the headwaters of the streams that emptied into the head of Hood's canal, was first determined upon, for the reason that it was supposed to be somewhat less known, and for this last reason (though not very clear why) richer in minerals. In this direction we again took up our march, following the backbone of the divide, between the Dosewallips and Elwha for several miles, and made a dry camp upon the mountain top, which proved, though dry, unspeakably uncomfortable, it being impossible to keep from sliding down in our sleep.

Facing the Southeast

The next morning we had an early start, our faces still to the southeast and Union City, but progress upon the comb of the mountain was extremely difficult and slow. We then resolved to again descend to the water of the Dosewallips, but here we again found all our efforts thwarted, unless we retrace our steps of the last two days, and this was impossible. The memory of the perils of the ascent rendered the entertainment of the idea somewhat unpleasant. Therefore the entire day being exhausted in futile efforts to get down, and having made but little progress forward, we picked another dry camp to consider our exodus by another line than that we proposed.

After consultation it was determined to proceed by the valley or canyon of the Elwha, for Port Angeles. We took an early start, our first stage being over a snow field of about six thousand yards, with an incline of 45 degrees. For vehicles of transportation we improvised toboggans of our knapsacks. Getting in place, taking our seats, loosening brakes, and presto, we were at the bottom, sometimes with our apparel slightly disarranged, a skinned knuckle, or bruised shin. But these trifling accidents only added zest to the pleasure of our toboggan experience. We made very good progress down to the creek, though very steep, and the brush very thick. We crossed to the west side and were proceeding through a small park-like valley, when suddenly and unexpectedly we stepped into the midst of a herd of 18 or 20 elk, lying down resting. They immediately arose and gazed at us, apparently in stupefied amazement at this sudden intrusion. The boys, as soon as they had recovered their presence of mind, opened a fusillade, at the first shot bringing down one stately monarch, and wounding two others, disabling one of them so badly that we had to dispatch him by another shot. By this time the rest of the herd had sought safety in flight and disappeared. As our subsistance was getting low this opportune supply determined us to make camp and replenish the commissary. Water and wood being abundant at hand we, with alacrity, set about to skin and cure meat for future use. But scarcely had we commenced, and whilst every one was engaged at something of these duties, one heard a twig snap, and looking up, an enormous black bear stood within twenty feet of him. The meeting, I infer, was quite as unexpected by him as us, for he incautiously took to flight and set about clambering up a steep cliff, but the deadly Winchester was upon him and ere he disappeared in the brush its angry crack went reverberating down the canyon and Mr. Bruin, the king beast of this region came down the cliff, a huge and helpless black mass, at our very feet.

The Third Bear Killed

This is the third bear we have shot. The second we have skinned, on getting away. The is a magnificent fellow, very fat, weighing between 300 and 400 pounds. Having cured all the meat that we would probably need we again proceeded upon our way down the west side of the Elwha for several miles, but finding it very difficult, and our lame man being

200

almost unable to proceed, we felled a tree and recrossed and found a little better way, but still very rough. We had thus far seen no evidence or trace of any human beings, since we had left the foot of the gorge of canyon of the Dosewallips upon the east side. We had begun now to speculate upon the probability of falling upon the trail of the Press expedition, knowing that it had gone in by the Elwha, but night overtaking us we again pitched camp and made a hearty supper upon stewed elk, of which we had an abundance. After a reasonable night's rest and breakfast of the same bill as supper, we continued on our course under the usual difficulties, steep climbs, dense underbrush, great burns and slides, and fallen timber, crossing one or two small valleys or bottoms upon the river, which, from its many tributaries from all directions, is rapidly growing larger; timber only middling and of all varieties indigenous to mountain regions. Having made several miles and completely worn out, we again pitched camp, upon the east bank of the Elwha, and spread our hospitable board of boiled elk and a little coffee. A miserable night's rest enables us to rise early, to greet the dawning of our country's natal day, this being the 4th.

The Fourth in the Mountains

The boys welcomed it. A national salute, which awakening the slumbering embers of patriotism (which hard usage and deprivation of the last few weeks had well nigh entirely quenched,) and we made those eternal mountain peaks and crags, glens and grottoes echo the glad acclaim and it went reverberating up and down the canyon until lost in the pure ether above. The memories that swept upon us of many preceding Fourths and the clear sky made us more cheerful as we started upon our tiresome journey. We accepted them as a harbinger of coming good, an omen presaging luck and eagerly proceeded to verify it.

The Press Trail Found

After several hours of severest labor, we lunched on jerked elk and cold water, and again resumed our course. After an hour or two, as we emerge from the almost impenetrable jungle of a most precipitous gulch, through which we had descended from the top of the mountain, we found ourselves upon a very distinct and recently made trail. And then again the canyon rang with joyous Fourth of July shouts. Again we fired salutes, and resolved that, farther on, when we reached camp, to complete the commemorative exercises of the occasion.

We had no doubt now that we had struck the trail of the Press expedition, and after a mile or two more our conjectures were confirmed. We fell upon their cache, and here

I trust the gentlemen will pardon us, but honesty compels us to admit that never a sneak thief went through a private room with more celerity than we rifled those sacks, hoping against hope that we would find something to assuage the cravings of empty stomachs, forgetful of the fact that it was not usual for expeditions of this character to embark with the commissary of a palace hotel. We were therefore somewhat disappointed when the quest produced nothing.

Press Trail Followed

Replacing everything carefully we again took up the trail, glad that we were once more upon a path that had been trod by our kind. After making some distance we pitched camp. Completed the contemplated exercises by another salute and the recitation of the immortal declaration of independence, we supped sumptuously on jerked elk, went to bed, got well wetted but no sleep. Arose, started huge fires under the branching cedars, and awaited the dawn. Cached some of our utensils, breakfasted lavishly upon jerked elk. Starting again we soon lost our trail, it being obliterated by the snows and rain, only where chopped and blazed, first by the river and then hillside, both very hard. Pass over some very nice bottom land, the timber not of the best, fires having devastated some immense tracts; rain at intervals all day. Make several miles and camp, wet and hungry and about worn out.

Supped and breakfasted on jerked elk, an abundance of anything else we did not need for, you know, "man needs but little here below," and we did not know how long we would need that little for we were hopelessly at fault as to a probable trail, and the country extremely difficult. After diligently searching river bottom and hillside, making poor progress, after several hours spent in these fruitless efforts we scrambled to a high summit to take a survey, and behold in sight the straits, as a distant apparently as they were five days previous, but the river bottoms from this point seemed to be a little more passable. We therefore again descended, and just as we broke through the jungle upon the river bank we were again upon a new cut trail, which led us to the pine bottom, where we saw the largest trees of our experience. Cedars, some 30 or 40 in number, from 8 to 12 feet in diameter. We found one that some predecessor and locator had made his cabin and camp, and we concluded to appropriate it to our use for the night.

A Deserted Cabin Appropriated

While we were starting the fire one of the boys had wandered out picking salmon berries and discovered a recently built though empty cabin, which, upon examination, proved

201

to contain the remains of a sack of flour—a few pounds. Upon his report it took us but a brief time to strike camp and transfer ourselves thither, and in a few minutes we had the "flapjacks" compounded of flour and water spluttering over the fire, each awaiting with drooling lips and keen expectancy his turn, as we had cast lots as a first, second, third, etc. Never gourmand enjoyed with keener relish the most delicate morsel than we this flat, insipid and half-baked paste. After this sumptuous repast we made our bed in the cabin and had a good night's rest. After breakfasting upon flap jacks we felt greatly refreshed and strengthened for the efforts to reach the straits. Having now a plain trail and concluding that we would occasionally pass cabins, we took nothing with us but what we wanted to carry home. We were again soon upon the trail, every mile or two passing a cabin, some of them empty, others inhabited, the people only temporarily absent. After making several miles we reached McDonald's, seeing the first human face other than our own party, since entering the wilderness at the mouth of the Dosewallips, on Hood's canal. After a short rest started again, with the purpose of reaching the sawmill, five miles distant, and get something, if possible, to fill this "cavernous void" within us. The trail being pretty good, and our hearts and tracks somewhat lighter, and buoyed by the hope of something to eat, we tripped along at a frisky gait, and made better time than we expected, and we reached there at 3:30. The first house we approached happened to be the cook house.

Mistaken for Tramps

John Chinaman gave us a glance through the window as we passed. Our appearance, I take it, did not inspire a great deal of confidence, for in response to our knock of summons he opened the door with a degree of hesitancy that would have been amusing, had it not been a matter of seriousness to us, as it raised doubts in our minds as to whether we would not have to reach Port Angeles yet on the reserved force stowed away in our marrow and muscle. Still holding the door, he gave us another searching glance of inquiry, and in reply to our request for something to eat, he asked; "You got money? You pay?" All of which being answered in the affirmative, with the addition of showing him lots of money, he said, "Come in," and opened the door. A little adroit and judicious flattery soon mellowed and opened this Confucian, and we fared right royally. He was most hospitable and as loquacious as a jay. He heaped upon us everything the larder of the house afforded. After the substantials, coffee, tea, cake, pie and pudding had disappeared in great quantities, we gave him two bits apiece, lots of jerked

bear meat, and our thanks, and bid him good-bye, with a hazy idea that even this almond-eyed heathen was not as black a devil as fancy painted him. He got quite confidential before leaving. He had been four years in the navy during the war, and showed his enlistment and discharge papers. This was somewhat of a surprise to us, as none of us knew that Chinese were enlisted in the army or navy. But all the same that particular "John" will always have a warm corner in our memories.

Five miles more of good road to Port Angeles, but after the rest and bracing-up received at the hands of "John" this appears but a bagatelle, and as it was only 4 o'clock we concluded to essay it, bid "John" good-bye and started on our way, and arrived at Port Angeles at 7:30. Awaited a short time the arrival of the steamer George C. Starr. Go aboard and to bed, and sleep. Arrived at Port Townsend at 9 A.M., changed to steamer North Pacific, and were at home at 2 P.M., the 8th of July, after an absence of 24 days.

Resume of the Trip

As a resume of the trip or of the conclusions with reference to the country and its resources that we passed through, all can be told in a few words. It is the most difficult place to explore and prospect of all our experience, owing to the great amount of fallen timber, dense undergrowth, precipitous hills and beetling cliffs. One has to pass through many eminent dangers and hairbreadth escapes of flood and field, and deep wilderness, rocks and hills whose heads towered heavenward. No great area of agricultural land, but some very beautiful and fertile small bottoms and valleys, the largest containing not more, than perhaps two or three thousand acres. Neither did we see any very great areas of good timber, yet some small patches of first class. Though the whole country is wooded, it is rather of an inferior quality, and as far as we could judge of the north and western slopes, much inferior to that of the eastern.

No Minerals

As for minerals we saw no evidences of their presence. The formations are volcanic and barren of minerals. Among the foothills there may be and we have no doubt there is prolific veins of mineral. Game is very abundant, bear, cougar, elk, deer, woodchucks and grouse. Of fur-bearing animals such as beaver coon etc., we never saw a trace. We killed four bear, five elk, and five deer while upon this trip.

We had no instruments with which to measure altitude or distances, but we could arrive at the relative height of the various peaks by a very simple device, which for the informa-

202

tion of future explorers, we will describe. Extemporize a plumb, with anything conveniently at hand—a key, nail, pebble or bullet attached to a thread, and tie to the middle of your gun barrel, taking sight from the peak you are on at the top of the one you desire to know. If higher than you the relative angles of your gun make the plumb line immediately indicate whether you are shooting up or down. This may not be quite so accurate, but it is much easier and convenient than to go to the top of each.

We were reading a few days since an article, copied I think, from a Grays Harbor paper, claiming that as the best route and entrance to the Olympics. This may be all true, if people only wish to pop into them and return by the same way, but if they go to explore and pass over them we would think it would be best to attack the worst part of the road first, whilst in full possession of one's strength, vigor, resolution and enthusiasm, and not leave it until starved weak and spiritless. You very easily detect the difference in the traces of parties going in and those coming out; the first have cigars, boxes and grocers' paper bags and wrappings; the other picks, shovels and cooking utensils, old clothes, beds etc. The difference is about as easy to distinguish as that between a bear and an elk track.

John Conrad

THE PRATT/THOMPSON PARTIES 1890

Two of the exploration parties that departed soon after the return of the Press Party were the Pratt/Thompson Parties. Their reports were presented to the public by the Seattle Post-Intelligencer, *which seemed not about to let the* Seattle Press *corner the market on Olympic reporting. The* Mason County Journal *reported the first Pratt trip, which included outfitter Norman Kelley.*

MANY RICH MINES[4]

A Trip Through the Olympics Reveals Great Wealth.

All the Metals Except Gold.

Norman R. Kelley's Explorers Tell the Story of Their Journey—Correcting the Map.

George A. Pratt, Theodore H. Thompson and Ira Crawford have just returned from a prospecting tour in the Olympic moun-

tains, fitted out by Norman R. Kelley, of this city, who accompanied them on a previous trip. They traveled directly through the range from north to south and have added much to the public information about this little known region. They have made valuable mineral discoveries and will shortly return, accompanied by Mr. Kelley, to begin development of them.

The party started from Shelton on June 26 and went up the Satsop river, arriving on July 4 at the cache made on their previous trip. They found the provisions somewhat mildewed, but otherwise undamaged. On the 6th they killed a bear, and thus laid in a stock of bear meat. On the 7th, while moving their packs to a camp on the ridge between the Satsop, the Wynootchee and the Skokomish rivers, they treed a she bear and two cubs, all of which were killed by Mr. Pratt. Mr. Crawford was standing on a log gazing up at them when he slipped and had a bad fall, spraining his ankle and being disabled for two days. The night of the 10th was a miserable one, as it rained all night and the party were chilled to the bone. All of the 11th was spent in drying blankets, and all the provisions were found to be mildewed by the damp.

On the 12th and 13th, camp was moved to the east side of the Wynootchie, where the cache made on the previous trip was found to have been broken into by bears, which had eaten all the meat and apples. The rest of the provisions were found all right. To repair the damage done by the bears, the party went hunting, but though they saw numbers of deer and elk, they returned to camp without any spoils. On the 14th the balance of the camp was moved to the Wynootchie and then another hunt for supper began, this time with better success. The party found a herd of about sixty elk, of which one was killed. Mr. Pratt also shot a wildcat and a cougar. Mr. Thompson went after the wildcat, but foolishly caught it by the tail and got badly bitten on the arm. Another shot from Mr. Pratt killed it.

On the 15th everything had to be again laid out to dry. Mr. Crawford was left in camp to dry the meat, while the other two went hunting. They went up the river about three miles above camp, on a good trail, passing one mile above a beautiful waterfall, which is about 100 feet high and is pronounced by Mr. Pratt to be the finest on the coast. They found a tree with the names of Lew Shelton and Turpin and the date 1875, and the name Lewark, 1871, carved on it, besides other names dated from 1871 to 1887. They cut their names and date on the tree. The 16th and 17th were spent in moving to a second camp on the Wynootchie and making a cache.

On the 18th the travelers took their packs up a gravelly valley to the forks of the river, the main stream flowing from the west and the branch from east of north. At the forks they

203

[4] Author unknown, *Seattle Post-Intelligencer*, August 14, 1890.

found gold running about 20 cents to the pan. They went up the main stream on an old Indian trail and camped about one mile above the forks, where they found snow still lying in the valley. They also found indications of former mining operations—some diggings, and some old planks which had been used in sluice boxes.

The next day everything was moved to the head of the Wynootchie, where they were entirely surrounded by snow. They went to the summit of the range and had a fine view of the country, the ridge running east and west. To the south they could see Gray's harbor, and could clearly distinguish two columns of smoke towards Aberdeen, forty miles; to the west they saw the Quiniault river, six miles distant, and the Pacific ocean beyond it. The Sound was hidden from view by the mountains. One fork of the Quiniault was found to run due north, about one mile from the Wynootchie, but Quiniault lake could not be seen.

On the 20th the three travelers started with half their pack for the Quiniault and had a terribly hard time. In a mile's progress they descended 3,000 feet along the face of an almost perpendicular precipice, being often compelled to let themselves down with ropes. They made a cache and returned to camp. The next day they took the balance of the outfit and started at 4 A.M. for the Quiniault. They reached the cache at 1:30 and traveled onward till dark through a terribly rough country, down canyons, and among windfalls, and still they had not reached the river. Worn out with traveling, the party were prevented by swarms of mosquitoes from sleeping at night.

An early start on the following morning brought the party to the Quiniault about noon. Messrs. Pratt and Thompson took a trip up the river and while on a jam of logs, saw a man. They hailed him and found that his name was Benton, and that he was the last settler on the Quiniault. This was found to be a large stream, larger than the Snoqualmie at Falls City, and as they were only on the east fork they inferred that the river was still larger further down. While the other two were absent Mr. Crawford picked two pails of blackberries, and as Mr. Pratt killed a bear weighing about 600 pounds, they had no lack of provisions. The next day they moved the remainder of their camp, and returned to the river at dark, tired, hungry and played out. At camp they saw a bear, which was promptly converted into meat by Mr. Pratt's rifle.

On July 24th they went over the ridge to the main stream, which proved to be not quite as large as the east fork. This stream runs about magnetic south, while the east fork runs westward. They found good quartz and some colors of gold in both streams. The valley has fine bottom lands about five miles wide, overgrown with alder and vine maple, but not much timber. All the camp outfit was moved over to the main stream on the following day and the ascent begun. The bottom lands continued wide and rich, but were all cut up by the river. On the 26th they started up the river, which is a torrent, falling about 150 feet to the mile. They traveled mostly on the sandbars, and found large quantities of [illegible] quartz. The broad bottom lands continued, but the timber, which was fir and spruce, was not very extensive. Some old, but no new, elk trails were observed.

July 27, being Sunday, was spent in camp in repairing clothes, the party being in rags and almost naked. They washed out a few pans of dirt, but only got colors, and tried fishing, but found none in the river.

They moved on next day until they came to a large stream flowing from the northeast, and then made camp. They tried to pan, and found lots of color, but no quartz. The country continued to be rough and the stream very swift. There was fine timber on the northeast, but no game. Here the first indication of the Christy party was found— one of their camps. Mr. Pratt located a gold mine on the northeast fork of the river.

On July 29 Mr. Pratt sent his two companions up the north fork of the river with two packs, and followed the other pack coming in from the west. Two camps of the Christy party were found by Messrs. Thompson and Crawford, and next day Mr. Pratt joined them and found at one of the camps indications that the explorers had killed an elk there and devoured it in the eagerness of semi-starvation. There also they found a cache in which were 250 40-65 Winchester cartridges and a pair of snowshoes. The next morning, the 30th, the party arrived at the forks at 11 o'clock and panned some dirt, but found no color of gold. They traveled with heavy packs on bad trails, mostly on the sides of the mountains, which rose high on all sides. They traveled about five miles and made camp, longing for fresh meat but without any signs of finding any.

The party started early on the 31st, and crossed on a log to the west side. Two miles from camp two streams came in from the west. The canyon was grand in the extreme, being almost a tunnel, 100 feet wide, 500 feet high and the walls almost meeting at the top, so that a man could stand with one foot on each side. One waterfall succeeded another, the height ranging from six to ten feet. The Christy camp was reached at 10 o'clock and camp was made at a new fork coming from the east and very nearly the size of the north fork. The pan was tried and about twenty colors of gold were found.

On August 1 the party turned up the north fork and

followed an elk trail and came to another camp of Christy's expedition, where, judging by the appearances of the stumps, the snow must have been six feet deep. Snow still lay on the ground in the gulches. They climbed a high mountain and camped, all wet and weary, rain having fallen all day. The tramp up the elk trail was continued next morning and the summit reached at 10 o'clock. Several wide openings were passed, covered with grass knee high, while high peaks rose both north and south. After a hurried lunch Messrs. Pratt and Thompson ascended a peak to the southeast of camp, about 6,000 feet high, which was named Kelley's peak, in honor of Mr. Norman R. Kelley. There they got their bearings and had a wide view in all directions. They could see the ocean to the west, the straits to the north and the Sound to the east, while ten miles west-northwest towered Mount Olympus. The west fork of the Elwha river runs northeasterly for about five miles, then swings to the north. The Quiniault runs from the pass westerly to the forks, about six miles distant, then swings to the south to the main fork, thence a very little south of west. In the pass were two lakes of about 100 acres each, about 200 yards apart. A camp of the Christy party was found and it appeared that they came up the east fork of the Elwha. They found quartz mixed all through the mountains in small seams. On August 3 the homeward journey began, the party tramping down the Elwha on a good elk trail, and making a descent of about 2,000 feet. They passed through fine bottom lands and vast stretches of splendid timber, clear of brush. At night the mosquitoes again swarmed and caused much profanity. On the 4th the march was continued down stream for about three miles, until a very deep canyon was reached, which it was hard to get around. An idea of the depth of the canyon can be formed when it is stated that a stone dropped from the tip took eight seconds to reach the water. About two miles below this canyon a large stream flows into the river from the east. Camp was made at a point where the river splits and forms a large island. There a number of trout were caught, some of them weighing as much as four pounds. No gold or quartz was seen on this day, nothing but slate rock being found. The whole day's march was through an unbroken forest of splendid timber. On the 5th the journey was continued down the elk trail until a canyon was reached, to avoid which the party took to the hills. Then another canyon was reached, at the foot of which, where another fork of the river flows in from the east, an old camp was found and a cache of Christy's party, where were signs of a bear having been killed. There camp was made, the cache opened and some tea taken out. All the contents of the cache were found to be safe and undamaged.

On August 6 Christy's trail was struck and followed all day. The traveling was bad, the main canyon of the Elwha, which is 1,500 feet deep, being passed. Six of Christy's camps were passed on this day's march, and the party camped where Jack Crumback had staked a claim and put up the foundations of a house.

The next day's march was up mountains, down canyons, through thickets, brush and briers the whole time. An old "burn" was traversed, the worst place for traveling I ever saw. At 4 o'clock Christy's trail was again struck, and an hour later his last camp was reached. The party arrived at Port Angeles at 5 o'clock on the evening of August 8.

Mr. Pratt says he found that several serious errors had been made by Christy's party in regard to the topography of the country. He says that Christy passed southward on the east side of Mount Olympus instead of the west, and that the head of the Elwha is about eight miles northwest of Mount Olympus, instead of on the east side, as represented in Captain Barnes' map. He also says that the Quiniault heads on the northwest side of Mount Olympus, a quarter of a mile from the head of the Elwha. Mr. Pratt went to the land office on his return to have the map corrected in these particulars.

According to Mr. Pratt, this region abounds in almost every mineral except gold. He found a five-foot vein of cinnabar on the Wynootchee and silver on the main Quiniault. On the Satsop an extensive vein of brown hematite iron ore eight feet thick was found and a claim located. On the Wynootchie, a seven-foot vein of grey copper, running right through the mountain, and probably assaying about 30 percent copper, was found. A large deposit of tin was also found on the Satsop. A quarry of splendid grindstone was struck on the Quiniault, a piece large enough for a pocket whetstone having been chipped by Mr. Pratt with his knife. The gold prospects are pronounced poor, as there is no black sand, and he does not think any quantity will be struck.

The statements of previous parties in regard to the abundance of elk are fully confirmed by Mr. Pratt. He says that they are so tame that they do not move when a man comes among them lying down on the grass, but stare as wonderingly as cattle, while their young followed them rubbing their noses against the coats of their strange visitors, and accepting caresses without fear of evil intentions. Mr. Pratt says that he could have killed any number of them with his ax, but avoided slaughtering more than were needed for food.

The timber is the subject of Mr. Pratt's greatest enthusiasm. He says that that along the Elwha is larger and more abundant than on the Snoqualmie.

The party will again start into the mountains in a few

205

days with the intention of working some of the mining claims he has located.

THE KELLY/PRATT PARTY 1890

THE OLYMPICS[5]

Norman Kelly and party composed of Geo. A. Pratt, Theodore H. Thompson and Robt. Crawford, returned Saturday from a seven weeks cruise in the partially unknown country west of Shelton, at the base of the Olympics, just now attracting much attention. In their tramps they found several fine valleys, one on the west fork of the Satsop river, about 8 miles long and four in width, at an elevation of about 600 feet above tide water, they believe to be one of the best in Western Washington, with fine agricultural land, covered with a growth of alder, maple and the bushes that indicate a good soil. On the Wynooche and the numerous other streams passed to the Humptulips which is nearest the ocean, such tracts are plentiful, although smaller in extent, in which the grass was two feet high. The party was mainly on a prospect of the mineral wealth which we all know lies abundantly through all this vast region, awaiting search and development. They found gold, silver, cinnabar, tin, coal, iron and copper specimens as well as granite and marble ledges, and are going back to the region as soon as they have made proper filings on several of the prospects, one of which, an excellent ledge of high grade silver ore, they claim is immense.

The falls of the Wynooche, lying in the range about 60 miles from Gray's Harbor and 25 miles from Shelton, are about 100 feet high, and out rival the Snoqualmie Falls near Seattle. The volume of water is thrice as large as that of the Satsop river. The entire section contains fine large timber, in abundance,—in fact, it has always been claimed by the few who have entered the "divide" very far, that there grows the finest timber of Washington.

The region is unsurveyed, therfore there is nothing official to show the topography of the country, but between this and Gray's Harbor is a progress of any railroad from that quarter. There is but one entrance to this vast natural "divide"—the one used by the prospectors, for they have endeavored to get there from points on the straits, Hood's Canal and Gray's Harbor. This is by way of Shelton, and the entrance is already commanded by the Satsop Railroad, which extends to within ten of the 25 miles that lays between. Therefore it is but a matter of a short time when the vast mineral and timber riches will be drawn from, and, the valuable tracts of agricultural land opened for settlement. A few years will see that section one of the most valuable and lively as any on Puget Sound, and Shelton people who are interested, realizing its great importance to this young city, have aided as well as furnished prospectors to search the field.

THE DeFORD PARTY 1890

EXPLORING THE QUINAULT[6]

Canoeing Far Up an Unknown River. A Skeleton Found.

At this time when so many people are watching for the signals to be sent out from the summit of the Olympic mountains by the Seattle Press exploring party, and when so much interest is being aroused in the success of the undertaking and its results, the following account of a trip along the Quinault lake and the Quinault river by three hardy prospectors will prove of special interest. It was printed upon their return home by the Aberdeen Herald.

Messrs. DeFord,[7] Buckley and Scammon have returned from a long cruise in the Northern country, where the white man's footsteps seldom go. They had many interesting bits to tell of their explorations. The trip was a prospecting tour for mineral. Leaving the Indian reservation they traveled by canoe up the Quinault river, alive with the famous Quinault salmon, blue-backs and steelheads. The Quinault lake they crossed in the direction of its greatest length and are enthusiastic in their description of the natural beauties of the scenery. The waters are as clear, they say, as crystal, and lie in the heart of a beautiful country that some day will be the finest summer resort in all of Northwest Washington.

Above the lake they found the canoeing difficult, it being necessary in many places to drag their canoes over the

---

[5] Author unknown, *Mason County Journal* [Shelton], June 27, 1890.

[6] Attached to Banta's diary was this newspaper article (author unknown, newspaper unknown, 1890). The *Mason County Journal* [Shelton] reprinted the article from the *Aberdeen Herald*, May 2, 1890.

[7] The *Mason County Journal* attached the following paragraph to its reprint of the DeFord piece in the *Aberdeen Herald*: "Mr. DeFord mentioned above, was in Shelton last week, and claimed to have discovered a magnificent copper lead in this county, which he filed and recorded in the Auditor's office last Saturday. He has been prospecting in the mountains for several years, and has frequently come across boulders of copper ore, but now he has found the lead, and has men at work opening up the mine, which is not far from Hood's Canal and easily accessible for transportation. Silver and gold, he says are abundant in the foot hills although he has not yet been lucky enough to find a lead. He thinks he has something as good as anything on Lake Superior."

shoals and jams. They traveled for an entire day above the lake by canoe. After leaving their boats they continued on foot for three days to the hills of the Olympic, and had the experience of a snow storm on the 25th of August.

In several localities the party washed out specimens of gold, and all are of the opinion that gold can be found in paying quantities when the bedrock of the river is reached. The party discovered in the foothills a human skeleton, and as the Indian who was with them was sure no Indians visited that locality, they concluded it was the remains of some whiteman who had got lost in endeavoring to cross from the Sound.

Mr. DeFord, of the party, who has no doubt cruised in this little unknown part of the world more than any other man, is a great believer in its wealth of mineral resources. He claims to know of the existence of free milling gold ore one day's travel from salt water on the west side that will assay $9 to the ton, and also the location of similar ore not far from Hood's canal that will yield $3 per ton. He has had assayed red iron ore that was brought from this unknown country that assayed 80 per cent pure iron. Some day, when this part of Washington is no longer a terra incognita, the wealth of this locality will be one of the wonders of the world.

It must be remembered that others have crossed over this same route. One party who did so included Ben E. Mastick of Port Angeles. The party he was a member of climbed up the Olympics by the headwaters of the Upper Quinault across the divide to the source of the Dosewallips river and down that stream to Hood's canal. The unknown regions which the Press party will explore lie between the region visited by the above named prospectors and the Quilayute river. Wonderful results are expected from this exploration, but it is expected that this vast area will prove to be agricultural and grazing lands, and one part of the work of the party will be to discover the best way for settlers to get into the country explored.

About the only prairie land in this northwest country suitable for agricultural purposes and not yet taken up by white men is on the Quinault Indian reservation. About ten miles from the coast there are several large prairies that are very similar to the Quilayute prairies and contain several thousand acres. These prairies are used by the Indians only to hunt elk on, and it is a shame that the government does not throw them open to settlements as the Indians will never use them for any other purpose. These Indians are rapidly dying off and it is doubtful if their tribe now numbers over two hundred, and yet they have the largest and finest reserve in Washington.

When this reserve was first set off the Quinault tribe was one of the largest in the territory, and nearly all the reserve was occupied by their villages, but at present there is only one village, and the village and the land used by the inhabitants will not cover in all fifty acres, while the reserve contains something in the neighborhood of 300 square miles.

The valleys in the foothills at present are useless, as any cattle that might be put in them in the summer would freeze to death in the winter unless some arrangement were made in the latter part of the fall to winter them. In these valleys, numerous bands of elk feed, but they are not much hunted, as they cannot be taken out and are only shot when the prospector wants fresh meat.

THE MURPHY PARTY 1890
IN QUILLAYUTE VALES[8]

A Summer Excursion Over the Olympic Mountains.

Sketches of a New Arcadia.

One of the Fertile and Promising Sections of the Northwest. Descriptions of the Valley.

The reports of the various exploring expeditions which have lately entered the Olympic mountains have been read with interest by the inhabitants of the whole Puget sound country. The accounts of the large number of elk, deer and bear encountered by these parties were enough to fire the soul of a sportsman, and enough was said about the existence of minerals in the Puget sound Alps to warrant a prospecting trip among them. Moreover, people do not generally realize the fact that the only considerable body of arable government land subject to entry by settlers in the United States is now confined to Northwestern Washington, and the disappointed hunter or prospector might still make his trip a profitable one by taking up a claim.

Moved by the three considerations mentioned above, the writer, in company with a friend, resolved to pay the much-explored region a visit. The route outlined was as follows: From Port Townsend to Pysht by steamer, thence across the northern part of the Olympic range, into the Quillayute valley, passing southward through the valley to Lapush, on the seashore, and thence up the Quillayute river into the mountains.

Settlers have been taking up claims in the Quillayute valley for the past eighteen years, and it was natural to expect that old residents of Port Townsend would know

207

---

[8] Thomas Murphy, *Port Townsend Leader*, no date. Reprinted in the *Seattle Post-Intelligencer*, September 4, 1890.

something about the country, but inquiry proved that in this we were mistaken, and we were unable to obtain much serviceable information respecting our proposed route.

On July 20th we boarded the steamer for Pysht. There were about thirty passengers on board, most of whom we learned during the day were either land-hunters or settlers returning to their claims. The vessel made brief stoppages at Port Angeles and Port Crescent to take on and discharge freight and passengers.

We reached Pysht, situated at the mouth of the Pysht river, about 5 o'clock in the evening, and found it a rather picturesque little place, consisting of two houses inhabited by white people, half a mile apart, and three or four Indian cabins, the latter situated under the lee of Pillar point, a bold headland which shelters the little village somewhat from the force of the winds. An antiquated canoe and a whaleboat, both clumsily handled, put out from shore, the latter receiving the freight and the former the passengers.

The Pysht river valley is surveyed, and contains some of the finest timber and rich bottoms in the country, most of the bottom land being easily cleared. There are, however, but about half a dozen settlers in the valley, the bulk of the land being owned by one man, whose policy it seems to be to let it lie idle for the present. If the fertile acres of this valley were divided up between actual settlers, vast quantities of produce would be raised yearly, and Pysht would become a town of considerable importance as a logging center and shipping point. Grouse and rabbits abound in the brush along the river, and deer tracks are plentiful on the trail.

A short distance from camp the trail again crossed the river, which crossing we made without mishap on another log. About two miles more of traveling brought us to the end of the valley, and the ascent into the mountains commenced.

Beaver Lake

Having reached the summit we began to descend, and reaching a small mountain brook, and unstrapping our packs, cooked dinner and threw ourselves on the ground for a much needed rest. Taking up the trail again we trudged on, and after a steep climb over the mountain were cheered by the sight of the Fifteen-mile house, situated on Beaver lake. This is a beautiful little sheet of water, bounded on one side by a high mountain about 500 feet in height. The lake has for an outlet Beaver creek, a swift and sparkling mountain stream, having a beautiful waterfall not far from the lake. Fine fishing is to be had in both lake and creek. Early the next morning we started on our way again. We were now entering the Quillayute valley. The trail forks here, one branch leading over a high mountain, the

other running along-side the creek. We kept to the latter, and about 4 o'clock reached Beaver, a rolling prairie a few hundred acres in extent, where there are two houses, one of which is a store and the other an eating house. The trail again led into the timber. By pushing ourselves we made Higgins' prairie, containing about 200 acres, by 7 o'clock. Here is situated another small lake, which has no visible outlet. It looks as though it ought to contain plenty of trout, but the folks there informed us that there were no fish in it except a mongrel species which would not bite.

Forks Prairie

We arrived at Forks prairie (so named from the forking of the Colower at that point) early in the afternoon. The prairie contains some twenty-five hundred acres, which was originally covered by a dense growth of fern, much of which is still standing, in which bands of cattle, sheep and hogs find excellent pasture. The surface of this land is easily cleared, but then the cultivator's work has only begun. The roots of the fern strike deeply into the ground, necessitating the work of years to thoroughly kill them. Nevertheless, patient labor has cleared much of the prairie, and fine crops of hay, oats, potatoes, hops and berries are raised on the cleared land. The farmers, however, have no inducement to clear more of the land than is sufficient to raise produce for the consumption of their families, as there is no practicable way of shipping their produce at present at a reasonable cost.

Forks prairie is located within the survey and is occupied by fourteen settlers, and has the advantages of a postoffice and sawmill. The prairie is bounded on the south and east by the mountains, on the north by the Colower river and on the west by the Bogochiel, the latter being navigable for canoes for fifteen or twenty miles from its mouth. The ground is perfectly level, and is admirably adapted for a townsite. A simplicity of manners prevails that is truly Arcadian. Robust physiques denote the healthfulness of the settlers, and they take life in a leisurely manner that is refreshing to one used to the keen competition of the city. We found them remarkably courteous and obliging to strangers, and neighborly among themselves. About two miles from the Bogochiel we came out on the Quillayute prairie, considerably larger than the Forks prairie, and the eldest settled district in the valley. The first settlers arrived there about twenty years ago. Like all other prairies in the valley, the ground is covered with a dense growth of fern, which in some places is ten feet high. Considerable gravel is found here, and the soil is not considered first class, although fair crops of hops, potatoes, beans, hay and oats are raised. Settlers on these prairies have

208

endeavored to raise tobacco, but whether from lack of experience in cultivating this plant or climatic difficulties, the product was very inferior. Like Forks, Quillayute prairie has a schoolhouse and postoffice. The prairie is perfectly level throughout its entire extent.

At about 4 P.M. we passed into the timber again, and at 5:30 we ferried across the Quillayute river, the longest and broadest stream in this section. This river and its tributaries, the Soleduck and Bogochiel, constitute the highways by which the settlers throughout the whole valley receive their supplies, although many light articles come by the way of Pysht by mail and pack horses.

Lapush is situated at the mouth of the Quillayute river, and consists of a store, a house inhabited by whites and an Indian village. A long and narrow point of rocks runs out into the sea on either side of the village site, forming a small bay, in which the water is comparatively smooth. A rock a few acres in extent rises boldly out of the sea about 800 yards from the village, which is called James Island. The surroundings are rough and wild, and being exposed to the heavy sea fogs, Lapush would not seem to be a desirable place of residence.

At Lapush we found ourselves compelled to relinquish the idea of going up the Quillayute into the northern part of the Olympics, as from previous experience with the difficulties of the country we realized that in the short time allotted for our trip it would be impossible to accomplish anything. Besides, our claims demanded attention; so the next morning we started back for Forks, packing our supplies, and reached the prairie late in the evening.

Country of Great Promise

The country watered by the Quillayute and its tributaries I regard as a most promising section of Western Washington. It has magnificent possibilities, unexcelled by any country on the Pacific coast. The rich bottoms and prairies will grow a great diversity of crops, the pasturage for cattle, sheep and hogs is excellent, and the never-failing abundant rainfall renders a crop failure an impossibility. The slopes of the mountains are covered by splendid timber. The existence of gold, silver, copper, coal and iron in the mountains in paying quantities has been repeatedly proven by the discoveries of prospectors. The difficulty of obtaining supplies and the thickness of the country, however, combine to make unusually hard work of prospecting. The seeker after minerals must pack his supplies and tools on his back, and not being able to take much with him, must return for a fresh supply before covering much ground. Coal has been found by almost every one who has looked for it, but I could hear of no case where a

prospector had sunk a shaft for any distance. Should the projected railroad through this country be built, the Quillayute valley will become celebrated for the amount and diversity of its products.

The soil is either black or sandy loam, and will raise almost anything. The high land, though sometimes gravelly, often shows rich soil in places. In the Quillayute country it is considered risky to take up a timber claim as such, as it can be generally proved capable of growing a crop, whether on high land or low.

The winters are long and wet. but are not usually cold, and a snow-fall is rare. The summers are cool and delightful. Heavy dews fall in the summer season.

I heard considerable complaint while in the valley of men taking up claims for syndicates, being provided by the latter with supplies, and receiving a few hundred dollars for their claims after proving up. This dodge was attempted some time since on a section, which, it was understood, was to be shortly surveyed. Information was filed at the surveyor general's office of the crookedness of the matter, and as a consequence the survey has been postponed for an indefinite period, on account of which there is much wailing and gnashing of teeth.

There are still many good claims to be taken up on the upper portions of the Soleduck, Bogochiel, Dickey and Quillayute rivers, but it is probable that the end of the present summer will find the whole country pretty well run over. It is estimated that a couple of hundred settlers have located along the Quillayute and its tributaries since January 1st. Good claims are still to be had but the land-hunter must move quick to secure one, as the woods are full of cruisers. A person starting out to find a claim should have plenty of time at his disposal and a few hundred dollars, otherwise he may return disappointed, as many have this summer. The intending settler will seldom get a pointer for nothing. A good many of the settlers calculate to make their supply and proving-up expenses out of locating strangers, and if they know of a good piece of land unclaimed expect fees ranging from $10 to $100 for guiding the stranger to it and finding his lines for him. Sometimes, being familiar with the country, the time and labor they can save the inexperienced land-hunter is well worth a reasonable fee. But the intending settler should beware of trusting every locator who comes his way. Many cases are on record of men being shown a valuable claim, and then, being ignorant of their whereabouts, located on a worthless one. These crooked locators are late arrivals in the valley, and should the services of a locator be required, one who is recommended by the old settlers should be applied to.

CHAPTER NINE.
THE WICKERSHAM EXPEDITIONS 1889 AND 1890

James Wickersham's Olympics exploring efforts are inordinately important in the history and development of Olympic National Park. Once he concluded that the area should be made into a national park, he actively pursued that goal over several years, predating by nearly a half century its successful conclusion. During his 1890 excursion, Wickersham continually interacted with Lieutenant Joseph P. O'Neil and other members of the O'Neil party, giving us a picture of the tone and character of that expedition as well.

Judge Wickersham's family expedition into the then little-known Olympic Mountains in 1890, and his trip deep into the range the preceding summer, were the basis of his enthusiastic article about his vivid wilderness experiences and observations in the eastern Olympics. His party was the first to explore some of the high river-source region and to descend the Dosewallips River. Greatly impressed by what he saw, Judge Wickersham made the first known proposal for an Olympic National Park in letters dated

November 3 and 8, 1890, to Frank Leslie's Publishing Company and to the Century Publishing Company. He wrote: "A more beautiful national park cannot be found. . . . A large number of prominent people in this State of Washington and Oregon are interested in the establishment of an Olympic National Park."

Wickersham also sent a day-by-day report of his 1890 Olympic exploration, along with detailed recommendations for an Olympic National Park, to the Tacoma News, which published both together in January 1891. The following April, he sent his article to Century magazine, but apparently it never was published there. Anxious to have a park established without delay, in July 1891 he sent his maps and article "descriptive of a proposed Olympic National Park" to Major J. W. Powell, superintendent, U.S. Geological Survey, and said: "I am informed that you are now preparing to recommend several reservations, under the Act of March 3 [1891], and I send you this with the hope that you may be induced to make the proposed park."

While exploring the upper Skokomish in July 1890, Wickersham met Lieutenant O'Neil's party, which was engaged in making the first extensive reconnaissance of the Olympics, and the first trail across the range. O'Neil provided extensive support to the Wickersham party, including the loan of a mule for part of the trip. O'Neil also had a deep appreciation of the beauty and the fauna of the mountains and, with a backhanded but prophetic compliment, his Report of the Explorations of the Olympic Mountains[1] provided to the government concluded with this: "I would state that while the country on the outer slope of these mountains is valuable, the interior is worthless for all practical purposes. It would, however, serve admirably for a national park."

Whether it was Judge Wickersham or Lieutenant O'Neil who first thought of an Olympic National Park, or whether they did so simultaneously, undoubtedly they exchanged views and information when they met in the mountains and after their return to civilization. The stage already had been set by Washington's first governor, Elisha P. Ferry, speaking of the Olympics as a "great unknown land like the interior of Africa," and the six-month Press Expedition that started December 8, 1889.

Judge Wickersham was accompanied in 1890 on his 125-mile, twenty-day foot-trip by his wife, Deborah Susan Bell

(Wood, The Land That Slept Late, 78)

---

[1] 54th Cong., 1st sess., published January 8, 1896 (dated November 16, 1890), S. Doc. 59.

James Wickersham as he appeared at the time of his Olympics explorations, 1889–90
Courtesy Manuscripts, Special Collections, University Archives, University of Washington Libraries, Seattle, UW14349

Wickersham (for whom Mount Susan was named); his sisters Clyde Wickersham and May W. Taylor; May's husband, Charles E. Taylor; and Charles E. Joynt, soon to marry Clyde.

Wickersham's life was filled with public offices and causes. He was probate judge, Tacoma City Attorney, member of Washington's state legislature, and after moving to Alaska in 1900, a U.S. District Judge and Alaska's delegate to the U.S. Congress. In the latter position, he introduced and worked for the passage of the Mount McKinley National Park bill and for the establishment of Alaska's first legislature, and was a leading advocate of Alaskan statehood.

An enthusiastic outdoorsman, he made numerous climbs in the Olympics and in the Cascades with his wife; walked from Cape Flattery along the beach to Grays Harbor; studied Indian customs with understanding and sympathy and visited many of their camps; took long winter trips in Alaska; made the first recorded attempt to climb Mount McKinley, and even adjourned court once to climb mountains in back of Valdez. His 1903 McKinley climbing party got to the 10,000-foot level, where they

were stopped by a sheer ice face that was later named the Wickersham Wall.

Born in 1857, James Wickersham would have been in his early thirties when he began his Olympics explorations and national park promotions. He both was married and was admitted to the bar in Illinois in 1880 at twenty-three. He died in Juneau in October 1939 at eighty-two years of age. A year before Wickersham's death, an Olympic National Park bill finally passed, forty-eight years after he began his agitation for a park. He lived to see it happen.[2]

A TRIP TO THE OLYMPIC MOUNTAINS [1889][3]

In June 1889, in company with Mr. John Mayo Palmer and Chas. E. Taylor, I boarded the "Meta" for a trip to the Olympic mountains. Tired and overworked in the office, we were off for a holiday and no boys off for a lark ever looked after guns, fishing tackle, ammunition and knives with more real pleasure. After the boat had departed on our trip a meeting of all parties was held and Mr. Taylor was unanimously elected "Commodore" out of regard for his past experience on the "briny deep." Mr. John Mayo Palmer was elected secretary and recorder. James Wickersham, who was armed with a small camera, "scientist." Previous discussions had settled the route which was to include a trip to Balches Cove, thence across to North Bay, thence overland to Hoods Canal and via same to Lake Cushman on the Skokomish River in the Olympic Mountains.

The weather was all that could be desired, clear and warm, and cool nights.

From the railroad wharf to point Defiance is rapidly filling up with manufacturing enterprises.

When I first saw this front of land in 1883, the only enterprise from the head of the bay to the Point was the Old Tacoma or Hansons Saw Mill and the old coal bunkers besides the R.R. wharf. Now all has changed: Large new coal bunkers are created and great grain warehouses are being built. Other mills are completed; one of these—the Pacific Mill is shown in the cut hereto pasted. From the new city wharf at the foot of McCarver Street in old Tacoma, the only buildings on the water front to Point Defiance are the Pacific Mills, and the first beginning of what is called the Smelter for smelting and working ores. No residences appear upon these bluffs which may some day be covered with the homes of the people of Tacoma.

211

[2] Adapted from James Wickersham, "A National Park in the Olympics 1890," *The Living Wilderness*, Summer/Fall 1961.
[3] James Wickersham, unpublished journal, courtesy of the Washington State Historical Society, Tacoma. Transcribed by Carsten Lien from a photocopy of the original handwritten manuscript.

Between the Pacific Mills and point are two places when the Indians camp on their annual fishing trips from their various reservations and the many colored costumes now on the beach inform us that the aborigines are in camp at that place. Many of the Klootchman, as the squaws are called, were out on the beach digging clams with a sharp pointed stick, while many of their peculiarly built canoes were drawn up on the bank. Dogs, babies, and stenches (not those of "blest Araby") filled the balance of the space just around the wigwams or "raucharies," as their board houses are called. As we passed their residences, I caught a photo from the deck of the vessel.[4] A mile farther is Point Defiance: so named I am informed from the bold precipitous banks and the wild rush of the waters of Puget Sound, which whirling around this point twice in twenty four hours create eddies, currents, whirlpools and dangerous tides that may well have filled the early explorers with the idea that he was defied. No residence or buildings of any kind are down in this vicinity, but as Congress has recently given the U. S. Reservation at this place to the city for a park, the day may come when it will be cleared, cleaned, graded and made to look civilized. That is now the expectation of our people and I hope they may realize the fullness thereof. From Tacoma to Gig Harbor a little steamer now makes a trip every day which is a great accommodation to the people living across the Narrows. Heretofore the residents across the Narrows were compelled to come to town in their small row boats, and it was a two day trip to come from Wholloachet Bay to Tacoma and return. Now they can walk to Gig Harbor and go over in the morning and back the same day. At the west side of the entrance to Gig Harbor lives "Sam, the Fisherman." Sam is an Austrian who followed the Fraser River gold excitement to B.C. some years ago: bought an Indian girl and settled down to fishing. He has a drove of half-breed children around him and his purchased bride has made a most exemplary wife. Out of respect to public opinion they were married a few years ago by a neighboring justice of the peace, a proceeding which legitimized six children then born.

A town has been secretly laid out at Gig Harbor and probably 1000 people live there being dependent for support on the sawmill established at that point. As early as 1850, ships came into Gig Harbor to load piles for foreign trade. About a mile south of Gig Harbor on the west side of the Narrows is the home of ye scribe. The picture opposite was taken from a point near Pt. Defiance and shows the wild and uncivilized appearance of the shore at this time. From Gig Harbor to Pt. Fosdick, there are only two houses, one of which is shown above and the other is a small shanty in the brush. One the east side of the Narrows there are but two or three houses from Pt. Defiance to Steilacoom. They are claim shanties, except at Byrds ranch and Westons.

March 3rd 1888. I went from Tacoma to Point Defiance with Debbie and our son, in a rowboat. The tide was so strong that we had a very dangerous crossing. We got across, went up the bank and there in the primeval forest we dug up some ground, chopped a small tree and then and there made the first settlement on our pre emption. There was no house from Gig Harbor to Point Fosdick—an unbroken forest of dense fir and cedar, and so filled with sallal brush and huckleberries that only an animal could crawl through. The climb up the bank was only to be accomplished by catching the brush and pulling up and then getting another brush. In June, 1888 we had had some land cleared and a small house built and moved over. The only way we then had to get up the bluff was by a road up the gulch. We built a small house, hired a good Swede man by name of Charlie Sundborg, bought a dog by name of "Daisy," got some pigeons, names "White Wings" and "Snow Flake" and Debbie, Clyde and Darrell took up their permanent residence. I stayed in Tacoma except Saturday and then went back Monday. We now have two acres or more cleared, 30 ft. tree, cow and calf, high steps etc. The loggers are cutting our timber and the above picture shows the log "roll way" just south of the house. We now live on the place from which we get fine views and good potatoes.

Our boat made a fine journey with the tide from Gig Harbor through the Narrows, Hales passage and across Henderson Bay to Balches Cove. We passed the entrance to Whollachet Bay in going through Hales Passage. This bay was once the hunting ground of the up Sound Indians and many traditions hang around it. About 1854 a fleet of British Columbia Indians came sweeping around Point Fosdick into Whallachet Bay and then attacked the resident Indians, killing some and frightening the balance away into the woods. Committing many other depredations the government sent an armed vessel against them. Several small steamers joined them and they came up with the Indians at Port Gamble and after considerable parley a fight ensued. The Indians were beaten, their canoes destroyed, their warlike spirit broken and never more did the Sound Indians fear the deadly swoop of their northern cousins in their great war ca-

212

---

[4] Wickersham's manuscript had thirty-three round photographs of very poor quality, about $2\frac{1}{2}$ inches in diameter, pasted onto the pages of handwritten text. They were meant to illustrate the text of his story as it unfolded. The condition of the photographs makes it nearly impossible to reproduce them meaningfully.

noes loaded with warriors and bent on plunder and slavery.

On the south side of Hales Passage, near the Fox Island shore is a small island known as Grave Island. Fox Island was the great camping ground of the wandering warriors of canoe Indians and Grave Island was the great burial place. A visit to the island a year or two ago revealed broken canoes containing bones, skulls, etc. The mode of burial of these Indians was what is known as "canoe burial." If a chief or owner of canoe dies, he is put in his best canoe, set up with his paddle in his hand, furnished with spear and food, and propped up where the canoe is put up in two trees near the water, prow out to sea, and left to await the day when he will go to the "happy fishing grounds." Sometimes a slave was killed with him and put in the canoe to attend the master.

The only signs of life on Fox Island are at the "Fox Island Brick Works" which are recently established and make both brick and tile. There is no other mill or business enterprise on Henderson Bay except a small shingle mill at Westmorelands on Scholalum Creek.

Balchs Cove is the nearest point to North Bay and our boat stopped there and let us off. We then shouldered our packs and started off across the portage to Vaughn Bay. The day was hot, the packs heavy, and the three miles of journey were the longest of any on our trip. There are two or three houses on Balchs Cove and we hear that they will soon start a brick yard. On the road over to Vaughns Bay, we passed a new ranch but old enough to have a strawberry patch and the farmer being a clever man asked us to eat and the packs seemed lighter afterwards. About 2 oc. We arrived at Vaughns Bay tired and worn out. Hiring a boy and his boat, we loaded our luggage into it and started on our way to Eberharts at the north end of North Bay, catching a picture of Vaughns Bay from the sand bar as we passed. We reached Eberharts late in the evening and put up for the night after sending our boy and boat back home. Eberhart lives near the north end of North Bay, about half a mile north of the mouth of Sherwood Creek which is the outlet of Lake Mason, some seven miles in the interior.

The first settler on this bay was _____ Sherwood,[5] who settled there many years ago, married an Indian woman, erected a sawmill run by waterpower, and now lies buried just north of the mouth of the creek in the orchard of great apple trees planted by his hand so many years ago. His old water mill is now a ruin but the waters of Lake Mason run through the old dam and make music for the wayfarer while

examining the most beautiful picture of broken age, moss and decay. The bay is silent except for an occasional visit of a Co's boat to get logs at the end of the logging railroad at the head of the bay. This road is now shut down, however, and the bay is as deserted as it was when Sherwood died and his mill which stopped forever. His half breed sons have erected a white stone monument over his grave and there he lies alone in the wilderness, surrounded by fast decaying signs of his early efforts to bring civilization to the Indians while his family and troop of Indian "tilacums" have paddled away to another "illahee."

Somewhere in an Eastern State a family graveyard is minus one grave. Brothers and Sisters lie with father and mother, buried with the evidences of Christianity so comforting to the Anglo Saxon, but one brother is missing— his grave is on the green banks of North Bay but surrounded yet by signs of a busy life. May he not rest uneasily by reason of his distance from mouldering kindred! May his spirit wing its way as unerringly from Puget Sound and lonely woods as from the crowded city cemetery! Rest in peace, pioneer, your work is done! On the spot you hallowed by a life of toil and exposure, coming thousands of your kin will build a city, erect great mills, pave streets, burn great gas and electric lights, and produce all the evidences of a civilization whose advance skirmishes you were! Your logging roads and trails shall lead railways towards points of commercial importance, your clearing shall furnish room for schools, stores and homes, your judgment in a choice of location shall be proven good by those persons who shall erect a city over your bones.

The only settler now on the west side of North Bay is John N. Eberhart and his sturdy family of boys and girls. At the north end of the Bay live two or three families of Squaxin Indians who make a living by picking lucious oysters from the tide flats and sending them to Olympia and Tacoma. This small remnant of a once powerful tribe live yet on the site of the tribe greatness. I am informed by an old Indian that the true name of the Bay is the "Squaxin" Bay. That Squaxin Island took its name from the tribe which lived on this bay and that when the tribe was given a reservation at the time of the Medicine Creek treaty of 1854, they were located on "Squaxin" Island. At the head of the bay the Coulter logging road is built up Coulter Creek for five miles, and great fir and cedar logs are hauled down from the uplands and rolled into the salt water to be towed to the sawmills or windlassed into

---

[5] Wickersham apparently did not know or had forgotten Sherwood's first name and may have intended to fill it in later, thus the empty space in front of his last name.

ships for transportation to foreign countries. The bay is silent and deserted otherwise.

Eberhart is a frontiers man: sharp, rather talkative, and always after the best end of the bargain, yet warm hearted and generous. He was born in Indiana and has moved toward the setting sun as fast as settlers crowded from the populous East. He has lived in nearly every state west of the Mississippi and hails from Texas to Puget Sound. His great delight is to talk and hunt corners of some section of government land with a view to earning an honest dollar by locating a settler. He is not adverse to a little "claim jumping" if there is an extra dollar in it and no great danger.

After a good nights rest we have a hearty breakfast of bread, coffee and grouse and prepare to march. One days experience with our packs taught us that they were heavy so we borrowed a horse and packed the baggage on him. Mr. Palmer and I carried our guns and such Mr. Taylor across to Lake Mason for Charles Joint, Esq. who was to make one of our party from Hoods Canal.

On the way across on the trail to Hoods Canal, I had a long talk with Eberhart about a project that I had long had in my mind, about establishing a town at the north end of North Bay. I found him willing to listen if the town could be located on his land. I had previously looked the locality over, and had concluded that owing to the condition of the flats his place would be the proper one for the town and then and there on the trail made the agreement to lay out a town at his place.

The agreement was that I should do the necessary surveying, clearing, advertising, etc. and build a mill. I should then have three lots out of every five. I determined to perpetuate the name of Sherwood also in our town and thought of calling it "Sherwood."

Mr. Palmer and I stayed all night at Morins logging camp and all bunks being full of loggers, we were politely given leave to sleep in the hay in the ox stable. We pitched our tent, ie., we spread our quilts in the hay and went to sleep. No better nights sleep ever visited me than the one that night. It was cool, we were tired, the hay was soft and how we slept.

The next morning we could not get away. Our plan was to go down to Union City by boat but no boat could be had for love or money. From North Bay to Hoods Canal, there are no roads and none to Union City. There is only a trail across to Hoods Canal until we struck Morins logging road. Then the walking was good. About a week before Eberhart had made the journey across with an ox team and wagon but he climbed over logs through brush and declared he would not try it again. There being no conveyance to be had, we

were obliged to wait. During this interval the scientist took a photo of the camp and its heavy ox teams and load of logs. There are about ten or twelve men at work at the camp and a Chinese cook. There is not a woman in sight but we are told that a Sister of Mercy and a companion are in an outhouse where there is a bed and some other comforts waiting for passage down to Union City. Logs are cut way back on the hill, fastened end to end on the skids. The great team of 8 yoke of oxen is hitched to it and move off slowly for the Canal, dragging 500 ft. of length behind. Arrived here the logs are rolled down the skid way into the water. The skid road at Morins is the finest one I have seen. It runs back to the hill land and across gulches, through deep cuts, over bridges, all the way on a level grade and over skids kept slick with grease.

About ten oclock we got a chance to get a boat by paying liberally for it but alas it would only hold four persons and the Sister of Mercy and her lady companion must go. There was no road along the Canal, it is twelve miles to Union City and walk would be impossible. While we were gravely debating how to get six persons in the leaky boat capable of carrying only four, an Indian Canoe came in sight. Hailing him in Chinook, one of the loggers got him to come ashore and engaged passage for me in his canoe. We found another small leaky boat, our transportation being now assured we embarked—I with the Indian "canim" and the others divided between the other boats. I found myself in a boat—canoe with "Union City Bill," a famous fisher of the oily tribe of Skokomish—or in the plain way—"Skoko" people. Embarking with care while two friends held it to prevent its overturning until I became seated in the bottom as ballast, we were shoved out into deep water and I was safe at sea on Hoods Canal. Smells do not disturb the olfactory nerves when confined under the water but if allowed full play above the waves they are considered "strong." If the full strength of the smells coming up from Bills boat were spread out over the waters and would not sink the whole of our party could have ridden in safety to Union City without any other conveyance. New smells, old smells, clean smells, dirty smells, fish smells and smells! Between the desire to preserve an equilibrium and stay close to the bottom of the boat and not to suffocate with the fishy smells, we sped along at a good speed.

The Indian canoe "canim" is the natural boat, long narrow and with elegant lines, it skims the water like a bird. In making them, the Indian shows an expertness that is his one redeeming quality. He has a mechanical eye thus far and no further. He cannot build a house but he can a boat. His habitation is a rough accumulation of poles and mats, put up gen-

214

erally in the most untidy and unmechanical way possible, while his boat is a delight to the eye of a master mechanic. The Indians down about the Straits of Juan De Fuca make theirs large enough to hold 60 men and they go to sea in them to hunt whales. "Bills" boat was a small one but under his management and by his quick steady stroke we rapidly left the other boats behind and by the time we were 6 miles from Morins camp, they were not in sight.

It was a beautiful day. The sun shone bright and the water was glassy. Not a house was on the other shore from Morins camp until we drew near Union City. A vast unbroken wilderness stretched away at either hand, while the deep clear waters of the Canal were unruffled except by the gentle breast of gull and ducks. Overhead an eagle lays white headed and hungry winged his way from shore to shore, a veritable bird of freedom, a grand larcenist, who steals from his weaker but more lucky feathered cousins. A seal sticks his head out of the salty water and looks at us in mild surprise. Until satisfied, he doubles up like a jack knife and disappears. How quiet everything is. No human voice, no human sounds, no sign of civilization, only high woody shores and solitude. In my lonesomeness I tried my gun on some ducks floating, apparently between sky and water at a considerable distance but without effect. "Bill" was greatly delighted at the "skookum" gun and the speed at which it operated.

About half way down to Union City (it seems) is a narrow place in the Canal called by some the "Diamond Gate." I could acknowledge its peerless beach but why it should have that name I could not imagine. About one P.M. we drew our canoe out on the beach at this point and ate a lunch and permitted "Bill" to rest. Soon we pushed off again before the others appeared in sight. "Bill" assured me that the "Boston" who was rowing the boats behind us was "cultus" and could not paddle along with him. "Bills" bump of vanity was equal to that of a "Boston" and his praises had to be sung even if he had to do it. He told me great stories in his broken Chinook jargon and English and was considerably in importance when I took a photo of him at the beach at Union City. After charging two dollars for his services, he paddled off Skokomishward, a wiser and richer man by reason of his few hours ride with a "Boston man" who carried the mysterious photo "box." On parting with my siwash voyager, I went to the hotel and rested for an hour or so until the others came up. I spent some time in taking a survey of the City and taking views of the scenery. The view of the Olympic Mts. is grand across the waters of the "Heel" of Hoods Canal. A large hotel, a store, an old decayed wharf, a small school house and two or three old dwellings constitute Union City. The principal business around, (in fact the only

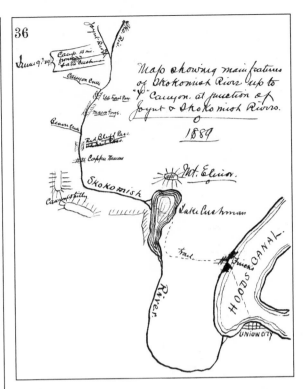

Map from James Wickersham's handwritten account of his 1889 exploration of the Skokomish Valley
Courtesy Washington State Historical Society, Tacoma.

215

one) is John McReavy, a logger. He keeps a large supply of logging outfits and everything needed by that class of people, runs the hotel and saloon, democratic politics and other small matters. Just west of Union City is the Skokomish Indian Reservation. The reserve stretches across the mouth of the Skokomish valley and includs a large area of fine land. The tribe now numbers some 100 people—a boat load of whom just now lie on the beach in front of the hotel and I get a picture of the boat and some of the "Klootchmen" or squaws. When Mr. Palmer and the Commodore and Mr. Joint arrive we proceed to lay on a supply of bacon, tin cups etc. for use in camping as this is the last place when supplies can be purchased. After laying in a full supply of everything used in camping, fishing and hunting, both meat and drink, we secured passage across the bay toward Lake Cushman. Jim McReavey, a younger brother of the storekeeper, very politely invited us to go across in his sail boat. The sisters of Charity were crossing to the north and east side of the Canal and he first put them off at their destination after which he carried us across to Finch's house. These Sisters of Charity are attached to the Catholic hospital at Olympia and were travelling through the logging camps collecting funds for their institution from the loggers, many of whom go to the Hospital when sick or hurt.

Finch's is about six miles from Union City on the west side of the Canal, where the trail for Lake Cushman strikes for the interior. His house is built at the mouth of a beautiful stream of water coming down from the high lands and in the little valley just above, he raises garden. Years ago, about 1850, one Andy Atkinson had a donation claim at this place when he lived with a Skokomish Indian woman and raised a family. With the proverbial shiftlessness of the early settler he failed to perfect his title. His half breed children and these facts will some day produce a first class law suit but lawyers are made for that purpose.

Mr. John Mayo Palmer and some little folk gathered among the rose bushes and I took a Kodak view of the only house at this place in 1889. We were landed here and after making up our packs, started on foot for Lake Cushman about 10 miles away. We followed up the bluff to the left hand or south of Finch Creek and thence over the high lands. Our route lay along a log or skid road to the top of the bluff and thence along a trail. About half a mile back from Finchs we found large bushes of what we termed Oleander but what afterward proved to be the Rhododendron in full bloom. Its gaudy flowers served to give a decidedly southern aspect to the character of the forest and it was a great surprise and pleasure to us to find it.

We started late in the afternoon and by dark had only four or five miles where we found a settler in the deep forest "holding down a ranch." His name was John Dow and his log house was our resting place for the night. With true western hospitality, he set out the best in the house for us and we were agreeably surprised to find him a man of more than ordinary intelligence. He had a small library, many newspapers and magazines and talked of matters of public interest in an appreciative way. His half breed wife was neatness itself and we enjoyed a good supper, a clean bed and a warm breakfast and gathering our packs set out on our journey before sun up for the lake. The rest of our party had remained at Finchs over night but overtook us just before we reached Lake Cushman. We enjoyed the walk through the great virgin forest reaching to the lake, as yet untouched by fire or axe and only traversed by one foot trail, used, however, as a horse trail at times but extremely rough. Our resting place for the night is the only house on the trail except for one or two small deserted cabins which were used to "prove up on claims."

Our first view of the Skokomish River, about a mile below the lake was such a pleasure that we caught it with the Kodak and here it is. By noon we had all arrived at the lake, and the boys had brought a tent with other things from Finchs by a horse pack and we right joyfully crossed the lake in a dugout canoe and camped on the west side in the valley near a fork of the in-flowing Skokomish river which finds its way into the lake through several mouths—but two I think. Lake Cushman is a mile and a half long by three quarters wide and is but an enlargement of the Skokomish river which flows in at the north and west side and out at the south end of the lake. It is very deep and full of fine trout. On the north side of the lake Mt. Elinor rises about 4000 ft. and on the west side the mountain spur comes down to the waters edge. A dense forest of magnificent fir and cedar lines the east shore of the lake and stretches away to Hoods Canal, the finest body of timber probably in the United States. It has recently been entered under the various acts of Congress by persons in the employ of the Stimpsons who then purchased it and have thus acquired this grand domain in defiance of the laws of the United States by fraud.

We unpacked our things and sent them across the lake to make a permanent camp. We then dispersed each to hunt and fish and enjoy life as best suited him. For two days we lived at this place fishing and roving and we enjoyed it immensely. Civilization has penetrated to this lake in the family of one who came here two or three years ago and settled on the flowery meadows between the forked mouth of the Skokomish and began to hew out a home in the wilderness on unsurveyed land. On a trip to Seattle he caught the small pox and died here on the west shore of the lake leaving his wife and small family the only residents of the region. Now, however, the wife has in her employ a big lout of a fellow who is making love to her and working as little as possible. Like many another fool woman she can see charms in him that no one else can see. Verily love is blind and if he dont propose soon she will. There are one or two rough canoes on the lake which they charge a big price for and then between selling eggs to prospectors and raising garden and stock, they make a pretty good living. The dead husband had considerable nerve and accumulated quite a band of live stock, sheep, cattle and horses and I suppose the "hand" has his eye on these as well as the "widdy." We were very successful in catching trout and many a fine skillet of crisp fish did we eat. So enjoyable a treat was it that Mr. Palmer who is a good and consistent Methodist fished on Sunday! He pleaded necessity and said that if the fish had not ceased to bite about noon that he had no idea how long the necessity would have lasted. We also dispersed our party over the valley and killed many a fine grouse. Saw signs of deer and elk but did not succeed in killing any. We climbed a point of the mountain on the west side of the lake, south of the river, and found

216

near the summit an old broken down log cabin. The oldest settler knew nothing of its history and it is probably the decaying shelter of some miner or trapper but why did he camp 1500 feet above Lake Cushman? We erected our tent on west side of the lake in a magnificent grove of cottonwood trees and passed a pleasant week.

June 8th 1889. We had a desire to know something more of the interior than we could see from Lake Cushman so on this day I (James Wickersham) and Charles W. Joint (my boyhoods chum) left Lake Cushman at 6 oclock A.M. for a two days trip up the Skokomish river. No one had, so far as we could ascertain at the lake, ever penetrated into this region up this river above a few miles, and no one had any idea of the character of the country a days march into the interior. A rumor seemed to be afloat that in the center of the Olymics was a great plateau of level country from whence flowed the Skokomish and other rivers but no one had seen the region but many "knew a fellow that had seen it" from a mountain peak on the outer circle of the mountains.

We each carried a gun and ammunition, hunting knives, compass and food for two days. Our food consisted of crackers, hard tack and canned beef and salt for game. Matches plenty. No blankets nor bedding of any kind.

Following up the river due west, about a mile through a dense body of fine fir and cedar timber, we came to the house of a settler by the name of Whitley. Nationality, Missourian, married with one child, wife, mother in law and a dozen dogs. They (the family) lived in a neat log house, deep in the dark forest but had succeeded in clearing a small garden about a yard square. We named (all explorers from Columbus down have that undoubted right) a great mountain canyon just back of his alleged ranch, "Canyon Whitley,"[6] after which act intended to immortalize our "Joy hawker" friend, we left some clothes that Mr. Joynt found superfluous with him and struck off north up the valley, following a dim trail through the woods.

Our friend Whitly [sic] walked a short distance with us and we were pleased with his appearance. He is a typical frontiersman—a bee hunter, bear fighter and a hunter of deer and elk. Tall, strong and muscular, wears a broad brim yellow hat, spotted with bear grease, slow of speech but frank of manner and a great "terbacker chawer."

A mile or so above Canyon Whitley, the river is choked with huge boulders, the remains of some mighty avalanche

from the snow capped Olympics thousands of feet above us. The river is broken into rapids and falls and roars between massive rocks, impassable for logs or anything except water. Just above these rapids we came upon three new unoccupied log shanties in very small clearings. No signs of life. We strapped on our things tightly, took a last look at civilization and plunged into the forest without path or guide, above any known point.

9:40 A.M. Arrived at the foot of Red Bluff Pass at 9:40. Distance from Lake Cushman 5 miles. Fine timber all along the route. Good wagon road can be built this far without expense. Signs of elk becoming abundant. We find at this point on west side of river extending from river water upward great masses of red stone. It seems to our slight examination to bear iron or some other mineral, probably copper. We are forced to go up over the point of mountain to get along. We have just passed a tree and an old camp. On the tree is written "F. C. Ward C. E. Kehoe & C. A. Billings of Olympia. Mt. Olympus or Bust July 12th 1887."

1:30 P.M. At one thirty P.M. we arrive at a large brook emptying into the Skokomish from the west. It is beautiful clear stream and from beaver sign on the banks, trees 6 in. in diameter cut off a foot above the ground, we named it, after drinking of its clear and rapid current, Beaver Creek.[7] At noon we camped at head of pass. Down this "rocky road to Dublin" the Skokomish dashes itself to spray over a series of pretty rapids formed by the water cutting away a channel in the rock. Great boulders fill the stream, which is here contracted and roaring through a narrow chasm. In the course of half a mile the river falls probably 100 feet. Good water power. Because of the regard we have for the youthful "Commodore," we name these the Taylor Rapids.[8]

2:20 P.M. At this hour we have arrived at the foot of a gorge where the walls of rock rise perpendicular on each side hundreds of feet and but 30 feet apart. Large waterfall in the canyon. It is going in the right direction for a R.R. etc. While we cannot approach the water we view the beautiful scenery from the canyon walls above. The clearcut and bold appearance of this gorge reminds me of the character and business like abilities of my friend Allen C. Mason, Esq. Hope he may some day see it and appreciate the beauties of "Mason Gorge."[9]

3:20 P.M. After a hard struggle of one hour we have succeeded in passing the mountain and have safely arrived at

217

---

[6] Canyon Whitley is called Dry Creek on today's maps.
[7] Wickersham's Beaver Creek is called Four Stream today.
[8] Unnamed today.
[9] This is the first gorge on the Skokomish upstream of Four Stream. Unnamed today.

the upper end of Mason Gorge. After a view from the upper end, I am more than satisfied that Mason is highly honored by so beautiful a monument, created and fashioned by an artist whose poorest work is far beyond mans power while this, one of the most beautiful, is beyond my poor description. Have seen several water ouzel on the rocks in the stream.

About a half a mile above Mason Gorge is another mountain chasm through which the river forces its way noisily. The mountains here close in and only by reason of a plain and well beaten elk trail were we enabled to get across the great barrier at all. In view of the beauty of the scenery and after great assistance rendered by the elk trail, I have concluded to name this the "Elk Trail Pass." By this name I seek to perpetuate our thankfulness for an elk trail when weak, sore and ready to drop which enabled us to continue our journey without much loss of time. We are now on the grand trail of the elk from the upper mountain regions to the valleys where the herd in winter escape the rigors of the higher altitudes.

At 5 oclock we rounded the mountain and the valley made away to the west and south. Continuing to follow the elk trail we arrived at the top of the small mountain and thence saw directly north what appeared to be an opening in the mountains. As this was the direction we desired to go we concluded to descend the mountain, cross the river and go off in a northerly direction. Descending we found that the stream that bore away to the west was not the river but a smaller stream which from its issuing from a deep canyon we named "Canyon Creek."[10]

5:30 We ate supper at 5:30 P.M. of one hard tack and some canned meat each. Have seen no game today other than some ducks on the river, grouse and small squirrels, none of which we shot at. Road possible so far. Mr. Joynt is now fishing but will not meet with success. The Skokomish bears away north west. We will soon make camp.

Ate supper at mouth of Canyon Creek and there being no good camp here, we crossed the creek on extemporized bridge of poles and rocks and after considerable difficulty climbed the opposite side of the canyon wall. We tramped about a half mile in a N.W. direction and from the top of the canyon wall got a view of the country to the north. We saw the river here divide, one stream continuing to bear away to the north west while the main stream came down from a due northerly direction. Our view at this point was unobstructed and far up the direction of this largest fork we saw what we so desired, a pass northward.

At a few minutes past six P.M. we climbed 150 ft. down the canyon wall, at a point where this feat could be accomplished hardly by a goat and found ourselves in the canyon of the west branch of the river about 100 yards above the junction. After taking (or attempting to take) some view of the wild and raging waters in this gorge we ascended the bluff half way and built our camp fire and prepared for a nights rest.

The larger of the two streams at this point runs due north and is the proper Skokomish River. The smaller is impassable for even a trout. It is full of great boulders, is confined in a narrow channel between great walls of rock and down this narrow passage it thunders and plunges over falls and rapids in a never ceasing hurry to the sea below. We could not ascend (or descend for that matter) without climbing entirely out of the gorge. From the peculiar shape of the canyon we have called it the "Y Gorge." The left hand river deserves a name and my genial friend Charles W. Joynt, being one of the first discoverers, I have named "Joynt River."[11]

June 9th 1889. Our camp on Joynt river was just a little too steep for comfort. The angle of the hill was about 60° and only by lying against a fallen log could we maintain a place on the ground at all. The force of gravitation tended at all times to drag us down hill and even with the assistance of our log we found it extremely difficult to lie in one spot long. We kept our fire going all night and by wrapping in our rubber coats we managed to sleep pretty comfortable.

[Hand drawn map of Skokomish located here]

Woke at 5:30 and at 6 oclock broke camp and started on our return journey. We do this feeling that one half a days journey more northward would not add much to our knowledge for we can see probably 15 miles up stream on the main river from the top of the canyon wall and the low looking pass due north convinces us that a road can be run that far at any rate. Packed and started on our return at 6 oclock. Made Canyon Creek after half an hours walk and with much difficulty descend the wall and cross the creek. Here we camp at the same spot where we ate supper last night and eat our breakfast. Repack and begin our homeward march at 8 oclock. 8:45 Soon after leaving breakfast camp we struck a large elk trail that went our direction and by following same at 8:45 arrived at summit of small mountain, probably 2000 ft. high. Here we rest and view the country. This summit is a weather worn rock 200 ft. long by 50 wide, devoid of vegetation except mosses and a few small flowers now in bloom. Find plenty of elk sign

---

[10] This is Five Stream today.
[11] Six Stream is the current name of this creek.

on top. The view is grand. Towering peaks surrounded us except off to the south east where the valley of the Skokomish breaks away to the sea. From our high perch we hear it beating and roaring below on its way to the sunny flower covered meadows around Lake Cushman. A fringe of timber extends above our perch and gives us a welcome shade while a gentle south wind comes up over the piney woods and cools our blood heated by the laborious climb to the summit. Our enjoyment of this novel situation is exquisite for it is my first visit to even a minor mountain summit. A few poor strawberries are making a struggle for existence while flowers of unknown varieties are growing. 10 A.M. On the tramp down the mountain toward camp—trout, bread and meat, rest and sleep. 12 P.M. Have just finished dinner at upper end of Taylors rapids.

1:30 P.M. Have passed the first barrier met with yesterday and now will have good walking back to camp. Notice a great many wild columbines, Indian pink and other old time Mississippi Valley flowers in open places. Below the copper mines found a great beaver dam in the river and gathered beaver cut club for specimen. At 6 oclock we got into camp at Lake Cushman, weary and worn out with our two days journey on hard tack, water and canned beef but with the feeling that we had seen a country heretofore unknown to white man. Every thing at camp OK and after a hearty supper, we turned into the tent and had a full nights rest under a blanket which refreshed us very much. A rest for a day or two, more fishing and great pleasure and our summers outing was ended. We packed up and left Lake Cushman's peaceful meadows and walked out to Finchs. When we arrived there we first learned of a great fire which had burned all the business part of Seattle.

We went across to Union City and after a nights good rest took the stage for Shelton and from thence by steamer home. We passed out the Big Skookum, passed by Squaxin Island covered with its ohauties, inhabited by Indians and onto Olympia, the territorial capital. Thence to Tacoma and home.

James Wickersham

The Unknown Olympics[12]

Jack Shants will take a trip through the Olympic range in the near future. He will go by water to Pysht, and thence south through the Quilliute country and endeavor to cross over the range to Lake Cushman and down the Skokomish to Hood's canal and Union City. It is a perilous trip and will take nerve to accomplish it. The writer in company with Judge Wickersham, of Tacoma, traveled eighteen or twenty miles up the Skokomish from Lake Cushman last summer. Elk trails were followed for miles through a dense forest skirting the banks of the river, with no evidence that human steps had ever before gone that way; anon scaling high rocky cliffs almost perpendicular, with little tufts of grass growing like steel from the crevices, making it possible to ascend; then again finding in the lower level grounds windfalls and boulders covered with moss eighteen and twenty inches thick, that had not the elk worked a trail through these barriers with their heavy, sharp hoofs on their semi-annual trips from the upper to the lower ranges for years past, it would have deterred stronger wills than ours from making the attempt. After climbing to the top of a high peak that was covered with a long, heavy grass, miles beyond Mount Olympus, a splendid view was had of the surrounding country.

Looking into the deep and hazy distance to the north we discovered that the oft-repeated legend of the Indians was not altogether a myth, but in all probability a fact. We could plainly discern that a large crater-like table-land lay to the north of us, bounded on the south and north by a backbone or summit of a few hundred feet high. Having run short of grub and time, we had to retrace our steps without having learned whether this level land was a fertile plain, as is claimed for it, or whether it is a barren waste. Mr. Shants will be able to answer this question on his return to Buckley. He has the time, the nerve and endurance, and will find his grub where he makes his bed—on the trail of the elk and the grizzly bear.

—Banner

The Olympics[13]

A party to explore the source of the Skokomish, cross the summit to the head of the Elwha and down that stream to Port Angeles will leave Tacoma July 10, consisting of Judge Wickersham, John Mayo Parmer[14] and Robert Parmer of Tacoma, Charles W. Joynt of the Banner and Charles E. Taylor of Buckley, Mr. Wickersham, Mrs. Parmer, Miss Ida Allen, the Misses Nannie, Clyde and May Wickersham will

219

---

[12] Charles W. Joynt, *Buckley Banner*, no date. Reprinted in the *Mason County Journal* [Shelton], May 23, 1890.
[13] Author unknown, *Buckley Banner*, no date. Reprinted in the *Mason County Journal* [Shelton], July 4, 1890. The *Seattle Press* chose this article to create conflict between this party and the O'Neil Expedition, which was then getting underway. The Wickersham party had close, cordial relationships with the O'Neil Expedition whenever they had contact with them. See "Belittling Lieut. O'Neil," below.
[14] The name "Parmer" should have been "Palmer."

accompany the party as far as Lake Cushman, where they will remain in camp for several days and then return home by way of Hood's canal and the Sound. This trip is a continuation of one taken a year ago by the same party, at which time Messrs. Wickersham and Joynt traveled about 20 miles up the Skokomish, when they ran short of grub and time and had to retrace their steps—however, not until they had gained an eminence from which they could see across the summit to the north and which confirmed the belief that a large table-land lies between the two ridges of the summit. Lieut. O'Neil and party will travel west from Lake Cushman to the Quinaiult country through that part of the mountains that has been traveled many times before, but the Banner party will travel north from Lake Cushman to the straits of De Fuca, right through the heart of the Olympics, skirting the base of both Mt. Olympus and Mt. Constance, through a country that no man has ever before trod as far as can be ascertained from the old settlers and Indians of the mountains. The party will take along an old mineral prospector, and a large lot of specimens will be gathered and brought back. A kodak will also gather specimens of a picturesque nature. All pleasure will be left behind at Lake Cushman, where the party will take up a line of march prepared for hard and thorough work.

—*Buckley Banner*

BELITTLING LIEUT. O'NEIL[15]

The Buckley "Banner" Insinuates That His Expedition Is Going To Do Nothing More Than Hunt Elk On a Well Known Trail—The Same Paper Brags About an Expedition Going Out In Command of Judge Wickersham.

A favorite way of running down the work of others is to profess greater work or brag about what is going to be done by themselves. The *Buckley Banner* takes occasion to belittle the efforts of Lieut. O'Neil and his staff of competent scientists by asserting that they are simply going to work on a trail from Lake Cushman to Lake Quinaiult, a road that has been traveled for a score of years. This is not true. Mr. O'Neil and his party have gone into the mountains to explore them and to bring out information of value to the people of this state. He will give particular atten-

tion to the corners in the southeast and northwest of the Olympic region, which corners were not reached by the *Press* explorers. He has not gone on a hunting excursion over an old well-known trail, but he has gone to look up unknown regions.

The *Buckley Banner* in its attempt to belittle Mr. O'Neil's purposes sends out the usual brag. Following is the article which appeared in its columns:

A party to explore the source of the Skokomish, cross the summit to the head of the Elwha and down that stream to Port Angeles will leave Tacoma July 10, consisting of Judge Wickersham, John Mayo Parmer[16] and Robert Parmer of Tacoma, Charles W. Joynt of the *Banner* and Charles E. Taylor of Buckley, Mr. Wickersham, Mrs. Parmer, Miss Ida Allen, the Misses Nannie, Clyde and May Wickersham will accompany the party as far as Lake Cushman, where they will remain in camp for several days and then return home by way of Hood's canal and the Sound. This trip is a continuation of one taken a year ago by the same party, at which time Messrs. Wickersham and Joynt traveled about 20 miles up the Skokomish, when they ran short of grub and time and had to retrace their steps—however, not until they had gained an eminence from which they could see across the summit to the north and which confirmed the belief that a large table-land lies between the two ridges of the summit. Lieut. O'Neil and party will travel west from Lake Cushman to the Quinaiult country through that part of the mountains that has been traveled many times before, but the Banner party will travel north from Lake Cushman to the straits of De Fuca, right through the heart of the Olympics, skirting the base of both Mt. Olympus and Mt. Constance, through a country that no man has ever before trod as far as can be ascertained from the old settlers and Indians of the mountains. The party will take along an old mineral prospector, and a large lot of specimens will be gathered and brought back. A kodak will also gather specimens of a picturesque nature. All pleasure will be left behind at Lake Cushman, where the party will take up a line of march prepared for hard and thorough work.

It will be only a few weeks before the people will be enabled to judge between the work of these two expeditions, the one under the command of Lieut. O'Neil and other under the command of ex-Judge Wickersham of Tacoma.

220

---

[15] Author unknown, *Seattle Press*, July 16, 1890.
[16] The name "Parmer" should have been "Palmer."

OLYMPIC MOUNTAINS[17]

Explorations Made by the Wickersham Party.

An Olympic National Park.

A Wonderful Journey Accomplished by Three Ladies—Glaciers, Flowers Snow, Deer, Elk New Rivers

Hairbreadth Escapes of the "News" Exploring Party

Mountain Meadows–Mines–Timber–Alaska Cedar– Mountain Ranges–Mississippi Valley Mayflowers are August Flowers on Olympic Summits. Preparations and Start

A party composed of James Wickersham, Mrs. Deborah S. Wickersham, Miss Clyde Wickersham, Charles E. Taylor, Mrs. May W. Taylor and Charles E. Joynt, [the] editor of [the] Buckley Banner, left Tacoma July 19th, under the auspices of the Tacoma News and the Buckley Banner, for the Olympic mountains for the purposes of exploration, hunting, fishing and pleasure. The party[18] was expected to cross the mountains from the lower end of Hood's canal by way of the Skokomish river to the headwaters of the Quiniault and Elwha rivers and down the last named river to Port Angeles, on the Straits of De Fuca. Considerable interest was taken in the trip, for the reason that no woman had ever before attempted to scale the lofty and broken peaks of the Olympics or even to break through the almost impenetrable forests at their base. It was not to be expected that these ladies could make a journey that had deterred many hardy mountaineers and had cost the Seattle Press people six months' hard labor. But true American grit and enterprise was not to be scared by rumors of danger and fatigue, but rather spurred on to the accomplishment of a feat that promised not only to be rare but to yield pleasures equal to their rarity.

Our ladies dressed for the trip in soft felt hats, blue ducking short skirts, blue ducking overalls, drawn tight around the ankle, and heavy leather shoes, with soles filled with hobnails. The men dressed similarly, all wearing rough, heavy, strong clothing.

On the afternoon of July 19th we took the Fleetwood for Olympia, arriving there at 6 P.M., where we chartered the steamer Jessie to take us to Shelton, on the Big Skookum. Started at 8 o'clock and got to Shelton at 12 o'clock midnight, when, after walking about half a mile through the Ethiopian darkness across a railroad trestle, we reached a hotel, where a dance was in progress. The gentlemanly clerk was attending to the hotel register between the times when he was dispensing liquor over a bar at the back of the hotel disk. His bright Hibernian "Hev yez re-gistered?" with a motion towards the hotel register, caused us to quickly enroll our names among the guests of the house and submit to be shown to bed on the third floor. Before retiring we engaged a stage for early morning to take us across country to Union City.

A Bridal Tour

A short time before our journey began, Mr. Charles E. Taylor and Miss May Wickersham were married at Buckley, and resolved to make this Olympic trip their bridal tour. They came down and met the party the day of their marriage, and had the unique experience of tramping more than a hundred miles through an unexplored mountain range as a bridal trip. It is to be hoped that the remainder of their lives will be less rough and tiresome than was the first few weeks.

Shelton, July 20.—On the 20th we had breakfast at the Central hotel, Shelton, and took the stage for Union City. Shelton is the county seat of Mason county, and is a thriving little town. It has two railroads, the Mason County Central and the Satsop R.R., and expects the Port Townsend Southern to be built through there soon. It is situated on the elbow of the Big Skookum. "Skookum" in the Chinook jargon means strong; "Big Skookum," then means the big strong which is to be applied to the force and speed of the tide rushing through this narrow place in its endeavor to seek its level. Our ride from Shelton to Union City, over the old stage road, was a treat. The morning was cool; glimpses of the mountains could be seen once in a while as we passed through little open glades or prairies the piney forests cast off a grateful and resinous perfume, the birds chatted in the morning sunshine and all seemed peaceful and happy.

Union City—Hood's Canal

At about 11 o'clock we arrived on top of the bluff above Union City. From this point can be obtained a fine view of the Olympic mountains.

221

---

[17] James Wickersham, *Tacoma News*, January 2, 1891.
[18] The Wickersham party consisted of James Wickersham, Tacoma; John Mayo Palmer, Tacoma; Robert Palmer, Tacoma; Charles W. Joynt, Buckley; Charles E. Taylor, Buckley; Susan (Mrs. James) Wickersham; Mrs. Robert Palmer; Miss Ida Ellen Wickersham; Miss Nannie Wickersham; Miss Clyde Wickersham; May Wickersham Taylor; and Deborah S. Wickersham. John Palmer, Robert Palmer, Mrs. Palmer, Ida Ellen Wickersham, and Nannie Wickersham remained at Lake Cushman.

We found the little burg, Union City, filled with teams, graders' outfits, tent saloons and all the other paraphernalia of railroad building. The Port Townsend Southern railroad has sent a large force here to begin at once on the construction of their road. Of course this has touched the sleepy old "city" to a new life. Corner lots are for sale, talk of business houses, mills, trade, etc., begins to circulate. Something else now is heard besides the talk of "logging," the only subject of interest in this primitive "city" for the last thirty years.

We went to the hotel—and by the way, it is the best hotel in that region—and were surprised to find it under charge of "mine host" Whitney, of the Carlton house, Olympia, who is staying here now with his family. His hearty welcome was appreciated, and when at dinner we found the dining room in charge of faithful old "William," we were prepared for a good dinner and were not disappointed.

After dinner we went out and purchased our supplies of food for our trip, this being the last store on our route into the mountains. Mr. Joynt, superintended the purchases, and they consisted of 20 pounds of flour to the man, 10 pounds of meal, five pounds of salt, 15 pounds of bacon, three cans of baking powder, six tin plates, three tin cups, fish hooks, chewing gum, French harp and tin whistle, and a long-handled frying pan. Add to these three blankets, guns, ammunition, knives, kodak, knapsacks, 100 feet of rope and extra clothing, and you will have an idea of the loads that we three men started out with into the mountains. We again chartered a steamer—the "Delta" to convey us across the end of the canal to Hoodsport, a new town just starting up on the west side. This steamer with the "Josephine" make regular trips from Union City to Seattle, going to nearly all points on Hoods Canal, a daily communication with the outside world, and taking the new and energetic trade of this region to Seattle. I cast a longing eye up and down the canal, and from my knowledge of the number of settlers in that locality, their needs and their preferences for Tacoma, I felt our business men were and are very short sighted indeed not to do something to get at least that portion of the Hoods Canal trade that is naturally tributary to Tacoma, and naturally inclines this way. But no effort is being made in that way. As soon as I get home I shall go to work myself on the project of a road across Wilkes Portage from North Bay to Hoods Canal, with steamer connection at each end and by this means I am sure a large portion of this valuable trade can be diverted Tacomaward.

We arrived at Hoodsport about 3 o'clock, when we met Lieutenant O'Neil, commanding United States Olympic exploring party, sent out by General Gibbons to make a thorough reconnoisance [sic] of these mountains. The lieutenant met us very kindly, and offered to carry our packs in as far as his camp on the Skokomish river on his mule pack train. He also loaned us a little black mule "Trix," to assist our ladies in as far as Lake Cushman. Hoodsport, the base of supplies for this expedition, is a new town, composed of two or three dwelling houses, but with a great future before it—according to the boomers. Really, however, it promises to be a good little town, being at the elbow of Hood's canal and the outlet of the Skokomish country. Some of our party started on afoot for Lake Cushman; others assisted in loading our packs on a mule, and the rest were engaged in borrowing a side-saddle, and getting one of the ladies on "Trix." The United States chief packer shook his head gravely and advised us to watch the little mule; but we had no trouble with her until we were nearly half way to Lake Cushman, when in ascending a little hill she ran into a yellow jackets' nest. The little yellow bees stung her, and she kicked—she reared and kicked—and the young lady on her back lost the bridle—lost her head—her balance, and the usual result followed. We caught her (that is the mule) loaded our small bundles on her, and one of our men rode her to Lake Cushman, the ladies declining to risk the "gentle animal" that Lieutenant O'Neil spoke so feelingly about, any further, by again mounting. The ladies got into Lake Cushman that night afoot, at 10 o'clock, having traveled by stage, steamer, mule back and afoot from Shelton to that point since breakfast—a distance of 25 miles. We crossed the lake in a canoe and found a settler's house on the opposite side where we applied for a bed for the ladies, to be told by the owner that he was not able to keep them, his beds being full. At this juncture a gentleman shouted out from up stairs and asked if we had ladies with us, and on being answered affirmatively said he would give up his bed. This two of them did, and very thankfully the ladies climbed up into the loft and retired, while we men folks went out to the barn and slept logs in a bed of sweet smelling new hay.

Lake Cushman, July 21.—Lake Cushman is situated about six miles west from Hood's Canal just at the entrance into the Olympic mountains. The Skokomish river runs through it; properly speaking it is an enlargement of the river. Great mountains rear up from the north and south sides thousands of feet, while the valley of the Skokomish extends either way to the northwest and southeast. The lake is half a mile wide by two miles long, and is a beautiful sheet of water. On the west side a great grove of cottonwood grows on the valley at a level with the lake affording a beautiful camping ground, while back of this grove is a meadow belonging to a settler, yielding fine hay for his stock. The scenery here is very fine, being rural, forest and mountain; the fishing first-class and as a resort Lake Cushman has no superior in Washington if it only had a man at the helm who had some idea of the method of conducting such affairs.

Some five or six years ago a settler moved his family to this spot, it being unsurveyed land, and "squatted" on a homestead. After living there four years, building him a good home, clearing land and getting stock and everything around him so that he could maintain his family comfortably, he contracted smallpox on a trip to Seattle, and now lies buried on the sunny banks of Lake Cushman, on the land cleared by his own brawn and muscle. His widow again married, and now a great big second husband is lying around waiting for the land to be surveyed by the government so that he can file on it as "first settler"—and thus the children of the dead father will be robbed of a rich inheritance. The new land officers at Olympia should prevent this injustice—the land belongs one-half to these infant heirs and the other to the widow, and the probate court at Shelton ought to protect them in the matter.

We found a "gin mill" running here full blast, with only a government license in sight, and the vileness of the liquor, the poor accommodations and the extortionate rates charged for everything make it all but impossible for tourists to stop at this place. They seem to have banded together to rob everybody coming that way, charging Lieutenant O'Neil 75 cents a meal for dinner for his men, and outrageous prices for everything else he obtained. Eden was occupied by a serpent, and it is not very surprising even if disappointing that this second garden of peace should be so occupied. A good hotel run by a competent man would get a large trade at this lake, beginning with the spring of 1891.

We camped at Lake Cushman until 2 P.M. and had an elegant dinner of trout caught with trolling hook. Lieutenant O'Neil got in from Finchs' and ate dinner with us. On account of the poor accommodations at the lake he suggested that in the afternoon we move up the river to the copper mines, about five miles, where there was a new shake house that we could occupy. As his pack train was going up, we did so, loading our pack on one of his animals. We arrived at the mines in the afternoon late, and were obligingly allowed to go into the unfinished house mentioned, when in the moss and shavings we made a good bed for the night.

Backwoods Post Office Service

All through this unsurveyed and heavily timbered country there are "squatters" and settlers holding down claims. Blazed trails, not to be followed except by trained eyes, lead from cabin to cabin and to the main trail out to the great busy world. These dwellers in the cool primeval forest shades must needs get letters and papers from "home" and a journey to

the "city" for the mail is quite a labor. To save this and at the same time get mail as frequently as possible, they put a box—cracker or coffee box, anything in the shape of a box, with a cover—at the point of junction of this trail with the main trail and write their name on it. The neighbor who goes to the city brings the mail for all the people having boxes along this road home, and delivers it as he goes by the boxes. No one asks questions, perfect faith exists, and Uncle Sam's public mail is not delivered with more care and honesty than is this backwoods free delivery by these squatter "mail carriers."

Camp Copper Mine, July 22.—Our beds of moss last night were in most cases comfortable. The extra care we took gave our ladies good sleep, but Mr. Joynt and I slept poorly, and were obliged to get up about 5 o'clock, build a fire and thaw out, when I again turned in but he went hunting, returning at breakfast time without game. There are several miners here working their copper claims which are yet undeveloped and not of much value. One of these men, Mueller, a six footer, tells us that he has been away above where Mr. Joynt and I went on this river last year, and talks very discouragingly about us getting through with our ladies—says it is impossible. At this camp an old prospector came to see us, having just returned from Lieutenant O'Neil's camp up the river, and gave us some big yarns about his explorations and prospecting tours in the Olympics. He offered to go with us as guide, but we declined his services, whereupon he gathered his pack, posed for a Kodak picture and bid us good bye. During the day Samuel B. Sweeney, of Walla Walla, and Charles A. Hungate, of Seattle, came into camp from up the river. They told us there had been on the headwaters of the Skokomish hunting elk, and had been with Lieutenant O'Neil's party also, and were then on their way home, having been unsuccessful in finding game except bear. They kindly gave us all the information they could about the route, but looked doubtfully at the ladies.

During the day we fished, rested and examined the copper mines, and at 3 o'clock shouldered our packs and started on our march up the river, turning our backs on the last house on the trail. We had now plunged into the forest, and knew that from this on, we must camp out, and depend absolutely on our own resources. We travelled on up the river on the new trail made by O'Neil's party, crossing the river twice on foot logs, and pitched camp in the evening in an open glade on the rivers' margin. On our way up we met one of Lieutenant O'Neil's men after a mule which had deserted back to the juicy pastures on Lake Cushman, and soon after we met another one taking a disabled mule down to the same luscious pasture. This last mule had tumbled over a precipice with a pack and hurt himself and was on his way to the mule

223

hospital. Caught some nice trout in the river today.

Camp May Taylor, July 23.—Our camp last night was made by setting up frame work of poles four feet high in front, and reaching to the ground back and covering it with cedar boughs. Our bed was pure river sand, and were covered with our blankets. A bright fire in front of the camp kept us warm all night and every one got a good sleep.

Before breakfast this morning Messrs. Joynt and Taylor went out fishing and Joynt lost his large hunting knife in the river. They could see it at the bottom in about four feet of water, and Taylor laying aside his outer garments took a plunge bath in the icy cold water and recovered it. He laid out in the sun an hour or two to dry out, while the rest of us loaded our packs and started on our journey up the river. After climbing over the points of the mountain to escape the canyons on the Skokomish we arrived at Lieutenant O'Neil's camp at noon, and went into camp about a hundred yards from him. He sent down an invitation to lunch which we accepted promptly, and sitting in a circle around his camp fire we ate a hearty dinner of bacon and beans, bread and coffee. Our ladies especially apreciated this courtesy and were loud in their commendation of his cookery.

After lunch we moved our baggage past O'Neil's camp, out across the south fork of the river[19] and went into camp for the night. He is having a hard time to cross the river at this point as it is confined in a deep canyon with no way of getting down or up. He has sent many trees across the canyon, but with one exception they cannot stand the strain and break and fall into the depths below. The one exception is a large cedar upon which we crossed and above which he is now engaged in making another attempt to cross. We carried our flour from O'Neil's pack train across the river, and tonight we are beyond him and ready tomorrow to cut loose from everything and dive into the deepest recesses of these forest ranges. Lieutenant O'Neil sent over an invitation to supper, and we again accepted his hospitality, having coffee, bacon, and "son-of-a-gun." For the benefit of the cooking club, col. Lindsey explained to us that "son-of-a-gun" was the soldiers' name for a boiled mess of bread and crackers, meat, onions, etc., a kind of a bread hash as it were! It was good as we all can testify, and later on in our travels we essayed to make a similar dish very successfully too.

Camp O'Neil, July 24th.—We slept last night in true camp style—with our feet to the fire, and nothing over us but a blanket and the diamond studded sky. Everybody slept

well but two confirmed coffee topers, who had imbibed too freely of the "cup that cheers but not inebriates," at supper. Last night the ladies were promised coffee for breakfast; and sure enough, it came over while we were breakfasting, and the ladies took their last draught of coffee until we shall return again to civilization and dyspepsia. We prepared our packs for carrying with the following load: 62 pounds flour, 10 pound meal, 10 pounds crackers, 2 guns, 1 revolver, 3 knives, hatchet, 60 rounds of ammunition each, 3 blankets, Kodak, etc., making a pack for each man of about 50 pounds. Our altitude at this camp is 1000 feet above sea level.

United States Exploring Party

During the summer of 1885, General Gibbons[20] sent Lieutenant O'Neil in charge of a party to explore the Olympics by way of Port Angeles. The expedition was successfully conducted, and made a thorough map of the region around the Elwha river, reaching well up into the interior, but for want of time the larger portion of the region was unexplored. It was determined to complete the reconnoisance [sic] this summer, and Lieutenant O'Neil was again selected to head the party as commander. This time he penetrated mountains from the south, by way of the Skokomish river, fully equipped for exploring and ascertaining in detail the character of the country. The expedition consists of 10 United States regulars, several members of the Portland Alpine Club, and scientists specially invited to join the party. They have been provided by the government with six months' rations, a pack train of 10 or 15 mules, and everythig necessary for a successful conduct of the enterprise.

Commanding, Lieutenant Joseph H. O'Neil, 14th infantry.
Mineralogist, Col. Linsley.
Taxidermist, Dr. Church.
Naturalist, Mr. Brotherton.[sic]
Artist, Mr. Fisher.
Botanist, Professor Henderson

There is no question about the successful outcome of the expedition, and western Washington is to be congratulated on account thereof. The result of its labors will be a complete map of this hitherto unknown region, as well as a thorough knowledge of its resources. Lieutenant O'Neil is a young man, energetic and ambitious, and has a thorough command of his party. He knows well what he is after, and

---

[19] Five Stream.
[20] Wickersham should have said General Nelson A. Miles.

will succeed in getting it, and the people of the state of Washington will never be able to appreciate his labors. His modesty will prevent his obtaining the proper recognition from the press for his services, as he declines to permit newspaper correspondents with his party. The practical effect of his exploration will be to make the Olympic mountains as easily travelled in the future as the best known parts of the Sound region. Settlements will follow at once, the rich valleys will be opened, the great quantities of fine timber brought out, towns and railroads built, and development of the Olympic region will be advanced ten years by his labors. The state of Washington should recognize the value of his services and follow him up by building a wagon road over the first class trails left by him.

We broke camp at 7 o'clock, with all our packs on our backs, and from that point onward depended on our compasses and individual efforts to get through the mountains. We soon reach the junction of the river where Mr. Joynt and I camped last year, and found one old camp. Mr. Joynt went down into the canyon to look for a crossing, and during his absence Colonel Linsley came up with us and told us that if we would go up the river half a mile we could cross above the canyon.

Calling Mr. Joynt we did this and arrived at the head of the canyon at about 11 o'clock, when we made dinner camp. Here the river is in a little valley, but suddenly contracts into a very narrow space and falls in three breaks a hundred feet or more into the canyon. These falls of the Skokomish are beautiful beyond my power of description, and are well worth a visit by tourists. (Lieutenant O'Neil has since named these falls Honeymoon Falls, in honor of Mrs. and Mr. Taylor, the bridal couple of our party.)

We cooked a lunch at the falls, and marked trees with the names of our party, after which we packed our traps and began mountain climbing in earnest by going up the mountain northward, between the forks of the river. We climbed northward and upward, until late in the afternoon, when seeking a camp and water we were obliged to descend to the east branch of the river. The descent was over a mountain side very steep and covered with fine rock, and gave us much labor and many hard falls. After a severe journey we reached the valley about four miles above the forks and went into camp for the night.

Camp Linsley, July 25.—Colonel Linsley is the mineralogist of Lieutenant O'Neil's party. He is a retired army officer, a gallant old gentleman, and out of respect we named our last night's camp after him. We built a big fire of logs, cut some cedar boughs and spreading our blankets over us, soon slept the sleep of tired children. Messrs. Joynt and Taylor went out hunting at 4:30 this morning, but at 6 o'clock they got in for breakfast without killing anything. Packed and at 6:30 were marching up the river. We had good walking until about 10 o'clock, when in crossing some logs with my pack I sprained my ankle, which gave me much pain. At about 11 o'clock we came to a patch of vine maple bushes intermixed with vines and high grasses, and for more than an hour we floundered in great confusion. After much hard labor we got out of it about noon, and arriving at an open place had lunch. Here I was engaged in rubbing my ankle with liniment, and found that I was very nearly past going any farther. The girls are completely fatigued and have not the strength to get dinner, which Mr. Joynt kindly cooks. Notwithstanding our unhappy condition we have some pleasures before us. To the west the mountain rises abruptly several thousand feet, and from these lofty summits come down four or five beautiful waterfalls. The water comes from snow which we can see once in a while way back on the summits, and the falls look like ribbons of silver coming down over the great, bare, black mountain walls.

My ankle grew so much worse that I really felt laid up, but an internal application of hot pancakes and an external rubbing of hot liniment enabled me to put my foot into my boot and continue my journey, not without much pain, however. After starting we found an old elk trail leading up the river, and had a good afternoon's walking. We found snow in the valley which shows that we [were] getting up in the world, and spring flowers begin to be abundant. At 6 o'clock we encamp in the timber on the west side of the river at a point where the small streams are coming down from the summits like fingers to the hand. We judge we are now near the headwaters of the Skokomish, and expect to begin the ascent out of this valley tomorrow. Can see a great snow-covered peak ahead apparently at the head of the valley. Our girls are tired, but bravely determined to go onward to the summit and down the other side, which journey I now believe we can accomplish. They are better walkers and stronger limbed than I expected, and difficulties seem to fade as we get nearer. The girls are now getting supper. An empty flour sack spread on the ground serves for a table, three tin cups, six tin plates and a frying pan constitute the crockery, while we eat with three hunting knives and one pocket knife, together with our fingers. My wife is mixing bread in one of the tin cups, while a sister is frying fat bacon on the coals. The boys are making a bed of fir boughs and the packs are scattered around a tree—in all it is a gypsy camp [come] to life. Mr. Taylor has just tried to "flip" a flapjack, but failed to catch but half when

225

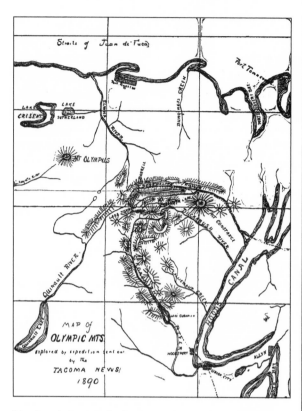

Map drawn by James Wickersham to accompany the report of his 1890 exploration of the upper Skokomish, Duckabush, and Dosewallips Valleys (Tacoma News, January 2, 1891)

range at the head of the Skokomish and deep northward on the same until we strike the Elwha (all of which we found afterwards to be entirely misleading as we should have kept to the west). Found fine heavy timber on the Skokomish and good land, but little brush and traveling good. We began to get fine views of the mountains from points reached by noon, and as the snow fields and mountain meadows began to show up on the opposite range we became impatient to get to the summit. Ate our lunch at noon half way up the mountain, and after a fatiguing journey arrived at what we thought was the summit at 4 o'clock, but on crossing found that we were only on a point of the mountain where the Skokomish makes a great sweep to the eastward.[22] We were some 2000 feet above the river, and from the point could see its valley disappear in the distance southward, and could also see its headwaters gathering all around from the snow fields. We were forced to retreat, to turn southeast and climb the higher mountains,[23] so as to go far enough east to get around the very head of the river. This we proceeded to do; but after some very rough and dangerous climbing over rocks, we camped for the night in a little meadow on the west brink of the mountain and in the snow fields. We made camp between two great snow beds on the little meadow, and after supper turned in under our blankets to sleep. Before sundown dense masses of storm clouds came piling up on the west side of the valley from Olympus, and it looked as if the great Storm King would attack us from these impregnable battlements for our temerity in encroaching on his domain. Possibly he concluded it beneath his dignity to marshal his greatest forces for an attack on pigmies. However, during the night these clouds floated across to our mountain, and settling around us in dense fogs, we were soon wet to the skin by the dampness which penetrated everything. A roaring fire failed to keep us warm, and we were uncomfortable until daybreak.

Camp Brotherton, July 27th.—Mr. Joynt and I were up nearly all night making fires and keeping the girls warm and dry. They did not get a very comfortable sleep, but enough to give them a rest. We broke camp early and started up for the summit. Arrived there at 8:30, to find it a great double peak, with snow everywhere. Owing to the density of the clouds which yet hung about, we were obliged to stay on the summit until the sunlight should drive away the fogs and enable us to see our way down again. Built a fire, erected a cairn of stones, and called the mountain "Saddle mountain,"[24] be-

226

it came down, losing the other half in the sand, which discharges him as cook.

Camp Henderson, July 26.—We had a good night's rest at Camp Henderson, which we expect to be our last one in the valley. We intend to cross the river this morning and climb the mountain side gradually as we go north. The river here roars and rushes down its rocky bed with great force and velocity. Falling over log jams and rocks it falls about one foot in four for miles. It roars like a great storm, and it is impossible to wade it owing to its swiftness, and we cannot hear each other speak only in a loud voice. Roaring, rushing, grinding, valley-making, earth-building, mountain-wearing, ceaselessly day and night with no human ear to hear, it goes on forever, a great work by the Creator, home making for generations yet unborn.

We broke camp at 7 o'clock, crossed the river and at once began to climb northeast up the mountain side.[21] We do this because we are told that we must get on the high

---

[21] Climbing up toward Mount Henderson.
[22] Could be the flank of Mount Henderson or Mount Duckabush.
[23] Mount Skokomish or Mount Stone.
[24] A portion of Mount Henderson.

cause of the two horns at the north and south ends, and the depression in the middle. We concluded that his Satanic majesty had used it when tending the volcanic fires that evidently once raged in the earth's interior in these mountains. Saddle mountain is the extreme double peak on the east and south side of the main branch of the Skoko-mish river, where it turns eastward to its headwaters. It is not the highest peak in the vicinity,[25] but from its position at the turn of the river will always be a landmark. Being the first persons to climb it we felt it was proper that we might name it, and did so while resting on the extreme point waiting for the clouds to roll by. Great banks of snow, a keen air, deep silence, drifting fogs like a driving snow storm gave one a feeling that it was the 27th of December instead of July. Just below us to the east and south we can see fine mountain meadows, with here and there snow fields, running brooks, beautiful flowers, a spring verdure and a delightful perfume. Across these meadows great frowning mountains rise above our perch, while around their summits clouds swirl and one shivers as the sight of the great snow banks and driving storms burst on his vision.

At 10 o'clock the clouds suddenly lift and we are able to locate ourselves, and find that we are like a certain great army that marched up the hill and then marched down again. We found we must go down all the mountain we had traveled in the last 48 hours, down into the valley of the Skokomish and thence up its head and to the summit.

While sitting on this peak Mrs. Taylor called our attention to a mountain at the head of the Skokomish saying, "There is a glacier." An examination with our glasses revealed a large mass of what certainly looked like ice. We will visit it when we cross, but for the present take Kodak views of it. We descended the east side of Saddle mountain into that branch of the Skokomish which runs southward, find it a beautiful little valley, with innumerable waterfalls of surprising beauty, leaping from the surrounding walls. The descent was very laborious, the last part being accomplished by the use of ropes. We reached the valley in time for dinner. Found footprints of deer, elk and bear, in great numbers. We followed this stream down to its junction with the main stream, which here runs due west. Following up the main stream for 200 yards, to our surprise and pleasure we beheld it issuing from a great

Snow Glacier

For miles above the river ran under this great mass of snow and issued out of the tunnel mouth with a roar. We got fine kodak views of the river as it issued from underneath the glacier, and then climbing up on the snow followed up over it for a long distance. Snow-clad mountains, glacial rivers, rock moraines, water falls and beautiful flowers of every hue springing out of the snow, all set in an evergreen forest and flooded by the red rays of the declining sun, make a picture worthy of a master painter—a scene to be appreciated and revisited.

Camp Church, July 26th.—We made halfway up the river to the summit last night walking on the frozen snow tunnel over the stream. Camped on the north side, up in the bushes where we made a bed of boughs. We cooked both supper and breakfast out over the frozen river where we could get wood and before breaking camp this morning set up a pole, naming it Camp Church, after the very gentlemanly and pleasant doctor and taxidermist of O'Neil's party. We started from Camp Church at 8:30 following up the glacier toward the big mountain upon which we saw the ice glacier yesterday. After a two hour's tramp up over the snow glacier, under which roared and ran the farthest head waters of the Skokomish river we reached the summit.

We are now passed up over the head of the Skokomish river and are standing on the divide between that and another river, which, beginning at our feet, flows directly north.[26] We are above the timber line, in the region of snow, ice, mountain meadows, flowers and humming birds. We are also at the foot of what we took to be the ice glacier yesterday—will examine it. It lies in an extinct crater on the west side of the summit of a large mountain, from which spring the waters of two rivers running north and east, and the Skokomish running west and south.[27] Down the divide north of us lies three small ice-covered lakes.[28] The summer's sun has partly loosened King Winter's grip, and between the great cakes of ice the water shows up as blue as indigo. Into these lakes falls a small stream, issuing out of the top of "Crater mountain," and on account of their peculiar color we name them "Blue Water lakes."

We reached the summit at abut 11 o'clock and made camp on [the] divide. To the south lies the valley of the east fork of the Skokomish[29] and to the north the valley of an unknown river,[30] but which may be the Dunginess, the

---

[25] The northwest ridge of Mount Henderson.
[26] Crazy Creek.
[27] Mount Stone.
[28] The Hagen Lakes.
[29] Called the North Fork today.
[30] Crazy Creek.

Quilcene, or some other of the rivers running northeast. Mr. Taylor went out hunting and soon returned saying that there was a bear over the mountain a little way from us in the meadow. Mr. Joynt returned with him, but they found they would have to descend into the valley of the Skokomish to get to him and did not do it. At this point we had promised Lieutenant O'Neil we would have a flag, and, one of the ladies furnishing a handkerchief, it was appropriately marked, hung to a pole and flung to the breeze. A cairn of stones was erected around the flagstaff and a small tree by it was blazed and marked with the name of our camp and with the names of our party. After lunch Messrs. Joynt and Taylor climbed Crater mountain, which we judged to be 5000 or 6000 feet high. They crossed the great crater on the ice and snow and climbed the narrow, sharp ledges of rock to the highest peak.

While they were gone I went hunting to the westward. Climbing the mountain, I got a good view, and found that the stream in front of us runs northeast instead of to the west. It may be the Dungeness, or—well, we can't tell what it is. We all arrived in camp about the same time. The boys saw great mountains all around us, with but little chance to correctly tell where the rivers run. They advise us to go west on the divide a few miles and then north on a chain of mountains running north, and that likely we will strike the Elwha over there. We conclude to camp here, as we have nearly spent the day in climbing Crater mountain and making maps.

Banner Camp, July 29.—This camp was called after the "Buckley Banner," of which Mr. Joynt is one of the proprietors. Mr. Joynt placed a pencil banner on a blazed tree with our names plainly printed thereon. We built a "lean to" or rude roof of fir boughs to sleep under, and started a fire in front at our feet. After supper last night, Mr. Joynt went hunting, where they saw the bear yesterday, and found him again. He got four shots at him at long range but failed to bring him down. On coming down from the mountain yesterday evening, the boys report that what we took for an ice glacier in the extinct crater on top of "Crater Mountain" was really such, and brought us some of the old ice in proof. To the southward we also locate another ice glacier on the north side of a great peak.

During the night the dense masses of clouds came down on us again and we were rudely awakened by the great drops falling in our faces. By replenishing our fires, drying our blankets, and again turning in we passed the night—but not comfortably. This morning I broke the ice to get water for breakfast and to wash our faces. Our camp is on an is-

land of green trees and bright flowers in a sea of snow.

Bear

Before breakfast Mr. Joynt and I went out to hunt. I got back for breakfast but he failed to appear until at 9 o'clock we heard him shooting, and Mr. Taylor went to meet him and found him coming into camp with the hind quarters of a fine fat bear. We are all rejoicing at getting fresh meat, and will stay in camp until noon cooking it to carry in our packs.

Birds

I am very much surprised at seeing so many birds on the summits, but more particularly at so many beautiful humming birds. I had always supposed that this elegant bird was of tropical life, but we find them in great numbers on the highest peaks of these wild and broken mountains hovering just over the snow and ice. Have also seen and heard many song birds, snow birds and eagles.

Timber

A magnificent body of timber extends from Hood's Canal to the headwaters of the Skokomish river. The valley and mountain sides are covered with a dense growth up to 2500 or 3000 feet. Fir, cedar, spruce, Sitka cedar, white pine and hemlock abound in merchantable quantities and will give work for an army of loggers for many years to come. It can be taken out by a railroad or a flume.

A Dangerous Slide

We left Banner camp at 11:30 and went northwest, keeping on the comb or top of the mountain. While going across a great snow field, which lay on the north side of the razorback summit at an angle of about 40 degrees, my sister Clyde suddenly slipped, fell and started down at a terrific speed.[31] Being near I grasped her hand as she fell, lost my own footing, and hand in hand, side by side, on our backs, loaded with heavy packs and a gun, we shot down the incline at lightning speed. Luckily we soon struck a place where the snow was lying less steep, and here, by using our heels and gun as brakes, we stopped, to our intense relief. If the incline had continued as steep serious results might have followed, for a short distance below the snow fell over a precipice hundreds of feet—to go over which meant instant death.

A little farther on we came to a place where the snow went down some 40 or 50 feet at a very steep incline then became flat. Here we sat down and slid to the bottom—we

---

[31] She slipped on the ridge southwest of the Hagen Lakes.

went fast and the snow flew. It was jolly fun, and put us in mind of our young days.

We kept on the summit, crossed on divide[32] and the great slope of a mountain and down into a divide between the north branch of the Skokomish and some other river running in a northeasterly direction, and forming a junction to the northeast with the one running north from Crater Mountain.[33] We now suppose, but we do not know, this river to be the Dungeness.[34] We crossed the divide from the Skokomish, leaving it behind to be seen no more—bidding it a long farewell, and make our camp on the headwaters of our new found river of unknown name.

Camp Tacoma News, July 30th.—We undertook to improve on our sleeping apartments last night by making a tent out of a large blanket for the ladies but about 12 o'clock the wind changed, blowing the smoke and sparks into the mouth of the tent in such clouds that they came out through the top spouting fire. We then changed our fire to a large log, and tore the tent down, using it for covering. With our feet to the fire on the ground, covered by the blankets, ladies and all slept on, while fields of snow lay deep all around us and the keen wind from over the pass whistled through Mr. Joynt's fine, large whiskers—which are now two weeks' old and getting older.

We packed up and started at 7:30 to climb the mountain south of us, so that we might get into the valley to the west and go around a great mountain[35] which is in our path. Could not climb the mountain and turn back. The valley of this river breaks where we are, one part being 200 or 300 feet above us, from which the stream descends with a sheer fall of that distance. A more beautiful view of a "broken valley" could not be found; it would be very enjoyable if we could get up into it, which we find we cannot. We turn to the right and begin the laborious task of going around the mountain to the north.[36] At noon we found ourselves thousands of feet above the valley, going westward around the roughest mountain we have yet found. We had to climb it to get along at all, and when near the top we were forced to cross a dangerous snow field, tipped at an angle which was frightful, being as it was on the verge of the tremendous precipices.

A Lady Falls

while going over this frightful incline, Mrs. Wickersham, the truest footed of our party, suddenly slipped and rolled over and over down the snow to the very brink of the precipice. She struck the rocks there, and after rolling over some of them caught on the others and stopped her fall, within a dozen feet of a precipice five hundred feet or more perpendicular. She soon regained her breath and upright position, and did not even seem frightened by her experience, but it might have been because, as an old sea captain afterwards explained to her, "women never do know when they are in a real danger."

Mount Susan

On this mountain we had the hardest and most dangerous climbing met with so far on the trip, but the handsome mountain meadows across the valley to the northwest, dotted with snow fields, green pastures, streams of pure snow water running through groves of gorgeous trees and falling in beautiful cascades over the mountain sides, make such a pretty picture that we are anxious to get across. After a day's hard work we found ourselves at evening camping time yet on the west side of this precipitous mountain[37] with the land of promise in sight, but so far away that we must wait another day to reach it. If we had climbed into "Broken Valley" we might have saved nearly a day's travel and fatigue.

Geysers

The Seattle Press expedition which went up the Elwha river and part way down the Quinault reports that it heard geysers or boiling springs near the headwaters of these rivers, but did not see them. They even went so far as to give the times and duration of the discharges of these eruptions, and wrote quite learnedly on the subject. It was very interesting to me and I resolved to pay particular attention to geysers and find them if possible. I found none and none exists except in the very vivid imagination of the young man who wrote for the Press from Indian Creek, back of Port Angeles. This young man heard a noise that he could not explain and concluded to call it geysers as it sounded nearer to that than anything he could think of. I found his geysers—they exist all though the mountains, and the following is a complete explanation of the sounds heard by him. One evening just after reaching the summit of Crater mountain, I called the attention of our party to certain intermittent sounds, like the escape of steam. All

---

[32] First Divide.
[33] Crazy Creek.
[34] It was the Duckabush.
[35] Mount Steel.
[36] North side of Mount Steel.
[37] Mount Steel.

listened attentively, and we could hear distinctly, as it seemed, the roar of geysers. We could hear it for a few moments at times and for many minutes at others, coming seemingly from the other side of the valley, or over the divide; we could not exactly locate it. The wind was light and variable, the atmosphere being clear and dry. We were between two great mountain walls, with an open valley leading down each way—on a natural sounding board, with every string set and the forces of nature in full tune. About half a mile away a waterfall tumbled over a precipice in white foam, and distinctly I heard it for a few moments,, and then, as the wind died out the sound ceased. Again as a current of air reached me, from even a different direction, the sound returned, at first indistinctly and doubtfully connected with the waterfall. After an hour's careful listening, and thorough examination we ascertained that the geyser sounds—steam escaping at irregular intervals—were positively made in this echoing way by this roaring mountain torrent falling hundreds of feet down the rocky walls in great sheets of spray, while the currents of air brought the sounds to our ears at irregular intervals, thus producing with startling exactness, I must admit the very sounds described by the Press said as geysers. In other words, here was an Eolian harp of Dame Nature's fashioning, calculated to even mislead the young man who jumps at scientific conclusions for the Press, and who saw blazes on trees that had grown 16 feet long. During our stay on the mountains we heard these geyser noises many times, and each time I took pains to verify my first conclusions, and in each case found the sounds to come from the same source—waterfalls, light variable winds, echoes—in short, an Eolian harp producing music from the waterfalls according to natural laws of sound.

Camp Deception, July 31st. —We named this camp because we were deceived by the appearances of the mountains into rounding this great peak[38] from the north instead of coming across "Broken Valley" and saving a day's hard travel. Had good night's rest and enjoyed our bear steak supper and breakfast. It tasted like good beef, is tender and keeping well. We fry it and also make famous stews, which with flapjacks and fried fat bacon constitute our bill of fare. We will cross at the head of the river this morning and then go north in the mountain meadows. Overhauled our provisions this morning and found we had eaten one-third.

Whistling Marmots

The first day or two in the mountains above the heavy timber line, we are startled at hearing whistling from many quarters. Our ladies insisted that it was made by some kind of a bird, but we soon got them a point of vantage when they could see the marmot sitting at his front door uttering his note of alarm at the approach of strangers. The marmot belongs to the rodent family is about the size of a large rabbit and of greyish yellow color. His habits are very similar to those of the prairie dog. He lives in burrows, has a flat place on the front of the burrow upon which he sits to chatter with his neighbor or watch for enemies, gives a shrill whistle of warning and whisks his tail and disappears into his hole when alarmed in a way very much like his smaller cousin, and he travels around among the neighbors and gossips, makes love and fights all in a way to remind one of the true prairie dog.

About the middle of September the marmot, being then fat, retires to his den, closes up the entrance from within and enters into the lethargic hibernating state like the bear, and does not again appear until about the first of April. His home is at the line of perpetual snow. We killed two or three and examined them carefully.

During yesterday's trip over the high mountain we were enabled to complete our maps of the streams in the vicinity, as well as of the direction of the mountain chains. We also made a careful location of glaciers, having now seen several on the north sides of lofty mountains.

We left Camp Deception early and went south and then west around the head of the river,[39] being compelled on account of perpendicular mountain walls to go down some 2000 feet into the valley. By noon we reached the big mountain meadow on the west of the river, passing on our way at the head of one of the branches of a small lake, clear and deep, with a small island in the center. This beautiful little gem is situated in a small meadow and trails of elk and other animals surround it, while wild flowers in the greatest profusion scent the air with perfume. After our smallest sister we all agreed to call this spot "Lake Jenny."[40]

Mountain Meadow Park

The large meadow is about five miles long by two and one-half wide.[41] It extends from the very summit of the mountains on the west to the mountain wall on the east when it drops 2000 feet perpendicular into the valley. On the north and south

---

[38] Mount Steel.
[39] The Duckabush near O'Neil Pass.
[40] This is Marmot Lake in Duckabush Basin.
[41] LaCross Basin.

230

it is shut off by high mountains. This magnificent natural park is covered in the greater part by green grassy meadow land with here and there stately groves of evergreen trees and bunches of smaller shrubbery. At just the proper distances apart are large pure white snow fields, in striking contrast to the light and dark green of the pastures and woodlands, while rippling streams of clear singing waters meander across the meadowlands or fall in white cascade over rocky walls. Beds of beautifully colored flowers charm the eye, while their sweetest scents perfume the air and birds, bees and insects chirp and buzz merrily in the sunshine. In the center of this wild Olympic park lies a pear-shaped lake, covering about 20 acres, upon the deep blue bosom of which yet floats ice cakes and snow, grim reminders of the last visit of the grizzly Frost King. This beautiful pear-shaped lake we named "Lake Darrell"[42] while standing on its banks gazing over it eastward at the most lovely landscape. No old English castle ever had a more beautiful park around it than this, and one instinctively looked but in vain, for signs of civilized inhabitancy.

Ate our lunch on this plain and climbed the mountain ridge to the left, only to find it nearly straight down for 2000 feet and impossible to descend it. We then started to the north, intending to go across the mountains at a pass, but the clouds gathered in battle array on the summits and came down on us in such dense masses that at 4 o'clock we were forced into camp for the night.

Camp in the Clouds, August 1st.—Flying clouds like a blinding snow storm, the shades of falling night, snow banks and floating ice made an arctic scene last evening that drove us to build a big, roaring fire of logs and keep it going late. In spite of the fire and blankets we got wet, but by building a barrier of wide bark we managed to keep pretty comfortable until at nine o'clock it cleared away. The wind sprang up strong and fresh from the north and the rest of the night was clear and cold. The full moon rose over the big meadows and the jolly bright face made every frost crystal on ice or snow sparkle, while the reflections in the lake, the shadows of the trees, the moonlight on the circle of mountains back of us and the heavens ablaze with a myriad of diamond lights, made an August night picture never to be forgotten. We started early and soon reached the summit, where leaving the rest Mr. Joynt and I climbed to a high peak to our left. At our feet, 2000 feet below us, flowed the white glacial waters of the Quinault river. We could see it as it leaped from a glacier some miles to the northeast, flowed down a great canyon at our feet, and onward for miles, until lost in the distance to the southwest. We could

not be mistaken about this river, and from it and the Skokomish we began to get our maps in definite shape. We found trouble to get down into the Quinault canyon, as the walls were perpendicular in nearly all places, but finally by climbing down hand over hand for hundreds of feet, hanging to points of rock, small bushes and grass, we managed to reach a snow incline. Down this we went for a mile or two and at lunch time we found ourselves on the headwaters of the east branch of the Quinault river which takes its rise in three great glaciers on the mountain sides near us. After lunch gathered spruce gum—everybody chewed gum for once. Our ladies are standing the trip splendidly—they take to rocky walls and steep snow fields like goats, and work like pack horses. They bravely go over places where one false step means death on the rocks below, yet decline to use the life line, and use hobnailed shoe soles as well as our strongest man. Since dinner the clouds have filled the Quinault basin with so dense a mass of dampness that we cannot break camp, and are compelled to lay up till tomorrow under some heavy-topped trees.

Flowers

We found many old friends among the flowers of the mountains. In the valleys and in the timber we found none, but when we got into the first mountain meadow, up above the timber line on the snow fields, we found them in the greatest profusion. The greatest variety exists—of all colors—old friends and new acquaintances—spring up in the wake of the disappearing snow beds, so close in fact that they come up under the ice and snow, and reflecting and gathering the heat of the sun, they bore holes through the ice and spring out of the holes, fling their blossoms to the breeze while their stalks are yet surrounded by ice. You may lay in beds of beautiful bending bluebells, and gather flowers with one hand and snow with the other—not little rifts of snow from under a rock, but banks a hundred feet thick, reflecting the rays of the noonday sun, until you are obliged to leave it to cool off. Familiar flowers were gathered as follows: Buttercups, columbine, Indian pink, yellow and blue violets, bluebells, yellow and white deer tongue, marguerite, lady fingers, roses, and mosses and ferns of infinite variety, besides dozens of beautiful kinds unknown to us.

The ladies were delighted with the great variety, perfume and color of such a mass of lovely homelike plants. We are Illinois folks, and in our young days, columbine, blue bells, Indian pink and deer tongue were our spring flowers at the opening of the season.

231

---

[42] This is Lake LaCross today.

Camp Quinault, August 2nd.—It rained all yesterday afternoon and until 10 o'clock tonight. Without a tent we got wet, of course, but a blazing fire kept the dampness from doing us injury—in fact, while we all lay down on the ground, within 20 feet of a great snow bank, and cover our six persons with three blankets, not one of us has even caught cold. Not even a case of sniffles has resulted, all owing to the purity of the air and the regular temperature to which we are all the time exposed. We find that it is not near as cold on the mountain tops at night, even by the side of the snow, as it is in the damp valleys. Here the sun strikes us from early in the morning, the first ray, until it disappears behind the distant peaks at night. We have twice the number of hours' sunshine here that we had in the valley. About 10 o'clock at night the rain ceased, and it again turned cold, the wind coming from the north, but our protection is much better than last night on the summit.

Started on the march at 7:30. The brush and weeds are so damp that in a few minutes our clothes are wet to the skin and our shoes full of water. We had to climb again over a high point of mountain and thence down into a horrible rocky chasm before reaching the waters of the Quinault. We went up the main fork of the river which comes down from a prodigious glacier on the mountain top ahead of us. The valley here is an incline of debris brought down by glacial action lying at an upward angle of 30 degrees. We intended to leave the river before going far and by sticking to the east climb into the low pass between the Quinault and the river heading with it on the east, but we went up too far and were forced to climb a high bank of slick sliding slate rock and then a perpendicular mountain wall which we accomplished only after much labor, danger and use of our lines. At 1:30 we got to the top where we struck a small prairie, just above the summit and ate our midday lunch.

While climbing up the glacier today our girls saw something moving on the plains east of us and across the river. On examination with our glasses we found the objects to be elk. A great band of magnificent brown-coated, prong horns grazing on a mountain meadow. They were probably three miles away, across the valley filled with heavy timber, and up the opposite mountain side, so we could not go after them, as it would be dark before we could get to them. A day or so ago we also saw deer, while trace and trail of these animals are everywhere. In going through the dense timber we simply follow elk trails and such is the unerring instinct of these animals that they make no mistake but always choose the best road.

The Quinault Glacier

The east fork of the Quinault river springs full-fledged from underneath a great ice glacier on the mountain top.[43] It plunges down a fall of 500 or 600 feet, the largest volume of water we have yet seen at a glacial head. It is eroding and cutting away the mountain rapidly, and the whole process of glacial action can be studied here to the best possible advantage, for the glacier, while high, is easily approached and well exposed for examination. It is the largest glacier yet seen, the parent of a river—the great mother breast from which flows the white glacial waters of the Quinault—a river from the time it leaps from its glacial home over 500 feet of mountain wall, striking in spray on the rocks beneath.

The former outlet of these glacial waters was to the east down the Dosewallips river, but in time the forces of the glacier carried great masses of rock to the Dosewallips outlet and finally dammed it up, when the force of the accumulated snow, ice and water broke the rim of the old crater on the south and a great flood of accumulated waters poured down the Quinault river, which has since been the outlet. The terminal moraine stands 100 feet high nearly full across the old outlet, and is composed entirely of clean boulders carried down by the ice. Since the breaking away a lateral moraine has also been built for several hundred yards in length inside the old outlet and reaching nearly across to the Quinault outlet. I believe this to be the great glacier of the Olympics—certainly none could be more interesting, and a sketch was prepared of its outlines and principal points.

Camp Elk, August 3rd. —We are now in the home of the elk, and as we saw the first band yesterday afternoon we named our last night's camp in remembrance thereof. From the Quinault glacier to Camp Elk we went along the mountain side on the east side of the Dosewallips river. We crossed flat, smooth bench of rock in the afternoon that had once been the site of a glacier. It had extended from the east side of the summit down to this bench and had worn two great pot holes in the rocks which are now occupied by lakes. This flat bench is probably 1500 or 2000 feet above the valley directly underneath, and was worn smooth by the movement of the ice, which accumulating at the top and gradually shoving down towards the valley, had in time worn away the rough rocks which held it back until possible the whole great glacier had toppled over into the valley with a prodigious crash.

[43] Anderson Glacier.

Certainly the site of the glacier remains, the smooth, rocky floor, covering a hundred acres or more, the glacial striations or marking, the pot holes and lateral moraines, yet attesting beyond question that at one time on that high mountain bench a glacier existed for ages. It is gone now and in the pot holes, beautiful blue lakes reflect the mountain views, the old glacial outlet yet forming a channel for the waters of the lakes to reach the perpendicular walls in front, where they leap 1500 or 2000 feet to the valley below. We camped on the north side of the site of this old glacier, on the mountain point which turned it into the valley below.

A beautiful, bright Sunday morning! We slept good last night and feel refreshed and well able to travel today. Left Camp Elk at 7:30 with good walking over the snow directly north toward the lowest summit that will permit us to get over to the north side of the range which here runs northeast. A great glacier lays on top and we make a bee line for it over the snow fields.

A Mother Bear and Cub Attack Us

Just before we reached the summit and the glacier Miss Sharp Eyes Clyde, who discovered the elk yesterday, called our attention by saying, "Oh, see, there is a bear." Sure enough about 200 yards above us, on the top of the glacier, sat an old bear with a half grown cub on her back. Her bruinship had evidently spied us before, for she sat on her haunches facing us with a look of wonder at the new form of enemy coming on her. By the time we saw her she had determined in her mind that we were enemies to race and cub, and giving it a toss from her back she elevated her hair a la Pompadour, and charged on us at a heavy plunging gallop, with the cub following close behind her.

We had been for hours climbing along the snow fields, and at this point were going up the snow to the glacier. Between the snow and that edge of the glacier where we first saw the bear was a meadow, and across this level ground but sloping downward, she came at a rapid gait. Quickly dropping our packs we formed a skirmish line with the girls behind us, and the battle began. As soon as she arrived within distance we fired a volley, and one of the shots struck her, but only to wound and make her more angry and active. She approached us as fast as possible, while we kept up as rapid a fire as our Winchesters and revolvers would permit. When the bear got near us she got behind some rocks and for a time we could get no shots at her, but when she made a rush from her rocky cover we are again prepared for her with another volley. She got probably within 50 feet of me, when, on raising my rifle and pulling the trigger it snapped. I had no more

ammunition in the gun and called to the girls to bring me some. My sister Clyde crossed the rocks to me with cartridges, while I stood facing the bear near Mr. Joynt with only my hunting knife as a defense. He had a revolver, but was rather waiting for me to shoot, as my gun was heavy, not knowing that my ammunition was gone. When I had reloaded we again opened fire and in a short time had ended her career.

During the fight with the old bear the cub had run around to the left and into a patch of small brush. While the old one was behind the rocks I had taken a shot by her at the cub and knocked it down. We supposed it could not then escape and, as the mother bear had by this time charged again, we gave her our attention. In the meantime the cub, not being seriously hurt, had started down the meadow across the snow towards the timber. Our girls were by this time taking as much interest in the fight as any of us, and shouted for Charley Taylor to catch the cub alive. He dropped his gun and started after it on a run. He was obliged to go near the old bear behind the rocks for the cub was farther away than she was and when she made her rush from the rocks he suddenly deployed to the left with an agility and style that would have caused Co. C of Tacoma to hug him with delight. Our volley, however, caused the old bear to stop, and he saw that he could again run after the cub which had now passed around nearly behind us, and he continued his race after it across the snow, cheered by the girls as well as by the calf like bleatings of the cub. It ran in a spraddle legged manner, but considerable faster than its pursuer, and got to the brush and safety ahead of him. We now gave the bear a shot or two that ended her life, and everybody gathered around to offer congratulations on our success in killing her without being hurt. It transpired that our girls had at the beginning of fight unsheathed the knives and climbed behind a rock ready to fight in case the bear succeeded in getting by us, but thanks to our Winchesters they had no necessity for using their Bowies on bruin's vitals.

We quickly cut out the hams of the bear, which proved to be young and very fat, and carving the meat into steak, salted it away, and in short time were on our way up the mountain with the tingling sensations of having had a bear fight under such circumstances as would leave a pleasant impression for the future in the minds of all of our party. The ladies in particular are delighted; the thought of a real bear fight in which they each bore a part, and saw all, was to them a delight and a source of never ending talk.

Motherhood! All the better instincts of animal—aye, even of a human mother—were displayed by the old bear in this final struggle against her enemies. Even in the throes of death she raised herself on her fore paws and gazed across the snows at her cub in its race for life from its pursuers. Her whole being was wrapped up in its defense—she had no fear of man, but boldly marched to attack him, and to death, to protect her offspring. And he, young scapegrace, probably came back and picked the bones we cut from her carcass, for his dinner! How very like some human animals that would be.

Saddle Flap Glacier

The glacier on which our bear was found was soon reached, and we walked across it towards a great rent on its north side. Arriving at this rent we were surprised to find that the glacier was in the form of a great saddle, with two flaps, one hanging toward the Dosewallips, and one into a river north of us,[44] which we instantly proclaim "The Elwha." The rent or connection between these two flaps is about 100 yards wide, and is a great split in the mountain chain, which here runs nearly east and west.

Passing into this gateway between the great mountain walls we were delighted to see running due north a river directly out of the north flap of the glacier upon which we stood. From all our information and our knowledge of the country we believe this to be the Elwha. It runs in the right direction and is in the place where we expect to fall upon that river.

The descent of the north flap of this glacier was a very ticklish piece of walking. The snow was laying at an incline at the top, at about 70 degrees, and Mr. Joynt was obliged to go ahead kicking his heels into the snow and making steps into which each of us put our heels and by this slow laborious and very dangerous process of stair making we managed to go down over several hundred yards of bad snow field. We then got on more level snow and by noon arrived below the glacier and camped for dinner in a beautiful valley, under a shining warm sun, in an atmosphere perfectly delightful. Surrounded by flower perfumed meadows, with handsome streams of water meandering through them, natural parks, snow drifts, evergreen groves and all flanked by high mountain walls, we are as happily situated as travelers could be, cooking fresh bear steak and flap jacks.

Oh, ye city dyspeptic, try one month's roughing it in the glorious mountain meadows of the Olympics in July and August, live upon bear steak, flapjacks and water that you can get nowhere else in the world, and come home with a good digestion and a contented mind. Our ladies, carefully

housed all their lives, have roughed it on this journey with us, have slept above the clouds, on the ground, in the rain, two under a blanket, bathed their blistered feet in the ice water just issuing from under the glaciers, and have for nearly a month climbed over high mountains, into deep valleys, crossed glaciers, snow fields and rivers, have wrung the ice water out of their garments each night before turning their feet to the camp fires to sleep, have walked eight days with their feet wet on the snow fields, have fought yellow jackets and bear, lived on flapjacks and fat bacon—and have not even had a sore throat or cold. Not one of our party has yet suffered except from bruises or fatigue, and health, strength and contentment is the lot of every one now lying in the little meadows at the foot of the glacier in the bright August sun, waiting for dinner. Does it really pay to be civilized—to huddle into Five Point city dens of filth and disease, or live confirmed dyspeptic invalids in gilded palaces, when we could be free and healthy in the mountains in close communion with Mother Nature? This question brings a unanimous voice from our ladies: "Oh! Let's get home—we haven't a change of clothing, and lost our soap two weeks ago"—so I guess the communion business must wait.

After dinner we continued our journey down the river, it getting larger as we go and running in a northeasterly direction. We now feel quite certain that it is the Elwha.[45] All the way down the river this afternoon we have been bothered by timber thrown into the valley by avalanches of snow, damming the river in some places and obliterating the trails, which has been a plainly marked elk trail from the summit down. We go into camp tonight way down the valley, having made the best day's journey on our trip. We have traveled for 10 hours today and have made probably as many miles, which is a big day's work as compared to our shortest—one mile. We are now way below ice and snow in the dense timber and out of the fogs or clouds.

Camp Clyde, August 4.—It would do Chilberg's chief cook good to see our girls mix flapjacks in a tin cup and when browned on one side in the skillet toss them into the air and catch them on the other side as they come down. Flapjacks, bear steak, mountain air, exercise, cold water, freedom and sleep under a blanket on the ground in the open air—what health restoratives! Mr. Joynt is suffering last night and this morning with swollen limbs, but what causes it we cannot imagine, as he has received no serious injury. My sprained ankle is giving me some pain, while Mr. Taylor ripped his

---

[44] Flypaper Pass.
[45] They are actually going down the North Fork of the Dosewallips.

clothes in such a manner that he was forced to retire early and cover up with a blanket, while his bride of two weeks is trying to repair damages with a needle and raveling from a fishing line for thread.

Left Camp Clyde early and travelled down the river expecting soon to see it turn northward. The canyon is now bad, being full of avalanches and fallen timber, rendering it almost impossible to get through it. The timber is not even merchantable and no valley. We are making no headway today, and everybody is tired of climbing logs and through brush, while Mr. Joynt is swelling over until his clothes will hardly hold him. The river continues east, with no sign of turning north.

An Unknown River Discovered

Camp Avalanche, August 5.—We were very much disappointed yesterday afternoon at not striking the main river running north. The stream we are on ran all day straight east, and this morning we can see it down the dim distance travelling eastward. We are now pretty well convinced that we are not on the Elwha, but have struck the Quilcene or Dociwallips, in which case, however, we will not turn back but will go on to the mouth. We will do this for several reasons, one of which is that Mr. Joynt's condition is such now that we can do nothing else. He is frightfully swollen, and is suffering severe pain, his feet being so swollen that he cannot get his boots off, but is obliged to sleep with them on. Another reason for going on down this river is that the Elwha was pretty thoroughly explored by Lieutenant O'Neil in 1885 and by the recent Press expedition, and while we intended to go down it on account of the trails, yet we are more than satisfied to explore this new river and gain some real new geographical information. While we are not yet satisfied that this will turn out to be the Elwha, yet we do not believe it is and are prepared to go over an entire new route to salt water. If Mr. Joynt does not fail us we will not have a hard trip we hope.

Since the return of our party Lieutenant O'Neil's expedition has advanced and they are now evidently wrestling with the same problems concerning the new river that troubled us. Under date of August 24, the Post-Intelligencer published a letter from their correspondent with O'Neil, in which they speak of the same river we had so much trouble with as follows:

Headwaters of Unknown River Discovered

On August 11, Colonel N. S. Linsley, our geologist, in company with Mr. Fisher, left headquarters, then at camp on the middle fork of the Skokomish river, for the purpose of finding the most advantageous route to cross the divide. Journeying up the North fork until they came to a point where it divides into two branches, they then followed up the one that leads off to the southeast until they came to a creek coming in from the northeast, which they followed up to its head and from there climbed into a ridge running to the northwest and after traveling along this for a distance of nearly a mile then climbed down on the other side and came to a lake, out of which a creek flowed. Crossing the creek they pursued their way in a northerly direction and came to another lake out of which another stream flowed. Then turning to the west they climbed to a high peak, showing an attitude of 5350 feet, and from which they could see three large lakes to the east of them, out of which flowed three streams that joined a large river, flowing on a course 20 degs. North of east. Mount Constance bore 52 degs. South of east, Mount Olympus 30 deg. West of south and Quiniault lake 48 degs. South of west.

Although we suppose that this river is either the Hamahama, Dacqueboose or Ducewallips river, our bearings do not fit to either one of them. But as no maps agree on either the locations of these rivers or the mountains, it is impossible to tell. And for the purpose of deciding this point, Lieutenant O'Neil has detailed B. J. Bretherton, the ornithologist of the party, and Sergeant Yates to make the descent down it to its outflow, and they will start in the course of two or three days. The lakes they saw and passed near by were our Lakes Jennie and Darrell, and the river to the east, bearing north, is the south fork[46] of the Docewallips, but they will only find this out by doing as we did; exploring it to the canal. At the time of seeing these lakes and river they must have been in the big mountain meadow upon which we camped on the night of July 31st.

Camp Ella, August 6th.—We made camp last night on a flat bench on the south side of the river where we had plenty of wood and water and a pretty good camp ground. Mr. Joynt is swelled out of all shape, and besides suffering severely keeps the party back by his inability to get along. Provisions are running low, everybody is tired of the sameness of climbing down this rough, rocky, brushy river gorge, and we are looking anxiously for the canal. Hope to get there tomorrow. Mountain meadow, snow fields and all the varied and beautiful scenery of the summit kept our courage up, but now that we are getting nearly out, and can see nothing new, have not pleasant surprises, only hard work, we are rapidly losing energy and interest.

235

---

[46] This fork of the Dosewallips is called the West Fork today.

Short Rations

We have only one more meal of meat and only a few of flour, and, having been on short rations for several days while working very hard, we are beginning to experience some of the vagaries of starving people. Our ladies talk of nothing only what they will cook when they get home—cakes, chocolate, rare steak, roast chicken, etc. They dwell on the delights of a well ordered table and discuss with a longing, hungry look the merits of different vegetables, meats and pastries. While no one goes hungry, we are experiencing some of the torments of Tantalus, for we have now been in the mountains 14 days with only 10 days' provisions.

Traveled down the river until noon, and the sentiment of the party regarding the hog trough sewer is anything but favorable. It is only an outlet for the great mountain meadow country of the interior and lacks everything to make it interesting to either the farmer, logger or sportsman. High mountain walls on either side of the river, without a stream coming in from either the right or the left, the valley choked frequently by avalanches, which render the walking next to impossible, dense masses of rhododendron through the stiff branches of which we stumble at times and actually crawl on our hands and knees, at others while we carefully pick our way along a hillside sloping at an angle of from 45 to 60 degrees.

This afternoon we arrived at the meanest, narrowest, crookedest, deepest gorge of the whole lot, through which the river ran roaring, leaping from fall to fall, filled with driftwood, snow and rocks, while the mountain walls rose straight up thousands of feet. We are forced by the perpendicular walls to go down, down, down to the river and here we were obliged to go across the rotten snow of an old avalanche and thence up the bank to where some little trees had fallen from one wall across the river striking the other rocky wall way above the demoniacal roar of the waters. We crossed on these small bushes, and from their topmost branches against the north wall of the canyon we again climbed the rocky walls to the summit. The river at this point had cut under the wall on the north side, leaving a bench nearly across it, and against this bench the small trees had fallen upon which we crossed. After crossing this frightful chasm we reached the summits of some small spurs inside the great gorge, and found better walking down to the water.

Camp Devil's Cauldron, Aug. 7.—Camped last night on the side of the river, where the roar of its falls almost drove one frantic, in a region never before trod by human foot, and where neither man nor animal could enjoy existence. The great rough mountains rear their angry and cloud capped crests thousands of feet above us; rocky gorges en-

compass us; sickness and privation overtake us, and our situation is anything but pleasant. Mr. Joynt has been ailing for some days, evidently suffering resulting from exposure and great fatigue and he is now sick and utterly exhausted. He retired—or rather fell on the ground in an exhausted condition—and now lies in a troubled sleep, groaning in pain. He is swollen almost beyond recognition, and can only remove his clothes or boot with much pain. The ladies are strong and active—good for the trip—while I am the strongest one of the party, but suffering with my ankle. Mr. Taylor's shoes are gone, but he is able to keep the soles under his feet like sandals. We ate our last bit of meat this morning, and today we start out with only bread and water. If Mr. Joynt gets unable to travel I will take the girls and make forced marches down the river with them, leaving Mr. Taylor with him until I can return with provisions, when we can get him out. Hope he will be better in the morning.

At noon we came down off the high canyon points on our elk trail into a little valley, and a cheer went up from the party as we came in sight of an old camp. Evidently the campers were hunters going into the mountains to hunt elk, and a rough note pinned on a tree was left possibly as a guide to a detachment of their party which were behind. It read, literally, as follows: "Saturday, 21. "follow the new trail, we have gon on slow hav got a laim man with us good buy."

The trail which we have been following during the most of the forenoon came down off the mountains, and the party had evidently passed to the northward of the Devil's Cauldron out to the mountain summit after a few days' camping at this point. This camp, the little valley and the general feeling that we are nearly out to the canal induced our girls to cook us an extra dinner, which consisted of water and flapjacks.

Poison Oak

Left Camp Devil's Cauldron at 7:30 with Mr. Joynt almost beyond the point of standing up. He is evidently poisoned by poison oak, which grows in these mountains and being, we are told, the only poison plant growing in these vast rocky solitudes.

Had bad traveling down the river for about a mile when we struck a great elk trail which led us over a fair road until noon, although we were obliged to go up and down the mountain points. During this forenoon trip I went ahead and in a little grove heard the chuck of a grouse. Never did necessity press harder—no meat to eat and a sick man to feed—the old ground hog and preacher story came to my mind, but I could only laugh a sickly smile, while I leaned my gun carefully up against a tree and after deliberate aim shot the grouse's

236

head off. The shot and my triumphant cheer was soon answered by the party, all of whom were delighted at our good fortune in again securing some meat.

Mush and Flapjacks

We expect to cook the grouse for supper. After dinner, with renewed courage, we traveled down the stream, which here had considerable valley on each side, and to our great delight we struck into berry patches—huckleberries, strawberries, blackberries, gooseberries, salmon berries and thimbles in abundance; and a grouse supper in prospect! This is what Mr. Joynt calls "marmalade." What more could hungry and tired travelers ask, with the gateway to Hood's canal looming up just before them? Saw red rock in the river like that so abundant at the copper mines on the Skokomish. From our present calculations and maps we are able to say pretty accurately that the river we are now on rises about 12 miles west of a line drawn north from Lake Cushman and about 35 miles north of that lake, and flows east and then southeast into Hood's canal.

Camp Ida, August 8th.—Made camp in the bottom under vine maples last night, and barring short rations, hunger and fatigue we slept well. During yesterday afternoon we had miserable traveling through vine maple mazes. This tree is small and its branches grow to great lengths, fall on the ground take root and spring up again. In this way a network of brush is formed that even a bear avoids if possible; and the very worst patches of vine maple we ever saw happened our way. We actually crawled on our hands and knees yesterday for long distances. This morning we breakfasted on half a flapjack apiece, without meat or gravy, and will have no more until we get out of the wilderness. Mr. Joynt is some better than yesterday, but yet fearfully swollen and stiff, while my sprained ankle is getting worse. The valley is about a mile wide and is the winter camping ground for elk and deer and bear signs are abundant.

Grand Forks of the Docewallips

At noon today we came to the grand forks of this river, one of which we are on and the other coming in from the southwest. High mountains press together here, and the rivers are only seen from the canyon walls deep in the abyss, a line of white foam, roaring and beating like an imprisoned monster. We came out on a high point of rock between the rivers, with the water several hundred feet below us, and the opposite canyon wall not over 50 feet away. It was necessary, however, to get down into this deep bed, which we accomplished after infinite labor and danger by the use of

ropes. Cooked our dinner of flap jacks and a grouse, in the canyon, while Mr. Joynt rested his swollen limbs for climbing the opposite wall. We found a pole across the rapid current and Mr. Taylor stretched a rope across over it, and by holding to the rope and walking the slick pole we got across in safety, and then climbed the almost perpendicular wall out of this dreary, dark canyon. Country is no good so far—no valley nor timber.

Civilization

About a mile below Camp Ida we saw a new cabin on the opposite side of the river. In great excitement we gathered on the bank and shouted until we were tired but received no answer. No signs of life could be seen except the new cabin itself, which appears to be the advance guard of the pioneers invading the mountains. The farmer who built the structure probably visits it once in six months so that some other agriculturist cannot "jump his claim." This is the first house we have seen since leaving Lake Cushman, and we sit on the bank of the river and gaze across at it with a feeling of homesickness; indeed, we are so tired and hungry that we feel like the boy—"I want to go h-o-m-e." We don't yet know what river we are on, or where we are, but hope to get out today or tomorrow and solve the conundrum.

At 11 o'clock today we came upon another new log cabin, but this time on our side of the river. It is rough built, no floor, no window, and not daubed. On the side of the door was written "J. G. Luckey's claim," with a description of the land embraced therein. A few trees were cut, and marks of a camp fire showed that at some time in the near past the claimant had rested from his labors at his shanty and cooked his meals under his own vine and fig tree.

We had a bad afternoon's traveling on account of the dense thickets of tangled vine maple. At times it would be impenetrable in front, and either a side or backward movement would have to be made, and many a hundred yards we went on our hands and knees. But about noon we smelled smoke—a faint odor of civilization—and refreshed at once we plunged into the vine maple thickets with renewed strength and courage. At nightfall we came out on the level river bottom, and just across the river we were delighted to behold

An Inhabited Log Cabin

A hearty yell from our excited crowd brought a boy to the door, followed quickly by his father and mother. To say that they were surprised to see a party of men and women coming down the river out of the mountains is to put it mildly. Their

237

surprise was not greater than our delight, for we were hungry and might reasonable expect a square meal, with a greater variety than water and flapjacks. The settler, accompanied by his family, rushed half way down to the river, when his wife ran back, but he came to the river bank and shouted for us to go down the river to a log and cross. He kept along even with us, and finally we found a great cottonwood tree across the river, and, assisted by the hardy pioneer, who had removed his boots, we crossed the river on the log and took up the line of march for his cabin.

Horner's Ranch

The settler's name was Horner, and his family consisted of wife, boy and girl. They are Philadelphia people and are pluckily on the advance guard into the heart of the Olympics, building a home in the narrow valley that now skirt the rapid waters of the Dosewallips, which dances and leaps along in the sunlight as smilingly as though it were never confined within canyon walls and leaped hundreds of foamy waterfalls.

Mrs. Horner tells us that her first impulse on seeing our ladies was to run down to the river to greet them, and the next, born of lonesomeness, was to run back to the house and cry. She was delighted to have visitors and bustled around lively to get us something to eat. The first pious act that each performed was to wash as well as we could with soap and warm water. We had lost our soap more than two weeks ago on the south side of the mountains and had been using sand instead, but—well, we enjoyed soap after a two-weeks' vacation.

Our first inquiry was about the name of the river we had so painfully followed for six days, and we were informed that we were only about six miles from Hood's Canal and on the

Dosewallips River

This river rises in the center of the Olympic mountains about 12 miles west of the line drawn north from Lake Cushman and at a point nearly northwest of where it empties into the canal. It is quite a large river after passing the Grand Forks canyon, but is not navigable for even a trout a greater part of its length owing to falls, rapids, drifts and rocks. It cannot be used to bring out timber, and it would be difficult to even run a road or railroad up it owing to the canyons. It is just about as near not account as can be imagined.

The word Dosewallips is of Indian origin and signifies a river with two mouths. The river forks a mile or two from salt water and finds its way to the canal down two outlets, hence the application. Of course in the Indian pronunciation guttural sounds are given the word that no white man can imitate, but the spelling given is the best that can be done.

Out hostess flew around her little home getting our supper, while we were talking to her husband and washing, and directly we sat to an improvised table of cedar boards out in front of the cabin by a fire and began the first hearty meal we had made since leaving O'Neil's camp on the Skokomish river many days before. The Horner house is a small, unfinished log cabin, and they cook in front of the log cabin over an open fire, but the brown, crisp bacon, the light loaves of bread, good coffee, butter and molasses, set before us in unlimited quantities, seemed sweeter than the most elegant spread. How we did enjoy some potatoes boiled with their jackets on! It is painful at this time to dwell upon the gastronomic feats of that meal. Sufficient to say that one of our party has been afflicted with rheumatism ever since.

After supper and a rest before the fire, Mrs. Horner made a bed for our girls in the house, while we men folks wrapped ourselves in blankets and slept in a great pile of cedar shavings out by a big log.

Brennan P. O., Aug 9th.—At four o'clock this morning we got up for breakfast so that we could get down to the canal to catch the steamer "Josephine" for Seattle. Mrs. Horner stirred herself and gave us another square meal, but we all suspected that our six individual appetites tried twice on her supplies must have reduced them considerable, so we paid as liberally as we could for our accommodations. Mrs. Horner stood in the door to see us depart, and soon a wave of the hand, as we lost view of the cabin in the trees, was the last sight of the plucky little Philadelphian who has followed her husband to this outpost of civilization to make a new home—long may she wave, and continue to dispense mealy potatoes, aromatic bacon, and skillet baked bread to weary and hungry travelers.

At five o'clock led by our host we started on our journey down to the canal, over a good trail the entire distance. All the land below Horner's is "squatted on" and we passed several little cabins. At 8 o'clock we reached the canal to be informed that the tide was out, that the steamer would pass on the opposite side of the canal, and owing to the low tide we could not get their row boat out of the creek to the salt water.

While we were talking the matter over, the Josephine put in an appearance across the canal and passed around the point out of sight, leaving us without hope of getting to Seattle this day.

The Dosewallips river empties by its two mouths into Hood's canal just west of the south end of the Toandos peninsula. The valley here is some two or three miles wide and is a very fertile tract of land. Many "old settlers" live here, including the Brannons and Captain Clements, an old sea captain. This old "salt chuck" captain is a character and is full of sailor yarns from the time he left New Bedford "for whales, back in the thirties," until he run his last lumber vessel into Puget Sound some 15 years ago. He offered to row us across the canal to a trail leading to Port Washington, where he assured us we could catch a boat at 2 o'clock to take us to Seattle. As we could do nothing better we agreed to this programme and left his house at 9 o'clock in a row boat. He told us many happy stories during our ride and, being a jolly old fellow, we enjoyed his company very much.

British Cannon at Seabeck

He told us about the British cannon at Seabeck which were left by a British man-of-war back in the forties, and have ever since been used by patriotic Americans to boom their Fourth of July celebrations. There are two of these old cannon put ashore as condemned guns, but which have ever since been able to belch forth smoke and noise on behalf of rather than against their enemies of 1812.

Duke of York's Sister

Tread lightly when at the mouth of the Dosewallips river, for you are in the presence of royalty itself. The Duke of York was for many years the chief of the Clallum Indians at Port Townsend, and was an exception to the rule that the only good Indian is a dead one. In 1850 he paddled Theodore Winthrop from Port Townsend to Fort Nesqually in his royal canoe, and such was his reputation among the white people that when he died a short time ago many of the old settlers at Port Townsend turned out and gave him a fashionable burial. Fine carriages followed the old chief to his grave, and many of the old people who bore the brunt of pioneer life of 40 years ago, felt that a true friend to the whites had passed away. Long live the memory of the Clallum Duke of York! His name will go down in history along with those of Samoset, Pocahontas and other friends of the whites. His race is dying out rapidly and it will be only a short time until the noble tribe of Clallums will be no more, but he will live in history as a representative of this people because he was as true a man as one could expect a savage to be—better than many who are not called savages.

But it was of the Duke of York's sister we were speaking. In an early day white women were scarce, and venturesome white pioneers, who never expected to see white women in any numbers on Puget Sound, married dusky maids of the forest. Possibly they followed the then prevailing fashion and purchased their brides with so many horses or blanket; but whether they were purchased upon the aboriginal or European plan, many of them made exemplary wives and mothers. A prominent and respected "old settler" at the mouth of the Dosewallips, following the early fashion, met, wooed and won (or purchased, as the case may be) the sister of the Duke of York, of the oily and fishy tribe of Clallum.

History does not record the details of the royal marriage—whether it was celebrated with pomp and ceremony by a "Boston le plet" in the house of some pioneer, or whether the bride stood, as usual, barefooted on the wet sands of Whulge as the tide was going out at even and amid the smells of fish, whale oil and blubber, and surrounded by the greasy tribes of Clallum, pledged her life, her strength and her royal honor to dig clams for her "Boston man" until he should see fit to depart for "the states."

Whatever the ceremony the neighbors of the sister of the Duke of York all speak of her at this date as an exemplary wife and a good neighbor. She is now getting old, but her kind disposition, neighborly ways and love for children have endeared her especially to all the old settlers on Hood's Canal.

A Bear vs. the United States

It is seldom that an officer representing the United States government is attacked or resisted, for stringent laws have been made to punish such offenses. Notwithstanding these criminal statutes officials upon whom dignity weighs and who represent the principal branches of the government are sometimes attacked, but seldom by bear.

Recently, however, the mail carrier from Brannon, who, by the by, is the jolly old sea dog, Captain Clements, was going along the road engaged in toting the mail bag on his official back and representing in his grizzled person Mr. Wanamaker himself. In crossing a little bottom he saw a cub bear and in his official character he undertook to catch it, which he did, as he remarked, "too darned easy." The cub bleated and scratched the representative of the postal department, and while the doughty captain was wrestling with it the old mother bear came upon the scene and fearing neither the law nor Mr. Wanamaker, willfully, maliciously and feloniously attacked and resisted an officer of the postal department contrary to the form of the statute, etc.

The old bear even went so far in her disregard of the majesty of the law as to chew the mail sack, when she could not get near enough to chew Captain Clements any more. He returned to the scene of action a little later with reinforcements and rescued his chewed up sack and scratched dignity and does not now interfere, in the name of Wanamaker, with cub bear.

239

Port Washington

Captain Clements landed us on the east side of Hoods canal about four miles above Seabeck, and bidding the jolly captain good bye we once more shouldered our packs and started on our journey. At 1:30 we reached the water of Port Washington which is a part of Dye's Inlet, and got dinner at the house of another settler, William H. Stillwood. We were disappointed again, for they informed us that no boat went to Seattle until the next day, and we were forced to content ourselves with resting until the next morning.

Home, August 10, 1890.—This morning we boarded the steamer, Sarah M. Renton, for Seattle. Passed Tracyton, and the chosen site of the United States navy yard opposite, Sydney and Port Blakely, and arrived in Seattle at noon. After lunch we caught the steamer Fleetwood for Tacoma, and arrived home at 3 o'clock Sunday afternoon, a tired, hungry, dirty crowd, but feeling amply repaid for all our labor.

THEY WENT OUT AFTER ELK[47]

Two Hunters Return From the Olympic Mountains.

They Saw the Wickersham Party.

Great Scope of Work Being Done by O'Neil—The Hunters Find Queer Plants, Etc.

The hunters returned last night from the Olympic mountains. They tell of some great experiences and bring news of the O'Neil party. They also met the Wickersham party near Lake Cushman. The hunters are Samuel B. Sweeney of Walla Walla, and Charles A Hungate of Seattle. They are old friends and have hunted together for the past 14 years. When they read in the Press of the remarkable herds of elk found in the Olympic mountains they determined to go there for an elk hunt. This was the sole purpose. They did not thirst for glory as explorers, nor did they dream of fabulous wealth in gold mines. They went out on a hunting trip, expecting to have some fun, and to use one of their own expressions, they "just found barrels of it."

They started from Seattle on July 11th and went up to Lake Cushman by the Lillewaup trail, which they pronounced as most damnable. The road from Hoodsport is in fine condition, and it is understood that the Lillewaup trail will soon be repaired, but when these hunters went in the trail was almost impassable. This coincides exactly with the report sent out by the O'Neil party after nearly swamping on the Lillewaup trail.

Headquarters With O'Neil

The two hunters found the O'Neil party in the mountains in their camp, while they went out on a long hunting trip in the mountains. When Mr. Sweeney approached the O'Neil camp the lieutenant came up, and, with a quizzical look on his face said: "Well, say, I know you. Seems to me when I saw you last you wore pretty good clothes." And as he spoke he glanced at the torn rigging of the hunter. "Yes; and I remember that you too were dressed in different style than what you are now." The two men had met at Vancouver and the last time they were together was at a reception in Portland, when both appeared in low cut vests and spike tail coats. As they confronted each other in the mountains they wore overalls, flannel shirts and slouch hats.

Lieutenant O'Neil Sends Out a Message

The hunters were with the O'Neil party as late as Thursday of the week; the camp was then about 11 miles back of Lake Cushman. Lieutenant O'Neil sent out word that though they were going slowly they were doing thorough work and would accomplish what they went after; and from what Mr. Sweeney says this promise will be completed.

"Why," says the hunter, "you would be astonished to see the way Lieutenant O'Neil handles that party. They all like him. They think the world of him and still he keeps them all hard at work. He works too. I tell you none of them work any harder than he does. Sometimes when we came into camp we would only find two men in camp. All the rest were out in the hills working, hunting and exploring. The work is being done in a most thorough manner, and the map of the country is being completed as the party advances."

Two Mule Loads of Botanical Specimens

"And there are scientists of the party," continued Mr. Sweeney. "They are hard at work, too. Professor Henderson, the botanist, is collecting specimens of all kinds of plants found there. He will have over two mule loads of botanical specimens before he comes out of the mountains, and some of the specimens are rare and beautiful, too." The ornithologist is collecting many birds and finding out all he can in that line, and so it is with every branch of science represented in the party.

---

[47] *Seattle Press*, no date. Reprinted in the *Tacoma News*, January 2, 1891.

Queer Birds and Animals

"Mr. Hungate and I saw some queer birds, plants and animals during our hunting trips into the mountains. One day we were having a steep, hard climb when I heard what I thought was someone whistling at me. I answered, and the whistling was repeated. We then sat down under a tree and began to call up this mountain whistler. Soon some birds put in an appearance. They resembled mockingbirds very much and were of a slate color. We whistled with them for a long time and they answered us quickly and freely."

The Whistling Marmot

"One day Mr. Hungate came into camp with the exclamation, "Sam, I killed two of the biggest squirrels today I ever saw in my life. One weighs about 25 pounds, and the other must weigh nearly 40 pounds. They whistled just like a man. I fetched a head on one of them." "As quick as he showed it to me I remembered it as the whistling marmot which I had seen before. We afterwards saw many of the marmots. In some places we found where they had burrowed up out of the snow. They are a good deal like a land beaver, living on about the same kind of food."

Headwaters of the Skokomish

"After some remarkable climbing, in which we were compelled to stick our bowie knives into the cracks in the rocks, we reached the summit of the mountains and could look over into an open space beyond. We found the headwaters of the Skokomish, and it is not at all like it is indicated on the maps. The maps show the south fork of the river branching off to the southeast and taking its rise in a remote direction from the rise of the other fork, of which Lake Cushman is a part. This is not correct. When we ascended the river beyond Lake Cushman we found that the south fork curves toward the north, and we could almost throw a stone from the headwaters of one branch into the headwaters of the south fork.

It has been generally supposed that the largest rivers of the Olympic peninsula took their rise at the base of Mounts Olympus and Constance, but such is not the case. Mt. Olympus only sends down a small stream into the Elwha river, the headwaters of which come from a point many miles farther south. The same is true of Mt. Constance and the Dosewallips river. All the streams of the Olympic peninsula rise at a point near the center of that region, and they generally start full fledged rivers, leaping far down over rocky walls, from underneath an ice glacier resting on the mountain top. The Skokomish, Quinault, Dosewallips and Elwha, and others will all head within a space of fifteen miles square, in the center of the Olympic mountains. It is the spot that should be selected as a park.

Five Little Lakes Discovered

"The north fork of the Skokomish, which flows through Lake Cushman, divides into three branches. The largest one comes from the northeast. It has its rise in a beautiful lake about 700 yards long. The middle branch flows from the northwest and its rise is in a group of five little lakes in which the water is ice-cold, and just as blue as any water ever saw. They are certainly the most beautiful little lakes I know of. The other branch comes from almost due west.

A Scene Unsurpassed

"At sunrise one morning we enjoyed a treat in the scenery line that never was equaled anywhere. Now, I have travelled about Mounts Shasta, Hood, Jefferson, the Blue mountains in eastern Washington, the Salmon River mountains, the Bitter Roots, Selkirks in British Columbia, and of course, the Rockies, and nowhere have I met with scenery to equal what we saw there in the Olympics.

"Gazing to the southeastward we beheld Tacoma and all its beautiful surroundings. Then we could trace the blue line of the great Puget Sound, and all around us were majestic mountain peaks, but the treat was not is this sublime aspect of the scenery. We had reached the brink of a crater-like meadow. The walls were overhanging. We could not see the base of the cliffs on which we stood, but beyond was an immense snowslide, and down that we proposed to descend. Before starting I leaned over the brink and looked into the meadow. I cannot begin to tell you how beautiful it was. There were wild flowers in great profusion and lillies of almost every shape and shade; great gardens of the most lovely wild flowers and grasses. While enjoying this scene a beautiful doe stepped out into the meadow, followed by two little playful fawns. Fancy my feeling now, after having been enticed by the scene before. While the doe slowly walked out into view I noticed two magnificent bucks with branching, velvet-covered antlers striding out into the natural garden. This was too much for my hunter nature, so, after drinking in a little more of the beauty, I raised my rifle and secured the larger of the two bucks.

Killed a Fine Big Bear

"Just then I heard rifle shots in quick succession from the vicinity of the snow-slide, and hurrying to the scene for fear my partner had got into close quarters, I found he had killed a fine big bear. Then we feasted on the choicest kinds of fresh meat.

241

Had to Return

"If my business, grain shipping, did not require return, I should most certainly have remained with the party and continued with them as hunter to the end of the exploration. We went after elk, but it was too late in the season. We found great broad trails just like wagon roads. They were fresh ones, too, but the elks themselves had all gone over the divide into the interior of the mountains. So our main ambition was not satisfied, though the sport we did have was simply magnificent."

Women Dressed for Exploring

"At the copper mines," continued the hunter, "we met the Wickersham party, composed of three men and three women. The latter are standing the fatigues of the journey remarkable well. They are dressed for the occasion. On their heads they wear soft felt hats. Their blouses are made of blue cotton drill and their skirts are very short, while their limbs are protected by overalls, which are tucked into their shoe tops. I gave Mrs. Wickersham a pair of corduroy leggings which I had found very serviceable, and she accepted them gladly. The ladies are ambitious to go clear through the mountains.

—*Seattle Press*

The two articles that follow were drafted by Wickersham to promote his Olympic National Park efforts. The first, which appeared in the Tacoma News along with his exploration report, was designed to entice public support for the concept of a national park in the Olympics. The second was aimed at the Washington, D.C., bureaucracy in the hope that the power of the presidency could be used to immediately declare park status for the Olympics. These two articles launched the half-century campaign of citizen activism that culminated in the park boundaries that were, for the most part, what they are today.

OLYMPIC NATIONAL PARK[48]

A Wonderland in the Olympic Mountains.

Glaciers and Mountain Meadows.

Congress Will Be Asked to Reserve a Large Olympic National Park.

Supposing that the population of Washington and the Pacific Coast does increase in population as the United States has for the last century, 50,000,000 people, it is apparent that they will require many things that the present small number of people do not need. It will require the building of other large cities, the opening up of every mine, farm, factory, and every natural resource upon the coast. Armies of laboring men must be raised, protected and maintained. Each one of this vast population will require just what every other individual of this or that day will demand—just what the health, strength and prosperity of every person demands—food, raiment, lodging and recreation. No civilized person is in a normal condition who does not take sufficient food to keep up his strength, wear sufficient clothing to be orderly and comfortable, maintain a house to protect himself against the inclemencies of the seasons, and last, but far from least, take such outdoor recreation as will preserve his health and his mind. There need be no fear but all these matters will be attended to by the coming people, except possibly the last. The growing tendency of our race is to "rustle" for wealth at the expense too often of health. This individual infirmity should be counteracted as far as reasonably proper by the encouragement of those resorts, parks and pleasure grounds, beaches, bathing places and outdoor sports and exercises which are in themselves harmless and intended rather to rest and recuperate the hard-working "rustler" or laborer, the minister or the merchant. No man can be a Christian or a good member of society with a disordered liver. This coast then will need food, clothing, shelter and recreation for a large population in a comparatively short time.

Public Resorts

It is an instinct as natural as that of going west for people of our race to love the sunlight, birds and bees, and the beauties of nature—the forests, mountains and plains. This natural feeling is exhibited in the care given to the smallest yard in the crowded city, even in the time bestowed by the poorer individual, whose whole wealth of land consists of a box of earth at the window, and whose only park is a few poor, struggling flowers tended and cared for daily.

Every box of earth containing flowers, in the laborer's home, every well-kept yard, every flower garden, every private and public park, is a standing and unanswerable argument in favor of the establishment of national parks. No people ever raised a protest against any reasonable appropriation of the public lands for that purpose, and no man in congress feels it necessary to apologize for voting for any reasonable bill to protect or beautify the few parks established by the government.

242

[48] James Wickersham, *Tacoma News*, January 2, 1891.

Public national parks are as necessary to the future of our people as either of the other necessaries mentioned. The government provides agricultural lands for the people, mining claims and timber lands; it should, without fail, also provide parks for their recreation. It can do nothing more, for it cannot, under our system of government, maintain public festivals and games, but it can control the public domain in the interests of the people, and their interests demand public national parks.

Public Parks on the Pacific Coast

There is no national park on the North Pacific coast. There are no large public grounds reserved for the people west of the Rocky mountains and north of California. In all the great commonwealths of Montana, Idaho, Nevada, Oregon, Washington and Alaska there is not a permanent national reservation of the public domain for park purposes, nor a public or private park worthy of mention. The forests are being felled and fired, the game slaughtered, the mountains washed down and every natural and beautiful object destroyed. The tourist comes to our coast only to find the beauties of our mountains, our forests, valleys, rivers, glaciers and summer snowfields hidden away where he cannot find them. No line of travel includes them, no accommodations could be had near them. He takes a trip on the Columbia river, or rides in a swift steamer over the waters of Puget Sound, or maybe on the route to the shores of Alaska, and then flies at lightning speed over the dusty plains to this eastern home, without at all seeing the glorious mountain, lake and forest scenery of our coast. Some provisions should be made for protecting at least a portion of this natural scenery and the game, and directing people in that direction. Thousands travel to the Yosemite park and the big trees of California because the natural beauties of these places are preserved and accommodations prepared for the traveler. California owes no little part of her prosperity to these parks.

An Olympic National Park Wanted

The increasing tourist travel to the Pacific coast is proof that its attractions are such, generally as will continue in the future to draw the eastern people. Not only this, but the number of people in the east who have either money investments or friends on the coast is constantly growing. These people do not consider a trip to the coast finished until they have seen Puget Sound, and lately Alaska is also included. The Straits of Juan de Fuca will be the line of travel for the tourist of the future.

Not only the people of the Atlantic coast, but of the Mississippi valley, and even of the states of Montana, Idaho and the Dakotas will feel that they too, can take a vacation and run out to Puget Sound for a week's rest and fishing. These transient guests of the Pacific will require our attention and courtesy. Our own people have a right to demand a place of rest and recreation, and there being no general public resort where either visitors or residents can go, it is not too much to ask that one be established. In this behalf it is asked that congress establish a national park on the public domain, at the headwaters of the rivers centering in the Olympic Mountains on the west side of Hood's canal, in the state of Washington.

Olympic Range

The Olympic mountains extends from Hood's canal and the west shore of Puget sound to the Pacific ocean on the west and the straits of Juan De Fuca on the north, and is very nearly square, containing about 5000 square miles or 3,200,000 acres. The country is very diversified, being largely a forest of magnificent fir timber. The census of 1880 shows that this region has the heaviest forest covering of any portion of the United States. It is also rich in minerals, copper mines of fine quality and vast quantity being now worked. The valleys of Skokomish, Lilliuwaup, and Dosewallups, leading into Hood's canal, the Elwha, Lysle and Pyseht into the straits of De Fuca, the Quallayute, Quinault and others into the ocean, and the Satsop, Wynoochu, etc., leading into the Chehalis river and into Gray's Harbor, all contain much fine farming land. Besides these fine agricultural valleys, the brush land around the mountains are rich and productive when cleared.

No well defined mountain range can be said to exist in the Olympics. It seems as if the volcanic forces had upheaved on large mass of the earth's surface, nearly round—a great blubber of hot air escaping—and this disturbed portion settling down has broken into hundreds of irregular peaks and ridges. Mount Olympus, about 15 miles south of the mouth of the Elwha river, and Mount Constance, about the same distance from Hood's canal, are the highest peaks, being respectively about 8500 and 7500 feet high.

Size of Proposed Park

The Olympic National Park should be 30 miles square, containing 900 square miles or 576,000 acres. This space is small as compared with the Yellowstone Park which contains 3375 square miles or 2,228,000 acres. The size of the park would enable one keeper to look after it and protect public property and game. It would not withdraw from settlement one

243

foot of land which could be classed as agricultural or mineral and the larger part of it would be above the line of good timber. It would include the highest land of the Olympics, the headwaters of all its rivers, the glaciers, snow fields, and homes of the last remaining elk, deer and bear. It would include a region that is absolutely worthless to the government or to the people except for use as a park. The 900 square miles in the park would not contain probably one square mile of tillable land, which is not covered snow the year around.

The Olympic mountains were caused by a recent upheaval. They are in the morning of their life. And the craggy rough broken surfaces have not yet been rounded and worn by the hand of time. Rough, precipitous and serrated, yet they are of easy approach along nature's highways—the river valleys.

The best routes into the heart of these mountains to the spot intended by nature as a park, lie up and along the Skokomish, Elwha and Quinault rivers, the Skokomish being by far the best. A railway will soon be built to the head of this river, to bring out the magnificent wealth of fir, cedar, Alaska cedar and copper which line its banks, and will furnish easy and rapid communication to the park from Hood's Canal. A railway is also projected into the same region from Port Angeles, up the Elwha, and another up the Quinault, and when these highways shall be built no park could have better facilities of approach. Two hours' travel from the shores of Hood's Canal, the Straits of De Fuca or the Pacific ocean, would land the tourist in the center of the park.

The park would be about 20 miles south of Port Angeles, 30 miles from Port Townsend, 50 miles from Tacoma, Seattle and Olympia, and about the same distance from Gray's Harbor. It could be easily approached from any of those points, and no one town or point would or could have a monopoly of approach to it.

The great timber wealth on the regions around about the park will build cities on the straits, Hood's Canal and the ocean. The fine stretches of ocean back to the westward will be an additional attraction to the people, while Crescent Lake on the north, Lake Quinault on the west, and Lake Cushman on the east, with the myriad of smaller lakes in the mountains will furnish bathing and fishing resorts of the finest character.

Description of the Park

The Skokomish, Duckaboos, Dosewallips, Quillayute and Quinault rivers all head on the summit in the park. They all spring full fledged rivers from glaciers on the mountain tops, and fall into beautiful cascades a thousand feet or more over the mossy rock walls. The water then generally flows for a mile or two down a bare, steep valley, built recently by the debris from the summits and then the milky stream finds its way into the dense timber in the lower canyon only to reappear in the sunlight when it reaches the salty waters of the ocean, the straits or the canal. The timber line is far down in the valley, away below the glaciers, the snowfields and the meadows, and below the location of the park except in the upper ends of the valley. Into these densely-wooded valleys the deer, elk, bear and other animals descend in winter, when the snow covers the upper country and renders their living precarious. Enough of these valleys will be included in the park to give a home for game, and to furnish the park with fuel and timber forever, if fires are kept out.

The average height of the land in the park will be about 6000 feet above sea level. Roads can be easily constructed connecting all parts of the park, reaching from river to river, from glacier to glacier, and all points of interest. It will be necessary in building roads for convenience in the park to go around the heads of the river, but they lie in such a position to each other that one general road north and south will enable all parts to be reached easily by branches. Considering the roughness of the country it will be easy to build roads. The passes from river to river are low, round and easily crossed with vehicles or horses.

Above the timber line are handsome mountain meadows. They are sparingly covered with groves of evergreen trees, patches of snow, foamy white cascades, beautiful flowers of every variety and color, green watered deep lakes and every variety of mountain, forest and prairie scenery. One moment the imagination locates the beholder on the plains of Dakota, the next in a well kept park in old England, and the next, the clouds having intervened, in the icy regions of the North pole. All kinds of landscape scenery will be met within a few minutes' time, from a grassy nook filled with warm sunshine, flowers, bees and humming birds, to a bleak, barren rock, surrounded by ice and snow, and obscured from the sun's rays by the dense clouds which cover everything with dampness—from the tropics to the polar circle is only a step on this wonderful height of land.

Between the headwaters of the Quinault and the Skokomish, on the head of the Duckaboos, above the timber line, lies one of these mountain meadows. A description of it is a description of hundreds of such spots in this Olympic wonderland.

It is about four miles long by two broad and lies on the east and south slope of the mountain. At the west side the bluffs of stone rise nearly perpendicular 500 to 1000 feet, and on reaching this summit the beholder is struck with amazement to find this wall only from 20 feet to a few hundred thick, and that on the west face it descends perpendicular a thousand feet and more to the canyon of the Quinault. This high, thin wall of stone runs the full length of the north and west side of the meadow, cutting off any approach from the Quiniault, even to elk and deer, such is its steepness. The meadow stretches from the base of this high wall to the edge of the canyon wall, at the bottom of the [?] which flows the Duckaboos. This canyon is 1000 feet deep and its bare and colored walls are enlivened at many places by ribbon-like streams of water pouring down its sides in snow white cascades. From the west wall of the meadow to the "jumping off place" the meadow slopes just enough to afford good drainage and beautiful views. To the west and north of course nothing can be seen but the serrated top of the mountain wall, shutting off the park from the rest of the world effectually. To the south can be seen glaciers, snow fields and mountains and all the small streams which, joining in the canyon below, form the river. To the east far away, can be seen the snowy summit of Mount Constance proudly rearing his head above all near neighbors, while to the southward of Constance can be seen "Washington's Face," a mountain having on its summit an exact profile of the father of his country. (This mountain and the profile can be seen distinctly from the prairies south of Tacoma, 56 or more miles away.) The valley or deep wooded canyon of the river stretched to the eastward until, rounding a mountain in the distance, it is lost from view.

About the center of the meadow it is beautiful. Lake Darrell covered yet, in part by its winter coat of ice, but now broken and melted enough to show the deep blue waters beneath. From the pebbly beach of the lake the meadow stretches away with graceful curves over rounded grassy hill, while in little valleys the great snow banks remind us of the reign of King Winter. Flowers bloom in profusion, springing up on the spots just made bare by the sun's rays melting the snow—even in some instances working their stalks through the snow and spreading their beautiful foliage and flowers over the icy crystals. Groves of evergreen trees, small but graceful, enliven the landscape, while streams of crystal water come dashing down over mossy boulders to find temporary lodgement in the lake. From the lake springs the headwaters of a river, and flowing across the meadow, through all this beauty, sunshine and life suddenly leaps over the precipice a thousand feet into the dark canyon beneath, from which it flows eastward into Hood's canal. Stretching from the summits to the lower levels are snow fields covering hundreds of acres of great depth. These generally occupy the low ground between the grassy knolls, which are themselves covered with a summer verdure and evergreen groves. From these grassy tracts will be found well-beaten trails, and well-marked tracks of elk, bear and deer. You may stand on a grassy bank, half buried in blue bells, with deer tongues and a thousand varieties of flowers, overcome by their delightful perfume, and lulled to rest by the busy buzz of the bees and humming birds and within sight count a dozen great glaciers of ancient ice, and cast the eye over immense fields of pure white snow below you.

I am sure that never a human foot was set in this great meadow before we came upon it. Since the first ice crystal formed, through all its changes by time and seasons, it was one vast solitude. Even when it became a paradise no human voice was heard, and no sound save that of glacial grinding broke its stillness. With our party civilization had come, and in its wake death and destruction. We seized on an old log, moss covered and dried with age, and a fire rapidly reduced it to ashes. A whistling marmot, bent on a personal inspection of this newcomer, yielded up his life for his rashness, and a new order of events for this virgin world was established.

About four miles north of the big mountain meadow lies the great Quinault glacier in the crater of an extinct volcano. In place of clouds of smoke and fire now find you a mass of ancient ice hundreds of feet thick covering perhaps 200 acres and surrounded by high rocky walls. Ages ago the waters from the glacier had flowed out eastward into the canyon of the Dosewallips, but in time a great terminal moraine was thrown across the channel and a new opening was broken through on the south side, and out of this new outlet springs the east branch of the Quinault river to the valley below, a distance that makes the brain dizzy to contemplate. Deep crevices, lateral and terminal moraines, old ice and new as well as old and new snow, and all the sights and sounds of glaciers, here greet you. In every direction we could see smaller glaciers, and probably nowhere short of Alaska can glacial action be so well and thoroughly studied as in the Olympic National Park. Probably a hundred glaciers of all sizes will be found to be embraced in the area mentioned as proper for the park and every mark or station left by ancient glaciers will be found on the mountain benches and summits nearby made by the present glacier age, which is in the height of its power in the land of sunlight and shadow.

From the mountain meadows, as well as from glaciers, one has a panoramic view of the whole Olympic range. It stretches away in every direction in tumultuous array like the storm-swept waves of the sea. No well defined range, but

245

a mass of dog-toothed mountain peaks everywhere, rough, serrated and new. To the west you can see the blue waters of the Pacific Ocean, and to the east the thread-like tides of Hood's canal. Everywhere lies snowbanks, glaciers, flower beds, lakes, meadows and groves. Magnificent waterfalls roar and splash down the mountain walls, reaching the bottom in many cases in the form of a fine spray, and, with the action of the winds, playing music on Nature's own Aeolian harps. Here, flowers, music, birds, sunshine and spring; there, fogs, ice, rocks and dreary winter. Every variety of scenery and climate in a moment from a given standpoint.

In the Olympic mountains there are probably 300 elk. With the exception of a few small bands this is the last of that noble race. In two years more without protection there will not be living one wild elk in the United States. A recent expedition into the Olympics reports that one of their men stood out of sight and shot ten of these magnificent creatures out of one band in one hour. Their carcasses were of course left to rot on the ground. Such acts of vandalism should be punished severely, for when this stock is gone, like the buffalo they will never again be found in our mountains. Something should be done at once to protect them and nothing better can be done than to place a keeper there to protect them. Bear and deer also need protection, but they can care for themselves better than the lordly elk, which were reported so tame that the sight of man would not cause them to run.

In conclusion the Olympic National Park should be established while the wild game is there to be protected and before any private rights intervene to make difficulties. Its magnificent scenery of glaciers, rivers, lakes, mountains, snow fields, meadows, cascades, canyons, flowers, fogs, sunlight, birds and bees, its tropical and polar scenes, and its splendid water and health-giving air make it a natural resort for the weary and sick. The tourists will find there a far greater variety of beauty than in the Yellowstone or Sequoia Parks of California. Its proximity to all the cities of Puget Sound will enable tourists to reach it easily, and being in the most distant corner of the United States, it will be visited by larger numbers of eastern and foreign people. Even our British Columbia friends can join us in this beautiful tract and discuss annexation and other friendly subjects.

If all those who have any information relating to this immediate tract in the Olympics will kindly send such to the writer, it will be used to the best advantage to secure a national park in the Olympics. Write to our senators and congressmen in favor of it, and get your chambers of commerce to pass resolutions in favor of its establishment. California has two national parks, and Washington is entitled to one. Truly,

James Wickersham

A NATIONAL PARK IN THE OLYMPICS[49]
By James Wickersham

In 1774 Juan Perez saw a snowcapped mountain range stretching eastward from Cape Martinez, and named it Sierra de Santa Rosalia. In 1790 Francisco Eliza, the Spanish Commander at Nootka, on the west coast of Vancouver Island, sent an expedition under Manuel Quimper down to the "Straits of Anian" [Juan de Fuca Strait]. Here Nunez Gaona was established by the erection of a brick fort surrounded by a stockade. But the colony remained only a short time. One day in the fall the colonists hoisted sail, deserted their brick fort, and left the Indian tribes again in possession of the shores of Anian, under the shadows of Sierra de Santa Rosalia. Old Tatoochatacus, the celebrated Makah war chief, burned their house, threw the brick into the stream, and, to show his contempt for the white man, planted potatoes on the site of the fort. The Spaniards sailed away; Captain James Cook changed the name of Martinez to Cape Flattery, Sierra de Santa Rosalia became the Olympic Mountains on all modern maps, and the descendants of Tatoochatacus occupy a reservation on the site Nunez Gaona and call it Neah.

In ancient times, the Wynoochee River, on the south side of the Olympics, fell into a wide and beautiful valley where the Indians during the golden age held potlatches, or friendly meetings. Enemies left their weapons on the summits before descending into its peaceful shades, and on the banks of its placid river they smoked the pipe of peace around the same camp fires. Strife and enmity were forgotten, the climate was a continual summer, game and fish abounded, the elk roamed the woods, and salmon filled the stream, while the pleasant prairies were gay with sweet-scented flowers. The tribes met here for trade and barter, and many a maiden listened to the new-old story, while her parents were critically examining the "iktas" with which the suitor sought to win their consent.

But Seatco, a god of the mountains, was filled with anger at these signs of happiness, and caused a mighty convulsion of the earth: a flood of waters descended, the mountains toppled, fire and smoke escaped from the ground, the voice of Seatco thundered in anger and exultation, the once happy

246

---

[49] *The Living Wilderness,* Summer/Fall 1961. Reprinted from the National Archives.

valley was destroyed with all its inhabitants, and snow-covered mountains now stand upon the spot. The Indians have not since that awful event penetrated into the interior, for it is said that the few who did so were slain and served by Seatco at cannibalistic feasts.[50]

The Olympic Mountains extend in broken, dogtoothed masses from Hood's Canal to the Pacific Ocean and northward to the Straits of Juan de Fuca. They are drained by the Skokomish, Docewailopsh [Dosewallips], Elquah [Elwha], Quillayute, Quinault, Satsop, and Wynoochee, and by many other smaller streams. No well defined mountain range exists; it seems as though Seatco threw up a large mass of the earth's surface—a great blubber of molten matter—and that this disturbed portion, settling back, broke into hundreds of irregular peaks and ridges. Mount Olympus, with its dozens of glaciers, is one of the highest peaks, while near Hood's Canal, Mount Constance proudly rears her mantle of perpetual snow.

The Skokomish, Docewailopsh, Elquah, Quillayute, and Quinault rise in the center of the mountains, and their valleys afford splendid opportunities to reach the magnificent park region high on the Olympic plateau. These spring as full-fledged rivers from glaciers on the summits, and fall with mighty leaps over mossy walls to the valleys below, where they must yet roar and beat their way through deep, dark canyons and the dense forest before joining their waters to the ocean.

The timber line is far down the valleys, away below the glaciers, the snow fields, and mountain meadows; occasionally, however, in a well protected nook in the meadows the lovely fir forms beautiful groves. The forests end at about 3,000 feet, except for a stunted evergreen which grows in clumps even to the summits. Into these densely wooded valleys the deer, elk, and bear descend in winter when the snow covers the meadows and the Arctic winds blow over their summer range.

Until last summer [1890] these mountains had remained unexplored since the dreadful day of Seatco's wrath. The density of the forest growth at the base and the frightful canyon walls at every point kept out all the white explorers, and so little was known that no map had located the streams falling out of these mountains. In July and August six of us—three gentlemen and three ladies—made a journey through the range, reaching the height of land in the central plateau from which flows the four large rivers. Our party examined all the rivers, high peaks, and hitherto unknown beauties of the Olympics. For 20 days we climbed mountains, waded torrents, slept above clouds, and, for the last seven days, lived on water and flour cakes, carried our provisions and luggage on our backs, and braved the wrath of Seatco, as well as all the usual fatigues of such a journey.

In all of the great commonwealths of Idaho, Montana, Nevada, Oregon, Washington, and Alaska, there is not a national public park. The forests are being felled, and destroyed, the game slaughtered, the very mountains washed away, and the beauties of nature destroyed or fenced for private gain. The beauty of Switzerland's glaciers is celebrated, yet the Olympics contain dozens of them, easy of approach and exhibiting all the phenomena of glacial action. A national park should be 30 miles wide, north and south, and 40 miles, east and west, containing 1,200 square miles or 768,000 acres, which is about one-third the size of Yellowstone Park. It would include the highest lands of the Olympics, the headwaters of all its rivers, the glaciers, Olympus, Constance, the snowfields, mountain meadows, grand canyons, and the homes of the last remaining elk, deer, and bear. It should include Lakes Cushman, Quinault, and Crescent. The average height of land in the park would be about 4,000 feet, while many peaks would reach 8,000 feet.

The Skokomish river rises in this region and flows down a mountain valley for several miles before it turns south on its way to the flower-covered meadows around Lake Cushman. From the mountain tops to the timber line it flows through an old snow tunnel, issuing at the foot with a mighty roar and plunging into the forest shades. From the summits on the south, cascades fall in many instances a thousand feet or more, and at the bottom strike under the glacier and join the gathering waters of the river. Immense boulders lie on this glacier. Trees, earth, and sand, dropped down by wintry avalanches, are all on the way to the valley below to fit it for the abode of man in ages to come. To the north spreads a beautiful meadow, reaching from the glacier to the summits and covered with grass, flower beds, and groves of evergreens, and enlivened with streams of water issuing from the new fields lying around the peaks. Along the sides of the glacier where the summer heat had uncovered the earth, waving masses of blue-bells and sweet-scented flowers spring up in wild profusion. Between the fields of flowers, in full view of this varied landscape on a hot July day, we toiled up this glacier till we reached the summit just west of Crater

247

---

[50] See the *Seattle Press*, July 16, 1890, "Semple's Striking Report," for the same story about Seatco. While Semple was governor of Washington Territory, he told the Seatco story in detail in a section of his annual report for 1888 entitled "The Olympic Mountains." The *Press* reprinted the story exactly as Semple had reported it because the tale affected the Press Expedition's views about the presence of Indians in the mountains.

Mountain, and beheld down on the other side three green lakes with snow and ice yet floating on their surface, and out of which sprang another river flowing northward.

Between the head of the Skokomish and Quinault, Mount Susan towers 7,400 feet high and from its sides spring waters that flow into those rivers and into a large branch of the Ducqueboose [Duckabush]. This mountain is very precipitous, but at a distance is a symmetrical peak. In rounding its snowy summit, a plucky member of the exploring party missed her footing, fell, and rolled down the snow at a frightful velocity toward the mountain wall, which drops perpendicularly hundreds of feet. Her life was saved at the brink of the precipice by the bare rocks which arrested her progress. Then and there the peak was named Mount Susan[51] with

hope that no future geographer would feel it necessary to change the name.

Within the limits of the proposed park above the timber line, extending in many instances to the very summits, are many large meadows. They are sparingly covered with groves of evergreen trees, snowbanks, fields of flowers of infinite variety and color, streams of pure water, cascades, green water lakes, and every variety of mountain, forest, and prairie scenery. One moment the imagination locates the beholder on the plains of Dakota, the next in a well-kept park in England, and the next, the clouds having descended, in the icy regions of the Arctic. All kinds of scenery may be encountered within a few minutes—one moment a grassy nook filled with sunshine, flowers, bees, and humming birds;

248

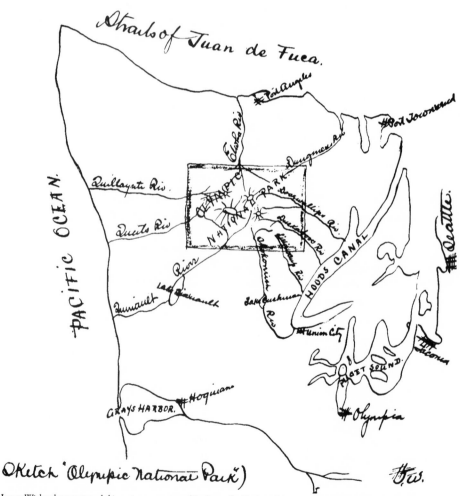

FIRST KNOWN MAP PROPOSING AN OLYMPIC NATIONAL PARK DRAWN 1890 BY JUDGE JAMES WICKERSHAM. FROM JAMES WICKERSHAM COLLECTION.

James Wickersham prepared this map to accompany his plea to the Geological Society to set aside the Olympics as a national park. (The Living Wilderness, Summer/Fall 1961. Reprinted from the National Archives.)

---

[51] Mount Susan is the mass of Mount Duckabush and Mount Steel together.

the next, a bleak and barren rock surrounded by ice and snow and obscured from the sun's rays by the dense clouds which enshroud everything. From the tropics to the polar circle is only a step on this wonderful height of land.

One of these large meadows near the summit is at the headwaters of the Ducqueboose, between those of the Skokomish and Quinault. It is four or five miles long, and two or three wide. At the west and upper side of the meadow the bluffs of stone rise almost perpendicularly several hundred feet. Upon reaching the tip of this wall, one is struck with amazement to find it only a few hundred feet thick, and that it descends on the opposite side more than a thousand perpendicular feet to the canyon of the Quinault. This high wall of stone runs the full length of the north and west side of the meadow, cutting off any approach to the Quinault, even to the elk.

The meadow stretches from this Cyclopean escarpment eastward to the verge of the canyon wall at the bottom of which flows the Ducqueboose. The canyon is a thousand feet deep, and its highly colored walls are further enlivened by numberless ribbon-like streams of water, pouring down in snow-white cascades and disappearing in the abyss. This magnificent natural park is covered for the greater part with grass and meadow land, with here and there groves of stately evergreens and thickets of smaller shrubbery. Rippling streams of water meander across it and fall in white cascades over the canyon walls. Beds of beautifully colored flowers charm the eye, while their sweetest perfumes fill the air, and birds, bees, and insects seem to sport merrily in the sunshine. To the west and north the vision is limited by the ragged mountain wall; to the south can be seen the glaciers of Mount Susan, snowfields and mountains, and all the small streams which gather on the summits and join in the canyon below to form the Ducqueboose; to the east, far away, can be seen Mount Constance proudly rearing its snowy summit above all others. South of Constance is "Washington's Face"—a mountain having a profile of that patriot's face on its summit. The valley or deep wooded canyon of the Ducqueboose stretches to the eastward, until rounding a mountain in the distance it is lost to view.

In the center of this wild Olympic Park, lies a pear-shaped lake upon the blue bosom of which floats great cakes of ice covered with snow, grim reminders of the reign of the winter king. From the pebbly beach of the lake—which we named Darrell—the meadow stretches away with graceful curves over rounded grassy knolls, while crystal snowfields lie piled on the north hillsides. Flowers in endless profusion are springing up on spots just made bare by the melting snow, even in some instances working their stalks through the ice crystals and

spreading their foliage and flowers over them. Groves of evergreen trees, small but graceful, enliven the landscape, while streams of pure water come dashing down over mossy boulders to find temporary lodgment in the lake. From the latter spring the headwaters of a river which, flowing across the meadow, suddenly leaps over the precipice into the canyon through which it dashes and roars on its way to the sea.

Stretching from the summits to the lower levels, snowfields occupy spots sheltered from the "chinook winds" by surrounding hills which themselves are covered with summer verdure and evergreen groves. From these small meadows well beaten trails of elk, bear, and deer lead to others of equal beauty and extent. You may stand on a grassy bank half buried in bluebells and an infinite variety of flowers, overcome with their delightful perfumes and lulled to rest by the buzz of bees and humming of birds, and within sight count a dozen great glaciers of ancient ice, and cast your eye over immense fields of snow below. I am sure that never a human foot was set in that green meadow before we came upon it. Since the first ice crystal formed, through all its changes by time and season, it was one vast solitude. Even when it became a paradise, no human voice was heard, and no sound save that of glacial grinding broke its stillness. With our party civilization had come, and in its wake death and destruction. We seized an old log, moss-covered and dry with age, and a fire rapidly reduced it to ashes. A whistling marmot yielded up his life to satisfy curiosity, and a new order of events for this virgin world was established.

From the escarpment above the Quinault on the west side of the meadow one has a panoramic view of the whole Olympic Range. It stretches away in every direction in tumultuous array, like the storm swept waves of the sea; no well defined range, but a mass of mountain peaks, rough, serrated, and new. To the west, way down the valley of the Quinault, one can see the blue waters of the Pacific, while to the east appear the thread-like tides of Hood's Canal. Everywhere lie snowbanks, glaciers, flowery meadows, lakes, and groves. Magnificent waterfalls roar and splash down the mountain buttresses, reaching the canyon bottom in fine spray, and with the action of the winds, make music on nature's own aeolian harps. Here music, flowers, birds, sunshine, and spring; there fogs, ice, rocks, and dreary winter—every variety of scenery and climate in a few minutes from our high porch.

We gathered familiar flowers: buttercups, columbine, Indian pinks, yellow and blue violets, bluebells, yellow and white deer's-tongue, marguerites, lady fingers, and roses, and gathered mosses, ferns of infinite variety, and dozens of other plants unknown to us.

249

The east branch of the Quinault springs a full-fledged river from underneath a glacier on the mountain top. This glacier is rapidly eroding and carrying away the mountain, and the whole process of glacial action can be studied here to the best possible advantage, for the glacier, while high on the summit, is easily approached and well exposed for examination. It is the largest glacier yet seen in the Olympics, the great mother breast from which flows the white glacial waters of the Quinault—a river from the time it leaps from its glacial home over 500 feet of mountain wall, striking with a roar on the rocks below. Ages ago, the waters from the glacier had flowed eastward into the canyon of the Docewailopsh, but in time a terminal moraine was thrown across the channel on the brink of the summit, the accumulated waters broke the rim of the old crater on the south, and out of this new outlet springs the east branch of the Quinault. This terminal moraine of great boulders stands a hundred feet high full across the old outlet, and inside a lateral moraine has since been built a quarter of a mile long, equally high, and reaching down nearly to the new outlet.

The Quinault glacier is the most interesting feature of the Olympics. It occupies a crater-like cavity on the summit of Mount Allyn at the head of the Quinault and Docewailopsh rivers. In place of fire, smoke, and lava, however, you find a mass of ancient ice, of unknown depth, covering a large area and surrounded by a high rock crater rim. Deep crevasses, lateral and terminal moraines, old ice and new, beds of snow, and all the sights and sounds of glaciers greet you. In every direction, too, you can see smaller glaciers. Probably nowhere short of Alaska can glacial action be so well and thoroughly studied as in this proposed Olympic Park. Probably a hundred glaciers will be found within the area mentioned as proper for the park, and every mark or striation left by glacial action will be found on the summits near by. The glacial age of the Olympics is drawing to a close; we passed mountain benches that had but yesterday, speaking geologically, been the site of glaciers. One immense rock floor, a thousand feet above the valley of Docewailopsh was worn smooth by the ice which had rested upon it. The accumulated ice at the upper end had caused it to travel until it had worn away the projecting rocks, and finally the whole was toppled into the valley below with a prodigious crash. The occurrence was so recent that the site is yet a smooth rock without debris or vegetation, and the glacial striations, the potholes, and lateral moraines prove beyond question that at no distant day a glacier existed here for unknown ages. It is gone now, and in the potholes blue water lakes reflect the mountain views, the old glacial outlet yet forming a channel for the waters of the lakes to reach the perpendicular walls in

front where they drop into the valley below. We camped on the north side of this old glacial site on the mountain point which had turned it into the valley.

An August night on one of these summits is indeed a change from a comfortable home in the city, and one in particular, passed on the upper side of the Duqueboose meadow, will long be remembered by our party. Great masses of storm clouds came floating up the Quinault and over the high rock wall on the upper side of the meadow and settled down on us about dusk. The driving mists, like blinding snow storm, the shades of falling night, the surrounding snowfields and icebergs in the lake, made an arctic condition that drove us to build a roaring fire of logs. The moisture, however, penetrated our very bones and, being without a tent, we erected a shelter of bark that but poorly protected the three ladies. We were blue, cold, and uncomfortable, without any prospect of rest until daybreak. However, about 10 o'clock the wind sprang up strong and cold from the north and the clouds went flying away leaving the sky without a blemish, while the north wind rapidly turned the moisture to ice and frost. About 11 o'clock the moon rose over Mount Susan, and its first bright rays discovered our whole party energetically exercising to keep warm.

The great meadow, now covered with frost, seemed to be carpeted with diamonds. The moonlight made every crystal on ice or snow, as well as on the waving trees, sparkle and flash like the richest jewels, while the floating icebergs in the lake, the long shadows of the trees, the moonlight on the circle of mountain wall back of us, the distant glaciers, glistening like burnished silver, and the heavens ablaze with a myriad of diamond lights made an August night picture never to be forgotten.

Our life on these great meadows around Mounts Susan and Allyn was one continuous surprise, not only at the beau-

"'Sketch of summit of Olympics' sent by Judge Wickersham to Major Powell, 1891." (The Living Wilderness, Summer/Fall 1961. Reprinted from the National Archives.)

250

ties of nature constantly before us, but on one occasion at least, by the appearance of a mother bear with her cub. We discovered her sitting on the edge of the glacier about a hundred yards away, eyeing us with evident alarm and displeasure. She had been playing with the cub, and when we first saw them the cub was sitting on her back. A little patch of meadow lay between us. Presently she threw the cub from her back, and growling, sprang toward us with a lumbering gallop, each individual hair on her back standing forward. Two good Winchester rifles and a heavy revolver were brought into action and we killed her at our feet, but only after a great number of shots. The half grown cub had run behind her, bleating like a calf, and when the mother was dead, one of our party threw his gun down and chased it across the meadow, but luckily for him did not succeed in catching it.

In the Olympics are probably 300 broad-antlered elk—the last remnant of an animal once numerous. In two years more, without protection, there will not be one in the United States. Something should be done to protect them, and nothing would be more effectual than a national park. Bear and deer, and the whistling marmot, also need some security. A reservation, as proposed in this high Olympic breeding grounds forever.

The Solduck River falls from the glaciers of Olympus and empties into the Pacific through the Quillayute. Near the headwaters of the Solduck at the base of Olympus are several large hot sulphur springs, which are located on the public domain and should be included in the reservation. Many persons who have penetrated that region report that geysers exist near these springs, but the report lacks verification. Crescent Lake, taking its name from its peculiar shape, is 15 miles long and lies buried deep in the north foot of

Olympus. Quinault Lake, about the same size, is really only a wide part of the river, as Lake Cushman is of the Skokomish, and all these lakes are flanked by precipitous mountain walls. The valleys of the rivers, however, afford an easy approach to each of the lakes, where there are splendid camping places, and unequaled hunting and trout fishing. Bear, elk, deer, and cougar, wild cat, beaver, and many smaller animals are numerous, while the streams and lakes are filled with trout and salmon—a veritable hunter's and fisherman's paradise.

The President of the United States has ample power under the twenty-fourth section of an Act of Congress, approved March 3rd, 1891, entitled, "An act to repeal timber culture laws, and for other purposes," to withdraw this region from disposal under the public land laws, and set it apart as a reservation. There are no surveyed lands within its boundaries and no private rights yet acquired. It would not withdraw any agricultural lands from settlement. Within its limits are large tracts of Alaska cedar, a very rare and val-uable wood, as well as dense forests of cedar, spruce, hemlock, and pine. The census reports of 1880 contain full information concerning the dense forests on the foothills of the Olympics, which extends in many instances far into the interior, along valleys and lower levels. The heaviest forest growth in North America lies within the limits of this region, untouched by fire or ax, and far enough from tidewater that its reservation by the government could not possibly cripple private enterprise in the new state, and by all means it should be reserved for future use. The reservation of this area as a national park will thus serve the twofold purpose of a great pleasure ground for the Nation and be a means of securing and protecting the finest forests in America.

251

Part III: The O'Neil Expeditions 1885 and 1890

Lieutenant Joseph O'Neil did more than anyone else to make the Olympics known, to sweep away the ignorance that prevailed regarding the backcountry of the region. His reconnaissance in 1885 provided a preview of what the interior of the peninsula was like. Then, in 1890, he completed the task of exposing the heart of the mountainous peninsula, but his goals were achieved only by "exertion, hard work, and the sacrifice of many comforts." Although his men faced danger almost daily, they explored the country thoroughly, cutting a trail as they did so "over the almost impenetrable Olympics." This trail, destined to become a main route of entry into the mountains, was one of the party's important achievements, and O'Neil hoped it would become "a monument to the expedition."

Together with his contemporaries—the Press Expedition, the Wickersham party, the Gilmans, and others—O'Neil lifted the veil of mystery long associated with the Olympic Mountains. After 1890 the region could no longer be called terra incognita, but regional magazines and newspapers still capitalized on the old legends and for many years thereafter printed stories about men going into the "unknown Olympics."

O'Neil was the pathfinder, the one who really found the key to the region. His second expedition, an in-depth survey of the southern half of the peninsula, encompassed the watersheds of nine major rivers, plus the headwaters of the Elwha. Because the lieutenant's 1885 reconnaissance had taken in the northeastern Olympics, this left unexplored only the northwestern quadrant—the valleys of the Hoh and the Quillayute.

One can best evaluate O'Neil's work by comparing it with the accomplishments of his rivals. On both of his expeditions—but particularly the second—he explored the mountains much more thoroughly than did his contemporaries. Although the Press Expedition was the first to cross the Olympics, exploring a narrow swath as it did so, James H. Christie and his men of the Press Party limited their scouting to locating a direct route across the mountains. The Wickersham party's wanderings in the southeastern Olympics contributed knowledge of that area, but James Wickersham's exploration was not extensive and he would not have reached the interior ahead of O'Neil had he not utilized the lieutenant's trail. O'Neil's investigations revealed what the mountains really were like, and added much to the knowledge of their configuration, topography, geology, flora, and fauna. This was apparently his goal and purpose. The scope of O'Neil's work exceeded the collective contributions of the other explorers.

Both O'Neil and Wickersham recommended national park status for the Olympic Mountains, in November 1890. We do not know if they arrived at the idea independently, or whether they discussed the subject around the campfire at Jumbo's Leap when they met there on July 23. Regardless, the lieutenant not *only advocated a national park whenever he lectured about the Olympics, but he also expressed the thought in his official report to the government. O'Neil did live to see his wish come true. On June 29, 1938, just four weeks before his death, O'Neil saw the creation of Olympic National Park, nearly a half century after he proposed it.*

Historians are fortunate that the O'Neil party included a number of participants, including Frederic J. Church, Bernard J. Bretherton, Nelson Linsley, Louis F. Henderson, and Harry Fisher, who recorded their experiences in diaries and subsequent newspaper and magazine articles. Their writings are presented here to supplement the official reports of Lieutenant O'Neil. [1]

Lieutenant Joseph P. O'Neil
Courtesy Robert B. Hitchman

---

[1] Each of these members of O'Neil's party is introduced to the reader in turn with a short biographical sketch beginning each chapter.

CHAPTER TEN.
LIEUTENANT JOSEPH P. O'NEIL

Lieutenant Joseph Patrick O'Neil was born during the Civil War, on December 27, 1862, which would have made him twenty-eight years old during his 1890 Olympics expedition and only twenty-three on his first Olympics penetration, in 1885. He died on July 27, 1938.

O'Neil was educated at St. Mary's College, a Jesuit school in St. Mary's, Kansas, 1873–79, and at the University of Notre Dame, South Bend, Indiana, 1879–83. He received a bachelor of science degree, with honors, at the Infantry and Cavalry School, Fort Leavenworth, Kansas, 1885–87, and attended the Army War College, Washington, D.C., 1914–15. He married Nina M. Troup, daughter of a steamboat captain, in Vancouver, Washington, on January 15, 1891, just after his return from his second Olympics exploration. They had no children.

Joseph O'Neil began his military career, which spanned more than half a century, by serving as an officer to the cadets at the University of Notre Dame when he was a student. On February 4, 1884, he was commissioned a second lieutenant in the Regular Army and assigned to the Fourteenth Infantry. Except for detached service at the Infantry and Cavalry School in Fort Leavenworth, he was with the regiment until mid-1891, first at Fort Sidney, Nebraska, then at

Fort Townsend, Vancouver Barracks, and Fort Canby, all three in Washington. While stationed in the Pacific Northwest, he conducted his explorations of the Olympic Mountains.

He was promoted to first lieutenant in 1891, and with the Twenty-fifth Infantry, a Negro regiment with white officers stationed at Fort Custer, Montana, he did duty "among the Cheyennes, best fighting Indians of America, and the Crows." O'Neil was also a diplomat, and during the railroad strike in 1894 he quieted the mobs in Livingston, Montana, without bloodshed.

When the Spanish-American War broke out, O'Neil's Twenty-fifth Infantry was sent to Cuba with the Fifth Army Corps and participated in the Santiago de Cuba campaign. O'Neil declared later that he survived the rigors of the campaign only because of the "spartan athletic training" he received at Notre Dame.

When the war ended, O'Neil was promoted to captain, placed on detached service, and assigned to general recruiting duty at Portland, Oregon. On July 1, 1899, his regiment was dispatched to the Philippine Islands, where it participated in "the bitter insurgent warfare." Anxious not to miss the action, O'Neil "sent out a barrage of wires" that resulted in his rejoining the Twenty-fifth Infantry on Luzon Island. He then distinguished

254

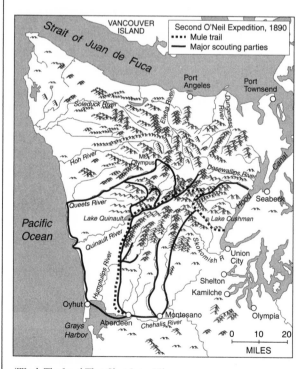

(*Adapted from Wood, The Land That Slept Late, 25*)

(*Wood, The Land That Slept Late, 98*)

himself by leading an expedition into Zambales Province, and for his "gallantry in action" O'Neil was awarded the Silver Star.

He returned to the United States in 1902, was promoted to major in 1907, and was assigned to the Thirtieth Infantry. He saw duty again in the Philippines before being promoted to lieutenant colonel in 1912 and sent to Alaska for two years, where he engaged in garrison duty "mixed with some surveying and exploring."

After leaving Alaska in the summer of 1914, O'Neil was a student at the Army War College in Washington, D.C., for a year, then saw duty in New York, Texas, and California. He was promoted to colonel in 1916. America's entry into World War I provided a golden opportunity for the "wild Irishman." Appointed brigadier general in the National Army, O'Neil organized and trained the 179th Infantry Brigade, 90th Division, which participated in the St. Mihiel and Meuse-Argonne campaigns, and O'Neil was awarded the Purple Heart with Oak Leaf Cluster. The government of France conferred upon him the Croix de Guerre and Croix de Guerre with the Palm.

O'Neil returned to the United States in May 1919, and was honorably discharged from the National Army on August 31, reverting to the grade of colonel in the Regular Army. After service in Michigan, Pennsylvania, and Oklahoma, he was transferred to Portland, Oregon, in connection with recruiting. He retired as a brigadier general on June 21, 1930, but remained on active duty in charge of the recruiting office in Portland until August 15, 1932. He lived another six years but was a semi-invalid, crippled by heart disease, the last two years.

O'Neil's nephew, the late Frank Keller Jr., has given us what is perhaps the best description of the man who did more than anyone else to explore the Olympic Mountains:

I can think of one word which my memory uses to tabulate my uncle, and that is "cocky." I mean the ready to go, go to Hell sort of attitude that stands there ready and eager to back up his views. . . . He was short, active, loved to tease, and never in all the time I knew him gave an equivocal answer. He said "yes" or "no" with no attempt to hide his opinions, which were generally strong. His living room was lined with pictures, all autographed, of ball players, actresses, boxers, priests and ministers, politicians, and old Army friends. I sensed at the time that he was a real live character, and a story teller of great fame.

—Robert L. Wood
Adapted from Men, Mules and Mountains
(pp. 386–91, 440–42)

O'NEIL'S EXPLORATION[1]

Record of His Trip Back of Port Angeles in 1885

The First Man to Scale the Mountains and Push Along Their Summits to Where the Water Runs into Hoods Canal—Many Exciting Hunts and Adventures—A Man Lost on a Field of Ice—A Perilous Leap Over a Crevasse—Game Abounds—Iron Discovered—Big Elk Yards Found—Visited by Friends— The First White Woman in the Olympics—Return Home.

While stationed at Fort Townsend in 1884 and 1885 I was attracted by the grand noble front of the Jupiter hills, rising with their boldness and abruptness, presenting a seemingly impenetrable barrier to the farther advance of man and civilization. Inquiries about them elicited very little reliable information, and it seemed to me that Jupiter hills and the Olympic mountains were almost as unknown to us as the wilds of Alaska.[2]

A few bold, adventurous spirits, for the sake of a shot at game, or lured on by the thought of mineral wealth, had made some endeavors to penetrate the outer barrier of forest and underbrush, and the steep ridges and passes of the interior, but their efforts seemed crowned with so little success that their undertakings were wither given up or the results so barren that the termination of their adventures are unknown to us.[3]

Exploration by Col. Chambers

Col. Chambers, of the Twenty-first infantry, commanding at Fort Townsend, did endeavor in the years 1881–82, to penetrate the mountains back of Fort Townsend and construct a trail from that fort into the mountains. The summer months were given up to this work and the colonel gave personal attention to the undertaking. Had it succeeded great benefit might have been derived by Port Townsend and that part of the country on its

---

[1] Joseph P. O'Neil, Seattle Press, July 16, 1890. O'Neil's name was misspelled as "O'Niel" in this headline as it appeared in the Press.

[2] "The highest peak on the peninsula had been known as Mount Olympus for more than half a century when the United States Exploring Expedition, commanded by Lieutenant Charles Wilkes, added Roman to Greek mythology in 1841 by giving the name Jupiter Hills to the northeastern Olympics." Wood, Men, Mules and Mountains, p. 393.

[3] "Prospectors and hunters had, of course, worked around the edges of the Olympics for a number of years prior to the exploring expeditions, roaming the foothills and occasionally penetrating the mountains to considerable depth. But they were not explorers in the strict sense of the word, and since they were looking solely for mineral wealth or game, they left no records or trails. Many followed the lieutenant's 1890 expedition into the Olympics, to the point where the mountains became 'infested with miners, and it was no uncommon experience to meet three or four parties a day.'" Wood, Men, Mules and Mountains, p. 437.

completion. After six months, I believe, of weary labor a trail was cut to and across both branches of the Dungeness river, but in getting to the last range of foothills the way seemed so difficult and the undertaking so impracticable that the attempt was abandoned and the trail from then till now known only to military authorities and perhaps a few hunters and woodsmen.[4] Though I have never been on this trail and cannot speak authoritatively yet I believe, from the lay of the country and my knowledge of the existence of a trail from Dungeness, that this abandoned endeavor could be utilized as a cross country road between Dungeness and Townsend.[5] The only communication existing between these places during the year I was at the latter place was by means of a small tug, or at times of extreme low tide it was practicable to travel on horseback.

The country passed through by Chambers' trail is much the same found on the foothills all around the mountains. Dense forests and almost impassable underbrush are the main features but not the only difficulties, for windfalls, precipices and canyons abound. That the undertaking was carried on with such determined and persistent endeavors speaks well for the intentions of the originators of the idea to succeed in penetrating the mysteries of the Pacific slope. There have been other attempts to explore these mountains, but up to the year I made my reconnaissance I was unable to obtain any reliable information.

Vague and Useless Information

People had reported to me on the whole interior of the country, but their accounts I found in many cases to have originated in their imaginations from a distant view of the mountains. One man particularly insisted that he had poled up a certain river without difficulty, had come almost to its head, then shouldering his canoe, he, with a party of three others, crossed a divide and came down another river into the Pacific ocean. I did not hear from the others, but his plan seemed so feasible that had I been a sailor and not a soldier I would have deserted terra firma and trusted my party

and myself to the route by water.

A Wonderful Story Exploded

A few weeks later, after penetrating the mountains, I found that this party had accomplished the wonderful feat of poling a canoe up a fall of fifty feet and rapids of several miles. Another informed me of the existence of prairies of great extent inclosed in these mountains. Proud of the idea that I might be the first to canter over these plains I brought with me two saddle animals. One I left at Port Townsend; the other, after being in the mountains for some time, I took the first opportunity of returning to the fort. So many reports of this kind are circulated that it is with suspicion one listened to the narratives of men who claim to have been in and traveled through these mountains.

Gen. Miles Is Surprised

One evening Gen. Miles, then the commanding general of this department, having heard some of these wonderful stories, in the course of conversation expressed surprise that in so prosperous a country so much seemingly valuable territory should be unknown. He determined to send a party to make a reconnaissance and find out, if practicable, what the country was, its character and its resources, in case of military emergency.

The Party Organized

I was fortunate enough to receive the detail. The summer was then half gone, and as time was of importance, the party was hastily organized and within three days started from Vancouver barracks for Fort Townsend, the supply base. The engineer corps consisted of as bright, talented men and expert engineers as it is the good fortune of one man to secure— Mr. H. Hawgood, now chief engineer of the Southern Pacific, in charge of the Los Angeles and El Paso division; Mr. R.E. Habersham,[6] now constructing engineer of the South Coast railroad, and Mr. Norman Smith.[7] These men, together with Sergeants Heagraff, Green and Gore and Private Johnson of the Fourteenth infantry, made

---

[4] "In May, 1884, six weeks prior to O'Neil's arrival at Fort Townsend, two second lieutenants of the Twenty-first Infantry—Charles M. Truitt and Willson Y. Stamper—left with four enlisted men on a ten day reconnaissance in the Olympics, 'surveying trail to Snowy Range.'" Wood, *Men, Mules and Mountains*, p. 393.

[5] "The Twenty-first Infantry had been stationed at various posts in Oregon, Idaho, and Washington. Only Companies B and D had been garrisoned at Fort Townsend, and they left the post on June 26, 1884. O'Neil arrived at the fort on July 8, twelve days later. However, Lieutenant Wittich and three enlisted men who had worked on the trail remained at the post on detached service until July 18, and O'Neil probably talked to them." Wood, *Men, Mules and Mountains*, p. 393.

[6] "This name appears in O'Neil's manuscript as R. E. Habersham, but in his notes as Richard Wickersham—obviously a confusion with James Wickersham, whom O'Neil met on the 1890 expedition. (Conversely, in a dispatch printed in the *Seattle Post-Intelligencer* on August 6, 1890, B. J. Bretherton called Wickersham's group 'the Habersham party.') Polk's Portland, Oregon, Directory lists a Richard P. Habersham (1886, as an artist; 1889, as a civil engineer) and Richard L. Habersham (1889, as a civil engineer). Habersham later became constructing engineer of the Astoria & South Coast Railroad, and Hawgood rose to the position of chief engineer of the Southern Pacific." Wood, *Men, Mules and Mountains*, p. 394.

[7] "Smith was a great advocate of Port Angeles and destined to be elected its mayor in 1891. He promoted the building of a railroad from the town to Grays Harbor in 1903, but the project failed. Disillusioned and discouraged, he left Port Angeles and made his home in California." Wood, *Men, Mules and Mountains*, p. 394.

up the party.[8] We had with us a pack train of four mules, which we afterward increased to eight. There was some little hesitation in selecting a starting place. Taking into consideration the seeming nearness of the mountains to Port Angeles, we chose that place, and on the evening of July 16 arrived at the long dock at that port.

The Trip to Port Angeles

The trip from Port Townsend to Port Angeles is a beautiful one and on this day the sea was calm, and the woods, bluff and sky were beautifully reflected in the cool, calm depths below. About 1 P.M. we passed the old town of Dungeness. It was founded in the fifties and now has about 500 inhabitants. It is noted chiefly for it fine dairy, good timber and miserable harbor. The country behind it had been explored for probably five miles. A trail runs south from here to Last Mountain, and I think this and Col. Chambers' trail could be connected. When a good road is established between Townsend and Dungeness, I have no doubt that the whole north coast of the Peninsula can be traversed by a wagon road. Port Angeles itself was then a town with a hotel, United States Signal Service office and about 40 people, but each man, woman and child was thoroughly convinced that their town was to be the metropolis of Washington, and their harbor the safest and easiest of access on the coast. It may be now a rising city, but her hopes then looked to be dead sea fruit. Her harbor is indeed very easy of access. Ships can sail in at any time or with any wind. It is formed by an elbow shaped sand spit, varying from a quarter to three-quarters of a mile in breadth running into the strait. The body of water thus inclosed, the harbor, is called Port Angeles bay. The sand spit, although it breaks the sea, is no protection against the wind, but this is compensated for by the claim of magnificent anchorage at any part of the bay. Many years ago, some time in the sixties, this old town bade fair to become the metropolis of Washington. Victor Smith was then collector and had it made the port of entry. A custom house was to have been built, but the loss of the ship Brother Jonathan, together with Victor Smith's death, were blows from which

the town is only now recovering.[9]

A Big Event for Angeles

On our landing here the whole town turned out to see and help us. Our animals were soon pastured, our stores put up and our party established at the hotel. From this hotel there is said to be a road, running in a southeasterly direction about four miles. This was then a thing of the future, but, as a proof of their intention, a clearing, varying from three to 20 feet, had been made, except that logs of three or more feet in diameter were sometimes left as a reminder of what the road had been. I intended to follow this road and then take a trail which was used many years ago by Indians in packing game from the foothills.

The First Day's March

On the 17th we made our first day's march from Angeles, stumbling through underbrush, cutting and clearing logs, frequently stopping to tighten packs, averaging perhaps a mile in an hour and a half, until we were stopped by a marsh. One mule's curiosity was strong, and in his attempts to investigate the conditions of the herbage, went down, and it was only with the assistance of the other mules that we finally succeeded in getting him out. Here we were forced to camp, without grass or forage for the animals, and water neither the best or easy to get, and to add to our discomfort about one hundred yards beyond, our trail disappeared nor did we find it again except every now and then we would come across a few blazed trees. We pitched our shelter tents, floored them with cedar bark, and then camp assumed something of the appearance of a pigmy tent city. Shelter tents, though the name may sound well, are simply pieces of canvas two yards long by four or five feet broad, two of these buttoned together, fastened to a stick at each end of the center line and raised to the height of two feet is the shelter for two persons. To make an entrance to these dwellings you are not expected to be either stately or graceful.

257

---

[8] "According to O'Neil, a fourth enlisted man accompanied the party, but after noting 'Sergeant Gore' was a member, the lieutenant makes no further reference to him. No such person is shown in the regimental returns as having been with the expedition. Special Orders No. 110 (authorizing the trip) state that 'a detail of three enlisted men' would accompany the lieutenant, and Post Orders No. 155 (detailing the men) specify only Green, Weagraff, and Johnson. Moreover, the Registers of Enlistments, United States Army, do not contain anyone named Gore who was serving in the Fourteenth Infantry during this time period. One must, therefore conclude that O'Neil's statement is erroneous.

"The name Weagraff is generally misspelled Heagraff in the lieutenant's account of the 1885 trip as published in the Seattle Press in 1890, but this is a printer's error, the typesetter having misread O'Neil's handwriting. However, in some of his notes, O'Neil called the sergeant Updigraft and Updidraft. Apparently he confused the name Weagraff with that of Private Edward C. Updegraff, Company C, Fourteenth Infantry, who was a member of a United States Geological Survey party sent to Crater Lake, Oregon, in 1886." Wood, Men, Mules and Mountains, p. 394.

[9] "[O]n July 30, 1865, Victor Smith. . .lost his life when the sidewheeler Brother Jonathan struck a reef near Crescent City, California, and sank." Wood, Men, Mules and Mountains, p. 15.

Prospecting a Trail

The next morning Messrs. Hawgood and Smith went forward prospecting a trail and a party was sent back for the stores we were forced to cache on the last days' trip. About sunset all returned to camp, the engineer reporting the road before us very difficult.

Disturbed by a Panther

This first night the sleep of all was so sound that once when the cry of a panther within a few feet of our tents produced a wild disorder and almost a stampede among our mules. I had to awaken one man to help look after the train.

First Range of Foothills

The first range of foothills are about five miles south of Angeles and are about twelve hundred feet high. I made my way to the top of the knoll from which I could get a magnificent view northward. Before me were the straits of Juan de Fuca, Vancouver Island with its green hills, tinged with the golden hue of the setting sun. Up the straits two vessels with sails all set flying before a stiff breeze on their way to port. The distant smoke of a steamer marked its progress. The white tower of the lighthouse, indicating the end of the dangerous reef which surrounds the harbor seemed to rise at my feet, and twelve miles eastward lay Dungeness.

Prospecting for Gold

The Yennis or White Creek, a beautiful stream clear and cold, filled with trout flowed on toward the bay. When I descended I wandered along its bank looking for gold bearing specimens. Capt. White, of the revenue service after whom this creek is sometimes called, many years ago owned a ranch near its mouth,[10] and while prospecting found gold in quantities sufficient to pay for the working, but he was ordered to San Francisco, and though others have worked they have been unable to make it pay. I think it was due to the inexperience of those who made the attempt.

Sunday Spent in Hunting

The next morning (Sunday) all hands went hunting—some for trails or opening, to avoid bush cutting, and the others for game. Mr. Hawgood went up the creek, and found it impracticable to proceed in that direction. Mr. Smith crossed it, and found a better route on the farther side. Mr.

Habersham, when returning to camp stopped on the creek bank, and with his rod and fly secured a fine mess of trout, and in crossing got a good ducking by losing his footing.

A Bear in Camp

I was not able to get out this day, so remained to keep camp, and the only incident to mar the delightful monotony of the day was the advent of a bear in camp. I had been sleeping, and was awakened by a commotion among the mules. Hastily jumping from under my shelter tent, I was confronted, not by a mule, but a huge, black bear. Being unarmed, I started for the ammunition tent for a rifle. The bear made for the woods, and I made no attempt to molest him. The remainder of the day was spent in gathering together the frightened mules.

Trail making was continued the next day. We succeeded in cutting and grading nearly a mile, and two dangerous hills were overcome.

One Member Is Taken Sick

Sergt. Weagraff was taken sick. He seemed to suffer greatly, and small, red spots broke out all over him. My medicine case had no preparation for such a case. Fortunately, remembering some salve that an old lady had given me as a cure for everything, I had him thoroughly rubbed that day, and next morning he was entirely recovered. Since then I have always carried the salve on my mountain trip, and found it invaluable. On the 21st we moved camp a mile and a half further to the bank of a small creek tributary to the Yennis.

Skull Creek Camp

While clearing ground for the camp a well-preserved human skull was found, so we named this place Skull Creek camp. Next day cutting work began again. The hills were much steeper; the first one was about an angle of forty degrees and a three hundred feet climb. Late in the afternoon of the 23rd we again moved camp to the "Three Holes," a distance of two miles. These "Three Holes" are large springs which seem to have no outlet, still the water is not stagnant, but clear, sweet and cold. On this day's march two of the mules behaved badly.

Mules and Profanity

During their antics near the top of Skull creek hill, one lost its footing and tripping the other, both rolled down into the

---

[10] "An item in the July 16, 1885, *Seattle Post-Intelligencer* stated that Captain White arrived in Port Townsend on July 13, en route to San Francisco under orders of the Treasury Department to organize a Board of Revenue Marine officers to appraise the value of the dismantled cutter *Richard Rush*, but upon his arrival at Port Townsend he received a telegram rescinding the order. Modern maps show White Creek as a tributary of Ennis (Yennis) Creek." Wood, *Men, Mules and Mountains*, p. 394.

stream. I gave them up for lost, but the packer, with the assistance of one of the men and a large amount of profanity, succeeded in releasing their packs, they then got up and began to graze as if nothing had occurred. I have had many occasions to notice that the gift of volubility in strong, terse and emphatic language is a specialty with men accustomed to handling mules, but had I never known it before it was very forcibly forced upon my mind this day. On the next hill the mule "kicker" attempted the same performance. This time it did not escape so luckily, for in this roll, its hind leg was frightfully torn, and was so badly hurt that we were obliged to unpack and abandon it.

Old Windfalls

Up to this point we would now and again strike the old Indian trail, which was a very peculiar one, consisting simply of blazes on trees, so that a person could keep the direction, but it ran straight with utter disregard to windfalls, precipices, or other little inconveniences of mountain travel. Often we would come to a windfall 20 or 30 feet high, which seemed to have been the result of winds of hundreds of years.

When we reached camp two of us were laid up from bruises and over-exertion, and camp took somewhat the appearance of a field hospital.

The next morning the trail was prospected and cleared to the junction of the Yennis and Annis creeks. This point is just past the foothills and near the foot of the first range of mountains. We moved camp in the evening to the junction on a little promontory between the creeks.

Grub Getting Scarce

On the 25th our provisions were low. Sergeant Green was sent out to supply our larder, the others to work on the trail. It was a gloomy day and hard work told on the men now almost fasting. The sergeant had poor luck and returned with only two grouse.

On this part of the trip we did not find game in any great plenty. The next morning, taking Mr. Smith with me, I

started for the mountains to look out a trail. Mr. Hawgood was left in charge. A hill I thought impossible to ascend and recommended a backward move. To try to avoid it was the engineer's problem for that day. Mr. Hawgood felt that a backward move would delay us many days and proceeded to fix a trail here. With the sense, judgment and good luck he has always had in railroad construction he surmounted this obstacle and we passed without any loss, even of time.

Sherman Miles Range

Mr. Smith and myself followed an elk trail for about six miles and came into a most beautiful valley, surrounded by lofty peaks, completely enclosed by the mountains, and forming one of the finest grazing grounds I have ever seen. These mountains seem to be a distinct range. I called them the Sherman Miles range, for Mrs. Gen. Miles. On the north side traces of the dense undergrowth still exist, but at our elevation of about 2000 feet the tangling underbrush disappears.

Traces of Alaska cedar are found here, and one of my engineers reported a quantity growing near our camp; all our firewood for several days was this valuable wood. Hemlock and spruce are also found on this range. On the ridge a vein of quartz is laid open by a slide of the rock and earth of the mountain side. The general direction of the range is almost parallel with the strait. It is broken here and there by peaks rising in some instances almost abruptly from and sometimes to an elevation of 3000 feet above the surrounding ridges.[11] Two of these peaks are noticeable. I called them the Sister peaks. One is about 6500 feet high, and the other about 1000 lower. They are just at the head of the valley, and, from the mountains looking toward the strait, appear to be joined together. They are, however, separated by a pass which is about 3000 feet below the highest point;[12] and is on the narrow ridge that divides the head waters of the Annis creek from the Chamber creek. This pass or divide, for it is in reality both, we called Victor pass, after Victor Smith, the collector at Port Angeles, who lost his life in that ill-fated cruise of the ship Brother Jonathan.

259

---

[11] "O'Neil indicated in his 1890 expedition report (which contains remarks about the 1885 reconnaissance) that he called 'the northern district' the Miles Range, in honor of Major General Nelson A. Miles. However, his account of the 1885 trip (published two weeks after he began the 1890 explorations) states that he called the first line of peaks 'the Sherman Miles Range for Mrs. Gen. Miles.' This statement is ambiguous and opens the door to speculation [see "Nomenclature of the O'Neil Expeditions" in Appendix to the O'Neil Expedition Reports at the end of part 3].

"Together with the Jupiter Hills, the Miles Range was separated from the main part of the Olympics (named the Gibbon Range by O'Neil in 1890). The principal peaks were Constance, Clay Wood, and Sherman. By 1890 the latter was called Mount Angeles by the people living in Port Angeles. (O'Neil probably named Mount Sherman for Senator Sherman rather than his famous brother, General Sherman. About a month before the lieutenant began his 1885 trip, General Miles and Senator Sherman visited Port Townsend while looking for sites to build fortifications on Puget Sound.) O'Neil stated that only a portion of the Gibbon Range was visible from Puget Sound, but nearly the entire extent of the Miles Range could be viewed from the steamers on 'any bright day.' He noted, however, that the Gibbon Range showed well from the ocean." Wood, *Men, Mules and Mountains*, p. 395.

[12] "O'Neil's estimate was grossly exaggerated. The pass, crossed today by the Mount Angeles trail, is the low point between Mount Angeles and Klahhane Ridge. Chambers Creek is now called Morse Creek; Annis Creek was a tributary of Yennis Creek." Wood, *Men, Mules and Mountains*, p. 395.

Indications of Iron

On this ridge, near the Sister Peaks, I found the strongest indications of iron. While leaning against a rock taking my bearings, the iron ore, which must have been of the magnetic quality, was so pure as to deflect my needle over 15 degrees. This spot I marked at the time with a slab, as it was a point from which I took observations. I did not notice the rock itself at the time for I was not looking for mineral wealth of any kind, but to find out where I was, and I did not discover the peculiar effect it had upon my compass needle until when at some distance from the rocks, again looking at my compass I found that my course was over 15 degrees from the proper one, and in platting my work found that the compass readings varied about the same. The valley itself nestles beneath the Sister Peaks and is a little gem. The sides rising abruptly are the mountain sides and through a gap in the north end runs the Annis creek. It is well wooded, the grass is luxuriant and of the blue joint variety.

Trouble From a Curious Little Animal

A curious little animal found here in these mountains was first discovered here. We called it the Whistling Marmot, though I am not sure that that animal is found in this part of the country. The resemblance, however, is striking. One was killed by a member of the party, but I did not see it, nor did I have a chance at any time to examine this animal closely. It has the peculiar school boy whistle, and was the source of much discomfort to two of the party who went out after a bear. They separated, each getting on either side of the woods, with the understanding that should anything occur requiring the presence of the other a whistle would be given. A whistle was given and each hastened to the other; meeting, both were surprised and for a moment doubted the other's veracity; thinking it a practical joke, when the same whistle sounded from the side of the mountain, and after a time it was discovered to come from this peculiar little animal.

A Peculiar Haystack Rock

There is a curious rock about the center of the valley, which at a distance closely resembles a haystack. The peaks around show strange, fantastic figures. The place could well be called the mountain of the Gods. Near the highest point of the highest peak sits Jove on his chair of state, thunderbolt in hand. Prometheus, too, seems to have been transported from his Caucasian rocks to be chained to the cold rocks of Mount Mars: and Mars, equipped for war, seems to stand in solemn gloom on the highest point.

Group of High Mountains

Passing through this valley and climbing a steep ascent on the south, after a toilsome march we reached the summit of Victor pass, and here the scene changes. Looking east, west and south mountains, free from timber, some covered with snow, rise in wild, broken confusion. The grandest sight is of a cluster of mountains about thirty miles or so due south of Freshwater bay. This cluster I set down as Mount Olympus. For this mountain, famous as it is, seems to be a source of mystery as to where it really is located; sailing around on the ocean a mountain, or rather cluster of peaks, is seen, and very probably some mariner gave that name to these. I have never found or heard of any one who had, up to this time, been on or near it. This cluster is snow covered, and seems to be the center of a mountain range, the formation of which much resembles a coil. It has no pronounced direction, but seems to circle on itself, and guard, as the walls of a citadel, the great gem, the pride of the particular territory, its central peaks. The formation of the mountain itself, if you choose to call it one mountain, as seen from my point on the Sister Peaks, is that of a huge ridge running about northwest and southeast, broken here and there by peaks, the entire ridge elevated considerably above the surrounding snow-covered mountains. There seems to be a river running by the outer circle, whose canyon is lost to sight in the center of the mountains. This river I pronounced to be the Elwha,[13] and then and there resolved to use my party so that one division could trace it up and give light on that most interesting part of these mountains.

Our intention was to strike the Elwha where it penetrated the range, so we prepared to descend the south slope of the ridge, then gain the ridge on the southwest and travel westward. This was necessary, as the Sister Peaks rose so abruptly that in no possible way could we pass on this ridge.

Chasing a Band of Elk

While descending, we saw a band of elk about two miles away, across the valley of the headwaters of Chambers creek. As fast as possible we made our way towards the coveted game, for we had tasted fresh meat only once since leaving Port Angeles. Mr. Smith was somewhat in advance and was lost to my sight in a small cluster of trees; he suddenly came out with an excited air, an accelerated pace and the informa-

---

[13] "Viewing the central Olympics from Victor Pass, O'Neil saw a curving chain of peaks (named Bailey Range five years later) superimposed against Mount Olympus and paralleled by the Elwha River." Wood, *Men, Mules and Mountains*, p. 395.

tion that a large bear had disputed passage with him. When we got to the copse the bear was hastily disappearing down the ravine, concealed from us, except for a passing glance, by the trees and brush in the bottom. In our excitement we sent a hasty shot after him, but failed to stop him. The report, however, frightened the elk, and the reverberation in the valley so confused the startled band that they headed directly for us. The excitement proved too much for us, and, not waiting for them to come within sure range, we sprang from our concealment, fired a volley and missed them. Mr. Smith's second attempt was more successful, for he brought down a yearling doe, breaking its back. Here we camped for dinner. After our dinner we felt more in the humor for traveling and continued our trip until dark, when we camped on a hill side in a deserted bear's den. The night was bitterly cold and we had but two blankets. The only way we could keep comfortable was to have a large fire, and this was a necessity as well as a luxury, for we were not sure at what moment Mr. Bruin might wish to reclaim his quarters.

Rifle Practice on a Wolf

Just before going into camp we practiced with a rifle on a large wolf. Mr. Smith took him in the leg. We supposed there were many around, but that was the only specimen of the wolf tribe I saw on the entire trip. The next morning we followed the ridge until we came in sight of the valley of the Elwha. This famous valley is at this point a canyon or at best a narrow ravine, and the river seems filled with rapids. We did not enter it, contenting ourselves with locating the gap through which it passed, and turned to retrace our steps. I found that had I begun my trail from a point between Angeles and the Elwha we could have passed into the mountains with much less trail cutting and fewer steep hills to climb; the timber, too, had been burned and the aggravating work of cutting through the dense, tangling underbrush would have, to a great extent, been avoided. The country is magnificent for grazing, and wild game is found in the greatest of plenty. Many traces of hunters were here, and a little old log cabin in which they slept still stood under the brow of a protecting hill.

Down a Mountain in the Dark

The home trip was very dangerous, for it is far safer to ascend than to descend a mountain. About dark we reached Victor's

pass, and here we decided to make for our camp in preference to spending another night on the mountain.[14] To go down at a reasonable pace a steep mountain side is at any time a slightly risky undertaking, but to travel thus on a night so dark that it is hardly possible to distinguish an object nine feet away, is by no means a trip devoutly to be wished for. Mr. Smith had one serious fall, and I thought at first that his back was broken, but after a long delay he was able to proceed with a little assistance. His injuries were not severe, but he was very much bruised and sore.

The last time camp was moved a bay mule had undertaken some antics on the steep mountain side, and had shared the fate of the "Kicker." Both mules were so badly crippled as to be unserviceable, and the horse brought along with the vain hope of cantering over the prairies, was useless as a packer, and an ornament for which we would have no use. Feeling it necessary to replace these, I left for Port Angeles, taking Mr. Smith with me. We had also determined to hire an Indian as a guide and courier. Town was reached on the 28th and we shipped the condemned animals to Townsend. New ones were hired and after much parleying, an Indian engaged and early next morning we started for our camp in the mountains.

Fires in the Forest

Early in the summer someone had set fire to the timber in the foothills and fire had gradually worked its way to the foot of the mountains and was creeping toward the straits. As I passed into town I noticed the fire gradually coming upon our trail and I feared it would cut our communication. We reached camp at Skull creek at dark and halted to await the coming of the moon.[15] After delaying about two hours we again resumed the march. Ahead of us the whole woods were lurid and the glare of the fire shone higher and higher until it seemed to almost reach the heavens. We began to have grave doubts about getting back to our party but pressed on as fast as possible. At the water hole the fire was on our trail and was burning fiercely. We sat and watched it for a long time; it was indeed a grand sight. A great quantity of dead timber and twigs here fed the flames, and the blaze next caught a huge dead fir tree filled with pitch. It was a magnificent sight to watch the flaming sheets wrap around it and rise until there seemed to be one huge

261

---

[14] "Although summer days in the Olympics may be quite warm, the nights are usually cool, frequently cold. According to the June 21, 1892 issue of the *Seattle Post-Intelligencer*, the temperature in Seattle on July 27, 1885, reached 97°, thus it was an unusually warm day in the Pacific Northwest." Wood, *Men, Mules and Mountains*, pp. 395–96.

[15] "The moon rose about 9:00 P.M. at the latitude of the Olympics and was in the waning gibbous phase, having been full on July 26, three days earlier." Wood, *Men, Mules and Mountains*, p. 396.

column of fire. Suddenly with a crash and roar like the thunder of a huge cannon, it broke and fell. After a time we attempted to pass, but for nearly two hundred yards the flames were well nigh scorching us. The mules we had hired seemed accustomed to brush fires, and we had but little trouble with them.

Camp All Alert for an Outlaw

Shortly after midnight we hailed camp. It was fortunate I had thought to announce our coming, for on this day a noted outlaw had escaped the sheriff and was in these woods, supposed to be desperate for want of food. Posses from Dungeness and Port Angeles were after him, and our camp was notified and requested to see that he did not cross our trail. About 9 o'clock that evening it was reported in camp that a prowler was around, so close watch was kept and directions given by Mr. Hawgood, who was in charge, to halt any one who approached or attempted to pass. The camp was on the alert, and to add to the smothered excitement, a panther persisted in haunting the vicinity. Roaming about its outskirts much to the serious discomfort of the animals and no little disturbance to the men. Several times during the night that wild, weird, almost horrible howl broke the stillness and it seemed to come from the picket line. The camp was wrought to such a pitch that when our advance mule came crashing through the brush, had it not been for a timely call, he would probably have been stretched on the trail with a bullet through his brain. We were joyfully received as we brought back provisions, and an impromptu feast and war-dance was celebrated after midnight.

Panthers and Legends

The camp was aroused several times after this by the panther's cry resounding through the woods. If there is anything that will make a man's blood creep it is to be suddenly awakened in the night by that terrible salutation of our king of the mountains.

There is a curious legend among some Indians that a God, a bird of some kind, as eagle or raven, makes its home in these mountains, and it will inflect a terrible punishment on those who by entering them desecrates its home.[16] Among what

Indians or tribes this exists I know not, but when our copper-colored friend saw where we were and found out where we were going, neither big pay or the fear of being shot, both were promised him, could detain him. He reluctantly camped with us but during the night folded his tent and quietly stole away.

Visited by Friends

The First White Woman in Those Mountains

On the 4th of August we had finished the trail up to the mountains and were making preparations for breaking camp when Mr. Chambers, a brother of Col. Chambers, accompanied by his son and daughter, visited us, having made the trip to this point in about 10 hours, a distance by the trail of probably 12 or 14 miles. They were the first who crossed the trail after us. Miss Chambers was, I believe, the first white woman in these mountains, and we all admired her pluck in following such a road.[17] On the 5th we moved camp to the valley of the Sherman Miles range. During the afternoon, in company with Mr. Chambers, his son and daughter, I climbed to the summit of the lesser of the Sister Peaks, and while there a fog came down upon us and we experienced great difficulty in finding camp.

Mules in the Mountains

We had trouble in making a trail from the valley over Victor pass. Near the summit of the ridge there is a ledge of rocks about five feet in width, over which our animals had to pass. On one side the mountain rose almost abruptly; on the other was a sheer fall of a thousand feet. It was enough to make one feel the risk of handling animals in the mountains. Mr. Hawgood's engineering qualities again came into play, and with not tools but mattocks, in an hour we had passed the ledge without accident. There is a peculiarity of mules always noticeable in mountain work, that they will always walk near the edge of a precipice; it seems to be their instinct to keep so far from the wall that there is no danger of their packs swinging against it. In building a trail the outer edge should always be made solid. On this day we successfully passed the first ridge of mountains and crossed into the val-

---

16 "This was, of course, a variation of the thunderbird myth found among so many North American tribes." Wood, *Across the Olympic Mountains*, p. 23.

17 "The statement in O'Neil's manuscript that the Chambers party was 'the first who crossed the trail after us' conflicts with his notes: 'Up to now [Victor Pass] we had no dearth of visitors. I did not encourage them nor was I a hail fellow well met, for it was work enough to provide food for hungry trail builders, and a tramp to my camp did whet the appetite of visitors. But I did enjoy the visit of Mr. Chambers, his daughter and son. They had been so good to us that the entire party outdid themselves to be nice to them. A big trip was planned [to] our highest near peak.' Many years later, O'Neil could still recall 'the coolness and precision Miss Chambers showed in passing most dangerous and difficult climbs,' and he stated that , if still living, she could 'claim the credit of being the first white woman to penetrate the outer barriers of the Olympics to the interior.'" Wood, *Men, Mules and Mountains*, p. 396.

ley where heads the Chambers creek and reached the second range. We had been from the 17th day of July to the 5th of August cutting our way through the dense forests and undergrowth which clothe the foothills.

The Party Is Divided

On a prominent point of this second range of mountains[18] our camp was made. This was to be the main cache camp, and here all clothing, blankets and provisions not absolutely necessary were deposited. A good view of the numerous ranges could be had from this point, and we planned our courses from our tent. The party was to be divided. Mr. Hawgood, with one division, was to take direction of the Elwha, make his way to that river, then follow as nearly as possible to its head, travel southward and come out on the south southwest slope. I was to take the other, strike southeast, find the head of the east fork of the Elwha, and then make my way out to Hood's canal.[19] The main stream of the Elwha was about twelve miles from our position, and intervening were several ridges.

Mr. Hawgood Has Bad Luck

Mr. Hawgood, after traveling about a week, found it almost impossible to proceed. An accident occurred on the trail which deprived him of part of his train, all his instruments and provisions. In crossing the east fork of the Elwha and climbing the bluff on the farther side, one of the mules in the lead missed its footing; it and nearly all the others were almost lost. The one carrying the instruments rolled from the trail, the pack became loosened, all the provisions, mess outfit and instruments went into the river, and it was impossible to recover them. The poor animal, after rolling some distance, was stopped by a clump of trees, and they succeeded in getting it to camp. No one had any hopes of its recovery, but I believe it is still alive on Mr. Chamber's farm near Angeles. This party, hungry, tired and discouraged, returned to the Cache camp.

Following a Ridge

The ridge followed bore in a southeasterly direction, and was often broken by sharp peaks. Away below me was the valley of one of the creeks which head in these mountains and flow into the straits between Port Angeles and Dungeness. The valley was beautiful and might have been mistaken for one of the prairies the people had spoken of. Some places it was several miles in width and grass as luxuriant as I have ever seen. Our mules, worn and thin by constant travel, and no food except what they could pick from tender shoots of the brush in the foothills, here began to pick up, and notwith-standing the hard travel climbing and descending remained in good condition, and on my return to Angeles were as strong looking as when they were taken from their stables at Port Townsend.

Some Clear Valleys

Some of the valleys we passed were densely wooded but most of them were clear and capable of immediate cultivation. On the right of the ridge ran one of the tributaries of the east fork of the Elwha. The stream below looked dark and turbulent and the grade was so steep that none cared to venture to take the water. On the second day's travel we were stopped by a peak so sharp and steep as to defy the making of a trail. Here we turned to the right and made camp in a canyon of a tributary to this tributary of the Elwha.

Two Bears With Three Shots

After camp was pitched Sergt. Heagraff started hunting and had not left the camp five minutes before three shots in rapid succession were heard; as that was our signal for assistance, we all rushed to his rescue, and found that he had killed two bears with those three shots.

I had never seen this feat accomplished before. We had a very comfortable camp that night. On our mountain work we had become accustomed to break the ice on the water before making our not very elaborate toilet, and here it seemed strange to find clear running water. The next morning we regained the ridge and by cutting eastward passed the peak. This route took us into another valley, and we crossed the headwaters of the Dungeness.

Our old ridge bore off southward, so, making our course southeast we struck another parallel to our original direction.

263

---

[18] "The 'second range' was Hurricane Ridge. The exact location of the camp cannot be determined, but it must have been on or near Big Meadow, the site now occupied by the lodge." Wood, *Men, Mules and Mountains*, p. 396.

[19] "O'Neil's references to the 'East Fork of the Elwha' are vague. . . . Viewing the Olympics from Hurricane Ridge, and not having maps showing the topographic configuration, the lieutenant may have confused Long Creek for a 'West Fork,' and the Hayes, the Lillian, or the Godkin for the upper course of the 'East Fork.' . . . He describes the 'East Fork' as having a length of 'about 35 or 40 miles'—much longer than the Hayes, the Lillian, or the Godkin—and states that it headed in a 'small but very pretty' field of ice; but in other notes he refers to the source as a 'snow field.' Quite likely he considered the Hayes and lower Elwha together as the 'East Fork' and the Lillian as its tributary. O'Neil traveled some distance beyond the Lillian. This is confirmed by his notes. 'We got to Mount Anderson—recalled to go to Fort Leavenworth.' And again: 'We arrived at a very prominent mountain I called Mount Anderson to honor the Colonel of my regiment. From the top of this mountain a good sketch could be made of the interior.'" Wood, *Men, Mules and Mountains*, p. 397.

While crossing this valley of the Dungeness, Sergeant Heagraff and myself, being considerably in advance of the train, came suddenly upon three large elk lying in the shade of a small cluster of trees. After carefully selecting our game we fired, and each finally brought down his elk. The flesh was a little tough and we afterwards became such epicures in the matter of game meats that we wondered how we could have so demeaned ourselves by eating it, but as many days had passed since we tasted fresh meat we relished it then. The camp was near the spot where we had killed the elk.

Game Plenty From This On

That evening the hunting party brought in a calf and from that time our larder never wanted for fresh meat.

About eight miles from this camp another peak arose. The descent this time was so steep on all sides that it was unsafe to try to bring the mules down, so, leaving them in camp, I resolved to tramp until we could find a place to get them over or discover the head of the Elwha's east fork. During the last two day's march we noticed that all streams ran eastward instead of northward, and knew from that the ridge on which we traveled was the divide between the stream's tributary to the strait on the north and Hood's canal on the east. Not being familiar with either the names or location of these streams I could not readily place them.

Mr. Pilcher had joined us in the valley of the Sherman Miles range; taking him and Private Johnson, each of us packing to a weight of about 40 pounds, we started from camp at 5 A.M., and marched nearly 11 hours, when we camped in a bear's den, very tired. From here we could see the source of the east fork of the Elwha and the field of ice from which it started. The monotony of the day's travel was varied every now and then by a band of elk, a bear, or a deer perched on one of the peaks. We made no attempt to shoot the game, but we gave no respite to the bear when we came across one.

Rather a Dangerous Fall

Late in the afternoon, while trying to get from a mountain to the valley below and following the bed of a dry creek, whose banks were covered with brushes, which overhanging, concealed the pathway to a great extent, I lost my footing and fell. The incline was so great that my fall started the loose dirt, and after sliding with it some distance my pack caught between two rocks and stopped my headway for the moment. This gave me time to recover myself, and with the assistance of the shrubbery on the bank I pulled myself out. Glancing around, I discovered that just below me, and not ten feet away, was a fall where, in the spring, I suppose, the water

made a magnificent jump. The fall was at least 50 feet deep, and the huge, ungainly boulders at its base did not look inviting. With great difficulty I got below the falls, and made the creek again.

Grand Scenery

The scenery in these mountains is grand—waterfalls and canyons, valleys, and snow-covered mountains. One fall attracted my special attention. It was of a stream about 10 feet wide, with a descent of about 150 feet, then seething and foaming for a short distance, made another leap nearly as large as the first. Large fields of ice and snow were often passed, and trees dotting a landscape of green in the valleys.

During the several days we traveled on this trip we passed numerous bands of elk and small game in great plenty. They were all so tame and almost confiding that it was like going into a herd of domestic cattle, selecting your beast and killing him. Orders were very strict and no one was allowed to shoot at any game unless the camp needed a supply of meat. Many a time did I long to shoot and it required a strong repression of my inclinations to pass within fifty yards of a band of elk and content myself with gazing at them.

An Exciting Bear Hunt

One day I saw a bear lying on a rock sunning himself. He was a huge fellow and I was anxious to have him. With great care I drew a bead on him, aiming at his heart. I struck him fairly and he tumbled from the rock. I afterwards found that the bullet had passed through the fore shoulder and not the heart, but at the time I thought him dead. Dropping my rifle and drawing my knife I made for the rocks behind which he had rolled. When I got there the bear was up and made for me. Fortunately he was crippled and got the better of him in my race for my carbine. When I recovered my gun I managed to dispatch him by using the Apache's tactics, that of circling around my game. He carried thirteen pieces of lead before he gave up life. This was my most exciting hunt.

Big Elk Yards

While traveling in the valley you come every now and then to what I called an elk yard, the winter home of the elk. These yards are sometimes hundreds of acres in extent. The trees are denuded of their bark, the bushes cut down and the ground as trampled as the picket ground of a cavalry troop. They seemed to be always found on the southern slope of a ridge or mountain, and so hemmed in that they are, to a great extent, protected on all sides. Elk are generally found

264

in the valleys in the morning or evening. During the heat of the day they climb a mountain side and rest in a cool snow field. Deer are seldom found in the valleys except in the very early morning or late in the evening.

Estimating the Length of the Elwha

The head waters of the east fork of the Elwha I would roughly estimate to be about 25 miles from our main cache camp, and the length of this fork is about 35 or 40 miles. I did not go to the river itself but traveled for some days on the ridge overlooking it, and it has a very sullen appearance. The field of ice in which it heads is a small but very pretty field with an incline somewhat too steep for easy travel. Passing this we continued on our way towards a peak from which I wished to take observations. This we gained about noontime, and ascended with some difficulty. From here I could see Mounts Baker and Rainier rising in their massive grandeur. Mounts Constance, Adams and St. Helens were distinctly visible, as was also the Sister Peaks of the Sherman Miles range.[20] We found ourselves about 10 miles south and 12 miles west of Constance. Having made no provisions for camping out we returned to the last camp, where we had left our packs. Mr. Pilcher had a few days before going to the pack train camp. Johnson and myself in making our way back came to the snow field, in which rises the east fork of the Elwha.

A Perilous Leap Over a Crevasse

Here I had an irresistible desire to cross and not follow the trail around the ridge, which was much longer; so leaving Johnson with instructions to watch me for a signal to come if it was thought best, or to go around by trail if not, I started. The snow was hard packed and in many places pure ice, and very slippery about halfway down, and the incline was rather steep. Here a crevasse about 10 feet wide yawned before me. It was impossible even to estimate its depth; to return, was on account of the steepness of the grade, the smoothness of the ice, and lack of spikes in our shoes, impossible, so taking the only alternative I leapt it.[21] In alighting I lost my balance and fell, sliding down I reached the bottom much quicker and more bruised than I had anticipated in starting. But on recovering myself immediately signaled to Johnson to go back by trail.

A Man Lost in the Hills

He was much excited by my mishap, and in trying to come to me as quickly as possible, attempted to take a shortcut, but got bewildered among the many ravines and wandered away, lost. After waiting a sufficient time for him to come up, I slowly made my way to camp, thinking to find him there, but when I found the camp deserted my anxiety was aroused, and, lighting huge fires on all the points around sought by this means to show him to camp. The night slowly passed but no Johnson came, and after wandering around firing off my gun and doing all things else that could possibly attract attention started for the pack train camp with the hope of finding him there. I was disappointed. Every one was sent out to look for the missing man, thinking that he might have fallen and injured himself, but on searching every part of the trail over which we had passed, felt that he was lost and his only chance of safety lay in his own judgment. He might perhaps follow down the Elwha and cross Mr. Hawgood's trail, or cross it and reach the ocean. Hastening back to the main cache camp, we found the other division of the party. A man was sent to watch the river and all the others to search for the missing man. After several days of fruitless search no signs of Johnson were found.

Return to Port Angeles

When I arrived at camp I found a courier with an order directing me to proceed to Fort Leavenworth for duty. I delayed as long as I possibly could looking for our lost man, so leaving the party in charge of Sergeant Weagraff to continue the search, I left for Angeles and on the 26th of August took the boat to return.

Repaid for the Toil

We had been at work in these mountains from the 17th of July until the 26th of August. The travel was difficult, but the adventures, the beauty of the scenery, the magnificent hunting and fishing amply repaid all hardships, and it was with regret that I left them before I had completed the work I had laid out for myself, and there is no doubt in my mind that my object could have been accomplished had I the time.

---

[20] "The peak the men climbed may have been near the source of the Dosewallips River, more likely was closer to Mount Anderson, which blocked the way like a massive fortress. O'Neil estimated they reached a point 'about 10 miles south and 12 miles west of Constance,' but he must have been mistaken. This would have placed them beyond Anderson and near O'Neil Pass, the gap used by the 1890 expedition when crossing the Grand Divide. Mount Clay Wood, one of the peaks at the head of the Dosewallips, was named by O'Neil for Major Henry Clay Wood (1832–1918), Assistant Adjutant General, Department of the Columbia, who signed the orders authorizing the 1885 expedition." Wood, Men, Mules and Mountains, pp. 397–98.

[21] "O'Neil had good precedent for leaping the crevasse. During his last year at Notre Dame, he won the 'running jump' by leaping 17 feet 2 inches, and he placed second in the 'running hop, step and jump' with a total distance of 37 feet 7 inches." Wood Men, Mules and Mountains, p. 398.

Wealth of the Valleys and Mountains

I have spoken at length of the valleys and streams of these mountains. I had no special object to look after; all I wished to learn was the character of the country and its topography. There must be, however, great mineral wealth here, for gold has been found in the foothills, as has also coal. There are now two claims which have first class coal located near Hood's canal. Iron ore is in some places most abundant and very pure. I also carried a specimen out which was pronounced by a learned man to be copper. The formation of these mountains seems to speak plainly of mineral wealth.[22] There is no regularity about their formation, but jumbled up in the utmost confusion, and the only regularity which does exist is that the ranges nearest the Strait and Sound seem to run parallel to those bodies of water, and with all their irregularity, ruggedness and at present difficult of access, the day will come when the state of Washington will glory in their wealth and beauty.

Joseph P. O'Neil, U.S.A.

UNTITLED[23]

The party under Lieutenant O'Neal [sic], which started out some weeks ago to explore the Olympic Range, was recalled before completing the trip across the mountains. The Lieutenant confirms the previous reports of an extensive and fertile rolling country back of the foothills south of Port Angeles. He explored the country spoken of for about forty miles in length, parallel with the Straits of Fuca, and reports that he found good range for thousands of stock. On the lower levels a kind of blue grass grows rank and tall, and on the elevations this is varied by patches of genuine bunch grass. The probabilities are that exploration of this region will lead to its occupation by stockmen ere long.

Intense local interest in the newly exposed Olympic Mountains continued for years after the first serious bursts of exploration that occurred in 1890. Five years later, in 1895, the president of the University of Washington, Mark W. Harrington, requested of Washington's Senator Watson C. Squire that Lieutenant Joseph P. O'Neil's reports of his Olympic explorations be made available to the public. Squire, in turn, requested that the Army provide them, but the Army's files failed to yield anything about the 1885 expedition, which by then had occurred ten years earlier. Senator Squire handled Harrington's request by entering O'Neil's 1890 Olympics report and comments into the public record of the U.S. Senate, which made them permanently available nationwide in all of the libraries designated federal depositories. Following is the official report as entered into the Senate records, as well as notes O'Neil used for his lectures and some added remarks that contain references to his 1885 expedition.[24]

54th Congress 1st Session Senate Document No. 59[25]

In the Senate of the United States

January 8, 1896.—Referred to the Select Committee on Forest Reservations and the Protection of Game and ordered to be printed.

Mr. SQUIRE presented the following

Letter From the Assistant Adjutant-General, Transmitting Copy of the Report of Lieut. Joseph O'Neil, Fourteenth Infantry, of His Exploration of the Olympic Mountains, Washington, From June to October, 1890.

War Department
Adjutant-General's Office
Washington, January 7, 1896
Sir: In compliance with the request of Prof. Mark W. Harrington, president of the University of Washington, Seattle, Wash., on November 14, 1895, returned to you with letter from this office of December 3, 1895, I have the honor to transmit herewith a copy of the report of Lieut. Joseph P. O'Neil, Fourteenth Infantry, of his exploration of the Olympic Mountains, Washington, from June to October, 1890.

The photographs, map, and reports of members of the Alpine Club, referred to therein, were not received here with

---

[22] "O'Neil apparently changed his opinion about the presence of valuable minerals in the Olympics. His notes state: 'Hawgood and I in our youthful wisdom, as we both had recently acquired pieces of sheepskin which said we were engineers, and we both believed we were, decided that the country was a result of a recent volcanic upheaval and too youthful to have concealed about its person precious metals. Strange to say that five years later, during the 1890 trip, Colonel Lindsay [Linsley], one of the greatest mining experts in the United States, . . . pronounced the doom of ambitious prospectors in practically the same words.'" Wood, *Men, Mules and Mountains*, p. 398.

[23] Author unknown, *West Shore* 11 (October 1885): pp. 319–20. This appeared without a headline, and seems to be the only known newspaper or periodical comment on the 1885 O'Neil Expedition.

[24] The names of rivers and other proper names (peculiar by today's spellings) have been left as O'Neil wrote them in his report. The obvious typesetting errors in his report have been corrected.

[25] Serial no. 3349, vol. 3.

266

this document from the headquarters Department of the Columbia, and the department commander says the report of Lieutenant O'Neil on this subject, of 1885, is not on file at his headquarters.

Very respectfully,

J. C. Gilmore, Assistant Adjutant-General.
Hon. Watson C. Squire, United States Senate.

Vancouver Barracks, Wash., November 16, 1890
The Assistant Adjutant-General,
Department of the Columbia,
Vancouver Barracks, Wash.

Sir: I have the honor to submit herewith my report of the exploration of the Olympic Mountains, Washington.[26]

On the 9th of June, 1890, under the direction of the department commander, I left this post to visit the Sound, in order that I might make such preparations for the trip as were possible. At Port Townsend I engaged the steamer *Enterprise* to tow a covered scow down Hoods Canal to Union City. I had procured a scow large enough to carry the entire party and outfit. This service was not rendered. An accident happened which left her in an unfit conditon to perform the service, and I was, on my return, forced to hire another vessel. I made diligent inquiries to gain all information possible; but little had been done toward the exploring of these mountains since my trip of 1885. The *Seattle Press*, however, had sent out an expedition in December, 1889. I anxiously awaited this report, which was promised me.[27] Their full account was published in the issue of July 16, 1890.

It was a mistake to send out such an expedition at such a season of the year in such a country. This party spent six months or about that time in traveling up the Elwha and down the north fork of the Quinaiult to the lake. An idea can be had of the progress they made by a comparison with our trip up the Quinaiult. They were seventeen days in passing over ground which we passed over in not quite three days. Their work, though performed under the most difficult circumstances, is very nearly correct, as long as they confined themselves to recording notes of the country actually passed over by them; but their mistakes of some landmarks render the general map

of the country which they publish not entirely correct. As I had been over the northeastern section of this peninsula before, under direction of General Miles, my desire was now to penetrate from Hoods Canal to the Pacific.

The plan I submitted to the department commander after my return from the Sound, June 16, was to go up the Skokomish River to its head, to try to find the terminus of my trail of 1885, then to proceed westward, coming out at the Quiets River, Grays Harbor, or whatever point I could make. The intention was to make one main trail—detached parties sent in various directions were to discover as much as possible of the surrounding country. This plan was approved by the commanding general and followed. There is a trail over which mules carried from 100 to 200 pounds each, from Hoods Canal to Grays Harbor via Lakes Cushman and Quinaiult. This trail is about 93 miles in length, and was in itself an Herculean undertaking. No one not conversant with the nature of this country—the windfall, the tangled undergrowth, its steep, almost precipitous character—can appreciate the immense amount of patience and labor spent on this comparatively small portion of the work of the expedition.

In this regard I can not mention too highly my appreciation of the energy, push, and interest of the Board of Trade of Hoquiam, on Grays Harbor. At a very large outlay of capital they hired a gang of men to cut a trail from their city to connect with and meet my trail in the mountains, and of this 93 miles of trail fully 30 was cut by them. Too much credit can not be given to the men who accompanied the expedition. These men I had spent much time in selecting, and in every way came up to my expectation. Of Sergeant Marsh, Company G, I feel called upon to make special mention. Any direction I gave them I felt sure would be executed, and that promptly. Private Fisher I made an acting corporal, and he was placed in charge of detached parties, and after the departure of Prof. L. Henderson, the botanist, was acting in his place. The party consisted of Sergeants Marsh, Yates and Haffner; Privates Barnes, Kranichfield, Danton , Hughes, Higgins, Fisher, and Krause. Private Krause had a severe attack of rheumatism, brought on by the continuous exposure and rain, and was incapacitated for service and sent back. He was relieved from duty on the 8th of July, but was unable to leave until about the 20th.

267

---

[26] "The record consisted of three parts: first, an account of the 'incidents of the trip'; second, the lieutenant's 'remarks and conclusions'; third, photographs taken on the journey. Among the photographs O'Neil submitted with his report were a number of views taken from Mount Seattle in May, 1890, by Charles A. Barnes of the Press Expedition. The pictures show the mountains covered with snow, thus contrast sharply with photographs made by Bretherton in late September. Although O'Neil neglected to credit the Press Party, he probably included the pictures to illustrate the explored country more thoroughly, not to represent them as the work of his expedition." Wood, *Men, Mules and Mountains*, pp. 380, 436.

[27] "O'Neil did receive the Press Expedition report but more than two weeks after his party left for the mountains. O'Neil had, in fact, asked one of the Press explorers to join his expedition. He received a terse but positive reply: 'Never again!'" Wood, *Men, Mules and Mountains*, p. 400.

At Port Townsend the representatives of the Oregon Alpine Club reported to me. I showed the letter of instructions sent to me, and all agreed to its provisions and promised compliance. The representatives were B.J. Bretherton, naturalist; L. Henderson, botanist, and N. Lindsay, mineralogist.[28] After the departure of Private Krause Mr. Church, a settler, asked to join, and as his services were voluntary I allowed him to accompany us, and he more than made up for the man I had relieved. J. Church, M.D., was added to the strength of the party on the 25th of July. M. Price, an employee of the quartermaster's department, accompanied the expedition in the capacity of chief packer.[29] At various times, actuated by the absolute necessity of the case, I employed men as packers. These were professional carriers of Indian extraction, and were engaged when we were forced to have more supplies than we could carry on our backs at a certain place by a certain time.[30] A matter of great importance was the foraging of the animals—these had very severe labor when employed—and as grazing was not to be had in the Skokomish Valley they were kept back at Lake Cushman, or at Hoodsport, as much as possible.

Mr. Price, the chief packer, deserves great commendation for his watchfulness and care of the pack train, and it is due to him that is crossing one ford of the Skokomish River that we did not lose four of our best mules. The current carried them under a drift of logs, he plunged into the river, cut the ropes and freed the mules, and got them once more in quiet water. Three mules were the only casualties of the trip, and it was simply providential that to so large a party crossing so rugged a country in injury other than a broken finger was received. There was one mule branded, "B.C.," which we thought recorded his date of birth, on account of cold and exposure gave out; a good camp was selected and he was abandoned. Another mule, Sorais, fell from the trail and rolled into the gorge of the Quinaiult River; She had no bones broken, and we endeavored to save her, but all efforts were fruitless. The third, called "Weakback" maddened by yellow-jackets' stings broke from the trail, and before she could be stopped plunged over the precipice in the wildest part of the canyon of the Quinaiult.

Following the custom of explorers, I gave names to such places as I thought proper. I took the liberty of calling the main range of mountains the Gibbon Range, in honor of the commanding general. The northeast district, which is separate and includes the Jupiter Hills, the Miles Range, in honor of Maj. Gen. N.A. Miles, United States Army; the third range, the Hoquiam Range, after the enterprising city of Hoquiam, Wash. Mount Anderson, the most important mountain next to Olympus, after Col. T.M. Anderson, Fourteenth Infantry.[31] Two lakes at the head of the Ducquebusch received the names of Francis and John. A few mountains were christened. All names are carried on the map.

In the following I have arranged: First, the report of the principal incidents of the trip; second, my remarks and conclusions after careful examination; third, photographs. I also submit translations of the names of some rivers and places. The meaning of the names of the others I could not get. All rivers were named by the Indians who inhabited the country at their mouths. Also a few legends relating to this country, which show why this country was not well known to the Indians. The reports of the members of the Alpine Club are hereto appended.

Very respectfully, your obedient servant,

Jos. P. O'Neil, Second Lieutenant Fourteenth Infantry, Commanding Expedition Olympic Mountains

Report of the Exploration of the Olympic Mountains [1890]

On the 24th of June a pack train under charge of Sergeant Marsh, Company G, Fourteenth Infantry, accompanied by Packer Price and Private Barnes, left this post en route for Fort Townsend. The next day, the 25th, the remainder of the party, consisting of Lieutenant O'Neil; Sergeant Yates, of Company B; Sergeant Haffner, Company D; Privates Danton, Company K; Fisher, Company G, Higgins, Company F; Hughes, Company E; Krinichfieldt, Company B, and Krause, Company E, all of the Fourteenth Infantry, took their

---

[28] "Linsley was not a member of the Oregon Alpine Club, but he represented the organization in the capacity of 'staff geologist.' On September 8, while the expedition was still in the mountains, Linsley's name was submitted to the Oregon Alpine Club's board of directors for honorary membership in the club." Wood, *Men, Mules and Mountains*, pp. 54, 401.

[29] "More than fifty years of age, Price was the oldest man on the expedition and a civilian employee of the Quartermaster Department. He had also served as General Gibbon's private packer, having been with Gibbon at the Big Hole battle in 1872." Wood, *Men, Mules and Mountains*, p. 54.

[30] "Except for Indian teams hired to transport the men from the Quinault Indian Agency to Oyhut, this is the only reference in the records to packers other than the ones who were members of the expedition." Wood, *Men, Mules and Mountains*, p. 401.

[31] "This was the last 'big mountain' still unnamed in the new state of Washington when O'Neil christened it for his regimental commander. The mountain is double-peaked, and in the 1930's O'Neil told Anderson's grandson, Dr. Charles A. Gauld, that he named one peak for the colonel, the other for his lady, Elizabeth Van Winkle Anderson (1850–1914). Mount Anderson is the hydrographic apex of the Olympics. The mountain's glaciers and snowfields are the sources of three major streams—the East Fork Quinault, the Dosewallips, and the Hayes (a tributary of the Elwha), which flow, respectively, to the Pacific, Hood Canal, and the Strait of Juan de Fuca." Wood, *Men, Mules and Mountains*, pp. 420–21.

departure, and on the 27th arrived at Fort Townsend, without anything of importance occurring. As before mentioned the steamer *Enterprise* had been engaged to convey the party to Union City,[32] at the southern extremity of Hoods Canal. The day before our arrival an accident occurred by which her boilers were tendered unfit for use. A delay occurred in trying to get another steamer. We finally succeeded in chartering the steamer *Louise*, of Port Hadlock Mills.

On the 1st of July we steamed out of the Port Townsend Harbor, and after an all-night run landed at the mouth of the Lilliwaup Creek, about 6 miles from Union City. There being no dock, and the steamer unable to land, we were forced to transfer our supplies to the shore with small boats, and to jump the mules from the deck and swim them to the shore. This was accomplished without loss. The provisions were secured in a dry place under the bank until the pack train could move with the first load. As we were able to carry only about a quarter of our supplies a trip, we shipped the remainder up the creek to Mr. Taylor's ranch, to be stored until we could remove them.

The pack train in the meantime had been sent forward, lightly loaded, over the trail to Lake Cushman. The trail was represented as being good, and the lake only 6 miles distant. Thinking that the trip could be easily made in a few hours, nearly all the men had been sent ahead to clear what obstructions there might be, while three packers followed with the train.

The trail had been entirely misrepresented and was very difficult to travel; the almost perpendicular hills, heavy windfalls, miry swales, and to add to this the freshness of the mules, newness of the ropes and aparejos causing the packs to constantly slip, rendered this day's march about the most difficult of the entire trip. The party ahead had been almost worn out in trying to clear the way. To add to the disagreeable features of the day, heavy rain began in the morning and conscientiously followed us the entire day. About 9 o'clock that night camp was pitched in a swamp, as it was too dark to proceed any farther. Owing to the constant slipping of the packs, the falling of the mules, and heaviness of the trail, we had made about $2\frac{1}{2}$ miles this afternoon.

Early the next morning, July 3, the march was resumed, and Lake Cushman reached about noon. This lake is a beautiful sheet of water, nestling under the rugged peaks of the first range of mountains from the canal. It is about $1\frac{1}{2}$ miles in length by 1,000 yards in width and about 200 feet deep. It abounds in fish, the principal variety of which are the brook, lake, and bull trout.

Some five or six years ago a man named Rose squatted on a quarter section on the edge of the lake, and made for himself a beautiful home. Others have followed, and there is now no section of land not taken up or squatted on within 3 miles of the lake, or between the lake and Hoods Canal.

Rose had built for himself a raft on which he ferried his animals across the lake, and we were forced to hire this old and water-soaked collection of logs to cross or spend two weeks in cutting a trail around it. All our provisions, men, and animals were thus ferried across, and camp was pitched on the west side of the lake in Mr. Windoffer's field.

The pack train was sent back to the Lilliwaup for another load, and were thus kept busy until the 9th in moving up the stores. The trail cutters were set to work on the trail, which was cleared for a distance of about $2\frac{1}{2}$ miles from the lake.

The Fourth of July was observed, the usual order "all duty other than the usual guard and fatigue will be dispensed with," the result of which was a great increase to our larder, and among the others, Professor Henderson especially distinguished himself by a catch of a hundred trout, fine, large, beauties, in a few hours.

On the 5th, three mules were taken from the pack train to move the necessary bedding and provisions for the trail workers. Scouts were sent out to prospect for a trail up the Skokomish River, while I went back to find out the condition of the trail to Hoodsport, with a view of changing the route by which supplies would be brought in. This trail was found to be a good one, and was used by us from this time forward. The scouts sent out to prospect for the trail met with no very encouraging success, and the necessity of forcing our way through the dense forest and over precipitous bluffs dawned on us and placed us all in no very sanguine mood; and to add to the discouragement, an incessant downpour of rain had followed us from the time we left the Lilliwaup.

On the 6th, Mr. Church, a young man who had come out from the East, and had some time before taken up a squatter's claim, wishing for experience, asked to join us. And I, anxious for the assistance of good woodmen, readily

269

[32] "Union City, which boasted a population of 214 in 1890, began in 1858 as a trading post called Skokomish, although a blockhouse thought to have been used by traders for the Hudson's Bay Company had been built about 1830. The town experienced a boom in 1890 because the Union Pacific Railroad selected the site for its salt water terminus, and waterfront lots were held for $1000 in anticipation of the coming railroad. However, shortly after the construction crews arrived, they were recalled because of the bank failure in London that precipitated 'the panic of 1893.' The name Union City, which became the town's official designation in 1890, had no connection with the railroad." Wood, *Men, Mules and Mountains*, p. 401.

granted it. He continued with us throughout the trip.

July 7, a trail had been cut a distance of about 4½ miles, and Camp No. 2 there established. This camp is about 500 yards from a camp occupied by a set of miners. These men are now developing a copper mine. Some years before prospectors found hematite at this place and took up claims, expecting to develop an iron mine. In their work they came across small pockets of copper, and they are now developing, expecting to find a paying copper mine. The formation there is sandstone and slate, with veins of porphyry. The copper is found in these veins of porphyry.

At Camp No. 2 a bluff jutting into the river stopped further progress, and after vainly endeavoring to get around it we were forced to bridge the face of it. This was done by felling trees from the top in such a manner that they would lay so that when covered with dirt and boughs they formed a ledge of sufficient width to allow a mule to pass.[33] The entire strength of the party was occupied for four days and a half in building this bridge, but it was done in so substantial a manner that this piece of road, which some miners were afraid to cross, did not even delay the pack train. By the 10th all supplies were brought up, and were cached at Camp No. 1.

By the 11th of July a trail had been cut to Camp No. 3, a distance of about 7 miles from Lake Cushman. By this time we had passed several rough fords in the stream, and the water being quieter and more shoal, we undertook to travel up the bed of the stream in preference to cutting through the fallen timber. Our first trip over this new kind of a trail nearly drowned for us two of our best pack mules, and cost the loss of the supplies they were packing. We were forced to leave the river and continue to hew our way through the woods.

At Camp 3 I began the practice of sending out exploring parties, while the eight trail workers continued on the trail. Thus the party, while continuing to progress toward the center of the mountains, were enabled to discover the country on either side of the trail, and to locate prominent points called observation peaks. The first of these parties was found by Professor Henderson and Private Fisher, the botanists. They ascended a peak on the left-hand side of the

Skokomish Valley, about 10 miles from Lake Cushman. From this point they could locate Union City and Hoods Canal on the south and east, and the head of the North Fork and the Skokomish River to the north and west.

On the 14th Camp No. 4 was established in a little basin about a mile below the falls of the river,[34] at the east extremity of what is called the Canyon. Here another cache camp was made, and while the packers were bringing up supplies, the remainder of the party, trail makers and all, went out to look for a way over or through this canyon to make the divide.

The most dangerous part of the trip was experienced in scouting for trail and securing observation points, and this was no exception. Two civilians, out for a few days' hunting, had joined us and went with the party prospecting the North Fork. They were hardy men and good hunters, but they made no more requests to accompany any of our scouting expeditions.

The party of the North Fork, after very severe labor, succeeded in reaching a point we called Bruins Peak, and from here we gained first sight of what we then believed to be, and afterwards discovered was, the East or Main Fork of the Quinaiult River. This part of the country is very peculiar and deceptive. The main direction of the Skokomish River from its head to the lake is almost east—to be more accurate 12° south of east. About 11 miles from the lake, a branch called Jumbos Leap, comes in from the south, while a mile above this junction a branch comes in from the north. This last is the largest of the streams and a true main branch of the river. The North, Middle, and South forks are fed by numerous small streams and rills, each of which is separated from the other by steep, precipitous hills. This renders the country not only difficult, but dangerous for travel. After four or five days a route was blazed across the South Branch of Jumbos Leap, past the falls, to another supply camp called No. 6. This was about a mile above the junction of the North and Middle forks.[35]

The making of this trail was one of the most difficult and hazardous pieces of work of the entire trip. After cutting a zigzag trail up the steep side of the canyon and cutting

270

---

[33] "According to W. T. Putnam, Jr., the route over the bluff became known as 'The Devil's Staircase' during the 1890's after a visitor called it that upon returning from a trip up the river. Eventually the 'Devil' was dropped and the place became known as simply 'The Staircase.' Other theories have been advanced, however, regarding the origin of this name. About 1910 several miners blasted a ledge along the face of Fisher's Bluff, using powder provided by the Forest Service, thus eliminating the need to climb over the obstruction." Wood, *Men, Mules and Mountains*, p. 404.

[34] "This was Four Stream. Beginning with No. 4 and concluding with No. 9, where the mule trail left the river, each camp was located adjacent to a tributary of the North Fork. Although not so named, the various creeks later became known, through popular usage, as Camp No. 4 Stream, Camp No. 5 Stream, et cetera. Eventually the names were simplified to Four Stream, Five Stream, et cetera." Wood, *Men, Mules and Mountains*, p. 405.

[35] "The Skokomish was really two rivers—the *North Fork* and the *South Fork*—which came together near the Big Bend of Hood Canal. The expedition was traveling up the *North Fork*. This stream in turn had several 'branches'—the *West* or *Middle Branch*, now called Six Stream; the *South Branch*, known today as Five Stream (and sometimes as McKay Creek), and the *North Branch*, generally considered to be the main river (i.e., the *North Fork*). However, O'Neil refers, in both his notes and report, to the North and South Branches rather than to the North and South Forks, and he then speaks of the West and South Forks of the North Branch." Wood, *Men, Mules and Mountains*, p. 405.

through the woods about a mile and a half, we were confronted by the torrent of Jumbos Leap. This turbulent little stream rushed through a canyon not more than 80 feet in width and 80 feet in depth, and whose sides were perpendicular rock. Our scouts had crossed this by swinging to a tree which grew about 2 feet from the side, and, sliding down that, crossed the stream on a tree which we felled, and climbed the other perpendicular side with the assistance of trees and overhanging vines.

It was a difficult problem to cross our pack train, and we spent nearly a week in trying to bridge this, as there was no means by which to get around it.

The workers' camp had been moved from the supply Camp No. 4, to this point, which we called Camp 5. In bringing the supplies to this camp we had the first serious accident. Many mules had fallen and rolled down the steep hillsides, but none had heretofore been injured. On this move one of the best mules of the train, on the second pitch of the canyon hill, lost its footing and rolled to the bottom. When we got to her to relieve her of her load, we found her hind quarters so severely injured as to render her unfit for service for some time.

While at this Camp 5, a party consisting of Judge Wickersham and several members of his family came through with the intention of penetrating the mountains and coming out on the other side of Port Angeles. The Judge had been up the summer before, and had mistaken the North Fork for a pass, and thought it led direct to Port Angeles. His party, however, did descend the Dosewallips and, after almost incredible hardships, reached Hoods Canal and civilization. They were in the mountains about twenty days.

From this camp Mr. Church and Mr. Brotherton were sent to explore the main South Branch of the Skokomish River[36] from its head to where it empties into the main river, a few miles from the Skokomish Indian Reservation. We had been misinformed as to the size and length of this stream, and acting on the information received they had carried with them only three days' provisions. It took them, however, fifteen days to make the trip and they suffered somewhat from the scantiness of their larder.

The South Branch of the Skokomish is similar to the North, except that its valley is wider and contains very few narrow gorges. Its tributaries are very small until near its mouth, where it receives a very good sized stream.

Meanwhile the trail workers had been kept steadily at

the bridge, and after many failures succeeded in building a substantial crossing. The pack train was enabled to move the working camp to Camp No. 6. Here the same difficulty presented itself as faced us at Camp No. 4. We first made the attempt to work the trail up a ridge which lay on the divide of the Quinaiult River; and having cut over a mile trail up the steep hillside, the scouts returned with the information that it was impracticable to proceed farther with animals. All men were then taken from the trail and exploring parties sent out in every direction. After an absence of nine days a party composed of Sergeants March, Yates, and Fisher returned with the information that a route had been found to the head of the North Branch of the Skokomish. Here it was possible to gain the divide and descend to some valley on the other side. They were unable to tell whether this valley was of the Quinaiult, Elwha, or Duckabush. Up to this time we had no fresh meat, except a deer or a bear, which had been killed by former scouting parties. This party, however, ran across a band of elk, and killed several. Leaving Fisher to dry the meat, the two sergeants hastened back to report their success and show their spoils. All hands were immediately placed on the new trail. At Camp 6, we regretted the loss of Professor Henderson, who was called home on urgent private business.

During the next twelve days no incident of importance occurred. All hands were busy on the trail, except Packer Price and his two assistants, who were engaged in bringing up the supplies.

During this time we had several times sent back for supplies, our bacon having run short on account of the scarcity of game, and much wastage and loss was occasioned by the numerous falls of the mules while fording the streams, or losing their footing on the sidehills. The clothing of the men and their foot wear had also to be replaced.

On the 16th of August we arrived at Camp 9. Here we prepared to split up the main party, send off smaller expeditions, while sufficient numbers were left to carry the pack trains to the center of the mountains, where the smaller parties returning would report.

The Skokomish River, from the head of the North Fork to the lake, is a turbulent stream—a torrent at times, full of falls and rapids, until within a few miles of the lake. It is about 25 miles from its head to the lake. The Middle and South Forks are short streams, and their only interest is their turbulence. The Skokomish River, from the lake to its

271

---

[36] "The reader should not confuse this stream with Jumbo's Leap, the South Branch (or Fork) of the North Fork." Wood, *Men, Mules and Mountains*, p. 407.

mouth, is a very fair-sized stream, averaging in depth from 4 to 5 feet. Its great drawback is a gorge filled with rocks and boulders, through which it rushes. It is joined a few miles above the Skokomish Agency by the South Fork.

The formation of the upper river is massive slate, coarse sandstone, and a sprinkling of barren quartz and porphyry, carrying no mineral, with the exception of a small quantity of iron and the copper before referred to. The timber growth consists of fir, red cedar, Alaska cedar, hemlock, mountain hemlock, white pine, alder, and vine maple. The principal berry shrubs are of the heath, rosaceæ, and gaulthèria families. There was only one food plant found in the valley, which was a pucadenum, of the umbellifera family.

There was great difficulty in procuring forage for the animals. It was necessary to keep them back at the lake as much as possible, there they could get grass. The charges here were so exorbitant that I kept them at Hoods Canal as much as possible. We found no grazing until near the head of the North Branch, and even here it was dangerous to allow them to graze, as our botanist had found poisonous stagger weed (*Acconite montanus*).

Having come within a day's march of the divide, and feeling now that there was no doubt of the possibility of crossing it with a pack train, directions were given for the various parties to start on their respective trips. Mr. Church, with one assistant, was directed to proceed to the head of the South Branch of the Skokomish, from thence to the headwaters of the Satsop, to cross thence back westward, until he reached the Winooche, to go down that stream to its mouth, then to go up the Whiskan to its head. Mr. Brotherton, with Sergeant Yates, was sent down the stream first seen by the party of sergeants, while prospecting for a trail, and which I afterwards discovered to be the Duckabush, and to also find the headwaters of the Dosewallips.

Taking Privates Fisher and Danton, I started out to find the head of the east or main branch of the Quinaiult, to follow that stream to the lake. From the lake we were to cross over to the head of the Humptolips River. The thorough exploration of this stream was not at first considered necessary, but the conflicting reports as to the source of the stream, the mineral wealth, the timber and agricultural lands, the general characteristics of the country, together with the communication from the assistant adjutant-general directing that if possible a thorough examination of the Humptolips and Whiskan be made, decided me to make as accurate a map

and gain as good a knowledge of the country as possible.

Mr. Church had very rough experience, his assistant, Dr. Church, who had recently come from Washington, D.C., had volunteered his services and was sent on this trip. Mr. Church once, while trying to scale a bluff overhanging the west fork of the Satsop River, lost his footing and fell several feet, and though his injuries were not severe, he lost much of his provisions, ruined his compass, and was left in an almost destitute condition. For five days they were forced to exist on berries or whatever other food they could find. The doctor had his first taste of shoe leather as a food.[37] After many severe trials the mouth of the Wonoyche was reached. The doctor, who had been crippled, was left at a farmhouse, while Church proceeded as best he could up the Whiskan. He was assisted much by the kindness of the settlers, who have taken up all surveyed land in that district.

This party reported their trip as having been very severe; that the country around the head of the south branch of the Skokomish is very ragged and of no use except for timber. The Satsop River is formed by the junction of five small streams, these formed from numerous creeks and rills. The Wynooche rises back in the mountains, and is formed from many small streams. The Whiskan does not extend as far back as the mountains, and has been surveyed almost to its head by or under the direction of the Government, and all sections laid off taken up either under the timber law act, or homesteaded, or pre-empted.

The incidents of the trip undertaken by me and our two men were as varied and dangerous as those of the other parties, and a few words will suffice to illustrate the character of the country. Camp No. 9 in the Skokomish Valley, was the cache from which all parties started. This was situated about 5 miles from the headwaters of the Forth Fork in the creek bottom. About 2 miles away was the summit of the ridge— the divide of the Skokomish and Quinaiult rivers. The top of the divide was 3,500 feet above our camp.

At 5:30 A.M. we started, loaded with 50 pounds a man. The hillside was so precipitous that were it not for the huckleberry bushes, which grew in great profusion, we would not have been able to have made the ascent. At 11 A.M. we had accomplished 2,000 feet. We had come to a perpendicular cliff of slate; our only hope was to find some place to scale it. There was no possibility of gaining the height at any other place; careful inspection showed a ledge, some places nearly a foot in width, others hardly 6 inches. This we essayed, and after hang-

---

[37] "An indication of the rugged nature of the country they explored may be gained by noting the word 'cañon' appears twenty-four times in the section of Frederic Church's diary devoted to this trip." Wood, *Men, Mules and Mountains*, p. 416.

ing to this frail support for nearly an hour and a half, we finished this first part of the climb by 1:30 P.M., having gained nearly 2,500 feet. By the side of a small lake we took a rest and lunch, then again the perilous work. At 5 P.M. we first sighted the Gibbon Range, with its snow-crowned peaks,[38] from the summit of the long-wished-for Quinaiult Divide.

Descending into the valley of the Quinaiult we caught an elk trail. Following this some distance, passing a huge sugar-loaf mountain standing alone, we came to where a mountain, almost denuded of timber, seemed to be the home of bear and elk.[39] One of the strangest freaks I have ever seen forced its unwelcomed strangeness on us. An elk trail as broad as a wagon road, as well beaten as a towpath, stopped abruptly at the edge of a precipice. How many elk had been fooled as we were! This nearly cost the life of some of our party. We attempted to climb down the promontory-like cliff, but after a short distance were forced to seek the bed of a dry creek; this, after we had followed it for some time, ended in a fall of some 50 feet. Toiling back, clinging to every bush, we finally reached a place where a smaller stream joined. From this we made our way to the bed of the main stream. Selecting as level a place as we could find we camped, as it was now dark. Early next morning, again trying to reach the river bed, Private Danton nearly lost his life. He was swinging to a ledge on a cliff when his feet caught, and but for prompt assistance would have been thrown below.

A little before noon we reached the bank of the Quinaiult River. This river heads at the base of Mount Anderson. On Mount Anderson are three glaciers; from these, streams are formed which form the main stream.

Mount Anderson, if not the highest, is as important as any mountain in this district. It is the most prominent peak—much more so than Mount Constance—in the southeast part, and at its base four of the most important rivers rise, viz., Quinaiult, Duckabush, Dosewallips, and a branch of the Elwha. It stands the second peak in Gibbon Range and bearings can be taken on it from any point in the mountains.

After a very heavy tramp of five days we reached Lake Quinaiult. This is a sheet of water about 5 miles in length, by 3 in width, and is very deep, many places 300 feet or more. It abounds in fish, and the Quinaiult salmon—found only in this lake and river—is said to surpass the famous chinook of the Columbia. Trout of all kind abound.

The country of the Quinaiult is very different from that of the Skokomish, the bottoms are much wider, the stream is not as turbulent, nor canyons as numerous. After the junction of the North and East Forks, about 10 miles from the lake, the river becomes a large-sized stream, in spring very rapid. It was just below the junction that the party sent by the Seattle Press met with an accident, by the capsizing of their raft, which nearly ended in disaster. The North Fork is a stream nearly as large as the East Fork, rising just south of Mount Olympus. It has very little bottom land and is very boisterous. The valley from the junction is well adapted for agriculture. It is fertile bottom land, about 3 miles in width.

After spending a few hours as guests of a Mr. McCalla, which time was used in inspecting the lake and trying to get a photograph of it and the peak which stands like a sentinel over it,[40] we started for the Humptolips River. After a three-day jaunt we reached Humptolips City. This city has two houses and a name. Here I sent Fisher and Danton up the East Fork while I with an old trapper explored the North Fork. We spent altogether twelve days in this section, and then crossed over to the Hoquiam River.

My completing the Humptolips and the Hoquiam, finished the rivers on the southern slope of the mountains. A few words may give an idea of its resources, the resources of the country south of the main mountains. This extends from the Pacific Ocean to Hoods Canal, a distance of 65 miles. On the south it extends to the Chehalis River, a distance of about 25 miles. The soil, except in the southeast corner, is adapted for cultivation wherever cleared. The southeast, however, is very rocky. Timber is to be the great production for many years, and the supply does seem inexhaustible. The principal trees are fir, pine, red cedar, larch, alder, water maple. The red cedar and fir, however, are the most numerous. The soil where it has been cleared produces the first season, and requires but little cultivation.

273

---

[38] "O'Neil named what he thought was the main range of the Olympics for Brigadier General John Gibbon, commander of the Department of the Columbia in 1890. This range started near the southeastern corner of the Olympics and extended in a northwesterly direction until it 'sunk into low foothills.' The principal peaks were Olympus, Anderson, The Brothers, Ellinor, McMillan, and Lee. (McMillan, named for John G. McMillan of Hoquiam, was not identified as to location; Mount Lee, previously named Mount Meany by the Press Expedition, probably honored Major James G. C. Lee, the Chief Quartermaster at Vancouver Barracks.)" Wood, *Men, Mules and Mountains*, p. 414.

[39] "The second basin was the only one lying at the head of Upper O'Neil Creek, and the 'tall round mountain' was the peak northwest of O'Neil Pass. Many old, fire-killed trees still stand on its western slope, scattered among a thick growth of young conifers." Wood, *Men, Mules and Mountains*, p. 414.

[40] "McCalla's Peak was one, or perhaps all, of four summits rising in a compact cluster five miles east of Lake Quinault. The name did not last, and they became individually known as Colonel Bob (for Robert Ingersoll), Gibson Peak, Baldy, and Wooded Peak. On October 5, 1932, forty-two years after Joseph P. O'Neil first saw Lake Quinault, the Board of Geographic Names officially changed the name of Baldy to Mount O'Neil, although another mountain near O'Neil Pass was already known as O'Neil Peak." Wood, *Men, Mules and Mountains*, pp. 415–16.

There are some small patches of ground bare of trees, called prairies; these have all been taken; in fact, all surveyed land has been settled on and many squatters located on unsurveyed sections. But there is a great evil, one that will injure the development of the country; that is, large tracts of land controlled by one person or corporation. A large amount of this land is so controlled; three townships on the Humptolips has thus been kept from settlement. Besides this many other tracts are held from settlement unless settlers pay about three times the amount, or more, than that charged by the Government. This entire strip of country, about 60 miles in length by 25 in width, is what might be termed a rolling country, heavily timbered, but when cleared, very good agricultural land.

When we arrived at the Hoquiam River, we found it so affected by the tides that at high water steamers could navigate it for about 12 miles. At what is called the Hoquiam Landing, we found a small steamer and a party of engineers of the Northern Pacific Railroad under charge of Mr. Davis. They had been prospecting a route for a road from Grays Harbor to Crescent City or some point on the Straits. A point at or near Crescent City was thought by them to be the best point for a terminus. The road was found to be practicable. We traveled together on the steamer until Hoquiam was reached, where we separated, their party going to Aberdeen while we remained in Hoquiam to pass Sunday, as no means of transportation could be had.

The people of Hoquiam were very civil and hospitable, and make our stay very enjoyable. The day was spent in looking over the harbor and country around.

The resources of Grays Harbor are very great. Not only the country before spoken of, but the entire west coast north of it must here seek an outlet. The harbor is a good one. It has had very little assistance or work, yet vessels drawing 16 feet have sailed in.

It was now the 31st of August, and an immense amount of work remained, and I feared that I would be forced to abandon and send back the pack train for the sake of putting all men to work exploring, but the Board of Trade of Hoquiam offered to finish a trail into their town if I would use it. I accepted their offer, provided it was finished by September 25. I then started for Union City by steamer and rail. It would have taken me two weeks to have retraced my steps, whereas I could reach my mountain camp over my trail in a three days' march.

Mr. Bretherton and Sergeant Yates had a rough trip. They had followed the Duckabush divide, discovered the head of the Dosewallips, and traced the course of both streams to

Hoods Canal. Judge Wickersham's party had gone down before them, and had come out at the mouth of the Dosewallips some few days before. This latter party had suffered considerable from lack of food; one of the party had been poisoned, and was swollen almost beyond recognition.

There are only a few miles on the east side of the mountains—perhaps will average 5—fit for cultivation, the remainder steep hills or deep canyons. A large quantity of good timber is found, all of which is proved up on and sold to mills, but from the entrance of the canal little else of value is discovered. At the head of the canal the Skokomish Indian Reserve is laid out and inhabited by about fifty Indians. This is excellent land, and raises fine crops of hay, besides many cereals. These Indians are civilized, live in houses, own and cultivate farms, and are seemingly very prosperous; but their morals are the Indian morals—they are suffering from the effect of their animal life. In a few years they will be extinct.

The streams on the east side of any importance are the Skokomish, Duckabush, Dosewallips, and Quilicene; the minor streams are the Lilliwaup, Eagle Creek, Humma-Humma, and Fulton Creek; these last rise in the foothills and do not penetrate into the center of the mountains. Of all these the Skokomish is the largest and most important.

The mountains are more precipitous on this side; within 5 miles of the canal they are nearly as high as they are in the heart of the mountains. This stretch of country, rough, precipitous, cut by deep canyons and gorges, extends for about 35 miles; this country is absolutely unfit for any use except, perhaps, a national park, where elk and deer could be saved. The scenery is well suited for such purpose, and I believe that many views there are unequaled in the world.

By the 7th of September all parties had arrived in camp. While we had been scouring the country Mr. Lindsay and Sergeant Marsh had been left with eight others to complete the trail to the foot of Mount Anderson and get up all supplies. This had been finished by September 6, so that we now had an abundance of supplies in the heart of the mountains.

From Mount Anderson we were able to locate Mount Clay Wood, which I had located and named in 1885, while exploring in the northeast section of this district. Mount Constance, or the Three Brothers, can not be distinguished from the interior of this country. It is here where the party sent by the Seattle Press last winter made a mistake by attempting to locate points from these two mountains. They mistook Mount Anderson for the Brothers and probably Mount Clay Wood for Constance, and this miscalculation threw them probably twenty miles out of their course.

From our camp (14) at the foot of Mount Anderson, we could gain a fair idea of the general direction of the various directions of the different mountain ridges. There are three principal directions in which the mountains run, and form that number of distinct divisions. These ranges were called The Gibbon Range, the Miles Range and Hoquiam Range.

The Gibbon Range starts at the southeast corner at Lake Cushman and extends in a northwest direction to near the Quillayute River, where it sinks into low foothills. The principal peaks are Mounts Eleanor, The Brothers, Anderson, McMillan, Olympus, and Lee. The rivers are the Skokomish, Quinaiult, Duckabush, Dosewallips, Quiets, Raft, Ho, all branches of the Quillayute, and the Elwha. The lakes are Crescent, Quinaiult, and Cushman.

The Miles Range occupies the northeast corner of the district. The Jupiter Hills form the east part of this range. The principal rivers are the Quilicene and Dungenness; there are many small streams and creeks flowing into the Sound and Straits. Its principal peaks are Mounts Constance, Clay Wood, and Sherman; this last peak is now called Mount Angeles by the people at Port Angeles.

Only a portion of the Gibbon Range is visible from the Sound, while nearly the entire extent of this range can be seen any bright day from the steamers. The Gibbon Range shows well from the ocean.

The third—the Hoquiam Range—extends from Mount Anderson southward, then west until it loses itself in rolling foothills near the Pacific. Its northern slope is drained by the creeks flowing into the East Quinaiult, while the Satsop, Wynooche, Humptolips, and also the South Skokomish, drain its southern slope. The Whiskan and Copalis do not take their rise in this range proper, but in the foothills.

On our arrival at Camp 14, on September 6, we were all much worried at the report that it was impossible to proceed with the mules; they would have to be returned. Mr. Lindsay reported that he had used every endeavor to find a way out. In fact things did look gloomy, and it seemed as if nothing without wings could pass from that divide. Old tactics were resumed—every available man was sent out to prospect for a trail. My intention was to get into the valley of the Quinaiult. This meant getting down 3,000 feet from the divide—a feat that nearly cost the life of a man when we essayed it nearly a month ago. That time we had no pack mules to get down. After a search of thirteen days a place was found where, with

some work, a trail could be made passable. All hands were set to work. The river was 3,000 feet below us and the descent almost perpendicular, but by zigzagging—making nearly five miles to gain three-quarters—we finally reached the bottom. Camp 15 was made on the Quinaiult side of the divide. From this camp all extra baggage was ordered back. Each man was allowed one blanket and one piece of shelter tent; an extra pair of socks and one of under-clothes was to be packed in each knapsack. One month's provisions was reserved. Sergeant Marsh was ordered to take one man and the packers, bring the stores to Hoodsport, and be back at Camp 15 by the 22nd.

We had been much troubled by yellow jackets stinging the mules. The north slope of the Skokomish-Duckabush Divide, over which the trail ran, was so invested with these insects as to render it almost impassable. Numerous small fires were started to burn out their nests. These fires spread and when the train attempted to pass to Hoodsport the trail was almost obliterated. Two of the mules lost their footing and rolled over 100 feet, landing in the creek bottom. When they were again gotten on the trail they were found to be so badly injured that the packs were thrown aside and the mules abandoned. They followed the train as far as camp 6. The orders I had given to the chief packer were, should any mule in falling break its leg to kill it, but if injured and there was any hope of its recovery to try to leave it at any of our abandoned camps, so that if it recovered it could be reclaimed. When we had all gotten out of the mountains I sent Sergeant Marsh back to try and recover the mules and their packs. One mule marked B.C. had gotten as far as Lake Cushman and had died the day before the Sergeant arrived. The other he succeeded in bringing to Hoodsport. It died the day after its arrival.

The pack train on its return made two endeavors to pass this burning hill and failed. The men, discouraged, wished to abandon the attempt, and had a less determined man been in charge we would have been deprived of our pack train. Sergeant Marsh overcame all the difficulties, and returned at 5 o'clock of the day he was ordered to report.

On the 16th of September directions were given for parties to prepare for the final trip through the mountains. Two parties were formed. Mr. Lindsay, the mineralogist, a man who had spent many years in prospecting mountains, was given charge of the party going north. He was to find the source of the Elwha; to place the copper box of the Oregon Alpine Club[41] on the summit of Mount Olympus,

---

[41] "Since its inception in 1877, the Oregon Alpine Club had been placing copper boxes on the major peaks of the Pacific Northwest in order to 'keep a systematic record of all trips made to the summit of these mountains, either for pleasure or scientific study.' Climbing parties were expected to register their names in the books kept in the boxes and to write accounts of their ascents, recording such observations as might be 'of interest or scientific value.'" Wood, *Men, Mules and Mountains*, p. 401.

if possible; then send parties down the Ho and the three branches of the Quillayute. The party was to assemble some place on the Solduck and make for Port Townsend and await my arrival. This was one of the most important expeditions of the entire trip,[42] and I thought I had selected a competent leader. Mr. Lindsay was given Sergeant Yates, Privates Fisher, Danton, Kranichfeld, Hughes, and Mr. Bretherton, the naturalist. They carried twenty-five days' provisions with them.

I took the other party. Its purpose was to get the pack train to Tade Creek, a tributary of the Quinaiult, where the Hoquiam people were to meet us, then up the North Fork of the Quinaiult, over some of the country explored by the Seattle Press party, to find the head of the Quiets and Raft rivers and follow them to the ocean. The pack train, after we left it, was to follow the trail which had been cut by the Hoquiam people to Hoquiam, and there take a steamer for Portland. Coming down the divide was a dangerous piece of trail for the mules. Looking at them from below they seemed like flies coming down a wall. They had become accustomed to this kind of travel, however, and no mishap occurred. Soon we were traveling down the valley of the Quinaiult. The country was so comparatively open that in five days the train was able to make the forks, and for two days traveled behind the trail makers.

The day before arriving at the forks we lost another mule. We had passed the dangerous places on the trail, and were congratulating ourselves on having passed safely through the canyon, when we noticed a commotion among the mules. They had run into a yellow-jackets' nest. Blinded with pain, they broke from the trail; four made for the bluff. We succeeded in stopping three, but one passed, and with one bound was over the edge, and a dull thud told us that she had struck on the first ledge nearly 200 feet below. Under ordinary circumstances I would not have allowed anyone to undertake a climb so dangerous for so little gain, but this mule, in her pack, carried the coffee and some public papers of mine. By the aid of the omnipresent huckleberry bushes I swung down to her, followed by the packer, the doctor, and Haffner, and reached the place where she was held to the side of the cliff by two trees, which she had fallen into. It was impossible to recover anything except a small bag of rice

which had loosened in her fall. Her neck was broken. We continued our march, nothing of note occurring until we separated from the pack train the next day.

The 22nd of September was the day we sent the pack train back to civilization, while with Mr. Church, Dr. Church, and a Mr. West I took my direction for the head of the North Fork of the Quinaiult. Sergeant Marsh, with a man named McCarty, was directed to cross the Hoquiam Range and try to strike the head of the Humptolips River. We found the traces of many camps of the Seattle Press exploring party, and comparing their report, which I had with me, I found that it was a very accurate description of the country passed over. Their map, however, is not entirely correct, from the fact that they took bearing on mountains which they supposed were Mounts Constance and The Brothers, which were Mounts Anderson and Clay Wood. These mountains are much farther from the canal than the mountains they supposed they were sighting at. This threw their map and their position much out of its proper place. They must have traveled very slowly, for in three days we passed over the distance that they traversed in seventeen days.[43]

At the mouth of the main canyon we sought to make the divide, but were forced by the steepness of the mountain into the bed of a creek which joins the main stream at the canyon. This creek we called Canyon Creek. Its banks rose perpendicularly from its narrow bed, sometimes to the height of 200 feet. At every few rods cascades varying in height from 10 to 50 feet and the damp walls of porphyry presented a spectacle which might have at any other time pleased us, but now only wearied us. Wet through to the skin, and tired and hungry, we made camp in this rocky bed, having progressed only $2\frac{1}{2}$ miles since 10 o'clock A.M. The next day a little after noon we made a lunch camp in a beautiful park about 500 feet below the ridge of the divide. After lunch we pushed on to gain the summit, and here we behold far in the distance the sinuous course of the Quiets River wending its way to the ocean.

Mount Olympus, with its forty glaciers, loomed up above the jaggy mountains that surrounded it; its height has been heretofore greatly over estimated. The actual height, as taken by our aneroid while our party was at the summit, is only 7,875 feet, but its immensity make the mountains around it,

276

---

[42] "Although more than a century had passed since Captain John Meares named Olympus, no one had been near the mountain, unless one accepted the seriously questioned contention of B. F. Shaw (the discoverer of Lake Cushman) that he, in the company of H. G. Cook, Michael Simmons, and two Makah Indians, climbed the peak in 1854." Wood, *Men, Mules and Mountains*, p. 422.

[43] "This statement is both erroneous and puzzling. O'Neil did not go as far north as Low Divide, but he must have computed the seventeen days from the time the Press Expedition arrived there on May 5 until the party was picked up by Frederick Antrim on May 21 near Lake Quinault. The Press Expedition did not leave Low Divide until the afternoon of May 9, and reached the forks of the Quinault on May 17, eight days later." Wood, *Men, Mules and Mountains*, p. 435.

though they are only from 1,000 to 1,200 feet lower, seem insignificant. The Quiets River rises on the southeastern slope of Olympus, but it has large tributaries coming in from the south and the north; its general direction is almost due southwest. Mr. Church and the doctor were sent down this river. Mr. West and myself turned back to find the head of the Raft River. I was much disappointed, expecting to find the Raft one of the largest of the western rivers, that I had passed its source, which was so insignificant that I had overlooked it. On our return we found it and traveled on the ridge some distance to observe it and set its general direction. We then turned eastward to strike a stream on the other side of the divide which we knew to be the North Fork of the Quinaiult, or one of its tributaries. We reached it, but were unable to travel either on the ridge or hillside, and again forced into the bed of the stream.

Down grade is always more dangerous than uphill work. We had several narrow escapes. In the most perilous place we lost our footing and rolled together to the brink of a precipice, where we were stopped by a small tree that had fallen there. The only injury, besides some bruises, was a broken finger. This was the most severe accident that happened to any member of the expedition, and it was providential that traveling with so large a party over so rough a country no more serious accident should have occurred. Once again that day, in descending a place where the water fell about 15 feet, we attempted to slide down the rocks in a shallow part of the stream, of course, intending to go down feet first; but my spike catching in a crevice, I reversed my intention and position, and dove into a deep pool of water. It was fortunately so deep that I sustained no injury, other than breaking my watch and losing all the provisions I carried.

This stream increased in size very rapidly, fed by its numerous tributaries, and I was puzzled to know where it joined the North Fork of the Quinaiult. But what puzzled me more a little later was where the stream we had been following, a rushing, foaming body of water, fully 30 feet wide and from 6 inches to 5 feet in depth, disappeared and as completely as if it had never existed; and for three hours we tramped along in its bed, which was as dry as if water had never touched it. We dug several feet but found no water. At last we had about resolved to make a dry camp, when just in front of us flowed the stream, much larger than where it disappeared. We afterwards noticed a great many

of these freaks, the water sinking and again rising some 8 or 10 miles distant.

We had mistaken the location of this stream, for instead of flowing on to the North Fork it makes a curve and joins the main Quinaiult River about 5 miles above the lake. I called this stream the West Branch, for Mr. West. He proved himself a thorough mountain man.

On the 28th we arrived at the lake and were glad to get under shelter once more, for we had been in a drenching rain for three days and nights. After drying ourselves, we started in a canoe across the lake and down the river to the ocean.

The Quinaiult Indian Reservation extends to and includes the waters of the lake. It contains about 30 square miles and about 100 Indians.

The Quinaiult River from the lake to the ocean is about 35 miles in length, but it is rendered this long by the great number of bends, it being a very tortuous stream; with comparatively little expense it could be rendered navigable for steamers. The agency is situated at its month on the left bank of the river. It is a rather neat looking village.[44] The Indians all live in frame dwellings, some of which are very comfortable in appearance. There is no agent there at present, and the school superintendent, Mr. Sager, is now in charge. The Indians are well-behaved, orderly, and have attained a higher state of civilization than any I have seen, and they seem contented. One of the saddest sights is the number of Indians that are blind, or nearly so. This is caused to a great extent by the smoke in their shacks.

When we started on the lake in our frail bark the rain accompanied us and was a constant companion during the two days we were paddling down the river; many times we were forced to land and bail out. About 7 miles from the agency the Indian habitations appear; they are spread with great scarcity down the river from this point. We stopped over night at Ha Ha a Mally's place; this place was occupied by Charley High as man Chow Chow and Ha Ha a Mally, and their squaws and papooses. It was any port in a storm, and the rain had given us such a thorough drenching that I was willing to go anywhere. I was agreeably surprised at the neatness of everything, and especially the cooking, the squaws even washed their hands before beginning the preparation of the meal, which consisted of dried fish, boiled potatoes, coffee, and bread. The rain had continued during the night, and was raining torrents when, after a warm breakfast—an unusual thing—we

---

[44] "O'Neil's impression contrasted sharply with Fisher's, the latter stating that he was 'disagreeably surprised with the appearance' of the agency. 'Instead of the neat and freshly-painted cottages that Uncle Sam usually supports,' he wrote, the village was 'a group of rookeries in sad repair.'" Wood, *Men, Mules and Mountains*, p. 435.

continued our way down to the agency, where about noon we arrived. We were treated very kindly by the superintendent, given dry clothing while ours were drying, and a good dinner. In looking over the reports of prior agents I found the reservation classed worthless land by many. The present superintendent seems to have inspected it more closely, and agrees with me that this land is exceptionally good.

The Indians are anxious to have their lands allotted in severalty. This would be advantageous, for at present there are very few Indians occupying this immense tract, and none of it is cultivated or worked, except a few acres near the agency. The reservation contains exceptionable land and very good timber; there is some swamp land near the center, but it is only about 8 miles in extent.

I had arrived at the agency on the 30th of September. At dinner I was informed that the party under Mr. Lindsay had passed through the day before, on its way to the O He Hut, to take steamer for Hoquiam, so instead of delaying here to rest I immediately started to overtake the party and arrived at Hoquiam on the 1st of October.

The party to explore the northwest section had suffered considerable hardships, and the travel was very rough. I do not feel satisfied, however, by the work done by them, and on account of the early camps made and the time wasted in them, they were unable to carry out their instructions. And I was much disappointed that I had no explorers of my party to go to the railroad engineers' trail at the mouth of the Bogachiel and Solduck rivers, where they unite and form the Quillayute. Still, this lack was supplied by Mr. Davis' notes, which were sent to me, and which I have freely used in compiling my map of this portion of the country. Mr. Bretherton fixed the copper box, containing records of the trip and records from the pages of the Oregon Alpine Club, on the summit of Mount Olympus, where, I believe, human foot had never trod. From this summit they could descry the Ho in the far distance. Private Fisher, who had been acting, and with much success, as botanist since Professor Henderson's departure, got separated from the party, struck the head of the Quiets, and followed it down to its mouth.

Two days later Mr. Lindsay got on the same river, and

having mistaken his bearing, thinking it was the Ho or one of the branches of the Quillayute, followed and got traces of Fisher, who had by that time become convinced that this must be the Quiets. The foot wear of the men, however, had given out, and the rations were low. Mr. Lindsay thought best to bring the party down to Hoquiam, where the various other parties I had sent out were to meet. Had this trip no results other than ascending the height of Olympus, it would have been a success, but though it failed in its exploration of the Ho and the Quillayute,[45] it located the head of the Elwha and the Ho—this latter from a distance, however—as I was afterwards able to supply most of the missing data of the Quillayute district. The Ho is the only river of the West that we must pass with no remark.

The country on the west side of the mountains is capable of great possibilities; though the undergrowth is rank and luxurious, and the entire country heavily timbered, it is no more difficult to clear than are the farms of western Washington. There are many patches of so called prairie land on all the rivers. The river bottoms have very rich soil, and are mostly covered with alder and vine maple in the valleys. All the country will eventually make good farm land. Before this is accomplished many million feet of timber will have been taken from it. With a market for the lumber there is hardly a quarter section that would not almost pay for itself. Our explorations or the reports received from auxiliary parties did not extend north of the Quillayute River, but from that river to Grays Harbor, a distance of about 80 miles, and for 25 miles back, the country is the same as that on the south slope of the mountains before referred to.

I have the honor to be, very respectfully, your obedient servant,

Jos. P. O'Neil, Second Lieutenant Fourteenth Infantry, Commanding Olympic Mountains Exploring Expedition

Remarks on the Olympic Mountains

In the summer of 1885, under the direction of General Miles, then commanding the Department of the Columbia, I made

---

[45] "The party sent to Olympus was directed to explore the Hoh and Quillayute, but failed to do so, and O'Neil was therefore displeased. 'This was one of the most important expeditions of the entire trip,' he wrote, 'and I thought I had selected a competent leader.' Although Linsley's men ' had suffered considerable hardships, and the travel was very rough,' O'Neil did not feel satisfied with the work done by them. He charged that 'on account of the early camps made and the time wasted in them, they were unable to carry out their instructions,' a criticism having some merit. He was also 'much disappointed' that none of the men had gone to the 'railroad engineers' trail' where the Bogachiel and Soleduck united to form the Quillayute. This lack was supplied, however, by the notes of Davis, which were forwarded to him, and which he freely used in compiling his map 'of this portion of the country.'

"As a whole, the assignment given [Linsley] was a difficult, comprehensive one, and he failed (perhaps justifiably) to carry it out in its entirety. Both he and O'Neil were probably at fault. The lieutenant expected too much but it is also apparent that Linsley could have made an effort to explore the Hoh and the Quillayute. O'Neil conceded, however, that Linsley had lost his bearing upon reaching the Queets and thought the river was 'the Ho or one of the branches of the Quillayute.'" Wood, *Men, Mules and Mountains*, pp. 437–38.

my first trip into these mountains. The strength of the party was eight men, and we had eight pack animals. We spent about six weeks, when I was ordered back to Leavenworth, and the entire party returned.

That time I started from Port Angeles. The trail was cut from that town southward to Mount Sherman. The name of this mountain has since been changed by the people of Port Angeles to Mount Angeles. Near this peak we found a pass which led across the first ridge of mountains to the head of what we called Hawgood Creek. The mountains of the northern slope, like those of the eastern, come close to the water. The first range is only about 9 miles from the Straits.

The trail from Victors Pass goes straight south until the ridge on the south side of Hawgood Creek is reached; it there tends southeast about 12 or 15 miles. In passing on this trail from the summit of any of the peaks the Dungeness River can be seen, while south of it the most eastern and northern branch of the Elwha runs.

The southeasterly direction of the trail is stopped by a very sharp peak; at this point it turns almost south for about 10 miles, when it was abandoned. On this trail some very fine but small valleys are passed. Game—elk and deer—were found in great abundance, and after passing the first divide, until the slope to this tributary of the Elwha, no undergrowth was found. There are three small valleys that at the time I believed would be valuable for small ranches.

The timber in all sections is much the same. Alaska cedar was found on the first ridge, south of Angeles, near its summit; a few trees of Port Orford cedar were found there as well as on the slope.

There is, I believe, no precious mineral in these mountains; some few specimens of gold have been found, but entirely placer. Captain White many years ago owned a place on White or Yennis Creek, near Port Angeles. He tried washing for gold. I have lately discovered that he stopped because it did not pay expenses. Gold has been panned on the Lilliwaup Creek in the southeastern section, but only a few colors were found. Old experienced miners prospected this place, and it is on record that a man panned $1.50 in one day. Even the most sanguine abandoned their prospecting trips. An article was shown to me saying that an assayer had determined that a piece of ore brought from these mountains carried $200,000 to the ton (estimate of Mr. Everett, of Tacoma, Wash.). I would unhesitatingly pronounce this bosh. Such ore never came from there. I found one man with some magnificent specimens of silver in the mountains. I took him with me, made him all kinds of promises, and at last found out that they were the products of a mine in the Cascade

Range. Many unprincipled men have done this and reaped rich harvests from speculators.

Quartz, porphyry, slate, and such gold-bearing rocks abound. In the valley of the East Quinaiult I found a vein of quartz fully 3 feet thick, but barren. Because quartz is found in gold fields it does not follow that gold is found in quartz fields.

The reason I assign for the absence of precious minerals here is that these mountains bear every indication of being of very recent formation, and I fully believe they are.

There is, however, a ledge of copper. I first discovered it in the Skokomish Valley, and afterwards found traces of it on the Wynooche, Whiskan, and Humptolips rivers; the ledge appeared to be the same, and was in the same formation. Parties are now prospecting this in the Skokomish, Wynooche, and Whiskan valleys. There have been no favorable reports of this yet received. The best indications I saw were at the head of the Humptolips River.

While out in 1885, south of Angeles, I found strong indications of iron. This was of magnetic quality, and its effect on the needle of my compass was marked. I did not, however, at the time examine it, and lost by a mule's fall all my specimens. Though many reports have been sent out about the quartz of coal of this district, I have seen no specimens, nor have I ever come across any indications. I made a diligent search for any trace of limestone and found none. There is in the copper ledge an agate that at first I thought might be some crystal of lime, but the mineralogist decided that it contained no trace of lime. I was also informed that on the Prairie River, a small branch of the lower Quinaiult, limestone was to be found; but in passing down by it I could see no formation to induce me to waste time in prospecting it, especially while I had three experts who passed within 10 miles of this creek, through a canyon where the walls had been cut several hundred feet, and while they were looking for it did not discover the slightest trace. As I reached Humptulips City great excitement prevailed because of the report that in the canyon, some 20 miles above, granite had been found. I took with me an expert I had sent to me for this special trip. I got down into the canyon, at the imminent risk of my neck, and the nearest approach to granite was porphyry.

There is a great wealth in this district, and that is its timber. It seems to be inexhaustible. A story was told by a man sitting near me in a dining room. He said that they tried to dissuade him from coming to Grays Harbor, saying that there was nothing there, and elk walked across the mouth of the harbor at low tide without wetting their bellies. "When I came," he remarked, "and found a vessel drawing 17 feet in the harbor and 22 feet of water on the bar, I concluded that a country that grew timber 12 feet in diameter, and elk with legs 22½ feet long was good enough for me." I could not quite agree as to the elk, but I have measured many trees over 40 feet in circumference, and some over 50 feet. The foothills are nearly all covered with fine fir and red cedar timber. On the Humptolips larch is found. At the head of the Quiets is an immense quantity of red cedar. Should the Alaska cedar in the Skokomish ever be gotten out it will prove more valuable than a coal mine.

As before mentioned, the land in the southeastern corner is not very favorable for agriculture on account of the stony soil, but with this exception the soil is very good, and a glance at the map will show how well watered it is. In the Quinaiult Valley, near the lake, an old gentleman invited me into his garden to help myself. I had had no vegetables for over six weeks, but from one turnip I made a hearty meal. The place where this garden stood was last winter a tangle of trees and underbrush. Near the Humptolips, in August, I was offered some magnificent strawberries, and that night we fed on peas, cabbage, and potatoes; yet last winter this place was a wilderness.

The game is very plentiful, particularly elk and bear; deer are somewhat scarce. I did not see as many elk on this trip as on my former. All the large game seeks the higher altitudes during the midday, but may be found in the valleys morning and evening. We were entertained one night in the latter part of September, when the elk were beginning to run, with the whistles of the bulls. This is sweet music in the wilds.

The black bear are the only specimens of bruin's family we ran across, or saw signs of; no new species were seen. This bear is cowardly and will on the slightest noise make away. We came across two exceptions, however; one disputed the possession of an elk with Fisher, who was armed with a small-caliber revolver; Fisher concluded to let the bear have the elk. Once again a she bear was walking with her cub; a rifle shot wounded her; she turned, her hair, like the quills of the porcupine, showing her anger; she was killed, however, before she reached the party. Cougar are found in the foothills; I have seen none in the mountains. Beaver, mink, otter, and skunk abound in the valleys. The whistling marmot is found on the rocky mountain sides. A small animal much resembling him, called the mountain beaver, if found

in soft places on the mountain sides. These are very industrious little animals and adept engineers; they dig canals to bring water to their holes and cut drains to prevent themselves from being flooded.

Trails

The trail made in 1885 before described is, I understand, still in use. This leads from Port Angeles to Noplace, in the heart of the mountains. [46]

There is a trail from the Quilicene to near the mouth of the Elwha River. Leading from Pisth southwest over the hills to the Pacific, near the Quillayute, is another trail.

Our pack mules traveled from Hoods Canal across the heart of the mountains to Lake Quinaiult and then to Hoquiam in nine days. This trail I hope will be a monument to the expedition. It is over 93 miles in length, through forests, across chasms, up and down almost perpendicular mountains, across rivers and torrents, and, worst of all, quagmires.

There are two termini on the east of the trail that may be taken at either Lilliwaup or Hoodsport, on Hoods Canal, to Lake Cushman; from thence it travels almost west for about a mile, crosses to the right bank, which it keeps until the miners' camp is passed about 3 miles. The river is then forded several times. Each ford is prominently marked. It follows the right bank after the sixth ford and continues until it passes the North Fork about 1 mile.

Jumbos Leap (the South Fork) is bridged. This might be now carried away, but the foot log will last for ages. From the camp (No. 6) the trail turns after crossing the river, strikes for the North Fork, and follows it for about 10 miles. At this camp (No. 9) it turns northwest, takes up the divide, and passes over into the Duckabush, which it follows about 6 miles, then turning southwest crosses the branch it had followed, and travels up the main fork about 4 miles, crosses this fork and ascends to the Duckabush-Quniaiult Divide; crossing this divide it descends into the Quinaiult which it follows to the lake; from the lake it turns south to Humptulips City, then southeast to Hoquiam Landing. A steamer can here be procured to Hoquiam. The trail is well blazed throughout its entire extent.

The expedition called much attention to this country. Since its organization the towns of Lilliwaup, Hoodsport, and Quinaiult City have been established and are on the trail. Last March there were 2 settlers on Lake Quinaiult; today there are over 125. The Quiets country has now about 60

280

---

[46] Noplace was perhaps an appropriate name for this camp—its exact location can not be determined today. Most likely the camp was in the vicinity of Cameron Basin.

settlers. Men were going into the mountains as I was returning. One of the great inconveniences of the trip was that a number of prospectors and others followed, and a guard had to be left at each cache camp to protect our stores.

The rare bits of scenery, the hunting and fishing, will always attract numbers to these mountains for a summer outing.[47]

In closing, I would state that while the country on the outer slope of these mountains is valuable, the interior is useless for all practicable purposes. It would, however, serve admirably for a national park. There are numerous elk—that noble animal so fast disappearing from this country—that should be protected.

The scenery, which often made us hungry, weary, and over-packed explorers forget for the moment our troubles, to pause and admire, would surely please people traveling with comfort and for pleasure.

I have the honor to be, very respectfully, your obedient servant,

Jos. P. O'Neil, Second Lieutenant Fourteenth Infantry,
Commanding Olympic Mountains Exploring Expedition

Following is a transcription of notes, written on plain, unlined paper with lead pencil by Joseph P. O'Neil, presumably as "aids" for a lecture to be given about his first expedition in the Olympic Mountains. The notes are undated, and are from the Robert B. Hitchman Collection[48] and from Mary Kegg, grand-niece of O'Neil. Hitchman obtained the notes from Mrs. O'Neil after General O'Neil's death.

The notes were transcribed by Robert L. Wood, as part of his preliminary research before writing Men, Mules and Mountains: Lieutenant O'Neil's Olympic Expeditions *(Seattle: The Mountaineers, 1976). In transcribing O'Neil's handwritten notes, Wood produced a literal transcription, including O'Neil's phonetic and sometimes illiterate spellings of common words. Even though O'Neil was an honors graduate of Notre Dame, he could not claim skills in English as one of his many accomplishments in life. The compiler has opted to bring, as precisely as possible, to the readers of this collection Wood's rendering of O'Neil's notes— bizarre spelling, lack of punctuation, and all, without the editing*

that would have made reading easier. O'Neil paid no attention to how the individual members of his party spelled their names. Bretherton is Brotherton, Linsley is Lindsay, and so forth. To those readers for whom such matters are important—beware. The strikethroughs are O'Neil's. Bracketed notes in the text are Wood's. Wood's longer transcription notes are in footnotes.

LECTURE NOTES OF LIEUTENANT JOSEPH P. O'NEIL FOURTEENTH INFANTRY

O'Neil's Notes—Set #1

[page 1]

In the summer of 1885 pursuant to orders of the Dept Comdr. Gen Miles.

Composition of the party

Harry Hawgood, C.E. S.P. Ry
Richard Wickersham Eng & Artist
Victor Smith —Port Townsend & Port Ang.
Eight Enlisted Men & 8 pack mules.[49]

Port Angeles Starting point—Smith invaluable

[page 2]

Tentative Route
    up the Elwha—down the Quinault.
    Started for the head of the Elwha—via the Tumwater and one party across country to the Elwha.

Cliffs, precipices and windfalls made going too hard.
Col. Chambers Brother for the S.E.

Port Angeles people gave help in cutting trail as it would be their County Road

[page 3]

Country not so difficult

White Creek

---

[47] "O'Neil's appraisal was valid. Within five years, Lake Cushman boasted a post office, stage line, and hotel accommodations. Guides were employed to conduct parties into the mountains, and visitors were urged not to fail to take the trip across the Grand Divide via the expedition trail." Wood, *Men, Mules and Mountains*, p. 436.

[48] The Robert B. Hitchman Collection is located in the library of the Washington State Historical Society, Tacoma. The Robert L. Wood Collection in the Manuscripts, Special Collections, University Archives division of the University of Washington Libraries, Seattle, also has O'Neil Expedition materials.

[49] Transcriber's note: Although the date of the notes is not known, apparently O'Neil either wrote these notes hurriedly, or his recollection was faulty. The name Habersham is given as Wickersham—apparent confusion with Judge Wickersham, whom he met on Skokomish in 1890; Victor Smith is substituted for Norman Smith, who was actually on the expedition, Victor Smith having earlier perished on the shipwreck of *Brother Jonathan*.

Proceedings—General plan laid down. scouts going out to Map trails—The route most promising selected —Trail cutters put on the job—Pack train move supplies from one Camp to the next.

The General plan was to strike the head of the Dungeness River cut south on the

[page 4]

divide that Separated the waters of the Elwha and Quinault from the waters of the Quilicene, Dosewallips and Duckabush, go down the Quinault to the Ocean, down the Coast line to Grey's Harbor.

After penetrating the Mountains to the interior to Explore by Means of scouting parties Mount Olympus

[page 5]

and other land marks and Key Points—

We got to Mount Anderson—recalled to go to Fort Leavenworth.

The rest is detail—Can be told in 5 minutes, can be told in 5 hours.

Elk Shoot
Outlaw
Cougar
Trail cutting

O'Neil's Notes—Set #2[50]

In the Summer of 1885 under orders of General Nelson A. Miles then Commanding the Department of the Columbia at Vancouver Barracks Wash I made my first trip into the Olympic mountains. The strength of the Party was Eight Soldiers of the 14th Infantry,

Mr. Harry Hawgood after Chief Engineer S.P.R.R.
Richard Wickersham an Engineer and Artist still living in Portland, Oregon
and Victor Smith the famous fighting Collector of Customs of Port Townsend who was lost at Sea many years ago.[51]

Eight of the Army's best friends of those days were with us a Careful pick from the famous Mule Pack train then assembled at Vancouver Barracks. I had been in Port Townsend and admired with youthful enthusiasm the Olympics—noth-

ing was known of the interior of the Country. The indians of the Coast would not pass the foothills and it looked as though the jumble of Jupiter Hills as the North East Portion of the Olympic Peninsula was Called would be a difficult trail cutting proposition. Mr. Smith had moved to Port Angeles, where there was a magnificent Harbor and saw mill two stores and a few shacks. He came with all the Knowledge he had gleaned from years of living on the North & North East fringe of the Country gave of his Knowledge and Volunteered his personal Services.

The Elwha the largest river in the North seemed to head in the center of these mountains. We knew the Quinault flowed in the Pacific in the South Western edge of the district. It would be a pleasant Weeks End trip up the Elwha cross the divide and meander down the Quinault. Four years later the Seattle Press did send a party over that route. It took six Months and most of the Vitality of carefully picked wood Men. I after the trip met one and asked him to join the party I was organizing for the 1890 trip—His answer was terse and positive "Never Again"—

Port Angeles was selected as the base. The Elwha-Quinault the route. We started bravely up the Elwha, ran into a windfall. We went around it and Came to another. We had gotten into a precipitous Country—where there were no windfalls there were cliffs and we had a pack train. Time was taken out for prospecting a route. The inhabitants were helpful. They explored and advised. A Mr. Chambers a brother of Colonel Chambers of the Army was most helpful. He had explored to the North East and knew the Country was much easier than the Elwha and after a careful study we decided it was; The Port Angeles people offerred to build 3 Miles of their County road for us—a route was prospected—the Port Angelenes and we started trail building. The trail ran approximately South East to near the forks of the Dungeness River. One of the points of interest on this part of the trail was White's Creek. Some years before a Captain White of the Revenue Cutter service had a ranch here was alleged to have found gold on the creek—many weary prospectors tramped all the stream beds but no gold was found. We did not stop—Mr. Chambers naratives made us prefer productive work on the trail to useless work on the stream. Hawgood and I in our youthful wisdom as we both had recently acquired pieces of Sheepskin which said we were Engineers and we both believed We were de-

---

[50] Transcriber's note: Another set of lecture notes: Also undated; handwriting poorer than preceding set, and shows lack of control, indicating elderly hand. Probably written many years after expedition.

[51] Transcriber's note: In these notes O'Neil persists in using the name Wickersham for Habersham and Victor Smith for Norman Smith. He refers to Smith as "Collector of Customs." Check date of shipwreck of *Brother Jonathan*. O'Neil's recollection must have been faulty.

cided that the Country was a result of a recent Volcanic upheval and too youthful to have Concealed about its person precious Metals—Strange to say that five years later during the 1890 trip Colonel Lindsay one of the greatest mining Experts in the United States an expert retained by the great Mining Co operations at Spokane Wash then in the heyday of its Wonderful Mineral development pronounced the doom of ambitious prospectors in practically the same words. Scouts were always Kept ahead prospecting trail route. Some days we would progress a quarter of a mile. Some days 5 or 6 miles, depending on the density of the timber, the fallen timber and the steepness of the ridges to be topped. Like the Buffalo trails on the plains forming the ground work of our great transcontinental roads of today the Elk trails were our great reliance in our progress into the Mountains, but like the buffalo trails the Elk trails did not always anticipate our wishes as to direction and after a few miles of comparatively easy travel we were often forced in our own devices to cut through wilderness Windfalls and build zig zag footpath to the summit of some frowning pass. The first twenty days we were forced to live on government rations, game was scarce around our Cook tent. This was probably due to the intense devotion to trail building and to the noise of the work and workmen. But Pork & Bacon, flour, beans, Coffee, though they are sustaining are sometimes improved by variety. Sgt. Updigraft and I took a day off to look for game. We traveled on a ridge and about 5 Miles from Camp came on the most magnificent Bull Elk I have ever seen. His perfect antlers are now in a Museum in Boston, Mass.

[Page 12 of the Notes is missing]

Elk then at a mountain near by then at the ground at my feet. I knelt to aim—with no better success, then laid prone and finally got the rifle mussle quieter. All this time the Elk seemed to have no interest in the proceeding. I fired—the Elk flinched, got to his feet and started to amble away. I use the rifle as a pump gun, Emptied the Magazine and the Elk kept on going. Sgt. Updigraft sympathised— We followed the trail—about 75 yards down the hill we saw the Elk—went to him—he was dead. The first shot had pierced the apex of his heart, all the others had missed. Have you ever had "Buck Fever"—well see your first 800 pound Bull Elk and try to shoot. We ran across three bands that day. One band across the Valley feeding. I fires one shot in the Air. Evidently the Echo confused them for they stam-

peded direct toward us. After a little they quieted and went on, grazing. The Elk at this time would not scare of [off?] and later on the year, the rutting season, would attack a man. My bull was tough but was Meat. Shooting was then prohibited except to Certain detailed hunter, who was required to Keep the Camp supplied with young Elk, deer, bear, pheasants or ducks and even he could not Kill while there was fresh Meat in the larder. On this trip we were tenderfoot boys from the plains tramping through the mountains, our first Experience of them. Many things were strange. Sargeant Updidraft and Sargeant Green once almost came to blows. They were out prospecting for trail and would signal by whistle. Green heard the whistle, rushed around a mountain to rescue Updidraft. Updigraft was rushing to succor green and they met. There were some recriminations and unfriendly feelings. Neither believed the other. When things began to reach a climax the Whistle sounded again. A little animal was sitting on the side hill. He gave the Whistle. Prairie dogs of the plains were Common to us and their peculiar squeak was well Known to these two men. The animal Whistled once More, his last. Updigrafts rifle killed him. He was brought to Camp and afterward discovered to be the Whistling Marmot. These animals were safe after this and it is pleasant when traveling through the wilds to hear their cheerful call.[52] My dairy [sic] shows Breakfast 5 A.M. trail cutting, supper 6 PM. Bed. The dairy gives these details in full but it is awfully dull reading. It is my dairy so not so good. Later in this paper I will give the Notes of Mr. J. Church on one of his exploring trips from the Main party of the 1890 Exploration. It may give you an idea of the details we go in while fighting our way through virgin Country. One or two days from this 1885 exploration may give a fair idea of our Sorrows and pleasures. On the 18th day we left our Camp at three holes at 6 A.M. This camp we named from three large deep holes very near together. At the bottom of each hole was a spring. There seemed to be no outlet from any of these holes yet the quantity of water never increased and the quality was pure, sweet and very Cold. Well we left Camp at 7 A.M. Five days had been spent in cutting trail for about six miles to Victor Pass a short distance from Camp was a stiff climb, about 1200 feet the trail zigzaged up. Just as the lead mule reached the top he refused to budge one step forward. He would back [brack?]. The Packer lost his patience and temper, there was a fight between Man and Mule, the halter broke, the mule fell backward rolled

283

---

[52] "How the confrontation between Green and Weagraff would have concluded, had the marmot not whistled again, is debatable. Green was six feet tall, Weagraff only five feet five and one-half inches. The latter is known to have been an expert shot, but Green may have been equally proficient." Wood, *Men, Mules and Mountains*, p. 396.

down the trail to the first turn then continued down the mountain. I believe I would have been glad had he gone on down alone and broke his neck but no such luck. In rolling down [erased] he made a clean sweep of all the mules following, knocking them from their feet and we stood watching our freight transportation rolling away from us. Strange not an animal was hurt bad enough to prevent it working. After expenditure of much time, energy, and language we got back on the trail and made Victor Pass that night. From the peaks on either side of Victor Pass we had our first good view of Olympics—exterior and interior. We could see Hoods Canal on the east, The Straight of Feucea on the North, a mass of Snow Capped mountains to the south and to the southwest a collection of peaks—no single one dominating the others but all dominating the surrounding country. This we called Mount Olympus. I determined to find which was Mount Olympus but was forced to wait another day and another exploring trip. From Camp at Victor Pass we continued trail cutting and exploring. With Mr. Smith I took the route east. From a high point sketched in the topography. Mr. Smith from a high point about $\frac{1}{2}$ a mile away also drew a sketch. Our orientation was the most divergent two reputed intelligent men could produce. I checked on him then he checked on me. To make a long story short I had selected a Mountain of Magnetic Iron. A compass was useless on or near it. That is the only mineral or metal of value I ever saw in that entire Peninsula. Up to now we had no derth of visitors. I did not encourage them nor was I a hail fellow well met, for it was work enough to provide food for hungry trail builders and a tramp to My Camp did Whet the appetite of visitors. But I did enjoy the visit of Mr. Chambers his daughter and son. They had a good view of the beautiful scenery—but a dense fog rolled in and it was difficult to make our way back to Camp. I remember the coolness & precision Miss Chambers showed in passing most dangerous & difficult climbs and if she still lives She can claim the credit of being the first White woman to penetrate the outer barriers of the Olympics to the interior. At Victor pass we checked our work. Then onward a general S.W. course. The going was fairly good. The trail was blazed perfectly. We arrived at a very prominent mountain I called Mount Anderson to honor the Colonel of my regiment. From the top of this mountain a good sketch could be made of the interior. It could not be accurate for this Peninsula is the result of a recent upheaval, and the force which threw them toward

O'Neil's Notes—Set #3[53]

Mr. Smith came suddenly on a bear cub. He attempted to capture it. The mother suddenly appeared, showing no appreciation of Mr. Smith's endeavor to pet her offspring. Mr. Smith did not stop to explain but broke the record of a 500 meter dash in coming back to me. The bear was not far behind. It was necessary to stop her with a bullet. We never saw the cubs again and Mr. Smith had lost all interest in them. We got back to camp late that night. We had been successful in our quest of the divide and having decided to spend next day in camp was not particular to be quiet and not awaken the sleepers. It is hard to find a shelter tent camp on a dark night so we yelled and made quite a racket. Lucky we were noisy, for on this day the camp had received notice that a noted outlaw had escaped, robbed a cabin in the woods below us and was now desperate for food. Posses from Dungeness and Angeles were scouring the country for him, and our camp was on the qui vive with the finger on the trigger. Our trail had cost much energy, hardship and work. It was so clearly marked that a novice could in a few days travers[e] the country it took us so many weeks to penetrate. I was soon to regret that our trail was so good as to make it possible for messengers from the outside to reach us promptly. Mr. Hawgood had about the most important job of all the parties sent from camp. He was to locate the headwaters of the Elwha. Some tiresome work was spent on these explorations and we were gathered around the council fire putting on a map the data collected. This work was interrupted by a messenger from Department Headquarters. I had been selected to go to the Infantry & Cavalry School at Fort Leavenworth to spend two years studing [studying] the Art of War on the banks of the muddy Missouri river. This trail was well made. For years it was called O'Neil Trail, then the name changed to government trail, and I understand there is now a well built road following some portion of the trail called government road. The Olympic Mountains when once you know them you love them, their grandure, ruggedness, & beauty. Wild life and plant life, the forrests, and glades, their streams and lakes, all that can entice the interests and desires of live he men they have, ready and willing to give you their joy of living if you have the manliness to desire it.

In 1890 unable to resist the siren call of the Olympics, I succeeded in having another exploration ordered and was

[53] These notes, which begin with page 26, apparently follow one set of notes owned by Robert Hitchman, which stop with page 24. Page 25 is missing.

lucky enough to be given command.[54] The party consisted of Colonel N. Lindsay, mineralogist, a noted mining engineer, Professor L. Henderson, botanist, B. J. Brotherton, naturalist, F. Church, mineralogist, Dr. J. Church, medical officer. The last two were recent graduates of Princeton University and foot ball squad. M. Price, chief packer, Sgt. Marsh, Yates, Haffner, Privates Barnes, Kranichfield, Danton, Hughes, Higgins, Fisher, and Krause. The last name broke down under the hardships and was forced to be carried outside. Mr. A. West [A Mr. West?] joined us in the interior. On the 24th of June 1890 the pack train left Vancouver Barracks and the next day the party followed. I let a friend read this manuscript. He said you are not mentioned as being in this party. Sorry I forgot to mention it. I was. This is just like the names I stuck on peaks and rivers. Every one had something named for him except me. I forgot to name anything O'Neil. We based on Port Townsend. On July 1st with a scow and a tug we steamed out of Port Townsend bay and after an all night run landed at the mouth of the Lilliwaup Creek. There being no dock and the steamer unable to get near shore we landed our supplies using row boats and canoes and threw the mules overboard and herded them to land. The provisions were shipped up the creek and stored at Mr. Taylor's Ranch. The pack train was sent forward loaded. The trail was represented as good. Lake Cushman six miles distance, a matter of only a few hours travel. The trail was not passable. The men sent ahead to clear the trail worked to exhaustion, a heavy rain came down to welcome our arrival and at the end of the second day still accompanied by the rain we raised our shelter Tent Camp on the bank of Lake Cushman. The was a beautiful sheet of water nestling under rugged peaks about $1\frac{1}{2}$ miles long by about 100 yards wide and very deep, abounding in fish, brook, lake and bull trout. A Mr. Rose had built a home near the edge of the lake, others had followed and squatters were on all sections of land between the Lake & Hoods Canal. Mr. Rose had built a raft on which he ferried his animals across the lake.[55] We used this to get our men, provisions and animals across and camped in Mr.

Windoffer's field. This was our first supply camp and all provisions were moved here.

July 5th the serious work of [the] trip was started. Scouts went up the Skokomish river to prospect for a trail. The landing was changed from Lilliwaup Creek to Hoodsport. The scouts report was that it would be to force our way forward. We started with saw, axe, brush hook, mattox, pick & shove[l] and I would advise Jack Dempsey to take up this line of exercise to come back. About 5 miles from Lake Cushman was a camp of copper mines. Their trail was a godsend to us. They were developing a copper mine. I sent Colonel Linsey to investigate for the chance of finding mineral in paying quantities. His report was brief. "None." I have never heard of that mine from that day to this.

On our 15th day the scouts on the North fork of the Skokomish succeeded in reaching a point we called Bruins Peak and saw what we afterward knew was the East or Main Fork of the Quinault river. The North Fork of the Skokomish we considered to be the main branch of the river. Making trail up this stream engaged our undivided attention, and bringing up supplies after the trail was built was scientific work. Chasams [chasms] had been bridged, trails cut up and cut around perpendicular clefts and at many places one false step by man or mule ment [meant] fini. From the head of the North Branch of the Skokomish we made Camp No. 7 and saw a stream on the other side. What stream it was puzzled us, then we later found that it was the Duckabush. Camp 6 Prof. Henderson was called home and Private Fisher was our only remaining botanist.

O'Neil's Notes—Set #4

[Note: Page #1 is missing]

The aborigines are of the great Coast tribe which extends from the Columbia River to Alaska. They are distinctively a fish eating people and pay little attention to the chase. Their legends and miths are very poetical. The raven represented their Chief, hero or god. Their contact with the

285

---

[54] "The record is not clear whether the idea of the 1890 exploration originated with O'Neil or Steel. The lieutenant was the prime liaison between the Army and the Oregon Alpine Club, since he was an officer in both organizations, and he obviously played an important role in the matter. The two men may have arrived at the idea simultaneously. The Oregon Alpine Club had been 'intended merely as an organization among half a dozen friends who were in the habit of seeking adventure and recreation in the mountains,' but rapid expansion led to reorganization in 1889, with its object the 'foundation and maintenance of a public museum, and advancement and encouragement of amateur photography, alpine and aquatic exploration, and the protection of . . . game, fish, birds and animals.' The club was divided into four departments—exploration, photographic, game protective, and museum. Steel was president of the exploration department, the branch affiliated with the Olympic expedition. Steel was a 'publisher and entrepreneur of real estate and natural scenery.' He promoted the creation of Crater Lake National Park, helped organize the Oregon Alpine Club (and its successor, the Mazamas), and intermittently published *Steel Points*—a little magazine dealing with 'various geographic and scenic subjects'—from 1906 to 1925." Wood, *Men, Mules and Mountains*, p. 400.

[55] "Rose died from smallpox in January, 1889, and the county took possession of his property, burned the house and barn, and paid the widow $1500. She moved to Olympia but later returned and the county built her a new home. Shortly afterward she married Windhoffer, who now operated the raft." Wood, *Men, Mules and Mountains*, p. 402.

whites have sadly demoralized them. I believe it was owing to their superstitious dream of this Country, for they formerly claimed it to be the Raven's home, that prevented them from making rails through it. Even to this day it is related by them that many years ago two powerful tribes went into the mountains to the head of the Wishkal river to hold a Council, and while there the ground opened and the mountains fell on them destroying all but one, who less timourus than the others would not venture into the valley.

The Country remained a terra incognita until 1885, when General Miles ordered my to make an attempt to explore it. Again in 1890 by direction of General Gibbon I was sent to complete the work left in 1885. Several attempts had been made between these years to find the secrets of this Country and an Expedition sent by a Seattle News Paper did penetrate from North to South.

Up to 85 no one could say what the country was, but when I came out of it that year I knew it was the last home of the Elk. The dense forests and denser undergrowth around the base of these mountains extending about twenty miles back from the water render all attempts to enter, but the most systematic trail cutting, abortive. The Rivers can not be ascended to the interior of the mountains on account of the swiftness of the Current and the numerous impassable falls, and it is to this that some portions are alive with game having no fear of man.

The country is rugged and abrupt. In the valleys run beautiful streams even in the heart of the mountains only seven or eight hundred feet above the sea and towering above them rise the mountains 7000 feet in the air. It seems to be but a collection of saw toothed ridges capped with snow crowned peaks crossing each other in every direction. Every now and then the forests on the mountain side disappear and plateaus sometimes 400 yards square and again several miles square, dotted with lakes and streams runing from the eternal snow on the mountain tops. These plateaus are ideals of beauty, the view of them picturesque beyond description. A dozen snow capped peaks sparkling in the sun before you and down in the dimy valley, the silver thread of water winding and turning in its tortuous way to the ocean.

The stories of the people about these mountains led one to believe there were vast deposits of mineral wealth, awaiting only the coming of a discoverer. I do not know but what this idea made me more anxious to explore this unknown wild than even the delight and adventures of a new country.

But the provoking coolness of my chief mineraligist, with his invariable, "Nothing here but sandstone" or "Nothing here but basalt," every new range we would come to , at last dampened my ardor as a prospector, but the wonderful beauties of the Country increased my ardour as an explorer.

In selecting the men for my party I was always fortunate in procuring one or two good shots, men who with a Springfield Carbine could cut the head from a grouse at 50 or 75 yards five time out of six. The first part of the trip meat was scarce as the constant chopping, sawing and shouting of the trail makers scared even the grouse. But when we got fairly into the mountains game was plenty. More so however on the northern and ~~western~~ slope than on the southern.

The first game I came across was what we call a panther, he was an immense fellow and followed the train for three days, getting bolder and bolder but keeping out of reach during the day. The third night he came almost to the picket line, and I was suddenly awakened from sleep by the long, weird howl not twenty feet from my canvas shelter. Our animals stampeded and our hunters feared to shoot. Wegraff the squirrel shot as we called him [two words illegible] fired at the place a second howl was heard.

The next day parties from the Coast visited us. They had a small spaniel and to test the truth of the story that Panther will not come near a barking dog we kept the little fellow. The dog was almost as disturbing as the panther but the latter gentleman never came near us again. Several weeks after one of the hunters brought in a panther skin but it was abandoned at a Cache Camp. I did not hear of a panther during my trip through the southern part of this Country, except along the Pacific Coast and Greys Harbor. On the [illegible; could be "7th A," meaning August 7] we had been trail cutting six weeks[56] and had at length gotten into the mountains out of the dense undergrowth. We had made camp early that day in a rich grassy bottom. Sergeant Weagraff and myself with our rifles started out prospecting for the next days trail. We had hardly gone a half a mile from Camp when we came across three Elk lying in the shade of a clump of pines. ~~They seemed comfortable in the shade, it was a hot August day.~~ Not looking for or expecting game we had come upon them without warning, and were not a hundred feet away. To my surprise they made no attempt to escape but calmly watched us as though we were objects of curiosity to them. Hastily selecting the largest one I fired. He rose seeming uninjured and walked about

---

[56] This is erroneous. Check the date the party started from Port Angeles, and add six weeks: July 17 to August 27—six weeks would be after the expedition was over.

50 feet away then fell dead. I had just touched the lower edge of his heart. The sergeant also brought down his elk. The third one seemed surprised, but made no attempt to run. I had pity for the magnificent creature and allowed him to escape.[57] The antlers of the one I killed stood nearly five feet ten inches long, and were the finest I have ever seen. They still adorn a dining room in Portland, Or. We had not tasted fresh meat for weeks, and hurriedly cutting a piece of Porterhouse we retraced our steps to camp for an early supper. The meat was quickly broiled, but our enjoyment was not great for it was the texture of leather and of very rank taste.[58] In examining his skin twenty scars were counted showing that he must have had some terrific battles in his day. Immediately after supper the Sergeant went a short distance from camp and shot a Calf. I went to him and there was a herd of about thirty cows and calves looking around in alarm, but seemed to pay no attention to us, after a while went on quietly grazing. When we walked to the edge of the heard [herd] where the Calf lay they started off, ran about a hundred yards and began grazing.

From that time on we ran across a heard almost every day. But no member of the party was allowed to kill an Elk without special permission, and this was given only when meat was necessary. One ~~morning as I was~~ day about noon as I was walking on the ridge I suddenly came on a band lying in a snow field. There were probably 50 or sixty animals. When they saw me they rose but did not run. There was only one old bull in the band and he was the most magnificent creature I have ever seen. He eyed me curiously. The sudden discovery gave me what is known as the buck fever, I threw up my gun and fired and missed him. The shot brought me to my senses and I was glad to see the band trot off down the hill unharmed. My party came up from below at the sound of the shot and we feasted our eyes on the noble band. It required the greatest amount of self restraint to keep from following and decimating the band, such is man's nature. But we were explorers, not hunters.[59] Five years later while on the south side of the mountains my hunters ran on a very

similar band. They could not restrain themselves and eight of those magnificent creatures fell in as many minutes. The party was delayed five days curing the meat which afterward formed [the] chief source of supply. Several weeks after this slaughter our meat again ran low and a hunter was sent out for fresh meat. Just across the ridge from the camp he shot an Elk, brought some meat into camp and early next morning a party started out to pack the supply into camp. While working Mr. Brotherton our Naturalist happened to glance toward a clump of timber and there asleep was a bull Elk. Mr. Brotherton went up to him with his camera, we then woke him up. He roused himself, with a half defiant look turned on us, stood as if posed, and when the camera snapped turned as leasurly as if he were the commandant of a parade and trotted off down the hill.

Deer are not so pleantyful in ~~these mountains~~. It is easy to find the Elk at any time in the Early morning or late in the Evening they are in the valleys near the head waters of a stream, during the day they gradually ascend until at noon they are found on the plateaus of the mountains or in the snow fields. During the spring and summer months the gulls seperate from the Cows. In the later part of September after the velvet has entirely disappeared from their horns they again join the band of cows which have been following a patriarchal old bull. During the nights of September and October is heard the whistling of the Elk the whistling of the Elk is most often heard. It is a most peculiar call, sweet and clear. Many a night have I laid on my bed of boughs on the mountain side, listning to the calling in the valley below. It is a pleasure one does not soon forget.

In this as yet almost unknown country the Elk are not the only attraction to the sportsman. There are not very many deer. But every mountain is the home of a family of bears. On Mt. Olympus while my party was on it, they saw twenty five in one day. So numerous were they that two of my best shots bought their discharge from the service and have established a very profitable [word illegible] Camp on the Q. River.

287

---

[57] "O'Neil wrote a different version of this incident in his [official report]. While the explorers were crossing a valley tributary to the Dungeness, he and Weagraff were traveling 'considerably in advance of the train' when they stumbled upon the three bulls and killed one. The party camped that night near the spot, and as soon as the steaks were ready, the men 'fell to it with a will.'" Wood, *Men, Mules and Mountains*, p. 397.

[58] "O'Neil's [official expedition report] . . . states: 'The flesh was a little tough and we afterward became such epicures in the matter of game meats that we wondered how we could have so demeaned ourselves by eating it, yet at the time we relished it, for it had been many days since we had tasted fresh meat.'" Wood, *Men, Mules and Mountains*, p. 397.

[59] "The lieutenant's [official expedition report] gives a somewhat different version of this (or perhaps a similar) incident: One day he and Weagraff took leave of expedition duties and went out 'to look for game.' They traveled on a ridge and about five miles beyond their camp came upon 'the most magnificent bull elk' O'Neil had ever seen. The animal was lying down, unaware of their presence. Stricken with 'buck fever,' O'Neil became highly excited and agitated. He began to shake badly and found it impossible to hold his rifle still. One moment the muzzle would be pointing at the elk, then at a nearby mountain, and a second or two later at the ground by his feet. Attempting to control himself, he 'knelt to aim, with no better success.' He then lay prone upon the ground, and 'finally got the rifle muzzle quieter. All this time the elk seemed to have no interest in the proceedings.'" Wood, *Men, Mules and Mountains*, p. 397.

But next to the Elk the greatest treasure of these mountains are its streams filled with trout. Prof. Henderson our Botanist was a thorough diciple of Isac Walton. He could gaze unmoved at a band of Elk but a line, a fly, and a quiet pool would lure him away from his morning's forty winks, even though a hard days march was before him. And our gratitude is due him for many a change from the regulation bacon breakfast to delicious fresh mountain trout. The streams are filled with these speckled beauties. The lakes are even as interesting as the streams. One morning before breakfast the Prof. took two men with him and within two hours brought back one hundred fish. Lake Quinault on the southwestern slope of the Mountains is particularly a paradise for fishermen, the lucious salmon trout are found in great numbers. Like all other streams that enter the Pacific Ocean in that latitude these streams are also alive with salmon, the magnificint Royal Chinook salmon, the delight of both sportsman and Epicure.

How long will this home of game be spared to us from the ruthless hand of pelt hunter. Settlers can find no lodgment in this rugged precipitious country, they will be confined to its outskirts. The miner will find his labor in vain. The timber is its greatest natural product. Vast forrests of fir, cedar, and some Alaska cedar clothes its slopes, but here will be difficulty to get at it. It has no geysers but every other requisite for a national park, as many wonders and natural beauties as can be found in any localities, and it is today the last home of the noble elk, where he is found untamed, and fearless of man. In a few years at most he will be missed from this home. Without some protection he soon will be what the Buffalo is to day, almost forgotten.

O'Neil's Notes—Set #5

[Pages 1 through 4 are missing]

blank phrases uttered in a quiet sotto sotto voice and the mule like a Cable Car shot up the hill. I felt satisfied and left the train to go ahead and select a Camp. The trials of that day were severe, and the party had to Camp along side the trail, and some had their first meal on Flap jacks and Water. A mountain flap jack consists of Flour, salt and water, and is when extremely hungry very palatable. It required until the 7th of July to get our ~~8000~~ 5000 pounds of supplies, over this trail with our pack train and cache them at Lake Cushman.

This lake a beautiful sheet of water about two miles in length by 1000 yards in width, and average much over 100 ft. in depth, seems to have been formed by the Skokomish river flowing into a deep basin and forcing its way out through the S.W. extremity. It is filled with fish principally Trout,

mountain and brook, which rise to the fly, though not particularly gamy. Our Proffessor (Henderson) in one morning Captured over one hundred.

The Skokomish river from the lake to the Canal is a large sized stream but rendered useless for all practical purposes by a very bad gorge through which it rushes. The scenery along it is very pretty and the fishing good and gamey.

[Page 6 is missing]

to procure lumber, and all building material had to be taken from the tree by splitting shakes, and a tunnel of nearly eighty feet run, and this by means of moderate circumstances and doing the work almost entirely without assistance.

Up to this point our traveling & trail making had been comparatively easy but from here on every step was gained by honest and persistent toil. Just outside of Camp 2 rose Fishers bluff coming down to the river's edge and the river in this place at this time a torrent. After some days spent in prospecting a way to move on we finally decided to bridge the bluff by building a ledge around its face sufficiently wide for mules when packed to pass, a rather large undertaking but a successful one. After going farther up the river we found it necessary to ford, and it was here that the expedition came near returning without a leader. A few rods below the ford the river narrows some, a tree was cut to fall across. I attempted crossing on it but a misstep sent me into the water and the current carried me under the tree. I got out, and made for camp, the trail was continued by the others. Sever work and constant fording brought us at last to Camp 4 but not without dangers. One of the coolest acts on the entire trip was when in making one ford the current threw one mule and carried it under a pile of drift and the packer a man of over 50 the one whos ability I doubted the first day lept from his mule into the foaming water and to his eminent risk cut the ropes holding the packs and freed and saved the mule. Little Frenchy it was called and he served us well.

From Camp 4 exploring parties were sent North, South, East to look for a way for a trail, to find the nature of the Country and study the mineral formation. After many days fraught with hardships and dangers a trail was blazed to the North branch of this branch of the river and by the 26th we had reached Camp 6 a distance of about 11 [?] miles from Lake Cushman.

During this time continual scouting was kept up, and many laughable, many serious incidents occurred. One of the scientists after ~~creeping hundreds of~~ creeping a hundred yards or more on his hands and knees to get a shot at a deer spent ten minutes, much strength and lots of profanity in trying to

288

pull off an Army gun at half Cock. He was not used to the safety notch. Messrs. Church & Brotherton had been sent to explore the main south fork of the Skokomish, and after many dangers and great privation having taken only 5 days provisions and were gone 15 days on very short rations finally getting over [out?] at the Skokomish Indian reservation. They arrived at Camp 6. the day the most discouraging news came. Our Scouts had been unable to find a trail over which we could bring the mules. We had been 26 days chopping & digging and were still in a valley where a man could not see 20 yards in any direction except directly upward so dense was the forest and undergrowth. But there is always a way to do a thing if you choose, still it looked as though the invention of a flying machine was the only solution to this problem. Every man however was sent out on a five days scout looking for a route, and when 17 men actuated by the same desire and working together on one plan they must succeed and we did get out of the valley or rather the cañon of the Skokomish after 45 days incessant work.

The bit of trail from the Canal to the divide between the Skokomish was a very heavy undertaking and cost much suffering labor and privations, but brought its recompense in the feeling that henceforth nothing was impossible. Its effects still linger around me for I essay a more difficult task tonight than the trip through the devils gulch.

After finding the possibility of surmounting the divide and getting my pack train into the heart of the mountains preperations were made for the great work of exploring. With supplies in the center and supplies easily obtainable on the outskirts we could work without fear of the dread enemy of adventure, hunger. This left us the privilidge of working from the center outward in any direction.

The Ducquebusch & Docewallups rivers puzzled us, we could not make them out. Reports made them little foothill streams, & here in the mountains they were large streams. Parties were sent down them to examine and report upon them.

(Show some Duckabusch & Doscewallups Views)

Parties were also sent down the Wishkan, Wynoochi, Satsop & humptulips rivers, the East Quiniault to the lake, this was to close the first half of the expidition.

These trips where the main party is broken up into bands of two or three are always fraught with danger. Mr. Brotherton & Sgt Yates twice barely escaped with their lives. Mr. Church fell from a cliff and but for striking in a deep pool must have been badly mangled by the rocks and bowlders. Our Doctor eat shoe leather for the first time and was so badly used up that when his party did reach civilization they were forced to leave him at a farmhouse for a week to recuperate. The

Quinault & Humptulips expedition I took Charge of, and the recital of the trials of this is a fair sample of the others.

Leaving Col. Lindsay in charge of Camp the Party moved out about 5.30 A.M. We were packed full 50 pounds each. The Camp was in the valley on the bank of the stream the ridge was only $1\frac{1}{2}$ miles away and 3000 feet above us, for the first 1000 feet rising in a rather gentle incline it seemed so to us, but it was nearly half again as steep as the Portland Heights Cable road way, going up the heights, the remainder was almost perpendicular or where any slope could be hoped for broken by rivines. This ridge never could be ascended were it not for the omnipresent Huckle & salal berry brush, but by clinging to these as we each time renewed our foothold we succeeded in passing the first 1000 feet. Here we confronted by a gulch flanked on the oposite side by a perpendicular cliff of slate. We paused for rest, and to examine [changed to look] for the best place to scale it. A ledge running diagonally across the face of the Cliff from top to bottom in som places as much as a foot in width and many others not six inches we essayed. I remember now so distinctly that climb. I had not attempted one like it for 5 years. The ascent of Mt. Hood, with out packs that twice before I had made was childs play. We moved, like men with their lives in their hands at stake. A miss step and there would not be enough left of one to weep over With hand and foot and eye in unison up, we breathed lightly as if in fear that the least extra weight would break our frail support and hurl us into an abyss below, litterally a bourn from whence no wanderer could return. No word was spoken but we moved as quietly as spirits, and when the top was reached Thank God would have been forced from an Infidel had one been there. We ascended 2500 feet by 1.30 P.M. and stopped for lunch. A comparison my be drawn between these climbs and Mt. Hood. Two years ago on Aug 12 we left our Camp at an altitude of 5000 feet. at 4.45 A.M. and reached the summit alt. 11,620 by 11.15. This day we left at 5 30 and gained 2500 feet by 1.30 and we climbed as steadily and were much better able to stand the fatigues on account of our two mounths roughing it. After a hasty lunch we moved on and reached the summit. Crossing we were on the land drained by the famous Quiniault. A mountain now called Arlene loomed in front of us shutting off all view of the river.

(Show Climbing Rocks)

Keeping up on this ridge we traveled until a Burned timber mountain was crossed, and attempting to descend. we had trouble we had in first gaining the ridge and we camped that night in Devils Gulch at Camp Purgatory, which was a rocky bed from which the stream had partly receded, we were

289

along side a water fall whose constant spray drenched us, to procure water one of us would anchor himself to a tree then form a line holding hands so that one could dip up a canteen full, without slipping into the deep gorge below, for it was impossible to hold on to the slippery rock with out assistance. Not other place could be found where we could lie down. In the morning we were up long before the sun and started on our climb to get out of this hole as soon as it was light enough to see. By noon we made the Quinault river. At this pint 5 miles below its head it is 1150 feet above the sea. The Skokomish at about the same distance from its source is about 1800, the Duckabusch & Doscewallups are nearly 2000, the Elwka 1650. While the height of the mountains around are about the same, this shows that the Quinault must have cut deeper than the other streams.

Tramping down the stream was quiet easy work for a day then because of our not crossing to the South side we experienced the difficulties of traveling the length of a Cross Cut saw, with mountains for teeth and the sea level for the blade. I have often thought of the Ant on this trip. An Ant makes a straight line for home. Should it come to a blade of grass it will climb one side and down the other, accomplishing much work and little gain. It was thus with us. After a half days march to find ourselves ten minute walk from where we started. We were under the disadvantage of it being impossible to go around. The Ant however had one advantage of us, it was possible for it to go around but all ways were equally difficult to us On account of Carring a Camera with 15 days provisions we did not feel justified in loading ourselves any heavier so no blankets were carried but in their stead a two and $\frac{1}{2}$ pound piece of Canvas by each. And rain with its usual perversity overtook us the 2nd day out, and for 5 successive days we had the unprotected benifit of it. Mark Twains advice to stand under a tree till it got wet through, then go to another was eminently practicable. Lake Quinaiult a beautiful sheet of water 2 M by 5 M long, surrounded by bare rugged peaks was shut in by the fog and rain, and its beauties we could not see. Securing a skiff we got across to where there was a settler a Mr. McCalla, who treated us cordially. We had slipped many times on the trip, which together with the dense undergrowth tended to render our clothing a little rugged and make more apertures than absolutely required for sanitary measures. When he found out that we had come in from the Mountains he asked if O'Neil's party were still in the Mtns (still in there). I informed him that part of it was Near Mt. Anderson at the head of the East Quinaiult, but when in answer to a question he was told that the Headquarters were in his cabin he mistook us for wags

290

joking at his expense, he would have been at least unpleasant for a while had I not informed him that I was the Lieut O'Neil and he Complimented me by saying I never would have thought it. We were all disreputable. The Clouds, rain, and mist played tag with each other all day, but I was unable to delay so went on the lake to take its picture after waiting for an hour the Clouds lifted slightly for one brief second, then closed down again. This is the result. A beautiful scene was found by the sun struggling through the Cloud and illuming the summit of McCalla's Peak for just thr [?] second and then the mist closed in and a heavy rain poured down all day. But we were forced to move on, for nearly two days we had been traveling wet Constantly to the skin, first by fording the river then the steady downpour. For three days the rain continued and we travelled for We finally reached Humptulips City. This City contains two houses and one family, and is situated on the Humptulips river about 18 miles above Greys Harbor. A rather large prarie covered with fern lies just west of it which is utalized for grazing a large number of Cattle. Here we ate our first civilized meal cooked in a civilized method, since leaving Hoods Canal, and the good people did no more than cover expenses when they Charged us 25¢ each. I really felt ashamed of taking so much and tried to slip in an xtra half dollar but his fraud was detected and I was given back the xtra change. Though I cannot say much for the size, business and general City appearance I must say that while their substantial Country food cured the inner man, and their honesty, hospitality, and evident desire to assist wanderers like ourselves was even a far better welcome back to civilization. Here I was joined by Surveyors of one of the trans-Continental R.R. we joined forces, and Continued the tramp 16 miles further to The party was here divided. Fisher & one man sent up the East Fork of the Humptulips, while I with an old miner started for the head of the W. fork. My original intention was to take a hasty look about the stream and pass on for time was important but the reports of great mineral wealth recently found there Changed my plans and the two parties spent 15 days Carefully examining the stream. I will refer to this later under the head of Minerals. When we returned to the metropolish we found surveyors Engineers of one of the trans-continental R.R.s awaiting our Coming. We joined forces and set out for the Hoquiam River to take the steamer for Hoquiam. Money had been an article absolutely useless to us, we therefore carried little with us depending on getting someplace where we could use Checks when we needed funds. The last 15¢ I had was used in ferring across the Humptulips river, but that did not trouble me for I felt that at Hoquiam any of the dealers would be glad to accommodate ~~me~~ us. Hoquiam was in my opinion a town of about 7 houses, 4 saloons a blacksmith shop, a Salvation Army Barracks and a Church. When we reached the town I was surprised to find such a neat, orderly, well laid out place. Lighted with electric lights, well kept streets, board sidewalks, a first class Opera house, and a hotel I have never seen equalled in a town ten times its size. Greays Harbor has been much misrepresented. The Sound, and Columbia River's mouth are the only harbors north of California state line surpassing it in the Amount of territory tributary. The building of large interests here both in lumber & manufacture must surely come in time.[60] A good Story was told there by one of the old settlers. He asked at Olympia how to get to Greys harbor. his friend tried to discourag him saying that the Country was no good, and Elk walked across the mouth of the harbor and did not wet their bodies at low tide. I came, said he, and found trees 12 to 16 feet in diameter and 22 feet of water on the bar, and a Country that Can grow such timber and Elk with legs 22 feet long must amount to something. He was not entirely correct for there is at low water only 16 feet on the bar in many places.

In the Army we are Nomads, here today and perhaps a thousand miles away next month. People may say what they choose for the East, but it is refreshing to see the push & Enterprise of the North West. While discussing my plans in Hoquiam I expressed a doubt of being able to push my pack trail through to the Pacific on account of taking away too many of my ~~explorers~~ scouts from Exploring work. The next morning I recieved a communication from the Board of Trade that if I would use it they would cut a trail to Tade [?] Creek in the Quinault Country. My answer was if it was done by the 17 of Sept I would accept it. The guaranteed it would be done by that day, and it was. Out of the 94 miles of trail cut while on the trip the people of Hoquiam cut over twenty five.

One day spent in Hoquiam and then all haste back to our Mountain Camp. The Camp had by this time been located near Mt. Anderson, and virtually in the center of the mountains, for within a radius of 5 miles were the head waters of the Skokomish, Ducquebusch, Docewallups, Elwha and East Quinault.[61] The advantages of having camp thus located are evident. Other attempts to explore these mountains were not successful because the adventurers took their supplies through and there only hope for more was to reach

civilization again, while we could leasurly look about in the very heart of this hitherto impenatrable range and feel sure of plenty near at hand. I reached my main Mountain Camp on Sept. 8 having been gone nearly a month from the main party. All parties had returned and reported except the Churches, who took in the Southern rivers ~~except~~ but the Humptulips. They did not return until the 22nd. The main party had during our absence become discouraged, finding no way to get down into the Quinault with the Pack train. This stream is very difficult to reach from the divide, and nearly a month before my two Companions and myself nearly lost our lives in trying to reach it. The old tactics were resumed, every man was sent from camp and every mile for fifteen miles carefully prospected and success crowned our efforts, a place was found after 13 days of Continued search.

All extra baggage was now ordered packed and allowing each men one blanked all other bedding was placed with superfluous stores and sent back to Hoods Canal. Perhaps a little incident which occurred here will show why this expedition was a success. The pack train had orders to be back by the 20 if possible but it must be back by the 22nd. The steep incline from the divide between the Skokomish & Ducquebusch was called Yellow Jackets' hill on account of the great number of these ~~pestiferous~~ natural history curiosities. A small fire had been started on the trail to burn out a particularly ~~large~~ nest which had rendered itself particularly obnoxious, this fire spreading the entire hill was ablaze when the train reached it. After a few unsuccessful attempts to pass it one of the train men discouraged argued to give up the attempt. The Sgt. in Charge quietly told him that they would reach my Camp or Hell by the 22. and at 5 P.M. on the 22., begrimed, bruised and exhausted they came to us. Two poor faithful mules blinded by smoke and wild from the stings of the insects stipped [stepped] from the narrow slippery trail and their bones are laid to rest in those hills over which they were the first of their kind to pass.

Here on the divide of the Quinault the party was to make its last meal togather, on the following Morning they were scattered in all directions, still keeping Organization. The district North of the East Quinault was given to Col. Lindsay who was to send parties down the Hoh & Quilihute rivers, the district south I retained to work the train to lake Quinault and then explore the Queets & Raft rivers.

291

---

[60] "Grays Harbor had been discovered by Captain Robert Gray in 1792, visited again in 1824 by Hudson's Bay Company men, and in 1841 by the United States Exploring Expedition. Settlers began arriving in the 1850's by way of the Chehalis River. Slowly but surely the area grew, development accelerating rapidly after the building of several sawmills in the mid-eighties." Wood, *Men, Mules and Mountains*, pp. 418–19.

[61] "The source of the Elwha was about a dozen miles to the northwest, but the heads of two major tributaries—the Godkin and the Hayes—lay within this magic circle. O'Neil probably considered the Hayes as the East Fork of the Elwha." Wood, *Men, Mules and Mountains*, p. 418.

The Colonel's party were to ascent Mt Olympus if possible and plant the box Containing the records of the Oregon Alpine Club, on the summit, and it is there, there where living man had never before placed his foot, and those who choose may not go & write their names on the roll of the Oregon Alpine Club. Speaking of mountains it seems strange to me why people go to foreign Countries for scenery. On Mt. Olympus are 40 Glaciers the smallest more than 2 miles in length. Forests were trees measure as large as 53 feet in Circumferance, Water falls some 3 and 4 hundred feet in heighth. ~~Elk, deer, Bear, Marmot, Cougar, Wildcat, Marmot, Minx, Beaver, & Many other are found. Fish the delight of many a Walton has been hid for ages in these mountains~~ Scenes that cannot be surpassed even if you should travel the world over.

If to us, tired & overpacked Explorers, Scenes were so grand as to enforce our attention and make us for the moment forget our trials, What effect would they have on pleasure seekers traveling with comfort and for pleasure. Had I the power of a Craddock to draw a pen picture of mountain scenes, I could entrance you. These Cold lifeless views, taken by amatures, Carried through rain, fog, & mist, tossed about at rude Camps, knocked among cliffs, with all their rough experiences, I hardly thought it possible to reproduce them. ~~Still they give only an idea~~ Still they give only an idea of scenes difficult to surpass.

But explorers could not live on scenery and the Colonel, finding the provisions decreasing rapidly felt it best to make his way out as quickly as possible, his party made the Queets river and followed it to its mouth.

While the others were enjoying Olympus, short rations and rain, we were dragging pack mules out of the mire and working like Trojans to get the train to Lake Quinault. The Hoquiam trail had been cut, and every thing was running smothely, we were almost out of the mountains when another faithful pack mule was killed by a fall. When I selected Mr Price as packer I inquired into his experience. He had followed General Gibbon in the Big Hole fight Campaign had gone with mules where no one had dared go before, and when I quietly told him to look out for his mules on this trip he had an air of cinicism. No trip could equal those he had been on. He changed his mind and statement before he had been out two months, and on the Quinault, where the trail climbs a sharp point where one con stand on the narrow three foot trail and see a roring torrent 200 feet below, on oneside,

and a black abyss on the other, he following the last mule up, when the dangerous pass was Crossed, the expression of relief that passed ~~over~~ his pale face made a lasting picture on my mind.[62] All seemed plan sailing now for I had run the trail back from the bluff, but the best laid plans are often frustrated. A yellow jacket's nest raised a stampeed among the Mules four in their blind agony headed for the Cliff, three were Caught but Weakback passed the men, one bound she went over the Cliff and struck a tree 150 [170?] feet below. I brought a pistol to shoot her, but there was no need her agony was short, and before we reached the place where she was held to the perpendicular Cliff by three trees she was dead. Under ordinary Circumstances I would have hesitated in sending any one down to where she lay, hardened to such climbing was we were, so dangerous was it, but three of us went to her, to save what we could of the pack. But our trouble was useless. ~~Now that the trip is over it seems providential to me that our only loss was three mules. I could take up hours this evening doing nothing other than relating perils and narrow escapes. But we all came back safe & sound.~~

At the junction of the N. Quinault & the East Quinault I bade good by to my pack train, sending it to Hoquiam & civilization while I with the two Churches and Mr West turned northward up the N Quinault, to find the Queets & Raft rivers. After 5 days difficult travel in three days of which we passed over the same ground that the Press party passed over in 17 days, we reached the Queets. The Churches were sent down this river. I was then ignorant that Col. Lindsay had mistaken and gone down this stream with his entire party a short time before. Mr West and myself retraced our steps to find the Raft river, this we found after some days of hard travel, and explored it until we could see its direct shoot to the Ocean, then we turned to find the head of big Creek, a tributary to the Quinault. We were successful in this also, and descended it. After a time the travel became so difficult that we were forced into the bed of the stream. We had two narrow escapes in this tramp and one incident which then did not seem ludicrous to me. We had come to where the stream jumped about 20 feet, the banks on either side rose precipitously a hundred feet or more. All we could do was select the most shallow part of the stream slide down with the water into a basin about 50 feet in Circumferance below, then swim for the rock. My original intention was to set down and go feet first but my heel spike catching a Crevice in the rock my intention was reversed and I went head first, the

292

---

[62] "The pack train had already filed through O'Neil Pass when traveling from Camp No. 14 to Camp No. 15. The 'sharp point' referred to was probably the difficult place in the elk trail on the western spur of the 'burnt timber mountain,' perhaps a mile beyond O'Neil Pass." Wood, *Men, Mules and Mountains*, p. 431.

depth of the water saved me from injury but Oh! it was so Cold. I lost in this slide several important official papers, with a notebook. I expect in about 2 years hens to carry on an animated correspondence with the 3 [?] Comptroller of the Treasury about this same fall and those papers.

This dry creek, I called after Mr West, who behaved so gallantly on this trip is a very peculiar stream, a body of water about thirty feet wide and at places 4 to 5 feet deep, disappears so suddenly that you doubt your senses for ten miles you can walk in a dry rocky bed and never dream that a large stream should run here 'til suddenly your progress is barred by a stream almost as large as the N. Quinault coming from the ground at your feet. The rain had kept us company during most of this trip and we were glad to get under shelter of a roof for a night. The next morning we took a canoe crossed the lake and started down the main Quinault river. This is a beautiful stream, and but for a few log jams & riffles would by navagable for small boats fro the lake to the ocean, a distance by water of thirty five miles. About 7 miles from the Quinault Agency which is on the Ocean beach, the indian habitations begin to appear. We stopped that night at Ha-Ha Mallay's Boston (white man's like) house. The squaws cooked us a very nice supper, and we laid by the fire place and slept that night. Outside it was raining pitchforks, and I was satisfied with my lot, though it did seem strange to be near the bounds of civilization and sleep on the floor by a kitchen fire, but we get used to many things in this life, and I found Ha Ha Mallay's Kitchen fire much more Comfortable than a log fire out in a pelting rain an hotel the entire party had during the trip. Next day Sept. 30 about noon we reached the Agency and how it did rain. I was in the bow of the Canoe looking out for bad places and guiding to good water, the rain Came down in such a deluge that were it not for the law of gravity the Canoe would have sailed upward. At length we reached the Agency, wet and chilled to the bone. Mr Ager the supt. treated us kindly allowed us to dry our selves and told us what had been going on in the world during the past month. Among other things that Col Lindsay of my party had passed the day before on the way to Hoquiam. I then surmised that the Col. had taken the wrong route and that my pet river the Quilihute was unexplored. My surmises were not entirely correct, for an auxillery party in the employ of a R.R. had taken in that river and their report Came a week or so ago. So that in my comming will take in every corner of the hither to unknown land.

The agency team was about to start for the Ohe-hut a distance of twenty three Miles, and being heartily tired of tramping we took passage on it and after a good days drive made the landing and took a sail boat for Hoquiam. Once more the party was united. We were feasted and made much of until the str. [steamer] Alliance hove in Sight then we disbanded again one part going on her to Portland while I had to go back to Townsend to gather up baggage that had been shipped from the Mountains.

A few words about the resources of this district and I have done.

About 4 Miles above Lake Cushman a Copper mine has been opened. It now bids fair to be profitable. This Copper belt is on the Southern slope of the Mountains Continues and Crops out again on the Winooche, Wishka & Humptulips rivers, that this will ever become one of the resources is a question on which our experts are divided— but should it be developed and found to pay it will become one of the richest districts in the world. Farther up the Skokomish Iron Crops out abundantly but it will be there for ages as it is so difficult to get at. Along the Lilliwaup Creek gold has been panned as high as $1 50/100 to the pan but it is found only in packets. After passing the divide slate is often found ground up with rotten quartz and many inexperienced persons are lead to believe that they have found galena but precious Metal is very rare. Though Quartz, Slate, Porphory and other mineral bearing rocks are found in great quantities, no indication of gold or silver was found. ~~I do not believe that~~ These Mountains bear every trace of being of recent formation, & I believe they were the last piece of our Country from which the ocean receded.

In timber it contains great wealth, the Alaska, Port Orford, and Common Cedar, White Pine, fir, spruce, Hemlock, Larch, Maple and found.

The Animal is represented by the Bear, Cugar, Elk, deer, Wild Cat, Marmot, Mountain Beaver, Bever proper, Minx, Otter Coon.

The streams are alive with fish the principal being Mountain, Lake Bull & Salmon trout. the various families of the salmon.

~~I have one wish~~ This is a progressive Country. Oregon & Washington have been heard of the world over. There ~~is a district of 2000 sqr. miles~~ is a country ~~nearly~~ absolutely worthless except for its scenery, and game, ~~the Noble Elk will soon be what the buffalo is today, known only from hearsay This territory flanked~~ This entire Olympic district except on the East by a 5 mile strip of land on the south and west by a strip of 0 miles and on the north by about ten miles, suitable for agriculture will remain unused.

Though we have no geysers (that I could find) there,

we have every other inducement, and as many wonders and natural beauties as can be found any place. We need protection for our game, the noble Elk will soon be what the buffalo is today almost forgotten.

[Fragments of two paragraphs, which could be called Set #6]

While making my first trip down the Puget Sound I was attracted by the noble front and snow clad heights of the Olympic Mountains. The Western tourist and the Alaskan sightseer are to day as I looked upon the beautiful creature who had fallen a victim to my rifle,—my heart was moved with pity to think of his untimely fate, and yet even in death ~~he was beautiful~~ He gave me an idea that living He must have been a dangerous antagonist. His antlers measured 5 feet from [two illegible words, written in different ink]

O'Neil's reports and notes conclude here, and what follows are newspaper accounts of the expedition.

Untitled[63]

A member of the O'Neil party, now engaged in exploring in the Olympic mountains, writes as follows of the Skokomish falls: These beautiful falls are at the head of the gorge through which the Skokomish river runs for a distance of about three miles. The whole body of water is here gathered into a space of about five feet, falling over a ledge in the form of a veil a distance of twenty-five feet into a very deep pool about thirty feet wide and forty feet long. At the end of this pool it makes another drop of thirty feet, and turning slightly to the left passes through a chute formed in the rock, and striking the opposite rock wall descends in a cloud of spray a distance of sixty feet, falling in a solid body into a rocky bowl, which causes the water to be thrown up again like the petals of a flower. From the foot of the falls perpendicular walls of rock rise 200 feet high on both sides.

Out of the Olympics[64]

Arrival of O'Neil, the Explorer, at Gray's Harbor.

Hills Adapted to Farming.

Splendid Timber and Fertile Soil—A Broad Trail Cut—Thoroughness of the Investigation.

Gray's Harbor, Wash., Sept. 3. Lieutenant J. P. O'Neil, of the United States army, who for the past two months has been in charge of an expedition exploring the Olympic mountains, was in Gray's harbor last Sunday, having arrived in Hoquiam the day before from the camp of the party down the Quinaiult and Humptulups rivers and across from Stevens prairie to the Hoquiam landing. In an interview with a reporter of the *Post-Intelligencer*, Lieutenant O'Neil gave an account of the work already done by the party.

We started from Hood's canal seventeen in number, on the morning of July 5, and cut our way by trail over the mountains nearly north across the divide and in the direction of Mount Constance. The trail was of sufficient width to admit the passage of pack animals with their loads of provisions. The trail was cut with a great deal of difficulty, but was finally completed to a length of forty miles and the main camp established on the Quinaiult, at Mount Anderson, just west of Mount Constance. Here are the headquarters of the party now, and the point from which the several smaller expeditions radiate.

My plan of work, mapped out before I entered the mountains and scrupulously carried out since, has been to assign a certain region of the country to smaller parties under the head of a chief, and to have them thoroughly traverse their respective territories and report in detail as to their characteristics at the main camp. For instance, various parties, numbering two and three each, have been sent down the rivers emptying into Hood's canal. One party, dispatched down the Skokomish, has completed its task. The last sent out is under charge of the assistant mineralogist and has orders to go to the Wynoochee river, get its general course and the character of its tributary country, and then to cross to the Wiskah river and follow its course to the mouth. This party, which started on August 14, has not yet been heard from. I took my course down the Quinault river to the lake and then crossed to the Humptulups at Stevens prairie. Here my party divided, and the mineralogist and a companion were sent up the east fork of the river, while a mineral expert and myself went up the west fork. You can imagine that we made careful scrutiny of this region, for we spent nineteen days in our investigations, whereas I had expected to devote only two to the Humptulups.

The sub-exploring parties now at work completely cover the eastern and western portions of the Olympics.

294

[63] Author unknown, *West Shore* 16 (August 30, 1890): p. 43.
[64] Author unknown, *Seattle Post-Intelligencer*, September 4, 1890, p. 9.

Their instructions are to report to headquarters at Mount Anderson, and thence they will immediately be dispatched to the north and west. You may remember that five years since I began explorations of the mountains from Port Angeles. It will not be necessary to traverse again the regions then explored, and not so much remains to be done in the north on that account. On the west, however, I expect to send parties down the Raft, Queets, Hoh and Quillayute rivers, emptying into the ocean. The largest of these rivers is the Quillayute and the strongest party will be sent to it, that it may divide and take in its three branches. It may be expected that all parties will have completed the tasks assigned to them by October, and they are instructed to report to me at Fort Townsend. I think we will be through by October 15.

What do I think of the Olympics? The country has unlimited resources of timber. The southwestern quarters from the mountains to the waters of Gray's harbor are exceedingly fine either for timber or agricultural purposes. I do not hesitate to say that the main slope of the mountains is toward the Pacific, and that its most valuable part is directly tributary to Gray's harbor. I have gone over a great deal of comparatively level land that can be described as magnificent for agricultural purposes. Of the rivers flowing down the mountains, the Humptulups is the most even. The bottom land tributary is covered with a light growth of timber, easily cleared. The hills back are heavily timbered with the same wonderful growth that thickly clothes the whole southern and eastern range of the mountains. Prominent among the trees are larch and Alaska cedar. The former is very fine for finishing purposes. All the timber is of the most magnificent kind and is easily accessible.

As to mineral resources of the Olympics, I can not yet say much definitely. To be frank, they have not come up to expectations. The assayer of the party, however, is now engaged in testing some copper ore taken from the Lake Cushman district. I am very hopeful that it will turn out to be valuable, and that the mineral resources of the Olympics may be very rich and varied.

Lieutenant O'Neil's main party with its pack animals will move down the Quiniault river to the lake on its way out via Gray's harbor. The route will be across from the lake to Stevens' prairie, on the Humptulups, and thence across to the Hoquiam landing on the Hoquiam river. A trail cut from this city to the Hoquiam landing will allow the party to reach here with facility, and to that end the Gray's Harbor Company offers to build a trail from here to Hoquiam landing, as well as to complete the partial trail from Stevens' prairie to Lake Quinault.

Another offer has been made by the people of Hoquiam to complete the trail at Quiniault lake and to bring the party across to Hoquiam landing and thence to Gray's harbor via Hoquiam. It is probable that the latter will be the route accepted, inasmuch as it was the first to be suggested.

Lieutenant O'Neil started Monday morning for Hood's canal. He will there follow the trail cut by himself and go into the main camp at Mount Anderson.

Hoquiam, Sept. 3. Lieutenant J. P. O'Neil, in charge of the United States survey in the Olympic region, left Hoquiam Monday morning on his way to join his supply team at the foot of the Lake Cushman trail. The lieutenant reports three facts of great interest to the people of the Gray's harbor basin: First, that rich indications of copper and iron are found in the southern and western slopes of the Olympics; second, that the highly-valued Alaskan cedar is found in large quantities in the western slope, and third, that the most natural outlet to this wonderfully rich and almost wholly unexplored region is down the valley of the Quinault river and the Humptulups to the north shore of Gray's harbor. The lieutenant has made arrangements with parties at this place to bring his mule train out from the Olympics and ship them to Portland from this point.

O'NEIL'S CARAVAN EMERGES[65]

The Pack-Train Arrives at Gray's Harbor from the pleasant Olympics

Olympia, Sept 27—[Special]–A Hoquiam special says: The pack-train of Lieutenant O'Neil's exploring party, in charge of Sergeant Hoffner, reached Hoquiam today. They crossed the heart of the Olympic mountains via the upper Quiniault river and the Quiniault trail to the Hoquiam river in charge of Sergeant Hoffner, who will proceed from this part [point?] by the steamer Allicane to Portland and Vancouver Barracks.

Lieutenant O'Neil, with the remainder of the party, will reach this point the 4th or 5th of October, and about the 6th a grand reception will be tendered the explorers in the Hoquiam. General John Gibbon and other distinguished guests are expected to be present.

295

A Trip Through Olympics[66]

A Young Englishman's Experience in the Mountains

Mr. F. Leather, who has been associated with Sanders & Houghton, the architects, returned last evening from a trip into the Olympics.

He started from Seattle on September 6, on board the steamer Josephine, destined for the Olympic mountains on a general exploring expedition, in company with Mr. Higgins and son, Mr. Hartney, Mr. LeBar, and Mr. Will Lawton. The whole party went as far as the Grand Divide. There Mr. Leather left the party and proceeded on to Lake Quiniault, took canoe and went down the Quiniault river, having a most exciting ride down the rapid stream, finally reaching the Quinault Indian reservation agency, which lies on the ocean. From there the party walked to Damon's Point, following the coast, and accompanied by two Indian guides, proceeded to Gray's harbor City, reaching it on Sunday last. [September 28, 1890] They found plenty of small game in the mountains, and lived high. Mr. Leather says they passed through some very wild country on the summit. The land in the Quiniault valley is very rich for farming.

At one place on the side of a bluff they found a mule lodged in a tree, where it had fallen from the trail above. It had a pack and blankets on its back. It was impossible to reach it on account of the dangerous position in which it was lodged. [O'Neil's Mule]

Two of the party were lost for two days on the divide. The party were without provisions, living on raw partridges for two days. The most experienced woodsmen and hunters frequently get lost, as owing to the peculiar rugged and irregular formation of the mountains, mistaking one peak for another. A member of the party found the rifle that the Barnes exploring party had dropped in the river. It was almost impossible to reach the summit on account of provisions giving out and the difficulty of packing provisions. Mr. Leather traveled alone for two days, moving very cautiously, as there was no trail to follow, but he finally reached the O'Neil expedition at the forks of the Quiniault, eleven miles above Lake Quiniault. [Reached pack train there?] The remainder of the party are still in the mountains, at the head-waters of the Quiniault river.

Mr. Leather's home is in London, where for some time he was associated with the London papers.

296

---

[66] Author unknown, *Seattle Post-Intelligencer*, September 30, 1890. Harry Fisher mentions the same Englishman in his diary entry for September 26. See part 3, chapter 15, Harry Fisher/James B. Hanmore.

CHAPTER ELEVEN.
FREDERIC J. CHURCH

Frederic J. Church was a pickup member of the O'Neil Expedition. He was living on the squatter's claim that he had taken up, near Lake Cushman, when the O'Neil Expedition came through. He asked O'Neil if he could join the expedition and O'Neil readily agreed. At twenty-four, Church was in vigorous good health and had prior experience in the Olympics from hunting trips, matching what O'Neil was looking for—"the assistance of good woodmen." Church also had completed three years of college, where he had acquired some background in mineralogy. He agreed to help in investigating the rock formations as well as writing dispatches about the expedition for the newspapers.

Church was born in Hudson, New York, in 1866 or 1867. After leaving the College of New Jersey in June 1887, he traveled all over the country for six months, ending up at Seattle, Washington, where he worked at sundry occupations. Church went east on a trip in May 1889, returning to Seattle in July. Because the fire of June 6 had destroyed the firm that last employed him, he went to Lake Cushman and took up a quarter section of government land. He was living on the claim when he joined O'Neil's expedition.

Church worked at various occupations throughout the West after the expedition, then entered the produce shipping business in Alabama. He died in Hurricane, Alabama, on August 14, 1914, at the age of forty-seven.

—Robert L. Wood
Adapted from Men, Mules and Mountains *(pp. 458–59)*

THE DIARY OF F. J. CHURCH[1]

Satsop, Whiskahl and Wynoochee

[Sunday] Aug. 17. Trip from Camp 9 O.E.E.[2] down the Satsop to Grays Harbour. F. J. Church & Dr. J. R. Church. We left camp 9 at 9:30 A.M. and reached camp 7 at 11:45 A.M. Taking dinner there. Immediately after dinner crossed the creek & took the hog-back travelling 10° W. of S., reaching the abandoned camp of the Expedition at 4:30. Dr. trav-

elled very slowly & being played out we camped. The ridge runs 10° N of W from camp.

[Monday] Aug. 18. Left camp at 7 A.M. & travelled due West along the divide all day; Passing the Bruin peaks[3] & The Cathedral rocks just West of Mt. Adelaide by descending to the South. Shortly after starting the Dr. shot a beautiful young martin. Took dinner by snow bank on ridge 2 m. from camp just E of Bruin peaks. Ridge runs 5° S. of W. Bearings from this point are—Mt. Churton 5° W. of S. The west peak of the Three Sisters (Between the Middle & South branches of the Skokomish) 15° E of S. 3 miles distant. High peak on the divide north of the West branch (that has a low saddle to the W. of it) 40° E of N.

Bearings from top of Mt. Adelaide—Bruin peaks, ¼ mile away 55° E of N. The divide between the West branch of the Skokomish & a river that the Dr. said was the Quinault but which I am pretty sure is the Wynooche runs due N from Bruin peaks. The West peak of the Three Sisters 40° E of S. Course of divide 60° S of W. A high peak which I christened Mt. raven on the divide north of us bears due N from Adelaide. Cathedral rocks 300 yards beyond Adelaide. descended & after skirting them reached the top again. Below us on the right the source of the Wynooche (?) rising in a beautiful lake. On the left a broad grassy valley with two small lakes[4]—the source of the middle fork of the Skokomish—The Wynooche (?) & the Middle fork of the S. run parallel, but in opposite directions for about one mile. Right below us on a snow field were four elk, one of which the Dr. shot. Packed some of the meat down a good elk trail to the lake at the head of the Wynooche (?) & camped. Christened lake & valley "Wapiti" lake valley & high peak 35° W. of S. from lake we christened "Wapiti peak. After shooting the elk we had a fine spectacle, one of the huge bulls refusing to run. We got within 30 ft. of him, holloed, threw our hats in the air & stones at him. After gazing at us for 20 min. he went off down the snow field with slow stately strides.

[Tuesday] Aug. 19. Dr. spent day in drying & smoking

297

---

[1] Transcribed by Robert L. Wood, December 1967. Strikethroughs are Church's. Bracketed notes in text are Wood's. Wood's longer transcription notes are in footnotes.
[2] Olympic Exploring Expedition.
[3] Bruin's Peak or the Bruin Peaks—the name is given both ways—was the high point on Six Ridge about 600 yards northwest of today's Camp Belview.
[4] The McReavy Lakes, or possibly two small, unnamed lakes just east of them. Church sometimes refers to Six Stream as the "West Branch" of the Skokomish; sometimes as the "Middle Fork." The McReavy Lakes were named in the 1890s for John McReavy of Union City, who accompanied the "Lake Cushman college boys" on a trek through the Olympics. The name has been corrupted since then to McGravey Lakes.

elk meat while I ascended Mt. Wapiti & took bearings. Ascent extremely dangerous. Bearings from summit are Mt. Adelaide 85° E of N. West peak of 3 Sisters 125° E of N. Mt. Churton[5] 145° E of N. Mt. Church due S. Mt. Constance 40° E of N, Mt. Olympus 35° W of N. Saw a number of ravens, who had a curious flight, turning over on their backs much like a tumbler pigeon & uttering shrill crys. Also saw a number of black swifts with an extraordinarily rapid flight. Raven peak bears 30° E of N. The mt. & ridge consisted of large masses of metamorphosed granite—often strongly resembling gneiss.[6] The blocks were full of minute particles of mica schist. Could find quartz & feldspar in only small quantities. The mt. slopes were covered with beautiful wild flowers in the greatest variety, most of them having a delicious odor.

[Wednesday] Aug. 20. Awoke in a dense fog. Waited an hour in hopes it would clear & then started up the divide. Spent 2 hrs. in getting over as we had great difficulty in finding the pass on acct. of the fog. Descended to the S.E. of Mt. Wapiti into the valley of the middle fork—passed along the foot of the cliffs—Most of the time being spent in scrambling over the huge blocks of granite. Shortly climbed up to the top of a high peak, as the fog seemed to be clearing. Waited some time, but being unable to see anything continued along the ridge. From the top of Mt. Wapiti,[7] and from a glance I got from this peak I felt sure that the river at whose head we camped last night swings to the south instead of the N.W. & runs past the W. slope of Mt. Church. My observations since & information that I have gathered strengthen that belief. Descended from ridge & lunched at foot of big snow bank right at the head of the middle fork. The geology of the whole region consists of great masses of muscovite—granite filled with mica in minute particles. & milky quartz. The stone is somewhat gneissoid of a light grey color. The cliffs at the head of the river consist of ledges of a fine limonite or brown hematite iron ore that seemed to be very rich. A little higher up were several croppings of light grey shale. After ascending we continued along a very narrow ridge, with a good elk trail along it, its course being 30° E of S. & apparently swinging still further to the East. Tried to descend in a westerly direction sev-

eral times, but found impassible cliffs. Could not see 50 yds. in any direction on account of the fog. Finally the divide about $1\frac{1}{2}$ m. from Mt. Wapiti ran almost due E & W[8] & descending a low saddle we came to a small stream running due S. Followed down stream on right bank & soon struck a good elk trail. This trail played us false, leading us on to a flat rock on a pt. between two cañons that dropped off 500 ft. on all sides,—what possible object the elk have in going down there I am at a loss to conjecture. Were forced to go back to the head of the river, and took down the left bank of the river. In about an hour came to another cañon almost as bad as the first with a stream coming in from due E. Decided to descend & had the most dangerous bit of climbing I have ever had; in 3 places had to drop some 10 ft. & trust to Providence to stick to the small ledges below. At last after several narrow escapes we reached the bed of the creek. Followed down the river, its course being S.E. for $\frac{1}{2}$ m—& made Camp in a good sized bottom covered with fir, on the right hand bank of the stream. In the bed of the river quantities of float of a red colored rock, almost exactly similar to the rock in the copper belt at lake Cushman. Broke several pieces & found two minute particles of native copper & a little iron sulphate.

[Thursday] Aug. 21. Arose at 5:30 & after cooking b-fast & doing a little mending started down the river. A short distance below camp a small stream comes in from the W., flowing due E. A half a mile from camp found a trail on the right bank with numerous axe marks as if it had been roughly cut out. Valley wide with good bottoms. Fog so dense that we could not see above the fir-tops. Just after striking the trail the stream sinks utterly & for nearly half a mile we travelled in the dry gravel bed. This bed consists of a very slippery bluish grey & greenish grey rock with milky quartz scattered through it in a beautiful spider-web like formation. There are also large masses of a green conglomerate. The body being green & the pebbles almost coal black. The course of the river S.E. most of the time varying from S. to S.E. At 9 A.M. it commenced to rain & was soon pouring down. One & one quarter miles from camp we came to the forks. The main river running a little N. of E. The river just below the camp ran due E. into a cañon & we followed the trail down the

298

---

[5] Churton was one of several peaks that would appear superimposed against each other when viewed from Mount Wapiti.

[6] Church's references to "granite" are puzzling. According to geologists, granite is not found in the Olympics except for glacial erratics left on the northern and eastern slopes by the Ice Age glacier that came down from Canada into the Puget Sound basin. Church probably mistook sandstone or quartzite for granite.

[7] A careful study of Church's diary in conjunction with today's topographic maps leads one to the inevitable conclusion that Church was in error. Observing the terrain from Mount Wapiti, he evidently mistook the upper canyon of Graves Creek to be a continuation of the canyon of Success Creek, thus gained the impression that the stream circled to the left, then flowed south. He therefore concluded that it was the Wynoochee.

[8] This short east-west ridge, just south of Sundown Lake, connects two north-south ridges, one lying between Six Stream and the South Fork and the Wynoochee. The north slope of the east-west ridge drains to the Quinault via Graves Creek, the south slope to the South Fork Skokomish.

right bank. After running E for $\frac{1}{4}$ m. the river turned & ran S. again, continuing a little E of S. all the rest of the morning. At 12 P.M.—reached a spot of the river which I recognized as being on the South Fork of the Skokomish. We the [then?] struck due West by compass & for the rest of the day & night were more miserable than we ever were before—It rained in torrents & we were bitterly cold, being wet to the skin. Dined off of dried Elk Meat, sitting in the rain—For one hour we travelled over a big rocky bottom, covered with small fir saplings. Shortly we started up a mt. side & until 5 P.M. struggled up the mt. Very steep & precipitous. At 5, being apparently no nearer the top than we were when we started we made camp on the mt. at an angle of 50°—Built a wall of rocks underneath a leaning hemlock & scratched enough dirt to make a level place 5 x 5 ft. Where we were comparatively dry. Got water by shaking the bushes into the frying pan—Christened camp Camp Foulweather—Passed a very miserable night being unable to sleep.

[Friday] Aug 22. The whole mt. is one mass of loose reddish grey gravel and shale. Awoke to the same miserable wet, rainy weather & again started up the mt.[9] In an hour reached a rocky peak, & the fog lifted affording a magnificent view. The valley of the S. fork extending 30° S of E below us. 70° E of N. Mt. Henderson, 110° E of N Hoods' Canal & far beyond the Sound.[10] Due west Mt. Church $\frac{1}{2}$ m. with very narrow rocky ridge connecting us. Travelled along the ridge the fog closing us in again and at 5 P.M. reached a huge snow bank. Camped. Soon began to rain, so built a shack of cedar bark.

[Saturday?] Sun., Aug. 23. Awoke with sun smiling on us but valley full of fog. From camp Mt. Churton bears 30° E of N. High peak due north of us $1\frac{1}{2}$ m. Mt. Constance 45° E of N. Mt. Eleanor 70° E of N. West peak of the 3 sisters 30° E of N. Before we got through breakfast the fog closed in on us again. Spent two hours trying to ascend Mt. Church but failed. Then descended to the South, and took West along the foot of the cliffs. Travel very dangerous. The Drs. shoes very much played out—patched them with cedar bark. On the East slope of Mt. Church we found numerous good ledges of specular iron ore or black hematite that was broken had a perfect metallic lustre. Course during the morning a little West of South. After dinner struck

due west, reaching the top of the divide in $\frac{3}{4}$ of an hour.[11]

It was raining hard and the fog was so dense that we could see nothing. Descended the western slope of the divide, and in a short distance came to a meadow with a stream running due North. We started up the stream, soon finding a good elk trail which within $\frac{1}{4}$ of a mile brought us to the ridge again, which runs N. & S. Followed elk trail in a S.E. direction down the other side, and within $\frac{1}{4}$ m. came to a stream flowing due South. Followed this down for $\frac{1}{2}$ mile & came to a very pretty lake & there camped. Christening lake & camp "Margaret" after the girl I left behind me.

[Sunday] Aug. 24. Awoke to a clear sky, but the bushes very wet. Around the lake were large quantities of penyroyal. In the bed of the river, above the lake fine blocks of a light pink sandstone that wd. make a fine building stone. Upon starting found that Lake Margaret has no outlet. the South end being surrounded with a high gravelly bank. Struck due S.W. by compass & for $1\frac{1}{2}$ m. passed through a wonderful country, rolling, but constantly descending towards the south, full of small ponds with streams running into them., but no outlets—The whole being covered with very fine fir & hemlock, the red fir predominating. In an hour & a half came to a stream flowing 20° W. of S., but afterward found that it ran due S., both above & below us, we being on a bend. Just above bend a beaver dam. The Dr. shot a duck, using his last round of ammunition and for dinner we had a stew consisting of flour, dried elk meat, bacon, duck, salmon, huckleberries and water. Very fine. After dinner started down the river, it flowing S. all the rest of the day through broad bottoms covered with magnificent fir. Travel very slow because of the numerous windfalls & dense undergrowth. At 3 P.M. I fell off of a windfall & broke my compass, the subsequent bearings being taken from the sun. They are fairly accurate as we had two watches. Made camp on left bank of stream at 6 P.M. The water in the river is much darker and less cold than that in the Skokomish. Fished without success.

[Monday] Aug. 25. Awoke to a beautiful day & found at last that the bushes were nearly dry. Started down the river at 7:30. One half mile below camp we found a good sized stream flowing in from the East. Course of river S.W. all the morning or rather S.S.W. Travelled about 3 miles during morning. 4 miles from camp river ran due West for $\frac{3}{4}$ of a

---

[9] Transcriber's note: Up to this point, the diary had been written with a blue-leaded pencil. At this point Church shifted to a pencil with hard black graphite, and the diary, though dim, is still legible.

[10] "This is the only reference to Mount Henderson in expedition diaries, notes, and other records, but the peak was obviously named for the [expedition's] botanist. However, Church either mistook Mount Ellinor for the peak or erroneously recorded the bearing in his diary. Mount Henderson should have registered 45° east of north, whereas Mount Ellinor would have been '70° E. of N.' When he took bearing the next morning from a nearby point, Church did, in fact, record that Mount Ellinor was '70° E. of N'." Wood, *Men, Mules and Mountains*, p. 417.

[11] Transcriber's note: At this point, Church shifts back to the blue-leaded pencil, and the diary is much clearer to read once again.

mile, then turned & ran due South. At 3 P.M. we came to a cañon & it took us all the rest of the afternoon to travel $\frac{1}{2}$ a mile. At 5 P.M. came to a good sized creed [creek] running into the main river in a S.W. direction. Descended & camped just below the forks. Just before striking the cañon saw two black bears wading the river, but having no shells were forced to let them go. The geology of the cañon is much the same as in the river above, consisting of sandstone & porphyry.

[Tuesday] Aug. 26. Left camp at 6 A.M., and were almost immediately forced to take to the side of the mountain on account of the cañon. All day long, we struggled along, making a bare 3 m. & having the hardest work we have ever had. The banks were so intersected with small cañons that it was impossible to walk on the ridge while the river was too deep to wade. The sides were always at an $\angle$ of 45° often of 70° & the undergrowth very dense. All the morning the river ran a little East of South. At dinner smoked our last tobacco & were forced to take to dried tea leaves. $1\frac{1}{2}$ m. from head of cañon river changed its course & ran due East for $\frac{1}{4}$ of a mile, then south, then south west: which it continued to the ft. of the cañon. At each of the angles a good sized creek comes in through a deep cañon, flowing S.W. The travel during the afternoon was worse than the morning travel. At 5:30 P.M. finding no place to camp descended to the river, and camped on a small gravel bar. The cañon, formed of very black rock, found several lumps of black oxide of manganese, on the gravel bar. Since striking the river have been living on half rations & now only have 2 half ration days provisions left.

[Wednesday] Aug. 27. Immediately after breakfast commenced to wade the river, and although at times we were in up to our arm pits & the water was bitterly cold we made the foot of the cañon & a broad smiling valley by 9 A.M. The river here resumed its general course, running 10° E. of South. Was certain by this time that it was the Satsop, but was afraid to go across without a compass & with no food. The river winds through broad bottoms of alder & vine maple. Many of them containing rich agricultural land. In the river bed I found large quantities of the B. oxide of manganese & a beautiful yellow sandstone which would make superb building stone. About 11 A.M. we passed some high clay cliffs with beautifully stratified formation, the strata running north & south, with a dip of 15° to the south. During the afternoon we passed numerous cliffs of a yellow ferruginous and argillaceous sandstone. The cliffs being some 200 ft. in height & first on one side & then on the other. I found also large quan-

tities of plumrose [?] gypsum or hydrous calcium sulphate. At 6 P.M. we camped on a bend of the river, dubbing the camp "Camp Hope"—About 2 P.M. we found the first signs of man, a bed of leaves and remains of a small fire—Just below this camp a very large beaver dam, a half a mile long, 30 ft. deep & filled with a dead forest, the trees having been killed by the rising waters—Along the shore numerous fresh signs of the intelligent animals—at the foot of the cliffs are great piles of a curious argillaceous stone, bright red on the outside, but pure white on the freshly broken surface. This stone was very soft, being easily whittled with the knife. On the plateaus all along the river on each side we saw beautiful fir timber. Travelled about 8 m. during the day.

[Thursday] Aug. 28. Left camp at 8 A.M. and travelled all day down the river. The character of the country & course of the river remaining the Same. At 10 A.M. passed a Small camp, in the which were the bones of the hindquarters of an elk. Two miles below camp "Hope" a small stream comes in from the West and one mile further another from the East. Here all along the river bed & in the cliffs we found Some very beautiful granitic concretionary, fossiliferous Sandstone, full of pure white shells of various sizes & shapes. Some of them would be 3 inches in diameter. The cliffs all along the river consist of a friable, argillaceous stone of a blue clay color. Saw numbers of ducks consisting chiefly of Mallards. ~~Mergans~~[12] Sheldrakes—What are known as "fish-ducks." The elk signs are fast dissapearing but bear, cougar, & raccoon fresh & in plenty. Do Beaver. At the base of each cliff is almost invariably a ~~cliff~~ shelf from a few in. to 20 ft. in width, raised only a couple of in. above the surface of the water & as level as a sidewalk. During the aft. we passed cliffs of a different character, being composed of a course, friable, pudding stone. 5 m. from camp Hope we came to a good sized stream running in from the N.E.—that is flowing S.W.—This we afterwards found is "The forks," but it cannot compare in size with the main river. Across the mouth of this stream was a chopped cedar log, one end of which had been sawed. About 3 P.M. we got out of the clay cliffs into some magnificent bottom lands covered with spruce, fir and curley maple. At 5 P.M. came to a small clearing on the left bank & found a small cabin with the following on the door—Notice —Satsop June 7, '90 Any & all persons are requested not to molest anything on these premises—John G. Foster—Any persons wanting this place can have it by paying John G. Foster for the improvements. John G. Foster, Administrator of Estate for L. A. Gates, June 24, 90—

300

[12] Transcriber's note: Apparently Church started to write "mergansers," then drew lines through "mergans" and wrote above "Sheldrakes."

Here we camped, calling the cabin, "Camp Realization." While cooking supper heard about a dozen rifle shots below us. Hunted all over the cabin for something edible, but only found 32 beans on the floor, which we carefully boiled.

[Friday] Aug. 29. Left Gates cabin at 6 A.M. & travelled for a short distance on a trail, but soon lost it, and for an hour were forced to wade the river again. Finally halloed & received an answer. In a short time perceived a little cabin perched upon a bluff & met Mr. John Singer, who took us in & treated us most hospitably. We spent the day at Singers resting & getting filled up. We found that we were on the West fork of the Satsop on the Township line between 19 & 20, N. R. 7 West. Mr. Singer has lived there over two years, and never heard of anyone ever having crossed before. Mr. Gates had been killed last spring by a falling tree.

[Saturday] Aug. 30. In the morning we, in company with Mr. Singer, followed the T.P. line East across to the East fork of the Satsop,[13] there finding a beautiful place owned by Mr. Etzeleski, who gave us a great treat in the shape of some new milk. From there we followed the road south, Mr. Singer kindly taking our packs on his pony. Took dinner at Mr. Turners, who gave us some information concerning Kelly—Kelly, Geo. Pratt & two others passed Mr. Turners about 6 Wks before—i.e., about the middle of July—Claimed to have explored the headwaters of the Satsop & Wynooche, in trying to reach Shelton, got lost & wound up on the E fork of the Satsop. Said that they left two rifles, & a shot gun & 100 lbs. of food up the Satsop. Found iron & copper, with large quantities of silver in the iron. Intend to go back & take a saw & a frow. Said they had found enough to make them all rich men. Gave Mr. Turner a description of the source of the Satsop which is absolutely false. Walked all day & reached Montesano at 6 P.M. Worn out. Put up at the Montesano house and were very hospitably treated.

[Sunday] Aug. 31. Sun. Spent in town, as we couldn't get out there being neither Steamer nor train. Met Mr. A. C. St. George Kemp who so ably assisted the Press Party. Mr. K. treated us with royal Kindness, let me a compass, gave us drawing paper & materials, placed his office at our disposal

& in general treated us as kindly as he could. Mr. C. E. Jamison, Mr. Bridges & others were very Kind to us. Mr. Jameson presented me with the original copy of the field notes of the survey of the Quinault & Quillieute Indian Reservations, dated Sept. '61.

Trip Up the Whiskahl and Down the Wynooche Rivers
[Monday] Sept 1st.—On account of the Drs. slow travel I decided to make this last trip alone & accordingly Sent him up the Wynooche to stop with a rancher named Est until my return—Left Montesano at 5:30 A.M. on the Str. [steamer?] Aberdeen & reached Aberdeen safely. Immediately went to see Mr. Fred Antrim[14] who treated me with the greatest Kindness, neglecting his business & devoting his whole morning to me. Outfitted & as the Whiskahl Chief was laid up for repairs was forced to hire a small boat, & reached The Forks, distant 15 m. & Mr. Fairfields at 5 P.M. where I spent the night. On the Aberdeen I met Col. Wilroy [Milroy?] who supplied me with the following information—14 yrs. ago the indians used to bring lumps of native copper from the head waters of the Wynooche & hammer them out into bracelets. Lumps of coal (a Lignite) as big as a mans head have been found in the beds of both rivers, but never anything but float. The indians say "Hiyu Coal" in the Mts—but refuse to say where—60 yrs. ago there was an indian village of 1,000 inhabitants on the ~~Wynooche~~[15] Whiskahl—that a medicine man got lost, became a bad Sewash & came & killed them all—For that reason the indians cannot be persuaded to go up the Whiskahl to this day—Whiskahl means "Stinking Waters" from the putrefaction of the slain indians[16]—They used to go up the WhisKahl, drag their canoes across & then go down the Wynooche. They now go up the latter river & on one of its branches obtain quantities of red & yellow ochre, with which they paint their faces & canoes—15 ys. ago an indian named "Teweet" [?] found a gold nugget worth $9.20 on the Wynooche. 18 yrs. ago the indians obtained a natural oil on the Humptulips river. The oil exuded from the ground & lay on the surface of the pools. The indians lay their blankets on the oil & when thoroughly saturated squeeded

301

---

[13] "This stream was later named the Tornow Branch for John Tornow, the 'Wild Man of the Olympics,' a bearded giant who sought seclusion in the southern foothills from 1910 to 1913. After escaping from a mental institution, Tornow shot two nephews he suspected were looking for him, although they were hunting bear. He killed several more men who were attempting to capture him before he, in turn, was dispatched by a deputy sheriff." Wood, *Men, Mules and Mountains*, p. 417.

[14] Frederick Antrim and his Indian guides were the first persons seen by the Press Expedition on the North Fork of the Quinault as they approached Lake Quinault the preceeding May. It was he who took them down the river in his canoe.

[15] Transcriber's note: Church had written "Wynooche," then ran a line through all except the "W" and wrote above "hiskahl."

[16] "This story resembles the legend reported by Governor Eugene Semple in 1888 that a great catastrophe occurred in the mountains during an Indian festival. The Indians had offended the 'chief of all evil spirits,' and most of them perished. Since that time, ages ago, the Indians had shunned the upper Wynootche." Wood, *Men, Mules and Mountains*, p. 417.

[squeezed ?] them out into cedar-bark buckets. The Whiskahl up to the Forks is a beautiful bottom valley, full of flourishing farms with fine timber on the hill-sides. Mr. R. informed me that all the trees having about 300 rings are charred inside within about 8" of the center. This would seem to indicate a great forest fire ages ago. Saw great quantities of wild geese flying south during the afternoon & evening.

[Tuesday] Sept. 2nd. Left the forks, in company with Aflred Clark at 9 A.M. feeling very miserable. Rheumatism in my back & limbs so bad that I could hardly travel. Reached a ranched [ranch ?] owned by two brothers named Boyce at 6:30 P.M. & was warmly welcomed. Fine agricultural land all along the river & by all odds the Finest Timber that I have seen.

Wed. Sept 3rd. Was so sick that I could not travel & spent the time at the Boyce's.

Thurs. Sept. 4th. Was still very sick, but left Boyce's at 9 A.M. & in $\frac{1}{2}$ a mile reached the forks. Took up the left hand stream—the main river, and soon came to huge sandy flat, very marshy & full of small pools. In this marsh the river heads, running off into innumerable small branches— this flat is 2 m. long & $1\frac{1}{2}$ m. broad & covered with fine spruce & hemlock & a few cedars. Head of the Whiskahl about 6 or 7 m. above the Boyce's cabin which is in the North end of 20 N. R. 6 W. After lunch struck a little N. of E. & travelled steadily all the afternoon, reaching the Wynooche at the head of the big Cañon at 7 P.M. Country between the rivers rolling, fine land, & covered with hemlock & fir—the timber as a whole not amounting to much— the underbrush is very thick, making bad travelling. Mr. Boyce says that 10 m. N. of his place there is a high fir-covered Mt. between the Humptulips & the Wynooche. The Boyce bros. are hand logging their own claims, the last 162 trees that they had cut before I met them averaged 7500 ft. of lumber to the tree. The last half mile of the way was through a marsh in the [?] which I sank up to my knees at every step. Upon trying to cook supper found that my flour had so much baking powder in it that I couldn't eat it, which added to the rheumatism brought my misery to a climax. Just before reaching the marsh I passed 7 elk within 50 yards—2 Bulls, 2 cows & 3 calves.

Thurs, Sept. 4.[17] Still very lame with rheumatics but left camp "Miserabill Dictu" early, started to wade up the river. General character much the Same as on the Satsop,

but the bottoms broader of river [upriver?]. Of course the usual clay cliffs with the little side walks underneath. About $\frac{1}{2}$ m. above the Cañon I saw numerous great slabs of a bluish green sandstone, some of them being over ten feet long—Just at the head of the big cañon, a short distance above camp a good sized creek runs in. course 12° S. of E—About 1[18] m. above the Camp the river makes a big bend. Course E for $\frac{1}{2}$ m. S. $\frac{1}{4}$ m—W. $\frac{1}{2}$ m—Just above the bend another Cañon. Much smaller than the first—About $\frac{1}{2}$ a m. long—Camped at head of 2nd Cañon—

Friday, Sept.5.—Shortly after breakfast met a man named Hamen [?] en route from the Humptulips to the Satsop, who Kindly changed flour with me—Traveled for two hrs. through some fine bottom land & then came to a third cañon at the head of the 3rd cañon the river forks. the main stream flows S.W. the left hand fork almost due East. Just below the forks a good sized creek flows in from the East, course 5° S. of W—Between the forks a high rocky peak with a large bank of snow on the N.E. side. This I climbed. Mt. Church bears due N.W.[19] The main Wynooche flows past the West side of the mt. The West fork seems to be about 3 or 4 m. & beyond the divide at the head is a cañon running S.W. in which must be the Humptulips. The mineral formation the same in every respect as on the Satsop. Camped at foot of the high peak that night.

[Saturday] Sept. 6th. Went up the river about 2 m., but as it got pretty small & my supply of provisions was exceedingly low I started down. Reached old camp at head of 1st cañon & as I felt very sick decided to remain. While cooking supper cougar came around, hit him with a fire brand & he howled & bounded off, but I sat up all night & kept the fire going.

[Sunday] Sept. 7th. Only got to the foot of the Big cañon, distance about 3 m. Cañon runs in the shape of a letter S, the sides consisting of black perpendicular rocks. At the ft. of the big cañon I found an old hut with some blankets in it.

[Monday] Sept. 8. Left camp feeling better. River continued its S. course, but greatly winding—at 3 P.M. reached a claim in Sec. 14, T.P. 20 owned by a Mr. & Mrs. Hayes. Remained there that night.

[Tuesday] Sept. 9. Travelled down river by trail, at night reached Mr. Carters and was most hospitable treated.

[Wednesday] Sept. 10. Picked up the Dr. at Mr. Estest

302

---

[17] Transcriber's note: Church had written "Friday," then wrote "Thurs" over it; also "Sept. 5" with a "4" written over the "5"—apparently the same day as the preceding one.
[18] Transcriber's note: Church had written "2," but wrote "1" over it apparently.
[19] "Church was obviously mistaken in his note of the bearing of Mount Church, which would have had to be directly east or slightly south of east. Perhaps because he was ill he misread his compass or recorded the observation incorrectly." Wood, *Men, Mules and Mountains*, p. 417.

& reached Montesano at 3 P.M. At Carters met a Mr. Bernston who says he has a claim on the Wynooche above the cañon.

Queets Trip

[Thursday] Sept. 25. Lieut. O'Neil, Mr. West, Dr. & F.J. Church left the Forks of the Quinault. Alt 375 ft. & travelled up the N. fork. Took dinner on a gravel bar. $3\frac{1}{2}$ m. from the Forks—Course of river from 35° to 22° W. of S. 4 m. from forks first cañon—Stillwater Cañon—Just above cañon river runs due south. $\frac{1}{3}$ m. above S. Cañon came to Hornet [?] Cañon—good elk trail up the left bank. $\frac{1}{4}$ mile above Hornet C. the forks—of the N fork. The left fork runs S.E., the right fork 55° W of N. 8 m. from Main forks—S. fork locally called The Rustler. Camped $\frac{1}{4}$ m. above the Forks—On the left hand Fork.

Sept. 25.[20] Shortly after leaving Camp came to a big cañon. Found elk trail on the left hand bank & blazes of the Press Party. At the head of the cañon $1\frac{1}{2}$ m. found an old camp—course of cañon due E, course above cañon S.E. alt.1700 ft. 1 m. above this camp came to the Foot of the Grand Cañon. 5 m. in length. here a stream, Cañon Creek runs in. Took up the creek. Creek formes a V with the points towards the S. general course during the aft. N.E. At night came to where the Cañon forked 3 times. Camped in Camp Paradise Lost, alt. 2675 ft.

[Friday] Sept. 26. $\frac{1}{2}$ m. from camp came to a broad plateau covered with heather—2 small lakes—Went west over the ridge, along an elk trail & over a second ridge. Camped at small lake at the head of the Queets river—Camp of the last parting [party?] Alt 3300 ft. [probably "last party" reference to Brother's trip to Olympus?]

[Saturday] Sept. 27. Party split—Lieut & Mr. West going down the Raft. Dr. & F. J. Church down the Queets. The two C's travelled along the ridge south of the Main Queets—Camped by two small lakes at night. Alt. 3800 ft. Trinity Mt.—30° E of N.

[Sunday] Sept. 28. Continued along divide, heard roaring of some huge water fall on smaller branch of Q—on our left—Came to where the ridge forked & took the right hand fork. Descended a hog-back reached the river at 11:20—Alt. 725 ft. Course of river W.S.W.

Mr. Brotherton's notes cover the whole river from here; and so I will not give a resume unless requested—

F. J. Church

OLYMPIC EXPLORERS[21]

First News From the Government Expedition

The Wild Grandeur of Nature

Tough Experience of Lieutenant O'Neil's Party up the Lillewaup trail Lake Cushman and the Grand Canyon Above Lake

---

The first news from the government exploring expedition in the Olympic mountains, under the charge of Lieutenant O'Neil, of Vancouver barracks, comes to the *Seattle Press*, through its correspondent, F. J. Church, who is also the guide of the party. Mr. Church writes:

On the morning of July 2 the steamer bearing our explorers stopped at the mouth of the Lillewaup creek, where they were told that was the proper beginning of the trail to Lake Cushman.

Too much can not be said in censure of such a statement. In the first place the people there knew perfectly well that the proper trail ran from the flourishing little townsite of Hoodsport—four miles to the southward, shorter than the Lillewaup by some six miles—and in perfect condition, both as to the grade and the absence of logs, and the second place they likewise knew that on account of bog-holes, or morasses, and precipitous inclines, the Lillewaup trail was neither safe for man nor beast. On account of this willful misstatement the expedition has been delayed at least three days; one of the mules was hurt falling down the trail, and several were almost lost in some of the swamps on the route.

Arrival at Lake Cushman

The lieutenant and scientists arrived at the lake and made camp one on Mr. Windhoffer's ranch on the west shore.

Lake Cushman, paradise for the followers of Issac Walton, is one of the most beautiful spots in this glorious land of ours. Nestled among the foothills of the Olympic range, at a height of four hundred feet above the sea, with the rocky crags and snow peaks hanging over it, and reflecting themselves in its placid bosom. The Skokomish river, forming outlet and inlet, runs through a valley of the most fertile agricultural land and covered with forest of gigantic fir timber. The lake itself is a mile and one-half in length, by half a mile in breadth, being of almost perfect oval shape, and abounds in two species of brook trout, which grow to a

---

[20] Transcriber's note: Church repeats the date of the preceding day.
[21] Frederic J. Church, *Oregonian* [Portland], July 19, 1890.

gigantic size, the red spotted variety running as high as fifteen pounds.

The Famous Copper Deposits

The trail from the lake runs up the south bank of the river for some four miles to the famous copper deposits, and from there all signs of civilization cease; the valley being a succession of fine bottoms and precipitous mountain sides, which in places approach the grandeur of a canyon.

Camp two is some two miles above the milling camp of the Mason County Mining and Development Company, and about six above the lake—although the trail has been cut some two miles further, a portion of it over cliffs and gulches which had to be bridged, the pack train now being engaged in bringing the remainder of the supplies to camp two.

On July 6, Colonel N. E. Linsley, the geologist, and Mr. F. J. Church, his assistant, were sent by the commanding officer as an advance well up toward the Grand divide.[22] The course led up the river bottom for some five miles, naught of interest being seen until an impassable canyon was reached, the water rushing forth from between two perpendicular cliffs at least 100 feet in height. Our travelers then breasted the side of the mountain on the left, following the well beaten elk trails where practicable, and ascending the ridge to a height of 1100 feet above the lake, or 1620 feet above the sea, according to the barometer.

A Grand Canyon

Last September a party of six followed the river to its source or rather thought they did, but our mineralogist proved them wrong, for it was simply a small fork of the river that they followed up, the main stream flowing from the northwest through a canyon inexpressibly grand. Black perpendicular rocks, dripping with moisture and covered with mosses and fern rise on either side, while far, far beneath the river roars, its waters at one time as blue as the sky above and then anon tossed about the rocks in sheets of foam as white as the driven snow. The explorers crossed the smaller fork on a small and slippery foot log, skirted the mountain and went up the main river, being forced to keep at a high altitude on account of the inaccessible canyon beneath. After proceeding constantly upward and onward for a distance of three miles, passing

through forests of fir and hemlock, with yew tree and white pine scattered here and there, a descent was ordered, and down they went, down, down—for fully two hours—being so situated that a single misstep would have meant instant destruction. At last the bottom was reached, and all that was found was snow—snow in huge drifts and snow in patches, and the river, naught but melted snow, tearing its way through the midst of the little narrow valley. There we made our second camp, the first night have been spent on the mountain, high above the Grand canyon.

Monarchs of the Forest

The whole valley was full of the most beautiful white cedar and red fir, trees that would cut 15,000 or 20,000 feet each; such monarchs of the forest as one does not often meet with. At daylight the next morning we were up and onward, crossing the river on a log jam, and then for two or three hours walking in the virgin forests with nothing to bar our progress except an occasional windfall. About noon this lovely valley was left behind—for lovely it must be when grim winter has loosened its hold—and climbing up over the mountain and descending the other side, we came to another and still larger fork, set in a canyon of black, forbidding rocks, much resembling the others that we had passed before.

A Real Tug of War

There was nothing for it but a descent, which was easily made—at times much too easily—and then came the tug of war. For two continuous hours we climbed that cliff, helping one another along and lifting up Tige, the canine member of the party, he finding it absolutely impossible to follow us. Forced to bear our whole weight on a small huckleberry bush or a branch of a yew tree, while every few moments some boulder, dislodged by our exertions, thundered down the mountain side and plunged into the cataract beneath. We found no sign of life of any description, even the small gnats and mosquitoes seeming to have deserted this barren region. At last the top of the canyon was reached, and after long rest we once more held on our way, our direction being southeast. With the Black canyon we left all trouble behind, the remainder of the journey being comparatively easy, and camp No.2 was reached about 6 P.M. on the 9th, where a very welcome supper greeted us.

---

[22] "Frederic J. Church was about twenty-five years old and had 'taken up a squatter's claim' near Lake Cushman after attending the College of New Jersey for three years. He had asked to join the expedition and O'Neil, who was 'anxious for the assistance of good woodmen,' had readily granted his request. Since he had some background in mineralogy, Church would help Linsley investigate the rock formations and he also agreed to write dispatches for the newspapers. His chief duty, however, would be to act a guide and scout since he had been on hunting trips in the Olympics before. Like Norman R. Smith in 1885, Church apparently exaggerated his familiarity with the mountains. He claimed that in 1888 he had gone as far as the 'Grand Divide' at the head of the Quinault; but, strangely enough, he was unable to direct the scouts as to the best route to run the mule trail, and they later experienced great difficulty in locating a way." Wood, *Men, Mules and Mountains*, pp. 83–84, 404.

One Blue Grouse

The only game we saw on the whole trip was one blue grouse, whose head the colonel knocked off with a bullet from his Winchester, although we passed elk and deer signs in plenty. The highest point reached was some 2200 feet above the sea and the distance traveled over only some twelve to fifteen miles but the difficulties to be encountered may be imagined in that the very inhabitants of the river valley supposed that the main body of the river above the Grand canyon was the small fork explored last summer and as far as can be found out the regions above described are absolutely unknown to the civilized world, at least, the copper regions above the lake are too well known to need a description. Above them were found principally basaltic formation in the cliffs and ledges. Above the Grand canyon a belt of red slate containing iron, black oxide of manganese and some copper was crossed, while still further up the river we discovered alternate belts of slate and porphyry with here and there a boulder of metamorphosed granite. The trail from there on will be explored by the geologist Colonel Linsley and your correspondent.

Above Lake Cushman[23]

The Progress of the Olympic Exploring Expedition.

Climbing Up a Huge Precipice.

A Tough Experience Up the Lillewaup Trail. Struggling Through Forest, Mud and Rain.

Olympic Exploring Expedition, Camp 2, July 6, 1890.

As is probably well known by our readers, an important scientific expedition has been sent out by the government for the purpose of exploring the unknown fastnesses of the Olympic range, and making a complete report on the geology, botany, zoology, ornithology, etc., of the surrounding country. The party, commanded by Lieutenant J. P. O'Neil of the Fourteenth infantry, consists of a geologist, mineralogist, botanist, naturalist, photographer, a guide, who is also the *Press* correspondent,[24] three sergeants, six privates and a packer. The personnel of the party, together with an account of the expedition up to July 2, has been published, and being

known to the public, will not bear repetition. On the morning of July 2 the steamer bearing our explorers stopped at the mouth of the Lillewaup creek, where they were told that was the proper beginning of the trail to Lake Cushman.

Too much cannot be said in censure of such a statement. In the first place the people there knew perfectly well that the proper trail ran from the flourishing little townsite of Hoodsport—four miles to the southward, shorter than the Lillewaup by some six miles—and in perfect condition, both as to the grade and the absence of logs, and in the second place they likewise knew that on account of bog-holes, or morasses, and precipitous inclines the Lillewaup trail was neither safe for man nor beast. On account of this willful mis-statement the expedition has been delayed at least three days; one of the mules was hurt falling down the trail and several were almost lost in some of the swamps on the route.

The lieutenant and scientists arrived at the lake and made camp one on Mr. Windhoffer's ranch on the west shore.

Lake Cushman, paradise for the followers of Isaac Walton, is one of the most beautiful spots in this glorious land of ours, nestled among the foothills of the Olympic range at a height of 400 feet above the sea, with the rocky crags and snow-peaks hanging over it and reflecting themselves in its placid bosom. The Skokomish river, forming both outlet and inlet, runs through a valley of the most fertile agricultural land and covered with forest of gigantic fir timber. The lake itself is a mile and one-half in length by half a mile in breadth, being of an almost perfect oval shape and abounds in two species of brook trout, which grow to a gigantic size, the red-spotted variety running as high as fifteen pounds.

The view from the east bank is grandly beautiful, the mountains rising on every side, abruptly from the margin of the lake almost to the line of perpetual snow. The lake was crossed on a raft belonging to Mr. Windhoffer, who has a ranch on the west bank, and the party partook of a plentiful and very welcome meal at his house. After a short rest camp was pitched and every person busied himself in getting things in shape. The next day being the Fourth of July, no move was made and the day was spent in fishing in the lake. Professor Henderson distinguished himself by a catch of nearly 100. The trail from the lake runs up the south bank of the river for some four miles to the famous copper deposits, and from there all signs of civilization cease; the valley being a succession of fine bottoms and precipitous

---

[23] Frederic J. Church, *Seattle Press*, no date. Reprinted in the *Tacoma Daily Ledger*, July 20, 1890; in the *Oregonian* [Portland] as "Olympic Explorers," July 19, 1890; and in the *Mason County Journal* [Shelton], August 1, 1890.

[24] Church here is referring to himself.

mountain sides, which in places approach the grandeur of a canyon.

Camp two is some two miles above the mining camp of the Mason County Mining and Development company, and about six above the lake—although the trail has been cut some two miles further, a portion of it over cliffs and gulches which had to be bridged, the pack train now being engaged in bringing the remainder of the supplies to Camp two.

On July 6 Colonel N. E. Linsley, the geologist, and F. J. Church, his assistant, and who also serves the *Press* as correspondent, were sent by the commanding officer as an advance well up toward the Grand divide. The course led up the river bottom for some five miles, naught of interest being seen until an impassable canyon was reached, the water rushing forth from between two perpendicular cliffs at least 100 feet in height. Our travelers then breasted the side of the mountain on the left, following well-beaten elk trails where practicable, and ascending the ridge to a height of 1100 feet above the lake, or 1520 feet above the sea, according to the barometer.

Last September a party of six followed the river to its source, or rather thought they did, but our mineralogists proved them wrong, for it was simply a small fork of the river that they followed up the main stream flowing from the northwest through a canyon inexpressibly grand. Black perpendicular rocks, dripping with moisture and covered with mosses and fern, rise on every side, while far, far beneath the river roars, its waters at one time as blue as the sky above, and then anon tossed about the rocks in sheets of foam as white as the driven snow. The explorers crossed the smaller fork on a small and slippery foot log, skirted the mountain and went up the main river, being forced to keep at a high altitude on account of the inaccessible canyon beneath. After proceeding constantly upward and onward for a distance of three miles, passing through forests of fir and hemlock, with yew trees and white pine scattered here and there, a descent was ordered, and down they went, down, down—for fully two hours—being so situated that a single mis-step would have meant instant destruction. At last the bottom was reached, and all that was found was snow—snow in huge drifts and snow in patches, and the river, naught but melted snow, tearing its way through the midst of the little narrow valley. There we made our second camp, the first night having been spent on the mountain, high above the Grand canyon.

The whole valley was full of the most beautiful white cedar and red fir trees that would cut 15,000 or 20,000 feet each; such monarchs of the forest as one does not often meet

with. At daylight the next morning we were up and onward, crossing the river on a log jam, and then for two or three hours walking in the virgin forests with nothing to bar our progress except an occasional windfall. About noon this lovely valley was left behind—for lovely it must be when grim winter has loosened its hold—and climbing up over the mountain and descending the other side, we came to another and still larger fork, set in a canyon of black, forbidden rocks, much resembling the others that we had passed before.

There was nothing for it but a descent, which was easily made—at times much too easily—and then came the tug of war. For two continuous hours we climbed that cliff, helping one another along, and lifting up the canine member of the party, he finding it absolutely impossible to follow us. We were forced to bear on a small huckleberry bush or a branch of the yew tree, while every few moments some boulder, dislodged by our own exertions, thundered down the mountain side and plunged into the cataract beneath. We found no signs of life of any description, even the small gnats and mosquitoes seeming to have deserted this barren region. At last the top of the canyon was reached, and, after a long rest, we once more held on our way, our direction being southeast. With the Black canyon we left all trouble behind, the remainder of the journey being comparatively easy, and camp No. 2 was reached about 6 P.M. on the 9th, where a very welcome supper greeted us.

The only game we saw on the whole trip was one blue grouse, whose head the colonel knocked off with a bullet from his Winchester, although we passed elk and deer signs in plenty. The highest point reached was some 2200 feet above the sea and the distance traveled over only some twelve or fifteen miles, but the difficulties to be encountered may be imagined in that the very inhabitants of the river valley supposed that the Grand canyon was the small fork explored last summer and as far as can be found out the regions above described are absolutely unknown to the civilized world. The copper regions above the lake are too well known to need a description. Above them were found principally basaltic formation in the cliffs and ledges. Above the Grand canyon a belt of red slate containing iron, black oxide of manganese and some copper was crossed, while still further up the river we discovered alternate belts of slate and prophyry with here and there a boulder of metamorphosed granite. The course of the expedition will be up the south bank of the river to the Grand divide. The trail from there on will be explored by the geologist, Colonel Linsley and your correspondent.

—*F. J. Church in Seattle Press*

The Lake Cushman Copper Mines[25]

Lake Cushman, Aug. 2.—The copper leads in the Skokomish bottom, above Lake Cushman, were first discovered in September, 1888, by J. D. Dow and A. H. Rose, of Mason county. Several claims were located but nothing was done toward developing the mines until this spring, only occasional trips being made there by the various claim owners. In March, 1890, the Mason County Mining and Development company was organized with F. H. Whitworth of Seattle president, and C. M. Brooks of Union City secretary, the company being composed of claim holders in the copper belt.

Since March the development of the mines has been pushed as rapidly as it possibly could be. A fine trail has been cut and graded from Hoodsport to the mines, a distance of some 18 miles; two large camps have been built and quantities of explosives, mining tools and supplies carried thither. A shaft is being sunk and a gang of men are, at present writing, hard at work blasting and working out the rich red ore, gleaming with its yellow freight. Out side of the company 15 claims have been located, many of them now being worked.

A Grays Harbor company, headed by Mr. John S. Soule, controlling seven of them.

The ore is a porous iron ore, containing copper in all its veins, with pockets of the black oxide of manganese. Several exhaustive analyses of the ore have been taken at the expense of the company, both in Seattle and Philadelphia, which have shown as exceedingly rich copper ore containing both native copper and the oxides, red and black, which should bring a mint of money to the fortunate owners of claims. The leads belonging to the company are as follows: "Hoodsport," 1500 feet, with 220 foot vein; "Sheriff," 1500 feet, 140 foot vein; "Mascot," 3000 feet, 350 foot vein; "Olympic," 1500 feet, 4 foot vein; "John Mac," 1500, width of vein unknown; "O.K.," 1500 feet, 80 foot vein, and the "Dakota," 1500 feet, with 300 foot vein. The company are daily expecting a large shipment of dynamite from Seattle, and as soon as it arrives work will be pushed with still greater vigor. Within a few weeks a smelter will be started at "Hoodsport"; also a narrow gauge railroad to the mines, and our readers may in the near future expect to see scow loads of the purest copper landed on the Seattle wharves for shipment to the various factories where the valuable metal is used. In a succeeding letter I will send maps of the mines with still further particulars.

—*F. J. Church in Seattle Press*

---

[25] Frederic J. Church, *Seattle Press*, no date. Reprinted in the *Mason County Journal* [Shelton], August 15, 1890.

CHAPTER TWELVE.
BERNARD J. BRETHERTON

Bernard J. Bretherton was one of the four civilian "scientists" supplied to the O'Neil Expedition by the Oregon Alpine Club. He had prior experience as a naturalist, taxidermist, and zoological collector, and was sometimes known to the exploring party as the "bird stuffer."

Bretherton was born on January 26, 1861, in Birkenhead, England, the youngest of eleven children of Edward and Alice Bretherton. He emigrated to the United States about 1885 and lived in Portland, Oregon, with the family of an elder brother. He was first employed as a baggage man for a railroad, but by the

time the exploring expedition was organized, he was curator of the Oregon Alpine Club and a "collector and preparator of zoological specimens for museums and taxidermists."

After admission to U.S. citizenship on January 24, 1891, Bretherton went to Alaska to collect specimens of the flora, fauna, and fishes for the British Museum, the Smithsonian Institution, and the U.S. Department of Agriculture. He was in Alaska about three years.

In about 1900, he served as assistant keeper at the Yaquina Bay Lighthouse at Newport, Oregon, then as keeper at the Coquille River Lighthouse at Bandon, Oregon, where he died in 1903.

—Robert L. Wood
Adapted from Men, Mules and Mountains *(pp. 457–58)*

THE DIARY OF BERNARD J. BRETHERTON[1]

[Note: The first page and the top of the second page have been obliterated, by reason of scrapbook items having been pasted over the original writing.]

& skinned the Elk and jerked the meat. Hughes and I camped there.

Sept. 8. Spent all day dressing Elk hide. Linsley came over and helped. Saw a young bear.

Sept 9. Finished elk skin and sent Hughes home. Fisher and Kid reached my camp about noon and after dinner we started for camp and took meat and head. Very hard untill got to

2. After supper Sgt Marsh brought me in a jumping mouse. After supper wrote to Griff & [erased]. Fisher gave me some fine crystals.

Sept. 10th. After Breakfast went with Yates & Fisher and brought in Elk skin, took all day.

Sept. 11th. Broke Camp at N 14 and moved over divide to valley of Quinault River. Col Linsley and myself remained over night in old camp.

Sept 12th. At 10 Oclock the pack train pulled out for

Bernard J. Bretherton
Courtesy Robert B. Hitchman

308

---

[1] Unpublished diary, courtesy of Olympic National Park. Transcribed by Robert L. Wood, February 16–18, 1968. Bracketed notes in the text and transcriber's notes in footnotes are Wood's.

Transcriber's note: In preparing this transcription, I have had available for my perusal a transcription made by June Maguire for the National Park Service, in whose custody the diary presently resides. Mrs. Maguire's transcript was very helpful and time saving, and allowed me to concentrate my efforts on words and phrases that she found illegible. In a few instances I believe certain words are different [from how] Mrs. Maguire has transcribed them. Also, I have endeavored to retain Bretherton's original spellings; for example, "beutifull" for "beautiful"; in some instances, "untill" for "until"; "@" for "at" and "&" for "and."

Hoodsport. After dinner Col and Self went to main party and got ready to start.

Linsley Detch [Detachment?], Sept 13th, 1890
Left ONeils camp with party of 6, namely Hughes, Kranichfelt, Fisher, Yates, Higgins and Col Linsley @ 8.20 A.M. each man carrieng [carrying] 60 lbs.

After leaving camp took directly down to Quinault River through a large burn. Descent very steep, reached river at 11.30.

[Note: Next page of diary is missing, and apparently contained several entries, because the beginning entry of the succeeding page is apparently part of the entry of September 15, 1890.]

[**September 15.**] One of the men in making a fire to warm himself let the woods on fire and as there was a strong wind it soon spread. To north west of us stretched a fine broad valley which we took to be the valley of the Elwaha [Elwha] called "Chester Valley" by the Press party.[2] After resting a while we worked our way to the west and in about a mile and half we came to a fine pass in the divid [divide?] between the headwaters of a river flowing to the north and those to the south. Here is a beutifull level saddle extending between two high rocky peaks in which are situated two beutifull little lakes named Lake Danton and Lake Etta. Leaving our packs here we scattered out in every direction to try and find a route out and also to see if we could find any traces of former visitors, but in vain. Yates and I climbed to the summit of the peak to the north from which we could see Mt Olympus while between it and us was a fearfull broken country in which the gods had been at war.

Camp Pass, Sept 16th. At 8.30 A.M. we were again on the move, the morning was cloudy and a fog was comming in from the sea. Leaving the party I hurried ahead up to the mountain we had seen the night before and just gained the summit in time to see Mt Olympus bearing 320° and [Anderson][3] Mt 60°. After we had all gained the summit we took a due west course along the ridge intending to pass to the west of the highest pinnacle and round its base but before we had got to it the fog became so dense that Linsley decided to go into camp. Before the fog closed in however we had a beutifull view of the range. We were on one of the highest [higher?] mountains on the divide between the head of a branch of the Quineault and a branch of what we took to be the Elwha. At an altitude of 5000 ft. to the S.W. of us was a very prominent mountain which towered far above <u>its heirs</u> [others?] shaped like a castle with a turret on its N end. While all around us were rugged bare rocky peaks in the gulches of which were glasiers of varied size & far below us on either sides seemed to be large beutifull valleys all heavily timbered. As the fog showed no signs of lifting and it had begun to rain very hard we made camp on a level grassy spur on the S end of the mountain and passed the remained [remainder] of the day in our little tents singing and telling yarns.[4] On a tree at Linsley camp I drew pictures suppose [supposed] to resemble the different men here of our party in various states of damp misery. During the afternoon a good many birds came on to the mountain, namely [mainly?] pigeons going south. Varied thrush, snow birds and a small green warbler. Yates killed a varied thrush & on dressing it I found it had been gorgeing itself on huckleberrys. While climbing yesterday I had the misfortune to fall with my gun under me and bent the left barrell so as to effect [affect] its shooting. By bed time the fog was no better.

[Sketch, labeled "Our Eastern Horizon, 4 A.M.]

Sept. 17th. The morning broke fine and clear and by 8 A.M. we were on the way to the top of the ridge which we crossed @ 5300 feet and climbed down on to the glasier on the North side, down the face of which we went for about a half a mile then took to the ridge to the East and followed down its crest arriving at a branch of the Elwha at 5 P.M.

September 18th, Camp Lowland. Leaving Camp Lowland we crossed the stream and traveled along the side hill in a northernly direction trough [through] a country bare of underbrush and covered with very streigh [straight] but small timber. At noon we had lunch by a beutiful little stream & while strolling round I picked up a piece of paper the following[5]

Cock Robin vas a liddle Bird
Vhat lives oop mid de sky
Und Greenbaum was a lost dutchman
Vhat soon oxpects to die.

He roamed the Olympic's vide vild vhaste
Und stormed the Elwhas tide
Nor drink nor morsel did he taste
But oop und onwards glide.

---

[2] The Press Party named an area of the North Fork of the Quinault River "Chester Valley," so Bretherton is in error here.
[3] This word is illegible, but undoubtedly was intended to be "Anderson" because Bretherton so indicates in his article on the trip to Olympus, published in *Steel Points* in 1907.
[4] "Linsley called it simply 'Camp Fog,' and Bretherton referred to it as 'Linsley Camp' in his diary." Wood, *Men, Mules and Mountains*, p. 423.
[5] See two articles following the diary for background on this poem.

The wild beasts gaze did on him dwell
That drilled his bones to marrow
Till happy thought of Wm Tell
Und his little bow and arrow

A robin soon was lying dead
And ts blood he drank
Which gave him strength to raise his head
When lo!! 300 yds. was camp.[6]

After dinner we traveled on until about 5 Oclock we saw a large open glade on the other side of the stream and to this we crossed & made camp. About two thousand feet above us were two large glasiers from which fell in a very large waterfall of about 500 ft. This camp we called Camp Glasier.

Sept 19th Friday. Left Camp Glasier @ 7.30. We followed up the right hand of the stream through a timber belt for about ¼ of a mile and came out at the foot of a long canyon entirely filled with snow[7] on which we traveled all forenoon, comming out about 1 P.M. on a large glasier at the base & to the east of Mt Olympus. Here we stopped at an alt of 4300 ft[8] while one party ascended a high mountain to the left and one to the right and reported as follows. 3 large streams take there [their] rise on Olympus flowing east, west and northeast. Here we saw [illegible] black bear & killed one. Afterwards we went down into the creek bottom & made camp. Calling it Bear Camp.

Sept 20th, 8 day, Sat. Leaving Bear camp in the morning we crossed the stream which we found to be a great deal smaller than in the evening previous. These creeks flow through deep gorges and have there [their] head in the glasiers of Mt Olympus. Climbing out of the canyon we came onto a beutifull level plateau of about fifty acres in extent and this we called the Garden of the Gods. Laying in a basin @ an alt of 4000 ft it is entirely surrounded by wild rugged mountains the sides of which are coverd [covered] by large glasiers, the waters from which join to form the headwaters of the [left blank] Riv. Here we made camp calling it Garden Camp.

Sept. 21st, Sunday, 9th day. Left Garden Camp in the

A.M. We took a southerly course. Crossing a deep canyon we followed rou [round?] the side hill with the intention of getting to the West Side of Mt Olympus. After passing through a long swail [swale] of alder we came to were [where] a rock slide ran down clear from the top of the range and up this we toiled up for [from?] 12.20 to 5.30 making camp @ an alt 4750 ft to the east & south and at the base of Mt Olympus. While passing through the swail we lost Fisher but saw his fire below us at night & signeled [signaled] him and got answer.

[Sketch: Trinity]

Sept 22nd, 10th day, Monday. Contents of box, pencil, glove of the ladies of the Banner party, deck of cards, 2 army buttons, 1 beer ck [check], shoe lace, piece of Quartz, 1 card, 3 tellegrams. Made ascent in 2 hours and 45 minutes. Left Box @ 6840, summit to [too] pointed & no place to put it. Elevation of Summit (Albine [Alline? Alpine?] Peak) 7250. Ascent easy. After returning to party made our way back down to river and made camp. No sign of Fisher. Called this Camp B.F.

Sept. 23rd, 11 Day, Tuesday. Leaving camp @ 7.30 we made our way down the ridge and by 9 Oclock we reached the bed of river @ an elevation of 1200 ft. Here we crossed a large creek & climbing up the bluff on the other side came out on a level flat which gradually descended untill on a level with the river. Here we found a good Elk trail that led us all day through fine level Bottoms devoid of underbrush. The river here is very broad & the Bottoms on both sides are wide and covered with a fine groth [growth] of timber. Here we saw a ceder that 8 men could not reach round. We did not see and [any] game but the sand bars were all tracked up by Elk, Deer, Bear, Wolf and Otter signs. In the afternoon we passed a small working Beaver Dam, and about one hour before we made camp we came on to the tracks of an indian & dog and about 5 P.M. we shot a duck and went into camp for the night.

Sept 24th, 12th Day Wednes. Left camp Pollard @ 7.30 and traveled all forenoon through fine large bottoms containing enorous [enormous] trees. About 4 P.M. saw lots of Salmon and shot two then went into camp for the night. All day saw lots of game signs and old indian camps.

310

---

[6] "Bretherton pasted the 'scrap of paper' in his diary, also copied the verses on another page, making a few insignificant mistakes. The poem as published in *Steel Points* in 1907 varies slightly from the two versions in the diary. According to his diary, Bretherton made the discovery during lunch on September 18, but in *Steel Points* he states he found the composition at Camp Lowlands on the night of September 17. The poem, which must have been penned within a few weeks prior to that date, proves that during the summer of 1890 men were penetrating deeply into the Olympics by following the trail blazed by the Press Expedition. On August 3, 1890, the *Seattle Post-Intelligencer* printed a story detailing the ordeal of one William Greenebaum, who in late July was lost several days in the mountains. Apparently the author of the poem had read this story, or perhaps he was in the rescue party." Wood, *Men, Mules and Mountains*, p. 424. The Greenebaum account, as told in the *Post-Intelligencer*, can be found following this diary.
[7] "This was the Elwha Snowfinger, which in 1890 had the characteristics of an active glacier, including blue ice with potholes. Today it is classed as a permanent snowfield." Wood, *Men, Mules and Mountains*, p. 425.
[8] "The men variously estimated the altitude of this gap on the divide between the Elwha and Queets from 4000 to 4600 feet, but the true elevation was 4750 feet. In 1907 several men from the Explorers Club, who were on their way to Olympus, named it Dodwell-Rixon Pass because they believed the 1898–1900 survey party headed by Arthur Dodwell and Theodore F. Rixon was the first to use it." Wood, *Men, Mules and Mountains*, p. 425.

Sept. 25, 13 Day, Tuesday. Did not sleep well last night. Were disturbed by mink and weasels trying to steal our provisions & also by mirriad [myriads?] of small gnats that bit us, besides the salmon did not agree with some of us. Took trail @ 8 A.M. and traveled through fine bottoms @ [all?] day, made camp at night in open flat. Got mole [?].

Sept. 26th, 14 Day, Friday. Left camp @ 8 A.M. and made our way through dense tangle of vine maple looking like S American forest untill noon. River very crooked, running southerly. Stopped at noon on sand bar for lunch. After took to wood again. Saw many fresh signs of Bear, Cougar, Otter, Coon and mink. Saw two Bear traps. Saw many Salmon spawning. @ 2 P.M. came to a large spawning bed and shot nice small salmon. @ 4 P.M. came to 2 small cabins and by the lower one made camp for the night. Saw all of Fishers camps. Saw Blue Herons, Ravens, Mergansers, Pollard, and linnetts.

Sept. 27th, 15 Day, Saturday. Left Camp Salmon @ 8 A.M. continuing down stream wading from Bar to Bar untill 10 A.M. when we came to a Cabin and as there was no one @ home we stole some turnips. Further on we came to a house on the opposite side of the stream & crossed over and found out we were 10 miles from the mouth of the Quiets River. Met two men in Canoe going up stream. They said it was 12 miles to the mouth. Before noon came to another house. Stole some Potatoes and crossed the River and cooked dinner. After tried to follow trail and got lost. L [Linsley] in a bad temper. Snappy all night, grousing about grub, etc.[9]

[sketch of a potato]

Sept 28th, 16th day, Sunday Potatoe Camp. Left camp @ 8 A.M. We soon found a good trail and soon came to a cabin were [where] we were told that it was 5½ miles to the Sea. From this trail was bad [lead?] in about 2½ miles came to Indian Ranch and got indian to put us across River there, forded again below & had dinner. Found good trail for 1 mile and came to another Indian Ranch and hired Indian to take us to the Ocean (1.50), got to Ocean @ 3.20 and started down Beach and made mouth of Raft [i.e., Raft River] by 4.30. Crossed this and made camp about ¼ mile below.

Ocean Camp. Sept 29th, 17 day Monday. Left camp @ 6 A.M. in order to catch the tide round the rocks, this was no inconveniance as our camp was in a beastly damp hole behind a big root on the edge of a bluff. The coast here is wild and rugged with large rocks standing out in the sea, some taking the form of castles while others form large arches and all alike are covered with cormorants and gulls. Our first essey was a steep climb over a projecting headland then a stretch of level beach for about 3 miles where we were obliged to take to the bluff again for a stretch of a mile. A trail runs along here and this led us again to the beach. Here again we had good traveling for about five miles which we found ourselves in perilous possition. Unnoticed we got to a part of the beach that was shut off from the main land by high perpendicular bluffs leaving a space of about 20 ft at its base not yet covered by the rapidly approaching tide. Before we had proceeded any distance we perceived a point of rocks jutting out into the Sea, while on looking back we saw that our retreat was already cut of [off] by the approaching tide. Hurring [Hurrying] our pace we to [took] the oppertunity afforded to us by a receeding wave and made a dash through an arch formed in the rocks by the action of the Sea, but this was "out of the fring [frying] pan into the fire" for on gaining the other side we found ourselves in a rocky basin, with another headland shutting us of [off]. Over this we had to climb and about 20 minutes after came to the mouth of the Quinaielt River on the opposite side of which the Agentcy stands. Hailing an Indian, we were soon on the other side and dring [drying] out by the stove in the school house. We stayed here all night.

Agency. Sept 30th, 18 Day Tuesday. Left reservation @ 6 A.M. in two indian wagons and traveled along the beach until 11 A.M. when we had to stop on account of the tide being to [too] high to allow of our crossing the Chopalis River. We stopped at a house on the beach opposite Copalis Rocks. These rocks are a great nesting place for Sea Birds & on the largest one is built a small hut for the purpose of hunting Sea Otter. The fur of this animal has a very high market value and in consequence all along the beach @ intervals of perhaps a half mile apart, both indians and white men have raise [raised] high tripod box stand in which they sit and watch for them. This is also a great ground for both ducks and geese in winter. The beach from Copalis Rocks to Oyhut is beutifully level and according to the reports of the settlers it is a splendid beach for bathing as no undertow is felt. Add to this that there is an unlimited supply of Razor, Cohog [i.e., Quahaug] and Eastern Clams. At 6 P.M. we reach the place designated as "Oyhut" which is really nothing but a sand road across the neck of land seperating Gray's Harbor from the Ocean, and here we remained for the night. Only had 1 squar [squall?] today.

311

---

[9] "Apparently Linsley was easily irritated. In 1915, when responding to a request from the Bureau of Pensions for additional family information, he wrote: 'In conclusion permit me to say: That there appears to be no good reason for the data ask[ed] for, unless the Department considers that every soldier that survived the Civil war is a d—n scoundrel.'" Wood, *Men, Mules and Mountains,* p. 434.

Oct 1st, 19 Day, Wednesday. Left Oyhut @ twelve noon on a sailing scow called the Economist owned by Capt Chas White. The Economist is not a fast sailer but what she lacks in this respect she makes up for in her commodious accommodations, having a cabin 25 x 12 well lit with side windows and a good cook stove on which we cooked dinner. After dinner the wind died out and we did not pass nest rock untill 3 P.M. By 5.30 P.M. we arrived @ Hoquiam, a small thriving town. After we had deposited our things @ the hotel we hunted up Mr. McWilliam [McMillan?] and succeeded in making a raise on P.O. and as there was a meeting of the Board of trade we went by invitation.

THE GREENEBAUM INCIDENT

Bretherton reports both in his diary and in his article "Ascent of Mount Olympus," in Steel Points *(presented later in this chapter), the finding of a poem on a piece of paper in Elwha Basin. This satirical poem was inspired by "the Greenebaum incident," which was reported in two articles in the* Seattle Post-Intelligencer. *The poem was so appealing to Bretherton that he recorded it verbatim in his diary. Greenebaum, identified as a San Francisco merchant on a hunting trip with friends, became lost in the mountains while the O'Neil Expedition was underway. After being lost for four days without food, he was finally found, resulting in a happy ending for all.*

ESTRAY IN OLYMPICS[10]

Parties Scouring Hills for a Missing Explorer

Port Angeles, July 29.—Last week Frank Wimilski, C. J. Gibson, J. F. Gibson and J. B. McFall reached Port Angeles with the intention of making this the starting point of an exploration into the Olympics. They came from San Francisco, but are old Colorado explorers. Their object was to test the capacity of the Olympics as a mineral producing country. Friday last they were joined by William Greenbaum, Ed Rewin, M. N. Frank, Charles Douglas and H. D. Pellin, and that day started on the trip.

Saturday they reached the headwaters of Morse's creek and went into camp. During the day Greenbaum went out to find one of the horses that had strayed. He was in sight of the party until about 3 P.M., and as he did not return his companions became alarmed and instituted search. They fired guns, hallooed and built fires, but no response came.

One of the party returned to Port Angeles and secured sixteen men to aid in the search, and a tug was brought from sea with four cruisers, and the search is now being pushed thoroughly. Friends in Seattle, San Francisco and Aberdeen have been communicated with.

Greenbaum has a brother in San Francisco who is quite wealthy, and funds are not lacking to push the search. From the lay of the country it seems incredible that he should have lost his way, and the supposition is that he fell and either killed himself or was so badly injured as not to be able to make outcries. His brother will reach here tomorrow, and the search will be conducted until he is found, dead or alive.

LOST IN OLYMPICS[11]

Adventures of Greenebaum in the Mountains.

Four Days Without Food.

The San Francisco Merchant Tells of His Terrible Experiences and of His Discovery of Friends.

William Greenebaum, the San Francisco merchant who was lost July 21 from an exploring party in the midst of the Olympics, reached this city at 3 o'clock Friday afternoon, after having wandered about in the mountains four days without food.

It will be remembered Greenebaum left this city July 16 as one of a hunting party composed of himself, Edward Lewin, Frank Wischenyski and Charles Dugas, to make a trip through the Olympic mountains, prompted by the spirit of adventure and a desire for hunting.

Learning that Greenebaum had safely returned, a POST-INTELLIGENCER reporter called on him at 214 South Eleventh street last evening and got the story of his trip and adventures.

The party, bound for the Olympics, reached Port Angeles July 17, at 3 o'clock in the afternoon. Here a jack [pack?] train with supplies was formed, and the party started the same evening for the range, taking the old government trail. They crossed the first main range on the 19th, at 5 o'clock in the evening, and made permanent camp in Bunch Grass valley. Three prospectors from Colorado were overtaken there, but the two parties kept distinct.

Greenebaum's party spent the time hunting and exploring this valley until the evening of the 26th. They had de-

---

[10] Author unknown, *Seattle Post-Intelligencer*, July 30, 1890.
[11] Author unknown, *Seattle Post-Intelligencer*, August 3, 1890. Bracketed notes are Wood's.

cided to break camp and go to Port Angeles on the 28th.

One of the pack horses had strayed from his stake and the whole party went in search on the afternoon of the 26th. Greenebaum became foot-sore and paused to rest within a quarter of a mile from the camp.

The others pushed on after the horse and left Greenebaum on the side-hill near a canyon.

While the latter was resting a mountain lion attacked him. The animal came crawling up and Greenebaum was driven about in various directions in trying to escape. He did not dare to run until he reached More [Morse] creek in the canyon below, when he waded into the water up to his waist, thus keeping the animal at twenty yards distance from him.

This was on the evening of the 26th, at 5 o'clock. Greenebaum had to move very cautiously to keep the lion from springing upon him. He waded down stream followed by the lion on the shore.

It was fast growing dark. Watching his chance when the lion was extricating himself from a swampy point in front of which were high boulders, Greenebaum swam to the opposite shore and hastily built two bonfires against the base of a high cliff.

Between these two fires Greenebaum spent the night watching for the reappearance of the lion, which had been frightened off by the flames.

Greenebaum began search for the camp the morning of the 27th, and hunted diligently all day. By night his efforts were a failure, and he was obliged to kindle a fire, which he did with one of the three matches in his possession, and spent a second night without sleep or food. This was at a point supposed to be within five miles of where Greenebaum's party had first camped.

He spent the next day, also, in fruitless search, and at night he was again forced to lie down on the bank of the creek by a bon-fire, built with the next to the last match he had.

Greenebaum wandered about with no better success the following day, and on the morning of the 30th his condition was desperate. He had been three days without food or sleep, and had no weapons all the time but a pocket-knife. He now resolved to follow the creek, which he had kept near, to salt water, and there hail a passing steamer.

Luck greeted him at last. He was fortunate enough to find a tough piece of yew wood out of which he made a bow and arrow, with which he killed a robin and drank the blood. As he was fishing in the stream at 4 o'clock that afternoon he was found by a search party, organized at the instance of E. H. Emanuel, of this city, and taken on horseback to Port Angeles, whence he arrived in Seattle yesterday afternoon with the other members of his party who had reached Port Angeles after fruitless search just one hour before him. Greenebaum is the son of a wholesale dry goods merchant of San Francisco, who is represented by A. H. Emanuel, of Seattle. The latter organized a search party on the 28th upon receipt of a telegram from Port Angeles to the effect that Greenebaum was lost in the mountains and chartered the tug Rainier for that place.

Greenebaum is safe and sound, except that he is nearly famished. The former reports that he was at any time out of his head or delerious were entirely false.

GATES OF THE RANGE[12]

Entrance to the Olympics Reached by O'Neil's Party.

Climbing Up a Precipice.

Beginning of the Government Exploration—A Struggle Through Forest, Mud and Rain.

From a Staff Correspondent of the Post-Intelligencer.[13]

Camp Nellie Bly, July 9.—On the morning of July 7 the party sent out by the government for the purpose of exploring the Olympic range, accompanied by the scientific corps of the Oregon Alpine Club, landed at the mouth of Lillewauk[14] creek, and shortly after the advance party took the trail for Lake Cushman.

The party is commanded by Lieutenant J. P. O'Neil, Fourteenth infantry, and consists of a geologist, mineralogist, botanist, naturalist photographer, three sergeants, six privates and a packer.

The pack train, consisting of twelve mules, took the trail for Lake Cushman at 11 A.M., but though the trail has been packed over before, it was found necessary to do considerable clearing, and in consequence only three miles were covered that day. The trail, after leaving the shores of Hood's canal, leads up the flat at the mouth of Lillewauk creek past

---

[12] Bernard J. Bretherton, *Seattle Post-Intelligencer*, July 14, 1890.
[13] This was Bretherton.
[14] The *Post-Intelligencer* typesetter misread Bretherton's handwriting on this proper noun throughout. It should be Lillewaup.

Mr. Taylor's ranch and climbs up a very steep ascent to the first ridge.

Here trouble was encountered for the first time, one mule making the ascent three times and each time losing his footing and rolling to the bottom of the hill.

After gaining the summit of the ridge the trail runs due west, crossing Big creek, and leads through a heavily-timbered country to Lake Cushman. Lieutenant O'Neil, realizing that the pack train could not cover the remaining seven miles to the lake that night, pushed on and overtook the advance party on the east bank of the lake. Five members of the advance then returned to the pack train, which in the meantime had kept steadily on its way.

That first day and night will long be remembered by every member of the party. The mules, green from a long spell of idleness, were slow to assert themselves when caught in a bad situation, and, as the trail crossed many small creeks, making soft, muddy swails, a greater part of the day was spent in getting mules out of the mud. Add to this that none of the party had eaten anything since an early breakfast, that almost every roll of blankets in the outfit was either smeared with mud or wet through, and you will have the situation which might have found us on July 2.

The trail had been represented as being good and the distance only six miles, and in consequence preparations had been made to camp at Lake Cushman that night, but the trail was found to be bad and the distance at least ten long miles.

On the morning of the third, the march was resumed and the party reached the lake at 1 P.M. Lake Cushman is a body of water covering an area of about 1,000 acres, fed and drained by the river Skokomish, its waters forming a paradise for lovers of angling, as the finny beauties are gamy, large and plentiful. The view from the east bank is grandly beautiful, the mountains rising on every side, abruptly from the margin of the lake almost to the line of perpetual snow.

The lake was crossed on a raft belonging to Mr. Windover, who has a ranch on the west bank; and the party partook of a plentiful and very welcome meal at his house. After a short rest camp was pitched and every person busied himself in getting things in shape.

The next day being the Fourth of July, no move was made, and the day was spent in fishing in the lake, Professor Henderson distinguishing himself by a catch of nearly 100.

The following day Lieut. O'Neil started on ahead to locate a trail, and the scientific corps started in to gather material for their report. So far the weather has been fine,

but it commenced to rain on July 4th and has continued ever since. The pack train in the mean time was engaged in bringing up the remainder of the supplies from Lillewauk, and in this way four days were consumed.

On the morning of the 7th, camp was struck and the march resumed. From the Windover ranch the trail led up the right bank of the Skokomish river, crossing several small creeks and passing some four or five cabins. No trouble was encountered here, as the trail was good and level, following along the river bottoms.

Five miles from the lake further progress was barred by a perpendicular bluff rising from the bed of the river. Here camp No. 2 was pitched and dubbed "Nellie Bly."

The next day [July 19] all hands fell to to cut a zig-zag trail up and over the bluff, and are still occupied in doing so.

So far the only game encountered has been two or three grouse and a few pigeons, and fish has been our chief diet.

At camp No. 1 the party was joined by Mr. Church, a mineralogist and extensive traveler in the Olympic range. At Camp Nellie Bly all signs of civilization end and the next move will be into an entirely unknown region.

B. J. B.

THE RANGE CROSSED[15]

Lieut. O'Neil's Scouts Have Reached the Quinault.

South Fork of Skokomish.

Two Members of the Expedition Journey Along That Stream to Hood's Canal and Nearly Starve.

Hoodsport, Aug. 4.—Professor Henderson, of Lieutenant O'Neil's government exploring expedition, has arrived here on his way to Olympia. The main party is now camped on the middle fork of the Skokomish, while members of the party exploring have reached the headwaters of the Quiniault river.

On July 12, the trail having been completed over Fisher's bluff, Lieutenant O'Neil's expedition moved on. After leaving this point the Skokomish river takes a slight bend to the north, the left bank being very steep and rugged, while the right bank runs through a large bottom for about two miles. It then comes over a small cataract, and here both banks are very rough on account of the large boulders, and sharp rock points rise abruptly out of the ground. The trail, after com-

314

---

[15] Bernard J. Bretherton, *Seattle Post-Intelligencer,* August 6, 1890. Bracketed notes are Wood's.

ing down the western side of Fisher's point, leads up the left bank to this point, where the river is crossed, the mules fording it and the party going over on a foot log, then passing well to the south of the rocks, comes down to the river again through a beautiful bottom covered with fine timber, with a light undergrowth of vine maple. Here the river was again crossed, and camp pitched on the left bank, in the bed of an overflow. This camp we called Camp Rest on account of Sunday rest being taken there.

While at this camp Professor Henderson and Mr. Fisher made a trip to the summit of a very high mountain on the other side of the river, returning late at night with wonderful accounts of what they had seen, and a fine collection of botanical specimens.

On July 14, while still at Camp Rest, Mr. C. A. Hungate and Mr. S. B. [?] Sweeney joined us. These gentlemen were on a hunting trip, having heard so much about the large game of the Olympic mountains that they had decided to come and see for themselves.

On July 15 we again moved camp to a large bottom about one mile up the river. Between these camps we did not cut any trail, as we found it practicable to travel up the river by crossing from bar to bar. About a quarter of a mile above this camp the river runs through a large gorge, at the head of which, though still in it, it forks, one branch running north and the other south.

With the intention of ascertaining which of these would be the better route to take, Lieutenant O'Neil sent out the following exploring parties: To the north—Lieutenant J. P. O'Neil (chief), L. B. Sweeney, C. A. Hungate, Sergeant Marsh, Private Fisher. To the south—Colonel N. E. Linsley (chief), Professor Henderson, Sergeant Yates. The writer, with Private Berriens, started for the highest peak he could find to the southwest, to make a general survey of the surrounding country. These parties were out three days, when they all returned, with the exception of Mr. C. A. Hungate, who had got astray from his party and did not return for four days. Sergeant Marsh had killed a deer, and in consequence there was fresh meat in camp. The results of these expeditions showed that the branch to the north, after leaving the gorge, forked again, the largest fork running to the westward, and this was decided on as the best route to follow. Hungate and Sweeney had gone off on a hunting trip about this time, from which they returned on the 22d, having killed a bear and two deer. These gentlemen reported having seen on the south side of the divide a large stream flowing to the eastward, which we took to be the little [middle?] fork of the Skokomish river, [South ?]

and as this had long been a matter of dispute among the settlers here Lieutenant O'Neil decided to send a party from its rise to its junction with the main river, about eight miles from Union City. For this purpose he selected the writer and Mr. Fred J. Church, and as our experience is a good sample of what travel is in these mountains, I will give it in detail.

Exploration of South Branch of Skokomish River

At 7:00 on the morning of July 25, the writer, in company with Mr. F. J. Church, left headquarters, then opposite the north fork of the Skokomish river, with instructions to travel to the southward until they came to a large stream running east, and to follow it down to its outflow, then to make our way to Hoodsport, on Hood's canal, and from there by way of Lake Cushman back to the main party. The trip we were told would take us two days; but mistrusting this statement we took four days' rations. Our provisions consisted of flour, bacon, tea, sugar and salt, besides which we took a shelter tent, one double and one single blanket, a shotgun and rifle, beside cooking utensils, hatchet, etc.

Leaving the Skokomish river we followed up the branch running to the south. For the first mile the travel was extremely bad on account of numerous windfalls and large boulders, so crossing the river, we took to the other bank. This we found better, though far from good, but we followed it until noon, when we arrived at a fork coming in on a course 40 degrees west of south. Here we stopped to cook dinner. We had now traveled about five miles, and were at an altitude of 1,600 [1,000?] feet.

As we had traveled this route before, we knew pretty well where to go; so, keeping well up the hillside of the left bank we traveled in a southwesterly direction until we came to a place where the creek falls over a rock about twenty feet, and here we crossed in order to gain the plateau on which the lakes are situated in which this branch takes its rise. To do this we had to climb up the face of a small cliff about forty feet high. Take into consideration that we each had a pack of about thirty pounds, and you will understand that this was no easy matter, but foot by foot we worked up, sometimes flattened against the rock on some narrow crevice, at others hanging to the shrubbery within reach until we gained the plateau above.

We were now in the snow and traveling was a great deal better. So far the only game signs we had seen tended to show that this was their winter range, but at present the stillness was only broken by the twitter of some flock of chickadees, snow-birds, and at times mountain finches. But on this plateau elk, deer and bear signs were both fresh and plentiful.

The lakes in which this fork takes its rise are all within a few hundred yards of each other on this plateau. They are small, shallow sheets of water of a crystal clearness, inhabited only by water beetles and newts.

Proceeding on our way, we clambered up a steep incline of snow and in due time reached the summit of the ridge. From here Mount Rainier and the Pacific ocean can be seen, also a large mountain that we took to be Olympus. Making our way along the ridge to a camping place that we had occupied when on our ornithological collecting trip three days before, and where we knew there was plenty of snow and wood, we soon had a fire going and settled down for the night. We had not been here long when the barometer began to fall, and inside of twenty minutes we had passed from summer to winter. The greater part of the night was spent in trying to keep warm.

On the morning of July 26 we were up early, and after a light breakfast, Mr. Church started for a high peak to the southwest of us to get a general survey of the country, while the writer took notes of the birds at an altitude of nearly 4,000 feet. I found the rufus humming bird (Sataphrous ? rufus) very numerous, also the Oregon snow-bird (Junco Oregonus), and also saw two moose-birds (Perisorius? Canadensis, var. obscurus), all of which showed no fear of me, coming close to me to see what kind of an animal I was.

On the return of Mr. Church we both climbed to the summit of a high peak about 500 yards from camp, on gaining the summit of which we had a good view of the river we were in search of. The summit of this peak showed an elevation of 4,000 feet, and from it we could see a large body of water bearing thirty degrees south of west from us, distant about twenty miles, while intervening between it and us were three large fires. As it was now nearly noon, we decided to have dinner and descend to the river we had seen. We gave this peak the name of Churton peak,[16] as it was from here we saw the head waters of the south fork of the Skokomish river.[17] After a tedious climb down a very steep hillside for three hours, we reached the river bottom, and shortly after we found an Indian trail leading down stream. Following this we came about 5 [6?] o'clock, to where it crossed a ford and here, at an alti-

tude of 1,125 feet, we made camp for the night. On the morning of the 27th we forded the river and took the trail down the right bank. The water was so cold that wading with bare feet, even for a short distance, was very painful. After about twenty minutes' travel we came to a creek coming in from the northwest, and below this the river ran through a canyon for about a mile on a course twenty degrees south of east. Below this canyon is a large bottom about a mile wide, and heavily timbered with fir, cedar, yew and, along the river, alder, cottonwood and vine maple. Here we saw no signs of game, except what were old, but all vegetation was a great deal farther advanced than on the north side of the divide. The Indian trail that we were on, although a good trail while in use, was very poor now, on account of its not having been used this year, and being filled with last winter's windfalls, and in consequence, we did not gain anything by following it.

At noon we came to a gravel bar grown over with willows, and here we found a patch of ripe strawberries. The Indian trail was good here, and so we followed it until we came to another ford, where we stopped for dinner. While the writer built a fire, Mr. Church took a line and flies and tried for a trout, with the result of catching three small ones, but which were very welcome, as we had nothing else but bacon. After dinner we again forded the river and took the trail on the opposite side, and made good traveling until we came to a grassy opening, where we again lost the trail. We now began to lose confidence in this trail, for whenever we followed it, it led us into a bad place and there it seemed to stop. A short distance below this we again crossed to the right bank, this time on a log. The bottom here is very wide, being formed of a rich loamy soil covered with a luxuriant growth of herbage, and beautifully timbered with large, straight trees. Below this we came to a place where the river ran through a wide gravel washout, with high-sandy banks on either side, and here we stopped for the night, making our camp in the edge of a large cotton-wood grove. Our supplies were now beginning to look small, so we tried hard to catch more fish, but could not. Either they were not hungry or they did not like our style of fishing, for we could see them quite distinctly in this clear water, but although we tried both flies and different kinds of bait, we could not get a bite. All this evening numbers of jumping

---

[16] "Churton was one of several mountains at the head of Jumbo's Leap that vary in elevation from 4500 to 5000 feet. The most likely candidates are Peak 4851 and Peak 4666, near the national park boundary, but Churton may have been the peak we know today as Wonder Mountain." Wood, *Men, Mules and Mountains*, p. 407.

[17] "Bretherton wrote two accounts of the trip down the South Fork. The stories vary slightly as to some details. For example, in one account he mentions shooting a solitary tattler (a species of sandpiper) but in the other he states that they had killed two little sand snipes and from them they 'made a sort of broth.'" Wood, *Men, Mules and Mountains*, p. 407.

mice played around our camp-fire, staring at us with their large black eyes, and making off in great haste, clearing two feet at a jump, only to return again in a few minutes for another look.

On the morning of the 28th we were up at daylight and again tried to catch some fish, but without success, so strapping on our packs we started on again. As yet we had seen nothing to indicate that we were getting near any habitations or how far we had yet to go. The river here has an average depth of about two feet and a width of from twenty-five to fifty feet, while most of the way there are large gravel bars alternately on one side or the other. The traveling on these bars is good, and so to gain the advantage of them we took to wading from one to the other, and in this manner we were able to travel along at a good speed.

While taking a short cut across a bottom where the river formed an angle, we shot two old grouse and one young one, so that there was no danger of our starving for the present at least. After eating one old grouse and the young one for dinner, we resumed wading again. Here the river widened out, filling the whole of its bed, but it was only a few inches deep, so we waded down the middle of it. Below this we passed through a second canyon formed by high sand and gravel banks on each side. This canyon is almost one mile and a half in length, and at the lower end of it the mountains again recede back from the river, forming a large level bottom, with a creek coming in on the left bank, down a large canyon from the north. About a mile and a quarter below this again another creek comes in on the left bank, also from the north, down what appears to be a very large bottom.

Here we stopped for the night and while looking for a place to make camp we found the following inscription on a tree:

Sunday, Sept. 19, 1880.
As long as there are mountains there will be dam fools that will climb them. CPN

We agreed with C.P.N., but did not admire his mode of expression. After supper on the remaining grouse we summed up our situation as follows: We had traveled twenty-two miles from the divide. Our provisions had got down to three-quarters of a pound of flour, a little tea and sugar and a piece of bacon about as big as a hen's egg, and we could not tell how long we had yet to go before reaching the main river.

On July 29 we were out at daylight, and again tried to catch some fish, with the same results as before, so we ate a piece of bread each, with a cup of tea, and started, wading as on the previous days. About noon we came to a place where the river formed a letter S, where we saw a good many fresh beaver signs, and soon after the track of a man and dog. Below this the river made a sharp bend. To save distance we crossed with the intention of making a short cut. On going up the bank we came on to a clearing of about 15x30 feet, with logs laid for a house, and on a tree near by a notice that read as follows:

Notice.
This homestead is taken by William Weller, described from this point as follows East 160 rods and from the river north 160 rods. All parties are warned not to trespass.
William Weller
Witnesses: John Cardwell
Albert Wallace
July 8, 1890

About half a mile down we came to another clearing with "John Clark" written on a freshly-cut stump. Passing on to a sandbar we found the frame for a tent and part of a loaf of bread, which we ate, after which we felt much better.

But our spirits drooped somewhat when on turning a sharp corner we saw the river enter a large gorge, the perpendicular walls of which rose to a height of 300 or 400 feet on each side. But there was no help for it, and only one thing to do, namely, to go on. So down this gorge we went, wading when we could, or clambering along the rocks and boulders. In this way we made about three miles, all the time expecting to come to the end, until we came to a place where all progress was stopped on account of there being no place to get a foothold. We had now only two alternatives, either to go back or find some place to climb out, and this latter we did, climbing up a crevice that had been made by water running down in winter, and in which some bushes had grown. Clinging to the brush and rocks, we worked up this 300 [?] feet, where to slip was to be dashed to pieces on the rocks hundreds of feet below.

At length we gained the top, which was a small plateau, in which we had not traveled ten minutes when we came to another gorge, caused by a large creek coming in at right angles to the river. Climbing down this, we tried to make our way back to the river again, but came to a deep pool that we could not pass, so up we went again. We soon found that we were on a sort of hogback that grew narrower as we got higher, until at a height of 200 feet it was so narrow that we had to walk with a foot on each side, and could drop a stone from the outstretched arm into the water below. On gaining

317

the summit we had not gone a quarter of a mile before we came to another canyon, but smaller than the last. In this way we crossed two more, and in the third we stopped for the night. We had killed two little sand snipe, and of these we made a sort of broth, and this, with about six ounces of bread, was all we ate that day.

On the morning of the 30th we baked the last scrap of flour we had, which made a cake about as large as a saucer, and divided this between us. Climbing out of the gulch in which we had slept, we found ourselves on an extensive table-land, falling gradually to the south. Over this we traveled all the forenoon. We had not been able to properly dry out our clothes in the night, and they now hung heavily round us, but to make matters worse this plateau was covered everywhere with a heavy growth of salal, which made walking extremely bad. We were now getting pretty weak for want of food and would often fall. The whole of this day we did not see a living thing to shoot and all we could do was to eat berries. About 4 o'clock in the afternoon we came to the end of the gorge, and here we climbed down to the river bed again. Here the river spreads out over large gravel bars in many small streams. We saw here a deserted cabin on the right bank that had been about knocked down by the snow last winter. Along about 5 o'clock we noticed a trail on the other side of the creek, which was well-worn, and evidently led to some ranch, but which way we did not know, and of course we took the wrong one. The trail soon led up a steep hill, and we followed it more because there were lots of wild berries there than for any other reason. We had nearly got to the top and were sitting down in a berry patch when we heard some people talking. We soon made ourselves heard and in a short time we were standing beside Mr. Reynolds, who was on his way to the mountain for a pleasure trip, and was now waiting for the rest of his party to come up with the wagon.

On hearing our story these gentlemen did all in their power to relieve our sufferings and in a short time we were busily stowing away bread and cheese at a great rate. After we had satisfied the inner man we all repaired to the ranch of Mr. Kichland, where Mr. Reynold's opened his supplies and we soon had an excellent supper under way. We remained here over night, and after breakfast Mr. J. Cardwell, who was a member of the party, went with us for about two miles in order to put us on a trail that was a short cut to Union City. With heartfelt gratitude to this gentleman for his kindness we bade him goodbye and according to his instructions followed the trail till we came to a log jam, on which we crossed

the river into the Indian reservation and made our way through Union City to Hoodsport, reaching there that evening.

We had completed the work entrusted to us, and it only remained for us to make our way back to the main party.

The day before we left headquarters the camp was visited by the Habersham [Wickersham] party, consisting of Judge J. Habersham, Mrs. and Miss Habersham, Mr. Charles Joint and Mr. and Mrs. Taylor, the latter couple being on their honeymoon.

B. J. B.

OLYMPIC EXPLORERS[18]

Interesting Narrative by One of Gen. Gibbons's Expedition.

Source of the Skokomish River

Many Narrow Escapes and Privations—Scaling Precipices and Wading Streams

---

[Special Correspondence Sunday Ledger.]

Union City, August 1, 1890.—The expedition sent out by General Gibbon and accompanied by the scientific staff of the Oregon Alpine Club is now getting down to real work. They have thoroughly explored the Skokomish river from its mouth to its source of icy lakes in the heart of the rugged Olympic mountains and hillsides, having cut a first-class bridle trail into the interior.

With the exception of Messrs. Church and Bretherton's privations from want of food while exploring the South fork the party has not suffered any great hardships, although the trip has by no means been a picnic.

The party left the Lilliewaup bay on Hood's canal on July 2, and proceeded by way of Lake Cushman to the forks of the Skokomish river, a distance of some twenty miles, which occupied them for three weeks. Here a halt was made and exploring parties sent out in every direction. Each of these parties, consisting of from two to four men, go fully equipped with compass, barometer, route book and everything necessary to make a thorough and accurate map of the country over which they travel and on their return make a report of all they have found and seen to the secretary from which he compiles a general report and map.

---

[18] Bernard J. Bretherton, *Tacoma Daily Ledger*, August 10, 1890.

The result of their work so far is as follows: The Skokomish river after leaving Hood's canal takes its course in a south-westerly direction for a distance of ten miles through a fine agricultural country to a point on the southern boundary of the Indian reservation, where it divides into two forks, one running south, called the south fork, and the other running west which is termed the main river, which flows through Lake Cushman. Along the river from the forks to the lake is one long canyon with very little agricultural land except small bottoms, but splendid timber is found everywhere.

After leaving Lake Cushman the river has a course almost due west for a distance of ten miles.

Here about four miles from Lake Cushman, the copper mines of the Mason County Mining and Development company are located, which show a very good prospect for copper. About five miles above the mines the river runs through a deep gorge, at the head of which, though still in it, it forks again, one branch running due north and other south. The north branch, after leaving the main river forks again, the largest stream running to the westward and rising in a lake to the southwest of the "Three Brothers." The branch running to the south forms two small forks also rising, one out of one lake and other out of five lakes, situated on the opposite side of the Three Brothers. It is on this south branch that the Alaska cedar is found to be plentiful, growing very large.

Large game has been so far found to be scarce except at high altitudes, but Lake Cushman and the river below the gorge abounds in large trout of several varieties.

On July 14 the party was visited by C. A. Hungate and S. B. Sweeney, who were on a hunting trip, and remained until July 22, killing a bear and several deer.

On the 23rd of July we also had as visitors the Wickersham party, consisting of Judge J. Wickersham, wife and daughter, Mr. and Mrs. Taylor and Charles Joint, who left on the 24th, traveling up the north branch.

A fair idea of the difficulties of travel and hardships endured in these mountains may be gained from the following account by Bernard J. Bretherton, the naturalist of the party, while exploring the south fork, in company with Fred J. Church, both gentlemen being experienced travelers and therefore selected by Lieutenant J. P. O'Neil for this work.

At 7:30 in the evening of July 25 Mr. Fred J. Church and myself left headquarters, then opposite the north branch of the Skokomish river, with instructions to travel to the southward until we came to the first large stream flowing east, and to follow it to its mouth, then to make our way to Hood's Port on Hood's canal, and from thence by way of Lake Cushman back to the main party. Leaving the Skokomish river, we followed up the left bank of the south branch. For the first mile [unintelligible word] banks on either side rose at a steep grade from the water's edge and the traveling was extremely bad on account of the windfalls and large boulders. Crossing the river on a log we took to the other bank. This we found to be better, though far from good traveling, so we followed it until noon, when we came to a branch leading off to the west in course 40° west of south. We had traveled a distance of about three miles and were now at an altitude of 1500 feet.

Here we cooked dinner of bacon and pan bread, and after a short rest proceeded on, keeping well up the hillside, but within sight of the creek. We traveled in a southwesterly direction until we came to the fall, where we crossed again in order to gain a small plateau on the opposite side, to get on which we had to climb up the face of a small bluff some forty feet high. Take into consideration that we each carried a pack of thirty pounds besides our guns, instruments, etc. and it will be understood that this was not an easy matter. But foot by foot, we walked up, sometimes flattened against the rock on some narrow crevice, at others clinging to the bushes within reach until at last we gained the plateau, on which is situated the five small lakes in which this branch takes its rise.

These lakes are all within a few hundred yards of each other and are beautifully clear, while the only living thing seen in them was one "newt" or water dog.

So far the only indication of game that we had seen showed that this was their winter range, but at present the woods had an oppressive stillness broken only now and again by a band of chickadees with their noisy chatter, but after leaving the lakes elk, bear, deer and cougar signs became plentiful. Proceeding on our way we clambered up a long snow bank and in time reached the summit of the divide. Mount Tacoma and also the Pacific ocean could be plainly seen from here and a large mountain that we took to be Mount Olympus.

Making our way to a camp site that we had occupied three nights previously, when on an ornithological collecting trip, we doffed our packs and started in to make camp. We were now at an altitude of 3775 feet, and soon after making camp the temperature began to fall, and inside of twenty minutes we had passed from a hot summer's afternoon to a winter's evening, for the clouds rolled in, shutting out the sun, and it soon became dark.

Most of that night was spent in trying to keep warm.

On the morning of July 26 we were up at daylight, and after a light breakfast Mr. Church started for a high mountain to the southwest of us, in order to get our bearings, while I took notes of the birds seen at an altitude of nearly 4000 feet.

I found the Rufus humming bird very plentiful, feeding on the blossoms of the mountain plants that were now in full bloom.

From their actions it was plain that I was a stranger in these parts, for they would come and hover within a foot of my face, eyeing me over in the most [unreadable word] manner.

The Oregon junco was also numerous, feeding on the insects found on the heather. I also saw two moose birds, as they are here called.

On the return of Mr. Church, we both climbed to the summit of a peak about 500 yards from camp. On gaining the summit we had a first rate view of the river we were in search of. The summit of this peak showed an elevation of 4005 feet, and as this was the point from which we discovered the south fork, we gave it the name of Churton peak. From here we could see a large body of water, distant about twenty miles and bearing 30° west of south from us, and which we took to be Grays harbor. And intervening between us and it were three large fires. As it was now nearly noon, we decided to have dinner and then make our way down to the river on the other side of the ridge. This we did descending on the other side. The pitch of the hillside was tremendous. At the place we went down there was no undergrowth and the ground was as slippery as glass, on account of the coating of pine leaves on it. At one time I lost my footing and shot down about ten feet, when I caught a root with my left hand, almost dislocating my arm. Holding with my left hand, with my gun in my right, I was unable to get a foothold to raise myself and had to sling my gun by its strap and drag myself up with both hands.

While going down we saw deer, at one of which I shot with my 16-bore collecting gun, causing him to cut some funny capers and then make off.

On this side of the range we saw only one small patch of snow, and all the vegetation was farther advanced than on the north side.

After a tedious climb of three hours we reached the bed of the stream that here is at an altitude of 1125 feet above sea level.

Shortly after we found an Indian trail which we followed until we came to a ford, and here we made camp for the night, and on the morning of the 27th were out at daylight and forded the river and took the trail on the other side, following down the right bank, and in about twenty minutes traveling came to a creek coming in from the northwest. Below this the river runs through a gorge on a course 20° south of

east, then into a large bottom about a mile wide, heavily timbered with fir, cedar, yew, and by the river alder and vine maple. All game signs seen here were at least a week old. The head of this bottom is at an altitude of 700 feet, and here we began to lose confidence in the Indian trail, for it was plain that it had not been used this year, and it always seemed to lead us into the middle of a bad windfall and then get lost.

At noon we came to a large gravel bar grown partly over with willows and here the trail again crossed the river, and so we stopped for dinner, and while I got the fire going Mr. Church took my line and flies and tried for a trout.

When detailed for this trip we had just returned from a previous one of three days, and in consequence our food had been very similar for some time, namely bacon and pan bread. Therefore, great was our joy when three mountain trout lay flapping their lives out on the sand. True, they were small but they were good.

After dinner we again crossed the river and took the trail on the other side, but soon lost it in an open where the grass was fresh grown.

The bottom here is very wide being formed of a rich red loam, with a luxuriant growth of herbage and fine timber.

Here we again crossed to the left bank and stopped for the night, and as our supplies were getting very low we tried hard to catch some fish but could not, although we could plainly see them.

Great numbers of jumping mice played around our camp fire all the evening and they would come and look at us with their large black eyes wide with wonder and then hop away in their peculiar manner clearing two feet at a jump, but always returning for another look.

On the morning of the 28th we were out early and again tried to catch some fish with the same result, so we ate a very light breakfast and started on again. All along the river here there is a gravel bar either on one side or the other. In order to gain the advantage of these for travel we took to wading the river from one bar to another, and in this way made very good traveling.

In going across an angle in the bottom that the river made we killed two old grouse and one young one, so for the present at least there was no fear of our starving, and we stopped for dinner at the first good place where dry wood was to be found, and baked one grouse in what is commonly called a "tin oyster," (which is a sort of combination tin dish and frying-pan supplied by the government)and made broth of the young one.

After a good dinner we traveled on, wading from bar to

320

bar as before. Here the river is very broad and shallow and sometimes we would wade for a mile at a time down the middle of the stream. Here the hills on both sides came down to the water, forming high banks on each side, which soon formed into a sort of sand canyon, as we proceeded. Below this another large creek comes in from the north down a deep canyon, and about one mile and a half farther another creek comes in from the north, down what appears to be a large bottom. At the mouth of this creek we made camp, and while hunting for fire wood we found that it had been used for a camp before. We found one large elk horn, and the following inscription on a tree:

Sunday, Sept. 19th
As long as there is mountains there will
be d—n fools that will climb them.
C. P. N.

We agreed with C. P. N. but did not admire his style of expression.

After a hearty supper of the remaining grouse, we summed up our situation as follows: We had traveled about twenty-two miles from the divide. Our supplies had got down to three-fourths of a pound of flour, a few ounces of tea and sugar, a little salt and a piece of bacon as big as a hen's egg.

At daylight on the 29th we were out again and tried for a trout without success, so after a breakfast of half a piece of bread as big as a saucer, and a cup of tea, we started on, wading down the river as on the day previous. About noon we came to a large bar on which we could see many fresh beaver signs, and shortly after we saw the tracks of a man, horse and dog, and below this about one mile we crossed the river on a log and came upon a clearing about 15x30, with logs laid for the foundation of a house, while on a tree near by was posted a claim sign showing that it was the intention of William Weller to squat on this land. About a quarter of a mile further we found another for one John Clark. We now supposed that we were nearing a settlement and must be near the main river.

Passing through a willow swale I killed a beautiful specimen of the solitary tatler, and we both felt in much better spirits when, coming onto an old camp site, we found a portion of a loaf of bread, which we ate. But our spirits fell with a crash when, turning the next bend of the river, we saw it enter an immense gorge, the perpendicular walls of which rose to a height of 500 feet on each side.

But there was nothing for it but to keep on and so we did, for we thought that most likely it was only about three miles long. By clambering along the edges and wading from side to side we managed to get along about three miles when the water became so deep and rapid that at every crossing we were in danger of being swept into the pool below. At the last crossing we made, the water came up to our waists and Mr. Church had a narrow escape, being turned completely round and flung against a rock. After this we decided to give it up and look round to find a way out. We could not go back for wading against such a torrent was not possible. There was a place where water had run down the cliff in the winter and formed a crevice in which some bushes had grown and up this we went, hanging to projecting rocks and bushes. Lumbered up as we were with packs and guns this was a dangerous climb. We had not had a meal all that day and were fagged out and our soaked clothes hung heavily round us. Had a bush or rock given way certain death would have been the result.

In this way we climbed up 500 feet and gained what seemed to be a small table-land, but great was our disgust when after traveling almost fifty yards we came to another gorge, caused by a large creek coming in at right angles to the river.

Climbing down this was not so bad, but up the other side was very rough.

We crossed two other gulches after this, each getting smaller than the last, and in the third we made camp. That night I sacrificed my specimen and we made a cupfull of a sort of broth out of it, which constituted our supper.

On the morning of July 30 we ate our last piece of bread at about 5 A.M. and started on in a very weak condition. Our only hope was to get to some ranch. To do this we knew we must reach the forks of the river, but how far that was we did not know. We had been told that we could make the trip in two days and we had been out five now, and we knew that we were not near our destination yet because of the high altitude we were at. All the forenoon we traveled on a sort of plateau which would have been good traveling had it not been that was covered with sallal that came above our knees.

We did not see a living thing to shoot, and all we could do was to eat berries, which though they did not strengthen us at least stopped the cravings of hunger.

About 4 in the afternoon we came to the end of the canyon, and here we descended to the river bed again. Here the river fans out over a long succession of broad sand bars, and is surrounded by extensive low bottoms. We were now very weak and had got into a sort of "don't care" style. Any little obstacle would throw us down, and it required more mental than physical exertion to get up again. In this manner we traveled about three miles, when we saw a good trail on the other side of the river. So through the water we went, perfectly indifferent to the fact that it came above our waists.

The trail was well worn, and we knew that it led to a house somewhere; but it soon led up a steep hill, and up this we went, three or four yards at a time, till at last we got nearly to the summit, and seeing a fine lot of blackberries, we sat down to eat some. When we heard somebody speak we soon made ourselves heard, and in a few minutes we were standing beside Mr. Runnells, who was on a trip to the mountains and had stopped at the top of the hill waiting for the rest of his party with the wagon to come up, which they did, and we soon were regaling ourselves on crackers and cheese.

When we were somewhat satisfied we all repaired to the ranch of Mr. Kirkland. Here we had an excellent supper, bed and breakfast. To these gentlemen we owe a great deal as they did everything in their power to help us out.

In the morning Mr. Cardwell went with us a distance of two miles, in order to show us a short cut to Union City. With heartfelt gratitude to this gentleman for his kind treatment, we bade him good-bye, and, according to his instructions, we followed the trail down the river to a place where a log jam had formed, which his men were engaged in cutting out.

Mr. Cardwell is at work clearing the south fork, in order to drive logs as soon as his land is surveyed. We had now completed the work intrusted to us, with the following results:

We had ascertained that the south branch of the Skokomish river rises in a lake to the westward of the main river, at an altitude of 2000 feet above sea level. That for a distance of twenty-five miles in a southeasterly direction it flows through a splendid timber country, with very fine agricultural bottom. It then runs through a deep gorge, in which it runs a distance of seven miles, coming out on the low bottom land and almost three miles below joins the main river.

At present there are no settlers above the gorge, but there are some few ranches below it. The time is not far distant when this beautiful valley will be dotted with comfortable homes.

Fall and winter elk, deer, bear, cougar and wolves are plentiful in here and in autumn splendid fishing may be had at any time, the trout in these waters growing to a very large size.

B.

ACROSS THE DIVIDE[19]

Progress of Pathfinder O'Neil and His Party.

Falls of the Skokomish.

Band of Fifty Elk Encountered and Ten Slain—Trail Now Cut to Summit of the Olympics.

In The Olympics, Aug. 9.—On the evening of July 15 the O'Neil party, then camped on the Skokomish river just below its south branch, dropped their canvas, hauled down the stars and stripes and pennant of the Oregon Alpine Club, and again the jingle of the bell-mare broke the oppressive stillness of this wilderness of timber as she picked her way down the newly-cut trail, followed by the straggling string of loaded mules. The route led up the south branch for about half a mile to a point where a bridge had been thrown across the stream. This crossing is worthy a word of notice. Formed of felled timber, and filled in with broken rocks, it spans the mountain torrent not three feet above its seething surface, while a beautiful waterfall gives out its everlasting roar not twenty feet away, making a sight worthy an artist's pencil.

After crossing the stream the trail follows down the opposite bank, crossing to a point one mile up the main river. Here on the bank of the stream camp No. 6 was pitched, about a quarter of a mile below which are situated the falls of the Skokomish.

These beautiful falls are situated at the head of the gorge, through which the Skokomish river runs for about three miles.

The whole body of water is here gathered into a space of about five feet, falling over a ledge of rock in the form of a veil a distance of about twenty-five feet into a very deep pool about thirty feet wide and forty feet long. At the end of this pool it again makes another clear drop of thirty feet. Then taking a slight turn to the left, it passes through a chute formed in the rock, and striking the opposite rock wall, falls in a cloud of spray a distance of sixty feet, striking on a ledge, and falls in a solid body into a rock below that is shaped like a bowl and causes the water to be thrown up again like the petals of a flower.

From the foot of the falls perpendicular walls of rock rise on both sides to a height of 200 feet.

With the intention of viewing these falls to the best

---

[19] Bernard J. Bretherton, *Seattle Post-Intelligencer*, August 14, 1890. Bracketed notes are Wood's. The O'Neil party's wanton slaughtering of elk reported by Bretherton in this article caused James Wickersham to comment in his Olympic National Park piece that "such acts of vandalism should be punished severely." Wickersham included the article as an addendum to his Olympic report, which the *Tacoma News* published on January 2, 1891. See part 2, chapter 9, The Wickersham Expeditions 1889 and 1890.

advantage, and also in order to represent them to the public in a proper manner, Colonel H. E. Linsley and the writer climbed down to the foot of them. Here we found another of nature's wonders, namely, a small subterranean creek flowing under this great wall of rock.

It is regrettable that the photographer of the expedition is unavoidably detained in Portland, and so we cannot procure a photograph of these falls, but photographic apparatus has been telegraphed for, and as several of our members are adepts in this line we may yet be able to get a picture of them.

On the left bank of the river, opposite the falls, we found the Joynt river camp of the Wickersham party, which had led us to suppose that they did not know that this river already had a name, and so had called it after Mr. Joynt, a member of their party. To compromise the matter, we gave the falls the name of Honeymoon falls, in honor of Mr. and Mrs. Taylor, who were members of the party and on their wedding tour.

Our exploration party that have been over the divide report large quantities of snow still in the higher ranges. With this in view Lieutenant O'Neil made camp No. 6 permanent headquarters for some time, while parties were sent out in every direction to ascertain the most advantageous route to cross the divide.

While on one of these trips Sergeant Yates, Marsh and Assistant Botanist Fisher had the good fortune to come across a band of fifty elk, out of which they killed ten.

The party had been sent out to see if there was a crossing by the head of the North Fork, and also to get some game if possible, as meat was wanted in camp.

On the second day out they got to the headwaters and found it impossible to get mules over this way. They here killed a whistling marmot which they had served in different styles for three meals. That day they passed several camps of the Wickersham party, and slept that night under a large glacier. In the morning they crossed over into a canyon that contained five lakes, and here they separated, Fisher remaining on the summit, while the other two started in different directions down the canyon.

After separating Sergeant Yates soon saw a very large band of elk crossing to the east which, on gaining a large snow bank, all lay down. Yates then made his way back to Fisher, and posting him in a position where he could watch them and also signal to him if they moved, he started out and soon found Marsh. The elk lay on a bank of snow just under a small bluff, and onto this bluff the hunters got, and picking out an old bull and two cows that lay side by side, so that in case they overshot they would hit the farthest and if they undershot they would hit the nearest, they drew a bead on the old bull that lay in the center and opened fire at 250 yards, killing the farthest cow dead and mortally wounding the bull. The elk then got up, and not knowing where the shots came from, they came right down under the bluff the hunters were on and in this way they were able to kill three bulls and seven cows.

Taking all the meat they could carry and leaving Fisher to look after the rest, they returned to camp and the following morning all hands left with knapsacks to bring in the meat, returning on August 6 with about 200 pounds of meat.

They reported having seen a great number of bears, and during their absence Fisher seeing a bear had darted after it with his revolver and followed it into a brush patch where there were five more. This he thought was rather too much of a picnic and so resigned his claim to any bear meat.

On arriving at the elk camp Samuel [Lieut.] O'Neil, taking Fisher and his dog Max, started on across the range. The main business of the camp is now to jerk the supply of meat on hand. On Sunday, August 3 [?], our botanist, Prof. L. F. Henderson, was obliged to leave us.

As far as he had got the professor had found the flora identical with the Cascade range, excepting only the Alaska cedar, which is found here. The work so well begun by the professor will be carried on by his assistant, Mr. Henry Fisher.

In fact in all the branches of natural science the conclusions have been about the same, nothing of importance having as yet been found.

On August 8, Lieutenant O'Neil and Mr. Fisher returned to camp and reported having found the camps of the "Banner Party" up to a point on the headwaters of one of the rivers leading into the Sound.

On the divide they found the flag left by the ladies for Lieutenant O'Neil and bearing the figure 14 in honor of the Fourteenth infantry, his regiment, but having found it he had not the heart to take it, thinking it better to leave it on its pinnacle of snow as a memento of three ladies' pluck and daring. May all good fortune go with them.

The Skokomish river, with all its branches and tributary streams, has now been explored and platted, and our next work will be in a new country with rivers flowing to the southwest. The trail is now cut to the divide and our exploration parties have been on the Quiniault river, and we are now only waiting for the last batch of supplies to come up, and then in one long reach we will clear the divide.

B. J. B.

323

OLYMPIC ADVENTURE[20]

The Entire Skokomish River Explored and Mapped.

Coming on a Big Band of Elk.

Ten of Them Killed and the Meat Dried—Venturesome Ladies—No Minerals Found.

Special Correspondence, Sunday Ledger:

Union City, Wash. Aug. 15.—On July 25th the O'Neil party left camp No. 5, on the south bank of the Skokomish river, and moved to camp No. 6, on the Middle Fork. After leaving camp No. 5 the trail follows up the south branch of the river through a very rough country, all the time descending until it reaches the bed of the stream about a mile from the main river, where the stream is crossed on a bridge built by the party, just below a very picturesque fall. The trail then leads down the left bank of the stream, and a short way up the main or middle fork on the right bank, camp No. 6 is located, while a little below on the opposite side of the stream is the "Jayut River" camp of the Wickersham party, named after Mr. Jayut a member of their party. And it was here that one of the most beautiful waterfalls in this country of beautiful scenes is located.

The inner falls are situated at the head of the gorge through which the Skokomish river flows for a distance of three miles. Here the whole volume of water is gathered into a space of five feet, falling over a ledge of rock in the form of a veil for a distance of twenty-five feet, diving into a large and very deep pool, at the lower end of which it again makes another fall of about thirty feet; then turning slightly to the left, the water passes through a rock chute, and, striking the rock wall on the opposite side, falls in a sheet of spray a distance of sixty feet to a ledge below, over which it falls in a solid body onto a large block of rock formed like a bowl, out of which the water rises again like petals of a flower. The foot of these falls is in a chasm, the perpendicular walls of which rise to a height of 200 feet on the other side.

It is to be regretted that the photographer of the expedition is still detained in Portland, and in consequence many beautiful views are lost, but two cameras have been telegraphed for, and as several members of the party are adepts in this line, many good views will be taken. A large camera will be used for views and a small one (No. 2 kodak) for camp scenes. Our naturalist is also making a specialty of pictures of birds and animals taken from life. Exploration parties that had been sent out over the divide reported lots of snow still on the upper ranges, and with this in view Lieutenant O'Neil decided to make camp No. 6 headquarters for some time while parties will start out in all directions to find the most advantageous route to cross the divide.

One of these parties composed of Sergeants Yates and Marsh accompanied by Assistant Botanist Fuller left camp August 1 for the head of the North Fork, and after traveling two days came onto a herd of fifty elk, ten of which they succeeded in killing. Taking as much meat as they could carry they returned to camp and the next day all hands started out and brought in the remaining meat. On this trip several bear were seen and Mr. Tisbee, who had remained as a guard over the dead elk, had seen five large black bears altogether in a space of fifty feet.

When here Lieutenant O'Neil and Mr. Tisbee went on over the divide and the remainder of the party returned to camp and busied themselves jerking meat.

While at camp No. 6 the party was visited by Messrs. Williams and Gray, who left us August 6. On August 3 the party mourned the loss of Prof. Henderson, our botanist, he being obliged to leave us. His work is now being able carried on by Henry Tisbee, his former assistant.

So far the flora has been found to be identified with the Cascade range, the Alaska cedar being the only exception. Several parties of miners, hunters and pleasure seekers are already taking advantage of the O'Neil trail, and pass our camp daily, pushing on ahead and generally returning in a day or two, and all telling the same tale, namely, that they have been all over the mountains, though a little questioning always goes to show that they have only been in the next canyon.

So far no minerals in paying quantities have been found in this district, the formation being chiefly volcanic, trap, talcues, hornblendic schists and slate.

In fact, the only thing of value seems to be the timber, of which there is no end.

A trail is now cut to the foot of the divide, and it will only be a matter of a few days before the party is over the divide.

The camps of the "banner party" have been traced to a point where they crossed the divide, and where the ladies of the parties had fulfilled their promise to Lieutenant O'Neil

---

[20] Bernard J. Bretherton, *Tacoma Daily Ledger*, August 17, 1890.

by leaving the flag of the Seventeenth infantry on the summit, and here he found it a few days afterward, and there it still flies, a monument to the pluck and bravery of Misses Wickersham and Taylor the first ladies to cross the Olympic range. To fully appreciate what these ladies have done a person must travel in this country. A member of the monkey tribe might enjoy himself here, but a woman hardly, for it is almost a constant climb, not only on the hillsides but on what small bottoms there are you are either wriggling over a log or squirming under one, not to mention devil clubs and vine maple; in short, these ladies have succeeded where many "would be" explorers have failed.

All the meat from the elk killed by Messrs. Yates and Marsh is now dried, and orders issued forbidding the killing of game except by exploration parties for their own use.

Every branch and tributary of the Skokomish river is now explored and mapped, and the next river to be explored will be the Quineault.

B. J. B.

OLYMPIC EXPLORATION[21]

Further Results of the Work of Lieut. O'Neil's Party.

Game and Fish Are Plentiful.

The Headwaters of an Unknown River Discovered. New Trips Laid Out.

On August 11th the Olympic Exploration party, commanded by Lieutenant James [sic] P. O'Neil, made one more move into the unknown region of the Olympic mountains, and leaving camp No. 6 on the middle fork of the Skokomish river we crossed the stream and over a small sloping foothill down into the canyon of the north fork, and followed up its right bank. The north fork comes into the main river about twelve miles above Lake Cushman, in the center of the gorge through which the main river flows. For the first half mile it flows down a steep, rocky canyon, at the upper end of which a beautiful waterfall comes in on the left bank. Above this the banks are low and in places open—that is if a jungle of salmonberry bushes higher than a man's head can be called open. Up this stream we journeyed a distance of two and one-quarter miles, and made camp No. 7 about two in the afternoon. This, at first glance, may seem to be very poor

traveling, and a word of explanation is therefore required. This country is full of two things, namely, windfalls and landslides, and the traveling is perpetually on a side hill. When we strike a landslide we have either to go up around it or down below and wade up the river; while though we might saw out the fallen logs before winter, we prefer to go round the big ones, cutting out only the smaller. In this way, it will be understood, that in order to go two miles in a given direction with the pack train we have to travel over about six.

At camp 7 we only remained two days and the only incident of note there was a visit paid us early one morning by a large black bear; but on account of the clamorous welcome tendered him by Max, Jumbo, and Tige, our canine night-watch, he did not remain long enough to be entertained by the other members of the party.

At this camp we found the fishing to be fairly good, but the trout were all small. On the morning of August 13, we again made a move of three and a half miles, camping on a large gravel bed made by a creek that came in on the right bank, falling down a perpendicular bluff in a series of small waterfalls of about ten feet each, and there we had good fishing and made the discovery that eight-tenths of the fish caught were males.

Early in the morning of August 14, Lieut. O'Neil, who had been away buying supplies, returned to camp, bringing with him two cameras, one large one and a kodac for the writer. The camp was visited the same day by three gentlemen who wished to see our mode of life. They greatly admired the air of comfort prevailing everywhere, and were surprised when told that the whole encampment could disappear any time at twenty minutes' notice.

August 15 we again made another move up to the falls, a distance of a little over three miles, and within two miles of the summit of the divide. This move was without incident, and camp No. 9 was pitched between the two forks of the river in a beautiful little bottom, surrounded on all sides by high perpendicular bluffs.

These bottoms are mostly all covered by a dense growth of salmon berry, the fruit of which grows to a very large size and are of a delicious flavor. Huckleberries are also very plentiful here, while in the creek trout are large and numerous, but the birds are very scarce, while bear are seen every day and deer are to be found within a half mile of camp, but in order to find elk a higher altitude must be reached and nine out of ten of the hunting parties that pass our camp come back empty handed. On the journey up this North fork we have seen many

325

---

[21] Bernard J. Bretherton, *Tacoma Daily Ledger*, August 24, 1890.

fine cedars, one of which we measured and found to be fifty-two feet in circumference and perfectly sound.

Headwaters of Unknown River Discovered

On August 11, Colonel N. S. Linsley, our geologist, in company with Mr. Fisher left headquarters, then at camp on the middle fork of the Skokomish river, for the purpose of finding the most advantageous route to cross the divide. Journeying up the North fork until they came to the point where it divides into two branches, they then followed up the one that leads off to the southeast until they came to a creek coming in from the northeast, which they followed up to its head and from there climbed onto a ridge running to the northwest and after traveling along this for a distance of nearly a mile then climbed down on the other side and came to a lake, out of which a creek flowed. Crossing the creek they pursued their way in a northerly direction and came to another lake out of which another stream flowed. Then turning to the west they climbed to a high peak, showing an altitude of 5350 feet, and from which they could see three large lakes to the east of them, out of which flowed three streams that joined and formed a large river, flowing on a course 20° north of east, Mount Olympus 30° west of south and Quiniault lake 48° south of west.

Although we suppose that this river is either the Hamahama, Dacqueboore or Dulewallips river, our bearing do not fit to either one of them. But as no maps agree on either the locations of these rivers or the mountains, it is impossible to tell. And for the purpose of deciding this point, Lieutenant O'Neil has detailed B. J. Bretherton, the ornithologist of the party, and Sergeant Yates to make the descent down it to its outflow, and they will start in the course of two or three days. At the same time two other parties will leave as follows: To make an exploration of the Quinault river and its tributaries; Lieutenant James P. O'Neil and Messrs. Fisher and Danton.

Down the Humptulips River to Its Outflow, the Messrs. Church

All these parties, after fulfilling their several missions, will make their way back to Union City, and from there by way of Lake Cushman to the main party, which, in the meanwhile, will be pushing its way west under command of Colonel N. E. Linsley.

This is almost the exact programme that will be gone through with all the water courses encountered.

The O'Neil party are not going through these mountains against time to get to a certain point but their object is to put before the public a true account of the country as they see it.

ON THE DUCKABUSH[22]

———

Trip of a Camping Party in the Olympics.

———

Exploring the Docewallips.

———

Colony of Whistling Marmots—An Elk Kodaked—Notes on Geology and Botany.

———

Hoodsport, Sept. 1 On the morning of August 18 the writer, in company with Sergeant F. W. Yates, left the headquarters of Lieutenant J. P. O'Neil with instructions to find the river reported by Colonel N. E. Linsley; to locate its rise and follow it down to its mouth. Of what river this was, or how long we would be in reaching its mouth we had no idea, except that we supposed from its general direction that it flowed into Hood's canal somewhere.

Our supplies consisted of each twenty pounds of flour; bacon, five pounds; sugar, two pounds; tea, half a pound; salt, four ounces, and a little pepper. Besides our supplies, we carried between us one army carbine and twenty-five rounds of ammunition, one 16-bore shotgun, a No. 1 Kodac camera, skinning tools, curatives, specimen case and blankets, frying-pans, etc. So it will be seen that we were not lightly loaded.

Directly after leaving camp we commenced traveling in a northwesterly direction. For the first two hours our work consisted of climbing through dense thickets of young fir with an occasional swale of vine maple and devil's clubs for variety, but after gaining an elevation of about 3,000 feet we were able to follow up a sort of grass meadow, through which a small stream ran.

These meadows are formed by heavy landslides in the winter, which carry all the timber and brush to the valley below, leaving a bare place where the slide started; over this, in the course of time grows, what at first appears to be a grassy meadow, but on close inspection proved to contain very little grass but a great profusion of wild flowers and a sort of wild bean or vetch. These meadows are very plentiful in the higher ranges of these mountains, forming at this season of the year the chief feeding grounds for both birds and animals.

Following up these meadows, which lay in cups [?] up the

---

[22] Bernard J. Bretherton, *Seattle Post-Intelligencer*, September 3, 1890.

mountain side, separated by small timbered bluffs, we kept on until noon, when we stopped for dinner. The view from here was wildly grand, below us in panoramic view lay the valley of the Skokomish river with all its branches and tributary streams, while around us rose the rugged monarchs of the Olympics, their jagged summits towering towards the sky.

After dinner we again pursued our journey on up, and in the course of about one hour arrived at the summit. Below us and about three miles distant lay the river we were in search of, while nearer to us ran one of its tributaries. Descending we came on to a small plateau, in which were situated two small lakes, and at the western end of one of them we found a camp of the "Banner Party" indicated by the following inscription on a tree:

"Banner expedition, July 29, 1890. Soldier Camp., James Wickersham, Deborah Wickersham, Clyde Wickersham, Chas. E. Taylor, May W. Taylor, Charles W. Joynt. From Lake Cushman to Port Angeles."

And under this the register of one of our own parties, as follows:

O.E.E., August 11, 1890. Colonel. N. E. Linsley, H. Fisher. ⁄ Alt. 4,250."

To a person not understanding its use this system of registering and naming camps of small parties may at first seem foolish, and so I will explain. When a small party is sent out in any direction every night they blaze a tree, and giving the camp some name, they write it, together with the date and their own names, on the tree. The use of this is obvious. Should a man not return to camp in a reasonable time a search party can trace him by his camps; or, should it be necessary to send any one to a place on their route afterwards, by giving him general directions and telling him which of their camps to go to he is then able to tell for certain when he is on the right ground.

It was by this means that we were able to tell in which direction to proceed. Climbing down the southwest slope we came to a snow lake lying in a large, loose rock basin, which was alive with whistling marmots, sometimes called mountain beaver. This member of the great family of rodents, though of repulsive appearance, is very interesting in its habits. In size it equals the badger, attaining a weight of about six pounds. In its winter coat it is a yellowish red, and the hair is very long and shaggy, changing in summer to a dark silver-gray and the hair becoming short and thick. Its dwelling is a burrow in the ground, the entrance generally being

situated between large rocks. It is an herbiferous animal, collecting a supply of food for the winter, which it first dries and then stores away. On the approach of danger to their warrens they give a shrill scream of alarm that so much resemble the whistle of a man as to give the animal its name. Here we killed three grouse, and also obtained some fine specimens of the crossbill (Loxia curvirostra Americana), this bird now being very plentiful here.

After leaving the snow lake we had a smart climb down to the creek bottoms below, and after following down the creek for some time we camped on a small grassy island.

All through the day the writer had suffered from the stings of insects, and could not sleep in consequence, for the pain and itching was terrible, so he was obliged to spend the greater half of the night bathing his arms and face in the creek.

August 19.—After breakfast we took some photographs and then wended our way down the stream. The geological formation here is chiefly slate, and a conglomerate of sand and gravel, and the timber is fir, pine, hemlock and Alaska cedar.

After traveling down stream for about an hour we came to where it entered a deep canyon, and all further progress was barred in that direction, so we had to take to the ridge, in [on?] which we found good traveling. In the course of an hour we arrived at the river and took our route on the right bank, at noon stopping for dinner on a sand bar. After dinner, while I took some pictures of the river, Sergeant Yates, who is an expert fisherman, tried to catch some trout, but without success; the stream being seemingly too cold for the fish, while another feature of this stream is that it is of a milky white color, a feature not met with in the other streams.

In the later half of the forenoon we had traveled a good game trail; so after dinner we again took to it and traveled steadily until 6 o'clock. On our way we passed many large land slides, one in particular attracting our attention, and the conclusion we arrived at in regard to it was as follows: Sometime in the winter storms a spur of the mountain had become detached and started down the hillside, gathering speed as it went and carrying everything before it, trees, shrubs and earth, so that in its wake nothing but the bare rock was left, and crashing through the river had spent itself in [on?] the opposite hillside, there raising miniature hills and valleys, 500 to 800 feet in height.

That night we made camp in the "Docewallip Camp" of the Linsley party, and in the morning took our way up the game trail, which now led straight up the bluff to our right. After a hard climb of several hours we came to the crest of a

327

small plateau, and here in the soft mud on the trail we found the print of a lady's foot and knew that this must have been the route of the Banner party. This plateau lay about 1,000 feet below the summit of the grand divide and contained a beautiful, round lake with an island in the center, while its banks were covered with a profusion of wild flowers. Of this lake I took two pictures, and here we again found Col. Linsley's register on a tree, giving the lake the name of Marmot lake, and an altitude of 4,725 feet. While resting here we saw something up a glade to our right that looked like a grouse, and on bringing the telescope to bear on it we were sure it was, so while I kept him in view Sergeant Yates took my shotgun and stalked him. The actions of the bird were interesting to watch. He had seen me and was on the watch, standing rigidly erect, every faculty on the alert for the first sign of danger. Suddenly his bearing changes, his head sinks lower and lower until he sits crouching on the log, while a stealthy form emerges from the bushes on the right, a puff of smoke, and a dull boom wafted on the mountain breeze and the tragedy is ended.

After getting our packs in shape again we continued on in a northwest direction and arrived on top of a small table land, a point of which ran out in such a manner as to give us a grand view of the river below, and to this point we went, and were enjoying the view when we were startled by a noise like the trotting of a hundred horses. With momentary visions of a charging host of light-foot Indians we turned in the direction from which the sound came and saw one of the grandest sights it has ever been my good fortune to see.

Headed by an enormous bull, charging down the slope, came a band of at least sixty elk, until within thirty feet of us, when they wheeled eight and ten abreast round a clump of firs to our left.

So engrossed had I been in watching then that I had forgotten we were wanderers in an unknown country, and should not lose an opportunity to replenish our larder. But luckily my companion was more practical, and the crack of the rifle called me to my senses. The next thing I knew he was going through a wild fandango to rid himself of his pack, and I at once proceeded to imitate him, and in a few moments I was racing after him over the heather, my shotgun in one hand and camera in the other, and arrived a "good second," in at the death of a yearling cow. After cutting up the cow we went into camp and "smoked" the meat, and this occupied the rest of the day. That night we lived high on elk liver and broiled grouse.

August 21.—We were up at sunrise and found that the band of elk had passed back close to our camp during the night. Our meat was not dry but was sufficiently smoked, so after making up our packs we strung it on the outside of them and started. A queer sight we must have been, but there was no one to see us and one was as bad as the other, so we could laugh at each other.

We now found ourselves in a deep basin containing two large lakes from the banks of which loose rock slides ran up in every direction, the only outlet being by the way we had come in, and this accounts for the elk passing us in the night. A remarkable feature of these lakes is that they all swarm with frogs and their young, but not another living thing is found in them. Following up this basin to its northern extremity we climbed to the summit and found ourselves in the heart of the ruggedest part of the Olympic mountains, known as the Jupiter hills. On our left hand and almost below us flowed another large river that we afterwards found to be the Docewallips, while in the mountains around us we could see five large glaciers glistening in the sunlight.

To the southeast of us we could see the seven beautiful lakes that form the headwaters of the river we had orders to descend. The first part of our mission was now executed, we had found the river's rise, we had now to descend it and ascertain what river it was.

Descending to a lower middle of the ridge we saw a lake in a deep pocket, the waters of which were of a beautiful indigo in color, and on this account we called it Indigo lake. To get down to this lake was not an easy matter, for it was at least 800 [300?] feet below us, and the walls of the basin in which it lay were almost perpendicular, but by careful climbing we were able to make the descent in safety. By this lake we had dinner, and after dinner tried to find a way along the ridge, but could not, and so were obliged to climb down. This we did, hoping to be able to find a route at the lower elevation, but we soon found that we were on the edge of the large slide seen on our second day out, and that it was impossible to pass.

There was now nothing to be done but to make our way straight down to the river again. This we did by so steep a route that by the time we reached the stream we were both sore and tired by the many bumps and bruises we had received. Crossing the stream we made our way back to the point at which we first had struck it, and here we made camp for the night.

All that night we slept the sleep that only those who labor can enjoy, and awoke the next morning feeling ready for another hill. For breakfast we had the remains of the Elk liver, resolving to save our dry meat to the last.

For the first three miles the trail led through lightly tim-

328

bered bottoms, over a light, rocky soil that bore no underbrush, and we were able to travel at a good round pace. Our first obstacle was a good-sized landslide, and this and another smaller one was the only trouble met in the forenoon.

But while at dinner our luck changed, and it began to rain in torrents. That afternoon was the most miserable we either of us have ever experienced since we have been in these mountains. Slide after slide we clambered over, and had to ford the river four times, until at 4 o'clock, cold, wet, and hungry, we stopped to make camp. To make a fire in a heavy rainstorm in the woods is no easy job, but to make a camp is worse, and it may interest the reader to know how we made a shanty against a large fallen log by driving two uprights into the ground then to these we tied another pole, then cutting two more poles, we laid one end on this and the other on the log. This we covered by pulling the bark off a cedar tree and placing it shingle-fashion, bark side down, the smooth under surface shedding the rain splendidly.

In front of this we made a very hot fire, and, cutting fir limbs, dried them over the fire and made a bed of them.

August 23.—The morning sun making a sickly attempt to penetrate the damp, gloomy woods, aroused us from our morning nap. Our fire had been put out by the rain, and a more dismal prospect could hardly greet the waking vision of two lone travelers. About ten minutes after starting we were again wet through, but it now began to clear up and the sun shone out strong.

The canyon now began to get very narrow and rough, but by following the game trails we were able to avoid the worse places.

About 10 o'clock we came to a place where the trail turned up a very steep hill, and the cause of it was a very heavy landslide that it was impossible to pass. Thinking the trail led up and round the head of the slide we started up it. All that forenoon we climbed up a slope of about 1 to 1, and at noon had not got to the top. The afternoon was the same, until about 4 o'clock we arrived at a small grassy plateau about 200 feet below the summit of the range. Here we dropped our packs and climbed to the top of the ridge. Here we again came on the trail of the "Banner party," which we knew by finding a leaf from that well-known novel, "Put Yourself in His Place."

After watching the sunset and picking out the route to travel next day we went to our camp again. On the way we killed a marmot for supper, for these rodents can be eaten.

Sunrise Camp, Aug. 24.—This morning the sun topped the divide with a smiling face, and it was with light hearts we shouldered our packs and climbed to the summit of the ridge.

In the valley below us lay solid banks of white fog, and nothing was visible. Traveling along the ridge we found it to be composed of a slate formation, lying in perpendicular layers, while almost all the loose rock was of a beautiful white fine-grained sandstone. After traveling along the ridge for an hour we came to a ragged pinnacle, over which we had to climb. This was very dangerous work, the crest was not wide enough to walk upon, so we were obliged to climb along the side, hanging to the upright ribs of slate, while below us was a clear drop of several hundred feet.

After an hour's climb we landed on the other side, and here the ridge was broad and tolerably level, but at the other end was a high pinnacle similar to the one we had climbed over, only that on one side was a grassy ledge, so that passing it was comparatively easy; coming round a sharp corner on this ledge we came onto a band of three whitetail deer, and, as we had eaten all our elk meat, we shot one, and, as the others did not move, I resolved to take a photograph; so, dropping on my side, I called to Sergeant Yates to get out my camera from my pack, which he did, and, having got all ready, I commenced to approach the two remaining deer by walking up to them in full view. The dead buck lay between me and them, and at thirty feet I took a picture of the group, and then walked up closer until within fifteen feet of them and ten of the dead one, when they walked towards their fallen comrade, and so did I, until we were not ten feet feet apart, when I took another picture of them, then yelled and flung my hat at them; there and then only did they condescend to trot off.

Before we had dressed the deer the fog gathered around us so thick that we could not see fifty feet away from us, so we decided to remain here until the fog lifted and in the meantime cook dinner, but it did not raise, and so we continued our way guided entirely by our compass, having many narrow escapes of walking over the edge of bluffs, until late in the afternoon we found ourselves in a basin containing water, and here we camped for the night.

Camp Fog, Aug. 25.—The fog was thick yesterday, but it was nothing compared to what met our waking gaze this morning as we crawled from our blankets, cold and stiff, at 5 A.M., but as by the time we had cooked our breakfast it began to clear we decided to go on. Climbing along this rugged crest of rock soon became tiresome, and we tried to get down to the river but could not, for it seems that below us at varying distances there was a perpendicular bluff down which we could not climb. Had it been clear we no doubt could have seen a way, but the fog was still too thick to see any distance. While traveling along the ridge we saw many grouse and one band of eight deer.

329

About 10 o'clock the fog shut in around us again, and in about one hour we came to a pinnacle of rock towering above us in the fog. Climbing around this was terribly risky work, both footing and hand hold being hard to find, while the slightest slip meant death.

After passing this we had not gone two hundred yards before we found ourselves looking down a cliff about five hundred feet. This was a climax, and I now determined to go to one or the other river, and with that idea started down the west side of the mountain.

Climbing down was worse than it had been going up, but it had to be done, and by 8 o'clock that evening we had got about one-third of the way down, and so decided to camp.

At 6 o'clock the following morning we again started down, and about 9 o'clock we struck a good game trail. On the way we also saw more traces of the "Banner party." The trail led us down a little gulch to the water's edge, and we found ourselves about the middle of a deep, rocky canyon, through which boiled a deep and powerful stream, and how to get across was now the question. The only way seemed to be to ford, and this we resolved to do. So securing our guns on top of our packs, we cut each of us a good stout stick and waded in. The water reached our waists, and it was with great difficulty we kept our feet, but by carefully working from the shelter of one large boulder to another we at last reached the shore in safety.

After wringing the water out of our clothes we again took to the trail, and in the course of half an hour came to a place where a blaze had been made on a tree. While commenting on this aloud we saw a man sitting on a log, and a few minutes later made the acquaintance of Mr. A. D. Olmstead, who had been on a prospecting trip. The first question we asked him was what river this was, and he told us it was the Docewallips. Then we knew that the other river was the Duckabush.

That night we slept in a cabin, the highest one up the river, and the following day reached the mouth of the river, and bidding a reluctant good-bye to Mr. Olmstead, took passage on the steamer Josephine for Hoodsport.

B. J. B.

OLYMPIC EXPLORATION[23]

Lieutenant O'Neil's Party on the Duckabush River.

Many Hardships of the Trip.

Coming Across a Band of Sixty Noble Elk—Magnificent Scenery but No Agricultural Lands.

[Special Correspondence Sunday Ledger]

Union City, Aug. 29.—The morning of August 18 saw the writer in company with Sergeant Yates leaving the headquarters of the United States Olympic Exploration expedition under Lieutenant O'Neil, with instructions to find the river seen by Colonel Linsley, to locate its rise and follow it to its outflow into Hoods canal, then to return to the main party by the way of Hoodsport and Lake Cushman. Directly after leaving camp we commenced a climb through devil clubs and vine maple and this continued until we gained an altitude of 3000 feet, when the country became more open, leading through small, grassy glades, separated from each other by small belts of timber and a little bluff. At 2 o'clock in the afternoon we arrived at the summit, and after starting to descend on the other side, we came on to one of the camps of the "Banner Party," called Soldier camp, and bearing date of July 29.

Climbing down the southwest slope we came to a large basin in which was a small lake and a large mass of snow. Passing over this we took a westerly course and for the next two hours spent our time hanging on for dear life to the bushes and shrubs that grew on the face of a small precipice, down the side of which we were obliged to climb. On gaining the bottom we found ourselves in a fine grassy meadow, through which a creek flowed toward the north, and here we made camp for the night.

August 19 we were awake and up with the sun, which is not very early when you are camping in a canyon with perpendicular walls at least 1000 feet in height. After breakfast we took our way down the stream.

The geological formation we here found to be chiefly slate and a conglomerate mass of sand and gravel, and the timber was mostly fir, pine, hemlock, Alaska cedar and vine maple near the water. After following down the creek for some way we came to where it ran through between two perpendicular walls of rock having an average height of 500 feet. This, of course, stopped all further progress in that direction, and so we were again obliged to scale the bluff on our right and gain the summit of the ridge again. This we did with no little difficulty or risk, but after a climb of some thirty minutes we again stood on level ground.

We now took our way down the crest of the ridge, which

[23] Bernard J. Bretherton, *Tacoma Daily Ledger*, September 7, 1890.

fell at a gentle slope down to the river, and about 11 o'clock arrived at a point where the creek we had been following flowed into a large river coming from the west.

From its direction and its bearing from "Soldier Camp" we knew that this was the river we were looking for, and so we followed up the stream.

Experience had taught us that in every river bottom somewhere there is a game trail, and that these trails are the best routes to travel, and, after a little hunting around, we found a very good one here and took our route along it to the west, for our first business was to locate the source of this river. At noon we stopped to have dinner on a sandbar in the river bed, and, after dinner, while the writer took some photographs of the stream, Sergeant Yates tried to catch some fish, but although this gentleman is an expert fisherman he was unable to get a bite. This, and the coldness of the water, led us to believe that the fish did not come so high up.

Again we took to the game trail and after many hard climbs, up hill and trail crossed the river, but as good luck would have it a foot-log lay across, and this time we escaped a wetting. On gaining the other bank the trail led up through a grassy glade and into a belt of large timber at its head. Here we found one of Colonel Linsley's camps, named "Docewallip Camp," and here we remained for the night.

August 20.—As the writer had some ornithological specimens to prepare, we did not get started on our way until after 10 o'clock.

The trail turned directly from our camp up a very steep bluff, and this proved a rather tedious climb, but after an hour's plodding we arrived at the crest of a large plateau containing a beautiful lake with a small island in the center and surrounded by fine sloping banks covered with a beautiful profusion of wild flowers.

Here in a muddy part of the trail we saw the print of a woman's foot, and knew this must have been one of the ladies of the "Banner party."

Here again we found that Colonel Linsley had been before us and given this lake the name of Marmot lake. After resting a time we again took to the trail and climbed to a still higher plateau. Here we had a fine view of the river we were about to descend; a peculiar feature about this river is that for about twenty miles of its course it flows in a perfectly straight line. While standing on the edge of this cliff we were startled by a noise behind us like a band of trotting horses which continued to increase until the ground fairly shook beneath us. Turning around a magnificent sight met our gaze.

Headed by an enormous bull, trotting down the slope not forty feet from us came a band of over sixty elk. They had winded us but did not know our whereabouts, and almost ran over us before discovering our presence. The sight was grand indeed, but it was lucky for us that there was one with an eye to our larder in the party, and I was brought to a realization of the situation by the crack of Mr. Yates' carbine, and the next moment he was going through a first-class contortion act in a wild endeavor to rid himself of his cumbersome pack. Then the writer joined in and in a few minutes was racing over the heath, a kodac camera in one hand and a collecting gun in the other, determined to see the fun if there was going to be any, but only succeeding in coming in a good second at the death of a yearling cow.

After dressing the elk we climbed down to a creek in a large basin below us and made camp, built a smokehouse and proceeded to "jerk" the meat. That night our bill of fare contained stewed grouse, deviled elk kidneys, elk liver and bacon, and unlimited dodgerwaullip. We did not sleep well that night.

August 27th we were up early and found that the whole band of elk had passed our camp in the night, this, as afterward learned, being the only way out of this basin. Our elk meat was not yet dry, but sufficiently smoked, so we converted ourselves into traveling drying racks by stringing the meat on our packs and started for the northwest extremity of the basin.

This basin is at an elevation of about 4000 feet, and is surrounded entirely by bare, rugged peaks, from the feet of which almost to the center of the basin reach long slides of loose rock. In the center is a large, deep lake, the margins of which are covered with a profuse growth of mountain wild flowers. A remarkable feature of these lakes is that, although they are so cold that fish will not live in them, they swarm with frogs and their young.

On gaining the summit of the ridge at the western end of the basin, a magnificent view opened before our eyes. Below me, almost at our feet, a large river flowed, and from this point we could see five large glaciers, seven lakes and two rivers.

Descending, we took our way in an easterly direction we again climbed to the crest and found ourselves looking down into a very deep basin containing another lake. The sides of this basin were extremely steep, and it was with great difficulty that we were able to make the descent. At this lake we stopped for dinner, and gave the lake the name of "Indigo Lake," on account of the color of the water.

After dinner we tried to follow along the ridge, but soon came to a tremendous precipice. To pass this we started down hill, but after two hours traveling we found that at the foot of

331

it there had been a large landslide which had cut a gully all the way down the mountain side, cutting so deep as to leave a good-sized cliff on each side.

There was now nothing to do but to go down again to the river, which we did, reaching the point at which we had first struck it two days before, and camped there for the night.

August 22 we slept the sleep that only those who labor can enjoy, and after breakfast on the last of the elk liver we shouldered our packs and hunting up our old friend, the elk trail, we started down stream.

For the first three miles the trail led through lightly timbered bottoms on a shallow soil that bore no undergrowth, and we were able to travel at a good round pace, the only obstacles we met in the forenoon being two large landslides.

While at dinner it began to rain and soon turned into a gloomy, wet afternoon. Of course we were soon wet to the skin, when, to add to our misfortunes, the trail led across the river and we were obliged to follow it. This fording chilled us to the bone, and after we had crossed four times, which we did in the course of two miles, we considered we had done enough for the day and so made camp for the night.

The morning of the 23rd dawned gloomy and cold. The rain had ceased, but not before it had put our fire out. Our clothes were still wet and stiff and cold. We crawled from our damp blankets, wishing ourselves anywhere but in our present situation. But we must keep going as our provisions were beginning to look small, and as yet we had no idea how far we had to travel.

It is needless to say that we had not gone half a mile through these wet woods before we were again in a dripping condition. The canyon now began to get narrower and very rough, and it was only by carefully following the elk trail that we could make any headway at all. The trail in places was very dim, but where it led up around bluffs it was as large as a wagon road.

After traveling about three hours we came to a point where the trail led directly up a very steep hillside and appeared to be going to the summit of the ridge, and not wanting to go this way, we kept on down the river, but had not gone 200 yards before we found ourselves looking over a cliff several hundred feet high. This was caused like the one encountered on the 21st, by a heavy land slide, and, like the former, had started from the summit of the ridge.

Making our way back to the trail, we commenced what we knew would be a long and hard climb. It was now 10 A.M., and at 4 P.M. we threw off our packs in a small grassy basin about 100 feet below the summit.

Leaving our packs here we climbed to the crest of the ridge and found ourselves looking down into a large rocky basin but the ridge itself seemed to be good traveling. Here we found traces of the "Banner Party," showing that they must have camped near here, but we could not find their camp.

Making our way back to our packs we killed a whistling marmot, which we tried to eat.

August 24. — This morning the sun topped the divide with a smiling face, and it was with light hearts that we strapped our packs for an early start. The valley below us was hidden in a dense white fog, above which the snow-capped monarchs of the range rose in majestic grandeur. We were now on a sharp ridge, which sloped down on our left to Dosewallips river, and on our right to the Duckabush. This ridge we found to be composed chiefly of slate and beautiful white sandstone, the slate laying in perpendicular layers, making it very difficult to walk on.

After traveling on the summit for about an hour we came to a high pinnacle, around which we had to climb. Below us was a deep precipice, while all we had to cling to was the broken edges of slate; this was about the most risky climbing we did. After passing this pinnacle we had a good level ridge to travel on for a long distance, but at the end of this was another pinnacle like the first, except that on this one was a grassy ledge along which we could travel. This ledge lay on the south side of the mountain and on its outer edge grew a small grove of firs.

As we rounded the point we saw three fine white tail deer, all males, lying in the shade of these trees. At the crack of Sergeant Yates' carbine the largest one staggered to his feet, but at the next shot fell dead. In the meantime I had been watching the other two, and, seeing that they made no attempt to get away, I got the sergeant to get my kodac out of my pack, and commenced to walk boldly up to the two remaining deer. At thirty feet I took one picture and then, when about twenty feet from them and fifteen feet from the dead one, they commenced to walk toward their dead comrade, and so did I, until we were not more than ten feet apart. At this range I took three more pictures, and then threw my hat at them in order to make them run, as I wanted one photograph of them "on the jump."

After dressing the deer we made our way to a snow bank on the north side of the ridge and cooked our dinner, but before we had finished eating it began to rain a little and the fog got so thick that we could not see fifty feet from us.

That afternoon we floundered along in the fog until 3 P.M., at which time we came to a place where there was running water, and, fearing we might not find any more before night, we here made camp.

332

"Camp Fog." Aug. 25.—The fog yesterday was nothing compared to what met our waking gaze, as we crawled from under our blankets at 5 this morning. Everything we had was wet through and we felt both disheartened and miserable.

After breakfast we continued our way along the ridge. We could not see either of the rivers below us, but their constant roar told us only too plainly that traveling was bad in the canyon.

Traveling along the ridge now became very dangerous on account of the fog being so thick, our only guide being our compass, to follow the indications of which we were obliged to keep a straight line, climbing over everything we came to.

About 10 o'clock we came to a level stretch, and, the fog lifting a little, we saw eight deer feeding quite close to us. We also saw a great many grouse (*canace obscurus*). I had hoped to find the ptarmigan (*lagopus*) here, but so far have been unable to. Once in the fog I shot *canace obscurus* in mistake for him, the bird having assumed the squatting attitude of the ptarmigan. All day large bands of crossbills (*laxia curvirestra*) passed over our heads.

About 11 o'clock we came to a deep cliff, beyond which we could not pass, and so were obliged to climb down; first we tried the south side, but on this side we found a fearful precipice reaching away down into the impenetrable fog, and so we tried the north side with better success, as we were able, by hanging to the bushes, to climb down. After descending about 500 feet we stopped and had dinner by a large snow bank. After dinner we continued down, hanging on for dear life.

This continued all afternoon until at 8 o'clock in the evening we at last found a patch of level ground about twelve feet square, on which we made camp, one of us having to go back up about a quarter of a mile in order to get a block of snow to cook with as there was no water.

The next morning we continued on down, and about 9 o'clock came in sight of the stream, but to our dismay we found that it flowed through a deep canyon, the wall of which rose from the water to a height of five or six hundred feet. The opposite side seemed better traveling, but how to get there we did not know. In this dilemma we were moving up stream when we came on to a game trail, which soon led us down a small ravine to the water's edge, but still we encountered difficulties; the water was too deep and swift to ford, but after scrambling over rocks ups stream aways we came to a place not so deep and here, with great difficulty we crossed. After rubbing our limbs and feet, for the water is so cold in these streams that it almost stops the circulation, we again

took to the game trail and had not gone far before we came to blazes on the trees, and soon afterward we found a gentleman sitting on a log, who proved to be A. D. Olmstead of Seattle. In company with this gentleman we made the remainder of our trip, arriving at the outskirts of civilization that night.

At 4 o'clock in the afternoon of the next day we boarded the little steamer Josephine and in due time arrived at Hoodsport, where we delivered ourselves into the hospitable hands of Mrs. Finch and for three days lived on the fat of the land, at the expiration of which time we again took up our packs and started back to the main party.

Summary

The Duckabush river has its main source in five lakes and one glacier at a point situated half way between the Skokomish river and the Dosewallips. For the first twenty miles it flows on a course 20° north of east, afterwards swinging gradually to the north until within ten miles of its mouth, when it takes a bend and empties into Hood's canal on a south-east course.

There is no land on it suitable for agricultural purposes, and it is a very bad route to travel.

EXPLORING THE OLYMPICS[24]

———

How O'Neil's Party Crossed the Divide—New Work Mapped Out.

———

Union City, Sept. 18.—On August 19 the government expedition under Lieutenant J. P. O'Neil, moved from Camp No. 10, situated on the west slope of the divide between the north fork of the Skokomish river and the Duckabush river to Camp No. 11, on the headwaters of one of the tributaries of the Duckabush. Camp No. 11 was at an altitude of 4,100 feet, and situated in a rocky basin beside a large snow bank.

The next day Colonel N. O. Linsley, who was in charge of the party, went out to locate a trail down the stream. This was no easy matter, on account of the rough nature of the country, but with skillful engineering the work was accomplished, and on the 24th camp was moved on to the right bank of the Duckabush river. During this time the weather had been very bad, raining on and off all the time.

The same day Colonel Linsley killed a young elk, and in consequence there was great rejoicing in camp; for so far we have not found game very abundant in these mountains.

[24] Bernard J. Bretherton, *Seattle Post-Intelligencer*, September 19, 1890.

The weather now began to clear up and every man was put to work cutting a trail up to the forks of the river. With such good will did they work that on the 28th , camp was again moved to No. 13 on the headwaters of the river.

While cutting trail here we were greatly tormented by "yellow jackets," which infested the woods, and many amusing incidents occurred to break monotony of trail-cutting.

Camp No. 13 was in the river bottom, and on all sides the mountains roll at a very steep grade right up to the summit of the divide, and the talk of getting the trail up onto the summit was one likely to puzzle the brain of a railroad engineer, but here again Colonel Linsley showed himself equal to the occasion, and four days later the bell mare poked her nose over the crest and sniffed the salt breeze of the Pacific ocean.

Camp No. 14 was pitched in a large grassy valley on the divide between the headwaters of the Quiniault and Duckabush rivers. This basin contains about seven hundred acres of fairly level land, but mostly rocky soil, on which nothing but the hardy mountain plants will grow, but the balance is grown over with wild grasses, which affords very good feeding for the stock. It is in the form of a horseshoe, with the open end toward the Docewallip river, while all around it the ridge rises to a very sharp crest, forming beautiful peaks, from any of which Lake Quiniault, Mt. Rainier and Mt. Constance can be plainly seen.[25] On September 5 Lieutenant O'Neil returned to camp from his trip down the Quinault river. He reported having found a good route down that river, and declared his intention of going out by that route.

On September 10 Lieutenant O'Neil called the party together and stated to them that it was now his intention to divide the party as follows: Colonel N. E. Linsley, B. J. Bretherton and six men would take the northern part of the range, descending the Hoh, Quillayute, Dickdochtedar and Ozette rivers, and also crossing the headwaters of the Elwha. This party will make an attempt to plant the Oregon Alpine Club box on the summit of Mt. Olympus.

The pack train, under Sergeant Marsh, will push through to Gray's harbor, while Lieutenant O'Neil will explore the rivers to the southward. The party will all join at Fort Townsend in about four weeks.

B. J. B.

ELK AND CAMERA[26]

A Photographing Adventure
By Bernard J. Bretherton

We were camped on the second divide, in that part of the Olympic Mountains known as the Jupiter Hills. There were fourteen soldiers and two civilians under Lieutenant J. P. O'Neil, constituting the Olympic Exploring Expedition. We had been in the range over two months, and at this particular date we were out of food. In fact, this had become a chronic state of things about this time.

Sergeant Yates and the writer had just returned from an exploration of the Duckabush River and Mount Constance, and as the sun sank over the western ridge we lay on our blankets chewing our discontent and growling at things in general, when a shout from the ridge to the north of us called our attention to two of the boys who had been out on a hunt and were making down the ridge toward camp. On their arrival they reported having killed a large bull elk in a basin about four miles to the north of camp. Much to our delight and comfort, they had brought the liver with them, and after the feast we arranged to go out next morning and pack in the meat.

Our camp was peculiarly situated in a saucer-like depression of about thirty acres in extent, open on the southeast, where it overlooked the valley of the Duckabush River, but surrounded in all other directions by a circular ridge of loose rock rising about six hundred feet above us to a sharp ridge. This basin was devoid of timber excepting a long row of bull-pine which straggled down the ridge from the east and one lone fir-tree on the crest of the ridge to the northwest. The winter gales had so broken and twisted this tree as to give it the resemblance of a cross. Directly under it in the basin was a small lake which, on this account, we called "Lake of the Cross." Over the ridge to the north, on the southern

---

[25] "As in the case of 'Camp Docewallups,' the statement 'with the open end toward the Docewallip river' is obviously erroneous and possibly stemmed from the men's initial confusion as to the identity of the rivers, or perhaps was due to carelessness on Bretherton's part when he wrote the account. The basin faces the Duckabush." Wood, *Men, Mules and Mountains*, p. 418.

[26] *Overland Monthly* 35 (February 1900): pp. 112–15. This article appears exactly as Bretherton wrote it, complete with nineteenth-century spellings.

"Unfortunately, Bretherton appears to have mixed the events of two visits to the basin (on September 7 and 10), perhaps to embellish the story, or possibly because of faulty recollection due to the passage of time. Therefore, the article cannot be relied upon insofar as it conflicts with the details in his diary, recorded at the time of occurrence. For example, he states in this article that on September 7, when he approached the elk with his camera, Yates covered the bulls with his rifle, but the naturalist's diary and Fisher's narrative both indicate the sergeant was then with another group in the vicinity of O'Neil Pass. Yates did, however, accompany the party that returned to the basin on September 10." Wood, *Men, Mules and Mountains*, p. 420.

slope of Mount Anderson was Lindsley Glacier, in which the Quinault River, flowing to the west, and the Docewallups River, flowing to the east, have their origin.

Sunrise next morning found us astir and soon on our way, heading for Mount Anderson, at the foot of which lay the dead elk. Yates and myself, being in the lead, crossed the basin in which we were camped and made our way leisurely up the ridge, taking occasional shots at the whistling marmots that annoyed us greatly, heralding our approach with their shrill whistle, and thereby spoiling our chance of seeing game.

On one of these occasions an incident occurred which tends to show the ferocity of these giants of the rodent tribe. We were making our way across a rock slide, which was no easy matter, as we were both carrying heavy packs, and by this time the sun was glaring down unpleasantly warm. I had not had much experience with the army carbine,—which is harder to hold than a bucking bronco,—so when a large marmot suddenly appeared at the mouth of his burrow, not ten feet from me, I threw up the carbine and let drive without taking the necessary precaution of bracing my feet and setting my teeth, and in consequence found myself flat on my back in less time than it takes to think. The heavy pack prevented my "springing to my feet" in true Leatherstocking fashion, and the next thing I knew that marmot was right on top of me. My best weapons of defense were my heavy mountain boots, and these I used with the greatest precision and rapidity I could command. But a man on his back with head downhill at an angle of forty degrees is not in a good position to kick, and so the marmot had the advantage, particularly as I was scared and he was not. However, I kept him off until he sank his teeth in the extension sole of my boot, and Yates, with a hatchet, put an end to his fury.

While we were getting cooled down, Private Fisher, who had killed the elk the day before, caught up with us, and together we proceeded on our way up the slope to the summit of the ridge. Under the guidance of Fisher, we reached the summit at one of the few points where it was possible to descend on the other side, and even here it was one of the steepest and most leg-wearying descents we had undertaken, being down a gully filled with loose shale and snow and standing at so steep an angle that it was almost impossible for a man to keep his feet with a pack and without the aid of a staff.

The gully broadened out into a little mountain meadow on a bench about eight hundred feet below us, and through the center the melting snow had cut a deep ditch, on the side of which nearest to us lay the object of our tramp. As we sat on the ridge in the shade of a great slab of loose rock,

Fisher drew from his pocket a small telescope, with which he carefully scanned the scene below. After a few minutes he calmly announced, "I see another elk." And sure enough, there at the edge of the timber was a splendid bull! We watched him for a while through the glass, and then held a consultation as to what our procedure should be. We could not handle any more meat, and we had our work cut out to care for the one already killed; so we concluded to let him go in peace. Having so decided we slid off the ridge and began the long descent.

Much to our surprise the elk did not seem to notice us, although we must have been plainly discernible against the snowfield. From time to time as we made our way down we would stop and look at him through the glass, and we noted that he was feeding out from the end of a large fallen tree.

We had nearly reached the bench upon which he was feeding when we saw him lie down, and the tall mountain grass then hid him from our view. I sat on a snow-bank and thought; for an idea had come into my head, and I racked my brain for a plan to carry out the same, which was to photograph the elk. Such things, I knew had been done, but perhaps not quite in the same way. The "subject" had usually been cornered, or the photographer had lain in wait. But to approach and photograph this wild elk became my sudden and strong ambition.

My plan was to get into the gully and make my way down it until opposite the elk; then climb out and stalk him through the lone grass.

From where we sat on the snow-bank the bottom of the gully could be plainly seen; so I left Fisher here, having arranged with him a system of signals by which he could warn me when I had arrived opposite the fallen tree. Taking out a pair of moccasins and the camera, I left my pack with Fisher, and in company with Yates worked down the gully.

Sergeant Yates was as near a dead shot as it is possible for a man to be, and to his skill I intrusted my welfare. He took his position behind a large bowlder, at a point where, he assured me, he could kill the elk with ease if need be; and we agreed that should I raise my hand above my head, on that signal he must shoot. Everything now being arranged, I stripped to trousers and shirt, removed my boots and put on the moccasins, took off my hunting-knife, and emptied my pockets of anything that might rattle. Then taking my camera (a No. 4 folding Kodak) in my hand, gave one last look around and slid into the gully. I found that traveling therein was not so easy as I had anticipated; the stream that looked so insignificant from above proved to be both deep and strong, and to add to my discomfort the gully was cut through a strata

335

of soap-stone compared with which a banana-peel is easy to walk up. But bending all my energy to the safety of the camera, I slowly worked my way down the gully, first on its sloping side, then in the water.

As I neared what I thought was the point at which to climb out, I kept looking back to Fisher for the signal, and at the same time noted with pleasure that the formation under foot changed, the soap-stone being confined to the creekbed, and the sides of the gully, which at this point were about twenty feet high, were formed of a loose gravel containing many large bowlders, projecting in such a manner as to form a fairly good foothold. At last, after I had gone so far that I felt sure of having passed the point at which I should ascend, Fisher gave the signal to stop, and followed up with "All's well!" which assured me that so far I had been successful. However, the real work was ahead, and before climbing out of the gully I took every precaution that occurred to me to aid my success.

The camera was the first consideration. I opened it, drew out the front, and set the focus at a hundred feet. Everything being ready, I began to climb up, the large projecting rocks in the side making it comparatively easy. Half-way up, in some unaccountable way, I dislodged quite a large bowlder, which went banging and crashing down with so much noise that I was sure my chance would be gone. But no signal came from Fisher; so I went on.

Arrived at the top, I cautiously crawled on to the plateau, pushing the camera ahead of me, only to find my caution unnecessary, as the grass was so high that I could neither see nor be seen. Slowly raising my head and holding my camera ready for instant use, I peered over the grass. Having located the fallen tree, I dropped down on hands and knees and began crawling toward it, parting the grass with one hand and holding the camera with the other.

So far I had succeeded in keeping my nerves pretty well under control; but as I crawled through the grass, not knowing at what moment I might come upon the elk, or he upon me, the strain began to tell. Perspiration saturated my clothes and ran off my face in a steady stream, getting into my eyes and obstructing my sight. My joints seemed to creak at every move, and nervous flushes ran up and down my limbs and spine.

Having made my way about fifty yards in this manner, I noticed through the rank grass a brown object, and looking at it more intently, recognized the hind limbs of the elk. There he lay on his side, fast asleep, his limbs stretched out toward me, not more than eight feet away. For more than a minute I remained spellbound; then realizing my position cautiously backed away.

Now that the time for action had come, nervousness entirely left me, and although I had not yet accomplished what I had set out to do, I felt reasonably sure of being able to do so.

There were two imperative reasons why I could not succeed in taking a picture from where I was. First, the sun was almost directly in my face; and second, I fully expected the elk when aroused to bound to his feet and make for the timber at full speed, and therefore I needed a larger field on my plate than I could get at that distance. With this end in view, I worked my way around to a position with the sun behind me, and where the elk would have to pass before me to regain the timber.

I had half risen from my knees when I noticed a large bowlder standing above the grass a few feet to my right. Thinking it a better point of vantage, I dropped down again and crawled to it. Mounted on this rock, facing the elk, my camera on my knees, I had a splendid position with a clear field all around. Judging the distance at fifty feet I set the focusing dial, gave a hurried glance at Yates to see that he was ready to shoot in case of danger, and gathering myself together I gave a sort of mild war-whoop.

The effect was magical. Before I had time to shut my mouth that elk was on his feet. There was no getting up about it. It was a though a huge spring had shot him into position.

But here was indeed dismay; for he had risen with his back toward me. A picture in that position would be out of the question; so I gave another yell, fully expecting him to bolt for the timber, and kept my eyes on the view-finder of the camera. Suddenly it showed him facing me, and I snapped the shutter.

Then I looked up, and the sight before me caused my heart to stop and a clammy sweat break out upon me; for instead of the mild-eyed, timid animal I had expected to see I found myself face to face with a picture of incarnate fury, imbued with the animal instinct of self-preservation.

There he stood so near! his great black mane with hair erect; his eyes two living coals, and nostrils expanding and contracting with every breath. His nervous ears worked back and forth, sometimes singly and sometimes together, and his grand majestic pose was expressive of acute alertness, but indicated no sense of fear. It was such a sight as a man will carry with him to the grave.

I have looked on the death struggles of most of the large American carnivora; seen Bruin make his last desperate stand against overwhelming odds, and the mountain lion treed; but such sights pale to insignificance when compared to the superb, majestic beauty of an elk at bay.

336

In the contemplation of this picture everything else was forgotten,—my camera, Yates, my rear guard, and even my own danger, until I was reminded of the latter by the elk giving an angry shake of his fine head and advancing a few rapid steps toward me. Hastily winding on another film, I snapped the shutter again, when with another shake of his huge antlers he made a nearer advance and I exposed another film.

I now fully expected him to charge, and had half-raised my hand to give Yates the signal to shoot, when to my utter surprise and astonishment, the elk turned and trotted leisurely off toward the timber, stopping at the edge to give one last look back, and with a parting toss of his head disappeared in the woods.

It only remains to be said that of the three negatives taken only one was good, the last two being out of focus. Such is the luck of the amateur photographer!

Seventeen years after Bretherton was involved with the O'Neil Expedition, an article by him appeared in which he recounted the experience of climbing Mount Olympus in the late summer of 1890. This firsthand account of a participant of the events discussed is apparently the only published account of this climb. Robert L. Wood points out in Men, Mules and Mountains *that the article appeared four years after the author's death and was partially rewritten by W. G. Steel from an unidentified newspaper clipping. It must therefore be considered suspect. Wood further suggests that much of the confusion regarding the ascent of the O.E.E. party stems from this article's ambiguous references to the "grand glacier of Mount Olympus," together with a heretofore unclear description of the mountain. Significantly the diary Bretherton kept during the Olympus trip does not mention a "grand glacier."*

ASCENT OF MOUNT OLYMPUS[27]
By B. J. Bretherton

On the morning of September 13, 1890, the writer, in company with Colonel N. E. Linsley, Sergeant F. W. Yates and four men, left headquarters, on the headwaters of the east fork of the Quinault River, for Mount Olympus. They carried with them a copper box and a record book of the Oregon Alpine Club, to be placed on the summit of the mountain. From camp down into the valley was a long and tedious descent, but by 11:30 A.M. we gained the bed of the stream. The valley of the Quinault here is very narrow, hills rising on both sides directly from the water's edge, while the stream itself is only about ten feet wide, very rapid and of a milky color. The valley is all heavily timbered with fir, pine, cedar and yew, while the ground is covered with a thick carpet of sheep sorrel.

After eating lunch we wended our way down the right bank of the river until we came to a stream entering from the north, which we called Fire Creek, on account of a slight accident. Here we camped for the night.

Next day we started up the left bank of Fire Creek and found the ascent to the divide comparatively easy, the only unpleasantness arising from the stings of yellowjackets, of which there seemed more than were needed. That night we camped on a small marsh just under the crest of the divide and next day gained the summit at 10 o'clock and found ourselves looking down into a splendid valley, which we took to be the valley of the Elwha River. The head of this valley was distant about three miles to the west. Thither we wended our way, and by 4 o'clock arrived on a beautiful level saddle, having all the appearance of a park. A fine, broad game trail crosses it, making an easy route from the headwaters of the Elwha to the headwaters of the west branch of the Quinault. This was the only pass through the range that we found, and we called it "Bretherton's Pass."[28] Here we camped, as the range seemed very rough to the north, and we considered it advisable to send out scouting parties.

On the northern end of the pass is a high peak, containing three glaciers, and which is often taken for Mount Olympus. On its side is a large game trail, which we took next morning on our march to Olympus. By 9 o'clock we gained the crest of the ridge, and just in time to see Mounts Olympus and Anderson enveloped in a cloud of mist, which now began to gather about us, and within two hours it had become so thick as to make traveling dangerous. It began raining, so we made camp near a small clump of trees and waited for the fog to clear, which it did not do until next morning.

September 17 dawned fine and clear, and by 8 o'clock we were on our way over the ridge, which was crossed at an

---

[27] *Steel Points* 1 (July 1907), pp.148–53. The article as presented in *Steel Points* contained the following footnote attached to the title: "This article has been partly rewritten from a newspaper clipping, and we do not know to whom to give credit."

[28] "They were now crossing the Elwha-Quinault Divide or Burke Range, so named by Charles A. Barnes on May 6, 1890, when he viewed the line of peaks from Mount Seattle. He called the peak north of the pass Mount Taylor, after Charles Taylor of the Boston *Globe*. The other, directly south of Bretherton's Pass, and near the head of Pyrites Creek, was a peak that O'Neil's men 'had often noticed from afar.' They named it Capitol Mountain because, when viewed from the east, it resembled the Capitol Building in Washington, D.C., but from other directions 'lost its form and beauty.' Another mountain near the head of the Wynootche is called Capitol Peak today." Wood, *Men, Mules and Mountains*, pp. 422–23.

elevation of 5,500 feet. We then climbed down the face of the glacier on its northern slope, coming out on a lower ridge that ran north and south between two tributaries of the Elwha. Down the crest of this ridge we traveled, until by night we had reached the Elwha just above its forks. Here we found sign of a former camp,[29] and picked up a scrap of paper, bearing a recent date. It contained the following original poetical composition:

> "Cock Cobin [Robin] was a liddle bird
> Vat lives oop mid the sky,
> Und Greenbaum vas a lost Dutchman
> Vat soon expects to die.
>
> "He roamed the Olympics' vild vide vaste,
> Und stormed the Elwha's tide,
> Nor drink nor morsel did he taste,
> But oop and onward hied.
>
> "The vild beasts' gaze did on him dwell,
> Und trilled his bones to marrow,
> Till happy thought of William Tell,
> Und his liddle bow und arrow.
>
> "A robin soon was lying dead,
> Und from his blood he drank,
> Vich gave him strength to raise his head,
> When loo; three hundred yards vas camp."

Next morning we crossed the stream and again took a northerly course, following a ridge until we came to the foot of a glacier on the southern slope of Mount Olympus, where we camped for the night.

September 19 we started up a long glacier, on which we traveled until 4 o'clock, when we arrived on the summit of the glacier from which the Queets receives its main supply of water.[30] This glacier faces the southwest and is oval in form, about three-fourths of a mile in width, and a mile and a quarter in length. Its eastern end is the highest, and it connects on the north side with the grand glacier of Mount Olympus, which reaches from here to the summit of the mountains, a distance of over three miles, with an average width of about three-fourths of a mile. In all there are fifty-three glaciers that can be counted from Mount Olympus. These glaciers are constantly moving and displacing vast quantities of rock, which makes it dangerous to pass below them. The writer spent several nights this summer on the opposite side of the Quiniault from the great glacier of Mount Anderson, and was often awakened by avalanches that shook the very mountains themselves as they tore onward to the valleys below.

Next morning we climbed out of Pluto's Gulch on its western side, and, after making our way through a belt of timber, emerged on a beautiful level plateau of about one hundred acres. Great pinnacles of rock were scattered over it, and huckleberries were found in great profusion. On every hand immense fields of ice sparkled in the sun, and in the midst of all the air was filled with the twitter of song birds. It was an inspiration and we called it the "Garden of the Gods." Here we pitched our tents, then tried to find a route up the mountain. It was no use, so we decided to move to the west and try that.

Next morning we left the Garden of the Gods and made our way over a very rough country, round the northern side of the mountain. While passing through a dense alder swale Private Fisher got separated from us, but as he was an old woodsman we did not feel alarmed, but kept on expecting him to overtake us. After getting through the swale we followed the

338

---

[29] "The record is not clear whether the men first struck Delabarre Creek or the Elwha. Bretherton indicates they reached the river at nightfall 'just above its forks' (confluence of Delabarre Creek and the Elwha?) and states that the next day they traveled parallel to 'a tributary of the West Fork,' but they were actually following the Elwha. The 'former camp' was located in the vicinity of Chicago Camp, but on the opposite side of the Elwha, near the base of Low Divide, thus was not a Press Expedition camp. According to Fisher, the altitude was 1700 feet, but Linsley indicated 2025 feet. The correct figure is about 2200 feet. On this occasion, and for several days thereafter (including the climb of 'Olympus'), the party's aneroid consistently registered altitudes up to 500 feet lower than the true elevation, although the instrument 'was correct at sea level before and subsequent to the ascent'." Wood, *Men, Mules and Mountains*, pp. 423–24.

[30] "This was the upper Queets Basin, a cirque bordered by Mounts Queets and Barnes and spurs of the Mount Olympus Range where it abuts the Bailey Range. The basin contains numerous snowfields today, but in 1890 must have supported either a glacier or unbroken snowfield. One of the expedition photographs, taken near Dodwell-Rixon Pass and showing Olympus in the background, is captioned: 'On a glacier of Mt. Olympus.' Bretherton described it as follows in *Steel Points*: 'This glacier faces the southwest and is oval in form, about three-fourths of a mile in width, and a mile and a quarter in length. Its eastern end is the highest, and it connects on the north side with the grand glacier of Mount Olympus, which reaches from here to the summit of the mountains, a distance of over three miles, with an average width of about three-fourths of a mile.' Alpinists have puzzled over this description for years, thinking the naturalist referred to the Humes, but that glacier does not face the southwest. Obviously, however, the men considered the unbroken expanse of snow in the upper Queets Basin to be a glacier, although this may or may not have been the fact. After winters of heavy snowfall, the basin is sometimes entirely covered in late August, the snowdrifts spilling over Dodwell-Rixon Pass and merging with the Elwha Snowfinger. The winter of 1889–90 was exceptionally snowy, but the late date (September 19) the explorers visited the basin makes one hesitate to conclude the presence of what appeared to be a glacier was due solely to the deep snows of the preceding winter. One must remember, too, that glaciers were larger and more numerous in 1890 than they are today and many of the smaller ones have since disappeared." Wood, *Men, Mules and Mountains*, pp. 425–26.

bed of a small creek, clinging to the rocks and dragging each other up, until we made the summit of a level bank of snow, in which the creek had its rise, and here found we had made an ascent of 5000 feet in three hours. That night we camped on the edge of a precipice 5,200 feet deep and saw Fisher's fire away down in the valley, and attracted his attention by firing guns, but he was unable to get to us, and, after trying most of the following day, gave it up and made for the ocean. We were now more than half way up Olympus, and everything was made ready for the ascent on the morrow.

We made an early start on the morning of September 22, and by 9 o'clock the entire party had gained the edge of the grand glacier. From this point Colonel Linsley, Private Danton and myself climbed alone, taking with us the Alpine Club box and flag and camera. We found the best traveling on the western side, as there was a ridge of decomposed quartz and slate running along the edge of the precipice, which gave us a better footing than ice. In two hours we had gained an elevation of 7,240 feet, and half an hour later made the summit, where we remained long enough to place the box and take a few pictures. The Alpine Club box is made of copper and contains a book in which future climbers can record their names and describe their trips. There is also a compartment for small trinkets, in which we left the following articles: One lead pencil, a glove belonging to one of the ladies of the Wickersham party (found by us on the north fork of the Skokomish River), a deck of cards, two army buttons, a beer check, shoe laces, a visiting card and three cablegrams.

Olympus is a double-peaked mountain, entirely covered on the eastern side by a large glacier. The northern slope also contains a glacier, separated from the larger one by a high comb of bare rock. Its southwestern side is a sheer precipice, making the mountain appear from the south as if half of it was cut off. It towers considerably above any other mountain in the range, although its elevation is only 7,550 feet.

CHAPTER THIRTEEN.
NELSON E. LINSLEY

As a part of its commitment to the Olympic Exploring Expedition (OEE), the Oregon Alpine Club provided Nelson E. Linsley as one of the civilian "scientific" staff. He was a noted mining engineer, mineralogist, and geologist. Linsley was billed as "staff geologist" of the club, although he was not a member.[1]

Nelson E. Linsley was born April 23, 1842, in Greene County, New York. Apparently restless by nature, Linsley went west after the Civil War and "followed the mining industry in the several mining states and territories." He arrived in Virginia City, Montana, in 1866, "when that rich placer field was in its heyday," but left in 1869. He then wandered from place to place—living at various times in Salmon City and Boise, Idaho, then in Salt Lake City, Utah, for several years. Eventually he moved to Spokane, Washington, where he was living when the 1890 exploring expedition was organized.

When the Olympic trip ended, Linsley returned to Spokane and "devoted his energies to mining activities, as a promoter and engineer." He served in the Ninth State Legislature in 1905, elected to the House of Representatives on the Republican ticket. His wife died in 1909, but Linsley continued to reside in Spokane until his death January 23, 1925, at the age of eighty-two. He was survived by a son and two brothers.

—Robert L. Wood
Adapted from Men, Mules and Mountains *(p. 462)*

EXPEDITION REPORT

Hoquiam, Wash.
Oct 3rd 1890
Lieut J. P. O'Neil U.S.A. in charge of O. E. E.[2]

Dear Sir

I herewith submit a report of our trip from Camp 15 via Mt Olympus and the Quiet R. to this place. We left Camp 15 on the morning of the 13th of Sept droped down on the Quinault about five miles from the head waters 2,700 feet lower than Camp 15 thence down the River to Smokey Creek distant about three miles and camped for the night. On the morning of the 14th we broke camp left the Quinault and followed up Smokey in a northernly direction all day could not keep near the creek on account of the impassible cañon. The route was a dificult one as we had no game trail to follow and our packs would average not less than Sixty pounds per man. When we camped at night I found that we wer about four and one half miles from the Quinault and had mad a rise of 2,600 feet for the day. On the morning of the 15th after traveling about 1½ miles we reached the summit. The lowest pass showed that we wer at an alt. of 4,400 feet and near the head waters of the main fork of the Elwha River. After dropping over the divide and marching west about 1½ miles we camped for dinner on the head of the Elwha R. The afternoon was consumed in exploring the pass between the north fork of the Quinault and the Elwha and camped for the night just over the divide on the Quinalte side in order to get some shelter. This is one of the finest passes I have seen in the mountains about 80 acres of fine prairie lies on the divide alt. 4,200 feet.

On the 16th we started at the usual time 8. A.M. traveling to the north and west to gain the summit of a divide between two works or branches of the Elwha. We made about two miles and then wer compelled to go into camp as we wer so befogged that it would be folly to undertake further travelling until the fog raised which did not occur untill the next morning so we spent the day at Camp fog Alt 5,180

17th The fog was far below us this morning early and I went up a Mountain peak just 1,000 feet higher than Camp fog to pick out our route for the day but the fog raised rappidly and only the highest peaks was visible so nothing could be gained but direction for Olympus so we droped over the backbone on a large glacier and by chopping steps in the Ice gained after a time an easy grade[3] and reached the top of the ridge

---

[1] "O'Neil wrote that he sent Linsley 'to investigate for the chance of finding mineral in paying quantities.' His report was brief. 'None. I have never heard of that mine from that day to this.' Linsley's judgment was valid. After several years of feverish activity and promotion by the Mason County Mining and Development Company, the mines at Staircase fizzled out." Wood, *Men, Mules and Mountains,* p. 404.
[2] Olympic Exploring Expedition.
[3] "Fisher referred to it as 'a mammoth glacier'; Linsley called it 'a large glacier.' Although current maps do not so indicate, a glacier does cover the northeast slope of Mount Taylor, at the head of Delabarre Creek, but this icefield was undoubtedly larger in 1890 than it is today. Only by descending onto the glacier could the party gain the ridge between Buckinghorse and Delabarre Creeks, because the precipitous terrain barred access where the ridge abutted the eastern flank of Mount Taylor." Wood, *Men, Mules and Mountains,* p. 423.

running north and south and had very good walking for five miles. This ridge divides two branches of the west fork of the Elwha. We reached the north end of the ridge at 1. P.M. average alt. 4,400 ft. After lunch we commenced the descent to the Elwha in a Westernly direction and camped on the west fork alt. 2,025 ft at "Camp Lowland."

18th We broke camp at 7:30 A.M. and travelled nearly in a N.W. course parallel to a tributary of the West Fork that we called Glacier Cañon a very dificult trail and at 3:30 P.M. went into camp for the night having made about four miles from "Lowland."

19th At 8. A.M. we continued our march up Glacier Cañon to the divide the last mile and a half over a large glacier alt 4,600. at the head of Glacier Cañon there is a large basin nearly a mile either way across it. One solid glacier fills this basin of unknown depth. Here we took some photos and for the first time had a good look at Olympus about four miles distant to the N.W.[4] This great basin is drained by both the Elwha and the Quiet Rivers. Here we spent the afternoon in exploring the sorounding country taking course of rivers & camped for the night in one of the cañons of Olympus through which flows one of the tributaries of the Quiet. The camp was so disagreable that we called it "Plutos Box." On the morning of the 20th moved camp about one mile west at the base of Olympus in a beautiful place we called "Garden Camp." All the men remained in camp to repair shoes and clothing except Fisher and I. We spent the day in prospecting for a route to the Summit of Olympus reached an alt. of 5,800 and found the route a very

dangerous one as we had to cross two large Glaciers full of immense cracks from one to three feet wide some of them over one hundred feet deep.[5] On the 21th we traveled all day to mak two miles to the West had to drop down to the river and then climb up again and made camp at the base of the Peaks alt. 5,050 feet. Fisher strayed off to day and at night we could see the smoke from his campfire about 3,000 ft below us and near the Quit R. On the morning of the 22nd Bretherton Danton and I went to the summit of Olympus where we deposited the O.A.C.[6] record box Alt 7,140 ft There are four peaks we named the highest one (alt 7,550) Alpine Peak but there was no safe place there to place the box. After completing our observations and taking some Photos we returned to camp for lunch and thence down to the Quit and made camp for the night. On the 23rd we made the best days travel on the trip about 12½ miles here I intended to divide the party and take in the Hoh and Quillayhute but an inspection of the Shoes changed the programe as three of my men wer nearly barfooted and right here I wish to call your attention to the fact that the government shoe is worthless for a campaign like this. My boots had been in use over a year when I started on this last trip and they are good for two more of the same kind.[7] From the morning of the 23rd until the night of the 28th we wer travelling down the Quiet R. takking the course of the River every mile or so and carefully estimating the distance and find it to be 59¼ mi. long. On the night of the 28th we camped just south of the Raft R. on the Coast and from there made our way along the beach to the Quinialte Agency here we

---

[4] "They were justifiably impressed. The mountain covered more than thirty square miles lying above the timber line (about 4500 feet). The highest point was more than five miles from Dodwell-Rixon Pass, in a direction slightly north of west. Fisher wrote that Olympus was 'due west about one mile,' but he was deceived by the terrain. The lower ramparts of the mountain, adjacent to the terminus of the Humes Glacier, were about two miles west of the pass." Wood, *Men, Mules and Mountains*, p. 426.

[5] "The ridge edging Humes Glacier on the south forms a Y-shaped pattern, with the top to the east, the base to the west. The 'arms' of the Y enclose a triangular, sloping area of snowfields, forest, and meadowland, in the lower or eastern part of which Garden Camp was located. Fisher and Linsley apparently climbed the 'north arm' to near the point where it joined the 'south arm.' Linsley's statement about 'two large glaciers' evidently refers to two parts of the Humes. A rock rib extends northward about 600 yards from the ridge, thus partially dividing the glacier, and the men could have had the impression they had crossed two distinct icefields." Wood, *Men, Mules and Mountains*, p. 427.

[6] Oregon Alpine Club.

[7] "When Linsley learned that O'Neil was dissatisfied with his efforts to explore the northwestern Olympics, he virtually exploded. On November 14, 1890, he wrote an irate letter to Will G. Steel, in which he countered the criticism by claiming that on the Olympus journey he had time for little else than picking out a route. 'I wrote O'Neil a pretty sharp letter and I told him that if he had paid less attention to cheap newspaper notoriety and more to business we might have accomplished more, and I don't think he feels friendly over it.' (A year later, in another letter dated October 25, 1891, Linsley stated, 'O'Neil was furnished ample field notes to make a good map but lost them.')

"Linsley also stated in the November 14, 1890 letter that he had been delayed in writing his report on the geology and mineralogy of the Olympics, and that he had been waiting for O'Neil to ask him to forward it, but he didn't think the lieutenant would so request at that time; therefore, since the Oregon Alpine Club might need the report, he would send it to the club first.

"The report Steel received from Linsley was in the form of a letter, dated November 13, but on October 3, while he was still in Hoquiam, Linsley had written a report to O'Neil on the trip to Olympus. Apparently he intended to write another on the geology and mineralogy to submit to the Army, in compliance with the terms of the agreement with General Gibbon, but other than the letter to Steel no such report is known to exist today.

"Linsley was still bitter four months later. On March 19, 1891, he wrote to Steel that he had just heard that O'Neil had made a report in which he said that Linsley was the cause of the expedition having been a failure, also that the lieutenant had been circulating reports in the Puget Sound country that were detrimental to the colonel's character. He asked for a copy of the report and requested that Steel tell him what he knew about the matter. 'O'Neil cannot afford to have his doings investigated,' Linsley charged, 'neither can I afford to let him make me the scapegoat of his incompetency.'

"Unfortunately, we do not have the reply letter, if any, that Steel and O'Neil sent to Linsley, and therefore cannot assess the merit to Linsley's charges." Wood, *Men, Mules and Mountains*, pp. 437–38.

hired two Indian teams to bring us to Oyhut thence by sail boat across the bay to the point where we arrived on Oct 1st 5 30 P.M.

On our trip we took in six tributaries of the Elwha, the north fork of the Quinalt the headwaters of the Hoh & the Nile and the entire main Quit River from source to mouth. Mr. Bretherton took many photos which will be very interesting. Mt. Olympus is sorounded by Glaciers some of them at least three miles long from one Peak on Olympus I could count forty seven Glaciers some of them at an alt. not to exceed 3,000 feet.[8] I make this report brief as the map which will be handed you by Mr Bretherton will greatly aid you in your final report[9]

Very respectfully etc

N. E. Linsley

342

[8] "Most of the 'glaciers' were permanent snowfields or small bodies of ice. Olympus has nine distinct glaciers, plus many snowfields and ice patches." Wood, *Men, Mules and Mountains*, p. 434.

[9] "Although the [Oregon Alpine] Club's Board of Directors expressed satisfaction with the expedition's success, Henderson and Linsley later complained they had not been reimbursed for certain expenditures. . . . On November 14, 1890, [Linsley] penned a letter to Steel, in which he stated: 'Through [O'Neil's] carelessness I have not yet been able to get my extra baggage sent out and there are in it many things I can never replace, and besides that I furnished him in money and supplies about $80 that he agreed to repay me when we got out of the woods. As I lost the entire summer I want him to settle unless I was expected to furnish myself and pay something for the privilege of going.' Linsley couldn't resist a parting shot. He added: 'I saw by the *Oregonian* that O'Neil had handed in his financial report and it had been accepted. I would like to know what it was like. It ought to make a curiosity for the museum.'" Wood, *Men, Mules and Mountains*, p. 436.

CHAPTER FOURTEEN.
LOUIS F. HENDERSON

Louis F. Henderson, a botanist, was one of the four civilians provided by the Oregon Alpine Club as "scientists to the expedition."

He was born in Roxbury, Massachusetts, September 17, 1853. After graduating from Cornell University in 1874, Henderson emigrated to California, where he taught languages for a year, then joined his brother in Oregon, and taught botany, history, and modern languages. He was living in Olympia when the exploring expedition was organized.

About a dozen plants bear his name in one form or another, among them the endemic spirea of the Olympic Mountains that he found while traveling with O'Neil.

In 1890, with the plants he had collected sitting on the table in front of him, Professor Louis F. Henderson, the O'Neil Expedition's botanist, wrote a summary of the six weeks he spent with O'Neil in gathering his botanical specimens for classification and evaluation. This paper, "The Flora of the Olympics," was first published in ZOE, *a biological journal, in October 1891 and again in* Steel Points *in 1907, seventeen years after the expedition. In 1932, forty-two years after the expedition, when Henderson was seventy-nine years old, he wrote about the expedition again in the paper "Some Early Experiences of a Botanist in the Northwest," which included a section on the 1890 O'Neil Expedition.*

Henderson was a member of the Academy of Sciences and published a number of monographs. In 1926 the University of Oregon awarded him the honorary degree of master of arts in public service, as a "distinguished pioneer botanist and one of the leading authorities upon the flora of Oregon." An athletic man, Henderson continued to climb on the high peaks until he was well past eighty. On his seventieth birthday he swam across the Columbia River at Hood River, Oregon. He was also a scholar, a student of Shakespeare, gave readings, and acted in plays. When he died in Tacoma, Washington, on June 14, 1942, he left behind "a large circle of friends" in Idaho and Oregon, where he was "loved for his kindliness," and for his efforts to create a greater interest in the native flora.

—Robert L. Wood

Adapted from Men, Mules and Mountains *(pp. 461–62)*

THE FLORA OF THE OLYMPICS[1]

Report of the Botanist of the O'Neil Expedition from Observations Taken During Six Weeks Stay with the Party and Incidents of General Interest

L. F. Henderson.

"Parturiunt montes, nascetur ridiculus mus."[2] Shall I be able to blame the reader if, after the perusal of this very meager report, but extravagant heading, Horace's caustic remark occurs to him? I have been laboring hard with this heading, trying to reconcile my desire to give a very brief announcement with a greater desire to impress upon my readers the fact that it is a very incomplete report, partly due to my necessarily short stay with the party, partly to the rather surprising similarity of the flora of this region to that of the Coast and Cascade Ranges. In this latter fact I was much surprised, perhaps without reason. I had thought that a pile of mountains so isolated, so nearly surrounded by water, must have a remarkable endemic, or peculiar flora. But in my wild expectations that new forms, if not new species, or even new genera would be peeping out from the crevices of every succeeding mass of rocks, smiling down upon me from every cliff, or being crushed by every other step upon those green, sunny banks, which always border the perpetual snows, I forgot, or perhaps would not remember, that the Olympic Mountains are but the gigantic and chaotic ending of the Black Hills and Coast Range; that they are but sixty miles distant from the Cascade Range; that birds have flown, that waters have carried; that winds have blown for ages past, as they are doing today, all assisting in the constant dissemination of seeds; that, lastly, the same glacial age acted upon the Olympic Mountains that did upon the Cascade Range, scattering and leaving a largely similar flora on both ranges as it disappeared toward the north. I might have found many treasures could I have stayed the whole summer with the party, which the limited time at my disposal forbade my finding I

343

---

[1] ZOE 2 (October 1891): pp. 253–95. Reprinted in *Steel Points* 1 (July 1907): pp. 160–98. Henderson's 1891 report in ZOE, when reprinted in *Steel Points* in 1907, was seriously marred by a printer's error. Lines of type were misplaced at random in two places, creating sizable, unreadable *non sequitors*. Robert L. Wood deciphered the text in *Steel Points*. His corrected text accurately reflects the original text as it appeared in ZOE and that appears here.
[2] Henderson's opening Latin quote is from Horace's *Epistles*, Book 2, Number 2, line 139: "The mountains will be in labor and a ridiculous mouse will be born." Virtually the same quote appears in the Aesop fable *The Mountain in Labor*: "A huge gap appeared in the side of the mountain. At last a tiny mouse came forth."

might have found, had not a large collection made after my return by one of the soldiers been lost by some unaccountable means, that the flora is much more varied than I think it at present. Furthermore, it may be found that I am greatly mistaken in my statements, when more careful research shall have disclosed all that continuous pile of rocks holds within its inhospitable recesses, when several as energetic young explorers as Charles V. Piper of Seattle shall have gone over the ground as carefully as he did after my return this summer. I had hoped to excite envy in the breasts of many of my botanical friends by my rare "finds." I see on the table before me, as the result of my six weeks "cruise," two or three possibly new species. I had hoped to write a paper which should attract the notice of many scientific men to this flowery El Dorado; I find that I must content myself with the description of a flora trite in the extreme to those who are acquainted with the plants of the northwest. If, however, I shall have established an acquaintance between some of our pretty, modest flowers, or grand trees, and any lovers of Nature technically unacquainted with them; if I shall have brought home to any heart those beautiful lines of Bryant's Thanatopsis:

> To him, who in the love of Nature,
> Holds communion with her visible forms,
> She speaks a various language. For his gayer hours
> She has a voice of gladness, and a smile
> And eloquence of beauty; and she glides
> Into his darker musings, with a mild
> And gentle sympathy, that steals away
> their sharpness e'er he is aware,

I shall take pleasure in thinking that these six weeks were not lost time.

After a vexatious, unavoidable, but none the less aggravating delay to the writer, who had but a limited time at his disposal, the little steamer Louise landed us, men, mules and merchandise, on the beach at Lilliwaup, then a mere landing place, now a "flourishing townsite" (God save the mark!), on the beautiful and romantic Hood's Canal, and about eight miles from Union City. Here was "the best and nearest trail to Lake Cushman," as we were told by the veracious officers of the boat, who, we were afterwards informed, had quite an "interest" in the townsite, and who were, naturally, we may imagine, entirely opposed to our landing at Hoodsport, four miles further down the canal, and from which "rival town," as we afterwards found out, there was a beautiful and well cleared trail to Lake Cushman. May the officers of that boat and the "townsmen" of that first "site" be forgiven for the

vexation, exasperation, delay, disappointment, and. to our animals, suffering, that first eight or ten miles caused us and them, coming as they did from the fresh pastures and "dolce far niente" life of unbridled license enjoyed at the Post at Vancouver.

While the packs were being sorted, the different parties assigned their duties by the Lieutenant, and the animals fed and packed, I amused myself by seeing how many plants I could collect in a radius of one hundred yards. I first collected those which had "escaped from cultivation," as our dear and common teacher Dr. Gray would have quaintly remarked; then those camp followers of the cultivated army, following as they do wherever man tills the ground, and, lastly, the indigenous or native plants. Amongst the first were the two clovers, white clover (*Trifolium repens*), and red clover (*T. pratense*), timothy (*Phleum pratense*), June grass (*Poa pratensis*), orchard grass (*Dactylis glomerata*), soft grass (*Holcus lanatus*), and foxglove (*Digitalis purpulea*) with its various colors, white, blue, pink and purple. It is remarkable how this plant takes possession when once well started. Indigenous, I certainly cannot think it as some do for I have never found it save along road sides, paths, or running wild about old homesteads. I have, however been frequently and pleasantly informed that I was approaching a home a mile or so before I reached it by meeting these handsome flowers waiting for me, as it were, by the road or by path. Amongst the second class, the introduced "weeds," I collected the common little yellow clover (*Trifolium procumbens*), sow thistle (*Sonchus asper*), mouse-ear chickweed (*Cerastium vulgatum*), "little" cranesbill (*Geranium pusillum*), curled dock (*Rumex crispus*), ribwort or rib-grass (*Plantago lanceolata*), plantain (*P. major*), cheat or chess (*Bromus secalinus*) (how often have I heard the remark by the more ignorant of the farmers of the Willamette Valley, "I planted that field in first class winter wheat. and it came up all cheat!"), Yarrow (*Achillea Millefolium*), false blue-grass (*Poa compressa*), hedge mustard (*Sisymbrium officinale*), lamb's quarters (*Chenopodium album*), sheep sorrel (*Rumex Acetosella*), door-weed (*Polygonum aviculare*), self-heal (*Brunella vulgaris*), chickweed (*Stellaria media*), cup-weed (*Cotula coronopifolia*), a ballast-waif from South Africa which has made itself "at home" along the salt marshes everywhere in the Sound country, goose-grass (*Poa annua*), shepherd's purse (*Bursa Bursa-Pastoris*), common vetch (*Vicia sativa*), nettle (*Urtica Lyallii*), thyme-leaved speedwell (*Veronica serpyllifolia*), and "Mother Carey" (*Matricaria matricarioides*).

The third set, the native plants, yielded me in trees first *Pseudotsuga mucronata* ("red or yellow fir" vernacularly, but

344

more properly Douglas Spruce). This tree is not a true fir as may be known from its pendant cones which fall from the tree in one piece, like the cones of the pines. In the true firs the cones stand erect, or nearly so, and the outer pieces (scales and bracts) fall off from the central column, which remains perpendicular upon the branch for years, the erect "spikes," presenting a most peculiar appearance to any daring climber who will mount to the top of one of our white or balsam firs in the late fall, after the cones have—what shall we call it—moulted? Next I found the hemlock (*Tsuga heteroplylla*), with its soft delicate leaves and handsome, symmetrical trunk. This tree is one of our grandest evergreens. Some of the trees of this species whose girth would not be far outdistanced by our large Douglas Spruces, were found in the rich, alluvial forests about Lake Cushman. Near by and always present except upon the rocky slopes, was the western arbor-vitæ, called commonly "cedar" (*Thuja plicata*). These trees about Lake Cushman, together with the Douglas Spruce, are of gigantic proportions, rivalling the famed redwoods of the Californian forests. The size of some of the fallen monsters of these two species can best be realized when you have to saw one after another out of the trail to make a way for your pack animals, or when occasionally one has to be felled over some chasm as a bridge for yourselves, or, possibly, for your animals! "Hic labor hoc opus," you sigh with Aeneas of old![3] I have before me at this instant the photograph of a cedar stump which attracts widespread attention near the town of Snohomish, Upper Sound. It is nearly eighteen feet in diameter at the ground. It is planked over and easily accommodates a quadrille set with their accompanying musicians. A fir tree near Olympia was cut this year which, as I am informed by truthful parties, "scaled" 12,460 feet of lumber. Add to this, according to the lumberman's measure, one-quarter for waste, and this single stick contained 15,575 feet of wood. It was fifty-two inches in diameter at the smaller end, seventy-four at the larger, and was 102 feet long without a visible knot. I myself have seen much larger trees of this last species, but it is rare to find any of quite such regular proportions, or so nearly columnar. Near by was found the yew. To one acquainted with the way this plant appears in the Eastern States it might seem a misnomer to call this a tree. It is hardly ever more than a bush in the East, but our species (*Taxus brevifolia*) reaches a diameter of three or even four feet in moist, dark ravines. Its wood is extremely tenacious and almost as heavy as mahogany, at least when green. On the shady, moist slopes of the Olympics it forms, at

times, such dense thickets that it is almost impossible to force or even cut a way through, especially when bent down to almost a trailing condition by the weight of winter snows or the violence of spring avalanches. Near by and always to be found in moist ground along the shores of the Sound, was the white fir (*Abies grandis*). This is a beautiful tree, with its long leaves, regularly two-ranked, glossy and dark above, light gray or white beneath—its trunk white and regular till well advanced in years—its cones clustered at the summit of the tree, looking like bunches of erect red bananas, at times gemmed with drops of balsam which glisten like diamonds in the sunlight. To the lumberman, however, it stands the tree to be avoided, for its wood is probably the most worthless, foot for foot, of any of our western trees. Near by, and always present along the Sound banks, just above high-water mark, was found a red alder (*Alnus Oregona*). The common name is a misnomer, for the only time it ever looks red at all is when the reddish catkins are swinging on the trees in early spring. White is more proper on account of its white bark; possibly it may have derived its name from the wood, which assumes a reddish tinge when cut and exposed. Near at hand was the large-leaved maple (*Acer macrophyllum*), common all over our hills, and yet always a favorite from its generous foliage during the hotter months. Its wood is handsome and is highly esteemed by furniture dealers on this coast. The "burls," formed on these trees by various causes, furnish some of the most beautifully marked wood and capable of the finest polish of any found on the coast. Near at hand, and almost always in the company of the latter, was to be seen the vine maple (*Acer circinatum*). This plant in moist, rich bottoms, well merits its name of "vine," for if any plant, pretending to be a tree, ever simulated more the "viny" nature, I should like to know what it is. Furthermore, does the mountaineer know a more exasperating tree to deal with when engaged in cutting trail? Here is a clump of them bordering upon or overhanging this soft, miry-looking spot in your path. They are growing thickly together and offer a complete barrier to your further progress, unless hewn away, sprawling out as they do in every direction, but generally down hill. With your keen axe or brush-hook you strike the first one a strong, sharp blow, just where it commences to bend, and your tool goes through it as if you were cutting a piece of cheese. "Very well," you mutter, "if it is all accomplished like that, this little job will not last long." Ah, little do you know this Machiavelli among trees! You attempt to lift it out of your path, and you find that its top, some thirty

345

---

[3] "This is our task," from Book 6 of the *Aneid*.

feet away, has taken root and is firmly fixed in the ground. A half dozen blows are now required to cut in two the limber, lively, snake-like remnant. You throw it out of the trail and strike another; you find that its elasticity has been by no means lost on account of its apparently lifeless posture, and the severed end thwacks you over the shins or in the face. You slash another, and succeed in cutting it through just far enough to have the remaining whip-like portion split down to or below the surface of the ground, where a dozen blows among the stones or rotten logs finally severs it. You think they are all out of the way now, and lead over the first mule, which, in plowing through the quagmire, loosens a before unseen stem. It rises, like the typical Banquo's ghost, just under the legs of your mule. Mule becomes entangled in its folds, and rolls over, burying your pack deeply in the soft mud.

Everywhere common along the clay banks of the Sound grows a small tree (which I there found abundant), the white elder (*Sambucus glauca*). This plant is called "white" because of its fruit. This is, when ripe, really black, but so covered with a "bloom" is it that it appears always whitish, at times nearly snow-white. A pretty tree it is with its flat cluster of cream-white flowers in late spring, or in fall its handsome fruits, which remain on the stems till late in the winter, if not taken by the birds. The berries are held in good repute among our housewives, on account of its pie and wine-producing virtues. Close at hand was its blood relative the red-berried elder (*Sambucus callicarpa*). This hardly ever approaches the proportions of a tree, but rather a large shrub, while the former attains an occasional diameter of two feet. The red-berried elder is not a particularly pretty plant, except when covered with its pyramids of scarlet fruit. This latter is intensely disagreeable to the taste, but seems to be greatly relished by wild pigeons, for their diet is almost entirely confined to this fruit where it grows plentifully.

Next I found a not very common tree, Pursh's buckthorn (*Rhamnus Purshiana*). This seldom grows larger than a large bush, though I have occasionally seen it a foot and a half in diameter in the salt water marshes back of Long Beach, Ilwaco. Its large, handsome leaves, its smooth, mottled trunk, and its medicinal properties save it from the charge of insignificance.

Hard by I came upon one of the commonest of our small trees, the early willow (*Salix Scouleriana*). If the law of contraries holds good, if the most delicious odors are compounded from the most disagreeable substances in the famed city of Cologne, as is said to be the case, there should be some virtue in this tree, sanitary or odoriferous; for a more fetid, horrid smell can hardly be imagined than that from the broken twigs of this tree in early spring

In strong contrast with this Mephistopheles among trees stood near the Ithuriel of our northern woods, the western flowering-dogwood (*Cornus Nuttallii*). This tree is never commonplace, whether putting forth its green buds in the early spring, whether lighting up the forests with its captivating contrasts of light green leaves and milk-white flowers, or whether in fall it dyes the woods with the purple, saffron, or crimson of its leaves, and the scarlet of its fruit clusters. I have traveled through miles of woods, between Portland and Eagle Creek in Clackamas County, which have been rendered entrancing from the beautiful effects of its flowers and the intoxication of their delicious odor. I know of no scent so far reaching and yet so delicate, unless it be that of the wild grape or the yellow jasmine of the Southern woods. The wood is very fine-grained and would "work up" well into smaller articles of utility under the turner's lathe.

The last tree found here was the red-berried cherry (*Prunus emarginata villosa*), noticeable from its small, smooth, slender trunks, its medicinal properties and wood fine for the turner.

The salt marsh near by, and the shores of the canal, yielded me quite a number of plants, very few of which, however, are in any degree attractive, save to the enthusiast. These were sand spurrey (*Tissa rubra*), cud-weed (*Gnaphalium purpureum*), *Gaertneria bipinnatifida* (a kind of trailing burdock, common along the beach from Fort Canby to the recesses of the Sound), salt marsh plantain (*Plantago maritima*), silverweed (*Argentina Anserina*), a pretty plant with its large, yellow flowers, large compound leaves of a bright green above and silvery below. *Chenopodium rubrum*, *Puccinellia distans*, *Orthocarpus castilleioids* (a little plant which saves itself from being overlooked by the pretty white tips to its bracts), *Ranunculus Cymbalaria*, a delicate little trailing buttercup, common in salt mashes as well as along the borders of pools in Eastern Washington and Oregon, and *Sagina occidentalis* (?). This plant I mark with a question mark, for though returned me as this species by an eminent authority, I cannot but question it. *Sagina occidentalis* away from the coast, that is, as we know it commonly about Portland and throughout the Willamette Valley, is a very delicate, upright thing so delicate as only to be seen when the head is bent toward the ground, for it seldom grows over an inch in height. The sea coast form, if form it be, grows flat upon the ground. and forms a mat two or three inches broad, when exposed to the salt spray along the rocky points that extend into the ocean. I am even inclined to believe that it is a biennial, if not of longer duration. Near at hand, rising two or more feet out of the soft mud was the arrow-grass (*Triglochin maritimum*), and mingling with it arose the graceful and beautiful hair-grass (*Deschampsia cespitosa*), its plumes waving with every breath of wind, and sending out a sheen of gold, bronze, purple or green from its ever-varying tassels. It is a commoner below, but from the middle to the tip of its plume, I know of no more aristocratic grass. When you stand in some hollow or in a boat at low tide in a locality where this plant covers hundreds of acres, as it does at Tillamook Bay—when the sun is shining brightly and the sky is of a deep blue—when the wind is coming in strongly from the ocean and acre after acre billows under the passing breeze—when each clump sends forth its own peculiar color, but all equally glistening—I know of nothing more peacefully beautiful nor more like fairyland. The only other marsh plants here seen were a beautiful wild clover (*Trifolium involucratum*), the most beautiful with which I am acquainted in this country of wild clovers, a delicate little umbelliferous plant (*Lilaeopsis occidentalis*), sheep fescue (*Festuca rubravar*), and the omnipresent skunk cabbage (*Lysichiton Kamtschatcensis*). This plant is not to be despised, for its yellow chalices light up the otherwise ugly swamps in early spring, its green and generous leaves are as handsome, if so large, as those of the banana, its fruit and leaves are eagerly eaten by horses, hogs, deer or bear, while its odor is nearly so overpowering as its name, whether English or Latin. The last marsh plant was the peculiar burr-reed (*Sparganium simplex*).

The hill-side plants were very numerous and kept me busy for an hour or more. First came the gorgeous Turk-cap lily (*Lilium Columbianum*), with its inverted and turban-like flowers, yellowish red and mottled with brown; *Psoralea physodes*, an inconspicuous plant, nearly a foot high, bending over or reclining, and covered with an abundance of small cream-colored flowers of the ordinary pea type; *Osmaronia cerasiformis*, the representative of the almond sub-genus on this coast, was just ripening its fruit near by. This is a pretty bush, with its bright, elliptical leaves, racemes of drooping white flowers, and later its handsome clusters of indigo-colored fruit, which contrast prettily with their scarlet stems. The fruit is eaten with avidity by birds, bears, Indians, and occasionally by white people. Then I collected our commonest western lyme-grass (*Elymus glaucus*), growing too isolated ever to become valuable as a forage-plant. The more noticeable among the other plants were red-flowering currant (*Ribes sanguineum*), black-berried gooseberry (*Ribes divaricatum*), monkey flower (*Mimulus Langsdorfii*), a handsome plant, with its large, irregular, funnel-shaped flowers, bright yellow and

mottled with brown within; musk plant (*Mimulus moschatus*), prized as a potting plant on account of its remarkably strong musky odor; "tall" thistle (*Carduus edulis*), a very variable plant—sometimes nearly destitute of prickles and tall, reaching ten or twelve feet along the streams tributary to Yaquina Bay; at others low and very prickly as usually found along the sea-shore, the young shoots said to be eaten with a relish by the western Indians; the three brambles, red-cap (*Rubus parviflorus*), a handsome bush, with its wide soft leaves, snow-white flowers and red fruit; black-cap (R. *leucodermis*),and dew-berry, or, as it is commonly called wild blackberry (R. *macropetalus*); the delicate and sweet-scented yerba buena of the California Spaniards (*Micromeria chamissonis*), its dried leaves used by many as a tea plant; the delicate little enchanters' nightshade (*Circaea Pacifica*); the red berried and evergreen huckleberries (*Vaccinium parvifolium, and V. ovatum*), the fruit of the former tart and pleasant, and a splendid substitute in uninhabited districts for puddings and pies; the second yielding a delicate and delicious berry, found in great quantities along the ocean or Sound country, and a staple article of food and sale among the Indians, the fruit lasting fresh and good until December or January, and quantities being consumed in the cities of the Sound; the snowy everlasting (*Anaphalis margaritacea*), four fine ferns—deer-fern (*Struthiopteris Spicant*), its fertile fronds towering above the sterile like the protecting antlers of the buck over the lesser herd of fawns and does; the beautiful maiden's hair (*Adiantum pedatum*), with its smooth stems, glossy-black or bluish, and its delicate drooping fingers of divisions to the frond; the armed shield-fern (*Polystichum munitum*), a graceful plant especially from a distance; its dense cluster of bending fronds looking like some inviting foot-stool; the lady-fern (*Athyrium cyclosorum*), always of graceful form, whether rising but a few inches along some mossy rill-bank, or towering up from some rich swamp to a height of six or seven feet, when it remarkably resembles *Dryopteris Filix-mas*. Next flamed up the tall stalks of the giant fire-weed (*Epilobium angustifolium*), always at hand the year after a fire in the forests, though how it gets there so quickly is a mystery to the scientific world, its pink-purple flowers making a mass of color where it occurs abundantly; the modest little western blue-bell (*Campanula Scouleri*), though "bell-flower" would perhaps be more appropriate to this species, since but a delicate and varying shade of blue dyes its otherwise white flowers, as if you had by chance mixed a little bluing in a bowl of milk or white paint, and taking thence a spoonful had made a flower; the dark trailing vines of the kinnikinick (*Arctostaphylos Uva-Ursi*), its berries, a beautiful red, contrasting

347

strongly with the dark green of its leaves, the leaves themselves being dried and smoked by the Indians, and (shall I confess "sub rosa"), no less eagerly by many of our party as their store of tobacco decreased; our two wild roses (*Rosa Nutkana*, and *R. Gymnocarpa*), the first the analogue of the Eastern Rosa *blanda* or thornless rose, except that it will not do to imagine ours "thornless," for with this idea in one's mind, one might get into a bad "scrape" if he came in contact with its terrible, hooked thorns; the second a delicate, little rose, much smaller and generally lighter in color than the last, its branches sometimes perfectly smooth but generally thickly beset with straight, harmless prickles; the wild pea (*Lathyrus polyphyllus*), a fine forage plant in open woods where better ones are lacking; close at hand and scrambling over bushes, ground, old logs or fences, the black-pea (*Vicia gigantea*), so called on account of the coal-black color of its pods when ripe; American vetch (*Vicia Americana*), was found near by; the low strawberry (*Fragaria Chiloensis*), grew upon the open clay-banks; in the fields and open ground, the tarweed (*Madia racemosa*), was everywhere; too common for easy locomotion along the trail was the salal (*Gaultheria Shallon*), the fruit of which forms a staple article of diet among the Coast Indians, occurring as it does in great profusion, and being not at all unpalatable (though with a tinge of the Indian or Chinese in its flavor!); lastly, the peer of any of them, though modest withal, the twin-flower (*Linnaea Americana*). Many think our great master, Linnæus, should have had his name identified with a grander member of the plant-world. To me it is peculiarly appropriate, representing the purity of his life in the beautiful mossy banks where it is found, his unassuming manner in its bowed heads, and the sweetness of his disposition in the delicious fragrance it exhales. I know of nothing more refreshing than, when tires with the long trail and heavy pack, to throw oneself full length upon a bank covered thickly by this little vine, and with head pillowed in its soft embrace, drinking in the "honeyed nectar" of its scent, and view the blue sky or masses of snowy clouds through the overarching branches of the firs. Along the shaded rills were several other plants more or less remarkable. These were the spring beauty (*Claytonia Sibirica*); Bishop's cap (*Tiarella trifoliata*), its ripened pods looking remarkably like the caps worn by the popes and bishops of old; the silver leaf (*Adenocaulon bicolor*), the dark, smooth, green upper surface being wonderfully different from its satiny under surface; avens (*Geum macrophyllum*)—perhaps we should call it the "little bayonet plant," since the ends of the styles are so bent to one side as remarkably to resemble a mass of fixed bayonets; the magnificent goat's beard (*Spiraea*

348

Aruncus), its tall tassel of minute white flowers lighting up the dark dells or shady banks; near by the hazel (*Corylus Californica*), its green fruit clusters covering the ends of the branches and containing their nearly ripe nuts.

These were the more conspicuous plants; the inconspicuous were many and need only be mentioned—three bed-straws (*Galium triflorum, G. trifidum,* and *G. aparine*); tall chickweed (*Alsine borealis*), two Epilobiums (*E. coloratum,* and *E. minutum*), *Agoseris laciniata*; the two wood-rushes (*Juncoides glabratum,* and *J. parviflorum*); speedwell (*Veronica Americana*), *Oenanthe Californica, Ranunculus Bongardi, R. Bongardi Greenei,* the smallest flowered butter-cup; white-flowered hawk-week (*Hieracium albiflorum*), sweet Cicely(*Washingtonia purpurea*), western tall dock (*Rumex occidentalis*), five bog rushes (*Juncus tenuis, J. effusus,* and var. *hesperius, J. ensifolius, J. bufonius*); several grasses, the graceful *Trisetum cernuum, Festuca subulata, Agrosits microphylla, A. exarata*; wild barley (*Hordium nodosum*), a handsome nodding brome-grass (*Bromus eximius umbraticus*), and *Cinna latifolia*; a bull-rush (*Scirpus microcarpus*); one sedge (*Carex stipata*); two mosses (*Polytrichum juniperinum,* and *Bryum* sp.) and a lichen (*Cladonia furcata*).

Certainly no one can say from this showing that our flora is poor. It would look so to one not intimately acquainted with it, on account of the lack of color or size in the flowers of Western Washington and Oregon. Everything in the plant kingdom seems to be overpowered by the unending, majestic but gloomy fir forests that cover plain, valley and mountains to far up their slopes. Even the birds lack the merriment of the songsters of Eastern woods, and a certain plaintiveness or harshness pervades their notes. Far different is it with the flowers of Eastern Oregon and Washington, or with those that bloom above the timber line on our higher mountains. Life is short with them, whether from the dry, hot climate of the country east of the Cascade Range, or from the short summer natural to the high altitudes in the neighborhood of perpetual snows. Nature is prodigal, especially in the latter regions, with her paint-pot, and gorgeous colors meet the traveler at every step.

Leaving the larger number of the expedition with the "mule-train," and preceded by another party composed of axe-men and hunters. I started along the "fine trail" to the lake, which I anticipated reaching in about three hours, as it was described to be about five or six miles distant, and a botanist doesn't travel fast when there is anything to be collected. I started at half past eight o'clock, alone and with no lunch in my pocket, and reached the lake after a slow but continuous march of ten hours and a half! The mule-train reached it in installments at the end of the second day! After the first half mile the trail commenced to ascend the hills very abruptly, and a mere half hour's travel brought a great change in the flora. As I toiled up the steep, sunny path, the first plant not previously met with was the manzanita (*Arctostaphylos tomentosa*) of the northern slopes and plains, now collected in the unsatisfactory state of green fruit. Next the common prince's pine (*Chimaphila umbellata*) was very abundant, its waxy, whitish flowers always appearing rather out of place in the midst of the dark, leathery leaves. Scattered here and there were the bright, handsome stems of the madrone (*Arbutus Menziesii*). This tree well merits the praise bestowed upon it by Bret Harte, for though it does not grow as large as in Middle California, it occasionally reaches a diameter of two feet, and when the outer loose bark has fallen off, as it often does, exposing the smooth, bright cinnamon color of its inner bark, when the deluge of pearly flowers lights up the glistening large leaves, or the ripened fruit causes the whole tree to look like a great tongue of flame, it is a picture in itself. Next I was surprised to find a bush generally found high up in the mountains and along creeks, *Pachystima Myrsinites*. Its growing in such a location convinced me more firmly than ever that this plant is destined sometime to be largely used, and to become a favorite when used, as a border to walks in handsome grounds. As the firs grew thicker, the beautiful and fragrant false Solomon's seal (*Vagnera amplexicaulis*) raised its white clusters of flowers, and near at hand was the Western wintergreen, *Pyrola bracteata*, a very unmeaning name, but the only one it has. Then a still greater surprise was in store for me, for here was the elk-grass (*Xerophyllum tenax*) in great profusion. This striking Liliaceous plant had never before been found by me at such low altitudes. It is most frequent upon our snow mountains just as one is emerging from the timber and nearing the snow line. It is a wonderfully handsome plant with its mass of long, gray, recurved leaves, which are as tough as leather and cut like a knife—its long stalk shooting upward as the flowers gradually expand to a height of three or four feet, and surmounted till late in the season by a tuft of snow-white flowers, which are constantly renewed by fresh ones higher up as those below wither away into the fruiting stage. Never on the whole trip did I so miss the camera, which should have been with us (and arrived after I had left the party) as when I came upon whole fields of these plants several weeks later, near the snow-line and just in their prime. It is hard, when looking upon a whole "park" of these plants to realize that they have not been planted by the hand of man and tended by his care. Next I found the service-berry (*Amelanchier*

florida) and the star-flower (*Trientalis latifolia*).

Passing from the hill into a ravine, I was again surprised by finding at so low an altitude the Western white pine (*Pinus monticola*). This handsome tree, with its moderately long leaves and narrow worm-shaped cones. Its wood is soft and of a fine quality, but the scarcity of the trees forbids its ever becoming marketable, or in any way rivaling its prototype the white pine of the Michigan and Maine forests. Near at hand was the "sweet herb" (*Achlys triphylla*), as good a thing to put in a "clothes press" or bureau to scent linen as anything that I know.

In a dried lakelet, where I threw off my pack to rest, and the floor of which was thickly carpeted with the handsome moss *Fontinalis Neo-Mexicana*, I found the marsh violet (*Viola palustris*) in profusion, though now in fruit, the sweet two-leaved Solomon's seal (*Unifolium bifolium kamtschaticum*), and then a fern I had never seen growing in this country before, though common near Seattle—the moonwort (*Botrychium silaifolium*), the hard-hack (*Spiraea Douglasii*), and one of the handsomest, when not too old, of our sedges, *Carex Sitchensis*. Then came the pride of Hood's Canal, as it is of many other places, the beautiful pink-flowered Rhododendron (R. *Californicum*), still in flower though past its glorious prime. The firs then grew denser and higher, though the quality was still poor and the trees small. Here began to appear in great profusion mosses and lichens, only the most remarkable of which I shall mention here, or elsewhere in my narrative, as the description of them would but tire the general reader. One of the most noticeable mosses of our country, and here abundant and unusually well-fruited, is *Hypnum splendens*, its frond-like sections fern-like and reproducing themselves from near the top, year after year. Here also was another Pyrola (*P. picta var. dentata*), and high goat's-beard, or arrow-wood (*Schizonotus discolor*), a beautiful bush when in flower, its cream-white small flowers hanging in clusters like the grape, while its straight, tough shoots form shafts for the arrows of the Indian, or tips for the rods of Isaac Walton's disciples. Then appeared the peculiar "barber's pole" (*Allotropa virgata*), an Ericaceous plant, its white stems regularly striped with winding bars of red up to and among it white or pinkish flowers, with which latter the red-brown anthers form a striking contrast. Sparingly appearing was the other prince's pine (*Chimaphila Menzesii*), a much more delicate and pretty plant than C. *umbellata*.

Soon on every hand occurred an orchid, the rattlesnake plantain (*Peramium decipiens*), from the mottled leaves of which the name was probably derived, though some say the Indians use the plant as a remedy for the bite of the rattlesnake. Then the common wood-rush (*Juncoides campestre*) put in an appearance, and next, one of our most beautiful ferns, the spiny shield-fern (*Dryopteri spinulosa*). The common wake-robin (*Trillium ovatum*), was just coming into fruit, while the two mosses (*Hypnum loreum*, and *H. triquetrum*), and in the swamp itself were the nine-bark (*Opulaster opulifolius*), the beautiful trailing pine (*Lycopodium clavatum*), whose stems are such a favorite in the New England States for decorating during Christmas, the twist-stalk (*Streptopus amplexifolius*), and the dreaded "Devil's walking-club" (*Echinopanax horridum*). This plant, about five or six feet high ordinarily, is covered on stem, leaves and flower clusters with long, fragile prickles. When one carelessly presses through a clump of these plants, the prickles enter the flesh and break off, and, being of a poisonous nature, cause swellings which are painful, if not at times dangerous. On returning to camp late one evening, being unable to tell one kind of bush from another in the darkness, we passed through quantities of this bush. Our knees were filled with the troublesome prickles, though we were quite thickly dressed, and for a week or more to kneel or sit was torture.

As the woods grew deeper and the ground richer, an occasional bunch of the strange, ghostly Indian pipe (*Monotropa uniflora*), was just appearing above the ground. On my return, six weeks later, it was in its prime and most abundant. With it, and earlier by a month, was the brown Indian pipe (*Monotropa Hypopitys*), and with it grew a single specimen of the strange Orobanchaceous plant (*Boschniakia strobilacea*), the specific name of which is very good, for nothing more like an open pine cone ever existed, unless it were another pine cone. Then appeared another of this strange set, the leafless Pyrola (*P. aphylla*), and then another, Merten's coral-root (*Corallorhiza Mertensiana*), sending up its numerous shoots to the height of a foot and varying in color from pure white to rose-pink or purplish-brown. A strange crew they are, these sun-despising, fungous-looking plants! Plainly do they show us that the forest, dark and shadowy even in the midst of a sunny day, render it necessary for them to live differently from the majority of plants. The lack of sunlight and consequent absence of green coloring matter, or chlorophyll, show them to be in character, the "tramps" of the vegetable kingdom. They must either steal the elaborated juices of other live plants, or depend upon the decaying matter of others which are dead. Then came two other delicate little orchids, the two tway-blades, almost always found the one in the company of the other. These are the greater tway-blade (*Ophrys convallarioides*), and the lesser (*O. cordata*).

Suddenly the firs gave place to a rich maple-bottom and more open hillside, and there appeared the wild ginger (*Asarum caudatum*); the strange Saxifragaceous plant (*Leptaxis Menziesii*), one of those peculiar plants that disclose their seeds through the opened pod long before they are ripe; another of the same family whose fringed petals are as delicate as, and similar to, the crossed lines in a spider's web, namely the leafy mitre-wort (*Mitella caulescens*); the beautiful palm-tree moss (*Mnium Menziesii*), one of the finest on the coast, and more like a delicate little tree than a moss. Upon the moist bank grew the Virginia waterleaf (*Hydrophyllum tenuipes*), its flowers sometimes a pale lavender, sometimes a whitish-green; and with it the pretty squirrel-corn (*Bikukulla formosa*), whose flowers closely resemble both in form and color the "bleeding-heart," to which it is related.

Plunging immediately into the densest timber I had yet met on this trip, the ground of the fairly gloomy forest, which would have been dark and dismal in the extreme, was suddenly lit up as if I had come out into the open sunlight, or like stars in an otherwise black heavens, by acre upon acre of the snowy Canada dog-wood (*Cornus Canadensis*), and the fairest flower of the higher forests (*Clintonia uniflora*). This pure, Liliaceous plant, with its snowy or creamy flowers, delicate scent, glossy soft leaves in twos or threes from the root, and later its dark blue fruit is a favorite with everyone, and I have yet to find the person, no matter how much or how little he valued botany as a science, who has not asked me the name of this pretty, and in English, nameless flower.

At six o'clock I rounded a point in the woods and came suddenly in sight of the lake and of the party of pioneers who had preceded me. There was not a morsel of food in the camp and no chance of seeing the remainder of the party that night, as we well knew from the quality of the trail we had left behind us. Two had been sent out to forage, and soon returned with a small piece of bacon and a large loaf of bread. By careful division we had about finished our frugal fare, when a whoop was heard and soon the Lieutenant appeared with a full haversack slung over his shoulders. More help was needed for those with the pack animals, and all returned save the Lieutenant and myself. We went down to the lake, and after firing two shots, the approved method of letting those on the other side know that a "fare" was in waiting, we were ferried across and made arrangements with one of the farmers for bringing over the animals on a raft when they should appear. When! It was six o'clock the next day before three of them arrived, and later before all came in. What a sight! They had been relieved of half of their packs, half of the whole "outfit" had been left at our landing place, and with the burdens they bore they looked tired enough, and the men looked no better. Three of the mules had rolled down hill, so steep were the hills and so untried were their muscles, and one had so wedged itself under a large log that the log had to be cut off and the mule cut out! On account of this miserable trail it was four days before baggage enough had been collected to allow us to proceed, and weeks passed before the whole of the baggage was in camp with us. Poor trail, the never-ending delay caused by enforced ferriage across the lake on a miserable raft, and lack of almost all wild forage-plants for the mules, actually threw a damper over the spirits of the party which only vanished as we left all traces of man and extravagant tolls behind us. The next day no "driers" being on hand, or likely to be for a day or two, I determined to do no more collecting till they arrived, but spent part of my time in exposing those already collected to the sun to keep them from "burning," and the rest in trout-fishing. I was always very successful, especially toward evening, for fish are abundant in the lake, both brook- trout and "bull-trout." The latter take the spoon greedily, even after a hearty meal. I caught one about two feet long, and on preparing it for the cook I found in its stomach a whole trout eight inches long.

Lake Cushman is a body of water well worth visiting. It is about one and a half miles long by one-half or three quarters of a mile broad. It is very deep, and has probably been formed by a grand landslide in long past ages, or possibly a dyke from some fiery overflow. The mountains rise abruptly on two sides, and the one on the northeast was covered with snow on our arrival, but when I returned was bare. They are densely covered with firs to the very top, and magnificent timber most of it is. The Skokomish, a rapid, dashing stream, flows into it from the northwest, and goes out a sluggish but icy cold stream, at its southeast extremity. Could the obstructions at the falls be removed by blasting, thus giving as open "roadway" down the river for logs, the timber interests of this country would be very considerable. Moreover the land is generally good, and would be of no secondary value when the timber was removed. The bottom land to the west of the lake, though only about one mile wide and five or six long, is of wonderful fertility, owing to the almost yearly overflow of the upper Skokomish, and the "backing-up" of the lake. Vegetables grow here most luxuriantly, and a better stand of timothy I never saw in my life than on one of the lake ranches.

The afternoon of the 5th of July I spent in botanizing, for, though my presses and driers had not yet put in an appearance, I felt certain they would be at hand on the 6th. I went first to the rich alluvial bottoms and along a small creek that flows into the lake. Along the sandy banks of the latter

I found the turtle-head (*Chelone nemorosa*). In the mud grew the common cress (*Roripa nasturtium*, probably introduced) and the tall culm of a drooping grass (*Cinna latifolia*). Next were found *Mertensia Sibirica*, with its beautiful drooping lapis lazuli flowers, and close by, the bitter-cress (*Cardamine kamtschatica*). In the mud and water flourished the manna-grass (*Panicularia pauciflora*), and on the bank, the handsome flesh-colored flowers of the tall flea-bane (*Erigeron Philadelphicus*), lit up the dark green of the surrounding foliage. Close at hand shot aloft the tall shoots of a wild lettuce, not yet in flower, but on my return found to be *Lactuca spicata*. While looking down intently to see where I was putting my foot—for the lesser rills are often deep and muddy and covered over by the thick but none the less treacherous growth of the salmon-berry (*Rubus spectabilis*) the fruit of which was even then ripe and varying in color from corn-color to a black-brown—I was pleased to find for the first time in my life a magnificent specimen of the Virginia moonwort (*Botrychium Virginianum*), which measured over two feet from the tip of its elongated fertile frond to the ground. In vain I searched for more; it was a "solitaire" as far as my observation led me. On the sunny banks of the rill were the large mitre-wort (*Tellima grandiflora*), and the prickly gooseberry (*Ribes lacustre*), one of the handsomest of the genus, with its glossy green leaves and its black fruit. Close at hand rose the gigantic umbel known as the cow-parsnip (*Heracleum lanatum*), then just in flower, while cowering at its feet were the delicate plants *Cardamine oligosperma*, and *Alsine crispa*. The St. John's-wort (*Hypericum Scouleri*) was just preparing to open its yellow cluster. The alum-root (*Heuchera micrantha*) and the snow-berry (*Symphoricarpos racemosus*), were in full flower everywhere, while many mosses, such as Hypnum, Dicranum, Neckera, Mnium, Dichelyma, Racomitrium and Grimmia, covered trees and ground. I soon came out of the dense, rich forests on to a gravel-bar of one of the arms of the river, and here an entirely different flora awaited me. First was the delicate, red-stemmed Polygonum (*P. minimum*), the four-leaved Galium (*G. Kamtschaticum*), and the gorgeous plumes of the painted-cup or Indian pink (*Castilleia angustifolia*). The two rock-cresses (*Arabis hirsuta* and *A. glabra*) were abundant, as were the winter-cress (*Campe barbarea*), the various-leaved Collomia (*C. heterophylla*) and the graceful Gilia (*G. gracilis*). The beautiful Penstemon (*P. diffusus*) fairly covered the bar with its royal purple, while, as if to vie with royalty, flamed out the red flowers of their more modest colorings were the fruit and flowers of the wild strawberry (*Fragaria platypetala*), the pink blossoms of the delicate creeping spring beauty

351

(*Claytonia parvifolia*), the golden yellow flowers and the white stems of the "gold and silver" (*Eriophyllum lanatum*), probably the most variable plant on this coast, the greenish-white flowers of *Phacelia heterophylla*, and the minute blue flowers of the little "innocence" (*Collinsia tenella*). On the deciduous trees near by, and in fact along the whole trail so far, though nowhere else in such profusion, were festoons composed of the two pretty mosses *Neckera Douglasii* and *N. Menziesii*. Some of these draperies were three or four feet long, and resemble in all save color the Tillandsia or long-moss of the South, when seen at a distance. This moss, commonly collected for "stuffing," grows in such abundance there that were it nearer a market it would give quite an income to its gatherers. In these rich, warm bottoms, amongst the gigantic firs and cedars, the greenness of the plants and the size of the more perishable species are remarkable. The size of the moon-wort has recently been mentioned. The enchanter's nightshade here grew two and one-half feet high, while the leaves of Tolmiea were found over six inches in diameter. On my return to camp I found the delicate Saxifragaceous plant (*therofonelatum*), a sedge (*Carex festiva*), the hedge nettle (*Stachysciliata*), and the beautiful pink monkey-flower (*Mimulus Lewisii*), evidently a "waif" from the regions of the moraine and glacier.

352

The following day, armed with a rake, I proceeded to the lake. I paddled about for some time looking for aquatic plants, but met with poor success. A Potamogeton (*P. Robinsii*), covered the bottom of the lake in places where a depth of water from two to six feet obtained. In the shallower parts of the lake were growing abundantly mare's-tail (*Hippuris vulgaris*), mud-rush (*Iquisetum fluviatile*), two sedges (*Carex utriculata*, and *C. aquatilis?*), the latter too young for accurate determination, and the long, ribbon too young for accurate determination, and the long ribbon-like leaves of the bur-reed (*Sparganium angustifolium*), floated upon the waters. The shores were lined with the trees prevailing on the lake-borders of this country. These were the cottonwood (*Populus trichocarpa*), marsh willow (*Salix lasiandra*), long-leaved willow (*S. longifolia*), Oregon crab (*Pyrus diversifolia*), tall bush-honeysuckle (*Lonicera involucrata*), besides the firs, hemlock, arbor-vitæ, maples, buckthorn and alder, which here grow right down to the water's edge. Seeing an abrupt dyke of basalt rising almost directly out of the lake to the south (?) I rowed to it, landed and climbed up its steep face. Besides many mosses and lichens, I found the smooth maple (*Acer Douglasii*), Merten's saxifrage (*Saxifraga Mertensiana*), and the gray fescue-grass (*Festuca rubra*).

On the morning of July 7, the necessary part of the bag-gage having arrived, we struck camp, and taking up the trail, soon left behind us the last vestiges of civilization. I found but few plants along the trail not previously discovered. In moist sandy places under the willows and poplars appeared the little grove-lover (*Nemophila parviflora*), and an Epilobium, probably (*E. alpinum*), though approaching (*E. origanifolium*). Here also grew the valerian (*Valeriana Sitchensis*), filling the woods with its peculiar odor, while along the bottoms grew the bee-willow (*Salix Sitchensis*), a tree or shrub whose flowers are much frequented by the honey-bee in early spring. The female catkins were just disappearing, while the next plant found, the meadow-rue (*Thalictrum occidentale*), had dropped its ripened fruit. Here also was a delicate grass (*Agrostis exarata*). Soon succeeded an old gravel-bar, and there was the beautiful blue-bell (*Campanula rotundifolia*), in full bloom, while covering whole patches of ground were the green cushions of the alpine phlox (*Phlox diffusa*), a plant likewise away from home, for never before have I seen it at any other place than on banks at or above the timber line and even above the glaciers. About noon we reached the end of the trail, and the goal for which the trail was cut out—the copper mines, as they are called. Claim marks were abundant, but if there is not a greater showing of copper than was generally found in the specimens examined by our mineralogist, Colonel Linsley, there will be no fear of their claims being "jumped." A few specimens were tolerably rich in copper, but the majority showed much more of iron than the other metal. The various camping places were numbered consecutively and marked very distinctly "1," "2," "3," etc. From our present camp, No. "2" to "3," there intervened only about three miles, and yet so great was the labor in making trail and occasional bridges for the mules; in cutting or sawing gigantic fallen trees and in looking for suitable fords (for the river was at this time deep and swift), that six days were consumed before we reached the next camp. My attention was entirely diverted from botany to the uncongenial but none the less necessary handling of axe, saw, shovel and pick, for shirks were not in favor in the camp, and all worked with a will.

The only plants collected during this period were the pretty little bird's-foot bramble (*Rubus pedatus*); several mosses, notable among which was the handsome black-moss (*Scouleria aquatica*); the Western blue-berry (*Vaccinium ovalifolium*), whose berries are too sour to gratify the taste, but "make up well" into puddings and pies. One of the high-altitude firs first put in an appearance here, and though the cones were too young for accurate diagnosis it bore resemblance to one found in abundance two weeks later, namely the "lovely fir" (*Abies amabilis*), one of the many reminders that we were reaching a higher altitude. The other reminders were: *Rubus spectabitis*, with fruit half-grown; *Ribes lacustre*, in blossom, and the female cones or "catkins" of *Alnus Oregona* hardly at all awakened from their winter's sleep. That evening after the work of the day, and supper was over, I wandered along the gravelly and beautiful banks of the river and collected a few strangers to my trip so far. These were the large-leaved sand-wort (*Moehringia macrophylla*), the large leaves of the Western colt's-foot (*Petasites speciosa*), the fruit of the tall yellow violet (*Viola glabella*), strangely enough now seen for the first time on the trip, and lastly, the mountain bush-alder (*Alnus sinuata*), the delicious odor of whose leaves always prepares me for its presence before I see it. This bush or small tree, common enough in most of the mountains, is even more abundant in the Olympics and sometimes for a mile or more offers an almost impenetrable barrier to the traveler, unless he is armed with an axe. Nearly always inclining strongly down hill, owing to their six or eight months weight of snow, sometimes partly covered by humus or moss, they are the cause of more serious falls than any other tree, unless it be the vine-maple.

The next day a halt was ordered for mending clothes, resting and bringing up the remaining baggage from the last camp. Accompanied by one of the soldiers, Mr. Fisher, I started soon after nine o'clock to ascend a high peak which began just across the river and ended—no one knew where. A light breakfast with several good strong cups of coffee, a cool morning and beautiful sky, all conspired to put us in excellent spirits, and we went up mile after mile with very little sense of fatigue. The slope was most of the way of an angle of fully forty-five degrees and some of the time at that of sixty-five or seventy, while near the top it was not far from eighty. Nearly the whole of the route lay through a tolerable thick growth of conifers, thus diversifying the way, deceiving us as to its length, and giving us many a soft resting place. It was a continued scene of beauty, for so steep was the slope that at any time we could look down upon the tops of high trees not a hundred yards distant, thus allowing us to examine at will every variation of leaf, branch or cone. The forest was made up of a jumble of Douglas spruce, arbor vitæ, white pine, white fir, balsam or lovely fir, yew, Western hemlock, and far up the slopes, alpine fir and alpine hemlock. We had not proceeded a half-mile from the camp before we came upon a large snow bank protected from the warm rays of the sun by the thick forest at this place. Then came one of those surprises, not infrequent in the mountains, but seen nowhere else that I am aware of—an entire change in the

flora. From this snow bank and thick woods we passed almost immediately to an exposed dyke of basalt, upon whose scant patches of earth the sun was now throwing its slanting but mid-day rays. The earth, such as there was, was almost as dry as an Eastern Oregon slope in summertime, and here were the very plants common on the sunny banks of the Willamette River, though some of them I had not seen since leaving Oregon, and many not since I had joined the expedition. Nearly the entire surface of the rock for a hundred yards or more was thickly carpeted with the boulder-moss (*Racomitrium canescens* Brid.), while the poison-oak (*Rhus diversiloba*) was just coming into fruit. The mock-orange (*Philadelphus Gordonianus*) was just budding, while the plains-grass (*Merathrepta Californica*), mouse-ear chickweed (*Cerastium arvense*), stone-crop (*Sedum spathulifolium*, "moss" in the vernacular throughout Oregon and Washington), five-finger (*Potentilla glandulosa*), *Hosackia parviflora*, small-headed clover (*Trifolium microcephalum*), few-flowered clover (*T. olganthum*), and rock club-moss (*Selaginella rupestris*), not only all plants new to the trip, but the only plants here growing. How did they find this, to them, little oasis in the desert of forest? Certainly it supports the theory advanced by some, if theory it can be called, that the various methods in which seeds my be scattered cannot be measured, that where you find the suitable habitat and environment, there you will be sure to find the plant. Here also were a few plants seen at our landing on Hood's Canal, and not seen since, namely, the cherry (*Prunus emarginata villosa*), and the yellow Composite (*Agoseris laciniata*). Near the dyke was out common early violet (*Viola sempervirens*) and strange companion for this little friend found only about Portland, the snow-loving bramble (*Rubus nivalis*), a pretty thing with its glossy, evergreen leaves and lurid-red flowers. Rare mosses, lichens and fungi now began to appear on every hand, the most noticeable of the first class being the caterpiller moss (*Hypnum robustum*), so named on account of the yellowish-green and exceedingly worm-like branches; while the "barber's poles" (*Allotropa virgata*) and coral-root (*Corallorhiza Mertensiana*) were sticking up everywhere. Here first appeared the myrtle-leaved huckleberry (*Vaccinium macrophyllum*), the fruit of which is a luscious berry equally prized by white or Indian, though the bush was now hardly past the flowering stage. As we mounted higher and higher, the trees grew more scanty and stunted, with glades here and there. Presently were found occasional shoots of the small-leaved huckleberry (*Vaccinium scoparium*), the modest little mountain wintergreen or salal (*Gaultheria ovatifolia*) and the downy bramble (*Rubus lassiococcus*). In the more open, loose soil were grow-

353

ing a pretty sedge (*Carex Rossii*), and one of the showiest and most common Lupines near the snow line, *L. rivularis*. Steeper and more arduous grew the ascent, for a fire had killed the now scattered trees, thus taking from us all shelter from the intense rays of the sun, and making the soil so loose that our feet sank ankle deep at every step. The fire had gone through this place the previous year, and though it had destroyed nearly all vegetation, the deep roots of the elk-grass had not been injured, and it was out in thick magnificence. The beauty of this plant I have previously described. Veritable snow-balls they appear perched upon the summits of their green and purple stems. Soon vast banks of snow were reached, as the slope went down toward the north, and immediately a new set of flowers appeared. On a little sunny bank, peering out of the snow like an islet from the sea, was the pretty alpine buttercup (*Ranunculus Eschscholtzii*). Then began one of the most singular mixtures of mountain and valley flowers that I had ever witnessed; common yellow violet (*Viola glabella*), white adder's tongue (*Erythronium revolutum*), yew (*Taxus brevifolia*) in flower, a lily (*Disporum Oreganum*) just flowering, baneberry (*Actea spicata arguta*), meadow-rue, just flowering, sweet-herb, Western barberry or Oregon grape (*Berberis nervosa*), all low altitude plants, common all about Portland or Olympia, there grew in strange incongruity with the goose-berry (*Ribes lacustre*), an alpine currant (*Ribes laxiflorum*), alpine valerian (*Valeriana Sitchensis*), alpine wood-rush (*Juncoides parviflorum*, an alpine form, and the two alpine mitre-worts (*Mitella trifida* and *M. Breweri*). The two next found, smooth maple (*Acer Douglasii*), and an umbelliferous plant, *Washingtonia ambigua*, seem equally at home at the snow line or along our rivers at low altitudes.

The mountain slope now grew rocky and far more steep. Where a scant covering of earth overlaid the otherwise bare rock were great patches of the sweet mountain pink (*Phlox diffusa*), the soft cushions of whose intermingled leaves and branches, seconded by the delicious scent of its white or pink flowers, offer as luxurious a pillow to the warm head and panting frame as any Sybarite could choose. Then, as with body stretched out its full length at an angle of twenty or thirty degrees, bathed in the warm rays of the afternoon sun, with eyes looking upward and outward and meeting nothing but the blue sky, except it be a majestic white cloud-pile moving across the field of view not far overhead, or a butterfly flitting just above; hearing nothing but the plaintive whistle of

the mountain marmot, or the roar of some Alpine cataract far below, all cares of the world vanish for the instant; one seems to be upon some vast, quiet sea, and instinctively some such soothing couplet as that of Buchanan Reid's occurs to the mind:

> *My soul today is far away,*
> *Sailing the Vesuvian Bay.*

But with a start I realize that I am getting cold, that the evening is advancing, and that the top has not yet been gained. Near at hand, my senses steeped in the incense from its leaves, was the bush-alder (Alnus sinuata), just in flower, and right under it the yellow adder's tongue (Erythronium grandiflorum parvifloram); next the pretty mountain-ash (Pyrus Sitchensis). Just here a bear started up and went plunging down the steep slope at a fearful gait, and altogether too quickly for the expert pistol of my companion. Up a little ravine, at an angle of fully eighty degrees, ran the trail, well marked and even scored by the feet of deer.[4] How do they possibly ascend such slopes? Had it not been for the almost continuous assistance given us by bushes, plants or jutting rocks, we would have been compelled to beat a retreat a number of times. The whistle or cry of the marmot grew more frequent; where a combination of soil and crevices of rock would admit of it, were numerous holes of the mountain beaver. Jutting out from the cliff-faces was a plant belonging to a class much sought after by the Indians for its food-producing roots, called "cous," and botanically Lomatium. This species (L. Hallii) we found no exception to the rule, and we ate or rather chewed several of its figrous, parsnip-like roots with a relish. Then appeared the peculiar Menziesia ferruginea, and the undeveloped buds of the white azalea (Rhododendron albiflorum). Next, in strange contrast, the common blue violet (Viloa adunca), and low strawberry (Fragaria Chiloensis) put me in mind of home. The young shoots of Pedicularis bracteosa) were just appearing from the ground, while from a rich handful of earth was growing a clump of the pretty alpine form of our waterleaf (Hydrophyllum tenuipes). Soon a delightful surprise was in waiting for me. As we scaled the now almost vertical wall, slowly and with the utmost care, for a misstep would send us rolling hundreds of feet down the steep and rocky defile, my face, almost in contact with the rock, came suddenly upon a dash of color almost as vivid

354

---

[4] "Henderson made an error common to the pioneer explorer; i.e., grossly exaggerating the steepness of the mountains. However, in fairness, it should be pointed out that slopes inclined at forty-five to fifty degrees often seem to be almost vertical to experienced mountaineers." Wood, *Men, Mules and Mountains*, p. 405.

as if some one had overturned a pot of crimson or carmine, and covering an area of a foot or more. It was the beautiful alpine Douglasia (D. dentata), probably, though at the time I thought I had found an unknown treasure. Soon this plant occurred in great abundance, and as these brilliant patches of red fell upon the eye from a distance, one could hardly dissuade oneself from thinking this some Lookout Mountain up which an attacking force had been clambering and though the bodies had been removed the stains bore witness of the bloody fray. Clinging to the overhanging rocks was the handsome Penstemon Menziesii, while Antennaria Howellii, Saxifraga Marshallii (early Saxifrage), Saxifraga punctata, Allium Tolmiei, Arabis hirsuta, Pachystima Myrsinites, in full bloom, and the beautiful western heather (Phyllodoce empetriformis) yet in bud, took hold wherever a handful of earth was to be found on the otherwise bare rocks. Bordering the snow-banks, near the summit, were thick beds of another plant closely related to the last Cassiope Mertensiana, the beautiful white bells of the latter forming a pretty contrast to the pink buds of the former. Next came a violet, handsome both in leaf and in flower, the name of which is totally unknown to me. There was but one bunch of it, and though I scanned the cliffs far and near not another did I find. (This plant is called V. Howellii by Mr. Watson.) Near the summit appeared Lewisia Columbiana, where sufficient disintegrated rock had given it a bed, while near by was Saxifraga Bongardi in bud.

After traversing a few more snow-fields and rounding several cliffs, we came to the extreme summit, and, in order to rest, sat down upon a three-foot mountain hemlock (*Tsuga Mertensiana*), which supported me like a spring bed, and from whose top, as I drank in the splendor of the scene, I cut the flowers both male and female. Then I bent over toward me a six-foot alpine fir (*Abies lasiocarpa*), and cut from its top the female flowers and half-developed cones. What was the age of these dwarfs would be difficult to calculate, as the rings are so near as to be almost unrecognizable without the aid of a microscope; but from the cut end of one about the same size on Mt. Hood I made out fifty rings and possibly more. The dwarfish nature is only natural to them when inhabiting the extreme tops of the lower mountains, or above the snow line on the higher. On the slopes near the end of the main timber belt they reach generous proportions and are both objects of beauty. The fir is sometimes nearly one hundred feet high and is almost cylindrical from the bottom to the top, so short and thick are the branches. The hemlock is the exact opposite, and when half-grown is a perfect cone and the most beautiful conifer with which I am acquainted.

It seems at times as if the tree must have been subjected to the pruner's shears, so perfectly regular is its form. Add to this its very dense, pretty clusters of leaves, giving it the appearance of being thickly covered with green rosettes, and it is a delightful object to gaze upon. Even when age has given it a diameter of three feet, it does not lose its beauty, for a pleasing majesty takes the place of its charming regularity, like a beautiful girl ripened into regal womanhood. No room was given me at this time for these reflections, for while my companion had kindled a fire in a little clump of dead hemlock, and the bacon was sizzling thereon, preparatory to being sandwiched between slices of bread, our frugal, but after such labors, appetizing meal, I was busy making a rough map. I spread out a sheet of clean paper upon a flat boulder, and, placing upon it my compass to get the cardinal points, I traced thereon the main trend of rivers and chains, and located the highest peaks. This was all done to enable our friends below to judge somewhat of the unexplored country beyond us, and where it was most probable a trail could be run, for this purpose alone, for had the time been altogether at my disposal, I should have done nothing but gaze. A more magnificent scene had never presented itself to my eyes, and I doubt whether anything in the higher Alps or the grand ice-mountains of Alaska could outrival that view. To the south and east, and apparently right at my feet was the narrow, blue ribbon of Hood's Canal, and at the heel of this watery boot stood out like a large flake of snow in the distance, the village of Union City. Then came a narrow neck of land, and then succeeded one another like fingers to a gigantic hand North Bay, Eld Inlet. Totten Inlet and Budd's Inlet. The hand became an arm and lost itself in the hazy distance toward Tacoma. Mt. Rainier was visible from top to bottom, and never before was I so struck with its magnificence as when looking upon it from this height and being able to compare it with every intervening object. But it was the opposite view which captivated me most. Canyon mingled with canyon, peak rose above peak, ridge succeeded ridge, until they culminated in old Olympus far to the northwest; snow, west, north and south; the fast descending sun bringing out the gorgeous colorings of pale-blue, lavender, purple, ash, pink and gold. Add to this the delightful warmth of a summer sun in these altitudes—the awful stillness broken every now and then by the no less awful thunder of some distant avalanche—a fearful precipice just before us down which a single step in advance would hurl us hundreds of feet and one can form some slight idea of the reasons that compelled us to gaze and be silent.

But it was now after four o'clock, and a long, steep journey lay between us and camp. Regretfully we turned our eyes away from this scene and swiftly passing back to the east slope of the mountain, we were surprised to find that evening had already set in there. Slipping, sliding, running, jumping where the trail was easier—crawling backwards and holding tightly by every bush or bunch of grass where the way was dangerous, we finally reached the timber line. Then running, jumping, slipping again, the miles flew swiftly behind us until at half-past nine, and after several shots had been given by our friends in camp, who were uneasy at our prolonged stay, and answered by us—dripping with perspiration and trembling like aspens our legs almost giving way under us at every step owing to the fearful strain upon muscles unaccustomed to such a descent—foot-sore and happy with the success of the trip, we entered camp and there detailed the circumstances of the day to a group of listeners, while beside the blazing camp-fire we refreshed ourselves with a good supper and pints of hot coffee.

The next day owing to the mass of material I had collected the previous day (for I aimed to gather at least one specimen of every species I saw on the whole trip, that the Alpine Club might have as complete a collection as possible) I spent the whole of the time in sorting and drying the plants, and arranging with some of the men to attend to my "pack," for the following three or four days were to be given up to "scouting" for trails. At eight o'clock July 15 we again broke camp and moved up the river two or three miles, the mules making good use of the shallow fords on this part of the river as well as the long stretches of gravel bar. At nine o'clock "Camp 4" was reached, where vertical walls, a swift and deep river, and numerous falls revealed to us the fact that the serious work would now begin. Three scouting parties were quickly formed, and orders given by the Lieutenant as to the ground we were to "cover." Our party consisted of Colonel Linsley, our mineralogist; Sergeant Yates and myself, to be increased shortly after our departure, and much to our disgust, by our mastiff-hound "Jumbo." We went very "light weight," owing to the severe climbing we knew was in store for us, our stock of supplies and equipments being one haversack of hardtack, tea and coffee, a pound or two of bacon, a hand axe, a rifle and a small press. For this reason was Jumbo's society not only undesired, but the dog came to be actually abhorred, till famine toil and heroism proved his staying qualities and changed our antipathy into admiration. As we toiled up a mossy cliff the flowers of *Rubus spectabilis* were just opening from bud; the fruit had vanished months ago around the Sound. Further on the ground was carpeted with the green leaves and bright with the snowy flowers of the little bramble (*Rubus pedatus*), while quantities of the

pink twist-stalk (*Streptopus roseus*) were on every hand. We were soon driven by the steep bluff to the river-bed of the South Branch, more of a creek than a river, and rushing and roaring a constant succession of rapids, pools and occasional falls. Here I came upon a little friend I had not seen since leaving the Columbia River at Rooster Rock, the delicate *Romanzoffia Sitchensis*, while a little further up the stream, and growing from the snow *Vaccinium ovalifolium* was just blossoming. On a bank in the woods, but recently abandoned by the snow, was growing *Lycopodium lucidulum*, its leafy spikes just ripening their spores. The trail was followed with the utmost difficulty. The severe winter that had just passed, with its accompanying and unheard-of mass of snow, followed by severe storms and avalanches in the spring, had prostrated trees in every direction, piling the giant cedars and firs sometimes four or five deep. It was probably due to the unusual depth of snow and quantities of "wind-falls" that game had been so scarce during the whole trip so far, for its absence puzzled the "oldest inhabitant." If it had not been for the fallen timber the way would have been comparatively easy, for a deeply cut elk-trail led along the river, which would have been as plain as a cattle-path had the successions of fallen trees, dislodged stones, landslides and at times deep snow allowed any trail to be followed for more than a hundred yards. Soon we abandoned all thought of trail and took boldly to the timber, keeping the stream always in sound if not in sight, and skirting, while ascending, the steep slope to the north of the creek. After several miles of wind-falls, snowbanks, vine-maple, huckleberry brush and alpine alder we came suddenly upon one of those dykes often found on mountain sides, and there my delight was great in finding a pea whose whole aspect was new to me, even to its generic characters. From one slightly formed pod I judged it might be a Desmodium, but have discovered since that it is *Hedysarum occidentale*. On taking again to the forest, as my eyes were fixed upon the ground noting the various mosses and lichens, my attention was suddenly arrested by a little cone about the size of a very large pea or small cherry. I glanced up and there over my head were the pretty, pendant branches and white trunk of the Sitka or yellow cedar (*Chamaecyparis Nootkatensis*). This valuable tree, valuable alike from its strong scent, light yellow wood, close grain—so close that the mere blow of a sharp axe leaves a surface as highly polished as if it had been planed and oiled—is here found in great abundance, and at times reaches a diameter of eight or nine feet. The most of these large trees, however, are more or less wrecks, the heavy snows, landslides, old age, or what not, having laid no gentle hands upon them, but leaving them gnarled and dead at the top or broken off half way up. On a slope facing the south, reached on a succeeding day, we found the wood much more perfect and the trees smaller, but very numerous. In fact, nearly one-half of the timber was of this species. the remaining timber was composed mainly of white pine and "lovely fir," the trees of both kinds being very large and fine. The company which first invents some way to get these trees to market (now it seems almost an impossibility) will make a fortune here, for I am told the logs of the Sitka cedar fetch a very high price at Victoria, in such high repute is the lumber in Europe. On the same slope where I first found the Chamæcyparis, *Silene Douglassii* was growing in great clumps, and out of the rocks near by quantities of lace-fern (*Cheilanthes gracillima*). Higher came the little Saxifrage (*S. bronchialis*), and the handsome shield-fern (*Polystichum Lonchitis*).

Here night threatened to overtake us and we were forced to camp, though there was no water, and nowhere could we find a slope which could afford us a couch at a less angle than thirty degrees. Right against a huge boulder, however we built our fire, and as we had no blankets and some of us no coats, we collected wood for an "all night's session." Fortunately this was abundant, as it is everywhere in these mountains, and soon a roaring fire was blazing upward. We collected great cakes of snow, and putting into our quart cup handful after handful of this substance, in lieu of water, we soon had tea. As we sat around our camp-fire, partaking of our delicious repast of hardtack, bacon and tea, the pleasure of the moment was rather clouded by thoughts of the coming night to be gone through, and I for one involuntarily repeated the words from a well-known selection, slightly amended:

> "Few and short were the prayers we said,
> And we spake not a word of sorrow,
> But we steadfastly gazed" on the snow all around
> "And we bitterly thought of the morrow."

By constantly replenishing the fire all night, and by constantly changing our freezing and our roasting sides, we managed to keep moderately comfortable, and five o'clock the next morning saw us up, and shortly after, continuing our upward course. As we neared the top of this particular peak I came upon a very interesting plant, new to me, and I had hoped, new to science, the Alaskan Spiraea (*Spiraea Hendersoni*), springing out from the top of vertical walls, in this respect very unlike its relative, *Lutkea pectinata* which ordinarily grows in loose moraine material. I hear that Professor Eaton thinks it a new species. In slopes on the summit

was the dwarf huckleberry (*Vaccinium caespitosum*) then in flower. Next came the yellow *Arnica Chamissonis*, and a grass (*Trisetum spicatum molle*) with a sedge (*Carex leporina*). In thickets near by were the delicate little flowers of the wood wind-flower (*Anemone nemorosa*), a remarkably small form with flowers varying from white to blue. This little plant seems worthy of a varietal name, but I have been told by eminent authorities that intermediate forms are found. However this may be, I never have found them, neither have I ever found the small form in the neighborhood of the larger. The only times I ever found this form were in its present situation and in an "oak-prairie" five miles southeast of Portland. On a moist, sunny bank near by was *Epilobium alpinum*, and further on I collected a solitary specimen of Drummond's wind-flower (*Anemone Drummondii*), the alpine meadow-sweet (*Spiraea densiflora*), Drummond's rush (*Juncus subtriflorus*), and *Saxifraga Bongardi* now in blossom. The only other plant found by me not previously described was the pretty grass, *Deschampsia atropurpurea*. The travel of this day was the most provoking I ever experienced, the most dangerous and very fatiguing. It was one constant succession of climbing up one wall, down another; up one snow-bank, down another, creeping along a precipice, or walking along a sharp "backbone" upon the tops of eight-foot trees. Some idea can be had of the nature of our advance when I state that we left the former camp at six o clock A. M., stopped one hour at noon, and at six o'clock in the evening camped on a flat ledge of sandstone rocks not two miles from our "covert" of the night before. At six the next morning, after having blazed a tree and written thereon the object of our search, we were again on the way, my botanical pack swelling visibly hour by hour, but the contents of the haversack reduced to a slice of bacon, a handful of sugar and about a quart of cracker crumbs. We had accomplished the object of our mission, however, which was to satisfy ourselves that a trail up this south fork would be not only difficult and long, but hazardous, as the other side of the ridge seemed most forbidding for pack animals. We were convinced that the trail should go farther to the north, and this view being fixed in our minds, the next thing was to get back to camp as quickly as possible since our store of provisions was reduced to a minimum. Passing down the north side of this ridge, crossing the creek at the bottom, and ascending the opposite ridge to the north, we found no small undertaking, and six hours were consumed in making, on a straight line, not over one mile and a half. On the cold, wet bottoms of the north slope I found growing abundantly Jeffrey's mosquito-bills (*Dodecatheon Jeffreyi*), and the white marigold (*Caltha biflora*), the latter blossoming right out of the snow, so late was the season and so deep had been the snow. Along the rills lower down, the delicate corymbs of *Trautvetteria grandis* were abundant. After arduous toil we reached a point well up the opposite ridge, and took there a very hasty and meager meal, the last one in the haversack. Camp was about eight or ten miles away, but we had luckily struck a fine elk trail and an open hillside. This trail we kept for several miles, till the fallen timber of the bottom compelled us to seek the creek-bank. Here I collected the only other plant not yet seen, the graceful rein-orchid (*Limnorchis stricta*), though one other plant was seen, not yet fit for collection. The tall stalks of the "stagger-weed" (*Delphinium trolliifolium*) were in their prime stage for being cropped by animals, and acted as another motive to cause us to abandon this route, as I have too frequently seen the deadly effect of this plant upon cattle and horses. At nine o'clock, wearied, hungry, and our lower limbs filled with the poisonous prickles of *Echinopanax horridum*, we caught the gleam of the camp-fire and were welcomed by a chorus of shots, yells and the baying of hounds. All of the other parties had returned, and one of them with a fine, young deer. I will not tax the reader's credulity by enumerating the number of slices of fried venison, cups of coffee or slices of bread we severally devoured that night. Passing this immaterial part of the record suffice it to state that nothing of great value had been discovered as to the most feasible trail, but it was determined to reach the Upper Falls, about six miles distant, before sending out more parties.

This trip consumed the 15th, 16th, and 17th of July. From the 18th to the 27th we were engaged in making trail, and on the morning of this last day were encamped at a beautiful spot above the Falls, "Camp 6." Here another scouting party, consisting of Colonel Linsley and Private Fischer was sent out. During their absence the remainder of the party was engaged in continuing the trail up a steep but more open slope, and "Camp 7" was reached the evening of the 28th. Here a tree had been blazed by the exploring party sent out on the previous morning, and we were surprised to find the reading of the Colonel's barometer registered only 2,300 feet. How different from the Cascade Mountains! Here we were camped by a great snow-bank the last of July, and our altitude only 2,300 feet above the sea. These same surroundings in the Cascade Range would have given us an altitude of not less than 6,000 feet.

Here, after a three weeks' handling of saw, axe, pick and shovel, and not having received a scratch or bruise the whole time, I inflicted a severe cut upon my wrist while cutting fir boughs for the beds, and was rendered immediately a "useless

member" for days to come. To add to my disgust, and that of our "advance working gang," word was brought us from "Camp 6" that the explorers had returned and announced the fact that farther progress along our present line was not only impracticable, but even impossible, and that we must return to the lower camp and explore for a northerly trail. The evening of the 30th saw us all reassembled in "Camp 6," not, however, before I had collected at the former camp a few more plants. These consisted almost entirely of mosses, lichens and fungi; but the berries of the several huckleberries were just ripe enough for good collecting, and the sweet flowers of the white azalea were here seen, for the first time this season, in full bloom. A forced rest for the next two days was a necessity for the party, as the Lieutenant had been compelled to go to Hoodsport for supplies and to learn of our photographer, who had not yet put in his appearance, though this had been promised for several weeks. This rest would have been appreciated by me in my present useless condition, if I had not been constantly annoyed by the thought that the time at my disposal was oozing rapidly away. The Lieutenant returned on the evening of the 31st, and plans were immediately formed to send out three more parties on the succeeding day. From "Camp 4" a party consisting of our naturalist, Mr. Bretherton, and our engineer, Mr. Church, had been sent out by the Lieutenant over the divide to the south, with instructions to explore and carefully to map out the South Fork of the Skokomish River, the longer and possibly the larger fork of the main river, and which joins the one that flows out of Lake Cushman a few miles west of Union City and the Canal. They had now been gone since the 18th, and as they had taken only five days' rations, we began to feel uneasy about them. I was to learn the cause of their long absence a few days later.

The morning of the first of August broke dark and gloomy. The scouts were divided into three parties, and were told not to return till they severally found the route taken by them either utterly impracticable or absolutely safe. They were provisioned for a five to seven days' trip. My hand having healed sufficiently to cause me less inconvenience, I was anxious to accompany one of the parties, since at the utmost I had but a few weeks at my disposal before I should be compelled to return. Both the Lieutenant and the Colonel, however, spoke strongly against my proposal, and unwillingly I gave it up. At ten o'clock, three hours after their departure, it commenced to pour, and glad enough I was then that I had not accompanied them in my disabled condition. Before the party started I intimated to the Lieutenant that I should return to the Canal before he got back, explaining the position fully to him. So "good-byes" were given and returned, and August 3 saw me on my return, accompanied by one of the soldiers, Higgins, while my collection and few belongings were tightly strapped to the back of the faithful little mule "Frenchy." As it was about twenty miles to Hoodsport, and as we wished to reach that point the evening of this day, we took one other mule to help us on our journey, and by riding in turns render it less tedious.

I found nothing to collect till I reached Lake Cushman. There a three weeks' absence and the lowering of the waters of the lake had brought a few more flowers into view. These were *Oenanthe sarmentosa*, an Angelica (*A. Lyallii?*) in flower, the creeping buttercup (*Ranunculus Flammula reptans*), a sedge (*Carex stipata*), a pretty aster (*A. foliaceus frondeus*), the blue-flowered lettuce (*Lactuca spicata*), now in full bloom, and the tall, drooping grass (*Cinna latifolia*). In the dark fir forests bordering the lake, and for the ensuing two or three miles, the woods were thick with the ghostly stalks of the Indian pipe (*Monotropa uniflora*). Nothing else was seen to collect till we reached a gravelly, burnt plain, almost entirely devoid of underbrush, and with but few firs and other trees. The ground was thickly covered with salal and kinnikinick, while clumps of the Lupine (*L. rivularis*), *Psoralea physodes*, and *Hosackia crassifolia*, occurred at intervals. Then came quantities of the black pine (*Pinus contorta*), which differs here, as it does in the high mountains, from the ordinary seacoast form, possibly enough to merit the specific name that some give it of *P. Murrayana*. It struck me, as I looked at this tree, that it took just the intermediate ground between the coast and high mountain forms, and made even the var. *Marrayana* of Engelmann unnecessary. The coast tree is a low, bunchy tree, thickly covered with very enduring cones; the mountain tree is a very tall tree for its size, at times more resembling gigantic bamboos than trees. This form occupied the middle ground. It is never very bunchy, but bears cones, as does the coast form, when quite low. As I rode along the cones on the tops of some of these trees or bushes did not reach my shoulder. Here it is always symmetrical, and at times reaches goodly proportions. As I rode in the stage between Union City and Shelton, I observed many over two feet in diameter, and one old decrepit hero, broken off half way up, measured nearly three feet. As we dropped off from this bench

the firs and hemlocks again took the place of the pines. Along the hillsides near Hoodsport I found the small-headed cudweed (*Gnaphalium microcephalum*) abundant, and as I came down upon the beach I collected several specimens of the last plant gathered on this trip, *Grindelia Hendersoni*. I was rather doubtful about this name when it was sent me, or about this being a new species, but from the specimens collected this year, both flower and fruit, I am convinced that it is neither *G. cuneifolia* nor *G. glutinosa*.

When I reached Hoodsport I found Mr. Bretherton and Dr. Church looking rather pulled down. On my inquiring what the matter was, they told me as follows: Relying upon what false statements they had heard from miners and Indians, they had crossed the divide with only three days' rations, since they had been assured that a good trail and a short day's trip down the south fork of the Skokomish would bring them into the Indian reservation, and thence an easy trip into Union City. They were out seven or eight days, and for the last three days with hardly a morsel to eat. Had it not been for timely succor given them by a party of hunters from Olympia, it is doubtful whether they would ever have been enabled to reach their journey's end to tell the tale of their hardships. They were to follow after the party the next day, and wishing them good-bye and a successful termination to the whole expedition, I hired a sailboat and was soon over at the little but beautifully situated village of Union City. There I took stage the next morning for Shelton, and after a four hours' drive over a fine road, and picturesque but rather poor country, I reached the latter place, whence I took the steamer for Olympia.[5]

As one of the youngest soldiers, Mr. Fisher, seemed much interested in my work, I left him my press, driers and plenty of paper, asking him to finish what I had barely begun. This he agreed to do, and from what I was told by the Lieutenant and by other members of the party, he kept his word well, and had gathered for me many plants which he knew I had not. By some untoward accident this bundle, carried with so much difficulty all through the mountains, miscarried somewhere on the way to Gray's Harbor, to which place they went when taken upon the western coast. This is greatly to be regretted, for it must be that the most interesting flora and time of collecting came after I left the party, both on account

359

---

[5] "Henderson had hoped to collect many rare and unknown plants in the Olympics but had been surprised by the absence of unique species. After he returned home and checked over the 300 or so specimens he had gathered, he saw 'two or three possibly new species.' Although he had planned to write a paper that would attract the attention of scientists to the Olympics, he had to be content with describing 'a flora trite in the extreme to those . . . acquainted with the plants of the northwest.' He did not, however, consider his few weeks in the Olympics lost time, and he felt his report was 'very incomplete.' He had been rather surprised by the similarity of the flora to that of the Cascade and Coast Ranges, perhaps without reason." Wood, *Men, Mules and Mountains*, p. 409.

of the mountains growing higher, the distance as they advanced being farther removed from salt water, and the snow disappearing from the slopes and leaving more of the ground uncovered. This unfortunate circumstance may have been largely mended by the good collections made by Mr. Charles V. Piper, who followed some weeks later along the route taken by the party, and reached a point much further inland than did I. If reports from his collections sent, when unknown, to the different authorities for identification, come back at about the same time that mine do, I shall incorporate the additional plants collected by him in this report.

As yet a great deal is to be learned about the flora of these mountains, and when several such fine trails as were cut by our party are made into their hearts they will not long be a terra incognita.

List of Plants From the Canal to the Snow Line

Those seen by Charles V. Piper and not by me are followed by his name. I am indebted to Messrs. Sereno Watson, George Vasey, L. H. Bailey, J. Cardot, O. F. Cook, H. Willey and Charles H. Peck for the identification of many species. Some were too fragmentary, some of the grasses were too old, and some of the carices too young for exact identification, and all such are unnamed in whole or in part, or given with a question mark. The list enumerates nearly five hundred species:

Thalictrum occidentale Gray.
Anemone nemorosa L.
    Drummondii Wats.
occidentalis Wats. (Piper.)
Trautvetteria grandis Nutt.
Ranunculus Eschscholtzii Schl.
Flammula L., var. reptans Mey.
Ranunculus tenellus Nutt.
    Cymbalaria Pursh.
Caltha biflora DC.
Trollius laxus Salisb. (Piper.)
Aquilegia formosa Fisch.
Actæa spicata L., var. arguta Torr.
Berberis nervosa Pursh.
Achlys triphylla DC.
Dicentra formosa DC.
Barbarea vulgaris R. Br.
Erysimum arenicola Wats.n sp (Piper)
Arabis hirsuta Scop.
perfoliata Lam.
Cardamine oligosperma Nutt.
hirsuta L., var. sylvatica Gray.

pratensis L.
Lepidium Virginicum L.
Viola palustris L.
Howellii Gray (?).
glabella Nutt.
sarmentosa Dougl.
Silene Douglasii Hook.
Cerastium arvense L.
Stellaria borealis Bigel.
crispa Ch. & Sch.
Arenaria lateriflora L. (Piper.)
macrophylla Hook.
Sagina occidentalis Wats. (?)
Lepigonum medium Fries.
Calandrinia Columbiana Howell.
Claytonia triphylla Wats.
cordifolia Wats.
Sibirica L.
parvifolia Moc.
Hypericum anagalloides Ch. & Schl.
    Scouleri Hook.
Pachystima Myrsinites Raf.
Rhamnus Purshiana DC.
Acer macrophyllum Pursh.
glabrum Torr.
circinatum Pursh.
Rhus diversiloba Torr. & Gray
Lupinus rivularis Doug.
Trifolium involucratum Willd.
pauciflorum Nutt.
microcephalum Pursh.
Hosackia crassifolia Benth.
parviflora Benth.
Psoralea physodes Doug.
Hedysarum boreale Nutt.
Vicia gigantea Hook.
Prunus emarginata, var. mollis Brewer
Nuttallia cerasiformis Torr. & Gray.
Eriogynia pectinata Hook.
cæspitosa Wats. (An sp. nova?)
Spiræa Douglasii Hook.
betulæfolia Pall.
discolor Pursh. var. ariæfolia Wats.
Aruncus L.
Neillia opulifolia B. & H.
Rubus nivalis Dougl.
spectabilis Pursh.
leucodermis Dougl.

Nutkanus Moc.

pedatus Smith.

ursinus Ch. & Schl.

lasiococcus Gray.

Geum macrophyllum Willd.

Fragaria Childensis Ehrh.

Virginiana var. Illinoensis Gray

Potentilla Anserina L.

gelida Mey. (Piper.)

glandulosa Lindl.

Sibbaldia procumbens L. (Piper.)

Rosa gymnocarpa Nutt.

Nutkana Presl.

Pirus rivularis Dougl.

sambucifolia Ch. & Sch.

Amelanchier alnifolia Nutt.

Saxifraga bronchialis L.

bronchialis var. cherleroides Eng.

Mertensiana Bong.

occidentalis. Wats.

stellaris L.

Leptarrhena pyrolifolia R. Br.

Boykinia occidentalis T. & G.

Tiarella trifoliata Hook.

Tellima grandiflora R. Br.

Mitella caulescens Nutt.

Breweri Gray.

trifida Graham.

Heuchera glabra Willd. (Piper.)

micrantha Dougl.

racemosa Wats. (Piper.)

Tolmiea Menziesii T.& G.

Parnassia fimbriata Koenig. (Piper.)

Philadelphus Lewisii Pursh.

Ribes divaricatum Dougl.

laxiflorum Pursh.

sanguineum Pursh.

bracteosuni Dougl.

lacustre Poir var. parvulum Gray.

edum spathulifolium Hook.

divergens Wats.

Hippuris montana Ledib. (Piper.)

vulgaris L.

Epilobium origanifolium Lam.

spicatum Lam.

luteum Pursh. (Piper.)

minutum Lindl.

coloratum Muhl.

Circæa Pacifica Asch. & Mag.

Glycosma ambiguum Gray.

Osmorrhiza nuda Torr.

Œnanthe Californica C. & R.

Crantzia lineata Nutt.

Selinum Hookeri.

Angelica arguta (?) Nutt.

genuflexa Nutt. (Piper.)

Peucedanum Hallii Wats.

Martindalei C. & R. (Piper.)

Coelopleurum Gmelini Ledeb.

Heracleum lanatum Mx.

Fatsia horrida B. & H.

Cornus Canadensis L.

pubescens Nutt.

Nuttallii Aud.

Sambucus glauca Nutt.

racemosa L.

Linnæa borealis Gronov.

Symphoricarpos mollis Nutt.

Lonicera involucrata Banks.

Galium trifidum L.

Aparine L.

Kamtschaticum St.

triflorum Mx.

Valeriana sylvatica Banks.

Sitchensis Bong.

Chrysopsis Oregana Gray.

Grindelia Hendersoni Greene.

Aster foliaceus var. frondeus Gray.

Engelmanni Gray var. paucicapitatus B.L. Robinson n. var.
    (Piper.)

modestus Lindl. (Piper.)

Erigeron salsuginosus Gray.

Philadelphicus L.

compositus Pursh. (Piper.)

Antennaria plantaginifolia Hook.

Anaphalis margaritacea B. & H.

Gnaphalium microcephalum Nutt.

purpureum L.

Adenocaulon bicolor Hook.

Franseria bipinnatifida Nutt.

Madia sativa, var. racemosa Gray.

Eriophyllum cæspitosum Dougl.

Artemisia vulgaris L.

Petasites palmata Gray.

nivalis Greene. (Piper.)

Luina hypoleuca Benth.

361

Arnica Chamissonis Less.
latifolia Bong. (Piper.)
Senecio Bolanderi Gray.
triangularis Hook. (Piper.)
Saussurea Americana Eaton.
Cnicus edulis Gray.
Hieracium albiflorum Hook.
Prenanthes alata Gray. (Piper.)
Troximon laciniatum Gray.
Lactuca leucophæa Gray.
Campanula aurita Greene. (Piper.)
rotundifolia L.
Scouleri Hook.
Vaccinium cæspitosum Mx.
Myrtilloides Hook.
ovalifolium Sm.
Myrtillus var. microphyllum Hk.
parvifolium Sm.
ovatum Pursh.
uliginosum Gray. (Piper.)
Arbutus Menziesii Pursh.
Arctostaphylos Uva Ursi Spreng.
tomentosa Dougl.
Gaultheria ovatifolia Gray.
Gaultheria Shallon Pursh.
Myrsinites Hook. (Piper.)
Cassiope Mertensiana Don.
Bryanthus empetriformis Gray.
Menziesia glabella Gray. (?)
Rhododendron albiflorum Hook.
Californicum Hook.
Chimaphila Menziesii Spreng.
umbellata Nutt.
Pyrola aphyla Smith.
picta Sm. var. dentata Sm.
rotundifolia var. bracteata Gray.
     secunda L.
Pterospora andromedia Nutt. (Piper.)
Allotropa virgata T. & G.
Monotropa Hypopitys L.
     uniflora L.
Newberrya spicata Gray.
Dodecatheon Jeffreyi Moore
Douglasia nivalis var. dentata Gray.
Trientalis Europæa var. latifolia Torr.
Fraxinus Oregana Nutt. (Piper.)
Phlox Douglasii var. diffusa Gray.
Gilia heterophylla Gray.

gracilis Hook.
Polemonium humile var. pulchellum
Willd. (Piper.)
Hydrophyllum Virginicum L.
Nemophila parviflora Dougl.
Phacelia sericea Gray.
circinata Jacq.
Romanzoffia Sitchensis Bong.
Mertensia Sibirica Don.
Collinsia parviflora Dougl.
Chelone nemorosa Dougl.
Penstemon Menziesii Hook.
diffusus Dougl.
Mimulus moschatus Dougl.
luteus L.
Lewisii Pursh.
Veronica alpina L.
Americana Schw.
Castilleia miniata Dougl. (Piper.)
parviflora Bong.
Orthocarpus castilleioides Benth.
Pedicularis bracteosa Benth.
contorta Benth. (Piper.)
Boschniakia strobilacea Gray.
Pinguicula vulgaris L. (Piper.)
Micromeria Douglasii Benth.
Stachys ciliata Dougl.
pubens Gray. (Piper.)
Plantago maritima L.
Asarum caudatum Lindl.
Chenopodium rubrum L.
Oxyria digyna Hill. (Piper.)
Rumex occidentalis Wats.
Polygonum Douglasii Greene.
Bistorta L.
minimum Wats.
Callitriche autumnalis L.
Urtica gracilis Ait.
Corylus rostrata Ait.
Alnus viridis DC.
rubra Bong.
Salix Barclayi And. (Piper.)
flavescens Nutt.
Sitchensis Sanson.
lasiandra Benth.
Populus trichocarpa T. & G.
Taxus brevifolia Nutt.
Juniperus communis var. alpina Gray.

Chamæcyparis Nutkaensis Spach.
Thuja gigantea Nutt.
Abies grandis Lindl.
amabilis Dougl.
subalpina Eng.
Pseudotsuga Douglasii Carr.
Tsuga Pattoniana Eng.
Mertensiana Carr.
Pinus contorta Dougl.
monticola Dougl.
Lysichiton Kamtschatcensis Sch.
Sparganium simplex Huds.
simplex var. angustifolium Gray.
Potamogeton Robbinsii Oakes.
Triglochin maritimum L.
Habenaria gracilis Wats.
Goodyera Menziesii Lindl.
Listera convallariodides Nutt.
Corallorhiza Mertensiana Bong.
Allium Tolmiei Baker.
Smilacina racemosa Desf.
sessilifolia Nutt.
Maianthemum bifolium DC. var.dilatatum.
Lilium Columbianum Hanson.
Erythronium grandiflorum Pursh
var. (?) revolutum Smith
Streptopus amplexifolius DC.
roseus Mx.
Prosartes Oregana Wats.
Clintonia uniflora Kunth.
Trillium ovatum Pursh.
Veratrum viride Ait.
Stenanthium occidentale Gray.
Tofieldia occidentalis Wats.
Xerophyllum tenax Nutt.
Luzula parviflora Desv.
comosa var. macrantha Wats.
parviflora Desv. (Alpine form)
spadicea DC.
Juncus Mertensianus Meyer.
tenuis Willd.
Parryi Eng.
xiphioides, var. triandrus. Englm.
effusus L.
effusus var. brunneus Engelm.
Scirpus sylvaticus var. digynus Boeck.
Carex (too young)
stipata Muhl.

festiva Dewey.
Deweyana Sch.
deflexa var. media Bailey.
leporina var. Americana Olney.
utriculata Boott.
Sitchensis Prescott.
Mertensii Prescott.
Phleum alpinum L. (Piper.)
Agrostis scabra Willd.
       Scouleri Trin. (?)
Agrostis exarata Trin.
exarata Trin. var. pallens.
microphylla Steud.
canina L.
Agrostis vulgaris With.
Cinna pendula Trin.
Deyeuxia Canadensis Beauv.
var. (?) Howellii Vasey
Deschampsia cæspitosa Beauv.
latifolia.
elongata Monro.
Trisetum canescens Buckley.
subspicatum var. molle Gray.
Danthonia Californica Bolander.
intermedia Vasey, "form."
Melica brodoides Gray.
Harfordii Bolander.
Pleuropogon refractum Benth.
Poa alpina, var. purpurascens Vasey.
Cusickii var.
gracillima Vasey. (Piper)
Glyceria pauciflora Presl
distans Whl.
Festuca Jonesii Vasey.
sublata Haeck. (?)
rubra L. var.
ovina L., var. brevifolia Wats.
ovina L., var.
occidentalis Hook.
Bromus ciliatus L.
Hordeum nodosum Hudson.
Elymus Americanus V. & S.
Sitanion Schultz. (Piper.)
Equisetum robustum Braun.
Telmateia Ehrh.
limosum L.
Botrychium Verginicum Schw.
simplex Hitch. (Piper.)

ternatum Schw.
Polypodium falcatum Kell. (Piper.)
vulgare L. var. occidentale.
Adiantum pedatum L.
Pteris aquilina, L. var. lanuginosa Bong.
Cheilanthes gracillima Eaton.
Cryptogramme acrostichoides R. Br.
Lomaria Spicant Desv.
Asplenium Filix-f œmina Bernh.
Phegopteris alpestris Mett. (Piper.)
Dryopteris Fee.
Aspidium munitum Kaulf.
Lonchitis Schw.
spinulosum Sch.
Cystopteris fragilis Bernh. (Piper.)
Lycopodium lucidulum Mx.
Selago L.
clavatum L.
Selaginella rupestris Spring.
Jungermannia cordifolia Hook.
Scapania Bolanderi Aust.
Fimbriaria pilosa (Wahl.)
Conocephalus conicus. (Dum.)
Porella vavicularis. (L. & C.)
Frullania Asagrayana. var. Californica Aust.
Kantia trichomanis L., var. tenuis.
Ptilidium Californicum. (Aust.)
Metzgeria pubescens. (Schrank.)
Dichodontium Olympicum Ren. & Card. sp. nov
Decranum Howellii Ren. & Card.
fuscescens Turn.
Ceratodon purpureus Brid.
Distichium capillaceum B. & S.
Barbula cylindrica B. & S.
Grimmia apocarpa var. rivularis B. & S.
apocarpa Hedw.,var. rivularis
B. & S. "forms."
Scouleria aquatica Hook.
Racomitrium varium Mitt. (R. Oreganum Ren. & Card.)
varium Mitt. "forma foliis squarrosis R. & C.
aciculare Brid.
canescens var. ericoides Brid.
heterostichum Brid.
Orthotrichum leiocarpum B. & S.
Encalypta cilata Hedw.
Tetraphis geniculata Girg.
Bartramia pomiformis Hedw.
Bartramia OEderiana Schwartz.

Webera nutans Sch.
Bryum capillare L
psiudotriquetrum Schw., var. gracilescens Sch.
Mnium venustum Mitt.
punctatum Hedw.
Menziesii Muell.
Aulacomnium androgynum Sch.
Oligotrichum aligerum Mitt.
Pogonatum alpinum Roehl.
urnigerum Roehl.
Polytrichum junperinum Willd.
Fontinalis Neo-Mexicana Sul. & Lesq.
Chrysophylla Card.sp. nova.
Dichelyma cylindricarpum Aust.
uncinatum Mitt.
Neckera Douglasii Hook.
Menziesii Drum.
Antitrichia curtipendula Brid.
Climacium dendroides W. & M.
Heterocladium heteropterum B. & S.
"forma an sp. nova?"
Clayopodium crispifolium Hk.
Camptothecium lutescens B. & S.
megaptilum Sulliv.
Amesii Ren. & Card. "forma?"
Scleropodium obtusifolium R. & C.
Isothecium stoloniferum Brid.
myosuroides Brid.
Eurynchium Stokesii B. & S.
Oreganum Sulliv.
Plagiothecium denticulatum B. & S.
undulatum B. & S.
Harpidium uncinatum Hedw.
Hypnum robustum Hook.
circinale Hook.
Dickii Ren. & Card.
plumifer Mitt.
ochraceum Turner.
Schreberi Willd.
Hylocomium splendens B. & S.
triquetrum B. & S.
loreum B. & S.
Sticta Oregana Tuck.
Stickta pulmonaria L.
anthraspis Ach.
Alectoria jubata (L).
jubata var. sarmentosa.
Sphærophorus globiferus L.

Peltigera aphthosa Hffm.

venosa Hffm.

polydactyla Hffm.

Cladonia furcata Huds.

pyxidata L.

gracilis L.

gracilis var. elongata Fr.

gracilis var. hybrida Schær.

rangiferina L.

bellidiflora (Ach..)

Stereocaulon tomentosum Laur.

Umbilicaria Muhlenbergii (Ach.)

Cetraria glauca (L.)

glauca, var. Polydactyla.

Parmelia physodes (L.)

Physcia pulverulenta Schreb.

Thelotrema lepadinum Ach.

Heterothecium sanguinarium.

Lecanora pallescens L.

subfusca L.

Placodium ferrugineum Huds.

Graphis scripta Ach.

Buellia geographica (L.) ?

Lecidea tessellata Flk.

Pilophorus cereolus, var. Hallii Tuck.

Exobasidium Cassiopes Peck, n. sp.

Nidularia candida Peck, n. sp.

Mycena strobilinoides Peck, n. sp.

Otidella fulgens (Pers.) Sacc.

Polyporus varius Fr.

piccinus Pk.

versicolor Fr.

hirsutus Fr.

Pluteus cervinus.

Mycena galericulata Scop.

Bovista pila B. & C.

Daldinia concentrica Boet.

Pluteus cervinus.

Mycena galericulata Scop.

Bovista pila B. & C.

Some Early Experiences of a Botanist in the Northwest[6]

Henderson's 1932 comments about the 1890 O'Neil Expedition

In the summer of 1890 the "O'Neil Olympic Expedition" was organized for the purpose of passing through the Olympics from east to west, climbing Mt. Olympus en route, and making abundant side trips. To Mr. Will Steel, once a resident of Portland, now of Medford and Crater Lake, must be given the honor of organizing this expedition. It was a mixed expedition, the army represented by Lieutenant O'Neil of Vancouver and about a dozen non-commissioned officers and privates forming the complement of the army. They also furnished a quantity of mules to transport the baggage and supplies of the expedition. The old Oregon Alpine Club, the father of the present Mazamas, furnished the scientific staff and most of the money.[7] This staff consisted of Col. N.E. Linsley, once an officer in the Civil War, at the time an assayist and prospector living in Seattle and Spokane. During the whole time of my connection with the expedition this delightful man regaled us round the camp fires with his stories of his expeditions, either scientific or military. A second member of the staff was B.J. Bretherton, a pleasant young man and cartographer of the expedition. To him was the work of plotting the country, and naming unnamed mountains and streams. The writer was the botanist of the expedition. We soon found out that much scientific work must give way to making trails, for none existed than a few miles above Lake Cushman. How I grew to hate those poor innocent miles! Day after day and week after week we were engaged in sawing through and rolling out of the way sections of fallen trees from three to seven feet through, in order that the animals might transport the food and bedding of the party. So a vicious circle was established: go back with the mules to Hood's

---

[6] Paper (the section on the O'Neil Expedition) presented at a meeting of the Oregon Audubon Society in 1932 (Special Collections, University of Oregon Library, Eugene).

[7] "Although the club's Board of Directors expressed satisfaction with the expedition's success, Henderson and Linsley later complained they had not been reimbursed for certain expenditures. On November 6, [1890?] just three days after the special meeting of the Board to receive an accounting of expenses, Henderson wrote Steel, stating he had understood the O.A.C. had agreed to 'pay all traveling expenses.' He therefore submitted a bill for $21.75, covering expenditures from Olympia to Port Townsend, via Seattle, and for a two-day delay at the latter place, as well as the party's delay at Port Townsend. 'A good deal of this could have been saved,' he wrote, 'as well as much of my time, had Lieut. O'Neil told me to meet him in Union City instead of Seattle, and had he not come two days after I was notified that the party would assemble in Seattle; but according to 'my orders' the expense could not be avoided.' Henderson again wrote Steel on January 30, 1891, and suggested that, should the Oregon Alpine Club desire to publish his report on the botany of the Olympics, he was willing to accept, in lieu of the reimbursement, 100 copies of the pamphlet. Apparently the offer was not accepted; Henderson's article was published in the October 1891 issue of ZOE, a botanical journal, then reprinted by Steel sixteen years later in Steel Points." Wood, Men, Mules and Mountains, p. 436.

Canal to bring in more fodder and food for animals and men, so that the men could cut more logs to let through the mules and consume more food to cut more logs. So gigantic were many of these logs and so impenetrable the vine maple and devil's club thickets, that often we all worked with saw, axe and brush-hook, to gain a quarter of a mile in a day. Then the delay caused by the numerous expeditions which the Lieutenant was forced to send out to scout for terrain suitable for trails. This was absolutely necessary, as much of the country stood so on edge that the mules could not get along, even if no logs were in their way. Once, when exasperated by the delays, I heard Col. Linsley say, "Curse this country! I have prospected all the mountains of the United States and I never saw one to equal this in difficulty of progression and at the same time in lack of any valuable minerals!"

Some of these side trips were of intense interest to me, as the flora was abundant and no one had ever collected there before. One of these trips stands out in my memory, and will give you some idea of what we had to overcome. It was composed of Col. Linsley, Sergeant Yates and the writer. The first night we had to camp on the side of a tremendous slope, so steep that we slept with feet down hill, a standing tree on one side and a big log on the other to keep us from rolling down the slope, and not even a blanket under or above us! But if that day's trip was hard, the next day's was to be so much worse, as to make the first seem easy by comparison.[8] Soon we were proceeding along a very knife-blade with a river sending a faint roaring a thousand feet below us on the left, while a rock-strewn, icy slope was at our right. One misstep and down we went on one side or the other to a certain death, even worse, a severe injury which would render it almost impossible to take one out alive. Finally towards noon we came to a spot that seemed at first impassable. The edge of the knife-blade was here covered by a string of alpine firs, without a bit of foot-way to right or left. When we reached the first of these little trees, we saw to our surprise that some prospector had been here this year or the year before, and had with a little saw or sharp hatchet cut off the tops of all these trees to within a foot of the ground, and had thus succeeded in passing them, we imagined with his legs dangling on each side. So good a job had he done, however, that by cutting each of us a walking stick, we were able to step on each little tree and thence to the next one, and so gradually across. I know not what would have happened to any one of us, had he been subject to vertigo, but each man simply glued his eyes to the next tree, and thus we all crossed safely this 30 or 40 foot space. Just beyond this place, I was repaid for my whole hazardous day's work by finding a little Rosaceous plant which proved new to science. This was a tiny shrub named by Canby *Friognia Hendersoni*, and changed by Greene to *Lutkea Hendersoni*, and eventually by Piper into *Spiraea Hendersoni*.

As we had expected to be out only one day, our food supply was very low. It consisted now of ground up crackers, from our constant slips and falls. So we poured this out carefully onto a paper from the sack, and then divided the mess scrupulously into three small piles. We then nibbled on this slowly to make this, our dinner, last longer, while an old hound, that insisted on following us from camp, stood in front of us, gazing longingly on the fast disappearing crumbs, while abundant saliva dripped from his mouth. Not a crumb did he get, however, for we knew we had to reach camp while our strength lasted, and we did not know whether this would be this night or the next day, so uncertain were we of its location. Having found that it was vain to try to get mules through where we had been started down a draw, and from now until dark our trip was easier and more interesting, as for the first time in all of our lives we went through a solid forest, consisting almost entirely of Alaska cedar, *Chamaecycaria nootkatensis*, many of the trees of gigantic proportions for this species. As night approached, we were traveling down first a rill, then a small creek, and the flats on both sides as well as the slopes were a tangled mess of Devil's Club, known scientifically as *Echinopanax horridum* by some botanists, or *Eataia horrida* by others. My kind friends, did any of you ever have the doubtful pleasure of forcing your way through Devil's Club by night. If you haven't, you still have one experience you will never forget. By 9 P.M. we were every now and then firing off our rifle to see whether we could be answered from camp. Finally we were delighted to hear answering shots in the distance. By 10 P.M. we had reached camp, but not to sleep. The next day we spent most of the time in pulling out or even cutting the prickles of Devil's Club from our faces, hands and arms, and rubbing the parts with bacon rind, as we had not other curatives. For the next week our faces and arms were swollen and sore, and I suppose it was due to our splendid health that none of us was affected by blood poisoning, as is the fate of many who pass through this cursed brush.

366

---

[8] "After spending the night together, the two parties apparently went separate ways the next morning. The records do not indicate what Bairens and Bretherton did, but they probably returned directly to Camp No. 4 while Linsley, Henderson, and Yates crossed over the ridge into the valley of the West Branch." Wood, *Men, Mules and Mountains*, p. 406.

We hadn't advanced our camp ten miles from this spot, when one evening when cutting boughs and trimming them for by bed, I was unlucky enough to cut my wrist very severely with my hatchet, just missing a large artery, but severing several veins. Not a thing did we have in camp, either for sewing up the wound or for a germicide, so I resorted to that wholesome material I had so often used before for small cuts or contusions, namely, the pure, clear balsam from fir-blisters. The following morning, as the time I could spend with the party was nearly up anyway, the Lieutenant sent me out on one of the mules, accompanied by my good friend and occasional assistant, Corporal Fisher. At the end of the second day I was home, where I let a surgeon look at my wound.

So perfect had been the curative and antiseptic properties of the balsam, that the doctor decided to let well enough alone, and my wound was soon healed, after he had, however, taken a few stitches to hold it together. It was a source of regret to me not to have continued with the party, as the Lieutenant finally saw, as had most of us for a long time, that the only way to get through was to send back the mules, take packs upon our backs, and then make the ascent of Olympus and thence go down the rivers to the west. Far greater was my disappointment at not continuing, and thus finding many more new plants. However, this was rectified by Professor Piper's going over all the ground a few years after, when several new plants were found.

CHAPTER FIFTEEN.
HARRY FISHER/JAMES B. HANMORE

The "Harry Fisher" who served in Company G, Fourteenth Infantry, and who was a member of O'Neil's Olympic Exploring Expedition, was really James B. Hanmore, born in New Albany, Indiana, in 1856. Fisher was a druggist by trade and was not known to have been married while in the service, or otherwise.

He served almost eight years in the Regular Army, enlisting as Hanmore on October 5, 1883, at Fort Omaha, Nebraska. He served in Nebraska and in Washington Territory for five years before being honorably discharged. Then he reenlisted November 2, 1888, at Fort Sherman, Idaho Territory, for what was to be five years, but he was court-martialed and dishonorably discharged August 3, 1889, in Utah. Hanmore next surfaced in San Francisco, California, on August 13, 1889, to enlist as "Harry Fisher."

James B. Hanmore and Harry Fisher first came in proximity to each other at Fremont, Nebraska, on July 2, 1886, when units of the Fourth Infantry from Fort Omaha (Hanmore's station) and Fort Niobrara (Fisher's station) joined forces to travel together to Fort Spokane, Washington Territory, which was reached on July 11, 1886. On December 13, 1887, both men were transferred from their respective companies (B and F) to the Hospital Corps. Each completed his five-year enlistment and was honorably discharged at Fort Spokane—Fisher on September 12, 1888, Hanmore on October 4, 1888. Fisher did not reenlist, but Hanmore did, ending up at Fort Douglas, Utah Territory.

Shortly after he arrived at Fort Douglas, Hanmore became involved in serious trouble. On two occasions he was too intoxicated to perform his duties as an acting hospital steward at the post hospital. When threatened with a court martial, he pledged not to drink again, but one week later he was again intoxicated, the post surgeon filed charges, and Hanmore then aggravated the situation by leaving the hospital grounds for a few hours.

Hanmore was charged with being drunk on duty, absent without leave, and "conduct to the prejudice of good order and military discipline." He pleaded guilty to drunkenness and the related bad conduct, but not guilty to the other charges.

The court found Hanmore guilty of all the charges, except the time he had been absent without leave was determined to be less than had been charged. He was then sentenced to be dishonorably discharged from the service and to forfeit all pay due, but no prison term was imposed. The sentence was duly executed at Fort Douglas on August 3, 1889.

Ten days later, Hanmore showed up at the Presidio of San Francisco and enlisted in the Fourteenth Infantry, using the name "Harry Fisher." During the two years that his fraudulent enlistment went undetected, Hanmore participated—as "Private Harry Fisher"—in Lieutenant O'Neil's 1890 expedition in the Olympics. His deception came to light about a year after the exploration ended. The original Harry Fisher, upon returning from a trip to England, visited the Adjutant General's Office in Washington, D.C., to report that he wished to reenlist and requested a certificate in lieu of his discharge papers, which he had lost while in Europe. After he had fully indentified himself, the certificate was issued, and with the permission of the A.G.O. he reenlisted on September 9, 1891. However, the A.G.O. then discovered, to its chagrin and embarrassment, that its records showed Fisher was still in the Army, presently on duty at Vancouver Barracks, Washington. When confronted, the "Fisher" at Vancouver Barracks admitted that he was really Hanmore. On October 15, 1891, Hanmore/Fisher was summarily discharged for "having enlisted under false pretenses."

It is interesting to note that, except for the signature "Harry Fisher" on his enlistment papers, Hanmore always went by "H. Fisher." This is the name that appears on his manuscript about the expedition and on the map of the Olympics published by William G. Steel, and it is also the byline on several articles he wrote for the Oregonian in 1892.

On October 18, 1891, three days after he was discharged, Hanmore—still using the name "H. Fisher"—left Portland with two other men for the Olympic Peninsula, to winter on the Queets River. Because he was interested in botany, Fisher intended to devote considerable time to studying the flora and gathering specimens. During March and April, the men explored the upper Queets and the Clearwater, then returned to Grays Harbor. Fisher next journeyed to "the frosty Cascades," where he prospected in the Snoqualmie Valley in the summer of 1892. Here his trail vanishes.

Explaining why he had returned to the Olympics, the former soldier wrote: "Mr. Yates, Cranmer and myself, having spent the summer of 1890 exploring the Olympics with Lieutenant O'Neil, were charmed with the country and concluded to pass the winter here and improve our claims." Where and when he died is unknown.

—Robert L. Wood
Adapted from Men, Mules and Mountains (pp. 446–50)

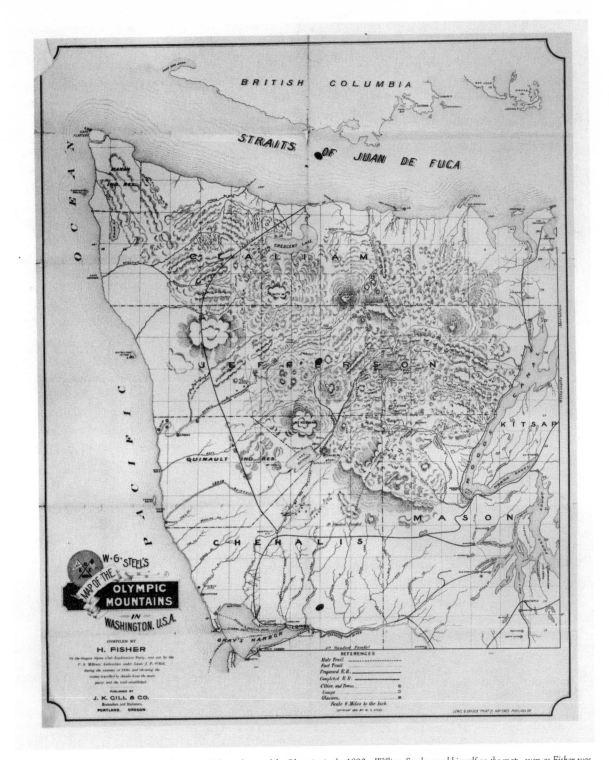

This map, compiled by Harry Fisher, was the most widely used map of the Olympics in the 1890s. William Steel named himself on the map, even as Fisher was credited for compiling it.
Courtesy Manuscripts, Special Collections, University Archives, University of Washington Libraries, Seattle.

Lt. Oneils [sic] Exploration of the Olympic Mountains[1]
By H. Fisher

With Map and Illustrations

~~Copy right applied for~~
1890

A True history in detail of the Exploration of the Olympic mountains and thrilling adventures of Lt. Oneil and his party of intrepid mountain climbers accompanied by a correct map of the country.

Handsomely illustrated from photograph and sketch setting froth the mountains in all their wild beauty and splendor.

The Animal & vegetable kingdoms has been thoroughly considered as well as the formation and mineral resources of the country.

Instructive

Entertaining

and interesting information

pertaining to a country that has been unknown for 398 years.

Lt. Oneils Exploration of the Olympics

Preface

Gentle reader: in opening the pages of this book understand that it is no novel written from the imagination of a wild fancy, but a true history of the travels and thrilling adventures of Lieut. J. P. Oneil, U.S.A., and his band during their exploration of the Olympic mountains in connection with a correct map of the country whose surrounding were taken from the government coast survey, and the interior from the work of competent engineers. The geological formation as well as the animal and vegetable kingdoms will be duly considered and finely illustrated in all their wild beauty and splendor for which I am indebted to our able Professors of the different sciences and last but not least I will be ever grateful to our Chief who during the entire trip was noted for his kindness and constant vigilance for our general welfare. So much has been said of these lands that a geographical description may prove tiresome to some, but beneficial to others uninformed. The Olympic mountains are situated in the most north-western portion of the U.S. and north-western corner of the state of Washington. (Alaska Ter. excepted) The boundaries are the straits of San Juan de Fuca on the east. Pacific Ocean on the W. Grays harbor & Chehalis River principally on the South.

In area they are about 100 miles E. & W. at the N. and 60 miles at the S. & about the same as the crow flies. Possessing some abilities as a botanist, mineralogist and assayer and naturally being imbued with the spirit of the pioneer, induced me to keep notes of every days events. Upon my return home members of the party persuaded me to give them to the public, in book form. My education being the fruits of my own efforts; and as is generally the case neglected in the use of our language; and my first efforts for publication, I would ask you dear reader: to overlook my imperfections, and try to be content if I succeed in explaining my self by the use of ordinary language. In spelling the names of The streams, I have spelled them as pronounced by the Indians e g Quinailet is Quinault.

Introduction

In the course of common events 399/400 years fraught with their joys, sorrow, griefs, and calamities, have passed over

---

[1] Unpublished diary and illustrations courtesy of the Mazamas, Portland, Oregon, Manuscript #001-2001. The original of Fisher's journal is in the Mazama Club Library, a gift of William G. Steel on October 1, 1923. A microfilm copy is available in the Manuscripts, Special Collections, University Archives division of the University of Washington Libraries, Seattle.

William Steel attached the following statement to the front of Fisher's account before he transmitted it to the Mazamas: "GOD: The fool hath said in his heart, There is no god. Then I looked upon the earth and beheld a bit of green, breaking through the moist ground and watched it grow, until it arose to a great tree, with wide singing branches spreading over the lawn. It became a giant of the forest and defied the winds and the storms that swept over it. Then I reached forth and plucked a leaf and ground it to bits, one of which I placed beneath a microscope, where it was magnified and showed an atom of nature rounded and shaped to perfection and beauty and all other leaves and all other trees were like unto it.

"I looked upon the heavens above and the stars thereof and gazed through a telescope to planets of untold magnitude and distance, away off to systems of worlds, the light of which required thousands of years to reach the earth and could I have plucked a bit from one of them and crumbled it into dust, one atom placed beneath a microscope would have shown a perfect scene of Nature's handiwork, beautiful and perfect.

"Through all creation billions of laws govern these things, without conflict or confusion, so must proceed from one center, for were there more it must conflict and I stood amazed at the infinity of it, in wisdom and power, and trembled as I thought, What is man that art mindful of him. For this is God."—William Gladstone Steel, Eugene, Oregon, May 1, 1928.

The transcription of Fisher's handwritten pages presented here is the work of Robert L. Wood, who spent the winter of 1967–68 at the task. Wood's notes are bracketed in text, with longer transcription notes in footnotes.

Transcriber's note: In transcribing, I have attempted to be as accurate as possible, but have used my discretion. For example, Fisher often starts a sentence with a lowercase letter, omits apostrophes, and frequently capitalizes words that obviously should not be. In many instances the rendition is exact; in others, in the interest of making the document read more easily, a correction has been made; i.e., those sentences beginning with lowercase letters have been capitalized; certain capitalized words in the journal have been transcribed as lowercase, to avoid confusion; etc.

mother earth since Columbus landed upon the American continent, and since that time all nations have flown thier colors, upon all most every inch of the surrounding water, bringing people of all races to her shores until America long since, became one of the leading powers of the earth. Between the migrations of the plainsman, the pioneer, the trapper, and the read man, it was thought that scarcely a quarter section of land remained untrodden by one or the other, in their lust for gold, or love of sport and adventure. But with in the last few years it was whispered from one to Another, that the Olympics were as yet unexplored, and that as little was known of their character, as of Stanley the great. It is true there were maps for sale, and taught in all the school rooms of all nations, upon whose face were printed, in bold type, OLYMPIC MOUNTAINS. Mt. Olympus, and Mt. Constance were as commonly spoken of as were proud old Shasta, or Mt. Hood, but who enquired the Press in 1889, was prepared to come forth and inform the public of this small chain of mountains. Was it rich in minerals? Was it a prairie country? Or a timberland? There were some individuals who came forward and attempted to satisfy an inquisitive people, (i-n-q-u-i-s-a-t-i-v-e?) but from limited information, it was very evident that they had explored those mountains at long range, or in their imagination. Great cities e. g. Seattle and Tacoma whose histories are a marvel, whose wares and productions are in all channels of commerce, and whose ships sail to all ports of the world, had grown up in the very shadows of these mountains. With every mornings sun rise, their populations might see Olympus beneath her crown of snow, but who had ever been there?[2]

The red mans people, who have lived, and died, in their very foot hills for many generations, were questioned. Their answer a deep guttural mumbling, in their peculiar dialect, suggestive of ignorance, or indifference as to their knowledge of the country. The pioneer prospector, and sailor, were alike sought and questioned, with the same unsatisfactory results.[3]

Many were the legends said to have been handed down by the red man, which magnified as they traveled until the pot of inquisitiveness was in a state of ebulution [ibulution?].

Lieut. J. P. Oneil, 14th Inf., U.S.A. while stationed at Fort Townsend, Washington, in 1885 had penetrated the forest for some miles up the Elwha river, but owing to the loss of one man brought the favorable season so near its close, that he decided to return to civilization, and abandon his purpose for the present, but time has shown that there remained within him, a plucky determination to again attempt, what had for so long remained unfinished. The Mr. Gilmans had explored in the Quinault valley. The Seattle Press sent out a party in the fall of 89, who disappeared in the mountain fastness, to emerge with the spring time, in a Robinson Crusoe garb. Following their appearance were incredulous reports, and wildest rumors, such as one of their party, had stood upon a dizzy prominence, like a knight of old, sweeping the Ocean, sound, and strait, at a glance. While another had seen beautiful table lands and prairies, over which Indians tipping the beam at 300# avoirdupois, chased the buffalo & Elk, and whose mother tongue was as strange as it was unknown to all races.[4] Strange red bear as ferocious as the bengal tiger, were met and mountains of gold, silver, Iron, & tin, with coal to smelt them, overlooked the streams that drained them. Such reports as these aroused our gallant Lieut. from his state of lethargy, and the summer of 1890 found him making preparations which have resulted to favorably. The following is a true history of the trip and country, by one who kept notes in detail, nicely illustrated from photographs, actually taken from the country.

It was in the columns of the Morning Oregonian bearing dates of April & May, that Lieut. J. P. Oneil, U.S.A. under the auspices of Gen'l John Gibbon, U.S.A., assisted by a corps of scientific gentlemen, in combination with the Oregon Alpine Club, were soon to fit out an expedition for the purpose of exploring the Olympic mountains. During the warm days in June it was officially announced, that the names

---

[2] "Viewed from Puget Sound, the mountains presented an imposing skyline and many persons mistook Constance or The Brothers for Olympus, but the latter could not be seen, hidden as it was by intervening peaks nearly as high. Nevertheless, Olympus was the first geographic feature in Washington to be named by white man. Apparently no one had been near it, despite a claim that five Caucasians and four Makah Indians approached the mountain in 1854, and that several members of the party climbed the peak. However, no one conversant with the nature of the country now takes this contention seriously." Wood, *Men, Mules and Mountains*, p. 398.

[3] "The exploits of Billy Everett, son of trapper John Everett, were a notable exception. While Lieutenant O'Neil was reconnoitering the Olympics in 1885, young Everett, who was then only sixteen years old, hunted elk on the Bailey Range. He is believed to be the first man to see Cream Lake Basin. On the other hand, interesting but incredible stories were rampant. Among them were the tales of one L. L. Bales, who alleged in 1889, after Governor Ferry issued his call for exploration, that he had 'crossed and re-crossed' the Olympics, 'alone and with a companion.' According to Bales, in the summer of 1882 he made a solo trip across the mountains because he 'found it difficult to obtain anyone willing to encounter the hardships and dangers of traveling an unexplored region.' He had followed the Duckabush River to its headwaters, and on August 26 he crossed the Grand Divide at 6000 feet, negotiating slopes inclined at an angle of 90° (i.e., vertical) with the temperature 10° below zero!" Wood, *Men, Mules and Mountains*, pp. 398–99.

[4] "Fisher was alluding to a story, entitled 'Strange Indian Tribe,' that appeared in the *Oregonian* on March 11, 1890. The reporter apparently had accepted without question, a wild story spun by a trapper who had been in the Olympics." Wood, *Men, Mules and Mountains*, p. 399.

of the entire party were enrolled upon the roster which proved to be the case. By permission and as each and every member of the party must frequently appear in the succeeding pages, I will order a roll call, which thanks to our Chief we found unnecessary during our struggles in the mountains.[5]

Lieut. J. P. Oneil, U.S.A., 14th Inf, in Command
Col. ____ Linsley of Fairhaven, Wash, Mineralogist.
B. J. Bretherton, Naturalist and a member of the Oregon Alpine Club, Portland, Oregon
Proff. L. F. Henderson, Botanist, Olympia, Wash. Also a member of the O.A.C.
Mr. ____ Yocumb, Photographer and member of the O.A.C.
Mr. ____ Price, Chief Packer for the U.S.A. at Vancouver Bks.
Sgt. William Marsh, Co. G, 14th Inf, U.S.A.
Sgt Walter F. Yates, Co. B, 14th Inf. U.S.A.
Sgt. John Heffner, Co D, 14th Inf, U.S.A.
Pvts. John Bairnes, Co. B, 14th Inf, U.S.A.
Edward Danton Co K, 14th Inf. U.S.A.
H. Fisher, Co. G, 14th Inf, U.S.A.
J. Higgins, Co. F, 14th Inf., U.S.A.
Wm. Hughes, Co. E, 14th Inf., U.S.A.
J. Kranichfield, Co. B, 114th Inf., U.S.A.
I. (?) Krause, Co. E, 14th Inf., U.S.A.

11 mules and a bell mare, last, but not least, our overgrown hound called Jumbo who was the occasion of much laughter and of about as much importance as Handy Andy was to squire Egan, out rivalling all of his good deeds with his awkwardness. It is suffice to say that the scientific branch of our party were men of means and prominence and it was not small sacrifice for them, to launch forth upon such a perilous trip. Neglecting business, and loss of time, not considering the denial of many luxuries, such as feather beds, pies, cakes, & tarts, which the Olympics do not produce. Our boys in blue weary of the monotony and dull routine of garrison life, volunteered in great numbers, from which our Chief selected his men, principally through the recommendations of his Non Com Officers. Having no field service with them of a trying nature, there was little to be considered, more than to select men of will and determination, and men whom had former experience in the mountains since all of Uncle Sams men

are supposed to be models of strength, and endurance. The 21st day of June, found the Lieut. and his party, busy in gathering together their many articles of camp, and garrison equippage, the election of which required careful consideration. We needed many things, but had no means of transportation for any extra pump handles. June the 24th found our truck and turn-over, all upon the dock at Vancouver, Wash. consisting only of the substantials, in the way of edibles, excepting a small box of canned preserves that a lady kindly presented to our Chief, and 4 gallons of spirits of Frumenlt (Frumenti) to be used strictly for snake bites, and upon no other occasion. Our tools invoiced as follows: 7 axes. 12 hatchets, 5 brush hooks, 2 picks. 3 mattocks. 3 spades, a cross-cut saw. Files, hammers, and shoeing kit, for the mules. For arms we had 4 Spring field Carbines, Army pattern, 1 revolver, same pattern, Colts patent, to be used for camp purposes. While Mr. Bretherton, Sgt. Yates, and Bairnes carried breech loading shot guns, Fisher existed night and day, with a large revolver and belt, from which were suspended numerous pouches, ladened with fishing tackle, salmon spears, telescopes, Microscope, sun glass, Compass, shoemaking out fit, assaying apparatus, garden seeds, medical supplies, stationery, spare wire, and other things too numerous to mention. Col. Linsley also carried a revolver, of 38 Cal. Our supplies were calculated to last us for 100 days and amounted to 8000# in heft—tools & all,—so it may readily be seen, that we could not move the entire amount at one nor two loads upon 10 animals, for we found places where we could not proceed with 100# per mule. I hope not to tire the reader, yet it is necessary to enter into some details that I will be brief with, in order that you may more thoroughly comprehend our plan of operation. Since every one can not be so situated in life as to become acquainted with mountain life, and the pack train method of transportation. In every well controlled pack train a bell is attached to a mare, or leader, to which the mules become so attached, that they will follow her over a precipice, thereby saving much time and labor in preventing the animals from straying away from the trail or during the night, when they may be turned out to grass, providing the Bell mare be tied up. One animal is also selected by the chief packer for saddle purposes, in order that he may at all times, be at an advantage to over look his packs. Should he detect

---

[5] The names of the soldiers as they signed them on their enlistment papers and as they were entered in the regimental returns were used by Robert L. Wood in his book on the O'Neil explorations (*Men, Mules and Mountains*, p. 401) and therefore were presumed by him to be correct. However, he offers the following cautions: "Apparently Fisher omitted their given names in his manuscript, leaving space for them to be inserted later. They were written in darker ink than the original writing and may have been added by someone else. This appears to have been done carelessly, as some of the names do not agree with the official records. (The names as given in Fisher's manuscript that vary from the official records are Walter F. Yates, John Heffner, John Bairnes, Edward Danton, P. Kranichfield, and I. Krause.) The various records (official and otherwise) include seven different spellings of Bairens, six of Kranichfeld."

an animals pack coming off, he rides swiftly to its side, throwing a blind over the mules eyes, it halts upon the spot, remaining until recinched, and the blind removed. Another peculiar feature I will mention is that in every pack train there is one animal that will be next the bell mare, despite the efforts of the others to crowd it back. It is upon this animal that we load the amunition that it may at all times be readily at hand. Each of the 10 animals remaining after the Bell mare and saddle mule was selected carried an apparejo or Government pack saddle, and each and every man of our party was drilled to throw the diamond hitch in all of its mysterious loups, a peculiar & Complicated, but secure method of lashing packs upon the Apparejo.

During the evening of June 24th Mr. Price & Pvt Bairns,[6] with the animals in charge of Sergt. Marsh set sail from Portland Or, for Port Townsend, Wash. upon the steamer Alliance. On the day following, Lt. ONeil with his party remaining, boarded the cars from the same place, via Seattle & Tacoma, traveling over the sound pr Steamer Kingston.

Frid. June 27th found us of Uncle Sams denomination enjoying ourselves among the comrades of our Regiment, i.e. Co. a, 14th Inf., U.S.A., which was then stationed at Ft. Townsend, in command of Capt. Bainbridge, and I must say that we were kindly received and well treated by every one in Co. A from top rank to rear file.

Lieut. ONeil with the civillian branch of the party were in the city of Pt. Townsend, 5 miles across the bay from the Fort, where they were anxiously awaiting opportunity to continue on our journey. The Lieut. after an extensive correspondance, added to his former experience, decided to approach the mountains at the s.e. border, hence it became necessary to charter a steamer to convey us to the head of Hoods Canal. There being not steamer running in that trade it was with much difficulty that we succeeded in finding any that would contract to cancel our wants. While the Pt. Townsend branch of our party were enjoying themselves one moment, and pacing the dock in their impatience the next, We of the blue coats were also taking a nip on the sly occasionally & meeting chums of other days. During the morning of this day, Sergt. Marsh went out to train his gun. Fisher & Krause thirsting for first blood, ground a couple of scythe blades that they called hunting knives and the re-

mainder of our party down the bay for a clam bake. As the twilight gathered, so did we and in comparing notes, we all agreed that we had enjoyed the day and had been properly chaperoned by Sergt. Jones of Co. A, 14th Inf. Saturday June 28th the same sun came up and found us all in the same places. After the usual rough and tumble to settle our breakfast we odorized the room with Tobacco smoke, while taking a few lessons in mountain travel from a particularly peculiar character, whose existence with our party was destined to be as brief as he was then attempting to make it brilliant. Mr. Price during the oration walked to the door looking wise in a wisdomotical manner, as he lit the same old identical pipe that he smoked in the 77[7] when he was following the pack train with Gen'l Gibbons Command which was following Chief Joseph & his warriors whom were following every thing but the law,[8] and gasped. But as I was saying Mr. Price made his exit while We were all attention, with great beads of liquid astonishment oozing from our brows as we listened to a lecture from a member (that we will give the Sobriquette of Potato bug Pete) upon the ways and means of existing mid all of the exigencies of camp life, from the small task of finding the big bear upon a cloudy night, to the large one of finding water with a forked stick. Yes we took it all in and mused him in his weakness until he attempted to stuff it down us, with bad german, that he could ascertain the where abouts of the sun at any hour during the day or night by manipulating a common pin upon his left Thumb nail, and that he could also ascertain the true north by the pine limbs that grew upon the S.W. side of a hemlock tree. These last declarations were the fragments that broke the Campbell down so we caressed him with our snow shoes, and deserted the school room for that day. Some of us went fishing, some gathering berries; while others enjoyed Themselves in various ways. At 9 Oclock A.M. Lieut. ONeil visited the post, and enquired after our welfare—satisfied that we had every thing comfortable, he returned to the City—Pt. Townsend/ Sergt. Marsh became seriously nauseated after dinner, presumably from swallowing a fly, and no thanks to the Hospt. Steward who relieved him by not doing any thing, but giving the nurse a growl. Later in the day a message came over the wires from Lieut. O. for Sergt. Marsh to go to Hadlock landing, some 7 miles, to charter the steamer Louise. Sergt Marsh who had

373

---

6 "On June 19, five days before he left with the pack train, Bairens married 19 year old Elizabeth E. Huckins in Vancouver, Washington." Wood, *Men, Mules and Mountains*, p. 401.

7 Transcriber's note: At this point in the diary, the following six lines of the diary someone had attempted to eradicate by erasing, then circling lines through. Careful viewing of the microfilm, however, enabled me to transcribe the eradicated matter, and I believe this is a correct transcription.

8 "Gibbon had fought in the Civil War as a brigadier general and major general in the Volunteers. After being mustered out, he continued in the Regular Army as a colonel—the rank he held during the 1877 Nez Perce campaign—and in 1885 he was promoted to the permanent rank of brigadier general." Wood, *Men, Mules and Mountains*, p. 402.

not entirely recovered under the Stewards peculiar treatment, sent Sergt. Yates in his stead.

Sgt. Yates, not wishing to walk enlisted a small mule to do it for him. Vaulting astride of the cross tree, he took the guy lines and set sail for Hadlock's landing, his legs being too long, or the mules too short he left a peculiar trail in the dust, for which the corral boss was going to chastise some one for causing a mule to draw such a large sled in the summer time. Potato bug Pete strained his back carrying in the stones that the Sergts feet had scraped, thinking that he had found a gold mine, but when he ascertained that his gold came from the brass tacks in the Sergts brogans, he repaired to the thick Jungle and prayed long and loud. We next persuaded him to go fishing, where he broke the record by eating clams, cockles, and sea crabs raw. While fish and crabs were plentiful, we were not favorably impressed with the sport at that date. The varieties caught were sand eels, Tom cod and flounders. Also a chuckled headed cat fish (pided like a rattle snake) caught along the N. pacific Coast, and its tributaries. During the 29th & 30th nothing unusual occurred to mar our pleasure, until late in the day. Jumbo was reported absent without leave, and one mule sick. Mr. Price and Fisher understanding the Chinook jargon and mule-ology repaired to the bushes and after a brief consultation administered a dose of Epsom Salts, and other medicaments that we could remember connected with unhappy hours in boy hood days. The mule continued to grow no better, so we kindly exchanged him for a sound one with the Q.M.s[9] permission. Some of our boys were on Jumbos trail. While others basked in the sun shine, gazing upon the snow clad peaks that we were soon to explore. This being the last of the month, and muster at the post. We visited the dock where a strange craft was landing which proved to be the revenue cutter Rush, coming in to give the crew opportunity to cleanse up with fresh water preparatory to a cruise in the Northern seas. It was quite amusing for us to witness the salt water soldiers operating their queer washing machines, untill one give another a plug in the eye about a bucket, which was entirely wrong, but we did not tell him so, after witnessing his willingness and abilities to back it up. We had no calls to answer at the post but made it a point to be present when mess call was sounded, for Co. A was supporting a table with a lavish hand.

July 1st dawned forth in all its glory with a warm sun shine mellowed down to a pleasant temperature by a gentle sea breeze blowing from the west. Believing that the boat would soon arrive, the morning was partially spent in doing up our private bundles, which were supposed to contain a change of clothing, 2 blankets, and 2 pair of shoes each, which the post Q.M. kindly had transferred to the dock. The noon hour found us mules and all upon the dock as the Louise steamed into port. Thanks to Sergt. Yates success. Everything was placed aboard with out mishap untill it came to the mules, which we had to persuade down a schute by means of a long rope, and sheer awkwardness. They were all forced down but one who displayed all of the pure cussedness (belonging to his flop eared variety). In the melee Potato bug Pete entered the ring in a catch as catch can tussle. During the first round they landed heavily upon the steamers deck in a dog fall. Pete of the Potato bug variety was first up and the manner in which he navigated to this corner evoked a merriment of laughter from the lookers on that rang far out upon the waters. At 2-30 P.M. we steamed over to Pt. Townsend and spent about two hours in loading our supplies and rallying the different members of the party. Upon examination of the ships calender it was ascertained that we were two men and one dog short, of the Jumbo family. Unfortunately too one gentleman proved to be our photographer, Mr. Yocumb, who was detained at his home upon legal matters. At 4.45 P.M. the Louise slipped her cable and steamed across the sound leaving many individuals behind whom would have gladly joined us with our Chiefs permission. In passing a fleet at anchor in the harbor the revenue cutter Corwin saluted by dipping her colors, and we responded by whistle. Swinging to the S.W. we entered Hoods Canal and continued on our journey. Having purchased an out fit for calking shoes with steel spikes such as loggers and mountain climbers use, a man handy at the shoemakers bench was called for. Potato bug Pete promptly responded as an adept at the craft. One pair complete, and the owner pulled them on with an air of pride, but alas: the wrong end of the spikes were sank into the leather soles and as my bold man crossed the deck he left the spikes behind him much to the handy mans chagrin. After a substantial supper which a celestial prepared from the boats stores, we strolled about in search of Camping grounds. The steamer being a log tower, had sleeping accommodations for her crew only. So we contented our selves by stowing away in any vacant place and slept like troopers on the march (in boots & spurs). When day light appeared upon July 2nd we were anchored at Lillywaup landing 10 miles N. from the head of Hoods Canal. Lillywaup was a town of one house near the mouth of a mountain creek from which it took its indian name. The water being shallow we were 50 yds. from the beach and were compelled to Jump the mules overboard,

374

---

[9] Quartermaster's.

and convey our luggage in small boats to the land. Unfortunately the tide was going out and before we were all a shore the boat was unable to clear her self, and was left high and dry to await the flood tide. We were quite sorry for their misfortune untill the man what operates on the down stairs floor prayed long & loud which in some measure relieved our sorrows. By this time one of those atmospheric irregularities set in (called rain in other localities) just to help us along, which it did as you will soon learn. We assembled our truck and turn over upon the beach, just near enough to tide water to have to remove its fell the mules in time and got ready for business. Being informed that it was only 6 miles to lake Cushman over a good trail and fine country, we had not the least doubt but that we would lunch early upon its mossy banks. In compliance with the Lieuts. orders Mr. Brotherton the bird stuffer Sergts Yates & Marsh, with Fisher, Krause & Kranichfield (who by the way we will know hereafter as the Kid in order to save ink) preceded the pack train, arrived with axes to inspect the trail. We had not proceeded far until we unearthed a nest of business Yellow Jackets and two large logs in the trail lying in such a shape that we could not remove them nor cut through. Fisher returned and exchanged his instrument for a spade and cleared a passage under neath the logs. The next point of prominence was a steep hill of some 500 ft. Alt. which we surveyed with much dissatisfaction but continued on our way. Crossing Lillywaup Creek about 3 miles from the Canal forming a canyon at this point it was any thing but a good trail however we hurried on fearing that the pack train would overhaul us and share the troubles that we suspected they were having. Untill now the timber had been of fair growth but here it grew to large size and so dense as to almost shelter us from the rain that continued to fall. The varieties were fir, Cedar, Vine maple, Alder & hemlock, while the shrubs were principally Huckleberries and salal, so thick as to entirely hide the earth from our view. Sergt. Yates who being some yds. in advance gave a cry as if in distress, hurrying to his side expecting to behold him the cavtive [captive?] of some wild animal we were dumfounded to find him serenely gazing upon some 25 or 30 large small and indifferent logs lying across the good trail. Viewing the situation we concluded to swing the trail up hill by cutting the brush and undergrowth away, but go where we would an impassable barrier of Windfalls and brush Confronted us, with an occasional marshy swale to brush or cordoroi over, that the animals might pass over in safety. Thus

we worked untill the middle of the evening when we came to a fork in the once good trail. While soliloquizing two gentleman came up in our rear, and through them we gained the following information. The right hand trail led to their ranch one mile to the N. while the left one led to lake Cushman 2 miles to the West. They further informed us that the Lillywaup trail had been abandoned some three years, and that a better and shorter route had been established between Hoods port and lake Cushman. Drawing a map the gentleman illustrated to our satisfaction that it was only 6 miles from Canal to lake as the crow flies, but by tracing the serpentine course of the trail it increased to 10 or 11 miles. Hungry and fatigued, with bad news from the pack train, which they had passed near the Canal, we accepted an invitation from the generous gentleman who introduced himself as Mr. McCabe to accept a lunch. Sergt Yates & the Kid[10] volunteered to go by his house and meet us at the lake while the remainder of us pushed on with the trail. Posting a notice upon a tree to inform other members of the proper trail and distance we proceeded to the lake arriving at a small hour in the evening. True to their promise Sgt. Yates, Mr. McCabe & the Kid were there with the lunch consisting of fresh bread and bacon. While kindling a fire Proff. Henderson came up who had botanized the country so far, carrying a monster pack of specimens upon his back. Mr. Brotherton had brought down a grouse and while preparing lunch some tried fishing which proved unsuccessful owing to the brush and need of a boat. While the lunch was not a square meal I do not think we ever ate with more relish or were ever so generously inclined as we were to Mr. McCabe who positively but pleasantly refused payment for his Kindness. We were in the act of lighting pipes when Lt. O. approached, with a large pack upon his back looking much fatigued and careworn. He had foreseen our unpleasant predicament and rushed over the 11 miles of trail with a lunch for us. Of course we could not do otherwise than dine again in Exhibition of our appreciation. Lunch over and looking about us we had struck the Hoodsport trail some 200 yds. S. of the lake (See Map) approaching it at its S.E. shore. Lt. ONeil & Prof. Henderson set out through the brush which entirely closed the lake in from our view and succeeded in gaining the open water attracting Mr. Windhoffers attention who resides upon the west side of the lake, rowing his boat over the twain embarked with him for the purpose of remaining over night and making arrangements for our future welfare.

---

[10] "Fisher and Bretherton both refer to Kranichfeld as 'the Kid.' He was the youngest member of the party, smallest in physical stature (with the possible exception of Lieutentant O'Neil), and his behavior often indicated emotional immaturity and instability. During the forty-three months he served in the Fourteenth Infantry, Kranichfeld was court-martialed a dozen times." Wood, *Men, Mules and Mountains*, p. 402.

The Lieut. knowing the condition of the pack train sent us back to order it into camp on the spot, as it was impossible to make the lake. The main party, under the impression that I had gone forward, while I was off getting a drink, rushed forward over the Hoodsport trail thinking to overtake me before dark, in their hurry they over looked the place where our trail intersected and on they went, a mile or more before discovering their mistake. I under the impression that they were ahead of me, great beads of perspiration ran over my face as I leaped over logs, up hill & down, & I concluded I was growing old at my inability to overtake them. Onward they rushed pell mell untill Potatoe bug Pete gave out and darkness forced them to go slow. With me beneath the dense foliage it was so dark mid rain & fog that I lost the trail, entangled in the brush, wet to the skin, and no food. I sat down upon a log and thought of the empty bed at the post, at the same time making preparations to go into camp. Jumbo came dashing over my trail and after making sure of his not being a bear I was right glad to see him, notwithstanding he had never yet done me a good deed I thought it time for some of his good points to leak through his worthless hide, encourageing him to go forward. I followed him and discovered the blazed trail again, when he deserted me as suddenly as he came, returning to the rear party. On I stumbled for some moments meeting Col. Linsley alone on the trail who informed that the pack train was scattered along the trail from the Canal, 6 miles out. We returned to the foremost of them and it was then about 10 Oclock at night and hopelessly stuck in a low muddy bottom, heavily timbered and well brushed with a rich growth of devils Club, the most poisonous and aggrivating of the nettle family that I have ever met with. So long with our exorcise, or work to speak of dear reader you can imagine our situation. We had all previously seen something of camp life but this days events were crowding on hardships faster than we were prepared to meet them.

The pack train party had perhaps more cause for loud prayers than had we. The animals having done nothing for a 12 month were raw and unruly, the ropes new and kinky, ever ready to stretch and grow loose caused much trouble. Mule after mule rolled down the hill I first mentioned untill 2 gave out and their loads which were our bedding were left by the trail. While some of us were kindling a fire other willing hands were busy in relieving the mules of their loads, who were as sadly in need of attention as were we. Mr. Brotherton and Co now joined us in a state of perspiration

and reported l line similar to what I had experienced, in keeping the trail. By careful examination of The Log Book it was ascertained that we were 2 men and 3 mules short and that we were all snake bit. The Col. opened the sideboard and administered antidote. Sergt. Heffner who was in charge of the mess with assistance was preparing supper. Volunteers made their way some 500 yds. back over the trail finding 2 mules too much fatigued to move farther with their loads. They were unpacked upon the spot and brought into camp. Not a blade of grass grew in this locality so dense was the larger growth. Consequently there was nothing to do for the animals but tie them up with out food. Jumbo made him self useful by getting in every persons way and taking up two men's room in front of the fire, in trying to be popular with the cook. Pounding up some coffee in a boot leg we soon had a fair kettle of hot coffee but no sugar, and Bacon with flap jacks minus yeast powder was the bill of fare to which we did ample Justice[11]—a smoke and a forced laugh at our awkward position and hardships, we repaired to the thick jungle and prayed long and loud for the good people that had inveigled us into opening up the Lillywaup trail, instead of informing us of the Hoodsport route. The rain continued falling in a gentle spray as it can only upon this northern pacific coast.

A few blankets were found among the packs and we distributed our selves to the best advantage and slept with a troubled conscience for I think it weighed heavily upon every ones mind more for the poor mule lost early in the day than for the two men who were more able to take care of themselves.

Thursday, July 3rd came much the reverse of yesterday. The sun shone brightly but little we seen of it beneath the thick growth of vegetation which was saturated and as bad as rain to us. Sgt. Yates went back to where we had unpacked the two mules, whose packs proved to be our sugar and bacon, taking a supply to camp. Sgt. Marsh and Fisher proceeded back on the trail to gain some information of the lost mule and two men. About one mile out upon the trail we met Higgens & Bairnes with our little mule Trixy [Frixy?]. Pushing on for camp. They had found the mule late the evening before where she had gave out, relieving her of the pack they camped there untill morning and set out to overtake us. We were much relieved to learn that the mule was properly looked to but not so with the two men who were out all night in the rain with out supper or breakfast. Return-

---

[11] "According to O'Neil, this was the 'first meal on flapjacks and water' for some of the men. 'A mountain flapjack,' he wrote, 'consists of flour, salt and water, and is when [one is] extremely hungry very palatable.'" Wood, *Men, Mules and Mountains*, p. 402.

ing to camp, breakfast was the same as supper with the addition of sugar to our coffee. More dead than alive with clothing wet and plastered with black muddy mud we packed up and set out for the lake. The mules again too fresh for good service, in their crowding for first place in line, frequently upset one another in the mud and water, and the nearest trooper was invited to wade in to help them up, which usually resulted in the mule getting up and knocking the trooper down in his struggles. Thus we continued to struggle through the mud and muck untill noon when we reached the lake. Following the east shore to the N for 300 yds we discovered a narrow trail cut through the jungle to the lake shore, where the Lieut. had secured a <u>large</u> <u>raft</u> of <u>primitive order</u>. There being no trail around the lake it was decided to ferry across the lake. Getting aboard with our freight, we exereted about 200 dog power for something like an hour before we ceased to dip the clumsy car that wafted us over to the other shore. Here quite a patch of ground was cleared and clothed with a rich growth of clover and timothy. Back to the west was Mr. Windhoffers house of log structure, substantially built and comfortably furnished. Contracted brows from yesterday's hardships gave way to smiles when the Lieut. notified us that dinner awaited us at the house where had succeeded in making himself quite a favorite. Proff. Henderson who is an inveterate and scientific fisherman as well as botanist had just returned from the lake with a large catch of speckled beauties (brook trout) and it was then & there that we enjoyed many good things that we were not destined to taste soon again. Gaining some information of our host & hostess I will state here that she has proven herself a lady of much nerve and pluck. She had lost her husband soon after settling upon the claim and had resided for months in those wild woods with only her two small children, at one time for a period of two years with out seeing or speaking to one of her own sex. May prosperity be distributed freely in her pathway by the hand of providance to gladden her declining years. Later Mr. Windhoffer was captivated by her many charms. They now own what will in the near future form a pleasant summer resort.[12] Engaging Mr. W & his team to convey our luggage from the lake to the rear of his home, upon the banks of a beautiful stream that rippled by, we went into camp untill such time as we could bring up the balance of our supplies

from the Lillywaup landing. Thus far there was nothing strange in the Vegetable Kingdom. The common plants of the country were Osier, Huckle, and salmon berry. Sallal, Elk & deer ferns, epilobium, tea plant, Kinnikinnick & etc. The formation was of a sandy loam with a rich covering of decayed vegetation and growing moss. While a strong producing soil and lying favorable it would be a gigantic undertaken to prepare it for cultivation. I have since been informed that all of that portion lying east of the lake has been bought up by a syndicate from timber cruisers i.e. parties who make it a business of proving up on timber claims and selling out their rights. Such proceedings should be prohibited by the government & laws which are not rigidly enforced in some sections. Lake Cushman of which we will now speak is a beautiful sheet of water which the skokomish river flows through and so into Hoods Canal (See Map) in dimensions the lake is $1\frac{1}{2}$ miles long 1000 yds wide and 200 feet deep. Fish abound in plentiful numbers and of three varieties viz. brook trout, Lake trout and the large Bull trout or Charpie. The first two take the fly readily and the latter rise for the spoon or trolling hook. Here the mountains rise abruptly from the northern lake shore almost precipitous in out line—general formation sand stone coarse and sharp with light veins of milky quartz (SiO) but barren. To the west one wall of rock over looks the lake but upon the S.W. side the rise is more gentle for some two miles before the elevation becomes mountainous. To the South it is broken here & there with level bottoms intervening especially along the water courses. The skokomish from this point flows with a gentle fall through a flat bottom being generally wide and shallow with many trees whose boughs over hang the water whose course is so tortuous, all things considered, will prevent rafting a success upon this stream.[13] During the afternoon we put up our tents which were of the Army pattern composed of 3 light pieces of canvas 6 ft. square, that button together standing 4 ft. high with the front gable open and covering sleeping room for two men. That done our luggage in camp and feed conveyed across the lake for the mules we posted up the log book and found that we were all happy but he of the insect name who was practicing vodooism against the rheumatism. The game killed up to this date was one rabbit, one grouse and a moss [?] wildcat to the credit of Mr. Brotherton. When night closed in we

377

---

[12] "According to W. T. Putnam, Jr., the avocation of Victor Muller, one of the pioneer settlers at Lake Cushman, was recruiting prospective spouses for the community's bachelors, widows, et cetera. Muller brought Windhoffer to Lake Cushman and introduced him to Rose's widow. Windhoffer deserted her, however, about a year after their marriage, leaving her with still another child. She became discouraged, sold the property to William T. Putnam in 1891, and went to live elsewhere." Wood, Men, Mules and Mountains, p. 402.

[13] "The unscheduled bivouac on the Lilliwaup trail was not given a number. Beginning at Windhoffer's ranch, the mule trail camps were numbered consecutively—Camp No.1, Camp No. 2, et cetera—up to and including those on the Grand Divide, ending with Camp No. 15." Wood, Men, Mules and Mountains, p. 402.

were prepared for inclement weather but the sky was clear this night, and the stars twinkled merrily over a camp fire that burned out early, while we enjoyed the much needed sleep. Morning came with the memmorable 4th day of July. Doubtless more than one of us lie in deep meditation reviewing their different trails through life since boyhood days, from the hour of tin guns, fire crackers and candy to maturity—mid passions of sunshine and sorrow. Onward through the rugged paths of life from the hour of parting from the maternal hearthstone to the present site of camp life— but enough dreaming—it was not through idle fancies that George Washington raised the flag of independence, so with the little hatchet we must be up and doing if that same banner be borne over the lofty peaks of the Olympics. Emerging from our dog tent in dog fashion we found our cook dodging about the fire with his weather eye upon Jumbo who was about to flush a side of bacon. The Proff and his fishing rod were absent. Not remembering the last date that we performed our ablutions and water so handy, there was no excuse this morning. Breakfast over the pack train accompanied by Mr. Price, Sgt. Yates, Hughes and Higgins returned to Lillywaup to bring up the supplies. Sgt. Marsh went out for the double purpose of hunting and prospecting our route which lay up the skokomish river N.W. The remainder of us went fishing or sketching. During our absence Proff. H. came in with a catch of 100 fine trout, remaining long enough for lunch, away he went botanizing and fishing. We all made a fair catch and returned for dinner. Mr. Brotherton sought a level spot— a place fit for a lovers tryst, intending to bathe his weary limbs in the balmy air, but his stay was as brief as his movements soon were comical—Mad dogs—Wild Cats—and circus performances flashed upon our minds as he dashed through the wilderness, his striped jacket standing well to the wind like a tin can to a yellow curs tail we thought. Before we could find a lasso he brought up in a thick jungle and it proved to be a pronounced case of yellow jackets. He knelt down before his tent, we thought to pray, but he disappeared

378

in his dog tent dog fashion and remained in silence. Deep were his thoughts which developed themselves later at our Chief's expense. Knowing that our Chief had business in Union City at an early date, and that there were young ladies there, he conceived the Idea of assisting the Lieut. to a secure spot where he could arrange his wardrobe. The aforesaid spot was a patch of tall weeds and the afore said weeds were business weeds or Bull nettles equally as painful as yellow jackets in their sting. So we leave you to imagine the sequel and join in the laugh with Mr. B. who now considered him self as equal with all mankind again.[14] As twilight gathered, so did we around a pleasant campfire, pipes produced and yarns spun that would have sent the Arabian nights to McGinties long resting home. By this time the few settlers living in the vicinity had gathered in, which I introduce to you as Mr. Muller, Church, Stebbins, Davis, McCabe & Windhoffer, who all had claims near the lake, and Missus [Messrs.?] Smith & Hays two prospectors then operating in the mountains adjacent a small logging camp upon the S.W. shore with the above named constituted the entire settlers about the Lake,[15] excepting a mining camp $4\frac{1}{2}$ miles up the skokomish that I will refer to later. All told we formed quite a large circle and a merry one around the camp fire. Someone with Yankee ingenuity produced a violin well knowing it would do much toward aggrivating the snake poison. The Violin went around the circle in silence until it came to Fishers corner who proved himself a proffessor of the barrell head order. Air after air upon the puncheon floor system rang out upon the mountain air, with our effect, untill (Give the fiddler a dram) was rendered which broke the Chorus & the seal as well upon a long necked bottle after which we sang songs to the national airs untill weary of the pass time where upon we crawled into our tents for a nights repose.[16]

Sat., July 5th came and with it another atmospheric irregularity. Lieut. ONeil set out to inspect the Hoodsport and Union City trail with a view of using it instead of the Lillywaup trail, in case we came in need of fresh supplies.

---

[14] "This bit of horseplay is indicative of O'Neil's extraverted personality. He was fun loving, liked to play practical jokes, and was a great tease. Nicknamed 'the Marshal' while attending the university, he was a popular student and received considerably more than his share of attention in the Notre Dame Scholastic. Although polite and considerate, he was somewhat quick tempered and inclined to settle an argument with his fists. Described as 'indefatigable and irrepressible,' he was active in several literary, dramatic, and musical societies, gave many declamations and public readings, and frequently engaged in debates. He participated in a number of dramatic plays, generally assuming a major role, usually that of a villain, brigand, or conspirator. His performance in a harlequinade was described as 'inimitable': He 'appeared in the most grotesque of all costumes—that of a faded Negro beauty—and excited much merriment by his well acted part.' He was also an accomplished dancer." Wood, *Men, Mules and Mountains* pp. 402–403.

[15] "Fisher's statement that this was everyone who lived near the lake requires clarification. A number of men had taken claims in the vicinity of Lake Cushman in the late 1880's and many of the properties had changed hands, some on more than one occasion. The majority of the settlers had little or no interest in living on their claims merely to 'prove up' on them in order to acquire the timber rights, which they promptly sold to lumber companies." Wood, *Men, Mules and Mountains*, p. 403.

[16] "Although he no doubt participated in the singing, O'Neil may have refrained from sampling the contents of the 'long necked bottle.' As a student at Notre Dame, he sang bass in various musical entertainments, played in the cornet band, and was also active in the Notre Dame Total Abstinence Union and lectured on temperance. The song mentioned by Fisher was a rollicking Kentucky fiddle tune that began with the words: 'Dance all night with your bottle in your hand, and long before day give the fiddler a dram.'" Wood, *Men, Mules and Mountains*, p. 403.

Sergt. Marsh made his report from yesterdays experience, while not successful in finding game reported a good trail for $4\frac{1}{2}$ miles to the mining camp which lay in our direction, consequently we could move up with out further labor on the trail when the animals returned.[17] Proff. Henderson was so interested in fishing, despite the rain that continued falling all day, that we had trouble in getting him into his meals. But thanks to his rod and success as a fisherman the camp was well supplied with trout of the finest quality. We also learned that our packers were successful in fishing in the Lillywaup Creek and all well excepting Mr. Price who was slightly ill for a day. Someone in trying to make a Black berry pie like his mother used to make had made a mistake which was perhaps indigestible but we never learned the pie builders name. Extending our travels to a wider circuit—we found salmon berries ripe, rich, and juicy, wild pigeons were flying over, quite numerous. Shotguns were produced and quite a number brought down by different parties, which gave us an excellent pot pie for supper and work for Mr. Brotherton who prepared some specimens for the museum of the Oregon Alpine Club. Fisher took a jaunt up the river fishing with fair success and also found a mallard duck upon a nest of 9 eggs. Later on we conveyed more hay across the lake for the animals and busied ourselves in various ways making life happy and camp comfortable. When our cook called supper a circle of happy faces gathered around a large dutch oven full of pigeon pie, fresh butter, trout in abundance with many other good things that would make you hungry to hear mentioned, all cooked to a Queens taste, for our cook was no novice nor upon his maiden trip with the Alpine Club.[18] Darkness came and closed us in with her vaporous folds, as it rained us up it rained us to bed, and continued to fall as we soundly slumbered, with naught to disturb the music of the patter of the rain, except an occasional set to between some member of the party and Jumbo, who was constitutionally opposed to sleeping out in the rain.

Sun. July 6th next appeared upon the calender and with

it the rain continued, down it came in large drops and small ones. Now it came in mists then in streams. Tired of coming straight down it came in diagonal shoots from all directions, as if there was some unseen opening in our tents that it had not yet penetrated, but we were bound for Olympus or bust, and all of the web foot family and we continued with banner afloat. Our cook in dipping up a pail of water accidentally tumbled into the river and deprived us of a good laugh in choosing such an appropriate time for his mishap. So we nursed a feeling akin to anger more than of pity for him. As matters appeared in a wet state so did Lieut. ONeil and a Gentleman introduced as Mr. Fred Church, Assistant Mineralogist & Engineer to the party. They had came from Union City through the rain. Two dogs were also registered upon the logbook as Tiger, and Max.[19] Jumbo received them quite friendly untill mess call, when they all entered the ring dogs burg rules tearing down several tents in the melee and the owners there of prayed long & loud. Next in order was the pack train returning with an other load of supplies which were ferried over and brought to camp. The trail east of the lake was now very muddy and cut up necessarily reducing the loads, and many a hard hours labor was spent in getting through at all.

Mon. July 7th being a fine day and the 1st of the week we must have a good start to keep time with the old superstition, at an early hour, in compliance with the following programe, Col. Linsley and the other rock picker Mr. Church,[20] set out for a 4 days jaunt in order to learn the nature of the country that we were to go over. Lt. ONeil the boss Soldier with Proff. Henderson, The Weed-Puller, Mr. Brotherton the bird stuffer, Bairnes & Fisher set out over the trail to remove any obstructions. Sgt. Marsh, Mr. Price, Hughes and Higgins returned to Lillywap with seven mules, while Sgts. Yates & Heffner and the Kid remained in the present Camp No 1. to follow us with 3 animals that we had ferried over. Krause had distributed himself among some of the setlers, vodoo medicine, rheumatism and all. The Lieuts. Party made the mining camp early, over a

---

[17] "This statement by Fisher conflicts with O'Neil's report which indicates work had to be done to make the trail usable by the mules: 'The trail cutters were set to work on the trail, . . . July 7, a trail had been cut a distance of about $4\frac{1}{2}$ miles, and Camp No. 2 there established. This camp is about 500 yards from a camp occupied by a set of miners.' O'Neil also refers to the miner's path in his unpublished notes: 'Their trail was a godsend to us.'" Wood, *Men, Mules and Mountains*, p. 403.

[18] "Haffner normally was in charge of the mess, but this statement indicates one of the scientists cooked the dinner on this occasion." Wood, *Men, Mules and Mountains*, p. 403.

[19] "On October 19, 1890, the *Oregonian* reported: 'Three dogs accompanied the party, one a cross between a blood hound and a deer hound, used in trailing members of the party whenever they got lost, a bear dog, and Lieutenant O'Neil's Irish setter.' On several occasions Fisher refers to four dogs, but he names only three—Jumbo, the hound, Max, the Irish setter, and Tiger, the bear dog." Wood, *Men, Mules and Mountains*, p. 403.

[20] "Fisher's comments regarding Church are confusing. Although he mentions that a settler named Church attended the campfire festivities at Lake Cushman on July 4, he also indicates Church accompanied O'Neil when the latter returned from Union City on July 6, and states that he was then introduced to the explorers. O'Neil also gives July 6 as the date Church asked to join the expedition, but he notes, additionally, that the request was made 'after the departure of Private Krause.' This, however, may refer to the date Church left for Union City to arrange his affairs. 'As his services were voluntary,' O'Neil wrote, 'I allowed him to accompany us, and he more than made up for the man I had relieved.'" Wood, *Men, Mules and Mountains*, pp. 83–84, 404.

very good trail, soon followed by Sergt. Yates party who made two round trips this day with 3 mules. From this point on there were no more settlers nor trails. The mine upon investigation proved to be one of free Copper deposited in a formation of slate, sandstone & quartz but not in quantities to excite our rock samplers. By noon we had pushed the trail on to a distance of 5 mile from the lake, keeping the left bank of the stream. Here we approached a formidable looking bluff (named for Fisher) and went into Camp No. 2 or Nelly Bly. Our course lay to the N.W. but we were in the rivers basin with only two ways of getting out, which was at either end. Here the stream was 100 ft. wide, 4 ft. deep, ice cold, and too swift to ford. After falling several large trees we succeeded in lodging one for a foot log. It was here that the weed sampler proved himself a thorough axeman. During the eve excepting the cook, the entire camp turned out in search of a passage. Cross the river we could not with animals, and the left bank rose perpendicular from the river bottom of a deep hole. A thorough exploration resulted in but one passage over Fishers bluff which crossed it at 500 ft. elevation. The incline 45 deg. with good footing, excepting one wall of solid stone just below the summit 12 ft. high and another at the northern descent, dropping over another perpendicular wall some 15 ft. in to a muddy creek, the opposite side of the stream being a mass of fallen timber many feet deep and well brushed. It was a case of dig and bridge. Returning to camp in time to remove the bark from some large Alders to sleep upon and making some shakes from a fallen cedar for a table, we turned in for the night.

Tues. July 8th. Getting down to business now and becoming some what inured to hardships. 6 Oclock was the breakfast hour and 7 for supper, with one hours rest at noon.[21] Sgt. Yates & Bairnes returned to the lake with 3 animals, removing Camp No. 1. to No 2. and the east division made another trip to the lake and returned to Lillywaup. The remainder of us worked on the trail removing many large logs from the trail, by sawing them through twice and removing the section. Our saw having been smashed up by a falling mule, the Kid set out in search of another with no success. No band of men ever worked with more spirit than we did, logs lay so thick you could step from one to the other while between over & under them were loose stones tangled up in the brush, while great roots protruded from the earth and rock requiring the greatest care to preserve our tools. Camp No 2. while pleasant in dry weather, was now saturated with

Perched upon the rock with bent rod

continuous rains. Fir & cedar grew here to monstrous heights and 12 ft. in diameter, while hemlock was not so large it was greater in numbers. The earth and undergrowth was completely covered with moss and the trees completely draped from top to bottom, hanging in clusters & bunches of many feet in length. Living night and day excluded from the sun, little as it shone, we were like insects existing with in a saturated sponge. The days were yet long and there was some light untill 9 Oclock. Tired as we were we ate hurriedly, gathered rods, and hurried to the stream. At this camp in a deep & seething hole, there seemed to be but one size of trout as we caught none other. Each and every one was the picture of the first caught, weighing $2\frac{1}{2}\#$. A very large brook-trout, and to land one trout, dear reader, repaid us for all the days work such trout as these and in such a place was worthy the angling of the Gods of old, leaping a foot in the air they took the fly from above, and in no single instance did they every miss taking a good hold of the hook, up & down, across & back, they shot through the boiling foam while we perched

---

[21] "The explorers usually referred to their three daily meals as breakfast, dinner, and supper. Occasionally, however, they called the midday meal lunch and the evening meal supper." Wood, *Men, Mules and Mountains*, p. 404.

Great trees were fallen

upon <u>the</u> <u>rock</u> <u>with</u> <u>bent</u> <u>rod</u> and nerve strung to a pitch of excitement. At last behold him landed safely, casting again and again until darkness drives us in. Lt. ONeil learning that Krause was sick proceeded to the lake to investigate his case which he easily diagnosed prescribing more rest and a pleasure trip to his station which met with general approval, and henceforth we had no bugs in camp to eat our potatoes but those with brave hearts and willing hands.[22]

Thurs. July 9th came bright and as clear as a marriage bell. The kid again set out in search of a crosscut saw and returned with success after a jaunt of 12 miles. During the while, the inmates at camp Nelly Bly worked on the trail. <u>Great</u> <u>trees</u> <u>were</u> <u>fallen</u> up hill, lodging their tops upon the cliff before mentioned, brushed over and covered with earth carried from a distance. Presenting a steep incline, our bridge was complete. Pushing on with the trail, and second bridge, Fisher was consigned to the mattock work. Returning to the bottom he dug a zigzag toe path which by night appeared as if we might succeed in our triumph over an at first doubtful undertaking. Here the earth carried an iron stain with an occasional grain of copper, and at one spot a granulated read slate was unearthed, beautiful in color, due to Iron Oxide (FeO) but use less in the arts in its shattered state. So near camp was our work that we returned for dinner with hands blistered and bruised from familiarity with axe helves. Imagine my wrath when I learned that some one had unthoughtedly tied Jumbo to my tent where he had spent the morning in chewing ropes to fragments, tearing down tent and scattering all that I owned helter skelter

in his frolicsome sport. My education had been too much neglected to do justice to this occasion so I said nothing and soon forgot my injuries when I observed green peas and clams for dinner, that some kind soul had brought from slat water. Every spare moment of the noon hour was now utilized in making camp comfortable, washing our clothing & etc. not that we were compelled to rush matters thus but each and every man was inspired with the same energy and strong desire to reach the divide, and gaze upon the topography of this strange Country. While there was no Top notch Tim's or ear less Rube characters, so vividly represented in the ten cent terribles hanging by the chin from the horn of the moon. While scalps flew like autumn leaves from their hob-nailed brogans, these were men who labored for our common cause, and whom heard not, needed not, harsh commands or vulgar compensation (money) to stimulate their blows. A suggestion was law, and forward the watch word and thought. During the evening the Col and Mr Church returned from their explorations which had been directed to that territory up the west bank of the Skokomish R. Their report ran as follows. A continuous rank forest, dense undergrowth, and miry, where there was earth, from melting snow and many scattering springs, while the general character of the higher elevations were fretted— ragged, and saw toothed, to the extreme, ending in cones and pinnacles whose angles were as sharp as the laws of cohesion and gravition [gravitation] versus the elements would admit. Elk, bear, and deer sign, of recent date, was abundant, but none were sighted. Their bag was one grouse. They had spent one half of their time in dragglng their selves over cliffs and windfalls and the other half in assisting Tige (the dog) after them, who was unable to climb as they were, assisted by swinging limbs and creeping vines. We had now accumulated four as worthless dogs as ever howled at the silent moon, yet we caressed and fed them well, knowing that they were full of good points since not one had yet left them. Lt ONeil with two men and 3 mules went to the lake this eve, and camp followers became visible. While we had no extra supplies, we extended a generous welcome to as many, in fact more than we could well afford. The Lt with a keen fore sight kept our camp as much isolated as courtesy would permit, well knowing that pleasure and toil such as we experienced never travel hand in hand. Perhaps some were offended at what they may have pronounced selfishness, but with due consideration no man should undertake

---

[22] "Krause apparently did not like Army life. Less than six months later he purchased his discharge for $90 under provisions of General Orders No. 81, Adjutant General's Office, dated July 26, 1890, which permitted such action. This was no mean sum, since Krause's pay as an artificer was $15 a month." Wood, *Men, Mules and Mountains,* p. 404. This date in Wood's footnote is in error. See p. 479, note 81, in *Men, Mules and Mountains.*

a ten days trip with 3 days provisions and seven days bedding, which is invariably the case with a tenderfoot and many too that wear corns from well earned experience. Messrs Church & Muller by the way claimed to have been with in gun shot of salt water previously but this short trip proved that they were deceived by the deep Quinault basin and fog which during their observations hung like a curtain over the vast expanse of Country beyond the east of the Ocean.

Thurs July 10th found us early on the trail. Mr. Bretherton to day went to Lake Cushman and back, after agents in which to pickle insects, having now turned entomologist and bug catcher. I here in a measure lifted one sin from my shoulders by persuading him to rob the ducks nest for which I was rewarded by an olfactory shock of Carburetted and sulphuretted hydrogen $(CH)(H_2S)$ instead of the dainty pudding down upon the Menu Card. However another specimen was added to the Museum in the form of an embryo Mallard duckling. Lt ONeil returned with 3 mules loaded, and later the main branch of the pack train arrived with loads, reporting all supplies up from Lillywaup, with some yet remaining at Lake Cushman. There being no feed for animals to subsist upon, it was necessary to return them each day to the Lake, or carry hay (no grain to be had) as occasion required, which frequently found our men upon the trail until late at night. Mr Church having decided to join us for the summer returned to Union City to arrange his affairs accordingly. Mr Wright, a settler who with his son had been some miles to the west prospecting, passed through our camp half clad, having lost his son in the forest, and had carelessly burned hat & shoes to a crisp. A fine string of trout and two ducks fell to our prowess to day, and Jumbo the object of much mirth through falling off the foot log into the roaring torrent which at this point was a continuous rapid lashing its water into foam against the many obstructing boulders. Four and one half days we had toiled upon Fishers Bluff and now we were rewarded with a toe path zig zaged like the lightnings glare over the formidable hill where fallen logs, boulders, and brush had so recently held sway, deposited as they partially were by the snow slides mad chaos.[23]

Frid July 11th. The weather now appears settled and our forest home becomcoming [becoming] more pleasant as we grow accustomed to the death like silence of this forest of stately trees, and silicious cones. To day Sgt Marsh, Higgins, and Danton came in with 4 mules loaded, the latter being one of our party at Townsind who had missed the boat and was now rejoining us. All hands at the trail, and the woodsmans axe rang merrily. By noon we had made one and one half miles. Here another impassible barrier confronted us, and we were forced to make an about turn to the north, crossing the river which was admissible at this point. After cutting down the banks, Lt ONeil cut a foot log in order to cross over and examine the country and took a russian bath, very reluctantly too, as it was as cold as snow could make it. Proff Henderson & Sgt Yates crossed over and as they stepped upon the opposite shore down went the foot log, borne onward by the mad water. Mr. Bretherton now appeared with our lunch, and well they earned their portion by cutting a large fir in order to rejoin us again. Mr. Bretherton by this time had added many curios to his collection, such as water oozles nest, bright plumed humming birds, Quail, robbins, Camp robbers, & etc. Hughes & Higgins were now permanently assigned to the mysteries of the diamond hitch, and with Mr Price were soon to follow us with equippage from Camp No 2. Mr Wrights son, who was lost up the river, came through to day accompanied by a gentleman sent out to search for him. Our cook was being sorely tried in patience and endurance with 14 hungry men and 4 dishonest dogs to look out for. Detachments of the pack train coming and going at all hours, extra lunches and regular meals, kept his reflectors ovens continually before the fire, from which great loaves blossomed from the leaven flour. Yet he fought his battles nobly and commanded the respects of the camp. After supper we angled again for the finny tribe, and made a rustic wash tub from a cotton wood log. Our camp to night has the appearance of a farm yard upon wash day.

Sat July 12th. We set out on the trail. Crossing the river, we were compelled to cut the trail to the north for a mile or more from the stream to avoid obstacles and return again to recross the river as the bottom changed from side to side with the rivers tortuous curves. Here we had made more than 2 miles of trail in a V shape, gaining not more than 1000 yds in our course. The river here had formed an ugly canyon through which the water plunged with a deafening roar over the many terraces of the river bed.[24] Approaching the stream again it was necessary to fall a very large tree and

[23] "O'Neil stated in his report: 'The entire strength of the party was occupied for four days and a half in building this bridge, but it was done in so substantial a manner that this piece of road, which some miners were afraid to cross, did not even delay the pack train.' According to both O'Neil and Fisher, the bluff was first approached on July 7 (Fisher says at noon) and the bridge completed on July 10. This, of course, was less than the four and one-half days both men say were required." Wood, *Men, Mules and Mountains*, p. 405.

[24] "The terraces became known in later years as Staircase Rapids, an adaptation from the settlers' name for the route over Fisher's Bluff." Wood, *Men, Mules and Mountains*, p. 405.

382

a small one lapping their branches for a foot bridge over the now wide but shallow stream. Four ducks were brought down, and we kindled a fire upon the gravel bar to prepare our lunch. What a pleasure to emerge from the silence of those dark forests into this warm sun shine, its rays seem to penetrate the body with a pleasant effect not unlike the soothing effects of an opiate. Here small willows fringed the high water line. Birds chirped and warbled their wild songs, flitting from bush to tree, while bright winged butter flies went skimming near the water as if in defiance of the wily trout in his brooklet home beneath. It was now that we enjoyed camp life, surrounded as we were by natures grandest charms. No woodmans axe had as yet despoiled the forest. No red mans moccasin had tracked the earth. In the poets language it was like leaving this mortal vale of tears to enter the enchanted lands. Lunch over and our sun bath must end. Danton was sent back to guard Camp No 2 since camp followers were numerous and some helping them selves to supplies which we could ill afford to spare. The narrow bottom that skirted the stream being upon our side now, we were again in full force opening up the narrow passage that must take us to the Ocean. All who had been out far enough to see what lay before us turned back for other lands to hunt in, and while they said we could never succeed, we thought:

George Washington with his little axe cut down the cherry tree
and lived to push his ink stained quill that set our country free.
Greely sailed the gallant ship that came so near the pole, and
lived to hear his honored name around this wide world roll.
Stanley cross'd the Congo land, and made the savage tame,
He now in England lives in state, mid laurels, ease and fame.
May ONeil and his chosen men be spared to cross this land
and live to reap a ripe old age, caressed by daughters grand.

As yet no changes have occurred in the formation or Vegetable Kingdom, with one unbroken mass of timber and brush through which an occasional columbine or tiger lilly struggled in vain to greet its love, the sunshine. The pack train came in loaded. Tents were raised and camp assumed her natural aspect. Mr Price was now some what out of spirits, one of his animals had fallen from the bridge on Fisher's bluff, and a second one rolling in the ascent, bruising them up some and causing much extra labor in extricating and returning them to the trail again.

Sun July 13th. As we had pushed, toiled and struggled with unceasing energy and in this beautiful camp where all was enraptured, The Lieut though young in years was in command of the Olympic country by virtue of power invested.

Consequently it became him in his worthy position to issue an appropriate proclimation which displayed his finer feelings toward his God and fellow-man, in announcing that this the 13 would be a holiday. Which announcement was received with pleasure and taken advantage of, with the exception of the pack train party who were anxious to catch up with their work. I suppose, dear reader, you will imagine we slept untill the noon hour and rested our weary limbs in the sunshine during the evening. But No! Better attempt to still the Oceans ever restless tide than the Spirit of natures child who breathes the mountain air. Sgt Yates & Marsh did not await their breakfast in their eagerness to go hunting. Barns soon followed suit with his shot gun, while Prof Henderson and my self waited for breakfast. Leaving the Lieut et al in camp drawing maps and balancing up the log book, we set out North, heading for the group of highest peaks in this locality. Crossing the river and tearing our way through the brush and over fallen logs 2 to 5 deep for some 1000 yds, we approached the foot hill and began the ascent. Choosing a modest gulch that marked the mountain side, we continued up untill it widened to a gentle draw growing smaller and more narrow until it carried us out upon one of the phalanx like ridges that sloped away from the main elevation. The ascent was now so difficult that we must assist our selves by the friendly bushes that grew in abundance. Quicker than thought a huge black bear dashed by with in 15 feet of me. Thin in flesh, having but recently left their winter homes, it went like the wind. 2 leaps only and it disappeared in the brush again. I afterwards learned that the two Sgts were above and were the cause of its fright. Oregon grape root, Salal and the large huckle berry now grew scattering and small openings appear here & there with a perceptible change in the vegetation. Mountain Ash, Wild Cherry, dutchmans pipe, beautiful mosses, lichens & fungi, Wild pea, Indigo plant, and at this point 3 or 4 specimens of poison oak—(rhus Toxicodendron) the only that we found in the entire range of mountains.

At about 3000 feet altitude a short stretch of dead timber crossed our trail, which was significant of a fire having at some time visited these hills. No charred particles remained to verify our presumptions so much as did the fire weed growing here which by some freak of nature soon follows the wake of a fire, as if to gladden and beautify the firey monsters trail. Seldom do we meet it except in burned districts. Upon either side and ahead of us now are thousands of blossoms from the mountain asphodel or Elk grass which form a sea of white built up as they are of snow balls imparting their fragrance, until the air becomes heavy with their sweet perfume.

383

Beyond this and we are upon the top of a bench. Here we changed our course to the west, crossing a bank of snow beneath the hemlock and firs whose foliage protect it from the summer sun. Here a field of lillies greet the eye and most strange of all as if not to be out rivaled by their neighbors they actually grew and blossomed in the snow and in pools of ice water. Beautiful and as white as the snow its self, they turn violet with age. Now we meet a smaller variety, the Clyntonia. Passing on we reach the base of the peaks proper, skirted as they are by grassy slopes, and yellow lillies prevail here. Passing beneath the now perpendicular walls of stone we discover a large gap or fissure some 12 ft wide. Clinging to the bushes we go upwards. Though the sun light seldom kiss them, here are violets yellow and blue, pucadenums, pinstemons, Hellebore, valerian, flowering mosses and indian pinks, with many other bright hued flowers, all blended into one harmonious panorama. Wild onions next are found. Once more slinging our collections over our shoulders we continue up the narrow pass. Looking above, our hearts leap with joy. The entire face of the cliff is covered with a brilliant red. Perspiration streaming, and hearts throbbing with over exertion and excitement, we leap from stone to stone and gaze in admiration of that beautiful plant. A flowering moss, and a stranger to science, first feather in our caps. Higher up with its rootlets pinched in the almost imperceptible cleavage is a violet, also a stranger and another feather in our cap. One by one we continue to collect them until we are perfectly sure of three strangers and probably six. Now we have reached the lower summit, crossing a great bank of snow, steep but soft to the depth of two inches during sun shine. Now for the topmost point which is gained. Grand, Inspiring, think we, as we stand there in the golden light of the sinking sun. It is one vast field of cones, canyons, & cross canyons, cross'g at all angles like the twine of a seine whose meshes are filled with cones. Where is Olympus and Constance? Producing compass and paper we sketch. Five hundred peaks greet the eye and all are apparently of equal heigth. Better try to name so many drops of water and distinguish them one from the other than those peaks, think we. We know where we are and know where those two prominent peaks are located upon the maps, but in reality they are not there.[25] The day has been spent so pleasantly, led forward by the many changes in scenery & vegetation, like a child chasing the butterfly we have never thought of camp or lunch untill now. Hurriedly

kindling a fire from the dwarf mountain hemlock, which is perhaps the first fire that ever flashed upon those rocks, we each draw a crust. Since missing my dinner the first day out, a square of bacon had hung suspended from the belt of many pouches, and how its odor tickled our palates as it broiled upon the spits. Onions salt were also produced. With pure cold water from the melting snow, it was to us a feast, with nectar for the Gods. It was almost sundown now and the snow freezing. We must hurry if we reach camp to night, and hurrying down hill quickly cripples the knees. Taking a last look at Union City, and Hoods Canal, which was the only portion of salt water visible, we rushed down as speedily as the surroundings would allow, recrossing the snow safely. I shot a large blue grouse, and we rushed downward untill from the knees down were uncontrollable when we reached level ground again. Thinking we were brush foundered they gave us the camp signal (3 shots) but we were then near the river and arrived at 10 Oclock. The other parties had long been in with four grouse and three ducks. No large game sighted. Yet some fresh tracks were seen by them, as well as our selves. Thus ended our holiday which was hapily spent, but think of our legs in the morning. This being our first days climb, and a running descent will thoroughly use up a professional.

Mon July 14th. We five who had been out yesterday string halted, but like the drunkards remedy, that of using the dogs hair for his bite. Our supplies were now pretty well distributed in camps Nos. 2. & 3. Returning to our trail which led through a level bottom for some two miles. Where wind falls and brush became impassable the river bed was to be used. Keeping to the shallow places and ripples in crossing by this method Camp No 4. was reached, of which the Lieut had decided to make a depot Camp. Just above us the stream again formed a Canyon. Steep & ragged hills confronted us, with high mountains upon all sides in the distance. It was necessary to spend some time at this camp in exploring and seeking passes.

Sgts Marsh and Yates again went hunting and exploring to the south, where they climbed all day, making little progress and sighting no game. The pack train came in early, pushing through Camp No 3 they took the river bed trail for No 4, and made things lively for a few moments. 3 animals lost their footing and were carried down by the current, lodging against and under some drift. Old dry bones, the packer, ever watchful over his pets, was soon among them wielding

---

[25] "They had expected Olympus and Constance to rise far above the other peaks, but no mountain was dominant. Although Fisher stated the two peaks were not located where depicted on the maps, it will be noted that Henderson in his report noted that the scene 'culminated in old Olympus far to the northwest.'" Wood, *Men, Mules and Mountains*, p. 405.

his jack knife to good effect, and the mules were soon free and extricated with out much loss, but some damage to our supplies. Camp 4 was made and we all returned to Camp 3 for the night, making preperations for the morrow. Danton was sent to the lake to bring a portion of our arsenal that we had left to keep dry until needed. Arrived in camp Messrs. Hungate and Sweeney of Walla Walla, Wash. Outing. Seeing they were portly gentlemen we knew they were good natured and were glad to welcome them. Although we did not own the ground, we found a wet place for them to sleep, and did other friendly acts for them.

Tues July 15th. Col Linsley, Prof Henderson, and Sergt Yates set out early to explore the S. side of the West branch. Mr. Bretherton, the bug man, and Barnes to the S.W. Lt O'Neil, Messrs. Hungate & Sweeney, Sgt Marsh and Fisher to the N. & West. While in the meantime the pack train was to continue operations. Mr. Bretherton and Barnes headed the South branch (known afterwards as Jumbos leap) and met Col Linsleys party. Reaching the summit at sun down they all camped together upon the saw toothed ridge, alt 5000 ft, with snow for water and barely enough room to lie down upon the sharp rocks. Our party had crossed the main stream. Swinging to the North West we formed a skirmish line expecting to catch the North fork with in two or three miles travel. Mr. Hungate being upon the right flank drifted too far to the right and we saw him no more until our return to camp. Mr Sweeney informed us that Mr H was perfectly at home any where, and would keep up his flesh on pine bark, so we did not worry about him. We reached the N. fork at noon and learned that it formed a deep canyon from its junction for 3 or 4 miles. Observing some drift logs had lodged, forming a bridge, we descended to them by swinging limbs and hard climbing to the depth of 100 feet, with falls above and below us. We found room enough to prepare lunch, after which we crossed over and made the ascent. How, I don't know. I only re member that our lives hung upon very small tendrils that we clung to, working from one small projection to another. Appearing impossible to pass this way with mules we continued west, ascending deer mountain. While it was not more than 2000 feet from here to its summit, its character was such that we were untill night-fall in making it. Brush was the ruling obstacle here and steep as well. How our heads jumped at every pulsation beneath the heavy growth, close air, and excessive heat. Mr Sweeney jumping from a life of ease into this of toil, became sadly fatigued. Also carrying blankets which we did not. No importunities would induce him to allow us to share his load. It was now roosting time but the Lieut did not wish to halt. Sergt Marsh, rather than

acknowledge that he was ready to knock under, threw him self into a siwash attitude, motioning for us to halt. Poor Mr Sweeney, as tired as he was, threw pack and hat, as he bounded through the brush. Perhaps he had heard deer. Anyway, it was so late when he returned that we were compelled to camp where we were, and we gave him credit for springing an old soldier trick upon us. There was no water here but plenty of snow and wood. What more could we ask? A few specimens of white pine and many of the famous Alaska Cedar grew here. The latter we were much surprised to meet, accounting for its presence probably through the migration of birds that had transplanted it far away from its Alaskan home. This valuable tree I can not pass by with out some remarks. In appearance it grows straight and generally free of knots & low branches. Leaf as in the Arborvitae, but drooping in the older trees, bearing a cluster of fruit the size of 38 Cal shot, splitting in four sections, containing small delicate seeds. Upon each section, exteriorly, projects a small horn-like spine. Bark thin and red as in the Manzanita in the young trees, turning white as it grows older, and protected by long scales as in the shell bark hickory, peeling easily when Sap is up, tough and as pliable as leather. Sap never more than half inch thick, and white, while the wood proper is of a rich yellow color, fine grained & hard, taking a high polish. The entire tree is rich in oil of not unpleasant odor and may prove a valuable agent upon the druggists shelf. Particles that had lain for perhaps an hundred years, while some what weather beaten, positively refused decay by natures process of earth to earth and dust to dust. In our opinion too much can not be said in its praise, excelling rose-wood or mahogany for beauty, repulsive to insects, for chests and wardrobes. As strong as oak, and as lasting as a motherinlaw, with bark as inflammable as pitch pine, and asgood as ropes for general utility occasions. We are told that it is quoted at $300 per M. and well it is worth it. Returning to our camp from which the snow had but recently disappeared, the earth was wet and we endured a poor nights rest. According to ap'cs [appearances?] the pack train had been busy freighting, and bringing up feed for the mules. One mule weary of adventure in the Olympics broke the 47th Article of War by desertion. Hughes begot him self afloat of another mule and set out to arrest it in its mad flight. By a member of the party he was described thusly. Sat well upon the weathers [withers]. Mule jumed [jumped] log, rider located well astern. Hat gone to Davy Jones' locker, hair stood high, as the foot soldier disappeared upon his long eared charger.

Weds July 16th. We continued to the West upon the back bone of deer mountain because we could not descend

385

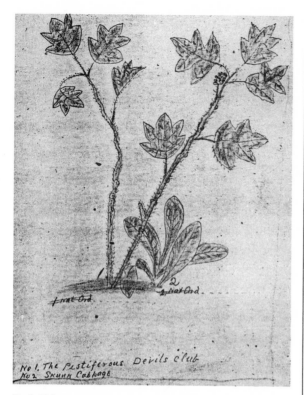

Devils Club

386

the deer in twain we set out for camp just as the Lieuts Huckle berry Watch struck 1. Oclock. Swinging down into the West branch of the Skokomish R opposite the Linsly party, taking notes of our own, we assembled two hours later in a large Elk yard upon the N. bank, fortunately where a fallen tree had bridged the stream, and in advance of the Linsley party. Not having a knap sack I was at a disadvantage, having to use one hand to steady the deers saddles. They kindly offered to relieve me of it, but having no gun to carry I declined. A hard looking country was this. ~~The devil upon one side and hell upon the other.~~ The stream formed a continuous canyon except where we crossed Nature had neglected to wall it in. Mounting the foot log we crossed and turned eastward. It was muddy from the start until you ascended the saw toothed ridge, and there sharp ridges & deep gulches fretted the mountains side. Again we descend to the mud & <u>devils</u> club. Our hands smarting from its poisonous sting, we thought language inadequate and ink not black enough to describe this wild chaos of vegetable growth and stagnant mud, outrivalling and taillngs of a country sorghum mill in a point of adhesiveness and repulsion. Travel or navigation as you might term it grew so difficult that we seperated in hopes of finding more favorable ground. Mr Sweeney and Sergt Marsh recrossed the stream upon a fallen tree. The Lieut up hill and I down the canyon. The dog Max which had heretofore beat time upon the Lieut heels with his chin, in his affection, now deserted his master, going from one to the other side as if in

either side. Col Linsleys party was traveling in the same direction upon a ridge some miles to the South. While our route was not plain sailing, theirs had the appearance of a cross cut saw, business side uppermost. During the day they headed the West fork and descended into its basin, skirting the banks in hopes of finding an Elk trail. Sgt Marsh and Mr Sweeney had gone forward in hopes of finding game. The Sergt had descended into a basin filled with snow and made him self a hero by bringing down a black tail buck of about 75# weight. Taking it between us we dragged it to the top and found Mr Sweeney who had followed the ridge untill it became so sharp he had climbed a tree in his efforts to get around it. We were Anchored. Leaving Mr Sweeney & Sgt Marsh to prepare lunch, Lieut ONeil & I dropped down after retracing our steps some distance. Hugging the cliff we succeeded in passing under the obstruction and ascended Brulns peak,[26] which over looked a branch of the Quinault R. Mt Ranier, Lake Cushman, and all to the east was visible, while fog hung over the N. & W. country, obstructing our view. After sketching and registering upon a blazed tree alt 4800 ft we descended and partook of a hearty meal. Cutting

Into the mud

---

[26] "Apparently the name was given to this peak eleven days later, when Linsley and Fisher killed a bear near the summit." Wood, *Men, Mules and Mountains*, p. 406.

quest of some one to lead him once more into Gods Country. The sun had now sunk until its light ceased to aid us in those stigean forests. We frequently heard but seldom saw each other. The old proverb Strength in unity had forsaken us, and it was every individual for him self. Great trunks of trees twice our heigth in diametor lie prone upon the earth, covered with slime and moss.

Grasping a bough for support to extricate our feet from the mire, we take a new direction. No use, those monarchs are ubiquitous. Occasionally we feel a sound footing. It is a buried log. Cautiously groping our way in the darkness, off we go and <u>into</u> <u>the</u> <u>mud</u>, receiving the 113th coat of boiler paint, reach out for support, and the ever ready devils club is there with its spines. The sound of rushing water to the front and below warns us of danger. This proves to be the S. branch. While only one and one half miles to Camp 4. it is equal to 20 good miles of open trail. With the S. branch in front and Main branch to our left, both in canyon, I set out up hill and meet the Lieut coming down. Upon examination we find the S. branch to be a continuous canyon 80 ft deep and 100 ft wide, at whose bottom the waters rush madly. No foot log to be found. We all-most despair of making camp to night, when we find a tree where the streams meet, growing up from below, and whose top branch lap out over the crest. Ascertaining that our packs will lodge safely (by dropping stones) we heave them into the dark abyss. With the dog between us, we descend from limb to limb, gaining the bottom. Here a treacherous foot log had been cut to span the stream which we crossed with much difficulty and ascended the opposite bank pretty much as we had came down. A short trail now led to a bark lean to that a Mr Wright, before mentioned, had formerly used for a hunting camp. This and the foot log having been cut proved that we had found the only point at which this stream could be crossed, and that by climbing down the tree. Faint and weak from hunger and fatigue, we continued, falling every few yds., until thoroughly exhausted. We asked for the camp sign~ but our own shot only echoed back. Where were the others? Then we knew not, but Mr Sweeney and Sergt Marsh were half a mile below us, the others [Linsley party] a mile above us, and Mr. Hungate far away in the mountains feasting upon dog or Whistling Marmots, which he called 30# rats.[27] We were now forced to camp. Kindling a fire it was now only 10 Oclock but had been dark with us for four hours. Although we had venison we were to [too] tired to cook it, and lay down with out blankets or blouse,

after eating a small cake of chocolate that we carried for such occasions as this. Wood was scarce with no axe to cut it, and we suffered for water rather than climb that canyon again.

Thurs July 17th. Up and moving before day light, hoping to make camp by breakfast time. The nature of my pack placing me at a great disadvantage and more dead than alive. The Lieut went in advance, intending to send me assistance if he made camp first. So weak & stiff from yesterdays struggles I had to rest frequently. So disgusted with log & brush climbing I attempted to reach the stream and take passage on a log or any means, in preference to this, but no use. I could not make the descent. Besides, a duck could not live upon those mad waters, and I must ascend again. I cut off the feet and some of the skin that I had until now tried to save, and had a good mind to heave the venison away. But shame, at the thought. If an Officer long used to high life could make a pack mule of himself so could I, and with renewed energy I proceeded again. At 8.15 A.M. I heard a human voice. It was the Kid whom the Lieut had sent out to meet me. It was only 400 yards to camp. Relieving me of my load, we were soon there. One long draught from the long necked treasure, a hearty meal, and I was soon with my blankets in the land of nod. Arising for dinner we found the entire party in camp who praised us for our courage and pluck, thankful for the juicy steaks. Mr Hungate had meandered off to the N. hunting with poor success, and made camp this morning. Sgt Marsh and Mr Sweeney had made camp soon after us, followed by the Linsley party. The Prof was elated over his success in botanizing, finding a strange pea, and the Alaska Cedar was added to his collection, among others. They had crossed the south branch by climbing down the tree and poor Jumbo, too large to handle, was left at its top <u>to</u> <u>howl</u> <u>in</u> <u>his</u> <u>loneliness</u>. With one wild leap he shot through the air and down into the mad waters. How and where he ascended the opposite side, no one knew, but the south branch was hence forth known as Jumbos leap, in honor of his daring skill as a mountaineer. It turned out that the Lieut & I had traveled over the most favorable ground, and Jumbo with his keen scent was a guide in leading them. Hence forward in stead of an ugly mans dog he was the pet and the hero of the camp. A gentleman was now introduced to us as Church the second & surgeon to our party. The reports of the different parties were all compiled, from which we gleaned the following facts. It was impossible to reach the head of the West branch with a pack train. No outlet to the south, which was not in our

387

---

[27] "Henderson's description implies that he, Linsley, and Yates were at least five airline miles distant at this time. This was probably correct, since the professor states they traveled about ten miles the next day (July 17) and did not reach Camp No. 4 until 9:00 P.M." Wood, *Men, Mules and Mountains*, p. 406.

direction, and as yet no pass had been discovered to the N. or N.W. No mineral had been found with the exception of Iron oxide (FeO) which was inaccessible and not in paying quantity. The timber growth was magnificent, especially up the West fork, where Alaska cedar grew in abundance between the altitudes of 2500 & 4000 feet. Skunk cabbage and stagger weed was plentiful along the streams, the latter very poisonous to animals which will eat it where feed is scarce, which was just our condition. Three lakelets were discovered upon a small table land of the saw toothed ridge by the Linsley party. The run away mule had also been captured by Hughes, the steeple chaser. The log book was now closed. During the evening Mr Price with 3 mules set out to Hoodsport after Mr Yocumb Our Photographer who was now expected, and we passed the evening in eating, and picking devil Club spines out of our flesh. Mr Sweeney attempted to count the abrasions upon his hands. Running it up to 35, he gave up in disgust, and when night came we were satisfied to turn in, dispensing with yarns & songs for one night.

Frid July 18th. Our tools by this time had suffered much among the moss covered stones and Barnes with the Kid was sent to the Miners camp to grind a portion of them. Mr. Church and the Doctor, Sgt Marsh, Danton & my Self were at the trail with the Col ahead blazing the route. Danton & I were again with the mattocks digging the toe path, while the others were removing the brush and logs. This stretch of trail led over two bluffs for a distance of two miles, descending to Jumbos leap. At noon time Mr Church mashed a finger and laid off. Our shoes and leggings were now well worn. It being one of the Lieut strong measures to keep his men well fed and strongly shod, Sgt Yates was sent around to learn our wants, which the Lieut set out to order from Ft Townsend, that being the most accessible point for Army supplies.[28] Game not having been plenty, extra bacon was also ordered, with other edibles, such as potatoes, on'ns & soup wrapped up in paper. When night came the route was blazed to Jumbos leap, and the wening [waning] hours were spent in various and useful pursuits. Fishing was not a success here. Mr. Brotherton having his bugs and birds to look after in addition to his duties as secretary and correspondant was always busy. The Prof in these damp woods had his hands full in drying plants. Some of us fond of the weed drying Klnnikinnick, which was held in preference to the original leaf.

Sat July 19th. Col Linsley, Sgts Marsh & Yates, Barns, Danton, the Kid and my self at work on trail which by noon we had finished to Jumbos leap, with the exception of the

mattock work. A bridge was now began, to cross Jumbos leap near its mouth. Tree after tree was fallen across it, until timber grew scare [scarce] near the chasm, and one log only had lodged. Notwithstanding they were from 2 to 5 ft through they had snapped in twain like reeds, to disappear in the canyon. Our only chance at this point now was to peel a log and skid it over with ropes, which we did not have sufficient in size. Noon time and the Prof appears with our lunch. After which we spent the evening in much hard labor, accomplishing little of importance. Returning to Camp found Mr Bretherton & Church gone south, upon another exploring expedition. Three prospectors passed through, bound for the divide.

Sun July 20th. Col Linsley, Prof Henderson, Sgts Yates & Marsh, Barns, Danton & Fisher at work on the trail which we completed by 1 Oclock to Jumbo's leap, while the Kid made the round trip to Lake Cushman for ropes and Augar per bridge. No ropes were to be had, and the bridge work was suspended for the present. Returning to camp and enjoying a late dinner. Sgt Yates went hunting, bagging 1 grouse. Dr Church to Camp No 2. fishing, with success. Work or no work, every one seemed restless in camp and embraced every spare moment to assist our efforts and make camp comfortable & the Cook was well employed. With our exercise and the bracing air we were always ready for mess call. Messrs Bretherton and Church now returned and we could guess all from their gaunt forms before they spoke. They had been in some hard country, disabling both guns by falling upon the stone. Sighting deer, Mr Bretherton had strained his arm trying to pull an Army gun off at the safety notch, which he was not accustomed to. The deer he said actually became tired of waiting for him and slowly walked away. Fishers black smith shop was opened and guns repaired.

Mon July 21st. Matters look serious to day. Jumbos leap a difficult matter to over come with our implements and appliances, and if we succeed in crossing it we do not expect to be able to proceed much farther in that direction. As we sum matters up, two gentleman outing approach camp and report poor success at hunting and fishing. They pass on and we observe that one has had the misfortune to loose an arm. We finally map out the days programme and close the book. Sgts Marsh, Yates & Fisher again explore up the N. fork while the remainder work at the bridge. We cross the main stream and travel over pretty much the same route taken before, to catch the N. fork, deploying with the understanding that we again meet upon the N. fork. Sgt Marsh bears too much to the

---

[28] "O'Neil apparently left on July 18 to overtake Price, who was on his way to Hoodsport." Wood, *Men, Mules and Mountains*, p. 406.

right, and follows up a side stream to its source, which is a small lake. Night runs him into camp with bacon only. We have the flour, sugar & Tea. Failing to meet the Sergt, Yates & I follow up the east bank, untill it is out of the question to make a trail farther. Here we cross over and examine a small branch coming from the west. It proves impassable and we swing to the west, ascending Deer mountain, in hopes of meeting Sergt Marsh at the spot where we camped previously. Arriving here at dark we go into camp on bread and tea. Lt ONeil returned this eve from Hoodsport with the news that Mr Yocumb could not join our party. A grind stone was now added to our implements of warfare against the forest. During our travels to day, we found a camp, made perhaps 3 years before, and upon a blazed tree was inscribed Balentine, Brodie, and McLaughlin, at Camp Comfort. Antlers and deer horns lay near a ripling brook which spoke of their success upon Deer mountain. Cut with an axe in large letters were M.W. and some writing now illegible, executed perhaps two years before. Bridge continues a failure.

Tues July 22nd. We decided to return to camp and Sergt Marsh was moved by the same spirit. We again descended into the West branch but at a different point in hopes of finding a better route, hard at its best. It was much better than the one we had formerly returned over, having kept upon the N. bank and at a greater distance from the river. Arriving near Camp No 4. we met Sergt Marsh who had just returned and on his way to Camp No 5 where they had removed to during our absence. Receiving this information we accompanied him, assisting with the mules, now upon the second trip that day, arriving at Camp No 5 in time for supper. This was one of our most miserable camps, situated as it was in a mud hole over looking Jumbos leap, but being the only place that we could get to water, which flowed from a stagnant spring, it must be endured. Although it was now dark the animals must return to the Depot Camp No 4. for feed. This had been a hard day for them, frequently falling upon the loose stones, one had cut an ugly wound upon the left hip, which was stitched and hurried away to Hoodsport by Danton before it became unable to travel. Messrs Hungate and Sweeney who had been out hunting since the 18th inst had returned killing two deer, and two black bear, bringing a heavy pack of the latter in with them. They were great lovers of natures beauties and enjoyed them selves very much in studying the formations and plant growth of these mountains. Having scarcely enough clothing left upon their per-

sons to dust a small fiddle and learning that there were ladies coming up the trail, they stampeded for home.

Wedns July 23rd. Lt ONeil, Col Linsley, Prof Henderson, Sgt Yates and Marsh, Barnes & Fisher again attack the bridge. We had now cut all of the available timber along Jumbos leap only to see it snap in two and disappear in the chasm. We had succeeded in falling one large fir that answered for a foot log and studied various plans to utilize it, but in vain. Disheartened with the out look I sought consolation in the quiet forest, and the pipe. Following up the stream a mile or so from its mouth I discovered a point where I could descend into the canyon by swinging boughs. Here was a water fall of some 50 feet, and above it the walls were lower, rising at an angle of 45 deg and of polished stone. We could bridge this, and build approaches inclining or in other words cordoroi the rocky walls, for our mules could now climb like Billy goats. Returning for Sgts Yates & Marsh, we inspected the point thoroughly and agreed to complete a bridge in two days if the remainder would abandon the first attempt and clear the trail to the bridge. The Lieut agreed and we set to work. It was an extra mile of hard trail to cut and a rough looking point to bridge. For once the right timber grew in the right place. Sgts Yates & Marsh being thorough axman, we soon had a number of trees fitted to gether, as if grown for the purpose. Returning to camp for lunch, which now had more the appearance of a parlor scene than an African jungle. The Banner Party of Tacoma, consisting of Judge Wickersham & Lady & Sister, Miss Ida Allan, Messrs Joyce and Palmer, whom were enroute from Lake Cushman to Port Angelos. The Lieut had kindly assisted them thus far with their luggage and gave one of the ladies who was indisposed a mule to ride. While there was no horn upon the aparejo there was all the room desirable. Every thing went well untill the mule waked up a nest of yellow jacks, and the lady descended from her pungi, preferring to travel upon her hob nailed slippers.[29] Our supplies being of the coarse substantial type I was some what embarrassed for the ladies as they sat down for lunch, but was soon relieved by seeing them manipulate the rusty implements as they lay in to the bear meat & beans with the grace of old soldiers. We heartily sympathized with the ladies and would have rejoiced to have seen them turn back from their undertaking, well knowing what lay before them. The Gentlemen of course were human, men of experience, who had been this far before upon Elk trails that we could not travel with mules, over foot logs

389

---

[29] "This metaphor was apparently meant to humorously compare the mule as a mode of transport with a pungy, a broad-beamed schooner used on Chesapeake Bay in the oyster and fish trade." Wood, *Men, Mules and Mountains*, p. 406.

and miry swales. It was as simple now to follow our trail as standing an egg upon end. Lunch over they crossed upon our foot log and went into camp. Danton now came in with the mail and immagine our surprise to learn through the columns of the press that we were out upon a pleasure trip, traveling Elk trails, living upon the fat of the land. We who had patched our clothes by the light of a pine knot in our eagerness to make every day a full one. Glancing down at the signature to learn who was so well informed, we found it to be fathered by the Buckley Banner party. We immediately transferred our sympathies to the masculine sex of their party who in their weakness had pricked us with the pen. However we passed it by, well knowing that our work would mark our course with brands more lasting than printers ink or serpents sting. Perhaps our feelings were wounded at this attempt to misinform the public, however, as our axes threw the chips we thought that

> The rich man hath the golden time
> The smart man hath the fame
> The Soldier hath no time at all
> But he'l get there all the same

We were getting near the haunts of game now, but in exploring we must seperate and continually keep halooing to each other, and make much noise in the brush, if we made any time. Consequently but few deer or bear were sighted, while their tracks were numerous. We had also come to thoroughly realize the nature of these mountains which was such that you must go over every foot of them to know them. All rules that held good in other lands failed. Here e.g. we look down upon a hill side whose slope is gentle, judging by the tree tops, whose surface is a solid sea of green, as continuous and unbroken as the calm Ocean's bosom. But descend and travel beneath its foliage, and we find that a storm at sea could not shake the waters in to more ragged uneveness than nature has left this same innocent looking hill side in one of her mad convulsions. The snow falls early here, and we must continue to use every exertion—utilize every spare moment to the best advantage. We must search every mound, crag and rivulet, ascend every peak and pinnacle of that rough but picturesque country, to surmount the many obstacles, and with muscles now like iron we must bend to our work. It needed no eloquent speeches nor stern commands to intoxicate our minds or stimulate our actions. We were volunteers for the mission which lay like the 15 puzzle to solve or aban-

don in bitter disappointment. We retired this night with light hearts, knowing that Jumbos awful leap, with its mighty cataracts and deafening roar, would trouble us but one day more. While it was wet and miserable in this Camp No 5. the wet soil fit us like so much feathers and we were not to be robbed of a nights sleep by any frivolous discomfitures. Side by side we lie peacefully dreaming All wrap in a coating of mud.

Thurs July 24th. Arising bright and early, hot coffee was taken to the Buckley Banner party who were also up and engaged in pistol practice. Thanking us, they did justice to the menu and departed, going up the N. fork of the Skokomish R. Hughes and Higgins came in with 3 mules loaded, joining Lt 0., Prof H., Sgts Yates & Marsh, Barns, Church, Kid, Danton and Fisher who were at work upon the trail. Dr Church having slipped a shoe set out for Hoodsport to be newly shod. The sun shone brightly upon the chloros sea above us as if to cheer us through where all was but recently so dark. Bright flashed the impliments and loud sang the end man Heave-ye-ho in measured tones, as stick after stick of bridge timber was launched to its home. The trail was now clear to the bridge and the log and brush crusaders pushed on down the descent.[30] Hughes, who had proven him self an adept at swinging the toe path, was left to assist Fisher in grading the bridge approach, which was complete at sun set. Although staunch and firm the bridge was not more than four feet wide and was like asking his long eared highness to cross the Niagara, over looking the falls as it were. Thus another day passed crowning our most difficult task with great success. Supper over we fit our forms into our mud canoes and voyaged to the lands of morpheus.

Frid July 25th. The time mill upon the month now registered one moon since we had left our homes with soft palms, and cheeks crimsoned with the glow of health, but how changed! Our health continued good, while hands were well horned and whiskers five a bag, which had so transformed our visages that we were strangers to our selves. Colored to vie with cheap sugar and as unkempt as the frazzled end of a gunny bag, I frequently thought of calling a convention to nominate the king of beauty but refrained since that honor was so equally distributed between all members of our party. One month had passed away and while only a short distance had been gained we were thankful to our maker and proud of the narrow opening that marked our course. Lt ONeil, Col Linsley, Prof Henderson, Mr Church, Sgts Yates and Marsh, Barnes, Danton, Kid and Fisher at work upon the trail. Descending we approached the river at the junction and S. of

390

---

[30] Transcriber's note: Several lines have been obliterated at this point and cannot be deciphered.

the N. and W. forks, making another V in the trail that cost us much time and labor, and covering but little distance in our true course. Here the streams were in ugly canyon and we followed up the narrow bench over looking the W fork until it run out, landing us at the waters edge. Having previously ascertained that it was useless to go farther up the W. fork, and no out let yet known in any other direction, it was decided to make this another depot camp and remove every thing up to it, while the scouts searched the country. Hughes and Higgins made one trip with three mules whom were now faring badly. It was a long trip to the lake for feed and we could not turn them out while seperated from the main pack train which was operating further east. We could only lariat them out where the devil Clubs were thickest and which they stripped it of its foliage in preference to other shrubs, hence we thought that the most poisonous snake might have

some important mission upon this earth, if science could but divulge its mysteries. At the noon hour lunch had been distributed to the different parties along the trail and Barns had in his search for water become estranged from his bearings. His cries were answered by the cook in Camp 5. below Jumbos leap. Being unable to sight, or learn each others wants, they indulged in many words spoken in the hoo-voo-ow-whow are you? language.

Moral
The cook burned his bread
Barns lost his dinner
And Jumbo disappeared into the jungle with much bacon.

Returning to camp found Messrs Bretherton and Church absent for some days to come. They had gone to learn some

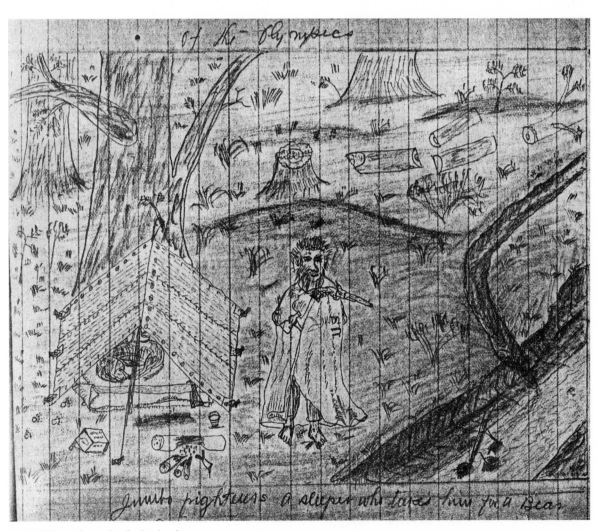

Jumbo frightens a sleeper who takes him for a bear

thing of that country between the lake and Union City, as well as to explore a branch tributary to the lower Skokomish R. While this branch had been hunted over by the settlers its true course had not been taken and the Lieut did not wish to omit it, nor make reports from any but positive information.

Sat July 26th. Danton was sent down this morning to guard Camp No 4. Sgts Marsh and Yates went hunting and exploring. Carrying their bedding up as far as Camp No 6., they directed their attention again to Deer mountain. Returning at night unsuccessful in finding an outlet, killing one grouse. The Lieut with the remaining party this day removed camp from No 5 to No 6. making three round trips with 3 animals.[31] Having sent for a . . . which arrived, it was set up . . . style, implements suspended, and a ford made across the stream for the animals and foot logs cut for the men.

Fishing unsuccessful at this camp also. The Col and my self had left camp early in the morning prospecting for a route. Crossing the West branch at Camp 6. we ascended Deer mountain which was very steep for 500 feet, after which its slopes became more gentle at this point, but well brushed. Finding that a trail could be made by ascending this mountain we returned to report the fact that they might proceed to work on the trail. There was no water to be had upon this mountain, but snow lie in great banks making a beautiful scene mingled with the heather that grew here, and now in blossom. Dr Church returned from Hoodsport this eve with two animals loaded with potatoes and onions. Dogs very noisy at night, probably bear prowling around camp.

Sun July 27th. While the party at Camp 6. completed the trail, ascending Deer mountain the Col and I again set out to hunt a point at which we could make the descent and continue the trail to the N.W. Ascending Deer mountain, blazing the route as we went, we followed its course west to Bruins Peak, arriving there at 3 P.M. A heavy rain now set in, stopping farther progress. Under the S.W. base of the peak grew 16 mountain hemlocks in a circular cluster making a natural camp, well sheltered from rain and storm. Here we pitched camp and while gathering wood the Col sighted a large black bear feeding to the S.W. some 150 yds away. Taking the carbine he disappeared in the brush to the left, while I descended a few yds toward bruin, who was busily engaged in regaling his appitite from the Elder, Huckleberry and mountain ash, which was now in blossom. The slope here to the W. & S.W. had been swept by a snow slide at some time, and brush grew thick in its track. I spent some moments of suspense in the rain awaiting the Cols fire. A dense fog now

swept by and closed every thing in from view. Five minutes more it passed over, disclosing bruin still at work among the flowers. "Bang" went a shot from the Col gun and bruin made one wild leap into the brush, appearing again in an opening with head pointed for my quarters. Another rift of clouds was coming over and I sent two shots from my revolver, as the Col fired his second, and all was dark again. Keep track of him, cried the Col. I could see neither, but seven hells seemed to be turned loose, and we in the suburbs of them all. Louder than the thunder sounded that bears squalls and he seemed to be rending heaven and earth with those huge paws for some moments, and all was quiet again. As the vapor lifted we took up his crimson trail and found him quite dead some 400 feet from where he was first shot. Although thin in flesh he would weigh good 300# and his hide was so tough that it was almost impossible to penetrate it with one of Sheffields best blades. One shot had passed through the back bone but had not unjointed the vertebra, while another had penetrated the stomach, which was the cause of his loud bawling. With a main artery severed, lung perforated, and spinal

Bruin was gathering the flowers

---

[31] Transcriber's note: These next three lines have been obliterated but are partially legible.

column punctured, he had lived 5 minutes and left a trail like the work of a derailed locomotive. It is all very fine, dear reader, to kill bear while entertaining company, or a round the camp fire, but when you meet him in the woods you are not the same man, nor is he the same bear that we have read about. Many tales have I read about knifing them and climbing trees to escape their fury. Being unaccustomed to the sight of man and very plentiful in these mountains, I had ample opper-tunity for studying their habits, from which I gleaned the following facts. They are not in the least afraid of man and can climb any tree with ease and speed from the size of a hoe handle to the California Giants, and as for locomotion while not a graceful mover they can get there just the same. As a pugillist and in use of their form I have defined him as an animal with out end that can with ease and freedom sit upon any portion of his body and gather berries with four feet at the same time, and with more speed than any Mongolian hop picker upon the Pacific Coast. Taking his hind quarters, liver and heart, we returned to our camp and made preperations for the night. The rain continued until midnight but we were well sheltered and dried our clothing out, making a very comfortable night of it in Bruins Camp, alt 4575 feet, with snow all around us.

Mon July 28th. Lt ONeil with Danton and three animals set out to Hoodsport for supplies, and the clothing he had ordered. Also taking in Messrs Hungate & Sweeneys baggage and a bear skin which the mules were indisposed to travel with. Those remaining in camp were to complete the trail and move camp upon the mountain which orders the Col and I were not aware of.[32] Having set out early to prospect a continuation over deer mountain. We ascended. We left our bear meat in bruins camp, and ascended Bruins Peak, where we had a pretty view of the surrounding country. The rising sun reflecting in the eastern sky threw a beautiful shade of orange and red behind Mt. Rainier,[33] while in front and beneath floated a sea of fog with fleecy clouds hanging above like curtains, forming one of the most charming views that I have ever witnessed. To the west and beneath us was one of the tributaries to the east branch of the Quinault R. making a gap in the earth more like a part in the cleavage than a natural water course, so dark and deep was its channel. The same fantastic cones and steeples that we had formerly looked upon met the eye at every turn. Tracing out the course of any one canyon or water course was impossible. Traveling upon Bruins Peak was much like a stair case, the one way up was the only

Ferry and raft Lake Cushman at Mr. Windhoffers

one down. We now knew that all efforts to go west were in vain. To the North appeared much the same from this point, as at this altitude it was one continuous bank of snow projecting over an ugly canyon, which we had set out to cross. Swinging to the east as we descended, we continued untill one Oclock before we arrived at the bottom, descending 2900 feet and going more than a mile eastward to get down by swing'g from bush to ledge. The Col at one time came near loosing his life. The heather that he was grasping gave way, and loosing his balance he made three quick jumps downward from ledge to ledge which were too narrow to regain his balance. He was precipitated to the snow below, clearing some 40 feet in the jumps and fall. Once on the snow he was sliding to his long home and I powerless to aid him, but his coolness saved him. Burying his light axe in the frozen snow, it answered for an anchor and arrested his descent. It was a miracle that he came out with only a strained back. We were now in the first west branch of the North fork whose water flowed beneath some 30 feet of snow extending the full length of the stream. Upon the snow were great boulders and trees, some with roots pointed

---

[32] Transcriber's note: The next few lines have been obliterated, but are legible.
[33] Transcriber's note: Tacoma had been written but lined out, and Rainier written above.

to the sky and tops down, the result of snow slides, the snow subsequently melting and setling away from the debris. Upon either side of the snow were narrow banks where the grass grew, mingled with butter cup, lillies, and violets. Selecting an open place we prepared lunch and enjoyed our smoke while viewing the walls of our prison. Precipitous as they were, vegetation had grown so thick that their rougness was hidden from our view. Mountain hemlock, fir and Sitka Cedar in those steep places had grown straight out from the walls some three feet, bending upward with a graceful curve, which enchances [enhances] their value for many articles of furniture and implements, having the required curve and parallel to the grain. This specie of mountain hemlock is also valuable for its timber in that it is a hard and close grained wood, very lasting and receiving a high polish. The humming birds here were more numerous than I had ever seen them. Lighting upon the bushes very near us we could admire their plumage at short range, as they sat viewing the strange visitors to their flowery kingdom. Blazing a tree we registered names, date and missions, with the act a custom that we all practiced, but I thought as I did so in this place that none but the imps would ever again come this way. We had now to travel to the west over an incline of snow to the head of the canyon, that we might ascend to the North. On our way up we discovered where five elk had lain the night preceding, but it was our misfortune to miss them. Bruins tracks were also numerous but we were not in quest of him now. It was late in the evening when we reached the summit opposite Bruins Peak which was not more than 1000 yds to the South. A low saddle here connected us with deer mountain but its slanting sides and sharp back did not present footing for a goat. To continue North was to descend into the branch of the Quinault about one and one half miles from its source, which we did by cutting foot steps in the snow, gaining the head where a pretty water fall leaped over the wall. We were completely shut in again. Here was a beautiful slope about one mile long with a water fall above and below and only one point to approach it from. Darkness drove us into camp and with bear liver, Bacon, onions and potatoes we were satisfied with our fare in this rough Country. This we christened Camp divide alt. 4200 feet.

Tues July 29th. The fog settled so densly that we could not see twenty yds. Remembering the exact direction we had came we traveled by compass and reached the base of Bruins peak by keeping under the west side of the saddle. Here we dropped in to the crevasse between the snow and rock. Work-

ing half way around in this manner, we emerged through a fracture in the cleavage and came out with in 50 yds from where we started from the day before. Calling at Bruins Camp for lunch, we skinned some bark from our friend, the Cedar. Making comfortable packs we set out for Camp 6 with a hind leg of bear each. We now knew every inch of the surrounding country and made better progress than the Lieut and had made over pretty much the same route. Making camp at sun down, imagine our surprise, expecting a good supper and blankets. Danton and Jumbo only were there to welcome us, and they were more hungry than we. Danton had just returned from Hoodsport with one mule loaded with sugar and onions. The mule had rolled down hill on the trail, dumping its load and knocking Danton in the stream. He had left the stores by the trail and came on with the mule. He had just arrived and knew nothing of camp having been moved. It was too late to do any thing but make a night of it. We rustled up enough for all hands to eat, made our lone mule comfortable, and turned in.

Weds July 30th. Danton took the trail at day light to recall them to Camp 6, as it was impossible to get over Deer Mountain with animals. They had found out their mistake in moving up and were only too glad to return and enjoy ready made water and the pleasures of Camp 6 again. The luggage was all brought down in two loads, and when our Cook appeared we thought they had captured a siwash. Compelled to melt snow for water with poor wood he was smoked untill he was sugar cured and carried the odor of buck skin. The three prospectors who passed through on the 19th returned to day and report it impassable to the West. They had been floundering in the Quinault below where the Col and I had doubled our trail. Prof Henderson had cut his wrist severely, disabling that arm for the present. All matters considered Danton and Dr Church were sent in with one mule, the former with a note to Hoodsport informing Lieut ONeil of our unhappy situation, while the Doctor was to return with the mule and sugar which we were in need of. Barns who was lonesome in Camp 5 returned with the mule and left the Doctor in charge of Camp 4.[34] Glad of an oppertunity to police up we proclaimed this a day in China and put out our wash. Jumbo lost a friend in the Professor by running through his specimens that were out to dry and made himself conspicuous by fighting, tearing down tents, and sampling the cooks work through out the day.

Thurs July 31st. All in camp laying off to day as noth-

---

[34] "Apparently Bairens returned the next morning to Camp No. 4 or No. 5, because Fisher states that when O'Neil arrived in Camp No. 6 on July 31, he was accompanied by Bairens, Dr. Church, Price, and Danton." Wood, *Men, Mules and Mountains*, p. 407.

ing can be done with profit until the Lieut returns. While the Cook was getting up an elegant bear stew the camp in general was mending shoes and clothing. Considering the country over which we had traveled, it was wonderful that we had any clothing left upon us, for the dogs had worn the hair away from their sides in crowding through the brush. Two gentleman loaded down with blankets and tin ware passed through camp today hunting and prospecting. We could generally guess how many days these parties would be out as two days struggling in the brush beyond where our trail ended usually satisfied them all. Huckle berries were ripe and plentiful at this camp which were quite a treat to us. Although we had an abundance of soap and water, we were soiled beyond the controll of detergents. Clothing all patched, we were a motley looking set. Mr. Bretherton, the bug catcher, was most rare of all, his curios, cast off leggings, boot tops and gunny bags mingled with our clothing in all of the grotesque fancies to be found upon a crazy quilt.[35] The party had about given up all hopes of proceeding farther with the mules and nursed the idea of sending the animals home, doing the packing our selves. We actually worked one full month upon the trail which was not exceeding 22 miles in length, and here we were like rats in a trap, seeing the sun only at noon time when it was straight up over us. Lt ONeil, Mr Price, Dr Church, Barns and Danton now entered camp with fresh supplies on the pack train from Hoodsport. Our shoes and leggings also. After receiving the reports and considering our condition he said we must and would get through some way and issued orders for all avilable men to draw rations for a week or more if necessary, and make preperations for an early start on the morrow to scout the country again. At this point most men would have gave in and pronounced these mountains impenetrable with mules, but not so with Lieut ONeil. The evening was spent in hob nailing new shoes and spiking them. Beans and bear stew, sang the Cook in his off hand manner of announcing supper. I was always a staunch friend of the Army bean, but now being in the advance of camp so much with out vegetables I could scarcely constrain my joy when I returned to camp and found beans in the dutch oven. Seldom enjoying the luxuries of camp and ready cooked victuals, I will inform you how we managed while out on a scout. In our knap sacks we each carried a small sack each, of flour, Salt, Sugar, tea, peice of bacon, an Army meat can and baking powder can, with an improvised wire bail. An Army meat can or Oysters as we call them are formed of two

oval shaped tins that fit securely together, closing like an oyster but detached. To one tin is a short handle used as a frying pan, or folding over forming a fastening when closed. Mixing our dough upon the flap of the knap sack, one tin is nearly half filled, closed and tossed into the fire. In ten minutes you have as nice a loaf as any charter Oak stove can turn out of the same material. Next the meat is fried or cooked with the lid on closing so tight that all juices and flavor is retained and you have a stew. Stirring some flour in the liquor or grease as the case may be you have gravy or artificial butter. While this is going on your cup of water suspended from a forked stick has boiled and tea drawn. Coffee boils over, wasting coffee and time. In twenty minutes after the fire is going your meal is ready, providing you have only bacon. For cooks we were all kitchen mechanics and those who were unacquainted with this little instrument of Uncle Sam's after a few times using pronounced it a camp fire indispensable. Each individual with his own supplies and equipments strapped upon his back could act independently of the others, in case of seperation. Having something on hand for the morning, we all retired happy.

Friday Aug 1st. As the sun climbed the eastern horizon, we were again climbing Deer mountain. Lieut ONeil and Hughes set out west to prospect thoroughly a descent into the Quinault branch. Dr Church and Danton also in the same direction taking a different route. They spent this day upon Deer Mountain doing some hard climbing and camped near where Sergt Marsh had killed the deer. Sgts Marsh, Yates & Fisher were to travel north. Crossing the stream at Camp 6 we ascended to the first bench, swinging to the east. Here we approached the N fork. Keeping well up from the steep banks of the Canyon, by careful work we discovered a route that could be made passable. Pushing on we discovered fresh Elk tracks and followed them perhaps two mile finding a route in that manner that we might never have otherwise discovered through the ugliest portion of the Canyon. Many mountain streams came in here and numerous springs making the earth soft and miry and undergrowth more rank. A narrow bottom bordered the stream upon one side or the other with a growth of large alders and a variety of brush and elk ferns beneath. For hours we battled against this, and a rain set in to make it worse. We had to ride them down with our weight and were some times compelled to use hatchets to get through at all. At noon time we approached a thicket of willow, alder and vine maple grown up like rip rap work.[36] In cutting our way through this we found marks of some one in advance of us. As

---

[35] "Although Fisher includes these comments about Bretherton in describing the situation on July 31, the naturalist had been away, exploring the South Fork, since July 25, and he did not reach Camp No. 6 until August 4." Wood, *Men, Mules and Mountains*, p. 407.

[36] "Vine maple was prevalent throughout the Olympics in the lower valleys and had caused the explorers no end of trouble in building the mule trail, as graphically described by Henderson [in 'Flora of the Olympics' in chapter 14]." Wood, *Men, Mules and Mountains*, pp. 407–408.

we proceeded a legging and a ladies glove was picked up with an occasional peice of light fabric hanging to the bushes. We had again struck the Banner parties trail. Taking lunch here at Camp Bacon we again set out. The marks of an abandoned Elk trail could occasionally be seen but it had not been traveled for some years and grown up with brush and obliterated excepting at an occasional spot of gravel formation. A great portion of the down timber here appeared as if lately fallen, no doubt accounted for by the unusual fall of snow last winter through out the west. Following the stream up some eight miles, its general direction was N. & S. Formerly under the impression that this was only a north branch, we now learned that it was the main stream. Here was three branches, one small one from the N.W., one from the N, with the main branch coming almost at right angles from the E by South. Drenched to the skin we began preperations for the night. A spot was cleared of the brush, bark peeled and a lean to built against a large log and supper prepared. This was another miserable night. The rain continued falling, with the brush and moss saturated. As fast as one side became dry the other became wet. Not belonging to any lodge of weak drinks we would in all probabilities have wet the inside also if—** let the imaginations flow. A cold wind followed the rush of the water, added to the wet and green wood, with the falling rain, a Kodak was all that was needed to illustrate mans contortions. While two were sleeping the third man was trying to roast them out into a wider circle to make room for his own tired frames. Even in our misery it was laughable to witness one in his sleep navigating with his head and heels to escape the scorching fire, and an hour later would find him wrapped around a stone or charred chunk like a star fish. We afterwards learned that the Lieuts party and the other two had met and were perhaps more uncomfortably situated upon a rocky prominence, awaiting some dry trees to burn down that promised to fall upon their chosen spot for slumber. Col Linsley having an inflamed eye was left in charge of camp with others, and the Proffessor unfortunately could remain away from his business no longer, was making preperations to leave us. It had also came to pass that Mr Yocumb who was to have been photographer to the party could not join us and other arrangements must be made to catch this territory upon card board.

Sat Aug 2nd. Lieut. ONeils party spent this day in work-

ing to the south of Bruins peak, finding a point where animals might probably be lowered down with ropes in case no other outlet could be found, and then it was a question of gaining the Quinault by this branch as its side streams are in narrow gulches with many cataracts. Hughes was out on his first scout in these mountains, and coming in contact with their roughness so abruptly, he expounded his opinion of their formation in many queer phrases, and traveled principally upon all fours. Nothing unusual occurred in the main camp to day. The mules were obtaining much needed rest and able to pick up some vegetation but grass as yet was not to be found except at the base of peaks on the S slope where no four footed beast could reach. Our party proceeded to the east and up the course of the main stream. Three mountain streams came in from the North, but we decided to follow the main lead to its source and return at a higher elevation and choose a route upon our return trip. Following this up, its water came down over stones and boulders at a fearful rate, falling some 5000 feet in the last mile, where it came from a north direction again. At an elevation of 4000 feet much snow remained in the Canyon, and Marsh Peak over looked a pass or point at which we could cross the Mt.[37] Gaining the pass which was 5000 ft alt we found the Banner parties 5th camp since leaving us, named respectively Camps ONeil, Linsly, Henderson, Bretherton & Church. Here we went into camp also. To the N and beneath us flowed a stream that proved to be the Ducquebusche R (see map). Marsh Peak was perhaps 1500 feet above us and clinging to its side was a glacier of solid ice apparently of many years formation judging by the layers that were visible upon the exposed face to the West. In looking about we found a bears foot, informing us that the Banner party had at least killed one. Screaming Marmots were making things hideous with their shrill cries. We killed one and tried it for supper. I should pronounce it equal to dog meat. A hankerchief belonging to one of the ladies was found here answering for a banner, but we left it undisturbed, to learn later that it was meant for the Lieut.[38] Much fresh Elk sign had been seen to day and one time we were very close to them, not knowing it untill our tearing through the brush alarmed them. Looking down into the Ducquebusche was a gentle slope covered with grass, but be-

---

[37] "Because of (man-made?) rock patterns in the heather, this pass is now commonly called 'The Great Stone Arrow.'" Wood, *Men, Mules and Mountains*, p. 408.

[38] "The Banner Party had named its last five camps for O'Neil, Linsley, Henderson, Bretherton, and Church, in that order. The men had now traced Wickersham's camps to the point where he had 'crossed the divide.' Here, according to Bretherton, the women 'had fulfilled their promise to Lieutenant O'Neil' by placing upon a 'pinnacle of snow' a flag 'bearing the figure 14, in honor of the Fourteenth infantry.' When O'Neil saw the banner a few days later, he did not have the heart to remove it but left it 'as a monument of the pluck and bravery of . . . the first ladies to cross the Olympic range. Concerning the women in the Banner Party, Bretherton wrote: 'To fully appreciate what these ladies have done a person must travel in this country. A member of the monkey tribe might enjoy himself here, but a woman hardly, for it is almost a constant climb, not only on the hillsides but on what small bottoms there are you are either wriggling over a log or squirming under one, not to mention devil clubs and vine maple.'" Wood, *Men, Mules and Mountains*, p. 408.

low that was a bench covered with snow and beyond was an abrupt drop of many feet. We estimated this <u>Camp</u> <u>Marsh</u> as being 15 miles from Camp 6. by the rivers course and seven miles from the head of the Ducquebusche as the crow flies. Night approaching and a heavy clouds settling about us we turned in after making all preperations for an early start in the morning. Having no protection this was a cold camp with much snow in sight. The Lieuts party had by this time worked down into the West branch of the Skokomish R, camping in good shelter. Nothing new had been found belonging to the Vegetable Kingdom excepting that grass grew more plentiful— principally wild red top, and heather was now found upon all of the high elevations, and some juniper. The formation was generaly the same porphory, slate and sand stone. Arising at mid night to replenish the fire found the clouds dispersed and the moon shining brightly. Consulting our memories it was the first time we had seen the moon since leaving salt water. Every thing appeared so beautiful toned down by its soft light that we spent an hour in gazing upon the surroundings before we again took to heather.[39]

Sun Aug 3rd. This promised to be an exceedingly bright day and we set out to the west keeping on top the mountain seperating the head waters of the Skokomish and Ducquebusche. To the east our view was entirely shut off by Marshs Peak which was not accessable from this side, its smoothness baffling all attempts to climb its sides. A portion of its S W side had fallen away, scattering fragments all over the mountain side, which was thoroughly prospected with out showing any signs of mineral save Iron Oxide which was only in small quantities. In the face of the mountain to our south was 3 large streaks of Iron stain but the float below did not warrant its value. Continuing our course to the west for a mile over a rough sand stone formation, a short ridge extended to the north over looking the country, which Sergt Marsh went out upon for a better look to the N. E. Sgt Yates and my self continued on to the west another mile. Ascending a bare point of rock, we had an excellent view. We were now at more than 5000 ft elevation and could distinguish Deer mountain with Bruins Peak at its westerm extremity, Olympus to the N.W., and hundreds of other tall peaks. Yet Olympus was easyly distinguished from others by its Monitor shaped top and numerous small pinnacles. Also carrying more snow than any of the others. This being an important point I proceeded to sketch the country but could scarcely do so for my eyes kept reverting to a beautiful basin that lay be-

Elk Basin

neath us and to the N.W. It was perhaps one mile across, perfectly clear of brush and timber, while immediately through its center ran a small stream. In fact the water ran from all directions to the center of this basin, where a small lake reflected the sun light. This lakelet being the head proper of one of the streams tributary to the Ducquebusche R. I had swept the entire country time and again in hopes of sighting game. Look, exclaimed Sgt Yates. Following his range I espied 3 or 4 small dark objects not larger than fleas down in the basin below. Taking the field glass my heart beat joyfully. 3 or 4 large Elk were crossing a small bank of snow and they were coming up the direction that we were located, but there was a drop of 2000 feet between us before the footing was at all to be thought of. One by one they emerged from the timber untill 60 or 70 were in sight. Watching through the glass, I could see the calves indulge in their morning play, dashing hither and tither, kicking up their little heels in ecstacies. This warm morning sun light after the rain, they had just finished grazing and were slowly moving toward us. Many a proud pair of antlers floated above the general level of the

---

[39] "The moon was then in the waning gibbous phase, having been full on July 31, two days earlier, and at the latitude of the Olympics it rose about 9:00 P.M." Wood, *Men, Mules and Mountains*, p. 409.

herd, and well might they move with out fear since no foe had ever disturbed them in their mountain retreat. For generations they had gamboled and sported in this pretty basin, coming with every spring time and the flowers, far away from the murderous foe. But now the tables were turned. Cain, as red handed as of old, with eyes sparkling and cat like tread, was advancing upon the unconscious herd. What sportsman could have feasted his eyes upon that lordly band with out hurling his concience [conscience] far into obscurity. For weeks we had toiled and wormed through the brush like serpents. Was it unnatural that we should go into ecstacies over a sight like this. They were full 4000 feet below us and to approach them we must drop back to the North east and discover some point of descent. Again leveling the glass I found Sergt Marsh working his way down from his difficult position. A map I must make. We decided that Sergt Yates would go down and meet Sergt Marsh, informing him of the game, and I would remain on top and telegraph with my hat the movements of the game. By the time they had gained safe footing my map was complete and the band had entered a gulch, lying down upon the snow. Telegraphing the fact by signal with my hat I reconsidered the situation. Suppose they became frightened and ran. There was only two outlets, one to the N.E. down the river, the other to the S.W. over a pass and into the Skokomish R. They would approach from the N E and I set out for the other. I knew I must run to get there in time. Setting out, I made the best time I could over the broken surface and snow. A strange moss met my eyes as I ran. Grasping moss, earth and all, I continued with knap sack pounding the breath out of me. An occasional grouse, bold now that I had no time, flew up in the scrubby growth that was thinly scattered over this ridge. Here & there a marmot gave a shrill scream and disappeared in his hole. A mile of this travel brought me to the pass which over looked one continuous slope, gentle in out line and carpeted with grass, gradually narrowing between two points at the bottom. If they came this route I would have a sight seldom occurring more than once in a life time, and at short range I was sure to drop one with my large revolver. Choosing my place of ambuscade I advanced a few yards to get another view of the valley or basin. It was indeed an eden spot in these wild mountains, and I could see up the gulch where lie the band. Again drawing my glass, I could see them as distinctly as though I

were among them. They were all gathered close and lying down upon the snow, save a few young cows that were standing as if on watch for the impending danger. I had forgotten the sergeants so interested was I in each pair of great horns as they swung them to and fro disturbed by the hemlock gnats. Presently the very heifer I was looking at plunged and dropped to her knees and the shots echoed in the far away hills. Jumping to their feet, they were distracted and knew not which way to move. Hearing numerous shots, I presumed that they could not get with in range and was trying pot luck at long range. The Elk at last became frightened and ran out through the N. E. out let, passing near where the two sergeants were concealed. At more than a mile distant I could not see any dead ones but observed one badly wounded trying to make the timber. Taking the direction I again set out at a run carrying my pack. This basin was carpeted with a velvety verdure, and I made good time untill I reached the opposite ascent. Gaining the scene of action Sgt Yates was cutting the throat of a huge cow. On I dashed after the wounded animal. Overtaking it, my feelings changed to pity. A large cow, round and plump, was scarcely able to drag its limbs after it, sick from its wound. Drawing, I fired three shots rapidly to end her suffering, and the lifeless form plunged down the hill side into the Ducquebusche basin. The excitement now over, I realized that I was thoroughly warmed up as well as fatigued with a two mile run. Returning to where the sport had first opened, I was surprised to find ten of those stately animals life less in this beautiful basin. The Sergeants claimed that there were so many of them, and so closely crowded together, that they could not see any drop, and were under the impression that they had erred in estimating the distance. Be that as it may, it was a sad spectacle for a true lover of sport to witness that death scene. A full grown Elk will weigh 800 to 1000 # and here was three large Bulls, three grown Cows and four yearling heiffers besides the wounded one that I had dispatched.[40]

There was work before us and we taken hold with a will. While the two Sergeants were removing the hides, I selected a good camp near at hand beneath some Sitka Cedar and joined them in the work. Blow flies, house flies and hemlock gnats were very numerous here and caused us much trouble through out the trip. The gnats and small flies were more aggrivating than mosquitoes with their bite. While it was

---

[40] "Fisher had good reason to doubt the sergeants, as both were expert riflemen. The previous year, Marsh had been a member of the Department Rifle Team and competed at Santa Cruz, California, in the Military Division of the Pacific contests. He had placed first in both the Department and Division events, winning two gold medals. In 1884, during a prior enlistment, Yates had been a member of a similar team at Creedmoor, Long Island, New York. O'Neil apparently shared Fisher's doubts: 'They could not restrain themselves and eight of those magnificent creatures fell in as many minutes.'" Wood, *Men, Mules and Mountains*, p. 409.

impossible to protect fresh meat by any method except a dense smoke. We dressed five pairs of saddles and suspended them over a smudge. I prepared lunch while they cut out all the tenderloins. I will not attempt to describe how we enjoyed that meal after a breakfast of dog meat and bacon.[41] It was decided that I would remain and cure the meat while they returned to Camp 6 and reported a passable route as far as the divide between the Skokomish and Ducquebusche. Taking about 75 of clear tenderloins they left me about 3 P.M. and crossed the beautiful basin, disappearing over the S.W. pass, alt 4050 ft. Erecting a smoke house from poles, sticks and large squares of green bark, I worked like a beaver untill bed time, jerking and hanging up meat. I had very little rations left me now, but with plenty of meat and of the finest quality, I could get along. Sgts Marsh & Yates made Camp Yates this day and went into camp, passing a more comfortable night than the first one at this camp. Lieut ONeil and party had passed through some hard country and returned to Camp 6. awaiting our return before taking any other steps. Proff Henderson could remain away from his duties at home no longer and was making preperations to return the day we left Camp 6. This day he set out accompanied as far as Hoodsport by Higgins and sufficient animals to carry in his equippage. In parting with the Proffessor we were loosing a jolly companion. A person of much experience in the mountains and a thorough good all round man was the Proff. Enjoying this life. Enthusiastic in his successful endeavors to promote the interests and science of his proffession. We were all sorry that he was called away before we reached the heart of these mountains. I was now nominated assistant weed puller and must acknowledge that I entered upon my duties with more zeal and pride than I had ever displayed in the post garden.

Aug 4th. Weather bright and a magnificent day. Sergts Marsh & Yates reached Camp 6. to day, and the inmates relished the fresh meat, especially such choice bits as these. 75# of Elk tender loin is not found in Jay Goulds pantry every day. Mr. Bretherton and Church arrived in Camp 6. to day, having completed their explorations of the lower Skokomish R. The nature of that portion was similar to what we had passed over. Lying near the sea level, there was perhaps a more shrubby growth of Salal causing travel more difficult. No large game was sighted during their travels, nor nothing new discovered. Yet Mr. Brotherton had made some important collections from the birds of the forest and had received

a Kodak which he had formerly ordered. To his work I am indebted for the greater number of the illustrations. Under the impression that the scenery would grow more beautiful as we penetrated further into the mountains, the country between here and the lake was not photographed to any extent. Those in camp well cared for we will return to the lone man at Camp Elk. With only a small hatchet to take the place of an axe, I had more than I could well attend to between cutting wood, gathering bark and fighting insects, all the while in the midst of a dense smoke. At 10 A.M. this morning Elk passed through the basin and loitered about all the day. There appears to be a great many bear about here, and loose stones frequently rattle down the mountain side. With so much fresh meat about I am expecting a visit from Bruin at any moment. I worked very hard to day, did not make lunch in my hurry to save the meat. By dark I had in the smoke house about 1000# of clear meat, cut and smoking. The remainder was so badly fly blown I concluded to let it go. About 3 P.M. while busily engaged with my work a peculiar loud noise attracted my attention. Not knowing what wild animals there were in these mountains, it was natural to suppose that a menagerie might appear here at any moment. Again & again I heard it, a shrill scream which I knew was not a marmot, followed by a terrific snort similar to that of a frightened horse. Loosening up my implements of war, I proceeded to investigate. It was all open ground toward the basin and open timber growing between me and the mountains above. I had about given up the task of finding the master of that queer noise and went to visit the elk that lie furthest down hill, and under a bench from Elk Camp. Upon looking over the bench I observed a cow and two calves. They were either snorting at the scent of blood or the dead animal, I could not decide which. They paid no attention to me. Now satisfied, I returned to my work, and they came with in 60 yds of camp, remaining quite a while, trotting about and snorting half in fright, and half in wonder at the strange scene before them. The young calves were the origin of the shrill noise, followed by a snort from the mother. I did not feel as if I ever wished to see another animal killed, and enjoyed their light graceful movements for several moments. They crossed the basin and grazed a short time before sunset, and lie down for the night. It was in this camp that I had a fine oppertunity for studying the habits of Elk and bear. The former did their feeding very early and late, lying upon the snow, generally where the sun could reach them during the middle of the

---

[41] "The reader should keep in mind that whenever the explorers refer to eating 'dog meat,' they are referring to marmot." Wood, *Men, Mules and Mountains*, p. 409.

day, as this was their only protection against the gnats and flies. I also noticed that quite a number of horse flies were left after the disappearance of this band of Elk. When night came I was too tired to sleep, and sat up late keeping up my smoke. I had no idea when I would hear from Camp 6. They might send me up some flour and sugar or they might leave me there untill they cut the trail out and moved camp up, which I rated as a ten days task at the least calculation.

Tues Aug 5th. Higgins returned to Camp No 6 having left the Proff enjoying himself among the suburbs of civilization again.

Rising early I was glad to see my meat was well coated and too dry to suffer from flies any farther. It was well covered in case of rain, as I had removed great squares of cedar bark forming a good water shed. After lunch I built slow fires and set out to continue explorations, leaving a note in camp stating that I would return in two days time, in case any one should come during my absence. They had left me a carbine and 5 cartridges but I left them in camp. The basin that I was in was drained by a branch running due N emptying in to the Ducquebusche R. By going down this branch was the

only outlet I could see for us to make a trail. Scanning the left bank closely with my glass I could see an elk trail leading from the bottom up the mountain side. Elk trails were numerous here and I set out to prospect the most favorable route. Descending with the stream I could find no trail as the grass grew almost waist high in the narrow bottom. This was indeed beautiful. Small open glades a profusion of grass and wild flowers. Where timber grew it was like parks, generaly clear of brush, with long narrow vistas here and there. The earth was inclined to be moist, and the many tracks every where with no general trail was indicative of a favorite feeding ground and the natural home of the Elk. I must go higher up to catch the trail that I had seen from afar, and proceeded to do so. After going up 300 feet I became entangled in a perfect jungle of Alaska cedar. After some hard struggling I gave up at this point and descended to the bottom again to hunt a more favorable point. Emerging from the jungle more by climbing and falling than by walking, pretty well warmed up and nervous from my exertion, I continued on down the stream. I noted an unusual amount of bear sign here and thought it time I was sighting some of his prowling family.

Bear jungle

400

Though very migratory, they usually fed among the young grass and roots along the lower streams in the morning, appearing higher up among the mountain huckle berry during the middle of the evening. Entering a small open of one acre in area I did not at first notice that I had company so near me, as I was looking up for an opening to ascend. Dropping my eyes, three bear reared up in the high grass and were intently considering my appearance. We were not more than 20 yds distant from each other and I could see the form of some animal in the grass which they had been eating from when I approached. Going closer I guessed that it was a portion of the elk that I had killed and seen roll down into this bottom. It was too late to back out now, but we wanted to very badly. I must go through where they were, or return to camp by the route I had come. I made a rush at them, making wild gesticulations with my hat & giving vent to several Commanche whoops. Two of them disappeared, one upon either side of me. The third one retreated about 10 feet and turned facing me. I never was much of a scrapper and came to a halt also. Bruin gave a snarl, showing his teeth, and came rushing for me. I drew knife and revolver and opened fire. The first shot had no effect but at the second the bear dropped to the earth. Arising immediately, he scampered off into the jungle. I reloaded and thought matters over. I was out hunting a mule trail and not bear. By profession and at heart I was a soldier and I was not going to take charge of the menagerie portion of this zoological garden.

He who fights, and runs away,
May live to fight another day.

I do not think the bear would have molested me except in defense of his food. He was then like a dog with a bone.

I was not loaded for bear and returned to camp and wrote down in my note book Bear Jungle. I passed the day here in sketching, rendering out tallow, and sewing up the rents in my clothing with Sinew. An abundance of snow was near at hand from which rippled a stream of water. I do not think I had ever enjoyed such water as we found in these mountains unless it was in the upper Cascades. While the temperature ranged between 80 & 90 deg Fahr during the day time, the nights were cool—more so under an open slope than upon top of the mountains—as the wind drew down during the night, and this proved a cold camp. I had just finished a brush shelter against the downward current and was admiring the beautiful sky in the west under a clear sun set, when I heard a far away but distinct whoop. If there was any one in these hills that could loosen the pegs in his shoes with a

Commanche yell, it was Sergt Marsh. Watching the S.W. pass with my glass I soon had the pleasure of beholding ten forms upon the opposite hill side. Catching sight of my smoke, they whooped in concert, much to my joy. It was music to hear human voices again. In due time they arrived in camp as follows. Lieut ONeil, Sgts Marsh & Yates, Mr Willlams, a resident of Union City (Outing), Dr Church, Barnes, Danton, Hughes, Higgins, and the Kid. They had set out early, coming over the 15 miles of mountain, brush, and windfalls. They had plenty of Sugar, flour, onions, and tobacco, and I was not long in making a boot jack of a fresh plug. Supper was began and a grand supper it was to be. Gathering up the oysters, I made the bread. Some prepared the tea and Barnes was chef deCuisine. A chopping bowl was improvised upon a fallen tree, and hamburg steak, Huckleberries, and other good things that tickle a hungry mans fancy. Heather, grass and flowers, two feet deep and as soft as feathers. Wood and water in abundance, and such water, too, sparkling like Champagne, frigid & clear. As the Rebel & Union man fought for freedom, a home and fire side, so might the red man fight for his freedom and forest home, thought I. During these reveries I often asked my self if I could give up companionship, surrender the excitement of city life, and deny my self social, and civil advancement. It was a hard question to answer. 401

But I love the rough Olympics
Where flowers grow in the snow,
Far out from civilization,
So free to come and go.

From one hand eating berries,
The other juicy steaks,
Upon a downy bed of heather
In the land where there are no snakes.

Where the Elk, bear, grouse and marmot
Eat bread crumbs from your hand,
Oh, carry me back to Olympus,
So beautifully wild and grand.

The boys were all tired to night and made preperations to retire early. None of them would hear of going through in one day, but Lieut ONeil is one among the best walkers I have ever traveled with. His manner of ordering men to do things was executed this day as was his usual custom. Follow me. This was the first night for some of them away from the trail and camp. Dividing up into squads of twos and threes, we kindled fires and sought our pillows. Hughes and I slept in front of the smoke house, and his clothing was well ventilated by popping hemlock. The Lieut and Sergt Marsh selected a higher alt, and complained of frost. Mr. Williams and the Doctor slept little and ate much, while the remainder buried themselves in the heather and snored under cover of the twinkling stars. Col Linsley, Mr Brotherton, Mr Price, Mr Church and Sgt Heffner were enjoying the comforts of Camp 6 and looking after the mules. All of the dog family were with us and it was a pleasure at one time in my life to see their appetites thoroughly gratified. In crossing Elk basin the entire party had passed near a single bear on the open ground, which did not verge from his course nor evince the least sign of fear.

Wedn's Aug 6th. After enjoying an elegant breakfast and gathering the ivory tusks from the Elk, nine of the party taking each 40# of the smoked meat, set out for Camp No 6. Lieut ONeil and my self, descending into the basin with them, turning to the N for the purpose of continuing our explorations. As we crossed the basin a young calf walked

leisurely along in front of us. The other calf and mother were no longer in sight. The two sergeants now thoroughly acquainted with the route to Camp No 6. made a forced march with their heavy packs, reaching camp at Sun down with the entire party. Dr Church suffered from cramps in his limbs and was frequently laid out upon the earth and severly chaffed to relax his contracted muscles. Mr Williams also unaccustomed to packing such loads grew weak, but bravely kept up with the party. The Lieut and I passed down into the branch flowing N and through Bear Jungle. Directly above the small opening where I had previously met the bear, and not more than thirty yards away, a large black bear was peering over a log at us, as he shuffled to and fro taking a great interest in the Lieuts bird dog Max, who was a thorough pointer and setter, and did not seem to notice the bear. We had a carbine with us but passed on, leaving Bruin in his mountain look out. Ascending the hill side to the left to an alt of 3500 feet we discovered scattering elk trails that soon led us to the large trail that I had seen from afar. Following it up, it led

Peering near a log at us

through open glades, vistas, meadows, and grassy plots, skirting the slope beneath the rocky and higher prominences. No prettyer sight ever charmed the eye of man than we beheld this morning. Indian pinks, Mountain Asphodel, Yellowed flowered moss, Violets, butter cups and Lillies decked the earth, with here and there banks of snow, a glittering back ground for the Spring time scenes. Patches of heather, hard hack and princess pine grew higher up as if struggling for supremacy. Dew drops were yet suspended from every leaf, bush, and twig, reflecting the sunlight like so many sparkling diamonds. Occasionally we could catch a glimpse of the rushing stream far beneath us, appearing as a silver thread winding through the forest. This was a well traveled Elk trail and passed over a more open timber country than we had found elsewhere. We had now came about four miles due N and the mountain ended abruptly over looking the stream, which we supposed to be the Docewallups. The trail descended into the basin which probably run N.E. judging by the general slope of the country. Any way, it was not in our direction for the mule trail, and we abandoned the trail and headed West by South, following the left bank over looking the stream. This soon became so precipitous that we were compelled to gain the summit. Facing the skye with a rough sand stone surface, it presented good footing, by swinging below an occasional pinnacle or saw toothed crest. We ascended five different peaks[42] during the evening, but owing to clouds or fog could never see more than five or six miles in any direction. Approaching another tributary of the Ducquebusche which formed a two third circle around a large round shaped mound like mountain, we attempted to cross it but were unsuccessful and headed South to gain its source. Belts of timber, meadows, and thickets were passed in succession, as varied in appearance as a fleeting panorama. A group of three lakes, where many marmots screamed from the rocks over looking, and we at last gain the head of this tributary. Its source was characteristic of all the streams in these mountains, heading in a basin shaped form perhaps 1000 yds across it and walled in upon all sides except the outlet by massive walls of rock. At first glance one would scout the[43] . . . at the mention of climbing them, but generally we could find winding fissures filled with snow. Up some of these we could usually climb, aided by the rough slate formation. Looking down in to the basin from our location

above, much water and snow was in sight, and we pitched camp where we were. A large band of elk were grazing below us some 500 yds but they were not disturbed. During the day we had found a strange member of the mushroom family. While of an edible specie it was infested with numerous white worms. Its appearance was similar to a well developed cauliflower of a rich cream color. A specimen was retained and we enjoyed a good nights rest after a hard days jaunt.

Thurs Aug 7th. Descending into the basin we examined the organic as well as the inorganic formation, with one addition to our herbarium. This was the only spot at which I found water cress in the mountain streams and these were very small, too insignificant for table use. It looked very much as if we were stuck here but by perseverance we gained the divide again between the two streams. A very pretty and tall cone over looked the country, and we unslung our packs and began its ascent. Upon this peak I collected two plants in flower that were entirely strange to me. Gaining the apex we commanded a fine view. To the S.E. and under neath us was Elk basin. Leveling the glass I could distinctly make out a deer in the lake, playfully splashing the water. Further on was the lone calf and higher up was bruin who, I have no doubt, added this calf to his greed before morning. We could trace the Ducquebusche quite a distance and also distinguish that one ridge of broken mounds and peaks only seperated it from another water course lying North of it but flowing parallel. General direction N.E. Later explorations proved these to be the Docewallups and Duckquebusche Rivers. Tracing the Ducquebusche to its source, an open country formed the divide between the East branch of the Quinault and main branch of the Ducquebusche. This open country appeared comparatively level, generally free of timber and brush, extending 8. or 10. miles N. &. S. and a mile or more in breadth, excepting the narrow places between the direct water sheds. The mountain upon which we now were extended to the S.W. some four miles from this point, and many small streams had grooved either side in many places, while only two large gullies masked the South slope showing any pass through the saw toothed crest upon top.[44]

It was our intention now to move camp, as rapidly as we could make trail, to a point near Camp Yates, and explore further. Mt Constance was keeping watch at 62 deg, Mt Baker at 45 deg and Mt. ~~Tacoma~~ Rainier at 103. Completing

403

---

[42] "The 'five different peaks' were various high points on the ridge running northeast from the mountain that overlooked Elk Basin from the north. A few years later this peak was named Mount Hopper by the settlers at Lake Cushman for Roland and Stanley Hopper, who homesteaded above the lake in the 1890's." Wood, *Men, Mules and Mountains*, p. 410.

[43] Transcriber's note: Apparently a word was inadvertently omitted, as there is no continuity with the beginning of Fisher's next page.

[44] "The 'range' included Mounts Hopper, Steel, and Duckabush. The two gaps were North Pass and the one leading into Elk Basin." Wood, *Men, Mules and Mountains*, p. 410.

our sketches we descended to our packs. While adjusting our paraphrenelia a deer was sighted descending below us. Thinking we might find a good route down into Elk basin, we allowed it to go undisturbed and followed its trail. While passing over a damp spot [something erased at this point] a strange wild onion was discovered. Silver skin and of peculiar shape, while blossom and odor was natural. The bulbs grew in clusters as in artichokes, firm and very rich in albumen. Sufficient was gathered for lunch and farther down very pretty specimens of Ranunculus Rhomboideus was collected. Upon reaching Elk Camp it was 3 P.M. We prepared lunch, made about 40 packs from the smoked meat and set out for Camp No 6. Instead of following the tracks of the other party over the pass and down into the Skokomish, we kept well up on the slope beneath the S Side of the crowning ridge, in order to get some idea of the surface and probabilities of a trail. A greater portion of the timber was dead at this alt (perhaps fire had spread) allowing the sun to kiss the earth which supported a thrifty growth of wild red top. Melting snow from above created a dampness in the soil which was burrowed as thoroughly as a prairie dog town. The inhabitants were to us a mystery. Marmots were bold and inhabited dry and rocky slopes, generally the track of a rock slide, while these animals choose wet places, frequently irrigating their holes by digging ditches. Their holes were much smaller than the Marmot and none of them were ever sighted. We called them mountain farmers from the fact that they gathered grass and herbs, distributing them in regular and even bunches upon logs & rocks to cure. This was all done at night and taken in when cured. Whether mountain beaver, wood rats or a specie of the marmot we were unable to decide accurately. The mountain lower down was a continuous fret work of gulches and ridges, but we were nearing the point where we must descend to catch the N or main branch of the stream. Selecting the most favorable looking ridge we descended into a forest of the heavyest timber that I know of in those mountains. The growth was principally fir here, and many trees were in sight measuring 10 & 12 feet in diam. The gathering twilight drove us into camp near a little brooklet. This was the warmest night of all. Sheltered by hill & forest, we slept with out replenishing the fire. Mr Price and Church went into Hoodsport with mules to bring out supplies and the remainder passed the day in resting up and making preperations for trail work.

Frid Aug 8th. We were not long in gaining the stream this morning, having almost made the descent yesterday eve. Passing through Camp Yates we registered the alt here, which was 1750. Pushing on we could follow the tracks of the preceding Party excepting where they had traveled upon logs. There we frequently lost them, and had to ride the brush anew. I realized that we had gone further from Camp 6 than I at first thought, and was eager for lunch when we reached Camp bacon. Lunch over we got along fairly until we entered the canyon under Deer Mountain. Here we lost their tracks and were unable to discover where they had passed. Fatigued and eager to make camp, we were inclined to leave the main stream too early, and were aggrivated by continually running into the cliff, and that meant to descend again. Thoroughly disgusted, we at last gave up short cuts and returned nearer the stream where the travel improved. Observing a blazed tree we discovered that those in camp had blazed the route for two miles. Following them up we made camp at 6.50 P.M., in time for supper, and found all in camp with the exception of Messrs Price and Church. I had now been away from the main camp 8. days with out removing my clothing and enjoyed a change and a night in the blankets.

Sat Aug 9th. Sgts Yates & Marsh, Barnes, Danton, Hughes, Higgins and the Kid at work on the trail. Carrying the meat upon our backs had warmed it up and in this shady camp it was inclined to grow soft again. Barnes was sent in to re-smoke it. Mr Price and Church arrived from Hoodsport with supplies and the mules were all driven across the stream to pick up what they could. They were yet in good flesh and standing the trip quite well under Mr Prices care. One or two had suffered slightly from the cinch ropes, but were not minus one half of their hide and hair as you generaly find animals upon an expedition of this magnitude. Our packer was a veteran at the business, and I dont doubt but that he had packed mules when Pikes Peak was a hole in the ground. Very slight form and 100# from being fat, I thought that his mule might loose him out of the saddle with out becoming the wiser. Yet those dry bones were linked together with sinew stronger than the cinch ropes them selves. He had pulled at the ropes so long I fancied that he slept with that grin of grim determination upon his face. If ever amused he laughed inwardly, giving no demonstrations of passions mingled with joy or care. I spent this day resting up and made a pair of Elk skin moccasins that I might have some thing in which to rest my feet while sleeping with out blankets. Sergt Marsh came in during the evening suffering from the cholic. Squibbs Mist did not relieve him, and he sought solace by fitting his form upon a log. The party made a fair showing upon the trail to day and we were all happy to know that we would soon leave Camp No 6 behind us.

Sun Aug 10. Lieut ONeil after issuing his wishes set out to Hoodsport, and Union City, to obtain a large sized camera. Sgts Marsh, Yates, Mr Church, Barnes, Danton, Hughes, Higgins, and the Kid, out at work on the trail, and the Doctor remained in camp until noon to carry lunch out to the working party and continue on up the N branch sketch'g the country, assisting Mr Bretherton in <u>making</u> a <u>map</u> of <u>the</u> <u>country</u>. The Col and I left Camp 6. early, to be gone four or five days in seeking a route N. and N.W. at the first passable point. Three parties also passed up the trail hunting. The Col had an attack of colic during the day. Having no medicine along with us for that complaint, He ate straw berry and blackberry leaves for lunch, which gave him relief. Not feeling well we went into camp at Camp Yates. The Doctor as usual fell over another precipice and bruised an arm severly, and carried a larger map of the country upon his ribs than he had made upon paper, and the Winchester had also suffered severely during the mishap. The trail to day was complete for a distance of three miles which placed them opposite the falls in the N fork and here a spot was cleared of brush upon which to establish Camp No 7.[45]

Mon Aug 11th. Sgts Marsh, Yates, Barnes, Hughes,

F. Church drawing maps

Danton and Mr Church pushed on with the trail cutting, and reached the alder thicket to day, while Mr Price, assisted by Higgins and the Kid, moved camp from No 6. to 7. Mr. Bretherton was now sorely tried with these moves, having so many collections that required careful handling. Sergt Heffner in the capacity of cook had cured like a pumpkin rhine and was proof against horse flies, rain or devil Clubs. He had made wry faces at the smoke untill his features had assumed a set caste like a well shaken before taken trade mark. Seventeen days had been spent before we could select a route to take us from Camp No 6., and that just after loosing a week at Jumbos leap. People might travel that trail now and wonder why we attempted any other route at the out set. We might also wonder why some other party had not preceded us years ago, blazing a trail for us. Returning to the Col & I whom we left in Camp Yates last night eating charcoal to keep away the colic, we were much improved this morning. It was clear in the river bottom this morning, with clouds hanging low upon the mountains. Beneath the clouds and umbrageous growth, we had much trouble in selecting the draw that appeared most favorable to the Lieut and I, while above the country and looking down at it. We might as well have been hooped up in a barrell, for all we could see from here, and it is an unprofitable pursuit to climb half of the day to learn where you had came from. Deciding to trust in fate, we followed the main stream up untill the first stream of note came in from the N after leaving Camp Yates. Keeping its course I ascended upon the W. bank of it while the Col choose the east side. We each had the good fortune to discover an elk trail leading up over a very steep incline but good footing for a zig zag toe path. At an elevation of 4000 feet the stream had narrowed to an innocent branch, flowing through a small meadow, closed in by a growth of alder. The trail upon which I had traveled now crossed over and joined the Col's by an easy ascent. Here it played out so to speak but we headed to the N.E. beneath the hemlock growth, and caught it again in crossing a small gulch. Though narrow there was fine grass growing in it. Gaining the east bank, a snow slide had spent its fury in a cedar jungle. Only that it was a narrow strip we would have dropped below again, but the slope being gentle we crossed it and gained quite a large meadow, in some places grown up with brush, in others open and giving nourishment to a rank growth of red top. A massive wall of rock some 100 feet high over looked this slope and seemed to be devoid of any opening or fracture. In looking up the incline,

405

---

[45] "The reader should not confuse this camp with the original Camp No. 7, established July 26 on Deer Mountain and abandoned two days later. The new camp was located on the North Branch, close by the tributary now known as Seven Stream. Apparently the 'falls' alluded to were the 'bridal veil' created by Madeline Creek where it plunges down the east canyon wall into the river." Wood, *Men, Mules and Mountains*, p. 411.

something white attracted our attention. A Bear skull, remarked the Colonel. I advanced to examine it, and was some moments before I defined it as a mushroom. For the benefit of my readers I give the notes that I wrote down then. A. Fungii Shapeed as a flat dutch Cabbage—diam 6 x 10 inches, weight about 8#, supported upon a short root stock $7\frac{1}{4}$ in in diam enclosing a single stone upon which it had grown. Splitting it transversely into four quarters, it was as firm as cheese & of a rich cream color, having no core or general centre, a thin skin resembling tanned buck skin covered the plant entire, peeling easily. I ate of it freely before and after cooking and found it to be the finest flavored and most firm of any fungus specimen that I ever met with. Samples retained dried perfect, with out loosing but little in shrinkage or changing color. I consider it a rare and important addition to that prominent family, and hope that it may be successfully hatched out. Taking a liberal amount of it along, we continued to the N.E. and soon beheld a narrow streak of light peeping through the stone wall. It was an easy pass, but grown up with mountain hemlocks, until it was almost hidden from view. Alt 4500 ft.[46] Thus far, so good. We could bring the animals here. Although it was noon we were too eager to see more of the country to stop for lunch. There was perhaps 10 acres of open ground sloping gently toward the Ducquebusche which we crossed and headed N.W. Here was another round shaped mound, much the same as the one alluded to lower down this stream. We could drop down into the Ducquebusche but we had now gone several miles out of our desired course, and were anxious to gain the level plateau seperating the Quinault and Ducquebusche. It was necessary to drop some and in doing so we found a camp of the Banner party, bearing date of July 29th 1890. The woods had caught fire and to all appearances of the camp they had passed a restless night. We made lunch here and spent the evening in climbing among some of the most ragged peaks that we had previously came in contact with. Here was where the innocent snow flake had left a trail more lasting than the waters course below it. Mountains of hard slate and quartz were alike worn down as smooth as a polished slab, while the uneven projections and loose boulders had been comminuted to dust and gravel, and lie heaped in pyramids like the tailings of some great stamp mill. Here was a tall bare peak that must be passed by some method. We drop beneath it and to the north, by keeping between the

wall and snow that had melted away from it. Gaining a fissure where some great shock had fractured and caused it to seperate, the Col ascended in this, while I choose the comb, which was rough and sharp on the N.W. angle. It was necessary to head back S.E. and gain the head of the stream which as usual formed in one of those basins peculiar to these mountains. We climbed in all directions for some hours. The Col had succeeded in finding a tunnel in the snow while I gained the uppermost point. It was a rounded comb of slate with scarcely enough surface for a bird to light upon. Going hand over hand, I swing my body to a part in the cleavage, working my self down like a glut to the snow, and joined the Col who accounted to me for his long silence by pointing to the hole from which he had emerged. We were now in a long steep gulch half filled with snow, and soft from facing the evening sun. It was growing late and we ran down the soft descent hoping to reach a good camp before dark. Gaining the stream near its head we crossed and found a beautiful camping ground which we called Camp Docewallups.[47] Camp No 6 was removed to No 7. to day, an unpleasant camp, surrounded by thick brush and upon very uneven and damp soil.

Tues Aug 12th. Mr Price, Higgins, and the Kid were now busily engaged with the mules in removing supplies from Camp No 6. to 7. while the remainder of the party were cutting through the rip rap alder thicket. Yellow jackets and hornets were becoming more numerous and it was a frequent occurrence to witness some unfortunate charge through the brush with arms flying about his head like the fans of a wind mill. The Col and I examined the stream for fish this morning but found none. The glaciers over looking the many tributaries were settling, and grinding the earth and stone, until the water was of a milky appearance from the sediment. Ascending to the N we discovered an elk trail making the ascent. Once out of the river bottom, fallen timber was not so plenty and while steep there was good footing. These elk trails while guiding you over the most favorable parts for travel could not be followed through out with pack mules. Consequently, we had to build new trails, avoiding mud, terraced walls and other obstructions that the Elk managed to pass over. We reached the level Plateau after a circuitous route and were at last able to deviate our course to the W. We were now well north upon this level, the general alt being about

---

[46] "Subsequently, the men referred to this low point on the divide between the Duckabush and Skokomish as 'North Pass.' They called the ridge itself the 'First Divide,' because it was the first one crossed by the expedition. The 'Grand' or 'Second Divide,' reached later, was the main watershed of the Olympics, rising between the heads of streams flowing east to Hood Canal and west to the Pacific." Wood, *Men, Mules and Mountains*, p. 410.

[47] "Why the men gave this name to the camp is puzzling. They were on the Duckabush, not the Dosewallips: but, uncertain as they were of the river's identity, they may have assumed it was the Dosewallips. The expedition's Camp No. 13 was later established at this point." Wood, *Men, Mules and Mountains*, p. 410.

Heart Peak

appeared more beautiful and grand. A lake of some 500 yds in width and length, having the form of a heart, lie directly under this lone peak and to the S.E. of it. Ascending the peak whose alt was 5100 ft. we commanded a view to be had from this peak only, isolated as it was. To the S.W. and probably 25 miles Lake Quinault flashed up like a heliograph in the sun light. Nearly due S. and at the Southern extremity of this plateau a majestic peak rose higher than any in this locality. Majestic in appearance and perfect in its outline, resembling the bell of liberty as we viewed it. In the distance a line of snow well representing a crack as illustrated in the grand old bell. About four miles to the N a glacier furnished the first water to form the east branch of the Quinault. This was known as Linsleys Glacier in honor of the Col who had first sighted it while exploring the west branch of the Skokomish.[48] The Quinaults general course between here and the lake of same name ran due S.W. While either of the slopes over looking this branch were of a precipitous nature, the northern slope for a distance of 10 miles was one continuous wall of Slate perpendicular, with glaciers crowning the crests, and in line like soldiers prepared for battle. Numerous streams of water leaped over this wall to the depth of 4000 feet, some striking its face while others were atomized to spray and vapor, plunging through the aerial ocean, out rivaling the beautiful Bridal Veil of the Columbia, or any other that we had ever witnessed. At the northern end of this plateau the great wall of stone curved to the south, forming a bulwark around the level below, and enclosing another good sized mountain lake which we gave the name Lake of the holy Cross from the fact that the trunk of a once large tree over looked it, and upon either side of it at right angles there extended a limb, forming a cross which was richly festooned with moss, and whose image was reflected from the calm clear water beneath.[49] To the N.E. the Canyons of the Docewallups and Ducquebusche could be traced to the Canal where they disappeared beneath the fog which was ever hovering over the sound, strait and ocean. For two hours we stood enjoying this marvelous arrangement of natures work, and the longer we gaze the more enchanting it grew.[50] Col

4000 ft. The first point of beauty was a mountain lake some 200 x 500 yds with an oval shaped Island or mound of stone directly in its center, from which mountain hemlock grew. Blazing a tree and registering we gave it the name of Marmot lake. Continuing to the N.W. over an open country with here and there a group of hemlocks thickly clustered, we ascended a small butte and beheld one lone peak reared up as if sentinel over this beautiful table land. Heather and mountain Huckle berry was the principal small growth, relieved in many places by wild red top which grew to a degree of perfection. While this plateau appeared level from a distance, once upon it you could see it only by sections, gaining our admiration with frequent out bursts of surprise, as each changable scene

---

[48] "This glacier (nameless on today's maps) occupies a cirque northwest of Anderson Glacier and directly south of the mountain's West Peak. The two glaciers are the source of the East Fork Quinault." Wood, *Men, Mules and Mountains*, p. 410.

[49] "About ten days prior to the arrival of Linsley and Fisher, the Banner Party discovered the 'pear-shaped lake'—upon which floated 'great cakes of ice covered with snow'—and called it Lake Darrell. Lieutenant O'Neil stated in his report that his expedition named it Lake Francis. Portus Baxter, a prominent Seattle newpaperman, referred to it in 1899 as the Maltese Cross Lake. An article by Bretherton, published in 1900, states the men called it Lake of the Cross. All these names were short lived, but the euphonious appellation Lake of the Holy Cross survives to this day in corrupted form, the tarn being labeled on today's maps as Lake LaCrosse." Wood, *Men, Mules and Mountains*, pp. 410–11.

[50] "Visitors in later days were also bewitched and today the upper canyon of the East Fork Quinault is known as the 'Enchanted Valley.'" Wood, *Men, Mules and Mountains*, p. 411.

407

As if some statesman before a camera

deviated as if dodging the squares of a chequerboard. There is no necessity for artists, tourists, and summer resort loving people, to visit Europe or even Alaska in search of season, scenery, or climate. Here are the four seasons at one glance in all the various stages. Slopes covered with snow and verdure. At one point the snow has just disappeared and we find venation in its infancy. A few yds lower down we find the same specimen in blossom and can trace it all down in twenty moments, finding the same plant with fruit matured in 50 yds of its infant neighbor. Our sketches complete, though loth to leave, we descended to our packs and prepared lunch. Passing by Hearts lake, which we named from its shape, we examined it for fish, but found none. We saw no reason why the brook trout would not multiply in any of these lakes, which were of unknown depth.[51] Throwing bright fragments of slate, we could trace their wavering decent [descent] for one minute, reflecting the sun light through the clear water. I have no doubt that this lake is 100 feet deep. Lying under the very walls of the lone peak. A small hemlock upon the crowning point bears the synonym of <u>Hearts Peak</u>. Upon the banks of Marmot Lake we had seen tracks made by the Banner party but they had ceased to bulletin their trail and had no doubt gave up reaching Port Angelos after once looking down into that ugly canyon of the Quinault which they must cross. These were the last tidings of them for many days. We now headed south to explore the entire level and seek for a more favorable route for the trail. Passing again by Marmot lake I made an excellent shot, sending a bullet from my revolver through a young dogs head at 50 paces. Continuing on to the South many beautiful scoop outs and basins. Mounds of pure quartz as white as the snow were passed in succession. Emerging from a small thicket of Rhododendrons and Mountain Ash, we espied a half grown bear directly in front of us and very close. Rising upon its other end, it lightly rested one paw upon a large stone, standing in an attitude <u>as if some statesman before a camera.</u> Sorry we were that we did not have a Kodak. We had dog enough for supper and left him undisturbed. Continuing over snow, earth, and heather, we ate a late hour in the evening cross'd a large scoop out beneath the great peak, which we will call Skookum for

Linsley was a person of much travel, having crossed the plains in early days, and had spent the principle part of his life since in locating and operating mines, which avocation has led him through and over the rugged parts of America, Mexico, and British Columbia. He remarked that though the mountains were not high they were the most precipitous, ragged and saw toothed that he had ever beheld, and that there were few ridges extending more than one or two miles with out breaking. Thus causing you to descend from an alt. of five and six thousand feet to that of 1500 to 2000 ft above sea level, and then your course

---

[51] "Fisher's statement clearly indicates the origin of the lake's name, but today the spelling is usually corrupted to Hart, possibly to distinguish the tarn from another Heart Lake (also heart-shaped), or perhaps because of a mistaken belief that a man named Hart had something to do with the nomenclature. Fisher may have caused the confusion by writing Hearts instead of Heart. (He did not insert apostrophes in his writing.) . . . The name has been spelled Hart only in recent years, however, and is a classic example (as is LaCrosse for Lake of the Holy Cross) of how, with passage of time, names often become distorted. O'Neil wrote in his official report: 'Two lakes at the head of the Ducquebusch received the names of Francis and John.' An expedition photograph indicates Lake Francis was Lake of the Holy Cross. Lake John must have been either Marmot or Heart Lake." Wood, *Men, Mules and Mountains*, p. 411.

the present,[52] meaning (Strong or great in Chinook). We had now left the level country behind us, having traveled over 10 miles of country very rapidly, and I will remark here that it is the only spot in the Olympic range where you can travel with ease and enjoy the sun shine all the while. The basin alluded to was drained by a short tributary of the Quinault, and just over a low ridge to the south lay another, similar in size and appearance, surrounded upon three sldes by a grassy slope circling like an amphittheare [amphitheater] to the centre, where lie a quantity of snow, and upon which seven bull elk were rest-

Viewing live elk at short range

ing. A narrow line of timber grew upon the crest of the surrounding hill where the projecting slate would admit, and just below timber line a faint trail coursed through the grass. By following this it would save descending and climbing the grade to the S.E. again. Dropping to with in 50 feet of the trail, we hallooed loudly in our attempts to frighten the elk. Knowing their habits, we were under the impression that they would come our way to leave the basin. They would not rise from the snow, and the Col fired a shot from his revolver. They sprang to their feet in an instant looking up as if expecting an avalanche from above. Lazily stretching their limbs, they came slowly to ward us, brousing upon the grass. Slowly they came up the narrow trail until with in 50 feet of us. We sat like statutes [statues] in plain view, gazing upon those seven proud monarchs of the forest. Three pairs of antlers were out of velvet, and three retained their pretty clothing, while the 7"enth had partially removed the velvet, which hung suspended about his ears. Although only one ridge seperated us from the Skokomish R we never thought of shooting, having a~reed to embrace this oppertunity of <u>viewing live elk</u> at <u>short range</u>, and feast our eyes upon their beauty. They scented us and snuffed the air, tossing their heads high in the air, and at last they detect us. Step by step with caution they approach us, inquisitive as to our character. Occasionally nipping the grass, unconscious of lurking danger, they drew up in line and studied us. We could see their eye leashes [lashes], and trace natures filligree work upon their antlers, so close were they. Gnats and flies reaped a harvest. I scarcely think we would have moved for a rattle-snake. For 5 moments we enjoyed this charm, gazing as if in a trance. The sun was setting in the western sky and we must move. Arising to our feet, they scampered away about 100 yds and continued feeding. They were so fat and round that we could detect the loose flesh shaking with their movements. Never again in civilized America do I expect to behold a scene like that.

---

52 "This peak, adjacent to O'Neil Pass at the head of the Duckabush, had been tentatively identified as Skookum by Linsley and Fisher on August 12, less than two weeks after Judge Wickersham named it Mount Susan for his wife, Deborah Susan Bell Wickersham. The names Susan, Skookum, and Arline were short-lived. Before the turn of the century common usage had established the name Mount Duckabush.

"O'Neil and Fisher both misspelled the girl's name—as Arlene and Irlene. However, the references to 'Mount Irlene' in Fisher's manuscript have been changed (apparently in W. G. Steel's handwriting) to 'Mount Steel,' despite the fact that name was given, at an early date, to another peak less than two miles distant. The two mountains are clearly distinguished—in both pictures and text—in the February, 1898 issue of *Recreation* magazine. The southwest peak is identified as Mount Duckabush, the northeast one as Mount Steel. . . . Portus Baxter, a newspaperman who visited the Olympics in 1899, also notes a distinction: 'The two mountains are connected by rough, snow-dotted peaks.' However, the men who wrote about the 1890 trip (O'Neil, Fisher, Bretherton, Henderson, Linsley, and F. J. Church) do not refer to two peaks, and they may have considered them to be one mountain.

"The name Mount Steel honors William G. Steel (1854–1934), who helped O'Neil organize the 1890 expedition. It is not clear, however, whether this name was given to the mountain during the exploration or after its conclusion, and at whose instance. The name does appear on Fisher's map of the Olympics published by Steel in 1891." Wood, *Men, Mules and Mountains*, pp. 414–15.

A Kingdom for a Kodak

Swinging to the left and around the basin landed us upon top of the ridge, at this place dividing the Skokomish and Quinault tributaries. This ridge was perfectly sharp upon top, but finding where a great stone had lost its balance and gone thundering down the mountain, we pitched camp in the excavation, large enough to keep us from rolling over board. We registered alt 5150 at Camp Quinhomish.[53] Bringing up a square of snow for water, we yet had some of the mushroom, and dog for supper. It was now pitch dark and we were not exactly sure of our location over the Skokomish R. Notwithstanding we were up pretty high, it was a calm night and we slept comfortable and warm.

Wedns Aug 13th. We were up early and enjoyed a beautiful sun rise and took our bearings. We were due west of the sharp bend in the N fork of the Skokomish and looking almost down at the location where Camp Yates was, but there was 2000 feet of a precipice beneath and east of us and we must go south to hunt a pass. Dropping back on the west slope to avoid the saw toothed ridge, we did not go far untill we discovered a narrow pass that would lead us down over terrace and bench for a thousand feet, and after that we must trust to fate. Stopping to take a last look at the land to the west, five deer were sighted making their way across the basin. Upon examining the pass where snow remained yet, we learned from fresh tracks that they had came through from the east. We were now very anxious to find a route to this pass for if we could once gain it, at least 18 miles of trail cutting would be saved, and that over a very rough country. A rock rabbit was jumped up and several shots fired from our revolvers, but Jack made his escape. We succeeded in finding a route for about 1000 feet down, but here we became hopelessly stuck. After once dropping from the crest a massive wall confronted us upon the N and was impassable at all points between Camp Quinhomish, and the pass some 7 miles N.E. leading into the Ducquebusche. We worked over the terraces through vine maple and brush, going south about three miles ere we reached the stream, spending the greatest portion of the day, and gave up getting out by this route with animals. We found Mr Church, Sergts Marsh, Yates, Barnes, Danton at work upon the trail, and Mr Bretherton, who had brought their lunch out. They informed us that the Pack train had removed camp from No 7. to 8. and 500 yds brought us

to it. A beautiful camp in the sun light upon a gravel bar, formed by a mountain stream that rushed through camp. We were now informed that the most of our elk meat had soured and made them all very sick which accounted for the Col being sick when we set out. The dogs again grew fat and lazy. The boys had done excellent work in getting this far and the country was more favorable from here to Camp Yates. Nothing new had as yet been discovered of importance. Some one had picked up a small showing of asbestos along the stream, but that territory had been too thoroughly explored to have passed much of it. I had added several new specimens to the herbarium which were strangers to me. The formation through-out had continued the same with the exception that quartz was more plentiful, but barren. The three Gentleman who had passed up a few days previously returned homeward to day and right glad to travel up on the trail again.[54] B. C., a raw boned cadaverous pack mule, came charging through camp with head and tail up, and came near stampeding the other mules. We presumed that he had met a bear while grazing above camp. Fishing became excellent in this stream again from Camp No 8 to Camp Yates, though none were seen or caught in the N fork below Camp No 8., which was something we could not account for. Grazing for the animals improved some from here, and they managed to hold up with what hay they got when upon the east end of the trail. For supper we had brook trout, Beans, and stew from Elk that had been saved by dipping in strong brine, and blankets for all to night.

Thurs Aug 14th. Lieut ONeil arrived in camp before breakfast having laid out half a mile below, where darkness had over taken him. Unable to keep the trail, there was nothing to do but pitch camp. He had carried a large 35X camera from Hoodsport and was accompanied by four gentlemen, out to see the country. They pronounced the Lieut a good traveler and were shaking yet from having witnessed the Lieut take a bath in the ice cold water before sun up, splashing in the cold water with an air of indifference as to temperature. Breakfast over, Mr Price and the Kid, with three mules set out to Hoodsport to bring up some bacon, which was running short. Mr Church, Sergts Marsh, Yates, Danton, and Barnes at work on the trail. The Col and Mr Bretherton compiling maps, while I arranged and dried my plants. Mr Bretherton carried lunch out on the trail at noon, and I as-

---

[53] "This name is a combination of Quinault and Skohomish, the latter being an archaic spelling of Skokomish." Wood, *Men, Mules and Mountains,* p. 411.

[54] "On August 10, Bretherton sent a dispatch to Union City, via Lieutenant O'Neil, for the *Tacoma Ledger,* in which he wrote: 'Several parties of miners, hunters and pleasure seekers are already taking advantage of the O'Neil trail, and pass our camp daily, pushing on ahead and generally returning in a day or two, and all telling the same tale, namely, that they have been all over the mountains, though a little questioning always goes to show that they have only been in the next canyon.'" Wood, *Men, Mules and Mountains,* p. 411.

sisted during the eve with the mattock work. Much work was done near the river, and continually crossing, the men were wet through-out the day. After supper different parties went fishing and the catch numbered thirty good sized brook trout. The trail was complete up to the sharp bend in the stream, and at the junction of a west & north tributary. About 500 ydes west and down stream from Camp Yates was located Camp No 9. The Lieut, after receiving our reports and considering the distance that could be saved by gaining the level plateau at the south extremity, decided to explore the country thoroughly before attempting the N.E. route crossing the Ducquebusche Canyon. While almost sure that we could not gain this point, we were all very willing to settle it permanently by another exploration. [Thur, Aug 14th All up early and breakfast over.[55]] The Lieut. had arranged his tripod, and photographed Camp No 8., men, mules, dogs, and all. Sgts Marsh set out to explore for a pass to the N.W., taking his gun and the bear dog Tige. Sgts Yates, Mr Church, and my self soon followed upon the same errand. Passing through Camp 9 Sgt Marsh had left two grouse, and began the ascent to the left of the west tributary, while we began the ascent upon the right and N side. The best that we could do was to assist our selves by grasping the bushes. We continued upwards to an elevation of 3000 feet and became hopelessly stuck under a cliff, and were trying to assemble, when Sgt Marsh opened fire, with Tige barking loudly, to the S.W. and above us. We could not see out of the growth that surrounded us, but afterwards learned that he had wounded a bear, which made good his escape, and Tige had fallen into a hole and was barking for aid. We dropped into the water course, which was in a deep and rocky gulch. Crossing to the south we explored until the middle of the evening, and returned to Camp 9. and found a late dinner awaiting us. Those left in Camp 8 during the day made two trips to Camp No 9. with 7 animals, bringing equippage sufficient to make our selves quite comfortable. After dinner Sergt Yates went fishing. Col blazing a route. The Dr gathering berries for supper, and the remainder of us laying off. It was useless to attempt an ascent with the trail [train? i.e., pack train], and the N.E. route was the only course left us. A bear was seen in the trail to day by Sergt Heffner and Danton, but as we preferred bacon to bear they did not disturb it. After a supper of grouse, trout and stewed berries, we busied our selves in the elk ferns, and enjoyed a good sleep.

Frid Aug 15th. All hands out on the trail. There was much work to be done for one mile until we could connect with one of the trails leading up through north pass and into the Ducquebusche. While the Col and I had passed over easly enough, it was not so with animals. The trail was very crooked, and winding. One steep bank was to be dug down, and many large logs to cut. Although every man had worked hard, we had not gained the stream up which the trails led.

Sat Aug 16th. All hands out at the trail and connected with the elk trail by noon. The trail which I had followed up the left bank was selected as the best route. Sergts Marsh, Yates, and myself pushed on cutting the logs and brush, passed through the first meadow and gained the gulch where the grass grew. Selecting a place for Camp No 10. we returned and found the remainder well along with a zig zag toe path that had to be dug for about 400 yds in the steepest place. The party of Citizens who had gone through Camp No 8. returned home this evening with no success in sighting game and disgusted with brush and log climbing. Mr Price and the Kid returned with two hundred # potatoes, one hundred # sugar and 60# bacon. They never had more than 50 or 75# of bacon at a time in Hoodsport or Union City and we were compelled to make trips in more frequent. Jumbo had for some time considered him self an addition to the pack train and frequently took a lay off at Hoodsport, coming up to camp alone when it suited his convenience. He had remained behind upon this trip and it was the last time he was seen for many days. The Lieut now called camp together, and after the identical pipe was well under way, He seated him self upon the central blanket and talked as follows. We had surmounted all obstacles so far and there was no doubt now but that we would reach Hearts peak with the animals and all supplies, and once there we were in the centre of the mountains, and if we could proceed no further, animals could be sent in and we could take our grease and flour upon our backs and strike out from the hub in different directions and finish the explorations. We were all complimented for our attention and interest displayed in the work. We had found Mt Olympus and Constance to be all of 30 miles distant from each other instead of 10 as the existing maps had illustrated. We were unable to determine what streams the Docewallups and Ducquebusche were and knew the Quinault by the lake only, as the Col & I had seen it. To morrow morning, said he, Col Linsley will take charge of Camp, with Sgt Heffner, Mr Price, Barnes, Hughes & Higgins. Sgt Marsh had leave to visit Hoodsport, and Union City, for a day or so, and would return and join the Cols party, who would during our absence cut the trail and move all equippage and supplies to

411

---

[55] Transcriber's note: This sentence was eradicated.

Hearts Peak, or in that neighborhood as far as they could. Sgt Yates and Mr Bretherton would gain the two streams flowing N.E. and trace them to their mouths, and explore the country in that direction, and upon gaining the Sound or Canal, reach Hoodsport and rejoin the Camp, which would be in the vicinity of Hearts peak. Mr Church and Dr Church were to return to Jumbos leap and cross the mountains finding the head of the Wishka and trace its course,[56] as well as explore the country in that direction. Upon gaining salt water on the west they were to rejoin the main Camp via Montesano, Kamilchee, and Union City. Lieut ONeil himself would take Danton and Fisher and trace the Quinault, perhaps the Humptulips, and explore the country in that direction. We were all to draw as much supplies as we deemed fit, and be sure and take enough, said he. Each party retired and slept their last night under blankets for almost a moon.

Sun Aug 17th. One after another the parties left camp, leaving the Col and his party making preperations to move to Camp No 10. to day. The Mr Churches carried light rations for 20 days, a Winchester, and small axe. Mr Bretherton & Sergt Yates carried 20 days rations, a shot gun, carbine, and a hatchet each.[57] We having the large camera to carry decided to risk the trip upon 10. days rations, and trust in being able to renew our supplies at Lake Quinault. Our limited supplies of victuals and necessary accoutrements now amounted to 40# @ and we could not carry any bedding, and our party would not carry a gun, save the large revolver that I carried. The two men of the meeting house gender in compliance with instructions set out for Jumbos Leap. I never met them again to learn the particulars of this trip and can only give the extracts taken from their report, with additions to the map, formation & etc. They succeeded in finding the Wishkah R. and some very rough country South of Jumbos leap. After once gaining the Wishkah, the country sloped to the Pacific Coast in gentle modulations, with a more stunted growth of vegetation. Larch, Balm of Gilead, with Cottonwood along the streams, were an addition to the timber growth. While the formation was much the same as what we had passed over, slate predominating with porphory varying

in color from bright red to chocolate and occasionally green. They had lost their bearings and worn their clothing and shoes to shreds, and had no doubt experienced a rough trip, pushing through salal and crab apple, indigenous to the Coast bottoms. They were both large men with hearty appetites, and of some five and twenty summers. Fred Church was inured to hard ships, while the Doctor was cutting his eye teeth as a mountaineer, added to a tinge of carelessness, very frequently placed him in embarrassing predicaments. They were unsuccessful in finding game, which with one article negligently left behind to day, and another to morrow. We were not surprised to learn that provisions had advanced in market value as they had reached civilization, and reported our approach. Returning to Mr. Bretherton and Sergt Yates, we will follow them up during their travels. They were men who had slept many nights in the wilds of other lands, which was plainly evident upon short acquaintance, seeing how natural the moss took to them. There was no danger nor fear of accident from this quarter, unless they mistaken each other for some rare curio, as either of them in their Davy Crockett costumes might have passed for the missing link. They followed the trail up, passing through the location of Camp No 10., continuing on through the N pass. They perhaps carried more in their packs than the others. Mr Bretherton had his Kodak and instruments pertaining to taxidermy, and no doubt thought of home and fire side before night. They passed down the slope and discovered the Banner Camp as we had. Instead of keeping to the west over the rough country that the Col and I had passed over, they dropped down into the Ducquebusche basin and camped upon a low ridge near where Camp 12. was afterwards established, at camp B No 1.

Monday Aug 18th.[58] Continuing the descent they gained the Ducquebusche R., killing some grouse as they went, and preparing lunch at a log jam in the stream. Heading west up the stream they by accident came upon Camp Docewallups where the Col and I had camped. Camp No 13 was afterwards pitched at this point. Remembering our description and direction of the Elk trail that led up to the level plateau, they had no trouble in gaining it. Passing Lakes Marmot and

[56] "This name is spelled several ways: Hwish-kahl, Whiskahl, Whiskan, Wishka, Wishkah, and Wishkal. The Indians had no written language, and the various spellings are attempts to anglicize the name, which means 'stinking water.' Note also the varied spelling of other rivers: Wonoyche, Winooche, Wynooche, Wynoochee, and Wynootche; Humptolips, Humptulip, Humptulips." Wood, *Men, Mules and Mountains*, pp. 411–12.

[57] Transcriber's note: Several words are erased here.

[58] "Fisher and F. J. Church state that the various exploring parties left Camp No. 9 on August 17, but Bretherton indicates that he and Yates began their journey on August 18. Apparently Fisher and Church were correct. With reference to the Duckabush-Dosewallips trip, Fisher combines in the second day the events that Bretherton says occurred on the second and third days. Thereafter, Fisher has each day's events occurring two days earlier than Bretherton does. Although Fisher's account was second-hand (except with regard to the starting date), he apparently would have had the various dates correct had he not made the mistake of combining two days in one. Thus, both men appear to be in error by one day, the correct date being the one between. This view is strengthened by the schedule of the steamer Josephine which traveled between Seattle and Union City." Wood, *Men, Mules and Mountains*, p. 412.

Holy Cross, they ascended the divide seperating the Quinault and Ducquebusche Rivers, but were unable to gain the Docewallups owing to the precipitous nature of the mountains at this point. Returning to a point S.E. of Lake of the Holy Cross where Camp No 14. was afterwards established, they sighted a band of Elk numbering in the neighborhood of 90. Killing one they pitched camp and spent the day and night in curing what they could carry with them.

Tues Aug 19th. Finding they could not get any further N at this point, they headed N.E. making another ascent which landed them upon a spur between the plateau and Ducquebusche R. Dropping down to the east they discovered a mountain Lake which they named Indigo Lake from its color, walled in as it were and excluded from the light. Here they were again baffled in their attempts to travel N and gain the Docewallups. By a circuitous route they returned to where they had first struck the Ducquebusche and camped. Mr Bretherton had one bad fall during the day, bruising him self badly and damaged his shot gun. The country about here was very precipitous. The timber growth and abundance of brush was here as elsewhere. While they could have followed the river bottom out, it was their wish to gain the ridge seperating the Ducquebusche and Docewallups and if possible trace the two streams out at the same time.

Wednes Aug 20th. This morning they concluded to follow the stream down some distance and look for a more favorable ascent to the N. Crossing the stream at Camp 12. they followed down upon the N side untill noon when a hard rain set in. Here they halted and prepared lunch. Wet to the skin, and cold, they were more miserable at ease than while traveling. Rain continued falling and they set out, making poor headway, but reached a good bottom late in the evening, and went into camp near the stream. It threatened to be a bad night and a bark lean-to was erected and a fair nights rest enjoyed, though it rained all night and made one feel miserable in these dark and damp woods. Moss, as in every portion of these forests, had clothed trees, logs, stone & earth with a covering one and two feet deep, and from the boughs it hung suspended like streamers, of many feet in length.

Thurs Aug 21st. following down stream, frequently wading as the stream curved from one side of the bottom to the other, they traveled until 10 Oclock A.M. The bottom now ran out, the stream formed a canyon, and they began the ascent to the N. By four in the evening they were at the summit of the ridge. Leaving their packs they ascended the peak and com-

manded a fair view of the country to the east, fortunately too as this was a clear day at the right time for them. Descending to their packs and prospecting for a camp, they discovered signs of the Banner party having passed, which was the first learned of them since leaving the level plateau. Pitching camp here where all was open to the east and expecting clear weather, this was blazed and registered as Camp Sunrise.

Frid Aug 22nd. This morning contrary to their expectations a dense fog floated over the entire country. However, they attempted to gain the Docewallups which lay N and beneath them, but got stuck by the abrupt and precipitous walls of the Canyon. Working back to the crest, they again made the N bank of the Ducquebusche R. While upon top of the ridge and in the dense fogg they saw three white tail deer and killed one. Continuing east they made some distance in the fog but could not see much of the surrounding country. Approaching a basin they camped for the night with the vapor hanging dense, and saturating earth and growth more thoroughly than rain.

Sat Aug 23rd. They ascended to the crest of the ridge seperating the two rivers, traveling east until 11 A.M. when eight white tail deer were sighted. Successful in bringing down a fawn, they carried it along with skin complete, as Mr Bretherton wished to retain it for a specimen. The fog remained with them and made traveling more difficult and uncertain. During the evening they attempted to descend into the Ducquebusche and failed. They now returned to the Docewallups and were successful in reaching the stream, but camped some distance up the mountain side. This had been a hard day, carrying the extra weight. Mr Bretherton worked untill 11 P.M. fleshing and preparing the fawn skin and Sergt Yates, economical with his tobacco, was drying Kinnikinnick.

Sun Aug 24th. Dropping to the stream they forded it and followed down upon the N side until 11 A.M. when they fell in company with a Mr Olmstead, who was on his way to the Sound country. According to his statement he had been over on the head waters of the Elwha, trying to reach Mt Olympus, but had failed and was returning. He was under the impression that there was a mountain of Asbestos in the vicinity of Olympus, but I did not learn from what source he had gained this information. At any rate they described him as a man who had passed many days in the mountains, judging from his appearance. He carried bedding and supplies in abundance and was in general more thoroughly equipped for camping and prospecting than any they had met in these mountains.[59] As unfortunate as our party, he had seen no

413

59 "Olmstead was one of five prospectors who, in the summer of 1890, went up the Dosewallips and over the divide to the Elwha, then followed down the Press Expedition trail. This may have been the first party to cross Hayden Pass." Wood, *Men, Mules and Mountains*, p. 412. Their account is found in the July 16, 1890, edition of the *Seattle Press*.

mineral indications of a prominent character. The country was now less precipitous than it had been, but owing to the rain and clouds, they could not see for any distance. The general character of these two streams were similiar to the Skokomish, receiving the water from the mountain tributaries at an elevation of about 1500 feet, presenting a great fall and forming many canyons. The greatest fall in these streams was one of about thirty feet in the Docewallups, which stream rushed madly against the base of <u>Mt Constance</u>, whirling abruptly to the South. They did not attempt to ascend Mt Constance as the face over looking the stream rose perpendicular from the water to a heigth of many feet. Striking a cabin about night fall, which was untennanted at the time, they were comfortable despite the rain.

Mon Aug 25th. The river bottom now presented a level surface, but supported a rank growth of brush and difficult traveling. Bidding Mr. Olmstead good day they headed more to the N.E. Leaving the stream they crossed a ridge and made the beach on Hoods Canal at 1.30 P.M., just in time, the steamer Josephine was then going by, and a gentleman passing in a boat. They employed him and his boat to row them out to the steamer, upon which they secured passage to Hoodsport,[60] arriving at 9 P.M. They were allowed to wear their shoes so long as they remained upon the lower deck, but they were invited to remove their shoes before entering the Cabin on account of the spikes mutilating the floor. Removing their shoes was removing their stockings also, if they were as holy as ours at about this date. There were not many settlers located up either of the streams that they had explored. They considered it about 28 miles from Heart Peak to the mouth of these streams and they learned that the northern-most stream was the Docewallups and the next

south of it the Ducquebusche. They had watched closely for the Banner parties Camps but could not find any marks announcing that they were from Lake Cushman to Port Angelos. No tidings could be learned of their coming out. Not a line in the news papers announcing their safe return, and they began to grow uneasy, when by accident they met a gentleman who had seen them emerge from the mountains, approaching Hoods Canal with the ladies in advance. We thought it fortunate that they selected this route after leaving the level plateau, as in language applicable to the bad lands of the North West, Hell with the fire out lay between them and the Elwha River.

Aug 26 & 27th. Was spent in resting up at Hoodsport, enjoying the hospitality of Mr. Finchs.[61] Added to his collections Mr Bretherton had one fawn skin complete for mounting, marmots, cross bills, Finchs, Moos birds and a hawk, with bugs and worms which were beyond our knowledge, excluding the fish bait question.

Sat Aug 28th. They set out at noon arriving at Lake Cushman at 6 P.M. They had been cordially invited by Messrs Lake and Putnam (who had erected a restaurant) to call and be welcomed.[62] They did call and slept where the floor may be some day.

Sun Aug 29th. It rained hard all day. <u>Lunch</u> was enjoyed in Camp Three where they were successful in fishing. During the after noon they made Camp No 4. and camped for the night.

Mon Aug 30th. Camp No 7 was made by noon time. Here they were again successful in fishing. The fish would not rise at this point before, notwithstanding there were many deep holes in which they are generally found. Rain set in again after noon and continued through out the afternoon,

---

[60] "According to Bretherton, the men reached Hood Canal and boarded the southbound Josephine on Wednesday, August 27, but Fisher gives the date as Monday, August 25. However, according to the schedule published by the Hood's Canal Transportation Line, which operated the steamers Delta and Josephine, the latter left Union City for Seattle on Mondays, Wednesdays, and Fridays, and sailed from Seattle for Union City on Tuesdays, Thursdays, and Saturdays. Therefore, it is probable that Bretherton and Yates boarded the vessel on Tuesday, August 26." Wood, *Men, Mules and Mountains*, p. 412.

[61] "Ida Robbins Finch (1864–1950) was born in Maine but became a self-reliant pioneer on Hood Canal. . . . [Her] family . . . were the first settlers at Hoodsport. Ida Robbins then married a logger, John Vincent Finch (1853–1936). The Finches took a 200 acre homestead on Finch Creek, where Captain Robbins built a New England style home for his daughter and son-in-law (on the site of the present day fish hatchery). During the Klondike gold rush, Finch went to the Yukon, then settled in British Columbia. His wife refused to leave her home on Hood Canal, however, and she continued to operate the place as a boarding house or hotel until about 1909. She called it the 'Gateway Inn,' meaning gateway to the Olympics, and it became a well-known supply point for hunters, surveyors, and prospectors going into the mountains." Wood, *Men, Mules and Mountains*, pp. 412–13.

[62] "William T. Putnam (1866–1957) was a graduate of Trinity College in Hartford, Connecticut. He came to Seattle, Washington Territory, in July, 1888, at the 'insistence' of Frederic J. Church, who had been a classmate at St. Paul's School in Concord, New Hampshire. While in Seattle, Putnam became acquainted with Elton Ainsworth and William B. Lake, and in the fall of 1888 the men took claims at Lake Cushman. Later Frederic Church and Carl Stebbins—another classmate at St. Paul's—visited Putnam, and they, too, acquired claims near the lake. Together with Putnam, they became known to the other settlers as 'the college boys from the East.' Because Lake Cushman was famed for its trout, many people came to camp and fish. Putnam and Lake took advantage of the opportunity and established Cushman House, the restaurant referred to, in July 1890, 'in a tent on the east shore of the lake, near the terminus of the Lilliwaup trail.' They leased the site from a company 'which owned several thousand acres of timber in the neighborhood.' The following year they acquired the old Rose place from Mrs. Windhoffer. This tract, on the lake's west shore, contained 300 acres, 'embracing practically all the farm land in the valley.' Here they built a hotel (also known as Cushman House) 'not a stone's throw from the lake in a clump of immense cottonwoods.' Putnam acquired Lake's interest in 1892, thus becoming the sole proprietor of the establishment, which he operated until 1923." Wood, *Men, Mules and Mountains*, p. 413.

414

and night. Camp No 9. was reached where they put up for the night.

Tues Aug 31st. Following up the trail they found that it led through their camp of Aug 17th in the Ducquebusche basin. Having killed some grouse, they prepared lunch at this point. Following up the trail which had been recently traveled by the animals, they had no trouble in making Camp No 14. where the Col with his party had arrived a few days previously, having done good work. This though a hard trip was a successful one in that they had traced the two streams ascertaining which was which. They had killed an abundance of game for the two and were never in want of food. They had made maps of, and photographed the country, in addition to the specimens that may long remain in the museum as momentos of their work. The Col expected the Lieut et al into Hoodsport at any day, bacon was needed in the main camp, and Mr Price was sent in with three animals, to await the Lieut appearance at Hoodsport. Consulting the log book, the party had done much hard work on the trail, and the mules had rolled many times, but were not seriously injured. After going through North pass they found it necessary after descending the first large basin to swing to the east in making the descent. Gaining a small meadow with fine grass, they turned north and west following the course of the Ducquebusche R. The stream unfortunately formed a canyon here, and they were compelled to lead the trail up the mountain again, leaving the river for some three miles. The canyon was continuous almost to its source, but they descended and found a heavy bank of snow that spanned the gulch. Crossing upon this, they followed up the North bank about two miles, making Camp No 13. at our former <u>Camp Docewallups</u>. From here the greater part of the work was digging a toe path up the ascent leading to the plateau upon which were the three lakes and Hearts peak. In crossing this there was no work of any consequence. The Col had killed one elk up to this date. Being a calf it did not last long. The Bacon had run out, no large game could be found, and they were eating dog meat instead. Flour, Coffee, tea, and salt were in abundance, but men that had worked up such appetites as we all had, craved meat as well. Having traced them all back to camp except the Lieuts party, we will return to Camp No 9. and follow them up.

It was Sun Aug 17th that The Lieut with Danton and Fisher set out to explore the S.W. and Quinault Country. Heading west we began the ascent where we had attempted to make the short cut with the trail. Our packs were heavy, and we followed the most direct route up. It was a little more than 3000 feet to the summit and almost every inch of the

first 2500 feet was gained, every inch of it, hauling our selves up from one bush to the next. The greater portion of the route was over the track of a land slide some years before, and had now grown so thick that a snake would have tied himself into a knot in getting through it. Perspiration streamed in our eyes, and our hearts throbbed like a stranded locomotive with the violent exertions. It was 1. P.M. before we found enough level ground to build a fire and prepare lunch. This was at the small lake seen from Camp Quinhomish by the Col & I. After lunch we set out, crossed the divide, dropping into the basin where we viewed the seven elk. This branch of the Quinault appeared similar to the road to China that we had heard of. Heading N.W. we gained the elk trail and followed it up over a tall round mountain upon which all the timber was dead. While resting here the Lieut was admiring the majestic mountain that we had defined as the liberty bell. A tree was blazed and the mountain located and named after Col Andersons daughter as Mt Irlene. Continuing to the W & N.W. over the trail, it rounded the mountain and turned N & east, making a half circle around the deadning [?]. The Lieut & I differed very much in opinion. While he would follow an elk trail regardless of its course, I followed the course, ground permitting, but all rules failed in these mountains. I wished very much to leave the trail and attempt the descent but would not make any bold advances for fear I might get stuck, as it yet looked as black as an ink bottle below. Continuing upon the trail we completed the half circle around the dead timber mountain. While the surface of it sloped away from the apex, gently, for a quarter of a mile before it came [became] precipitous, the N.W. face of it seemed to have dropped away, and two deep gulches dreaned [drained?] the scoop out. The timber had also suffered from some cause in this hollowed out region, and we could survey it plainly from where we were, upon a Comb of Sandstone that formed the Southern wall of, and over looking the great scoop out. A large black bear beneath us crawled out of the gulch, and turned the hair forward upon his back. In other words, he had his back up at our appearance. We ignored his presence and it slowly moved away. It did not seem reasonable to descend upon this Comb that appeared to end in a precipice at no great distance. We were about four miles S.W. of Heart peak, and south of the Quinault R over looking its canyon. This great scoopout extended from here to Heart Peak. We were at an elevation of 4000 ft and it appeared easy enough to drop in to the scoop out and descend, as the slope was very gentle as far as we could see. We descended to the gulch, examining either for trails. Many cross trails ran from one gulch to the other. At last, crossing both of them we found an elk trail as large, and as well worn, as a mail route. We rejoiced at this discovery and set out.

Often down in ashes deep
Are living coals of fire asleep

The farther we followed it the broader it grew until at last it ended abruptly,over looking a precipice of at least 60 feet drop. A mountain stream had cut deep in the Stone upon either side and our ridge had come to an end, and very abruptly too. What had brought those elk down there or why this trail had been traveled more than any other is one question among others remaining for solution. We swung out by the bushes and examined the point and two sides of this ridge. There was no descent. Moss grew upon the faces of the stone and no debris below indicated a fracture, or breaking away of any portion, yet elk had recently left foot marks upon the very brink, where they had slipped in their sudden halt.[63] We retraced our steps some yds and swung over into the east gulch and followed down a short distance. The farther we went the worse it grew untill now it was but a dry water course, where the water had leaped from one terrace to another like a continuation of great steps. Portions of logs were standing up in some places as the mountain torrent had left them, and it was by clasping our arms and sliding that we descended. The fissure at last closed to a mere crack in the slate and faced over a drop of 100 feet. To get out we must return, and climbing these logs on end, slick with slime and moisture, was like climbing a greased pole to get up again. It was impossible to go west and we did some trapeze work to the east in swinging from one gulch to the other, which was smooth stone from the action of the water. The different gulches all seemed to lead into one large one, coming in at every 10 feet. Some were dry while others carried water. We reach the last small one leading into the large one, and descend some thirty feet over a fall by sliding down a large log standing upon end, the water having subsided since the freshet now sheers to one side and drops upon the solid slate bench, only to plunge onward to the next one, a cataract of thirty feet fall above us and a greater one below. Night sets in and we have about a ten foot circle to camp upon, with water splashing upon us all night. We gathered some poor wood left by the freshets, as it was washed to one side, and managed to get supper. We joined hands and let one down over the shoulder of rock, to

Camp Purgatory

dip up water. Thus when one wished a drink, it taken [took] all hands to get it. There was no tree here to blaze and we were not prepared for stone engraving, but I wrote down in the note book <u>Camp purgatory</u> and thought that I could enjoy the heat next door, after this night in the neighboring city. Complaints from the members of our party were unheard of. I do not think that any of them would have accepted their transportation home, but this camp out rivaled any ancient mode of torture. Henceforth I thought we would prefer a cave with bear and rattle-snakes, a drift upon the ocean, or any thing before a ten hours russian bath.

Mon Aug 18th. When day light found its way into this satannic camp we prepared a hasty meal and worked our way up again.[64] Heading to the east we cleared this canyon. Consulting the anaeroid we were yet 3000 feet above the Sea. The drop below, as far as we could see, resembled one grand stair case, with each step rounded off. Mountain hemlocks

---

[63] "The explorers had stumbled upon an unusually dramatic example of a common phenomenon in the Olympics—the 'disappearing elk trail.' Three weeks later, Marsh, Yates, Bairens, and Higgens discovered that the elk had indeed gone this way, and by following their path they located what turned out to be the only possible route that mules could travel from the Duckabush to the Quinault." Wood, *Men, Mules and Mountains*, p. 415.
[64] O'Neil's description is equally interesting. See earlier, p. 289, chapter 10, "Lecture Notes of Lieutenant Joseph P. O'Neil Fourteenth Infantry," set #5.

grew rank with much tangled huckle berry beneath. By swinging from bough to brush, we worked to right and left gaining downward as a ship tacking against the wind. Our friend the Alaska Cedar had deserted us upon this descent where it was most needed. A rope from its tough bark would have aided us very much. It grew so dangerously rough and precipitous that we deployed in hopes by covering more ground that one of us would succeed in finding a better route. But No! It grew worse, if worse it could be. The Lieut and Danton in bearing to the right were stuck and sang out in the familiar Hey—oh to learn my where abouts. It was so steep and brushy I could not discern what the next step would divulge but responded and eased down, anchoring above a tree to await their arrival. I was not more than one hundred yds from them, yet it was 30 minutes before they appeared upon the cliff above. I directed them to a mass of fallen logs under which I had descended bear fashion, but they preferred the boughs and brush. The Lieut landed safely. Danton being hampered with the Camera became entangled in the brush, hanging suspended from a limb with legs dangling in search of friendly footing. It might have been the last of a more delicate individual. The Lieut directed him to let go with the left hand which swing him into a shelf rock, and footing. The Lieut had fore seen that two packs containing our supplies would grow lighter, while the camera would remain the same. This was remedied by exchanging packs every 6 hours. The next act was one remindful of boy hoods days and Grimes cellar door. There was 75 feet of wet surface beneath a blind spring, too steep and slippery to walk upon, and richly ornamented with devils Club offering no support. We sat down with wry faces, and played Otter, until we brought up against the timber below. In disgust we looked from our bleeding hands to the shreds from our tattered garments hanging to the bushes above. It was a continuation of these varied performances fraught with danger until 10. Oclock A.M. we reached the narrow bottom of the east Quinault valley. Ripe red & yellow Salmon berries grew in profusion, some as large as one and one half inches in diameter. Cool and refreshing, we gathered many. Reaching the stream at a point about three miles from the glacier named for the Col, we consulted the instrument which registered 1425 above sea level, but this was not a fair estimate. Being as yet only a mountain stream 1000 feet would be a fair estimate for this branch of the Qinault as

against 2000 for the Skokomish and 1500 @ for the Ducquebusche and Docewallups streams, showing that this stream had cut much deeper in the earth than the eastern water courses. Crossing to the N. bank we found an elk trail and followed its course parallel with the stream. Some seven miles below the Glacier a good sized stream came in from the N. Carefully prospecting this as we had the main stream for float, we discovered light crystals of Iron Pyrites in the slate cleavage and small quantities of spar, no doubt a calcium carbonate ($CaCO_3 + Ag$) judging from its form of crystal's. During the day we passed through an old camp occupied one year previously by one of the parties who had claimed to have followed up the east branch of the Quinault, dropping over in to the Skokomish and going out by the route that we had came. A Mr. DeFord visited our camp and informed us that he was one of the party, but having been imposed upon by parties offering them selves as guides who were ignorant of the country and were desirous of prospecting at the parties expense, these solicitations were kindly rejected. Never the less Messrs DeFord, Shelters, Pratt, Brown, and an indian by name of Fred Pope had came from the Quinault Lake to the source of the east branch of the Quinault river,[65] as will be shown by connecting circumstances. Preparing lunch at this spot, we found a tree blazed and registered were F. P. L. W. & DeFord. Here we cast for trout unsuccessfully. The Glaciers above were grinding violently, and the water was contaminated to a milky whitness [whiteness] with fine sediment. At this point the Aneroid registered 1150, a drop of 275 feet in two hours travel. Pushing on until dark we approached a mammoth log jam where it had filled up the river bed & which had turned the stream to the left. Unslinging our packs we pitched camp and registered Camp Jam, alt 950 feet. So far, there had been no canyon nor falls but a continuous decline over which the water dashed at the rate of 12 miles an hour. We judged that we had traveled 8 miles to day, which is an excellent days travel in this country.

Tues Aug 19th. Seven Oclock was our hour for setting out and 5 P.M. for camping when location would permit. The trail for the first mile was entirely grown up with brush. The elk evidently do not use these bottom trails only in the winter when the snow drives them down from the mountains. Consequently the trails are almost invisible under the tangled brush. By about 10 A.M. probably two miles were covered and at this

417

---

[65] "Dennis DeFord was one of the best informed men on the Olympics at that time. He had prospected them extensively, and he was credited by the settlers in Mason County with having 'cruised in this little unknown part of the world more than any other man.' He was the discoverer of the 'monster copper lead' in the foothills, about twelve miles west of Hood Canal. Fisher variously refers to Shelter and Shelters, and it is not clear which is the correct spelling of this name. Apparently more than one party had been on the East Fork of the Quinault prior to O'Neil. The Gilmans had traveled up the river to the vicinity of Anderson Pass in the autumn of 1889, but Fisher does not mention having seen any of their camps." Wood, *Men, Mules and Mountains*, p. 415.

point another camp of the Shelter party was found, and a small stream emptied here, coming from the east. No change had as yet occurred in the timber growth, excepting an absence of the Sitka cedar, which is poorly represented upon the western slope of these mountains. The undergrowth was as usual huckle berry with Devil club in wet places. No grass is to be found, but much epilobium and large leafed sorrell. This valley was painfully silnt [silent]. With the exception of the rushing water, not the song of a bird nor chirp of insect was heard to releive the monotony. No animal tracks marked the earth, and save our own existence we seemed to be painfully moving down the valley of death. Until noon time a single raven circled above our heads, croaking in mournful tones over the deserted valley. We thought that these birds usually remained near the lakes and were in hopes this might prove true, as no Salmon had yet been sighted to bring them up. Passing a small stream coming in from the North we noted a strong Sulphurous odor. A steep and high bluff now confronted us, and we crossed upon a number of fallen trees forming almost a jam. Soon after gaining the south bank we found the trail had crossed also. Here we found another camp that had been occupied by the Shelters party, bearing date of June 20th 1889. The stream here formed a Canyon and we followed the trail which led to the South, and ascending some 800 feet. The formation as we ascended changed from sandy loam to Argillaceous and the trail more distinct. Also two strokes of an axe marked an occasional tree, no doubt the work of the Shelter party. The next point of importance was a spring at which they had camped, and upon a tree was a death scene of an elk, and registered Van B. & Pratt. By night fall we came out upon the brink of a steep bank over looking the Canyon. Looking up its course we could indistinctly see through the gathering twilight beautiful falls. The channel was very narrow between high and perpendicular walls of stone. The timber was of small growth here but thick upon the ground, tall and straight. At this point another of Shelters camps marked their course. In this we pitched camp just as a rain set in, and fog hung low. This camp we registered as Camp Raven in honor of the only form of life that we had witnessed since leaving the mountains crest.

Wedns Aug 20th.—Setting out we descended to find quite a large stream coming in from the east.[66] This we judged to be the stream that headed at Bruins Peak. It was rather early to bathe, but there was no other oppertunity offered than to get in and wade. Once across, trails all led to the south, leaving the bottom. After a couple of hours struggling in the tangled brush, we returned to the stream, having gained but little distance. The stream was much divided and the little islands densely covered with willows and driftwood. We passed the remainder of the morning in wading down its course, crossing and re-crossing to advantage. Three medium sized Salmon were sighted. I drew and fired, lifting the dorsal fin from one, but it reached deep water and disappeared. The stream when all collected was about 30 yds wide and 2 to 4 ft deep. At noon time we kindled a fire upon a gravel bar, prepared our lunch, adding Chocolate to the bill of fare for dessert. Removing our shoes and stockings, we dried out to some extent. Rain continued to fall at intervals through out the day, and made it miserable enough in the brush. We had long since learned that there were no snakes in these mountains, nor along the streams, hence we used the last of our antidote at this point and looked upon the dead soldier with sorrow and regret. Soon after lunch to our utter dismay we were forced to take to the water again. Covering about two miles we approached the first cabin, unfinished and with one acre of ground cleared. No one at home, nor visiting card out. From this point a trail had been blazed and some brush removed. It soon left the east branch and we being upon the right bank made about five miles, approaching the North branch about one mile above its junction with the east branch, and at a point where several large trees had been cut and fallen across for foot logs. Consulting the compass this north branch which we could trace for some four miles came from due north which was not in accord with the Seattle Press Partie's map. The branch known as the east branch held its general course from source to mouth S.W. Crossing upon these logs and considering that there was a wide bottom to the west, and the main stream below inclined to flow more west than south, we made a sad mistake in attempting to make a short cut. Striking due west following some blazes they proved to be the land marks of some claim, instead of a trail. What we met here excelled any rip rap or willow basket work that we had ever beheld. The growth of timber, principally Fir and red cedar, was extraordinarily heavy, and beneath it vine maples had grown, taking root upon every thing it came in contact with, equaling any Banyan tree growth upon Mother earth. Great cedars lay prone upon the earth, while numberless other trees grew upon top of them with roots forming an arch, and in the interstices Salmon berry, huckleberry and elk ferns until a chipmonk, had there been any, must needs seek a hollow tree to reach the earth. We worked our selves into a state of excitement climbing, falling, and crawling. There was no sun to guide us and we soon

---

[66] Graves Creek and its principal tributary, Success Creek (the latter heading near Bruins Peak).

came out at the point we started in from. Down the stream or west, said I. West, said the Lieut, and in we went again. We had not gone far untill we discovered that we were going east again. It was impossible to keep any direction. Carrying open compasses, we set out again and then we could keep no one direction, avoiding obstacles. We turned S.W. and got into a Beaver swamp with mud, water, brush and logs. It was beyond description. Keeping our course to the S.W. in hopes of reaching the stream again, we came to the beaver dam, and the growing darkness reminded us of the camping hour. Working below the dam, we found that we were upon the head waters of a small tributary. Following it a short ways, we went into camp. If ever moss grew to perfection it did here in this Banyan like forest. I blazed a tree and registered Camp Africa. We were wet now night and day, but fatigue over came misery and we slept despite the surroundings.

Thurs Aug 21st. Following this small stream south about one mile we gained the main stream which had grown much deeper by the confluence of the three branches, but not much wider. Crossing to the left bank we found a trail and passed cabins upon claims posted by Daniel Peterson, Olson, Chesney, and Clough,[67] at some distance from the stream with a wide gravel bar to our right. We were in the act of entering the brush in search of the trail when I espied a dog in the distance. A white man's dog, says I. A gentleman and boy appeared next and upon meeting introduced him self as Mr. Clough and Nephew. We were very fortunate in meeting him too. Crossing over the bar, he led us over a log jam, gaining the right bank. Upon that pile of drift, said he, the Seattle Press Party went to wreck. Mr. Gilman & West had passed down the day before, finding a gun and other sundries that they had lost. He informed us that it was only three miles to Lake Quinault and considered by the settlers as 10 to 12 miles from the Lake to the forks above.

The rain had fallen at intervals all day and we did not complain of the wading that we had done. Mr. Clough being on his way home kindly offered to guide us over the trail, which offer we gratefully accepted. He was a man of six feet four and his shoes though as long as a pick helve were in proportion to his form. His nephew while only thirteen summers was a third larger than either of us. We were anxious to reach the lake and bravely kept up, but it was a long three miles. We passed cabins, around which grew excellent vegetables, speaking for the soil, and learned that they were

claims taken as follows by Mr Bell, Mr Cloughs Bro, Messrs Bruce & Bro, and Harry West of Hoquiam, a gentleman of newspaper fame in the N. West. Nearing the lake we met Mr West, who informed us that he had just returned from a trip up the north Quinault branch in company with Mr Gilman. Engaging Cloughs son to take us over the lake we passed an indian camp. This being the first indians or first signs of indians in or about these mountains. As it was raining hard we merely passed the <u>Kla how ya six</u>, and passed on, anxious to reach our destination, which was the site of Quinault City, some three mile south, and across the N.E. corner of the lake. Here we found a small house of one room, built from split boards and owned by the City authorates [authorities], Mr McCalla being an active member. He had several men employed to clear the town site but as yet they had not let sun light to the earth. We were invited to share his cabin but we were chilled through and longed to feel the genial warmth of a large camp fire, and kindled one upon the beach. When we rang the supper bell the Lieut came with a spider filled generously with our first love, Boston Baked Beans. We had seen no game on the way down and were tired of the bacon straight. We passed a very good night, glad to meet strange faces again.

Friday, Aug 22nd. Mr McCalla kindly offered his services and boat in showing us around the lake. While the Lieut and He were out making the rounds I accepted a small boat and trolling hook and was soon enjoying a pleasure that I had long promised my self, that of casting in Lake Quinault. Salmon were jumping in all directions. One of perhaps 25# came to the surface, and I drew in hopes of a shot at the next. No more than ready than one cleared the water in eight feet of me and I dropped it a dead fish. The boat I was in would not carry more than 160# and I weighed with in 10# of that. While attempting to secure it with a string, it escaped me and sank. I was not only fishing for pleasure now but on the ground hog principal also, i e for fish. I swallowed my sorrows and set the spoon to spinning. A small trout of 1# was hooked but no management would keep it in the water. As soon as it struck the surface it shot in the air again and again, until it broke the hold and was lost. Rounding to, I passed by the same gravel point again and hooked a 10# Bull trout. Drawing in the slack, I could see every spot upon his pretty back 12 feet beneath the surface. I played him untill I grew anxious to see it landed and much more so when I found the hook was cutting deeper with

419

---

[67] "According to Ernest Olson (as related in *Trails and Trials of the Pioneers of the Olympic Peninsula* [Lucile H. Cleland, Humptulips, Wash.: Humptulips Pioneer Association, 1959]), his father, John A. Olson, and James Peterson 'came west in the year 1893' to establish new homes in the Pacific Northwest and located on the south bank of the Quinault about eight miles above the lake. He also states that Dan and Frank Peterson, brothers of James, took claims on the north side. The men later returned to Minnesota for their families. Ernest Olson appears to have been mistaken as to the year the men came west, since O'Neil, Danton, and Fisher traveled down the East Fork in August, 1890, and Fisher's manuscript, written that year, indicates that Olson and Daniel Peterson had already taken claims above the lake." Wood, *Men, Mules and Mountains*, pp. 415–16.

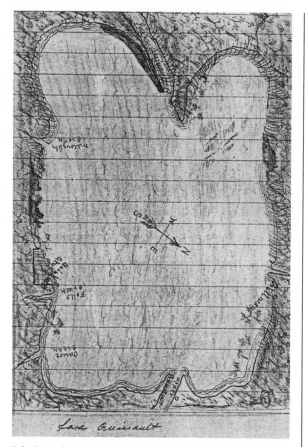

Lake Quinault

420

through to the east upon some route. We now accosted an old indian who was digging canoes from large cedar logs. Examining them, they were pretty models, and very accurately made, and their measure is their eye. His prices were from Seven to Twenty Dollars per Canoe. Gradually weakening in his attempt to keep silent, he eventually dropped his mallet and chisel and replied to our questions, speaking good Chinook. Finding that his knowledge of the mountains extended only to the foot hills, we returned to the Canoe and the Lieut mounted his Camera and, after an hour of patience, caught the mouth of the upper Quinault, and back ground, consisting of the bordering timber and McCallas Peak, named in honor of the gentleman who had and was now rendering us kind and valuable service. The fog we were informed remained over the lake until 10 A.M. every day, despite the sun shine, and we were long delayed this morning in waiting for it to raise. From here we paddled about the lake, sketching its shape and points by the compass, learning the names of the different inflows, which were six, with one out flow, which is shown on the map, as well as location of Mr Gilmans claim and cabin, Mr Zeigler's and the Town site of Quinault City. There is no doubt but that the point is out-rivaled by no spot in the west as a town site, in many respects, e g its fishing is not excelled if equaled. The surrounding forests are and will be for many years a source of inexhaustable revenue, and as a healthful and pleasant summer resort too much can not be said. Returning to the town site, and our Camp. Danton had dinner ready and as usual the last fish was always the best. The Lieut wished to investigate reports stating that mineral, lime stone, coal, and granite, had been found on the Humptulip River. We knew we could head east and find the stream but we dreaded the brush. Laying in fresh supplies which were very high with freight at 6¢ pr # we made preperations to set out. It was 35 miles down the lower Quinault to the ocean, 18¼ to Humptulip City. The trail was partially blazed to the latter, while canoes were the only method of gaining the ocean. The Lieut decided to call at Humptulip City, which lay 10 points W of south from the lake. Mr McCalla conveyed us some distance down the lake and as we skimmed over this beautiful sheet of water we had ample oppertunity to admire the charms of nature at its best. Not a ripple save what we made disturbed the placid water, and what you could see above was more brilliantly reflected from below. The beach generally was flat, but at some points the border was of stone and perpendicular but never of great elevation. The depth was as yet unknown. 34 soundings had been made in the centre with no bottom. In rounding a point our conversation was interrupted by a yell from the shore asking us where was Quinault City. Inform-

each effort. I drew and playing him to the surface sent a ball through his body just in time, as but a frail portion was held by the hook. The large boat now returned and The Lieut wished me to go to the indian camp and find out what the indians knew, as well as do some photographing himself. We paddled across to the camp which was inhabited by the Pope family, from Quinault Agency, up on a fishing tour. But alas, the old man had gone up the north fork early. Consulting his son, Fred Pope, we learned that they did not know but little of the Olympic Mountains, seldom going up as far as the foot hills, since they could obtain all the game and fish desired nearer home. However, of the bottom country next the coast they were well acquainted, as well as the Whites. Upon questioning him as to who had crossed these mountains, He said that his Father had remained in these foot hills many snows, and the only ones red or white that they knew of going entirely across was that the Seattle Press Party came down the Quinault, and that he was one of the Shelter party. He had gone as far as the head of the east Quinault branch. He had returned from there in company with Van Brown & Pratt, leaving J L Shelters & Dennis DeFord at the divide, and he thought they went

ing him that he was then parading the boulevard we glided on, Mr McCalla promising to return as soon as we were landed. Pointing out the trail to us, we bid him a friendly good-bye and rather sorry that we must leave Quinault, to Boondle up our thraps and welt the road again. It was now late in the eve ening and we made about three miles, and pitched camp near a second small creek that we had crossed. It now began raining again, and very little wood could be gathered here. Making the best we could of it we recapitulated the log book and remembered that we had neglected one item and that was that there were then about 60 claims taken in the Quinault Valley. This night we registered at Camp McCalla.

Sat Aug 28th [23rd]. Fog and rain hung so dense there was no room for any more to fall, bushes wet to a point of saturation, trail ran out and vegetation baffled all descrip-

tion. Rain continued falling and we pushed on like steeple chasers. One moment wind falls lead us so high we reach the earth again by climbing down a tree, the next we are on hands and knees, crawling in muck, and mud, wishing that the bug collector was in front to point out the harmless from the mischief making bugs, and worms that dropped down our shirt collars. This was growing worse than Banyan thicket and Camp Africa. We climbed over logs until it sickened us to look at them. We were just preparing for a rest when Danton gave a whoop, disappearing in the brush, soon followed by the Lieut using his hat like a jockey upon the home stretch. It was Hornets this time.

This kind of traveling lasted until sun down, at which time we passed two cabins, and met a gentleman that owned one of six claims in that vicinity, returning from Humptulip City with a pack upon his back. He informed us that it was

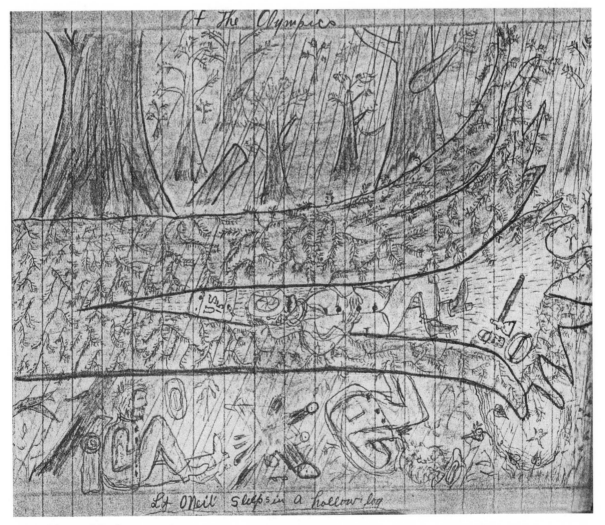

Lt O'Neil sleeps in a hollow log

only seven miles to the City and that we could easyly make it. Darkness was now gathering, but the Lieut was determined to make it, and according to directions we set out again. It grew too bad, and we camped in the suburbs of a mud hole. The rain dropped industriously, the wood refused to burn, and water gathered where we meant to have slept. The sap had gone down and a bark house was out of the question. Danton selected the best place in choosing the ashes. I took second by propping up against a tree, and the Lieut took third place by crawling into a hollow log, rotten, and as wet as water could saturate it. This was a night equal to the first night out near Lillywaup, the less said the better thought.

Sun Aug 24th. We had, so we had been informed, about two miles to cover and this route would develop into the County road. Emerging from the timber we crossed a Swamp about one mile in width. We approached a cabin, rapping at the door a gentleman ran his head through an aperture and replied to our questions. This was Mr McCarthy and he was the most distant of any from civilization that had as yet brought his lady with him.[68] A very pretty garden graced the front yard, and in it grew some of the most thrifty Straw berry plants that we had ever seen. Following his directions we reached Mr Boyds ranch. This gentleman was most happily situated of any. It was civilization again and the first that I had seen for two months. There were three ladies at this place, children playing about the house, roosters crowing, and dogs barking at our approach. Although he had not much ground cleared he had done some hard work in cutting a road out for a distance of five miles, which connected him with Humptulip City. Parting company with this place, we followed the road which to us was a boulevard after what we had passed through. Passing through some four miles of timber we came out upon a prairie of perhaps five hundred acres. It was grown up with ferns and but little grass. A herd of cattle were brousing in the distance. Near the border of this prairie flowed the Humptulip River, and upon the west bank was the City of same name, consisting of one store and one hotel conducted by Mr Davis. This prairie was known as Stevens prairie. The soil was considered no good for farming, being of a hard gravely nature. Taking dinner at the hotel, it was necessary that we make some demonstrations toward improving our appearances and in the attempt we approached a mirror. I knew that the Lieut & Danton looked hard and had grown accustomed to them, but when I witnessed my own reflection I thought I might well have been King of the hobo tribe.

Over the door fluttered a domestic sign announcing Meals and lodging 25¢. Allow me to add that we sat down to a better meal than any Sound city had ever placed before us for double the price, and this twenty six miles from the nearest town or City. Fresh butter, milk, sweet and sour, coffee, tea, and an endless variety of vegetables, fruits and cake, served in the good old fashioned way, much to our advantage as we were not compelled to blushingly ask for the thirteenth biscuit. Dinner over we returned to the small store and renewed our supplies, to last four men for six day's. The Lieut had mapped out a new programme, as follows. A Mr Landers of Chicago was to join us. Upon reaching the forks of the Humptulip R we were to seperate. The Lieut and Mr Landers were to trace up the Humptulip's west branch, while Danton, and my self, operated upon the east. Had the Lieut been out for unearned notoriety as had been formerly intimated he would no doubt have enjoyed a recreation here, with these people, who were kindness unexemplified. Mr. Landers was of small statue [stature] but proved a good traveler and brilliant conversationalist. He had operated in many of the important mining districts of America, and was a judge of mother earths constituents, and had visited the vicinity for the purpose of investigating reported finds of Coal, Granite, and noble metals. While we were unable to find any one that knew any thing of the true source of this stream, we did not consider this an exploring trip, but one of investigation. We headed N.E. to reach the stream near its forks, some two miles above the town site. Arriving there, a pretty falls met our view. Passing through several small fern meadows, and alder thickets, we arrived at George Kerns claim, and decided to seperate. The Lieut & Mr Landers were to follow up this the west stream and Danton & I were to cross and travel east untill we caught the east branch. It was now late and the Lieut concluded to remain here for the night, and Danton & my self accepted an invitation from A. J. Clark, a resident of Aberdeen, to remain at his cabin across the stream. Both parties enjoyed a good nights rest. Thus far the country was rolling and not as wealthy in timber as we had expected. Very good trails had been cut through the thick salal and a party of surveyeors were then at work up on this section.

Mon Aug 25th. Mr Clark had a route by which we could get on a trail leading to the east branch. He kindly acted as guide until this was reached, much to our advantage. Passing two cabins representing claims of Mr Parker et al, we reached the east branch at Mr Myers cabin. Here we met a gentle-

[68] "This may have been Neil McCarthy, a pioneer hunter, trapper, and woodsman who helped locate settlers near Lake Quinault in the summer of 1890. However, Neil McCarthy was supposed to have been a confirmed bachelor." Wood, *Men, Mules and Mountains*, p. 418.

man who was packing for the surveying party and was perhaps good authority, so far as he had traveled. He judged it four miles between the two streams at this point, and 14 miles to the forks following the course of this stream. Farther north he knew nothing of it. Finding a foot log, we crossed over to the east bank and followed up stream, after probably two miles travel we passed two cabins. While there was no one at home, Two brothers had left their names upon the door as claimants, answering to the name of McGillicuddy. Upon the opposite side of the stream was another cabin, but the stream was in canyon and we could not cross. However, we approached as near as possible and held a conversation with Mr Roberts, formerly a soldier in our regiment. He was the only well informed gentleman that we met, with regard to this country. He had been to the head of this stream, which was not more than six miles above here. As to reports, he had heard them but had seen nothing but sedimentary formation, and no coal nor lime stone indications. We declined his importunities to remain over night and pushed on.[69] The character of the country was more level now, with a decided improvement in the timber growth, which was fir, Cedar, and pine,—Huckle berries were more numerous and larger than I had ever seen them. Here the stream made almost a circle and resumed its former course N.E. At this point we camped for the night.

Tues Aug 26th. We set out upstream and traced it to a small creek. Another cabin was located near its head occupied by people of both sexes. We learned that three ladies were living in this vicinity, which was the farthest that any one had penetrated. By going east from here we were informed that nine miles travel would bring us upon the east branch of the Wishkah R heading the West Wishkah branch. There was no elevation high enough to look over the timber growth, and we having fulfilled our mission, set out on the return as we had came. In crossing from the east to the west branch of the stream we met Mr Shell, who resided half mile above Mr Kerns place. He was entertaining some Lady at his house and now upon her husbands trail to inform him of the happy event, viz the arrival of his wife. It was no doubt the first of the fair sex that he had met for some time, as he was well warmed up with running, and in his excitement had became turned around upon the trail to his own home. At sun down we reached Mr Clarks place, who kindly ferried us over, and we camped about half a mile below his place. There were no

animals in this country, consequently everything had to be packed in from Humptulip City, or canoed from Grays harbor. A canoe could be poled up as far as Mr Shells place, by dragging it around the many log jams and some falls. These people would not think of accepting compensation for entertainment and we declined pressing invitations to ride a free horse too hard. The Surveyors had just finished Mr Clarks claim over which he was highly pleased at being one of the few living upon a Surveyed Claim, more definite than squatters rights. Two Claimants passed up the trail stating that they had claims between the two streams.

Wedns Aug 27th. We set out down stream meeting a Wild Bill appearing youth loaded for bear, who was seeking his fortune. One or two trails branched off at different points and sign boards were up upon which were written trail to Walker's, Hes's, and Baungardener's. Also one industrious man of the Siwash family had his sign upon the trail opposite his ferry. We registered along the trail, that the Lieut might know we were at Humptulip City, which we made at 1 P.M. Arriving at the store we met 12 men, all loaded with supplies enroute to their different claims. Each one carried a Winchester, and some large revolvers but we had seen no game, no recent signs of any, but no doubt the game descended during the winter to these bottoms. Here we met a gentleman, Mr Ferguson by name, who had followed our trail to Camp No 4 on the east side, and was now cruising here for timber land. We were informed that there was an organized band of claimants holding lands for the timber, in case the projected R.R. should come through this locality. They being staked by parties in Aberdeen et al towns who gave them a certain price for their rights when accepted as bona fide. Leaving word at the store where we would camp, we pitched upon the river at a large log jam, where wood was plenty, and I wrote up the Humptulip Country as follows. East branch heads about 21 miles N.E. of Humptulip City flowing S.W., joining the west branch to form the main stream at a point two miles above the City. Here were the only falls of any importance. The bordering country was generally undulating and of sandy loam. Fir, larch and cedar grew thickly upon the ground. While there was a wealth of it, it does not compare with the Quinault and other mountain valleys. Several small streams flowed into the east branch but only one of any importance, which came in at McGillicuddies claim, and known as the large east branch. The streams from the forks

---

[69] "This appears to be a reference to the Thomas Roberts homestead in Township 21 N., Range 9 W., but according to Frank Roberts, as related in *Trails and Trials of the Pioneers of the Olympic Peninsula* [Cleland, 1959], the family did not arrive in the Pacific Northwest until 1891 and settled on the homestead the next year. Either his recollection as to when the family arrived was faulty or the reference is to another family." Wood, *Men, Mules and Mountains*, p. 418.

upward coursed through a glen, lying from forty to one hundred feet below the level. The main stream was about 20 yds wide, averaging one foot deep in low water, descending over many ripples at a gentle speed. We had carefully prospected the route and stream traveled by us, finding no mineral indications. Float of a friable nature was found along the streams but lacked adhesiveness peculiar to good clay. About four miles below the head of the east branch some heavy croppings of chocolate colored porphory confined the water to its channel, but generally the banks were coarse gravel, firmly cemented, whose fracture displayed a transparent agent, no doubt Sodium, holding Silicon in solution ($NaSiO_3$) with Calcium sulphate ($CaSO_4 + Ag$). Along the gravel bars were stones worn round by the action of the water and whose face showed numerous colors. One a gray variety, when broken resembled granite in appearance, but an expert would readily determine its sedimentary formation. This was no doubt the reported granite. Some float a bright red porphorous rock resembled cinnabar very closely in some respects, but subjected to agents verified its worthlessness as a mineral bearing rock. In the east branch were very small trout. Game at this season was limited to a few grouse. This stream no doubt at one time was the home of many fur bearing animals, such as mink, otter, Beaver and raccoon. Some remained yet but not in plentiful numbers. The choice lands were mostly filed upon and we did not see much to induce the filer beyond the timber. We had selected a cluster of bushes for our camp, which was upon a gravel bar, enjoying either Sun shine or Shade. We had carried a small bit of soap with us, which we now utilized in washing our clothes, wearing one half while the other dried, and by the middle of the evening we considered our selves respectable, despite our rags, and unshorn locks. Leaving Danton to keep house I cast with great success, landing fifteen trout for supper. Expecting the Lieut in at any hour we did not make any preperations farther than leveling down the gravel. Our trip was not at end yet and we knew the result of sleeping one night in bed and the next upon earth. With this precaution we refused to accept even a barn to camp in.

Thurs Aug 28th. The Lieut did not appear to day, and we spent the time in fishing and lounging about the corner grocery. Four gentlemen from Seattle passed up the river, outing in a canoe. We informed them that they would be mostly out in the river wading, or pulling around a log jam, but they went on their way. Another party of land & timber cruisers arrived, and later, some of the stock holders of Quinault City, enroute to Lake Quinault. Every one left speaking words of praise for the genial and generous inmates of Humptulips Hotel, and well they might, after several days out upon bacon and sobby [soggy?] rolls.

Frid Aug 29th. We again employed the rod to good use, landing thirty five trout. At 3 P.M. we heard the Lieuts familliar Hey—o-h and proceeded to the store. Here we made many notes. The Lieut and Mr Landers gave us a discription of their trip. Arriving at Mr Shells, they had secured a canoe and waded some miles pulling it after them, and were at a disadvantage. Leaving the canoe they went on pushing their way through the Salal. No trails had been formed up the banks of this branch and few settlers above Mr Shells. The nature of the country was very similar to what we have noted regarding the east branch—with the exception that they had found traces of copper. The west branch was about 15 miles longer than the east one, and carried a third more water. They had seen a number of grouse, one cougar, and caught very fine trout. While ascending the stream, they over taken a gentle man who was travel in a light canvas canoe. They placed their packs in the canoe and helped him tow it. Our trip had been a pleasure compared to theirs, for traveling in Salal is equal to scrubby Osage Orange. It was decided that reports of minerals in the Humptulip Valley were very much exagerated.[70] A party consisting of A.F. Wilbur of Tacoma Wash, J. M. Davis of Tacoma Wash and Set I Davis of Pysht Wash had just arrived. They had set out from Port Crescent on the straits, traveling S.W., striking the trail at the Swamp near McCarthys, before mentioned. They had been 12 days in coming through and their clothing beggared description. All there was left of Mr Wilburs Trousers was a breech clout. They had came over the western foot hills, encountering a jungle of Salal, crab apple, and Huckle berry, and were not favorably impressed with the timber growth. They had crossed the Solduck, Queets, Hoh, Raft, and Quinault streams, as well as the small tributaries of the Quillayute. The greatest alt gained was 2700 feet, illustrating that they had not gone far enough east to join the mountains proper. They carried specimens of Good Kaolin, greenish and white quartz, showing free gold, and one stone we thought carried nickle. They informed us that they found them upon the Queets, but they reminded us very much of the Cascade ores. Another gentleman also displayed some pocket pieces, no doubt from cabinet collections. Asking if it was any secret where he found

---

[70] "Perhaps the greatest incentive to exploration were the persistent but highly inaccurate reports of rich deposits of valuable minerals that lay waiting discovery by some lucky prospector. The newspapers of the day were filled with accounts of rich mineral strikes in the Olympics, none of which proved out." Wood, *Men, Mules and Mountains*, p. 399.

them, he swept the Olympics with an answering nod. Perhaps a boom or similar enterprise was his object, but we were not heralding reports of weak foundation, and lost our interest in his imported stones. The Lieut mounted his camera and photographed the <u>party</u> as <u>they</u> <u>stood</u> in front of the store. Enjoying a good supper at the Hotel we parted company with Mr Landers and in company with the Crescent party set out for Hoquiam Landing 16 miles distant. It was now 6 P.M. and we were anxious to arrive on the tide, and catch the boat to Hoquiam. Our companions were jolly, witty, and interesting, especially Seth Davis, who was a Sut Loomgood character, an Original source of queer phrases. The Lieut had made a good days travel, and was now traveling upon his uppers. The funny Davis was tip toeing it and Mr. Wilbur sadly laffed. We carried 30# each, while they had only about 5# each. Mr. J. M. Davis, taking the lead over a newly cut waggon road, ran most of the time. A family of indians set us across the stream in a canoe and we continued at this heel and toe, go as you please, making ten miles the first two hours. It now became so dark that it was impossible to keep in the road. We kindled a fire and laid over until 11 P.M. waiting for the moon to rise. We were all very thirsty but could not find any water. Setting out again we made perhaps one mile and were compelled to go into camp. A pretty sight we were. We had fallen into muddy holes time and again, and were in a deplorable condition to enter Societies brilliant circle. We seperated into two parties and slept a few hours.

Sat Aug 30th. Rising at early dawn we traveled four miles, arriving at Hoquiam Landing, verifying the old adage

Luck in leisure,
Truth in measure.

The tide was at its lowest, exposing a flat muddy river bed, with small row boats scattered about in the mud, and one small family boat upon the bank. Arousing the inmates who were two partners running row boats between this and Hoquiam, we learned that they traveled with the tide and we must wait. We enjoyed a very good breakfast which we cooked our selves while the boatment [boatmen?] righted up their boats. The country between this and Humptulips City was not of a promising character, the soil was poor clay, and gravel formation. The timber growth was not of the best, and few cabins that faced the road side were empty. The country was inclined to hills and hollows. One saw mill was in

operation near Hoquiam Landing and many stumps denoted the removal of much timber from these woods. A small dock had been erected at the landing with accommodations for storing freight. A native was hauling hay from this to his claim and we thought him the most ill natured individual that we had met in many a day. His horses, the only ones we saw in these lands, and his dog as well, suffered the torments of his violent temper. Asking a few simple questions, we were answered in the style of a Council Bluff (Ia) Baggage smasher and moved beyond range of his foul tongue. The steamer Romp, a pretty little craft, came with the tide at 1 P.M. and as we boarded her, Mrr [Mr] Roberts, the gentleman whom we had talked with on the east Humptulip R. arrived, reminding us of our meeting. Putting his lady aboard we glided over the muddy waters of the Hoquiam river for a distance of 10 miles, arriving at the City of Hoquiam at 3:30 P.M., fare ¢50. The country bordering the Hoquiam stream was inundated by high tides, but some good timber fringed the shores. There being no trail, boats are the only means of transportation. Gaining the dock in our wild west uniform, we noted our bearings. Hoquiam was a pretty little town of 3000[71] population, located upon a tide flat point near the head of Grays harbor, and at the mouth of the Hoquiam River. At high tide Ocean vessels could enter and land in the heart of the City. We were the objects of much interest and were plied with many questions. Repairing to the Coronado Coffee house which was conducted by Mr. White, we satiated our appetites and sallied forth upon the streets where our locomotion was awkward to the extreme. Minus our packs we were inclined to pitch forward while our step was as sadly water logged as Jack Tar's. I think the traditional elephant had tramped upon the Lieuts purse of ready money, but he carried his character with in his pocket and approached a bank. The inmates removed the golden tray from the tellers wicket, and I think were expecting an attack from the James gang. The cashier glancing at the time mill apparently in hopes that it would contrary to regulations lock the great vault prematurely. Our Lieut swallowed a few times, and broached the subject, and succeeded in establishing connections with his bank a/c. He now proceeded to the Hotel Hoquiam and found a guard of colored servants at the door. Accustomed to guard duty, he removed his shoes with the horrid spikes and was passed to the register. It was soon known who we were, and we were welcomed to the town. Meeting a few acquaintances of former days we were soon at home and passed a pleasant evening.

---

[71] "The appearance of Fisher's manuscript indicates he left a blank space for the population figure and that the number '3000' was inserted later, perhaps by someone else. Official figures of the United States Census for 1890 give the population of Hoquiam as 1302. Aberdeen had a count of 1638, and Grays Harbor City, 523." Wood, *Men, Mules and Mountains*, p. 418.

Sun Aug 31st. No boats were running our way, and we were compelled to lay over. The Port Crescent party had gone on to Montesano, but could get no farther until Monday. Mr Gilman of Quinault was met and notes compared of the Quinault valley. The Lieut had appeared in a bran [brand] new suit of clothes, and Richard was him self again. The board of trade called a meeting and proposed to extend the trail from Mr Boyds ranch to a certain point upon the east Quinault, if the Lieut would bring the mules out upon this route. They appeared to have the interests of their City at heart and were speareing no expense to improve every oppertunity that offered its self.[72] They farther invited us to lay over and accept an excursion around the Harbor. The Lieut agreed to the arrangements regarding the trail, but was too anxious to rejoin the Camp to indulge in any pleasures. Strolling about the town, we noted that all buildings were new and handsomely designed. The Hotel Hoquiam was a $40,000 building, conducted upon the most improved system, and would have credited either Portland or Frisco in affording style or comforts.[73] The streets were raised above high tide, and were well side walked through out the town. A large saw mill and sash and door factory supported a large pay roll and many large mercantile firms displayed a prosperous front. Numerous steamers and sail boats were passing to and fro, upon the harbor. Among others were the Str Alliance and Fleet Typhoon of Portland, Oregon. We were well pleased with the appearance of Hoquiam and its surroundings when the tide was in, but when out the horrid mud flats were not in harmony with this pretty town.

Mon Sept 1st. At 7 A.M. we boarded the Str Montesano and steamed up the Harbor. I did not learn the cause of all the travel but it was remindful of a Kansas City or St Louis wharf, to witness such a throng of people, and in this infant as well as remote locality. Landing at Aberdeen some 4 miles up the harbor, a town dressed in prosperous colors, in honor of the coming R.R. then grading through its suburbs. Here the surroundings were like a Japanese picture. Scores of fishing boats clustered about, discharging their last nights catch of Salmon, Smelt and sturgeon. Leaving this point we left Grays Harbor and entered the Chehalis river, a stream of good depth. Passing Cosmopolis, we reached Montesano at 10 A.M. making connections daily (Sunday excepted) with the Puget Sound and Chehalis R.R.[74] Boarding the train we were at Kamilchee by noon time, where we enjoyed an excellent meal at the Kamilchee Hotel for 25¢. I am sure that I never in all of my travels west of the Mississippi R met a class of Landlords so generously disposed as we met in the small towns of this N.W. country. Taking the stage line, here operated by J. H. Long, we passed over a good road, but through an unsettled country, poorly timbered. During the middle of the evening Shelton, a small town, was reached. Changing horses we continued, reaching Union City at 7 P.M. A hot supper and we boarded a hay scow for Hoodsport. It is only three miles across the bay between the two places, which is generally traveled by sail, or row boats, but this night the steamer Tillie, a small tug, was billed to bump at Hoodsport, and Danton & I concluded to make that place this night, and await the Lieut's arrival on the morrow, He having to await a telegram from the Churches. While on the trail, we again met the Pt Crescent party and they informed us that the two Churches were in Aberdeen awaiting our arrival and it was necessary to assemble them again.[75] Among the few passengers aboard the scow was Smith, the Skokomish R prospector, and the genial Mr Finch, the moving spirit of Hoodsport. Arriving at Hoodsport at 10 P.M. we were snugly stowed away in Mr. Finchs barn loft, wrapped in an abundance of blankets. Finchs house, a neat little cottage, was inadequate to accommodate the unusual number of people drawn tither to learn what the ONeil party were doing. 27 men had been here for dinner this day and quite a number beside our selves were snoring loudly upon all sides of us. There were no rooms petitioned [partitioned] off in the hay loft, but in the N.E. corner one individual contrary to the rules of the house was indulging in a smoke and as he flashed a lucifer we observed that it was our comrade Mr Price and the same old identical pipe. He had been here a day or so awaiting our arrival. We were soon a sleep and pleasantly passed the night.

Tues Sept 2nd. Bang "Whang" came two missiles against the barn and we were informed that we were over sleeping

---

[72] "Another offer was made by the Gray's Harbor Company to build a trail for the expedition's use from Hoquiam to Hoquiam Landing, but this was apparently never done. The company also offered 'to complete the partial trail from Stevens' prairie to Lake Quinaiult.'" Wood, *Men, Mules and Mountains*, p. 419.

[73] "According to some accounts, the hotel cost $100,000." Wood, *Men, Mules and Mountains*, p. 419.

[74] "Frederic Church had left Montesano at 5:30 that morning, bound for Aberdeen on the steamer Aberdeen. O'Neil, Danton, and Fisher left Aberdeen at 7:00 A.M., headed for Montesano on the Montesano. The ships therefore passed each other en route to their respective destinations, but apparently neither party was aware of the presence of the other." Wood, *Men, Mules and Mountains*, p. 419.

[75] "The report the Churches 'were in Aberdeen' was false. The Wilbur-Davis party apparently met them in Montesano on August 30 or 31 and learned that Frederic Church was going on to Aberdeen. However, after sending the doctor to a ranch, Frederic Church left Montesano on September 1 and upon arriving in Aberdeen outfitted himself for a solo trip up the Whiskah and down the Wynootche." Wood, *Men, Mules and Mountains*, p. 419.

our selves. It was my first trip to Hoodsport and when seated at the breakfast table I became cognizant of the magnetism that attracted our boys to Hoodsport. These Finches were of the Golden variety and were endowed with that charming accomplishment of making every one feel at home. I never short of a banquet enjoyed such feasting as was crowded upon us by this whole souled gentleman. We have no time for particulars but gentle reader if ever you chance to wander upon the borders of Hoods Canal do not fail to call at Finch's. Breakfast over we amused our selves in the shadows of this pleasant picture. A mountain stream rippled close by the door yard and beneath a rustic bridge. Upon the south side was Browns logging camp, and in the boom near by were hundreds of logs, and fine one ones too, from Mr. Finchs claim. A small store, a dwelling of Mr. McCreavy, and a new building under way, these including the barn and boat house, completed the town. Salmon were now running and the children screamed merrily as they chased them, thrashing them over the back with poles. Eight oxen slowly came down the skid way with three large trees gliding along as noiselessly as a serpent. These skids are logs about 16 inches in diamator placed 10 feet apart and half buried and anchored by the earth. Instead of using waggons this style of road way is built, and logs are dragged over them by animals, from three to six logs are dogged to gether and one man walks by the foremost end of the log with oil can and swaub, lubricating each skid. The logs having been rounded at the end and bark removed are easily dragged. We were informed that this fir timber was rated at $6. pr M. feet in the boom or $14. at the saw mill.

Seating our selves upon a log with Mr Price, we had him relate all the news. Mr. Bretherton and Yates had gone up the trail upon the 29th ult and many parties outing had been up the trail, and now empty fruit cans and other marks of tourists were numerous along the trail. A party of prominent gentleman from Seattle consisting of Messrs. Caldwell, Brooks and et al were then making their way up the trail. One of the gentleman was in ill health and was out in these mountains for a breath of air, and pure water, while his friends were eager to meet the bear and elk. They had engaged Mr Windhoffer and three ponies at $100 pr day to carry their luggage and were sparing no pains nor expense to pave the way for a good time bye & bye. A row boat landed containing Messrs Williams and Gray with 50# of bacon which the Lieut had sent over, stating that he would follow next on boat. People were coming and going with packs and each one halted at the great refrigerator and quenched his thirst with cold milk. Every one drank milk, and the table groaned with milk, cream, and butter, yet we seen few cattle

from which it came.

Wedns Sept 3rd. The Lieut had no oppertunity to cross the bay this morning and we are in no hurry to leave this home like place. Basking in the sun shine and idly watching the sea gulls skimming over the glassy waters, we beheld the pretty little steamer Nellie McCreavy steering for the Hoodsport Dock. The Lieut leaped ashore and at 11 A.M. we left Hoodsport with three animals carrying all the salt meat to be had in the two towns, which was only 125#. We found the Hoodsport trail to Lake Cushman an excellent trail and in two hours we were at Lake Cusham [Cushman], noting the many changes. A new trail had been cut through from Lillywaup landing. Messrs Lake and Putnam, two eastern gentleman, had established a restaurant on the east border of the lake, and were prepared to accommodate the weary traveler with excellent meals at 50¢ pr meal.

A trail had been cut around the Lake, saving an hours toil upon the cumbersome raft. Heading the north end of the lake, we observed a new cabin representing a claim of Mr Hayes. Calling at Mr Windhoffers for hay we learned that tanglefoot was dispensed at the rural cabin. By night time we had reached the miners camp near our Camp No 2. Here three substantial cabins had been erected and the miners were sangine [sanguine] that the mines when properly developed would yield in paying quantities. We remained overnight and noticed a vast change since our passage two months previous. This spot then a howling wilderness now presented an air of civilization, and our now broad trail could be traveled at a trot, where we had so recently gained inch by inch through the almost impenetrable forest. Examining some specimens from the mine we noted the chocolate colored porphory, and spar found through out the Olympic range. The metalic copper was sparingly present in these samples. We were kindly entertained by the miners and passed a pleasant night.

Thurs Sept 4th. Set out up the trail making very good time. Mr Price rode over a good portion of the trail, the pack mules following with out any trouble, while we made some short cuts, and while passing near Camp No 4 I was reminded of an unpleasant incident that I neglected until now. I had some fishing tackle tied up in the crown of my hat. Vexed at a tangled mass of vine maple, I gave a violent jerk at a crooked branch which struck upon my head, and drove a large fish hook deep into my scalp. There I was with hat securely and painfully pinioned to my head. The Lieut turned the hat inside out, cutting the line, and proceeded to perform the first and only surgical operation necessary on the trip. Taking a large hunting knife he cut the hook out while I underwent the

427

He cut the hook out

ordeal as I thought attending the scalping operation. We prepared lunch at Camp No 8. We traveled during the evening with nothing to bother us, passing through the old camps that reminded us of many incidents fraught with toil and pleasure, camping this night beyond Camp No 10. where grass was good. We came near having a smash up at this point. Danton and I were up the mountain side rolling logs and limbs down for wood, and one large log beyond our controll went dashing for camp. The mules fortunately were up the gulch grazing. We gave them warning below and men and dogs flew right and left in time to save them selves. Rolling over the camp fire it scattered brands right and left, doing some injury to our equippage, such as mashing cups, pans & etc. A stiff breeze drew down the gulch this night and we spent a good portion of the night in making fires to keep warm. We heard a shot to the north late in the evening, and having passed some luggage left by some party, we presumed that we were nearing the Seattle party. We learned afterwards that a stiff wind had passed over Camp No 14. blowing tents down, and scattering articles of camp and clothing. This was the only hard wind that we experienced in the mountains.

Frid Sept 5th. Having but a short distance to reach the summit of the divide, we were soon descending into the Ducquebusch basin. This was my first trip over this part of the country since the trail had been cut by Col Linsley and his party. Descending into the second scoop out, we passed the Seattle party in camp at our Camp of No 11. They had now come to the farthest point reached by them. The trail beyond this was too difficult for Mr Windhoffer and his ponies, and the jingle of gold failed to tempt him to adventure any farther. They were well equipped and had a representative

of Ham to mix de bitters and do the Cooking. The Lieut halted here to converse with the party, while we moved on with the mules. A gentle decline faced this scoopout and was yet covered with snow. Mr Price here dismounted from his mule and attempted to drive it a head with the other animals. It would not be driven and run back to Camp No 11. giving me a chase of 1000 yds or more. I thought it strange that he choose this plan of proceedure but soon learned the cause of it. We were approaching Yellow Jacket hill, the point that frightened Mr. Windhoffer, also the spot where we afterwards had the sad misfortune of mangling some animals. The descent was almost precipitous over the track of a spring, rock and mud formed the treacherous footing in some places, and in others it was dry, brushy, and a live with yellow jackets. A fire had been kindled to burn them out. Ashes from the debris had covered the trail in places and the entire hill side was covered with a dense smoke, while many logs were burning brightly. This was the agent that persuaded Mr Price to abandon his mule. It was dangerous to go in front of a mule here for more than 100 feet. Threshing the fire out, we attempted to drive the mules down, but they stampeded, and scattered in the scrubby groth [growth] above. Tracking them up one by one we returned them to the trail and tried it once more with success. They slipped and fell from terrace to ledge, groaning and feeling their way. It was truly the most difficult portion of trail that we had ever witnessed a beast of burden pass over, but there was no help for it. We had done all in our power to improve it. It was most difficult traveling for nearly five miles until we had crossed and ascended the mountain side north of the Ducquebusche river. Here we struck the level plateau, having passed <u>Camp 12</u> & 13. where some of our equippage yet remained. We also passed one of the Seattle party and Mr Windhoffer near Camp No 12 who were out hunting and inspecting the trail. The Seattle party as yet had killed nothing but small game and fish. Killing three grouse with my revolver, we halted to rest the mules and await the Lieut, who did not appear. Setting out again we made <u>Camp No 14</u>. at 12 M and found them all glad to see us, with some bacon aboard. They had been unsuccessful for some days in finding large game and were out of bacon, with dog meat as a substitute. Sergt Marsh had been over to ~~Mt Irlene~~ Mt Steel[76] the day before, killing a black bear, and a party returned carrying it to camp entire. Their fur was now beautiful and it is to be regretted that we could not save any of them. It was a pleasure to be located upon these mountains again. Nature appeared more beautifully clad now than before, but little snow had disappeared since we were here before. We

---

[76] Fisher had written "Mt Irlene" but that name was stricken and "Mt Steel" was substituted.

turned all of the animals loose and they galloped away to join their mates near Lake of the Holy Cross, brousing in the sweet grass. It was a perfect paradise here, and strange it was that no game was sighted. While our thoughts ran thus, Sergt Yates cast his eye up the mountain side and beheld a bear carefully working his way around the rocky points. Sgts Marsh, Yates, and Mr Bretherton dashed away after him, while we watched him through the glasses. It seemed impossible for him to escape but it required an hours time for them to make the ascent, and when they arrived at the proper point bruin had disappeared, leaving no track to mark his course. A deer frightened at their noise dashed down the mountain side. Before they could fire, he was out of range, and away. They returned with two mountain grouse and we had supper, all being together again, excepting the Lieut and the two Churches. Once more with our blankets we turn in beneath the dog tents.

Mond [Sat] Sept 6th. I was up and out before any one in camp was astir, off to ward the north. I reached the summit by sunrise, and enjoyed a most beautiful scene. There were three different approaches to gain the summit dividing the Ducquebusche and Quinault rivers. Animals could ascend any of them from the south, but the descent in to the Quinault was impossible for animals and it was beyond our power to prepare the way any farther in this direction. The Col and other members of the party had scouted the country, unsuccessful in finding any point over which animals could be taken. The best of it was so rough that it required careful attention from the footman to make his way. I returned to camp in time for breakfast and the Lieut soon arrived. He had spent some time in the Seattle parties camp thinking he could make a short cut and over take us before night. In this he was mistaken and he camped alone in the Ducquebusche basin. The morning was spent in various pursuits. <u>The Lieut was sleeping in the heather.</u> Some posting up the log book, others greasing shoes. Mr Bretherton was preserving marmot skins and the Kid fleshing a bear skin. Dinner over we compared notes and estimated the distance by trail from this point, Camp No 14, to Hoods Canal via Hoods port. We had been two days in traveling it and with the matter uppermost in our minds we rated it as follows. First half-day from Hoodsport to Miners Camp 13½ miles. Second day from Camp No 2 or Miners Camp to Camp No 10 15. miles. Third half-day from Camp No 10 to Camp No 14. 14. miles. Some declared it 50 miles, as I had always been credited with under estimating distance. I recorded it in this instance at the lowest estimate as 42 miles by the trail. We had formerly judged it as only 20 miles from here

direct to Lake Quinault but after traveling it we estimated it at 25 miles and at 40 miles considering the windings necessary to follow a trail. This camp near Heart Peak being located in the heart of the mountains was a point of importance, and we also estimated the distance to other points. Olympus was considered 14 miles to the N.W. and Constance at least 20 miles to the east by north. From here we could look back to the south and with the glasses see a tree that the Col and I had blazed during a difficult descent while upon the first scout of the Ducquebusche basin. Also the sharp pointed peak that I had passed over, hand over hand, at an alt of more than 6000 feet, was in line and easily distinguished from others, was called Fishers Peak. Some one had found Slate carrying pyrites of Iron in the Ducquebusche stream but only in small quantities. At about one Oclock we were up and moving again. It was thought a settled matter by every one except the Lieut that we would get the mules no farther. But he clung to the idea of meeting the Hoquiam arrangements. With this in view, Sgt Marsh, Yates, Barnes & Higgins went S.W. to explore, and the Kid & my self were to go north and according to my judgement seek an outlet. I meant to descend into the Quinault and follow down its course, trying every trail or favorable point of ascent along the south side, as I could judge the country much better from below than above. Taking the same route I had gone before breakfast we made the ascent and gave up descending in to the Quinault through this centre one of the three approaches. The left was more dangerous and difficult and we spent an hour in gaining the right hand or east one. It was not more than a stones throw from one to the other but most difficult climbing unless we descended below the rocks and came up through the approach proper. Upon reaching the Quinault side we sat down to cool of [off] and view the country. It was a steep descent over stretches of snow and broken stones for 2000 feet and from there a very gentle slope led away to ward the Quinault. Upon either of three sides the mountains rose up to a heigth of 3000 feet, enclosing this gentle slope with rocky walls shaped like the letter U.[77] It was another of the scoop outs or basins common to all of the head waters of these mountains, and in many instances as in this one much snow remained in the centre. The growth in these bottoms was always the same rich carpet of grass and flowers and perfectly clear of timber until you began the ascent upon one side or the other. I was down looking and thought I observed a small object moving. Directing the glass I beheld a large bull elk crossing the basin, and a pair of beautiful antlers floated proudly with his graceful bearing. We watched until

429

---

[77] Fisher appears to have written a V and changed it to a U.

he gained the snow and two more dark objects (Bear) appeared not one hundred yds from and above the elk, and between us. This was growing interesting. Whether it merely happened so or whether they were patiently biding their time we could not tell, nor did we wait. Fresh meat was needed in camp and we began the descent. It was all open country between us and we walked boldly down over the snow and stone, halting occasionally to locate the game. The elk lay down upon the snow and we swung to the left, dropping into a gully and out of his sight. Following this small stream untill it leaped over a bench, we could go no farther. The elk was in plain view with the bear below us and mid way between us and the elk. The Kid carried the Carbine and I gave him first chance to kill his first elk. We found out afterwards that the elk was 500 yds away and 300 feet below us, but the snow and surroundings were deceptive and we estimated it at 200 yds. Lying close in the grass the Kid fired but the elk did not move and no bullet was seen to strike the snow. Again he tried it, raising the sights to 300 yds, with no better success, but the elk jumped to his feet, and looked in vain for the perpetraters. A third shot was fired falling several feet short and the gun was handed to me, as the Elk started to leave at a swinging trot Hastily raising the sights to 500 yds I fired and he halted, holding his left fore leg clear of the snow. I had shattered the fore arm just below the shoulder joint. Raising the sights I gave him another shot but could not tell where it hit. Handing the gun to the Kid, he fired again, breaking the right hipp bone. The snow was covered with blood and he reeled and fell heavily to the snow. Advancing to with in a hundred yds, he rose upon his two good legs and painfully limped ahead. The Kid sent a bullet through the centre of his neck and our amunition was gone. The elk had by this time limped dangerously near a deep gulch that drained the scoop out, and we were afraid to crowd him for fear he would go over. Giving him time to lie down again, I placed my self in range behind a large stone, and rushed up to with in 50 feet of him before he could rise. When he did so I let fly three shots in quick succession from my revolver, two taking effect in the left side. With the sound of the last report he dropped to the earth and died upon the very brink of the gulch. The bear had escaped to the west but we meant them no harm while elk was in sight. We removed the entrails and taking the liver and as much fat as we could carry, set out upon the return for camp, arriving in time for supper. The liver

weighed upwards of 20# and we were issued grog for our prowess. We had been very careful about cutting the throat. As this was a monster elk, weighing more than 1000# with good antlers, we were in hopes of preserving his skin. The dogs made much noise in camp this night chasing some animal to some distance from Camp. Our mules were rapidly filling out upon the good grass in this Camp, and with the exception of B.C. were looking well. B.C., like his master, the packer, positively refused to show his feed, and we often built castles with regard to his ancient pedigree. What did B.C. branded in sign-board letters indicate? Was it British Columbia, as some of the boys would have it, or had he wandered from the happy land of Jerusalem with a record reaching back to a period Before Christ? At any rate this trip was destined to be his last upon earth, and if John Lo is right in his Sunday teachings, we hope that B.C. may have a better time in the happy hunting grounds than he had upon these of the Olympics. The Sergts party in their explorations to day had followed the level to Marmot lake, taking the same course that the Col & I had first traveled, and swinging to the N.W. catching the trail leading around the mountain, where the Lieut, Danton & I had gone upon the Quinault trip. They had enjoyed great sport with bear which were numerous in that locality, feeding upon the sweet Huckleberries. Night drove them into camp before they reached a point of descent.

Sun Sept 7th. Mr Price and Danton set out to Hoodsport taking in some fresh meat to the Seattle party. They were to return with some sugar and Bacon that the Lieut had made arrangements for with the Seattle party. Lieut ONeil, Col Linsley, Mr Bretherton, Hughes, the Kid, and my self returned to the elk. Upon our way down we discovered an other large Bull below and to the right of the dead one, feeding upon the grass. In descending upon the snow, Barns in illustrating how he formerly traveled over such places in Germany lost his footing and went bounding over each little knowl of snow and ice, for a distance of 3 or 4 hundred yds before he could arrest his downward flight. Mr Bretherton next tried, using a flat stone for a toboggan. Matters did not work harmoniously and it was a race to see which would gain the bottom first, Mr B, the stone, or the gun. I caught the gun before it reached the rocks and Mr B checqued his speed after a good ride. No one was hurt but Barns had a severe head ache from the shaking up over the rough snow surface.[78] The elk we paid no

430

---

[78] "Fisher indicates this sport occurred on September 7, when several men visited the elk he and Kranichfeld killed the day before. However, Bairens was then with Marsh, Yates, and Higgins, searching for a route beyond O'Neil Pass. Fisher obviously misplaced the account in his narrative; the event must have occurred on September 10, when Bairens accompanied the men to the place where the elk was killed. This conclusion is strengthened when it is noted that Bairens does not appear in the photograph taken by O'Neil on September 7, showing the men grouped around the dead animal." Wood, *Men, Mules and Mountains*, p. 422.

Linsleys Glacier

attention to until we arrived where the dead one lay. The other had laid down in the grass some 300 yds below, and Mr Bretherton advanced cautiously with his Kodak for a photo.[79] Approaching with in 80 yds of it, there was naught but open ground between them, and he walked boldly up as near as he wished, swinging his arms wildly to frighten the elk into a standing attitude. The elk sprang to his feet and assumed a

proud bearing while his Photo was being taken. How I wished for an instrument to catch the two of them. Bretherton, hatless, coatless, and half pant less, swung his arms wildly to frighten the Elk, but he stood in proud defiance, striking the ground viciously with his feet. The bright morning sun streaming down in a flood of light. We were in the act of running to his assistance when the elk turned tail and trotted slowly away.[80] The Elk as in the Photo stood facing the S. W. and Mr B the N. E., showing the mountain in the back ground that lay at the head of the east Quinault branch. Mr Bretherton stepping the distance <u>which</u> <u>was</u> <u>47</u> <u>ft</u> now returned and we measured the elk as a tailor would measure for a suit of clothing. I only remember his length, which was 102 inches from nose to tail.[81] This was done at Mr Bs direction that he might know his exact dimensions for mounting, which may be seen by visiting the Alpine Clubs Museum in Portland, Oregon, Cor 2" and Washington str room No 43. The elk was now turned over <u>upon</u> <u>his</u> <u>back</u> <u>and</u> <u>Photographed</u> by Lieut ONeil, after which they set to work to remove his skin. The Kid and I were sent over to explore to the north of the Quinault, as well as to give the Kid some exercise in mountain climbing, he not having had oppertunity before. He had often expressed a desire to go out upon one of these picnics, as he termed them, and it was necessary to give him some experience preparatory to a trip then projected.[82] Mountain climbing, like all other pursuits fraught with danger, grows tame with experience, and it would be unfair to expect a novice to follow one with months of fresh experience. Lt ONeil & the Col assisted all day, returning to camp at night with a load of meat, leaving Hughes to assist Mr Bretherton in curing the meat. The Kid and I worked over to the N. E. and descended in to the Quinault immediately under Linsleys Glacier. Here we prepared lunch and began the ascent to

431

[79] "Bretherton wrote an account of this adventure, entitled 'Elk and Camera,' which appeared in *Overland Monthly* in 1900 [see chapter 12, Bernard J. Bretherton, in this book]. Unfortunately, he appears to have mixed the events of two visits to the basin (on September 7 and 10), perhaps to embellish the story, or possibly because of faulty recollection due to the passage of time. Therefore the article cannot be relied upon insofar as it conflicts with the details in his diary, recorded at the time of occurrence. For example, he states in *Overland Monthly* that on September 7, when he approached the elk with his camera, Yates covered the bull with his rifle; but the naturalist's diary and Fisher's narrative both indicate the sergeant was then with another group in the vicinity of O'Neil Pass. Yates did, however, accompany the party that returned to the basin on September 10." Wood, *Men, Mules and Mountains*, p. 420.

[80] "Bretherton's attention had been directed to taking the picture, and his reaction after snapping the shutter is interesting: 'Then I looked up, and the sight before me caused my heart to stop and a clammy sweat break out upon me; for instead of the mild-eyed, timid animal I had expected to see I found myself face to face with a picture of incarnate fury, imbued with the animal instinct of self-preservation. There he stood, so near! his great black mane with every hair erect; his eyes two living coals, and nostrils expanding and contracting with every breath. His nervous ears worked back and forth, sometimes singly and sometimes together, and his grand majestic pose was expressive of acute alertness, but indicated no sense of fear. It was such a sight as a man will carry with him to the grave.' O'Neil gives a somewhat different version of the incident. He indicates that the elk was not discovered until after the men were at work upon the dead elk: 'While working, Mr. Brotherton, our naturalist, happened to glance toward a clump of timber and there asleep was a bull elk. Mr. Brotherton went up to him with his camera. We then woke him up. He roused himself, with a half defiant look turned on us, stood as if posed, and when the camera snapped turned as leisurely as if he were the commandant of a parade and trotted off down the hill.'" Wood, *Men, Mules and Mountains*, p. 420.

[81] "The length from nose to tail proved to be eight and one-half feet but Fisher could not remember, when writing his account, the dimensions of the slain elk, except the length. The mounted specimen was later exhibited at the Oregon Alpine Club's museum in Portland." Wood, *Men, Mules and Mountains*, pp. 275, 420.

[82] "The ascent of Mount Olympus." Wood, *Men, Mules and Mountains*, p. 421.

gain the north side of the Quinault. It proved one of the most difficult tasks of any that I had attempted. While not more than 1000 feet above us, we spent the entire evening in reaching the comb seperating <u>Linsleys glacier</u> from another very large one to the east of it. I regretted many times that I had attempted the ascent but it was more dangerous to turn back than to go on up. Every finger and toe must be used now, and we had to go one at a time, dropping a stout cord back to the low man, hauling the carbine up, anchoring it for the next reach. By this method we made some 400 feet with empty space beneath us. Only that it was of massive slate with cleavage almost upon edge, we never could have ascended a foot, and this at times presented an unwelcomely smooth surface. Gaining the Glacier we camped upon the jagged comb between the two great bodies of snow and ice, finding wood sufficient from the scrubby groth [growth] of Mt hemlock that invariably finds a hold in and among the most barren rocks. This we registered as Camp Snow. Returning to the others, Sergt Heffner had been keeping camp alone, while the Sergeants party had continued operations in search of a route down into the Quinault. They had worked around to the very place where we had dropped in to the large scoop out. They had prospected the mountain all over and were despairing of success, when they were led by chance out upon the rocky point alluded to by us in our descent in to the scoop out. It surely did end abruptly, but by anchoring logs and stones against trees they could tack back to the S.W. & get clear of this point. Here they found that elk had scrambled down, though it looked impassible, and from here on down the thickly wooded hill side, they followed the elk tracks, finding good footing all the way to the stream, and returning to the great scoopout they camped beneath the rocky point where we had erred and paid so dearly for dropping down before examining the most absurd looking point for descent. This probably is the only point by which the Quinault can be gained with animals and this would frighten parties that were not impelled by strong motives.

Mon Sept 8th. Sergt Marsh and party returned to Camp 14. reporting their success. Mr Bretherton & Hughes continued working at the elk, and were visited by the Lieut and the Col taking in more meat. While at work a bear had came very close and viewed the scene, disappearing in the brush. By night they had all of the hind quarters cut up and smok-

ing and the skin and head thoroughly fleshed and under going the action of preserving agts. The Kid and I made several unsuccessful attempts to drop on to Linsleys Glacier but all in vain. We gave up the task. We could easyly reach the one to the east which we did and found it to be about one mile square, and man may never know how deep the snow, and ice, lay.[83] All hours day, and night, you could hear the rumbling, muffled noise of stones grinding beneath this slowly moving mass of crystalized fluid, and occasionly a rounded stone would drop with the escaping water, crowded from its home by the great weight. These Glaciers appeared to lie in funnel shaped receptacles upon the mountain top. During heavy snows they are no doubt filled to over flowing, but at this date they had settled until a comb of slate closed them in upon all sides, save a gap upon the lower side facing the streams, where the water escaped, invariably leaping over the stone face in a pretty fall. This large Glacier was generally level excepting the S. and N. sides. Toward the former it had slipped and jammed as it melted untill it was fretted most dangerously with many grooves about 10 feet apart. Some were shallow and others deep, and the ice honey combed in places, and running water could be seen and heard gurgling and splashing in all directions. At times a sink hole would be passed where the water dropped down in the well like hole to a depth beyond the sense of hearing. For a hundred yards of this fret work, it was most dangerous to move in any direction with out a long alpine stock, which we did not possess. By care we gained the solid surface beyond and scaled the eastern wall. We could see a small lake high up on a bench below us, and running N.E. was a branch of the Docewallups with a pretty but small park at its head. No water fell from this Glacier except at the one point and that into the east Quinault. Dropping to the Glacier we crossed to the N. side where hundreds of snow birds were feeding upon flies, mosquitoes, and other wingd insects that had came in contact with the snow, paralysing them with cold. Here the snow plant lay upon the ice in quantities that resembled the death scene of some large animal, staining a brilliant red for many feet.[84] The snow remained well upon the mountain side facing the south, that every days sun might shine brightly upon its face, but it yielded not to its warmth. Ascending until the snow played out, the Kid concluded that he had enough of this picnicing and would not venture any further. I disap-

---

[83] "Fisher and Kranichfeld had approached the glacier about midway on its western side, at a gap in the ridge that extends south from Echo Rock, a false summit rising between the upper parts of the two glaciers. Anderson Glacier was considerably longer in 1890 than it is today, and blocks of ice frequently crashed down the mountainside because the snout extended over a cliff. Expedition photographs indicate, however, that Linsley's Glacier has changed but little since 1890, although it is perhaps thinner." Wood, *Men, Mules and Mountains*, p. 421.

[84] "Occasionally snowfields in the Olympics exhibit shades of red. This is sometimes the result of wind-blown dust; more often, however, it is due to the presence of algae adapted to living in the harsh environment of the higher altitudes." Wood, *Men, Mules and Mountains*, p. 421.

peared amid the many windings and fractures between the slate walls, gaining a few feet at every turn, until I reached a slanting groove, like the Devils slide in Utah, and up this I made the top. I was more than 6000 feet above sea level astride of the slate comb. Another large Glacier lay beneath me and to the north whose water dropped into a tributary of the Elwha River.[85] This I could trace to the N.W some 8 miles where it joined a larger tributary, judging from its canyon, that came from the S.W. To the N. and between the Elwha, and Docewallups, one continuous spur ran east and west for a distance of some 10 miles, with out a break in its southern face.[86] But little timber or vegetation grew upon its face above an alt of 2000 feet. All about me was a mass of snow and ice, hemmed in by combs and pinnacles of slate, devoid of vegetation, and twirled in to indescriable [indescribable] forms, regardless of cleavage. In some places the cleavage was circular, resembling the annual growth of timber. This appeared to be one of the crowning points or nest egg of these mountains, dividing the waters of the east Quinault, Elwha, Docewallups, and Ducquebusche, and Olympus, as we afterwards discovered, was the other core from which radiated the large branch of the Elwha, the North Quinault, Queets and Hoh, while the Quillayute was formed from streams originating in a lower Country. No sign of mineral appeared in this formation, but one large heap of coarse sand stone lay piled up as if dropped from the heavens upon top of the slate. Veni, vidi, but I was conquered, and could go no farther with out long ropes, and I began a most difficult descent. Looking below I observed the Kid making gisticulations to the S.E. and looking out upon the field of snow I saw the object of his attention, a black bear making for our location. It certainly meant to cross, this being the most favorable point. I since my experience in Bear Jungle did not care to meet Bruin as friend or foe upon this uncertain footing, and I lost no time in joining the Kid upon a bench affording good footing, where we awaited its arrival, amused at its playful actions. Running and walking, by spells, like a child upon its way to school, it came, and when with in 200 yds I fired a shot from my revolver so as to tear the snow up in front of it. Standing high up on its hind legs it surveyed carefully for the cause of this.

On it came. Passing near us, it choose a more difficult point than I had to ascend. Stopping occasionally to note our movements, it continued upward with slow and labored progress. Returning to our camp of last night, we slung packs and descended at a different but difficult point. Passing 10 elk that were lying down, we continued on down the Quinault in search of some place of ascent. None was found, and I reached the spot where we approached the stream on our former trip. I knew that the Sergts party had explored by this time between this and lower down, where the Col and I had operated. At one point we found more Iron pyrites and spar than we had discovered elsewhere, but afterwards ascertained that it carried no gold. We saw some fresh elk sign in the Quinault basin made by one lone elk. From its very recent passage and abrasions upon the willows, we concluded that it was the same one that we had photographed and frightened out of the scoop out, and we returned up the stream to learn where it had came down. On our way up we found the last camp of the Shelter party in the Quinault basin. Upon a blazed tree was written (J.L. Shelters and Dennis DeFord, June 27th 1889. Crying for want of meat. Raining and rivers rising. Here with four days flour). We also discovered his mining tools that he had often referred to which consisted of one long handled shovel standing against the decayed side of a tree, and covered with bark. Many pieces of barren quartz lay scattered about this as did all of their camps. These two men had no doubt crossed these mountains by coming up the Quinault and going down one of the streams tributary to Hoods Canal. However, we were unable to find any marks of their camps after leaving the Quinault basin.[87] Another party had left camp fires, and removed bark for camp purposes from the trees. This parties work we judged to be about five years old, and traced it up the Skokomish and out to Camp No 14 loosing track of it, untill near the Quinault water, where we descended later with the mules. Here we lost all trace of them. No names or record was left to denote their nationality, any more than it was a white mans fire. In one place the charred ends of the once green sticks remained as they had left them. With the exception of these two parties, there were no signs or marks of any one ever having passed over this country,

433

---

[85] "Fisher saw the Eel Glacier. He had climbed to Flypaper Pass, or perhaps slightly higher on the ridge to either side. However, the glacier is the source of Silt Creek, a stream tributary to the Dosewallips, not the Elwha." Wood, *Men, Mules and Mountains*, p. 421.

[86] "Fisher was high enough to be looking down the lower part of the Hayes, which he mistakenly concluded had its source in the glacier at whose head he stood. The 'larger tributary' would have been the Elwha. He could not see the end of the glacier from his vantage point and apparently failed to realize that the stream flowing from it turned to the northeast to join the Dosewallips. The spur running east and west would have been the ridge extending from Mount Clay Wood to Wellesley Peak." Wood, *Men, Mules and Mountains*, p. 421.

[87] "If Shelters and DeFord did cross the mountains in 1889, they accomplished this prior to the Press Expedition's trip. In view of the rivalry then existing with regard to exploration of the Olympics, it is unlikely that, had they been successful, the achievement would have gone unpublicized, but for the fact they were prospectors, interested only in locating deposits of minerals. It may well be that they were the first to cross the mountains." Wood, *Men, Mules and Mountains*, pp. 421–22.

until we reached ~~Chester~~ a valley in the Elwha basin, where we state what we discovered and leave the readers to judge for them selves. Continuing on up the now small tributary we passed a dry gulch in the rocky wall but it was not at all inviting. We learned that the Elk had descended as we had done by ascending to the east, and swinging back to the S.W. We did not care to ascend at the same point that we had came down. So we swung more to the N.E. and were encouraged for a time by a gradual slope. Slowly but surely it assumed a steeper slope until we found our selves upon hands and knees, clutching at any frail object that presented its self. We had worked in to the track of a recent snow slide, where the earth and stone was wet and smooth, most miserably so. Darkness was gathering and there was no prospects of a camp in sight. We were too far from the bottom to return, and make the summit to night we could not. The groove we were in ran out with the ascent landing us upon a rounded angle of this peak. A scrubby hemlock growth set in and grew heavyer above. Hauling our selves up from tree to tree, we found a hole where a good sized tree had uprooted, falling uphill, and sliding down until its branches lay scattered about the hole that the roots had torn in the earth. The Kid had long been wishing to camp and we pitched in this hole and kindled a fire. Searching about we discovered a bucket ful of snow, perhaps less. This we melted from, and prepared our supper. I had sized up our surroundings while searching for snow, and found that we were upon the side of a most decidedly steep mountain. We were just preparing to anchor ourselves in the hole when the fire caught in the green branches of a scrubby hemlock. Up at this alt the moss was dry as tinder upon the boughes, and before we could realize our danger the atmosphere above was a seething, roaring, flaming mass of fire. As each tree caught, the roar of the burning foliage and moss was deafening. Limbs and frag-ments of bark kept falling, and spreading down the mountain side to the west, as a very light breeze blew in that direction. Loading up our traps, it was now as light as day and we crawled out to the east against the breeze to escape the heat and flying embers. Here we anchored for two hours before it was safe to return to our hole and indulge in sleep. The Kid declared that when he joined the camp again that he would go on the pack train and remain with it to the bitter end. The fire died out excepting a few dead trunks that burned dangerously near us all night. It was perfectly warm with out any more fire and we slept nicely.

Tues, Sept 9th. We did some desperate climbing to gain the top, and from here with the glass we look down and see them smoking meat in the basin. Descending some 3000 feet into the basin, we took up the elks trail from where he was photographed, and trailed it down the mountain side, but lost the trail, and could never learn how that Elk got down into the basin of the Quinault, but we found a dry gulch that a man could descend in, with careful climbing. We now returned to where they were smoking the elk and prepared lunch. Hughes had gone in to Camp 14 with a load of meat. Taking the wrong pass, he wandered all day amid the cliffs, getting to camp late in the evening. This was the fattest animal I ever saw butchered. The saddles were completely enveloped with three inches of fat. Lunch over we taken the horns, head, and what meat we could carry, and returned to Camp No 14. We could not well do any thing towards the trail until the pack train returned, bringing up some tools from Camp No 12. This proved an unusually cold[88] night, and frost lay thick and white upon the grass, with ice formed upon the small pools of calm water.

Wedns Sept 10th. Mr Bretherton, Sergt Yates, Barnes, Hughes, Higgins, and my self went over to the basin where our meat was smoking and descended into the Quinault branch, through the dry gulch, after some beautiful specimens of <u>quartz crystals</u> that we had discovered the day before, near Shelters last camp. They were beauties indeed. From shelving stone that projected over the water, many beautiful specimens were suspended like stalactites, and not far away they were in pockets in the clay of various and beautiful forms. Among others we found one a perfect cross, formed of large and small Hexagonal bars. Some were perfectly trans parent, while others were colored from yellow to green and amber. Gathering specimens for all, we returned to the temporary camp. Taking the remaining meat we set out for Camp No 14. Mr B, Sgt Yates & I bringing up the rear with the elk skin. The knee and hock joints, hoofs as well, were intact, and green as it were amounted to about 100# in heft. With this and 80# of meat, we had nearly 3000 feet of steep ascent to make, and as much descent upon the south side to Camp 14. The entire distance lay over treacherous footing, alternately of snow and loose stones. Exchanging packs to spell each other, you can well imagine the task was one of magnitude. We reached camp with it, and I have since had the pleasure of seeing it in the museum at Portland, Oregon. But the fawn skin that Mr Bretherton had carried for miles over

434

---

[88] Transcriber's note: Next page is sketch, apparently clipped from a magazine, depicting quartz crystals. Printed below is the legend, "Cluster quartz xls." Depicts several crystals, pointing in various directions.

the mountains was stolen by some unprincipled person. The pack train had returned with sugar, bacon, and the needed implements. The Seattle party they had over taken enroute home carrying one bear skin as a trophy of their prowess. In return for our kindness they had sent us a vessel protected by willow, with best wishes for our success. A pow wow was ordered to night. Beneath the twinkling stars and in the glare of the camp fire, the Lieut partially unfolded the following. We would break camp in a few days and again seperate into two or three parties, and finish our explorations, while some would go down the Quinault with the animals. The details were not made yet as we were to remain together until the trail was complete into the Quinault, where it was thought that a small party could manage untill they met the Hoquiam party, who had agreed to cut the trail as far as the mouth of the stream coming in from Bruins Peak.[89]

Thurs Sept 11th. We packed up every thing excepting what we meant to carry upon our backs. All except equippage sufficient to get along with was to be sent into Hoods port for ship ment to Pt Townsend where we intended to assemble. This done, Sergts Marsh, Yates, Danton, Hughes, the Kid and my self set out to work the trail. Heading south by west over the level plateau we passed by Marmot lake. Turning due S.W. here through a pass,[90] we dug a toe path zig zagging down a very steep slope in to the basin N. of Mt ~~Irlene~~ Steel.[91] Crossing a great bank of snow in the basin, we prepared a camp where we had been so close to the seven elk. This was the east Main Camp or No 15. We prepared lunch here and followed the trail, cutting a log out here and there. Just after passing the tree where The Lieut, Danton and I had passed, naming and registering Mt ~~Irlene~~ Steel, three bear were seen at once. One up the mountain side, one in front, and a third to the left of us, not more than twenty yds away. This was the largest black bear I ever saw. Loking [Looking] at us intently for a moment, it started to ward us and Sergts Marsh and Yates fired simultaneously. Bruin dropped with a bullet through his brain and never moved again. This shot setted [settled] a question that I have often heard contended. The bear held his head high with nose almost level with his fore head. The bullet nevertheless penetrated the frontal arch, not glancing as many contend that it would. This bear was in full fur and glossy black, an excellent specimen and worth all of forty Dollars, but we could not carry it with our work.

Continuing we completed the trail as far as the rocky point over which the trail descended. Dropping to the gulch for water, we pitched camp for the night in a patch of dead timber. During the day we had killed 5 grouse, a duck, and bear and were not in want of meat for supper. Hughes was preparing a pretty nest for the night when timber caught fire and burned him out of house and home, as it did all of us before morning. A laughable incident now occurred at the Kids expense, who was an expert at loosing pipes. At noon time a spoon was found with out an owner. The Kid denied it as his property and made us a very pretty little speech regarding his methodical and systematic manner of doing business in camp life. A spoon was our only instrument for preparing and eating our victuals, save our hunting knives, and was consequently an article of general utility in camp needs. Every man was now his own cook, and the Kid had no spoon to mix his flour with. An investigation proved that he had lost spoon, pipe, tobacco, needles, thread, and in fact almost every thing

Yellow Jacket Hill

---

[89] "This was Tade Creek, a name that does not appear on today's maps. The stream was probably Graves Creek, but could have been O'Neil Creek. Success Creek, which is the main tributary of Graves Creek, and O'Neil Creek both have their source near Bruin's Peak." Wood, *Men, Mules and Mountains*, p. 422.

[90] "Because this gap at the head of the Duckabush was used by the pack train in crossing the Grand Divide, it became known in later years as O'Neil Pass. The elevation is 4950 feet." Wood, *Men, Mules and Mountains*, p. 422.

[91] Fisher had written "Irlene" but it has been changed to "Steel."

of importance, and he laid it all to the poor dead bear, and refused to join us in the laugh. Sgt. Marsh returned to Camp 15, carrying as much bear meat as he could. There He found The Pack train with Lieut ONeil, Mr Price, Sgt Heffner and Higgins. Col Linsley and Mr Bretherton remained in Camp No 14 to perfect their arrangements.

Frid Sept 12th. Sgt Marsh, Mr Price and Higgins went into Hoodsport taking our blankets et al things from Camps 14. & 12. Yellow Jacket hill had now grown impassable for ordinary animals, and in making its ascent a sad accident happened. B.C., a pack mule, had almost gained the top of this bad place when his footing gave way, and he came tumbling down among the animals below. Tripping another mule, a half dozen of them were knocked down. Rolling for a distance, they gained their feet. B.C. and one other continued until they brought up in an ugly gulch, bruised and bleeding. They were unpacked and extricated from their prison, but were unable to travel from their injuries. Grazing and water was good below here and they were necessarily abandoned for the time, and the party moved on much saddened to leave two animals that had been our best friends in the many struggles of this adventure some trip. They reached Hoods port upon the third day and found the two Churches at that point, who now set out to over take the camp. Our party was overtaken by Lieut ONeil who joined us, and by noon we had completed the trail to the Quinault stream, connecting on to the elk trail that followed down the stream. While this was a passable trail there were many logs to be removed before the mules could travel it. Here we cached our tools and other articles. After preparing lunch we returned to Camp 15. Col Linsley and Mr Bretherton arrived just as we did, and we enjoyed an elegunt bear stew and the last beans for many days. The willow covered present from the Seattle party was given a place by the large camp fire and the parting address was delivered by the Lieut, embracing his instructions which were as follows. Col Linsley in command with Mr Bretherton, Sgt Yates, Danton, Hughes, the Kid, and my self, were to proceed to Mt Olympus, and there we were to take routes to be selected by the Col from Mt Olympus, which were to embrace the western streams. Mr Bretherton and Sergt Yates were to constitute one party. The Col with Hughes and the Kid, a second party, while Danton and I formed the third party. We were first to ascend Mt Olympus and plant the Copper Box of the Alpine Club, and then seperate, taking in the Hoh, Quillayute, and western country, in general. Lt ONeil, Sgt Marsh, Mr Price, Barnes, Higgins, and the two Churches, if they returned, would accompany the pack train, until they

were sure of getting through. When the Hoquiam party were met The Lieut would, accompanied by some one, explore the Raft River, sending the two Church [Churches] over to the Queets, and the animals with Mr Price, and sufficient men in charge, would be shipped direct from Hoquiam to Portland via Ocean steamer. Sergt Heffner would continue in charge of the mess, and cook for the party. Tobacco was issued to those in need, and we were told to take what rations we wanted, which was all we could carry. We taken each as follows, intended to run us one month if necessary, but if possible were to come out by October 5th.

Flour 25#, yeast powder 1#, salt 1#, Tea $\frac{1}{2}$#, sugar 4#, Bacon 6 to 8#, smoked meat 2#, Chocolate $\frac{1}{2}$#. In addition to this we carried axes, guns, amunition, our cooking utensils, with $\frac{1}{2}$ shelter tent each, Kodak, Copper box, and other necessaries. Our packs averaged about 60# each, and we soon discovered that we were loaded to the limit of our abilities. We passed a sociable evening and turned in upon the grass at several camp fires, passing this season. The place having been fired no doubt by the unknown party that had passed over this route, all brush had been killed out, and now only the mountain variety of Huckle berries grew here. They are very sweet and much sought by the bear, which could be seen at a long distance. We never passed this dead timber mountain with out seeing from one to three, and only one of the entire number met displayed any signs of fear. This one was most probably frightened by two dogs that we were trying to hiss on. Tiger, it was claimed by his master, was an excellent bear dog, and upon this occasion we proceeded to test his instincts as a bear dog. We pointed and run to wards the bear to attract their attention, but No! Max chased a butterfly, and Tiger could find nothing but a chip monk, which he put up a tree, and remained with it until the bear had ample time to make good its escape, and then he quickly found its trail but did not follow it beyond open ground. We found dogs a great nuisance through out the trip, at least such as we had, and no matter what their good points are they must be frequently helped where they could not climb.

Sat Sept 13th. Col Linsley, Mr Bretherton, Sergt Yates, Danton, Hughes, the Kid, and my self, set out over the trail. It was a long and tiresome descent of some 4000 feet and our knees were weak beyond controll when we reached the stream. Here we halted and prepared lunch, repacking and taking on the articles previously cached at this point. In the mean time Sergt Heffner was left in camp untill The Pack train should come on, and the Lieut and Barnes passed us, working the trail on down the river. We had formerly decided to follow down

436

stream until we reached the first stream of note coming in from the N. which was two miles from here or about six miles from Linsleys Glacier.[92] This we reached at 3 P.M. We unslung packs and scouted to learn if we could make the ascent. We scouted either side, and the canyon, and concluded to ascend here on the morrow. While preparing supper, Lieut ONeil and Barnes approached, having cleared the trail this far, and they pitched camp near us. Mr Bretherton asked the Col what he meant to call this camp. The Col, vexed at his oyster, replied indirectly in a chosen term, and the camped [camp] was named Odamit. We estimated our travel at four miles to day. No game was seen and while our packs were so heavy we ate freely.

Sun Sept 14th. The Lieut and Barnes pulled out early to work on the trail. Our party got started at 8 A.M., choosing the east side of the tributary to make the ascent. It was [a] warm day beneath the timber and brush, and so steep that we crawled from one object of support to another, and found it necessary to blow frequently, and cool off. We traveled untill 1 P.M. before we found water, which was at a small spring in a pocket upon the hill side. Here we prepared lunch and proceeded on to the N. By 3 P.M. we were almost as high as the pass, but more than a mile of country lay between us and the pass which was most difficult to travel over. Gulches whose sides were precipitous and crumbling had cut deep into the earth & stone, and it required 30 minutes to cross each one. Between them was a perfect jungle of shrubs. When night came we estimated that we were not more than one and one half miles from where we set out in the morning. But we had a most beautiful spot to camp upon. Alaska Cedar grew more numerous here than at any point upon the west slope of these mountains. A brook now almost dry and grown up in grass and flowers formed a vista for quite a distance down the hill side, and upon either side was clear of brush for a short distance. A small lakelet gathered the water, and near its margin were many elk and bear tracks, but no animals were sighted. The trees were entirely clothed with a covering of yellow moss and it required much care to avoid setting the woods on fire. A very pleasant night was passed and this was registered as Camp Comfort. Nothing new had developed in the mineral or vegetable kingdoms, nor had we seen any signs of a human being ever having passed this way. Sgt Yates carried a rifle, The Kid one, Mr Bretherton a shot

gun, and the Col and I a revolver each, but no object had been seen to shoot at.

Mon Sept 15th. We set out at 8 A.M. and run into a nest of cliffs. The Col a slow but earnest traveler hampered by heavy packs made slow progress, and I ascended a cliff for a look out. A pretty meadow lay upon the slope in front of and above me. Informing them of the fact, I crossed it, waiting some time for them to follow. They remained resting some moments and with the exception of Sergt Yates dropped into the canyon and brush to make the ascent. I continued and made the pass very easyly, waiting long for their appearance. A cool wind blew from the north, and moist with perspiration I kindled a fire. Uneasy at their long silence, I examined my situation by climbing a point of rocks above the timber and discovered that the canyon branched like a crows foot into three branches, and they might go through either of them, missing my route. I hallooed and was answered by Sergt Yates, who was going through the east pass, having followed me through the meadow. During my absence from the fire it had spread, catching in the dry moss among the trees, and away it went. I was uneasy that it might spread and interrupt the ascending party, but they emerged from the central gulch and we all assembled upon the summit, and considered the country ahead of us. The fire did not burn very far and the wind carrying the smoke south did not cloud our view, but from here we could see that a large fire was burning near the straits which gave off great clouds of smoke and obstructed our view of the north for several day's. The remainder of the morning was spent here, to no effect. There was but one way out, and that to the N.W. The water upon this side flowed into the west branch of the Elwha, and the slope was very precipitous. Dropping into a gulch we prepared lunch and set out to the west and entered a beautiful meadow of some 40 acres that lay under the N side of Capitol Mountain, a peak that we had often noticed from afar, shaped much as the Capitol building from the east, but from other directions it lost its form and beauty. Here we layed off a good portion of the evening. This meadow was perfectly level, richly carpeted with grass, and near the centre was an elk wallow, where the noble creatures had recently sported in great numbers. Mr Bretherton and Sergt Yates went North, following a ridge or saddle that connected us with a tall and important peak.[93]

437

---

[92] "On the trip down the Quinault with O'Neil and Danton, Fisher indicated the creek was seven miles below Linsley's Glacier. This tributary of the East Fork, now called Pyrites Creek, was referred to as Smokey Creek by Linsley, and he noted it was 'distant about three miles' from where they had struck the Quinault. Bretherton states the men called it Fire Creek, 'on account of a slight accident.' (The reader should note this is not the Fire Creek shown on today's maps.)" Wood, *Men, Mules and Mountains*, p. 422.

[93] "The description of this peak in *Steel Points* sounds very much like Mount Christie, but that peak rises three miles northwest of Bretherton's Pass. The mountain in question must have been Peak 6024 (the Press Expedition's Mount Taylor), located at the head of Rustler, Buckinghorse, and Delabarre Creeks." Wood, *Men, Mules and Mountains*, p. 423.

Danton and the Kid ascended upon a bench to the S.W. finding two mountain lakes, which were named Lakes Danton and Eda. The Col searched for signs of previous parties, but in vain. I scouted in the direction that Mr B. & the sergt had gone but taking the opposite side of the ridge from them. Gaining the base of the Peak, I swung to the left, and they to the right. Passing a small lake, I learned that this ridge was a dividing line between a tributary of the Elwha and one of the North Quinault branch. They swung to the east following an elk trail that circled again to the west and ascended the peak which had much fine grass upon the south side, and snow upon the north. From here they saw much rough country but indistinctly as there was smoke from fires in the north. We all returned to the meadow, and the Col dropped down upon the west side of the saddle to camp. Danton and I were not inclined to make any preperations or comforts for camp and always built a seperate fire, sleeping well regardless of rocks, feathers, or mud, while the remainder of the party erected canvas shelters of small dimension. The woods were open and in parks upon this saddle and we were much charmed with the surroundings, but were confidant that the snow in winter would clear it of animal life. Some grouse were seen this eve but none were killed. Three pairs of antlers much decayed were observed near this camp, but no other bones to represent the body were found. We blazed several trees that may be seen for quite a distance from this meadow and registered as at Camp pass, estimating distance gained to day at one and one half miles.[94]

Tues Sept 16th. Danton and I up early and breakfast over, we were sent ahead to prospect the peak. Reaching its Southern base, we unslung packs and ascended, swinging to the left. Loking [Looking] back toward Camp pass we could see a bear feeding with in 150 ydes of camp, but they did not observe him. Gaining the west side of this peak we could trace a good sized stream, and canyon to the S.W. turning south, that could have been nothing else but the north Quinault branch. We now observed that our party had passed our packs, taking the long and circuitous route of ascending, with out waiting to receive our report. We descended to our packs and followed them up over a very good trail, and at 10 A.M. we were with in a few yds of where Danton and I had been in the morning. Rain now set in and fog gathered until we could discern nothing to the N. or N.W. We laid off in

hopes the fog would raise but it grew worse, everything became saturated and a cold wind set in from the N.W. We went into camp having gained about 1000 yds in our desired course (N.W.). It was a miserable day and night in the cold rain. But little timber grew here, and that formed no shelter. A few Elk tracks marked the earth, which all pointed to the Quinault. We examined this locality thoroughly for signs of the Seattle Press Party but found no marks of man. We used snow for water and registered at Camp Be fog. Mr Bretherton was quite an artist at sketching, and left many comical drawings upon the trees.

Wednes Sept 17th. The sun came out bright but was some time in lifting the fog. The Col made almost to the top of this peak, gaining an alt of 5400 feet. At last we gain a view of the northern country and observe three ridges with as many streams running parallel to the north, tributary of the Elwhas west branch.[95] Descending over a mammoth glacier, we gain the west ridge and follow it north. A sand stone formation rises from the crest and makes travel difficult. Sergt Yates cripples a bear, but lost it, and by noon we have gained the north end of the ridge over looking the Elwha, and to the N.E. we could observe the main forks, or canyons, where this branch joins the one I had seen from near Linsleys Glacier, forming the main branch or Elwha proper. Beneath us was no doubt one of the valleys where the Press Party had camped during their sojourn in these mountains. We had been unable to find water or snow since leaving the Glacier, excepting a pool of highly colored, brackish water that was near at hand. They all ate lunch dry but my self. I made tea and found the water O.K. It was precipitous over looking the Elwha, but by heading to the west we descended and turned north again, approaching the main west branch by night. The timber growth had grown excellent again but many wind falls barred the way. We examined the woods for marks and found only a stick that some one had been whitling upon. This was no doubt the work of one of the Press party. We were not a great ways from the source of this stream, alt 1700, about the same as the Skokomish R. This we registered as Camp Lowlands and estimated to days travel at six miles. Mr Brethertor had collected some specimens from the feathered tribe. Otherwise there was nothing new. The stream presenting the same milky appearance as the others. We thought we were under the N.E. side of Olympus, but were mistaken,

---

[94] "Because they could not travel in a straight line, they had gone about twice that far—one and one-half miles from Camp Comfort to the divide, then a like distance to Camp Pass. But they had gained only one and one-half miles toward their destination." Wood, *Men, Mules and Mountains*, p. 423.
[95] "The three ridges were, from east to west, those lying between Hayes River and Godkin Creek, Godkin and Buckinghorse Creeks, and Buckinghorse and Delabarre Creeks. The explorers evidently considered the Hayes the East Fork of the Elwha and the stream flowing from Elwha Basin the West Fork or Branch, thus the river below their juncture would have been 'the main Elwha.'" Wood, *Men, Mules and Mountains*, p. 423.

and no doubt under the same that the Press party considered as Olympus, for, by crossing to the S.W. you would be over looking the North fork of the Quinault.[96]

Thurs Sept 18th. There was a flat bottom bordering the stream here and we scouted it thoroughly for trails. We found scattering ones all leading to the S.W. Had we followed them we no doubt would have found the Press parties trail.[97] We crossed to the N bank of the Elwha and skirted the mountain side until travel became impassable, and we dropped again, striking the stream in an open meadow of good grass and some alder thickets, of small growth. We pitched camp about four Oclock after a hard days jaunt, making about 4 mile, and the aneroid registered 2275 feet. Mr Bretherton and I set out to select a route for the morrow. Following the stream up untill the water came from under the snow, we learned that we could pass through upon the snow. Prospecting for other outlets we returned to camp, reporting our success. This we registered as Camp Glacier. The surroundings would suggest this as a favorite haunt for game, but none was seen, and we used the last of our sugar to night, and chocolate as well. During the night a rain set in and Hughes was making the rounds in search of a lantern. We expected he would ask for Electric lights next. He had left flour and all just as he had scattered things in getting supper, and was now most anxious to care for those precious stores. The rain however did not last long and we enjoyed sweet repose once more.

Frid Sept 19th. We set out following up the Elwha. A grassy slope bordered either side of the stream untill approaching the Canyon. Here it leaped down from bench to bench, and many side streams were received from melting glaciers that lay upon the mountain top. The walls of this Canyon were something grand, rising to a heigth of 3000 feet. The bed of the canyon lay almost N & south and was filled to a depth of 100 feet or more with ice and snow. It raised with a gradual ascent for a distance of two miles, and not with standing that every days sunshine had a clear sweep, concentrating its rays upon this snow, it remained firm and hard. Two views were taken with the Kodak while ascending upon the snow, and the first Glacier was gained at alt of 4000 feet.

Here one might well imagine him self with in the Arctic Circle. Great banks of snow, and ice, containing the fall of many years, met the eye in all directions. Numerous basins were filled with water forming lakes and lakelets. Gaining the summit we unslung packs and viewed the country. Due west about one mile was Mt Olympus. There could be no mistaking now. We had viewed it a score of times from afar. The ridge upon which we were formed a crescent with its bow to the north, its southern point connected with Glacier Peak, while the west point butted against Mt Olympus. Below and with in the circle of this ridge lay a beautiful basin carpeted with grass, heather, and small Huckleberry. All of the surrounding shoulders and pinnacles of stone were worn away and rounded like a monitors back, from the effects of sliding snow from above. The action of the snow must be something terrible here during the winter. Slate, quartz, and sand stone were alike ground down and polished by natures icy hand. Mr Bretherton and Hughes followed the ridge to the N. and the Col and I ascended Glacier Peak that we had first mistaken for Olympus. We reached an alt of 5300, which was the top.[98] The topmost portion was entirely of a course sandstone formation down to alt of 4000 feet, where slate set in. This variety of sandstone is very hard and coarse presenting a true cleavage, and we observed large and beautiful slabs of from two to many inches in thickness. From this Peak we had an excellent view. Looking back at the Elwha we could see its many tributaries and the peculiar course of this west branch, shaped like a fish hook, with its point joining the glacier that we had just left. To the S.W. we could trace a large stream or its canyon for a great distance, and beyond it lay a long low ridge which we judged to be at least forty miles away. I could also recognize the mountains around Lake Quinault to our south. I could clearly distinguish the canyons of the N and east forks of the Quinault. This stream running S.W. we could not make out. Some maps had the Quillayute rising east of Olympus, while others had the N branch of the Quinault rising here. Taking a sketch of the country we descended to our packs. Mr Bretherton and Hughes had returned and reported no streams in sight to the north except a tributary of the Elwha. They reported heavy

439

---

[96] "The statement regarding the Quinault was true, but their position was more than a dozen miles southeast of Mount Carrie, the peak the Press Expedition mistook for Olympus." Wood, *Men, Mules and Mountains*, p. 424.

[97] "The Press Expedition stayed near the site of Chicago Camp, on the north side of the Elwha, prior to making the climb to Low Divide. Although Linsley's party crossed Christie's path at some point in this vicinity, it is not likely the men would have detected evidence of the Press Expedition having passed, unless by accident they stumbled upon its camp. The ground had been covered with five feet of snow in May, and by then the Press explorers had abandoned trail building and they blazed a tree only occasionally." Wood, *Men, Mules and Mountains*, p. 424.

[98] "Apparently the reference is to an unnamed subsidiary peak (5819 feet) on the north ridge of Mount Queets (6480 feet), the mountain the men had mistaken for Olympus when they were in the Elwha Basin. Fisher gives two elevations for 'Glacier Peak'—5300 and 5350—thus placing it some 1300 feet higher than the pass, which he estimated at 4000 feet (750 feet too low). Linsley and Fisher did not have time to climb Mount Queets, but they could have attained this lesser summit one-half mile south of the pass." Wood, *Men, Mules and Mountains*, p. 426.

snow upon the north side and thought by keeping around the ridge that we could reach Mt Olympus with out any trouble. While we were out scouting, those remaining with the packs had sighted bear in the basin between Olympus and Glacier Peak and had descended in quest of them. We presently heard shots from Sergt Yates and the Kids gun's, and observed a bear making his escape. The country was all open for quite a distance and it was a pretty sight to see Bruin flying over snow and heather. This was the only bear that I had ever seen thoroughly frightened. Through the glass I could distinctly make out that if injured it was only a flesh wound. They who think that a bear can not run should have witnessed this one. It was but a very short time in covering two miles of territory and disappeared around the S.W. side of Mt Olypus. The Col was strongly inclined to drop very low towards night, in search of camping grounds, and usually by night we had lost all the heigths that we had gained during the day. Taking the extra packs we descended to the bear hunters. The Kid was under the impression that his gun barrell was crooked, as his abilities as a marksman were not to be doubted. Danton assumed the role of Big Injun, and boasted of his prowess as a bear slayer to Little Injun, the Kid, untill he worked him into a rage. Sergt Yates, in the meantime, had cropped down into the basin and redeemed his falling record by slaying a monster black bear. We removed a claw each as a momento of the occasion, made doubly romantic by our ghoal, Olympus. While we were removing the skin the Col, apparently not in love with bear meat, had set out across the basin, and disappeared in the gulch below. We taking a quarter each and wished very much to camp here, as the ground was favorable and wood and water plenty. Our bacon was running low and it was very essential that we make some additions to our larders. Darkness was coming and we set out to overtake the Col. He had gone on about one mile, dropping to the bottom of an ugly gulch through which the water plunged with a deafening roar, and following it a cool draught of air. There was no word of complaint but an air of dissatisfaction pervaded the camp which was established and removed again, to a point further down the gulch. Danton and I were satisfied anywhere, and remained where we were. Danton and the Kid now shook hands over the bear

controversy, and we entertained the Kid at our house for the night. Every thing seemed to go wrong this eve. Hughes had lost his footing and it was a race between him self and bruins hind leg to see which would roll the more rapidly. His belt dropped off in the race. His look was one of pity when he discovered its loss. I had picked it up, and returned it to him after enjoying his agonizing glance at the walls of this ugly gulch. The bear meat which we had carried along was now sampled and would have staggered a Digger Injun.[99] Its odor was the tripple extract of valerian, upon which it had been feeding, and its flavor was the same multiplied by ten. I had formerly eaten dog, crow, owls, and hawks, and considering the present stock of bacon, I must not long for pie. I made a meal of it very much as a novice would on limburg cheese, and was surprised that it did not make me sick. The others ate very sparingly. Three bear had been seen to day but no sign of other game. Elk nor deer had not been in this basin during the summer. We estimated that we had traveled four miles to day and called this Camp Pluto in Plutos Gulch.[100]

Sat Sept 20th. As usual our little party had breakfasted early and went down to the Cols Camp. They were in the mouth of a side gulch and like seals upon the damp and shelving rocks. There were three of these deep gulches draining the basins to form the main stream, which we afterwards learned was the Queets River. This headed between Mt Olympus alt 7500 and glacier peak alt 5350. Their highest altitudes were not more than a mile apart. Dropping to the Queets, of 1000 feet elevation, the readers can picture for them selves the character of the gap between and in which we were encamped.[101] Although we observed but little standing, a large Alaska Cedar had rolled down from Mt Olympus and bursted into many pieces. The snows of many winters had robbed it of its deep yellow color, but it retained its terebinthic odor. From this we split alpin stocks, and mine was a great friend to me in days to come. We ascended to ward Olympus and by 10 A.M. had gained an altitude of nearly 4000 feet which landed us up on a beautiful level bench at the east base of Mt Olympus. It contained perhaps 30 acres and many huge blocks of sandstone were distributed over its surface that had tumbled from Olympuss lofty summit. This basin at the head of the Queets was the largest of any

440

---

[99] "'Digger Indians' was a term used during the Nineteenth Century for various tribes living in the Great Basin west of the Rocky Mountains. The name, which had no ethnological significance, was generally used derogatorily and is believed to have been derived from the fact the people dug roots for food." Wood, *Men, Mules and Mountains*, p. 426.

[100] "According to Bretherton, after killing the bear they 'went down into the creek bottom & made camp, calling it Bear Camp.' Linsley wrote that they 'camped for the night in one of the cañons of Olympus through which flows one of the tributaries of the Quit. The camp was so disagreeable that we called it Pluto's Box.'" Wood, *Men, Mules and Mountains*, p. 426.

[101] "Although unintentional, this was a gross exaggeration, perhaps due to the abrupt nature of the terrain. Mount Olympus and Glacier Peak (Mount Queets) were six miles apart, and the elevation of the river in the lower part of Queets Basin was about 3000 feet." Wood, *Men, Mules and Mountains*, p. 426.

Mt Olympus from the east

we had discovered, and with the rocks terraced around its circular form [it] was remindful of a great amphitheatre with its vacant seats over looking this beautiful spot. Colorado had preceded us, but never-the-less, we christened this as The Garden of the Gods,[102] and well worthy is it of the name. Our object first was to ascend and deposit the copper box.

We pitched camp here and over hauled our much torn clothing and well worn shoes. A little brook rippled by and washing was soon out to dry. Huckle berries grew large and sweet and in a very few moments cans were filled for dinner dessert. After noon Mr Bretherton stuffed some birds that he had killed. The Col and I ascended Mt Olympus to select a route up and a place for the box. We choose the east face, and found it hard climbing. Snow slides had rounded the once sharp stones untill the footing was very dangerous, and with but few projections to which you could grasp for support. We became blocked once, and dropped some, bearing north. Here we succeed in gaining the top of this peak of 5500 feet alt, but it was not the highest. Between us and the crowning point were two needles side by side, as acutely formed as church steeples.[103] To the south of them it was precipitous, and we dropped to the snow upon the north of them, in hopes of passing by their bases. In this we were foiled as the snow was in precipitous banks clothing the north side, and in places had settled and parted like broken stone or ice. At one point we passed over one of these deep gaps which had been covered by about one foot of drifting snow. Thawing and freezing alternately had turned it to ice, which bore our weight. Observing what a dangerous crevasse we had passed over, we sounded it by dropping lumps of ice. It was no doubt more than 100 feet to bottom, and not more than three feet wide. The sun was nearing the western horizon, and we could get no higher on Mt Olympus at this point. Nor was there any point in sight at which we could ascend.[104] From what we could see of its character the S.W. side would be the most favorable point of ascent.[105] Viewing the coun-

441

---

[102] "The explorers variously estimated the level bench where they camped as ranging from 30 to 100 acres in extent. The forest west of Pluto's Gulch is broken by several such meadows, any one of which could have been the site of Garden Camp. According to Bretherton, the men called the meadow the 'Garden of the Gods,' but Fisher indicates the name referred to the entire Queets Basin, an area encompassing perhaps three square miles." Wood, Men, Mules and Mountains, pp. 426–27.

[103] "The peak attained, one of the pinnacles bordering Humes Glacier, was probably Icarus (6200 feet). The two needles were the Hermes Pinnacles (6800 feet)." Wood, Men, Mules and Mountains, p. 427.

[104] "Readers familiar with Queets Basin may find it puzzling why the explorers did not traverse—with little elevation loss, then little gain—directly onto Humes Glacier to make the climb of Olympus. Linsley's inclination to camp at lower elevations (thus the descent to Pluto's Gulch) may be the explanation, but a more compelling reason was the forbidding appearance of the glacier. In 1890 the Humes terminated in a steep, broken icefall—a serious challenge to an expedition not equipped with the climbing paraphernalia available in that day." Wood, Men, Mules and Mountains, p. 427.

[105] "On the journey from O'Neil Pass, the men had lost sight of Olympus when descending to the Elwha, and they did not see the peak again until they reached Dodwell-Rixon Pass. When they dropped down to Pluto's Gulch, Olympus—including the Athena Group, or 'South Peak'—again disappeared. As a result, Linsley and Fisher made a crucial mistake on September 20 during their reconnaissance above Garden Camp—an error that caused the party to climb the wrong peak two days later. Upon reaching a viewpoint on the ridge south of the Humes, the scouts could see the Athena Group and the Hermes Pinnacles ('two needles side by side') but the principal peaks of Olympus were hidden behind a peak that is now called Circe. Viewed from the east, Olympus and the Athena Group share a rough resemblance, and it is reasonable to conclude the scouts mistook the peaks they could see for those they could not.

"One cannot pinpoint how far the men went. Fisher speaks of attempting to drop to the snow below the two needles. This implies they reached the col between Circe and the Hermes Pinnacles by climbing over or around Circe, from where the Hoh Glacier and Olympus would have been visible. If so, they did not recognize them as such. Moreover, when viewed from Circe, the Hermes Pinnacles are superimposed against each other, not 'side by side' as in Fisher's sketch of 'Olympus,' which shows the pinnacles as they appear from the ridge south of the Humes.

"The time element strongly suggests the scouts did not go beyond Icarus, since they did not leave Garden Camp until after the noon hour and on September 20 the sun would set about 6:00 P.M. Fisher probably referred to an attempt to descend onto the upper Humes west of Icarus, an area difficult to reach in late summer because the ice pulls away from the rock, creating deep moats.

"Since the peak they mistook for Olympus looked too difficult to scale from the east, Linsley and Fisher decided the party should work around to the southwestern side to make the ascent, and this threw them off course for Olympus." Wood, Men, Mules and Mountains, pp. 427–28.

try in the distance, we were unable to see salt water in any direction. We located Mt Clay Wood, so named by Lieut ONeil during his explorations of 1885. We estimated it as Twenty miles to the North, by 28 deg east, but as it was smokey in that direction it may have been less. Descending to camp, we heard the days doings. Sgt Yates had been to the S.W. descending to ward the Queets, and had seen three bear. Danton had been out gathering berries and had seen a bear also. The others had remained in camp and supper was almost ready upon our return. Up to this time the game killed was only one bear, and to eat that was like taking a dose of worm medicine. We had husbanded our stores as much as possible after the first three days out, never the less the sugar was gone, and bacon running very short. We were growing some what anxious to know what the future had in store for us, but received no information. We knew that we were camped at Olympus and that it must be near fifty miles to the ocean. I was under the inpressin [impression] that we had headed and passed the N branch of the Quinault, and what stream this Queets R was we knew not at that time. A vigilant look-out for camp signs had failed to discover any, except the whittled stick picked up on the Elwha R. It was very evident that no human, white or red, had ever been upon or around Mt Olympus. We ate our bear meat with an ugly grimmace at each bite, and turned in, little dreaming what was in store for me upon the morrow, and for nearly a fortnight to follow. Although we had sampled every suspicious looking stone, no change had occurred in the formation, excepting that sandstone predominated instead of slate. The cleavage was wonderfully smooth upon Mt Olympus and great slabs stood up on edge, as large and as smooth as a flooring of tile's. Small particles of clear silica held the reddish brown sand together, forming a very hard and coarse stone. But little mica had been found through out the mountains and that in very small scales.

Sun Sept 21st. The Col decided this morning to descend until we could swing under Olympus, and gain the S.W. side, taking the route over which Sergt Yates had gone for some distance on the day previous. We had observed from the mountain top that the entire country above was one of snow, counting 45 different glaciers from one point.[106] From each of these small streams flowed, gathering into the three main tributaries to the Queets. It was down into the forks of these that we were heading. It was with out a doubt the most precipitous and weired looking country that we had discov-

ered. Below the junction of the three mountain tributaries we could discern the Queets bottom, and at one point observe the water like a thread of silver wending its way through the forest. The east bank of the stream was altogether impassable and to our right, or upon the west bank, nearly a mile of thick jungle had grown upon the slope between the stream and Olympus. It was to wards this that we were heading, and the descent was most difficult through brush, and the many windings. Col Linsley appeared inclined to rush this morning, and those carrying guns and other articles in their hands were straggling more or less. Having had more oppertunity than others to get the lay of the country, I remained behind and rendered some assistance in keeping all together, which was of the utmost importance now. It was impossible to hail by sight, as the brush closed in behind each passing individual, and the roar of many cataracts, and rushing streams, smothered all other sounds. It now become necessary to cross a deep gulch, and to avoid the danger of dropping stones upon each other, we selected different points at which to swing down by the bushes, and rocks to support us. I was on the right flank, or up stream, and began the ascent upon the opposite bank not more than 10 feet from the nearest party. I suppose it was some seventy feet to the top of the bank and when I gained it no one was in sight. I hallooed but received no response. I made a half circle but discovered no trail. My repeated cries were unanswered, and I descended into the gulch again, taking their trail up from the waters edge. I found in ascending they had swung down stream or to their left. Once gaining the brush above the gulch, there was no trail or marks to follow. I knew which direction they had meant to travel, and set out for the large jungle. When near its edge or northern border, I was answered, but amid the roaring rush of the water I could not locate them. Approaching nearer the river their cries were lost and I could hear them no more. Gaining the jungle I entered it with the intention of gaining the elevation beyond & ahead of them. Near its centre I obtained a view of the four points surrounding, and sent up a column of smoke with out effect. This meadow extended in a narrow strip from the stream to the precipitous face of Mt Olympus. It was an abrupt drop of 150 feet to the stream, and many ugly falls forbid navigation. To the S.W. and above me there was a gap or rocky gulch in the cliff and I knew that they must either come down through the thicket or hug the precipice and attempt a passage through the rocky gulch. I was thoroughly sick of this thicket of alders and Salmon berry grown

442

---

[106] "Glaciation was more extensive in 1890 than it is today. Linsley stated he counted forty-seven glaciers from Mount Olympus; Bretherton mentions fifty-three. Most of them were, of course, snowfields." Wood, *Men, Mules and Mountains*, p. 428.

tangled like riprap, but entered it once more. Gulches, boulders, brush and ferns all interlaced, I was thankful when I reached the opposite side. Here was exactly the place I was seeking. A large dome shaped rock rose to the heigth of the timber surrounding, and offered an excellent look-out. Gaining the up hill side I made the ascent. I commanded a view of the entire thicket. Scrubby pines grew here. Gathering an armful of green tops, I sent up column after colum of dense white smoke, and looked in vain for an answer. I had half a loaf of bread which I ate and remained upon my look out until two Oclock. I came to the conclusion that they had passed ahead of me, and set out to the S.W. again. I had not gone far until a gulch some 200 feet deep cut the slope in twain. I attempted to head it and was foiled by a perpendicular cliff. I sought the stream, which was no better. I had but little hopes of rejoining the party again. I could return, and go down the Elwha, but that country was known, and I concluded to make the pacific coast at any cost. I selected the most favorable point and commenced the descent. There were bushes to hold on to until with in 50 feet of the bottom. This was hard clay, and gravel, and if I could slide with out toppling over, I could bring up against the boulders with out any serious consequences. I tried and succeeded but the bosom of my trousers were rent like a paper baloon at a dog show. I quenched my first and followed to the main stream for a look. The muddy water was dashing between the rocky walls, with falls above, and below. Following the gulch to its head brought me deeper below the precipice that had formerly balked me, and the ridge to the south had grown taller and lacked but little of being a perpendicular wall. I returned to the main stream again, and began the ascent. The formation was slate upon edge offering a narrow foot hold here and there, and occasionally a tree had found footing and struggled for its life, upon this ugly cliff. I did some perilous climbing and once came with in 20 feet of the top. By throwing rocks over I ascertained that it was only a sharp comb of slate. It presented a smooth face here, impossible to scale, and as I swung to my right the ridge ascended, and I spent the entire evening upon these ledges, often not wider than two inches, clinging to any frail object of support. I frequently hung on to and passed over loose slabs of slate upon edge, which I expected to break away at any moment. In desperation I had held on to my Alpine stock suspended by a string, and many times it was of great assistance, where I could reach over head and wedge it in the cleavage for support. I gained the top just at sun down,

getting out near the source of this gulch. The country sloped to the South mostly of soil and bearing a thick growth of mountain hemlock. It was now growing dark and I kindled a fire and went prospecting for water. I was unsuccessful, and returned to my fire which had spread to a windfall, making a tremendous blaze. This was seen by the Party above. They had Gone up through the rocky gulch alluded to and gained the top of the cliff that I had been under. They were now more than one thousand feet above me, and they fired a signal of three shots which I heard, but faintly. I answered, and they fired again, informing me that they heard me.[107] With out water I could neither eat nor drink, and could only enjoy the sleep that never failed me.

Monday Sept 22nd. I was up early and fired a shot from my revolver, and in response an answering shot appeared to echo from the heavens. Crying at the top of my voice, I was answered by Sergt Yates. We now knew exactly where each other was, and I moved up the mountain, crying out at different points to inform them that I was not hurt, and able to travel. They were fully 1200 feet above me and only the loudest cries could be faintly heard. I moved on up the mountain side, in hopes of gaining a point at which I could ascend Olympus, but the cliff upon which they were continued to the S.W. Crossing another ugly gulch, tributary to the Queets River, Mt Olympus appeared like a fluted dome and I found it as impossible to ascend as they did to descend. It is true I might have returned by the route I had came, but the climbing was too perilous, and I might as well have searched for the hidden treasures of the sea, as search for men in those mountains. They might remain a day or so in the vicinity of Mt Olympus, and they might set out to day. Fearing they might loose time in hunting for me, and waste their limited supply of amunition, I returned to the spot where I had camped and signaled again. They had gone, and my own cries were echoed back to me. It was now 9 A.M. and I was thirsty and hungry. No water was to be found upon this ridge, and I conclued [concluded] to make the Queets. I blazed several trees with my hunting knife, and wrote upon them my intention of tracing this stream to the Ocean, and set out upon the descent. I had one more ugly gulch to cross. Dropping into it I gained the water and prepared breakfast. Taking an inventory of my supplies I had left about 13# of flour, 12 oz of bacon, 3 oz of bear fat, enough tea, and matches, to run me a month, and $\frac{1}{2}$# of salt. Danton had my hatchet, but I was fortunate in saving my amunition, and had left 36 cartridges for my revolver. My sugar sack was now a

443

Landing in a tree top

444

quence of the many snow banks and glaciers. At, and about, Mt Olympus natures convulsions had left the formation upon edge, assuming all of the acute angles and grotesque forms known to the laws of crystalization. Olympus and Glacier Peak differed from all others in having the sand stone formation uppermost the slate upon both the Elwha and Queets slope. Iron Pyrites was perhaps more plentiful than in the Quinault basin, while the porphory was more sparingly disseminated. I had kept a vigilant look out for Goat, and sheep, and am satisfied that neither are to be found in this range of mountains. The large game of the mountains were Elk, bear of the black specie only, white and black tail deer. Along the streams were Cougar, Otter, Beaver, Raccoon, Minx, Wild Cat, and perhaps Wolves, but none were sighted by our party. Among the ground animals were the Marmot or (Arctomys), different from the European species, and the smaller mountain farmer, perhaps a mountain beaver, whose habits and appearance we learned but little of. Chipmonks were plentiful and some gray squirrels. All varieties of grouse were represented, but no quail. Snakes were entirely absent excepting a harmless water snake near the salt water beaches. Wild fruits beyond the berry families, and food plants were poorly represented. One pucadenum and the fungi order were the only ones found in any quantities. Consequently, beyond the game and fish, hemlock bark and black berry shoots offer the only means of substance [subsistence] out of the berry season. A variety of frogs exist in the ice cold water of the mountain lakes and appear unaffected by the cold, as I have seen them leap from the edge of the snow, but no doubt they conform to the habits of their family when jack frost attacks the country in earnest.

Returning to the pack train party whom we left upon the 12th inst. They had succeeded in getting one of the crippled mules to Lake Cushman, and the other to Camp No 6. Time was precious, and they could linger no longer. Mr. Windhoffer was engaged to look out for one of the disabled animals and the other made its way to the Miners Camp, so that they did not suffer for want of attention. Sergt Marsh, Mr Price, and Higgins made Camp No 15. upon the 20th, having consumed 8 days in making the round trip, owing to the accident befalling them, with the animals. The two Churches had made Camp No 15 the day previous, finding Sergt Heffner in charge, having the mountains all to him self. Lieut ONeil arrived at Camp No 15. at sunset, impatient that the pack train had not followed on ere now. He was accompanied by Harry West, a Gentleman alluded to during our first visit to Lake Quinault. The Lieut and Barnes

useless piece of property, and I rein-forced my trousers with it, cut the tongues out of my shoes, patching them up, posted up my note book, and set out again. This proved the last gulch of importance that I had to cross. After climbing out of this, I discovered fresh elk tracks and followed them, which led me to the Queets, directly below where it left the canyon. In looking back up the canyon, its walls and the trees faded in the inky darkness, despite the sun light, and I was very thankful to be delivered from the most precipitous portion of country that I had ever passed over. The bottom though very narrow was level, and beautiful. Number less elk had kept the under growth down, and walls whose summits were invisble rose upon either side of the stream. No elk trails were to be found ascending more than 500 feet, and I am under the impression that elk are unable to make their way over the divide between the Queets and Elwha, and a mule trail over this divide would prove entirely impracticable.[108] No additions to the flora were to be seen upon the lofty heigths of Olympus—in fact, vegetation was limited more so than upon other peaks, in conse-

---

[108] "Fisher was mistaken. Elk regularly cross back and forth between the Elwha and Queets via Dodwell-Rixon Pass." Wood, *Men, Mules and Mountains,* p. 432.

had worked the trail almost to where the Hoquiam party had agreed to meet them. Leaving Barnes with Mr. McCarthy (formerly alluded to) who was now engaged with the Hoquiam party on the trail, the Lieut and Mr West returned to learn of the pack train. They remained at Camp 15 this night and were not far from a party of hunters whose names I never learned. One of their party, an Englishman, had spoken to Sergt Marsh for permission to accompany the pack train on through to the coast. He was informed that he could go along working as the others did. Upon the following morning Lieut ONell, Messrs West, and Price, the two Churches, Sergt Heffner, and Higgins, with the animals, set out over the trail but the Englishman did not appear, and was thought no more of. They estimated that they made about 12. miles this day, traveling until after dark. They pitched camp in an alder thicket and passed a miserable night, fatigued as they were. Several mules had rolled during the day, causing much trouble. One of their bridges spread, letting two animals through it, and one animal had been left behind upon the trail. Lieut ONeil and Sergt Marsh returned through the darkness, and brought it to camp. Wood of a combustible nature was very scarce here, with out cutting great trees, and it proved an all round disagreeable night.[109] Upon the following morning, which was the 23 of Sept (as near as I can judge), Mr West, Sergt Marsh and the two Churches set out over the trail to over take Barnes, and McCarthy helping them out with their work upon the trail. Two hours later Lieut ONeil, Sergt Heffner, Mr Price, and Higgins followed with the pack train. More trouble was experienced with animals rolling down the hills, and the long hill formerly alluded to where the trail left the stream to avoid the Canyon of the Quinault had become slippery from rain and was now difficult of ascent. They succeeded in crossing this five mile of mountain trail, and in the vicinity of Camp Shelters in descending to the stream that came in from Bruins Peak. Here another accident occurred. A nest of yellow jackets was stirred to action, and one animal made frantic by the stings leaped over a precipice, <u>landing in a tree top</u> below, meeting sudden death. It had carried 30# of coffee among other articles which were irrevocably lost. The descent into this canyon proved

more difficult than was expected, and a new trail had to be cut for a distance of 200 yards. It was sun down when the stream was reached and a camp location had been selected two miles below. Again they were long after dark in pitching camp, which paves the way for a disagreeable night.

Sept 24th. They traveled a distance of 8 miles over a nice bottom country, which they alluded to as pleasant valley. They spoke of it as generally clear of brush and under growth, and bearing an excellent growth of large timber. This night they camped upon a sandy bar with the pleasure of knowing that the trail was completed from this point on to the sea.

Sept 25th. They all set out over the same route we had taken in our first trip through this country, reaching the north branch of the Quinault at 12. P.M. Here they posted a notice signifying a redivision of the southern division of the O. E. E. Sergt Heffner, Mr Price, Barnes, and Higgins were to proceed with the pack train, reaching Lake Quinault this day if possible. Mr. McCarthy also accompanied them for the purpose of obtaining a compass at the lake. The remainder of the party remained at this point until the following morning. No game had been killed, in fact none sighted, as but little remains in the river bottoms at this season of the year, and they had no time for fishing.

Sept 26th. Lieut ONeil, Mr West, and the two Churches set out to the west with the intention of exploring the Raft River. Upon reaching this the two Churches were to proceed on to the Queets R which up to this time had been considered as only a short stream, not penetrating beyond the foot hills. Sergt Marsh remained in camp but a short time until Mr McCarthy returned from the lake with a compass, and together they headed N. by east following up a small tributary of the Quinault River. The Englishman now came yelling in a voice of distress. Rushing to his assistance they observed him coming down the trail, crying at every step, with head down, and eyes riveted upon the trail. They learned that he had followed their trail expecting to easily overtake them and had with this in view neglected to carry any means of subsistance. They gave him a square meal and sent him on, and he no doubt found his way to the lake settlement.[110]

---

[109] "This was the first of the unnumbered mule trail camps. After descending from the divide to the Quinault, the men failed to number the camps, but the reason why is not given." Wood, *Men, Mules and Mountains*, p. 431.

[110] "An athlete and journalist, Fritz-Herbert Leather was one of a party of six men who left Seattle on September 6, 'destined for the Olympic Mountains on a general exploring expedition.' The party traveled to Hoodsport, then took the trail to Lake Cushman and followed O'Neil's route to the Grand Divide, where it overtook the pack train. Leather requested permission to accompany the military expedition because he wanted 'to see about chances for a homestead' on the Quinault. After failing to join O'Neil when the lieutenant left Camp No. 15, Leather took leave of his companions and 'traveled alone for two days, moving very cautiously.' He finally caught up with the explorers at the forks of the Quinault, eleven miles above the lake. Leather intended to rejoin his party, but as he 'found his homestead' near the lake, he traveled to the ocean via the lower Quinault—'having a most exciting ride down the rapid stream' in a dugout canoe—and returned to Seattle by way of Grays Harbor. Meanwhile, his former companions became concerned for his safety, and two of the men—Alfred V. Higley and his son, Orte L. Higley—left the Grand Divide on October 2 (where four inches of snow had just fallen) and made their way to Lake Quinault to determine if the Englishman had gotten through. Impressed by the country, they remained to establish homesteads and became prominent settlers in the valley. Higley Peak is named for them." Wood, *Men, Mules and Mountains*, pp. 431–32.

445

They proceeded up this small stream, finding its source in about 6 miles travel. The country was now of a hilly nature, but not mountainous, well timbered, and an abundance of brush beneath. Heading more to the east they struck the Humptulip R. about 2 mile below its source and camped. The country to them was uninteresting. The information sought was to ascertain the distance from the Quinault to the Humptulip, also its source as compared to a certain point from the Quinault river. They estimated the distance between the two streams at 8 miles.

Sept 27th. They headed down stream wading and pushing through brush, as the Lieut and Mr Landers had done before them. They passed the forks, and falls, of the Humptulips stream, arriving at Humptulip City in time for supper, learning that the pack train had passed through at 11 A.M. of that day. Wet and cold, they retired to get warm, and spoke flattering words of the table set by the Humptulip people. Upon the following day in company with two other gentleman, they set out for Hoquiam Landing, traveling the 16½ miles by 12-15 in order to catch the boat. The pack train was awaiting a special barge upon which to ship the animals. This arrived at 3 P.M. with a delegation of Hoquiam people, represented by Mr. McMillan, who was acting in the interests of the O.E.E. as per an understanding of former date. Men, mules, and all, boarded the steamer and barge, landing at Hoquiam City in safety. Many people crowded the Dock to witness the approach of this party of men whom with animals were the first white, red, or black men successful in crossing the ragged Olympic Mountains. They were properly received, and kindly treated, by the Hoquiam people. Sergt Marsh spoke of Mr McCarthy as an excellent woodsman and untiring traveler. No steamers left here upon Sunday, and a lay over was necessary until Monday, Sept 29th. Mr McMillan in compliance with a request from the Lieut, shipped the mules direct for Portland, Oregon, per steamer Alliance, which arrived in due time. Mr Price, the veteran packer, headed the pack train through the busy streets of Portland, with the stars and stripes afloat, and long may the torn flag wave that we planted inch by inch from the Sound to the sea. Mr Price declares that in all his forty years of mountain life and experience as a packer, that he never saw mountains as precipitous as were these. He may be envied the honor in again reaching civilization with as many of his animals as he did.

Early on Monday morning as the Alliance left Hoquiam, Sergt Marsh boarded the steamer Montesano, arriving at Union City during the night. Sept 30th before daylight he was in Hoodsport, and after breakfast set out upon the trail in search of the crippled animals. B.C. was alive at Lake Cushman. Continuing up the trail he reached the Miners Camp and found the second mule there, kindly cared for by the Miners, remaining here overnight. He reached Camp No 6. upon the day following, in search of the apparejo, which was no where to be found. Returning to the Miners Camp the mule had left, and gone in to Lake Cushman. Arriving at Mr Windhoffers, B.C. was turned up dead in the door yard, and the other was with much difficulty got to Hoodsport, and left for ship ment but died later.[111] So ended the career of three faithful animals whose death we sadly regretted, for even Jumbo, encased in his worth less hide, had ingrafted his presence as an attache to our party until we marked his absence with regret.[112] Sergt Marsh now set out for Fort Townsend, reporting to Lieut ONeil, upon his arrival.

22 [i.e., September 22]. Returning to the Queets or Mt Olympus division where we left the main party upon the cliff, with my self in the Queets bottom. I wrote a note here explaining that I was going down this stream and that they need not be frustrated in their plans upon my account, as I could well take care of my self. I removed the bark from some saplings to attract attention, and placed the note in a split stick where it could not be over looked. Crossing upon a fallen tree to the left bank, I struck a good trail leading down the stream. The bottom grew wider as I proceeded. After a half mile's traveling, I recrossed with the trail to the right bank. Traveling until 3 P.M. I gained the open spot that I had seen from Mt Olympus. Considering this a good point to signal from, I sent up dense columns of white smoke, which was not answered. After preparing lunch with out meat I shaved off the side of a fragment of pine, and wrote another note for the information of my party, in case they came this way. I afterwards learned that the Cols party approached the river at this point and discovered my note. From here I continued and found that the trail, and best travel, was upon the right bank. A few moments before sundown I brought down a large grouse, at the first shot. More proud was I of this fowl than any large game that I had ever dropped with weapon. I trav-

[111] "O'Neil and Fisher both indicate the expedition lost three mules—Weakback on the Quinault; B.C. and another not identified by name on Yellow Jacket Hill. O'Neil also states that an animal named Sorais was lost on the Quinault, but this must have been the mule that died on Hood Canal after being injured on Yellow Jacket Hill. Otherwise, this would indicate four mules had been lost, which is not in accord with the records. O'Neil apparently confused Sorais with Weakback." Wood, *Men, Mules and Mountains*, p. 432.

[112] "This is the last reference to Jumbo in the expedition's records. On August 14, when Price and Kranichfeld left Camp No. 8 for Hoodsport, the dog accompanied them, but he failed to return to the camp and was not seen again 'for many days.'" Wood, *Men, Mules and Mountains*, p. 432.

446

eled until darkness set in and found a beautiful camping ground, at the mouth of a dry branch. Drift wood had gathered upon the gravel beneath the alders, forming a shelter from wind, and rain, with plenty of good wood near at hand. I did justice to one half of the grouse, smothering it in my oyster with a little bear fat, and was surprised how well one can manage when it is any port in a storm. This I blazed and registered as Camp Grouse. I kept a close lookout for signs of previous parties, or signs of indians, but no marks were left by animal life, save by the denizens of the forest. Some float containing Iron Pyrites but not to any extent. The timber growth was excellent and of the same species indigenous to the other streams. I estimated that I was seven miles from Mt Olympus. Small streams came in from either side, but they were all too small to be recognized as branches or forks of the main stream.

Tues, Sept 23nd. I set out early making two miles in good time. At this point the stream made a short dash to the west and continued on in its general course, that of S.W. The stream made many tortuous bends which I compared with the compass at frequent intervals. During the day I heard many grouse drumming, and saw some flying, but did not get a shot. About 10 A.M. I observed a large dog salmon under a log, but it was bruised up so I did not molest it. Taking this as a hint I fitted one of my spears to the alpenstock and <u>killed a large dog salmon</u>, reserving enough for dinner and supper. I never could, never was called upon to feast upon dog salmon before, but upon this occasion I made a good meal of it, and rejoined that it was far more excellent than either strong bear or dog flesh. I had no farther misgivings from this on regarding my means of subsistance. Having given up the idea of rejoining my friends, I regained my former spirits and found much to amuse me among the works of nature. The fog hung low all day and I could not obtain a good view of the mountains surrounding, above an alt of 600 feet, but one queer freak of nature was that the mountains and streams upon the east bank sloped and flowed to the north east, almost the reverse of the main stream. At a point of 12 miles from Mt Olympus the Elk trails all left the stream heading west, and from this on it was most difficult traveling through the entangled undergrowth of salmon, Huckle and Salal berry brush, with elk ferns filling up the interstices. Vine maple and moss was also well represented. Eagles, Ravens, and Cranes [Crows?] allowed me to approach quite near them before rising, and the sandy beach was literally covered with Cougar, Otter, Beaver, Minx and Coon tracks, with an occasional bear track. This I considered as a good omen as Salmon must be running in plentiful numbers. About 4 P.M. I discovered

And killed a large dog salmon

447

the first signs of Human existence upon this stream, which was in the form of a decayed rack upon which the indians had dried their fish. This had now grown to a beautiful stream and I was more charmed with its character as I proceeded down it. I had given up the bank and had since noon time kept upon the gravel bar [bars?] wading from side to side as occasion required. The stream carried a great amount of water, but was wide and shallow, so by keeping upon the ripples or shoals it was not more than from one to two feet deep. I had seen many salmon running but all of the dog variety, and I had enough of that in my pack for present needs. My shoes were suffering from constant wading, and rough footing upon the rounded stones. Selecting a good camp, I turned in, passing a good night, at Camp Salmon. I estimated to days travel at 10 miles, and I must have been at least 15 miles from Mt Olympus when I discovered the first signs of indians.

Wedes Sept 24th. Setting out early, many fish drying racks were passed to day, but none had the appearance of having been used this summer. The tracks of animals grew more numerous, with an occasional track of an indian. I could never catch sight of a Cougar but frequently approached near them, seeing where they had left a fish partially eaten, and scarcely dead, from which they were frightened at my approach. Eagles and ravens were quite numerous to day and dog salmon running lively. The fog continued hanging low and dense, giving me a poor idea of the hills surrounding. At noon time I waded out into water deep and swift and speared a large salmon and in the scuffle I lost my balance upon the slippery stones and was washed down with the current, loosing spear and salmon, but retained my staff. I had one other barb and used it to better effect. One stream 15 feet wide was received from the east after having traveled five miles. The main stream at some points to day was 100 yds wide but shallow. Passed an old camping ground at which were registered Mrs Julia Dickens and H. A. The name and work of the artist indicated that they were copper colored natives, which I afterwards learned was the case. At one point to day I passed a large log jam that had completely bloccked [blocked] the stream. The water had over flowed, cutting a new channel to the west, and returned to the old channel one mile below. The stream was gradually growing deeper as it gathered more water, and I was continually wet with fording, and wading at least one half of the time. Many times I attempted to take short cuts across the bends but grew sick of the brush, and was glad to reach the water again. The fog lifted late in the evening and I could distinguish that only foot hills were in sight and that a wide bottom, level and heavily timbered, bordered either shore. I passed a good night at Camp Eagle, having registered in many places for the information of other parties in case of any accident. I observed many trout jumping, but had no time to fish, as long as salmon were so easily caught with the spear. I was rushing over this country for more purposes than one. First, I had enjoyed better living and more society than I now mingled with, and next, I had not a penny nor transportation slip by which to reach home. I had came in the Army to avoid the avocation of tramping, and I was most anxious to head the pack train off, and ship as a pack mule, in which capacity I had been acting for some time. Sergt Yates had my transportation and I could not lay hands upon him at this date nor many others I feared.

Thurs Sept 25th. Set out as soon as it was light enough to see, stream was very crooked and running to all points of the compass. By observing map it will be seen that the portion of the stream traveled to day formed a horse shoe in two places. The wading was much deeper to day, and I was washed down with the current at one crossing. At one point I noticed much fresh beaver sign. A great many chips and stubs spoke plainly of recent work, and a road way over the sandy

beach had been formed by dragging brush to their dam. There were a great many grouse flying and drumming, but I did not waste any time in attempting to shoot them. Deer tracks were more numerous now than at any point over which I had traveled. At 4 Oclock in the evening I passed a cabin that had been recently erected, and upon a split board was written Chas Lawler 1514. D str Tacoma Wash. An excuse of a trail led down the right bank which I followed, soon approaching another cabin representing the claim of Samuel Spoerton of Tacoma, with the information written upon the door that he had gone for supplies and would return soon. In due time the third cabin was passed, belonging to Alma Thornton, and a fourth cabin upon the opposite side of the stream was passed. While none of them were at home their axe marks were fresh.[113] The trail that they had made was preferable to wading in the deep and cold water and I was in hopes that I could retire with clothing partially dry to night. I found a beautiful camping ground directly above the reception of a small tributary from the west. I had no fish on hand, and while dipping up water for supper I observed many large Chinook Salmon running. I returned to camp for revolver and spear and shot a fine one, but the current carried it to deep water before I could secure it. The fish here were more shy and I soon found my self in the middle of the stream with spear poised and again wet to the skin. I had not long to wait untill I had a Chinook Salmon weighing about 40#. Several water oozles perched upon the rocks near me as if realizing that I would leave them the lions share. This was the first occasion in which I ever heard a water oozle sing. One warbled beautifully and in clear notes, seemingly happy at the bounteous feast before them. Cutting off enough for supper and breakfast, I had scarcely moved ten feet away, before three of them were pecking at the flesh remaining. This camp I registered as Camp Skookum (an adjective of the Chinook jargon). Although warm and comfortable I might as well have selected a camp in Barnums Meanagerie so far as sleep was concerned. Located near a shoal in the stream, great Salmon threshed in the water all night long, in their efforts to ascend the stream. Wild animals which I could not see snapped the bushes in all direction, traveling up and down in search of fish. At every few yards was to be seen the remains of a fish where Cougar, Coon, Otter, or eagle, had made a meal. There was now a wide valley through which the stream coursed bearing much fine timber, and occupying space sufficient for many fine farms, when cleared of the growth. Bordering the stream for some yards back was only a growth of tall alders,

448

---

[113] See the diary of J. J. Banta in part 2, chapter 7, The Banta and Sharp Exploration 1889–90.

and Salmon berry which is very easly destroyed. In choosing one of these spots for a claim a spot of some ten acres can be cleared in one season, but cutting the growth which will burn in six months. Then it can be fired and the more valuable timber preserved for a market, which will not be many years in reaching this important valley. The fog lifted this night, and the stars appeared in the heavens, the first time to me since leaving Mt Olympus and my comrades.

Frid Sept 26th. The sun rose bright and I discovered this morning that I had left my match box about one mile up the stream. I had plenty of matches, but I had carried the worthless tin case, that I generally used as a salt can, for eight years. In the Ozarks, the Blue Mts, Rockies, Cascades and Sieras it had done me service and I could not part with it now for a two mile jaunt. Recovering it I crossed the creek and passed under a steep bank of the river. The adhesive nature and blue color of the soil here, attracted my attention. Examination disclosed a large bank of it which is defined by Dana as Kaolin or Blue shale. According to the Pt Crescent parties description it must have been further up this small stream that they had discovered the sample that they carried. I observed that it cropped out in more than one place. At a point lower down I found upon a blazed tree that a Mr Banta had filed upon 20 acres but his notice was faded so, that I could only make out his name, with date of April 3rd 90. A capital Q also led me to believe that I was upon the Queets river. In about 3 miles travel I passed another cabin untennated with a small garden close by. Soon after this I emerged from the timber into a small clearing and observed a gentleman at work, and a young Lady, his daughter, with a child. This was quite a surprise to meet whites, before the indians. I approached, glad to have met some one to talk to. I learned that this was Mr Hollenbeck of Tacoma, and his son in law was then down at Grays Harbor after supplies. I unslung my pack and remained an hour, gaining the following information. The entire settlement along this stream, which he informed me was the Queets, had came from Tacoma about one year previous. Some of them had very good cabins, and small patches cleared, upon which there were good gardens well matured. It was 12 miles to the Ocean. The trail was very good along the stream for a distance of five mile, but above and below no trail had as yet been made. Mr. H. informed me that quite a number of deer frequented this valley, but that they were very shy. The foot hills I estimated as seven or 8 miles from here, added to the distance to the Ocean minus the bends in the stream would, at least calculation, form a wide valley some 15 miles in length. South of the foot hills the small stream from the east alluded to, according to the indians statement, came from the direction of Lake Quinault. The

Indians claimed that there was an old elk trail leading up this stream and across to the lake, and for the consideration of 10^{00} had agreed to guide the whites over it. Their intention was to connect with our trail at the lake and bring their supplies in this way. It was considered about half days travel or 14 miles across to the Lake. Formerly, they had been compelled to land their supplies at O-E-hut on Grays Harbor, transport them upon waggons or sail boats in favorable weather up the Ocean beach, to the mouth of the Queets, and pole up in canoes from that point. These people were above the average farmer in point of intellect and refinement, and I spent an hour pleasantly in conversation. Declining an invitation to stop for dinner, I left here at 11 A.M., passing several cabins with good gardens, but only one at home. This was H. B. Lyman, who was at work grubbing upon his claim. Below this came Messrs Balls, and Sharps claims, also from Tacoma. None of them were at home except Mr Lyman. Below Mr Sharps cabin there was no trail and I must battle with the brush again, or take to the water. I tried the brush first. The stream ran close to a high ridge upon the right which I recognized as the one I had seen from Mt Olympus. It was this ridge that obstructed our view of the Pacific Ocean, and was that body of land between the rivers Queets and Hoh, or Ohalat as some maps have it. While struggling in the brush I caught a glimpse of two men poleing a canoe up stream, but did not hail them. I afterwards learned that they were Messrs Wilbur and Davis making their second trip through this coast bottom. Making about two mile with much labor and deep wading, I prepared lunch upon the beach, and set out again. I had not gone far untill I heard in a loud voice <u>Kar</u> <u>Mika</u> <u>Klatawa</u> (Where are you going)(in Chinook jargon). <u>Hyas</u> <u>Salt</u> <u>Chuck</u> (To the Ocean) I replied before seeing my red friend. At this his canoe shot out from beneath the lapping boughs and he paddled over, asking me to ride. He was alone and was out with gun and spear, in search of <u>Muck a Muck</u> (food) for the little ones at home. He was a Quinault Indian and spoke excellent Chinook, but no English of account. I inspected him thoroughly and noted his queer shaped head. His fore head was broad but sloped back from the brows, as it did forward from the Occipital, forming an apex at the crown like the roof of a house. I had no fear for my safety, but all indians have a weakness for <u>tenas guns</u>, or revolvers, and I had rather loose six months pay than an Army revolver. We became talkative and exchanged names. Giving mine as Fisher, it was necessary then and there that we meet in the centre of the floating canoe and shake hands, as by coincidence his name too was Pisher, as he pronounced it. We were now staunch friends, and I would not have exchanged my berth for a cabin passage upon an Ocean

449

steamer. He would not allow me to use a paddle, or pole, except in bad places, and I thorouohly [thoroughly] enjoyed this ride. Running in under some bushes, one by one he lifted six large Salmon from the water that he had speared on his way up. Gathering some boughs to keep my pack clear of the fish, we set out again, and I envied this nomad his happiness, as we sped before the current. The river was now of good depth, except an occasional shoal. At these shoals were abrupt bends, and this happy red man indulged in song, and yells, in cadence with each dextrous stroke of the paddle, controlling his canoe with the ease of a gull at sea. It was very evident that Mr Fisher with long hair was indulging in some vanity at the expense of my insignificance in handling this graceful moving craft. Many large salmon shot through the water as we sped by, but he only viewed them with pride, as a farmer would his cattle. He had killed sufficient for present needs, and the others were left to fatten for another day. No Dog salmon were to be seen this near the ocean, and my captain informed me that these salmon were all red and of excellent quality untill they had been in cold fresh water for a certain time. Then they turned white and became poor and bruised in their efforts to reach the very source of small streams to spawn, that their eggs might escape the greedy trout. I have formerly understood that Dog Salmon were so called from their great teeth. So far as this goes, the Chinook salmon has enormously large teeth, and I am inclined to think with my Couisin [Cousin] Fisher, that they are both one and the same salmon, as the Dog salmon is seldom found numerous near the Ocean, and the Chinook Steel heads, Silver sides, and Blue backs are upon rare occasions found retaining their color at any distance from the Ocean in mountain streams. Fishers theory was that they set out to spawn in their sixth year. At a point of [erased; appears to be "four"] miles from the ocean a fair sized stream came in from the west. This Fisher informed was Nellis Creek, and that ten Boston houses were located up the stream (meaning ten white families had taken up claims, erecting cabins). Instead of evincing a disposition to jealousy, he spoke of them with an air of pride, as if pleased to welcome them as neighbors.[114] He could not inform me why this was called Nellis Creek, any more than that it was a siwash name) but I have since learned that a Mr Nellis was the first settler here.[115] We soon arrived at his destination, which was a large cabin built from split cedar (puncheons). Judging by the moss, it had stood for many years. I

informed Fisher that I had no <u>chickamin</u> (Money) and made him some presents of fishing tackle, of which he was very proud. He had tried my pipe, a meerschaum that had done service in Africa and was rich in nicotine. About three whiffs satisfied him, much to my gratification. I was expecting to get clear of the cabin and pitch camp, as it was now growing dark, and I was wet, hungry and cold. In this I was much mistaken. My red cousin shouldered my pack, and trotted up the bank to the cabin, and I was rushed to the interior, little dreaming that I was to be made a hero of. This cabin or museum, as I might well call it, was about 40. feet long x 20. wide, and 12. feet to the eves, and sheltered by a well pitched roof. A rude ventillater was constructed upon the comb, more to allow the smoke to escape than upon hygienic principles. The frame work was rude but substantial, and upon cross bars hung many salmon properly cut for curing in the smoke. Along the entire side walls bunks were built two high, and the interior was lined with grass matting which excluded the air as effectually as paper. A fire burned upon the dirt floor of either corner, representing as many branches, or different generations of the Moses family. A platform 10 feet square and made of boards split from cedar was raised about one foot above the earth floor. This was covered with clean grass matting, and answered the purpose of table, chairs, sofa and etc. I was not long in folding my chilled limbs around the fire. Fisher klucked like a goose at an ugly squaw apparently of about ten and one hundred summers. In response, she began mixing flour for bread, aided by several others. In due time I had dried my clothing to some extent, and supper was announced. Pappooses, Dogs, Chickens, & Cats now emerged from under the bunks where they had flown at my approach, and in the midst of this motley crowd I folded my limbs for a seat and joined them in the following repast. Entree Boiled Salmon in abundance, dumped out upon a great dish. Using our fingers we each helped our selves, and were kept busy keeping dogs and chickens at a respectable distance. After fish came good yeast powder bread, Coffee, potatoes, Salmon Oil for gravy, and salmon eggs, all nicely cooked. A wash pan full of sugar was scooped up from among the mysteries of an old trunk, and the meal proper commenced. Digging down into my pack I brought out a spoon, whereupon they produced a knife and fork which I recognized as one of Uncle sams gratuitous distributions. Supper over all forms of animal life assembled around Fishers fire, and I was asked to talk. Two

---

[114] Transcriber's note: Next page, labeled at the top "The Queets River, 44." Notice sentence after the word in 4 "line." Referring to a sentence that had been inserted between lines

[115] "Fisher originally wrote another name, apparently an Indian one, but in all instances it has been obliterated and Nellis substituted. When making the change, Fisher should have stricken the phrase, 'any more than it was a Siwash name.' N. Nellis was one of the settlers who came from Tacoma in the spring of 1890. He took a claim on the stream, which is known today as the Clearwater River." Wood, *Men, Mules and Mountains*, p. 432.

of the men, Fisher and Charles Moses, understood Chinook, and Addie Moses, Charle's sister about 13 years old, understood english having gone to school at the Quinault agencey, but from some cause she would not divulge the fact, and I did not become the wiser until later on. I informed them that I was a Washington man, and had came across the Olympics from Hoods Canal. They were surprised to learn that the Queets penetrated so far into the mountains and they called <u>me</u> a <u>skookum</u> <u>tum</u> <u>tum</u> <u>man</u> (meaning brave heart) to cross these mountains alone. An old gray haired individual feeble with age was now led up, and the information was interpreted to him in their native tongue. His speech was laboured and with a decided impediment. His words I could not understand, but it was evident that he discredited my story, and a sectional map was produced by Iddie [Addie], who understood its meaning, and to test my veracity I was requested to illustrate to them some of the cardinal points. With the little squaw Addie at my back, I located Hoods Canal, our starting point, and traced our trail over the mountains to Lake Quinault, speaking of the Pope family, whom they knew. I traced the second route over Olympus down the Queets, locating the highest point at which I had seen their fish racks, for smoking salmon. After a great harangue between them selves I was requested to point out Ilwaco, Hoquiam, et al points, which I did to their satisfaction, with Iddie to my ignorance of her knowledge, interpreting all the while. A paper was now presented me in which Charles Moses, a Quinault Indian, had declared his intention to sever tribal relations and file upon the tract of land that we now were upon—reading this translated in Chinook, also a note from Mr Hollenbeck pertaining to a business transaction, they admitted me and my story in good faith, and made much of me, much to my embarrassment. One after another patted me upon the back, softly stroking my bare arms that were sadly scratched from the brush. My shirt was sleeveless and I was presented with a white calico shirt belonging to a feminine injun, but politely declined the gift, assuring them that mine was heap good until I over took my wardrobe. Fisher claimed me as his guest and I was assigned to his corner for quarters, and rations. I was kept up until a late hour answering questions, and at 11 P.M. we turned in. Despite my request to sleep by the fire, I was importuned to take a birth [berth] belonging to Mrs Fisher, in which I passed a restless night. I discovered that I was not alone and underwent the tortures of crawling insects. I made sure that I would have to anoint with Mercury and hid my head in disgrace. When morning came I was triply happy to learn that it was only fleas.

Sat Sept 27th. I observed that the squaws arose first, kindling the fire, and I played warrior, awaiting until the room became warm before rising. There appeared to be no cultivation or refinement among the males, they wearing only a shirt until after breakfast, when they completed their dress before going out. I was treated to an excellent breakfast of Fried potatoes, fried salmon, bacon, hot bread and coffee, with sugar, which alone to me was now a delicacy. They also prepared what I would term a sweet gravy by stirring sugar and flour to thick ness with boiling water. I watched them particularly in the preperation of this meal, and I was compelled to admit to my self that they displayed more care and nicety in their cooking than we had while upon the scout. After breakfast I was made aware of the family connections, and informally introduced to the four corners. Fisher and family occupied the S.E. Corner, Charles Moses and family the S.W. Corner. The old Gray haired man and Addie the N.W. Corner, and another branch, the N.E. Corner. Charles Moses was the possessor or ruling spirit, succeeding the old man, and was recognized as a chief by the indians. He was perhaps 25 years of age, intelligent, and a well to do indian. He informed me that he was going down to the Quinault Agency in a short time and that if I would wait he would consider me as a guest, and save me some trouble by guiding me through. I embraced this oppertunity, and abandoned my plans of proceeding further to day. One by one the majority of them disappeared in different directions, and Charlie invited me to accompany him around his possessions, of which he seemed greatly interested. First we visited his boats. Of these there were two very large canoes used for ocean sailing. They were dug from mammoth cedars formed as a double prowed skiff, and would easyly carry two tons. These I assisted in placing upon trusses for protection during the coming winter. They had many smaller ones, all prettyly modeled, and light. Next we went over his garden which consisted of the substantial vegetables. His potatoes in particular were very large and fine. From here we went to the fishery. About 100 yds below the house, and across the centre of a calm stretch of water, a rip rap formation of willows had been constructed from shore to shore, with sliding wickets that could be opened until fish had passed up, and closed behind them. Although the water was four feet deep in front of the house, the large salmon created a V shaped ripple, and some of the Children gave the alarm, and all rushed pell mell, eager for the sport. They possessed a fine gill net, but nets and traps were useless during the run of salmon, as they could be taken with the spear in endless quantities. The spears used by them were the barbs of bone or hard wood found with all fish eating indians. It consists of a long staff split for two and one half feet, forming a fork of two prongs. The barbs are

451

placed up on the forked ends. A thong secured to the spear points is also secured to the staff above the split. Poising the staff above their heads, it is thrown from 20. to 30. feet, very accurated-ly. The spear points driven through the fish now slip off and turn transversely, covering the wound, and no danger is incurred of breaking the staff, as in the white mans more clumsy weapon. From here we visited the woodland back of his cabin. His selection was a choice piece of land, and well timbered. We approached a large cedar over a poor trail, climbing over logs and through brush. Here he had made 430 clapboards, carrying them upon his back nearly 800 yds to the stream, for Mr Sharp, one of the Tacoma settlers. His price was $5.00 which was reasonable, considering the labor performed. A portion of the tree was blocked out for a canoe, and I made my self useful in assisting him until noon, in chopping and digging it out. I found him a superior axeman, using it effectually either right or left. His eye was as true as square and level, detecting the least deviation from the pretty curving model. This indian appeared surprised that I would stoop to work, and I was proud to know that there was an individual each of the army and forest that could scorn the hoodlums and the boot blacks railling cry of Soldier will you work. But few of the absent inmates had returned when we appeared for dinner, which was a substantial meal. The old and decrepit squaws were continually employed in making baskets and matting from the asphodel blades, and the smaller children playing in the water. One, an infant pappoose of not more than 20 months, waded near the shore, often falling, and was as frequently dragged to the shore by some of its play-mates. Of course I played the good samaritan and lectured them upon sanitary measures, but it was no use. They could not keep the little ones out of the water and made wry grimmaces representing a victim with the ague. They were all very particular to wash their hands after eating and thoroughly rinsing their mouths, cleansing their teeth. I spent the evening in lounging about the house, inspecting the many curios which they had collected. Queer shaped bladders floats and skins representing great gourds, bottles and demijohns, were filled with Salmon oil which they used as lard. Fragments of spars, chains, and all manner of wreckage from ships were to be seen here. Probably fragments of many an ill fated ship that had gone to pieces upon this dangerous coast was amidst their various collections. All manner of traps from the smallest newhouse to the No 6. Bear trap costing $210.00

per dozen was here. They were anxious to inspect my Belt and accoutrements, considering well every article. I was much surprised that not one of them begged for any thing. They now brought out their arsenal which consisted of many guns and one revolver. The old Army springfield and Carbine, Colts, Sharps, Marlin, Winchester, and Remington, were all here. A visitor appeared in the person of indian Dick. He was square built, weighing about 160#, lighter colored than my friends, and not a bad looking indian. He spoke a little english, and good Chinook. He run an eating house at the mouth of the stream, and with his boats carried people to any point desired. I had heard of him as an obliging indian from the people up the river. Several strange indians called during the evening and I was surprised at the familiarty [familiarity] taken by visitors. Those desiring victuals, with out a word took hold of any, and every thing in the house, and appropriated it to their use, which I learned was a custom common to these indians. A large kettle of boiled salmon was always in readiness and formed the most important dish with them. A peculiar arrangement across the stream attracted my attention and upon asking the nature they mutely hung their heads, uttering the word <u>Mem-a-loose</u> in sadness. It was their cemetry [cemetery] of which they did not wish to speak. Around five trees that formed a pentagonal square with out the graves were stretched long streamers of white, yellow, and pink calico, appearing more remindful of an arrangement for a May day gathering than the home of the dead. In accordance with the indian custom they had ingeniously drilled holes through every dish and other article belonging to the departed members, and nailed them upon the decorated trees, which resembled the displayed wares of a crockery merchant. I had a long talk with the old man regarding the Olympic mountains, and he informed me through a Chinook interpreter that He was perhaps the oldest of the old, and that he had never visited the mountains, and that he was not aware of any one white, or red, that had ever crossed them at this point. He had never been to the head of the Queets, or Quinault streams, but had passed his days in hunting and fishing near the coast. These indians were perfectly friendly and sociable to the whites. Of ordinary size and speaking Chinook, taken in consideration with their many cultured customs of the white man, completely explodes the Press Parties mythical reports of the Olympic indians, and other strange sights illustrated in the Seattle press.[116]

452

---

[116] The mythical tribes alleged to inhabit the mountain interior were supposed to be fierce cannibals, but the Indians who resided along the coast were, by the time the first settlers arrived on Grays Harbor, already influenced by the white man's civilization. They had blankets and firearms obtained from the Hudson's Bay Company, but they still migrated between various camps and villages in their quest for fish, game, roots, and berries. Although Fisher was slow to criticize others, he did on this occasion take the Press Party to task.

The more we heard of them, and witnessed of their six months exile in the mountains, the more plainly it appeared that they had enjoyed the hunting season hibernating in some pleasant valley. With the spring time appearing, puffed up to baloonic dimensions with bombastic ideas regarding what they saw but little of. Certainly it is and was a most difficult task to cross these mountains and it is not our intention to throw censure at any one or sweat beneath a cloak of Johnny Bull conceit. But to illustrate that we sought for information, and not for newspaper notoriety, Lieut ONeil as I have stated before would not allow a reporter to accompany us. The Alpine Clubs representatives sent in but few items, and out side of Fred Churchs limited correspondance gathered as a lichen gains its life, it was not untill my return home, that I entertained a thought of writing up the trip. Lieut ONeil was never known to fire a gun or cast a fly during the entire trip,[117] and I often wondered how he enjoyed this life and why he organized this and other expiditions fraught with toil and exposure, if not in the interests of science and in honor of the country the flag, and its people that he represented. With the setting sun all members of the different corners had returned, and none of them came empty handed. Some carried great bundles of grass leaves for matting, others had baskets filled with berries, and small crab apples, and others brought in fish, wood, and & etc. Charlies <u>Kloochman</u>, or his wife in our language, was cutting wood, a scene that I could never tolerate with my own people, and I relieved her of the task to the merriment of the male witnesses. Perhaps I had disgraced my self according to their customs, but I found that little acts of kindness were appreciated by these people, as by my own pale faced sisters. We were to set out about mid night in order to travel the Ocean beach at low tide, and we turned in early to catch a little sleep. About mid night I was aroused by Mr Pisher, and upon arising I found Fisher and Charlie attired in respectable clothing, and Addie spelling words in english from an illustrated primmer. This was the first that I learned of her english speaking qualifications. As it was evident that there were some reasons for her not using our language at home, I refrained from addressing her in my native tongue. A warm meal was awaiting us and we dined, and departed, Fisher, Charlie, his sister Addie, and my self. We were about 6 miles from the Ocean, by the stream, which made a great bend. Taking a canoe we crossed to the right bank and traveled 1000 yds through the woods, and thick

brush. Fearing I could not keep the trail, Fisher in his kindness dragged a white pole after him that I might follow his course. By this route we had saved some two miles travel. A fleet of canoes were near at hand. Boarding one we set out down the stream. Salmon were running and splashing in all directions. An occasional Indian hut was passed and we gained the Ocean beach. There were quite a number of houses that I could distinguish through the shadows of night, and Charlie informed me that there was a mission here. From this point, said he, it was 15 miles to the river Hoh, to the north, and 35 miles in the same direction to the Quillayute. To the south it was (8 miles, to the Raft river) (15. miles to the Quinault) (22 miles, to the Chopalis River) (23 miles, to the O-E-Hut) (28. miles to Damons point). We beached the canoe above high tide and set out over the beach which was flat and of firm sand, and fine to travel upon. The injuns carried their shoes in their hands. At some points the rocks form a cliff or promutory [promontory] which reached to the sea, and over these we climbed. I think there were five in all of these points. One continued for a mile and a good trail led over this. We reached the Raft river at day light and made preperations to wade it. They removed their clothing, and in we went, struggling with the current and yelling with the sport and cold. The tide was now rising, and we traveled very fast for what, I soon learned. The last point of rock affronted us and the only way by it was to await the receeding swells and dash through a tunnel that nature had formed through the cliff. Charlie, Addie and my self escaped the waves in safety, but Fisher was caught in a large swell, which soiled his Sunday clothing. Myriads of sea birds, ducks, and geese, lined the sea shore, and arose in clouds at our approach. We met two gentleman traveling up the beach, who informed me that the pack train had passed Lake Quinault, and before I could question them farther we had to fly in our opposite directions to escape the waves. These people were fine travelers and gave me all I could do in holding pace with them. With the exception of one mile of rounded, or live gravel, the beach was fine traveling, and by nine Oclock we were at the mouth of the Quinault. The Quinault and Queets were deep at the beach and effected [affected] by the tide, while the smaller streams spread, forming a shallow delta over the beach. The Queets I had traveled from the glacier that loaned it the first drop of water, to the Ocean, where it mingled its freshness with the saline fluid, and summing up the whole as a

453

---

[117] "The temptations O'Neil experienced on the 1885 trip were strangely at variance with his attitude in 1890, when he was 'never known to fire a gun or cast a fly during the entire trip.' This is puzzling, because on a number of occasions, both before and after 1890, O'Neil took 'hunting and fishing leave' from his post. During an interview in 1936, he stated he had always been fond of hunting, and recounted his experiences in shooting game and wildfowl at Fort Custer, Montana." Wood, *Men, Mules and Mountains*, p. 439.

country I was more favorably impressed with the Queets valley and stream, than any portion of the Olympic mountains. It forms no canyon after gathering its tributaries at Olympus, contains no falls, but presents one gradual decline. Canoes may be poled from the ocean to with in five miles of the summit of Mt Olympus. There is no reservation to usurp the choice land. And I have no doubt that ere this, the trail via Lake Quinault has been opened up to the Tacoma settlement. Game and fishing is plentiful up this stream. While Lake Quinault presents many inducements to the sportsman, and pioneer, I think I should prefer the Queets. As we traveled along, the indians pointed out Chapel rock, and various points where different vessels had gone to pieces, and appeared well posted with this portion of the coast. An indian police set us across the Quinault River to the Agencey, which was located upon the south bank and fronting the Ocean beach. I was disagreeably surprised with the appearance. Instead of the neat and freshly painted cottages that Uncle Sam usually supports, these ~~were~~ was rookeries in sad repair. I had learned that there was another impassable point, some two miles below, which I was anxious to pass, if possible, before the tide cut me off. I bid them a hurried good bye, promising

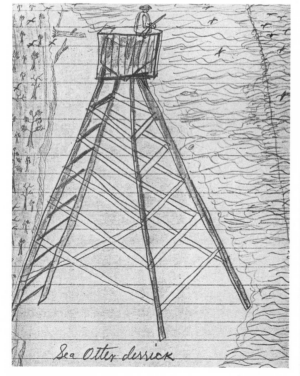

Sea otter derrick

to send them some presents. I left them in possession of a cabin, and contents, preparing their breakfast. I set out from here and made more than a mile when I approached the cliff over looking the ocean. The tide was thundering against the cliff, hurled on by a stiff west breeze. I prepared breakfast and ascended to the woods, attempting to pass beyond the cliff, and descend again. I worked my self into a passion mid brush, logs and holes, but it was useless. I had made about 800 [300?] yds and gave up. Kindling a fire, I slept until 3 P.M. Looking over I observed that some one had passed, and the waves now fell 20 feet short of the cliff. Rather than attack the brush again I endangered my life in descending to the beach. Dropping my pack, I eventually gained the beach and headed south again. Another great point ran out into the sea but over this was a good waggon road, no doubt a government road, for supplying the agency. Following it perhaps a mile it again descended to the beach. It was excellent traveling from this on, until near dark I had more wading across a swale that set in. I traveled until after dark, camping near a claim taken up several years previous, and abandoned. It had been retaken and was posted by a Mr Glover, but no one was at home. I found some stagnant rain water in a barrel beneath the eaves of the cabin and pitched camp between some fallen trees. I did not know what the character of the beach below was, and was anxious to set out with the tide. The rain awoke me at 3 P.M. and I prepared breakfast and set out down the coast.

Monday Sept 29th. Traveling until day light I saw a man near the beach moving his effects from one cabin to another upon a large wheel barrow. I learned something of the coast from him, and proceeded on in search of fresh water. There were quite a number of small springs emitting a sulphurous odor, and what slop it was to me, after having enjoyed the melting snow and ice, filtered to transparency through the mountain gulches. I came up with two gentleman, enroute for Grigsbys store, some five miles down the coast. One by one we joined school children emerging from the timber with dinner pails, going to school in the vicinity of Grigsbys store. I learned from them that there were quite a number of setlers along the coast but located back in the timber. They claimed that there was plenty of good land, but that the timber growth was scrubby for a mile or so bordering the beach.[118] Observing large <u>derricks</u> at every half mile, I enquired their use. The gentleman informed me that they were look outs from which they shot the sea Otter. This was new to me and I asked to be enlighted

---

[118] "According to an item in the May 5, 1890, *Oregonian*, all the beach from the Indian Agency to Grays Harbor had been taken. On January 1, 1890, John J. Banta recorded in his diary: 'The beach is all taken up by parties who think it will be a great summer resort some day.'" Wood, *Men, Mules and Mountains*, p. 433.

[enlightened]. They explained, as I could see, that four timbers about 30 ft long were secured upon end, slanting inward at the top, and securely braced and nailed together upon the top was a small platform about one yard square, and upon this four walls boarded high enough to shield the hunter from the ever vigilant Otter. A ladder was constructed by which the hunter gained his look out. The derricks were constructed near low tide line. Once the hunter gained his cache there was no escape from it until the tide receded. The skins of these animals, owing to the tough pelt and fine fur, bring upon the market from $75. to $150^{00} Dollars each, and the hunter who obtains as many as four in a season is considered fortunate. They seldom get a shot nearer than 600 yds, and that as the animal rides the swells, and it is estimated that not more than one shot in 100 proves effectual. A rule is established that each man is allowed but one look out and that no closer than half mile of his neighbors. Each hunter has his own private mark upon his bullets, and when one is supposed to have been wounded the beach is walked in that vicinity three or four times per day until the sea gives up its dead. I am told that but a short distance along the Pacific is frequented by these valuable fur bearing animals, and they are with each year becoming more scarce. I was shown the skin of a half grown pup at O-E-hut. It was shaped much as the land otter but much larger. This one was about 6 feet long excluding the tail and was of a beautiful drab color and silver tipped when exposed to the sun light. This one in the possession of Mr Axtelle was rated at $125^{00}. Quite a neat cottage was passed now, belonging to Mr Chapman. Here one of the gentleman, who was the school teacher, past [passed] company with us, and many children was now passed coming up the coast to school. The gentleman stated that there was only 3 months school as the expense came from their purses. One mile further and this gentleman turned off to Griggsbys store. The fog had by this time gathered densly, and a hard rain set in. I crossed the Chopailis by wading and met Indians and whites hauling freight to Grigsbys store. Reaching O-E-hut, which is the Chinook name for a trail or road, I stopped at one of three houses upon the beach to make enquiries. They were half breeds and well fixed. There were none of the males at home, and the women folks spoke poor english, but very good Chinook. This trail or O-E-hut turned to the east, crossing Damons point, at about 5 miles above its Southern extremity. The point here was about one and one half miles wide. I found a very good waggon road to the landing upon Grays Harbor. Several buildings faced the

Harbor and a Dock of small dimensions had been constructed but could be reached by boats at high tide only. A half dozen half breeds whom had severed tribal relations were loitering about the dock. Their business was fishing, hunting and freighting with sail boats from one point to another upon Grays Harbor. Messrs Axtelle and Conkling were the proprietors of the principal building. They were prepared to serve meals, furnish lodgings, or sail boats. I arrived 20 minutes too late to catch the sail boat, and had to lay over untill next day noon. I was informed that Mr Damon owned this entire point, from which it had derived its name.[119] The rain continued to pour down and I went into camp under a large tree for shelter, and prepared lunch. I estimated that I had traveled 50 miles from Mt Olympus to the coast and 40 miles from the mouth of the Queets to the 0-E-hut, making 90 miles, mostly alone with out a cent, and with less than a pound of meat beyond what I killed with spear and revolver. The indians had befriended me a great deal but now I was advancing upon civilization again, utterly deficient in that accomplishment of existing with out means, so proficiently mastered by many. It was presumed that I would next appear at Ft. Townsend or arrangements would have been made. I had to cross this bay, which was 16 miles across. I had about made up my mind to set out over the mud flats at low tide when different individuals invited me to remain over night with them, and assured me that I would get across tomorrow. Mr Damon was at this point assisted by his son in law in building a floating Dock, and I remained over night with them at one of their cabins, and highly appreciated their kindness. Mr Damon informed me that he had once been fond of hunting, and seen much of the country under that role. He was tall and straight, with pleasant features and flowing beard, perhaps of two score and ten, though apparently younger at a passing glance, jovial, witty and a brilliant conversationalist. I highly enjoyed the evening. He had been settled upon this point for 12 years and numberless cattle bearing his brand, I am told, are rapidly enlarging his already lengthy bank account. At any rate he was yet partial to his first love, the camp fire, tumbling in to a bed of straw preferably to returning home where the comforts of life awaited him. We were in no hurry to arise in the morning, and found the sun well up in the eastern skye. The fog and rain having passed away with the night, and the balmy atmosphere had the soothing effect of a spring time morn.

Tues Sept 30th. After breakfast we passed through an orchard belonging to mine host, principally of apples, and

455

---

[119] "Albert O. Damon settled on Point Brown (commonly called Damon's Point) in 1878. He ranged cattle over the whole point, and bought, sold, and traded land in various parts of the Grays Harbor country. He died in 1928." Wood, *Men, Mules and Mountains*, p. 433.

very productive. Filling my pockets we approached the dock and seperated, with many thanks to him for his kindness. I now accosted a half breed whose name was, of course, John. He had informed me upon the Ocean beach that if he succeeded in obtaining clams he would sail to Hoquiam. I offered him four or five dollars worth of fishing tackle & etc to take me over, but he spoke in doubts of the wind, perhaps in hopes that he would yet obtain my revolver. The fare was only 1^{00} and I had made arrangements with Mr Axtelle and Conkling whom were going over at noon. They now appeared with their boat and I set sail with them, leaving John Lo astonished at the sudden departure. He soon followed us with out a passenger and I wondered if he knew the popular song of never kick a man when he is down. This was indeed a beautiful day, and with a stiff breeze we sped over the waves with astonishing speed. Messrs Axtelle and Conkling were old river rats, and were acquainted with every inch of the Pacific Coast, and amused other passengers as well as my self with Salt water yarns and funny incidents. The Humptulip channel was passed and I now had the pleasure of looking upon the mouth of the Humptulips, whose head waters I had formerly traced to a rivulet. Rounding a point, we appeared in view of Grays Harbor City,[120] a thriving little town which boasted of fine buildings. In order to establish a dock at which vessels could land, they constructed a road way upon poles which projected one and a quarter miles out into the Bay at a cost of $33000. Dollars. We landed at Hoquiam at 4 P.M. and I for the second time upon this expedition walked its busy streets. One of the first parties I met was John McCalla of Lake Quinault, now a deligate representing Chehalis County. He kindly introduced me at the Hotel Brunswick, where I engaged accommodations. He also informed me that my friends with the mules left yesterday or this morning, he was not sure which. Had I have caught the Sail boat yesterday noon, I would now have been upon my way home. But it mattered not. I learned that the Lieut was yet up in the Raft river country, and I was sure that he would revisit Hoquiam.

I also met Messrs Smith and McCarthy, the latter having been with Sergt Marsh up the Humptulip, after leaving the pack train. From them I learned some particulars of the southern division. In my rags and soiled condition, I was as anxious to leave Hoquiam as I was to arrive, but there was no alternative but to await future developments, and I amused my self with the jolly boarders at the Hotel Brunswick.

Wedns Oct 1st. It was raining and miserable out side and I passed the morning at the Hotel. The topic of general conversation was Real Estate and the probable terminus of the projected R. Roads which were Hunts system, and the N.P.R.R. Co. Members of all the towns were present, and each party was prolific with solid points as to why his town should get it.[121] I was too rusty to know any thing of the news of the day, and was not sure of any thing except that I was yet in America, and a deplorable looking representative of the flag. Strolling out upon the street, Mr McMillan recognized me as one of the O.E.E. party and introduced him self, and many other prominent Gentleman of the City. Among others I met the Officers and directors of the Lake Quinault Improvement Company. For the benefit of parties wishing to know in particular of this paradise and the intentions of the wide awake stockholders, I submit the names of the Officers, representing a Capital of $64,000.^{00} for the purpose of developing the Quinault Country.

Directors

Wm. B. Ogden Sec
John F. Soule Treas
O.G. Chase Pres't
C. F. Lancaster Vice Pres't
C. T. Russell
W.S. Liebendorfer
John McCalla
John G. McMillan

Mr McMillan Informed me that he had received a note

---

[120] "Grays Harbor City was supposed to be the terminus of George W. Hunt's railroad from the Centralia coal fields to Grays Harbor. The site, three miles west of Hoquiam, was picked by eastern capitalists. Development began in 1889, and the promoters built houses, graded streets, and at a cost of $33,000 constructed a 'roadway upon poles' that extended one and a quarter miles to the deep water in the bay. The project boomed for a while, accompanied by feverish land speculation. The development affected Hoquiam, which was incorporated as a third-class city, a Board of Trade organized, and a large hotel built to handle the expected visitors. The railroad was never completed, however, because the Northern Pacific (which had offered to buy out Hunt) went into receivership due to the failure of its financial backer, and a few years later Grays Harbor City became a ghost town." Wood, *Men, Mules and Mountains*, p. 419.

[121] "Hunt was then operating a railroad from Hunt's Junction (on the Northern Pacific near Wallula Junction) to Pendleton, Oregon. Early in 1890 he had proposed to the Portland Board of Trade (on behalf of the Oregon and Washington Railway Company) to build a line from Hunt's Junction to Portland. He also had started constructing a line to Grays Harbor, but the Northern Pacific was bitterly contesting for the right to serve that area. Worried that Hunt would get there first, the company attempted to thwart him by negotiating a purchase of the Puget Sound & Gray's Harbor Railroad, a small line that ran from Montesano to Kamilchee. By so doing, the Northern Pacific could connect this road to its main line and extend the railroad to Grays Harbor, thus securing access to the port and at the same time head off Hunt, who was 'becoming troublesome.' Meanwhile, Hunt had 500 men and 150 teams working feverishly on his 'Gray's Harbor Division.' The engineer in charge of the construction was R. A. Habersham, who had been with O'Neil on the 1885 reconnaissance of the Olympics." Wood, *Men, Mules and Mountains*, pp. 433–34.

from the Lieut in which he stated that he would arrive in Hoquiam on or about the 5th. Any assistance that I needed was tendered, and Hoquiam was home to me. While perusing The Washingtonian, Mr Smith, a R. R. genius, remarked that those gentleman must be my friends. Looking out the window I recognized a half dozen individuals that in appearance were a credit to old Uncas Dunca from Coopers pen. They were all strangers except by reputation. Placing them in the hands of the generous McMillan, they were soon made comfortable and pitched camp at the Gamage Hotel. I now played reporter and interviewed them as to their wanderings since I had became seperated upon the 21st ult. They had prepared lunch in the vicinity of the jungle beneath Mt Olympus, thinking I would over take them. In the after noon they had passed up through the dry and rocky gulch that I had noticed, pitching camp up on a rocky cliff, after some hard climbing in reaching it. While upon this point they had observed the light far below, which as they thought was from my fire, and caused them to give the camp signal. Upon the day following, which was the 22nd, they headed to the west, ascending, and crossed some ugly Glaciers that encircled the peak of Mt Olympus.[122] Gaining the S. W. side of Olympus, Sergt. Yates, who was almost barefooted, with Hughes and the Kid were to pitch camp and await the return of the other three who would ascend and plant the box.[123] Among other articles placed within its hollow was a dispatch of Victor Hugos death by Col Linsley, a glove once the property of a Lady of the Banner party picked up by Sergt Yates near the head waters of the Skokomish. A deck of cards by Danton, besides other articles and the register formerly alluded to. The box was located as high up as a secure cache

could be found upon the S.W. slope of the peak.[124] Gaining the point the aneroid registered 7500 feet, instead of more than 8000, and the instrument was correct at sea level before and subsequent to the ascent. Nellis Creek was traced from the west slope of Mt Olympus toward the coast flowing in a south westerly direction & parallel to the Queets. From the general form of the canyon it was estimated that it, like the Queets, received no large tributaries, passing through a valley of liberal width.[125] Returning to the temporary camp where dinner was awaiting them, they lunched and descended to ward the S.W. They had considered it impossible to attempt a descent over my trail and came to the conclusion that I would take care of my self. Their rations were running distressingly short, some of them almost shoeless, and they concluded the sooner they made civilization, the better. Following down to some distance between the Nellis and Queets, night came on them before they reached the stream and they pitched camp for the night. Sept 23 they located a prominent spur that was christened as trinity mountain[126] and dropped to the Queets with much difficulty, arriving at the stream at 11 A.M. They had left notes for me in case I was in the rear of them. They approached the stream some miles lower down than I had, and found the block of wood upon which I had written to them my intentions. They seperated, some trying the brush, and others the water. After lunch they came together again and followed pretty much in my tracks expecting that they would over take me. Camping near the stream upon an ant hill, they registered at Camp Misery, in honor of the insects I presume.[127] Sept 24th they found another note from me, instructing them to look under logs for salmon, in case they came this way. During the afternoon

457

---

[122] "The 'ugly glaciers' were two parts of the Jeffers Glacier and/or related icefields. [A] photograph of Linsley, Bretherton, and Danton sitting on a rock rib at the head of the glacier, shows in the background the pinnacle now called West Hermes. Apparently the picture was taken before the men left for the summit or after they rejoined Yates, Hughes, and Kranichfeld. The photograph thus pinpoints the location of the temporary camp—at 5800 feet on the south ridge of the Athena Peaks, at the head of the Jeffers Glacier." Wood, *Men, Mules and Mountains*, p. 428.

[123] "The mystery of the copper box may never be solved. Many alpinists have looked for it, and in 1972, 1973, and 1974, members of The Mountaineers ascended Athena II from the head of Jeffers Glacier, thus reenacting the 1890 climb, but diligent search for the box proved fruitless. The Athena Peaks are composed of extremely rotten, crumbling rock that changes yearly. If not swept from the mountain by an avalanche, the box may still lie at or near its original location, perhaps covered by snow or fallen rock. Nor should the possibility be overlooked that someone may have discovered and removed the box years ago but the event was never publicized. If, however, the explorers climbed Athena I rather than Athena II, they must have left the box on an almost inaccessible ledge 400 feet below the summit on the sheer south face, where it may still await discovery by some intrepid mountaineer willing to risk the hazard of loose, unstable rock in order to make a search. The time factor suggests, however, it is unlikely the men could have climbed Athena I from the Jeffers Glacier in two hours and forty-five minutes, and certainly the ascent would not have been described as 'easy.'" Wood, *Men, Mules and Mountains*, p. 431.

[124] See "The Mystery of the O.A.C. Box" in Appendix to the O'Neil Expeditions Reports at the end of part 3.

[125] "The men may have seen the upper reaches of the South Fork of the Hoh. However, an expedition photograph entitled 'Discovery of the Ho River' was obviously mislabeled. The picture shows three men standing on Heart's Peak, the camera pointing down the Duckabush, with The Brothers on the horizon." Wood, *Men, Mules and Mountains*, p. 428.

[126] "Trinity Mountain was not Mount Olympus, as commonly believed, but The Valhallas. The men's temporary camp at the head of the Jeffers Glacier afforded an excellent view of the mountain, which had a triple-peaked appearance, and Bretherton sketched it in his diary, noting that it was '20° W & S' from 'Mt. Olympus' (i.e., Athena), a very accurate observation. (Olympus, on the other hand, could not be seen from the camp because it was hidden by the bulk of Athena.) Trinity Mountain is visible from the Grand Divide, and the men probably saw and named it prior to August 17. Bretherton and F. J. Church both refer to it in their diaries, and they had not seen each other since that date. Bretherton sketched the mountain on September 22; Church referred to it a week later, when he was crossing the Queets-Quinault Divide." Wood, *Men, Mules and Mountains*, p. 434.

[127] "This is according to Fisher. Bretherton called the place Camp Pollard in his diary." Wood, *Men, Mules and Mountains*, p. 434.

they shot three salmon but saw no game during the day. Traveling until night closed in, they pitched camp near the stream in a thicket, and called this Camp Menagerie. Wild animals had prowled around the camp all night, at times coming close enough that their blazing orbs were seen. To frighten them away Mr Bretherton shot at one that he considered a cougar. Sept 25th They experienced some of the difficulties that I had in deep wading, and kept to the stream pretty much all the day, killing what Salmon they needed. This night they called a second camp after the providential Salmon. Sept 26th They approached the cabins to day, finding them all empty. They camped with in 200 yds of Thorntons claim. Sept 27th they passed Hollenbecks, Lymans, Sharps, et. al. cabins & pitching camp upon the beach. During the day Mr Bretherton and Danton met Messrs Wilbur and Davis, and talked with them. Sept 28th they passed two men from Seattle who were no doubt the gentlemen that I passed upon the ocean beach. Fording many times, they at last reached the hut where I had but recently left. Sergt Yates could chew Chinook as fluently as he could tobacco, but there was no one at home who could interpret his meaning. The old man appeared in his night clothes, presenting them with a clap board upon which to write their wants. This done he placed the board under the bed for Addie to read when she returned from school, which would probably occur in the spring time. The boss of the N.E. corner now appeared, and by launching his canoe they made him understand that they wished to travel Mimee down the river. The indian transported them over the route that we had traveled. Reaching the beach, they dismissed him with his money and traveled down the coast, camping one mile below the Raft River, upon a bluff over-looking the Ocean. Sept 30th The same shower that was making it miserable for me at O-E-hut run them into Quinault agency where they took dinner, their supplies having run out. They laid off at the agency until the following morning, and while there they learned that I had gone through the agencey. Oct 1st Engaging the indians and their waggons they proceeded down the Coast at an early hour, and reached O-E-hut in the evening. Engaging Capt Miller with his Sail rigged scow, they reached Hoquiam at 5 P.M. They had not discovered any thing new pertaining to the mineral, animal or vegetable kingdoms, and like my self had passed down the coast so hurriedly that they had no oppertunity of gathering the razor backed clams, whose shells were in great numbers upon the beach. It is to be regretted

that our party did not personally pursue their explorations more to the N.W. However, we should be satisfied with what we accomplished in one summers work. As our trail leading over the mountains is the brunt of the battle, we trust that other parties may soon follow our foot steps.

Thurs Oct 2nd. The day was passed very pleasantly with every person eager to learn something of the Olympics. During the day a report was current that stock was rising at the town site of Quinault City, and later we were confirmed of the fact. As the first and second parties were gentleman of our acquaintance, we were informed of the transaction, which was that 40 shares of stock in the town site had been exchanged for and in consideration of $1000 Dollars. How does that sound, gentleman, for young and prosperous America, wild land, and the wildest of wilds. Scarcely had the foot prints of the first domestic animals received the sun light, before enterprising man, and their money, were speaking more than words. Will it pay? asks a bean raiser from the red hills of old Vermont, and the ever doubtful and mosquito persecuted individual of Jersey. Yea any thing, and every thing pay's in the infant state of Washington, the pioneers claim. As brief and as varied as the butterflies existence, like a flower from seedling to bud and fruit in one short season are the growth of towns and cities in this grand North West. Is it doubted? If so, only glance back ten yrs, five years, and travel over the then wild waste where now lofty spires, steeples and walls of polished granite blaze in the sun light, e-g Seattle, Spokane, Tacoma, Ellensburgh, Yakima, Hoquiam, and hundreds of others locations that excel some of these in wealth and population. What were they five and ten years ago but the play grounds of pappooses. Trails that then led the red man to the haunts of game now lead the Iron horse from town to city, laden with native bullion and produce. Washington, the home of small grain, vegetables and hops, not those of Frisco and Florida that hop to the peoples distress. I allude to these matters not in idle advocation of a country that needs not booming, but as the Oklahoma was, so will the fertile Valleys of the Olympics soon be, thronging with people in search of homes.[128] While meditating upon these pleasant facts, and admiring western enterprise at work, regardless of the falling rain, a couple of mud soiled individuals hove in sight, and we recognize our leader, the Lieut, and his companion, Harry West. Next in order is their travels, which I will endeavor to relate. It was upon the morning of the

458

---

[128] "Fisher's prediction was too optimistic, but a typical viewpoint of the time. The reference to Oklahoma concerns the land rush of April 22, 1889, when the territory was officially opened for settlement." Wood, *Men, Mules and Mountains*, p. 435.

26th of September that the Lieut with Mr West and the two Churches directed their travels north-ward from the Quinault, after leaving Sgt Marsh and companion with orders for the Humptulip country. They headed north west, exploring the north fork of the Quinault and that country between it and the Queets river. They found the Quinault as represented in our map flowing generally south, but making a decided curve at a point above its confluence with the east branch, also sweeping from the west at its source, with one mountain tributary from the north, which was no doubt the one that we headed by crossing the mountain at Camp Befog. They found the north fork more inclined to canyon than the east fork, and more difficult to travel along. There were no falls of magnitude, but at four different points it passed through canyons more naviegable for fish than boats. The tributaries to the north branch came principally from the west. Nothing was added to former discoveries from the floral field, nor from the mineral wealth. As I have before stated, the Lieut was not inclined to hunt, or fish, and but little attention was paid to the animals of the forest. They had passed over too far to the N.E. to strike the source of the Raft River, and approached the Queets, over looking it at a point where I referred to upon the 24th Inst as receiving a stream from the east. Noting the direction of this tributary, they were almost sure that it emptied into the Queets, and the two Messrs. Church were sent down this. While the Lieut and Mr West returned more to the south west in order to catch the Raft. They stated that they found some very rough country through here, and were occasionally almost non plussed, in searching for a passage. In one instance related to us by Mr West, the Lieut lowered him down with a slender but tough limb from the maple, and depended upon dropping to the ledge where Mr West was to assist him in regaining his balance. Mr West, too eager, caught the Lieut before he landed, and the full force of his weight sent the two of them down the decline, over a mass of broken stones. With bruises well distributed over body and limbs, they hobbled on and carried marks of this fall to Hoquiam with them. At this point they were crossing a precipitous canyon, and had nearly reached the bottom. Mr West in stead of parting the brush to choose a landing point, placed him self in a toboggan attitude and sang out to Clear the Way for old Dan Tuck-O-O-h— The Lieut fished him out with a long pole and spread him out in the sun light to dry. From here they continued on to the south west and struck the Raft River, tracing it out to the Ocean. They estimated this stream as not more than twenty to twenty five miles from source to mouth—rising at the base of the foot hills and flowing S.W. between and parallel to the Queets and Quinault. Struggling through the brush again, they recrossed the country, heading for Lake Quinault. The brush and fallen timber were some thing terrible to push through at this point. You abraid your Shins in climbing upon great logs and slide off to disappear in the depths of some hole that is hidden by the Heath that flips your hat back to the other side. Oh, but its jolly, and a few hours circling among the Heath brakes of these bottoms reminds one of a ride upon a mutmeg [nutmeg] grater. The timber through out these bottoms reach for the earth with great bench roots that shake hands with its next neighbor, and so on, from one to the other. Boulders and the trunks of great trees are heaped in wild confusion, and in all stages of preservation, and decompocition. The great Fir, the king of the West, and the alder whose growth are so rapid, decay as speedily and give back to nature, the great analysist. Many specimens of the red cedar baffled all processes of the elements and were as well preserved now as they were fifty, seventy five, and one hundred years ago, when the small twig, which [is] now a monster, gathered its nourishment from the fallen tree. The foliage and falling twigs from year to year had gathered to a depth of three and four feet, with a deep covering of moss upon the whole, attending each and every step with the misgivings of another fall. The Lake was finally reached and Mr West launched his canoe, in which, with the swiftly moving current, they glided to the sea down the lower Quinault. It is considered 35 miles via the stream from Lake Quinault to the agencey at the mouth of the stream. This agencey is for the benefit of the Quinault Reservation covering a territory of thirty miles square or 576,000 acres of valuable land and timber. There are only about seventy Indians occupying this reservation and complying with the Indian anuity [?] laws, which allow almost Dalrymple farm of more than 8000. acres per head.[129] Lake Quinault or Quinialet, as some will have it, is bordered by the Reservation, whose limits are defined by the north west corner of the lake as per official allotment. The Lake does not lay to the points of the compass as represented in maps of former date, and an ugly question arises between the setlers and Indian Authorities as to what point is defined as the north west corner of this body of water lying as it does

459

---

[129] "Fisher misunderstood or was misinformed. The reservation covered about 190,000 acres, and had a population of 453 Indians in 1890. By a 'Dalrymple farm,' Fisher meant large-scale. Oliver Dalrymple was the manager of the Northern Pacific's vast wheat-growing operations in North Dakota." Wood, *Men, Mules and Mountains*, p. 435.

illustrated in our map. Spending some time with the Indian Agent, Mr E., they followed in our foot steps down the coast and sailed from O-E-hut to Hoquiam with Messrs Axtelle and Conkling, arriving as we had met them, upon the evening of the 2nd inst. Fred Church and the Doctor during these days were toiling down the Queets, and with their appearance upon the evening of the 5th ended the work of an exploring nature conducted by The O'Neil Exploring Expedition.

> Seldom a rose with-out the thorn
> Never a bitter with-out the sweet
> God made mountains, and man was born
> So were we good times to meet

And the following few days in which we shall figure were made as pleasant for us as a generous people knew how to frame them.

Friday Oct 3rd. The day was passed in pleasure meet'g former and new acquaintances, and in watching the many individuals angling for tom cod from the Hoquiam dock. Women, men and children mingling in the sport, and how different. In our yum yum days of pop corn and kisses, we were bound by strongest ties of Cupid's code to bait, and free the game, but these western beauties feared not the worm nor grub. Before the incandescent sparks were twinkling, the City had been bulletined by the G.A.R., stating that Lieut J. P. ONeils, at the Rink, would entertain the public with a lecture, embracing his thrilling adventures in the Olympics. The house was filled to its utmost capacity and entertained by the Lieut for a time, after which Col Linsley and Mr Bretherton were importuned to burst the fountains, and augment the melifulent flow of language that was expected regarding this supposed new Eldorado. But No! Their courage wavered, and their voices faltered with excuses. Strange! yet true, but it was ever thus. Men that had stood face to face with menaced dangers, braving hard ships and toil, men whom had rocked in the cradle of adventure and imminent peril, with laugh and song, now with in the lines of civilization quailed before the ladies. And even the Lieut, at other times a shining light at social gatherings, and drilled from infancy by a strict disciplinarian to meet all emergencies with that calm resignation characteristic of an Army Officer, even he searched for holes in his trousers pocket for means of escape,

but he was much better known now than upon his first visit to Hoquiam, when he sought in embarrassment connection with his bank account.[130] We observed displayed upon many a manly breast the insignia, yea, the proud emblem of those that bivouced [bivouacked] through the stormy days of the G.A.R. Dr Chase, Col Burns (the City Mayor) et. al. we had met with the warmth of friend ship, that grew warmer still when they appeared with uniform and badge. Disappearing to our respective inns as usual, Lake Quinault and Hunts R. R. were the themes of conversation at the Brunswick, and one Oclock chimed the tinkling bells ere we broke the spell that held us, charmed, by the brilliant discourse of Col Barlow, a Lake Quinault enthusiast. Oct the 4th and 5 passed slowly by, as the time does to individuals in idleness after a lengthy stretch of adventure, and inspiring grandeur of choicest mountain scenery. The Alliance, a Coast steamer plying between Grays Harbor and Portland, was now in port, and it was upon her returning trip that we were to return to our stations. Upon this 4th eve of the month, a reception more grand than the writer can picture was to take place within the gilt flowered walls of Hoquiam's beautiful Hotel. The Board of trade of this infant Metropolis, to give vent to their feelings, their love of hearth and home, as they met us with axe and brush hook in the wilderness, proud that their city was the terminus of this mountain trail, they also met us in banquet regardless of our shabby attire.

> The warmth of France, and Mountain Dew,
> Tit bits sweet, and plenty too,
> Flowed as free as mountain rill
> From the old Kentucky still.

Given the freedom of their town with our Sergt. Grand Marshal (pro tem) we were honored beyond the power of thanks by this magnanimous display, impulsively grand. It was far beyond the other side of midnight when the safety valve of nature bid us follow home the moon. During the evening of the 5th the Messrs Churchs came in. There is little to be said of their travels since they had as the reader is aware gained the Queets near the foot hills and followed to the Coast, not knowing that we had by accident preceded them.

Monday Oct 6th. We were up at 4-30 A.M. in order to catch the boat. Lieut ONeil set out for the Sound, to gather up the remains of our equippage, and Sergt Marsh with the

460

---

[130] "Fisher surely did not intend this statement to be taken seriously. O'Neil could hardly have felt uncomfortable in appearing before an audience. He was an accomplished orator and had won many honors for his skill in public speaking while attending the University of Notre Dame, where he quickly became 'a brilliant elocutionary star.' When giving declamations, he 'displayed great dramatic force and power, accompanied by appropriate gestures,' and he was credited with having 'a charming and graceful delivery.'" Wood, *Men, Mules and Mountains*, p. 435.

animals, whose fates we had not as yet learned. Col Linsley, Mr Bretherton, and the Churches, boarded the Montesano, en route to their respective destinations, while we Soldiers took the steamer Alliance for Portland Or. A heavy gale was blowing from the west which was sufficient to reverse the condition of what the name Pacific would imply. However, as we were bulletined to depart on time, at 5 A.M. we steamed down the Harbor. The cabin was uncomfortably small, as were the state rooms, and the motion of the vessel was a signal that brought all passengers out to view. 43 passengers in all, more than could be made comfortable. It was raining and disagreeable upon deck and the majority remained within the crowded cabin. The Bar was approached at the mouth of the Harbor. One look from the cross trees at the breakers, one blast of the madened gale, was enough for the Captain, and we steamed back to the Hoquiam dock. One very portly gentleman tumbled from his state room in a rage, and swore that he had passed a night under bed clothes too small to cover a match. No one offered any sympathies, and the gentleman balanced himself between his grip sacks and deserted the ship. This surely was a day for ennui, we could only sit or stand as the occasion offered, and study our opposite passengers. A half dozen ladies were board. The pleasant faced matron and blooming maid, among others, was there. Our failure to proceed upon our journey appeared to have dampened our spirits with in, as the rain had dampened without. The boat set an elegant spread which lost much of its temptation through the misfortune that but one third of us could dine at once. The day was gone at last and night closed in with her mantle of fog, more dreary than before. Col Burns the Mayor paid us a visit and in his kindness stated that he was ready to hear our complaints or wants if we had any, but as it was beyond his jurisdiction to calm the angry sea, we could ask nothing else from the representative of these over kind people.

Tues Oct 7th. A [At] 5-30 A.M. we approached the Bar again. The wind and breakers rushed on to meet us, half way, and soon we imagined our selves from mountain to valley as of yore. The Alliance was too short for her work, and the screw half of the time whirling in empty space, was unable to stem the tide of wind and wave. It was too much like trapeze work upon deck, and watching my chance I tumbled into the cabin and joined in a walk around with the chairs and passengers. Some were disgusted with the sport, and spit upon their food, and with nearly all, the air became as salt as the sea. Once more the Captain headed for the Harbor and run into Ocosta, to remain until the storm subsided. Ocosta is an other embryo town, upon the

south shore of Grays Harbor. We remained here all day and night, and had ample oppertunity to have talked the few inhabitants all to sleep had they been of ordinary material, but a trip a shore settled all. There were ten houses, nine Real estate and one drug store. Sure, pop, if you escaped the former you were a subject for the latter. Ocosta scarcely above the tide and a salt marsh, it was just as it once was where Hoquiam now flourished. The mud flats extending far out into the bay, had necessitated them to building a dock, as we have described at Grays Harbor City. Here again the Jersey farmer might inquire through what channels that bread cast upon these waters would return. It was too much for us, but we knew that Washington towns as mush rooms grow while the sun is cheering China. Corner lots were $750 to $1,000.⁰⁰ Dollars. A saw mill was coming, and nothing short of a flood of misfortunes could dampen their ardor. We strolled upon the beach, and fished for tom cod, as the ladies had all been caught, and put in the day as best the stranded could.

Wedns Oct 8. Again at the unfortunate moment of 5.30 we slipped the cable and made for the trackless sea. The gale had subsided to a fair breeze from the N.W. Every person was brave this morn, and with renewed courage came upon deck, to enjoy the fresh air and rising sun. One by one the passengers caved in, a victim to that awful sickness, and disappeared below. A mid ship there was some hopes of saving your breakfast, but forward or astern it was worse than see saw days. I was doing well enough upon deck, not sick, but mouth a little salty, when I allowed my self persuaded below. When I reached the cabin floor I plunged over obstacles and stood upon my head, poised for the next lurch. With this I executed a back somersault and richochetted from the dining table to my state room door, and in I went with out a bow as is usual after an act in public. We crossed the bar at this trial and when once out in deep water, it was over beautiful rolling swells. The Sun shone brightly, with a pleasant breeze from the north west. Before sail, and steam, the Alliance made excellent time, and by 2 P.M. we were crossing the Columbia River Bar, which was nothing to compare to our former experience. Ft Canby & Ilwaco were passed to our left, and the light house standing sentinel over the sea. To the right were the government jetties in construction, that will some day remove this bar as the Delta of the Mississippi was channeled out. At 2.30 P.M. we landed at Astoria, the old Sea port town, laying over long enough to visit the main thoroughfare. Perhaps this is one of the most important fisheries in America, especially for salmon, both in quantity and

461

quality, yet Astoria was not our ideal of a town. The tumble down dock, and moss covered buildings, weatherstained and faded, did not vie well with the pretty scenery surrounding. The Columbia is about five miles wide near its mouth, with many pretty moss covered points of rock upon either shore. Watching the many Ocean and river steamers moving like ants with their precious cargoes, until darkness came, we repaired to the cabin and enjoyed the evening at whist with the ladies.

Thurs Oct 9th found us, before the sun, in the Willamette at Portland, Oregon. From Portland to Van-couver is only six miles a cross the point between the Columbia and Willamette Rivers, or 15 miles around over water, via the mouth of the Willamette. Taking the Portland and Vancouver R.R. which connects with the ferries at Portland and Vancouver every hour, we were soon at home in our respective Quarters. Upon the Sunday following Lieut ONeil and Sergt Marsh made their appearance, which were the last of the O.E.E.ers in arriving home. The Oregon Alpine Club not to be out done and in recognizance of returning members from this successful expedition, received the O.E.E. and a small circle of select friends in Banquet, at Portlands Pride, the Portland Hotel, Oct 22nd 1890 at 8 P.M. We assembled in the richly ornamented parlours of this magnificent building and were presented to Mr W. G. Steel, President of the O.A.C., many of its members, and all invited guests. Mr Bretherton had thoughtfully displayed a collection of scenes, photographed from the Olympics, which were interesting and pretty even to us who had been there. At 9 P.M. we marched in column of twos to the Banquet Hall, which was ornamented for the occasion to the highest degree of perfection. Thirty covers were spread, and at each was a name of the invited guests, and members of the Club present. Also the beautiful Menu card artistically gotten up for the occasion, hand-painted and secured to the toasts by an Alpine stock and ribbon, delicately arranged. Upon its face was Lieut ONeils Photograph with imitation of Olympic scenery as a background. In addition to all that is beautiful in vegetable life, handsome nose gays were distributed and the banquet opened, governed by an experienced hand with a score or more of trained waiters. The occasion was indescribably beyond the flow of ink. With R. W. Mitchell as Toast Master, each and every word richly clad in wit, and trimmed in sober sequel, beyond the power of Nye.[131] To his call responded Dr. J. W. Hill, To Our guests. Lieut J P ONeil, To the last corner of the U.S., The Olympics. W. G. Steel, Our Pioneer Law, The Hand

462

Maid of Civilization. T. F. Osborn, To Portland & Her trade. Col Lee, The Dept of the Columbia. Father Gibney, The Early Missionary & Our City Government. Col C. F. Beebe, Our Young Sister, Washington, and the National Guard. Hon Geo. W. McBride, Oregon. H. W. Scott, The Press. B. J. Bretherton, The Olympian Forests. Wm Huntly Hampton, Our Mineral Wealth. Proff L. F. Henderson, The Botany of the Olympics. C. M. Idleman, The Alpine Club. Yes! all responded in words of eloquence, between the intervals at which was served all of the palate tickling delicacies known to the aerial or aqueous ocean, and Terra Firmas of the five Great Nations. Glasses oer flowing that sparkled like the Seven Sisters, whose number they represented, formed a crescent around our spreads, and ever kept full to brim with choicest brands that ever Nabob drank. In the wee hours of the morn, faces radiant with pleasure seperated to dream as one enchanted. To those inclined to outing, or that may wish to visit any portion of the Olympics, to enjoy the many different pleasures and benefits that may accrue there from, I will drop the following hints. For a short and easy trip fishing, take a boat from any of the Sound cities, via Pt Townsend, up Hoods Canal, and do not forget to land at Hoodsport where Mr Finches Hospitality will induce you to run away from home. From here take the trail to Lake Cushman (9 miles). Pack animals, and boats, can be obtained at reasonable rates, at either place, from Mr Finch and Windhoffer. For fishing you need a spoon or trolling hook for large trout. For brook and lake trout, flies, principally Brown hackle, and White Millers, or Jungle Cock, for use late in the evening, and when all others fail to attract a rise, use fish eyes. If you would wish to meet Bruin and the elk in their homes, carry enough of supplies to last you a month and follow the trail up the north fork of the Skokomish. Instead of keeping the trail after passing Camp No 9 cross the mountains due west (steep climb) which will drop you into a basin north of Mt ~~Irlene~~ Steel.[132] Here you will catch our trail again, or from Camp No 9. turn due east. Following up the main stream to its source, it will drop you in to elk basin, and Bear Jungle, the most beautiful of hunting grounds. Were it possible to continue east by S. it would drop you in to the Hama Hama stream, the smallest of the eastern streams. A shot gun may often be used to advantage, but a trusty rifle of large Cal is indispensable. In lieu of an axe a small 2# axe with 2 foot handle is far more excellent to either axe or hatchet, in that it is much lighter than an ordinary axe and sufficient for all camp purposes. Each individual should be provided with a pack, and light cooking

---

[131] "Edgar Wilson Nye, a well known humorist, had been elected an honorary member of the Oregon Alpine Club in 1889." Wood, *Men, Mules and Mountains*, p. 435.

[132] Fisher had written "Irlene" but it has been changed to "Steel".

out fit, for branch scouting and hunting, say for a day or so at a time, away from the main trail. Do not forget a compass, and carry a pound or so of alum. You may wish to save some trophies. If so, flesh the hide well, and thickly sprinkle with powdered alum, which will answer until the Taxidermist takes it in hand. If a head or entire animal is desired to be mounted, measure the animal,correctly, as you would your self for a suit of clothes, and make notes of it, which is very important data for the Taxidermist. Horns and antlers must be left attached to the frontal or face bone complete, which may be sawed length wise between the horns for transportation. The lower jaw bones must also be saved and thoroughly fleshed to baffle the flies and prevent repulsion from tainted flesh. Heads intended for market are of more value with the hide as far as the shoulders, preferably splitting the skin up the nape of the neck. If the throat is to be cut, slit the skin length wise with the dew lap, never cross-wise. The bone in Elk and deer legs, from knee and hock joints down, may be left untouched, but in bear there remains too much flesh. For a neat mount of bird, or animal, Mr Bretherton, of Portland Oregon, enjoys the best reputation of any one upon the Pacific Coast. Address B. J. Bretherton, Cor 2nd & Washington str, Portland Oregon. After having once gained as far as Camp No 9. do not forget to gain the Level Plateau and its lakes, from which point if you wish you can go down (a foot) either the Ducquebusch, Docewallups, or Quinault streams. If Mt Olympus is the desired point I would advise you to follow up either the Elwha or Queets Rivers, according to which side you might choose to approach. If up the Elwha, take steamer to Port Angels on the strait, and follow up the Government trail made by Lleut ONeil and party in 85. Approaching the main forks some 15 miles as the crow flies from the strait, take your right hand stream and be careful that you are not led off upon one of the smaller tributaries. Your course will be S.W. until having passed ~~Chester~~ Valley. The stream makes a fish hook curve coming from the North. If you would go down the north branch of the Quinault, soon after passing Chester Valley head south up the tributary that is received near Camp Lowlands. Crossing the divide at this point will drop you into the North Quinault basin. But if the Queets is the point desired, follow the Elwha to its ultimate, through the gulch and to the glacier. The basin between you and Mt Olympus will lead you to the Queets, but keep well up under Mt Olympus until entirely beyond it before attempting to descend. Bearing from here to the N.W. after having passed Olympus will drop you into the Hoh. If it is your wish to approach from the west side, make Hoquiam your starting point, where you can also secure any supplies or paraphrenelia needed, and at reasonable rates. This town may be reached from Olym-

pia, Wash. by rail and steamers that connect on time. From here you can take the steamer Typhoon for Damons point, or sail boats to the O-E-hut, and follow up the beach by sail boats, in calm weather, or with an east wind. Otherwise, you can engage indian teams, and canoe it up the Queets or Quinault, as far as Lake Quinault. Here you can purchase supplies. Or Hoquiam can be approached by coast steamer, taking a steam yacht as far as Hoquiam landing, where the waggon road will connect you with our trail. There is good fishing and some trapping and hunting in the winter season, on the Humptulips. Reaching Lake Quinault, if desirable, you can cross upon a trail to the Queets, approaching it at the Tacoma settlement. There are more deer in the Queets bottom than in any other location. The Salmon run is greatest in the latter part of Sept to Oct the 20th. During this season they may also be caught with troll in Pugets Sound, or Hoods Canal. For spearing, have barbs or spear points made as per illustration on page 392. You can carry them in your pockets, cutting a staff when needed. For trapping Beaver and Otter, a No 4 New House trap is needed, net price $12 per doz. For Bear a No 6. must be used, $210 per doz net price. Fur animals are most numerous along the streams draining the west slope. Huckle berries do not ripen until September, the sweet Mountain variety lasting until November, and where these are found, bear may also be found quite numerous. Earlier in the season the bear frequent the tracks of the avalanch where blossoms of the Heath family are plentiful and the young grass tender and sweet. The roughness and precipitous nature of the Olympic Mountains are such that dogs, no matter what their traits, are a nuisance. Game is not shy of man, but if it should in time grow wild, dog, nor man, will ever over take it by following its trail. To those in search of claims and timber lands, my first choice would be the Queets, or Quinault, bottoms. The Humptulips has yet left some good lands, and all along the west coast the country is of a rolling nature, bearing many fine specimens of larch, Fir, and cedar. The Elwha has also good bottoms, and fine timber. After having passed Lake Cushman the timber holds good, but the bottoms are contracted to small patches. The Hama Hama according to Mr Mullers report is more of the nature of the Skokomish, but good lands are to be found in the Ducquebusche and Docewallups bottoms that are well timbered. The Dungeness, Quillayute, and Solduck, we have only the reports of the press, and what we learned from the Port Crescent party. The timber is no doubt good throughout all the valleys and glens, and coal is reported from reliable sources to have been found upon the Dungeness stream. To the timber cruiser a trip might prove beneficial up the Wishkah and over into the south tributary of the Skokomish. Lake Osett, in the Quillayute valley, may prove an interesting sheet of water, and we regret that we had no more time to include it in our tour. While stationed in Elk basin and in the Garden of the Gods it was natural that ones mind should wander with the beautiful scenery into lines of verse, and rhyme. As my thoughts ran now, they were blended to many incidents of the trip in the following.

Ode to the Expedition

A party of tried and trusty scouts,
From O.E.E. little band
Set out to scratch Olympia's head,
The mysterie of our land

Oer peak and cliff, down glen and glade
Where the flowers o'er looked Ocean, sound and strait
For many an hour, with our grease and flour
We moved at a toilsome gait

At last we stand upon the summit bold
And gaze oer the myriad of peaks
Where glaciers feed the roaring falls
Dashing down and down from crag to mound
In many an angry leap

Unfurled to the breeze wave the stars and stripes
And the Oregon Alpine box.
They will tell the tale whether we swallowed the whale
Or actually climbed the rocks

Our chief takes the mules from the sound to the sea
While we climbed the snow covered mountains
And long may our knee prints remain in the sand
Where we knelt by your pure crystal fountains

One last long look down the Elwhas banks
To Docewallups and the Ducquebusche
And we turn to gaze at the setting sun
Where the Quillayute waters rush
McCallas Peak and Lake Quinault
Flash up like a heliograph
The Raft, the Hoh, and the Solduck go
With the Moos birds mocking laugh

Now our foot steps point downward to streams yet unknown
That whirl from divide to the Ocean

"Farewell"—friendly hill tops. "Good bye"—noble hemlocks
We leave you to the snow slides commotion

The antlered Elk and the graceful deer
We will leave you in your mountain home
With the bear, the grouse and kangaroo mouse
Save those that we have willed as our own

By the red mans wild home and pioneers claim
Through lagoon and salal like an arbor
O er beach and tide wave through sun shine and rain
To Hoquiam the town of Grays Harbor

So kindly received and well entertained
Yes, banqueted in our shabby attire
By the warm hearted people whom live near the main
And we remember the G. A. R.

Again we must enter a friendly good bye
To ye warm hearted sons of the Coast
May you soon be connected by Railroad and tie
To again meet us and rejoin in this toast.

"Home sweet home" we approach once again
And a circle of friends warm and true
Let it blow, Let it snow, Let it hail, Let it rain
While we stand with the Red, White and Blue

The O.A.C. prompted by impulse so grand
Wined and dined at the Portland Hotel
This our most bounteous camp of the land
In woodland, the meadow or dell.

The End

Following his winter in the Queets Valley with two companions, Fisher wrote several short articles for local newspapers on the tribulations of living for a time in this rugged area.

IN THE OLYMPICS[133]

Settlers' Interesting Adventures

Hardships of Making a Home in the Mountainous Country During the Rainy Season—Scarcity of Provisions.

---

[133] Harry Fisher, *Oregonian* [Portland], April 15, 1892. Brackets in original.

Olympic Mountains. Queets River, Wash., March 10.—
[To the Editor]

Perhaps few of your readers have ever perused item from this isolated spot of beauty, where the songs of wild birds mingle with the murmur of rippling water in its whirl from the heights of Mount Olympus to the ever-thrifty sea. There are some forty claims represented in the Queets basin, principally by Tacomans, of which ten families are passing the winter here, the remainder having gone out for want of supplies. A 15 ton sloop usually supplies this settlement, but, owing to the roughness of the ocean last fall, an inadequate supply forced many to go where necessary substantials were more plentiful. However, the sloop came in during the latter part of February, bringing an abundance for all. There has been no sickness here to speak of, but four deaths, viz., Mr. Turner's little child, which was puny from birth, a siwash child from exposure and pulmonary troubles, and the drowning of two men, whose names I did not learn, who in attempting to cross the Raft river were upset in a canoe and swept into the ocean.

The weather has been magnificent for ducks, raining eighty days out of a possible 150, with one light snow and some hail; precipitation as much as the depth of a time can, which was in this case five and five-tenths inches in twelve hours. Winter we had none on the lowlands. There was no ice formed, and only a few frosty nights. Flowers were blooming in February. In fact, nature has worn her spring garments throughout the entire season for winter. The soil is rich and well watered by springs and mountain streams, producing enormous crops. The valley extends twenty miles from the ocean ere it encounters the mountains from two to five miles wide, making room for many families; but what is needed is a railroad from the Straits to Gray's harbor and this valley will form the pearl of Washington for lumbering, fishing and agricultural pursuits.

Accounting for my presence here: Mr. Yates, Cranmer and myself, having spent the summer of 1890 exploring the Olympics with Lieutenant O'Neil, were charmed with the country and concluded to pass the winter here and improve our claims.[134] Setting out too late in the season, our adventure has been fraught with many accidents, although fringed with a tinge of pleasure. We left Portland October 18, 1891, by steamer Alliance under charge of Captain Peterson, arriving at Hoquiam O.K. From there we crossed Gray's harbor by the tug Tillie, landing at Oehut in a driving rain and wind storm. From Oehut to Quinault agency, twenty-four miles, we freighted out supplies, which amounted to 1300 pounds, per wagon cost, $20. Crossing the Quinault river by canoe, we divided our stores into packs of seventy-five and 100 pounds each, and carried them over the ocean beach to the mouth of the Queets river, a distance of fifteen miles. Yates and I proceeded up this stream six miles, finding cedar from which we split boards and made a scow, celebrated neither for speed nor beauty. The twist of the grain true to nature, remained twisting in the boat as it had in the tree. She was 16x35 feet and 14 inches deep with her starboard bow cocked high in the air and port astern as deep in the water. After naming her the Mary Jane, instead of the Scythe-Handle, we left John Hyassman with his tawny braves and beautiful squaws laughing in their sleeves at our embarking in the strange craft. During the rainy season, this, as all other mountain streams rises and falls almost as rapidly as the ocean's tide. This was undoubtedly the rainy season and the central part of it. Consequently our progress up the stream was very slow.

December 8.—We made Camp Disaster upon an elevated gravel bar about fifteen miles up the stream. Thus far the water had been extremely swift and the course very tortuous, with log jams and cross currents at every bend. After the usual smoke was over we retired to sleep but briefly. During the night a southern zephyr produced one of those atmospheric irregularities so common to the Northwest,

465

---

134 "In a letter to William G. Steel, dated January 2, 1892, Fisher indicated that Sergeant Marsh had joined the party, but stated that he departed after the boat capsized on the Queets. The Cranmer referred to appears to be Corporal Thomas Cranmer, Company B, Fourteenth Infantry, but this soldier was not a member of the 1890 expedition nor was he discharged from the Fourteenth Infantry until November 4, 1891, after the men had left Portland. However, he may have taken leave prior to being discharged. Apparently he knew Yates well. Before serving together in Company B, Fourteenth Infantry, both Cranmer and Yates had been in Battery H, Fourth Artillery (1884–1889). Nevertheless, the peculiar circumstances cause one to speculate that the 'Cranmer' who went to the Queets may have been Jacob Kranichfeld. The latter was a member of the 1890 expedition, had traveled down the Queets with Yates from Mount Olympus, and was dishonorably discharged from the Fourteenth Infantry on October 1, 1891, only two weeks before 'Fisher' was summarily discharged. Perhaps 'the Kid' took a leaf from Hanmore's book and adopted Thomas Cranmer's name—because of its similarity to his own—as a means of escaping the stigma of the dishonorable discharge. The mystery is deepened somewhat by a statement in O'Neil's lecture notes: 'So numerous were [bears] that two of my best shots bought their discharge from the service and have established a very profitable [illegible] camp on the Q. River.' This could refer to Yates and Cranmer, both of whom were discharged in accordance with the provisions of an order of the Adjutant General's Office which provided for discharge by purchase; or, if the soldier had more than ten years service (which both Yates and Cranmer did have) 'by way of favor,' without payment. (Private Krause, who was a member of the expedition, purchased his discharge on December 16, 1890, but it is highly unlikely that 'Potato Bug Pete' would have gone back to the Olympics.)" Wood, *Men, Mules and Mountains,* p. 450.

swelling the stream seven feet in half as many hours. We were aroused abruptly by the water breaking through under our tent, sweeping away our fire and arranging camp in beautiful order. Mid rain, storm and darkness we cast our truck and turnover into the Mary Jane, to drift upon the angry water. We made a successful landing upon a high bank and indulged strong coffee and yawns until daylight. We were forty-eight hours drying out and awaiting the freshet's rundown.

The late swells had almost blocked the river with the drift, and in attempting to make a narrow passage we lost bottom for our poles and drifted back to capsize against the drift. The bulk of our stores went drifting with a ten-mile current, with us in the midst. Hauling a sack of flour upon one log and some other article upon another, we saved enough to tide us through the winter. Fortunately our guns were secured with ropes to the Mary Jane, and she remained pressed to the jam by the strong current. It was a day of general hardship for all. Bacon and heavy articles rolled upon the gravel bottom and could be captured only by watching the rapids and rushing into the water, which was a foot and thirteen inches deep and ice-cold.

We camped here many days, hoping that McGinty would relent and give up; but halo, our hopes were all in vain. An inventory found missing most all of our ammunition, traps, medicine, sugar, coffee, tea, clothing, shoes, tools, garden seeds, baking powder, rice, salt, matches, pepper and other useful articles too numerous to mention. We experimented with various roots and herbs until we succeeded in making good yeast and excellent light bread, which, in a measure, alleviated our troubles, and with a liberal knowledge of the food plants so plentiful in the Northwest, we fared very well, considering. Proceeding on up the river we reached our destination, and made permanent camp twenty-three miles from the mouth of the stream.

Did you ever see a scoop roof? It looks as if made from endless curves, and imbricated like warped shingles. Well, that is our house. Mishap No. 2: Roof fell in at 12 o'clock midnight and caught fire; roof weighed about four tones. but fortunately no one was seriously injured; the fire department deserved great praise for prompt and efficient service. Mishap No. 3: Roof caught fire, supposed from a spark; damage light; no insurance. Mishap No. 4: Dug a canoe, "Injun" model; practicing upon rapids, capsized; two men fell overboard, and the third jumped out where the water was deepest, presumably to avoid getting damp.

There is plenty of elk, bear and deer in the foothills; grouse, rabbits and duck on the lowlands. Steelheads began running March 1. While I could have wrapped our Christmas dinner up in a sheet of this note paper, we are faring sumptuously now, and I can assure you that there are times when none but the rich can enjoy this life.

We have one copy of The Oregonian, which we have read for five months. Thus you see we daily read the paper, if not the daily paper—but excuse puns. There are two stores in here: one five miles up the stream, by J. E. Tisdel; the second seven miles up, kept by Mr. Lyman. There are no postal facilities beyond Quinault agency, but mail matter directed in care of either store finds its way in occasionally by the incoming settlers. We may come out in April; if so have your kodaks loaded, for we lost our grips. For reference geographically see W. G. Steel's map of the Olympic mountains.

H. Fisher

March 28, 1892.—Since writing the above we have tied up the latch-string and sought higher lands. Making our way up the stream three miles over numerous rapids thickly dotted with bowlders, we landed upon the east bank and entered the dark jungle heading southeast. For one mile we struggle through salmon and salal. Crossing a small stream we ascend 500 feet to the first bench or level plateau—altitude, 1000 feet. For a distance of two miles it continues level to the base of the foothills. Ascending 1500 feet beneath giant spruce, fir and cedar, with medium-sized hemlock in abundance, we gain the ridge and prepare lunch. Here elk and deer have tramped the earth until it resembles a barnyard. Proceeding on we reach the summit of this, the first elevation of any consequence overlooking the Queets—altitude, 3000 feet. How different from the low land which was dark and dripping wet. Here all is bright, dry and crisp. Departed snow has leveled moss and debris to a perfect smoothness through which peep the twig and flower in tender beauty. The sun shines bright and cheerful. Swamp robins whistle merrily as we recline, producing the glasses to review familiar country. Toward the Quinault overlooking the sea of green it appears like waving grass upon a prairie. To the southwest and northeast we can trace the Queets for twenty miles like a tiny thread of silver wrought in slate as it disappears and dashes forth again from beneath the alder thickets. Raising our eyes heavenward, beneath the arch of blue are fields of spotless white domes, spires and steeples, o'er whose beauty we fondly linger, recalling hours of pleasant toil connected the those hoary points. A white-tailed deer disturbs our reverie. Cranmer is the first to press the trigger. A few bounds and drops dead, a 2-year old buck, shot through the heart. A sketch of the surrounding, our task is finished and we commence the descent. Many fine specimens of white fir and cedar are passed between 1000 and 2000 feet elevation, and a band of elk routed. It is too far to carry meat, and we allow them to go undisturbed. Recrossing the creek, more to the east, we observe numerous beaver dams. Willow and alder thickets resemble a woodman's slashing where the busy rodents have gamboled in former days, but the Indians are crowding them and all other varieties of game closer to the mountains and utter extinction. I am informed that they slaughtered many elk last summer for their skins, leaving the carcass with juicy steaks to the vultures, which we verify through finding the bones of four at one point. We are all of thirty miles northeast of the ocean from the mouth of the stream. This being the first ridge of any consequence, illustrates the area of this valley.

H. Fisher

DOWN QUEETS RIVER[135]

An Exciting Voyage in Canoes—Explorations in the Olympics

Olympic Mountains, Queets River, Wash., March 30.— [Special Correspondence.]

Former observations with the Queets river, 1200 feet altitude, at the base of Mount Olympus, gave the average fall of the stream twenty-five feet per mile, but from our starting point this morning, for a distance of two miles, is one continuation of rapids, thickly beset with boulders, over which the water flows with great speed. This is considered the most dangerous point upon the stream, a fall of fifty feet per mile. No one but Indians, with few exceptions, attempt this passage, as all attempts have resulted in shattered canoes. For, once you lose control of your boat, destruction is unavoidable. With coats off and perspiration streaming, we brace upon the quivering poles while the spray flies from the tapering model like a thing of life. With the uneven bottom and dashing cross-currents, it is no place to dwell upon idle thoughts. Having passed over nine of these

terraced falls, we pass the Indian's smoke house upon the left bank, and opposite a fair-sized side stream. This is the highest point reached by the Indians in their fishing and hunting trips, it being located just below the great log jam upon the Queets. Killing a fine bag of grouse and rabbits, we face the rapid stream again. After having gone over two more rapids, and making a portage around the jam, we had fair water for a distance of seven miles. The surrounding country grows more beautiful with every mile's progress. Landing to prepare lunch, we found Colonel Linsley's second camp upon the Queets after leaving Mount Olympus, bearing date of September 25, 1890. Grouse are very numerous and signs of large game plentiful. Many pans of soil and sand fail to show any deposits beyond base metals. While I believe that coal underlies the mountains, I am pretty well convinced that the noble metals are absent in this range of mountains. Continuing to within fifteen miles of Mount Olympus, we found the general elevation 3000 feet upon the mountains, giving an average slope of 200 feet per mile from the apex to this point. Having meandered the country through, though loath to leave such beautiful scenery, we drift with the current, slowing up at some bad points and dashing others. We were fifty-five minutes in running ten miles. One week out upon this trip, sleeping upon the wet ground, and can heartily join you in the familiar air, "Be it ever so humble, there is no place like home." Every day's sunshine darkens the forest with overhanging foliage, making travel very difficult in the bottoms. In our travels thus far we have traversed every gulch and hillside inclosing the Queets basin and will at an early date direct some attention to the headwaters of Willis creek, the greatest tributary to the Queets.

H. Fisher

OLYMPIC MINERALS[136]

Formation of the Mountains That Compose That Range

Olympic Mountains, Wash., April 1.—Heading north from our cabin, we cross that land between the Queets River and Nellis Creek,[137] which is terraced in level benches not exceeding an altitude of 1000 feet and free from troublesome

[135] Harry Fisher, *Oregonian* [Portland], April 21, 1892. Brackets in original.
[136] Harry Fisher, *Aberdeen Bulletin*, no date. Reprinted in the *Oregonian* [Portland], April 27, 1892, and in the *Seattle Post-Intelligencer* (first four paragraphs) as "The Olympic Mountains: Worthless as a Mineral Region but Productive of Magnificent Timber," May 20, 1892.
[137] "Nellis Creek is today known as the Clearwater River. N. Nellis was one of the settlers who came from Tacoma in the spring of 1890, taking a claim on the stream." Wood, *Men, Mules and Mountains*, p. 432.

undergrowth after leaving the river bottoms. The Nellis basin is a duplicate of the Queets, but not so large, deriving its name from the first settler, Mr. Nellis, who located there three years ago. Many extensive banks of excellent clay border either stream, from which we made pipes, crucibles, bullet molds and other useful articles, and pronounce it a good quality of kaolin. There are about as many settlers on the Nellis as upon the Queets River. Having spent ten months of constant travel in the Olympic Range, until the appearance of my work now awaiting the press, I sum them up in a brief synopsis, as follows:

The formation is of recent origin as compared to the Cascades. Felspathic and calcareous bases are absent, while massive slate predominates with much barren quartz and sandstone capping the higher peaks. Many points expose beautiful walls of red, green and chocolate porphyry. In the Skokomish valley cupric oxide and native copper is sparingly found, and at one point mineral oil exudes from the earth, though sparingly. Hematite and iron pyrites are found throughout the mountains but not in quantities to insure development. Asbestos of inferior fiber is sparingly distributed.

The Indians stated that they had found lumps of coal and nuggets of copper as large as walnuts, and exhibited ancient trinkets which they claim were made from those picked up on the Wishkah river. The Dungeness presents the only coal croppings that are known to exist, and they are of doubtful extent. From the surrounding beaches traces of gold, accompanied with much black sand, magnetic oxide of iron, and minute garnets, remain with the heavy wash, but entirely disappear as we approach the interior.

All summed up, the Olympics are worthless as a mineral belt but productive of the finest body of timber (i.e., white and red firs, red and Alaska cedars, spruce, larch and hemlock) of any locality on the continent. While the north and east slopes are very precipitous, the south and west is more gradual. From east to west it would require a marvelous piece of engineering to construct a railroad, but from north to south, from Point Crescent to Gray's Harbor, an excellent roadbed could be found by skirting the base of the moun-

tains ten to fifteen miles from the beach. The sea wall is at points 250 feet high, very broken, and covered with an impenetrable jungle of salal, stunted conifers and cedar.

Having overlooked the Nell's Valley, we once more board the Mary Jane and drift with the current. Landing at Mr. Turner's we were shown a wildcat, shot by the plucky little woman of the house. As we had run out of the national plant (tobacco), substituting the inner bark of the red willow, we dropped anchor at Tisdel's store for a new supply and viewed the strides of civilization. Mr. Belcher had cleared seven acres as smooth as a city park, with Mrs. Tisdel promoted to chief clerk in the store and masticating chinook as easily as a school girl chews taffy tolu gum. We reach the ocean beach without accident, and, as our former travels had been so hurriedly performed over the beach, we decide to move at our leisure and feast upon the juicy clam, of which the razor is the finest variety and in great beds along North Beach. Our last camp was near the Copalis River, and scarcely had the blue smoke begun to curl heavenward until we received a call from two ladies that were passing by. Formalities on the front are brief, and we were soon informed that their homes were near by and we were welcome to share the comforts of a shelter and food. Newspapers we eagerly accepted, and were surprised to learn that we had been honored by a visit from the Pacific's Grace Darling. This renewed our interest in the Ferndale's wreck, which was in front of our camp. We afterwards visited the Whites at their home, and found them pleasant, generous people. After reading the many newspaper comments upon her daring act of heroism, we were proud to lift our hats to the frail but brave little woman, proud to know that the Olympics could boast of a genuine heroine, ever watching the angry sea, and proud of Portland's people in responding so gallantly to a well-merited cause, and may the government in due time unroll its vermilion tape and follow suit.

Having again reached Gray's Harbor, we join the civilized whirl—hoping next time to address you from the frosty Cascades.

H. Fisher

APPENDIX TO THE O'NEIL EXPEDITIONS REPORTS

NOMENCLATURE OF THE O'NEIL EXPEDITIONS[1]

O'Neil stated in his report that, "following the custom of explorers," he gave names to such places as he thought proper. So also did other members of his expeditions. The following list of names given to geographic features is believed to be complete. The names of camps have been excluded. The majority of the names were short-lived; the few that have survived and appear on modern maps are indicated by preceding asterisks. Names given by the 1885 expedition are indicated by that date in parentheses after the name.

Mountain Ranges

Gibbon Range Probaby the Mount Olympus range. Named for Civil War General, John Gibbon.

Miles Range (Sherman Miles Range, 1885) Hurricane/ Klahane Ridge today. Ambiguously named for Major General Nelson A. Miles and Senator John Sherman or the son of a niece named Sherman Miles.[2] The principal peaks of the Miles Range were Constance, Clay Wood, and Sherman [Mt. Angeles].

Hoquiam Range These are the peaks around the East Fork Quinault.

(According to Dr. Charles Gauld, O'Neil told him in the 1930s that he named a ridge for General George Crook, but this name is not mentioned in the records. O'Neil often confused names, and he may have been thinking of the Gibbon Range when he referred to "Crook Ridge.")

Mountain Peaks

Adelaide Peak The peak between Six Ridge and Five Stream.

*Mount Anderson 7321 Named for Col. Thomas M. Anderson. Located immediately north of the divide between the Dosewallips River and the East Fork of the Quinault River.

Mount Arline Called Mount Duckabush today. Named for the daughter of Col. Thomas M. Anderson.

Bruin's Peak (or Bruin Peaks) The name is given both ways. It is the high point on Six Ridge about 600 yards northwest of today's Camp Belview.

Capitol Mountain 6019 Called June 10th Peak today. Located one mile S.W. of the headwaters of Pyrites Creek, on the N.W side of Enchanted Valley.

*Mount Church 4770 Named for Frederic Joseph Church, a member of the expedition. Located 2 miles west of the South Fork Skokomish River at the head of Rule Creek and the North Fork of Church Creek. Mt. Church is $1\frac{1}{2}$ miles due east of Wynoochee Falls Campground on the Wynoochee River road.

Mount Churton The word is a contraction of Church and Bretherton, both members of the expedition. Churton was one of several mountains at the head of Five Stream that vary in elevation from 4500 to 5000 feet. The most likely candidates are Peak 4851 and Peak 4666, near the national park boundary, but Churton may have been the peak we know today as Wonder Mountain.

*Mount Clay Wood (1885) 6836 Called Mount Claywood today. Named after Col. Henry Clay Wood, the Adjutant General who ordered Lt. O'Neil on his first Olympic expedition.

Deer Mountain Called Six Ridge today.

Fisher's Peak A part of Mount Steel.

Glacier Peak Called Mount Queets today. The reference seemingly is to an unnamed subsidiary peak , 5819 on the north ridge of Mount Queets, 6480.

Heart or **Heart's Peak** West of Heart Lake (Hart on today's maps). Probably named for its proximity to the heart shaped lake at its base.

*Mount Henderson 6000 Named after Louis F. Henderson, the expedition's botanist. Located nearly a mile southwest of Mt. Skokomish and $1\frac{1}{2}$ miles north-northeast of Mt. Gladys.

Mount Lee unknown

Marsh Peak Mount Stone today. A sharp, multiple-peaked

469

---

[1] Wood, *Men, Mules and Mountains*, pp. 438–39. The simple listing of the expedition names in Wood's book has been expanded here with the assistance of Wood himself.

[2] "Nelson A. Miles married Mary H. Sherman in 1868. She was the daughter of Judge Charles Sherman, niece of Senator John Sherman and General William T. Sherman. A son, christened Sherman Miles, was born in 1882. Did O'Neil call the mountains the 'Sherman Miles Range' to please the lady by honoring her infant son? Or should the name perhaps have been hyphenated (i.e., Sherman-Miles Range) to indicate joint honors to Generals Sherman and Miles, or the Sherman and Miles families? And why did O'Neil indicate, in his 1890 report, that the range was named only for General Miles? Nelson A. Miles (1839–1925) was an officer in the Civil War and an Indian fighter during the post war days on the western frontier. He attained the rank of lieutenant general in the Regular Army in 1900 and retired three years later." Wood, *Men, Mules and Mountains*, p. 395.

mountain located at the head of the Skokomish River, Crazy Creek, and Whitehorse Creek.

McMillan For a Quinault settler. Location unknown.

Raven Due north of Adelaide, a peak between Six Ridge and Five Stream named by Frederic Church.

Sherman (1885) probably after Senator John Sherman, brother of General William T. Sherman. Called Mount Angeles today. See Wood, *Men, Mules and Mountains*, p. 395, footnote 1.

Sister Peaks (1885) Perhaps Klahane Ridge, alongside Mount Angeles.

*Mount Steel (expedition name?) 6250 The mountain the expedition called Mount Steel is called Mount Duckabush today. Over time the name has shifted from the peak nearest O'Neil Pass. Named for W. G. Steel of the Oregon Alpine Club, participants in the expedition. Located at the head of Nine Stream, Upper O'Neil Creek, O'Neil Creek and the Duckabush River. Today's Mount Steel 6200 is a rocky peak about $1\frac{1}{4}$ miles west-northwest of First Divide.

Three Sisters Peaks on the ridge between Five Stream and Six Stream.

Trinity Mountain Called The Vahallas today. This little known group of peaks is centered $3\frac{1}{2}$ miles southwest of Mount Olympus, between the Queets River and the South Fork of the Hoh River.

Wapiti Peak

Lakes

Lake Danton Near the head of Pyrites Creek, $\frac{1}{2}$ mile south of Bretherton Pass, the pass between the headwaters of the Godkin and the Rustler Rivers. Named for Private John Danton.

Eda (Etta) Lake See Lake Danton above. Apparently named for a girlfriend of one of the expedition's men.

Lake Francis Called Lake LaCrosse today. It was O'Neil's name for this lake but party members Linsley and Fisher called Lake of the Holy Cross.

John Lake This lake must have been either Marmot Lake or Heart Lake.

*Heart or **Heart's Lake** Linsley and Fisher gave this name. See Wood, *Men, Mules and Mountains*, p. 411, footnotes for Chapter 19, for a discussion of the naming of the lakes in the Duckabush Basin.

Indigo Lake Called Buck Lake today. East of Lake LaCrosse.

Lake of the Holy Cross Corrupted to Lake LaCrosse today. O'Neil called it Lake Francis but other members of the party called it this or Lake of the Cross after its shape.

Lake Margaret One of the Satsop Lakes.

470

*Marmot Lake Named by Linsley and Fisher. Located in the Duckabush Basin below O'Neil Pass.

Wapiti Lake Located near Six Ridge pass.

Other Names

Annis Creek (1885) Ennis Creek today.

Bear Jungle Fisher's name for the meadow where he ran into three bears, near head of Crazy Creek on the southeast slope of Mount Hopper. (Today's maps have changed the location of Crazy Creek.)

Bretherton's Pass Pass between the headwaters of the Godkin and Rustler Rivers. After B. J. Bretherton of the Oregon Alpine Club.

Canyon Creek

Cathedral Rocks Located "300 yards beyond Adelaide" to the west. Adelaide was a peak between Six Ridge and Five Stream.

*First Divide The divide between the Skokomish River Valley and the Duckabush Valley.

Fisher's Bluff The bluff at Staircase, south on the west side of the river. After Private Harry Fisher, a member of the expedition.

Garden of the Gods A meadow on the west side of Queets Basin.

Grand Cañon (Quinault) Between Squaw Creek and Kimta Creek in the Quinault Valley.

Grand or **Second Divide** Called O'Neil Pass today. The pass between the Duckabush Valley and the valley of the East Fork of the Quinault.

Hawgood Creek (1885) Probably the Lillian River. After H. Hawgood, a member of O'Neil's 1885 expedition.

Hornet Canyon North of Wolf Bar on the North Fork Quinault, probably Kimta Creek today.

Jumbo's Leap Five Stream.

Linsley's Glacier The glacier west of Anderson Glacier. After Nelson E. Linsley, a member of the party.

Noplace (1885) Cameron Basin.

North Pass On First Divide a little west of where the trail goes today.

Pluto's Gulch or **Pluto's Box** Creek through Queets Basin, in a big meadow in the lower basin.

Skull Creek (1885) Located by Annis Creek.

Stillwater Canyon On the North Fork Quinault near Kimta Creek.

Three Holes (1885)

Victor Pass (1885) Between Mount Angeles and Klahane Ridge, where the trail goes today.

Wapiti Valley

West Branch Six Stream.

Yellow Jacket Hill North slope of First Divide, west of Home Sweet Home.

Glacier Canyon

Honeymoon Falls On Six Stream shortly before it flows into the North Fork about $\frac{3}{4}$ of a mile from the confluence.

Related Names

Names related to the explorations but not specifically given by the explorers include:

*****Mount Bretherton** 5960 Located south of Upper Lake Lena. After Bernard J. Bretherton, a member of the expedition.

*****O'Neil Peak** 5758 1½ miles southwest of O'Neil Pass.

*****Mount O'Neil** (1932) 4289 Commonly called Mount Baldy today. In the Colonel Bob cluster, south of Lake Quinault.

*****O'Neil Creek** Starts at Lake Ben and flows south of O'Neil Peak.

*****Upper O'Neil Creek** Starts near O'Neil Pass and flows north of O'Neil Peak.

*****O'Neil Pass** The pass between the Duckabush and the East Fork of the Quinault.

THE MYSTERY OF THE O.A.C. BOX[3]

The men gave various figures for the elevation of "Olympus." Bretherton recorded 7250 feet in his diary, and noted that the copper box was left at 6840 feet, or 410 feet below the top, because the summit was too pointed "& no place to put it." However, in *Steel Points* he uses the figure 7550 feet, the same one reported by Linsley. The latter's report to O'Neil states: "On the morning of the 22nd Bretherton, Danton and I went to the summit of Olympus where we deposited the O.A.C. record box, alt. 7140 ft. There are four peaks. We named the highest one (alt. 7550) Alpine Peak, but there was no safe place there to place the box." (O'Neil and Fisher give the elevation, respectively, as 7875 and 7500 feet, but their reports were based on hearsay.)

The four peaks Linsley referred to form, collectively, the Athena Group or "South Peak" of Olympus. They may be called, for the purposes of this [appendix], Athena I, II, III, and IV. Athena I has an elevation of 7350 feet. Athena II, adjacent to it on the southeast, is about a hundred feet lower. Athena III (West Athena) and Athena IV (East Athena) are lesser points, but they are prominent enough, when viewed from certain vantage points, to be called "peaks."

Although neither Bretherton nor Linsley states explicitly that they climbed the highest of the four peaks (Alpine Peak or Athena I), this is implied in their language. Both men indicate the copper box was left at a point 410 feet below the summit of the highest peak, but the record is not clear whether the box was secured on the side of the pinnacle or perhaps upon the crest of one of the lesser peaks. A photograph by Bretherton which was reproduced in *Steel Points* with the caption, "Placing the Alpine Club box and flag on the summit of Olympus," appears to have been taken from the top of Athena II, thus indicating this was the peak climbed. Clearly depicted in the background is a prominent ledge on the southwest side of Athena I, and beyond it the upper level of the Hoh Glacier extending from the direction of Middle Peak to Athena III, the crest of the glacier appearing to be slightly higher than the ledge on Athena I. To duplicate this scene today, the photographer must stand on the summit of Athena II or at some point less than a hundred feet below the top. (However, it is possible Bretherton could have taken the picture from a lower point and still show the glacier higher than the ledge, because the glacier may have been thicker then.)

So far as is known, the copper box has never been found, therefore one cannot be certain which pinnacle the men climbed.

"Ascent of Mount Olympus," an article by Bretherton in the July, 1907, issue of *Steel Points*, appears to be the only published account of the 1890 climb. Unfortunately, this story—printed more than four years after the naturalist's death—was partially rewritten by W. G. Steel from an unidentified newspaper clipping, therefore must be considered somewhat suspect. Much of the confusion regarding the ascent by the O.E.E. party stems from this article's ambiguous references to the "grand glacier of Mount Olympus," together with a heretofore unclear description of the mountain. (Significantly, the diary Bretherton kept during the Olympus trip does not mention a "grand glacier.")

The "grand glacier"—i.e., "large glacier"—is first noted in connection with a statement about another, "the glacier from which the Queets receives its main supply of water." Here the reference is not to the Humes Glacier but to the field of ice or snow in the upper part of the Queets Basin. When Bretherton and Hughes scouted the ridge north of Dodwell-Rixon Pass, they reported "heavy snow on the north side." A glacier still exists here, the easternmost link in the chain of icefields lying between the Hoh Glacier and Bear

---

[3] Wood, *Men, Mules and Mountains*, pp. 428–31. OAC stands for Oregon Alpine Club.

Pass. The men did not go far enough north to see the full length of the Hoh Glacier; they could see only the uppermost part. However, the other icefields they observed would have appeared to extend "to the summit of the mountains."

The other reference to the "grand glacier" is contained in the description of the "Olympus" climb three days later: "We made an early start . . . and by 9 o'clock the entire party had gained the edge of the grand glacier. From this point Colonel Linsley, Private Danton and myself climbed alone. . . . We found the best traveling on the western side, as there was a ridge of decomposed quartz and slate running along the edge of the precipice, which gave us a better footing than ice."

Having mistaken the Athena Peaks for Olympus, the men must have assumed, upon reaching the Jeffers Glacier—which they approached near its head—that it was the "grand glacier." The photograph fixing the location of the party's temporary camp leaves no doubt as to the route—along the head of the Jeffers Glacier, then directly up the "ridge of decomposed quartz and slate" to the top of one of the Athena Peaks.

The statement that the "grand glacier" swept all the way to the summit was valid. Although the ice is thinner today, an almost unbroken sheath still plunges down from the upper névé fields of the Athena Peaks and helps sustain the Jeffers Glacier.

The ambiguity regarding the "grand glacier" is eliminated if one assumes the first reference relates to the icefields near Bear Pass, the second to the Jeffers Glacier. Although

one is prone to conclude, initially, that Bretherton referred to the Hoh Glacier—because it is the longest glacier on the mountain—the facts do not support this conclusion. Except for a possible (not probable) glimpse by Fisher and Linsley during their reconnaissance above Garden Camp, the men never saw the bulk of the Hoh Glacier except from the top of "Olympus."

Bretherton's description of "Olympus"—i.e., the Athena Peaks—now makes sense: "Olympus is a double-peaked mountain [Athena I and II], entirely covered on the eastern side by a large glacier [Humes]. The northern slope also contains a glacier [Hoh], separated from the larger one [actually smaller] by a high comb of bare rock. Its southwestern side is a sheer precipice, making the mountain appear from the south as if half of it was cut off. It towers considerably above any other mountain in the range, although its elevation is only 7,550 feet."

The last statement leaves unanswered the question why the men failed to observe Olympus was higher, assuming it was visible and not obscured by clouds during the brief time the explorers were on the crest of the peak they climbed. If the men saw Olympus, they apparently did not realize it was higher; or else, perceiving that loftier peaks were inaccessible from the point they had attained, declined to note the fact or attempt to climb further because they were footsore and weary. At any rate, no one recorded having seen a higher point.

BIBLIOGRAPHY

Books

Bagley, Clarence B. *History of Seattle: From the Earliest Settlement to the Present Times.* 3 vols. Chicago: The S. J. Clarke Publishing Company, 1916.

Cleland, Lucile H., compiler. *Trails and Trials of the Pioneers of the Olympic Peninsula, State of Washington.* Humptulips, Wash.: The Humptulips Pioneer Association, 1959. Facsimile reproduction, Seattle: Shorey Book Store, 1973.

El Hult, Ruby. *The Untamed Olympics: The Story of a Peninsula.* Portland, Ore.: Binfords and Mort, 1954.

Grant, Frederic James. *History of Seattle, Washington.* New York: American Publishing and Engraving Company, 1891.

Kitchin, E.A. *Birds of the Olympic Peninsula.* Port Angeles, Wash.: Olympic Stationers, 1949.

Marple, Elliot, and Bruce H. Olson. *The National Bank of Commerce of Seattle 1889–1969.* Palo Alto, Calif.: Pacific Books, 1972.

Parratt, Smitty. *Gods and Goblins: A Field Guide to Place Names of Olympic National Park.* Port Angeles, Wash.: Self-published, 1984.

Warren, James R. *King County and Its Emerald City: Seattle.* Seattle: American Historical Press, in cooperation with the Museum of History and Industry, 1997.

Wood, Robert L. *Across the Olympic Mountains: The Press Expedition 1889–90.* 2d ed. Seattle and London: The Mountaineers Books and the University of Washington Press, 1976.

———. *The Land That Slept Late: The Olympic Mountains in Legend and History.* Seattle: The Mountaineers Books, 1995.

———. *Men, Mules and Mountains: Lieutenant O'Neil's Olympic Expeditions.* Seattle: The Mountaineers Books, 1976.

Periodicals

Bretherton, Bernard J. "Ascent of Mount Olympus." *Steel Points* 1 (July 1907): pp. 148–53.

———. "Elk and Camera: A Photographing Adventure." *Overland Monthly* 35 (February 1900): pp. 112–15.

Christie, J. H. "From the Leader of the Press Expedition." *The Mountaineer Annual* 19 (1926): pp. 37–39.

Gilman, Samuel C. "The Olympic Country." *National Geographic* 7 (April 1896): pp. 133–40. Published posthumously.

Henderson, L. F. "The Flora of the Olympics." *ZOE: a biological journal* 2 (October 1891): pp. 253–95. Reprinted in *Steel Points* 1 (July 1907): pp. 160–98 (reprint contains misplaced blocks of type, which in turn left *non sequitur* blocks of text in several places).

Himes, George H. "First Ascent of Mount Olympus." *Steel Points* 1 (July 1907): p. 159.

Hitchman, Robert. "Name Calling." *Mountaineer Annual* 52 (1959): pp. 6–17.

Majors, Harry M., ed. "The Press Party Expedition in the Olympic Mountains 1889–1890." *Northwest Discovery: The Journal of Northwest History and Natural History* 2 (February 1981): pp. 67–134; 2 (March 1981): pp. 136–99; 2 (May 1981): pp. 314–21; 2 (July-August 1981): pp. 465–74; 5 (August 1984): pp. 200–286; 5 (September 1984): pp. 288–364; 5 (October 1984): pp. 366–448.

Meany, Edmond S. "The Olympics in History and Legend." *The Mountaineer Annual* 6 (1913): pp. 51–55.

Semple, Eugene. "The Olympic Mountains." *West Shore* 14 (August 1888): pp. 428–29.

Smith, A. A. "The Olympics." *Steel Points* 1 (July 1907): pp. 141–45.

Smith, Norman R. "The Olympic Mountains." *West Shore* 16 (July 18, 1890): p. 907.

Todd, John Ronald. "A Selected Bibliography of the Writings of Edmond Stephen Meany." *Washington Historical Quarterly* 26 (July 1935): pp. 176–91.

Washington Historical Quarterly. "Newspapers of Washington Territory." *Washington Historical Quarterly* 13 (July 1922): pp. 181–95; and 14 (July 1923): pp. 186–200.

West Shore. "Description of Skokomish falls." *West Shore* 16 (August 30, 1890): p. 43.

———. "Elk." *West Shore* 17 (February 21, 1891): p. 130.

———. "A member of the O'Neil party." *West Shore* 16 (August 30, 1890): p. 43.

———. "The party under Lieutenant O'Neal [sic]." *West Shore* 11 (October 1885): pp. 319–20.

———. "Report of large mineral deposits." *West Shore* 16 (August 23, 1890): p. 27.

———. "Toll road on the Dosewallips." *West Shore* 16 (June 14, 1890): p. 759.

Wickersham, James. "A National Park in the Olympics 1890." *The Living Wilderness,* Summer/Fall 1961. Reprinted from the National Archives.

Wood, Robert L. "The Goblin Gates Refound." *Nature Magazine* 47 (October 1954): pp. 414–16.

———. "Have a Heart." *Signpost* 23 (July 1988): pp. 24–28.

———. "The O'Neil Expedition." *Columbia* 4 (Summer 1990): pp. 40–45.

———. "Sleuthing in the Past." *The Mountaineer Annual* 71 (1977): pp. 49–57.

Newspaper Articles

Aberdeen Herald. "Exploring the Quinault." *Aberdeen Herald*, no date. Reprinted in *Mason County Journal* [Shelton], May 2, 1890.

Aberdeen Semi-Weekly Bulletin. "In the Olympics: Return of a Brave Band of Explorers." *Aberdeen Semi-Weekly Bulletin*, May 25, 1890.

Bretherton, B. J. "Across the Divide." *Seattle Post-Intelligencer*, August 14, 1890.

———. "Exploring the Olympics." *Seattle Post-Intelligencer*, September 19, 1890.

———. "Gates of the Range." *Seattle Post-Intelligencer*, July 14, 1890.

———. "Olympic Adventure." *Tacoma Daily Ledger*, August 17, 1890.

———. "Olympic Explorers." *Tacoma Daily Ledger*, August 10, 1890.

———. "Olympic Exploration." *Tacoma Daily Ledger*, August 24, 1890.

———. "Olympic Exploration." *Tacoma Daily Ledger*, September 7, 1890.

———. "On the Duckabush." *Seattle Post-Intelligencer*, September 3, 1890.

———. "The Range Crossed." *Seattle Post-Intelligencer*, August 6, 1890.

Buckley Banner. "The Olympics." *Buckley Banner*, no date. Reprinted in the *Mason County Journal* [Shelton], July 4, 1890.

Church, F. J. "Above Lake Cushman." *Seattle Press*, no date. Reprinted in the *Tacoma Daily Ledger*, July 20, 1890, and *Mason County Journal* [Shelton], August 1, 1890.

———. "The Lake Cushman Copper Mines." *Seattle Press*, no date. Reprinted in the *Mason County Journal* [Shelton], August 15, 1890.

———. "Olympic Explorers." *Oregonian* [Portland], July 19, 1890.

Conrad, John. "They Found the Trail: A Party of Five Prospectors Return From the Olympics." *Seattle Press*, July 16, 1890.

The Daily Progress. "Olympics Opened." *The Daily Progress* [Anacortes], May 27, 1890.

Fisher, H. "In the Olympics." *Oregonian* [Portland], April 15, 1892.

———. "Down Queets River." *Oregonian* [Portland], April 21, 1892.

———. "Olympic Minerals." *Aberdeen Bulletin*, no date. Reprinted in *Oregonian* [Portland], April 27, 1892, and in *Seattle Post-Intelligencer* (first four paragraphs) as "The Olympic Mountains: Worthless as a Mineral Region but Productive of Magnificent Timber," May 20, 1892.

———. "The Olympic Mountains: Worthless as a Mineral Region but Productive of Magnificent Timber." *Seattle Post-Intelligencer*, May 20, 1892. Reprinted from first four paragraphs of "Olympic Minerals," *Aberdeen Bulletin*, no date.

Gilman, C. A. "Farms in Olympics." *Tacoma Ledger*, no date. Reprinted in the *Seattle Post-Intelligencer*, May 28, 1890.

———. "The Olympic Region." *Tacoma Ledger*, no date. Reprinted in the *Seattle Post-Intelligencer*, May 28, 1890, and *West Shore* 16 (June 7, 1890): p. 724.

Gilman, S. C. "Description of the Olympic Country." *Seattle Post-Intelligencer*, June 5, 1890. Reprinted in part in *West Shore* 16 (August 2, 1890): p. 975.

———. "The Olympic Peninsula." *Oregonian* [Portland], no date. Reprinted in *Mason County Journal* [Shelton], June 13, 1890.

———. "Unknown No Longer." *Seattle Post-Intelligencer*, June 5, 1890.

Jones, R. "A Trail That Is No Trail." *Whatcom Reveille* [Bellingham], no date. Reprinted in *Seattle Post-Intelligencer*, September 30, 1890.

Joynt, Charles W. "The Unknown Olympics." *Buckley Banner*, no date. Reprinted in *Mason County Journal* [Shelton], May 23, 1890.

———. "The Olympics." *Buckley Banner*, no date. Reprinted in *Mason County Journal* [Shelton], July 4, 1890.

Layton, Mike "The Men Went Over the Mountain: The First to Tame the Olympics." *Oregonian* [Portland], September 24, 1967.

Mason County Journal. "Alpine club expedition." *Seattle Press*, no date. Reprinted in *Mason County Journal* [Shelton], May 23, 1890.

———. "Press party reaches Aberdeen." *Mason County Journal* [Shelton], June 6, 1890.

Meany, Edmond S. "Beyond the Olympics." *Seattle Press*, January 1, 1890.

———. "A Chance for an Explorer." *Seattle Press*, July 16, 1890.

———. "The Olympics: An Account of the Explorations Made by the Press Explorers." *Seattle Press*, July 16, 1890.

———. "Press Exploring Party." *Seattle Press*, December 5, 1889.[1]

---

[1] The five expedition articles, written by Meany and appearing in the *Seattle Press* between December 5, 1889, and January 7, 1890, are apparently lost because no copies of the paper issued during that period have survived. Meany's articles are listed here in order that the record of his involvement in the expedition be complete.

474

———. "The Press Explorations." *Seattle Press*, July 16, 1890.

———. "The Press Trail." *Seattle Press*, July 16, 1890.

———. "Up the Elwha River." *Seattle Press*, December 17, 1889.

———. "Watch for the Signals." *Seattle Press*, December 20, 1889.

———. "The Whiteface Bear." *Seattle Press*, January 7, 1890.

Murphy, Thomas. "In Quillayute Vales." *Port Townsend Leader*, no date. Reprinted in *Seattle Post-Intelligencer*, September 4, 1890.

O'Neil, Joseph P. "O'Neil's Exploration, Record of His Trip Back of Port Angeles in 1885." *Seattle Press*, July 16, 1890.

Pollock, E. W. "The Wild Olympic Range." *Seattle Post-Intelligencer*, January 1, 1891.

Russell, Jerry. "An Exploration of the High Olympics." *Seattle Times*, March 18, 1962. Part one of a three-part series.

———. "Christie and Party Blazed Trail into High Olympics." *Seattle Times*, March 25, 1962. Part two of a three-part series.

———. "Olympic Pathfinders Finally Get Back." *Seattle Times*, April 1, 1962. Part three of a three-part series.

Seattle Post-Intelligencer. "Estray in Olympics." *Seattle Post-Intelligencer*, July 30, 1890. (The Greenebaum Incident.)

———. "Lost in Olympics." *Seattle Post-Intelligencer*, August 3, 1890. (The Greenebaum Incident.)

———. "Many Rich Mines." *Seattle Post-Intelligencer*, August 14, 1890.

———. "The Olympics Opened." *Seattle Post-Intelligencer*, June 5, 1890.

———. "O'Neil's Caravan Emerges." *Seattle Post-Intelligencer*, September 28, 1890.

———. "Out of the Olympics." *Seattle Post-Intelligencer*, September 4, 1890.

———. "A Trip Through Olympics." *Seattle Post-Intelligencer*, September 30, 1890.

Seattle Press. "Belittling Lieut. O'Neil." *Seattle Press*, July 16, 1890.

———. "The Olympics: An Account of the Explorations Made by the 'Press' Explorers." *Seattle Press*, July 16, 1890. Contains the edited trip journals of James Christie and Charles Barnes and supporting articles by Edmond S. Meany.

———. "They Went Out After Elk." *Seattle Press*, no date. Reprinted in the *Tacoma News*, January 2, 1891.

Semple, Eugene. "Semple's Striking Report." *Seattle Press*, July 16, 1890.

Stripling, Sherry. "Olympic Feats." *Seattle Times*, August 10, 1989.

Wickersham, James. "Olympic Mountains: Explorations Made by the Wickersham Party." *Tacoma News*, January 2, 1891.

———. "Olympic National Park." *Tacoma News*, January 2, 1891.

Public Documents

U. S. Congress. Senate. *Exploration of the Olympic Mountains, Washington*. Joseph P. O'Neil. 54th Cong., 1st Sess., 1896. S. Doc. 59, Serial 3349, Vol. 3.

Dept. of the Interior. Report of Eugene Semple, Governor of Washington Territory for the year 1888. "The Olympic Mountains." Washington, D.C.: U.S. Government Printing Office, 1889.

Manuscripts and Pamphlets

Author unknown. "Gilmans Return." Unidentified newspaper clipping, 1889. Attached to the J. J. Banta diary, which is contained in Lucile H. Cleland's *Trails and Trials of the Pioneers of the Olympic Peninsula* (see entry under Books in this bibliography).

Author unknown. "Exploring the Quinault." Unidentified newspaper clipping, 1890. Attached to the J.J. Banta diary, which is contained in Lucile H. Cleland's *Trails and Trials of the Pioneers of the Olympic Peninsula* (see entry under Books in this bibliography).

Bretherton, Bernard J. Diary kept during 1890 Olympic Exploring Expedition. Bretherton collection, Olympic National Park, Port Angeles, Wash.

Church, Frederic J. Diary kept during the 1890 Olympic Exploring Expedition. Robert B. Hitchman private papers.

Fager, Shirley. *Doctor, Miner, Explorer: Dr. H. B. Runnalls*. Unpublished pamphlet in Robert L. Wood Collection, Manuscripts, Special Collections, University Archives, University of Washington Libraries, Seattle, Wash., no date.

Fisher, H. "Lt. Oneils [sic] Exploration of the Olympic Mountains." Unpublished 1890 manuscript. Courtesy Mazamas (Mazama Club Library), Portland, Ore., Manuscript #001-2001. Transcribed by Robert L. Wood, 1967–68. Microfilm copy in Manuscripts, Special Collections. University Archives, University of Washington Libraries, Seattle, Wash.

Henderson, Louis F. "Some Early Experiences of a Botanist in the Northwest." Paper about the O'Neil Expedition of 1890 presented at a meeting of the Oregon Audubon Society, 1932. Special Collections, University of Oregon Library, Eugene, Ore. Copies in Robert B. Hitchman private papers and Manuscripts, Special Collections, University Archives, University of Washington Libraries, Seattle, Wash.

Linsley, Nelson E. "Report to Lieutenant Joseph P. O'Neil, October 3, 1890. On trip to Mount Olympus." Robert B. Hitchman private papers.

Meany, Edmond S. Collected papers (refer to box and folder numbers). Manuscripts, Special Collections, University Archives, University of Washington Libraries, Seattle, Wash.

Morse, Eldridge. "Notes on the History and Resources of Washington Territory." Handwritten manuscript, BANC MSS P-B 48, Bancroft Library, University of California, Berkeley, no date.

O'Neil, Joseph P. Manuscript on 1885 expedition in the Olympic Mountains. Robert B. Hitchman private papers.

———. Lecture Notes on 1885 and 1890 expeditions in Olympic Mountains. Five sets of notes, incomplete, plus fragments. Robert B. Hitchman private papers and Mary Kegg Collection, contained in Robert L. Wood Collection, Manuscripts, Special Collections, University Archives, University of Washington Libraries, Seattle, Wash.

Wickersham, James. "Lake Mason in 1889." Washington State Historical Society, Tacoma, Wash.

———. "A Trip to the Olympic Mountains [1889], an account of Wickersham's 1889 Olympic Exploration." Washington State Historical Society, Tacoma, Wash.

Wood, Robert L. "Memorandum on Place Names in the Olympics: Comments about Statements Contained in *Gods and Goblins: A Field Guide to Place Names in Olympic National Park* by Smitty Parratt (see entry under Books in this bibliography).

Worth, Grace. *Notes on the Life of James Halbold Christie.* Pamphlet in the Robert L. Wood Collection, Manuscripts, Special Collections, University Archives, University of Washington Libraries, Seattle, Wash., no date [1965?].

INDEX

Note: Page references to illustrations are set in italics. Page references to articles reprinted from specified newspapers or periodicals are set in bold.

Aberdeen 6, 31, 107, 301, 422, 426
Aberdeen Herald 206, **206–207**
Aberdeen Semi-Weekly Bulletin 138–139, **467–468**
Adelaide Peak 469
Adeline Cascade 79, 155
Admiralty Inlet 177
Alexander River 31–33, 99, 137, 155
Alexander Valley 33
Alpine Peak 471
Annis Creek 259–260, 470
Antrim, F. S. 102, 104–105, 107, 133, *133*, 134, 138–141
Antrim Range 156
Armstrong, Benjamin 13, 15–16
Athena Peaks 471–472

Bailey, William E. 10, 16, 18, 75, 79, 109, 139, 142, 158
Bailey Range 18, 32, 63, 65, 75, 79, *81*, 82, 84, 93, 156
Balches Cove 211–213
Banner Party 12, 327, 330, 332, 389–390, 396, 406, 413
Banta, J. J. and Sharp, S. Price Exploration 182–194
Barnes, Charles A. 8, *19*, 22–23, 25, 27–28, *28*, 35–109, 111–117, 120–127, 131, 133, 139, 141–147, 149, 152, 158, 376, 380, 388, 394, 403, 410, 411, 434, 437, 445
Bear Pass 471–472
bears 11, 16, 23, 57–58, 91–93, *91–93*, 95–96, 137, 140, 179, 198, 200, 202–204, 207, 227–228, 233–234, 239, 241, 244, 258, 261, 263–264, 271, 280, 284, 300, 311, 315, 319, 322–324, 381, 383, 386, 389, 392, *392*, 399–402, *400, 402*, 408, 428–430, 435, 440, 466
Belle River 66, 84, 124, 155
Bellingham 182
Big Island 126
Big Skookum 221, 408
Black Canyon 304
Bluff Camp 195
bobcat 48, 137, 203
Bogachiel River 180, 183–184, 208–209, 278
Brace Rock Lighthouse 116
Bretherton, Bernard J. 253, *308*, 308–339, 341, 358–359, 365, 372, 375, 378, 382, 388, 391, 395, 399, 402, 405, 412–414, 427, 429–431, *431*, 434, 436–437, 458, 462–463, 471

Brethertons Pass 470
Bruins Peak 270, 297, 393, 396, 418, 435, 469
Buck Lake. *See* Indigo Lake
Buckley Banner 12, **219–220**, 220–221, 228
Budds Inlet 355
Bunch Grass Valley 312
Burke Gilman Trail 11
Burke Range 32, 156
Burnt Bean Camp 14

Calawa River 183
Call, The 10, 18
Canyon Camp 37, 151–152
Canyon Creek 218, 276, 470
Cape Flattery 170, 211, 246
Capitol Mountain 437, 469
Cascade Mountains 10, 20, 173, 181, 211, 279, 358, 468
Cascade Range 343, 348, 358
Cat Creek 48, 155
Cathedral Rocks 470
Chambers Creek 259–260, 263
Chapel Rock 454
Chehalis River 6, 17, 172, 175–177, 186, 188, 243, 273, 370, 426
Chester Valley 31, 33, 98, 137, 155, 309, 463
Chimney Peak 75
Chopalis River 311, 453, 468
Christie, James H. 8, *19*, 20, 23, 27–28, *28*, 36, 38–39, 41–42, 44–45, 47, 52–53, 55, 57–59, 66–70, 73, 75, 81–84, 86, *87*, 88–89, 92, 97–98, 102, 109–134, 139, 141–146, 149, 158, 204, 252
Chronicle, The 10, 18
Church, Frederic J. 253, 297–307, 319, 358–359, 379, 381–382, 388, 390–391, 394–395, 399, 402, 404, *405*, 410–412, 453, 459–461
Churton Peak 316, 320
Clallam Bay 180
Clearwater Valley 182
Coldfeet Creek 72, 125, 155
Columbia River 10, 16, 356, 462
Conrad, John 197, 203
Conrad/Olmstead Exploration (1890) 196–203
Conrad/Olmstead Party 11
Convulsion Canyon 63, 67, 82, 157
Copper Box of Oregon Alpine Club 275, 471–472

482

483

ABOUT THE AUTHOR

Carsten Lien is the author of *Olympic Battleground: The Power and Politics of Timber Preservation*. He is a former visiting scholar at the University of Washington and chaired the Advisory Committee for the University's Institute for Environmental Studies. He has served on the boards of several conservation organizations, including The Nature Conservancy and Olympic Park Associates, and is the former president of The Mountaineers, an outdoor and conservation club based in Seattle. He has also served in executive positions with the Peace Corps and the Stanford Research Institute.

THE MOUNTAINEERS, founded in 1906, is a nonprofit outdoor activity and conservation club, whose mission is "to explore, study, preserve, and enjoy the natural beauty of the outdoors...." Based in Seattle, Washington, the club is now the third-largest such organization in the United States, with 15,000 members and five branches throughout Washington State.

The Mountaineers sponsors both classes and year-round outdoor activities in the Pacific Northwest, which include hiking, mountain climbing, ski-touring, snowshoeing, bicycling, camping, kayaking and canoeing, nature study, sailing, and adventure travel. The club's conservation division supports environmental causes through educational activities, sponsoring legislation, and presenting informational programs. All club activities are led by skilled, experienced volunteers, who are dedicated to promoting safe and responsible enjoyment and preservation of the outdoors.

If you would like to participate in these organized outdoor activities or the club's programs, consider a membership in The Mountaineers. For information and an application, write or call The Mountaineers, Club Headquarters, 300 Third Avenue West, Seattle, WA 98119; 206-284-6310.

The Mountaineers Books, an active, nonprofit publishing program of the club, produces guidebooks, instructional texts, historical works, natural history guides, and works on environmental conservation. All books produced by The Mountaineers Books fulfill the club's mission.

Send or call for our catalog of more than 500 outdoor titles:

The Mountaineers Books
1001 SW Klickitat Way, Suite 201
Seattle, WA 98134
800-553-4453
mbooks@mountaineers.org
www.mountaineersbooks.org

The Mountaineers Books is proud to be a corporate sponsor of Leave No Trace, whose mission is to promote and inspire responsible outdoor recreation through education, research, and partnerships. The Leave No Trace program is focused specifically on human-powered (non-motorized) recreation.

Leave No Trace strives to educate visitors about the nature of their recreational impacts, as well as offer techniques to prevent and minimize such impacts. Leave No Trace is best understood as an educational and ethical program, not as a set of rules and regulations.

For more information, visit www.lnt.org, or call 800-332-4100.

Other titles you might enjoy from The Mountaineers Books

OLYMPIC BATTLEGROUND, 2nd Edition, *Carsten Lien.*
This new edition of the classic account of the struggle to create and preserve Olympic National Park is also an exposé of the National Park and Forest Services.

OLYMPIC MOUNTAINS TRAIL GUIDE: National Park & National Forest, 3rd Edition, *Robert Wood.*
A thorough guide covering every trail, short or long, easy or challenging, in Washington's magnificent Olympic Mountains.

FIELD GUIDE TO THE CASCADES & OLYMPICS, *Stephen Whitney.*
Describes and beautifully illustrates over 600 species of plants and animals found in the mountains from Northern California through Southwest British Columbia.

100 CLASSIC HIKES IN™ WASHINGTON, *Ira Spring & Harvey Manning.*
A full-color guide to Washington's finest trails by the respected authors of more than thirty Washington guides, featuring their personal picks of the best hikes in the state.

SNOWSHOE ROUTES—WASHINGTON, *Dan A. Nelson.*
The most comprehensive guidebook to prime winter hiking in Washington, written by an editor with the Washington Trails Association.

NORTH CASCADES HIGHWAY: Washington's Popular and Scenic Pass, *JoAnn Roe.*
A comprehensive, regional history of the people, landscape, and environment along the North Cascades Highway.

STEVENS PASS: The Story of Railroading and Recreation in the North Cascades, *JoAnn Roe.*
History of the exploration and development of this scenic region, including colorful first-person accounts.

NORTHWEST TREES, *Stephen Arno and Ramona Hammerly.*
Superb drawings enhance this study of the thirty-five conifers and broadleaves native to the Pacific Northwest.

MOUNTAIN FLOWERS OF THE CASCADES & OLYMPICS, *Harvey Manning & Ira Spring.*
Full-color photos and descriptions of eighty-four of the most common wildflowers of the region.

KAYAK ROUTES OF THE PACIFIC NORTHWEST COAST, *Peter McGee.*
Everything you need to know about kayaking routes and camping sites from Puget Sound to the Queen Charlotte Islands.

WASHINGTON WHITEWATER: The 34 Best Whitewater Rivers, *Douglass A. North.*
From the Spokane River in Eastern Washington to the Elwha River on the Olympic Peninsula, detailed route descriptions include mile-by-mile river maps, matching river logs, and information on water-level curves.